THE BUTTERFLIES
OF NORTH AMERICA

CONTRIBUTORS

DAVID L. BAUER

HARRY K. CLENCH

THOMAS W. DAVIES

JOHN C. DOWNEY

JOHN F. EMMEL

THOMAS C. EMMEL

GLENN A. GORELICK

WILLIAM H. HOWE

ALEXANDER B. KLOTS

ROBERT L. LANGSTON

PAUL A. OPLER

EDWIN M. PERKINS, JR.

STEPHEN F. PERKINS

JERRY A. POWELL

KILIAN ROEVER

JAMES A. SCOTT

JON H. SHEPARD

SIGRID S. SHEPARD

OAKLEY SHIELDS

FRED T. THORNE

C. DON MACNEILL

THE
BUTTERFLIES
OF NORTH AMERICA

———————◆———————

97 COLOR PLATES CONTAINING
2093 ILLUSTRATIONS AND 32 TEXT FIGURES

William H. Howe

COORDINATING EDITOR AND ILLUSTRATOR
&
Twenty Contributors

———————◆———————

1975

DOUBLEDAY & COMPANY, INC.

GARDEN CITY, NEW YORK

ISBN: *0-385-04926-9*

Library of Congress Catalog Card Number 73-15276
Copyright © 1975 by Doubleday & Company, Inc.
All Rights Reserved
Printed in the United States of America
First Edition After a Limited Edition of 200 Copies

Prologue

The purpose of Butterflies will not be found . . . in the few flowers they may inadvertently pollinate. Nor in the numbers of parasitic wasps they may support. And to peer beneath a microscope at their dissected fragments will in no way elucidate the reason for their being. Their purpose is their *beauty* and the beauty they bring into the lives of those of us who have paused long enough from the cares of the world to *listen* to their fascinating story. . . .

OUR BUTTERFLIES AND MOTHS
WILLIAM H. HOWE

Measurements of butterflies in this book are given in millimeters.

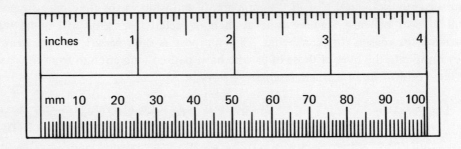

Preface

THE BUTTERFLIES OF NORTH AMERICA is a comprehensive volume on the butterflies and skippers of Canada and the United States, including Alaska and Hawaii. It is written for everyone who is interested in butterflies, from beginning student to professional. The numerous colored plates and line drawings are fully coordinated with the text, in which are given the most important facts about each kind of butterfly.

The first popular book on North American butterflies was *The Butterfly Book*, by W. J. Holland, published by Doubleday in 1898. It enjoyed enormous success and drew many into the absorbing study of these colorful insects. In response to continuing demand, Doubleday reprinted it many times and in 1931, shortly before he died, Holland completely revised it.

In time, however, even the revised version of Holland's book became dated and eventually went out of print. When I was asked by Doubleday if I would undertake to prepare a completely new and up-to-date replacement I readily agreed. Since Holland's day the extent of our knowledge of North American butterflies has so increased that the task seemed too great for any one person. I therefore enlisted a group of specialists to prepare most of the text, to accompany my colored illustrations. Throughout I have worked closely with Dr. Alexander B. Klots and several other lepidopterists.

Note. With the exception of a new subspecies of *Speyeria egleis,* no new names are introduced in this book.

The Contributors

This book owes it very existence to the generous contributions made by the many specialists in their particular fields. Below is a list of all who have prepared any part of this book, or who have assisted in its writing or scientific editing, together with an enumeration of the work they have done.

David L. Bauer, Lake Tahoe, California. Tribe Melitaeini (Nymphalidae).

F. Martin Brown, Colorado Springs, Colorado. Manuscript assistance.

Harry K. Clench, Carnegie Museum of Natural History, Pittsburgh, Pennsylvania. Introduction; genera *Oenomaus, Thereus, Allosmaitia, Ocaria* (Lycaenidae); *Vanessa* (Nymphalidae); manuscript assistance.

Mary H. Clench, Carnegie Museum of Natural History, Pittsburgh, Pennsylvania. Manuscript assistance.

Thomas W. Davies, San Leandro, California. Genus *Polygonia* (Nymphalidae).

John C. Downey, University of Northern Iowa, Cedar Falls, Iowa. Genera *Plebejus, Everes* (Lycaenidae).

John F. Emmel, Idyllwild, California. Subfamily Papilioninae (Papilionidae); genus *Satyrium* (Lycaenidae).

Thomas C. Emmel, University of Florida, Gainesville, Florida. Family Satyridae; genera *Ministrymon, Calycopis, Tmolus, Atlides, Euristrymon, Dolymorpha, Hypostrymon, Panthiades, Erora, Electrostrymon* (Lycaenidae).

Glenn Alan Gorelick, Citrus College, Azusa, California. Genera *Nymphalis, Precis* (Nymphalidae).

Ann Greer (deceased), Ottawa University, Ottawa, Kansas. Manuscript assistance.

William H. Howe, Ottawa, Kansas. All illustrations; families Danaidae, Ithomiidae, Apaturidae, Heliconiidae, Libytheidae, Liphyridae; subfamily Marpesiinae (Nymphalidae); tribes Coloburini, Ageroniini, Eurytelini, Epicaliini (Nymphalidae); genera *Hypolimnas, Euptoieta, Speyeria* (Nymphalidae); *Vaga, Lampides, Glaucopsyche* (Lycaenidae); family Pieridae (except *Colias*).

Alexander B. Klots, American Museum of Natural History, New York, New York. Introduction (part); genus *Colias;* manuscript assistance.

Robert L. Langston, Kensington, California, Genera *Brephidium, Leptotes, Zizula, Hemiargus, Philotes, Phaedrotes, Celastrina* (Lycaenidae).

C. Don MacNeill, Oakland Museum, Oakland, California. Family Hesperiidae.

Paul A. Opler, Berkeley, California. Genus *Lycaena* (Lycaenidae).

Edwin M. Perkins, Jr., University of Southern California, Los Angeles, California. Genera *Adelpha, Anartia, Siproeta, Hypanartia, Limenitis* (Nymphalidae): co-author with Stephen F. Perkins.

Stephen F. Perkins, Oregon Regional Primate Research Center, Beaverton, Oregon. Genera *Adelpha, Anartia, Siproeta, Hypanartia, Limenitis* (Nymphalidae): co-author with Edwin M. Perkins, Jr.

Jerry A. Powell, University of California, Berkeley, California. Family Riodinidae.

Kilian Roever, Phoenix, Arizona. Family Megathymidae.

James A. Scott, Lakewood, Colorado. Genera *Strymon, Callophrys* (subgenera *Cyanophrys, Callophrys*) (Lycaenidae).

Jon H. Shepard, Berkeley, California. Subfamily Parnassiinae (Papilionidae): co-author with Sigrid S. Shepard; genus *Boloria* (Nymphalidae).

Sigrid S. Shepard, Berkeley, California. Subfamily Parnassiinae (Papilionidae): co-author with Jon H. Shepard.

Oakley Shields, Davis, California. Genus *Callophrys* (subgenera *Mitoura, Incisalia, Sandia, Xamia*) (Lycaenidae), manuscript consultation.

Fred T. Thorne, El Cajon, California. Tribe Theclini (Lycaenidae); genera *Eumaeus, Chlorostrymon, Phaeostrymon, Harkenclenus* (Lycaenidae).

Acknowledgments

Without the cooperation of a number of museums and their curators, and of many private collectors, it would have been impossible to undertake this book. I take this opportunity to thank them, and list them below. Abbreviations of collections from which specimens are illustrated follow the name of the institution or individual.

American Museum of Natural History (AMNH), New York, New York. Dr. Frederick H. Rindge. Loan of specimens.

David L. Bauer (DLB), Lake Tahoe, California. Loan of specimens.

John M. Burns (JMB), Cambridge, Massachusetts. Loan of specimens.

California Academy of Sciences (CAS), San Francisco, California. Dr. Paul H. Arnaud, Jr. Loan of specimens.

Canadian National Collection (CNC), Ottawa, Ontario. Dr. Thomas N. Freeman. Loan of specimens.

Carnegie Museum of Natural History (CM), Pittsburgh, Pennsylvania. Harry K. Clench. Loan of specimens.

Thomas W. Davies (TWD), San Leandro, California. Loan of specimens.

John C. Downey (JCD), Cedar Falls, Iowa. Loan of specimens.

J. Donald Eff (JDE), Boulder, Colorado. Loan of specimens.

Thomas C. Emmel (TCE), Gainesville, Florida. Loan of specimens.

H. Avery Freeman (HAF), Garland, Texas. Loan of specimens. Most of Mr. Freeman's collection has since gone to the American Museum of Natural History and Carnegie Museum of Natural History.

L. Paul Grey (LPG), Lincoln, Maine. Loan of specimens; consultation on *Speyeria*.

John R. Heitzman (JRH), Independence, Missouri. Loan of specimens.

Roderick R. Irwin (RRI), Chicago, Illinois. Loan of specimens.

Stanley G. Jewett, Jr. (SGJ), Portland, Oregon. Loan of specimens.

John Lane (JL), Los Angeles, California. Loan of specimens.

Robert L. Langston (RLL), Kensington, California. Loan of specimens.

Los Angeles County Museum (LACM), Los Angeles, California. Lloyd M. Martin, Dr. Fred Truxal, Dr. Charles L. Hogue. Loan of specimens. Messrs. Martin, Truxal and Hogue also gave many valued suggestions and comments.

C. Don MacNeill (CDM), Oakland, California. Loan of specimens.

David V. McCorkle (DVM), Monmouth, Oregon. Loan of specimens.

Milwaukee Public Museum (MPM), Milwaukee, Wisconsin. Kenneth MacArthur. Loan of specimens.

Arthur H. Moeck, Milwaukee, Wisconsin. Loan of specimens. Mr. Moeck also checked the manuscript on *Speyeria* and furnished much valuable data. Mr. Moeck's collection has since gone to the Milwaukee Public Museum.

National Museum of Natural History (formerly *United States National Museum*) (USNM), Washington, D.C. William D. Field, Loan of specimens.

Edwin M. Jr. and *Stephen F. Perkins* (E&SP), Los Angeles, California. Loan of specimens. The Perkins collection has since gone to the Allyn Museum of Entomology, Sarasota, Florida.

John M. Plomley (JMP), Miami, Florida. Loan of specimens.

Jerry A. Powell (JAP), Berkeley, California. Loan of specimens.

Floyd W. and *June D. Preston* (F&JP), Lawrence, Kansas. Loan of specimens.

Walfried J. Reinthal (WJR), Knoxville, Tennessee. Loan of specimens.

Frank E. Rutkowski (FER), New York, New York. Loan of specimens.

Jon H. Shepard (JHS), Berkeley, California. Loan of specimens.

Oakley Shields (OS), Davis, California. Loan of specimens.

Don B. Stallings and *J. R. Turner* (S&T), Caldwell, Kansas. Loan of specimens. Mr. Stallings also checked the manuscript and illustrations for the Megathymidae and furnished additional assistance on this family.

Fred T. Thorne (FTT), El Cajon, California. Loan of specimens.

Ronald S. Wielgus (RSW), Phoenix, Arizona. Loan of specimens.

Last, but surely not least, I wish to thank Clara Claasen, Editor of Doubleday, who has given so much special attention to the special sort of editorial problems this book has presented.

WILLIAM H. HOWE

March 26, 1975   *Ottawa, Kansas 66067*

Contents

INTRODUCTION *by Harry K. Clench*

THE BUTTERFLIES OF NORTH AMERICA

PAPILIONOIDEA

CONTENTS

HESPERIOIDEA

INTRODUCTION

INTRODUCTION

HARRY K. CLENCH

What is a butterfly?

Butterflies and moths are scaly winged insects that make up the great order *Lepidoptera.* It is popularly thought that they are easily told apart. In actual fact butterflies and moths are quite similar, so the first order of business is to learn to distinguish between them.

All *butterflies* have antennae with a *club* or swelling at the tip. They never have the fore and hind wings coupled by a frenulum (see below), except for males of a single Australian skipper. Nearly all butterflies are *diurnal,* flying by day. A few are *crepuscular,* flying at dusk.

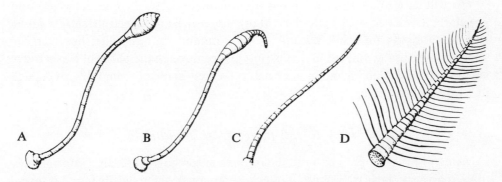

Figure 1. Antennae of Lepidoptera. A, B, butterflies; C, D, moths. A, *Euphydryas;* B, *Hesperia;* C, generalized filiform antenna of a moth; D, generalized pectinate antenna of a moth.

Moths have antennae of a variety of shapes: *filiform,* slender and unbranched, tapering to a fine point; *pectinate,* finely branched, looking almost like a tiny feather; or *clubbed.* Most moths have the fore wings and hind wings of each side linked together by a *frenulum.* This is a single, usually large, bristle or a cluster of smaller bristles, arising at the base of the leading edge of the hind wing. The frenulum is caught loosely in the *retinaculum,* a loop of chitin or fan of scales, or both, on the underside of the fore wing near its base. Most moths are *nocturnal,* flying by night, but some are crepuscular, and a surprising number are diurnal.

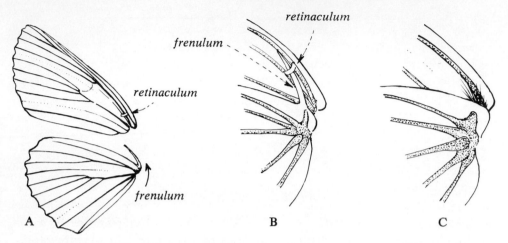

Figure 2. Frenulum and retinaculum of moths: A, entire wings of a male *Catocala lacrymosa* (Noctuidae), showing frenulum and retinaculum; B, detail of bases of wings of male; C, detail of bases of wings of female.

In addition to these traits, no butterfly has a tympanum, or hearing organ, but many moths do: situated on each side of the posterior part of the thorax or of the base of the abdomen.

You will notice that no mention has been made of color, the one character most popularly associated with butterflies. Many butterflies are indeed brightly colored, and many moths are assuredly dull. A large number of butterflies, however, are almost as dull as the dingiest of moths (just glance through the plates of Hesperiidae and Satyridae) and many moths are brightly colored, some of them brilliant enough to rival any butterfly.

How to tell males from females

Distinguishing the sexes of butterflies is often surprisingly difficult. Unfortunately there is no easy single way, short of direct examination of the mostly internal sexual organs. Each group must be learned by itself.

The easy ones. In many groups of butterflies males have patches of *androconia,* or special scent scales of peculiar form (Fig. 16), on their wings and in these groups the sexes are readily distinguished. Some of the Satyridae have such contrasting patches of androconia on the males, usually on the upperside of the fore wing. Nearly all the hesperiine skippers have males with a *"brand"* or *stigma,* a diagonal stripe (rarely a patch) of androconia, usually black or black and gray, again on the upper-side of the fore wing. Males of almost all hairstreaks have an oval or circular patch near the fore wing cell-end, generally called the *scent patch* if it is of vague outline and if there is no modification of the underlying wing membrane, or *scent pad* (also *stigma*) if it is sharply outlined and there is a thickened underlying area on the wing membrane. Occasional Pieridae have males with androconial scaling on the fore wing upperside, contrasting with the other scaling in texture and reflectivity, and some have a scent patch on the hind wing upperside near the base of the costa (*Nathalis,* some *Colias*). Male Danaidae have a patch or pouch of androconia on the hind wing upperside on vein Cu_2. Males of some pyrgine skippers have a *costal fold* containing androconial scales. This fold, however, is erratic in its appearance: it may be present in one species and absent in a near relative. Some Nymphalidae, chiefly *Speyeria,* have stripes of black androconia along the veins of the fore wing upperside.

The blues, many pierids, a number of skippers, some papilionids and some nymphalids do not have such conspicuous structural differences between the sexes but do have more or less conspicuous color or pattern differences. Nearly all blues (Lycaenidae) have very blue uppersides in males and much less blue, or none at all, in females. In *Colias* (Pieridae) males nearly always have sharp-edged, solid black borders above, while in females the borders are diffused and usually have yellow spots within. In *Papilio glaucus* and some others of the genus (Papilionidae) the female has a series of postmedian blue patches on the hind wing above that are absent in males. Males of the nymphalid, *Speyeria diana,* are orange above; females are blue.

In a number of species the female is dimorphic, and one of its two forms is usually radically different from the male. Most *Colias,* for example, have some females yellow, like the males, and some white. A white *Colias* is almost 100% likely to be a female. White male *Colias* are known but exceedingly rare. Female *Papilio glaucus* may be yellow, like the male, or entirely suffused with gray-brown, nearly black. A "black" *glaucus* is always a female. *Poanes hobomok,* a hesperiine skipper without a brand in the male, has some females orange like the males and some largely fuscous, the so-called female form "pocahontas."

The hard ones. In many butterflies—some papilionids, pierids, most nymphalids, some lycaenids, some satyrids, some megathymids, and a number of both pyrgine and hesperiine skippers—the sexes are largely without special, obvious distinguishing traits. The color and pattern of one sex are nearly identical to those of the other, and there are no visible male androconial patches. In most of these females tend to be a little larger than males, to have heavier abdomens, and to have more rounded wings. In most groups, especially satyrids and papilionids, the end of the abdomen is characteristic: the paired valvae of the male are distinctive and their ends, pressed together, form a vertical or longitudinal slit at the end. The female abdomen tends to have a more pointed end, and on the underside, just before the tip, a small, usually transverse, slit-like aperture (the vagina) is present. These traits are often visible to the naked eye but may sometimes require a lens. In North America all Libytheidae, Riodinidae and Lycaenidae have the fore legs much reduced in the males as compared with the females. With a little practice, and comparison of specimens of known sex, you can distinguish the sexes surely by this trait, but a lens or (better) a dissecting microscope is necessary.

Life history

Like most other insects a butterfly passes through four very different stages in the course of its life: egg, larva, pupa, and adult.

Egg. The egg is a compact, single unit, affixed on the proper food plant by the female. It is the structure within which the embryo develops from a single, just-fertilized cell to a small but highly organized larva. This process takes place in a few days, usually ten or so if development proceeds without delay. Some butterflies, however, may overwinter in this stage.

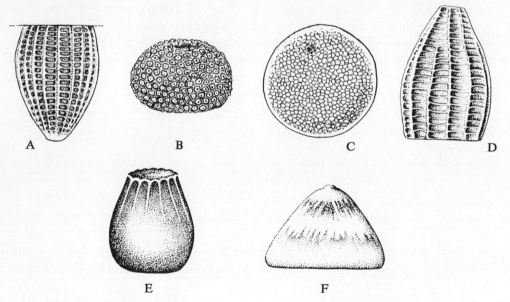

Figure 3. Eggs of different butterflies. A, *Danaus plexippus* (after Scudder); B, *Eumaeus atala* (after Rawson); C, *Euptychia mitchellii* (after Hubbell); D, *Anthocharis midea* (after Scudder); E, *Euphydryas phaeton* (after Scudder); F, *Atrytone arogos* (after Howe).

Butterfly eggs are heavy shelled and are usually a millimeter or so in diameter. They differ considerably in form and structure, so much so that if we knew them well enough we might be able to identify most butterflies to species from the egg alone. Some eggs are nearly spherical and smooth; others are wider than high ("turban-shaped") and with an elaborate surface sculpture; still others are higher than wide, more or less barrel or vase shaped, with longitudinal ribs and often cross ribs. Every egg has a small opening or pore at the summit, the *micropyle,* through which the sperm entered to fertilize it.

Larva. The primary function of the larva, or caterpillar, is growth, and eating is almost its sole activity. It grows exponentially in weight and at maturity is many times as heavy as when it first emerged from the egg.

Larvae are elongated and "wormlike." Each has a head, a three segmented thorax and a ten segmented abdomen. The *head* is heavily sclerotized and globular. On each side it bears a row of several, usually six, simple eyes (*ocelli*), a minute three segmented *antenna,* and a small *palpus.* There is a median "upper lip" (*labrum*) and a median "lower lip" (*labium*) which bears a median *spinneret* or silk extruding organ. Between these is a pair of massive, heavily sclerotized *mandibles,* each bearing a few strong, relatively large teeth: basic equipment for consuming quantities of food. The *thorax* has on each of its three segments a pair of multiple segmented true legs, each ending in a single claw. The *abdomen,* which hardly differs in appear-

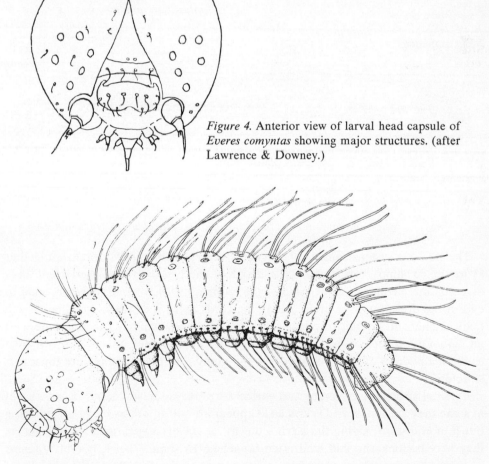

Figure 4. Anterior view of larval head capsule of *Everes comyntas* showing major structures. (after Lawrence & Downey.)

Figure 5. First instar larva of *Everes comyntas* showing major structures. (after Lawrence & Downey.)

ance from the thorax, has a series of false legs (*prolegs*), one pair each on the third, fourth, fifth, sixth and last (tenth) segments, the terminal pair called the *anal prolegs.* Each proleg bears on its plantar surface a series of tiny hooks, the *crotchets,* that enable the larva to grip silk threads or the surface or the edge of a leaf. On the first thoracic segment, and on each abdominal segment except the last two, is a pair of lateral *spiracles* which open into the internal tracheal system of air conducting tubes and tubules by which the larva breathes.

The internal anatomy of a caterpillar is basically simple. Not surprising in an animal whose life is spent eating, a larva is almost entirely a massive digestive tract. This tract is a tube comprising an *esophagus,* an enormous *mid intestine,* a small *hind intestine* and a terminal *rectum.* The circulatory system is simply an open dorsal tube with a pulsatile region (the *heart* or *dorsal aorta*) that pumps the blood forward, where it flows out the end of the tube and makes its way back through the body cavity to reenter the tube, partly at the tube's posterior end and partly through small lateral slits (*ostia*).

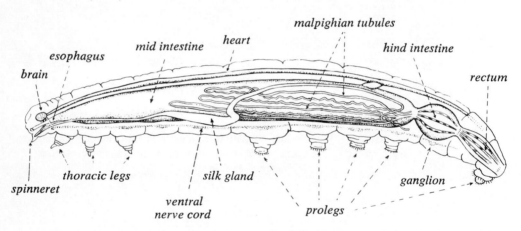

Figure 6. Major internal organs of larva of *Danaus plexippus.* (after Scudder.)

The nervous system consists of a pair of ventral nerve cords, so close together as to appear almost one, running the length of the body. At the anterior end they diverge, one passing on either side of the esophagus, then come together again to end in the dorsal, minute brain. Along the cords there is a pair of ganglia at each body segment from which branches diverge. The body wall is covered inside with an elaborate system of muscles. There are, of course, other internal organs, such as the malpighian tubules and the large silk gland, but the foregoing are the major structures.

External structures are many and varied. Most larvae have "hairs" or *spines,* but in some they are so few and sparse as to appear absent; in others they may be dense but thin and short, giving the larva a downy or velvety appearance; in still others they may be long and stiff, and often branched, In some species, notably *Danaus plexippus* and its relatives, there are one or more pairs of soft, fleshy *tubercles* of unknown function. The larvae of the Papilionidae have on the back, right behind the head, an eversible Y- or V-shaped organ, the *osmeterium*. Normally concealed, it is everted when the larva is annoyed or roughly handled. It emits a powerful, repugnant odor that is undoubtedly a defense mechanism, and probably an extremely effective one at that. The larvae of many Lycaenidae have posterior dorsal eversible "honey dew" glands that secrete a sugary liquid attractive to ants. Larval heads are mostly unadorned by special structures, but in some species they have various types of rigid *horns* or other processes.

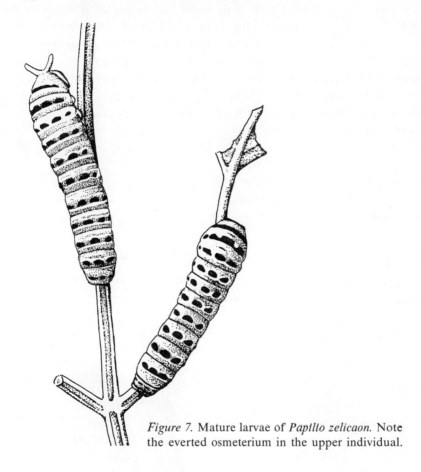

Figure 7. Mature larvae of *Papilio zelicaon.* Note the everted osmeterium in the upper individual.

A larva passes through a series of stages as it matures. At the end of each stage (*instar*) it casts off the old exoskeleton (*ecdysis* [compare "ecdysiast!"]) and for a short time thereafter the larva grows rapidly, then slows as it approaches the next ecdysis. The reason is simple: the exoskeleton is made of chitin, thin over the body but very thick on the head. Chitin, thick or thin, is not elastic and so cannot stretch after it has hardened. In order to increase in size, then, the larva must grow rapidly as soon as its old "skin" is cast off, until the new one has hardened. Most larvae complete four or five instars from hatching to maturity. As they do so they often change considerably in appearance.

Pupa. The *pupa* (*chrysalis*), like the egg, has a hard protective shell, and also like the egg it is fixed, sometimes immovably, to one spot. Compact and deceptively lifeless in appearance, it conceals a vast amount of remarkable activity inside. The life of a larva is utterly different from that of an adult, and the two require very different bodies to pursue these ends. A larva must chew and digest large amounts of solid food—usually leaves—while an adult butterfly lives solely on a liquid diet. A larva is a sexless, nearly sightless landlubber, while a butterfly's main purpose is procreation, and it spends much of its active life flying, for which it needs both eyes and wings. In some manner, therefore, the great digestive tract of the larva must be reduced; the massive jaws, no longer needed, must be gotten rid of; the eyes and the brain must be enlarged to cope with the complex visual and chemical signals soon to be needed and the more complex life the adult will lead; sex organs must be added; wings, and the muscles to propel them, must be provided. All of this takes place in the pupa. Incredibly it can occur in as few as ten days or even less. Most of the larval organs dissolve (*histolysis*) and the resulting fluid reforms (*histogenesis*) about small primordia of adult organs that had grown inside the developing larva. A remarkable event indeed!

The pupae of most butterflies are attached to the substrate by the *cremaster,* a few hooks at the end of the abdomen that are caught in a small pad of silk that the larva spun just before transforming. In addition, the pupae of many butterflies

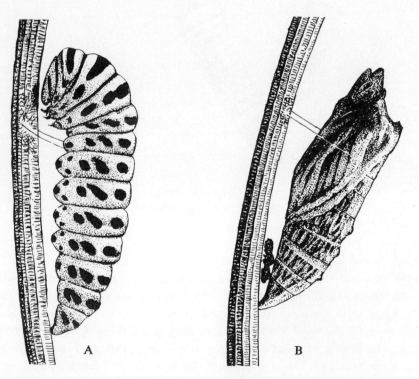

Figure 8. A, larva of *Papilio zelicaon* transforming to a chrysalis; B, the same individual, transformation completed (note the cast larval "skin" near the posterior end).

have a *girdle* or stout strand of silk looped over the back and attached to the surface beneath, like a window washer's belt.

Because of its hard covering (on which many of the body structures of the adult can be seen, fitted together like pieces of a three dimensional jigsaw puzzle), a subsidiary function of the pupa may be to carry the insect through the winter or through dry seasons. Like the egg, it is well designed to prevent the loss of water. Many butterflies, however, spend the winter in other stages.

Adult.   The *adult* (or *imago*) stage, as already noted, has reproduction as its primary function. The relatively long life and the many activities of an adult butterfly, however, require it to be much more than a simple reproducing mechanism,

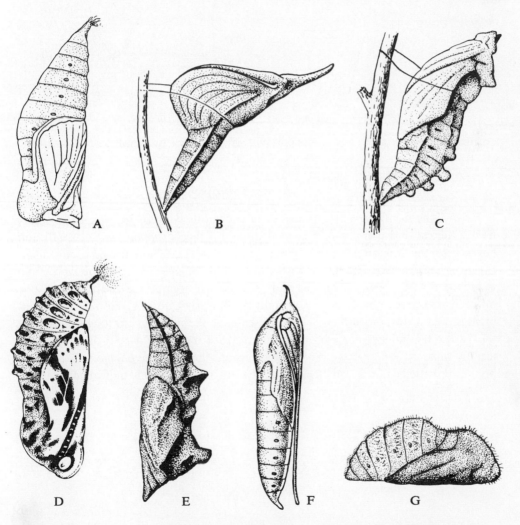

Figure 9. Pupae of various butterflies. A, *Euptychia mitchellii* (after Hubbell); B, *Phoebis sennae* (after Christman); C, *Battus philenor* (after Christman); D, *Euphydryas chalcedona* (after Essig); E, *Polygonia satyrus* (after Scudder); F, *Calpodes ethlius* (after Chittenden); G, *Callophrys henrici* (after Downey).

and its body is therefore rather complex. Like the larva it once was, a butterfly has three major parts: a head, a thorax and an abdomen. But there the resemblance ends. Each of these parts is far more elaborate and complicated than it was in the larva. If we skimmed over the larval structures rather briefly, not so here: we must go into considerable detail on the structures of an adult butterfly, not only because the subject is interesting, but because so many of these parts figure extensively in butterfly classification.

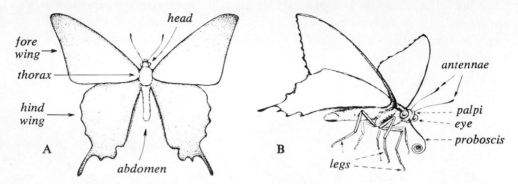

Figure 10. Major structures of an adult butterfly (*Papilio*). A, dorsal view; B, lateral view.

Adult morphology

Head. The adult *head* is dominated by enormous compound eyes, each nearly hemispherical and composed of several thousand facets (*ommatidia*) or small unit "eyes." At the junctures of the ommatidia minute hairs sometimes occur. Their function is unknown. The top of the head behind the eyes is called the *vertex* and is provided with a pair of curious and little-known organs, the *chaetosemata,* one on each side. Each chaetosema is a slight swelling that bears numerous short, stiff bristles, like a tiny pincushion. They are scaleless themselves, but long scales from the vertex behind usually arch over them. More mesially located on the vertex, usually more or less near the inner, upper eye margin, are the *antennae,* sometimes popularly called "horns" or "feelers." They are usually about half as long as the

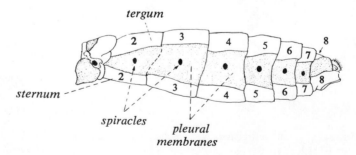

Figure 11. Abdomen of a butterfly (*Danaus plexippus*) denuded to show major structures. (after Ehrlich & Ehrlich.)

fore wing, and each consists of a globular *scape* (the single basalmost segment), an inconspicuous *pedicel* (the next segment), and a *flagellum* (all the rest). In butterflies the flagellum consists of a *shaft* and a terminal *club*. Beyond the club in most Hesperiidae and Megathymidae is a tiny, pointed continuation, usually bent at right angles, the *apiculus*. The flagellum is usually scaled, but various parts remain scaleless: sometimes the entire distal portion of the antenna; sometimes the ventral portion of the shaft and most of the club; sometimes only part of the club, in which case the scaleless part is often called the *nudum*. The club itself consists of the several enlarged terminal segments of the flagellum. Sometimes these are abruptly enlarged to form a striking and delimited club; sometimes the distal enlargement of the segments is so gradual that it is impossible to say precisely where the club begins;

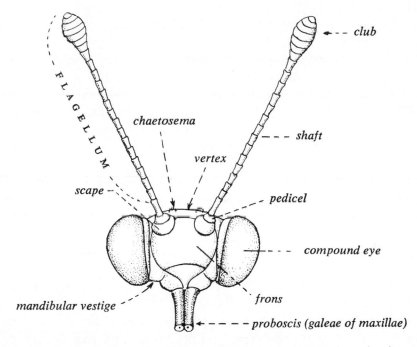

Figure 12. Head of a butterfly (*Danaus plexippus*) in anterior view, showing major structures. The head has been denuded of scales and the large labial palpi removed.

and in some the enlargement is so slight that the club is barely perceptible. The structure of the antennae, including the presence or absence of ventral ridges (*carinae*), or of various ventral pits, or scaleless patches, is important in higher classification.

Between the two eyes in front is the scaled surface called the *frons,* and at its ventral end is the buccal cavity where the mouthparts arise. These consist chiefly of a median *proboscis* and a pair of flanking *labial palpi*. The proboscis is a long sucking tube ("tongue") composed of two interlocking halves, one of the major distinctions of the order Lepidoptera. When not in use it is carried coiled up tightly

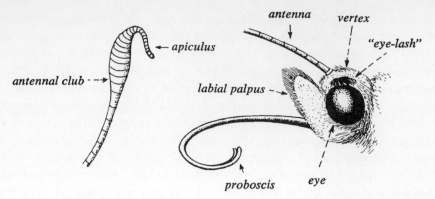

Figure 13. Head of a hesperiid butterfly (*Thorybes bathyllus*) showing major structures. Antennal club is to left.

between the palpi; in use it is extended to probe into flowers for nectar, or to suck up other liquids. On either side of the proboscis are the labial palpi, often called simply "the palpi." These are three-segmented appendages covered with scales and often bristles. The palpi are usually about one or two eye diameters in length, but in the Libytheidae they are enormous, particularly in our species, where they are about five eye diameters long, projecting beak-like far beyond the head. The libytheids are called "snout butterflies" for good reason!

Thorax. The thorax is the second major subdivision of the body, and in many ways the most complex. It consists of three segments, the prothorax, the mesothorax, and the metathorax. Each of these segments is composed of a dorsal *tergum,* a ventral *sternum,* and on each side a lateral *pleuron;* and each of these parts in turn is comprised of a number of sclerites. The thorax bears two important sets of appendages: the wings (one pair, the fore wings or primaries, on the mesothorax, one pair, the hind wings or secondaries, on the metathorax) and the legs (one pair on each of the three segments).

The internal anatomy of the thorax is relatively simple: the dorsal aorta, the digestive tract, the ventral nerve chord and the tracheae all pass through it. The major part of the interior, however, is filled with the massive muscles that power the legs and, most important, the wings.

The *wings,* large in proportion to body size, are roughly triangular in outline, the hind wing being usually somewhat more rounded than the fore wing. Each wing consists of a double membrane. The two layers are separate in early pupal development but later they fuse together to form a single transparent sheet. Through the wing run several veins, more or less radiating from the wing base. Like the rest of the body both surfaces of the wing are covered with minute, flattened, overlapping scales (a major distinction of the Lepidoptera), whose colors form the mosaic wing pattern.

The wings are particularly important in taxonomy and identification. The various terms for the wing parts are much used and should be familiar to anyone who works

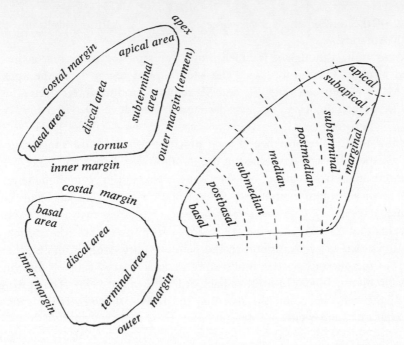

Figure 14. Wings of a generalized butterfly showing areas used in description.

with butterflies. These terms can be divided into four sets: wing areas, wing outline, wing veins, and pattern.

The wings, as already noted, are roughly triangular in shape. Each angle has received its own name: the *base* (nearest the body), the *apex* (the outer forward angle) and the *tornus* or *anal angle* (outer posterior angle). The margins between these angles are also specially named: the *costa* (between base and apex), the *termen* (between apex and tornus) and the *inner margin* or *dorsum* (between tornus and base). The latter on the hind wing is sometimes called the *abdominal,* or *anal, margin.* The central area of the wing is called the *median* area or *disc.* Various regions of the wing are identified in relation to these landmarks: *costal* (along the costa), *subcostal* (near the costa), *apical* (at the apex), *subapical* (near the apex), *terminal, subterminal, postdiscal, postmedian* and so on. The wing surfaces themselves, like all parts of the insect, are called *dorsal* (upper) or *ventral* (lower). The dorsal surface of the wings is commonly called the *upperside,* the ventral surface the *underside.*

The outline of the wings is extremely characteristic in many groups. The Heliconiidae are long winged; many Satyridae (such as *Coenonympha* and many *Euptychia*) are round winged; the swallowtails and many hairstreaks have quite straight sided wings; the species of *Polygonia* ("anglewings") have exceptionally irregular wings. Generally there are no special names for these variations, but two traits are distinguished by special terms, and a third ought to be.

When the apex of the fore wing is produced to a point that extends well beyond the level of the termen the wing is called *falcate,* a condition rarely encountered in North America.

A second trait, although it is much more frequent, for some reason has never acquired a name. On the fore wing the whole apical region from the apex down to vein M_1 or to between veins M_1 and M_2 may be produced, in extreme instances almost like a tab at the wing apex. It is particularly well developed in many Nymphalidae.

The third trait is the presence of long processes on the hind wings called *tails.* These are especially well developed in the Papilionidae, hence the name "swallowtails," and in many Lycaenidae, but they appear also in the Nymphalidae and even in blunt, atypical form in some Pieridae. Some of the pyrgine skippers have extremely long tails.

The veins that traverse the wing are basically simple, few branched, thick walled hollow tubes that (a) give support to the wing; (b) are conduits for tracheae and branches of the nervous system, innervating various sensory cells on the wing; and (c) carry circulating blood. In front-to-back order the major veins of each wing, each arising in the wing base, are the *subcosta,* the *radius,* the *media,* the *cubitus* and several *anal* or *vannal* veins.

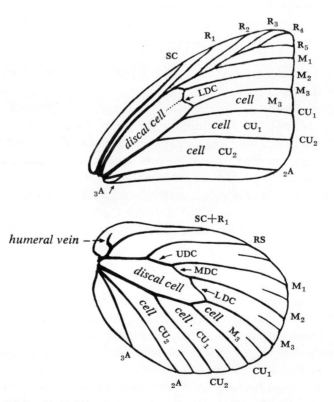

Figure 15. Wings of a generalized butterfly identifying veins and interspaces (see text).

On the fore wing these are as follows:

Subcosta (Sc): unbranched.

Radius (R): primitively five branched (R_1, R_2, etc.), but in many groups one or more may be missing, and sometimes R_1 may be partly fused with Sc.

Media (M): always three branched (M_1, M_2, M_3); M_1 is sometimes partly fused with R_5.

Cubitus (Cu): always two branched (Cu_1, Cu_2).

Anal or *Vannal* veins (*A* or *V*): primitively there are three in butterflies (1A, 2A, 3A; or 1V, 2V, 3V), but only 2A is always fully developed. The base of vein 1A appears in Papilionidae, and the course of the lost distal part can be traced in most butterflies through the middle of the Cu_2-2A interspace, often producing twinned spots or marks in that interspace (as in the postmedian spots on the underside of the fore wing of many blues, or the subterminal white spots of *Limenitis archippus*). Vein 3A is often absent entirely; even when present it is confined to the extreme base of the wing.

On the hind wing the veins are:

Humerus (Hum): a short spur vein in the extreme base near the costa, found in some groups (occasionally being forked: T- or Y-shaped), but not all.

Subcosta: in pupal wing development it can be seen that the first branch of the radius unites with this vein throughout, so the simple-appearing vein in the adult is actually a compound vein, symbolized as $Sc+R_1$.

Radial sector (Rs): in many groups of insects vein R_1 arises distinctly before the remaining branches of the radius and the latter are collectively called the Radial sector. In butterflies the latter is always unbranched on the hind wing.

Media (M): always three branched as on the fore wing, but M_2 may rarely be faint and underdeveloped.

Cubitus (Cu): always two branched as on the fore wing.

Anal or *Vannal* veins: 1A is always absent, as on the fore wing; 2A is always present, as on the fore wing; 3A is absent in most Papilionidae but present in all other butterflies.

Many entomologists believe that veins Cu_1 and Cu_2 as described above are really both branches of Cu_1, and therefore should be designated Cu_{1a} and Cu_{1b}; while in many moth families what has been called the first anal vein, 1A, is really vein Cu_2. These changes have been widely followed by British and European entomologists but have not yet gained wide acceptance in North America

In most Satyridae and a few Nymphalidae one or more of the basal veins on the fore wing are greatly swollen and bulbous. The function of these inflated veins is not known.

In addition to the above there is a vein on each wing that follows the margin all around: the *peripheral vein*. It is of value to the butterfly, but not to the taxonomist.

A conspicuous part of the venation of each wing is the *discal cell*, sometimes called the *discoidal cell*. This is an elongate space, more or less completely bounded by veins, from the base to about the middle of the wing. The discal cell on the fore

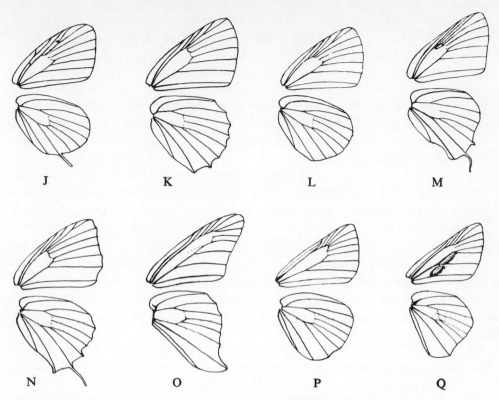

Figure 16. Venation of selected butterflies. A, *Papilio* (Papilionidae); B, *Parnassius* (Papilionidae); C, *Colias* (Pieridae); D, *Pieris* (Pieridae); E, *Danaus* (Danaidae); F, *Euptychia* (Satyridae); G, *Heliconius* (Heliconiidae); H, *Speyeria* (Nymphalidae), I, *Calephelis* (Riodinidae); J, *Everes* (Lycaenidae); K, *Lycaena* (Lycaenidae); L, *Celastrina* (Lycaenidae); M, *Satyrium* (Lycaenidae); N, *Hypaurotis* (Lycaenidae); O, *Epargyreus* (Hesperiidae); P, *Erynnis* (Hesperiidae); Q, *Hesperia* (Hesperiidae).

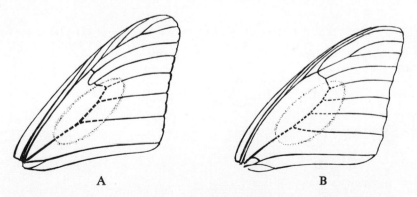

Figure 17. "Cubitus trifid" and "cubitus quadrifid" (circled areas). A, *Danaus:* cubitus apparently three-branched or "trifid"; B, *Papilio:* cubitus apparently four-branched or "quadrifid."

wing lies near the costa; that on the hind wing is about equidistant between costa and inner margin, and hence nearly central in the wing. Anteriorly the discal cell is bounded by the main stem of the radius and posteriorly by the main stem of the cubitus. Its distal end is formed by a series of cross-veins: one between radius and media (*r-m cross-vein;* also called the *upper discocellular, udc*), one between the bases of M_1 and M_2 (*middle discocellular, mdc*), and one between the bases of M_2 and M_3 (*lower discocellular, ldc*). The cross-vein between media and cubitus (*m-cu*) has otherwise no special designation. Sometimes the cell is "open:" the lower discocellular is absent (e.g., *Limenitis*).

In the development of the wings in the pupal stage the base of the media runs through the middle of the discal cell; but this part of the vein usually becomes suppressed in the adult. In some groups its distal end may persist in the discal cell, where it is then called the *recurrent vein.* Occasionally the suppressed parts of the media can be traced as faint folds in the cell. The remaining parts of the wing are viewed, for purposes of description, as cells or *interspaces,* bounded by veins. Such a cell or interspace may be identified in either of two ways: by the vein that forms its anterior border, or by designating both bounding veins. The interspace between veins M_1 and M_2, for example, would be called either "interspace M_1" or "interspace M_1-M_2."

In some groups vein M_2 appears more closely associated with M_1 than M_3, and the cubitus appears to have three branches (M_3, Cu_1, Cu_2). This condition is sometimes described as "cubitus trifid:" incorrect (because it comprises part of the media), but occasionally vivid and helpful. In contrast, other groups may have M_2 more closely associated with M_3, so that the cubitus appears to have four branches, and may then be called "cubitus quadrifid:" equally incorrect but similarly helpful.

The color pattern on the wings of butterflies is probably more genetically complex than that of any other group of organisms. It has, in fact, achieved the state of being a morphological structure. Through whole families homologies of various pattern elements can be traced. As yet, however, there has been little success in establishing homologies among families and therefore no single scheme of pattern terminology

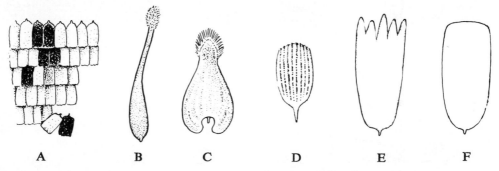

A   B   C   D   E   F

Figure 18. Wing scales. A, shingle-like arrangement of wing scales, *Papilio glaucus;* B, androconial scale, *Cercyonis pegala;* C, androconial scale, *Pieris rapae;* D, androconial scale, *Everes comyntas;* E, wing scale with toothed distal end; F, wing scale with entire distal end.

has been widely accepted. Such terms as are in general use are merely descriptive.

Butterfly wing patterns are true mosaics: the often extremely intricate and multi-colored designs are built of vast numbers of minute scales, each of only one color. These colors are of two fundamentally different types: *biochromes* or pigments, and *schemochromes* or structural or interference colors.

Biochromes are responsible for many colors, ranging from black through brown, red, orange, yellow to white. Frequently encountered pigment "families," each a group of chemically related pigment compounds, include *melanins* (blacks, browns, some reds), *pterins* (yellow, orange, red), *flavones* (ivory to deep yellow).

Schemochromes, in butterflies, are primarily the result of the ultramicroscopic division of the scale walls into thin sheets with fine air spaces between them. Schemochromes include iridescent purples, blues and greens. Often the color varies with the angle of incidence of the light and of the sight of the observer (e.g., in *Atlides halesus*) and frequently the color itself is perceptible only over narrow ranges of these angles. In some groups a schemochrome overlies a conspicuous biochrome, with spectacular effect.

Although green pigment occurs in some moths it is either absent or very rare in butterflies, and is found in none of ours. The green color in groups such as *Callophrys* (Lycaenidae) is a schemochrome; in *Anthocharis* and *Euchloe* (Pieridae) the marbled greens of the underside are produced by an optical blending of a mixture of black and yellow scales, both biochromes.

A final coloring effect is transparency. The wing membrane is thin and colorless. In some groups spots or patches on the wing are scaleless on both surfaces and hence transparent. This occurs most commonly among our species in the Hesperiidae. Transparency is more extensive in some tropical Satyridae and Ithomiidae, and in the sphingid (moth) genus *Hemaris*.

The wing pattern is produced by localized areas of contrasting shade or color. Ancestrally the most important of these areas consisted of dark transverse lines on a lighter ground color. The number and disposition of these lines is primitively the same on both surfaces of both wings and is basically constant at least within certain families and possibly within every family. Perhaps, in fact, a single basic pattern schema will be found applicable to all butterflies, although this remains to be done. The schema that Schwanwitsch (1924) developed for the Nymphalidae is among the best known.

The incredible array of patterns we see in the butterflies today all stem from evolutionary modifications of these relatively few primitive lines and the intervals of ground color between them. These modifications are many and usually complexly combined. They include (1) changes of color, both of lines and of ground color; (2) changes in thickness of lines; (3) changes of position of the lines as wholes, or of line segments separately; (4) changes in structural complexity of the lines themselves; (5) zonal changes of color and thickness (i.e., changes in certain areas of the wings only); and (6) differential wing surface changes, resulting in the fore wing being different from the hind wing, or the upperside different from the underside.

The *legs* are the second set of thoracic appendages. As in all insects there are

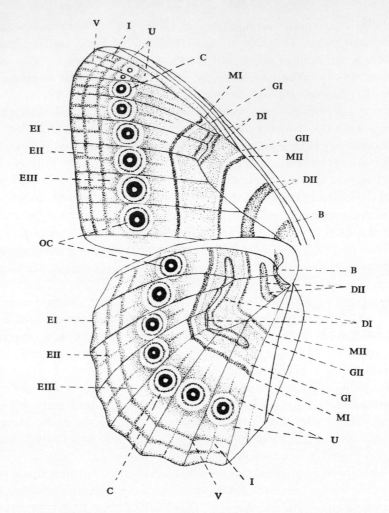

Figure 19. Nymphaloid wing pattern prototype schema. The abbreviations are: B, Basalis; C, Circulus; DI, Discalis I; DII, Discalis II; EI, Externa I; EII, Externa II; EIII, Externa III; GI, Granulata I; GII, Granulata II; I, Intervenosa; MI, Media I; MII, Media II; OC, Ocellata (eye spot); U, Umbra; V, Venosa. (after Schwanwitsch 1924, with his terminology.)

three pairs of them, one pair on each segment. The basic structure of these legs is the same: each consists of a series of segments, beginning with the *coxa* next to the body, then a *trochanter.* Both of these are short and rarely seen except under close study. If you should remove a leg from a butterfly the chances are that you would have only the next segments: the *femur,* the *tibia* and the *tarsus.* The first two of these are long and slender; the last is divided into five subsegments or *tarsomeres.* The first tarsomere, usually longer than the other four, is often called the *basitarsus.* At the end of the tarsus is a pair of terminal *claws* with an *arolium* between them and sometimes a pair of flanking *paronychia.* The tibia often bears

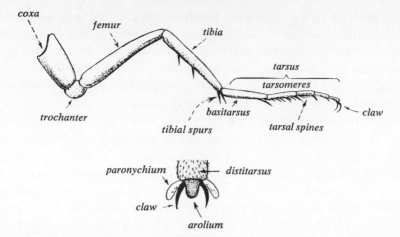

Figure 20. Leg of *Papilio polyxenes* showing major structures. Inset shows enlarged view of end of tarsus.

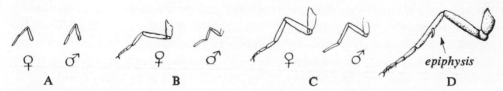

Figure 21. Fore legs of various butterflies. A, Nymphalidae (strongly reduced in both sexes); B, Riodinidae (female normal, male strongly reduced); C, Lycaenidae (female normal, male moderately reduced); D, Papilionidae (both sexes normal).

special structures, particularly terminal *spurs* (multicellular, articulating, spine-like processes): one pair in most butterflies, at the end of the tibia; two pairs in most Hesperiidae, one pair at the end and one pair just before the end; none at all in a few forms, such as the liphyrid *Feniseca tarquinius.* In addition to the spurs, the males of some Hesperiidae have, on the tibia of one leg on either side, a tuft of long hair-scales, the *tibial tuft* or *hair pencil.* (This curious, and in English almost nonsensical, term "hair pencil" probably arose from an inept translation of the German term for the same thing, *Haarpinsel,* which means an artist's paint brush, apt and descriptive indeed.)

The fore legs are always more or less modified. In all butterflies they are smaller than the other two pairs. In the Hesperioidea and in the Pieridae they are not otherwise different. In the Papilionidae the fore tibia has a curious blade-like appendage, the *epiphysis.* In the Lycaenidae the female fore leg is fully developed, though small, but in the male the tarsal subsegments are all fused together, claws included, into a single segment. In the Nymphalidae the fore legs of both sexes are extremely reduced, though somewhat differently in each sex, and are carried close to the body. The Libytheidae and Riodinidae have the fore legs of the male much reduced, as in the nymphalids, and those of the female nearly normal. Long ago this led to these two groups being combined, but it is now known that this similarity of fore leg structure has no such taxonomic significance: the libytheids are allied to the nymphalids, and the riodinids to the lycaenids.

Abdomen.   In comparison with the thorax the abdomen of a butterfly is a simple structure. In external view the abdomen (Fig. 9) is elongate and slender, sometimes nearly cylindrical but usually thicker in the middle than at either end. Most of the externally visible part consists of the eight pregenital segments. Each of these is composed of a strongly sclerotized *tergum,* or dorsal sclerite, an equally strongly sclerotized *sternum,* or ventral sclerite, with a *pleural membrane* between them on either side, in which the spiracle is located. These pregenital segments have no appendages and serve to house and protect the various internal organs: the digestive tract, the dorsal aorta, the ventral nerve cord, the tracheal system (with inlets at each spiracle), all as in the thorax. One additional system, however, is extremely important: the reproductive system, confined to the abdomen. This system, not unexpectedly, differs greatly in the two sexes. In both sexes the system consists partly of primary (internal) membranous structures and partly of secondary (external), mostly sclerotized, structures. The external genital structures, modified from the original ninth and tenth abdominal segments (which, accordingly, are often called the genital segments), are much used in classification and identification, particularly those of the male. This, incidentally, is not an example of male chauvinism, despite appearances. The external male genitalia are simply easier to dissect and study and usually have good, useful characters.

The *female genitalia* consist of two basic internal complexes which may be called the *primary genitalia,* for egg production and delivery, and the *bursa copulatrix,* for sperm reception and storage. Each has a separate opening to the outside. The primary genitalia consist of two ovaries, each a set of long tubules in which the eggs form and move down. The tubules of each ovary unite into a single *lateral oviduct,* and the two lateral oviducts in turn unite into a single *median* (or *common*) *oviduct.* Two *accessory glands* enter here, providing the adhesive material with which the eggs are attached when laid. The median oviduct then passes, via a section known as the vestibulum, to the outside (*ostium oviductus*) between the sclerotized *papillae anales* (highly modified ninth and tenth abdominal segments), just ventrad of the anus. The bursa copulatrix comprises a usually sclerotized *atrium,* opening (*ostium bursae*) on the eighth sternite, the surrounding specially structured sclerotized part of that sternite being the *genital plate* or *sterigma.* From the *atrium* the tube, now membranous, continues anteriorly as the *ductus bursae* and ends in a large sac, the *corpus bursae,* in which the sperm received in copulation are stored. The sperm are passed to the female enclosed in an elongate sac, the *spermatophore,* and this sac must be ruptured by the female to release the sperm. In the corpus bursae walls are one or more sclerotized structures, the *signa,* usually present and toothed, which appear to aid in rupturing the spermatophore(s).

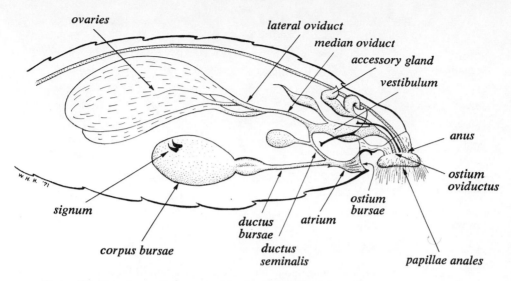

Figure 22. Female genital structures of a generalized butterfly. (after Klots 1970.)

Between the two complexes is a connecting tubule, the *ductus seminalis,* leading from the ductus bursae to the vestibulum. Sperm released from the spermatophore leave the corpus bursae, move down this tubule and fertilize the eggs as they pass down the oviduct. Rarely in some Pieridae a·fertilized egg may be retained in the vestibulum until hatching, when a so-called "live birth" may result.

The *male genitalia.* The visceral structures are quite simple and not unlike those of the female ovarian complex. Originally there were two *testes,* each with its own duct, the *vas deferens.* In butterflies, however, the two testes have fused into a single median globular structure. Two vasa deferentia, however, still leave this median structure, joining posteriorly to form a median *ejaculatory duct.* Just anterior to their union an accessory gland opens into each vas deferens, supplying the material with which the spermatophore is formed. The ejaculatory duct continues posteriorly and enters the penis, through which it passes to the outside.

Accessory to these primary reproductive organs is a complex of external sclerotized structures, the *genital capsule.* This complex is of extreme importance taxonomically and is usually what is meant when the term "male genitalia" is used in taxonomic writing. The base of the capsule is a sclerotized ring, the modified ninth segment, comprising the dorsal *tegumen,* the lateral and ventral *vinculum,* and a midventral anterior process, the *saccus.* Dorsally the *uncus,* the modified tenth tergite, is attached to the posterior edge of the tegumen, forming a sort of hood. It may be single lobed, usually ending in a hook, or bilobed. On either side at its base arises a pointed process or pair of processes, the modified tenth sternite, the *gnathos* or *falx* (pl.,

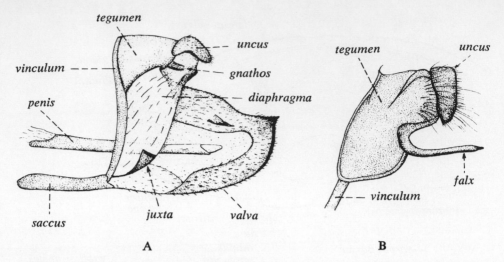

Figure 23. Male genitalia, showing major structures. A, generalized butterfly; B, dorsal structures of a lycaenid. (after Klots.)

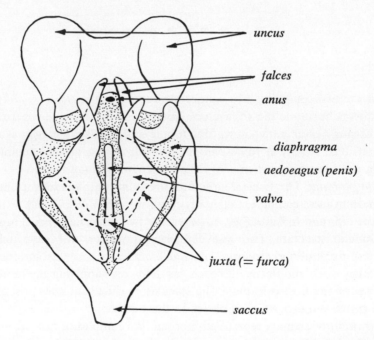

Figure 24. Male genitalia of a generalized lycaenid in ventral view. (after Ehrlich & Ehrlich.)

falces), that may be articulated or not, nearly straight or strongly curved. The anal opening lies just beneath the uncus, flanked by the gnathi. Sometimes the terminal membrane, just beneath the anus, has a small sclerotized area known as the *sub-scaphium.* On the ventral part of the capsule, articulating with the posterior edge of the vinculum, are the paired *valvae,* sometimes also called the *harpes,* the *harpa-*

gones, the *clasps,* or the *claspers.* These are derived from two primitive appendages, the *styli,* of the ninth segment. Of all parts of the genital capsule the valvae are probably the most taxonomically varied. They may be broad and rounded, or slender and elongate, or bifurcate, variously toothed or serrate, and sometimes provided with an articulating inner process. Between the bases of the valvae there often arises a median, usually forked, structure, the *furca* or *juxta.* In the Riodinidae it is usually firmly attached to the penis; in the other families they are separate. The furca apparently serves to guide the penis during copulation. The end of the abdomen is closed by a terminal membrane, the *diaphragma,* normally situated at about the level of the vinculum, which is provided with two openings: the anus, already mentioned, and the *penis* (also called the *phallus,* or *aedoeagus*). This is an elongated, slender, sclerotized tube. Its proximal end has an opening, either anterior or dorsal, where the ejaculatory duct enters. Inside is a membranous sleeve, everted during copulation, that is often provided with sclerotized structures, pointed rods or teeth, the *cornuti.*

In some Papilionidae, most notably the genus *Parnassius,* the male secretes a curious structure, the *sphragis,* onto the ventral part of the posterior abdomen of the female during copulation. It is claimed that it functions as a sort of "chastity belt," preventing a second mating by the female. Whether or not this is true, the configuration of the sphragis is species-specific and useful in classification and identification.

Butterfly biology

Mating. In order to mate successfully butterflies have to solve two major problems: a male and female must find one another; and they must be sure they are conspecific. Once these are done mating usually occurs.

Animals that range over an area large in proportion to their size could have serious difficulty finding each other and if they depended on random encounters many would never succeed in finding a mate. Location devices to improve the odds are essential. The phenomenon of broodedness, or voltinism discussed below, is one of these: it concentrates adults of some species into shorter periods of time. Congregating at flowers is also used, efficiently combining both feeding and mate location. Other species, such as the Cabbage Butterfly, may use a combination of highly visible, distinctive colors and flight patterns together with their usual limitation to particular habitat types. Individuals of even a small population dispersed in a large meadow would be readily seen by each other.

An important but still little studied location device is territorialism. It seems to work as follows, at least in some species. Both male and female recognize certain habitat configurations as suitable territories. Females wander from one to another of these areas in search of one that is occupied by a male. A male selects such a place and remains there, perhaps all day, perhaps only during a particular part of the day. When a butterfly, or often another insect, enters the territory it is investigated and identified by the occupying male. If it is another male of the same species it

Figure 25. A mated pair of *Graphium marcellus.* The upper individual is the male.

is chased away. If it is a female he begins courtship. If it is anything else he may give chase or simply abandon interest. Among the species that are territorial in this general manner are: *Thorybes pylades, Vanessa atalanta,* various *Hesperia* and *Limenitis archippus.*

A variant of this pattern which seems to be used by some species is a "common territory." Several males may occupy such a territory jointly and there wait for females to come.

After a male and female have found one another courtship begins. Butterfly courtship has one major objective: to insure that both individuals belong to the same species. Most butterflies live in a world with many more or less look-alikes and it is important to pick a conspecific partner. The device used, courtship, appears to be a sequence of alternating stimulus-response acts. The male makes a particular overt act that should elicit a particular reaction in the female. If she responds correctly he is then stimulated to make a second act, and so on. If each species has a distinctive sequence of these acts, which may be long or short, a conspecific pair will run through them correctly and then will copulate. If the pair is not conspecific, sooner or later a wrong answer will appear, the chain will be broken and the party is over. The acts involved seem to be in part behavioral, in part the release of odor (pheromones).

A female who for some reason is unreceptive to copulation may reject the first courtship overtures of a male. This *rejection reaction* may often be subtle, but one form is quite distinctive and has been seen in *Pieris rapae, Ascia monuste, Phoebis sennae* and possibly in a species of *Erynnis:* the female flattens her wings and elevates her abdomen vertically in the air at right angles to her thorax. Males that encounter such a response quickly desist from further courtship.

Copulation itself is a protracted process, lasting anywhere from a half hour up to several hours. The male employs the parts of his external genitalia, particularly the valvae, to engage firmly the end of the female abdomen, the penis enters the ostium bursae and the slow process of transferring the spermatophore begins. During copulation the pair rest on a branch or other perch and remain nearly motionless, facing in opposite directions. They are remarkably inconspicuous and relatively seldom seen.

If the pair is disturbed they will fly away, ponderously but with surprising speed. Only one of the two does the flying, and carries the other hanging passively from the end of its abdomen, wings folded together. Oddly, in most species and even most families the sex of the flying partner is consistently the same (Miller & Clench 1968). In the Pieridae and Danaidae the male flies; in the Satyridae and probably the Lycaenidae the female flies. In the Nymphalidae one sex may consistently fly in some species (*Phyciodes tharos,* female), while in others, such as *Speyeria nokomis,* either sex may fly.

The time of day in which copulation takes place varies considerably. In some species any daylight time is suitable if the weather is warm and sunny. In others mating may occur only in the late afternoon and evening.

Both males and females, at least in some species, are capable of mating more than once.

Broods (*voltinism*).   A *brood* (or *generation*) is a contemporary set of adults of a species or population. Typically they all represent the offspring of a single prior brood, but this is not always true. In *Celastrina pseudargiolus,* for instance, the spring brood produces offspring most of which will emerge as adults the following spring; but some of the progeny complete development rapidly and become adults of a summer brood, often called a *partial brood,* and these produce offspring which develop quickly into a late summer brood. These, in turn, produce young which will become adults the next spring. The spring brood in this species, therefore, is a mixture of "children" and "great grand-children" of the preceding spring brood.

Broods may occur in a surprisingly large variety of ways. Some butterflies have only one brood a year, regardless of where they are. Others may have one annual brood in the northern part of their range, two farther south, and so on. Certain species have discrete broods, with a marked interval between. Others have confluent broods, so that individuals may be seen anytime through the season. Some have brood patterns variously intermediate between these. In a number of species, especially in the genera *Nymphalis* and *Polygonia,* the brood that emerges in the fall flies briefly, then hibernates through the winter and flies again in the spring. They may even leave hibernation and fly on an exceptionally mild and sunny day in midwinter. Several arctic and subarctic Satyridae are biennial: they fly every other year, apparently taking two years to complete development. Oddly, in some of these species no individuals at all are on the wing in the intervening year.

Species or populations with only one brood a year are sometimes called *univoltine* or *monogoneutic;* those with two annual broods are called *bivoltine* or *digoneutic;* those with several broods are termed *multivoltine* or *polygoneutic.*

In the far north no butterfly has more than one brood in a year. In temperate localities the butterflies show a mixture: some are single brooded, some double or multiple; in tropical and subtropical areas most species are multiple brooded, and the broods often are confluent.

Life span.   We know very little about the length of life of an adult butterfly. Most broods in temperate regions have a flight period of from 30 to 40 days or so. Presumably no individual butterfly in a brood lives the full span of that time, but from the progressive worsening of condition through the course of the flight period we may suppose that some individuals can live up to 20 or 30 days. Several butterflies are believed to live no longer than about three or four days. Overwintering Monarchs, on the other hand, may possibly live up to six months.

Food habits.   The larvae of most species of butterflies are quite exacting in their choice of food. Many species are *host specific,* feeding only on one or a few closely related species of plants. Sometimes whole groups of butterflies favor a single family or a single genus of plants. Nearly all the Megathymidae, for example, can be divided into those that feed on *Agave* species and those that feed on *Yucca* species. Satyridae and Hesperiine skippers feed on grasses and sedges. The Pieridae and Lycaenidae have several trends of larval food choice in common: many members of each feed on Leguminosae; some of each feed on Ericaceae; and the only conifer-feeding butterflies in North America are the pierid genus *Neophasia* and some species of the lycaenid genus *Callophrys.* Many pierids, however, feed on Cruciferae, which lycaenids do not; and many lycaenids are oak feeders, which pierids are not. One butterfly, *Feniseca tarquinius,* does not feed on plants at all, but instead its larvae feed on woolly aphids.

The choice of larval food, of course, usually is not made by the larva but by its mother. She selects the plant and lays her eggs on it, and the larvae are stuck with it. Occasionally a female will blunder and lay one or more eggs on the wrong plant. The larvae usually die, but out of such mistakes a few probably work and ultimately become acceptable additional or substitute food plants. No doubt such successful "mistakes" in the past have given rise to the extensive diversity of larval food choice that now exists.

A much neglected aspect of butterfly nutrition is adult food choice. A larva feeds in order to grow; an adult butterfly feeds simply to obtain energy for its continued life and activity. It is possible, though not yet proved, that some butterflies may not feed at all as adults. The vast majority do, and among them we can distinguish many different kinds of food choice. Some species are exclusively nectar feeders, and are therefore important agents of plant pollination. They are seen only at flowers and many of them exercise a certain degree of preference for certain kinds, partly determined, of course, by what is available. *Satyrium calanus* shows marked preference for tall white flowers and avoids yellow flowers. *Amblyscirtes vialis* seems to prefer low, isolated, tiny flowers. In a general way common, large butterfly species favor common, large flowers with copious nectar. Certain flowers are known to be favorites of different kinds of butterflies: milkweeds (*Asclepias*) are favored by *Speyeria* and *Satyrium;* the purple flowers of vetch, and blue to purple flowers generally, are particularly visited by many Hesperiidae. The orange flowers of *Asclepias tuberosa* are a strong attractant for *Harkenclenus titus.* In the North *Rubus* flowers are much visited by many kinds of butterflies, but in Florida for some reason they are not. *Cercyonis oetus* is strongly attracted to flowers, particularly yellow ones.

Some butterflies rarely visit flowers. Such species, *Lethe portlandia* and most *Cercyonis,* for example, may feed at leaking tree sap, at carrion, dung, old urine patches on the ground. *Limenitis arthemis astyanax* has some very odd food choices, including all those just mentioned and in addition such things as the spittle of spittle bugs, fermented milk, and on occasion has been seen at the cold, presumably moist, ashes of old camp fires! Others, such as *Feniseca* (and *Hypaurotis* is suspected), may feed on the sugary secretions of aphids.

Certain butterflies, such as *Papilio* and *Celastrina,* have been seen "pumping:" imbibing water at moist ground and simultaneously ejecting or dripping it from the anus. It is suspected that this may have some nutritional or thermoregulatory function but nothing is really known about it.

Another curious trait has been seen in a number of skippers. They exude a drop of clear fluid from the anus onto the substrate (usually a person's finger, or even arm, but sometimes a stone or other object) and suck it up again. One guess is that they do this to acquire salts but, again, nothing is known.

Thermoregulation. It is now known that many of the so-called "cold blooded" animals are not really cold blooded at all. Instead of always conforming in temperature with their surroundings, as used to be thought, they maintain high and fairly uniform body temperatures while they are active by an assortment of behavioral acts, a practice called *behavioral thermoregulation.* Among the animals known to do this are the butterflies (Clench 1966).

A butterfly gains most of its heat by basking, which exposes its wings and body to the sun. Blood circulating in the wing veins is warmed and carried back to the body. Most butterflies use dorsal basking: they open their wings and expose the upper surfaces squarely to the sun. Some groups, such as *Colias,* use only lateral basking: they close their wings together and expose the under surfaces of one side squarely to the sun, even tilting to one side, if necessary, to accomplish this.

As soon as the sun is high enough in the morning a butterfly begins basking in order to build up its body temperature to operating level as soon as possible. In late afternoon, as long as the sun is shining with any intensity, it continues to bask, presumably maintaining flight capability for as long as possible. On cool days it will bask at every opportunity.

Not all thermoregulation is concerned with gaining heat. On hot days a butterfly will spend much of its time keeping cool. It may orient itself so that the edge of its folded wings is directed at the sun, thus keeping irradiation to a minimum, or it may force air in and out of the abdomen rapidly and deeply, the butterfly equivalent of panting. It may spend time drinking at a mud puddle or moist earth, drawing in cool water. The "pumping" mentioned above may have something to do with this. Finally, a butterfly may seek shade.

Enemies.   Butterfly larvae have many enemies and mortality is probably greater in this stage than any other. Most larval losses are caused by disease, parasites, predators, weather and accidents.

Little is known about diseases in butterfly larvae. Most of them are probably of viral origin. Two types of virus diseases, nuclear polyhedrosis and granulosis, are common and produce similar symptoms: the interior of the caterpillar liquefies, so that the body of the dead caterpillar appears as a limp sac of fluid. Butterfly larvae have been successfully inoculated with another virus, TIV (*Tipula* iridescent virus), but whether it occurs in them naturally is uncertain. It is one of the few virus species in insects that is not host specific.

Larval parasites are primarily the larvae of certain Hymenoptera (Chalcididae, Braconidae, Ichneumonidae) and Diptera (Tachinidae or Larvaevoridae). These larvae feed inside the growing butterfly larva which eventually dies, although it may live long enough to pupate. Punkies or no-see-ums (Diptera: Ceratopogonidae) occasionally suck hemolymph from larvae, but probably seldom with lethal effect. Information on parasites is badly needed and any parasites recovered in rearing should be saved, along with the larva and pupa (and its name, if known), and sent to the Entomology Department, National Museum of Natural History, Washington, D.C., where it will be identified and recorded.

Predators on larvae are primarily birds, although lizards may also take a toll, and undoubtedly small mammals—flying squirrels, shrews, mice, voles—find numerous larvae and especially pupae. The social Hymenoptera, such as *Vespa* and *Polistes,* are important predators on larvae. Some Heteroptera, especially the Reduviidae, may also attack them.

Weather may at times account for much larval mortality, both directly and indirectly. Dislodgement and drowning in heavy downpours, and freezing during unseasonable cold weather, are examples of direct action; indirect effects would include starvation from loss of foodplants during drought, or losses to viral disease favored by prolonged cool, humid conditions. A protracted period of cool, cloudy weather can also produce losses of adults emerging from pupae and unable to properly expand and dry their wings.

Larvae have only limited protection against their enemies. Passive defense, protective coloration and pattern, is their most widely used device. Larval papilionids have the osmeterium (p. 7) which, when everted in stress situations, produces a repugnant odor. Nymphalid larvae are commonly spinose, which may reduce their desirability as food. The larvae of many Lycaenidae are accompanied by ants, for which the larvae have "honey glands" as an attractant. It is likely that one of the advantages of this to the larvae is that the ants may protect them from insect parasites.

Adult butterflies suffer little if at all from disease or parasites, although latent viruses may be passed on by an adult to her offspring. Punkies of the genus *Forcipomyia* have been seen in Arizona attaching themselves to the wing veins of several species of Lycaenidae, presumably to obtain hemolymph.

Predators, however, are another matter. The principal predators on adult butterflies in our area include birds, lizards, dragonflies (Odonata), robber flies (Diptera), ambush bugs (Heteroptera: Phymatidae), crab spiders and a number of web building spiders. These predators are relatively infrequently seen at work, but their toll must nevertheless be enough to have generated the evolutionary development of a variety of protective devices, discussed under the next heading.

Mimicry and protective resemblance.   An unpalatable butterfly has a distinct advantage in being quickly identifiable to a predator, so the predator will not mistakenly attack it. Conversely, a palatable butterfly may gain an advantage by deceiving the predator so that the predator either does not know it is there at all, or misidentifies it as something else, or believes it to be somewhere other than where it is. Out of these facts selection has fashioned an immense array of protective patterns and behavior. The patterns can be grouped under two headings: proclamatory and deception.

Our most celebrated example of a proclamatory pattern (or warning coloration) is that of the Monarch, *Danaus plexippus.* Vividly and contrastingly colored, it makes no attempt to conceal itself or its pattern. Quite the opposite, it flies conspicuously, displaying its pattern in an unmistakable way. The Monarch derives its unpalatability from several poisons in its body acquired from its larval foodplants (any of various Asclepiadaceae). When the larvae have fed on *Asclepias tuberosa,* which they only rarely do, they are quite palatable, for that is one of the few plants in the genus *Asclepias* that lacks the poisonous compounds. Proclamatory patterns are many and varied but all agree in being conspicuous and in being conspicuously displayed.

An interesting variant of proclamatory patterns is *Müllerian mimicry,* far more common in the tropics than in temperate regions. A Müllerian association is a group of several unpalatable species, all sharing the same proclamatory pattern. It is believed that this reduces the amount of learning experience a predator must undergo, and that it simplifies the burden on the predator's memory: instead of learning two, three or four different patterns to be avoided, it need only learn one, with a great saving of mortality to all the species.

Deception patterns are of many different kinds. Perhaps the best known examples are in *Batesian mimicry* (or sometimes, wrongly, just "mimicry"). A butterfly that is palatable resembles one that is not, sometimes with startling fidelity, including even habits and behavior. Our celebrated Monarch has an equally celebrated mimic, the Viceroy (*Limenitis archippus*), with the same coloration and the same habits as the Monarch. Interestingly, in Florida the equally unpalatable *Danaus gilippus* occurs more commonly than the Monarch, and here the Viceroy exists in a different subspecies (*L. a. floridensis*), which is a striking mimic of *gilippus.*

Leaves are often about the same size as various butterflies and *much* less interesting to predators. A number of butterflies have made capital of this and resemble leaves closely. One of the most famous "dead leaf mimics" is the nymphalid genus *Kallima* of India, in which (on its underside) the leaf is copied in color and shape, even to the petiole; the leaf ribs are indicated by dark lines, and there are even transparent spots that resemble worm holes in the leaf! We have only a few dead leaf mimics, mostly in the genus *Anaea.* They do a passable job of it, but are not as good as the *trompe l'oeuil* masterpiece of *Kallima.* Butterflies of the genus *Phoebis,* and perhaps even our ubiquitous *Colias,* are generalized mimics of yellowed or yellowing leaves, and often perch, or roost for the night, in close proximity to yellow leaves of the right size and shade of color. Even green leaves are copied: species of *Callophrys,* which often perch on green leaves, match them closely in the green color of their under surfaces (subgenera *Callophrys, Cyanophrys,* and some *Mitoura*).

Butterflies that perch on tree trunks are often colored to resemble the bark closely, such as the species of *Polygonia* and *Nymphalis.*

A rather different type of deception is "flash and conceal." In the most general terms it works like this: an animal at the approach of danger, say a potential predator, leaves its threatened place of concealment suddenly and conspicuously, momentarily startling the predator. Its movement, however, is straight and obvious, usually because of bright and contrasting color, and the predator can track it to its next stop with ease. The predator follows and reaches the spot, but the animal is no longer there: it has moved inconspicuously, if only slightly, to one side. Frogs often do this when diving into the litter in a shallow pond. Grass moths do it as one walks through a meadow. *Catocala* moths often have vivid hind wings of yellow, orange or red, which makes them conspicuous when they fly to another tree trunk, only to vanish. Among our "flash and conceal" butterflies are *Nymphalis* and *Polygonia* species.

Several bizarre forms of deception, found chiefly in the tropics, seem to have their function in momentarily distracting a would-be predator so the butterfly can make use of that moment to escape. A number of hairstreaks have a false head design at the tornus of the hind wings below, complete with "eyes" (spots) and "antennae" (thread-like tails). In addition, the vivid and contrasting pattern usually consists of lines all converging on the false head, as if to say, "bite here!" A bite by bird or lizard in this part of the wing causes no vital damage and the butterfly escapes. It is, of course, useful to the butterfly only once, but specimens are frequently found with just this area torn from the wings. Several of our lycaenids have eye-spot-and-tail combinations that may function in this way (*Everes,* some *Satyrium*), although the deception is far less refined.

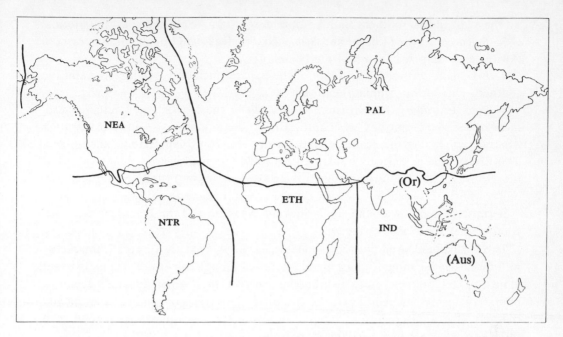

Figure 26. The faunal regions of the earth. NEA, Nearctic region; NTR, Neotropical region; PAL, Palearctic region; ETH, Ethiopian region; IND, Indo-Australian region (Or, Oriental subregion; Aus, Australian subregion).

Distribution

"The basic datum of biogeography," E. S. Deevey has said, "is conceived to be a map showing the range of a species." Biogeography, of course, is the methodical study of distribution. But what is the range of a species? Let us simply say, and it will do for present purposes, that a species' range is the smallest area within which the species occurs in appropriate environments and outside which it is absent entirely. For certain species we must make allowances for straying or other transient occurrences, perhaps by indicating separately its residential and transient ranges. Some species may have more than one discrete area on the map: they have *disjunct* ranges, true of many montane species, for example.

Faunal regions. Long ago it was observed that the animals within certain large areas had much in common taxonomically. These large areas roughly coincide with the world's major continental areas and are called faunal regions:

1. *Nearctic.* All of North America, excluding Greenland, southernmost Texas and southern Florida, but including northern Baja California and most of the Mexican Plateau down to the Isthmus of Tehuantepec. The area covered by this book is essentially the Nearctic region, but with bits of Palearctic, Neotropical and even Indo-Australian included (and of course Baja California and the Mexican Plateau excluded).

2. *Neotropical.* From Mexico south, including all of Central and South America,

all the West Indies, southern Baja California, southern Texas and southern Florida.

3. *Palearctic.* All of Europe and Asia, including Iceland, Greenland, and northern Africa; excluding Asia south of the Himalayas.

4. *Ethiopian.* All of Africa south of the Sahara, including Madagascar and the southern part of the Arabian Peninsula.

5. *Indo-Australian.* Southeastern Asia south of the Himalaya Mountains (and, more or less, the Tropic of Cancer eastward of these mountains), southward through Australia, including the islands of the Pacific. The Hawaiian Islands belong here. This diverse and extensively insular region is often divided in two: the *Oriental* and the *Australian,* the boundary between them (Wallace's Line) running from just east of Java north between Borneo and Celebes, then northeastward.

Because of many profound similarities the Nearctic and the Palearctic are often combined as the *Holarctic* region.

Two facts should be emphasized about these regions. First, they "work" remarkably well for nearly all animals in a general way, even though they were originally based almost entirely on vertebrate distributions. Second, they depart in small details of boundary position, depending on the group. The butterflies of southern Florida and southern Baja California, for example, are distinctly neotropical; the mammals of these two areas are just as distinctly nearctic.

Life zones. Practically every variable factor of the environment, whether it be the percentage of possible sunshine, the average date of the first frost in autumn, the incidence of thunderstorms, or whatever, limits the distribution of some kind of organism somewhere. Two groups of factors, however, have been found much more important than any others: temperature and precipitation. Note well that these are called *groups* of factors, for each can be extensively subdivided.

When C. H. Merriam devised his system of *life zones* in the 1890's he defined them in an overly complicated (and partially incorrect) way, he burdened them with some useless encumbrances and he grouped them in a needless hierarchy. Instead of being forgotten, however, they have persisted and survive today, only slightly modified in form, as one of the most simple and useful ways to map, describe and discuss the effects of temperature on distribution.

As modified, these zones are based simply on the mean temperature of the hottest month (T, below). In low latitudes this is not adequate, but since the inadequacy becomes marked only from about our southern border southward, it will not be considered here.

Each life zone except the Lower Austral and Subtropical spans 7.2°F (4°C) of midsummer temperature. This means that if we travel north or south in level country we would enter a new life zone roughly every 400 miles, and if we ascend a mountain we would pass into a new zone roughly every 2500 vertical feet. The life zones in mountains, however, are not horizontal. Looking at a north-south profile of a mountain with its life zones marked on it, we would see that a particular zone is about 2000 feet higher on the south (equatorial) side of the mountain than on its north (poleward) side.

Because of their altitudinal zonation, isolated mountain ranges behave biotically much like islands. Plants and animals of cooler climates are confined to the higher life zones and are hemmed in all around by a "sea" of uncongenial warmer climates below. Such cool-tolerant species are often present in widely disjunct populations in mountainous country.

The great effectiveness of the life zone system lies in the appropriate choice of three elements: (1) the base variable (mean temperature of the warmest month); (2) the particular size or temperature span, 7.2°F, of each zone; and (3) the location of the zone boundaries on the base variable. All of these were carefully chosen to coincide with the occurrence of important plant species. As a result, anyone acquainted even cursorily with the plants of a region can usually tell quite accurately what life zone he is in by the vegetation around him. An experienced lepidopterist can do the same with the butterflies. This should not be misconstrued. Only a few species of either plants or butterflies are rigidly confined to one life zone. Most occur over two or three and some are found over more than that. But a relatively large number have one distribution boundary or another coinciding rather closely with a life zone boundary, and by observing many species together one can usually tell what life zone he is in.

The life zones of North America are as follows, with their midsummer temperature limits given, where applicable:

Arctic-Alpine zone (T = 42.8–50°F). This is the zone of the "high arctic" and of high mountain summits above timberline. The Alpine areas, relatively small in extent, are not shown on the map (Fig. 27). They occur in many of the Hudsonian Zone areas shown. Tundra is the characteristic vegetation. The number of butterfly species is small and they tend to be rare in collections because the zone is hard to reach. Characteristic species: several *Oeneis, Erebia, Boloria; Lycaena phlaeas feildeni* and *L. p. hypophlaeas;* several *Colias.*

Hudsonian zone (T = 50–57.2°F). This zone marks the limit of trees, which are mostly fir and spruce. Most of the trees are low and at the colder reaches of the zone they become more and more stunted and scattered until they fade out altogether. Characteristic butterflies: several *Oeneis* and *Erebia; Plebejus optilete; Papilio machaon.*

Canadian zone (T = 57.2–64.4°F). Well named, this zone occupies much of Canada. It is also well developed in the Sierras, the Rockies, and even in small parts of the Appalachians. In the main its vegetation consists of fir and spruce forests, but under certain conditions aspen and birch may dominate. Characteristic butterflies: *Speyeria atlantis, Polygonia faunus, Colias interior, Pieris napi, Carterocephalus palaemon.*

Transition zone (T = 64.4–71.6°F). This widespread zone is well developed both in level regions and in most of our mountains. It is the principal zone of the great eastern deciduous hardwood forests of beech, maple and hemlock, sometimes also of eastern White Pine forest; and in the West it is the zone of Ponderosa Pine. A large number of butterflies are characteristic, including: *Cercyonis pegala nephele, Euphydryas phaeton, Boloria selene myrina, Chlosyne harrisii, Limenitis weidemeyeri, Hypaurotis crysalus, Satyrium acadica, Callophrys eryphon, Erora, Pieris virginiensis, Pholisora mejicana.*

Figure 27. Life zones of North America. AA, Arctic-Alpine zone; H, Hudsonian zone; C, Canadian zone; T, Transition zone; UA, Upper Austral zone (Upper Sonoran in the West); LA, Lower Austral zone (Lower Sonoran in the West); ST, Subtropical zone. (The Tropical zone does not occur in North America north of Mexico.) (Modified from map of Muesebeck & Krombein 1952, Syst. Zool. 1:24–25.)

Upper Austral zone (T = 71.6–78.8°F). In the drier West this is mostly known as the Upper Sonoran (a distinction based on reduced precipitation). Another widespread zone, oak-hickory-maple forests are typical in the East, oak-piñon-juniper scrub in much of the West. Characteristic butterflies include: *Cercyonis pegala alope, Cercyonis meadii, Euptychia rubricata, Speyeria diana, Limenitis astyanax arizonensis, Limenitis bredowii, Calephelis borealis, Euristrymon o. ontario, Callophrys mcfarlandi, Callophrys siva.*

Lower Austral zone (T = 78.8°F–?). In the West this is mostly known as the Lower Sonoran zone (see just above). This zone makes up the bulk of our southern perimeter. In the East the vegetation is predominantly a fire subclimax open pine forest, with hardwood (Live Oak, Sweet Gum, beech, magnolia) gallery forests along streams, usually hung with Spanish Moss; in swamps cypress forest is prevalent. In the West much of the Lower Austral is desert or semidesert, with ocotillo, Creosote Bush. Throughout most of this zone and southward some butterflies will be found on the wing all year. Characteristic species: *Euptychia areolata, Agraulis vanillae, Phyciodes texana seminole, Apodemia palmeri, Calephelis virginiensis, Atlides halesus, Calycopis cecrops, Hemiargus ceraunus, Papilio palamedes, Urbanus proteus, Ancyloxypha arene.*

Subtropical zone. This is our warmest zone and is found only in small areas along our southern limits: in southern Florida, southernmost Texas, in small areas of southern Arizona, and in desert parts of southernmost California. In Florida the marsh grasslands of the Everglades are typical (fire subclimax), with small patches or "hammocks" of subtropical hardwoods (including mahogany, fig, Gumbo-limbo). In southern Texas much of this zone is thorn forest, with acacias and other leguminous trees, but also with denser gallery forests and sparsely vegetated semidesert. Further west, in Arizona and California, most of the zone is semidesert and desert. Typical butterflies of this zone include: *Heliconius charitonius, Eunica, Phyciodes frisia, Siproeta stelenes, Lasaia, Chlorostrymon, Strymon acis, Strymon martialis, Strymon columella, Callophrys miserabilis, Phocides batabano, Polygonus, Asbolis capucinus.*

Tropical zone. No true Tropical zone occurs in our area, its nearest approach being in parts of the West Indies and in the lowlands of central Mexico.

Precipitation zones. These are by no means so well organized as the temperature zones or so widely agreed on, but they are no less important. Two aspects of precipitation are of particular significance: the total amount (mean annual precipitation) and its seasonal distribution (seasonality). The total amount tends to regulate the overall size of vegetation, from deserts where it is least to rain forests where it is most. Seasonality influences the kind of plants present: strongly seasonal precipitation in temperate and low latitudes is favorable to grasses and to sclerophylls such as conifers and oaks; non-seasonal precipitation is favorable to broad-leafed deciduous trees.

North America can be divided into three major regions on the basis of seasonality: (1) Winter Rain region, with strongly seasonal precipitation, most of which falls in winter: the Pacific coast; (2) Summer Rain region, with strongly seasonal precipitation, most of which falls in summer: the Rockies, prairie states, southeastern states (also most of Mexico); and (3) Non-seasonal Rain region, with precipitation fairly evenly distributed throughout the year: the northeastern states. Although these patterns intergrade broadly, the patterns themselves are independent of the total amount of precipitation and are stable over large areas.

Unlike seasonality, mean annual precipitation varies considerably, often over short distances. There is no standard, widely accepted, system of zones although one would be desirable. Solely as a rough guide, the following six "zones" may prove helpful (P = mean annual precipitation):

Desert (P = 0–8 inches).   Large expanses of bare ground and sparsely scattered low shrubs, tough and wiry, often spined, are typical. Ephemeral low herbs may be conspicuous after a brief rainy period. Few butterflies occur in such areas, and these are mostly in small places where the local water supply is increased (seeps, river borders, etc.). Areas of this type occur only west of the Rockies and in parts of Arctic America.

Semidesert (P = 8–16 inches).   Large areas of semidesert occur in the lowlands from the western plains westward, and over much of Arctic America, but not in the East. Bunch grass, sagebrush, rabbitbrush and *Opuntia* (prickly pear and cholla) typify this precipitation zone. Butterflies consist largely of wide-ranging "wanderers" such as *Pieris protodice, Eurema nicippe, Leptotes marina.*

Submesic (P = 16–32 inches).   Probably the largest zone in North America, the submesic occurs in localized small areas in the East (particularly the shale barrens of the Appalachians) and is widespread in southern Canada and from the Mississippi Basin westward. Vegetation varies from grassland (the tall grass prairie, probably a fire subclimax) to chaparral-like scrub, often in appropriate areas a pine parkland, and even forest. Butterflies are numerous.

Mesic (P = 32–64 inches).   Most of the eastern United States and southeastern Canada, but only small areas of the West, are in this zone, typified by forest everywhere. Butterflies are numerous, but mostly in natural or man-made open areas (glades, meadows, fields).

Humid (P = 64–128 inches).   Extremely localized, this zone occurs in a few small areas of the southern Appalachians, especially in the eastern Smokies, along the Pacific coast from northern California northward, in the Cascades of Washington and Oregon, and in the northern Sierra Nevada of California. Dense, tall forest, extensive shade, much fog and a high percentage of cloudy or rainy days all combine to make butterfly collecting a difficult and chancy thing. Species are interesting but not very numerous.

Wet (P = 128–256 inches).   This zone occurs locally, in the Olympic Mountains in Washington and along the Pacific coast of British Columbia and Alaska. Our only areas of true rain forest, these areas have few butterflies.

Zoogeography

The past history of North American butterflies, like that of the fauna of any continental area, has been long and complex. For millions of years our continent has been exchanging species with various surrounding areas in different ways and at different times. Being a large area it has also served as the nursery for many species and genera. With no useful fossil record in the butterflies to assist us, we can resort only to inference in unravelling this history, guided by what is known of geological events in the past, by the butterflies' systematic affinities, present geographic distributions and ecological associations, plus whatever other clues may be found. Although such a procedure is subject to error it is the only one we have and in properly cautious hands it is capable of suggesting much that happened long ago.

The four major areas adjoining North America with which faunal interchange has been at least potential, are: (1) Europe; (2) eastern Asia, via one or more land bridges in the Bering Straits; (3) South and Central America, via Mexico; and (4) the West Indies, via Cuba and the Bahamas.

(1) *Europe.* Little evidence exists that this region has given any species to our fauna, or received any from it, save by the hand of man. *Vanessa atalanta* is certainly derived from Europe, but is suspected of having been introduced. The same may be true of *Lycaena phlaeas americana* (but not of other subspecies of *phlaeas*). Both *Pieris rapae* and *Thymelicus lineola* are known introductions from Europe by human agency; they reached North America respectively in about 1869 and 1910.

(2) *Eastern Asia.* This is one of the most important regions, and faunal interchange apparently has been going on in both directions across the Bering Straits bridge for millions of years. It is clear that in the early history of this Bering transfer area conditions on both sides were much warmer than they are now, possibly equivalent to Lower Austral or even warmer (or more equable). The earliest crossers are now confined mostly to tropical regions and include the Ithomiidae (which probably arose in the New World, but has one remote genus, *Tellervo,* isolated in the Indo-Australian region), the ancestor of the little-known neotropical Plebejini (the genus *Hemiargus* is our only representative), the Strymoninae (whose ancestor probably crossed over to the New World from the Old, where relatives such as *Hypochrysops* and *Philiris* still exist), the Riodinidae (the vast assemblage of New World species and genera are probably all derived from two or three ancestral forms that crossed over from the Old World).

Somewhat later, but probably still in the Tertiary, the subgenera *Callophrys* and *Incisalia,* several *Satyrium,* some *Lycaena* crossed over from our area to Asia; *Speyeria, Lethe, Coenonympha haydenii, Hypaurotis, Habrodais, Everes comyntas, Celastrina, Feniseca, Zizula, Euchloe, Anthocharis* and probably several *Papilio* (perhaps including a derivative of the palearctic *Papilio alexanor* that was to become the ancestor of our *glaucus* group of species) all crossed from Asia into North America. This was both a later time (relationships are closer) and a cooler time (most of the forms are temperate, chiefly Transition and Upper Austral zone, species) and probably coincided with the great Arcto-Tertiary forest, with the remnants of which several members are still associated.

Still later, perhaps during the early Pleistocene interglacials, additional crossings were made, including many *Boloria,* some *Colias,* some *Oeneis,* some *Erebia, Lycaena phlaeas, Everes amyntula* and some *Parnassius,* all from Asia.

Later still, either in the last interglacial or even in post-Wisconsin time, have come our most recent invaders: several *Erebia, Boloria, Colias, Lycaena phlaeas feildeni, Vacciniina optilete, Papilio machaon* and some *Parnassius.*

(3) *South and Central America.*   Nearly or quite as important as Asia, this region has been the source of many of our species and genera and has in turn received a number from us. Dating the faunal movements, however, is much more difficult and even relative dates and sequences are still questionable. Among the early arrivals from the neotropical mainland are probably: most *Phyciodes,* all *Satyrium,* most of the subgenera of *Callophrys* and *Neophasia;* perhaps at about this time *Colias* and a few other groups made their way to South America from the north. Later arrivals from the neotropical mainland may include *Danaus plexippus, Euptychia, Calycopis cecrops, Eurema, Graphium marcellus, Epargyreus clarus.* Still more recently *Erora laeta, Panthiades m-album* and *Autochton cellus* came north, while *Anthocharis (midea), Limenitis astyanax (arizonensis)* and others went south. The most recent arrivals have come in chiefly as a result of post-glacial warming and include such groups as *Callophrys (Cyanophrys), Ministrymon, Myscelia, Mestra.* Most of them have barely crossed our border.

(4) *West Indies.*   Although the West Indies are really but a part of the neotropical region, their position, their insular nature and their depauperate fauna combine to give them a status distinct from the neotropical mainland. The Antilles have contributed so extensively to our fauna in Florida that as far as its butterflies are concerned southern Florida must be considered effectively a part of the West Indian faunal subregion. Among the many species apparently derived from the West Indies, via either Cuba or the Bahamas, are: *Strymon acis, Chlorostrymon maesites, Hemiargus thomasi, Papilio aristodemus, Phocides batabano, Epargyreus zestos.* A number of species, such as *Heliconius charitonius, Leptotes cassius, Eurema lisa,* have reached North America twice independently, both via Mexico and via the West Indies, often as different subspecies. Several species have gone in the opposite direction and have reached the West Indies from Florida: *Vanessa atalanta, Precis coenia, Phyciodes phaon, Pieris protodice, Papilio polyxenes.* An odd but marked peculiarity of this faunal element is its recency. Unlike the Asiatic and mainland tropical groups, nearly all the West Indian species in Florida appear to have reached our shores since the last glaciation, a mere yesterday in geological time. Indeed, some of them, such as *Eurema daira palmira* and *Asbolis capucinus,* probably arrived only a few years ago. The only possible exception to this recency is *Brephidium pseudofea,* which probably crossed to Florida during some prior interglacial.

Another source area should be mentioned even though its relationship to North America is not direct. At least three entities of our fauna are apparently from Africa:

Brephidium. Our two species, *exilis* and *pseudofea,* are probably both derived from a common ancestor that reached the West Indies from Africa. One species, *Brephidium metophis* Wallengren, still occurs on that continent, as does the related *Oraidium barberae* Trimen.

Leptotes marina and its relative *L. perkinsae* Kaye of Jamaica, are probably derived from a common ancestor that also reached the West Indies from Africa, where near relatives are still to be found.

Hypolimnas misippus is an African species that is also widely distributed around the West Indian region. It is popularly supposed to have been introduced by man during the days of the slave trade. There is little or no factual basis for this supposition, however, and it is just as possible that it reached the New World unassisted, probably by having been wind-transported as must have been the case with the preceding two.

The movements of animals over many millennia can become complex indeed. Even with our limited capacity to perceive the events of the past it is evident, for example, that a long time ago a species crossed from the Old World to the New and became the ancestor of all the New World hairstreaks (Strymoninae); that among its many descendants were such genera as *Callophrys, Satyrium* and *Euristrymon,* and that some members of each of these genera crossed back again to the Old World. The single species, *Lycaena phlaeas,* appears to have colonized North America on at least three different occasions. The earliest invasion was during an interglacial when the ancestor of most of the western populations (*L. p. hypophlaeas* and *L. p. arethusa*) arrived. After the last glaciation the far northern subspecies, *L. p. feildeni,* arrived. The last invasion, probably by human agency, was the eastern *L. p. americana,* which may have reached North America from Europe. The four species of *Vanessa* in North America require four different invasions to account for them. The earliest, long ago, was the ancestor of the *virginiensis* group, which crossed from Asia and went to South America (where most of the group is today), then produced our species, *virginiensis.* The next was the ancestor of *annabella,* also from Asia. The third was the species *cardui,* which could have come from Asia unassisted or from Europe by human agency. The last was *atalanta,* which came from Europe, probably introduced.

Movements within North America. During the past million years or so (some authorities say it was only some 600,000 years) the world has undergone four major periods of considerable cooling, the glaciations of the Pleistocene. During each of these periods temperatures were reduced world-wide by some five to nine degrees Fahrenheit, the distribution, if not the total amount, of precipitation was considerably altered, large ice sheets came down from the polar regions, and because of the vast amounts of water bound up in this ice, sea levels were reduced by some 300 feet.

We may never know how many butterflies became extinct as a result of these changes, but there are many clues to show that the survivors went through major changes of range. We are justified, in fact, in considering these glacial periods and the warm interglacials between them as among the most important architects of our present butterfly fauna. At the height of the last (Wisconsin) glaciation, southern

Florida had almost no West Indian butterflies at all, but instead had a fauna much like that of Georgia and the Carolinas today. Species now isolated in several different mountain ranges of the West occurred in the broad intervening basins. A considerable mixing of eastern and western species occurred as far south as New Mexico, and isolated populations of several eastern species may now be found in the mountains there as a result.

A curious aspect of our fauna is the great distinctness of the eastern and western parts of the continent. In general the eastern fauna is more depauperate than the western, a fact that is surely to be explained by the great difference in topographic, and hence ecological, diversity in the two areas. This, however, does not explain why so many eastern species are lacking in the West, or why so many western species and genera are absent from the East, even in life zones that are broad and continuous across the continent. A repeated pattern is a genus or subgenus that has many western species but only one or a few eastern species (*Coenonympha, Euphydryas, Speyeria, Cercyonis, Lycaeides, Anthocharis*). One possible explanation may be the difference in seasonality of precipitation: a pronounced dry season occurs in the West, not in the East. Adaptation to one or the other may be difficult to modify evolutionarily. In a few instances (*Lethe, Satyrium liparops* and *S. kingi, Feniseca tarquinius*) species now limited to the East have relatives in Asia, so we know that at some time in the past, probably in the Tertiary, these species or their ancestors must have ranged across the American continent, even though they have since died out in the West.

Classification and taxonomy

The people of the world are clustered mostly in towns and cities; these are, in turn, united into larger administrative areas (perhaps townships), and these into counties or their equivalents, while counties are grouped into states, states into countries, countries into continents. The continents collectively comprise our world. This may be called the hierarchy of human political and administrative organization.

In somewhat the same way the kinds of living things are organized into a *taxonomic hierarchy*. At the bottom are the individual organisms, plant or animal. These are clustered in smaller or larger groups, called *colonies,* whose individuals habitually interbreed with one another. Some colonies of butterflies may consist of only a few individuals and occupy an area no larger than a hundred square feet or so. Others may consist of millions of individuals and cover an area of hundreds, perhaps even thousands, of square miles. Colonies, in turn, are grouped in larger assemblages, usually called *populations*. Interbreeding between individuals from different colonies in a population is less than within a colony but still quite frequent, and gene flow within a population is considerable. Populations, in turn, are grouped into subspecies. Gene flow between the populations of a subspecies may be extensive, or it may be almost nil.

Up to this point all individuals are pretty similar to one another in appearance, whether we draw them from one colony or from different populations. There may be more or less individual variation but it will be much alike wherever we go. Careful statistical analysis of this variation would probably show differences in average values from one colony or population to another, but these differences would be slight, and without peeking at the locality label we would rarely be able to say where any one specimen came from.

The *subspecies* is the lowest taxonomic unit recognized by a formal scientific name. A subspecies shows enough visible difference between it and another subspecies that we could discriminate, without knowing the locality, from 75% to 90% or more of the individuals of one from a similar percentage of the other. Despite this, two subspecies are generally quite interfertile. Gene flow between subspecies may be virtually zero (if, say, they inhabit different islands or different isolated mountain ranges), or it may be moderate, if the two inhabit different but contiguous areas of land. In the latter event we generally have a *zone of intergradation* (or *blend zone*) between them. Zones of intergradation are interesting things and have been under increasing study in recent years.

Because of the interest in these zones and because, as collecting increases, more and more of them are discovered, it will be useful to digress a bit here and discuss them, so that when a collector finds one, or reads about one (and this book is filled with examples), he will have some idea of what the fuss is all about. The reader, however, should bear in mind that this is only a superficial account of a large and complex topic. For more details he should consult textbooks on systematics. The study and analysis of blend zones and their significance is necessarily a highly technical matter that should be undertaken by a beginner only with the help of a professionally trained colleague.

Zones of intergradation are basically of two different kinds, depending on the past history of the subspecies involved.

Suppose, first, that originally a species inhabited a given area, A, and that its northern limit was set by some limitation of temperature tolerance. Further, suppose that near the frontier a mutation arose that allowed its bearer to tolerate different, cooler, temperatures. Gradually this new trait would spread among more members of the population and the descendents eventually would be able to move into a new area, B, where formerly they could not have lived. As time passed the species, with additional mutations, would be able to move farther and farther, say to area C, gradually changing in appearance, because of these genetic changes, as it moved. Collecting shows that the individuals in area C are recognizably different from those in area A, and that those in area B are intermediate (*intergrades*). Such a situation would be called a *cline,* and the zone or area (B) between the two subspecies would be a zone of *primary intergradation.*

Now let us suppose that a species, sometime before the last glaciation, was distributed across the southern United States from Georgia to Texas. When the glacial period arrived the climate became colder and the species had to move south. Only two places were available for it, southern Florida and Mexico. During the long glacial period, then, it occupied these two areas, the populations separated from each other by many hundreds of miles. Evolutionarily they went their separate ways and became distinct subspecies. When the glacial period ended the climate warmed again and the two once-isolated populations moved north, recaptured their lost ground and came into contact. They were only subspecies, and were therefore interfertile, so where they met they hybridized. The band or zone between them where this hybridization now occurs is a zone of *secondary intergradation.*

How do we distinguish between these two types of intergradation? The only way to do so convincingly is by the use of statistics. We select a character which differs in the two subspecies and measure it carefully in (a) a sample of one subspecies; (b) a sample from the zone of intergradation; and (c) a sample from the other subspecies. Suppose such a character is the width of a band. In (a) it varies from 1 to 3 mm, in most of the individuals being 2 mm; in (b) it varies from 2 to 4 mm, most of them being 3 mm; and in (c) it varies from 3 to 5 mm, most of them being 4 mm. In this instance we would have a cline: the character is about as variable in the intermediate population as it is at the extremes. On the other hand suppose that in (a) it varied as before from 1 to 3 mm, and in (c) it varied as before from 3 to 5 mm, but when we measure (b) we find that it varies from 1 to 5 mm, most being 3 mm. In such an instance we would probably have an example of *secondary intergradation,* since the intermediate population is more variable, showing, in fact, the full range of variation found in both extreme populations. In practice one usually uses more than just three samples, and if possible more than just one character, but the principle remains the same. The reason for the different results in the two types of intergradation lies in their different causes: one intermediate population (in the cline) is an intermediate step in gradual evolutionary change; the other (secondary intergradation) is the result of combining two different gene pools.

To resume with the taxonomic hierarchy: the next step above the subspecies is the *species* (plural: species). But it is not a simple step, and requires yet another digression. More ink and paper have been expended on the question, "What is a species?" than probably any other in systematic biology. When we ask this question, what we really mean is "How can you tell a species from a subspecies?"

The answer, although basically straightforward, is often exceedingly complicated in practice. When individuals from two populations can interbreed successfully—with the production of a full complement of viable offspring—then they belong to one species; but if they produce no offspring at all, or only a few (usually of one sex) compared to the normal complement, or if the offspring themselves are inviable or sterile, then the two populations belong to different species. That seems simple enough: crosses within a species are fertile, between species are sterile. The complications, however, are many:

1. Two populations can be fully interfertile in the laboratory and yet still be *sympatric* (occurring in the same area; compare *allopatric* below) in nature, maintaining their separate identities. When it can be applied, the latter test is, of course, the ultimate court of appeal: two such entities that can coexist successfully in the wild are two different species. This is the main reason that *Colias philodice* and *eurytheme* are viewed by most lepidopterists as species, even though they hybridize and produce at least partially successful offspring.

2. Conversely, two populations can be externally extremely similar, even seem-

ingly identical, and yet be absolutely incompatible genetically. They are species, but difficult to discriminate. Such pairs of unusually similar species (*sibling species*) are turning up increasingly as butterflies are studied more carefully. Among relatively recent discoveries: *Satyrium calanus falacer* and *S. caryaevorus; Callophrys gryneus* and *C. hesseli; Lethe eurydice* and *L. appalachia.*

3. Intersterility is partly a necessary consequence of evolutionary divergence: the increasing genetic difference of two separately evolving forms tends to make their mixture more and more incompatible. Intersterility may also be selectively advantageous: a device to protect the genetic integrity (and hence to avoid population waste) of two forms occurring in contact and otherwise capable of living together. But when two populations are well isolated geographically there is no selective advantage to intersterility and it is possible for such forms sometimes to evolve in mutual isolation to a level of difference we would unhesitatingly call specific, and yet still be highly interfertile.

4. Interfertility and intersterility are not all-or-nothing states. Two populations can be just a little intersterile, or quite a lot, or absolutely incompatible. It would be possible theoretically to devise a scale of intersterility, based on all the varied ways in which genetic compatibility can be impaired, and find some pair of forms to occupy each tiny gradation along the scale.

5. In some critical instances we may lack the necessary evidence from which to reach a decision. When two forms are *allopatric* (occurring in different areas, without overlap) and, as is often true, we have no knowledge of what happens when they interbreed, our only recourse is to reason by analogy.

On a practical level, we decide whether two forms are species or subspecies by the following criteria:

(a) If their ranges broadly overlap and there are no, or few, hybrids, they are two species.

(b) If their ranges do not overlap but are contiguous, and if there are many intermediates in the contact zone, they are subspecies.

(c) If they do not overlap, but their degree of difference is at least as great as between other species that do, then we call them species and hope we are right.

(d) If they do not overlap, and have no contact zone, but look no more dissimilar than those that do meet and intergrade in a contact zone, then we call them subspecies and hope we are right.

There will always be a residue of forms that are not clearly either species or subspecies, and for these no solution is wholly satisfactory. One particular situation occurs rather frequently. Two or more forms, clearly related, are found to replace each other geographically and to hybridize at the zone(s) of contact, suggesting subspecies; but the hybrids are relatively few, perhaps inviable, and there may be morphological differences between the two (or more) forms, suggesting species. A possible example is the set of *Limenitis* that includes *lorquini, weidemeyeri,* and *arthemis* (with *astyanax*). When the components of such a group are relatively closely allied they may be called informally "semi-species," and treated taxonomically as subspecies; when the components are relatively well differentiated, the whole assemblage may be called informally a "superspecies," and the components treated taxonomically as species, as is true of the *Limenitis* just mentioned.

To summarize, then, species are collections of one or more subspecies whose individuals are relatively fertile with one another, but are relatively infertile with the individuals of other species. The taxonomic hierarchy above the species assumes a different character: the successive groupings are based on degree of morphological difference and become more governed by opinion and tradition than by objective qualities. This would seem to be a most unsatisfactory situation, but in truth it has withstood well the onslaughts of time and the idiosyncracies of biologists; it works quite well indeed.

Species, to continue, are grouped into *genera* (singular: *genus*), which are characterized by significant structural traits that the member species of a genus all share, and by which they can be distinguished from those of other genera. Over the years our ideas about the limits of genera have gradually changed. To Linnaeus, in 1758, all butterflies were in only one genus, *Papilio*. Some half a century later, Fabricius divided them more finely: his genera correspond roughly to the families of today. Later writers reduced the inclusiveness of genera still more, and by the end of the nineteenth century authors were writing of *Lycaena* (all blues), *Thecla* (all hairstreaks), *Argynnis* (all fritillaries), *Papilio* (all swallowtails), *Pamphila* (all hesperiine skippers), and so on. At about this time, Scudder, with remarkable (and at the time wholly unaccepted) views on generic limits, named scores of new genera that were promptly relegated to the synonymy by his contemporaries. We have still not caught up with Scudder, but the gap is closing fast, for generic "splitting" continues to become ever finer.

Genera in turn are grouped into *tribes,* and tribes into *subfamilies,* and subfamilies into *families.*

Tribes and subfamilies are being defined and used more often than they once were, a further consequence of the closer and more analytical study of recent years, and of the increasing need for the information that these groupings convey. Among other things, it is impossible to analyze zoogeographic problems without knowing the systematic relationships involved, and these relationships are indicated by such groupings. An excellent example of this is the recent revised classification of the family Satyridae by Miller (1968).

Families have shared the same "splitting" problems as genera. Even today, for instance, some authors use Nymphalidae for the butterflies that other authors would divide among the Satyridae, Morphidae, Ithomiidae, Danaidae, Heliconiidae, Apaturidae and Nymphalidae (strictly interpreted). There is no objective way to decide the merits of these opposing views, but time is probably on the side of the splitters.

Above the family the hierarchy continues: families are united into *superfamilies,* these into *suborders,* and these into *orders.* The butterflies, with which this book is concerned, represent two superfamilies, the Papilionoidea, or true butterflies, and the Hesperioidea, or skippers. These two, along with most of the superfamilies of moths, make up the large suborder Heteroneura. The two suborders, Heteroneura and Homoneura (the latter a small group of primitive moths) are combined into the order Lepidoptera, which consists of all butterflies and moths.

Orders, in turn, are united under *classes,* and these under *phyla* (singular: phylum); phyla are grouped under *kingdoms,* and all kingdoms collectively are called *terrestrial life.*

In this tour through the hierarchy of taxonomy several intermediate groupings have been omitted. One of the beauties of this hierarchy, and no doubt a major factor in its utility and durability, is just this sort of flexibility: there is room within its complexities for all kinds of simplification, for differences of opinion, for growth of knowledge with time. For those who may be interested, a relatively full classification is given below of a butterfly, showing many (but by no means all) of these additional categories. Opinions still differ widely as to just how many of these groupings there should be, and what each should contain, so this is no more than a distillation of a few recent ideas. Those who may think that all taxonomic problems are confined to genera and below will be pleased to learn that they are to be found at every rung of the hierarchical ladder. Many of us grew up with the easy and implicit belief, practically to be ranked with the sun rising in the east, that the world of living things was divided into two kingdoms, animals and plants. Not so at all, say many students of the problem. Whittaker (1969), whose higher classification (down to phylum) is followed here, recognizes no less than *five* kingdoms, and with good justification.

* *Terrestrial life* (includes all living things on earth; non-living things, viruses among them, are excluded; what, if anything, may occur on other planets we cannot even guess)
* *Kingdom:* Animalia (one of five kingdoms)
  Subkingdom: Eumetazoa (one of three in the Animalia)
  Branch: Bilateria (one of two in the Eumetazoa)
  Grade: Coelomata (one of three in the Bilateria)
  Subgrade: Schizocoela (one of two in the Coelomata)
* *Phylum:* Arthropoda (one of eight in the Schizocoela)
  Subphylum: Mandibulata (one of three in the Arthropoda)
* *Class:* Insecta (one of three in the Mandibulata)
  Subclass: Pterygota (one of four in the Insecta)
  Infraclass: Oligoneoptera (one of four in the Pterygota)
* *Order:* Lepidoptera (one of nine in the Oligoneoptera)
  Suborder: Heteroneura (one of two in the Lepidoptera)
  Division: Ditrysia (one of two in the Heteroneura)
  Superfamily: Papilionoidea (one of about thirteen in the Ditrysia)
  Section: Nymphales (one of four in the Papilionoidea)
* *Family:* Satyridae (one of seven in the Nymphales)
  Subfamily: Satyrinae (one of seven in the Satyridae)
  Tribe: Maniolini (one of ten in the Satyrinae)
* *Genus:* Cercyonis (one of six in the Maniolini)

Subgenus: (none in *Cercyonis*)
* *Species: Cercyonis pegala* Fabricius (one of four in *Cercyonis*)
  Subspecies: Cercyonis pegala alope Fabricius (one of about nine in *C. pegala*).

The major categories in the above sequence, the irreducible minimum, have been starred.

Polymorphism. Several types of variation occur, combined under the general term *polymorphism,* which have no place in the taxonomic hierarchy, but they are nonetheless widespread and often create serious practical problems of identification and understanding.

The most common type of polymorphism (which means simply the state of existing in two or more forms) is *sexual polymorphism* (perhaps more correctly sexual dimorphism), in which the two sexes are more or less markedly different, as in *Speyeria diana* and *Poanes zabulon.* It has happened repeatedly that the two sexes of a species were originally described as two different species (sometimes even genera!).

Another common type is *seasonal polymorphism,* in which the broods emerging at different times of the year differ in appearance. The genes of these seasonal forms are identical (they have the same *genotype*), but certain of them respond differently in development according to different external environmental conditions, producing a different *phenotype* (external appearance). Most of our seasonal forms reflect the temperature difference between cool spring and warm summer; but in many tropical regions there are seasonal forms, sometimes even more striking than ours, that derive from differences between wet season and dry. Seasonal forms have frequently been described erroneously as different species, one of the most celebrated instances being the European nymphalid, *Araschnia levana* Linnaeus. Its summer form is so different (black and white, instead of orange and white) that Linnaeus originally named it a different species, *prorsa.* Among the more conspicuously seasonally dimorphic North American butterflies are: *Papilio glaucus, Pieris protodice, Polygonia,* some *Phyciodes, Ministrymon leda, Celastrina argiolus.*

Individual polymorphism embraces many different things. In some species or subspecies two different forms may coexist, more or less in equal numbers, each presumably genetic. This is true in *Celastrina argiolus lucia,* for instance: dimorphic forms "lucia" and "marginata" occur about in equal numbers. Oddly, this dimorphism is not found in the more southern subspecies, *C. a. pseudargiolus.* In some species the dimorphism is expressed in only one sex, as in *Papilio glaucus* (females may be yellow or black) or *Poanes hobomok* (females may be orange or black). In other species a dimorphic form may occur more rarely and sporadically. In *Lycaena phlaeas americana,* for example, form "fasciata" occurs in some areas and apparently not in others, and usually in very low numbers even where it is found (in one locality in western Pennsylvania it is estimated to comprise not more than $\frac{1}{50}$ of the population, and perhaps much less). The form "pallida" of the introduced hesperiid, *Thymelicus lineola,* is even more sporadic and in even lower ratio, being found in probably less than $\frac{1}{1000}$ of the population. Finally, we come to forms so scarce that they have been seen only once or twice, these usually being called "aberrations." Actually, however, the term "aberration" ("*ab.*") is lepidopterists' jargon and has little if any currency outside the field; it is applied indiscriminately to any individual deviating strikingly in appearance from the norm, whether this deviation is genetic, environmentally induced (as in *Nymphalis antiopa,* aberration "hygeia"), or possibly even of pathological origin (known to be true of some in Europe), provided only that it is rare.

Scientific Names and Naming

ALEXANDER B. KLOTS

The part of the science of biology that deals with naming organisms is called *nomenclature.* Most of our butterflies have two kinds of names, common (or vernacular) and scientific. The vernacular names "just happened." They are useful in a way, but are not exact and are far from uniform. Some species have more than one. The Satyrid *Cercyonis pegala,* for example, is variously called Wood Nymph, Grayling, Blue Eyed Grayling or Goggle Eye. Such names change from country to country, language to language, and time to time. To an Englishman *Nymphalis antiopa* is the Camberwell Beauty; to us it is the Mourning Cloak. The butterfly that the English call a White Admiral is a very different species from the one (*Limenitis arthemis arthemis*) for which we use this common name. We now call *Vanessa virginiensis* the American Painted Lady; but a generation ago it was called the Hunter's Butterfly. It has also been called the Painted Beauty. Obviously such common names pose many problems. There are no rules governing them.

Scientific names of animals, on the other hand, are governed by the *International Code of Zoological Nomenclature,* which regulates the giving and use of scientific names in all countries and languages. The names are Latin or Latinized; even Russian, Greek and Japanese biologists use them, no matter how different their own alphabets may be.

Basically each scientific name of an animal is *binomial,* that is, double. It consists of a grouping, or *genus,* name which comes first and is capitalized; and a *species* name, which comes second, and is never capitalized. The name of our Tiger Swallowtail is *Papilio glaucus.* The name of our Spicebush Swallowtail is *Papilio troilus.* Species may differ from each other in many important respects; but the fact that they are in the same genus shows that they have many fundamental characteristics in common. Another of our swallowtails, the Pipevine Swallowtail, is named *Battus philenor.* It is in a different genus, from which we infer that it is more different from *P. glaucus* and *P. troilus* than they are from each other.

The first person to publish a scientific name properly is the *author* of that name. His name is to be given at least once in any publication in which the scientific name appears, and is written after the name that he proposed. The great Swedish biologist Carolus Linnaeus was the author of all three of the above swallowtail names. When he named them he put them all in the genus *Papilio.* Since we still keep *glaucus* and *troilus* in *Papilio* we write their names *Papilio glaucus* Linnaeus and *Papilio troilus* Linnaeus; but since *philenor* is now in a different genus, *Battus,* we write its name *Battus philenor* (Linnaeus), putting the author's name in parentheses as an indication that he originally described the species in a different genus than the one it is now in.

It has often happened (and still does) that more than one scientific name has been given to a species or genus. In this case the first name published has priority and is considered to be the valid name. A name published subsequently is considered invalid, and is called a *junior synonym* of the valid name.

Most species occur over a wide geographic range. Often it will be found that the population in one area differs somewhat from that in another (the species is *polytypic*). Such geographically distinct populations within a species are called *subspecies,* and their naming is subject to the same rules that govern species. These names are written *trinomially.* Thus the Viceroy, *Limenitis archippus* (Drury), is pretty much all the same from southern Canada to Georgia and Louisiana, but populations from peninsular Florida are distinctly darker brown. These populations are collectively recognized as the subspecies *Limenitis archippus floridensis* (Strecker); that leaves the northern and mainland populations to be called the subspecies *Limenitis archippus archippus.* Why a trinomial for it? By recognizing the existence of one distinct subspecies, we recognize that the rest of the species is also a subspecies (or perhaps more than one). Since the mainland subspecies was the first one named we call it the *nominate* subspecies and refer to it with a trinomial in which the original species name is given first, and then repeated as the subspecies name. When we speak of *Limenitis archippus* we refer to the whole species, including *all* of its subspecies. When we speak of *Limenitis archippus archippus* we refer to just one of its subspecies, the one that was named first. Summarizing, the species *Limenitis archippus* consists (in the East) of two geographically distinct subspecies, *Limenitis archippus archippus* and *Limenitis archippus floridensis.* A species may consist of a dozen subspecies; but one of these will always be the nominate one, the others will be those subsequently described.

Just as a species may consist of more than one subspecies, so may a genus consist of more than one subgenus. The subgeneric name is placed in parentheses after the generic name and, like it, is capitalized. The genus *Colias* Fabricius, for example, consists of quite a number of species which seem to fall into two groups in North America. Most of the species fall into one of these, the nominate subgenus, written *Colias* (*Colias*) Fabricius; but we have two species that are quite different, although not enough to warrant recognizing a separate genus for them, so we place them in a subgenus, *Colias* (*Zerene*) Hübner.

A final very important feature of nomenclature is the *type* concept. Each species name (whether we use it as a species, subspecies, or junior synonym) must have a type, which is a particular specimen. This type, or holotype (which may be either male or female), should be designated by the author of a new name when he describes it and must be one of the specimens studied by him at that time. The remaining specimens that he had then are called *paratypes.* If the original author failed to designate a type, all his original specimens are called syntypes (or cotypes), and one of these can later be designated as the type; it is then called a *lectotype* and the remaining syntypes become *lectoparatypes.*

There is a third possibility: the original type may have been lost or destroyed. In this case a later author may designate a *neotype,* a "new type," from surviving paratypes, if they exist, or even from some other specimens, if the original specimens are all lost. Some very special restrictions govern such a case.

Sometimes a paratype of the opposite sex from the holotype is designated as the *"allotype."* This may be useful. Names for other kinds of type-like specimens, such as topotype (from the same locality as the type); homotype (a specimen considered by someone to agree with the type) and a good many others have no status and should not be used. The *"type locality"* (TL), the place where the type was caught, is important for geographic studies. So, of course, is the exact date of the type's capture.

The type of a genus is the species (which must be one of those included in the genus in the original description) which is first designated in proper publication (preferably, of course, in the original description) as the *type species* of that genus. Every generic name, whether used as a genus or subgenus or placed as a junior synonym, must have its type species. As an example, the common European swallowtail, *Papilio machaon* Linnaeus, is the type species of the genus *Papilio.* The type specimen of a species-level name and the type species of a genus-level name give essential and immutable information about the proper usage of the names. It is important to realize that these types, type-species of genera and type specimens of species and subspecies, are simply reference standards for evaluating the names they bear. They need not be "typical," in the sense of representing average or normal appearance. Indeed, they often are not.

How to catch butterflies

People have caught butterflies in their fingers or in their hats, and have put them away in a bottle, in an envelope from an old letter, in an empty cigarette pack or in a torn-off piece of newspaper. Such methods may serve *in extremis* but they have nothing to recommend them otherwise. If you are going to collect butterflies you must provide yourself with certain basic items of equipment.

Net. Dealers in entomological equipment sell nets to suit nearly any purse. If you wish, you can make your own. Either way you will want to consider and decide on certain variables of design. The net bag should be made of tough, durable, snag-resistant, but fairly transparent, netting such as nylon or dacron. It should have a heavy muslin sleeve to fit over the net rim, and the bag should be from 2 to $2\frac{1}{2}$ times as long as its diameter and end in a blunt, rounded point. The rim should be made of sturdy metal: either flat spring steel strip (about $\frac{3}{8}$ inch wide) or heavy gauge wire (about $\frac{5}{32}$ inch in diameter). In general the strip is used for rims designed to take down flat for compact carrying, while the round wire rims are usually made to keep their circular shape. The rim of the net should be capable of separating easily from the handle, to permit changing the net bag when it is worn out. The rim may vary in diameter from about 12 to 17 inches, occasionally more. The larger the diameter the better chance you have of catching what you swing at and the less likely you are to damage a large specimen. On the other hand, a small diameter rim can get into and out of places too tight for a large one. The most commonly used diameter is about 15 inches. The net handle should be as light and as strong as possible, and about $\frac{3}{4}$ inch in diameter. Hardwood dowelling and aluminum tubing are both widely used. In general, a handle 3 to 4 feet long is the most useful. Some handles, however, are sectional, designed to add increments when needed up to a total length of 12 feet or so, for catching specimens up in trees.

Killing bottle.   After you have caught a specimen you must kill it. There are two schools of thought on this: one favors simply pinching the specimen; the other using a killing bottle. Pinching is quicker, easier and requires less equipment, but it takes practice to avoid smashed specimens. Sharp, moderate pressure between thumbnail and forefinger (only experience can teach you how much) applied to the thorax, stuns and mortally wounds the specimen, which may then be papered immediately.

A killing bottle should be of a size you can manipulate easily with one hand. It should be wide-mouthed, large enough to take even a large butterfly without damage, and have a lid that is both tight-fitting and easily removable. The butterfly is placed inside and the cover replaced. After ten minutes or so the specimen is dead and may then be papered. If, as often happens, the butterfly has "flipped" and is folded the wrong way (upperside out), you must carefully return the wings back up over the body with your forceps before papering it. The best killing bottles are made with potassium cyanide, *a deadly poison.* Whether you buy your killing bottles or make them yourself they should be treated with the utmost care.

If you wish to make your own killing bottle, proceed as follows: Into the bottom of a suitable jar place a thin layer of fine, *dry* sawdust, $\frac{1}{4}$ to $\frac{1}{2}$ inch thick. On top of this sawdust place a layer of about $\frac{1}{2}$ inch of granular cyanide, or a few nuggets if the cyanide is of this form. On top of the cyanide add another layer of *dry* sawdust, completely covering the cyanide to about one inch over the top of it. Cover this, in turn, with about $\frac{1}{2}$ inch of thickly mixed plaster of paris. Leave the bottle open until the plaster is *completely* dry. Afterwards, the bottle should always be kept tightly closed when not in use. The bottom of the bottle up to the plaster, or preferably the whole bottle, should then be wrapped with adhesive tape, to keep it all together in the event of breakage. Label the finished bottle, conspicuously, "Poison— Cyanide." It is also a good idea to write on the bottle the date that you made it. *Through the whole procedure be extremely careful, account for every bit of cyanide, work only out of doors or with windows all open, wash all table surfaces, and all tools, thoroughly with water afterwards, and wash your hands particularly well when you are through.* **Cyanide is a deadly poison.**

A well made and carefully used cyanide bottle should last several years. Moisture from the air, and from enclosed specimens, slowly combines with the cyanide and releases hydrocyanic acid gas, which is what kills. Always test the strength of the bottle by its speed in killing specimens, never by smelling at its mouth. If a jar seems very slow, and yet there is still cyanide in it, it may be too dry: a drop or two of water should restore its strength. A small amount of soft crumpled tissue inside the jar should help keep specimens from rubbing against the bottle or each other.

Forceps. These are indispensable for handling specimens in the field or in mounting, and it is a good plan to keep one pair in your collecting bag, and another on your work table. Some collectors prefer postage stamp tongs; most use forceps that taper to a fine, curved point. You should either attach your field pair with a length of string to your collecting bag, or tie a bit of brightly colored ribbon to them to help make them more visible should they fall into weeds or grass.

Envelopes. Most collectors "paper" their specimens in the field, either as they collect or at the end of a collecting stint. Specimens in envelopes can be stored easily, handled more or less freely without damage and shipped economically and with little risk of breakage. Three basic types of envelopes are in common use:

(1) Glassine envelopes. These are inexpensive and can be purchased in quantity from any dealer in stamp collectors' supplies. They come in a wide variety of sizes. Always insist on *ungummed* flaps. The chief virtues of glassine envelopes are their ready availability and their semi-transparency which makes sorting easier. The surface, however, takes ink badly and pencil hardly at all, so it is difficult to write data on the envelopes. Since the usual practice in relaxing and mounting (see below) is to put specimens in the relaxing jar in their envelopes, envelope data *must* be able to withstand prolonged moisture without flowing or blurring. Never use ballpoint pen: use pencil or india ink or a stamp pad with waterproof ink.

(2) Coin envelopes. These too come in several sizes, but one common size, $2\frac{1}{4}$ by $3\frac{1}{2}$ inches, will take all but the very largest butterflies. These brown paper envelopes are inexpensive, extremely easy to carry, store well and have a broad surface that takes ink or pencil perfectly and without running. They standardly come with gummed flaps, which should be *avoided.* Gumless flaps can be had on special order (through a stationer), but you may have to purchase a large number to get them: you may wish to pool your purchase with friends, or buy enough for several years at one time. These envelopes are, of course, opaque.

(3) Paper triangles. This is the standard form for home-made envelopes. Select cheap, absorbent newsprint (the cheapest "scratch" pads you can get), uncolored and unruled (the color or ruling may stain the specimen in the relaxer). Buy small pads of whatever size or sizes you prefer, or buy larger sheets and cut them into suitable sizes. Each piece to make a triangle should be a rectangle about $1\frac{1}{2}$ to 2 inches longer than wide. Common sizes are: $2'' \times 4''$ for small butterflies; $3'' \times 5''$ for average butterflies; $4'' \times 6''$ for larger butterflies. Almost any butterfly in North America will fit into the latter; in the tropics you may need some still larger. Make a diagonal fold of $45°$ so that one end of the fold is about $1''$ to $1\frac{1}{2}''$ from one narrow edge and the other end of the fold about half that from the other narrow edge. Fold over the projecting flaps: one will be much wider than the other, for writing data. Finally, fold over the projecting corners or snip them off (Fig. 28). With a little practice you can set up an "assembly line" and make large numbers at one sitting. It is wise to make up a good supply ahead of time and press them (a rubber band over a packet of 50 to 100 will do), so the folds "set."

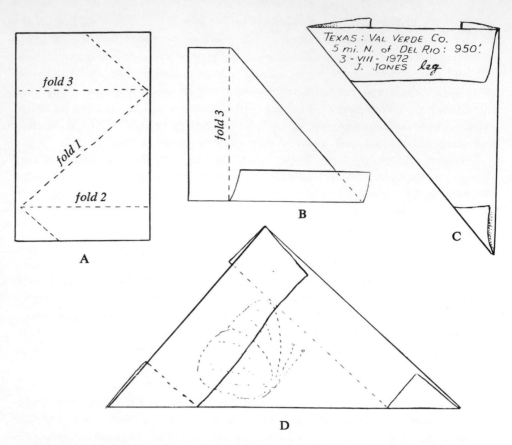

Figure 28. To make a paper triangle. A shows all folds needed; make fold 1; B, fold over shorter flap at fold 2, then fold over longer flap at fold 3 (shown unfolded); then fold over or snip off the small projecting triangles; C, finished triangle should look like this; write data on the wide flap; D, finished triangle showing butterfly inside.

Collecting bag.   A war surplus army musette bag, or something similar, is almost indispensible. It should have a strap so you can hang it over your shoulder. Use this bag to hold your killing bottle, a supply of envelopes, a container for papered specimens, a field notebook, forceps, perhaps a sewing kit (to make emergency repairs on a net torn in the field), plus whatever other things you may wish to carry with you. One home-made item is especially useful: take two one-quart plasticized cardboard milk containers, wash them thoroughly, cut them off to about 10 inches in height (or less, if your collecting bag is smaller), and tape them together, side by side, with lots of masking tape, including the rims. In one side you can keep a large supply of envelopes, and in the other you can place your papered specimens. This will fit in most collecting bags and still leave room for a killing bottle and other field paraphernalia.

Field notebook.   This is an essential item. See the section on data below.

Optional equipment.   In addition to the essentials above a few additional items of field equipment may be handy, depending on your interests and objectives. A *hand lens* (10X) is often useful in the field. As with forceps, either attach it to your collecting bag with a length of string or tie some colored ribbon to it. A *tape recorder* can be extremely useful for making extensive field observations. Small, battery-powered cassette types are light, fairly inexpensive, and the fidelity does not need to be high. Small cardboard *pillboxes* are essential for collecting larvae and have a good surface for writing data. A *vasculum* and a *plant press* for collecting foodplant samples are sometimes useful. A *field guide* to the wildflowers of your area is often extremely helpful and usually small enough to fit comfortably in your collecting bag. Equipment needed for data gathering and recording is discussed under the section on data below.

How to collect

When.   Almost any reasonably warm (over about 58° to 60°F) sunny day is suitable. Even in midwinter such a day is apt to have a few "hibernators" on the wing. Serious collecting, however, begins early in the spring, as soon as the first flowers have appeared, and may last until well after the first frosts. Few butterflies are out before the sun is well up in the morning, but a number of interesting species continue flying well after sundown, almost to dark.

Where.   All our butterflies must feed to keep alive and active, and feeding consumes a great part of their time. Some of the best places to look for butterflies, therefore, are at their food sources. Different kinds of butterflies feed on different things. Most of them are nectar feeders and should be looked for on flowers. Seek out preferably wild flowers such as blackberry (*Rubus*), milkweeds (*Asclepias*), dogbane (*Apocynum*), Viper's Bugloss (*Echium vulgare*), vetches, New Jersey Tea (*Ceanothus americanus*), spanish needles (*Bidens*) in the East; and penstemon, bee-balm (*Monarda*), rabbitbrush (*Chrysothamnus*) and many kinds of yellow composites in the West. Some butterflies avoid flowers and should be looked for at leaking tree sap, aphid sugar secretions on leaves, at carrion, dung, or old urine patches on the ground. Many butterflies supplement their diet with water and can be found, especially on hot days, at moist earth or at mud puddles.

Some butterflies occur almost anywhere, but most species show some degree of environmental preference. Some are found only in marshes or places where the ground is low and soggy; others occur only in open forest; still others like dry fields and meadows, while some are confined to lush, moister meadows. Woods edges are excellent places to seek many species. As you collect, therefore, develop an eye for different habitats and visit them not just once but repeatedly through the season.

Collecting techniques.   The art of collecting butterflies, like any other art, requires practice and a certain amount of skill. Only experience can teach you well. The following few suggestions may help shorten the process a little, but if you are so fortunate as to have a friend who is experienced, an hour observantly spent with him in the field will teach you more than all the books ever written.

1. To sweep or clap down.   Each of these two basic techniques is useful and each has its place. When a butterfly is perched on a flower or leaf a sweeping stroke

is usually best, keeping both hands on the net handle. Follow through by rotating the handle in your hands as soon as the butterfly is in the net, to fold over the net bag and imprison the butterfly inside. If your quarry is perched on or near the ground, and the ground is reasonably level, hold the net handle in one hand, the end of the bag in the other, under tension, then snap the net down quickly over the specimen by releasing the end of the bag. Immediately the rim is on the ground, raise the bag again: the butterfly will fly up into it, whereupon you swing the net and rotate the handle to imprison your specimen.

2. How fast to swing.   If you swing too slowly you will miss your specimen; too fast, you may ruin it. In principle, swing as slowly as you can to achieve your objective. You do not want to slice off the head of the flower you took your specimen on: it may be someone's prized garden beauty, or you may simply be killing the goose that could lay another golden egg for you. Some species, however, are faster in flight and more nervous in repose than others: they require fast swings. Again, only experience will teach you how best to approach a specimen, how long you can expect it to "stay put," and what it is likely to do next.

3. Removing a captured butterfly.   Once the specimen is in your net, immobilize it in a fold of the net so it will not batter itself, pinch it quickly, if that is the technique you use, then remove it and paper it. If you use a killing bottle, hold the net handle between your knees, insert the opened bottle into the net and over the specimen, holding the bottle lid in your other hand. Quickly close the bottle.

4. Running.   Cartoons always portray the lepidopterist in headlong pursuit after a flying specimen, which shows only that cartoonists know little about butterfly collecting. Instead of running after a specimen (you will rarely catch it anyway) it is easier and better to watch it until it lands, then approach it carefully for a sitting shot. If you miss a shot, and the specimen flies away and out of sight, be philosophical; but be smart, too, and return ten or fifteen minutes later to where you first saw it: it may well have returned by then. Experienced collectors watch their quarry, note what it is doing and plan sitting shots accordingly.

5. Wing shots.   You can wow your friends (and yourself) with a successful wing shot, but consider it comic relief, or sport, not a serious technique. Once in a great while a wing shot is necessary. If so, it is more apt to succeed if you *overtake* the flying individual with your net instead of meeting it head on.

6. Small butterflies.   Cultivate an eye for them. A hallmark of an amateur collection is a preponderance of large, showy specimens. Get these, too, of course, but make a particular effort to see and catch the tiny skipper flying inconspicuously down among the grass blades, the blue perched still and nearly invisible on a flower head, the hairstreak motionless on a leaf at the edge of a clearing. As you walk, keep an eye on butterfly "vantage points": a flower head projecting above the grass, a sunlit leaf outthrust into a small opening, a branch overhanging a woodland trail. When you come to a sunlit patch in the woods, approach cautiously and observantly: it may be the territory of an anglewing or a hairstreak. Wherever you go, use your eyes more than your legs. Walk slowly and avoid sudden movements, scan the area ahead and around you both for sitting and for flying individuals.

7. Whomping.   Some species, notably *Asterocampa* and many hairstreaks, frequently perch on leaves or branches of trees. Sometimes the trees are larval foodplants, sometimes they have flowers which the butterflies are visiting, or sometimes they may simply be favored perches. In searching such trees, "whomp" (shake it suddenly) and watch what flies out and where it lands. This is a favored technique for collecting *Callophrys gryneus* (on Red Cedar) and *Callophrys niphon* (on pines).

General.   Always respect private property. Ask permission if you want to collect on someone's private land. It will rarely be withheld. Always leave gates as you found them: especially, close them behind you if they were closed. Climb rail fences at the posts, where they are strongest. Cross barbed wire fences between the posts, where the wire can be spread (and pass your net through, carefully, first!). If you camp or picnic anywhere, leave the spot at least as clean as you found it. Exercising these ordinary courtesies takes almost no time and will assure you of a welcome if you wish to return.

9. Conservation.   "Game hog" collectors are anathema. If a species is rare, its very rarity may protect it from collectors. The most sensitive species are those that occur in small, localized colonies. Such a colony is easily extirpated by over-zealous collecting. Calculate your needs and never collect beyond them. Calculate, especially, the size of a colony and try never to take more than a small percentage of the individuals you *know* are there. It is far better to take ten specimens a year over a ten year period than to take a hundred at one time. Some species, notably several subtropicals in southern Florida (such as *Papilio aristodemus ponceana* and *Eumaeus atala florida*), are teetering on the brink of extinction. A collector fortunate enough to find such a species would do well to take only one or two males and no females at all.

How to make a collection

The aim of catching butterflies is to make a collection. The size of your collection can be as small or as large as your time and resources dictate, and its scope whatever your interests require. Some collectors limit their collections strictly to what they catch themselves; others just to one state or region; many encompass the whole of North America. Some collectors specialize taxonomically and limit themselves to just one or two families. Regrettably few collectors are interested in "exotics."

After your specimens have been caught, papered and the data written on each envelope (see below), you have two choices. You may mount them immediately, or you may store them. Specimens in envelopes, if kept reasonably free of excess humidity, will dry and keep thus indefinitely. They may be stored in ordinary cigar boxes until you are ready to mount or exchange them. You should, however, let them dry in a box that "breathes," to avoid mold.

1. *Relaxing.*   A freshly caught specimen that is still soft and pliable can be mounted immediately. If the specimen has been dried and stored it should first be softened (relaxed). *Relaxers* can be bought ready-made, but you can easily make one yourself. Any large, wide-mouthed, reasonably airtight can or jar will do. A

one gallon, wide-mouthed glass cooky jar with a glass lid is ideal. Place a few inches of clean sand in the bottom, add enough water to moisten the sand, and a teaspoonful or so of naphthalene flakes to deter mold. To relax specimens, leave them in their envelopes, sprinkle the envelopes with a little water and layer them in the jar with sheets of moistened blotting paper or paper towelling between. Be sure to put several sheets of blotting paper or towelling over the sand before adding the specimens. With the lid on the jar your specimens should be relaxed and ready for mounting in a day or two. Test for readiness by carefully spreading, with forceps, the wings of a specimen to see if they move easily.

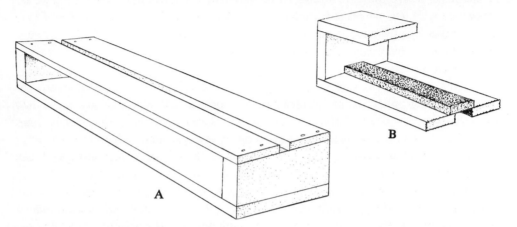

Figure 29. A simple home-made spreading board. You should make several, in different sizes, for different sizes of butterflies. Make sure the strip of polyethylene foam (or other soft pinning material) is firmly glued or bracketed in place. A, board as viewed from above; length may be anywhere from 12 to 18 inches, depending on your preference. (On longer boards collectors often start in the middle and work to either end.) B, detail of underside of board to show pinning material (stippled).

2. *Mounting.* For this you will need (a) mounting boards, (b) a few common pins, (c) a supply of insect pins, (d) some strips of good bond paper, and (e) forceps. Mounting boards can be purchased or you can make them yourself. They consist of two thin (about $\frac{1}{4}$ inch) boards of soft, fine-grained wood, such as basswood, placed side by side with a gap between them just a little wider than the body of the specimen you wish to mount. Different mounting boards are therefore needed for different sized butterflies. These two boards are nailed to two end-pieces that hold them strongly in place and elevate them high enough (perhaps $1\frac{1}{4}$ inches) to accommodate an insect pin. A strip of soft pinning material (entomological cork or polyethylene foam plastic) about $\frac{1}{2}$ inch wide is firmly glued under the gap. If you choose the height of the end pieces carefully, and nail or screw a solid board of wood to the bottom of the boards as shown in the figure, you will have a sturdier, safer mounting board and one that will automatically give you butterflies that are a uniform height on their pins. Insect pins you must buy. They are of standard length ($1\frac{1}{2}''$ or 37 mm), specially made for the purpose. The best are foreign made (Austria or Germany),

obtainable through U.S. dealers. These pins are made of stainless steel or well lacquered spring steel, have small, round, firmly attached heads and points that are sharp, but not too sharp. They come in a variety of sizes (thicknesses). You should always use the largest size practical for any given specimen. The largest-bodied butterflies will take size 4; most butterflies size 3 or 2; use size 1 (no smaller) for the smallest blues.

To mount a specimen, hold it at the thorax with your forceps, pressing them together gently just below the wing bases to spread the wings slightly. Carefully insert the pin, from the top, into the center of the thorax and push it all the way through, *perpendicular* to the body, to within about $\frac{3}{8}$ inch of the head of the pin. Holding the specimen by the pin, insert the pin vertically into the center of the groove of the mounting board and push it down until the wing bases are flush with the top of the board. Insert a $\frac{1}{8}$ or $\frac{3}{16}$ inch wide strip of bond paper between the wings and with it press those of one side down onto the board and pin the strip down lightly with common pins, one behind. Repeat with another strip on the other side. Now, remove the near pin on one side and, holding the strip down tightly with your fingers, use an insect pin, with its point behind one of the stouter costal veins near the base of the fore wing, and move the wing forward a little (being careful not to move it beyond the costa of the hind wing); then move the hind wing forward similarly. Push the common pin back into the strip, close to the hind wing. Repeat the process on the other side, moving the wings one at a time forward a little. Then return again to the first side and repeat, pushing the wings a little farther forward. When you finish—one or two "pushes" of the wings on each side should be enough—the inner margin of each fore wing should be perpendicular to the body axis and the hind wings should be far enough forward to leave a small angle between the hind wing costa and the fore wing inner margin. You can get a good idea of how your specimens should look by examining the plates of this book. When the wings are in proper position, draw the strips tight over them and firmly insert the common pins into the strips as close to the wings as possible, but not through the wings. Throughout the mounting process try to avoid piercing the wing with any pin. Sometimes, however, it cannot be helped. The last step is to spread and pin down the antennae (with insect pins), keeping them close to the costa of the fore wing on each side. If the abdomen needs to be raised or lowered to bring it in line with the thorax, this can be done by cross pinning (again, with insect pins) under- or over it. After the specimen has been pinned out, cut out the data from the envelope and pin it to the board beside the specimen.

By using one thin strip of paper as long as the board on each side, pinned down firmly at the head of the board, you can mount a lot of specimens easily and quickly on the same board. When the board is full, broad strips should be pinned down over the ends of the wings to prevent their curling up as they dry.

Freshly caught specimens may take several days to dry fully, particularly large ones. Relaxed specimens dry more quickly, in as little as a day for smaller ones. Data labels can be prepared while the specimens are drying.

3. *Storage.* Once the specimens have been spread and data labels attached, they

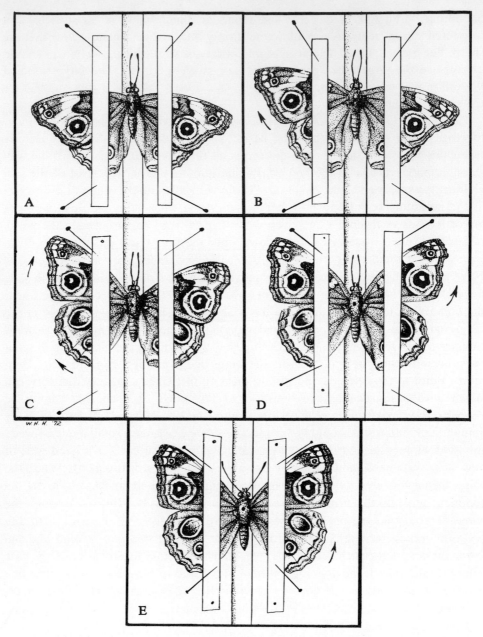

Figure 30. How to spread a butterfly. A, butterfly has been pinned in place in the slot of the board and its wings spread and pinned down with paper strips. B, wings on left side have been moved forward part way. C, wings on right side have been moved forward part way; those on left side are then moved into final position (inner margin of fore wing at right angles to body axis, hind wing far enough forward to make a slight angle or notch with fore wing). D, fore wing on right side has been moved to final position, hind wing is being moved. E, wings are all in final position; pins are repositioned close to all wings on each paper strip; antennae are spread and pinned down; pins (not shown) can be crossed over or under antennae or abdomen, if needed.

are ready for identification and then for storage and arrangement in your collection.

Permanent housing for a collection is a problem each collector must solve for himself. The better the housing, the more expensive it will be. The least expensive storage boxes are simply sturdy cardboard boxes, at least two inches deep and 20 inches or so on a side, with removable covers, of the kind commonly used as gift boxes by department stores. Each box should have a sheet of polyethylene foam plastic cut to fit and glued firmly into the bottom. Such boxes will work well, but precaution must be taken to keep them well fumigated. They are not airtight and not pestproof, so they must be stored in an airtight closet or chest which can be kept supplied with naphthalene or paradichlorobenzene (or a mixture of both).

Suitable wooden storage boxes ("Schmitt" boxes) can be bought over a wide price range, the price depending on whether the lids are detachable or hinged, whether the boxes are varnished or simply sanded but otherwise unfinished, and on the kind of wood and the quality of the carpentry. The better ones are quite expensive but are nearly airtight and virtually pestproof. They will still need to have fumigant kept in them, but it will remain in the boxes for a long time if they are not opened. Even the cheapest of these boxes are reasonably airtight and serve well.

The best housing for your collection, and the most expensive, are glass-topped museum drawers. If you are a good carpenter yourself, or if you have a friend who is, you can save considerably by making the drawers yourself. They must be tightly constructed, with a tight fitting, wood-framed glass lid, with a good pinning bottom of entomological cork or polyethylene foam. If you purchase these drawers, they come in three standard types: "Cornell", "U.S. National Museum" and "California Academy." If you make your own it would be wise to make them in the same dimensions, inside and out, as one or another of these three types. Then if you wish you can make use of the associated ready-made equipment that can be purchased for them, such as cabinets and unit trays. Give serious thought to unit trays if your collection seems destined to become large and if it includes a good proportion of smaller species. They give more protection to specimens and, most important, they greatly facilitate the addition of material to the collection.

A few words are appropriate here on the subject of pinning material. For lining the bottoms of storage or shipping boxes and cabinet drawers the ideal pinning material should be no more than about $\frac{1}{4}$ to $\frac{1}{2}$ inch thick, should accept a pin easily, hold it firmly, keep it rust-free and should not react with fumigants (naphthalene or paradichlorobenzene). It should also be inexpensive and readily available. Unfortunately, nothing meets *all* these requirements. *Entomological cork* is excellent on all counts but price. *Polyethylene foam* (6 lbs per cubic foot wt.) is extremely good, and the best inexpensive material available: it does not hold a pin quite as firmly as entomological cork, but in all other respects it is excellent and does not react with fumigants, as does polystyrene foam. Most kinds of *composition cork* (the kinds used as construction material) hold humidity and will rust a pin badly in a short time; they also accept and hold a pin poorly. In a pinch, or for reasons of economy, two thicknesses of *corrugated cardboard* placed crosswise will serve, but this material is much too hard to accept a pin easily.

It is best to arrange your specimens in taxonomic order, such as the sequence of families, genera and species used in this book. A small, neatly typed label giving the full name of the species and subspecies should be placed either at the head of the series or (preferably) at the end. Sort and arrange your series of each species geographically. An older generation mounted an occasional specimen of a species upside down to exhibit the under surface, a practice now uncommon and of little value. Another practice of former years was heading the species of each genus with a separate label. Such a label is not necessary if the species label includes the genus name, and a genus label takes up valuable space.

Study techniques

If you are bent on serious study of your butterflies, sooner or later you will want to examine the venation of various specimens and you will want to examine the genitalia. Both of these require special techniques.

1. *Venation.* For studying the venation of medium to large sized butterflies all you need is a small medicine bottle with a dropper. Fill the bottle with either 95% ethyl alcohol or with reagent quality xylol. To examine the venation merely wet the wing with a few drops of either fluid. This will temporarily clear the wing so you can see the veins (perhaps with the aid of a hand lens). The fluid will soon evaporate, leaving the specimen undamaged.

Smaller species or torn specimens may, however, be damaged by the weight of the fluid and for these a special gadget (Fig. 31) can be made that helps considerably. To a small ($\frac{1}{4}'' \times 2\frac{1}{2}'' \times 3''$) base of wood, screw an upright wooden block (2″ high, $2\frac{1}{2}''$ wide, 1″ thick) at one narrow end. To the top of the latter block glue firmly with epoxy (or even slide mounting medium) the ends of two micro slides, spacing them, like a mounting board, about $\frac{3}{16}''$ apart. To the wooden base firmly attach a large nut, heavy screw or other suitable counterweight. To use this venation block, remove the labels from the specimen to be studied, carefully lower it onto the slides so that the body falls in the gap and the specimen is supported by the wings on the slides. Move it to one side or the other so that the wings to be examined are fully on the glass. Moisten the wing with a few drops of fluid as before, and the specimen can be viewed as desired. The venation block is designed to allow transmitted light to pass through the wing, and is eminently suited to study of the venation under a dissecting scope. For more prolonged study a cover slip or another micro slide can be placed over the wing and fluid added between. When you have finished your examination, blot off excess fluid (without touching the wings) and allow the specimen to dry thoroughly before attempting to remove it. It should then come off easily, provided care is taken in lifting it off. This device is suited only to small specimens, but will work well even on "micros."

Sometimes a specimen is so dark in color that the fluid does not really clear enough to permit the veins to be seen. In such cases the wings must be carefully removed from the specimen, wetted with alcohol and then immersed in pure or diluted commercial bleach (sodium hypochlorite solution) until they are bleached enough.

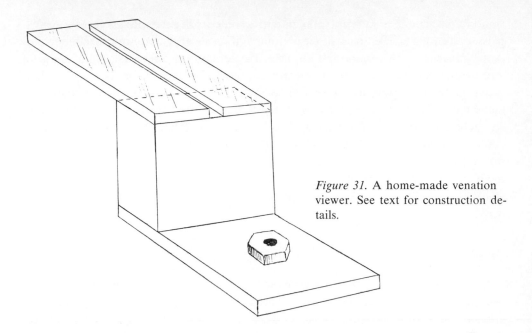

Figure 31. A home-made venation viewer. See text for construction details.

Then transfer them to water with a little white vinegar added, then to alcohol, then dry. They may be mounted on white card, or made into a permanent micro slide, using techniques similar to those for mounting male genitalia (see below).

2. *Genitalia.* The study of male or female genitalia is important in many groups, but it is by no means easy. It requires time, patience, skill and a fair amount of equipment. Most of the latter is inexpensive, but one item is not: a microscope. For preparation a binocular dissecting scope is essential. For study of medium to large sized species the same scope may be adequate; but for studying smaller species a compound (monocular) scope is also needed. You may sometimes be able to pick up a serviceable second-hand scope less expensively if you inquire of the biology department of a nearby college or university for the name of a second-hand dealer.

Only a brief description of genitalic preparation is possible here. If you plan to do this you will need more detailed information. The Section of Insects, Carnegie Museum, Pittsburgh, Penna. 15213, has a mimeographed set of instructions ("How to prepare slides of sclerotized parts of Lepidoptera," by H. K. Clench and L. D. Miller) which they will send you for fifteen cents (Cost of postage and handling). It describes in detail the process of slide making of male and female genitalia, wings, legs and other appendages, and larval integument. Or you can write to an experienced lepidopterist and ask him for help.

Briefly the procedure is as follows: (1) carefully break off the abdomen; (2) put it to soak in 95% ethyl alcohol; (3) in a test tube or small porcelain crucible heat to boiling about 5 cc of 10% potassium hydroxide solution (agitate tube continually while heating and always direct the mouth of the tube *away* from you and anyone near you: this is a poisonous and corrosive solution, always dangerous, and much worse when hot); (4) remove tube from heat, drop in the wetted abdomen and let stand for about one hour *only;* (5) pour entire contents of tube into a Syracuse watch glass, add enough water to cover the abdomen (if necessary), and under the binocular scope dissect out the genitalia; (6) transfer the genitalia to another watch glass with 95% alcohol, and leave for about one hour or more; (7) transfer genitalia to another watch glass with xylol, and leave for an hour or so; (8) transfer the genitalia to a micro slide, add mounting medium (Canada Balsam or preferably one of the newer synthetics), cover with a no. 2 cover slip; (9) add a slide label giving name of species, contents of slide, date of preparation and a permanent slide number; (10) add a pin label to the specimen giving the permanent slide number. Before step (6) the genitalia must usually be dissected, opened out, or otherwise arranged for optimum study, the particular manner depending on the group. Female genitalia are prepared in a similar manner, but the dissection and arrangement differ.

Data

A specimen without information about the time, place and circumstances of its capture—*data*—is a specimen nearly without value. At best it can tell us something about what that species looks like. With data, however, it can also tell us where and when that species occurs, and if the data are especially good, it may tell us something about its environment and habits. Recording this information entails a certain amount of work, but any good collector knows that a specimen worth the trouble of collecting is worth providing with good data.

The minimum data for a specimen should include all the following: place, accurate to within one mile or less; elevation, accurate to within about 50 to 100 feet; date of capture; and the name of the collector. All of this should be placed on a small label affixed to the pin that holds the specimen.

Nowadays we generally would like even more information than this. Where, exactly, was it taken? (You may wish to return to the very spot.) What was the environment like? What was the time of day? the weather conditions? What other species were taken with it? This amount of information is impossible to get on a pin label. The only way to record it is with a field notebook, which is so important and useful that it must be considered a necessity for serious collecting.

A field notebook can be organized in many ways. Some collectors simply keep a log book, a blank notebook in which they enter serially the dates and places they collect, along with whatever additional information they wish. This has the advantage of ease and flexibility, but you may overlook some item that later you wish you had recorded. If it is a bound notebook you must take earlier field notes into the field with you, with the risk of losing them. You can avoid this danger if you use a loose-leaf notebook and take only blank pages into the field with you.

One particular form of field notebook has proven extremely useful. It uses ring-punched, letter-size, pre-printed forms (field data sheets), with identified blanks to fill in or check, thus reminding you on the spot of all the things you want to keep a record of. You can design your own, to fit your own interests and needs, and have copies made at little expense. You take only blank forms with you into the field, leaving your previously filled sheets safely at home. A notebook of these sheets is too large to go into your collecting bag and is best left in your car. Take a small, pocket notebook with you to jot down observations while collecting. At the end of collecting you can transfer these to your data sheet.

What you put on your data sheets depends on your interests. The following should be a minimum.

Station number. The practice of numbering collecting stations is rapidly gaining favor. It has many advantages. Each collector keeps his own numbering sequence. You can begin it anew each year, but it is far wiser to start with number 1 and use a single, non-repeating sequence. Among the advantages of station numbering are these: (1) after your collecting at a given station you do not need to write the full data on every envelope, but simply the station number, thus saving valuable field time. This is particularly useful on a trip, when you may be making several collecting stops in a day. You can add full data to the envelopes at the end of the day, at your leisure. (2) You can use several different numbers at one locality if you want to segregate your specimens in some way. One number, for example, might represent specimens taken in a sedge marsh; the next number could apply to those taken on a wooded hillside nearby; or one number could apply to just a single lot taken at a mud puddle, with another number for routinely collected specimens. (3) If you use a non-repeating sequence, the numbers form an independent check on the rest of the pin label data. (4) Putting the station number on your pin label allows you to check back instantly to your data sheet for whatever additional information you wish.

Date. Write it out, or use a roman numeral for the month. *Never* use such designations as "3/6/71" (see labelling hints below).

Place. This is the most important item. Locality data are best viewed as consisting of two parts, locality designation and supplementary, or site recovery, data. *Locality designation* is what goes on the pin label (see below). *Site recovery data* are additional locating facts to help you, or someone else, to return to the actual spot where you collected, as for example, "depression, S side of state hwy 47 just W of jct with dirt road to N." If you are in mountainous country you should also identify the mountain or mountain range and the general slope ("west slope, Sacramento Mts.").

Latitude and longitude. While not necessary in the United States, this information is still useful and readily obtained from topographic maps. If you collect in sparsely settled areas, such as Alaska, northern Canada and many parts of the tropics, latitude and longitude (accurate, if possible, to the nearest minute) are indispensable.

Altitude. This is essential in mountainous country. You can sometimes get it from road signs, but do not count on it. Your best source is either a topographic map or an altimeter (see *data equipment* below). The significance of altitude depends partly on slope exposure, hence the importance of the latter.

In addition to the preceding items of basic data, you may wish to include space on your field data sheet for any or all of the following.

Time of arrival and departure (or of beginning and end of collecting). In filling this in be sure to include the time zone and whether Standard or Daylight Savings

Time. The military 24-hour notation (1:30 PM becomes 1330; 9 AM is 0900; etc.) is well suited to this, being simple, economical and unambiguous. Recording this information gives you not only the time of day when you collected, but also the duration of your actual collecting time, which can be useful in assessing the quality of collecting.

Weather. You can easily include spaces for: *cloud cover* (express in estimated percent), *wind* (express verbally: none; lt. breeze; gusty; etc.), *air temperature* (you will need a thermometer; and if you collect for a lengthy part of a day you may want space for several timed readings), *relative humidity* (you will need a psychrometer, and your field form should include spaces for three items: dry bulb reading, wet bulb reading, and relative humidity. The last can be determined and filled in later from tables with the two preceding readings.).

Vegetation. Most butterflies are more or less associated with certain kinds of vegetation. We still know little about this for most species, so a description of the vegetation of a collecting station is valuable. You need not have any special botanical knowledge to record useful data. "Desert: bare ground with widely scattered, low (4 ft.) shrubs" conveys a considerable amount of information whether you know that the shrub is Creosote Bush or not. In general the important things to describe are: height of vegetation, density of cover, leaf form (needle-leaf, broad-leaf, grass-like, etc.) and presence of epiphytes on trees. If you can add information like "second growth" or "recently cut-over" so much the better. Such descriptions of the vegetation are called *physiognomic* and, if carefully made, can be extremely useful. You can, of course, increase the value even more if you can also give the names—if only to genus—of some of the plants. If you are collecting in an open meadow describe it, of course; but if there is a forest nearby, this fact should also be mentioned.

Local topography. If is helpful to include a brief description of the local land configuration, the nearness and kind of any water, the color and texture of the soil.

Photographs. If you are a photographer, one or more pictures of the collecting site can be extremely useful. If you do make such photographs be sure to include a place on your data sheet for entering the information, perhaps including the roll and frame numbers.

Number of specimens. If you have a place on the field form in which to enter a rough estimate ("envelope count") of the number of specimens taken at the station, it will help you to determine how many pin labels to make, particularly useful if you wish to order the labels while the specimens are still unspread.

Species list. An important part of your data for a station should be a full list of all species observed. List separately those you *saw* and those you *took,* including how many, sexes and condition (which you may be able to do only after they have been spread and determined). Condition of the specimens can provide valuable information on how long the species had been on the wing prior to your visit. One easy method is to use a set of five letters: *a,* perfect; *b,* nearly perfect, but with some wear; *c,* fair; *d,* worn; *e,* badly worn, sometimes almost unrecognizable. Your note for one species might read "most *a,* a few *b,* one *c.*"

Companions. It is often interesting, at least to you, to have a note of who was with you in the field, and whether he actively collected but kept separate notes and specimens, or pooled his collecting with yours.

Empty space. Be sure to leave plenty of space for unscheduled comments, for these may sometimes be the major item on a field sheet. Suppose you see a migration: you will want to record what species, how dense they were, what direction they were moving in, how far above the ground they were, and so on. Pairs found *in copula* should not only have the basic information (time of day, sex of the flying partner) entered on the envelope that contains them, but it should be repeated on your field sheet. You should always keep a supply of blank paper in your field notebook for occasional extensive notes.

General. Obviously it will take some time and thought to fill out such a field form. It is best done in stages. In your pocket notebook jot down the time of arrival when you start to collect. Add any notes you wish to make while collecting, such as the species you see but do not take. When you have returned to the car fill out the form, adding the notes from your pocket notebook, *before you leave the locality,* as fully as you can. If you do not know exactly where you are, leave a space for the missing information until you learn. For instance, if you stopped on state highway 47 and you know you are east of Jonesville, but not how far, jot down the odometer reading where you collected, then proceed west to Jonesville and add the missing mileage there. Still later, after your specimens have been spread and determined, add a list of them to the sheet.

A good field notebook, conscientiously kept over the years, will be a source of great satisfaction to you. It will be a mine of information about the times, the places and the circumstances in which species fly; it will be a valuable aid in planning future trips; it will enable you to help a colleague who may be gathering information about some problem; and it will help you to relive the interesting and exciting experiences you have had in the field. You should consider it an important and integral part of your collection and your field notes should be passed on with the collection so that the information you have painstakingly gathered can continue to be used by others who come after you.

Pin labels. A small, printed or neatly lettered label bearing the essential data of place, date and collector should be affixed to the pin of every specimen. You should always include the state or province, the county, the town (or distance and direction to a nearby easily locatable town), the elevation (at least in mountainous regions) and the name of the collector. The additional information in your field notes may be too bulky for inclusion, although many collectors add a brief habitat description, such as "alpine meadow" or "pine-oak forest." In any case you can easily refer to the extra information by including your station number on the label. Most experienced collectors now favor the "inverted" form of label, giving first the state (usually in capitals), then the county, then the locality and elevation, and finally the date, collector and station number. This permits rapid scanning of series and is, further, the order in which one locates the place on a map. A suitable label might read as follows:

TEXAS: Val Verde Co.
5 mi N Del Rio, 950 ft.
3.vii.1963. leg. J. Jones
Sta. 10. Desert scrub.

Labels should be small but easily read, should always be on high quality (rag content or preferably 100% rag stock) heavy paper or thin card.

If you collect extensively in one place you can save hours of time and have neater, more legible labels if you have them printed, leaving blanks for the date and station number.

Some collectors purchase a small job printing press and print their own labels. A press with a 3″ by 5″ bed is quite large enough and not terribly expensive. You will need about two fonts of small (preferably 4 point), easily legible type. If you set up several labels in a single cross-wise row, you can feed in a 3″ wide strip of label paper, making a succession of closely spaced impressions which you can cut apart easily later.

Some hints on labelling. Always refer your locality to a town that is easily located on any standard road map. Avoid using township and range designations on pin labels (you can add them to your field notes, of course): they are absolutely meaningless to anyone without the specialized map on which they are given. You can write the date, "June 3, 1971" but "3 June 1971" saves you a comma and is just as clear. Better yet, write "3.vi.1971" which is still shorter and just as understandable. *Never* write "3/6/71," however. It could be either March 6 or June 3, and there is a vast difference! Roman numerals for the months are virtually universal in Europe, even among non-scientists, and widely accepted among entomologists everywhere. Always use black carbon ink for your labels (India ink, with a crowquill pen, if you letter them by hand). Never use a hectograph or similar device: the purple ink fades in time to absolute invisibility. If you have a "collected by" label printed, make sure that it has not just your name but also those words or their equivalent ("*legit*" or "*leg.*"—Latin for *collected* [*by*]), and never put your home town or address on it: it may later be mistaken for the locality of capture. In Europe many collectors print locality labels for all their collected specimens, whether they intend to keep them or exchange them. When they exchange a specimen they include one of the already printed labels with it. Few collectors on this side of the Atlantic do this as yet, but it is a fine and worthwhile custom, considerate, helpful and well worth adopting.

Data equipment. The proper gathering of field data requires certain items of equipment. Here is a list of the important ones.

Maps. For routine field work ordinary road maps are usually sufficient. If you plan to do considerable collecting in a single region, detailed topographic maps will be invaluable. With a little experience you can learn to read them: they not only tell you where you are, but also can guide you to potentially interesting places to collect. Detailed maps are a virtual necessity in sparsely settled areas.

Watch. An ordinary wristwatch or pocket watch is essential.

Compass. If you do much hiking you probably have one already. It is always a handy instrument in the field, and especially useful should you see a migration.

Thermometer. The best is a thin-walled bulb mercury thermometer with the degrees etched into the glass: it is accurate, stabilizes rapidly, reads easily and, although fragile, can be carried in a protective tube (which should be attached firmly in your collecting bag).

Sling psychrometer. This is used for determining relative humidity. If you have a psychrometer you will not need a separate thermometer because the dry bulb reading is ordinary air temperature. (*Note:* never measure air temperature or relative humidity in the sun: the readings will be quite erroneous.)

Altimeter. Altimeters for mounting inside an automobile are readily obtained. Smaller pocket altimeters are extremely useful but for some reason are difficult to obtain in this country. The best ones are of European manufacture. Both kinds operate on the same principle: they are essentially barometers and accordingly they fluctuate with the weather and need to be constantly adjusted to read correctly. The elevation scale is movable, and to adjust one simply correct the setting if necessary at a place of known elevation. This should be done at least once a day, and more often in changing weather.

Camera. Photographs of collecting stations are especially useful adjuncts to field records. Always keep a careful record identifying your pictures as you take them and note the pictures on your field data sheets.

Why collect butterflies?

The magpie disease afflicts nearly everyone. In mild form it manifests itself as a shelf of owl figurines or a drawer of match books. In more virulent cases it may appear as a house full of antiques, a study lined with madly ticking clocks, a stable of ancient cars or walls hung with priceless paintings. What you collect, how far you go and how much time you spend at it depend on your resources and on the severity of the disease in you.

Butterfly collecting is a broad spectrum solution: you can indulge in it as little or as much as you wish. Some collections consist of only a few hundred well chosen specimens. The collection of the late Lord Walter Rothschild, in contrast, numbered well over two million, housed in a specially built museum.

More than just a means of gratifying the magpie mania, butterfly collecting is also an excuse for getting out of doors with a purpose. It has the same attractions as hunting or fishing, and at least as many rewards. Like them, it offers a change from the routine of daily work and a chance to get away and enjoy the peace, quiet and solitude of the countryside. Unlike these pastimes, however, you are not so limited seasonally and there are no permits to get, no licenses to buy. In the spring, summer and fall you collect; in the winter you mount your specimens, exchange with others, and study what you have.

If your preoccupation is more than just casual you will eventually want to join the Lepidopterists' Society, an American based, worldwide organization of people with the same interests you have. You may correspond and exchange specimens with others and in the process may strike up abiding friendships.

Butterflies are the best possible souvenirs of travel. Often the kind you catch on some distant mountain range is found there and there alone. The more you learn about them, the more interesting and significant they become. This book was written to help you do just that.

Perhaps most important, your collection, whether large or small, if carefully made and with accurate data, will have permanent scientific value. If you pass it on eventually to another collector or to a museum, as indeed you should, it will be kept, valued and continue to serve the science you have espoused in making it.

Good hunting!

Disposing of your collection

Some day you will be faced with the necessity of parting with your collection. Let us assume that it consists of specimens in good condition, well mounted and with full data (including field notes), and that you have spent a lot of time and loving care building it up over the years. It is, therefore, both scientifically valuable and a monument to your efforts. You will want to assure that it is preserved and that it will be used by others after you are gone.

Most collectors consider that the pleasures of making and keeping a collection are ample remuneration for its cost and will pass their collections on, either as a gift in their lifetime or as a bequest.

Give serious thought to donating your collection to another private collector. If he is enthusiastic and active he could put your material to good use. You would want reasonable assurance that his collection in turn would pass into good hands when the time came.

Museums gladly accept the gift or bequest of private collections. Even if there is extensive duplication (and there is bound to be) they recognize the need for keeping long series and they welcome additions to their geographic representation, even of common species. If a museum receives your collection as a gift, it will be glad to evaluate it for you and the gift is tax-deductible. They will routinely have pin labels printed, identifying the collection and donor, and attach them to every specimen. Do not, however, place any conditions on your gift, such as keeping it housed as a unit, or restricting possible future exchanges of your material. Such conditions are ordinarily so difficult to honor that the museum may well have to refuse the collection.

Museums come in all kinds, large and small, private and public, university-associated or independent: almost any of them would be a suitable repository. Do avoid leaving your collection to small colleges with no entomological facilities and no permanent entomological staff, even if it is your alma mater. Small, essentially nonentomological institutions, such as local historical societies or public libraries, are also poor choices. Such places literally would not know what to do with your collection; few lepidopterists would even know it was there and could therefore not make use of it; and you seriously risk the chance that your cherished specimens would be stored away in a basement, forgotten, and eventually destroyed by mold or insect pests. Ideally you should leave your collection where there is already a substantial, well-known and permanently cared-for Lepidoptera collection. This will guarantee that working lepidopterists will see and use your specimens.

You may wish to sell. Museums, and sometimes private collectors, occasionally buy collections. Never expect to recover, however, more than a small fraction of what your collection actually cost you to make. If you are extremely lucky you may find a private collector who both needs and can afford a good price for what you have. Such opportunities are scarce. Your most likely purchaser is a museum. Museums, however, are chronically poor. They also have large holdings already and your material, though welcome, would contain extensive duplication for which they could scarcely justify purchase at full price.

Whatever you decide to do, make the decision yourself, in your lifetime. Do not leave such matters for your family to cope with. In all probability they would have no idea where to turn or how to go about disposing of your collection properly. Not knowing what to do, they may decide to keep it for sentimental reasons. Should they not know how to take care of it, the memento in only a few years could deteriorate to nothing. You, however, know your fellow lepidopterists and museum collections, and when you decide where you would like your collection to go, get in touch with the prospective recipient to be sure your collection will be welcome and put to good use, and make the necessary arrangements. With this small amount of forethought and effort on your part, the scientific value of your collection will be kept and passed on to generations of lepidopterists yet unborn. Remember, specimens gathered two centuries ago by Linnaeus, by Fabricius and by Cramer are still lovingly preserved in museums, still studied by lepidopterists.

Sources of equipment and supplies

There are many good firms that sell the equipment and supplies you will need. The following list gives only a few.

BioQuip Products, P.O. Box 61, Santa Monica, California 90406. Collecting and collection equipment and supplies; rearing cages; automobile altimeter (0–10,000 ft.); pin labels printed to order.

Fisher Scientific Co., 711 Forbes Avenue, Pittsburgh, Pennsylvania 15219. Microscopes; microscopic supplies; laboratory equipment and reagents.

Holubar Mountaineering, Ltd., P.O. Box 7, Boulder, Colorado 80301. Camping and mountaineering equipment; thermometer; compass; pocket altimeter (0–15,000 ft.).

The Kelsey Company, Meriden, Connecticut 06450. Printing presses; printing equipment and supplies.

United States Geological Survey, U.S. Dept. of the Interior, 1200 South Eads St., Arlington, Virginia 22202. Topographic maps (write first for an index map of the state you are interested in).

Wards Natural Science Establishment, Inc., P.O. Box 1712, Rochester, New York

14603; or P.O. Box 1749, Monterey, California 93940. Collecting and collection equipment.

Lepidopterists' societies and journals

The Lepidopterists' Society. Address inquiries about membership to the treasurer of the Society (consult a recent number of the *Journal,* or inquire of any member or of the entomology department of any large museum for the name and address of the current treasurer). If you have a serious interest in butterflies or moths by all means join this Society. You will receive two periodicals, the *Journal of the Lepidopterists' Society* and *News of the Lepidopterists' Society,* in which appear articles of value to both experts and beginners. Every other year the membership list is published, giving the names, addresses and interests of all the members. Among them you will find many who will be happy to correspond and exchange specimens with you and who will help you with problems of identification. The Society holds a meeting each year which you are welcome to attend and where you can meet fellow lepidopterists.

The Journal of Research on the Lepidoptera. Published by The Lepidoptera Research Foundation, Inc. Address inquiries about membership in the Foundation to Dr. William Hovanitz, 1160 West Orange Grove Avenue, Arcadia, California 91006. The Foundation publishes the quarterly *Journal,* which all members receive, but holds no meetings and publishes no membership list.

THE BUTTERFLIES
OF NORTH AMERICA

Superfamily PAPILIONOIDEA

Family DANAIDAE
(The Milkweed Butterflies)

WILLIAM H. HOWE

There are only a few species of Danaidae in the New World, although it appears that they may have originated here. The great stronghold for them now is the Indo-Australian region, particularly the Indonesian archipelago. Danaids are essentially tropical butterflies and only a few species of the genus *Danaus* are at home in the temperate zones. These peripheral species are inclined to be migratory, moving into the cooler regions as summer advances and retreating to warmer areas when winter returns.

The danaids that are found in the territory covered by this book are moderately large butterflies, bright fulvous brown to rich chocolate in color with black marginal bands that are dotted with white or yellowish. On some species the veins are lined with black scales. The undersides are much like the upper but paler. Males of *Danaus* may be recognized by the small black pouch of raised scales on vein Cu_2 of the hind wing. The males of all Danaidae have some sort of specialized patch of androconia. The position and structure of this patch is useful in recognizing the genera. Males of both *Danaus* and *Lycorea* have an extensible brush of black hair-like scales on each side of the abdomen near its end.

The butterflies of this family are distasteful to birds, lizards and other animals that prey on them. This quality is related to the poisonous juices of the plants upon which the caterpillars feed. These are mostly milkweeds (Asclepiadaceae). The chitinous exoskeleton of danaids differs from that of most other butterflies by being very tough and flexible. Thus when a predator does accidentally capture a danaid the pressure does not break the skeleton and the insect upon release is unharmed.

Early Stages: The eggs of danaids are conical and carry both vertical and horizontal ribs. The caterpillars are striped, usually transversely, and are brightly colored: blue, green, yellow, white and blackish brown. They feed on the surface of the leaves and make no attempt at concealment. Long soft filaments are found on the back.

The numbers of pairs of these is a good clue to generic and subgeneric placement. The pupae are stout and cylindrical, tapering abruptly to head and tail. They are suspended free from a pad of silk in which the cremaster is tangled.

Distribution: The Danaidae are found throughout the tropics and into the temperate regions of the Americas, Asia and Africa. Only stray specimens are found in Europe. It is interesting that the most frequent European stray is the North American Monarch.

Two subfamilies of Danaidae each are represented by a single genus in the region north of Mexico.

Subfamily DANAINAE

Genus DANAUS Kluk

This genus is common to both New and Old Worlds. There are several recognized division of the genus, two of which certainly warrant subgeneric standing. The type species of *Danaus* is *plexippus* Linnaeus: its caterpillars have two pairs of long blackish filaments, on the mesothoracic and eighth abdominal segments. The Queen, *gilippus,* has caterpillars with three pairs of filaments (the third pair on the second abdominal segment): it is classified in the subgenus *Anosia* Hübner. Other subgenera are recognized in the Orient.

The danaids have only two pairs of walking legs (mesothoracic and metathoracic). The first pair, on the prothoracic segment, is stunted and of little use. On the female these fore legs terminate in a spiny knob with which she scratches the leaf upon which she is about to lay an egg. Near the spines are chemoreceptors that respond to chemicals from the proper food-plant leaves and signal the female to lay an egg. This seems to be the way most female butterflies select the proper food for their young.

Early Stages: Very much as described for the family. The caterpillars of *Danaus* (*Danaus*) and *Danaus* (*Anosia*) are transversely striped.

Distribution: In the Americas members of this genus are found from central Canada to central Argentina, wherever milkweeds grow.

1. **Danaus (Danaus) plexippus** (Linnaeus). Plate 1, figure 1, ♂ (ssp. *plexippus*). The bright fulvous color of the wings interrupted by black along the veins immediately sets this butterfly apart from the others of the genus found in our territory. These butterflies pass the winter in Florida, Texas and southern California, and probably other southern states and Mexico. There they congregate in selected trees or groves and wait out the winter. As spring approaches these butterflies start migrating northward into cooler country. As they move northward they lay eggs on milkweed and the next lap is probably performed by the adults of that brood. Thus those that leave the southland are not the same as those that penetrate to the northern

limit of milkweeds in Canada. On the other hand, the last Canadian brood to emerge in the late summer may supply the majority of Monarchs that compose the hordes found in the winter places of refuge.

There has been debate about the number of subspecies of Monarch found north of Mexico. This has been brought about by the occasional capture of a specimen with pure white subapical patches on the fore wing. Such white patches are characteristic of the common sedentary tropical subspecies usually called *megalippe* Hübner. It is probable that the specimens from North America with white patches are variants of normal nominate *plexippus* (our subspecies) and should not be designated by the name *megalippe*.

Early Stages: These have been amply described many times. The mature caterpillar is sordid white with yellow and black transverse bands and two pairs of long soft blackish filaments. The pupa is green studded with golden spots and lines. The duration from egg to imago is about two weeks.

Distribution: The northern limit of the summer range appears to be from St. John, Newfoundland, across Quebec to near Churchill, Manitoba, and the foot of James Bay, thence southwesterly to Lloydminster, Saskatchewan, and Vancouver Island on the west coast. The winter refugia are in the southernmost parts of the United States and in Mexico. Autumnal migrants occasionally cross the Atlantic Ocean to England but never have become established there. The species has spread throughout the Pacific Ocean area and is well established in Australia.

2. **Danaus (Anosia) gilippus** (Cramer). The Queen is recognized by the uniform chocolate brown color of its wings and the black scales on the veins on the upper side forming very thin lines. In southeastern Texas and in southern Florida *gilippus* may be confused by some with the next species, *eresimus*.

Early Stages: These have been well studied. The mature caterpillar is darker than that of *plexippus* and not quite so brightly colored. It is brownish with dark brown and yellow cross stripes and a yellowish green lateral stripe on each side. There are three pairs of filaments.

(a) **berenice** (Cramer). Plate 1, figure 3, ♀. This subspecies does not have white edging to the black lines along the veins on the hind wing.

Distribution: From Florida and coastal Georgia around the Gulf of Mexico to the Mississippi; also in Cuba.

(b) **strigosus** (Bates). Plate 1, figure 2, ♂. This is the Mexican subspecies of *gilippus*. It can be recognized by the rows of white scales flanking the black ones along the veins of the hind wing.

Distribution: Texas to California, and occasionally north to Kansas, Colorado and Utah. In the Mississippi Valley this subspecies intergrades with *berenice*. In southern Central America it intergrades with *gilippus gilippus*.

3. **Danaus (Anosia) eresimus** (Cramer). This tropical species barely enters our region. The two subspecies that may be found in the United States can be confused at first sight with *gilippus*. The color of *gilippus* is uniform across the wing and a

duller brown than on *eresimus*. On *eresimus* the outer portion of the wings is paler than the inner and the brown color has a distinctly reddish tone. On the underside of the hind wings at the end of the cell there are conspicuous whitish patches on *eresimus* that are not found on *gilippus*.

(a) **tethys** Forbes. This West Indian subspecies has been found in extreme southern Florida. On the upperside of the fore wing there are a few more white spots than on *montezuma*. The additional spots are below veins M_3, Cu_1 and sometimes Cu_2.

Distribution: Antillean, very rarely in Florida.

(b) **montezuma** Talbot. Plate 1, figure 4, ♀. This subspecies is found regularly in extreme southern Texas. It has been erroneously reported as *cleothera,* a Haitian butterfly.

Distribution: From southern Texas southward to Panamá where it intergrades with *eresimus eresimus* of South America.

Subfamily LYCOREINAE

The butterflies of this subfamily are quite different in shape from those of Danainae, being long winged. In this respect they resemble *Heliconius,* but differ from that genus in many ways including the shape of the wings, which are quite rounded in *Lycorea* and apically produced in most *Heliconius.* The pattern of the one species that enters our territory is distinctive within the scope of this book. On the hind wing bands of black and bright fulvous brown parallel the wing margin concentrically.

Early Stages: These need to be studied since they are known for only one species from the Rio de Janeiro area. The caterpillars bear only one pair of fleshy filaments.

Distribution: This subfamily is confined to the neotropics and no closely allied subfamily is found in the Old World.

Genus LYCOREA Doubleday

There is some question how many species should be recognized in the genus *Lycorea.* There probably are only two, one of which is limited to South America.

Early Stages: The mature caterpillars are similar in coloring to those of *Danaus* but bear a pair of long filaments only on the mesothoracic segment. They feed on the leaves of *Asclepias curassavica,* the common red-flowered milkweed of the tropics. Reports of the larvae feeding on *Ficus* (fig) in Cuba and Mexico need to be confirmed.

1. **Lycorea ceres** (Cramer). Plate 77, figure 3, ♂. The two subspecies of *ceres* that may occur in southern United States are those of Cuba and of Mexico.

(a) **demeter** Felder & Felder. This is the Cuban subspecies, found upon rare occasion in southern Florida. It is darker than *atergatis*.

(b) **atergatis** (Doubleday). The Mexican and Central American subspecies is a little larger and much more brightly colored than the Cuban. It appears to be becoming commoner in Texas than in the past. It now is known from the southeast coastal plain west to the Big Bend National Park area.

Distribution: From Texas southward throughout Central America.

Family ITHOMIIDAE

WILLIAM H. HOWE

Most of the old books about the butterflies north of Mexico list one or more species of Ithomiidae. Holland included three in his "Butterfly Book" on the basis of Reakirt's statement, and noted for each that occurrence in our region is doubtful. Reakirt believed that his specimens came from Los Angeles. It now is clear that most of these records were based upon Panamá specimens. McDunnough (1938) continued to list the species in his check-list of Lepidoptera of Canada and the United States. Dos Passos (1964) omitted them and I consider this correct.

Family SATYRIDAE
(The Satyrs or Wood Nymphs)

THOMAS C. EMMEL

The majority of Satyridae are dull colored butterflies. A few of the tropical species are brightly patterned. Those that occur north of Mexico are brownish and grayish and in one group ochraceous or even whitish in color. Some of them have areas flushed with dull red and others have blue pupiled eyespots. The satyrs can be recognized by a combination of structural features. The fore legs of both sexes are poorly developed and not used for walking; the veins of the fore wing usually are swollen at the base; the cells of both wings are closed; very often males have patches of androconial scales on either the fore wings or the hind wings or both. A revised classification of the family has been published by Miller (1968).

The butterflies of this family are strongly sedentary. They do not partake in migrations nor do they wander far from the spot where they hatched. Some of our species are found only in open marshes, grasslands and meadows while a few others are restricted to woodlands and forests. Except for the forest dwellers, these butterflies are most active in bright sunshine. They have an erratic bobbing flight. Some—*Oeneis* and *Neominois,* for example—fly low and pitch suddenly to the ground. There they lean acutely and expose the cryptically colored underside of the hind wing. In that position these butterflies all but disappear from sight. Few of our satyrs regularly feed at flowers, but some *Cercyonis* (e.g. *oetus*) are attracted by rabbitbrush (*Chrysothamnus*) and other yellow flowers. Other species, such as those of *Euptychia,* are found sipping at leaking treesap, rotting fruit, muddy spots or on dung. The majority of species are rarely seen feeding.

Early Stages: Throughout the world the larvae of Satyridae feed on monocotyledons. Our species are grass and sedge feeders. The caterpillars almost always are green with longitudinal stripes that vary in intensity from species to species. The tail end of the caterpillar is bifurcate. This feature will separate them from caterpillars of grassfeeding skippers. The caterpillars of Apaturidae also have bifurcate tail ends but feed on dicotyledons, mostly trees.

The early stages of the genus *Cercyonis* have been most thoroughly investigated and considerable space has been devoted to them as an example of the work that must be done with the other genera.

North American distribution: No mainland state or province lacks Satyridae. The Rocky Mountain states with their abundance of varied habitats are host to large numbers of species of satyrs. The areas that are largely prairie grasslands are occupied by the least numbers of species. Because satyrs wander so little most species are distributed as discrete isolated colonies that occupy areas as small as an acre or as large as several square miles. Each colony probably develops minute differences from all other colonies. This has made the taxonomy of *Cercyonis* and *Coenonympha* confusing and difficult.

There is much to be learned about the Satyridae of our region. The details of life histories need to be studied. Enemies and parasites of the various stages are practically unknown. We have only a limited understanding of the distributions of the various species and know very little about the precise factors that control them.

Subfamily SATYRINAE

Tribe Satyrini

Genus OENEIS Hübner

The Arctics

Eleven species of *Oeneis* are found in the New World, and many more occur in the Old World. All are dull colored, medium to large butterflies which are characteristically found in arctic or alpine habitats. A few species are at home in temperate grasslands. All are extraordinarily cryptically colored on the under surfaces. When they settle into the tundra or prairie vegetation following a short rapid flight, their camouflage renders them almost invisible to the collector's eye.

Early Stages: Some data on the life histories of the species are recorded but much more needs to be learned. Diapause may occur in the first or third larval instar. All are probably grass or sedge feeders in the larval stage and all species are single brooded. Most species may require two years to complete a life cycle as their populations in many areas characteristically have flights of adults every other year.

Distribution: Members of the genus are found from the White Mountains of Arizona and the Sierras of California northward to the subarctic and arctic tundra. In the eastern United States the southernmost populations are on Mount Washington, New Hampshire, and near Bangor, Maine.

1. **Oeneis ivallda** (Mead). Plate 8, figure 8, ♂; figure 9, ♀. This is the least widely distributed of all the species of this genus. It is found only on alpine pinnacles in California from Sequoia north through Tioga Pass in Yosemite to Donner Pass (near Truckee). It is pale tan with whitish or yellowish areas around the fore wing spots. *Oeneis chryxus stanislaus* Hovanitz, a very dark, yellow-brown butterfly, inhabits the central part of the range of *ivallda,* from Tioga Pass to Echo Pass. Some authors have considered these two butterflies to be forms of the same species because the distribution of each color morph generally follows the distribution of light-colored granitic rock and dark volcanic rock in the Sierra. However, they are sympatric at several places and appear to represent two distinct species.

Early Stages: The egg and first instar larva were described and illustrated by Edwards; the egg is also figured in Comstock (1927: 259).

Distribution: The alpine zone of the Sierra Nevada in central California.

2. **Oeneis nevadensis** (Felder & Felder). This large arctic is characterized by its wood-brown upperside and almost unmarked underside. It probably has a two-year life cycle in most populations as the species flies in abundance only in alternate years.

Early Stages: These were described in part by Edwards and figured in Comstock (1927). The egg is the usual ovoid shape for the genus, gray-white in color. The larva is brownish buff with a black dorsal stripe and other longitudinal stripes of white or dark brown.

Distribution: Northern California (Coast Ranges and Sierra Nevada) to Vancouver Island and Washington, in Canadian and Hudsonian zone forests.

(a) **nevadensis** (Felder & Felder). Plate 6, figure 1, ♂; figure 2, ♀. Found in the northern counties of California and in Nevada, Oregon, and Washington, *Oeneis nevadensis* is characteristically a forest dweller, flying in little sunny glades. It is the most widely distributed subspecies. A synonym of *nevadensis* is *californica* Boisduval.

(b) **iduna** (Edwards). Plate 6, figure 5, ♂; figure 6, ♀. This form is found along the coast of California in the Coast Range south of Mendocino county. It is lighter than typical *nevadensis,* with pale yellowish brown on the outer half of the wings.

The discal band is less scalloped and the wings are larger than in typical *nevadensis*. It flies from late May to July in even-numbered years.

(c) **gigas** (Butler). Plate 6, figure 3, ♂; figure 4, ♀. This subspecies occurs on Vancouver Island in British Columbia and is larger and darker than typical *nevadensis*. Specimens have been taken in May and June. Several authors have noted the strong propensity of the males to gather at the tops of hills on Vancouver Island and to defend small territories.

3. **Oeneis macounii** (Edwards). Plate 6, figure 7, ♂; figure 8, ♀. This species is close in general appearance to *O. nevadensis* and may be simply a well differentiated subspecies. The males of *macounii* lack the prominent patch of scent scales on the fore wing. The scales are not wholly absent, as has been declared by some, but are greatly reduced in number and cluster along the veins. The species flies from late June well into July. The material from west of the Rocky Mountains needs to be studied critically.

Early Stages: Described by Edwards, they are similar to the others in the genus.

Distribution: British Columbia and the southern portion of Northwest Territories, Alberta (eastern base of the Rocky Mountains). Manitoba, western Ontario, and northern Minnesota and Michigan around Lake Superior.

4. **Oeneis chryxus** (Doubleday). This is a smaller yellow-brown species related to the previous three. It is the most widely distributed of North American arctics and has been divided into six subspecies. Most of these are found at relatively low altitudes for the genus.

Early Stages: Described by Edwards. The greenish brown striped larvae, covered with very short hairs, feed on grasses and hibernate in the third or early fourth instar.

Distribution: New Mexico and central California north through the higher mountains of the West and eastward across Canada into Quebec.

(a) **stanislaus** Hovanitz, Plate 8, figure 7, ♂. Inhabiting the central Sierra Nevada (Tioga Pass to Echo Pass) in northern California, this subspecies is quite dark brown in color. It flies in July at timberline and above.

(b) **valerata** Burdick. Plate 8, figure 4, ♂; figure 5, ♀. This subspecies, characterized mainly by less distinct dark and light markings on the underside, is found in the Olympic Mountains of Washington and on Vancouver Island. It flies in late July and August.

(c) **chryxus** (Doubleday). Plate 8, figure 1, ♂; figure 2, ♀; figure 3, ♂. This subspecies is found throughout the Rocky Mountain region from New Mexico to Alberta, and in the Dakotas. Specimens are also known from Mount Wheeler, Nevada. It flies from late June to August, from about 8000 feet to tree-line in Colorado, and at lower elevations in more northerly latitudes.

(d) **strigulosa** (McDunnough). Plate 8, figure 10, ♂; figure 11, ♀. Found in south central Canada (Ontario) and northern Michigan, *strigulosa* is characterized by its smaller size and brighter maculation. It flies in May and early June in areas where the soils are derived from limestone.

(e) **calais** (Scudder). Plate 8, figure 13, ♂; figure 14, ♀. This is the northeastern subspecies found in Quebec. It is found only where the soils are derived from the crystalline rocks of the Laurentian Shield. Mount Albert on Gaspé Peninsula is a well known collecting site for this butterfly. It is larger, darker and flies later (July) than *strigulosa*.

(f) **caryi** Dyar. Plate 8, figure 6, ♂. This subspecies flies in June and July in Alaska and the Yukon Territory. It has a strongly contrasting mesial band with white edges.

5. **Oeneis uhleri** (Reakirt). The wings of this species are somewhat different in shape and the insects noticeably smaller than any of the preceding species. The uppersides are gray-brown and the under hind wings marked with a linear black-and-white pattern.

Early Stages: These were described by Edwards in 1897. The larvae feed on grasses and hibernate in the fourth instar. Emergence is protracted in the spring giving rise to adults from May through July in Colorado.

Distribution: Colorado north through the Rocky Mountains and the Dakotas (including also western Nebraska) to northern Canada.

(a) **uhleri** (Reakirt). Plate 6, figure 9, ♀. The typical subspecies occurs throughout montane Colorado east of the Continental Divide, usually between 8500 and 10,000 feet in grassy forest glades and on dry hillsides. The mesial band is not well defined on the under hind wing of this race. It normally flies in June and early July, but in the Boulder region it flies as early as May.

(b) **reinthali** Brown. Plate 9, figure 3, ♂; figure 4, ♀. This subspecies, found on the western slope of the Continental Divide in Colorado, is larger and usually has a mesial band on the underside of the hind wings. It flies between 9000 and 11,900 feet in the mountains.

(c) **varuna** (Edwards). Plate 6, figure 10, ♂; figure 16, ♀. The types of *varuna* are from North Dakota and the subspecies ranges into South Dakota, western Nebraska, Montana, Manitoba, Saskatchewan and Alberta. It is a prairie inhabitant, smaller than the two preceding forms and generally has more ocellation on the underside and upperside of both wings. It flies in May and June.

(d) **nahanni** Dyar. Plate 8, figure 16, ♂; Plate 9, figure 13, ♀. The types are from the Nahanni Mountains 2500 ft. in the Mackenzie District of Northwest Territories, northern Canada. The original description states: "Hind wings below black and white coarsely strigose, somewhat as in *uhleri* Reakirt and *varuna* Edwards, but much more densely, the white of the wing being largely obscured." The median band is lightly marked.

(e) **cairnesi** Gibson. Plate 10, figure 5, ♂; figure 7, ♀. This is a little known subspecies of *uhleri* in which the adults are pale ochreous above with fine striations below on a solid white ground. It is distinct from *nahanni* as can be seen in the figures. The subspecies *cairnesi* is distributed in the boreal areas of the Northwest Territories.

6. **Oeneis alberta** Elwes. This butterfly is about the same size as the preceding species. It exhibits considerable variation in ground color. It is found in widely scattered colonies.

Early Stages: Described in Edwards.

Distribution: Arizona to Alberta, in the Rocky Mountains.

(a) **alberta** Elwes. Plate 8, figure 18, ♂; figure 19, ♀. This subspecies is widely distributed in the prairies of Alberta, Manitoba and Saskatchewan, and flies from late May through early June.

(b) **oslari** Skinner. Plate 9, figure 7, ♀; figure 8, ♂. This subspecies is found in Colorado (Jefferson, Park and Saguache counties) at around 10,000 feet and flies in early June. It is confined to mountain parks. The larvae feed on *Festuca* grasses.

(c) **daura** (Strecker). Plate 8, figure 12, ♂; figure 15, ♀. This is a mountain meadow subspecies found only in the White Mountains of Arizona, where it flies in June.

7. **Oeneis taygete** Geyer. This arctic-alpine butterfly is immediately recognized by the highly characteristic white lines on the veins and the bold mesial band on the underside of the hind wings. The wings are somewhat translucent so the underside pattern is visible through the brownish gray upperside.

Early Stages: Nothing has been reported about these in our region.

Distribution: In local colonies from Colorado north to Alaska and east to Labrador and the Gaspé Peninsula, Scandinavia in Europe, Kamchatka in Asia and in Greenland.

(a) **taygete** Geyer. Plate 4, figure 29, ♂; figure 30, ♂, underside; Plate 7, figure 18, ♀. The yellow-brown ground color is characteristic of *taygete*. According to dos Passos it is found in "Quebec, north of the St. Lawrence, Labrador, Ungava, south to James Bay, the islands on the east side of Hudson Bay, and on Baffin Island. It has not been seen from the island of Newfoundland." It flies from July to August.

(b) **gaspeensis** dos Passos. Plate 97, figure 12, ♂; figure 13, ♀. This subspecies is chocolate brown in color and occurs in Quebec south of the St. Lawrence. Thus far almost all specimens have come from Mount Albert in Gaspé National Park. The flight period is July.

(c) **fordi** dos Passos. Plate 10, figure 9, ♂; figure 10, ♀. Orange-brown in ground color, *fordi* is found in Alaska, Yukon Territory and the District of Mackenzie. The subspecies flies from mid June to mid July.

(d) **edwardsi** dos Passos. Plate 9, figure 1, ♂; figure 2, ♀. Gray-brown in ground color, this subspecies is found at high elevations in Colorado, Wyoming, Montana, southern Alberta, and southern British Columbia. A well known Colorado locality for this butterfly is Cottonwood Pass (12,000 ft.) in Chaffee county. It flies in July and early August.

8. **Oeneis bore** (Schneider). Two subspecies of this Old World *Oeneis* are found in northern North America. They resemble *taygete* but the subtriangular patches of androconia on the males are more prominent on *bore*.

Early Stages: These are well known in the European forms, the caterpillars of which feed on grasses in the genus *Festuca* and are not much different from the caterpillars of other *Oeneis*.

Distribution: In North America restricted to Alaska and northern Canada. In the Old World known from Norway, Finland and northern Russia.

(a) **hanburyi** Watkins. Plate 7, figure 17, ♂. This subspecies is found from the arctic coast about Coronation Gulf eastward to Hudson Bay. This subspecies and the following one resemble *O. taygete* closely in both general pattern and mesial band maculation. In *taygete* subspecies the veins are outlined in white on the underside while *bore* subspecies lack conspicuous white scaling along the veins.

(b) **mackinleyensis** dos Passos. Plate 7, figure 11, ♂; figure 12, ♀. This subspecies is larger than the preceding and the androconial patch is quite prominent on the upper side of the primaries. It has been collected in Mount McKinley National Park (around 3500 ft.), Alfred Creek Camp (3000 ft.), Boulder Creek and Teller, Alaska, in late June and July. One specimen is also known from the east end of Clinton Colden Lake, Mackenzie, Northwest Territories (August 10).

9. **Oeneis jutta** (Hübner). This species is circumpolar in distribution. It ranges farther south in the east (Bangor, Maine, and New Hampshire) than any other *Oeneis*. The nominate subspecies, *O. jutta jutta,* is Scandinavian. The species is a forest insect associated with spruce bogs (or lodgepole pine in Wyoming and Colorado.) The wings are much more opaque than those of the preceding two species and submarginally on the upperside there are interneural diffuse patches of yellow that may carry eyespots.

Early Stages: In eastern North America the larvae feed on sedge (*Carex*) and hibernate in the third instar. In Europe *jutta jutta* appears to feed on grasses.

Distribution: North America from Alaska across Canada to Newfoundland, with a few local colonies in the United States; in Europe and Asia in the more northern parts with similar southern isolated colonies.

(a) **alaskensis** Holland. Plate 7, figure 1, ♂; figure 2, ♀. Found in Alaska (American Creek; mountains between Forty-Mile and Mission creeks; Yukon Valley), this subspecies flies in late June to late July. It is smaller, has less scaling (more translucent wings), and is duller in color than the other subspecies.

(b) **leussleri** Bryant. Plate 7, figure 5, ♂; figure 6, ♀. This subspecies' occurs in far northern Canada in the Northwest Territories and flies in July.

(c) **reducta** McDunnough. Plate 7, figure 3, ♂; figure 4, ♀. A large brown subspecies with lighter tan marginal areas on the dorsal surface, *reducta* is known only from Middle Park, Grand county, Colorado, at 9000 ft. and in Hot Springs county, Wyoming, at 8600 ft. Both of these areas are lodgepole pine forest, and *reducta* flies about from trunk to trunk, where the dark bark perfectly matches its ventral surfaces. It occurs in late June and early July.

(d) **ridingiana** Chermock & Chermock. Plate 9, figure 15, ♀; figure 16, ♂. This subspecies is found in western Manitoba (Riding Mountains) in hilly country. It has a more ochreous and continuous submarginal band than either *reducta* or *acerta*. It flies in June and July.

(e) **acerta** Masters & Sorensen. Plate 9, figure 9, ♂; figure 10, ♀. This subspecies occurs from southeastern Manitoba and northern Minnesota eastward to Quebec and Maine. The light colored submarginal band on *acerta* is broken whereas it is continuous on *ridingiana*. The band is yellower (less ochraceous) on *acerta* than on *ridingiana*.

(f) **terraenovae** dos Passos. Plate 9, figure 14, ♂; figure 17, ♀. This is a large, dark subspecies with a cadmium yellow submarginal band on the dorsal surface of the wings. It is found in Newfoundland and flies in June.

10. **Oeneis melissa** (Fabricius). This species and *O. polixenes* usually have no ocelli on the wings, are small *Oeneis,* and have smoky, translucent wings. *O. melissa* is circumpolar.

Early Stages: These were described in part by Edwards.

Distribution: Alaska to Newfoundland, south to New Hampshire in the East and to Colorado and New Mexico in the Rocky Mountains.

(a) **semidea** (Say). Plate 6, figure 11, ♂. Known as the "White Mountain Butterfly" this is the most famous example of a butterfly population left isolated by retreating Pleistocene glaciers. It is found only on the alpine summits of the White Mountains, New Hampshire. The basal areas of the ventral surface of the wings are blackish while the outer areas are of a lighter shade. The rare form "nigra" has uniformly black undersides. *O. m. semidea* can be collected in early July on Mount Washington, where populations are most accessible by car. Boisduval's *eritiosa* is a synonym.

(b) **melissa** (Fabricius). Plate 77, figure 17, ♂; figure 18, ♀. The type locality is in Newfoundland, but the subspecies is more common in Labrador. The wings are pale brown and large. It flies in July. *O. oeno* Boisduval is a synonym.

(c) **semplei** Holland. Plate 15, figure 16, ♂; figure 17, ♀. This subspecies is known from the east and west sides of Hudson Bay. It is darker brown beneath and smaller than *melissa.*

(d) **assimilis** Butler. Plate 6, figure 13, ♂. This subspecies is found across the northern Arctic and is blackish gray with uniform marbling on the underside of the wings. It is smaller than *melissa.* Both *arctica* Gibson and *simulans* Gibson are synonyms.

(e) **gibsoni** Holland. Plate 9, figure 11, ♂; figure 12, ♀. Distinguished by heavy marginal markings on the underside, *gibsoni* occurs in the Kuskokwim Valley, Alaska (type locality).

(f) **beani** Elwes. Plate 6, figure 14, ♂; figure 15, ♀. The type locality of this subspecies is the high mountain peaks near Laggan, Alberta (8000–9000 feet). It flies in Banff National Park and other mountain areas in that province. It also occurs from 10,000 to 11,000 ft. on the Beartooth Plateau Summit in Park county, Wyoming.

(g) **lucilla** Barnes & McDunnough. Plate 6, figure 12, ♂. Found only in the Rocky Mountains in New Mexico and Colorado, this arctic is common above timberline from late June to August. It is dull gray with a brownish cast, and the underside is uniformly mottled with only occasional evidence of a mesial band.

11. **Oeneis polixenes** (Fabricius). This and the preceding species are very much alike. The wings of some of the subspecies of *polixenes* are so translucent that bold type can be read through them.

Early Stages: These were described in part by Edwards.

Distribution: Alaska to Labrador, and south in the Rocky Mountains to New Mexico; one isolated colony in the eastern United States on Mount Katahdin, Maine.

(a) **katahdin** Newcomb. Plate 7, figure 7, ♂; figure 8, ♀. This isolated subspecies is found only on Mount Katahdin, Maine. It is smaller than typical *polixenes* and the lighter colors as well as the dorsal submarginal spots are more pronounced. It flies in July.

(b) **polixenes** (Fabricius). Plate 7, figure 15, ♂; figure 16, ♀. Found in the eastern arctic south to Labrador, *O. p. polixenes* is a medium sized *Oeneis* with yellowish brown coloration, lighter towards the margins, and a row of suffused submarginal spots between the veins on the dorsal surface. It flies in July.

(c) **subhyalina** Curtis. Plate 7, figure 13, ♂; figure 14, ♀. The wings of *subhyalina* are more translucent than those of typical *polixenes*. It is found in the Northwest Territory, west of the range of *p. polixenes*.

(d) **peartiae** Edwards. Plate 9, figure 18, ♀; Plate 77, figure 15, ♂. A small subspecies with blackish translucent wings, *peartiae* bears a dark mesial band on the ventral surface of the secondaries. It is extremely rare and is known only from the far northern, central Arctic (type locality: Winter Cove, Cambridge Bay, Victoria Land, lat. 69°, long. 106°).

(e) **yukonensis** Gibson. Plate 9, figure 5, ♂; figure 6, ♀. The most northwestern representative of *polixenes,* this subspecies is found in Yukon Territory and Alaska. It flies in June. The mesial band is bordered by more white and the wing size is smaller than in *p. brucei* specimens from the Rocky Mountains.

(f) **brucei** Edwards. Plate 7, figure 9, ♂; figure 10, ♀. Frequently considered a distinct species, *brucei* seems to be the southernmost representative of *O. polixenes*. It is found in New Mexico and Colorado in the Rocky Mountains, above timberline. The translucent wings are dull smoky gray, with a well defined, darker mesial band. The larvae usually hibernate in the first instar and feed on alpine grasses the following spring. The adults fly in July and early August.

Genus NEOMINOIS Scudder

This nearctic genus contains only one species. It is closely related to the Asian genus *Karanasa*. Adult *Neominois* have flight behavior very much like that of *Oeneis*. They do not fly until disturbed and then travel a short distance at no great height above the ground. When the butterfly alights it leans to one side showing its cryptically marked underside.

Early Stages: Described by Edwards. The egg is barrel shaped, with about 15 raised vertical ribs. The larva has a globular head, cylindrical tapering body, and two anal projections. The pupa is formed underground.

Distribution: From the northern parts of New Mexico northward into Wyoming and thence west to the Sierras of California.

1. **Neominois ridingsii** (Edwards).   The only species in the genus, it is geographically varied in the Great Basin while the form that is found peripheral to this is surprisingly constant. There is no evidence as yet that the Rocky Mountain subspecies has continuous distribution with the subalpine Sierra form that so resembles it.

(a) **ridingsii** (Edwards). Plate 2, figure 23, ♂.   The name *ridingsii* is based upon prairie material from the eastern foothills of the Rocky Mountains in Colorado. Discrete colonies are found on the prairie and in the foothills of Colorado and New Mexico, especially where the ponderosa pines meet the grasslands. On the western side of the Continental Divide the insect seems to favor the sagebrush-grasslands habitat. A form that looks very much like *r. ridingsii* flies near treeline in the subalpine regions of the mountains of eastern California and western Nevada.

(b) **stretchii** (Edwards). Plate 2, figure 25, ♀.   This was a lost butterfly until William Burdick rediscovered it in 1935. The name still is frequently applied erroneously to the Sierra populations noted under *ridingsii.* This subspecies, *stretchii,* differs from *ridingsii* in having a very distinctly yellowish background color, much more so than any colony of *ridingsii* exhibits. Thus far true *stretchii* is only known from the mountain ranges in Nye and Eureka counties of Nevada and is quite rare. The figured specimen, though from Table Mountain in Inyo county, California, shows the *stretchii* coloration characteristic of the Nevadan populations.

(c) **dionysus** Scudder. Plate 2, figure 24, ♂.   By far the most distinctive subspecies of *ridingsii* is this one found in the deserts of northwestern Arizona, Utah and Nevada. Both Scudder and Strecker (*ashtaroth*) named the butterfly in 1878 with Scudder's name having a few months priority. It is larger than *ridingsii,* much paler and with the dark markings reduced and sometimes quite vague.

Tribe Pronophilini

Genus GYROCHEILUS Butler

There is but one species in this genus of satyrs, inhabiting the cool mountain forests of Mexico with a subspecies in our area. The genus is related to a group that inhabits the Andes. Our lone form is easily recognized from the illustration. The strongly arched costal margin of the fore wing, the scalloped margin of the hind wing and the row of ocelli on the underside of the fore wing are diagnostic.

1. **Gyrocheilus patrobas** (Hewitson). Plate 2, figure 5, ♂ (ssp. *tritonia* Edwards).   This butterfly, about the size of one of the larger *Cercyonis,* is dark brown with a series

of light submarginal marks on the upperside of the fore wing and a purplish red submarginal band on the hind wing. It flies during the late summer months.

Early stages: Not known.

Distribution: The subspecies *p. patrobas* Hewitson is found in the pine forests of southern Mexico. Our subspecies *p. tritonia* (Edwards) occurs in similar areas in northwestern Mexico and southeastern Arizona as far north as McNary.

Tribe Erebiini

Genus EREBIA Dalman

North America has ten species of *Erebia.* All are dark brown and small to medium in size. Several species fly below treeline, but most are true denizens of the alpine summits and arctic tundra. As with all arctic-alpine butterflies, the flight period is short, usually from June to early July; one species (*callias*) flies in July and August in Colorado.

Early Stages: The life history of *Erebia epipsodea* was studied by W. H. Edwards, but only fragmentary notes exist for the egg and other stages of any of the remaining North American species. The larvae have the usual satyrid form, with a cylindrical body tapering towards a slightly bifurcated terminal segment. All are probably grass feeders, and all species are single brooded. The larvae go into diapause at the end of the second or third instar to pass the winter.

Distribution: Found throughout the mountainous regions of Europe, Asia, western North America and in the subarctic regions.

1. **Erebia vidleri** Elwes. Plate 5, figure 13, ♂; Plate 78, figure 7, ♀.   The adults of this species have a distinctive yellow-red postmedian band, with a jagged distal edge, on the underside of the fore wing. Usually three ocelli are present in this band. The underside of the hind wing bears a grayish white postmedian band.

Early Stages: Unknown.

Distribution: This species is found in the Olympic and Cascade mountain ranges of Washington, and the mountains of British Columbia. It flies in July.

2. **Erebia rossii** (Curtis).   This and the next species, *disa,* can be confused. On the under side of the fore wing there usually are no more than two submarginal ocelli on *rossii* and four on *disa.* There are four bands on the under hind wing: grayish at the base, then dark, next gray and marginally a dark band. On *rossii* the outer gray band is narrower than the marginal dark band while on *disa* the two bands usually subequal. The fringes of *rossii* are almost as dark as the wing color, of *disa* they are checkered gray and brown.

Early Stages: Not known.

Distribution: This species occurs in eastern Siberia in the Old World. In North

America it ranges from the Arctic Ocean and Baffin Island southward in the mountains of Alaska and British Columbia and along the west shore of Hudson's Bay in the Barren Grounds north of timberline.

(a) **rossii** (Curtis). Plate 77, figure 13, ♂. Two ocelli are present on the upperside in the apex of the forewings. Dos Passos gives its distribution as "along the northern fringe of the continent from the Mackenzie Delta to southern Baffin Island, inland for an unknown distance in the Barren Grounds, and on Southhampton Island in Hudson Bay." Its flight period is mid-July.

(b) **ornata** Leussler. Plate 10, figure 12, ♀. Both *rossii* and *ornata* have an obscured marginal band on the underside of the secondaries. On *ornata* the two subapical ocelli on the upperside of the primaries are fused into one large ocellus. This subspecies is known only from Churchill, Manitoba.

(c) **kuskoquima** Holland. Plate 5, figure 1, ♂. This subspecies is known only from the Kuskokwim River Valley, Alaska. The marginal band is prominent on the underside of the secondaries.

(d) **gabrieli** dos Passos. Plate 77, figure 7, ♂. This race is close to *kuskoquima* in appearance but the marginal band is more prominent. It is found at about 3500 ft. elevation in the Alaska Range, especially in Mount McKinley National Park. Specimens have been taken between June 17 and July 26. Ehrlich says it occurs mainly below tree line in Alaska and "was plentiful along the highway in the valley of Teklanika River, in a heavily wooded area which supports a small moose population." He found it as low as 2500 ft.

3. **Erebia disa** (Thunberg). This is a circumpolar species. A conspicuous white patch below the cell on the secondaries beneath characterizes all races of *disa*. It is usually found associated with spruce woods or bogs, and has the earliest flight period of any *Erebia* save *discoidalis*. Ehrlich reports that its flight season in Alaska begins about June 7. *E. disa* is frequently associated with *Oeneis jutta* in spruce bogs, and has been reported by Ehrlich to congregate at mud puddles and damp spots. Three nearctic subspecies have been named.

Early Stages: Described only for *disa* in Scandinavia.

Distribution: Northern Europe and Asia and in North America: Northern Alaska south to southern British Columbia and east to Ontario and Hudson Bay. Single brooded, flying in June and early July.

(a) **mancinus** Doubleday. Plate 4, figure 28, ♂; Plate 10, figure 3, ♀. This subspecies is characterized by having reddish suffusion on the upperside of the fore wing and hoary gray scaling on the underside of the secondaries with very indistinct bands. It is found in the spruce forests of central Alaska, the mountains of British Columbia and Alberta and eastward to northern Ontario.

(b) **steckeri** Holland. Plate 16, figure 13, ♂. Named by Holland as a distinct species, *steckeri* is distinguished from the other *disa* subspecies by the very deep black mesial band on the underside of the secondaries, which is bordered by pale gray bands. It is found in the Kuskokwim River area in western Alaska.

(c) **subarctica** McDunnough. Plate 10, figure 8, ♂. This weakly distinguished subspecies is from the Mackenzie Delta, Northwest Territories, where the types were taken July 17. The upperside lacks reddish suffusion and on the under hind wings the bands are more evident than on the larger *mancinus.*

4. **Erebia magdalena** Strecker.   Our only large black *Erebia,* this species flies in precipitous rockslide areas at and above timberline. The ranges of the reputed subspecies are widely separated.

Early Stages: The egg and first instar larva have been described briefly and figured by Edwards.

Distribution: Colorado, Utah, Wyoming; Alaska and the Yukon Territory; and the Sayan Mountains of Siberia.

(a) **magdalena** Strecker. Plate 4, figure 27, ♂.   In the highest alpine regions of our central Rocky Mountains *magdalena* flies across the steep talus slopes above treeline where collectors rarely can capture it. Its large size and uniformly black pattern make it one of the most distinctive species of our North American fauna. It flies in July.

(b) **mackinleyensis** Gunder. Plate 10, figure 4, ♀.   This subspecies is found in Alaska, the Yukon Territory, and the Sayan Mountains in Asia. It is one of the rarest *Erebia.* The type was taken at Sable Pass in Mount McKinley National Park. This subspecies differs from Rocky Mountain *magdalena* in its reddish discal flush and rusty suffusion over the fore wings in the female (and occasionally the male).

5. **Erebia fasciata** Butler.   A true inhabitant of the arctic tundra, *Erebia fasciata* is found only in the far northern margins of North America and Asia. According to Ehrlich it is found "almost exclusively" in very moist grassy tundra areas, beyond treeline. The species is easily recognized by the four bold bands that cross both wings on the underside.

Early Stages: Unknown.

Distribution: Northern Asia and from westernmost Alaska east to Hudson Bay. It flies in late June and early July.

(a) **fasciata** Butler. Plate 10, figure 11, ♂; figure 19, ♀.   *E. fasciata fasciata* males are completely black on the upperside, while the females are somewhat paler. It occurs from Alaska to Hudson Bay.

(b) **avinoffi** Holland.   This subspecies is apparently recorded only from Kotzebue Sound on the eastern side of the Bering Strait, in westernmost Alaska. A broad, well defined rufous band across the black upperside of the fore wing distinguishes this butterfly.

6. **Erebia discoidalis** (Kirby).   Not a tundra species, *discoidalis* prefers open, dry, grassy areas in the same altitudinal and geographical range as *disa.* It is an easily distinguished species, with its underside pattern paling markedly from the base to the margin of the wings.

Early Stages: Unknown.

Distribution: Found in the high mountains of central Asia as well as the northern

Nearctic, *discoidalis* ranges southward from central Alaska to the Laurentides Park, with one record from Minnesota. It flies from late May to early July, depending on the locality.

(a) **discoidalis** (Kirby). Plate 5, figure 9, ♂. The typical subspecies is found in eastern arctic and subarctic America, principally on the western side of Hudson Bay south to central Minnesota (Itasca Park). Adults fly from mid May to mid June.

(b) **macdunnoughi** dos Passos. This subspecies is found from central Alaska south almost to the U.S. border, in the Hudsonian and Canadian zones. Most specimens have been taken in mid and late June.

7. **Erebia theano** (Tauscher). This small *Erebia* is characterized by submarginal rows of ochreous spots on both surfaces of both fore and hind wings. It is very local but where found it is abundant.

Early Stages: Unknown.

Distribution: In scattered colonies from northeastern Siberia to Hudson Bay and south in the Rocky Mountains to Colorado.

(a) **demmia** Warren. Plate 5, figure 16, ♂. Only in this subspecies are the spots on the hind wings larger on the upperside than on the underside; also, the butterfly is smaller than the other subspecies of *theano*. It is found only in the San Juan Mountains of southwestern Colorado, well above timberline (10,000 to 12,500 feet), and flies in mid to late July.

(b) **ethela** Edwards. Plate 5, figure 14, ♂. This subspecies has well developed tawny patches on the fore wings and a small red patch at the end of the discoidal cell. The type locality is Yellowstone National Park in Wyoming and its range extends to the Front Range of Colorado. It flies in late July and early August, almost always in bogs in Colorado.

(c) **canadensis** Warren. Apparently little collected, *canadensis* occurs from Fort Churchill, Manitoba, northward on the west coast of Hudson Bay. It is intermediate in characteristics between *alaskensis* and *ethela*. Strecker originally called it *sofia*, a preoccupied name.

(d) **alaskensis** Holland. Plate 5, figure 15, ♂. The home of this subspecies is Alaska and the Yukon Territory. It is characterized by a reduction of the size and number of the fore wing spots found in *theano ethela*, and the lack of the patch in the discoidal cell. It flies in July, around bogs in wooded areas.

8. **Erebia youngi** Holland. This far northern species resembles the widely distributed more southern species *epipsodea*. On *youngi* the spots or ocelli in the submarginal band on the fore wing, both surfaces, are more or less uniform in size and four in number. On the fore wing of *epipsodea* the band appears less wide; on the upperside the spots are ocellate with the third from the apex either absent or very much smaller than the others; and beneath there usually are only two spots.

Early Stages: not known.

Distribution: Central eastern Alaska and adjacent Yukon Territory.

(a) **youngi** Holland. Plate 5, figure 4, ♀; figure 5, ♂. The nominate subspecies was named for the Rev. S. Hall Young, who collected the types in the mountains between 40 Mile and Mission creeks, northeast Alaska, latitude 64°N. Dos Passos states that the general distribution of this subspecies is apparently in the basin of the Yukon River and its tributaries in northwest Alaska.

(b) **herscheli** Leussler. Plate 10, figure 6, ♂. This subspecies differs from typical *youngi* in its larger size (about 40 mm in expanse, compared to 33 mm) and in bearing two rows of spines instead of three on the clasp of the male genitalia. The type locality is Herschel Island, Yukon Territory, Canada. Dos Passos refers specimens taken at Aklavik, Northwest Territories to this subspecies also. It flies in July.

(c) **rileyi** dos Passos. Plate 77, figure 8, ♂. This subspecies is distinguished from the other two by its smaller size and by having only one row of spines on the costa of the clasp; coloration differences cited by dos Passos are not diagnostic but occur in series of the other two subspecies. The type locality is the Alaska Range, Mount McKinley National Park, where it flies at about 3500 feet elevation. Specimens have been taken from June 17 through July 15.

9. **Erebia epipsodea** Butler. The distribution and subspeciation of *Erebia epipsodea* has been thoroughly covered by Ehrlich (1955). It is the most common and widely distributed species of the genus in North America and occurs over a wide altitudinal range. Four subspecies are recognized, although as with most of the *Erebia* subspecies, differences are slight.

Early Stages: Notes on the life history of this species were made by Edwards, and partial rearing of the insect has been done by John F. Emmel. The eggs are deposited on thick-bladed grasses in wet meadows. The larvae feed until the end of the second or third instar, when they go into diapause for the winter.

Distribution: Northern New Mexico, north through the Rocky Mountains to Manitoba, Alberta and Saskatchewan, and northwestward from eastern Oregon to central Alaska. Flies from June to August, depending on latitude and elevation.

(a) **epipsodea** Butler. Plate 5, figure 7, ♂; figure 8, ♀; Plate 5, figure 10, ♂ (form "brucei"); figure 11, ♀ (form "brucei"). Most familiar to U.S. lepidopterists, the typical subspecies ranges from northern New Mexico north in the Rocky Mountains to western Alberta and eastern British Columbia. It is found throughout the forested belt in the mountains and just above treeline. It begins to fly in June in meadows in the lower zones and at the highest altitudes it may fly into mid August. An apparently genetic form, "brucei," with no ocelli on the upper surface, appears in *epipsodea* populations at high elevations in Colorado. The type locality, originally "Rocky Mountains," is now considered to be in the vicinity of Banff, Alberta. *Erebia rhodia* Edwards was described from Colorado and is a synonym of E. *epipsodea epipsodea.*

(b) **remingtoni** Ehrlich. Plate 5, figure 12, ♂. The most distinctive of the other subspecies, *remingtoni* bears reduced and fewer ocelli on both surfaces of both sexes, and the discal band is usually dark and prominent. Its range includes the extreme northwestern corner of British Columbia, southern Yukon Territory, and almost all of the southeastern part of Alaska. It flies from about June 10 to the third week of August.

(c) **hopfingeri** Ehrlich. Plate 16, figure 8, ♀. This subspecies is characterized by its large size, proportionately small patches on the fore wings, its complete set of ocelli, and very dark brown ground color. Populations occur in eastern Washington, northeastern Oregon, south-central British Columbia and northwestern Idaho. It flies from May to late July.

(d) **freemani** Ehrlich. Plate 16, figure 12, ♀. Ehrlich described this subspecies as differing from the other three subspecies of *epipsodea* in "the lighter orange color and sharper outline of the patches," especially on the underside of the females. The females usually bear a very heavy gray overscaling on the underside of the secondaries. It is found throughout the Canadian Prairie Parkland (Alberta, Saskatchewan and Manitoba). *Erebia sineocellata* Skinner was originally described from a single aberrant specimen taken at Fort Qu'Appelle, Saskatchewan, and is similar to form "brucei" Elwes, found in Colorado.

10. **Erebia callias** Edwards. Plate 5, figure 17, ♂ (ssp. *callias*). The nominate subspecies occurs above timberline in the mountains of Colorado and Wyoming; Asiatic subspecies occur in Iran and Mongolia, but not in intervening areas. In Colorado, the species flies in August in the mountain ranges comprising the Continental Divide. In the Palearctic region the species *callias* and *tyndarus* Esper are practically indistinguishable but differ markedly in chromosome numbers.

Early Stages: Unknown.

Distribution: In North America: along the Continental Divide in Colorado and Wyoming. Single brooded, flying in late summer.

Tribe Maniolini

Genus CERCYONIS Scudder

The Nearctic genus *Cercyonis* has had over thirty specific, subspecific, or varietal names applied to its members. There are four distinct species in our present concept of the genus. These are restricted to North America and range from just south of the Mexican border in Chihuahua north into southern Canada. Of the four species, only one (*pegala*) is found east of the Rocky Mountains.

Early Stages: All *Cercyonis* are single brooded and fly in June, July or August. *Cercyonis pegala* subspecies have six larval instars while the other three species—*C. sthenele, C. oetus* and *C. meadi*—have five larval instars. The larval food is grasses, and most subspecies do not seem to be narrowly restricted in host choice. Eggs are deposited singly on dried or living grass stems; a female may lay five to thirty per day for up to thirty days in the laboratory. Normal egg production is 100–150 eggs in *C. sthenele, C. oetus,* and *C. meadi,* and 200–300 eggs in *C. pegala.* The adult males and females can live up to forty-five days in the laboratory, but their average life span in natural populations is only five to ten days. Mating can occur almost immediately after the female emerges from the pupa, but the male is several days old before he makes any mating attempts.

On hatching, the first instar larvae of all species go into diapause immediately. In nature the site for this is likely in the base of grass clumps. During the fall and winter, larvae in diapause may shrink to one-half their former length. In late spring, probably April in most localities, the larvae come out of diapause and begin feeding. In nature, larvae reach maturity in two months for *C. oetus,* and two and one-half to three months for *C. meadi, C. sthenele* and *C. pegala.* Larvae destined to be females take longer to develop than do those that are males. This allows the males to emerge earlier and to be fully mature when the females emerge. The green or brown pupae are hung in grass clumps.

1. **Cercyonis sthenele** (Boisduval). The various subspecies of *sthenele* may be recognized by size and the patterning on the underside. The limbal band on the under fore wing is well defined and in males free of rusty flush (except on freshly caught *sthenele masoni.*) The mesial band on the under hind wing is gently irregular in outline, never deeply lobate on the basal margin as in *oetus.* On occasional specimens of *sthenele silvestris* the patterning is quite obscure but the above features can be recognized.

Early Stages: The egg is cream colored, almost spherical with flattened top and bottom, about twenty-six pronounced vertical ribs with fine horizontal connecting ribs. The mature larva is dull light green, marked with a dark median line on the dorsum, a thin white line latero-dorsally, and a broad white line laterally. In *silvestris* larvae, these latter four lines are yellow instead of white. The ventral surface is darker green. Head same color as body; entire surface covered with fine pubescence. The bifid tail above the anus is reddish. Foodplant: Various grasses, including *Poa pratensis.*

Distribution: This species, with four subspecies, ranges from northern Baja California to the Canadian border and east to the Continental Divide. It is characteristically a lowland species, flying in oakgrassland and hot semi-desert areas.

(a) **sthenele** (Boisduval). Plate 3, figure 13, ♀. The nominate subspecies was found only in the area now occupied by the city of San Francisco, California, and has been extinct since approximately 1880. There are very few specimens in collections. The only details of its biology that were ever recorded are that it flew in the month of June, had only one generation, and preferred to "settle on the ground" rather than on "the underside of oak branches" like *silvestris.* It is apparent that *sthenele* passed into oblivion through man's destruction of its restricted habitat. Grinnell's name *behrii* is a synonym (it was based on aged specimens of *sthenele sthenele*).

(b) **silvestris** (Edwards). Plate 3, figure 12, ♀. An early summer flier in the Upper Sonoran zone, *silvestris* is distributed intermittently from northern Baja California in Mexico north through California (west of the Sierra Nevada) and Oregon to Washington and perhaps southern British Columbia. The general light brown ground color and small number of ocelli on the ventral surfaces of the wings distinguish this subspecies. It is most active in mid morning and by noon has often settled under juniper or oak trees.

In California, fresh males appear in early June, and females may be captured through mid July at low elevations or through late August at high (5000 feet) elevations. Farther north, the subspecies flies mainly in July and early August. Oberthür's *okius* is a synonym of *silvestris*.

(c) **paulus** (Edwards). Plate 4, figure 5, ♀; figure 6, ♀, underside.   A denizen of the Great Basin country, *paulus* is found in eastern California, at scattered localities in eastern Oregon, throughout the state of Nevada, and in western Utah above the desert areas. The silvery gray mottling on the underside of the wings makes *paulus* quite distinct. July and August are its favored months of flight, and the collector can take large numbers of adults if he is fortunate enough to find sweet clover (*Melilotus*) in full bloom in an arid canyon.

(d) **masoni** Cross. Plate 3, figure 14, ♀.   This subspecies was described from the Colorado National Monument area in western Colorado, and occurs in similar sagebrush-canyon country in northeastern Arizona, eastern Utah, and western Wyoming. The striated, umber-brown underside with a strong mesial band and prominent ocelli distinguish this race. Freshly caught males often have a flush of rusty on the under fore wing at the apex. In this respect they resemble *C. meadii* and *C. pegala damei*. The rusty color soon fades on *masoni* but not on the other two. This butterfly flies at elevations ranging from 6000 to 7500 feet in July and is frequently sympatric with either *Cercyonis oetus charon* or *C. pegala boopis* or both.

2. **Cercyonis oetus** (Boisduval).   Occasionally, this western species is confused with the preceding *C. sthenele*. On the underside of the fore wing of *C. oetus,* however, the posterior ocellus is closer to the wing margin than the anterior eye spot. (In *C. sthenele,* the ventral fore wing ocelli are equally distant from the wing margin.) Another clue to this small species is found on the underside of the hind wing. The inner margin of the mesial band is strongly lobate on two subspecies. Rarely are members of *sthenele* as small as *oetus* and only *sthenele silvestris* may be confused with *oetus*. All other *Cercyonis* are noticeably larger than *oetus*.

Early Stages: Egg is barrel shaped, with about 28 heavy vertical ribs and very fine horizontal connecting ribs; cream in color. Mature larvae as in the description of *C. sthenele,* except that the dark green middorsal line is bordered by a thin white line on each side. Pupa as in other *Cercyonis,* except that it shows great variation in color, ranging from light green with no striations to dark brown with heavy linear markings. Foodplant: various grasses, including *Poa.*

Distribution: *C. oetus* is characteristically a Transition zone and Canadian zone butterfly, occurring in meadows or sage-grassland throughout the higher mountains of the West. The three subspecies are weakly differentiated and intergrade; the fourth (*pallescens*) is quite distinctive.

(a) **oetus** (Boisduval). Plate 4, figure 9, ♂; figure 10, ♀.   The underside of *oetus* is gray, and the mesial band is well marked by dark borders that are sharply indented in a zigzag pattern throughout their lengths. This butterfly ranges from the central Sierra Nevada and Owens River Valley in California north through almost all of Oregon to Yakima and Okanogan counties in Washington. It is also found in southern Idaho and in the mountain ranges of Nevada.

(b) **charon** (Edwards). Plate 3, figure 7, ♂; Plate 4, figure 7, ♀; figure 11, ♂. The mottled brown underside with an indistinct mesial band characterizes this subspecies. An inhabitant of the Rocky Mountains, *charon* occurs from northern New Mexico through Colorado and Wyoming to Alberta in Canada. It also flies in the higher mountains of northern and eastern Arizona, Utah, Montana, eastern Idaho, and the Black Hills of South Dakota. It is typically found in grassy mountain meadows, gathering on yellow composites (e.g., *Senecio*) in fair numbers.

(c) **phocus** (Edwards). Usually larger in size than the other subspecies, *phocus* is known from British Columbia and from scattered populations in Washington, Montana, and Idaho. The most characteristic feature is the uniformly colored, dark brown, "gravelly textured" underside of the hind wings. Occasional specimens from the mountains of Arizona and New Mexico resemble *phocus*.

(d) **pallescens** Emmel and Emmel. This highly distinctive subspecies was recently described (1971) following its discovery in the Reese River Valley area of Lander county, Nevada. The ventral surface is heavily suffused with white scaling, and in fresh specimens the dorsal surface is also noticeably lighter than the coloration in all other subspecies. The *C. o. pallescens* populations inhabit bright white alkaline flats where presumably the whitish coloration of these butterflies serves to help conceal them from predators.

3. **Cercyonis meadii** (Edwards). This species tends to be a little larger than *sthenele* and quite noticeably smaller than most members of *pegala*. The rusty flush on the fore wings is a good clue to *meadii*. Only *pegala damei* from below the rim of Grand Canyon show some permanent rusty scaling in the apex of the fore wing. Freshly caught males of *sthenele masoni* may have a rusty cast in the apex of the fore wing but this soon fades away.

Early Stages: The egg is almost spherical (about 1.05 mm in diameter) with flattened top and bottom, very faint, almost undetectable, vertical ribs and no horizontal ribs; cream in color. The mature larva is essentially identical in coloration and size to that of *C. oetus,* but the white laterodorsal line is as broad as the lateral line on *meadii* larvae. The pupa is dull green. Foodplant: grasses.

Distribution: C. meadii occurs in widely scattered, generally small colonies from Chihuahua, Mexico, to Utah and North Dakota, with its principal center of distribution in Colorado. There is one brood flying from late July into early September.

(a) **meadii** (Edwards). Plate 3, figure 6, ♀; figure 17, ♂. The few collections that have any *C. meadii* generally contain this subspecies. It is a mountain subspecies with blackish underside, found in Colorado at moderate elevations (7500–9500 feet) of the Rocky Mountains. It flies in August and seems to prefer valley bottoms where Shrubby Cinquefoil (*Potentilla fruticosa*) is in bloom, as well as along the forest margins of dry meadow areas. It is sympatric with *C. oetus charon.*

(b) **mexicana** (Chermock). Plate 3, figure 11, ♂.   This is a widely distributed but rarely collected subspecies with brownish, often heavily mottled, underside. It occurs in isolated and widely separated colonies from the mountains of western Chihuahua northward on both sides of the Rocky Mountains to central Utah in the west and to southwestern North Dakota in the east. Its habitat is the meeting place of the forest and the Upper Sonoran grasslands. Only in very favorable years does any one of the colonies produce enough individuals to allow a good series to be caught is an hour or two. Rattlesnakes in the juniper-piñon growth add spice to the search for this elusive butterfly. Wind's subspecies *melania* appears to be a synonym of *mexicana.*

(c) **alamosa** Emmel & Emmel. Plate 5, figure 2, ♂.   One of the most local North American butterflies, *C. meadii alamosa* is a race endemic to the San Luis Valley (8000 feet) of southern Colorado. Its distinctive silvery gray underside places it in the same relation to typical *meadii* as the pattern of *C. sthenele paulus* to normal *sthenele silvestris* or *sthenele masoni.* It flies in the latter part of August, after the summer rains have produced a rich growth of broad leaved grasses among the sage and saltbush. It avidly visits the yellow blooming rabbitbrush (*Chrysothamnus*) along Highway 17.

4. **Cercyonis pegala** (Fabricius).   This, the largest species of *Cercyonis,* can be recognized by a combination of features. It is the only species found east of the Mississippi River although it ranges from coast to coast. Very often the two ocelli (rarely one) on the fore wing lie in a field of yellow, ochre or orange colored scales. The inner margin of the mesial band on the under hind wing is poorly marked while on some the external margin is very well marked. There are usually up to six postmedian ocelli on the under hind wing.

Early Stages: The egg is larger than those of other *Cercyonis;* barrel-shaped but more rounded than the egg of *C. oetus,* with about thirty heavy vertical ribs and fine horizontal connecting ribs; cream in color. Mature larvae (sixth instar) are essentially identical in coloration and pattern to *C. sthenele,* but with the lateral band lemon yellow in color and the dorso-lateral band white. The pupa is green, with a white bar along the dorsal edge of the wing case. Foodplant: grasses.

Distribution: Cercyonis pegala subspecies are distributed throughout most of the United States and southern Canada; the species has not been recorded from Mexico, south Florida or much of Texas. Some of the western populations occur in arid regions, but all are found in areas where tall grasses grow. Apparently single brooded everywhere; flies in June in the southern U.S., and principally in July and August elsewhere.

Great variation in phenotype occurs, and the taxonomic treatment of this complex pattern of relationships poses many problems. In the following paragraphs, subspecies names are used as a convenient reference to well differentiated sets of populations.

(a) **abbotti** Brown. Plate 10, figure 1, ♂; figure 2, ♀.   For many years the name *pegala* has been used for this large and beautiful subspecies. Unfortunately, such use of the name is not supported by the original specimens described as *pegala.*

These are preserved in the University Museum at Glasgow, Scotland. True *pegala* is the coastal form later named *maritima* by Edwards, q.v. The subspecies *abbotti* is found from Mississippi east to northern Florida and Georgia on the Atlantic Coast. It is the largest subspecies of this species. It is recognized by the rich color of the yellow patch on the fore wing and the suppression of the posterior ocellus in that patch.

(b) **pegala** (Fabricius). Plate 3, figure 16, ♂ (form "alope"). From northern Georgia to Maine and eastern Quebec various phenotypes of *pegala* abound. The typical form *C. p. pegala* (type locality, Charleston, S.C.) is restricted to the coast. It is probably the same as *maritima* (Edwards) (type locality, Martha's Vineyard, Mass.) but tends to have only one ocellus on the fore wing whereas *maritima* has two and is usually smaller in size. These coastal forms with a dark orange-yellow postmedian patch on the fore wings intergrade with the inland form with a bright yellow patch which is called "alope." In turn in the north Atlantic states "alope" blends with a form that lacks the yellow patch and is called "nephele" (probably incorrectly!). In the northeastern part of the Midwest the "alope" form is somewhat paler and is called "ochracea" (type locality, Ohio.) *C. p. olympus* (Edwards) and *C. p. borealis* Chermock are synonyms. A larger paler form from the southern Appalachians has been dubbed "carolina" (type locality, Conestee Falls, N.C.).

As long ago as the 1880's W. H. Edwards demonstrated through breeding that all of the above forms are very closely related and intergrade. It is best that they be considered one subspecies that is strongly polymorphic.

(c) **texana** (Edwards). Plate 3, figure 1, ♂; figure 2, ♀. This large *pegala* subspecies has strongly marked undersides and is paler than the southeastern coastal subspecies. It ranges from central Texas (common near Austin in late May and early June) north to Kansas and Missouri.

(d) **Ino** Hall. Plate 3, figure 8, ♂; figure 9, ♀; figure 10, ♀; Plate 5, figure 3, ♂; figure 6, ♂, underside. A subspecies with washed out secondaries underneath and rarely with ocelli there, this butterfly occurs in Alberta and Manitoba, Canada, and in North Dakota and Montana.

(e) **boopis** (Behr). Plate 3, figure 4, ♀; figure 5, ♀; Plate 4, figure 3, ♀; figure 4, ♀, underside; figure 8, ♂; figure 12, ♂, underside. This is the oldest name available for the great complex of western *pegala*, large in size generally and with mottled secondaries and few marginal ocelli beneath.

C. p. boopis ranges from central New Mexico and Arizona north through the lowlands of Colorado to South Dakota and west to the Pacific Coast, from central California north to British Columbia on the coastal side of the Cascades and Sierra Nevada. Two smaller, darker forms ("incana" and "baroni") have been named from the Northwest and northern California, respectively, and many other odd colored forms appear in scattered populations in the West. Mercifully, lepidopterists have resisted the urge to put names on these local variants.

(f) **ariane** (Boisduval). Plate 4, figure 3, ♀; figure 4, ♀, underside. Figure 8, ♂; figure 12, ♂, underside. Plate 3, figure 15, f. **stephensi,** ♀. This subspecies has a strongly striated pattern on the underside with a diffusely edged yellow fore wing flush. It occurs in marshy meadows in the lowland areas of the Great Basin ("gabbii"), Owens Valley, California ("wheeleri," now believed extinct), north-eastern California, eastern Oregon, and eastern Washington (typical *ariane*). The heavily yellow washed female form, "stephensi," occurs mainly in northeastern California populations, but this phenotype also appears among females in Nevada and Oregon.

(g) **damei** Barnes & Benjamin. Plate 77, figure 16, ♂. The rarest of all extant North American *Cercyonis, damei* was described in 1926 from five male specimens and has been taken rarely since. It is found in numbers only below 6800 feet within the Grand Canyon of Arizona. Occasional stray specimens have been taken on both the North and South rims. It flies in Upper Sonoran zone vegetation among the oaks and scattered pines.

C. p. damei is larger than *C. meadii,* nearly the size of *boopis.* The coloration of the females is often very close to that of *C. meadii.* On the males, the burnt orange color is obsolescent, restricted to rings around the fore wing ocelli. On the underside, the burnt orange color is much reduced and largely replaced by brown, with heavy striations.

Both sexes have been taken from early June to late August.

(h) **blanca** Emmel and Mattoon. The lower surface of both the fore wing and hind wing of this recently discovered subspecies is heavily suffused with whitish or silvery white scaling, obscuring all brown areas except the principal striations. Described in 1972, *C. pegala blanca* has been found thus far only in Humboldt county, Nevada, around the Charles Sheldon Antelope Range. It flies in August. This subspecies is of special evolutionary interest because its development of white scaling matching its unusual white alkaline-flat environment parallels the white forms that have developed in *Cercyonis meadii alamosa, C. sthenele paulus,* and *C. oetus pallescens* under similar environmental conditions.

The egg, larva and pupa have been described by Emmel and Mattoon (1972). There are only five larval instars instead of the six instars found in the other *pegala* subspecies; also, the pupa may be entirely green, entirely black and white striped, or green with overlying stripes.

Tribe Coenonymphini

Genus COENONYMPHA Hübner

One of our most taxonomically confusing butterfly genera, the genus *Coenonympha,* is circumpolar in distribution and the approximately twenty-five species exhibit great geographic variation. In North America, they inhabit the western and northern states and the warmer parts of the Arctic. They are small, dull tan, brown or occasionally almost white butterflies with a variable number of ocelli on the underside of both fore wings and hind wings. The genus was revised by Davenport (1941).

Early Stages: The larvae, with the typical anal fork of satyrids, are greenish with a dark dorsal stripe. They feed on grasses (Gramineae) and sedges (Cyperaceae).

They are easily reared in the laboratory, yet little biological work has been done in this genus. Our species may be single, double or multiple brooded.

Distribution: There are two species complexes in North America—*haydeni* (a distinctive primitive *Coenonympha,* without any close relatives) and *tullia,* a super-species name applied to a great number of taxa that are separated here into six "species." The far western part of North America has *C. california, C. ampelos,* and *C. kodiak.* The central Rocky Mountain part of the continent is the center for *C. ochracea.* The northeastern portion is inhabited by *C. inornata* and *C. nipisiquit.*

1. **Coenonympha haydeni** (Edwards). Plate 2, figure 27, ♂. This is the largest of our *Coenonympha,* deep brown in color, and has five or more submarginal ocelli on the upperside that are surrounded by orange rings and pupiled with silver scaling. It occurs in open valley meadows at moderate elevations in the central Rocky Mountains, principally in western Wyoming (e.g., Yellowstone and the Grand Tetons) and southern Montana. It flies in late June and early July.

Early Stages: Unknown.

Distribution: Western Wyoming, eastern Idaho, and southwestern Montana, in local populations.

The *tullia* complex

2. **Coenonympha california** Westwood. A whitish dorsal ground color of the wings distinguishes this West Coast species from all others. Two or three broods occur in grassy hillside habitats in California and Oregon.

Early stages: Illustrated in Comstock (1927). At least two brooded, the larva is brown or olive, striped longitudinally, has a globular head, and an anal fork. The larvae hibernate in third instar in the fall. Grasses are the food plants.

Distribution: California to Oregon.

(a) **california** Westwood. Plate 4, figure 26, ♀. The southern to central California populations, in the coastal ranges and interior foothills and mountains, fall under this subspecific name. The spring brood (often starting in early February) has slaty gray shading on the undersides and small ocelli. The summer (late May and June) and fall (September) broods, called form "galactinus" (Plate 4, figure 25, ♀), are yellowish above and the underside is tan with well marked brownish ocelli.

(b) **eryngii** Hy. Edwards. Plate 78, figure 3, ♂; figure 4, ♂, form "siskiyouensis." In northern California and Oregon, the ventral ocelli are lacking in the summer brood, and this brood was originally named *eryngii* by Henry Edwards. The northern spring brood, with gray undersides and little ocellation, is called form "siskiyouensis."

3. **Coenonympha ampelos** Edwards. This species ranges from the Mono Basin and northeastern California north through Oregon, Washington and British Columbia, and east through Nevada and western Idaho to Utah. The name *ampelos* is the oldest in this complex of yellow forms. It is characterized by the rich yellow coloration,

the usual lack of ocelli on all wings (except in eastern Oregon), and on the ventral surfaces of the secondaries by the slightly darker basal area and the paler yellow extradistal area.

Early Stages: These were only partly described by Henry Edwards (1887). Much more work needs to be done on all the *Coenonympha* life histories.

Distribution: Northwestern United States and southern British Columbia.

(a) **ampelos** Edwards. Plate 5, figure 21, ♀; figure 25, ♂; form "elko": Plate 4, figure 13, ♂; figure 14, ♀; figure 15, ♀, underside; "mono": Plate 4, figure 18, ♂; figure 19, ♀. Described as above in the typical form, *C. a. ampelos* has its center of distribution in northern California, central and eastern Oregon and eastward. The form "elko" from northern Nevada and other areas is lighter in coloration and the underside pattern is more contrasting; however, there is complete intergradation between it and the normal *ampelos* form. The form "mono" is the representative of *ampelos* in the Mono Lake area of eastern California. Pale specimens from the northeastern part of the range of *ampelos* were named "sweadneri."

(b) **columbiana** McDunnough. This large subspecies is deep ochre on the upperside; the underside of the primaries is very bright ochre-brown which contrasts strongly with the gray-green apical section, and the undersides of the secondaries show more greenish color than in *a. ampelos*. *C. a. columbiana* occurs in the southern interior of British Columbia. It is single brooded.

(c) **insulana** McDunnough. Plate 78, figure 1, ♂; figure 2, ♀. This subspecies is found on Vancouver Island and similar populations occur along the northern coast of western Washington. It is very dark below, with gray-green scaling. It is single brooded.

(d) **eunomia** Dornfeld. Dornfeld applied this subspecific name to the double brooded *ampelos* populations of western Oregon (Willamette Valley) and Washington, west of the Cascades. It is characterized by brown ventral surfaces except for a slight gray-green margin, and no ocellation. *C. a. ampelos* in eastern Oregon almost always have ocelli as well as coloration differences.

4. **Coenonympha kodiak** Edwards. The northernmost of the western *tullia* complex is *C. kodiak,* found in the New World only in Alaska and northernmost Canada. It flies across the tundra for a few brief weeks in June and July.

Early Stages: Unknown.

Distribution: Northeastern Siberia: Alaska, Yukon Territory, and Mackenzie District in the nearctic.

(a) **kodiak** Edwards. Plate 4, figure 20, ♂, underside; figure 21, ♂; Plate 78, figure 12, ♂, not typical. The nominate subspecies is found only on Kodiak Island, Alaska, and shows a uniform dark gray coloration with no ochre appearing dorsally or ventrally.

(b) **mixturata** Apheraky. Plate 10, figure 23, ♂. This northern Siberian insect ranges eastward to Alaska, the Yukon and Mackenzie District at least as far as Coronation Gulf. Holland named it *yukonensis,* not realizing its identity with the Asian form. It is distinguished from *k. kodiak* by the ochraceous color of the upperside, the reddish basal area (not gray) of the fore wing beneath, and its whitish fringes. There is very little phenotypic variation among even widely scattered populations.

5. **Coenonympha ochracea** Edwards. This is principally a Rocky Mountain complex that extends north to the Mackenzie District in northern Canada and west to Arizona. The basic identifying features are a dorsal coloration of ochre-yellow and a ventral pattern on the secondaries involving up to six black ocelli and a very sinuous, broken or continuous, median band (often outlined in patches of lighter scaling) midway between the base and the hind margin. As far as is known, the species is single brooded with an extended emergence period in some localities. The subarctic subspecies, *mackenziei,* may not belong in this species.

Early stages: These are unknown, despite the widespread distribution of this frequently abundant *Coenonympha.*

Distribution: From Arizona and New Mexico north through the Rocky Mountain states to Montana, and again in the Mackenzie District, northern Canada.

(a) **ochracea** Edwards. Plate 5, figure 22, ♀; figure 23, ♂; figure 24, ♀. The nominate subspecies occurs in Colorado (from 5000 to 12,000 feet), Wyoming, Idaho, Montana, western Nebraska (Sioux county), South Dakota (Black Hills), New Mexico, and Nevada. The degree of hind wing ocellation varies greatly. It flies from early June to late July, depending on the elevation. The name *phantasma.* Burdick is a synonym.

(b) **brenda** Edwards. Plate 4, figure 22, ♂. This is the subspecies of *ochracea* in Utah. In *brenda* the ground color beneath is dark dusky gray with very pronounced eye spots on the secondaries. In many examples, however, the ocelli are "blind," (i.e., without a black pupil). Adults appear in a single brood from early June to early July at elevations between 5000 and 8000 feet.

(c) **subfusca** Barnes & Benjamin. Plate 4, figure 23, ♂; figure 24, ♀. This subspecies occurs in the White Mountains of eastern Arizona. It is brighter ochre-yellow on the dorsal surface than is *ochracea,* the underside is heavily powdered with black and the ocelli are more highly developed. It flies in late June and July.

(d) **furcae** Barnes & Benjamin. Plate 5, figure 18, ♂; figure 19, ♀. Known only from the South Rim of the Grand Canyon, northern Arizona, *C. o. furcae* is pale and semitranslucent so the strong markings on the ventral surface of the secondaries show through when viewed from above. The median band is quite prominent and six ocelli are always present on the males. It flies in early June.

(e) **mackenziei** Davenport. Plate 78, figure 13, ♂; figure 14, ♀. The range of this subspecies is the vicinity of Great Slave Lake in the Mackenzie District, northern Canada. This is widely separated from the range of the other taxa here grouped as *ochracea.* The upper surface is a bright tawny ochre and the fringes are sharply contrasting white. The undersides are gray-brown with a broken median band of white on the secondaries. Ocelli may or may not be present. The remaining races of *ochracea* are not found farther north than Montana, and the Alberta-Manitoba plains race *C. inornata benjamini,* which lies between *C. o. ochracea* and *C. o. mackenziei,* may represent mixing of *inornata* and *ochracea.*

6. **Coenonympha inornata** Edwards.   This northeastern species is ochre-brown or olive-brown dorsally, somewhat lighter toward the body. Ventrally, the fore wing is about the same color, with a transverse, sinuous postmedian band of paler color. The ventral surface of the hind wing is gray with a slight greenish tinge, darker from the body to the middle where a transverse, broken postmedian band of light color is present. All subspecies are single brooded and feed on grasses. The species was revised by Brown (1955). Adults fly in June.

Early Stages: These are described by Davenport (1941), and Brown (1961). The stages apparently resemble those of *C. california* quite closely.

Distribution: The spruce belt section of the eastern half of Canada, with western plains representatives as far as eastern British Columbia and into northern Montana and North Dakota. It is also found in Maine, New Hampshire and in northern New York.

(a) **macisaaci** dos Passos. Plate 10, figure 20, ♂; figure 21, ♂, underside; figure 22, ♀.   This far eastern subspecies is found only in southwestern Newfoundland and is much darker green-gray than nominate *inornata.* The ventral hind wing ocelli are absent.

(b) **inornata** Edwards. Plate 4, figure 16, ♂; figure 17, ♀.   As described above, this subspecies ranges from Labrador west through Quebec and Ontario to Lake Winnipeg (type locality) in western Ontario, and north at least to Hudson Bay. The name *quebecensis* Barnes & Benjamin is synonymous with *i. inornata.* There are usually one or two ventral ocelli in the anal angle of the hind wing.

(c) **benjamini** McDunnough. Plate 10, figure 13, ♂; figure 14, ♂; underside; figure 15, ♀.   This is the westernmost representative of the *inornata* group, and its center is the plains region of central Canada. It is distinguished by having brighter and lighter ochreous ground color than in *i. inornata,* and by a well developed apical ocellus on the underside of the fore wings. It is reported from Alberta, Manitoba, Saskatchewan, eastern British Columbia, northern Montana and the Dakotas. Brown believes *benjamini* represents a Pleistocene hybrid taxon of *C. inornata* crossed with *C. ochracea.*

7. **Coenonympha nipisiquit** McDunnough.   Though close in general coloration to *C. inornata* Edwards, this species is an August flier while *inornata* is a May–June flier. This late summer species occurs in only two areas of eastern Canada and adjacent northern New York.

Early Stages: These closely resemble the others in the genus.

Distribution: Northeastern New Brunswick and several of the Thousand Islands in the St. Lawrence River; not known elsewhere, but undoubtedly overlooked because of its resemblence to *inornata.* All late summer flying *Coenonympha* in the Northeast should be examined carefully.

(a) **nipisiquit** McDunnough. Plate 5, figure 20, ♂.   With a deeper ochre-brown dorsal surface than *inornata,* this subspecies is large and the pale postmedian hind wing band is quite prominent on a dark, greenish brown ground color. It is found in salt marshes in the maritime area of northeastern New Brunswick. It flies in early August.

(b) **heinemani** Brown. Plate 10, figure 16, ♂; underside; figure 17, ♂; figure 18, ♀. Similar in general coloration to *C. n. nipisiquit,* this subspecies has grayer fringes, a black spot at the apical ocellus position, and ventral hind wing spots (white or black points in the submargin) which the other eastern forms lack. It occurs on Picton and Grindstone Islands among the Thousand Islands in the St. Lawrence River, near Clayton, New York. It flies in August and September. On the same islands, *C. inornata inornata* flies in May and June. Rearing studies have shown that the summer flying insect (*heinemani*) does not result from eggs laid by the spring flying butterfly (*inornata*), so the two seem to be distinct species. Occasional hybridization may occur when a late flying *inornata* female mates with an early emerging *heinemani* male. This exceptionally interesting situation is fully described by Brown (1961).

Tribe **Euptychiini**

Genus **PARAMECERA** Butler

This genus is allied to *Euptychia;* only one species is known. Its pale, almost pearly ventral coloration and large apical fore wing eyespot will distinguish it readily from our *Euptychia* species. Six hind wing ocelli are present.

1. **Paramecera xicaque** Reakirt. Plate 2, figure 20, ♀; figure 21, ♂. Found in the pine forests of southern Arizona mountain ranges, *P. xicaque* occurs south through Mexico to at least the mountains of central Chiapas. It is a late summer flier in Arizona.

Early Stages: No information on its life history has been published.

Distribution: See above.

Genus **EUPTYCHIA** Hübner

These drab colored, usually small satyrids are a predominantly neotropical group that penetrates our area as far north as Michigan and southern Canada. All have ocelli on their brown or grayish brown wings. In 1964 Forster divided the neotropical butterflies usually called *Euptychia* among thirty-three genera! As yet not enough work has been done with the North American species to assign them to their proper places in that array. Therefore we adhere to the old generic limits of *Euptychia.*

Early Stages: The early stages of most of our species are known. The larvae are typical of satyrids, green to brownish with longitudinal stripes and bifid caudal appendages. They feed on grasses.

Distribution: From Chile and Argentina to southern Canada with the stronghold in the eastern Andes.

1. Euptychia hermes (Fabricius). Plate 2, figure 14, ♂ (ssp. *sosybius*). *E. hermes,* our smallest species, occurs from New Jersey to South America. The subspecies inhabiting the East Coast of the U.S. is called *E. hermes sosybius* (Fabricius). The fore wing ocelli are much smaller than those of *E. cymela,* a similar species, and the ground color is a dark brown. It is abundant in moist woods, and has two annual broods (perhaps three in Florida).

Early Stages: The larva is light green with darker longitudinal stripes. The abundant low tubercles on the larva are yellow and hairy.

Distribution: In the U.S., from south Florida and Texas to southern New Jersey on the East Coast. The species does not range farther north than Mazatlán, Mexico, on the west coast of North America, and thus seems to require moderately high environmental humidity.

2. Euptychia cymela (Cramer). This species is larger and lighter colored than *hermes* and the two eyespots on the fore wing underside are large; they are small or absent on *hermes,* and the northern species *mitchelli* bears four ocelli on the underside of the fore wing. The two recognized subspecies of *cymela* blend one into the other and only at the extremes of their ranges are distinctive.

Early Stages: The larva is pale greenish brown with the usual longitudinal stripes. The body tubercles are low and whitish. The pupa is pale brown with darker mottling. Various grasses are used as larval food.

Distribution: East of the 100th meridian from southern Canada into northeastern Mexico.

(a) **cymela** (Cramer). Plate 2, figure 10, ♂; figure 11, ♂, underside. The underside of this subspecies is brownish gray. It blends into the next in the coastal parts of the Gulf states and northern Florida. The range of *cymela cymela* is from the 100th meridian east to the Atlantic Coast from Ontario and Nebraska southward to Georgia and northeastern Mexico. Mostly single brooded in the north.

(b) **viola** (Maynard). Plate 97, figure 9, ♂, underside; figure 15, ♂. A distinctive subspecies occurs in the peninsula of Florida that Maynard called *viola.* The underside is almost violet-gray instead of being brownish gray. The farther south the insect lives in Florida the more evident is the violet color.

3. Euptychia gemma (Hübner). The underside of the hind wing of this species has brightly silvered, small ocelli grouped in a large, submarginal gray patch.

Early Stages: General markings as in other members of the genus, but the larvae bear two long, horn-like tubercles on the head and also on the anal segment. The larvae of the spring brood are pale green while the fall brood are pale brown in ground color. The pupa is green or brown and markedly bifid at the head.

Distribution: Southeastern United States, from southern Illinois to south Texas and central Florida; in Mexico south to the highlands of Chiapas. The species is found in areas of tall meadow grass.

(a) **gemma** (Hübner). Plate 2, figure 22, ♂; figure 26, ♂, underside. The nominate subspecies ranges from southern Illinois to Virginia, south to central Florida and the Gulf states. The ground color is yellow-brown.

(b) **freemani** (Stallings & Turner). Plate 2, figure 19, ♂. The ground color of this subspecies is reddish brown and the ventral striations on the wings are darker red-brown and more developed than in *gemma. E. gemma freemani* is found from southern Texas into tropical Mexico.

4. **Euptychia dorothea** (Nabokov). Plate 2, figure 16, ♂; figure 17, ♀. This southwestern species and *henshawi* are difficult to distinguish. Both are medium sized, dark reddish brown butterflies with a simple pattern on the underside. On the fore wing there are three dark lines more or less parallel with the outer margin. On the hind wing the outermost line is not parallel with the wing margin but the second and inner ones are. The second line on the underside of the hind wing of *dorothea* terminates on the costa outward from the termination of the outermost line on the inner margin of the fore wing. On *henshawi* the second lines on hind and fore wings terminate almost opposite each other. Look carefully at the illustrations for these features.

Early Stages: Not known.

Distribution: Arid canyons in southern Colorado, western Texas and Arizona southward into Mexico.

5. **Euptychia henshawi** (Edwards). Plate 2, figure 18, ♂. This butterfly occurs in the same range and habitats as *E. dorothea;* see the preceding discussion for the differentiating characters. One brood appears in June, the second in September.

Early Stages: Only the egg has been described, by Edwards. It is green, subglobular with a greater width than height, a flattened base, and virtually no sculpturing of the surface.

Distribution: Sonora (Mexico), Arizona, western Colorado, western Texas.

6. **Euptychia areolata** (Smith). This species may be recognized immediately by the prominent large strongly elongated ocelli on the underside of the hind wings. The two subspecies are not well defined and there is a broad blend zone.

Early Stages: The larvae are yellow-green with darker longitudinal stripes and low brownish tubercles.

Distribution: From coastal Texas and southern Florida northward on the coastal plain to central coastal New Jersey.

(a) **areolata** (Smith). This subspecies has larger and more elongate ocelli ringed with red than does the more northern one. It is found as far north as southern Virginia.

(b) **septentrionalis** (Davis). Plate 2, figure 12, ♂. The ring around each ocellus is yellowish and the ocelli are smaller and less elongated. It is found from Lakehurst, New Jersey, south into Virginia.

7. **Euptychia mitchellii** French. Plate 2, figure 13, ♀. This is a small satyr, a little larger than *hermes*. It can be recognized by the row of four ocelli on the under fore wing and six on the under hind wing. Its restricted habitat is a type of bog or semi-bog characterized by Tamarack. It flies only during the first two weeks of July, in a single brood. The species hibernates as a fourth instar larva.

Early Stages: There are six larval instars. The larva is light lime green in color with whitish striping. The numerous body papillae are whitish at the tips. The pupa is light lime green in color and has the typical satyrid shape.

Distribution: Usually in acid semi-bogs in southern Michigan, Ohio, Indiana and northern New Jersey. "Reclamation" is fast eliminating the habitat of this species.

8. **Euptychia rubricata** Edwards. This distinctive *Euptychia* is orange-brown in ground color and bears one ocellus near the apex of the fore wing, and one near the anal angle of the hind wing. Ventrally, the basal area of the fore wing is bright reddish. It is strictly a southwestern and Mexican species.

Early Stages: Unknown.

Distribution: Central America to Arizona, New Mexico, Texas and into Oklahoma.

(a) **rubricata** Edwards. Plate 8, figure 17, ♂, underside. The dorsal orangish patch in the adults of the nominate subspecies always includes the distal half of the cell of the fore wing, but is small on the secondaries. *E. r. rubricata* occurs in Texas (type locality: Waco), Oklahoma and New Mexico southward into Mexico.

(b) **cheneyorum** R. L. Chermock. Plate 2, figure 15, ♀. A weakly distinguished subspecies, *cheneyorum* has a reduced brick red patch on the dorsal surface of the fore wings, and a large red patch on the hind wings. It is known from many mountain areas in Arizona. It prefers dry, oak-bordered canyons.

Subfamily LETHINAE

Genus LETHE Hübner

The ground color of the adults is uniformly brown above with prominent, but usually "blind" ocelli. Beneath, the ocelli are highly developed and beautifully decorated with soft tones of pale lavender, blue and rich chocolate brown.

The species of *Lethe* require more or less humid environments. *L. portlandia, creola* and *appalachia* occur in shaded forest areas, *creola* and *appalachia* typically in riparian or swamp environments. *L. eurydice,* however, is found only in open, moist to wet grassy habitats, usually marshes.

The flight of the adults is swift and erratic. They often dart around trees and through dense vegetation, and are accordingly difficult to capture. Adults avoid flowers and feed largely at fermenting tree sap and at carrion, excrement and other nonfloral foods. They may be captured by using a screen trap baited with a fermented banana and beer mixture. The trap may be elevated by rope to at least four feet above the ground so the bait mixture will be out of reach of marauding raccoons.

Members of the genus *Lethe* are found in two widely separated areas of the world: in eastern Asia (including the Himalayas), where there are many species, and in the eastern United States and adjacent Canada, where there are only a few. This pattern of distribution is a familiar one and suggests that *Lethe* may have reached North America from Asia long ago in the Tertiary period.

Revisional studies in this genus have produced many important changes in recent years. These studies are still continuing, and we may expect further additions to our knowledge in the future.

Early Stages: The larvae are light green with a pair of horns, on the head usually marked with red, and an anal fork, usually red-tipped. The larvae feed on various Graminae (grasses) and Cyperaceae (sedges).

Distribution: From Labrador and Great Slave Lake south to the Gulf states, including northern Florida, and as far west as eastern Texas.

1. **Lethe creola** (Skinner). Plate 2, figure 1, ♂; figure 2, ♀; figure 3, ♀, underside. The male of this species is easily recognized by the more produced apical region of the fore wing and the conspicuous androconial patches on the fore wing above, absent in *portlandia*. Until recently females were not reliably separable from those of *portlandia* (especially those of nominate *portlandia,* which often occurs with *creola*). The only completely reliable way to distinguish them is in the configuration of the postmedian line on the fore wing underside. The costal part of this line, from costa to M_3, is irregularly convex, and the segment in M_1-M_2 strongly convex, in *creola;* in *portlandia* the costal part of the line to M_3 is straight or slightly concave, and the M_1-M_2 segment is straight. In addition, *creola* always, or nearly always, has a subterminal ocellus below vein Cu_2 on the fore wing underside, usually (but not always) lacking in *portlandia.*

Early Stages: Although these have not been studied it is reasonably certain that the larval foodplant is cane (*Arundinaria*), especially Switch Cane, *A. tecta.* There are two broods, one in late May and June, the other in August and September.

Distribution: From southern Virginia, southern Indiana and southern Missouri southward to Georgia and the Gulf states westward to eastern Texas. Strangely there are no authenticated records as yet from Florida, nor from West Virginia, Kentucky or Tennessee. More northern "records" of this species have been found to be based on misidentified specimens of *portlandia.*

2. **Lethe portlandia** (Fabricius). Males of this species lack androconial scaling above. Adults have a fast erratic flight, usually keep to the forest and often perch on tree trunks or other places where they are hard to capture. The species occupies a broad area from Maine to Manitoba, south to the Gulf states.

(a) **portlandia** (Fabricius). Plate 13, figure 14, ♀. Adults are brightly marked and females often have well developed ochreous above, as shown in the figure. This subspecies usually avoids sunlight and keeps to shaded woods and streambanks where cane (*Arundinaria*) is growing. Both *portlandia* and *creola* occur together and have similar flight habits, making them difficult to distinguish on the wing.

Early Stages: Undescribed, though the larval foodplant is known to be *Arundinaria*. There are three overlapping broods from May to September.

Distribution: Southeastern United States from central Georgia south, westward to eastern Texas. Northward it grades into the subspecies.

(b) **androcardia** (Hübner). Plate 13, figure 3, ♀; figure 4, ♂. This subspecies resembles the preceding but is smaller, duller colored, and has smaller ocelli.

Early Stages: The larvae probably feed on *Arundinaria*.

Distribution: Southern Virginia, southern Illinois and northwestern Arkansas, south to the latitude of central Georgia, grading into nominate *portlandia* southward.

(c) **anthedon** (Clark). Plate 2, figure 4, ♂; Plate 13, figure 10, ♀. This subspecies, probably the best known of all, is still smaller and duller than *androcardia*. Its flight habits are similar but it is often found in woods away from streams. It is possible that this and the next subspecies form a species distinct from the preceding two subspecies.

Early Stages: The larvae feed on *Muhlenbergia* (Kansas), *Brachyelytrum erectum*, and other forest grasses, but apparently never on cane. Single brooded over most of its range, from late June to early August; possibly double brooded southward.

Distribution: From central New England to southern Minnesota south to Virginia, southern Illinois and northwestern Arkansas.

(d) **borealis** (Clark). Plate 13, figure 13, ♀. This pale northern subspecies grades southward into *anthedon*. It is single brooded (late July) and occurs from Maine and Quebec westward to Manitoba and northern Minnesota, including the Upper Peninsula of Michigan.

3. **Lethe eurydice** (Johannson).

(a) **eurydice** (Johannson). Plate 2, figure 6, ♂; figure 7, ♂, underside. This species has the most northerly range in the genus. It occurs in open marshes and wet meadows with an abundance of sedges. There is only one generation a year, but the flight period is long, from late June through September.

Early Stages: Summer larvae have dark green longitudinal stripes on a pale green body. Hibernating larvae are straw colored. The two-horned head capsule has red side stripes which extend down the horns to the lower part of the head near the ocelli. The larvae feed on sedges (*Carex*).

Distribution: From Delaware westward to northern Illinois, northward to central Quebec and northwestward to Great Slave Lake, Northwest Territories.

(b) **fumosa** (Leussler). Plate 4, figure 1, ♂; figure 2, ♂, underside. Larger and darker than nominate *eurydice,* this subspecies is found in scattered colonies in permanent marshes in prairie regions.

Distribution: From eastern Iowa and eastern South Dakota westward to north central Colorado; now extinct in many parts of its range.

4. **Lethe appalachia** Chermock. Plate 2, figure 8, ♂; figure 9, ♂, underside.   Formerly believed to be a southern subspecies of the preceding, *appalachia* is now known to be a full species, its range broadly overlapping that of *eurydice*. It differs from that species especially on the under surface: in *appalachia* the ground color is darker, violet-gray, and the postmedian lines are only slightly wavy, while in *eurydice* the ground color is yellowish brown and the postmedian lines are deeply zig-zag. *L. appalachia* is found in wooded swamps, along streams through woods and in the shrubby, shaded perimeters of some bogs. Single brooded (late June to early August) in the northern part of its range; double to possibly triple brooded southward.

Early Stages: The larvae are like those of *eurydice* but the red side stripes on the head capsule do not extend ventrally below the bases of the horns. Larvae feed on *Carex.*

Distribution: From Maine and Quebec westward to southern Minnesota and eastern South Dakota, in and east of the Appalachians southward to northern Florida, west of the Appalachians south only to southwestern Pennsylvania and east-central Missouri.

Family APATURIDAE

WILLIAM H. HOWE

These butterflies usually are placed as a subfamily of the Nymphalidae. As long ago as 1840 Boisduval recognized them as a distinct family. In 1947 Clark revived this point of view and we follow it. The imagoes are very much like nymphalids in appearance but the immature stages are more like those of satyrids. The morphos and the apaturids bridge the gap nicely between the satyrids and nymphalids.

Early stages: The eggs are globose to ovoid and decorated with longitudinal and transverse low ridges. The mature caterpillars are quite like many satyrid caterpillars. The head is adorned with branching coronal horns and the last segment of the body bears a pair of subtriangular projections as do satyrid caterpillars. The pupae are unlike those of either Satyridae or Nymphalidae. Each of the two subfamilies of the Apaturidae, the Apaturinae and the Charaxinae, has its characteristic pupal shape.

Subfamily APATURINAE

This is essentially an Old World subfamily: only two of some twenty genera are found in the New World. The subfamily is an old one. A well-preserved fossil, *Chlorippe wilmattae* Cockerell, was found in the Florissant (Oligocene) shales in Colorado. The modern Apaturinae inhabit all the tropical and warmer temperate parts of the world. In the Americas the two genera, *Asterocampa* and *Doxocopa,* are quite distinct. The former is essentially a genus of warm temperate country and the latter is at home in the tropics.

Early Stages: The immature apaturines differ from charaxines in both larval and pupal stages. The apaturine larvae have no more than two coronal horns and the body is more or less cylindrical, tapering abruptly at both ends. The pupae of apaturines are rather elongate and thus resemble satyrid pupae but differ markedly in profile. In profile the venter of apaturines is straight and the dorsum is greatly and smoothly arched from head to tail. The wing cases do not break the profile.

Genus ASTEROCAMPA Röber

(The Hackberry Butterflies)

It has been customary to divide this genus into five or six species with numerous subspecies. Research currently being done by Dr. Walfried Reinthal suggests that most of the so-called subspecies are better considered full species in their own right. Accordingly they are so treated here, with all due credit to Dr. Reinthal and the hope that his intentions have not been misinterpreted.

The adult butterflies rarely stray very far from hackberry trees (*Celtis*). Usually they will be found sitting on the trunk or branches of the tree or adjacent shrubbery. They do not visit flowers but feed on decaying material—rotting fruit, fermenting tree sap, animal excrement and carcasses. Both sexes, but especially the males, are pugnacious and defend a territory against all comers, from other butterflies to lepidopterists. They are often quite crepuscular.

Early Stages: W. H. Edwards described these for a number of species in the 19th century. Dr. Reinthal has studied almost all species. Notes for *celtis* and *clyton* are given as guides.

Distribution: Throughout North America wherever *Celtis* grows and as far south as Honduras. One species is found on several of the Greater Antilles.

The species of *Asterocampa* can be divided into three groups. The *celtis* group has well developed ocelli on the upperside of the fore wing in the tornus and the markings in the apex of the wing are blackish rather than brown. The *clyton* group has the apical markings on the upperside of the fore wing reddish brown and lack ocelli on that wing. The *argus* group includes the tropical species and combines features of both of the temperate area groups: the upperside of the fore wing has a blackish apex and the wing is decorated with white spots (*celtis* features) but there are no ocelli on the wing (a *clyton* feature). This group may represent a primitive pattern. Within each group the pattern on the underside of the hind wing yields the best clues to the identity of the insect. In the *celtis* group the number of ocelli on the upper side of the fore wing will be helpful also.

The *Celtis* Group

1. **Asterocampa celtis** (Boisduval & LeConte). Plate 11, figure 11, ♀; figure 12, ♂; figure 25, ♂, underside. This is our most common and widely distributed *Asterocampa*. Males are variably hued above from gray-olive to olive-brown and both albinic and melanic forms occur. Females are larger and average paler in ground color than males. *Expanse:* Forty-five to fifty-five mm.

Early Stages: Egg; almost spherical, whitish, with nineteen to twenty-one vertical ribs. Mature larva: The head shield is either blackish brown with yellowish green markings, or green (little darker than the body) with whitish streaks. The coronal horns are small, four- or five-pronged. Body yellowish green with two solid or interrupted subdorsal yellow stripes with six to ten rectangular yellow spots on the dorsum. Chrysalis: the yellow-green head case is produced and subconic, the thoracic segments are depressed and the abdomen is arched and prominent dorsally. Two broods in the North and three in the South; hibernation as an egg (?). Adults appear from early June (Lat. 40°) until late September.

Distribution: Central New England to southern Minnesota southward to northern Florida and eastern Texas, wherever the foodplants are found.

2. **Asterocampa antonia** (Edwards). Plate 12, figure 11, ♂; figure 12, ♀. Adults resemble *celtis* but are more yellowish in ground color. It may be readily distinguished from *celtis* by two complete eyespots near the margin of the primaries in *antonia* (only one in *celtis*). *Expanse:* fifty to sixty mm.

Early Stages: Unknown.

Distribution: Central Texas and central Oklahoma westward to southern Colorado, New Mexico, southern Utah and Arizona. Occasional in southern Kansas.

3. **Asterocampa montis** (Edwards). Plate 13, figure 6, ♂; figure 7, ♀. Similar above to *celtis* but deeper ochreous especially in the males. Beneath, the ocelli on the secondaries of *montis* contain bright blue pupils and are well marked. In contrast the underside of the hind wing in *subpallida* is solidly pale ochreous or lavender-gray with very faint maculation and no ocelli.

A western Nebraska population may either be a subspecies of *montis* or a distinct species. It is figured on Plate 11, figure 21, ♀; figure 22, ♂.

Early Stages: These need further study.

Distribution: Mountains of southern Arizona, southern New Mexico and northern Mexico; possibly western Nebraska.

4. **Asterocampa subpallida** (Barnes & McDunnough). Plate 13, figure 8, ♂; figure 9, ♀. The differences between *montis* and *subpallida* are seen at once by examining the lower surfaces. Males of *montis* and *subpallida* are similar from above but the washed, immaculate lower surface of the secondaries characterizes *subpallida*.

Early Stages: Unknown.

Distribution: Less widely distributed than *montis*. Both species fly together in the Santa Rita, Baboquivari, Huachuca and Chiricahua mountains of southern Arizona.

5. **Asterocampa leilia** (Edwards). Plate 11, figure 13, ♀; figure 14, ♂; figure 15, ♀, underside. This butterfly may be confused with *montis* on occasion but one character always points to *leilia*: on *leilia* the basal area below the cell on the underside of the fore wings is very dark brown as indicated on the figure; it is never thus on *montis*. Expanse: forty-five to fifty-five millimeters.

Early Stages: Only partially known.

Distribution: Western Texas (Big Bend area), southern New Mexico and southeastern Arizona, south in the mountains of Sonora and Chihuahua. There are reportedly two broods.

6. **Asterocampa alicia** (Edwards). Plate 11, figure 9, ♂, underside; figure 23, ♀; figure 24, ♂. Large and bright in hue, with conspicuous ocelli, *alicia* may be confused with no other species. It is quite distinct from *celtis* to which some authors have erroneously assigned it. Adults of *alicia* frequently visit fermenting persimmons in Gainesville, Florida. *Expanse:* sixty to seventy-five mm.

Early Stages: Partially known.

Distribution: The coastal plain from southern South Carolina to Florida and westward to eastern Texas.

The *clyton* group

7. **Asterocampa clyton** (Boisduval & LeConte). Plate 11, figure 10, ♂, underside; figure 16, ♂; figure 17, ♀. Known as the Tawny Emperor, this species is much more widespread and abundant than would appear from collections. Apparently it is often overlooked, although it is frequently found around immature hackberry trees at the edges of woodlands. It is readily attracted to bait of fermenting fruit. The species is variable both above and beneath; some examples may be nearly solidly dark brown on the upper hind wing in both sexes.

Early Stages: Like those of *celtis* with these differences: the eggs have fewer vertical ribs; the mature larva has somewhat large and more branched coronal horns, a white or black face or any intermediate of black vertical bands on white, and a narrow, indigo-blue dorsal stripe; in profile the pupa is much less deeply notched at the dorsal junction of thorax and abdomen.

Distribution: Eastern area from central Massachusetts westward to Nebraska and south to Georgia and Texas. Locally abundant (especially in the South); two broods, one in June and another in August.

8. **Asterocampa flora** (Edwards). Plate 11, figure 8, ♂, underside; figure 18, ♂; figure 19, ♀. There is strong evidence that *flora,* larger and more richly hued than *clyton,* is a distinct species. There is no evidence to suggest that *flora* forms a cline with *clyton* in southern Georgia and the Gulf states.

Early Stages: Unknown.

Distribution: Southern Georgia, Florida, Gulf states, and Texas.

Type locality: Palatka, Florida. Two broods annually.

9. **Asterocampa texana** (Skinner). Plate 12, figure 7, ♂; figure 8, ♀. Although superficially resembling those of *clyton,* the lower surfaces in *texana* have a different pattern. Females of *texana* have a pale and washed appearance beneath.

Early Stages: J. A. Comstock described these.

Distribution: Found throughout most of Texas except the humid eastern region adjacent to Louisiana. Strays have been taken as far north as Kansas.

The *argus* group

10. **Asterocampa louisa** (Stallings & Turner). Plate 12, figure 9, ♂; figure 10, ♀. The underside of freshly collected specimens has a lavender or pinkish cast and the ocelli are subdued as in *texana*.

Early Stages: Unknown.

Distribution: Extreme southern Texas in the Rio Grande Valley and in northeastern Mexico.

Genus DOXOCOPA Hübner

Several generic names have been used for these butterflies: *Doxocopa* Hübner (1819), *Apatura* Fabricius (1807), and *Chlorippe* Doubleday (1844) are the most frequent. The types of *Doxocopa* and *Chlorippe* are neotropical species, while that of *Apatura* is European. There appears to be sufficient difference between the New and Old World species that they should be recognized by different generic names. The structural differences between *Doxocopa* and *Apatura* are slight but constant.

There are a great many species of *Doxocopa* in the neotropics. These have been divided into three groups on structural grounds, more or less paralleled by pattern differences.

Early Stages: A little is known about a few of the more common Brazilian species. The eggs are globose, green and longitudinally ribbed, not unlike the eggs of *Asterocampa*. The mature larvae also resemble those of *Asterocampa* but have slightly larger coronal horns and a more noticeable fine pile covering the body. Diagonal lines on the sides extend posteriorly to the dorsum from each spiracle. The pupa is more angular and "warty" than that of *Asterocampa*.

Distribution: Confined to the neotropics with a few species straying into the Brownsville, Texas, area.

1. **Doxocopa pavon** (Latreille). Plate 12, figure 5, ♀; figure 6, ♂ (ssp. *pavon*). The figures are sufficient to allow recognition of this Mexican species that on rare occasions has been taken in southeastern Texas.

2. **Doxocopa laure** (Drury). Plate 12, figure 1, ♂; figure 2, ♀ (ssp. *laure*). This common Mexican species has been taken once in numbers near Brownsville, Texas. The lower surfaces are brightly silvered.

Subfamily CHARAXINAE

The charaxines are essentially tropical butterflies found in both hemispheres. No genus is common to both Old and New World but some parallelism occurs. There are two well defined tribes found in the Americas and only one in the tropics of the Old World. In general the Anaeini (our only tribe) have peculiar venation along the costal margin of the fore wing. There the branches of the subcostal vein fuse with one another near the margin of the wing.

Only one genus, *Anaea,* enters the territory covered by this book.

Early Stages: These resemble the early stages of the apaturines, as might be expected. The most obvious differences are in the general shape of the caterpillars. Charaxine caterpillars have a much swollen thoracic or first abdominal segment, giving the insect a hump-backed appearance. In some genera this bulge is decorated with a pair of eyespots which, combined with the spineless coronal horns, produces the impression of an open mouthed demon. The forking of the terminal segment of the abdomen may be inconspicuous or consist of prongs as long as the head and thorax combined. The pupa is typically apaturid.

Genus ANAEA Hübner

(The Goatweed Butterflies)

This is a prolific neotropical genus. There is some question about its limits. W. P. Comstock (1961) brought together as *Anaea* all of the American Charaxinae with fused subcostal branches on the fore wing. This agglomeration he divided into eight subgenera. Others have recognized six genera among these butterflies. All that are found north of Mexico are placed by Comstock in *A. (Anaea)* or *A. (Memphis).*

Almost all species of *Anaea* that are found in the subtropics and warm temperate areas produce two distinctive forms, differing in the form of the apex of the fore wing.

Early Stages: These are outlined under the species for which we know them.

Distribution: From central United States to Argentina.

1. **Anaea (Anaea) aidea** (Guérin-Ménéville). Plate 77, figure 4, ♀.   The apex is falcate in form "morrisoni" (figured) and blunt in typical *aidea.*

Early Stages: Not known. This is an opportunity for someone living in the range of the species.

Distribution: From southern Mexico north to San Antonio and Jeff Davis county, Texas, west to southern California. Strays have been taken in Scott county, Kansas, and El Paso county, Colorado.

2. **Anaea (Anaea) floridalis** Johnson & Comstock. Plate 11, figure 3, ♂.   This butterfly was referred to as *portia* "Fabricius" for many years. The types of *portia* came from St. Croix, Virgin Islands, and are of a totally different species. The name *floridalis* applies to the winter form with the apex of the fore wing produced. The summer form, "floraesta," has a blunt apex.

Early Stages: The mature larva is green and dotted with many white low tubercles giving the insect a frosted appearance. It has a pair of yellow lateral stripes. The pale green head has seven tiny orange tubercles and two very low black coronal horns. Host plant: Woolly Croton (*Croton linearis*).

Distribution: Found from Miami southward through the Keys.

3. **Anaea (Anaea) andria** Scudder. Plate 11, figure 1, ♂; figure 2, ♀.   This is our most widely distributed and commonest *Anaea.* It has been confused with *glycerium* Westwood by W. H. Edwards and others and with *troglodyta* Fabricius by still others. According to Comstock the latter is a West Indian insect confined to Hispaniola. The ranges of *andria* and *glycerium* do not overlap. Both sexes of the latter can be recognized immediately by the outline of the fore wing. The winter form with falcate fore wing was named *andria.* The summer form, which in some areas flies as late as November, is called "andriaesta."

Anaea andria, in common with all members of the genus, is partial to decaying and fermenting fruit. It will be found from the first really warm days of spring until frost in old fields, in the edges of woodlots and along country roads. It is easily baited with a mash of fermenting fruits.

Early Stages: The mature larva is gray-green and covered with tiny tubercles giving the skin a granular appearance. The tiny orange coronal horns are more conspicuous because of their color than their size. When resting, the larva makes a hammock by drawing together the edges of a leaf. The pupa is green. Foodplant: goatweed (*Croton capitatum* and *C. monanthogynus*).

Distribution: From West Virginia and Ohio west to Illinois, Kansas and eastern Colorado thence south to Jalapa, Veracruz, Mexico. No authentic records are known east of the Appalachian Mountains nor west of the Rockies. The species hibernates in the adult state.

4. **Anaea (Memphis) glycerium** (Westwood). Plate 11, figure 6, ♂; figure 7, ♀ underside.   This is our only brown *Anaea* with the outline of the outer margin of the fore wing bulging outward from M_3 to Cu_2, as shown in the figures. All others have this region quite straight.

Early Stages: Not recorded.

Distribution: From the provinces of Sinaloa and San Luis Potosí in Mexico south to southern Colombia, Venezuela and French Guiana. A single stray is recorded from southern Arizona and the species is rumored to occur in the Brownsville area of Texas.

5. **Anaea (Memphis) pithyusa** (R. Felder). Plate 11, figure 4, ♂; figure 5, ♂, underside. This is the only blue *Anaea* reported from our territory.

Early Stages: not recorded.

Distribution: From Kenedy county, Texas, south to Bolivia.

Family NYMPHALIDAE

(The Brush-footed Butterflies)

This is the largest family of the true butterflies. Not only does it contain more species than any other but it probably is the most varied. Its members are recognized by the very reduced condition of the fore legs of both sexes. They are little more than stumps clothed in long hair scales, hence the name "Brush-footed Butterflies." The Nymphalidae is an old family. It is the best represented of all families among the few fossil butterflies known.

The structural features that set the nymphalids apart from all other families are varied and none alone is satisfactory. The antennae are never more than moderately long, are clothed with scales and terminate in a pronounced club. The palpi are hairy and robust. The venation is quite varied but the cell is open on one or both wings with few exceptions (when it is closed by a very weak vein). There are five radial branches on the fore wing and only one anal vein which never is bifurcate. The hind wing has two anal veins and a well developed humeral vein.

The subfamilies of Nymphalidae are best recognized in the immature stages. The features that set each apart will be found in the subfamily discussions.

Early Stages: It is easier to state how the larvae of nymphalids differ from other families than to succinctly state their features. There are no osmeteria as among Papilionidae, no soft filaments as among Danaidae, no bifurcation of the last segment as among Satyridae and Apaturidae, no "honey pots" as in many Lycaenidae. None of the nymphalid pupae are held in place with a silken girdle as occurs in the Papilionidae, Pieridae and most Lycaenidae.

Distribution: Common on all continents except Antarctica, from the polar regions and alpine heights to the equator and sea level.

Subfamily MARPESIINAE

(The Dagger-tails)

WILLIAM H. HOWE

The marpesiines are a small group of tropical genera more abundant in the Old World than the New. In the Americas the subfamily is represented by one genus, *Marpesia* Hübner, that can be recognized by the long, slender tail on the hind wing, something like that found on typical kite swallowtails. Marpesiines tend to be dark in color and not largely whitish, greenish or yellow as are the American kite swallowtails.

Early Stages: The Marpesiinae have mature larvae that are characterized by having only an incomplete dorsal row of soft spines on the body and a pair of long coronal horns on the head capsule. The primary larval foodplants belong to the family Moraceae.

Distribution: From extreme southern United States southward to northern Argentina.

Genus MARPESIA Hübner

There are a number of synonyms for *Marpesia* Hübner 1818. The most frequently met are *Athena* Hübner [1819], *Megalura* Blanchard 1840 and *Timetes* Doubleday 1844. Like many nymphalids, these butterflies are fond of feeding on decaying and fermenting matter. Unless somewhat drunken from such food these butterflies are difficult to capture with their tails intact.

A modern revision of the genus is needed. No one knows how many of the thirty-odd names that have been proposed are species, subspecies or seasonal forms. Three different *Marpesia* are found in the warmer parts of the Gulf coast.

Early Stages: The mature larva has a pair of long, somewhat curved coronal horns that bear stubby branches. The body has four middorsal spines, similar to the coronal horns but shorter, on segments 5, 7, 9, and 11. The pupa is somewhat conic and angular, and the thorax is somewhat swollen. The dorsal carina carries spines of unequal length, usually eight in number.

Distribution: Extreme southern United States to Argentina.

1. **Marpesia chiron** (Fabricius). Plate 15, figure 13, ♀. This species is commonly met in the tropics at mud puddles. It is often seen flying over open fields in early morning but spends the hotter parts of the day in the half shade of the forest edges. It is easily recognized by the longitudinal stripes on both sides of the wings.

Early Stages: Egg: subconic, longitudinally ribbed, placed singly on the buds of Breadfruit (*Artocarpus integrifolia*) and *Chlorophora tinctoria.* Larva: yellowish with a pair of black dorsal stripes and reddish black lateral stripes. Dorsal spines are in black patches. The face is greenish yellow with two black lines and a few dots. The horns are black ringed with white. Pupa: vari-colored—abdomen dark red brown, thorax and head gray, wing cases and ventrum yellowish white spotted with black—shaped as noted for the genus.

Distribution: From Argentina north to southern Florida and southern Texas, straying as far north as Kansas.

2. **Marpesia coresia** (Godart). Plate 15, figure 2. The common name for this butterfly, The Waiter, derives from the dark upperside and the bicolored underside, glistening white basally and darker outwardly.

Early Stages: Incompletely known.

Distribution: From Peru and southern Brazil north to Mexico and occasionally extreme southeastern Texas.

3. **Marpesia petreus** (Cramer). Plate 15, figure 4, ♂ (ssp. *thetys*). When a revision of *Marpesia* is undertaken it is probable that the name of this subspecies, *thetys* (Fabricius), will be changed. Both Cramer's name (*petreus*) and Fabricius's name apply to the same insect from the Guiana coast.

Early Stages: Similar to those of *chiron*.

Distribution: From Brazil north to central Florida and southeastern Texas, straying northward to southern Colorado and Kansas.

Subfamily LIMENITINAE

(The Admirals)

The clue to membership in this family lies largely in the decoration of the larva in the fifth instar. The spines are topped with a rosette of secondary spines. In addition to the usual paired rows of spines the Limenitinae show some evidence of the unpaired middorsal row that characterizes the Marpesiinae. Rarely are all rows of spines well developed; some are marked only with bristled tubercles, as in the genus *Limenitis.*

There is a goodly number of tribes within this subfamily. The special characteristics of the tribes that are found within our territory are given with each below. Some of the tribes, such as the Limenitini, are world-wide in range. Others are confined to a single major faunal region, for example, the Ageroniini in the neotropics.

Early Stages: These are quite varied and will be discussed below.

Distribution: The temperate and tropical parts of all continents.

Tribe Coloburini

WILLIAM H. HOWE

Of the seven neotropical genera that compose this tribe two enter our territory. Very superficial features have led to placing these butterflies among the apaturids. There is no structural support for this.

Early Stages: The larva varies greatly in decoration from three- and four-branched spines middorsal on *Smyrna* to almost spineless tubercles middorsally on *Colobura.* The three pairs of rows of spines are four- and five-branched. The pupa seen in profile is slender, with smooth ventrum and raggedly outlined dorsum. The larval foodplants generally belong to the nettle family Urticaceae.

Distribution: The neotropics with a few species invading the adjacent warm temperate areas.

Genus SMYRNA Hübner

Smyrna may be separated from other dark brown tropical nymphalids with a black apex on the fore wing by the intricately decorated under hind wing. The decoration is composed of blind and pupilled eyespots with blue, black and tannish swirling lines.

Early Stages: The mature larva carries nine rows of spines with those on the feet inconspicuous. The coronal horns are tubercle-like with five projecting spines.

Distribution: Mexico to Paraguay and Peru.

1. **Smyrna karwinskii** Geyer. Plate 16, figure 1, ♂. No other butterfly can be confused with this species in our territory.

Distribution: Mexico and Central America. Rare in the Brownsville area of Texas where it has not been reported for several decades.

Genus HISTORIS Hübner

The two species of *Historis* are large bodied, stiff winged butterflies. They are very tenacious of life. These are most at home in the half shade at the edges of the forest or in the forest crown. They are inveterate tipplers at fermenting fruit and tree sap. On occasion members of the genus migrate in swarms of other butterflies.

Early Stages: Egg: keg shaped, green with eighteen yellow longitudinal ribs and many fine cross ribs. Mature larva: two short, clubbed horns on the head; green and brown alternate transverse bands; dorsal and subdorsal spines black, lateral spines white. Pupa: laterally compressed, dorsum decorated with spinous processes, and two long double curved processes arising from the head.

Distribution: Throughout tropical America and straying into the adjacent warm temperate areas.

1. **Historis odius** (Fabricius). Plate 16, figure 4 (ssp. *odius*). This very large and easily recognized species has been recorded from Florida on several occasions. It may be a hurricane waif in that state.

Tribe Ageroniini

WILLIAM H. HOWE

In two tribes of Limenitinae, the Ageroniini and the Eurytelini, the butterflies have some of the veins of the fore wing swollen at the base. This is usually considered a satyrid trait, but it is not exclusively so. The Ageroniini are wholly confined to the American tropics. The other tribe, Eurytelini, occurs in both the New and Old Worlds. Of the four genera which we place in the Ageroniini only one, *Hamadryas,* appears in the southern borderlands of our territory.

Early Stages: Those noted for *Hamadryas* are descriptive of the tribe.

Distribution: Tropical forests from Mexico southward to northern Argentina. Strays occur in the Brownsville area of Texas.

Genus HAMADRYAS Hübner

(The Calicoes)

These lovely butterflies are forest dwellers and require a considerable extent of virgin forest to be common. When they are at rest on the trunk of a tree they are well camouflaged. As you disturb one and it flies off, the beating wings emit a click that may be a warning signal to others. The click is not produced in casual flight moving from one resting place to another. The recognition of the different species of the gray group of Calicoes requires careful attention to the structure of the ocelli on the hind wings. Reports of *februa* and *ferox* from Texas are unsupported.

Early Stages: Egg: white, globular with the sides marked by longitudinal sinuous grooves. Mature larva: variable, black to creamy white with longitudinal lines of yellow to green and less distinct transverse line of the same light color. There are nine rows of tubercles, the middorsal always spined, some of the others bearing bristles rather than spines. Coronal horns are black and pyriform. Pupa: very variable in coloring, the profile shows a strongly angular dorsal outline and two very long processes, half the length of the pupa, are on the head. Foodplant: *Dalechampia* species.

Distribution: Mexico to northern Argentina; straying into the Brownsville area of Texas.

Three species of *Hamadryas* appear to stray into the Brownsville area of Texas. One of these, *H. februa gudula,* is white on the under hind wing. the other two are yellowish (*fornax*) or buffish (*feronia farinulenta* (Fruhstorfer)). The best way to separate *fornax* from *feronia* is by the structure of the submarginal eyespots on the upperside of the hind wing. In both species the eyespots in the spaces between M_3 and Cu_2 are composed of a dark gray field surrounded by a single thin blue line and pupilled with white. There is a pure black cap on the pupil in *fornax* and no such cap in *feronia*. In *februa* the dark iris of the eyespot is surrounded by three concentric lines, a light colored one, a dark, and then another light one. The three species have been confused so frequently that all published records of occurrence are questionable. It is doubtful that the rare Mexican *ferox* (Staudinger) strays into the United States.

1. **Hamadryas fornax** (Hübner). Plate 15, figure 18, ♂. The strong ochre-yellow

underside of the hind wing is the best clue to this species. If the yellow is pale, then check the structure of the eyespots and look for the large truly black cap on the small white pupil.

2. **Hamadryas feronia** (Linnaeus). Plate 15, figure 12, ♂ (ssp. *farinulenta*).   Specimens of *feronia* from South America and southern Central America have the underside of the hind wing dirty grayish white. Those from British Honduras northward have the under hind wing buff colored. The white pupil of the eyespots on the upperside has no black cap.

3. **Hamadryas februa** (Hübner).   In this Mexican subspecies, *gudula* (Fruhstorfer), the underside of the hind wing is slightly grayish white. The eyespots on the upperside of that wing are much more complex than in either *feronia* or *fornax* as described above.

Tribe Eurytelini

WILLIAM H. HOWE

Westwood proposed the family name Eurytelidae in 1851 for a motley group of genera, some nymphalids and others satyrids. Aurivillius first used the tribal form of the name in 1898 and restricted it to nymphalids. In 1921 Seitz proposed Ergolini for a group of American genera. Since the Old World Eurytelini and the New World Ergolini have many features in common Munroe in 1949 combined the two and used the earlier name.

Three American genera can be clearly assigned to this tribe and a fourth is placed here with hesitation. Two of these enter our territory: *Mestra* Hübner, which is certainly a euryteline; and *Biblis* Fabricius, which is tentatively assigned to the tribe. The larvae of the Eurytelini all feed on *Tragia*. It is interesting that in Malaya where *Tragia* is not native the Eurytelini desert their native foodplant (*Ricinus*) to use introduced *Tragia* when the opportunity is presented.

The Eurytelini share with the Ageroniini inflated basal portions of the veins on the fore wing. The larval coronal horns appear to be absent on *Mestra dorcas* and often are absent on first and sometimes second instars of other genera in the tribe. There is too little known about the life histories of the American and African members of this tribe to attempt a summary.

Distribution: The tropical areas of Old and New Worlds.

Genus MESTRA Hübner

These small, delicate, pale colored butterflies wander extensively over land. Whether or not they do so over water is an open question. Only one species is found in the

United States. A second has been listed but is so questionable that we omit it. This is *floridana* (Strecker), which appears to be a synonym for a Guiana butterfly *Mestra cana* (Erichson). Apparently Strecker was misled by false locality data on the type specimens.

1. **Mestra amymone** (Ménétriés). Plate 15, figure 1, ♂. This may in time prove to be a subspecies of *hypermestra* Hübner, the common South American species. It appears to be specifically distinct from *dorcas* Fabricius, the only species of *Mestra* found in the Greater Antilles (Jamaica only).

Early Stages: Incompletely known and in need of detailed study.

Distribution: From southern Central America northward to Texas where it is common in the southern half of the state. Strays have been captured in Colorado, Kansas and Nebraska. Periodically great swarms are known to migrate, as happened in 1950.

Genus BIBLIS Fabricius

There is some question about placing this genus in the Eurytelini. The males have a pair of hair pencils at the sides of the middle of the abdomen, an unusual structure among nymphalids. The single species of *Biblis* varies throughout its range in the placement of the submarginal red band on the hind wing.

Early Stages: Egg: yellowish white with longitudinal irregular grooves and a whorl of fine hairs at the top. Mature larva: tapered to both extremities, with bright rose and brown spots on a green background. The earlier stages are almost uniformly gray-brown with lighter diagonal streaks. The coronal horns are large and the body spines moderate sized, mounted on red tubercles. Pupa: the wing cases dip below the ventrum and the dorsum in profile is irregular.

Distribution: From Paraguay to Mexico.

1. **Biblis hyperia** (Cramer). Plate 15, figure 8, ♂ (ssp. *aganisa*). This northern subspecies of *hyperia, aganisa* Boisduval, occasionally strays into the Brownsville region of Texas. Its range extends south to Panamá.

Tribe Epicaliini

WILLIAM H. HOWE

Müller proposed this group as a subfamily. Seitz later reduced it to tribal status. The tribe is large and may in time be split in two. The recognition features are found largely in the larvae. The coronal horns terminate in a rosette of spines; the dorsal row of decorations may be spines or tubercles; the subdorsal row of spines always is present; and the two rows that flank the spiracles rarely are complete, and one or the other may be reduced to low tubercles. The larvae usually are green. One group of genera utilizes Euphorbiaceae and the other Sapindaceae as larval food.

The several species of Epicaliini that occur in the United States all are strays from the tropics. One or two may get a temporary foothold and produce a breeding colony that lasts a few years. Several of the genera are very large and all of them are in need of study in the light of modern taxonomic techniques and theory.

Genus EUNICA Hübner

(The Purple Wings)

This large and confusing genus reaches its greatest development in the Amazon drainage area of South America. When a modern study of the genus is undertaken it may prove convenient to divide it into several subgenera, if not full genera. The purple wings are forest butterflies. They rarely attend flowers but frequent fermenting fruit and mud puddles. The base of the cubital vein of *Eunica* is somewhat swollen, variable in degree from species to species. Migrations have been noted in which a considerable number of *Eunica* took part.

Early Stages: Known for very few members of the genus.

Distribution: From extreme southern United States to Bolivia and southern Brazil.

1. **Eunica monima** (Cramer). Plate 15, figure 9, ♂. This is the smaller of the two *Eunica* that are found in the United States. The under side of the hind wing has only four, or rarely five, ocelli in the limbal zone.

Early Stages: Egg a truncate cone with ten or eleven longitudinal ribs. Mature larva: the black coronal horns are two or three times as long as the face; the body is orange or reddish green with a white lateral stripe; and it has three pairs of incomplete rows of spines. Where spines are absent there are white, bristled tubercles. Pupa green and rather smoothly contoured with a hump at the thorax and somewhat raised angles at the tops of the wing cases. Food plants: *Xanthoxylum* (Rutaceae) in Mexico.

Distribution: Costa Rica, possibly Colombia, north to southern Florida and southern Texas. Strays have been taken as far north as Kansas.

2. **Eunica tatila** (Herrich-Schaeffer).

   (a) **tatila** (Herrich-Schaeffer). Six or seven small white-pupilled eyespots form a row on the underside of the hind wing of *tatila*. This mainland form is larger and brighter than the Antillean form.

Distribution: Mexico and Central America. There is a single record of a wind blown stray from Kansas.

   (b) **tatilista** Kaye. Plate 15, figure 7, ♀. The eyespots on the underside of the hind wing of *tatilista* lack white or bluish centers. The white spots in the apex on

both upper and lower sides of the fore wing are smaller on *tatilista* than on *tatila*.
Distribution: Florida and the Greater Antilles.

Genus MYSCELIA Doubleday

This is an easily recognized genus of tropical forest butterflies. Recognition of the species within the genus is another problem entirely. Two species definitely are found in southeastern Texas.

Early Stages: Very much like those of *Eunica*.
Distribution: From southern Brazil and Peru to southern Texas, chiefly in forests.

1. **Myscelia cyananthe** (Felder). Plate 14, figure 14, ♂. The blue bars on the fore wing extend only halfway from the base to the margin of the wing. On the hind wing there is a tiny stubby bar at the base, two broad ones across the wing and a narrow shining blue margin.
Early Stages: Not reported.
Distribution: Mexico; strays into Texas in the Brownsville region.

2. **Myscelia ethusa** (Boisduval). Plate 14, figure 13, ♂. There are white spots in the apical third of the fore wing and the hind wing has three shining blue bands between the basal stub and the narrow marginal crescents.
Early Stages: Not recorded.
Distribution: Central America; sometimes quite common in southeastern Texas but doubtfully established there.

Genus DYNAMINE Hübner

This large tropical genus is sorely in need of serious study and revision. The fifty-odd species fall into three groups that certainly are worthy of subgeneric status. All of the butterflies in the genus are small. Thus far neither of the Cuban species has been found in Florida but one of the numerous Mexican species strays into southeastern Texas.

Early Stages: Not very different from those of *Eunica*. The larval foodplant appears to be *Dalechampia*.
Distribution: Throughout tropical America and straying into the adjacent temperate regions.

1. **Dynamine dyonis** Geyer. Plate 15, figure 11, ♂. This Mexican *Dynamine* cannot be confused with any other butterfly reported from north of Mexico. It appears to be getting more common in southeastern Texas or else more collectors are now working in that area than fifteen or twenty years ago.
Early Stages: Not reported.
Distribution: Honduras north to Mexico and southern Texas. Captures have been made as far north as San Antonio, Texas.

Genus DIAETHRIA Billberg

These pretty little butterflies are abundant and varied in the American tropics. Of the thirty-five or forty species only two stray into our territory.

Early Stages: Not very different from *Eunica.*

Distribution: The mainland tropics from Mexico southward to Argentina.

1. **Diaethria clymena** (Cramer). Plate 15, figure 3, ♂; figure 6, ♂, underside (both *D. anna*).   This species is a puzzle. Only two or three authentic specimens have ever been recorded from Florida. The last one was captured in February, 1944. What is puzzling is how the species gets to Florida. It is not known from the West Indies, the source of almost all Florida strays. It is a South American species and appears to be absent from Central America. The 1944 specimen may have hitch-hiked from South America on an aircraft.

The specimen figured (Plate 15, figure 3, 6) is actually *Diaethria anna* Guérin-Ménéville, not *clymena;* an error discovered too late for rectification. *D. clymena,* however, is similar in appearance, with these differences: the subapical spot on the fore wing upperside is light blue, not white; the sparse iridescent green sprinkling of scales in the base of this wing tends to be thickest along the posterior cell vein and vein 2A; the subterminal line of the hind wing is dull, pale blue and much thicker (about half an interspace). On the underside of the fore wing the inner of the two subterminal white bands is thinner and of more even width, the black area within it is thinner, and the discal red extends almost to the base, leaving practically no white in the base of the cell; and on the hind wing the black lines and spots are all much thicker.

2. **Diaethria asteria** (Godman & Salvin). Plate 15, figure 5, ♂, underside; figure 14, ♂.   The small amount of red on the under side of the fore wing, confined as it is to the cell, is diagnostic for this species.

Distribution: Mexico, straying into southeastern Texas.

Tribe Limenitini

The Limenitini have most of the spines on the larva reduced to tubercles, armed with a bristle or rosette of bristles. These butterflies are essentially an Old World group, but are absent from Africa and Australia. In the New World there are only two genera: *Limenitis,* which is essentially a temperate zone genus; and *Adelpha,* essentially a tropical genus. Chermock in 1950 suggested that only one genus is necessary. Others disagree.

Although the North American members of *Limenitis* are diversely patterned and each species easily recognized, biological divergence among them is slight. Wherever the range of two species overlaps hybrids will be found. The situation is quite different with *Adelpha.* The individual species in this genus are very difficult to recognize. In fact it appears that the only sure way to establish the validity of a species name is to have a full account of the immature stages. Among the larvae good species characters are easily recognized.

Early Stages: The egg is globular with a hexagonal reticulation. The mature larva usually has the coronal horns small and not particularly noticeable. The majority of spines are reduced to bristles set in tubercles that vary in size. The spines on the thorax and the last two segments of the abdomen usually are the best developed. Many larvae are cryptically patterned and formed to resemble bird droppings. The pupa in profile is rather smoothly outlined, with the tips of the wing cases dipping below the ventrum and an abrupt hump on the dorsum.

Distribution: Eurasia and the Americas in temperate and tropical areas.

Genus ADELPHA Hübner

EDWIN M. PERKINS, JR. and STEPHEN F. PERKINS

All neotropical Limenitini belong to this genus. With one exception, *bredowii,* the genus is confined to the tropics with very few species straying into adjacent warm temperate areas.

Early Stages: As for the tribe.

To the uninitiated the two *Adelpha* and *Limenitis lorquini* can be puzzlingly similar. The white band on the upperside of *lorquini* is boldly crossed by dark lines on the veins and the orange in the apex of the fore wing is a narrow tapered patch on the very edge of the outer margin. On the two *Adelpha* the orange apical patch is large, more or less rectangular and set in from the outer margin of the wing. On *bredowii* the white band across the fore wing is broken into patches; on *fessonia* it is solid.

1. **Adelpha fessonia** (Hewitson). Plate 14, figure 12, ♂. Until this genus is carefully studied the relationship between *fessonia* and its close allies is cloudy. Therefore we use a binomial for its name.

Early Stages: Not recorded.

Distribution: Southeastern Texas to Costa Rica.

2. **Adelpha bredowii** (Geyer).

(a) **eulalia** (Doubleday). Plate 14, figure 10, ♀; figure 11, ♀ underside. This subspecies intergrades with the next one in Arizona. It is found in typical form in southeastern Texas.

Distribution: From southeastern Texas and southern Arizona and central Utah south to central Mexico east of the Sierra Madre. From southern Mexico to Honduras nominate *bredowii* occurs.

(b) **californica** (Butler). Plate 14, figure 9, ♀. There is somewhat less violet on the under side of this subspecies. Other minor pattern differences help to identify this northern subspecies.

Early Stages: The eggs is typical of Limenitini. The mature larva is dark green above shading through lighter green to brownish below. The horns and tubercles typical of the tribe. The pupa is typical of the tribe with two divergent horns on the head, soft browns with darker irregular lines. Foodplant: oaks, especially *Quercus chrysolepis.*

Distribution: California to Oregon.

Genus LIMENITIS Fabricius

STEPHEN F. PERKINS and EDWIN M. PERKINS, JR.

Members of this genus are colloquially termed the Admirals. Five distinct species occur in North America; of these, only three range east of the 100th meridian, whereas all are found to the west of this longitude. Considerable interspecific hybridization occurs between members of the genus, e.g. *L. arthemis* x *L. astyanax* and *L. weidemeyerri* x *L. lorquini.* In the past, many names have been applied to such hybrids. Because hybrids are now considered infrasubspecific, however, their names are not recognized here.

Early Stages: The eggs are ovoid but flattened near their point of attachment to the foodplant, the surface finely hirsute and hexagonally pitted. The mature larvae have two prominent dorsal tubercles on abdominal segment II and smaller tubercles on segments III, V, IX and X. The spiracles are circumscribed by small protuberances. A lightly colored saddle usually extends between segments VII and IX.

The following key will serve to differentiate the 3 species:

1. More than 20 warty protuberances, situated above the spiracles, on each body segment . . . . *astyanax*
1. Less than 20 2
2. Secondary tubercles, posterior to large cephalic tubercles, well developed . . . . *archippus*
2. Secondary cephalic tubercles smaller, wider, and more confluent with larger ones . . . . *arthemis.*

The pupae have a characteristic postcephalic "saddle horn" and prominent, lateral wing cases.

A wide variety of foodplants is favored, including willow (*Salix*), poplar, aspen, cottonwood (*Populus*), and less often birch (*Betula*), oak (*Quercus*), hawthorn (*Crataegus*), gooseberry (*Ribes*), deerberry (*Vaccinium*), apple (*Malus*), cherry, plum (*Prunus*), and basswood (*Tilia*).

The prediapausal larvae characteristically construct hibernacula (small cylindrical overwintering shelters made of a foodplant leaf and silk). Numbers of annual adult broods vary from one to three or four, depending upon the species and its geographic location.

Although members of the genus are found in a variety of habitats, they are never far from their favored foodplants.

1. **Limenitis arthemis** (Drury).   The ground color above is a deep purplish black to black with rows of eight and seven white patches comprising the postmedian bands of the fore wing and hind wing respectively. The subapical area of the fore wing has two to four white spots; usually a row of seven red-orange spots, distal to the postmedian white band on hind wing is present. Bluish marginal and submarginal crescents are found on both wings. Beneath the ground color is maroon to reddish brown; the apical and subapical areas are of the same color. The area distal to the post median white band on the underside of the hind wing consists of an interrupted series of patches whose color approximates that of the ventral ground color. Bluish marginal and submarginal crescents are also present on the hind wing.

L. arthemis hybridizes with *astyanax* along a relatively narrow contact zone. Several inconsequential names have been applied to such infrasubspecific offspring. In the western limits of its distribution, *L. a. arthemis* intergrades with the subspecies *L. a. rubrofasciata.*

Open hardwood forests are the favored habitat of *arthemis.* It frequently glides high above wooded paths and along the brushy fringes that border the forest. Like *lorquini,* it often returns to favorite perches where it basks in the sun, well out of reach of a butterfly net!

Early Stages: The early stages of both *arthemis* and *astyanax* are similar to those of *archippus:* see the key above. Principal foodplants of *arthemis* include willow (*Salix*), birch (*Betula*), aspen and poplar (*Populus*).

(a) **arthemis** (Drury). Plate 14, figure 1, ♂; figure 2, ♀.   This is the butterfly described above. The nominate subspecies is recognized by the reddish brown coloring on the underside of the hind wing outside of the white band being restricted to a series of patches.

Distribution: Eastern Manitoba, east throughout southern Canada, south to Minnesota, Michigan, northern Pennsylvania, New York, and northern New England. Flight period between June and September.

(b) **rubrofasciata** (Barnes & McDunnough). Plate 13, figure 1, ♂.   This subspecies differs from nominate *arthemis* in that the maroon colored area, distal to the postmedian white band on the underside of the hind wing is not broken into distinct patches or spots but is confluent and forms a continuous band. The row of seven brick red spots distal to the postmedian white band of the hind wing above is well developed.

Distribution: Minnesota north to Manitoba, west across Saskatchewan, northern North Dakota, northwestern Montana, Alberta and British Columbia and north to the Yukon Territory and Alaska. Flight period between June and August.

2. **Limenitis astyanax** (Fabricius).   Recent studies suggest that *astyanax* is not a separate species but merely a southern subspecies of *arthemis.* However, for the sake of simplicity, *astyanax* is treated here as a species.

Where *astyanax* is not sympatric with *arthemis,* it may be distinguished by several characteristics: dorsal and ventral white postmedian bands are entirely absent; there are no red-orange spots on the upperside of the hind wings; a blue-green iridescent suffusion extends from the outer margin toward the basal area of the dorsal hind wings; the dorsal fore wings have two to four orange-red spots in the apical-submarginal area; the limbal area of the ventral hind wing is distinguished by a row of seven orange-red spots basad to the submarginal and marginal rows of blue-green crescents.

L. astyanax is a low flier that prefers open forest and forest edges. It is rarely observed in cultivated areas and seldom visits flowers.

Early Stages: See discussion under *Limenitis*. Favored foodplants include willow (*Salix*), aspen and poplar (*Populus*), hawthorn (*Crataegus*), wild cherry (*Prunus*) and gooseberry (*Ribes*).

(a) **astyanax** (Fabricius). Plate 14, figure 3, ♂. The eastern Red-spotted Purple is not purple but bluish black and can be recognized by the red spots in the apical part of the fore wing on the upperside.

Distribution: Ranges from central New England west to central Minnesota and adjacent South Dakota, south to eastern Texas and central Florida. Flight periods are between March and September; northern populations rarely emerge before late May.

(b) **arizonensis** Edwards. Plate 14, figure 4, ♂. The western representative of *astyanax* does not exhibit orange-red spots in the apical and marginal area of the dorsal fore wing. The submarginal row of large dorsal hind wing crescents is more white than blue-green. Ventrally, the submarginal crescents are comparably white and contrast sharply with the blue-green marginal row.

Throughout its range, *arizonensis* frequents arroyos, lower canyons, forested mountain trails and streambeds.

Distribution: Southern Arizona (May to September), southern New Mexico, extreme western Texas, south into Mexico.

3. **Limenitis archippus** (Cramer).   The upperside is uniform orange or orange-brown, the veins dusted with black scales. The hind wing has a narrow black postmedian line more or less parallel to the outer margin.

The Viceroy commonly inhabits riverbeds, wet meadows, marshes, drainage and irrigation ditches and gallery forests, wherever willow (*Salix*), poplar and aspen (*Populus*) occur.

Early Stages: The mature larvae of *archippus* closely resemble those of *arthemis* and *astyanax*.

(a) **archippus** (Cramer). Plate 1, figure 5, ♂. The Viceroy was given its common name because it mimics the Monarch. It has a much more restricted range than the Monarch and can be recognized by the dark line on the hind wing. Its ground color is lighter than that of *floridensis*.

Distribution: From southern Canada and New England south to Georgia and Mississippi, west to eastern Colorado and Montana.

(b) **floridensis** Strecker. Plate 1, figure 6, ♂. The figure will serve to identify this subspecies, whose dorsal surfaces are uniformly deep red-brown to rich mahogany. Generally, the ventral ground color of the fore wings does not contrast with that of the hind wings; rather, both are a vivid, deep reddish brown. Some specimens may have the basal to postmedian area of the primaries the same color as dorsally, the apical area and secondaries being a lighter, orange-brown. This does not appear to be a seasonal or individual variable, but occurs in all populations.

Distribution: Confined to Florida, where there may be as many as four annual broods between February and December; strays reported as far north as Virginia.

(c) **watsoni** (dos Passos). Plate 1, figure 8, ♂. Unlike *archippus* and *floridensis,* the fore wing ground color of *watsoni* contrasts somewhat with that of the hind wing; the fore wing is dark red-brown whereas the hind wing is a paler orange-brown. In addition, the spots in the apex of the fore wing are reduced in size and are orange-brown in color. This is a weakly differentiated subspecies.

Distribution: Described from Alexandria, Louisiana, *watsoni* also occurs in western Mississippi and Alabama, west to Texas and north to Arkansas.

(d) **obsoleta** Edwards. Plate 1, figure 7, ♂. Dorsally, this subspecies is characterized by a pale ferruginous ground color. A series of four white spots extends from the costal margin of the fore wings along outer edge of the postmedian area where black dusting is minimal. Unlike other subspecies of *archippus,* white spots or patches occur in cells along the postmedian black line of the dorsal hind wing, and black dusting of the ventral veins is greatly reduced.

Favoring willow (*Salix*) and cottonwood (*Populus*) associations, *obsoleta* frequents irrigation canals, water tanks and areas that border humid, semi-desert bottom lands. It is a frustrating experience to try to collect this subspecies because of its habit of flying twelve to fifteen feet above the ground, just out of reach of one's net!

Distribution: Southeastern California, southern Nevada, southwestern Utah, Arizona, southern New Mexico, and extreme western Texas. Flight periods range between April and October.

(e) **lahontani** Herlan. Plate 13, figure 11, ♂. Compared to the other members of the *archippus* complex, the black postmedian band on the hind wing of this newly described subspecies is conspicuously narrowed or absent; often this band, when present, is broken into a series of dashes that are most evident in cells Rs, M_1 and M_2. The ground color is a lighter orange.

In areas bordering canyon creeks, streams and rivers, *lahontani* is not uncommon, nor is it ever far from its favored foodplants, willow (*Salix*) and cottonwood (*Populus*).

Distribution: A Great Basin representative of the *archippus* complex, this race occurs in eastern Washington and Oregon, southern Idaho, western Colorado, Utah and central Nevada; it flies from July to September.

4. **Limenitis weidemeyerii** Edwards. Weidemeyer's Admiral may be confused with two other species of *Limenitis, lorquini* and *arthemis.* It lacks the orange patch on the apex of the dorsal fore wing of *lorquini.* It can be distinguished readily from *arthemis* by three characteristics on the underside: 1) the basal and discal regions of the hind wing are dusted with lightly colored scales (these areas are maroon in *arthemis*); 2) the fore wing has two marginal rows of eight or nine well defined,

crescent-like spots, the outer row of which is bluish white, the inner row distinctly white (both rows are bluish in *arthemis,* the inner row incomplete and diminutive towards the apex); 3) no extensive maroon ground color in the apical and subapical regions of the fore wing (present and well defined in *arthemis*).

The flight periods of *weidemeyerii* vary betwen May and August; habitats vary with the respective subspecies.

Early Stages: These have been described by W. H. Edwards. The mature larva is grayish, mottled with gray and white patches. Foodplant preferences include willow (*Salix*) and, at higher elevations, aspen (*Populus*).

(a) **weidemeyerii** Edwards. Plate 14, figure 5. The various subspecies of *weidemeyerii* are recognized by the width of the white bands and the submarginal markings on the upper side of the hind wings. The nominate subspecies has moderately wide white bands and rarely more than traces of red spots on the upperside near the margin of the hind wing.

Distribution: The original specimens of *L. w. weidemeyerii* were described from the vague locality, "Rocky Mountains." F. M. Brown recently designated a neotype and has fixed its type locality as Lakewood, Jefferson county, Colorado. This nominate subspecies occurs in a narrow belt that extends along the east slope of the Rocky Mountains from Colorado to central New Mexico. Examples from southeastern Wyoming are nearly typical, although this is an area of intergradation.

(b) **angustifascia** (Barnes & McDunnough). Plate 12, figure 4, ♂. Characterized by considerably narrower postmedian white bands and a darker ventral ground color, this southern race was formerly referred to as *sinefascia* Edwards. In size *angustifascia* is the largest subspecies of the *weidemeyerii* complex.

Distribution: Mountainous and wet valley regions of Arizona, southern Utah, western New Mexico and southwestern Colorado; it flies from May to August.

(c) **nevadae** (Barnes & Benjamin). Plate 13, figure 2, ♀. The Nevada Admiral is distinguished by suppression of the ventral red-orange maculation and the presence of bluish white scales on the medial part of the ventral hind wings. The latter trait is so pronounced that the row of red-orange spots distal to the postmedian band on the ventral hind wings is nearly obscured by these bluish white scales.

Distribution: The subspecies was described from the Spring Mountain Range of Clark county, Nevada; to date this is the only locality in which it has been found. Here, in an environment dotted by *Salix* and *Populus,* the Nevada Admiral glides up and down boulder strewn mountain washes. The flight period extends from June to July.

(d) **oberfoelli** Brown. Plate 12, figure 3, ♂. The distinctive feature of this subspecies is the presence of a row of bright orange to red-orange spots, located distal to the postmedian white band on the upperside of the hind wing. No other member of the *weidemeyerii* complex displays this trait as consistently or vividly as does *oberfoelli.* A brighter ventral orange coloring and lighter ground color also serve to distinguish *oberfoelli* from nominate *weidemeyerii.*

Distribution: Described from Slope county, North Dakota, *oberfoelli* ranges south to western South Dakota and northwestern Nebraska (June through August). Its habitat varies from the badlands of the Dakotas to the conifer-bordered stream beds of the Black Hills and the rolling sand hills of Nebraska's Pine Ridge belt. It never ventures far from its foodplants, *Salix* and *Populus*.

(e) **latifascia** Perkins & Perkins. Plate 13, figure 5, ♂. As implied by the name, this subspecies is characterized by exceptionally wide postmedian bands on both fore wings and hind wings. Such bands are one to three mm wider than those of any other race of *weidemeyerii*. In addition, the amount of white scaling on the ventral surfaces of both wings reaches an extreme in this subspecies.

In several localities of its range *latifascia* hybridizes with *lorquini*. The resultant interspecific hybrids have been named "fridayi" (Plate 14, Fig. 6). This name was originally applied to specimens collected at Mono Lake, Mono county, California.

Distribution: The type locality of *latifascia* is in Bannock county, Idaho. From southern Idaho this Great Basin representative of the *weidemeyerii* complex ranges into extreme western Wyoming, northern Utah, western Colorado, northern Nevada and east central California. It frequents streamsides, riverbeds or sage-covered flats that are contiguous with alkaline lakes and a *Salix-Populus-Artemesia* association. Adults fly from late June to August.

5. **Limenitis lorquini** (Boisduval). Described from California, Lorquin's Admiral is easily distinguished from all other members of the genus by its smaller size and orange apical patches on the dorsal fore wings. The area distal to the median white band of the dorsal hind wing is free of colored spots; orange colors on the underside are moderate to bright in intensity.

A minor form that occurs with variable frequency in typical *lorquini* populations was named "eavesii." It has a well defined row of orange spots on the dorsal hind wing and a more extensive suffusion of orange in the apical region of the dorsal fore wing.

Depending upon locality, altitude and climate, *lorquini* is on the wing between March and October. It should be sought in the vicinity of streams, rivers and lakes.

Early Stages: Dyar described these at length. Full grown larvae are mottled olive-green to brown. Secondary tubercles, posterior to the main cephalic pair, are reduced in size; otherwise the larvae are similar to those of *archippus*. Foodplants include willow (*Salix*), cottonwood and poplar (*Populus*).

(a) **lorquini** (Boisduval). Plate 14, figure 7, ♂. The apices of the fore wings of nominate *lorquini* are more broadly marked with orange and the creamy white limbal bands are broader than on the northern subspecies.

Distribution: Northern Baja California north throughout California (except desert regions and northern counties), central and northern Nevada, Utah and Colorado.

(b) **burrisonii** Maynard. Plate 14, figure 8, ♀. The dark red-orange apices on the dorsal fore wings are considerably restricted, the cream-white limbal bands are narrowed and a somber ventral ground color that often becomes very melanotic are the major traits which serve to distinguish this northern representative of *lorquini*.

The name *burrisonii*, described by Maynard in 1891 from "Landsdowne westward to Vancouver Island in British Columbia," is strictly applicable to a minor form that possesses a well defined row of burgundy red to orange spots distal to the cream-white median band on the dorsal hind wing. The more prevalent "normal" form was named "maynardi." Thus, *burrisonii* is to "maynardi" as "eavesii" is to *lorquini.*

Distribution: Northern counties of California, north throughout Oregon, Washington, and British Columbia, east to northern Idaho, western Alberta, Montana and Wyoming.

Subfamily NYMPHALINAE

WILLIAM H. HOWE

The spinous tubercles (scoli) on the caterpillars of the Nymphalinae either lack secondary spines or have them set randomly on the primary spines. This separates the subfamily from the Limenitinae. The presence of a dorsal row of spines, rarely reduced to low tubercles, separates the group from the Argynninae.

We recognize only three tribes among the North American Nymphalinae. One of these, Hypolimnini, is essentially pantropical. The other two, Melitaeini and Nymphalini, are world-wide but tend to concentrate in the temperate zones. As further studies are made of the tropical nymphalids it may develop that other tribes are needed to show the structure of the family and subfamily.

Tribe Hypolimnini

Four genera found in our area fall within this tribe: *Hypolimnas, Precis, Anartia* and *Siproeta.*

Genus HYPOLIMNAS Hübner

WILLIAM H. HOWE

This is an Old World tropical genus with strongholds in Africa and the India-Malayan region. There is every indication that the one species that occurs in the Americas is an import from Africa. It is reputed that this happened during the slave trade days.

Distribution: In the Americas confined to the Caribbean area.

1. **Hypolimnas misippus** (Linnaeus). Plate 16, figure 2, ♂; figure 3, ♀ (both ssp. *misippus*). The males of our subspecies, nominate *misippus,* are immediately recognized as moderately large blackish blue butterflies with a very large, more or less circular white patch edged with purplish blue centered on the hind wing, and similar patches but oval in shape on the fore wing, one across the end of the cell and a

small one in the apex. The females are strikingly different, resembling a danaid: fulvous, with an extensive black apical area on the fore wing and a transverse white bar just beyond the cell.

The females of *misippus* mimic a danaid species wherever the species is found in the Old World. Since the New World female specimens of *misippus* all mimic an African danaid, not one that is found in America, it seems most probable that our insect is an importation from Africa.

Early Stages: The butterfly has been raised on pusley in Florida (erroneously reported as parsley!) and on Malvaceae, *Ipomoea* and *Portulaca* in Puerto Rico.

Distribution: From the Guianas northward to Florida, mostly in the Antilles, nowhere common. There are five or six positive records from Florida between the 1880's and 1960.

Genus PRECIS Hübner

GLENN ALAN GORELICK

Members of the genus *Precis,* the buckeyes, are largely confined to the tropical regions of the world. The genus is characterized by angulate wing margins and the lack of hair on the eyes. Only two species occur in North America.

Early Stages: The eggs are broader than high with vertical ribs and the top flattened. The larvae have branching spines and are longitudinally striped; the chrysalis is strongly arched on the dorsum and concave on the ventral surface. In California adults exhibit mass movements in some years.

1. **Precis coenia** (Hübner). Plate 18, figure 9, ♀ (form "rosa"). This species, the Buckeye, is variable in size and color. A warm, dry environment produces smaller adults with reduced eyespots and a lighter ground color than those individuals inhabiting a cool, moist environment. The form depicted on the plate is the autumnal form "rosa," which may be recognized by its large size and pinkish undersides. The butterfly is found in many habitats, from sea level up to 9000 feet in the Tropical, Lower and Upper Austral, and Transition life zones (in the last two only as a casual). Two broods occur in northern and central U.S. (June to October); a third and sometimes a fourth in southeast and southwest U.S., including California. Adults hibernate in winter. The species is sometimes migratory.

Early Stages: Body dark olive-gray, striped or spotted with yellow or orange, with numerous short, branching spines all over the body, and one pair of spines on the head. Hosts: Plantaginaceae: *Plantago* (plantain); Onagraceae: *Ludwigia* (false loosestrife); Scrophulariaceae: *Mimulus* (monkey flower), *Antirrhinum* (snapdragon), *Gerardia* (gerardia), *Linaria* (toadflax); Crassulaceae: *Sedum* (stonecrop); Verbenaceae: *Verbena prostrata.*

Distribution: Southern Ontario and New England westward to California and Arizonia and southward to tropical America.

(b) **nigrosuffusa** (Barnes & McDunnough). Plate 18, figure 14, ♂. This subspecies, unlike *P. c. coenia,* is gray-brown to black. Many lepidopterists consider this darker form to be a distinct species and relationships between the two entities need further study. Its habitat is mountain canyons and riparian areas in the Lower and Upper Austral life zones. There are two or three broods per year.

Early Stages: Undescribed. Host: *Stemodia tomentosa.*

Distribution: Southeastern Arizona, southern Texas southward to central western Mexico.

2. **Precis evarete** (Cramer). Plate 18, figure 11, ♂ (ssp. *zonalis*). Our subspecies, *P. evarete zonalis* Felder & Felder, is often referred to in butterfly literature as *P. lavinia zonalis, P. orithya zonalis* or *P. genoveva.* The eyespots on the uppersides of the hind wings are very small in size relative to the corresponding eyespots on *P. coenia.* Adults are known to be migratory on occasion. They are found in open country, chiefly coastal, in the Subtropical and Tropical life zones. There are two or three broods per year.

Early Stages: The caterpillar is velvety black with tiny yellow spots and six rows of black branching spines with dark blue spots at the base of each spine; head black with spot of buff and a ring of bright buff around neck. Hosts: Verbenaceae: *Lippia* (in Cuba).

Distribution: Southern Florida and southern Texas (the species *P. evarete* occurs as far south as South America).

Genus ANARTIA Hübner

EDWIN M. PERKINS, JR. and STEPHEN F. PERKINS

1. **Anartia jatrophae** (Johannson). The White Peacock is widespread in the tropics, where it is divided into numerous races and varietal forms. Two subspecies enter our area.

Early Stages: The larva of *jatrophae* is described by Klots (1951): "Head shiny black with large, branching spines; body black with large, silvery spots and 4 rows of black branching spines." Brazilian, Cuban and Puerto Rican foodplants are listed as *Jatropha, Lippia* and *Bacopa,* respectively.

(a) **guantanamo** Munroe. Plate 18, figure 12, ♀. Ventral hind wing with black ocellus in cells M_1 and Cu_1 (M_3 rarely), each with blue-green pupil encircled by yellowish gold border. Cell Cu_1 of ventral fore wing contains another such ocellus. All ocelli are visible dorsally, but infrequently pupilled. Ground color varies from dark brown suffusion (summer form) to pale beige (winter form). Marginal and submarginal areas of upperside yellow to cream colored.

Distribution: Described from Guantánamo, Cuba, the subspecies extends into southern Florida. Occasional strays have been reported as far north as Massachusetts.

(b) **luteipicta** Fruhstorfer. This race is larger than *guantanamo* and the marginal and submarginal areas of its dorsal wings are white or cream colored.

Distribution: Described from Honduras, *luteipicta* ranges north through Mexico to southern Texas. Strays have been reported from Kansas. In Texas it flies between September and December; *Ruellia occidentalis* has been reported as its foodplant.

2. **Anartia fatima** (Fabricius). Plate 18, figure 15, ♂ (*form "venusta"*). The figure serves to identify the Fatima butterfly. Dorsally, the ground color is dark brown and the presence of four red spots in cells M_1, M_2, M_3 and Cu_1 of the hind wing is distinctive. The row of spots or patches in the median-postmedian areas of the dorsal wing surfaces is characteristically white in typical *fatima* but cream colored in form "venusta"; both phenotypes occur together.

Distribution: Common in Mexico, the Fatima is also well established in southern Texas where its two broods are on the wing from March to May and from October to December. Occasional strays are reported from Kansas.

Genus SIPROETA Hübner

EDWIN M. PERKINS, JR. and STEPHEN F. PERKINS

One species is represented in our area.

1. **Siproeta stelenes** (Linnaeus). Plate 14, figure 15, ♂; figure 16, ♂ (both ssp. *biplagiata*). Widespread and common in the tropical Americas, the Malachite is a large butterfly whose translucent, lime colored dorsal markings are offset by a dark brown ground color. Only one such lime colored spot occupies the forewing discal cell of the nominate subspecies which does not occur in our area.

Our subspecies *biplagiata* (Fruhstorfer) is similar to *S. s. stelenes,* but unlike the latter it possesses two lime colored spots in the fore wing discal cell. These cell spots are often unequal in size. Ventrally, the ground color varies between pearly and light reddish brown. Such variation commonly occurs within the same population. A prominent tail is present at hind wing vein M_3.

Distribution: This subspecies is taken in southern Texas from August to January; stragglers have been reported from Kansas. It also occurs in Florida, but it is uncertain whether as a resident or occasional immigrant.

Tribe Melitaeini

DAVID L. BAUER

This group of genera often is placed among the Argynninae. I disagree with this placement for many reasons. Structurally, in both immature and adult stages, these butterflies are closely related to Nymphalinae, especially the genera clustered around

Vanessa. The tribe is world wide in distribution with two apparent major centers of radiation. One of these is Eurasian and from that pool we have received one genus, *Euphydryas.* The Eurasian genera tend to be boreal. The second center is located in the Americas. These genera are essentially tropical and limited numbers of their species invade the adjacent temperate zones.

Habitats of the Melitaeini are extremely varied, from the steamy rain forests of the equatorial regions to the cold dry grasslands at treeline and at the edge of the tundra.

Early Stages: The eggs are roughly globular, flattened at the bottom, ridged in the upper parts and pitted below. They are laid in clusters of from just a few (*Phyciodes*) to several hundred (*Euphydryas, Chlosyne,* etc.) The larvae are rather well known and carry nine rows of branching spines or tubercles. The arrangement of scoli on the thoracic segments is helpful in making generic assignments. The pupae are pendant and varied in ornamentation. The host plants for the larvae are quite varied. In many instances the larvae appear to be host specific.

The arrangement of the species in genera is a result of a continuation of studies started by Forbes in 1945 and given further impetus by Higgins in 1960. The arrangement of the genera in a proper sequence must await further study.

Genus PHYCIODES Hübner

This genus is restricted to the Americas, and the vast majority of its species are tropical. Only twelve of the ninety-odd species that are recognized appear in our territory. The wing shape and color patterns are so diverse that they cannot be used either to summarize the genus or to set apart the three subgenera that we recognize. This must be done by examination of the posterior tip of the tegumen of the male genitalia. The subgenus *Phyciodes* has here two to four incurved hooks; in *Eresia* the valva terminates in two elaborate clusters of minute spines; and *Athanassa* has no armament on the end of the valva. The majority of *Eresia* and a few *Athanassa* resemble in a miniaturized way members of ithomiid and heliconiid genera, or the genus *Actinote.*

Early Stages: Largely unknown except for the species found within our area and those from southeastern Brazil.

Distribution: The genus *Phyciodes* is found from southern Argentina northward to the delta of the Mackenzie River on the Arctic Ocean. The great majority of the species are confined to the tropics.

Subgenus ANTHANASSA Scudder

The distinctive genitalic character of this large Neotropical subgenus has been given in the general discussion of *Phyciodes.* W. T. M. Forbes (1945) lists fifty species; only two cross the Mexican border into the United States.

1. **Phyciodes (Anthanassa) texana** Edwards.

Distribution: Found in the United States from Florida to Arizona and strays north to Nebraska. It is common to abundant throughout most of Mexico and ranges into Guatemala where it is found in the mountains from 5000–6000 ft. elevation.

(a) **texana** Edwards. Plate 45, figure 15, ♂. The Texan Crescent may be recognized by the orange-brown markings in the basal areas of the wings above being considerably obscured by dusky brownish black scales. The amount of basal orange-brown varies considerably from only a trace in many males to rather large spots in some females; however, it rarely approaches the unclouded confluent spots found in the subspecies *seminole*.

Early Stages: The host plants all belong to the family Acanthaceae.

Distribution: Nominate *texana* is the Mexican population. It is found as far north as southern Colorado (straying into western Kansas and Nebraska) and extends from Yuma county, Arizona, to Texas and south into Guatemala.

(b) **seminole** Skinner. Plate 44, figure 14, ♀. The upper surface of the wings has the same pattern as in *texana texana,* but all white or cream colored spots are larger, tending more to form bands; the basal orange-brown areas are brighter, clearer and slightly larger. The under surface of the wings is almost identical to *texana texana.* A blend zone may occur in central Kansas.

Distribution: Seminole is found from central Florida north to southern Georgia and west to Louisiana.

2. **Phyciodes (Anthanassa) ptolyca** Bates. Plate 44, figure 18, ♂. The figure is an excellent representation of the spring form in which the yellow spots are paler than in the summer broods. This species is readily separated from *texana* by the yellow areas which break up the dull orange-brown basal area on the under surface of the primary and also by the almost complete lack of submarginal dots on the upper surface of the primary.

Early Stages: Unknown.

Distribution: Several specimens of this species were captured at the Santa Ana Wildlife Refuge, Hidalgo county, Texas, in March, 1961. This is the only known record north of the Rio Grande. It has been taken repeatedly not far to the south in Mexico. It ranges south to Nicaragua.

Subgenus ERESIA Boisduval

See the general discussion of *Phyciodes* for the distinctive genitalic character of this subgenus. Many of the thirty-two species in the subgenus mimic heliconiids, ithomiids, and *Actinote.* Our single species, *frisia,* has the typical *Phyciodes* color and pattern.

3. **Phyciodes (Eresia) frisia** Poey. There are five named populations which vary in the color and size of the pattern of light spots. Two of these subspecies, and possibly a third, are found in the southern United States.

Early Stages: As far as is known, only those of *frisia frisia* have been recorded, and the information is presented under that subspecies.

Distribution: The species has a wide distribution from the southern United States to northern Argentina and in the Greater Antilles.

(a) **frisia** Poey. Plate 44, figure 16, ♀. The Cuban Crescent is small. The figure gives an excellent illustration of both the upper and under surface of the wings, and no description is necessary. The males are smaller and may be darker.

Early Stages: The eggs are deposited in clusters on the lower side of the leaves of *Beloperone guttata* (Shrimp Flower). The larvae are gregarious and feed at night. There are multiple broods.

Distribution: The type locality is Cuba. It is found in extreme southern Florida.

(b) **tulcis** Bates. Plate 44, figure 19, ♂. The figure shows the predominantly black-brown upper surface with creamy yellow spots so well that it can be readily recognized. The under surface of the wings is similar to *ptolyca*, but in the male *tulcis* is usually more washed out and paler.

The name *punctata* Edwards was given to specimens collected in southern Arizona. For many years no more specimens were found. In 1961 Roever captured one freshly emerged female in Sycamore Canyon, Santa Cruz county, Arizona. This specimen is identical with specimens from the states of Colima and Jalisco on the west coast of Mexico. Should a name be desired for this western population, *punctata* is available.

Early Stages: Not yet described.

Distribution: The type locality for·*tulcis* is Guatemala, and from there it ranges north to southern Texas and south to Panama.

Subgenus PHYCIODES Hübner

This, the nominate subgenus, contains only nine species. It is of greater interest to the student of Nearctic butterflies because all nine are found in the United States, and most of them also range north into Canada. One, *Phyciodes campestris* Behr, is the most northern melitaeine found in North America having, been captured near the shores of the Arctic Ocean in the Mackenzie River delta at about 68° North Latitude.

There is often considerable difference in the coloring of the under surface of spring and summer broods. This has resulted in names being given to these seasonal variations. The following arrangement of the species attempts to show relationships, but no linear arrangement can be very satisfactory. *Phyciodes vesta* Edw. is an isolated species, but the other eight species divide into three interrelated groups.

4. **Phyciodes (Phyciodes) vesta** Edwards. Plate 45, figure 14, ♀. This may be separated from the other species of the subgenus by the transverse black submarginal and postmedian lines on the under surface of the fore wings being connected by black scaling along the veins, resulting in the postmedian band being broken into three separate spots in cells M_3, Cu_1 and Cu_2.

Early Stages: These are being carefully studied by Roy Kendall, but have not yet been published. The foodplant is *Siphonoglossa pilosella.* There are multiple broods from March through September.

Distribution: It is common in southern Texas, strays north to Kansas, and ranges south to Guatemala.

The *tharos* group

In this group the costal and outer margins of the wings are quite rounded and are not angular or straight.

5. **Phyciodes (Phyciodes) phaon** Edwards. Plate 44, figure 7, ♀. A characteristic of *phaon* is the strongly contrasting coloring of both surfaces of the fore wing, as shown on the plate. Two other species of *Phyciodes,* which have a similar contrasting coloring on the underside of the fore wing, are *Phyciodes picta* Edwards and *Phyciodes campestris camillus* Edwards. Both of these species have a pale spot, or bar, near the end of the discal cell on the upper surface of the fore wing; and the orange-brown series of spots on the outer portion of the fore wing is reduced and broken into six or seven small separate spots of variable color, sometimes obsolete. In *phaon* the series is composed of four large spots with at most a trace of the other spots.

Early Stages: The eggs are deposited in small groups on the foodplants, *Lippia lanceolata* and *L. nodiflora.* Accounts have been published describing the larvae and pupae.

Distribution: It ranges from Florida north on the coast to southern Virginia, west to San Diego, California, north to Kansas, and south to Guatemala and British Honduras.

6. **Phyciodes (Phyciodes) tharos** (Drury). In spite of its variability, *tharos* can be consistently recognized and separated from other members of the subgenus by the extensive, relatively unmarked orange-brown basal and limbal areas as shown on the under surface of the fore wing in the figure. *Tharos* has adapted to a wide range of conditions, as diverse as Florida, Newfoundland and Arizona, but has not developed particularly distinctive subspecies.

Early Stages: The eggs are deposited on the leaves of asters and related Compositae in clusters of up to 200, often one layer on top of the first and sometimes three deep. The full grown larvae bear short, bristly, blackish to yellow-brown tubercles; the body is blackish brown with a yellow stripe along each side and yellow dots on the back. The larvae are gregarious, but do not spin a web. The pupa is ornamented with short abdominal tubercles and colored pale grayish to brownish, mottled with darker spots and lines. *Tharos* is single brooded in the north and has a succession of up to five or more broods in the south.

Distribution: Phyciodes tharos and its subspecies are found from central Canada to southern Mexico and from the Atlantic Coast to eastern Washington and Oregon and southeastern California. The species is absent from most of Nevada, California and western Oregon.

(a) **tharos** (Drury). Plate 44, figure 6, ♂; figure 8, ♀.   This is the well known Pearl Crescent. Its most distinguishing characteristic is the marked differences in the seasonal forms. The name *tharos* was originally given to the summer form with almost entirely yellow or cream colored hind wings beneath, as illustrated in the figure of the male; while the cool weather (early spring and late autumn) form, "marcia," has the under surface variously marked with light gray to brown scales. The nominate subspecies blends with the other subspecies around it to a considerable extent.

Distribution: The type locality is New York. It ranges north into southern Canada, west to the Rocky Mountains, and south to the Gulf States and Florida.

(b) **distincta** Bauer.   This subspecies has a complete pattern of fine lines on the upper surface, is very constant in wing pattern above, and rarely has the blotchy, irregular appearance so common in individuals of *tharos tharos.* The cool weather form is scarce and appears only during midwinter over most of its range. Similar individuals appear in colonies of typical *tharos,* and there is a broad blend zone of the two populations in Texas and northeastern Mexico.

Distribution: The type locality is Calexico, Imperial county, California. This is a predominantly Mexican subspecies, ranging south to the Sierra Madre del Sur and occurring in the United States along the lower Colorado River north to Moab, Utah, and in a blend zone with nominate *tharos* from southeastern Arizona into Texas.

(c) **pascoensis** Wright.   Plate 77, figure 9, ♂; figure 10, ♀.   The Pasco Crescent differs from *tharos* and *distincta* primarily in the lack of seasonal variation. Both generations have a light hind wing beneath similar to the summer form of *tharos,* but the ground color is deeper, more orange-yellow, and the brown area on the outer margin is small or obsolescent.

Distribution: It ranges southeast from Washington into northeastern Oregon and into Idaho; then south through Utah to the White Mountains of Arizona.

(d) **arctica** dos Passos.   The Arctic Crescent is the northernmost subspecies of *tharos.* It is single brooded. On the upper surface it has broader black margins than nominate *tharos* or *pascoensis.* It is distinguished from *tharos* by the deep orange-yellow color of the hind wings beneath. The females are somewhat paler beneath with a more prominent design of brown lines and spots.

Distribution: It is found in the Canadian and Hudsonian zones from Newfoundland west to British Columbia and the southwestern Northwest Territories. There are some colonies along the Canadian border in Maine and from Minnesota to Montana and south into the northern Rocky Mountains which resemble *arctica.* Their proper placement awaits future collecting and field study.

The *campestris* group

In this group the costal margin is straighter, but the outer margin and anal angles are rounded.

7. **Phyciodes (Phyciodes) batesii** Reakirt. Plate 44, figure 9, ♀. Although similar to *tharos,* Bates' Crescent is a distinct species allied to the western *Phyciodes campestris* Behr. It is single brooded where *tharos* has two or three broods. it coexists with *tharos* but remains distinct. Individuals of *tharos* with a heavy, dark pattern above have so often been confused with *batesii* that many published records are questionable. Bates' Crescent can be recognized by the median row on the upperside of the fore wing being a lighter shade than the other orange-brown areas; the heavier dark black brown transverse discal spots below on the fore wing; and the yellow, comparatively lightly marked hind wing beneath; and the prominent white fringes. As in *campestris,* the under surface of the hind wings is quite constant in the males but varies to a pattern approaching that of *tharos* form "marcia" in the females.

Early Stages: Larvae are reported to feed on *Aster.*

Distribution: It is found from New England, Ontario and Quebec west to Nebraska, southward in the mountains to Virginia.

8. **Phyciodes (Phyciodes) campestris** Behr. From the Great Plains to the Pacific Coast *campestris* is a familiar sight as it flies along streams, over meadows and abandoned fields, and grassy hillsides. Although *campestris* is variable, there is little evidence of seasonal forms. On the underside the males are rather constant in ground color, and the dark pattern varies only moderately. The females, unlike the males, vary greatly on the underside. Several distinct subspecies have been recognized and named.

Early Stages: The eggs are laid in clusters on the foodplant, *Aster foliaceus,* a widespread western species.

Distribution: This species occupies the area west of the Great Plains in the United States and Canada, and from the shores of the Arctic Ocean (near Aklavik, Northwest Territories) to the mountains of southern Mexico. It occurs from sea level to treeline.

(a) **campestris** Behr. Plate 44, figures 10 ♂ and 12 ♀. This northern and Pacific Coast subspecies bears the common name of Field Crescent. Its most consistent character is the rather bright (in fresh specimens) orange-yellow ground color of the under surface of the males as shown in figure 10. The females are variable in both the ground color and the amount of contrast in the pattern.

Distribution: This subspecies is found from near the shores of the Arctic Ocean in western Canada into Alaska, and south to Wyoming, central Nevada, and along the Pacific Coast to the San Gabriel Mountains of southern California. Adults appear from June through August in the north and from February to October in the south.

(b) **montana** Behr. The Mountain Crescent is about the same size and shape as *campestris.* It may be recognized by the greatly enlarged and more numerous orange-brown spots and bands above, particularly those on the outer half of the wings. There is a complete series of orange-brown submarginal crescents in the majority of specimens, and the marginal border is orange-brown on many females and a few of the males. On the hind wings above, the dark pattern tends to disappear and the orange-brown areas become partially or entirely confluent. On the under surface *montana* is very similar to nominate *campestris* but with dark brown markings reduced or entirely lacking. The females show the same variation in color and pattern on the under surface as described for *campestris campestris*.

Distribution: This subspecies inhabits the alpine regions of the Sierra Nevada from Kern county north to Mount Lassen and is found in the Carson Range in Nevada.

(c) **camillus** Edwards. Plate 78, figure 5, ♀. The principal difference between the Camillus or Rocky Mountain Crescent, *camillus,* and nominate *campestris* is on the underside of the wings: the fore wing has larger black-brown areas and usually a prominent irregular transverse black-brown band from the costal margin just beyond the end of the cell to the middle of the inner margin. The underside of the females is variable, but shows the same differences from the other subspecies as do the males.

Distribution: It is found from southern Wyoming and southeastern Idaho (where it intergrades with *campestris campestris*) westward to eastern Nevada and south throughout most of the higher mountains of Arizona and New Mexico.

There are numerous colonies of *campestris* in the western Great Basin which will not fit any of the above subspecies, but more specimens and field study are needed before their position and taxonomic standing are understood. In southern New Mexico some colonies show some of the characteristics of Mexican populations to the south.

9. **Phyciodes (Phyciodes) picta** Edwards. This butterfly averages smaller than most of the other *Phyciodes* found in the United States. The apical third of the fore wing beneath is broadly pale yellow and comparatively unmarked in *picta* and has the regular *Phyciodes* pattern of lines and spots in *phaon*. This characteristic of the apex of the fore wing along with the clear pale yellow underside of the hind wings with an obsolete pattern, and its smaller size, will also serve to separate it from *campestris camillus*. All three species inhabit some areas so careful attention should be paid to the identifying characters.

Early Stages: These have been described in detail by W. H. Edwards.

Distribution: picta is found from western Nebraska south into northern Mexico and west to south-central Arizona. There are two subspecies: one east of the Continental Divide; the other occupying a small area west of the Divide.

(a) **picta** Edwards. Plate 44, figure 11, ♀. This eastern subspecies of *picta* has received the common name Painted Crescent. The males are similar to the females on the upperside with a tendency toward more extensive black-brown areas. They differ from the females on the underside in that the light areas are a deeper straw yellow with very little dark pattern and in having the basal two-thirds of the fore wing similar to the same area of *phaon*.

Distribution: The Painted Crescent occurs in arid regions of western Nebraska,

Kansas, Oklahoma and Texas, in New Mexico, and is also found in the Arkansas and San Juan river basins of Colorado.

(b) **canace** Edwards. Plate 16, figure 11, ♀. The Canace Crescent differs from *picta picta* on the upperside in having the pale yellow and orange-fulvous spots larger and the bands broader, particularly in the females. Beneath the ground is straw yellow in both males and females and not pale creamy white as in females of *picta picta*.

Distribution: This subspecies is found in central and southeastern Arizona. The extent of its distribution to the south and east needs further investigation and documentation.

The *mylitta* group

The three species belonging to this group have the costal margin of the fore wing straighter and the wings more angular than the members of the two preceding groups.

10. **Phyciodes (Phyciodes) orseis** Edwards. This species is well illustrated by the figures, and no description is necessary. It is not common in collections and is considered a prize by lepidopterists. It lives primarily in canyons containing small streams. The males stake out an area where they perch on a favorite shrub and dart out, chasing other butterflies, particularly other *Phyciodes,* and then return to their chosen shrub. If the shrubbery is tall, they may perch six to eight feet above the ground, unusual for a *Phyciodes.* There are two distinct subspecies of this scarce butterfly, and little is known about them at present. They may prove to be separate species when further investigated.

Early Stages: Nothing is known.

Distribution: This species has two centers of distribution: one in the Coast Ranges, from San Francisco Bay north into southwestern Oregon; the other in the Canadian and upper Transition zones of the Sierra Nevada.

(a) **orseis** Edwards. Plate 43, figure 6, ♂. The Orseis Crescent is one of the rarest butterflies in North America. The determined lepidopterist who wishes to catch this prize can still find it in small numbers in the rugged Coast Ranges of northwestern California and southwestern Oregon. Nominate *orseis* is usually found flying with *campestris* and *mylitta.* The resemblance to *campestris* is so close that large specimens of *campestris* are often mistaken for *orseis* by collectors. On the fore wing of *orseis* the apex is more produced and more indented about midway on the outer margin. The hind wing has sharper outer and anal angles and is proportionately broader from the anal angle to the costal margin compared to the distance from the base to the outer margin. These differences between *campestris* and *orseis* combined with the *mylitta* type of pattern on both surfaces of the wings should help in recognizing *orseis orseis.*

Distribution: The type locality is Mount St. Helena, Napa county, California, but it has not been found in the San Francisco Bay area, or for many miles to the north, for the past fifty years. It extends north through the Coast Ranges into southwestern Oregon and has also been collected at Diamond Lake in the Cascade Mountains.

(b) **herlani** Bauer. Plate 45, figure 9, ♂; figure 10, ♀. The Sierra Nevada Crescent differs from its much scarcer Coast Range relative in the reduced dark pattern and more extensive and evenly colored orange-brown areas of the upperside. The Sierra Nevada Crescent flies in company with *campestris montana* and *mylitta* and resembles both species. The submarginal crescents on the under surface of *herlani* are more equal in size and rarely obscured with brown, and the postmedian series of dots are small, brown, and all of about the same size; in *mylitta* the dot in cell M_3 is generally much larger than the rest of the series, particularly the dots at each end of the row.

Early Stages: Nothing is known.

Distribution: The type locality is Glenbrook Creek, Douglas county, Nevada, at an elevation of about 7000 feet. Specimens usually are found in the Canadian zone of the eastern slope of the Sierra.

11. **Phyciodes (Phyciodes) pallida** Edwards. The species *pallida* has often been confused with *mylitta* Edwards, a smaller, but similar species with which it occasionally flies. the main difference between the two is biological: *pallida* is single brooded while *mylitta* is multiple brooded. The best pattern character is the prominent, often squarish, black spot at about the middle of the inner margin on both surfaces of the fore wing in the males of *pallida.* In *mylitta* this spot is orange-fulvous on the underside and, at most, edged with black or dark brown. The figure is not typical in this character. There appears to be no easy or constant way to separate the females except by association with the males. On the upper surface males of *pallida* are extremely variable, with a blotchy, somewhat uneven, pattern of black spots and lines, usually partially and sometimes extensively obsolescent. The females have the ground color of the upper surface varying from orange-fulvous to cream with a regular and complete black pattern. On the underside *pallida* varies in both sexes from ochreous yellow to whitish with a typical *Phyciodes* pattern of brown lines and shaded brown areas.

Early Stages: These need to be studied. The larval foodplants are thistles of various species. In the laboratory it has been raised on *Cirsium arvense* (Canada thistle).

Distribution: The species has been taken in the Fraser, Thompson, and Okanogan River valleys of British Columbia and southeastward to the Kaibab Plateau of northern Arizona, and from eastern Oregon and Washington to the eastern foothills of the Rocky Mountains in Montana and Colorado. It is absent from California, western Oregon, western Washington and western Nevada.

(a) **pallida** Edwards. Plate 44, figure 5, ♂. The figure on the plate and the discussion above under the species will enable ready recognition of the Pallid Crescent. It differs from the rather indistinct subspecies *barnesi* in the fainter and reduced pattern of brown lines and areas on the underside of the wings and more extensively yellowish appearance of this surface, particularly in the females. Many male specimens, however, approach *barnesi* in the heavier more distinct pattern below.

Distribution: This subspecies ranges from the eastern foothills of the Rocky Mountains in Colorado southwest to the Kaibab Plateau in northern Arizona.

(b) **barnesi** Skinner. Plate 43, figure 7, ♂; Plate 78, figure 6, ♀. Barnes's Crescent differs from nominate *pallida* in the more prominent brown pattern beneath and the greater prevalence of white on the hind wings, particularly in females from the northwest which have the entire underside of the hind wing white or pale cream without any yellow ochre.

Early Stages: The larval foodplant is thistle. The larvae and pupae are said to be quite distinct from those of *mylitta* by Dr. David V. McCorkle who has reared both species.

Distribution: This subspecies occupies the northwestern portion of the species range and becomes easily separable from *pallida* in Oregon, Washington, and British Columbia. It has been recorded also for Utah, eastern Nevada, Idaho, Wyoming and Montana.

12. **Phyciodes (Phyciodes) mylitta** Edwards. The figures on the plate should enable ready recognition of *mylitta* and its subspecies. Cool weather specimens have more extensive dark brown areas contrasting with whitish spots and bands. The warm weather form has the whitish color replaced almost entirely by yellow-ochre and a fine pattern of dark brown lines and much smaller brown areas. One of the important characteristics of *mylitta* is that it is multiple brooded throughout its distribution. Many species of thistles are used as foodplants by the larvae.

Distribution: This species has an extensive distribution in western North America, from the mountains of southern Mexico north to southwestern Canada. There are four subspecies; two are Mexican.

(a) **mylitta** Edwards. Plate 16, figure 9, ♂; figure 10, ♀. The Mylitta Crescent may be recognized by the reduced pattern of rather thin black lines on the upper surface and the consequent increase of the orange-fulvous areas. On the underside *m. mylitta* shows marked differences (more than in other subspecies) between cool and warm weather broods which are described above.

Early Stages: There are multiple broods from April to October in British Columbia and throughout most of the year in southern California and Mexico. It is double brooded at elevations of 7000 to 8000 feet in the Sierra Nevada. The larval foodplants are many species of thistles.

Distribution: The Mylitta Crescent ranges from Baja California to British Columbia and eastward into the mountains of Montana and the Wasatch Mountains of Utah. It has a wide range of habitats from near sea level along the coast to 9000 feet or more in the Sierra Nevada and to near tree line in the Cascade Mountains of Washington.

(b) **arizonensis** Bauer. Plate 43, figure 8, ♂. Specimens of the Arizona Crescent with reduced black pattern above often have been called (erroneously) *pallida* Edwards, while specimens having a more extensive black pattern have gone (equally erroneously) under the name *thebais* Godman & Salvin, a Mexican subspecies. Its smaller size and more yellow-fulvous ground color, combined with the much more regular and complete black pattern above, serve to distinguish it from *pallida* which is figured just above it on the plate. Typical *thebais* has the median band above narrow and broken into separate spots and is a much darker butterfly with an even heavier black pattern than that shown in figure 6 of *orseis*. The subspecies *mylitta arizonensis* is more like *mylitta mexicana* Hall from the east coast of Mexico than the west coast *m. thebais*. On the upper surface the more yellow-fulvous ground color combined with the rather broad median band and heavier black pattern in the basal and marginal areas will serve to separate most individuals of *arizonensis* from nominate *mylitta*.

Early Stages: Apparently unknown.

Distribution: The Arizona Crescent flies at elevations of 4000 to over 8000 feet in the mountains of central and southeastern Arizona and the adjacent areas of New Mexico and Sonora. The southern limit of distribution is not known. It has also been captured in extreme southwestern Colorado.

Genus TEXOLA Higgins

This is a genus of small neotropical butterflies which extend a few hundred miles north of the Mexican boundary. Higgins included three Mexican species in the genus, but the other species are about as close to *Microtia* or *Dymasia* as they are to the type species, *Texola elada* (Hewitson). Little is known about the early stages, but females of *elada* have been observed ovipositing on a small yellow flowered composite in Mexico and on a species of Acanthaceae in Texas.

1. **Texola elada** (Hewitson). The males expand 20 to 30 mm and the females expand 25 to 34 mm. Nominate *elada* is doubtfully found in our area. There is some question about the type specimen of the name *callina* Boisduval. Until the matter is cleared up the name should not be used. All *elada* populations can be recognized by the middle band of red-brown on the underside of the hind wings having the costal spot orange-brown, and the second spot white.

Early Stages: Undescribed.

Distribution: The Elada Checkerspot inhabits most of Mexico and the adjacent areas of the United States. The flight is rather weak, and they usually do not wander far from the home colony.

(a) **ulrica** (Edwards). Plate 41, figure 25, ♂; figure 26, ♀. The figures on the plate show the heavier dark network pattern above. The underside is also well illustrated. This population differs from *elada elada* in the narrow orange-brown spot band across the middle of the wings above. In *elada* this band is broader than the others and buff in color. There is a possibility that nominate *elada* might occur in extreme southern Texas.

Early Stages: The larval foodplant is reported as *Siphonoglossa pilosella.*

Distribution: The Ulrica Checkerspot is found from southern through western Texas into southern New Mexico and possibly extreme southeastern Arizona. The type locality is San Antonio, Bexar county, Texas.

(b) **perse** (Edwards). Plate 41, figure 27, ♂; figure 28, ♀. This subspecies has the same pattern above and below as *ulrica,* but the orange-brown is paler and the dark network pattern is finer resulting in slightly larger light spots. It is also paler orange-brown on the underside.

Distribution: The type locality is "Fort Grant and in the Graham Mountains, Arizona." This western subspecies extends from Arizona south into Sonora, Mexico. The northern limit is in Yavapai county, Arizona.

Genus CHLOSYNE Butler

This large and variable genus of butterflies is found from southern Canada to Patagonia. The subgenera and species groups are diverse and so variable that no generalization can be made. About all that the species have in common is the male genital structure which varies so little among some groups and species that in many instances it cannot be used for differentiation. For many years the North American *palla* group was placed in the Palearctic genus *Melitaea* while *gorgone* and *nycteis* were placed in *Phyciodes.*

This is a most interesting genus to study because subspeciation has been prolific. There are thirty-three species in the genus and twenty-one are found in the United States and Canada.

The early stages and life histories of most of the species are unrecorded. Where known, they arc useful in understanding relationships and recognizing species.

Subgenus CHARIDRYAS Scudder

Chlosyne nycteis (Doubleday) is the type species of *Charidryas* Scudder. This subgenus composes the northern branch of *Chlosyne* and includes nine species. In the past they have been divided between the genus *Phyciodes* and the Palearctic genus *Melitaea,* but they all have the characteristic structures of *Chlosyne.* All nine species inhabit the United States and seven of them range north into southern Canada. There are two groups: the western *palla* group of six species which lacks the postmedian series of black spots on the upper surface of the hind wings and has very plain, finely mottled pupae; and the eastern *harrisii* group of three species in which the postmedian series of black spots is prominent on the upper surface of the hind wing, and the pupae have a varied pattern of dark spots on a light ground color, similar to those of *Euphydryas.*

The harrisii group

1. **Chlosyne (Charidryas) gorgone** (Hübner). Plate 40, figure 1. The Gorgone Crescent, as it has been called in the past, is really a Checkerspot on the basis of the male genitalia. It is unique in the mostly pale silvery gray underside of the hind wings with little if any orange-brown. The figure on the plate is excellent. The male is similar to the female but smaller in size. Nominate *gorgone* appears to be an odd coastal subspecies found in eastern Georgia and is very rare. All of our specimens from central Georgia northward and westward are best considered *gorgone carlota* (Reakirt).

Early Stages: The egg is apparently undescribed. The mature larva is yellow with longitudinal black stripes, the tubercles blackish and bristly. The head is black and hairy, the legs are black and the prolegs yellowish. The pupa is light gray with lighter and darker spots and of the typical Melitaeine structure. The larvae feed on many species of Compositae.

Distribution: It is found from the eastern slope of the Rocky Mountains eastward to the Carolinas and Georgia, and from southern Manitoba to Mexico.

2. **Chlosyne (Charidryas) nycteis** (Doubleday). The Nycteis Crescent is also a Checkerspot by male genitalic structure. The species is somewhat variable in the amount of black above and the distinctness and completeness of the pattern on the underside of the hind wings. It can be easily recognized by the figures of the two subspecies shown on the plates.

Early Stages: The egg is ridged on the upper third, pitted on the middle third, and smooth on the lower third. The color is pale green when newly deposited. The full grown larvae are velvety black with a dull orange middorsal stripe and purplish streaks on the sides between the stigmata. Beneath the body is olivaceous brown. The entire body is speckled with whitish. The dorsal tubercles are dark brown or black with black bristles, except for the infrastigmatal tubercles which have yellowish brown bristles. The pupa is pearly gray marked in the typical Melitaeinae pattern with black-brown in varying amounts.

Distribution: This species is found from Arizona and Wyoming to the Atlantic Coast, and from southern Canada to Georgia and Texas.

(a) **nycteis** (Doubleday). Plate 40, figure 2, ♂. The excellent illustration of the Nycteis Checkerspot will enable easy recognition. This subspecies is characterized on the upperside by the wide orange-brown to fulvous band across both wings and the wide blackish marginal borders. On the underside of the hind wings and also in the basal area of the fore wings the pattern is rather washed out, as shown in the figure. There is considerable variation in the clearness of the underside pattern.

Early Stages: Described under the species above. The larvae feed on sunflowers and asters.

Distribution: This northern and eastern subspecies is found from the Great Plains to the Atlantic Coast across southern Canada and the northern United States.

(b) **drusius** (Edwards). Plate 40, figure 3, ♂. The Drusius Checkerspot has an increased black-brown pattern on the upperside as shown in the figure. The underside has slightly darker coloring and a more complete pattern.

Early Stages: Apparently undescribed.

Distribution: Colonies with the *drusius* coloring are found in Wyoming, Colorado, Arizona, New Mexico and Texas.

(c) **reversa** (Chermock & Chermock). Chermock's Checkerspot is a little-known subspecies in which the dark markings of the upperside are greatly reduced resulting in more extensive light areas. This subspecies is a parallel to *harrisii hanhami* Fletcher.

Early Stages: Unknown.

Distribution: This Checkerspot is only known from the type locality, Riding Mountains, Manitoba, and the immediate vicinity.

3. **Chlosyne (Charidryas) harrisii** (Scudder). This species is much more like the western members of the subgenus on the underside, but it differs on the upperside in the lack of a submarginal orange- or red-brown band which is replaced by a broad, black-brown margin similar to that of *nycteis.*

Early Stages: These are described in detail by Scudder and others.

Distribution: C. harrisii is found from Nova Scotia west to Manitoba and Wisconsin, and south to northern Illinois, Indiana, and Ohio, and in the Appalachian Mountains to West Virginia and possibly Georgia.

(a) **hanhami** (Fletcher). Plate 43, figure 9, ♂. Hanham's Checkerspot has broader orange-brown areas above than nominate *harrisii* and approaches *nycteis drusius* on the underside except that the silvery submarginal crescents are longer and not partially obsolescent as in *N. drusius* and *n. nycteis.*

Early Stages: Not described for this subspecies.

Distribution: The type locality is Bird's Hill, near Winnipeg, Manitoba, and the range of distribution was given as "eastern, central, and southern" Manitoba and northern Minnesota. It also has been taken in northern Wisconsin where it intergrades with *harrisii harrisii.*

(b) **albimontana** (Avinoff). This subspecies is not very different from many nominate *harrisii* specimens. It differs only in having more extensive orange-brown areas and reduced dark markings on the upperside of the wings. It somewhat resembles *hanhami,* but the underside is as in typical *harrisii.* It is not a very distinct subspecies.

Early Stages: Undescribed.

Distribution: The type locality is the White Mountains of New Hampshire. It ranges northeast through Canada's Maritime Provinces.

(c) **harrisii** (Scudder). Plate 40, figures 4, ♀. Harris' Checkerspot is readily recognizable from the figure on the plate. It is rather variable, and the two rows of orange-brown spots on the upperside of the wings tend to be partially fused but not to the extent found in *albimontana* or *hanhami.*

Early Stages: The best way to locate colonies is to look for the larval foodplant, *Aster umbellatus,* a white flowered aster of moist, brushy thickets.

Distribution: This subspecies ranges from New England southwestward.

(d) **liggetti** (Avinoff). Plate 45, figure 12, ♂; figure 13, ♀. On the upper surface the black areas are greatly expanded as shown in the figures, and the orange-brown areas tend to be paler and the spots well separated. The underside does not differ from typical *harrisii.*

Early Stages: These are undescribed.

Distribution: This dark subspecies has been taken from Ohio through Pennsylvania to Ulster county, New York.

The palla group

4. Chlosyne (Charidryas) palla (Boisduval). The species *palla* is widely distributed in areas of open forest in the Rocky Mountains and the Pacific states where it flies over hillsides, in canyons and along roads. The males are frequent puddle and damp ground visitors and may be captured readily while slaking their thirst. Both sexes spend much time feeding at flowers, and occasionally rest with wings spread to the sun. Their flight is moderately fast and usually just high enough to clear the lower vegetation. The males have a ground color of various shades of orange- or red-brown, broken into rows of spots by a network of black lines. The females are dimorphic. If the ground color is pale yellow, the black lines are greatly broadened and the light spots are reduced or even obsolescent (form "eremita"). As the ground color darkens, the black lines become progressively thinner, and some females with a red-brown ground resemble males in both color and pattern.

Early Stages: The egg is undescribed. The full grown larva bears shiny black bristly tubercles or spines. The dorsal half of the body is charcoal-black speckled with minute whitish spots so as to set off a black middorsal line with heavier concentration of white specks along each side and eight pairs of orange crescents on either side of the base of the middorsal tubercles. Two similar rows of orange spots extend along the sides below the rows of tubercles just above and below the spiracles. There is also a lateral whitish stripe of larger specks below which the body is grayish black. The legs are black and the prolegs are grayish black. The spiracles are black ringed with white. Pupa: The color varies according to the surroundings from pale tan to wood brown and pale gray to mostly black and is mottled with fine spots and streaks of lighter and darker shades of grays and browns.

Distribution: C. palla occurs in a broad arc around the northern Great Basin. This arc extends from the San Gabriel Mountains of southern California north to southwestern Oregon where it curves east of the Cascade Mountains. From there it extends eastward in a broad band across northern Oregon, eastern Washington, and southern British Columbia to the western edge of the Great Plains, and south in the mountains to central New Mexico. A study of the present variation of *palla* gives evidence of fragmentation of the species during a cooler glacial period into isolated subspecies which still maintain their distinctions, but have reestablished contact and in some areas apparently interbreed. Most of these subspecies have been given names and are treated below.

(a) **palla** (Boisduval). Plate 43, figure 12, ♂. Form "eremita," ♀, Plate 41, figure 7. This subspecies is characterized by the red-brown ground color of the males above with a moderately heavy and even black pattern. The females are dimorphic and vary from the very dark form "eremita" to specimens similar to males, with a mixture of red-brown to pale yellow bands and spots. In marginal colonies where contact is made with other populations, the ground color of some females resembles that of males more closely. Beneath the pale bands and spots are light cream to pale yellowish. The marginal band is red-brown, as are the basal and median spots on the hind wings. Most of the fore wing is red-brown in males and marked with contrasting pale and darker red-brown in females.

Distribution: At present the name *palla* is used for the slightly paler red-brown colonies found in the mountains of southern California, the typical coastal colonies of northern California and southwestern Oregon, and the very similar colonies of *palla* found in extreme southeastern Washington, northeastern Oregon, and in the mountains of Idaho just north of the Snake River Plain.

Early Stages: The food plant listed by Dr. J. A. Comstock is *Castilleja breviflora* (Scrophulariaceae), but *palla* must use other foodplants as it is found in many areas where *C. breviflora* does not occur.

(b) **whitneyi** (Behr). Whitney's Checkerspot differs from the other subspecies of *palla* in that both sexes have the wings above bright red-brown with thin, often partially obsolete, black lines. Beneath the pattern is as in nominate *palla,* but the red-brown is brighter, the pale areas yellowish, and the black lines thinner.

Distribution: Typical *whitneyi* inhabits the Canadian zone meadows and open hillsides of the Sierra Nevada and also the steep eastern slope canyons down to the lower limits of the Transition zone. It is also found sparingly in the spur ranges running out from the Sierras into Nevada. A somewhat disjunct population of *whitneyi* lives in the Canadian zone along the eastern slope of the Cascade Mountains in Oregon.

Early Stages: The larvae of *whitneyi* feed on rabbitbrush: three varieties of *Chrysothamnus nauseosus,* and *viscidiflorus* (family Compositae). The foodplant of *palla palla* is a member of the family Scrophulariaceae.

(c) **vallismortis** (Johnson). Plate 27, figure 15, ♂. The Panamint Checkerspot averages slightly larger than the other subspecies of *palla.* The ground color above is dull orange-fulvous, and the pattern is distinctive in its overall banded appearance caused by the heavy transverse black lines and bands and narrow or obsolescent dark scaling along the veins. Beneath the pattern is as in *palla palla,* but the colors are orange-fulvous and creamy white with a reduction in size of the basal pale orange-fulvous spots and a heavy invasion of cream colored scales.

Early Stages: Unknown.

Distribution: There are several puzzling populations of *palla* or *acastus* isolated in the higher desert mountain ranges extending from northwestern Nevada through eastern California to the Spring Mountains of southern Nevada. The name *vallismortis* was given to the Panamint Mountains population and has been used, probably incorrectly, for the others.

The Kyle Canyon population in the Spring Mountains, Clark county, Nevada, needs a great deal more investigation. From the specimens I have examined it appears that there are both *palla flavula* and *acastus* elements present. Whether the two separate species are found in the area of one conglomerate population, is not at present known. Therefore no name or placement is assigned.

(d) **flavula** (Barnes & McDunnough). Plate 77, figure 11, ♂; figure 12, ♀. The distinctive feature of the Flavid Checkerspot is stated so well in the original description that it is quoted below. "The underside of the secondaries is (as is usual in the group) the most characteristic portion, the pale banding being a very decided yellow, slightly deeper than in *palla*, . . . combined with this is the very fine nature of the black bordering lines, especially those of the broad median yellow band; the orange band of spots preceding the large yellow marginal lunules is rather reduced, leaving considerable of the yellow color visible, being in this respect more like *acastus* than *palla.*" In *Colorado Butterflies* (Brown, Eff & Rotger) a dark form of *acastus* was confused with *flavula,* for it is stated that the light areas beneath are often glistening white.

Early Stages: Unknown.

Distribution: Colonies with the yellow, washed-out appearance of *flavula* on the underside occupy the Wasatch Mountains of Utah and the mountain ranges of the upper Colorado and Green River Basins.

(e) **calydon** (Strecker). Plate 41, figure 5, ♂; figure 6, ♀. The Calydon Checkerspot flies in open, wooded canyons and hillsides. It differs from California *palla* on the underside of the fore wings of the males where it has a greater contrast in the light and dark orange-brown and fulvous bands and spots and heavier, more complete black lines outlining the dark orange-fulvous markings. The females have orange-brown and fulvous light spots and bands above, and only rarely do specimens have the pale yellow and predominently black pattern so prevalent in the *palla palla* populations.

Early Stages: Undescribed, but the larval foodplant is listed as Indian Paintbrush, *Castilleja.*

Distribution: Under the name *calydon* are included all the colonies of *palla* along and east of the Continental Divide from New Mexico north to Alberta and west to southwestern British Columbia and northeastern Washington.

(f) **sterope** (Edwards). Plate 40, figure 9, ♀; figure 12, ♂. This *palla* subspecies is found in the Palouse wildlife region and therefore is called the Palouse Checkerspot. It is the most distinct of the subspecies of *palla* and is unique in the following ways: 1) it is confined to an arid or semi-arid sagebrush environment; 2) it has maintained its distinctive characteristics without being isolated by present day barriers from the surrounding populations; 3) it combines a heavy, dark pattern above with a pale under surface. In this subspecies the females are more constant in color and pattern than the males, which vary from a heavy, dark pattern above with a pale fulvous ground to a light or thin, dark pattern and an orange-fulvous ground. Usually the ground is of two shades of fulvous in alternating bands and spots. The females are consistently the dark "eremita" form, which is normal for this population. Few females have orange-fulvous spots on the upper surface at the base of the wings or in the median band of the hind wings, and only about fifty percent have the orange-fulvous marginal band above. The pale areas beneath are chalk white, sometimes with a tinge of yellow, but not shiny or glossy.

Early Stages: So far the larvae have been found feeding only on *Chrysothamnus viscidiflorus,* to the exclusion of the other species of *Chrysothamnus* growing in the area.

Distribution: This subspecies appears to be isolated in the lowlands of eastern Washington and north central Oregon. Its favored haunts are the canyons and hillsides of the Upper Sonoran sagebrush country. The type locality, originally stated simply as "Oregon," has been restricted to the vicinity of Tygh Valley, Wasco county, Oregon. The name *hewesi* Leussler 1931 is a synonym.

5. **Chlosyne (Charidryas) acastus** (Edwards). The Acastus Checkerspot is at home in the canyons and washes of the Upper Sonoran zone. It prefers the lower portion of the Piñon-Pine-Juniper Belt, particularly where it is mixed with considerable sagebrush and rabbitbrush, but occasionally colonies are found in the washes in open sagebrush country. Males have the ground color above various shades of fulvous, varying from a pale ground color and heavy, dark pattern to a deeper fulvous with a partially obsolescent dark pattern. The ground color never approaches the orange-fulvous or orange-brown of the Rocky Mountain *palla* populations. Females have the same range of variation in pattern and ground color as the males, but usually present two shades of pale fulvous. Some populations have dark "eremita"-like females. Beneath the ground color of both sexes varies from glossy white to cream.

Early Stages: The egg is undescribed. The fully grown larva is similar to that of *palla* (see description under *palla*).

Distribution: C. acastus is found from the eastern foothills of the Sierra Nevada of California east to New Mexico and Nebraska, and north through eastern Montana to the Red Deer River, Alberta.

(a) **dorothyi** Bauer. Plate 40, figure 13, ♂; figure 16, ♀. The figures show the upper surface of Dorothy's Checkerspot so well that no comment is necessary. On the under surface figure of the male, however, the fulvous marginal band is too wide and too bright. Usually the marginal band on the fore wing is about half the width shown, quite pale, and invaded by dark scales along the veins.

Early Stages: The known larval foodplant is *Chrysothamnus viscidiflorus.*

Distribution: The subspecies *dorothyi* has a limited range in the isolated Burnt River and Snake River canyons of Oregon at the extreme northwestern limit of the species range.

(b) **acastus** (Edwards). Plate 40, figure 14, ♀, ssp.?; plate 41, figure 1, ♂; figure 2, ♀; figure 3, ♀ underside; figure 4, ♀. The figures on the plate and the description in the species discussion will enable easy recognition of this widespread subspecies. On the upper surface it differs from the subspecies *dorothyi* in the thinner dark pattern of both males and females and the fulvous ground color of the females.

Early Stages: The only plant the larvae have been found feeding on is *Chrysothamnus viscidiflorus.*

Distribution: Nominate *acastus* is at present considered to occupy the entire range of the species except for the range of *dorothyi.*

6. **Chlosyne (Charidryas) neumoegeni** (Skinner).   *C. neumoegeni* is difficult to define as a species because of the differences in color and pattern of the two subspecies. Both populations have the light areas of the underside shining silvery white; and males, and to some extent females, have most of the underside of the fore wing evenly washed with brick- or orange-red.

Early Stages: The eggs are light green and harmonize with the green of the leaves of the asters on which they are deposited in clusters. The full grown larvae are predominantly black. The body bears the usual number of shiny black bristly spine-like tubercles. The dorsal tubercles are not shorter and more cone shaped, as on the larvae of *palla, gabbii* and *acastus,* but are of the same slender spike-like shape and are about equal in length to the lateral rows. There may be a dull orange supra-stigmatal stripe, but in many colonies this orange stripe is obsolete.

Distribution: C. neumoegeni inhabits the deserts of southeastern California and southern Nevada, the mountains and desert south of the Colorado Plateau in Arizona, and also in southwestern Utah. It also occurs south into Baja California and Sonora, Mexico. The eastern limit of distribution is uncertain but *neumoegeni sabina* may occur in extreme southwestern New Mexico.

(a) **neumoegeni** (Skinner). Plate 40, figure 5, ♂; figure 6, ♀.   Neumoegen's Checkerspot is distinguished from all related members of the *palla* group by the characteristics given above for the species and from the subspecies *sabina* by the evenly colored brick- to orange-red ground color above and a strong tendency to obsolescence of the black network pattern. This is a true desert subspecies inhabiting some of the hottest and driest areas of the Southwest.

Early Stages: The foodplant is *Aster tortifolius.*

Distribution: Neumoegen's Checkerspot is primarily an inhabitant of the California microphyll desert. It is found as far north as 37° North Latitude in eastern California and Nevada. It also occurs in the Virgin River Valley in Washington county, Utah, (type locality). It ranges south through western Arizona and southeastern California into Baja California. The southern limit of distribution is not known.

(b) **sabina** (Wright). Plate 45, figure 5, ♂; figure 6, ♀.   The Sabina Checkerspot differs from nominate *neumoegeni* in the complete, rather heavy network of black lines on the upper surface of the wings and in the presence of two slightly different shades of red- or orange-brown in the bands and series of spots, and the pale yellow or buff color of the apical light spots on the fore wings in females and most males. It has been confused with both *acastus* and *gabbii* from which it can be recognized by the *neumoegeni* pattern and coloring of the underside, as described for the species. In two localities, the Hualapai Mountains near Kingman, Arizona, and along the Hassayampa River south of Prescott, Arizona, *n. neumoegeni* flies at the lower elevations and *n. sabina* at higher elevations, and complete series of intergrades have been taken.

Early Stages: Though the early stages are known, they have not been described in detail. The larval foodplant is *Aster.*

Distribution: The Sabina Checkerspot inhabits the Upper Sonoran zone chaparral and oak woodland, and to some extent the Piñon-Juniper areas of Arizona from Mojave county southeastward to Greenlee and Cochise counties, then south into northeastern Sonora. It is also found in the lower edge of the Transition zone, where it flies with the earliest spring butterflies and is often missed by collectors. Its occurrence in southwestern New Mexico needs confirmation. The name *pola* Boisduval may have to replace *sabina* as the subspecific name when more research and collecting are carried out in northern Sonora, Mexico.

7. **Chlosyne (Charidryas) gabbii** (Behr). Plate 40, figure 7, ♂; figure 8, ♀. On the underside of the hind wing the submarginal crescents and the median band of light spots of *gabbii* are exceptionally pearly in luster. The light spots between the two pearly spot bands are usually pale yellowish (not pearly as shown in figure 7) though commonly much obscured by blackish.

Early Stages: The larvae have been found feeding on *Corethrogyne filaginifolia* var. *bernardina,* and also on *Hazardia squarrosa.* The mature larva is predominantly black dorsally, speckled with dull white, and with a velvety black middorsal line. The middorsal row of tubercles has an orange-brown crescent on either side at the base.

Distribution: Gabb's Checkerspot ranges along the coast from northern Baja California to Monterey and in the San Joaquin Valley along the Sierra Nevada foothills to Tulare county. It has been found flying with *palla palla* at several localities and at least once with *neumoegeni.*

8. **Chlosyne (Charidryas) damoetas** (Skinner). *C. damoetas* is at home from near tree line up to 12,500 feet and is the only truly alpine species of *Chlosyne.* It is recognizable by the dull, pale orange-brown to pale yellowish orange ground color above, the more regular and less sinuous dark transverse lines on the outer half of the wings and a considerable dusky suffusion at the base of the wings. On the underside the usual *palla* pattern is present with reduced dull orange-brown areas particularly in the basal area of the hind wings as shown on the plates.

Early Stages: Unknown.

Distribution: C. damoetas has been taken from British Columbia and Alberta, Canada, south to the Rocky Mountains of Colorado and Utah and in the Sierra Nevada of California. In the north it is found at 8000 feet and in the Rocky Mountains of Colorado and the Sierra Nevada of California at 10,000 to 13,000 feet.

(a) **damoetas** (Skinner). Plate 41, figure 9, ♂; figure 10, ♀. Skinner based the name *damoetas* on specimens taken in the central Rocky Mountains of Colorado. Specimens from this area are characterized by considerable dusky suffusion in the basal area of the wings and a smudged, somewhat glossy or greasy look to both surfaces of the wings. Material from Utah, Wyoming and Alberta has less basal suffusion, but there are so few individuals from these areas that no conclusions on variation can be reached.

Early Stages: Unknown.

Distribution: The Damoetas Checkerspot has been recorded from timberline in the mountains of Colorado and Wyoming and from the Uinta Mountains of northeastern Utah. It is also recorded for the area about Banff, Alberta, and from Mount McLean, near Seton Lake, British Columbia. The original description mentions three localities: one in Grand county and two in Park county, Colorado.

(b) **malcolmi** (J. A. Comstock). Plate 40, figure 15, ♀; figure 18, ♂. Malcolm's Checkerspot is similar to nominate *damoetas* in appearance, habitat and habits. It differs from *damoetas* in the brighter, more clear-cut color and pattern with less dusky suffusion on the fore wing upperside. The glossy or greasy appearance so prevalent in *damoetas damoetas* usually is not evident on *malcolmi*.

Early Stages: Unknown.

Distribution: This subspecies is limited to the Sierra Nevada of California, from about tree line up to 12,000 feet.

9. **Chlosyne (Charidryas) hoffmanni** (Behr). *C. hoffmanni* is distinct from the other members of the *palla* group in the structure of the male genitalia. This is fortunate as its range is almost entirely within the range of *palla;* and in many localities it is sympatric with one or another of the *palla* subspecies. It differs from *palla* in wing pattern and color only in degree. On the upper surface, particularly of the hind wings, there are more extensive black-brown basal markings; the bands of spots on the outer half of the wings tend to be more regular; and the inner band is usually paler, sometimes markedly contrasting with the deeper shade of the outer bands of spots. On the underside the northern populations are very similar to *palla* while in California they tend to be more evenly and broadly banded on the hind wings.

Early Stages: So far only the Washington population has been described, by Mr. E. J. Newcomer in 1967. The eggs are deposited in masses on the leaves of *Aster conspicuus.* The larvae when full grown have black hairy heads; the body is black, speckled with white, with a cream colored, scalloped line just above the spiracles. Below this lateral line the body is brownish. The bristly tubercles above the lateral line are black circled with white at the base; those below this line are brown. The pupae vary in color from pearly white to brown with many irregularly shaped brown to blackish markings.

Distribution: C. *hoffmanni* has a wide distribution down the Cascade-Sierra ranges from southern British Columbia to the vicinity of Sequoia National park and also in the higher Coast Ranges of northwestern California and southwestern Oregon.

(a) **hoffmanni** (Behr). Plate 41, figure 8, ♂; figure 12, ♀. The figures should enable easy identification of Hoffmann's Checkerspot. The underside has much more regular banding and more extensive creamy yellow areas than the two northern subspecies. The name *hoffmanni* was given to the Sierra Nevada population, but it is also used for the north Coast Range population of California which differs only slightly in most colonies. Nominate *hoffmanni* is a butterfly of the Canadian zone in the Sierras and at times is very abundant in its favored haunts, along the edges of meadows and on open hillsides.

Early Stages: These have been described.

Distribution: Nominate *hoffmanni* is found in the Sierra Nevada, and a slightly darker but otherwise similar population is found in the higher north Coast Ranges of California from the Trinity Mountains north to the Siskiyou Mountains where it intergrades with *hoffmanni segregata.*

(b) **segregata** (Barnes & McDunnough). Plate 41, figure 11, ♂. This subspecies of *hoffmanni* has a complete network of dark lines on the outer half of the wings which is usually rather heavy on the hind wings and greatly encroaches on the center spot band. The inner spot band is generally considerably paler and quite prominent, although it is narrower than in *hoffmanni hoffmanni.* On the underside it resembles *palla* more than the Sierran *hoffmanni* populations.

Early Stages: These have not been described.

Distribution: The subspecies *segregata* is primarily a butterfly of the Oregon Cascades, but it is also found in the Siskiyou Mountains of southwestern Oregon.

(c) **manchada** (Bauer.) Plate 45, figure 17, ♀; figure 18, ♂. The Manchada Checkerspot resembles *palla* even more than does the Oregon subspecies *segregata.* The inner band of spots is narrower than in *segregata,* the middle band of spots on the hind wings is dark red brown and composed of larger spots than the rows on either side, and it is rarely heavily suffused with black as in *segregata.* The subspecies *manchada* varies considerably, from lightly marked colonies which closely resemble *palla* to melanic colonies in which the black brown pattern is much increased and the inner band of spots is pale cream.

Early Stages: Described under the species.

Distribution: The subspecies inhabits the crest and eastern slope of the Cascade Mountains of Washington and crosses the Canadian border into British Columbia. Just how far north its range extends into British Columbia is not known. The type locality is at 1600 feet in Tumwater Canyon, near Drury, Chelan county, Washington. The type colony is lightly marked, and not melanic as are the colonies about Mount Adams.

Subgenus CHLOSYNE Butler

This, the typical subgenus, is composed largely of neotropical species, commonly called patch butterflies because many of them have prominent patches of red or yellow on the hind wings. This widespread subgenus is composed of several isolated species and four species groups. None of the isolated species is found in the United States, but all of the species groups are represented. It is difficult to arrange the species phylogenetically as each character, such as wing pattern, genitalia, early stages, and distribution, seems to indicate different relationships and thus a different sequence. Actually, all the species or species groups not included in *Charidryas, Thessalia,* or some other subgenus, end up here. Though not very scientific, this must do until a thorough study of the entire genus *Chlosyne* has been completed.

The *lacinia* group

This group, composed of two or possibly three species, is the most widespread and abundant of American Melitaeini. The *lacinia* group character is a characteristic, though variable, wing pattern that always has an orange patch or spot on the inner margin near the anal angle.

Taken as a whole, the *lacinia* group is composed of a central conglomeration of variable populations occupying the area from southern Nevada to Colombia and Venezuela in northwestern South America. Scattered around these central, variable populations are four peripheral populations that are quite stable in color pattern and resemble each other more than they do the central variable populations separating them. These peripheral populations have become distinct subspecies; and one of them, *californica* Wright, has become a separate species that is now occasionally sympatric with *lacinia* without interbreeding. Further study may prove some of the other peripheral populations to be also specifically distinct. The entity *adjutrix* Scudder has the pattern and coloring of the peripheral populations, but is not specifically distinct from *lacinia*.

10. **Chlosyne (Chlosyne) californica** (Wright). Plate 43, figure 19, ♀. *C. californica* is very similar to *lacinia adjutrix* and is sometimes confused with it. The California Patch can always be recognized by the orange color of the discal cell on the fore wing underside and by the orange marginal series of spots on both wings above. The orange cell is never found in *adjutrix* and the definitely orange marginal spots only rarely. It occupies a different habitat from *lacinia,* being found along desert washes and canyons while *lacinia* inhabits the river bottom lands and towns, and is often abundant along irrigation canals where *californica* rarely ventures.

Early Stages: The eggs though apparently not described in detail, are said to be deposited in clusters at the base of the foodplant *Viguiera deltoidea* Gray. The mature larvae are not variable as are those of *lacinia.* The body color is black covered with white specks which are thicker on the lower half of the body. The tubercles are black and in some individuals have dirty orange areas around the base. The head is shiny black with white hairs, the legs black, and the prolegs pinkish gray. The pupa is variable tending to match its surrounding. The ground color is ivory and may have only a few dark dots and lines or be almost obliterated by extensive dark coloring. There are multiple broods from early March to October.

Distribution: The California Patch is found from southern Nevada south into northern Sonora, Mexico, and occupies most of Baja California including some of the islands in the Pacific Ocean. The type locality is given as the "Colorado desert," suggested by some to be the vicinity of Palm Springs, Riverside county, California.

11. **Chlosyne (Chlosyne) lacinia** (Geyer). This is probably our most variable butterfly, for there seems to be almost endless polymorphism of wing color and pattern.

Consequently, many names have been given to this species. One of the problems which needs much study is to find out whether these names represent individual color forms, subspecies, or possible closely related species. Two subspecies range north into southwestern United States: one along the Gulf Coast into the southern Great Plains; the other up the west coast of Mexico north into Nevada, and the Virgin River Valley in southwestern Utah.

Early Stages: The immature stages have been described and the larvae may be pests on sunflowers. The larvae are variable with the ground color and tubercles ranging from solid black to solid orange or red-brown with every gradation between. They feed on many species of compositae such as the sunflowers (*Helianthus annuus, H. cucumerifolius* and *H. ciliaris*), also on cocklebur (*Xanthium canadense* and *saccharatum*), *Verbesina virginica,* and *Ambrosia trifida.*

Distribution: As mentioned, *lacinia* is the most widely distributed of the American Melitaeinae, being found from the Pampas of Argentina to the southern Great Plains and southwestern deserts of the United States.

(a) **crocale** (Edwards). Plate 44, figure 15, ♀. The population that first received the name *crocale* is one of the variable central populations of *lacinia,* and almost any colony will produce specimens which have white bands and spots (*crocale*) or yellow to orange band and white spots (*rufescens* Cockerell) to specimens with obsolescent bands (*nigrescens* Cockerell). There are also many color forms that have not received names, one of which has both white and red spot-bands across the hind wings. Others resemble named forms such as *lacinia lacinia* and *l. pretona,* but all of these variations are part of the *crocale* population. The Crocale Patch intergrades on the east with *adjutrix* and in Mexico with *lacinia lacinia* and the melanic *l. quetala* Reakirt.

Early Stages: These are noted above.

Distribution: The Crocale Patch is found from southern Nevada and Washington county, Utah, south through Arizona and eastern California far into northwestern Mexico and Baja California. The type locality is the "White Mountains of Arizona."

(b) **adjutrix** Scudder. Plate 44, figure 13, ♀. This population is not as variable as those found in the center of the distribution of *lacinia.* It is well illustrated on the plate and can be recognized by the fairly wide bands of orange across both fore and hind wings. The color pattern is quite stable over most of its range but intergrades to *crocale* in west Texas and southern New Mexico and to *lacinia lacinia* in northeastern Mexico. It is a butterfly of the sunflower thickets found along roads, in abandoned fields and along streams.

Early Stages: In addition to the foodplants mentioned for the species, *adjutrix* larvae have been found feeding on *Verbesina enceloides,* and Mr. Roy Kendall reports larvae feeding on *Grindelia microcephala* and *Parthenium hysterophorus.*

Distribution: The Adjutrix Patch is common in much of Texas and southeastern New Mexico and strays north in late summer and early fall to Kansas, Nebraska and possibly southeastern Colorado.

The *definita* group

This is a rather extensive neotropical group of seven distinct species and a number of subspecies. All but one of the species are characterized by the band of orange or red-brown spots on the outer part of the underside of the hind wing with the center spot white, often reduced to a dot, while the two orange or red-brown spots on each side are large. Three species of this group are listed for the United States but one, *Chlosyne erodyle* Bates, is doubtful. The other two species, *definita* Aaron and *endeis* Godman & Salvin, are breeding residents.

12. **Chlosyne (Chlosyne) definita** (Aaron). Plate 46, figure 12, ♂. Aaron's Checkerspot may be readily recognized by the figure on the plate. The only other species with which it might be confused is *theona bolli* with which it flies in west Texas. *C. definita* can be separated from *bolli* by the three cream colored spots (two on the costa and one in the middle) in the orange-brown band of spots on the outer portion of the underside of the hind wing; in *bolli* all the spots from costa to inner margin are orange-brown. This species is not a strong flier and is not difficult to capture once a colony is found.
   Early Stages: Unknown.
   Distribution: The type locality of *definita* is stated as "inland from Corpus Christi," Nueces county, Texas. The species has been captured westward to southeastern New Mexico and eastern Arizona and ranges far south into Mexico.

13. **Chlosyne (Chlosyne) endeis** *Godman & Salvin.* Plate 44, figure 17, ♂. This species shows sexual dimorphism. The median band of males is dull ochre, and in females it is white. The upperside is mostly black with the fore wing having two rows of white dots parallel to the margin, and a median series of larger dull ochre spots and some markings of the same color at the base. The hind wing above is mostly black from the median band to the base, and the outer part of the wing is decorated with four or five orange-brown spots separated by a smaller whitish dot with two toward the inner margin and two or three toward the costa. The underside is very similar to *definita* except that the outer margin of the fore wing is black with two rows of cream color dots parallel to the margin. Also the basal area has no dark outlining of the pattern as is found in *definita.*
   Early Stages: Unknown.
   Distribution: The Endeis Patch was described from the Sierra Madre de Tepic in western Mexico and has a wide distribution in Mexico, entering the United States only in extreme southern Texas.

14. **Chlosyne (Chlosyne) erodyle** (Bates). Plate 46, figure 18, ♂. This is another Mexican and Central American species. It has been credited to the United States, but there are no known authentic records of its capture within our borders. It is figured so that should it be encountered in the future, it can be recognized. The white, spotted fore wing and yellow patch on the hind wing above are distinctive.

Early Stages: Unknown.

Distribution: It is found from Central America north at least to the state of Tamaulipas, Mexico.

The *janais* group

This is a small group of three species which have similar male genitalia. Largely neotropical in distribution, only one species crosses our border. All the members of this group are similar in pattern on the underside of the hind wing, which has a marginal series of yellow crescents followed by a series of white dots on a black ground, and a band of five red or orange-brown quadrate spots. In *janais* the basal area is yellow with black dots. In the other two species the basal area has black bands and spots or is wholly black. The members of this group can all be separated from the *lacinia* group by the orange or red-brown spot band on the underside of the hind wings not reaching the inner margin or anal angle as it does in *lacinia*.

15. **Chlosyne (Chlosyne) janais** (Drury). Plate 46, figure 11, ♂. The Janais Patch is one of the larger Melitaeini. The figure on the plate will enable ready recognition of this beautiful butterfly. The underside of the fore wing has the same pattern as above with all the spots larger. The underside of the hind wing has been described above under the group. It has often been confused with *lacinia lacinia* Geyer, but the red patch above never reaches the inner margin or anal angle in *janais* while it almost invariably reaches at least to the anal angle in *lacinia*.

Early Stages: In Mexico the larvae feed on *Odontonema callistachys* (Acanthaceae).

Distribution: The Janais Patch is a breeding resident of the Rio Grande Valley of extreme southern Texas, straying north during favorable years to central Texas and southeastern Arizona.

The *rosita* group

Since this manuscript was originally written one species of this group has been found as a breeding resident in the Rio Grande Valley, Texas: *Chlosyne rosita browni* Bauer. The character which distinguishes the members of this group is the total absence of the marginal series of spots or crescents on both upper and under surfaces. It is not figured but if you catch a butterfly that looks like *C. janais* Drury and there are no marginal spots it is *rosita,* and if the orange patch reaches the inner margin and costa of the hind wing upperside, it is *browni*.

Early Stages: In Texas the larvae feed on *Dicliptera bachiata* (Pursh) Spreng. var. *alternata*.

Distribution: Northeastern to central Mexico and Rio Grande Valley, Texas.

Subgenus THESSALIA Scudder

Chlosyne leanira Felder & Felder is the type species of *Thessalia* Scudder. The two groups in the subgenus are not closely related but are placed together primarily because the wing patterns of the underside are similar.

Early Stages: The larvae and pupae of both groups are distinctive in color pattern, from each other as well as from other *Chlosyne*.

Distribution: The subgenus *Thessalia* is found from southwestern United States to northwestern South America.

The *leanira* group

The *leanira* group is composed of four species. One, *cynisca* Godman & Salvin, is entirely Mexican; another, *cyneas* Godman & Salvin, enters the United States only in southeastern Arizona; and the other two species, *leanira* C. & R. Felder and *fulvia* Edwards, have a wide distribution in the southwestern states and along the Pacific Coast. *C. leanira* is variable and several subspecies have been named.

16. **Chlosyne (Thessalia) leanira** (Felder & Felder). This species divides into two main sections: the north coastal populations, which have yellow-orange antennae and predominantly black-brown uppersides; and the south coastal and Great Basin populations, which have the antennae black flecked with whitish at the ends of the segments and the dominant color on the upperside red- or orange-brown. These may represent separate species, but because they interbreed along the western edge of the Mojave desert they are here considered as one species. There is a considerable tendency to hilltopping in the Great Basin, and the species is often missed by collectors who collect in the desert canyons and washes but do not climb the ridges and hills. The dark coastal populations are not as frequent hilltoppers and are often found flying in the canyons, on hillsides and congregating at damp spots along creeks and roadsides. All the populations of *leanira* have males and females with similar coloring above, which will distinguish them from *fulvia* Edwards.

Early Stages: The eggs are deposited in clusters on the stems and leaves of the foodplants, various species of *Castilleja*. The larvae when full grown have the typical *Chlosyne* bristly tubercles, all of which are black, a paired row of dorsal orange spots located on the junctures of the segments (not at the bases of the spines) and along the sides two rows of smaller orange spots, one above and one below the stigmata. Ventrally the body color is slightly grayish black. In the coastal populations there is white on the segments between the orange spots at the bases of the tubercles.

Distribution: C. *leanira* ranges from western Colorado to the Pacific Coast and from northern Baja California into Oregon.

(a) **oregonensis** Bauer. Plate 40, figure 17, ♀. This insect differs from *leanira* on the upperside in the considerably smaller yellow spots, resulting in a darker appearance and causing the red apical areas of the fore wing, particularly of females, to be more prominent. In males the red apical areas of the fore wing tend to be small. On the underside the black basal and median bands of the hind wings are prominent in males and very broad and black in females. There is often a trace of a black line between the basal markings and the discal band enclosing the series of yellow dots.

Early Stages: Unknown.

Distribution: Most of the known specimens are from Jackson county in south-western Oregon. It has been recorded as far north as the Molalla River in Clackamas county, Oregon, and south in the Coast Ranges of northwestern California to Trinity county.

(b) **leanira** (Felder & Felder). Plate 41, figure 13, ♂; figure 14, ♀. Originally described simply from California, the name *leanira* gradually has been restricted to the populations found in the Coast Range north and south of San Francisco Bay and in the foothills around the Sacramento and northern San Joaquin valleys. Nominate *leanira* varies considerably in the size of the yellow spots, but they are usually considerably larger than in *oregonensis.* The red apical patch is sometimes completely obscured by black-brown. There are two local forms that have received names and deserve mention. The name *obsoleta* Hy. Edwards was given to the local form found at San Rafael, Marin county, California, which has the black pattern below obsolescent or wanting. The name *daviesi* Wind was applied to a population with the hind wings dark as in *leanira,* but the fore wings have more red. It was taken at Strawberry Lake, Tuolumne county, California, at an elevation of 5500 feet.

Early Stages: The mature larva has the typical pattern of orange spots on a black body described for the species, but differs greatly in having the spaces between the orange spots white so that the larva is definitely striped with black dorsally and laterally and stripes of alternating orange and white dorsally and along the sides.

Distribution: This subspecies inhabits the Coast Ranges north and south of San Francisco Bay and the foothills around the Sacramento and northern San Joaquin valleys. Southward it is reported to blend with subspecies *wrighti.* The type locality should be restricted to the San Francisco Bay area.

(c) **wrighti** (Edwards). Plate 41, figure 17, ♂; figure 18, ♀. The yellow spots above are larger than in *leanira leanira.* The antennae of Wright's Checkerspot are mostly black-brown above and yellowish orange below, but occasionally the yellowish orange shows above. The subspecies is fairly constant in the coastal areas of southern California, but it evidently intergrades along the western edge of the Mojave desert with the red Great Basin subspecies *cerrita.*

Early Stages: These have been described in detail by J. A. Comstock and C. M. Dammers.

Distribution: This subspecies occupies the coastal area from northern Baja California north into the lower San Joaquin Valley where it reportedly blends with *leanira leanira.*

(d) **cerrita** (Wright). Plate 41, figure 21, ♀; figure 22, ♂. The Cerrita Checkerspot is almost entirely red- or orange-brown on the upperside, and the light spots are often reduced or washed over with the orange-brown. The black-brown is confined on the upperside to the narrow wing veins, marginal line, and the apical area of the fore wing. Where it intergrades with *wrighti,* there is more black on the upperside. It differs from the following subspecies, *alma* Strecker, in the red-brown color of the discal cell on the upperside of the fore wing, which is usually clear and not dusted with black, and the more extensively red-brown basal portion of the wings. It can be separated from *fulvia* Edwards by the black markings in the basal area on the underside of the hind wings: at least a faint black bar occurs at the end of the cell; and at least a partial irregular black line crosses the middle of the cell and usually continues to the costa. In *fulvia* the hind wing has a Y- or V-shaped mark in the cell; if (rarely) there is a black area across the middle of the cell, it is indefinite and usually just a cloudy area of black scales.

Early Stages: The mature larva is black with large orange spots arranged as described for the species, and sparingly speckled with white.

Distribution: The Cerrita Checkerspot lives in the desert mountains and hills of the Mojave and Colorado deserts of southern California and southern Nevada and ranges north to Pyramid Lake in northwestern Nevada. The type locality, given simply as southern California, is probably somewhere along the western edge of the Mojave desert as Wright says it was flying in company with *wrighti.*

(e) **alma** (Strecker). Plate 15, figure 15, ♂; Plate 77, figure 14, ♀.   This subspecies of *leanira* is not well represented in collections, and many of the specimens placed under this name are really *cerrita* Wright or *fulvia* Edwards. To separate *alma* from *cerrita* and *fulvia,* see above under the Cerrita Checkerspot. The subspecies *alma* is like *fulvia* above but does not become as dark. The cell of the fore wing is mostly black-brown with a large yellow-buff spot at the end, below which there is a large black-brown spot. From this spot to the base it is mostly black-brown. Strecker says the underside of the hind wing is as in *leanira leanira* with "a small black mark or streak in the upper part of the discoidal cell and another at the costa." This makes it a member of the *leanira* complex and not the *fulvia-cyneas* group.

Early Stages: These are undescribed.

Distribution: The Alma Checkerspot was described from two specimens, one from Arizona and one from southern Utah. Colonies that match Strecker's figure and description have been found from western Colorado to Pershing county, Nevada.

17. **Chlosyne (Thessalia) fulvia** (Edwards). Plate 41, figure 15, ♂; figure 16, ♀.   The most outstanding characteristic of the Fulvia Checkerspot is its sexual dimorphism. The males are dark above and somewhat resemble *wrighti,* except that the discal cell is never red-brown. The females are predominantly orange-brown above with the dark pattern suffused and obsolescent, resembling the females of *cerrita* even to the orange-brown color of the discal cell of the fore wing. For the characters to separate *fulvia* from *cerrita* and *alma,* see the discussion under *cerrita.* Dark males of *fulvia* have been confused with *cyneas* Godman & Salvin. In males of *cyneas* the red-brown is confined to the marginal band of spots, and the basal half of the wings is more solidly black with reduced yellow spots. The two species can always be separated in females: those of *fulvia* are orange-brown above while those of *cyneas*

are very dark like the males. *C. fulvia* is found in canyons and frequents damp ground along roadsides.

Early Stages: The Larva and pupa have been described by J. A. Comstock and J. L. Sperry. The larval foodplant is *Castilleja lanata.*

Distribution: The Fulvia Checkerspot is found from Mojave county, Arizona, east to western Texas and north into southern Colorado. It has an extensive range in northern Mexico.

18. **Chlosyne (Thessalia) cyneas** Godman & Salvin. Plate 43, figure 10, ♂; figure 11, ♀. This butterfly is very dark above in both males and females as shown in the figures. The red-brown is confined to the marginal series of spots, and the yellow spots are small and absent to obsolescent in the basal area of the wings. The underside is marked as in *fulvia* and not as in the *leanira* complex. For separation of *cyneas* from *fulvia,* see the discussion under *fulvia.* The Cyneas Checkerspot is one of the most beautiful species of *Chlosyne.*

Early Stages: These are undescribed.

Distribution: The type locality of *cyneas* is given as the "mountains of Oaxaca," in southern Mexico. It ranges north to southeastern Arizona where it occurs in a few mountain ranges near the Mexican border.

The *theona* group

This group is largely neotropical and occurs in the United States only near the Mexican border. As understood now, the group includes four species. Two of them are found in our area and two are found mostly south of Mexico into northwestern South America. The species are characterized by distinctive male genitalia and wing patterns. On the underside of the secondaries there is a submarginal series of orange or red-brown spots that forms a broad band from inner margin to costa, and a postbasal band of the same color, often obsolescent and obscured by black. The known larval foodplants are *Castilleja* (Scrophulariaceae) and *Verbena* (Verbenaceae).

19. **Chlosyne (Thessalia) theona** (Ménétriés). Nominate *theona* is Mexican and not found in the United States. There are two additional subspecies found along the Mexican border, one in Texas and the other in Arizona. Both are the extreme developments of clines, one following up the Gulf Coast, the other up the Pacific Coast of Mexico, resulting in quite different looking insects. *C. theona thekla* and *t. bolli* are well illustrated on the plates and no descriptions are necessary except to point out the distinctive pattern on the underside of the hind wing. The ground color there is shiny creamy white, the veins and outer margins are narrow black lines. The postmedian band is composed of seven quadrate orange-brown spots reaching from the costa to the anal angle, and a postbasal band of the same color begins on the costa and extends toward the inner margin, divided in the discal cell by a shiny white spot.

Distribution: C. theona ranges from Central America north into Texas and Arizona.

(a) **thekla** (Edwards). Plate 45, figure 7, ♂; figure 8, ♀. There has been considerable confusion and lack of understanding of the difference in wing pattern of the subspecies *thekla* Edwards and *bolli* Edwards. The key differences are in the basal portion of the upper side of the wings. In the subspecies *thekla* the basal pattern of orange-fulvous areas is expanded toward the outer margins. This expansion is very noticeable on the fore wing at the end of the discal cell, where it becomes an elongated orange-fulvous area occupying half or more of the area between the end of the discal cell and the outer margin, and in cell Cu_2, just above the inner margin. In the subspecies *bolli* the reverse of the *thekla* pattern occurs. The two bands on the outer portion of the wings broaden, expanding toward the base of the wings, causing a reduction in size of the orange-fulvous basal spots. This reduction is particularly noticeable on the fore wing where the extensive orange-fulvous area at the end of the discal cell, so characteristic of *thekla,* is reduced to a spot no larger, and often smaller, than the paler fulvous spot near the end of the cell. Also in cell Cu_2, just above the inner margin, the postbasal orange-fulvous spot, so often prominent in *thekla*, is obsolete, being usually entirely obscured by the meeting of the dark lines on either side. Southward into Mexico the pattern difference between the east and west coast populations gradually diminishes as the *theona theona* coloring and pattern becomes dominant. The underside of *thekla* has the typical *theona* pattern and the subspecific differences described above are not as noticeable. *Thekla* is sometimes common in the canyons and hillsides of the southeastern portion of Arizona, and frequents damp ground along streams and mud puddles.

Early Stages: The mature larva has the head orange or yellowish, sparsely covered with black hairs. Dorsally the body is velvety brownish black sprinkled with whitish dots which are missing in the middorsal area, creating a black middorsal line, with the white dots more numerous on either side. The area at the juncture of the segments is not velvety but shining and purplish. Along each side is a broad longitudinal fleshy yellow band running the full length of the body, in which the black stigmata are set; and between the spines on segments 3 through 10 there are two or three large white dots. The true legs are glistening black; the prolegs are reddish brown with a black spot and black claspers. The ventral surface is rosy brown. The pupa is boldly marked with narrow black longitudinal stripes on a grayish white ground. Its structure is similar to the *leanira* group but smoother and more streamlined. Foodplant is *Castilleja lanata*.

Distribution: Thekla is found in Arizona from the Verde River Valley near Cottonwood southeastward into Sonora, and has been reported from the higher elevations of the Big Bend country of Texas. The type locality originally given as southern California, has been corrected by F. M. Brown to Fort Lowell near Tucson, Pima county, Arizona.

(b) **bolli** (Edwards). Plate 41, figure 19, ♂; figure 20, ♀; figure 23, ♂ underside. The illustrations make a lengthy description unnecessary. The identifying characters of the wing pattern are discussed under *thekla.* The underside has the typical *theona* pattern and reflects the same characters found on the upperside of the fore wing.

The subspecies *bolli* is locally common in the western third of Texas where it flies in canyons and on the plains.

Early Stages: Undescribed. The foodplant is *Leucophyllum texanum.*

Distribution: Boll's Checkerspot ranges from San Antonio, Texas (the type locality), westward at least to Pecos county, Texas, possibly into southeastern New Mexico and south into northeastern Mexico. Its relationship with *chinatiensis* Tinkham needs further investigation.

20. **Chlosyne (Thessalia) chinatiensis** (Tinkham). Plate 41, figure 24, ♂. The illustration shows the broad orange-brown areas of the upperside with little or no dark pattern except in the basal areas and the margin. The underside of the hind wings has the typical *theona* pattern with a tendency for the basal markings to become obsolescent. The Chinati Checkerspot has much the same habits as *theona bolli.*

Early Stages: Unknown.

Distribution: This species has a limited range in the mountains of west Texas.

Genus MICROTIA Bates

This genus contains only one species, characterized by having genitalia similar to those of *Chlosyne,* a long slender abdomen in the males, and fairly narrow, somewhat elongated wings. The sole species is a neotropical butterfly that has several forms based on variation in the extent of the orange markings. The wing pattern is extremely simple.

1. **Microtia elva** (Bates). Plate 1, figure 17, ♂. The simple dark brown and orange pattern above is reproduced on the underside with the orange changed to yellow on the hind wings and the apex of the fore wing. *M. elva* is a common to abundant butterfly in Mexico where it often frequents mud puddles. No other species of Melitaeini can be confused with it.

Early Stages: These have not been described.

Distribution: This species occurs from Nicaragua northward to southern Texas and Arizona, but the only authentic recent records of capture in the United States are in southeastern Arizona.

Genus DYMASIA Higgins

These butterflies have shape and structure similar to *Microtia elva,* but the color and pattern are much more typical of the Checkerspots.

1. **Dymasia dymas** (Edwards). Plate 41, figure 29, ♂. The figure illustrates the maculation of both surfaces and no further description is necessary. *D. dymas* is

scarce in collections. It differs from *chara,* with which it was formerly confused, in the more extensive but less distinct dark pattern above, and by striking sexual dimorphism.

Early Stages: Apparently these are undescribed, but the larval foodplant is listed as *Siphonoglossa pilosella* by Roy Kendall.

Distribution: The type locality is San Antonio, Texas. The range extends east at least to Corpus Christi, Texas. Investigation of the western and northern limits is needed as colonies exist in western Texas and southern New Mexico that are not typical *dymas* but are closer to *dymas* than to *chara.*

2. **Dymasia chara** (Edwards). This species is characterized by having the extra-discal band of spots on the fore wing paler and of a yellowish white or cream color. In the northwestern portion of the range of *chara* the pale area is often confined to the costal portion of the band. The sexes are almost alike. *D. chara* inhabits some of the hottest, driest portions of our southwestern deserts where, after abundant rains, it sometimes flies by the thousands.

Early Stages: These are described and figured for subspecies *imperialis* Bauer by J. A. Comstock and C. M. Dammers.

Distribution: It is found from central Arizona and southeastern California south at least to Tepic, Nayarít, Mexico. The extent of its range in Mexico is not well known.

(a) **chara** (Edwards). Plate 78, figure 15, ♂; figure 16, ♀. In this subspecies the males have rather broad black marginal bands on both wings above, which in some colonies obscure all the submarginal light spots except that in cell M_3 on the fore wing. In the females the marginal black areas are confined to the narrow marginal band except near the apex of the fore wing. On the underside of the hind wings the orange-brown bands and spots are rather broad and usually occupy as much or more of the wing area than the creamy white spots and bands. The Chara Checkerspot has a weak flight pattern and tends to stay close to the home colony.

Early Stages: Undescribed for this population. The known larval foodplant is *Beloperone californica.*

Distribution: The subspecies *chara* is found in the Verde River valley of central Arizona south along the west coast of Mexico to Nayarít. In the United States its eastern limit coincides roughly with the continental divide, and the Colorado River Valley is the western boundary.

(b) **imperialis** (Bauer). Plate 1, figure 18, ♂; figure 19, ♀. The Imperial Valley Checkerspot is the same size and has the same pattern of markings as *chara chara,* but on the upperside the black marginal areas are much narrower and the pale yellowish or cream spots are usually confined to the costal area. On the underside the light areas are shining white, particularly on the hind wings, not cream as in *chara chara;* and the orange-brown areas are reduced.

Early Stages: Noted above under the species. The larval foodplant is *Beloperone californica.*

Distribution: The type locality is Palm Springs, Riverside county, California. The subspecies ranges south in the canyons and washes along the west side of the Imperial Valley into Baja California. The limits of its range on the east and south need further investigation.

Genus POLADRYAS Bauer

This is a genus of strictly North American Checkerspots. In the past some have placed these butterflies in the Palaearctic genus *Melitaea* as part of the *didyma* group. There is considerable resemblance in the wing pattern to *didyma,* but the genitalia of *didyma* are more like those of *Phyciodes,* while those of *Poladryas* are a unique combination and stand between *Chlosyne* and *Euphydryas.* They differ from the genus *Chlosyne* Butler only slightly in the structure of the male genitalia; but the female genitalia are extremely simple, in marked contrast with the rather complicated female structures of *Chlosyne,* and resemble those of *Euphydryas.*

Early Stages: The larvae feed on *Penstemon,* a common foodplant of *Euphydryas,* but not used by any *Chlosyne.* The larval coloring is unique among American Melitaeinae. The pupae greatly resemble those of *Euphydryas* in color pattern.

Distribution: Two species are recognized in *Poladryas.* They have an extensive distribution from Nebraska to California, and from Wyoming south through the highlands of Mexico to beyond Mexico City.

1. **Poladryas arachne** (Edwards). This species has previously gone under the name *pola.* This butterfly is so well depicted on the plates that a lengthy description is not necessary. *P. arachne* has no black line between the fringe and the cream marginal area on the underside of the hind wing, while in *minuta* Edwards such a black line is present. This character separates all *minuta* from *arachne.*

Early Stages: The larva is described (as *pola* Boisduval) by the Sperrys, and the pupa by J. A. Comstock. The larval foodplant is *Penstemon alpinus.*

Distribution: It is found from California to Nebraska, and from Wyoming south into Mexico. The southern limit is uncertain.

(a) **monache** (J. A. Comstock). Plate 43, figure 13, ♂; figure 14, ♀. The subspecies *monache* has somewhat more orange-fulvous above than the low desert subspecies, but it shows a reduced black pattern on the upperside of the wings, with a tendency to obsolescence in some specimens. Also, the ground tends to be evenly orange-fulvous without the marked contrast found in other subspecies.

Early Stages: Not described.

Distribution: This subspecies inhabits relatively high elevations in the southern Sierra Nevada.

(b) **arachne** (Edwards). Plate 22, figure 13, ♂; plate 40, figure 10, ♀, and figure 11, ♂; Plate 1, figure 20, ♂ (form "gilensis"). This is well shown on the plate and needs little additional comment. Nominate *arachne* shows more contrast in the two shades of orange-brown and a bolder black pattern above than *monache.* The subspecies *nympha* Edwards has a heavier black pattern above combined with a greater contrast in color. The light areas of *nympha* are often cream or almost white.

Early Stages: Noted under the species above.

Distribution: The name *arachne* is in use for the Rocky Mountain population from Nevada to Nebraska and from Wyoming to the mountains of the northern portion of Arizona.

(c) **nympha** (Edwards). Plate 15, figure 10, ♂. This subspecies has a heavier dark pattern above. On the underside it is very similar to *a. arachne.* It is generally found from moderate to high elevations (5000 to 8500 feet), and like *monache* it is not as common in collections as *arachne.*

Early Stages: Undescribed.

Distribution: It is found from the mountains of southeastern Arizona, far south into Mexico. It will require further exploration to determine whether Holland's *gilensis* represents a mere aberration or a discrete population of *arachne.* Or, it may prove to be nothing more than a synonym. We have, nevertheless, included a figure of *gilensis* on Plate 1, figure 20.

2. **Poladryas minuta** (Edwards). Plate 46, figure 13, ♂. The discussion under the species *arachne* separates the two species. In addition to the fine marginal line at the base of the fringe, the underside of the hind wings also has a peculiar appearance of broad basal and discal bands, spots of leathery red-brown color and smaller creamy white, submarginal lunate spots. Some *a. nympha* approach *minuta* on the underside, but *minuta* does not have the strong color contrast and *arachne* pattern.

Early Stages: Undescribed, but the larval foodplant is reported to be *Penstemon.*

Distribution: *P. minuta* ranges from central Texas south to the vicinity of Mexico City. It has been reported from southeastern Colorado and Arizona but this needs verification.

Genus EUPHYDRYAS Scudder

This is our only melitaeine genus with a circumpolar distribution. The type species is *E. phaeton* of the eastern United States. There are no known tropical species.

Looking at the genus as a whole, we find nine distinct species that show relatively little variation. Seven of these are found in Europe and Asia and two (*phaeton* and *gillettii*) in North America. Contrasting with these fairly stable species are the highly polytypic *aurinia* complex in the Palearctic and the similarly polytypic *chalcedona, colon, anicia* and *editha* complexes in the Nearctic. The North American complexes are not well understood and much remains to be learned before acceptable order can be brought to them. The following arrangement is based on information available; it is tentative and subject to change. The early stages are discussed under the species and subspecies. Although they are similar in structure, there is considerable variation in coloring and habits and also in the foodplants used by the larvae. The majority of the species are single brooded; only the southern semi-desert and desert populations have regular second generations in late summer or early fall.

1. **Euphydryas phaeton** (Drury). *E. phaeton* (the Baltimore Checkerspot) differs from all the other *Euphydryas* by lacking the orange or red-brown band or row of spots across the middle of the underside of the hind wings. Compared to the western *Euphydryas, phaeton* is rather stable in wing pattern and color. Through the years several names have been proposed for variations among northern, central and southern populations. *E. phaeton,* described from New York, has the intermediate central coloring and pattern. The name *borealis* Chermock & Chermock 1940 (type locality Lincoln, Maine) was given to the northern color variation with larger, redder marginal spots and glossy jet black coloring above. The name *schausi* Clark, 1927 (type locality Cabin John, Md., in the vicinity of Washington, D.C.) is characterized as being blacker in ground color, with whiter light spots and narrower orange markings. The type locality is in a transitional area.

More recent and extensive studies of *phaeton* indicate dividing the species along different lines, according to larval foodplant intolerance. Experiments have revealed that before hibernation the young larvae from eggs deposited on *Chelone glabra* die when transferred to *Lonicera ciliata;* and those from eggs deposited on *Lonicera ciliata* die when placed on *Chelone glabra.* This seems a more consistent and practical basis for dividing the species, and is far less confusing. However, it must be remembered that in the spring after hibernation the larva can feed on either foodplant and also other species of plants. Some authors believe these foodplant intolerances indicate sibling species, others that they are subspecific. For the present they will be treated as subspecific.

Early Stages: These are described in detail by many writers. The eggs are deposited in clusters on the foodplants: *Chelone glabra* and *Lonicera ciliata.* The mature larva is black, striped transversely with orange and with a lower lateral stripe of orange. Beneath, the body is duller orange. The bristly tubercles are all black. The colonies are very local. The butterflies fly during May and June.

Distribution: E. phaeton occurs locally in wet meadows (northern population) or hillsides (southern population) from southern Canada south to Georgia and Missouri.

(a) **phaeton** (Drury). Plate 36, figure 18, ♀. This subspecies is thoroughly discussed along with its variations of pattern and coloring under the species. If names are desired for these variations *phaeton, borealis* and *schausi* are available; but it should be remembered that these names do not represent separate populations, only the two extremes and middle of a cline.

Early Stages: Described under the species.

Distribution: phaeton occupies the northern portion of the species range. It is found from Maine through southern Canada to Wisconsin. The southern limits are not well known, but it is found as far south as Maryland.

(b) **ozarkei** Masters. Not illustrated. The Ozark Checkerspot is recognizable in most of its range by the reduced orange marginal band of spots of the upperside of the wings, which sometimes are obsolescent on the fore wings. Also by the suffused or obsolete orange spots of the cell of the fore wings. The underside is almost identical with that of *phaeton phaeton . E. ozarkei* is the southern *lonicera ciliata* population.

Early Stages: Very similar to those of typical *phaeton.* It is in flight during May and June. The habitat is usually a dry hillside.

Distribution: The subspecies *ozarkei* is the southern population and seems to favor dry hillside habitats rather than wet meadows. It has been found in local colonies from Kansas to Tennessee. East of Tennessee there appears to be an overlap with the *Chelone glabra*-feeding *phaeton phaeton,* for nearby colonies have opposite early larval foodplant intolerances.

2. **Euphydryas chalcedona** (Doubleday).   The Chalcedona Checkerspot is one of the larger species of the genus. It has the typical pattern of light yellow spots on a ground that varies from entirely black to red-brown on the upperside of the wings. The figures on the plates illustrate the various populations, and no further description will be given because of the wide range of color variation of *chalcedona.* The only sure way to tell whether a peripheral area colony is *chalcedona, colon or anicia* is by the structure of the male genitalia. However, *chalcedona* is sympatric with *editha* over much of its range and *editha* can usually be separated from *chalcedona* by these features: by the more rounded apex of the fore wing; by the red of the post median spot band on the underside of the hind wing invading the adjoining area toward the base at least slightly; and, sometimes by its forming a double row of red or partially red spots.

Early Stages: The eggs and larvae have been described in detail by J. A. Comstock (1927). The eggs are pale yellow when fresh and are deposited in masses of up to several hundred, usually on the underside of the leaves of the larval foodplants. The larvae feed on many species of Scrophulariaceae, including Monkey Flower, penstemons and Indian Paintbrush, *Castilleja.* When the larvae come out of hibernation they occasionally feed on plants other than the original foodplant, sometimes members of the families Rosaceae and Caprifoliaceae, also *Plantago.* During the last three instars, the larvae have a middorsal row of orange spots at the base of the middorsal tubercles, which are also orange. There are also orange spots and tubercles along the sides. The color pattern of the body is of two types: black speckled with white, or black and white longitudinal stripes of varying widths.

Distribution: Populations with the *chalcedona* male genitalic structure and slight modifications of it are found from southwestern Oregon south to northern Baja California and eastward in the desert mountains of southern California and Arizona. There have been a few females taken in northwestern Texas that possibly belong to *chalcedona,* but we must await male specimens to be certain of the relationship of these Texas colonies. There are far too many blanks and gaps in our knowledge of the life histories of the *chalcedona* populations, so the subspecific treatment that follows is only tentative.

(a) **dwinellei** Hy. Edwards. Plate 36, figure 10, ♂; figure 11, ♀; plate 38, figure 17, ♀; figure 18, ♂.   Dwinelle's Checkerspot is described in the original description as having the fore wings "very much suffused with red, which color predominates over the discal portion, and toward the apices, almost obscuring the usual white spots, or rendering them a sordid, dull orange color." They also have an extensive black marginal field between the red marginal spots and the median band. Chermock & Chermock's *sperryi* is not a *colon* subspecies but a synonym of *dwinellei.* Dwinelle's

Checkerspot is an isolated subspecies and differs greatly in habitat from other subspecies of *chalcedona;* it lives in rather wet meadows surrounded by heavy forests.

Early Stages: The mature larvae feed on *Penstemon shastensis.*

Distribution: So far, typical *dwinellei* is only known from the area around McCloud fishing station, Shasta county, California (the type locality of *dwinellei*), and from a meadow 18 miles to the west near Bartle Lumber Camp (the type locality for *sperryi*).

(b) **chalcedona** (Doubleday). Plate 36, figure 3, ♀. The Chalcedon Checkerspot is the subspecies found in the Coast Ranges of California. It is often abundant, and the males often perch on a shrub in an open area and dart out after any passing butterfly, particularly their own kind. They also frequent damp ground. To find females, one must go to an area where the foodplants are growing, for they generally do not wander far from the breeding area unless there is a population explosion.

Early Stages: See notes under the species name.

Distribution: The Chalcedona Checkerspot is found from northern Baja California along the Coast Ranges to extreme southwestern Oregon.

(c) **quino** (Behr). Plate 36, figure 4, ♂; figure 7, ♀. Behr's Checkerspot has been confused with Wright's Checkerspot, which is an *editha* subspecies. *E. c. quino* is difficult to characterize as it is variable, ranging from yellow-spotted specimens with small amounts of red to very red specimens in some desert areas. True *quino* is found along the desert side of the mountains but intergrades to *chalcedona chalcedona* in the San Bernardino area. It is often abundant in the desert canyons where its foodplant grows.

Early Stages: The larval foodplant is *Scrophularia antirrhinoides* according to C. M. Dammers.

Distribution: The subspecies is found along the desert side of the mountains and in desert mountain ranges of San Diego, Riverside and San Bernardino counties in southern California.

(d) **klotsi** dos Passos. Plate 36, figure 16, ♀; figure 17, ♂. Klots' Checkerspot is a rather variable subspecies inhabiting the southwestern desert mountains. Colonies vary from specimens with mostly yellow, light spots above and a heavy black pattern, to those that are very reddish, approaching the coloring of *anicia hermosa*. The names *hermosa* and *klotsi* are considered synonyms in the dos Passos "Synonymic List of the Nearctic Rhopalocera," but differences in genitalia, life history and larvae indicate that they are valid subspecies, belonging to separate species (*anicia* and *chalcedona* respectively) and occupying different habitats.

Early Stages: The larval foodplant is *Penstemon.*

Distribution: The subspecies *klotsi* is found in the higher desert mountain ranges of the Mojave and Colorado deserts eastward into New Mexico; it is possible that the Texas colonies also belong to this subspecies rather than to *hermosa.*

(e) **corralensis** Bauer. Plate 37, figure 5, ♂; figure 6, ♀. The Corral Checkerspot is similar to *anicia hermosa* and would be considered part of that subspecies were it not for the male genitalia which have been examined by several entomologists and found to be of the *chalcedona* type. This reddish salmon colored subspecies, with considerably reduced black pattern, is well illustrated on the plate, and no further description is needed.

Early Stages: It has been reared by C. M. Dammers, whose breeding experiments with the desert *chalcedona* populations are published in the "Bulletin of the Southern California Academy of Sciences." He states that the larvae of all populations are "identical."

Distribution: The type locality is Rock Corral, San Bernardino Mountains, San Bernardino county, California.

(f) **macglashanii** (Rivers). Plate 36, figure 15, ♂. Typical specimens of Mac-glashan's Checkerspot are described as differing from coastal *chalcedona* in the more regular size and even spacing of the yellow spots above. Gunder described specimens with increased red coloring above from Truckee, California, as *truckeensis* and similar specimens from the Casa Diablo Hills, California, as *georgei*. Both are slight varieties of *macglashanii*. From the excellent description of the larvae given by Rivers in the original description, it is evident that the name *macglashanii* should be used for all the low to middle elevation colonies of *chalcedona* which have larvae with the longitudinally black and white striped pattern. This includes a wide range of variation in the butterflies from some that are quite red above to some very similar to *chalcedona chalcedona.*

Early Stages: The larvae are described in detail by Rivers in the original description. The larvae feed on *Penstemon breviflorus, P. lemmonii* and other species of *Penstemon.*

Distribution: Colonies with the *macglashanii* type of larvae and adults are found in the foothills around the north end of the Sacramento Valley, along both sides of the Sierra Nevada, north into Klamath and Lake counties, Oregon, and also in the spur ranges running from the Sierra Nevada into western Nevada. The type locality was restricted by Gunder to Truckee, Nevada county, California.

(g) **olancha** Wright. Plate 36, figure 6, ♀. The Olancha Checkerspot is characterized by having enlarged light yellow spots particularly on the outer portion of the upperside of the hind wing, combined with only a few spots of red in the discal cell of the forewing on the upperside. The name was given to specimens taken at about 11,000 feet on Olancha Peak on the Inyo-Tulare county line in the Sierra Nevada. There are numerous other high elevation colonies scattered along the crest of the Sierra Nevada, some with larger pale yellow spots above (Bishop Creek colony), others with heavier dark pattern and smaller yellow spots above (Sonora Pass colony). All of the high elevation colonies may properly be included under the name *olancha.* In the Sonora Pass area, *olancha* flies with a small form of the very red *chalcedona sierra* Wright. It also flies with *editha nubigena* Behr.

Early Stages: The mature larvae is very similar to that of *macglashanii* with slightly wider white stripes and feeds on alpine species of *Penstemon.*

Distribution: The Olancha Checkerspot is found in California from the area of Olancha Peak north to Sonora Pass at elevations of from 9000 to 11,000 feet.

(h) **sierra** (Wright). Plate 36, figure 9, ♀; figure 12; Plate 39, figure 11, ♂; figure

12, ♀. Typical *sierra* is a large red subspecies of *chalcedona* as shown in the figures; at higher elevations the specimens are smaller but otherwise maintain the same appearance. This alpine population is found from 6000 to near 11,000 feet in the Sierra Nevada. On the underside the black markings tend to be reduced and replaced by red so that in some specimens the red median band of the hind wings is very broad and invades the surrounding yellow areas as in some *editha* populations. In checking the male genitalia preparations of Gunder at the Los Angeles County Museum, I found that in two slides of *irelandi* there is a great deal of variation (not even the two valves from the same specimen being the same), but in spite of the variation they exhibit *chalcedona* characters similar to *sierra*. Consequently, the name is sunk as a synonym of *sierra* Wright.

Early Stages: The mature larvae are similar to those of *macglashanii* and *olancha*, with very wide white and narrow black longitudinal stripe with almost no white specks in the black stripes. The larval foodplant at the type locality is *Penstemon deustus*.

Distribution: The Sierra Checkerspot is found from Sequoia National Park north to Gold Lake, Plumas county, California.

3. **Euphydryas colon** (Edwards).   This species is almost as variable as *chalcedona* in the coloring and pattern of the wings on the upperside. There is no positive way to separate *colon* from the southwestern Oregon population of *chalcedona* except by male genitalia or larval coloring and foodplant. The larval habits also are different from those of *chalcedona* and are discussed below.

Early Stages: Distinguishing characteristics of *colon* larvae are the relatively abundant, fairly long, white body hairs and the white bristles on the lower half of the tubercles, giving the body a fuzzy white appearance. The head is black but covered with long black and short white hairs. In the color of the tubercles it is similar to *chalcedona*. The known larval foodplants are several species of snowberry, *Symphoricarpus albus* and *rotundifolius*. Sometimes in the spring after hibernation the larvae feed on species of *Penstemon*.

Larvae of *colon* differ from all other American *Euphydryas* larvae in the small, rather compact webs formed over the skeletonized leaves, the larvae remaining in the curled leaves even after the winter storms destroy the web and knock the leaves to the ground. It is therefore easy to collect the hibernating larvae from the Snowberry bushes until October or November.

Distribution: The species is northern in distribution and is found from southern British Columbia to northern California, east to northwestern Utah and the mountains of western Montana. It is not generally known that in many areas our western *Euphydryas* are sympatric. *E. colon* has been taken flying with *E. chalcedona macglashani* Rivers, *anicia veazieae* Fender & Jewett, *anicia howlandi* Stallings & Turner, *editha taylori* Edwards, *editha remingtoni* Burdick and *editha hutchinsi* McDunnough.

(a) **colon** (Edwards). Plate 36, figure 5, ♂; figure 8, ♀.   This subspecies has the same pattern as *chalcedona* and the coloring is very similar. About the only differences are the more extensive black pattern on the upperside of the hind wing where the submarginal light yellow spots are reduced in size, and the middle band of yellow being usually entirely obscured by black, resulting in a broad black band. The females show these characters also and have a more regular and evenly sized pattern of yellow spots than most *chalcedona* females. In border areas, such as southwestern Oregon and northeastern California, the only certain way to distinguish *colon* from *chalcedona* is either by the male genitalia or by the larval coloring and foodplant.

The Colon Checkerspot is a butterfly of open forested canyons, hillsides and roadsides, and exhibits much the same habits as a *chalcedona:* selecting a perch in an open area and chasing other butterflies as they pass, then returning to the favored weed stalk or bush.

Early Stages: The larvae of *colon colon* have a little less white on the body than some of the other populations.

Distribution: The type locality given by Edwards was Mount Hood, Oregon. F. M. Brown and J. D. Gunder have both suggested correcting the type locality, and Brown gives substantial reason for fixing Kalama, Cowlitz county, Washington, as one locality from which the Edwards' specimens came. The name *colon colon* should be used for colonies west of the Cascade Ranges in Oregon and southwestern Washington. In the Columbia River gorge, *colon* intergrades with subspecies *wallacensis* Gunder.

(b) **perdiccas** (Edwards). Plate 36, figure 2, ♀. The subspecies *perdiccas* is very similar to nominate *colon;* from the original description and the lectotype selected by F. M. Brown about the only differences are more red on the fore wing above and all of the red "dull and inclining to orange." After examining series of *colon* from the Puget Sound area, it is evident that *perdiccas* has more persistent red margins on the hind wings above, and at higher elevations intergrades to the subspecies *paradoxa* McDunnough.

Early Stages: It is suspected that the larval foodplant for some colonies is *Penstemon,* but snowberry is common in the type locality.

Distribution: As presently understood, *perdiccas* is limited to the Puget Sound area of western Washington. Edwards gave the type locality as "Mt. Hood, Oregon," but H. K. Morrison later corrected the locality saying he took the specimens he sent to Edwards in the "small prairies numerous near Puget Sound," and he stated that "it was abundant near Tenino." At present, *E. editha taylori* Edwards is often abundant in these small prairies, but no *perdiccas* have been taken there in recent years.

(c) **paradoxa** McDunnough. Plate 37, figure 3, ♂; figure 4, ♀. McDunnough's Checkerspot has the characteristic *colon* pattern. It differs from nominate *colon* and *colon perdiccas* in having the middle spot band on the outer portion of the hind wing above red and not obsolete or yellow as in other populations of *colon*. The fore wing above has more red and there may be some red in the basal area on the upperside of the hind wings. The red marginal band of spots is prominent and usually complete. The amount of red above varies considerably and some colonies have very red females.

Early Stages: The larvae are marked similarly to those of *c. colon* but usually have more white hairs and more extensive white markings. The white areas are often tinged with yellow and orange on the first three segments.

Distribution: The type locality is Seton Lake, Lillooet, British Columbia. The subspecies ranges south into the Cascade Mountains of Washington and east to the Idaho panhandle and adjacent Montana.

(d) **wallacensis** Gunder. Plate 37, figure 1, ♀; figure 2, ♂. Gunder's Checkerspot is very similar to *colon colon*. About the only differences according to the original description are: the smaller size (wing expanse of males 38 to 42 mm, females 43 to 45 mm); a more persistent marginal row of red spots; and larger pale yellow spots on the upperside. Some specimens, however, are as dark as *colon colon*.

Distribution: The type locality is Wallace, Shoshone county, Idaho. This subspecies includes the *colon* colonies of western Montana, most of Idaho, all of eastern Washington and Oregon and northeastern California. The name *huellemanni* J. A. Comstock is used for this subspecies in the dos Passos (1964) list; but, as F. M. Brown has pointed out, this is contrary to the *International Code*.

(e) **nevadensis** Bauer. Plate 42, figure 8, ♀. Plate 45, figure 11, ♂. The Nevada Checkerspot is the same size as *wallacensis*. The most noticeable difference between *nevadensis* and all the other *colon* subspecies is on the underside of the wings where the red ground is often of a paler pinkish shade, with the red areas reduced and the white areas increased. The basal half of the fore wings beneath is not evenly reddish as in most *colon* populations but is extensively washed with whitish along the inner margin and in the cell adjacent to it. It also has all the yellowish white spots of the upperside reproduced below and often enlarged. On the underside of the hind wings, the middle band of red is broken into spots and greatly invaded by whitish, often reducing the red to separate rounded spots. On the underside *nevadensis* resembles *anicia bernadetta* Leussler more than *colon* but differs from *bernadetta* in having less black and more red, particularly in the apical area of the fore wing. On the upperside, the pale yellow spots are generally larger than in other *colon* populations. Some specimens are quite red above even further reducing the black areas, while others resemble *wallacensis*.

Early Stages: The larval foodplant is Mountain Snowberry, *Symphoricarpus vaccinoides*.

Distribution: The type locality is Wildhorse Camp, ten miles south of Mountain City, Elko county, Nevada. So far, *nevadensis* has been found in the mountains of Elko county, Nevada; it also inhabits the adjacent areas of Idaho and Utah.

4. **Euphydryas anicia** (Doubleday).   Recent research on chromosomes by C. L. Remington, field studies and information concerning the early stages indicate that several closely related species with similar male genitalia may compose our present *anicia* complex. However, the information is so meager that for the present it is thought best to divide the populations into groups to show relationships and treat them all as subspecies of *anicia*. They vary greatly in color of the upperside of the wings from almost completely red-brown (Plate 38, figures 3 and 6) to a network of black lines enclosing whitish yellow spots (Plate 39, figures 15 and 18). The

subspecies are tentatively divided into four main groups on the basis of superficial resemblances, type of habitat or foodplant and larval affinities. These groups are: the *anicia* group, the *eurytion* group, the *wheeleri* group, and the *bernadetta* group. The subspecies of *anicia* are an interesting and rich field for life history studies and field observations. For instance, in one locality in Idaho there were thousands of *anicia effi* one summer; in the same locality a month earlier and three years later an entirely different type of *anicia* was occupying the area.

Early Stages: Little has been published concerning the early stages of the *anicia* complex. The few descriptions, both published and unpublished, indicate a great deal of variation in larval coloring and foodplants, although the pupae appear to be relatively uniform. The full grown larvae vary from an off-white ground mottled with black and having all the bristly tubercles black, to black larvae speckled with whitish in such a way as to give the appearance of indefinite, white, longitudinal stripes, with the middorsal bristly tubercles and the tubercles above the legs orange as in *chalcedona*. There appears to be every degree of variation between these two extremes.

Distribution: The *anicia* complex is found from the Yukon Valley in Alaska south to northern Mexico, and from the western edge of the Great Plains to the foot hills of the Sierra Nevada. It inhabits the Arctic-Alpine down to the Lower Sonoran life zones.

The *anicia* group of subspecies

These subspecies are northern and montane but do not necessarily occupy high elevations. Considered as a unit, we find in the extreme northwestern part of the range a subspecies with alternate red-brown and whitish bands of spots on the upperside of the hind wings and a complete network pattern of dark lines. At the southeastern limit of the group is a subspecies with predominantly brick red upperside and a tendency toward obsolescence of the network of dark lines. Two names have been given to the colonies inhabiting the area between these two extremes. Although they generally show considerable variation both from colony to colony and individually, in long series they are recognizably separable from each other as well as from the two extremes; but their standing as subspecies is doubtful and needs further study.

(a) **helvia** (Scudder). Plate 43, figure 17, ♂ and 18 ♀. Scudder's Checkerspot is the most northern *Euphydryas* found in the western hemisphere. The butterfly has alternating rows of red-brown and whitish spots on the hind wings above. It varies considerably in the amount of dark pattern on the upperside. This butterfly is not common in collections, and not much is known about it.

Early Stages: These are unknown.

Distribution: The type locality is "upper end of the Ramparts," Alaska. It has been taken in the upper Yukon River basin of Alaska and Yukon Territory, Canada.

(b) **anicia** (Doubleday). Plate 39, figure 3, ♂; Plate 45, figure 16, ♀. The species name *anicia* was given to a figure without description or a specific type locality. As the years passed and other names were proposed for one population after another, the name *anicia* came to be restricted to the subspecies found in the southern Canadian Rocky Mountains of Alberta and British Columbia. This subspecies is much like *helvia* but has more red-brown on the upperside of the wings and broader red-brown spots and band on the underside of the hind wings. Like most *anicia* populations it is variable, with some specimens very red above and others more like *helvia,* with alternating red-brown and whitish rows of spots.

Early Stages: Unrecorded.

Distribution: The type locality usually recognized is the Banff area of Alberta, and the name is given to the colonies found in the southern parts of British Columbia and Alberta. Along the United States border it intergrades with the next subspecies and there is no definite line where one begins and the other ends. In fact, there are no differences between many specimens from the northern Cascade Ranges in Washington and specimens taken in the area of 150 Mile House, British Columbia.

(c) **howlandi** Stallings & Turner. Plate 39, figure 7, ♂, figure 8, ♀. Howland's Checkerspot is described as having alternating red and white bands of spots on the outer portion of the hind wing above and to some extent on the fore wings. However, a paratype and a short series of topotypes show considerable variation in the amount of red in these areas. This subspecies differs from *anicia anicia* in the brighter deep red color above and the more clear-cut, brighter overall appearance. Many colonies are variable and the range in maculation is from near typical *anicia* to specimens resembling the next population, *capella* Barnes.

Early Stages; The full grown larvae have been observed in the Washington Cascade Mountains and in the area of Yellowstone National Park. At both localities the larval foodplant was *Penstemon barretae.* The Washington state larvae are mostly black with bristly tubercles, except the middorsal tubercles and the lowest lateral tubercles which are orange basally.

Distribution: The type locality is Polaris, Beaverhead county, Montana. The subspecies is found from the mountains of western Montana through northern Idaho and the mountains along the British Columbia-Washington border into the Washington Cascade Mountains on the eastern slope. Some colonies in the western portion of the range are extensively red above, but typical specimens and colonies also inhabit the area.

(d) **capella** (Barnes). Plate 38, figures 3, ♂; figure 6, ♀. Barnes's Checkerspot, one of the more distinctive subspecies of *anicia,* was described as "solid brick red, the white being entirely gone and the black reduced to the veins and the fine cross lines, the latter even being wanting in portions of the wings."

Early Stages: These apparently are undescribed.

Distribution: Barnes's Checkerspot was described from specimens captured around Denver and Manitou Springs, Colorado. It has a range along the east slope of the Rocky Mountains from Colorado northwestward into Wyoming.

The *eurytion* group of subspecies

This group occupies the Rocky Mountains from eastern Washington to New Mexico and Arizona. In Colorado it occupies the high elevations from 9000 to 12,000 feet, but northward it drops to intermediate or low elevations, whereas the *anicia* group of subspecies occupies habitats near treeline (Hudsonian and Canadian life zones). Along the eastern side of the Cascade Mountains of Washington where the canyon slopes are very steep individuals from *anicia* colonies sometimes wander down and are found flying with *eurytion* colonies, but the two have separate foodplants and differently colored larvae. A great deal more information on foodplants and immature stages is needed, and it no doubt will result in some changes in the present groupings.

(e) **hermosa** Wright. The Hermosa Checkerspot is predominantly reddish on the upperside. It is characterized by having the hind wing above almost entirely pale salmon red with the black line often reduced to a row of spots between the veins. This southwestern mountain subspecies has a modified type of *anicia* male genitalia. In Arizona there are two slightly different populations with the coloring of *hermosa.* The colonies in central Arizona resemble the desert *chalcedona* genitalic structure. The other type of genitalia is definitely of the southwestern *anicia* type and is found in specimens from Washington county, Utah, the Grand Canyon area, and from around Oracle north of Tucson in Pinal county, Arizona. These last mentioned populations match Gunder's figure of the genitalia of *hermosa,* so *hermosa* is placed with *anicia.*

Early Stages: The mature larvae in Oak Creek Canyon, Coconino county, Arizona, are of the black and white striped color pattern, and the larvae there feed on *Penstemon eatoni exsetus.*

Distribution: This subspecies is found from southern Utah to southeastern Arizona. W. G. Wright gave the type locality simply as "southern Arizona." Gunder's restriction to Camp Roosevelt, Roosevelt Dam, Gila county, Arizona, is questionable.

(f) **magdalena** Barnes & McDunnough. Plate 39, figure 16, ♀; figure 17, ♂. This readily recognized subspecies occurs at moderately high elevations and at times is abundant. The butterflies can be picked from the flowers by hand when the sun goes behind a cloud and they become chilled.

Early Stages: These have been described in detail by J. A. Comstock. The mature larva has an ivory ground color mottled with black. All the bristly tubercles are black; the middorsal row arises from orange-yellow spots. There is a narrow middorsal line.

Distribution: The subspecies *magdalena* appears to be limited to the White Mountains of Arizona.

(g) **alena** Barnes & Benjamin. Plate 38, figure 1, ♂; figure 2, ♀. The Alena Checkerspot is another of the Rocky Mountain members of the *anicia* complex about which there is much confusion. This butterfly of the *eurytion* group of subspecies has a fairly even, complete, thin network of black lines above, and considerable red-brown color. On the underside it somewhat resembles *capella* with brighter red tints than in the rest of the *eurytion* group. The figures on the plate do not show as complete and regular a dark pattern as does the type specimen.

Early Stages: Unknown.

Distribution: The type locality, originally given as "So. Utah," was later restricted by Barnes in a letter to J. D. Gunder to the "mountains between Parowan and Panguitch," Utah.

(h) **carmentis** Barnes & Benjamin. Plate 37, figure 13, ♂; figure 14, ♀. The figures on the plate show a distinct pattern with the outer portion of the hind wings red and the basal portion whitish and black with only a little red. There appears to be some confusion as to which is the true *carmentis,* so the brief original description is quoted: "Allied to the *alena* and to *magdalena,* intermediate in size, in this respect resembling *maria.* Upperside with the pattern and coloration nearly as in *alena* but tending to produce forms which are paler. Underside similar to *maria* but considerably paler, the contrast between the ground color and the yellow transverse markings much more distinct. The general appearance being more like that of *wheeleri,* but a considerably smaller and much neater looking species. Expanse: male 33–36 mm; female 40–43 mm."

Early Stages: Apparently undescribed. The Rev. Rotger discovered two populations of *Euphydryas* in Archuleta county, Colorado: one feeding on *Penstemon,* the other on *Castilleja.* The *Penstemon*-eating larvae are considered to be *carmentis.* The butterflies fly during June and July.

Distribution: The type locality is Pagosa Springs, Archuleta county, Colorado. Because of the confusion about true *carmentis,* the extent of its distribution is unknown at this time.

(i) **windi** Gunder. Plate 37, figure 17, ♀. Wind's Checkerspot is a little known subspecies whose exact standing and relationships need to be worked out. The males are identical in color and pattern to the females, but are smaller and have more pointed fore wings.

Early Stages: Unknown.

Distribution: The type locality is Timber Island, Teton Mountains, Teton county, Wyoming. Somewhat similar colonies occur in other Wyoming mountain ranges, but it is doubtful whether they should go under the name *windi.*

(j) **eurytion** (Mead). Plate 39, figures 1, ♂ and 2, ♀. The brief original description of *eurytion* states that "the yellow spots . . . are largely obscured in *eurytion* by fulvous," that it does not range to such high elevations as what Mead called *"nubigena"* (= *brucei* Edwards) and that it also flies with *"nubigena."* The name *brucei* is currently applied to the small, dark, high elevation color form. According to C. L. Remington there is genetic evidence that the low and high elevation populations are distinct and possibly of specific rank. The figures give a good representation of Mead's *eurytion* although most specimens are darker with more black.

Early Stages: The mature larva has an ivory-white ground mottled irregularly with black, and the bristly tubercles are black.

Distribution: Colonies of this subspecies are found from the higher mountains of northern New Mexico to southern Montana and Wyoming. Coloring varies considerably from colony to colony, and there needs to be a great deal more field and life history study of the colonies now going under the name *eurytion* and *brucei*.

(k) **maria** (Skinner). Plate 37, figure 15, ♂; figure 16, ♀. The figures on the plate will enable ready recognition of this subspecies. It varies, however, in the same ways as *eurytion* does, from red to quite black.

Early Stages: Undescribed. The larval foodplant, according to Kenneth Tidwell, is a blue flowered species of *Penstemon.*

Distribution: The type locality is Park City, Summit county, Utah. The Maria Checkerspot is the form found in many of the mountain ranges of Utah and north into adjacent Idaho. In southern Idaho similar colonies of *anicia* have received the name *effi*.

(l) **effi** Stallings & Turner. Plate 42, figure 6, ♂; figure 7, ♀. Eff's Checkerspot does not differ from *maria* in any way except for its slightly smaller size. All indications lead to the conclusion that *effi* is part of the *maria* population. In the original description, *effi* is compared with *hopfingeri* and *bakeri* and no mention is made of *maria*.

Early Stages: Previously undescribed. The larva is black with considerable white in the form of bands of spots and specks. Its foodplant is a species of blue flowered *Penstemon* similar to the foodplant of *maria*.

Distribution: The type locality is Corral Creek, Ketchum, Blaine county, Idaho. The form is found in the mountains along the north and east sides of the Snake River plain in southern Idaho.

(m) **hopfingeri** Gunder. Plate 39, figure 13, ♂; figure 14, ♀. Hopfinger's Checkerspot is much like *maria* and *effi* and shows a similar range of color pattern, from dark to reddish, but it differs from both in having a slightly salmon tint to the red, both above and below, and is not as pale and washed out on the underside.

Early Stages: On full grown larvae the dominant color of the body is black speckled with whitish spots, setting off a narrow middorsal black line by a concentration of white specks on either side that give the effect of whitish stripes. There is a double whitish band along the sides. The middorsal row of bristly tubercles is orange except for the last tubercle. Three rows of black tubercles occur on either side with a spot of orange at the base of the middle row of black tubercles. The row of small tubercles above the legs is orange. At Leavenworth, Chelan county, Washington, the larval foodplant is the blue flowered *Penstemon serrulatus*.

Distribution: The type locality is Brewster, Okanogan county, Washington. So far, *hopfingeri* has been taken along the Columbia River and surrounding hills from Kittitas county north to Okanogan county, Washington.

The *bernadetta* group of subspecies

This group has an extensive east-west distribution from the Black Hills and western Nebraska to eastern Oregon and Washington. The upperside of the wings has a bold black pattern with prominent pale off-white spots and rather limited amounts of red except in the population found on the Snake River plains of southern Idaho and extreme eastern Oregon. The general appearance is more like *Euphydryas chalcedona olancha* or *quino* than any of the *anicia* groups. The early stages are similar to those of *anicia hopfingeri.* There is a fairly good possibility that this group is a separate, but closely related, species instead of a subspecies of *anicia.*

(n) **bernadetta** Leussler. Plate 39, figure 5, ♂; figure 6, ♀. The butterfly is well illustrated on the plate and no description is needed. The figures are of light specimens; normal variation includes more extensive black markings and occasionally brighter red.

Early Stages: Undescribed.

Distribution: The type locality is Monroe Canyon near Harrison, Sioux county, Nebraska. From Nebraska it ranges north along the western edge of the Dakotas and westward in the sagebrush plains and hills of Wyoming and Montana.

(o) **veazieae** Fender & Jewett. Plate 39, figure 15, ♂; figure 18, ♀. The illustrations will enable easy recognition. Variation includes more black and brighter and a more complete series of red spots. This subspecies is so similar to *bernadetta* that they might be considered part of the same population were it not that considerably redder colonies are found between them. The genitalia differ from those of *bernadetta.*

Early Stages: The egg is unknown. The larva is mostly black with two dorsal rows of small white spots on either side of a narrow black middorsal line. The middorsal tubercles are orange at the base and black at the tips with black bristles. The other tubercles are all black and very bristly. The larval food plant is *Penstemon speciosus.*

Distribution: The type locality is the Jackass Mountains, Harney county, Oregon. Veazie's Checkerspot has an extensive distribution in the sagebrush country east of the Cascade Mountains from near Vantage on the Columbia River in eastern Washington, south to Pyramid Lake, Washoe county, Nevada. The eastern limits of the range need investigation.

(p) **bakeri** Stallings & Turner. Plate 39, figure 9, ♂; figure 10, ♀. This subspecies is similar to *veazieae* but, as the illustrations show, a red band of spots crosses the disc of the hind wing and the red spots on the fore wing are larger. Baker's Checkerspot intergrades with *veazieae* around Huntington, Oregon, but maintains the red markings in the type locality and surrounding areas. Although very local, *bakeri* is a valid subspecies.

Early Stages: Unknown.

Distribution: The type locality is Cave Creek near Durkee, Baker county, Oregon. Baker's Checkerspot has also been taken on the Idaho side of the Snake River Canyon near Oxbow Dam, Adams county, Idaho.

(q) **macyi** Fender & Jewett. Plate 46, figure 14, ♂; Plate 38, figure 16, ♀. The figures make a description unnecessary. Macy's Checkerspot is a larger insect than *bakeri* with less red on the underside of the hind wings. In other characters the two are very close.

Early Stages: Unknown.

Distribution: The type locality is Wildhorse Creek, Alvord Basin, Harney county, Oregon. This subspecies has also been taken in the Trout Creek Mountains, Harney county, Oregon, and at Glenns Ferry on the Snake River, Elmore county, Idaho.

The *wheeleri* group of subspecies

This group has an extensive distribution in the Great Basin eastward to Colorado. The colonies in the eastern part of the range have been largely missed by collectors because of the early flight period; they have also been confused with other populations belonging to the *eurytion* group. The members of the *wheeleri* group have a wide range of tolerance, being found from about 4000 ft. up to 11,000 ft. in the mountains of Nevada, with no noticeable difference in appearance between the low and high altitude specimens.

(r) **wheeleri** (Hy. Edwards). Plate 39, figure 4, ♂. The name *wheeleri* has been used for the colonies of *anicia* from the east slope of the Sierra Nevada at Mono Lake eastward into Utah. The figure on the plate shows the Mono Lake color pattern which is found along the western edge of the range of *wheeleri*. The original description calls for a butterfly with much more red. "It is wholly of a pale red ground color on the upper surface, except the base of the secondaries, which are cream white. The markings are as usual, but with very little black."

Early Stages: Undescribed. The larval foodplant is reported as *Mertensia ciliata* var. *stomatechoides*.

Distribution: The type locality of "Southern Nevada" and F. M. Brown's study of the Wheeler Expedition's travels would indicate a locality somewhere between Belmont, Nye county, Nevada, and Independence, Inyo county, California. The subspecies *wheeleri* is found throughout the mountains of central Nevada eastward through Utah to southwestern Colorado. The figures on p. 73 of Brown, Eff & Rotger, *Colorado Butterflies,* are *wheeleri* not *alena*. They report that in Colorado the larval food plant is a species of *Castilleja*.

(s) **morandi** Gunder. Plate 37, figure 18, ♂. Morand's Checkerspot is quite distinctive. It has a heavy black pattern in the basal area of both wings above; a predominantly orange-brown ground; and only small amounts of cream in the form of small spots on a black ground across the outer portion of the fore wing, and a trace, or none at all, in the basal portion of the wings. There is increased cream coloring in some colonies and individuals. A very local butterfly, *morandi* does not wander far from the particular colony area and is not generally distributed.

Early Stages: Unknown.

Distribution: Morand's Checkerspot so far has been found only in the Spring Mountains, Clark county, Nevada.

5. **Euphydryas editha** (Boisduval). Like *anicia, editha* is composed of many subspecies, most of which have received names. Our knowledge of this group is so spotty and limited that the arrangement and grouping of the named populations is only tentative. The *editha* subspecies can be divided into three main groups. The *editha* group is primarily found along the Pacific coast and has broader, more rounded wings, particularly the outer margin and apex of the fore wings of the males. The lárvae of this group are known to feed on *Plantago*. The *baroni* group, except for *rubicunda* and *baroni,* is intermontane. This group has a more produced apex of

the fore wing and sharper anal angles to the hind wings. It is not homogeneous and will probably be divided as more is learned about it. The larvae of some of this group feed on *Plantago;* others are reported to feed on Scrophulariaceae. The third, the *nubigena* group, is similar to the second in wing shape, but all its members are redder, and they inhabit higher elevations from southern California north to Washington state. The known foodplants of two of the members of this group are *Castilleja.*

Early Stages: The eggs are largely unknown. The larvae vary from longitudinally black and white striped to black, speckled with white or orange. The tubercles vary from short, cone-shaped and very bristly, to longer and more slender.

Distribution: Euphydryas editha ranges from Mexico to Canada along the Pacific Coast, and east to Montana, Wyoming and Colorado. So far there are no records for Arizona or New Mexico. Colonies are found from sea level to well above timberline and in a diversity of habitats from humid coastal areas to the semi-arid Great Basin and southern California hills.

The *editha* group of subspecies

(a) **wrighti** Gunder. Plate 38, figure 7, ♂; figure 8, ♀. This subspecies, when first considered different from *augusta,* went under the name *quino* until Gunder found that *quino* was a member of the species *chalcedona* and gave this subspecies of *editha* the name *wrighti.* The males do not have as rounded wings as *editha editha* or *editha bayensis,* the red color is more brownish and less distinct, the black heavier and the basal areas darker. This is the common, low elevation *editha* of southern California although here and there one encounters colonies that somewhat resemble *editha editha.*

Early Stages: Full grown larvae from the type locality, described by C. M. Dammers, have black head and legs and dull orange prolegs. The body is black, speckled profusely with minute orange dots. The bristly tubercles are all orange except on the first three and the last segments which bear black tubercles. The bristles are black on all tubercles. Larvae from the Gavilan Hills, Riverside county, are speckled with white and not orange. The larval foodplant is *Plantago pusilla.*

Distribution: The type locality is "San Diego, California." This subspecies extends south into northern Baja California and north to the Riverside—San Bernardino area, in brush covered desert hills.

(b) **editha** (Boisduval). Plate 37, figures 7, ♂ and 8, ♀. Edith's Checkerspot averages larger, with well rounded fore wings in the males. The wings are also quite broad. The figures on the plate do not depict *editha editha* well: there is not enough red above in the female and the wings are not as broad and well rounded as is typical of *editha editha.* Typical *editha* is rather rare in collections. Since the original description did not give a type locality, the naming of other *editha* subspecies has gradually restricted the name *e. editha* to the subspecies found in the foothills and mountains around the southeastern edge of the San Joaquin Valley and westward to the coast. Nominate *editha* is much redder above than the colonies about San Francisco Bay and not so red as those south of its range.

Early Stages: The full grown larvae are dull black. All the bristly tubercles are black, and those of the second lateral row arise from orange spots. The foodplants are reported as *Erodium circutarium,* clover and violets (?).

Distribution: It is found from the Greenhorn Mountains, Kern county, California, west to the coast in Santa Barbara county. The type locality has not been restricted as yet, but J. D. Gunder has suggested Cedar Creek, Greenhorn Mountains, Kern county, California.

(c) **bayensis** Sternitsky. Plate 38, figure 4, ♂; figure 5, ♀. The Bay Checkerspot is of the same shape and size as *editha editha* but with much less red on the upperside of the wings and a heavier black pattern. The figure of the male shows a little more red than average; the female figured is typical. This subspecies is often abundant in the hills along the east side and to the south of San Francisco Bay. C. Don MacNeill states that *bayensis* is confined to serpentine soils.

Early Stages: The larval foodplant is *Plantago erecta.*

Distribution: The subspecies *bayensis* is found along the east side and to the south of San Francisco Bay. Southward there is probably a cline with *editha editha.* It needs investigation.

(d) **taylori** (Edwards). Plate 38, figures 13, ♀. Taylor's Checkerspot is slightly smaller on the average than *editha editha.* The color pattern has heavier black lines and less red, and the light spots are not as yellow as in the *editha* group. The figure on the plate represents the subspecies well.

Early Stages: The full grown larva is black, speckled with white so as to form a double white middorsal line and a line along the side just above the stigmata. The middorsal and paired tubercles just above the prolegs are orange with black tips and bristles. All the other tubercles are entirely black. The tubercles are short, cone shaped, and very bristly.

Distribution: The type locality is Vancouver island, British Columbia, Canada. The subspecies ranges south along the coast to Oregon and in a slightly modified form along the east side of the Cascade Mountains of Washington and the mountain ranges of eastern Oregon.

The *baroni* group of subspecies

(e) **beani** (Skinner). Plate 46, figure 5, ♂ and 6, ♀. This small alpine form is similar in coloring to *taylori* but often is a little more reddish and has a somewhat suffused dingy appearance.

Early Stages: Undescribed.

Distribution: The type locality is "high elevations near Laggan, Alberta." The extent of its distribution is unknown but similar small alpine colonies are found at and above treeline in the northern Cascade Mountains of Washington State. The subspecies should be sought in the higher mountains between these two areas.

(f) **hutchinsi** McDunnough. Plate 46, figure 15, ♂; figure 16, ♀. This is a paler subspecies than most *editha* and has much more pale yellow color on the underside of the fore wings. The upperside is correctly illustrated and no further description is needed. The high alpine form (or subspecies?) on Mount Washburn, Yellowstone National Park, has been named *montanus* McDunnough.

Early Stages: The larva is quite different in coloring from those of other known *editha* subspecies. One larva collected at Wildhorse Camp, Elko county, Nevada, had a velvety black body boldly marked with white as follows: a prominent band of middorsal white spots of varying size, and a slightly broader similar band of white spots extending from the stigmata to the row of tubercles just above them. The middorsal tubercles are bright orange and arise from bright orange spots, as do also the row of black tubercles above the stigmata. The tubercles of the paired lowest row are also orange. The three rows of tubercles between are jet black. There are white specks in the black areas between segments. The overall appearance is that of black stripes with narrower white stripes spotted with orange.

Distribution: The type locality is Milligan Canyon, Jefferson county, Montana. The subspecies ranges south to northern Elko county, Nevada, and in a slightly redder form to Gunnison county, Colorado. Much more collecting of *editha* is needed in the Rocky Mountain States.

(g) **edithana** Strand. From the original description *edithana* did not seem sufficiently distinctive, so for years it was considered a synonym of *baroni* Edwards. Then J. D. Gunder obtained figures of the types and described them as "specimens which might at first thought seem redder and smaller *baroni*" (between *baroni* and *rubicunda*). This is about the best description that can be made of *edithana*.

Early Stages: Apparently unknown.

Distribution: The Edithana Checkerspot inhabits the Modoc Plateau of northeastern California. It is also found in the northwestern corner of Nevada and the mountains east of the Cascade Range north to central Oregon.

(h) **baroni** (Edwards). Plate 38, figures 9, ♀ and 12, ♂. Baron's Checkerspot shows the same range of variation as *bayensis,* but the red is redder and the pattern is brighter above. On the underside, *baroni* has much more red and less black. These differences, however, are not constant. The most consistent differences are the more produced apex and straighter outer margin of the fore wing and the more acute anal angle of the secondaries of *baroni*. The fore wing of the figured male is too rounded and not typical; also the red is too orange.

Early Stages: The full grown larvae are velvety black, dotted with small whitish specks. The ventral surface is smoky brown. The middorsal tubercles are orange with black bristles; those over the legs are yellow. All the other tubercles are black. The larval foodplant is given by Comstock simply as Scrophulariaceae.

Distribution: The type locality is Mendocino, Mendocino county, California. The subspecies occurs in the lower Coast Ranges from San Francisco Bay northward.

(i) **rubicunda** (Hy. Edwards). Plate 36, figure 13, ♂; figure 14, ♀. The Ruddy Checkerspot is the counterpart of *monoensis* on the western slope of the Sierra Nevada. It averages larger than *monoensis* at lower elevations (2500 ft.) becoming smaller at higher elevations. It differs from *monoensis* in the heavier black pattern above and smaller light creamy spots. The submarginal creamy spots particularly tend to obsolescence and infusion of red.

Early Stages: Undescribed.

Distribution: Known colonies of *rubicunda* are few: they tend to be local and difficult to find. The subspecies has been taken from Mariposa county south along the Sierra Nevada. It no doubt ranges north along the Sierras, but records are scarce or wanting. The type locality given simply as "Sierra Nevadas . . . 2500 feet to 7000 feet," was restricted to Mariposa county, California, by Gunder.

(j) **monoensis** Gunder. Plate 46, figure 9, ♂; figure 10, ♀. The Mono Lake Checkerspot was characterized by Gunder as having "all interior cream spots and lunate marginal cream spots fuller or broadened." The figures on the plate illustrate this distinctive character well and also the other characters of the upperside pattern. On the underside, *monoensis* is intermediate between *hutchinsi* and *lehmani* in coloring. The colonies of *editha* along the east slope of the Sierra Nevada are rather variable, but most of them show the distinctive pattern character quoted from the original description above. The paratypes of *fridayi* Gunder at the Los Angeles County Museum fall well within the range of variation range of *monoensis* colonies and are considered a synonym.

Early Stages: The larval foodplant is *Plantago*.

Distribution: The type locality is Rush Creek, near Mono Lake, Mono county, California. The Mono Lake Checkerspot has been taken as far north as Snyder Meadow in the Carson Range near Carson City, Nevada; in the spur ranges running out from the Sierra Nevada between Carson City and Mono Lake; and south to Bishop Creek, Inyo county, California.

(k) **lehmani** Gunder. Plate 37, figures 11, ♀ and 12, ♂. Lehman's Checkerspot is the subspecies in the Great Basin areas of central and eastern Nevada. Gunder describes it as looking "like a small *augusta* Wright but has its maculation less clear cut. The ground color is white, however, which makes it lighter than *augusta*." It differs from *hutchinsi* in having the basal and discal area of the underside of the fore wing largely red and not dusted and spotted with white like *hutchinsi*. It can be separated from both *hutchinsi* and *monoensis* by the broad continuous band of red spots across the fore wing above, and also from *monoensis* by the reduced light yellowish spots in the basal area of the hind wing above.

Early Stages: Unknown.

Distribution: Lehman's Checkerspot inhabits the higher Great Basin Ranges of Nevada from the Humboldt River Valley south to the central part of the state. The type locality is Lehman Caves Resort, White Pine county, Nevada.

The *nubigena* group of subspecies

(l) **augusta** (Edwards). Plate 37, figures 9, ♂ and 10, ♀. There is some confusion in the literature concerning the application of the name *augusta.* Edwards quotes W. G. Wright: "*M. augusta* is found on top of the mountains, elevation 5000 feet." Later Wright said he took it "in the foothills about San Bernardino" and used the name for all the southern California *editha.* Currently *augusta* is restricted to the rather red population found in the San Bernardino Mountains as illustrated on the plate. Whether this concept will stand the test of time is uncertain.

Early Stages: The mature larva is described as black, sparingly speckled with white, with the speckling more dense on either side of the middorsal line and in a line along the side just above the stigmata. The abdomen on the ventral side is black, speckled with white. The tubercles are all black except the middorsal and short lowest lateral paired row. There is a spot of orange at the base of each of the black tubercles of the middle lateral row from segments four or five to eleven. The wild foodplant is not certain, but eggs have been deposited on *Castilleja,* and larvae reared on *Penstemon.* If *Castilleja* is the natural foodplant, this suggests that *augusta* is allied to *editha nubigena* Behr.

Distribution: The type locality is the San Bernardino Mountains, San Bernardino county, California. This is the southern California higher mountain subspecies.

(m) **colonia** (Wright). Plate 38, figure 14, ♂; figure 15, ♀. The Colonia Checkerspot is a handsome red and yellow or yellowish white banded butterfly. Red coloring is often present in the submarginal yellowish spots. The figure of the male is typical, but the female on the plate is somewhat aberrant. Normal females of *colonia* are intermediate between females of *baroni* (figure 9) and those of *aurilacus* (figure 11). For separation from *taylori* compare figures 13 and 14.

Early Stages: Apparently unknown.

Distribution: The type locality is Mount Hood, Oregon. The subspecies *colonia* is a butterfly of the rocky ridges and openings in the alpine forests beginning just below treeline and extending down to where the dense forest commences. It has an extensive distribution from the Cascade Mountains of central Washington south through Oregon into the Siskiyou, Marble and Salmon mountains of northwestern California. About the only variation in this large area is the smaller average size of the northern specimens. Gunder mentions a series of specimens from the Priest River district in Idaho, which "really matches *colonia,*" and there are specimens from the higher elevations of the Wallowa and Blue mountains of northeastern Oregon which resemble both *remingtoni* and *colonia.* The identities of these Idaho and Oregon colonies are uncertain.

(n) **aurilacus** Gunder. Plate 38, figure 10, ♂; figure 11, ♀. The Aurilacus Checkerspot is similar to *colonia* but differs in having the submarginal series of spots larger and almost always completely red, not yellow as in *colonia.* The illustrations of *aurilacus* are good representations.

Early Stages: Undescribed.

Distribution: The type locality is Gold Lake, Sierra county, California. This subspecies has been reported from southern Oregon to as far south as the Lake Tahoe area in California. It is impossible to tell where *aurilacus* colonies end and *remingtoni* colonies begin, and the two names are probably synonyms.

(o) **remingtoni** Burdick. Plate 46, figure 17, ♂. The butterfly that has received this name is really only the northern portion of the subspecies that was named *aurilacus* by Gunder. The only differences are the slightly smaller size, darker red color, and reduced yellowish white areas.

Early Stages: Unknown.

Distribution: The characters given above are representative of the colonies found along the east side of the Cascade Range of Oregon from Klamath and Lake counties north to Deschutes county from 4000 to 6000 ft. The type locality is Mount Thielsen (below timberline), Douglas county, Oregon.

(p) **lawrencei** Gunder. Plate 43, figures 15, ♂ and 16, ♀. This small alpine subspecies is found on Mount Thielsen, Oregon. It is typical of many colonies found in our western mountains at and above timberline. These same mountains, however, also have larger but similarly marked and colored colonies on the lower slopes or at their bases. Whether these local dwarf alpine colonies deserve a name is uncertain. Lawrence's Checkerspot is the same size as *nubigena,* but of a darker red and has a heavier black-brown pattern. Many specimens are duskier than the figures on the plate.

Early Stages: Unknown.

Distribution: So far *lawrencei* is known only from the type locality, Mount Thielsen, Douglas county, Oregon.

(q) **nubigena** (Behr). Plate 46, figure 7, ♂; figure 8, ♀. The Cloud-born Checkerspot is small, the males only 28 to 35 mm in expanse and the females 30 to 40 mm. The predominant color of the upperside is red-brown to orange-brown. Many specimens are even more extensively red-brown than the figures.

Early Stages: A female was observed ovipositing on *Castilleja nana* at about 10,500 ft. near Sonora Pass, Mono county, California.

Distribution: The subspecies *nubigena* is found throughout the Sierra Nevada from about treeline up to 12,000 ft. The type locality is "the headwaters of the Tuolumne River and beyond, up to elevations of 11,500 feet."

6. **Euphydryas gillettii** (Barnes). Plate 36, figure 1, ♀. This species is unique in color and pattern among American *Euphydryas.* It is much more like the Eurasian members of the genus. If it were found in Alaska, we would consider it a recent arrival; but it is found in the heart of the Rocky Mountain system, isolated by thousands of miles from any Asian colonies with similar maculation. It is an inhabitant of mountain meadow lands and forest clearings.

Early Stages: In the fifth instar larva, the bristly tubercles are all jet black. The middorsal stripe is lemon yellow. The stigmatal stripe along the sides is clear white. The areas between these light stripes are dark brown, and the abdomen is soiled yellow with a middle stripe of brown. The eggs were deposited on Twin-berried Honeysuckle, *Lonicera involucrata.*

Distribution: The type locality is Yellowstone National Park, Wyoming. The species is found in the mountains of Montana as far east as the Judith and Little Belt mountains; it is also in northern Idaho and at several localities in Alberta, Canada.

Tribe Nymphalini

WILLIAM H. HOWE

This tribe is essentially confined to the temperate regions of the Holarctic. In the Americas only the genus *Hypanartia* is tropical; all other members of the tribe are temperate climate creatures. The genus *Hypanartia* is also known to be very old. It has been found as a fossil in the mid-Tertiary volcanic ash shales at Florissant, Colorado.

Coronal horns are usually absent on the caterpillars and there are usually four paired series of relatively simple abdominal spines. The plant hosts for larvae of the Nymphalini are usually species of Compositae and Urticaceae.

Genus POLYGONIA Hübner

The Anglewings

THOMAS W. DAVIES

The torn- and ragged-looking outer margins of these medium sized butterflies has given them the popular name "anglewings." All of the species in this genus are superficially similar in color and markings. The upper surfaces are of a tawny orange-brown color, heavily marked with dark spots and bars. The margins of the wings are bordered with black and sometimes a suffusion of black on the posterior wings. The under surfaces are soft hoary gray to reddish brown. All the species have a small silver colon or comma mark in the center of the underside of the hind wing.

Adult Habits: Species belonging to the genus *Polygonia* are forest dwellers. They seldom venture out into open fields but prefer sunny open spots in the woods. They rarely visit flowers but are attracted to exuding tree sap or fermenting fruit and plant juices. This attraction has been used to advantage to trap these butterflies. Anglewings overwinter in the adult stage, emerging at times from their hiding places to fly about on a warm winter day. They are quite pugnacious and are swift and erratic in flight. When landing they often pitch head down on a tree trunk with wings folded. The gray and brown underside patterns of the wings blend with the tree bark which makes them difficult to see.

Early Stages: The pale greenish eggs are laid singly or in strings or columns of two to six on the underside of the foodplant leaves. They are barrel-shaped, taller than broad and have eight to ten vertical keel-like ribs. The mature larvae are spiny, dark brown or green in color, and have pale longitudinal lines on the sides of the body. They are almost invariably solitary in habit. They usually live on the underside of leaves. In later life a larva may use a leaf to partially conceal itself by pulling the outer edges together with silken strands. The light brown chrysalis, rough and angulated in shape, has a conical protuberence and is covered with tubercles. The sides are streaked with gray or olive and a few metallic spots of silver or gold may occur in the dorsal region.

Distribution: The genus *Polygonia* is found throughout the Holarctic region, in the New World southward to central Mexico.

(1). **Polygonia interrogationis** (Fabricius). Plate 17, figure 10, ♀; figure 7, ♂ (form "umbrosa").   This is the largest of our *Polygonia* and is commonly called the Question Mark. The silvery mark on the underside of the hind wing is broken into a curved line and a dot. The wing margins are less angulated or excised than in other members of the genus. With its longer tails and bright reddish brown color it is easy to identify this species in the field. The Question Mark is attracted to the juices of rotting fruit and the sap of various trees; when feeding it can be captured easily.

There are two seasonal forms. The typical form is the overwintering pale *interrogationis.* From its eggs, laid in the spring, appears the darker summer form "umbrosa" which has the upperside of the hind wings broadly suffused with black.

Early Stages: The varicolored larvae are dull white to dark reddish brown. The sides of the body have a black stripe and light buff spots. The body segments bear two many-branched spines with a pair of spines on the quadrate head. In large colonies the young caterpillars are partially gregarious. The mature larva assumes a more solitary life. The angular gray-brown pupa sometimes has small spots of bright metallic color on the sides. As in all of the Nymphalidae the pupa hangs upside down, from branches of the foodplant or underneath fence railings. Its twisted curved shape has led to the suggestion that it, too, resembles a question mark. Food plants are various Urticaceae and Grossulaceae (nettle, hopvine, elm, linden and hackberry). The larva prefers hop and elm leaves.

Distribution: This common species occurs over most of the United States with the exception of the Great Basin and the Pacific Coast region. Found sparingly at low elevations along the eastern side of the Rocky Mountains, it ranges from southern Canada and Nova Scotia south through Texas and Florida. In the southern portion of its range it has three to four generations a year, but only two occur in the north.

2. **Polygonia comma** (Harris). Plate 17, figure 5 (typical form); figure 6, ♀ (form "dryas").   The reputation of this common species has suffered because of its fondness for hopvines in the eastern states. At times its larvae are so numerous that vines are stripped of leaves and pupae hang from every stem and branch. The Comma or Hop Merchant is a quick nervous insect, pugnacious in its habits, and will defend a territory. Numbers of individuals often gather at damp places in roads and forest openings and when disturbed return to the same spot.

The two to three generations of *P. comma* a year are seasonally dimorphic. The non-hibernating first generation, "dryas," is characterized by having the hind wings broadly suffused with black. Intermediates occur between *dryas* and *comma* in the second generation. The third generation is the paler typical *comma*, formerly known as "harrisii." It passes the winter in hibernation.

Early Stages: The pale green barrel-shaped eggs are laid in columns of two to nine eggs on the underside of leaves of hops or nettle. Upon leaving the egg the small larva does not seek concealment but lives on the underside of the leaf. As the larva matures it may loosely draw the edges of a leaf together with silk to form a crude shelter. The mature caterpillar may be snow white, greenish brown, or black with white spines. The light brown chrysalis resembles a bit of twisted dry wood. Along the dorsum is a conical protuberence and some small tubercles. At the base of the dorsal tubercles small metallic gold or silver spots may be seen. Foodplants are hops (*Humulus*), nettle (*Urtica*), false nettle (*Boehmeria*), and elm (*Ulmus*). There are two generations of this butterfly in the northern, three in the southern part of the range.

Distribution: Common in the eastern states from Canada to central Georgia, it ranges west to Kansas, Nebraska and Iowa.

3. **Polygonia satyrus** (Edwards). Plate 17, figure 8, ♂ (ssp. *neomarsyas*); figure 9, ♀. Wherever the stinging nettle (*Urtica*) grows in the low foothills of our western mountains this bright orange-brown species of *Polygonia* may be found. Common from early spring to late fall, it may be sought in any wooded canyon that has a stream. The Satyr Anglewing is readily recognized by the bright orange-yellow of its upper surfaces and the warm yellow-brown beneath. The dark borders so characteristic in the other species seem to fade away in *satyrus* leaving just the submarginal pale yellow spots. On the lower surface of the fore wing is a curved band of dark brown through the discal area. This band terminates in a blunt point just below the apex of the cell. The large marginal wing excision is bordered by a darker band of blackish brown. The discal band broadens on the hind wing and encloses the comma mark. Submarginal to the wing excision, below the tail, is another curved band of dark brown. The silvery comma mark is hooked or enlarged on the lower end in the form of an irregular "G."

In many females the bright orange-brown invades the upper surfaces, leaving the marginal borders indistinct and broken into bars. The wings beneath are unicolorus warm reddish brown with a median band of dark brown. The comma mark is thinner and not as prominent as in the male.

The subspecies *P. satyrus neomarsyas* dos Passos occurs in California. It was formerly incorrectly called *marsyas* (Edwards), a name that was based on incorrectly labeled European specimens.

Early Stages: Polygonia satyrus is multiple brooded and has been taken from late February to November. It does not seem to be seasonally dimorphic. The pale green eggs are laid on the underside of nettle leaves and the young larva makes a shelter by drawing the leaf edges together. The spiny head and body of the mature caterpillar are blackish brown. A greenish white dorsal stripe is anteriorly suffused with black and has a black V shaped mark on each body segment. The light brown angular chrysalis is seldom found on the foodplant but usually close by under rocks or on the rough bark of trees.

Distribution: This species is found at low elevations in riparian woodlands of the West from Arizona through Colorado, Wyoming and Montana, and east through southern Canada, New York, Ontario and Newfoundland.

4. **Polygonia faunus** (Edwards). Plate 17, figure 12, ♂. Across the upperside is a greenish luster that has given this butterfly the common name of "Green Comma." On the underside there are two rows of submarginal green spots. *P. faunus* has a much more "ragged" look than other members of the genus. The hind wings especially are deeply incised and indented. There are contrasting dark borders on the upper surface. On the hind wing this border encloses five small pale spots.

Like all members of the genus, *P. faunus* lives in woodlands. Seldom straying far from its chosen sunny glade in the forest it is yet audacious and quick to fly at the approach of an intruder.

From West Virginia to Georgia, in the southernmost part of the species range there is a larger and much darker subspecies, *P. faunus smythi* Clark. The subspecies *P. faunus rustica* (Edwards) occurs in the Northwestern states and is lighter and brighter. A third subspecies, *P. faunus arcticus* Leussler, found in the Northwest Territories is smaller than the nominate subspecies and has much more gray on the underside.

Early Stages: Only a few eggs a day are laid by the female. These are attached singly to the upper surface of the leaves of birch (*Betula*), willow (*Salix*), currant (*Ribes*) or alder (*Alder*). *Rhododendron occidentale* is said to be a foodplant of the western forms. Upon emerging from the egg the young larva crawls to the under surface of the leaf where it feeds in a solitary state. At maturity the caterpillar differs from *P. comma* larvae in having a small pale "W" mark on the front of the black head. The body is a dull tawny brown with a contrasting white patch on the posterior segments. The head and body spines are also white. Like the adult, the pale brown chrysalis is at times streaked with mossy green. There may also be a few metallic spots on or near the tubercles.

Distribution: The species is abundant in the Adirondack and Catskill mountains of New York, ranges southward to northern Georgia and north to Hudson Bay, then west through Canada to Vancouver Island and the Northwest Territories, and south to central California.

5. **Polygonia hylas** (Edwards). Plate 18, figure 3, ♂. The two species of *Polygonia* a collector frequently encounters in the mountains of Colorado are *P. zephyrus* (Edwards) and *P. hylas*. The latter is easily recognized by its smaller size and the more ragged appearance of the wings. It is also separable from *zephyrus* by the purplish brown and gray underside. The darker brown basal portion is separated from the lighter limbal area by a dark irregular band edged with black. Along the marginal areas of both wings is an indication of a few obscure greenish lunules. The upperside of *P. hylas* is a darker fulvous red with dark contrasting borders. The

borders of the hind wings are broader and encompass five small buff-yellow spots, in contrast to the large yellow lunules on the upperside of *zephyrus*. *P. hylas* has a sexually dimorphic female in which the underside pattern is uniformly gray-brown with darker fine longitudinal striations.

The Colorado Anglewing must be sought along the edges of mountain streams bordered by Quaking Aspen and a mixed undergrowth. It is restricted in altitudinal range from about 6500 to 9000 ft. Occasionally as a visitor to flowers, or while basking in an open spot, it may be caught with ease.

Early Stages: The life history of this species has never been studied. There is a question concerning the relationship of *hylas* and the western forms of *faunus* that eventually may be solved by study of the early stages of *hylas*.

Distribution: Encountered as a rarity in the higher mountains from Idaho to Wyoming, *P. hylas* is not uncommon in the montane districts of Colorado. Its range extends into New Mexico and Arizona. Northern California records of *P. hylas* are doubtful.

6. **Polygonia silvius** (Edwards). Plate 16, figure 6, ♀; Plate 17, figure 15, ♂; Plate 18, figure 6, ♀. From the time that William H. Edwards wrote the original description of *Polygonia silvius* in 1870 a considerable amount of confusion has arisen over the exact identity of this species. Edwards's male (the type) was a specimen collected by Lorquin, sold to Reakirt, and then given to Edwards. Edwards gave the type locality "California," now restricted to Yosemite Valley, Yosemite National Park, California. Edwards also had a female "type" which was from a population near the type locality of *rusticus*, i.e., Big Trees, Calaveras county, California. The male type (a lectotype) determines the status of the nominal species *silvius*. The female (a *rusticus*) does not affect this.

This is a large species, the male having a wing expanse of 51 mm, the female 61 mm. It is easily distinguished from other California *Polygonia* by the rich purplish brown under surface. The basal area is a mottled purplish brown with a darker irregular line of demarcation through the wings. The space beyond to the margin is tinged with soft gray. On the margins of the large excisions of both wings is a series of dark green confluent crescents edged with black. The discal silvery "C" mark is flattened on the curve and barbed on the upper end.

The sexually dimorphic female is a more uniform subdued shade of brownish purple beneath, the markings nearly obsolete, and the discal "C" spot reduced to a slight curve or scarcely distinguishable. A specimen is figured on Plate 16, figure 7.

Early Stages: David L. Bauer and John F. Emmel, have reared the Sonoma and Napa county populations of this species. It is with their kind permission I am able to give this brief account of the early stages: The egg is pale green in color, barrel-shaped, flattened at the top and bottom and slightly tapered toward the top, with eleven thin vertical ridges peripherally. The mature larva is 38 mm long. The head is black and bears two black branching spines, a few fulvous tubercles and hairs, and a fulvous inverted "V" or "X" in the center. Segments one to five are banded with black and fulvous. The spines are fulvous with the exception of the last lateral row which is white. The remaining segments are banded black and white and each segment has a black V shaped mark. Segmental spines are white with the last lateral row black. Two undulating lines of orange-fulvous run along the sides of all the segments. The chrysalis is tan, marbled with shades of olive and brown. It is slender and longer than the chrysalis of *satyrus*. The head case is elongated to form two horn-like protuberances. The mesonotum is high and keel like and a few silver spots appear on the tubercles of the abdomen. The larval foodplant is *Rhododendron occidentale*. In captivity larvae will also feed on nettle (*Urtica*).

Distribution: The species is found along the edges of streams wherever the food plant *Rhododendron* occurs, in north-central California and in the foothills of the Sierra Nevada of California.

7. **Polygonia zephyrus** (Edwards). Plate 17, figure 11, ♂. The Zephyr is easy to recognize by the soft overall gray or gray-brown of the undersides of the wings. The longitudinal wing markings are as in other *Polygonia* species but more subdued. Above the butterfly is light orange with a narrow marginal brown band and a submarginal row of prominent pale yellow lunules. It is one of the few *Polygonia* that feed at flowers (especially rabbitbrush, *Chrysothamnus nauseosus*) and the only one that ranges above timberline.

Early Stages. The larvae feed upon Squaw Currant (*Ribes cereum*), a plant found commonly as a ground cover in western forests from 5000 to 12,000 ft. The range of *P. zephyrus* coincides with that of this plant.

The inch-long, black caterpillars are armed with seven rows of spines. Those in body segments three to six are reddish buff, as are the basal areas surrounding them. The spines and upper surfaces from segments seven to twelve are white. The remaining black color on the back resembles a series of arrowheads pointing backwards. The chrysalis is slender with the head case elevated on top to form two short protuberances. The mesonotum is prominent and nose-like in appearance, the wing cases slightly elevated from the body. A few silver spots may occur on the upper tubercles of the abdomen. The pupal stage lasts two weeks. There is probably a succession of generations but no seasonal color forms of the adults are known.

Distribution: Essentially an upper Transition to Hudsonian zone butterfly, *P. zephyrus* is seldom taken below an altitude of 5000 ft.

Its range includes the Sierra Nevada and Cascade mountains of California, Oregon and Washington, the Rocky Mountains south to New Mexico, north and west to British Columbia and east to the Riding Mountains of Manitoba.

8. **Polygonia gracilis** (Grote & Robinson). Plate 18, figure 2, ♂. Seldom encountered or collected, this small, comparatively little known insect is one of the rarer species in the genus. It bears a close resemblance to *Polygonia progne* in the gray scaling of the underside, but can be separated from *progne* by a hoary band extending across the outer half of both wings. This white band contrasts sharply with dark ferruginous

brown of the basal portion of the wings. The upper surfaces are broadly bordered in black with small light yellow spots in the border of the hind wings. The markings and colors on the dorsal surface are very much like those of *P. faunus,* but the wing expanse is slightly less than the 51 mm of *faunus.* Like *Polygonia progne, gracilis* flies somewhat slower than others of the genus. It is rather shy and is met only singly and on rare occasions. Most of the *Polygonia* do not visit flowers but *gracilis* has been known to visit the blossoms of Everlasting (*Gnaphalium*).

Early Stages: Little is known of the life history of *P. gracilis.* The egg was described by Scudder.

Distribution: The range of this species is extensive. Specimens have been taken as far west and north as Alaska and Great Slave Lake. Its metropolis seems to be northern New England from Maine to New York then west to Michigan and Minnesota. A boreal species, it is found in the Canadian and Hudsonian zone regions of the northeastern forestlands.

9. **Polygonia oreas** (Edwards). Plate 18, figure 5, ♀ (*P. o. silenus*). The status of this species has been in doubt since W. H. Edwards's original description. The original types of both *oreas* and *silenus* were lost and disputes have arisen over the true identity of *oreas* and the relationship between *oreas* and *silenus* ever since. Recently neotypes have been designated for both and this may help to clarify many questions concerning them. The doubtful identity of *oreas* has been due in part to its rarity and its restricted range, associated with the Redwood regions of northern California and southern Oregon.

The butterfly is slightly smaller than our other West Coast *Polygonia;* above it is a light reddish fulvous, spotted and barred with black. The wings are deeply excised and the tail is prominent. Beneath *o. oreas* is much lighter than *o. silenus* with a definitely light brown color and a marked contrast in the basal-limbal area of both wings.

From northern Oregon to British Columbia there occurs a very dark subspecies, *silenus* (Edwards). It is distinctively dark black or blackish brown on the underside of the wings. The demarcation line of the dark band through the discs of the wings is indicated strongly in the primaries. Outside this band is a scaling of grayish white and along the costa are three grayish white patches of color. The band through the secondaries merges into the black basal color leaving the gray scaling indistinct. The discal silvery white mark is bent at right angles and is tapered at both ends. The upper surface is a deep reddish fulvous shading to brown in the basal region. The black bars and spots stand out distinctly as do the submarginal rows of pale fulvous lunules on both wings. This darkening tone of color in *silenus* may be influenced by humidity, and many intermediates occur between *oreas* and *silenus.*

Early Stages: Little is known of the early stages of *oreas* and *silenus.* The food-plant of *oreas* is known to be Straggly Gooseberry (*Ribes divaricatum*), found in shaded canyons and stream banks below 2000 ft, in mixed evergreen and redwood forest.

Distribution: The range of this pretty and rare species coincides with that of its foodplant, *Ribes divaricatum. P. o. oreas* has been found from Santa Cruz county, California, north to southern Oregon. Its preference for redwood forests in this area is marked. *P. o. silenus,* and forms intermediate between *oreas* and *silenus,* are found from northern Oregon through Washington to British Columbia.

10. **Polygonia progne** (Cramer). Plate 17, figure 13, ♂; Plate 17, figure 14, ♀ (form "l-argenteum"). One of the smaller members of the genus, *Polygonia progne* has grayish brown on the underside. The hind wings beneath are traversed by thin blackish parallel lines and the silvery comma mark is tapered at both ends. The butterfly is double brooded with the typical (overwintering) form being a bright fulvous orange above bordered with dark brown. The summer form, "l-argenteum," is much darker above with a suffusion of darker scaling across the hind wings. The lower arm of the comma mark on the ventral surface of this form has been shortened and suggests an "L."

Although associated with woods and forested trails, *P. progne* can be found around human habitations and often settles on the weathered wood of old buildings. It is an active butterfly but much slower in flight than other *Polygonia.* A wary insect most of the time, like all members of the genus, it is difficult to catch but is much attracted to baits.

Early Stages: The adult butterfly lays its eggs singly on the foodplants currant and gooseberry (*Ribes*), occasionally on elm (*Ulmus*). The eggs are pale green, higher than wide, and have ten vertical keel-like ribs. Mature caterpillars are yellowish brown with olive-brown variegated blotches and stripes along the sides. The brown head is crowned with two long branching spines. The body segment spines are shorter, blackish in color, and have many branching spinules. Fully developed larvae are more than one inch long. Chrysalids vary in color from dark brown to light buff streaked with brown and black. They hang suspended by the cremaster for ten to sixteen days before eclosing the adult.

Distribution: The range of the Gray Comma extends from Nova Scotia south to Virginia and North Carolina, and west to Kansas and Nebraska. It is reputed to occur in Alaska. It is rather common at low altitudes in the northeastern states and in the White Mountains of New England.

Genus VANESSA Fabricius

HARRY K. CLENCH

This nearly worldwide genus includes sixteen species in all. Some of them, like *atalanta* and *cardui,* have vast ranges and are among our best known butterflies.

Note: Glenn A. Gorelick prepared the original copy for *Vanessa.* In the last stages of editing this book, however, the important revision by William D. Field (1971) appeared. There was no time to refer the manuscript back to Mr. Gorelick for revision, so I undertook to rewrite the account of *Vanessa,* basing it largely on Field's revision.

Others are confined to exceedingly small areas, such as *tameamea* in the Hawaiian Islands or *samani* (Hagen) in the mountains of Sumatra. Five species occur in our area.

Members of *Vanessa* have a rather stout body and a characteristic wing shape with heavy triangular wings and a tab-like, produced apical region of the fore wing. The pattern of the hind wing underside is complex and includes a postmedian row of eyespots. These are often subequal, but in some species (including our *virginiensis*) the two in M_1-M_2 and Cu_1-Cu_2 are hypertrophied and the others suppressed. The upperside pattern is also rather complex and quite diverse among the species. All, however, share a dark brown ground color and a diagonal band of red, orange or yellow on the fore wing from near the middle of the costa across to the tornal area. This band is most band-like in *atalanta,* highly contorted, often broken, and with the addition of further, similarly colored markings on other parts of the wings in most other species. From one to five subapical white spots are found on the fore wing. Males and females resemble each other closely and are often difficult to discriminate.

These butterflies are powerful fliers and several species are migratory, *cardui* outstandingly so. Many species of *Vanessa* vary in numbers considerably from year to year. *V. atalanta* is known to be territorial, but I have no information on possible territorialism in any other species.

Early Stages: The eggs are barrel-shaped, with a variable number (see subgenera) of projecting vertical ribs, and are laid singly on leaves of the foodplants. The larvae are solitary and construct nests of one or more leaves attached together with silk. The larvae are variable in coloration, have short dorsal scoli and lateral spinules. Pupation is often in the larval nest. The brown or gray, gold-flecked pupae are suspended by the cremaster alone. Adults are multiple brooded.

Field has shown that the members of this genus are divisible into three distinct groups of species. He gave these groups generic rank but in view of their close interrelationship it seems preferable to treat them as subgenera. The subgenera *Vanessa* and *Cynthia* are found in the area covered by this book; the third, *Bassaris* Hübner, comprises two species found only in Australia, New Zealand and a few islands in the South Pacific.

Subgenus VANESSA Fabricius

The eggs have nine vertical ribs; larvae feed almost exclusively on Urticaceae. Adults have bifid paronychia on the tarsi (shared with *Bassaris*), and an apically bifid uncus (unique in this subgenus). Our two species have a conspicuous red or orange diagonal band on the fore wing. The subgenus as a whole is essentially palearctic, but with outliers in the Greater Sunda Islands, the Philippines, the Hawaiian Islands and North America.

1. **Vanessa (Vanessa) atalanta** (Linnaeus). Plate 18, figure 1, ♀ (ssp. *rubria*). Our

subspecies, *rubria* (Fruhstorfer), differs from nominate *atalanta* (western Palearctic) chiefly in the somewhat larger subapical white bar on the fore wing upperside, just beyond the cell-end. One of our best known butterflies, the Red Admiral can be confused with nothing else in our area and is readily identified from the illustration. *V. atalanta* occurs chiefly in shrubby fields (including suburban yards), woods edges and forest over a wide range of life zones from the Lower Austral to the Hudsonian. Possibly it is not resident in the Canadian and Hudsonian zones, and may migrate northward in spring and southward in the fall, as has been found true in Europe.

Early Stages: Larvae are extremely variable in color. They are found on a variety of Urticaceae, especially *Urtica* (nettle), *Boehmeria* (false nettle), *Parietaria* (pellitory). They also feed on *Humulus* (hops) in the family Moraceae. Adults are territorial, in the afternoon and early evening, and often take up territories on deserted roads, driveways and cement sidewalks well into dusk. Hibernation occurs as a pupa and, from the latitude of southern Pennsylvania south, also as an adult (at least occasionally).

Distribution: The subspecies *rubria* ranges in North America from the Atlantic to the Pacific and from northern Canada south to southern Florida and Guatemala. It is also found on Bermuda, on several of the larger islands of the West Indies (rare) and, introduced, the Hawaiian Islands. Nominate *atalanta* is found over all but northernmost Europe, including the Azores and the Canary Islands, south to northern Africa, and from the Atlantic Ocean eastward to Iraq and western Pakistan (rare) and the Altai Mountains, perhaps occasionally farther eastward. It also occurs on New Zealand (introduced).

2. **Vanessa (Vanessa) tameamea** Eschscholtz. Plate 18, figure 8, ♀;   The Kamehameha Butterfly is one of only two endemic butterflies in the Hawaiian Islands (the other is *Vaga blackburni,* a lycaenid), a majestic and interesting species whose nearest relative is the eastern Palearctic *Vanessa indica* (Herbst). It differs from *atalanta rubria,* which occurs with it, in its somewhat larger average size (*tameamea* is the largest *Vanessa*); in the paler, broader and more irregular diagonal orange band on the fore wing above, which surrounds and isolates a distinct, large black spot in the cell (fused with the ground color in *atalanta*); by the pale terminal band on the hind wing being about twice as thick in M_1-M_3 as it is below M_3 and separated from the termen by a distinct fuscous edge; and by the basal area of the hind wing above being orange-brown instead of fuscous.

Early Stages: The larva is pale green with a lateral white stripe on each side. The head has numerous short, white-tipped spines and a triangular maroon patch on the front. The thorax and abdomen have subdorsal scoli, those on the abdomen basally green, then red, then black. There are two or three broods per year. Larvae feed on various native Urticaceae. *Pipturus albidus* is the principal foodplant, but records also exist for *Boehmeria nivea, Neraudia, Touchardia* and *Urera.*

Distribution: The species occurs in montane forests only in the Hawaiian Islands (Kauai, Oahu, Molokai, Maui, Lanai, Hawaii).

Subgenus CYNTHIA Fabricius

The eggs have fourteen or fifteen vertical ribs; larvae feed principally on plants of the families Compositae and Malvaceae. Adults have simple paronychia on the tarsi (unique in this subgenus), and an apically simple, acuminate or bluntly rounded uncus (shared with *Bassaris*). The upperside is largely fuscous and orange (pinkish when freshly emerged) in a checkered pattern. A large quadrate orange spot is always present from vein to vein in the middle of the Cu_2-2A interspace on the fore wing above (often incompletely separated from the basal orange), absent or only weakly developed in the subgenus *Vanessa*.

3. **Vanessa (Cynthia) cardui** (Linnaeus). Plate 18, figure 4, ♂. The Painted Lady is one of the best known, most widely distributed butterflies in the world. It may be distinguished from *virginiensis* by the row of four or more small, subequal postmedian eyespots on the hind wing below (only two, and large, in *virginiensis*), and from *annabella* by the white, instead of orange, costal patch just beyond the cell-end on the fore wing above and the usual absence of blue centers in the post-median spots on the hind wing above.

This species occurs in open, sunlit environments but beyond this it seems to have little choice: it may be found on alpine mountain summits, in grassy meadows, desert lowlands, and is recorded from nearly all life zones. Our *cardui* is a great migrant. The migrations are often spectacular in the western states, much less so elsewhere. Its numbers fluctuate exceedingly from year to year and over most of North America it is probably not a permanent resident. Its only area of permanent residency may be the Sonoran Desert and adjoining desert areas, from which it migrates northward and eastward in greater or lesser numbers each year. It may occasionally overwinter outside its residence area, but not often. In Europe *cardui* has a similar pattern, with permanent residence in the Sahara Desert and perhaps in other low latitude desert areas.

Early Stages: The larva is yellowish green, mottled with black, the head black and hairy but not spiny; the subdorsal scoli are yellowish. In North America and Europe the larvae feed mostly on Compositae, particularly thistles, constructing a vertical nest near the top of the plant. Recorded foodplants include *Cirsium, Carduus, Centaurea, Arctium, Anaphalis, Artemisia, Gnaphalium* and others, all Compositae. Plants of the family Malvaceae (*Althaea, Malva* and others) are also used and in parts of the Near East (Iraq, Afghanistan, etc.) may be the principal food. *Borago* (Boraginaceae) is also reported. The species is multiple brooded.

Distribution: V. cardui occurs throughout the Palearctic; in isolated and probably non-migratory colonies in the mountains of the Malay Peninsula, Java and Sumatra; over the whole of Africa including Madagascar; in the New World from southern Canada south to Panama (probably non-resident in most of our area except southern California and southern Arizona); and on several of the larger West Indian islands (rare). Despite its wide range, no subspecies are recognized. A distinct but closely related species, *kershawi* M'Coy, is found in Australia and New Zealand, until recently believed to be a subspecies of *cardui.*

4. **Vanessa (Cynthia) virginiensis** (Drury). Plate 18, figure 7, ♂. The American Painted Lady (or Hunter's Butterfly) used to go under the synonymous name *huntera.* It differs from our other two members of the subgenus by having only two large postmedian ocelli on the hind wing underside, instead of four or five smaller ones. It is our only member of a group of five similar species (the *virginiensis* group) otherwise restricted to South America.

Like *cardui, virginiensis* occurs over a wide variety of environments, perhaps ranging a little more into forest edges, and over an equally broad span of life zones. Also like *cardui* its numbers vary a great deal from one year to another. It is not known whether *virginiensis* migrates, but if so it is certainly not to the extent of *cardui.*

Early Stages: The larva is black with narrow yellow cross-bands and a row of white spots on each side. The subdorsal scoli are blackish. The larva lives singly in a nest near the top of the foodplant, much as does the larva of *cardui.* Larval foodplants are chiefly Compositae (*Gnaphalium, Antennaria, Anaphalis;* less often *Artemisia, Senecio* and others). The species is also reported on Boraginaceae (*Myosotis*), Scrophulariaceae (*Antirrhinum*), Malvaceae (*Malva*), but these may be rare or exceptional. There are two or three broods per year, and hibernation may occur as adult or pupa.

Distribution: V. virginiensis occurs from coast to coast, and from southern Canada to Colombia, in the south only in the mountains. It is also known from several of the larger West Indian islands (rare), and has become naturalized (introduced ?) in the Hawaiian Islands, the Azores, Madeira and the Canary islands, with occasional vagrants in southwestern Europe and Great Britain.

5. **Vanessa (Cynthia) annabella** (Field). Plate 18, figure 10, ♂; figure 13, ♂ (ab. "letcheri"). Until recently the West Coast Lady went under the name *carye* (Hübner) and was believed to be a species that extended from western Canada south to Chile. Field (1971), however, found that two species were involved, one South American, one essentially North American. Since Hübner's name clearly applied to the former, Field described the one in North America as a new species.

V. annabella is similar to *cardui* in general appearance, but is slightly smaller (our smallest *Vanessa*). It differs further from *cardui* in having (1) an orange, not white, costal spot beyond the cell of the fore wing above; (2) an orange subterminal spot in M_3-Cu_1 on the same wing; and (3) blue centers to the postmedian spots of the hind wing above. From *virginiensis* it differs conspicuously in having four or five subequal small eyespots on the hind wing below, instead of two large ones.

This species is common in a broad range of environments, from alpine tundra down to sea level, but favors open, sunny areas.

Early Stages: The larva is variable in color, from tan to black with yellow lines; the subdorsal scoli are black. The larva lives solitarily in a leaf shelter. Larval foodplants are chiefly Malvaceae (*Malva,* the principal food; also *Lavatera, Althaea, Sidalcea* and others); also reported on *Ligustrum* (Oleaginaceae), *Lupinus* (Leguminosae) and *Urtica* (Urticaceae), perhaps only exceptionally. The species is multiple brooded, and in parts of California it is on the wing nearly all year.

Distribution: This is the only *Vanessa* in North America that is absent from the East. It is found from the Rockies (Alberta, Montana, Colorado [uncommon, in late summer; perhaps present only by periodic immigration], New Mexico and western Texas; occasionally vagrant eastward to Kansas) west to the Pacific Ocean and from southern British Columbia southward through most of Mexico to Guatemala, montane southward. It is replaced in South America (Colombia to Argentina and Chile, montane northward) by the closely similar *carye.*

Genus NYMPHALIS Kluk

GLENN ALAN GORELICK

The genus *Nymphalis* is primarily Holarctic. It is represented in the United States and Canada by four species whose ground colors vary from orange or brown to purplish black. The undersides are cryptically marked, appearing like dead leaves when the wings are held upright. The posterolateral margins of the hind wings and the apex of the fore wings are slightly angled. The head is moderately large, eyes hairy and palpi robust.

Early Stages: The egg is short and ovoid, broad at the base and tapering toward the apex. It also has longitudinal ridges with delicate crosslines. The eggs are deposited in clusters on the host plant. The larva has long, branching spines with bristles and are arranged in longitudinal rows on the body. The larvae lack dorsal spines on the head. The chrysalis is strongly angulate. The species are multiple brooded in North America, and adults hibernate in the winter. Mass movements have been recorded for several species.

1. **Nymphalis milberti** (Godart). Plate 17, fig. 2, ♂. According to W. T. M. Forbes Milbert's Tortoise Shell is probably a subspecies of the European *Nymphalis urticae.* The relationships between the two, however, still need to be clarified. The subspecies *N. m. furcillata* (Say) was described from the Great Lakes region and Fort William, Ontario. Specimens from a Colorado population were designated as *subpallida* Cockerell on the basis of the external yellow in the postmedian band on both wings. The name *subpallida,* however, was later synonymized to *furcillata.* Another subspecies, *N. milberti viola* (dos Passos) was described from Newfoundland.

Early Stages: In the first and second instars the larvae are gregarious and live in a silk web on the host plant; the more mature larvae, when single, live in folded leaves. The larvae are variable, black with a greenish yellow lateral stripe and a subdorsal orange stripe; they are covered sparingly with branching spines, white maculation and numerous fine hairs. Larval foodplants are chiefly Urticaceae

(*Urtica*: the principal host), Salicaceae (*Salix:* doubtful host), Compositae (*Helian-thella:* doubtful host). There are two or three broods per year, from March to September.

Distribution: The species occurs in riparian areas, usually at high elevations, in the Transition, Canadian and Hudsonian life zones. It is found from West Virginia (in the mountains) north to Newfoundland and west to the Pacific coast from California to British Columbia.

2. **Nymphalis californica** (Boisduval). Plate 17, figure 3, ♀.   Forbes states that the California Tortoise Shell is a relative of the European *Nymphalis polychloros.* The relationships between the two species, however, are still unclear. The name *N. californica herri* Field applies to those populations inhabiting the Rocky Mountains. Adults make periodic mass movements.

Early Stages: The body of the larva is black dotted with white and with yellow maculation above the dorsal spine bases; the lateral spine bases are blue. The food-plants include species of *Ceanothus* (Rhamnaceae), chiefly *Ceanothus thrysiflorus* (blue brush) and the ericaceous *Arctostaphylos* (manzanita; a questionable host). There are two or three broods per year, from about February to October. The adults hibernate during winter.

Distribution: N. californica is found in mountain canyons and riparian areas in the Upper Austral, Transition, Canadian and Hudsonian life zones. It occurs on the West Coast from southern British Columbia to southern California and eastward to the Rocky Mountains. According to Klots it was introduced into New York in the late nineteenth century but died out about twenty years later; it has also been recorded from Illinois, Iowa, Michigan and Pennsylvania. The records from these eastern states are all casual, and the species has not survived in any of them.

3. **Nymphalis vau-album** ([Denis & Schiffermüller]). Plate 17, figure 4, ♀.   The Compton Tortoise Shell is distinguished by the silver "J" mark on the underside of the hind wing. The subspecies *j-album* (Boisduval & Le Conte) is found in the eastern part of the range. The subspecies name *watsoni* (Hall) applies to those populations occurring in northern Wyoming, Montana, Alberta, British Columbia and Alaska. Nominate *vau-album* is Palearctic.

Early Stages: The body of the larva is light green, stippled with yellowish green maculation and with black, bristly spines. Larval foodplants include Salicaceae (*Salix,* and *Populus*), Betulaceae (*Betula alba* and *Betula papyrifera*). Larvae feed gregariously on the host plant. There is one brood per year, from June to April of the following year. Adults hibernate during winter.

Distribution: The species occurs in forested areas (chiefly in the Canadian and Transition zones) from eastern Canada and New England south in the mountains to North Carolina, and westward through Michigan and Minnesota to Wyoming, Montana, Idaho and Washington, north through British Columbia to Alaska.

4. **Nymphalis antiopa** (Linnaeus). Plate 17, figure 1, ♂.   The Mourning Cloak is subject to rare individual variation chiefly caused by temperature effects; many such

variations have been described. A subspecies, *N. antiopa hyperborea* (Seitz), occurs in Alaska.

Early Stages: Eggs are laid in a mass around a twig and the emerging larvae are somewhat communal in a silk web when immature, and remain gregarious or feed singly during the last two instars. The body of the larva is black with white maculations; there is a row of dorsal red spots and several rows of spines. Larval foodplants include *Salix, Populus, Ulmus, Celtis,* and *Rosa* (questionable host). The species has two broods per year, perhaps three southward; it usually occurs from January to December in California near the coast. Adults hibernate during winter.

Distribution: The Mourning Cloak is found in meadows, riparian areas and forests in the Upper Austral and Transition zones of the Holarctic region. In the Western Hemisphere it ranges from Alaska to Venezuela, diminishing in abundance southward.

Genus HYPANARTIA Hübner

STEPHEN F. PERKINS and EDWIN M. PERKINS, JR.

Although this genus is common and widespread in the tropics of the Americas, only one species may enter our area.

1. **Hypanartia lethe** Fabricius. Plate 11, figure 20, ♂. The figure serves to identify this species. A short tail extends from cell M_3 along the outer margin of the hind wing in this black and henna butterfly.

Distribution: Common in Mexico, *lethe* may occur as a straggler in extreme southern Texas. No valid records are as yet known.

Subfamily ARGYNNINAE

The Fritillaries and Silverspots

WILLIAM H. HOWE

The members of this subfamily are medium to large butterflies, bright fulvous or ochreous above. The pattern of black spots and markings on the upperside is characteristic, suggestive of a dice box (*fritillus*) from which the name fritillary was derived. They are also popularly known as silverspots because of the silvery white spots which appear on the ventral surfaces of many species. Adults of this subfamily comprise a conspicuous part of the summer insect fauna in many parts of the temperate zone. Three genera are represented in our fauna: *Speyeria, Boloria* and *Euptoieta.*

Genus EUPTOIETA Doubleday

WILLIAM H. HOWE

The adults of this genus are medium-sized, dull fulvous to orange, with a characteristic black dice box pattern above. The primaries are somewhat elongate as well as truncate. There is no silvering beneath. This neotropical genus has no representatives outside the Americas. Two species occur in our territory.

1. **Euptoieta claudia** (Cramer). Plate 1, figure 15, ♀.   This is the common and familiar Variegated Fritillary. Adults usually fly close to the ground in a hovering or darting sort of flight. Expanse: 55–60 mm.

Early Stages: The mature larvae are orange-red with a black lateral stripe enclosing white spots with six rows of black spines. The foodplants are violets and pansies, (*Viola*), both cultivated and wild, on which the larvae are occasionally destructive; also passion flower (*Passiflora*); purslane (*Portulaca*); stonecrop (*Sedum*); moonseed (*Menispermum*); and may apple (*Podophyllum*). There are continuous broods from early summer until autumn.

Distribution: The species occurs as a breeding resident in the southwestern, central and southeastern U.S. Migrants range northward to southern Minnesota, Manitoba and Wyoming each summer. Hibernation occurs in the adult stage in warmer latitudes (San Antonio, Texas). There is a strong northerly migration in spring in the Great Plains with individuals reaching eastern Kansas in late April. In the East *claudia* is rare north of Virginia. It is very common in Mexico, but occurs on only a few islands in the West Indies, notably Jamaica.

2. **Euptoieta hegesia** (Cramer). Plate 1, figure 16, ♀ (ssp. *hoffmanni*).   This butterfly may be recognized by the pale, unmarked basal region of the secondaries above. It is a common neotropical species which is rather abundant in the vicinity of Brownsville, Texas. The subspecies encountered in Texas and Mexico is *E. hegesia hoffmanni,* W. P. Comstock. Nominate *hegesia* is West Indian, but apparently does not reach Florida. Expanse: 55 to 60 mm.

Genus SPEYERIA Scudder

(The Greater Fritillaries or Silverspots)

WILLIAM H. HOWE

Members of this genus are the true fritillaries or silverspots. Seventeen more or less distinct species are encountered in our territory and a large number of subspecies have been named in our western states. The genus is entirely nearctic, with no species known to occur south of central Mexico. The taxonomic problems of this genus are several, and still unresolved as they have been for over a century. One of these is

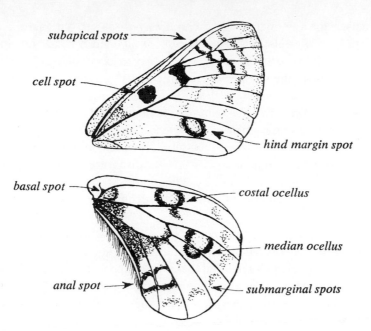

subapical spots

cell spot

hind margin spot

basal spot

costal ocellus

median ocellus

anal spot

submarginal spots

Figure 32. Generalized wings of *Parnassius* showing special pattern terms used in description.

the difficulty of establishing the limits of normal variation within a species. A related problem is the possibility of interspecific matings among our so-called species, which should be very low between biologically distinct species. Third, climatological events in the West have resulted in numerous montane "island" populations. Are these presently isolated populations species or subspecies? At one time many or most of them were united. These basic problems must eventually be resolved before the relationships in this genus can be properly assessed. Among the butterflies few groups have proven more baffling than our western *Speyeria.*

In the descriptions below I frequently use the term "disc" as a short way of saying "discal area of the hind wing underside."

I have made a number of taxonomic changes from the dos Passos & Grey arrangement of *Speyeria,* on the basis of new evidence discovered by western workers. *Speyeria adiaste* has been split from *S. egleis* and elevated to full specific rank with *atossa* and *clemencei* as subspecies. I have separated as full species the eastern and the western populations of *S. atlantis;* the eastern populations have been retained under the species *atlantis,* and the western subspecies are here placed under the species *electa* (= *cornelia* Edwards). *Speyeria nevadensis* has been removed from *S. callippe* and is here recognized as a full species. The subspecies with greenish discs, *semivirida, harmonia, calgariana, gallatini* and *meadi,* have all been placed with *nevadensis. Speyeria leto* is given full specific status (as it once was) and *letona* and *pugetensis* are assigned to it as subspecies.

I make no nomenclatorial changes in *zerene,* but I recommend that *pfoutsi* Gunder and *sordida* Wright be dropped into the synonymy, as is explained under *zerene.*

I see no reason for any changes in *Speyeria coronis* as yet but there is need for a thorough study of the relationships between *coronis* and *zerene.* Nor do I see any need for changes in *Speyeria hydaspe;* it is a fairly uniform and rather easily recognized species. Some of the subspecies presently recognized in *hydaspe* are of dubious worth as is also true in *coronis.*

The taxonomy of *Speyeria egleis* continues to be plagued with problems. It appears that we must continue to recognize *mcdunnoughi* Gunder even though I would prefer to see this name relegated to the synonymy. However, a valid, yellow-disced and geographically distinct population of *egleis* was discovered recently in the Toiyabe Range in Lander county, Nevada, by John Lane of Los Angeles. Altogether, I recognize over seventy subspecies among the seventeen species of *Speyeria* found in North America.

The interesting biological phenomenon of parallel variation may be observed in many areas such as Nevada where the trend in various species is to unusual pallidity. At present we can merely point out that these regional parallels exist, that their causes are obscure, and that they offer a good opportunity for research. These convergences appear to be especially marked in *Speyeria,* but they are observable in other butterfly genera as well.

The flight of all *Speyeria* is strong and rapid. In some instances males and females may not fly together but instead may usually keep to different areas. Despite their strong flight all *Speyeria* persistently visit many flowers such as thistle, Red Clover, Alfalfa, wild cherry, Golden Glow, Dwarf Woolly Sunflower, Western Penstemon, Butterflyweed, milkweed, dogbane and many others. In addition, many visit animal excrement and carrion, and in some areas (notably the Great Basin) mud puddles are visited by dozens of individuals.

Early Stages: The eggs are laid among the debris and dried stems of dead perennial violet or pansy leaves. The newly hatched larvae eat out the interior of the egg shell and proceed to hibernate immediately. They break diapause the following spring when the native violets put forth new growth. Both larval and pupal development at this stage is quite rapid. The adults emerge in early summer.

Distribution: Members of this genus are generally confined to cool, moist areas in which the host plant (violets) are found. Although distributed generally in the East and Midwest, they are more common in mountain ranges in the Great Basin, the Rocky Mountains and California. In the moister Pacific Northwest and British Columbia they are distributed more uniformly. Unlike *Euptoieta,* members of the genus *Speyeria* are seldom migrants and maintain a fairly close association with their host plants.

1. **Speyeria diana** (Cramer). Plate 19, flgure 3, ♂; figure 4, ♀. This handsome insect, the loveliest of the genus, is sexually dimorphic, as can be seen in the figures. Females begin to fly fully a month later than males, in association with *Battus philenor* in the southern Appalachians. During the month of August both sexes can be found at the flowers of thistles in this region. It has been suggested that female *diana* mimics *philenor,* which is also the supposed model for dark females of *Papilio glaucus* and for *P. troilus* and *Limenitis astyanax.* Expanse: 75 to 90 mm.

Early Stages: The larvae are black and spiny. They may be encountered along roadsides as they crawl about seeking a suitable site for pupation in late spring or early summer. The larval foodplant is violets.

Distribution: S. diana is a forest species inhabiting mountainous areas in the southern Appalachians and the Ozark Plateau. Its present distribution may be more restricted than formerly. Once widespread in Virginia, it is now rare. It is extinct from its type locality at Jamestown, Virginia, but may still occur in the nearby Dismal Swamp. It has grown scarce in Kentucky and West Virginia. it occurs widely in the Ozarks in Arkansas but may no longer occur on the Missouri side. It is still not uncommon in northern Georgia and extreme northwestern South Carolina at Caesar's Head.

The *cybele* group

2. **Speyeria cybele** (Fabricius). The *cybele* complex has the widest range of all nearctic *Speyeria* and inhabits much of the continent. It avoids the hotter areas such as the Gulf region and the arid Southwest but is common in most temperate localities across the United States and southern Canada.

Early Stages: These are well known and are carefully described in such popular works as Klots, Scudder and others. The larvae feed on violets.

Distribution: The species is found from the Atlantic coast to western Ontario and southward to northern Georgia, Kansas and northeastern Oklahoma. Nearly typical *cybele* occurs as far west as Great Falls, Montana.

(a) **cybele** (Fabricius). Plate 19, figure 1, ♂; figure 2, ♀. Although still widespread and relatively abundant, *cybele* is not the common butterfly it once was through much of its range. In eastern Kansas *cybele,* along with all *Papilio* species, has steadily decreased in numbers to the point where today it appears at a mere fraction of its former level. There is a considerable fluctuation in its numbers from one season to the next. It is a widespread and familiar species in the eastern states. Adults visit a number of wildflowers such as milkweed, Butterflyweed, Purple Cone Flower, thistles, Red Clover, and Joe Pye Weed. Males precede females in appearance by a full three weeks and it has been suggested that females do not oviposit until very late in their lives—possibly as late as early September. A north-south cline prevails in the East: adults are large and dark to the south, smaller and paler northward.

(b) **krautwurmi** (Holland). Plate 46, figure 4, ♀. *S. cybele krautwurmi* is a subspecies of imprecise status. It may be merely a color phase exhibited by females. In *krautwurmi* the ground is not fulvous but pale buff or ochreous on the outer parts of both wings. The basal portions are quite dark as the figure suggests. *S. cybele krautwurmi* was described from four females collected at Les Cheneaux, Mackinac county, Michigan. If we are to retain *krautwurmi* it is best to restrict its usage to specimens from the area of northern Ontario and northern Michigan. The name properly cannot be used for occasional females resembling *krautwurmi* which regularly turn up in normal *cybele* populations farther south.

(c) **carpenterii** (Edwards). Plate 31, figure 1, ♂; figure 2, ♀. Adults are smaller than eastern *cybele* but otherwise similar in pattern and hue. The subspecies inhabits cool, humid forest edges.

Distribution: It is found from Santa Fe Baldy in northern New Mexico northward into the La Plata and San Juan mountains in southern Colorado.

(d) **charlottii** (Barnes). Plate 43, figure 1, ♂; figure 2, ♀.   Adults of *charlottii* favor woodland edges. The females are quite shy and elusive.

Distribution: This subspecies occurs in western Colorado at elevations of 7500 to 8000 ft., seldom higher, in the Colorado River drainage. It intergrades with *carpenteri* in the Gunnison Valley. In Utah *charlotti* appears confined to the La Sal Mountains at similar elevations.

(e) **pseudocarpenteri** (Chermock & Chermock). Plate 43, figure 4, ♂; figure 5, ♀. Adults are small and pale. Males are pale fulvous above with reduced black maculation and slight basal suffusion; females are uniformly pale buff above with more basal suffusion above and below. The Turtle Mountains in North Dakota and Manitoba are an excellent area where intermediates between eastern *cybele* and *pseudocarpenteri* can be found.

Distribution: Typical *pseudocarpenteri* is abundant in the Riding Mountains of Manitoba and the Cypress Hills of Alberta. It also occurs in Saskatchewan.

3. **Speyeria leto** (Behr).   Three subspecies compose this beautiful western species, a favorite with collectors. This species is a member of the *cybele* group.

(a) **leto** (Behr). Plate 19, figure 5, ♂; figure 6, ♀.   Males are deep orange above with reduced black maculation and little basal suffusion. Females are strikingly different, characterized by a creamy white ground above with solid dark brown basal halves of both wings. The ground color is variable: some females are nearly milk white, others tend toward yellow. Both sexes are silvered beneath as shown. Adults fly rapidly and visit flowers as well as mud puddles. The sexes have contrasting flight habits; males fly in open sunshine while the females stay close to the protection of woods and visit only those flowers growing immediately adjacent. They fly in July and August. Expanse: 75 to 80 mm.

Early Stages: Eggs of *leto* are laid in August and hatch in two weeks. The tiny first instar larvae conceal themselves in dead violet or pansy stems in which they hibernate until the following spring. When feeding is resumed the caterpillars live in a semicommunal state with several larvae feeding upon a single stem. In the final instars they wander to more distant plants and feed in solitary fashion. At maturity the larvae wander still farther, often crawling many yards away from the host plant seeking a suitable site for pupation. The pupal state is brief, seldom exceeding two weeks.

Distribution: This subspecies extends from the Cascade ranges of California east to northern Nevada and northward from Oregon and British Columbia to northwestern Wyoming and Alberta. In the Cypress Hills of Alberta and in Blaine county, Montana, areas of intergradation exist between *leto* and its eastern relative, *cybele*. It may be common in one year and scarce or seemingly absent the next. In the California Sierras *leto* inhabits the lower slopes below 7000 ft. In southern Montana it inhabits canyons at 6000 to 6500 ft.

(b) **letona** dos Passos & Grey. Plate 43, figure 3, ♂. Adults of *letona* are only slightly distinct from *leto*. The essential difference is the somewhat reduced black maculation above in the outer marginal fourth of both wings in both sexes. Males are paler basally than in *leto;* females of *letona* are very similar to *leto*. Individuals are frequent in most low canyons of the Wasatch Range east of the Salt Lake Valley from early June (males only) into September. Females follow the males in appearance by two weeks but are generally more elusive and more difficult to locate than males.

(c) **pugetensis** (Chermock & Frechin). Plate 46, figure 1, ♂; figure 2, ♀. Adults of *pugetensis* are of striking beauty. The female is ivory yellow with heavy black maculation and a rich chestnut basal suffusion covering fully the inner halves of both wings. The disc beneath is deep reddish chestnut in both sexes with the silver spots reduced, compared with those of nominate *leto*. Expanse: 75 to 80 mm.

Distribution: This subspecies occurs in the coastal areas of Oregon, Washington and southern British Columbia.

4. **Speyeria aphrodite** (Fabricius). Adults are bright fulvous above and usually brightly silvered beneath. The disc is cinnamon brown to russet and it tends to either obliterate the outer buff band or suffuse it with reddish cinnamon scales (*alcestis*). Females tend to resemble *cybele* above but the ventral surface will readily distinguish the two. Not so easily distinguished are *aphrodite* and *atlantis,* particularly in areas where both species fly together. *S. aphrodite* lacks the outer dark marginal borders prevalent in *atlantis.* In *aphrodite* the fore wing veins of the male are narrowly lined with black while in *atlantis* they tend to be heavily suffused with dark scales. There is always a small black spot in the basal area between Cu_2 and 2A on the primaries above in *aphrodite,* while this spot is wanting in all populations of *cybele*. Females of *aphrodite* tend toward deep red basal shading ventrally on the primaries, and there is usually a rosy flushed area on the upperside of the secondaries just above the cell. While *aphrodite* is always silvered in the east, it may not invariably be so in certain sections of the west, notably in parts of Montana. In both the eastern and western areas pronounced and well documented north-south clines occur.

Early Stages: The egg is greenish, with seventeen to eighteen vertical ribs. The mature larva is velvety black with dorsal black spines that are yellow at the base. The chrysalis is reddish brown or gray, irregularly mottled and striped with black. The larva feeds at night upon violet leaves.

(a) **aphrodite** (Fabricius). Plate 20, figure 1, ♀; figure 2, ♂. Nominate *aphrodite* is eastern and may be recognized by the dark cinnamon brown disc usually only partially invading the outer band and seldom obliterating it as in *alcestis*. Males are paler above and below and not as deeply fulvous as *alcestis*. Females resemble *cybele* above but usually average smaller in size. Expanse: 55 to 65 mm.

Distribution: This subspecies ranges from central New York and southern Vermont southward to Pennsylvania, Maryland and Virginia (in the mountains). It intergrades with *winni* northward.

(b) **winni** (Gunder). Plate 20, figure 9, ♂; figure 10, ♂, underside; figure 11, ♀. Males are deep fulvous above and are heavily marked as shown. Females are paler above but, like the males, are heavily patterned with black. This subspecies is smaller than *a. aphrodite* but is otherwise similar in pattern and hue. Expanse: 50 to 55 mm.

Distribution: S. a. winni, the northernmost population of eastern *aphrodite,* is distributed from central New York and southern Vermont through Maine, Nova Scotia, the Maritime Provinces, New Brunswick and Quebec.

(c) **alcestis** (Edwards). Plate 20, figure 5, ♂; figure 6, ♀.   This midwestern subspecies occupies an area of similar latitude but west of nominate *aphrodite. S. aphrodite alcestis* averages somewhat larger, is deeper fulvous above and has lighter black maculation and less basal suffusion in the male. The secondaries beneath tend to be solid cinnamon red-brown because of the nearly complete suffusion of the buff band with cinnamon red scales. Expanse: 55 to 70 mm.

Distribution: The subspecies occurs from northern Ohio to southern Ontario, west to Minnesota and northern Iowa. It does not occur in Kansas despite published records to the contrary.

(d) **mayae** (Gunder). Plate 20, figure 12, ♀, underside; figure 13, ♀; Plate 32, figure 16, ♂. Adults are small, with reduced black maculation and somewhat paler ground color above, especially in the females; males tend to remain deeply fulvous above. In both sexes the disc is quite pale and the outer band is conspicuous and rarely invaded by any darker suffusion from the disc. Because of this, adults of *mayae* may be confused with *S. electa dennisi.* Intermediates between midwestern *alcestis* and *mayae* occur in the region where northwestern Minnesota, northern North Dakota and southern Manitoba adjoin. The name *manitoba* Chermock & Chermock is a synonym of *mayae.* Expanse 50 to 55 mm.

Distribution: This subspecies ranges from Manitoba and northern South Dakota westward to Alberta and eastern Montana, in the latter area intergrading with *ethne.*

(e) **ethne** Hemming. Plate 32, figure 1, ♂; figure 2, ♀; Plate 20, figure 3, ♀; figure 4, ♂ (**ethne**/*mayae* intergrade).   Don Eff of Boulder, Colorado, gave this account of his observations on *ethne* in *Colorado Butterflies:*

"Along with [*atlantis*] *hesperis, ethne* is probably our commonest *Speyeria.* Mainly it is a denizen of the grassy slopes and open ravines of the foothills. The males are especially common and easy to capture in the early morning hours as soon as the sun is up and warmed them sufficiently for flight. The females are a different story, and [are] never found in the places where the males are most common. Instead they prefer the flowers of the hillsides and the ridge tops of the foothills. Nearly to the exclusion of everything else they haunt the flowers of *Monarda.* The female is a striking insect, often surpassing in size the females of *edwardsi.*"

The southern Colorado population is larger and brighter as depicted. Individuals in the Bear Paw Mountains, Blaine county, Montana, may be unsilvered. Expanse: 55 to 75 mm.

Distribution: The subspecies *ethne* is found in the foothills of the Rocky Mountains, from southern Montana south to Utah and Colorado; it is absent from higher elevations.

(f) **byblis** (Barnes & Benjamin). Plate 31, figure 3, ♂; figure 4, ♀. The center of distribution of *byblis* appears to be near the Ditch Camp-McNary-Springerville area above the Mogollon Rim at 8700 ft. on the north fork of the White River in the White Mountains of Arizona. Adults appear after the summer rains in August and early September. In some areas *S. aphrodite byblis* is sympatric with *S. electa nausicaa* and *S. mormonia luski.* Adults of *byblis* favor marshy areas along the north fork of the White River in association with *S. nokomis nitocris* and both species may be encountered visiting thistles (*Cirsium*) and Golden Glow (*Rudbeckia*). It is also found about Hannagan Meadows in Greenlee county, Arizona. It may or may not be present in Oak Creek Canyon in Coconino county where it has been confused with *S. electa nausicaa* by some collectors. The insect is extremely rare in collections, but may be abundant enough in its proper locality. Expanse: 55 to 60 mm.

(g) **whitehousei** (Gunder). Plate 13, figure 12, ♂. Adults of *whitehousei* are large and heavily marked. The figure was drawn from a paratype. Much more exploration is necessary before the distribution of *whitehousei* can be learned. It is extremely rare in collections. Type locality: Jaffray, British Columbia.

(h) **columbia** (Hy. Edwards). Plate 20, figure 7, ♂; figure 8, ♀. The subspecies *columbia* occurs west of the Canadian Rockies in British Columbia. As the figures suggest, the adults closely approximate *ethne,* and the two subspecies intergrade in central Montana. *S. aphrodite columbia* represents the northwestern end of a weakly marked cline. Type locality: La Hache, British Columbia.

5. **Speyeria idalia** (Drury). Plate 44, figure 4, ♀. The Regal Fritillary needs no introduction. It has become rarer because of the destruction of the native prairie. In most areas it now is reduced to fragmented populations and has been largely extirpated from vast regions where it was once common, such as the Ohio Valley and the northern Midwest. Expanse: 75 to 90 mm.

Early Stages: The mature larvae are black with six rows of fleshy spines surmounted by black bristles. The spines on the two dorsal rows are white, tipped with black. The foodplant is *Viola pedata* (Bird's Foot Violet) and probably other *Viola* species. The larvae are nocturnal feeders.

Distribution: The species ranges from southern New England westward to southern North Dakota, southward to northern Virginia (perhaps to Georgia in the mountains), northeastern Oklahoma and eastern Colorado.

6. **Speyeria nokomis** (Edwards). Adults of *nokomis* are the largest of western *Speyeria.* Males are bright fulvous above; beneath, the ground color is golden ochreous with large, silvery spots. Females are cream above with heavy black maculation accompanied by much dark suffusion. Expanse: 75 to 80 mm.

Early Stages: Mature larvae are yellow-orange with numerous shining black spines tipped with coarse black setae. The host plants are presumed to be violets.

Distribution: The range of *nokomis* and its subspecies is much wider than was originally supposed; as more remote desert areas are explored by lepidopterists new colonies and range extensions undoubtedly will be discovered. Its present known distribution includes the southern and central Great Basin from eastern California to Colorado and southward into Mexico.

(a) **nokomis** (Edwards). Plate 45, figure 3, ♂; figure 4, ♀. The type locality of nominate *nokomis* was designated as Mount Sneffels, Ouray county, Colorado, at an elevation of 9000 ft. This may have to be reconsidered. I know of no locality in which *nokomis, apacheana* or *nitocris* inhabits an altitude this high. Moreover, collectors have repeatedly searched about Mount Sneffels without finding *nokomis* there. The type of *nokomis* may have been collected at Ojo Verde in east central Utah.

Distribution: Sedge bogs in the arid lowlands of the Colorado River system in Utah and western Colorado, and the Rio Grande drainage in central Colorado and New Mexico.

(b) **apacheana** (Skinner). Plate 44, figure 2, ♂; figure 3, ♀. Confined to spring fed marshes in desert areas, *apacheana* may be extremely abundant locally, frequenting the flowers of Dwarf Woolly Sunflower (*Eriophyllum lanatum*) by the dozens. Because of its limited, specialized environment this prized butterfly is subject to overcollecting. Lepidopterists should exercise restraint when encountering its colonies. It is extinct in the type locality, the vicinity of Camp Independence, California. Expanse: 75 to 80 mm.

Distribution: Colonies exist at Round Valley, Inyo county, and in the northern part of Owens Valley, California, and at Sweetwater, Lyon county, Nevada, ranging northward to the Carson Valley, Douglas county, Nevada.

(c) **coerulescens** (Holland). Plate 44, figure 1, ♀. Males of this Mexican subspecies resemble *nokomis apacheana* above but differ considerably beneath, being deep red-brown in the disc, in contrast with the yellowish buff disc of *apacheana* males. Females are bright blue above as depicted. A colony has been found at a spring-fed meadow at 7500 ft. near the summit of Sunnyside Canyon in the Huachuca Mountains, southern Arizona, the only known U.S. locality. The types were taken at the Head of the Rio Piedras in the Sierra Madre of Chihuahua, Mexico, between 7000 and 7300 ft. Adults fly in late August and September following the summer rains.

(d) **wenona** dos Passos & Grey. Plate 27, figure 13, ♂; figure 14, ♀. The sexes of this subspecies are colored alike. Its type locality is Cerro Potosí, Nuevo Leon, Mexico, at 12,000 ft. This Mexican subspecies is not found in the U.S. but was included here for completeness.

(e) **nitocris** (Edwards). Plate 22, figure 14, ♂; figure 15, ♀. Males are deeper fulvous above than in *apacheana* and with slightly heavier black markings above as well as a darker, redder, basal suffusion. They are darker ochreous to fulvous below with the silver spots reduced in size. The females have much darker orange basal suffusion beneath and a much darker disc tending towards indian red basally. The type locality of *nitocris* is the White Mountains of Arizona.

7. **Speyeria edwardsi** (Reakirt). Plate 19, figure 7, ♂; figure 8, ♀. Adults are bright fulvous above with characteristic light patterning and restricted basal suffusion. There

is a deep red or vermilion flush ventrally on the primaries. Both sexes are brilliantly silvered beneath. It is usually easily recognized but can be confused with *Speyeria coronis snyderi* in some areas of Wyoming. Adults visit the blossoms of alfalfa (*Medicago*), thistles (*Cirsium*), and Pink Spreading Dogbane (*Apocynum androsaemifolium*). Expanse: 60 to 75 mm.

Early Stages: The life history has been described by Edwards and other workers. The larvae feed upon violets and hibernate in the first instar to resume feeding in the following spring.

Distribution: This species is found principally in foothills and canyons of the east slope of the Front Range of the Rocky Mountains, extending eastward about twenty miles out into the high Plains (Colorado). It also occurs in western Nebraska in Scottsbluff National Monument area, in western South Dakota in the Black Hills, in the foothills of the Laramie Range in southern Wyoming and in the Big Horn Mountains, in the north central part of the state. It is abundant at low elevations (to 6500 ft.) in southern Montana on the eastern side of the Beartooth and Absarokee ranges, and also in both units of the Roosevelt National Parks in western North Dakota, and northward into Manitoba and Alberta. It reaches higher levels (8500 ft.) in Colorado than elsewhere in its distribution.

The *atlantis* group

This group contains two closely related species and twenty recognized subspecies.

8. **Speyeria atlantis** (Edwards). The *atlantis* group is a difficult taxonomic complex. As it exists today there appear to be two distinct species. The first, centered in the upper Appalachian region, we call typical *atlantis;* the second exists half a continent away in the central Rocky Mountains of Colorado at cool, forested elevations of from 8500 to nearly 10,000 ft. For the latter group we use the name *electa* (Edwards). The occurrence of pale *electa dennisi* and dark eastern *atlantis hollandi* together in the Riding Mountains has led to recognizing *electa* and *atlantis* as two species. Yet the richly silvered and dark bordered *electa* is, in many specimens, indistinguishable from upper Great Lakes and upper Appalachian *atlantis.* But if Colorado *electa* is really so similar to Appalachian and Upper Great Lakes *atlantis,* how did one get separated from the other? Or, put another way, what happened to the connecting populations that might have bridged the gap?

The assumed catastrophe that effectively separated them was probably the last midcontinental glaciation that extended as far south as northeastern Kansas and southern Ohio, pushing all insect life far southward. When the continent finally warmed and the glaciers retreated the midcontinent became too warm for either Rocky Mountain or Appalachian populations to rejoin. Today they behave as two distinct species, so altered has each become along the evolutionary post-glacial path each followed.

Early Stages: The larvae are velvety, dark brown with six rows of darker branching spines on both sides of the dorsum. Winter is spent as a first instar caterpillar. The pupal period is rather brief, averaging about twelve to fifteen days.

Distribution: S. *atlantis* occurs from Pennsylvania to the Maritime Provinces, westward to northern Minnesota and Manitoba.

(a) **atlantis** (Edwards). Plate 26, figure 1, ♂; figure 2, ♀. Adult males are fulvous above with rather heavy black patterning and heavy basal suffusion. Females are distinctly paler above but similarly patterned with heavy olive-green basal suffusion. There is a dark brown border above on both wings in both sexes. The disc is rich chestnut tending toward olivaceous in females and is strongly silvered. The heavily suffused venation in the males above distinguishes *atlantis* from S. *aphrodite.* Expanse: 55 to 60 mm.

Distribution: This subspecies occurs in Canada and the northern U.S. from the Maritime Provinces south to northern New England, New York and central Pennsylvania in the mountains and west to northern Minnesota, northern Michigan, and northern Wisconsin. There are old records from Highland county, Virginia.

(b) **hollandi** (Chermock & Chermock). Plate 26, figure 8, ♂. Adults of *hollandi* are similar to nominate eastern *atlantis* with these exceptions: males are smaller, more deeply fulvous above and with heavier basal suffusion; the silvery spots beneath are reduced in size; the outer band is narrow; females are darker but otherwise similar to those of *atlantis.* This is the western terminus of the *atlantis* cline in Canada. Expanse: 50 to 60 mm.

Distribution: Riding Mountains of Manitoba.

9. **Speyeria electa** (Edwards). As has been stated under *atlantis,* all western subspecies of this group are now placed under the species *electa* in which seventeen subspecies are recognized.

Early Stages: These have been thoroughly described for *lurana* only.

Distribution: Northern and central Rocky Mountains from Alberta and Manitoba southward to New Mexico and Arizona and westward to Oregon and Washington and the Sierras of California. In southerly latitudes *electa* is restricted to the higher and cooler elevations of mountains.

(a) **electa** (Edwards). Plate 26, figure 6, ♂; figure 7, ♀. Adults of nominate Colorado *electa* are admittedly indistinguishable from Appalachian *atlantis* and are not separable except by locality labels. It is presumed, however, that *electa* did not need to subspeciate for survival in southern Colorado as did other subspecies during post-glacial migrations and redistributions. For this reason *electa* has remained similar to original *atlantis.* The relationships among *electa, nikias,* and *hesperis* are not entirely clear at present. Expanse: 55 to 60 mm.

Distribution: This subspecies is found throughout the Rocky Mountains of Colorado at moderately high elevations (8500 ft. and up) and in the Laramie Range of southern Wyoming.

(b) **nikias** (Ehrmann). Plate 26, figure 13, ♂; figure 14, ♀. Adults are warm fulvous above; there is little or no dark brown on the outer margins and both sexes are brightly silvered below. This subspecies is sympatric with *hesperis* in many areas of Colorado and they are not believed to hybridize. The relationship is not under-stood at present and requires greater study. *S. electa nikias* is common on both the east and west slopes of the Rocky Mountains in Colorado but only at moderately high elevations (8000 to about 10,000 ft.). I have encountered males of *nikias* at sunflowers in open meadows and sun filled glades while females keep more closely to forest edges. Expanse: 55 to 60 mm.

Distribution: This subspecies is frequent in central and southern Colorado and in northern New Mexico.

(c) **hesperis** (Edwards). Plate 26, figure 11, ♀; figure 12, ♂. Adults are typically similar to *atlantis* above but are unsilvered below; the disc is brick red. This is the commonest Rocky Mountain form of *electa* and the most abundant *Speyeria* in Colorado.

Distribution: It is most prevalent in the Front and Park ranges east of the Conti-nental Divide; it also occurs in the Laramie Range of southern Wyoming. In Colo-rado *hesperis* is an inhabitant of high, cool forests at 8000 to about 10,000 ft.

(d) **dorothea** Moeck. Plate 26, figure 3, ♂; Plate 46, figure 3, ♀. Adults are fiery red-orange above with heavy veining and deep fuscous shading basally. The disc is brick red to purplish in females studded with rich silvery spots. Males are paler beneath. Adults of *dorothea* are large, females a third larger than the males and nearly equal to female *S. cybele charlottii*. Expanse: 55 to 70 mm.

Distribution: Confined to the Sandia and Manzano mountains, New Mexico.

(e) **nausicaa** (Edwards). Plate 32, figure 3, ♂; figure 4, ♀. Adults resemble the preceding both in coloration and size but there is usually some white overscaling discally on the underside of *nausicaa*. Also the disc is paler in *nausicaa* with somewhat greater dark suffusion in the outer limbal zone. Adults settle with wings horizontal against the ground in late afternoon sunshine along dirt roads in the White Moun-tains.

Distribution: The Arizona Silverspot is common generally in central and eastern Arizona above the Mogollon Rim at elevations above 8500 ft. It is frequent in the White Mountains in July.

(f) **greyi** Moeck. Plate 27, figure 1, ♂; figure 2, ♀. Adults are pale fulvous above tending toward ochreous, especially in the females. This subspecies represents the palest development of *electa* in the Great Basin. Adults of *greyi* are not as heavily marked as either *chitone* or *wasatchia* though individuals of *greyi* occasionally approach the latter. However, *greyi* is isolated from *wasatchia* by the Great Salt Lake desert. It appears that *greyi* is the westerly end of the Great Basin cline of *electa*. It is sympatric with *S. zerene cynna*. This subspecies of *electa* is named for L. P. Grey of Lincoln, Maine. Expanse: 50 to 55 mm.

Distribution: Moeck discovered this butterfly at altitudes of between 7500 and 10,000 ft. in the East Humboldt Range, near Wells, Elko county, Nevada.

(g) **wasatchia** dos Passos & Grey. Plate 27, figure 3, ♂; figure 4, ♀. Adults are larger than in *greyi* but are similar. They may be silvered or unsilvered and in this respect resemble *tetonia*.

Distribution: It inhabits elevations above 7500 ft. in the Wasatch and Uinta ranges in northern Utah.

(h) **chitone** (Edwards). Plate 26, figure 4, ♂; figure 5, ♀. Adults are larger than in *wasatchia* and have heavier black patterning above. There is little or no darkening in the outer marginal interspaces. Many examples of *chitone* are reportedly unsilvered though the figured examples are silvered, which conforms to the type. All specimens I have seen from the La Sal and Abajo mountains are also silvered in both sexes. Some examples of *wasatchia* may be confused with *egleis utahensis* but locality of capture should decide the point because *chitone* is confined to southern Utah.

Distribution: The type locality of *chitone* is the Cedar Breaks National Monument in Iron county, Utah. It is also abundant in both the La Sal and Abajo ranges in Utah.

(i) **shellbachi** Garth. Plate 31, figure 10, ♂. Adults are bright fulvous above with the limbal spot band greatly enlarged, forming a more or less complete heavy disjunct bar. They are dark basally. This subspecies somewhat resembles *chitone* and apparently is always silvered below. Its relationship with *chitone* and other members of the *electa* complex is still unclear. Expanse: about 55 mm.

Distribution: The type locality of *schellbachi* is the Grand Canyon National Park, Arizona.

(j) **tetonia** dos Passos & Grey. Plate 26, figure 9, ♂; figure 10, ♀. Adults are pale fulvous to ochreous above and not heavily marked, with little basal suffusion. Rarely is there any darkening of the outer borders. Adults are rather small and unsilvered beneath save for the outer marginal row of spots on the secondaries which may or may not be silvered. This subspecies somewhat resembles *Speyeria egleis* but may be differentiated by the ruddier disc in *tetonia* and its general brightness. The outer buff band in *tetonia* is broad and bright while in *egleis* it is narrower, more of a dead tan and more strongly suffused inwardly with brown scaling. Both *tetonia* and *egleis* fly together in many sections of Teton National Park and are sometimes a source of confusion, but in long series both appear quite different. Adults appear in early July. Expanse: 45 to 50 mm.

Distribution: The type locality is Jackson Lake, Teton National Park, Wyoming.

(k) **viola** dos Passos & Grey. Plate 27, figure 5, ♂; figure 6, ♀. Adults are rather small and slightly more heavily patterned above than *tetonia,* but are entirely unsilvered below. This butterfly is somewhat similar to the Pacific subregion *irene.* *S. electa viola* is a point on the cline from *tetonia* (Wyoming) to *dodgei* (Oregon) via the Snake River System. Expanse: 50 mm.

Distribution: Idaho and eastern Oregon. Type locality: Sawtooth Mountains.

(l) **dodgei** (Gunder). Plate 26, figure 15, ♂. Adults are deeply fulvous above; the black markings are heavy but there is only moderate basal suffusion. It is unsilvered below. The dark margins, characteristic of more easterly *atlantis,* appear completely lost in the populations of the Pacific region subspecies of *electa.* The disc is brick red with the outer band pink rather than buff, and these traits combine to give *dodgei* a look quite remote from the larger subspecies of *electa.* This and the next subspecies are atypical fringe populations. The butterfly was named for E. A. Dodge, of Santa Cruz, California.

Distribution: This subspecies is general in the Cascade Ranges of Oregon and southern Washington, eastward into Idaho.

(m) **irene** (Boisduval). Plate 27, figure 9, ♂; figure 10, ♀. Adults are not readily separable from *dodgei*. The butterfly also confounds the collector by its resemblance to sympatric *S. zerene*. It blends with *dodgei* northward.

Distribution: This subspecies occurs in the northern Sierras of California, south in restricted colonies to Yosemite.

(n) **beani** (Barnes & Benjamin). Plate 27, figure 7, ♂; figure 8, ♀. Adults are variable in size, usually smaller than in typical *atlantis* but generally a trifle larger than in either *tetonia* or *hutchinsi*. This subspecies is more heavily patterned above and has a darker disc below than in either *hutchinsi*, with which it blends to the south, or *helena* to the east. Solid dark borders, especially in females, are quite common in *beani*. It does not appear to intergrade in southern Washington with Oregon *dodgei* but it does blend with *hutchinsi* markedly in northwestern Montana (Glacier National Park). The disc is variable. In extreme northern Washington and in British Columbia it tends to be dark brick red with much encroachment into the outer band, ranging up to nearly solid suffusion in some individuals. Usually *beani* is silvered but some individuals are entirely or partially unsilvered. Expanse: 50 to 55 mm.

Distribution: The subspecies occurs in northern Washington, extreme northern Idaho, extreme northwestern Montana, British Columbia and the mountains of western Alberta. Type locality: Banff, Alberta.

(o) **helena** dos Passos & Grey. Plate 27, figure 11, ♂; figure 12, ♀. It is by no means clear whether *helena* and the next subspecies, *dennisi*, are really related to *electa beani*. We assume that they are but this may be difficult to prove. One disturbing, unresolved difference in *helena* and *dennisi* facies, as contrasted with that of western *electa* populations, is that adults of both *helena* and *dennisi* consistently lack the small black spot located basally between veins Cu_2 and 2A on the primaries above. This black spot is present on all other *atlantis* and *electa* populations but is consistently *absent* in all *S. cybele* populations. It now becomes necessary to go into the field and try to locate any populations of either *helena* or *dennisi* that might reveal possible intergrades to Manitoba populations of *cybele*. Here is an excellent opportunity for Canadian lepidopterists. Expanse: 40 to 45 mm.

Distribution: This prairie subspecies is found in Alberta on the dry side of the Rockies and in Saskatchewan. Type locality: Red Deer, Alberta.

(p) **dennisi** (Gunder). Plate 24, figure 6, ♂, underside; figure 7, ♂; figure 9, ♀; figure 10, ♀, underside. Adults are quite small, about 40 mm in expanse, the smallest of all *electa* subspecies. It is also the palest: the black patterning is greatly reduced and virtually wanting in many examples. The band is very wide and pale with a greatly reduced disc. There is no real distinction between *helena* and *dennisi* except that the latter concludes a cline toward pallidity in the Riding Mountains in Manitoba. Both *helena* and *dennisi* are silvered.

Distribution: *S. electa dennisi* occurs in Manitoba. Adults appear from late June into July. Type locality: Beulah, Manitoba.

(q) **lurana** dos Passos & Grey. Plate 31, figure 11, ♂; figure 12, ♀; figure 13, ♀ ("*atlantis* type"). Adults resemble *hesperis,* from which they have probably evolved. Unsilvered examples predominate but an occasional individual is silvered or partially so. In the Black Hills there is apparently a parallel to the situation in the Riding Mountains of Manitoba. In certain very moist areas of the Black Hills *atlantis*-like butterflies (Plate 31, figure 13) fly with *lurana,* but maintain their identity.

Distribution: This subspecies occurs in the Black Hills, South Dakota.

(r) **hutchinsi** (Gunder). Plate 31, figure 6, ♂ (unsilvered); figure 7, ♀ (unsilvered); figure 8, ♀ (silvered); figure 9, ♂ (silvered). *Speyeria electa hutchinsi* is so variable and intergrades so much with other subspecies throughout its range that the name is of questionable value. Because of its variability it was thought desirable to illustrate the extremes that may be encountered. Adults may be silvered or unsilvered with disc color variable from dark to light. Maculation above may be heavy or light. All these variants may occupy the same area. However, there is a trend toward pallidity eastward in Montana in drier environments and a deeper coloration in moister environments northwestward. Many examples in southern Montana are not distinguishable from British Columbia and Alberta *beani.* The big transition, where *tetonia* diverges distinctly to the northwest, is in Yellowstone National Park.

Distribution: This subspecies occurs in southern and central Montana and western North Dakota. It blends northward (Turtle Mountains, North Dakota) toward *dennisi* and in southern Alberta toward *beani.* This concludes the *atlantis* group.

10. **Speyeria coronis** (Behr). There are six recognized subspecies of *coronis,* most of which are isolated populations separated from each other by deserts. Very likely at one time their populations were joined. Today *coronis* is confined largely to cool, moist mountains, and the isolation results in intensive subspeciation as is true of many western *Speyeria.* Females of *coronis* often fly widely across open desert country during late summer and may be encountered many miles from existing colonies. Such wandering individuals may be seeking ovipositional sites.

Early Stages: The larvae of *S. coronis semiramis* have been beautifully rendered in watercolors by Dammers. They closely resemble those of *callippe comstocki* except that all spines are black with orange bristles.

Distribution: Present distributions suggest that climatic changes have greatly altered *coronis* and have forced many isolated populations into restricted areas. These areas are usually foothills, canyons or mountain slopes but at no place does any population of *coronis* appear to reach very lofty elevations. The diversity and discontinuity of the various *coronis* populations are in need of further study.

(a) **coronis** (Behr). Plate 23, figure 3, ♂; figure 5, ♀. *S. coronis* is palest to the south and darkest to the north, an apparent clinal relation. The subspecies does not intergrade to the south with either *hennei* or *semiramis.* The relationship of *coronis* with other Californian and Great Basin subspecies is presently under study. Warm, sunny chaparral-covered hills are favored places for *coronis.* It is sympatric with both *adiaste* and *callippe* in many areas. Expanse: 55 to 60 mm.

Distribution: Nominate *coronis* inhabits the coast ranges from central California,

Sonoma and Napa counties, south to the southern part of San Luis Obispo county. Adult males commence to fly in late May; females commence two weeks later and continue in flight until late August.

(b) **hennei** (Gunder). Plate 23, figure 9, ♀; figure 15, ♂. Adults of this subspecies differ from nominate *coronis* by a paler ground color above, finer black maculation and greatly reduced basal suffusion. There is generally more ochreous above and below. *S. coronis hennei* is silvered beneath as are all *coronis*.

Distribution: The type locality is Mount Pinos in Frazier Mountain Park at 7700 ft., Ventura county, California. Still paler versions of *hennei* inhabit the Tehachapi and Greenhorn mountains in Kern county, California.

(c) **semiramis** (Edwards). Plate 23, figure 13, ♂; figure 14, ♀. Adults are pale fulvous above with fine black maculation especially in the males. This subspecies is the palest of all California *Speyeria* except *S. adiaste atossa*.

Distribution: The butterfly is quite abundant in the San Gabriel, San Jacinto and San Bernardino mountains of southern California, and extends southward along the coastal ranges into San Diego county. Adults fly in July and August.

(d) **simaetha** dos Passos & Grey. Plate 42, figure 4, ♂; figure 5, ♀. This weakly differentiated subspecies of *coronis* has the appearance of a rather small, pale *snyderi*. The disc in *simaetha* is consistently paler, uniform olivaceous buff, more ochreous in males. The submesial band is ochreous as are the apices. Adults are on the wing in early June into July. Expanse: 55 to 60 mm.

Distribution: The subspecies *simaetha* inhabits the Cascade ranges of Oregon and Washington.

(e) **snyderi** (Skinner). Plate 45, figure 1, ♂; figure 2, ♀; Plate 23, figure 11, ♂; figure 12, ♀. This represents the population of *coronis* as it occurs in most of the Great Basin. Typical *snyderi* has a green disc below but in some sections of its range (notably northern Arizona and Wyoming) *snyderi* may have a brown disc. In Wyoming and southern Montana females are quite red basally on the underside of the primaries, the reddest of all *coronis*. Adults fly in association with *S. zerene garretti* in some places but the latter is consistently smaller and the disc is pale brown and not greenish. Long series are helpful in sorting out *coronis snyderi* from *zerene garretti*. Wyoming *snyderi* (Plate 23, figures 11 and 12) resembles Colorado *halcyone*. Adult *snyderi* visit alfalfa and thistle blooms in canyons and foothills and low sagebrush elevations up to 7800 ft. but are absent at higher levels. Widely separated populations suggest that they may once have been joined in a wider distribution than the insect now enjoys. It is the commonest *Speyeria* at low elevations and the earliest to appear. Expanse: 60 to 70 mm.

Distribution: Idaho: Sawtooth, Caribou and Lemhi ranges; Utah: Wasatch and Uinta ranges; Arizona: Apache and Coconino counties; Wyoming: Wind River and Big Horn ranges; Montana: Absaroka and Beartooth ranges. It also occurs in central and northern Nevada.

(f) **halcyone** (Edwards). Plate 42, figure 2, ♂; figure 3, ♀. Adults are large, with a reddish brown disc and are richly silvered. This is the largest of all *coronis* subspecies, with an expanse of 60 to 75 mm; females may average nearly the size of female *aphrodite ethne* (in Colorado) or female *edwardsii*. Adults frequent wild cherry blossoms, thistles and *Medicago*. This is a foothills butterfly which does not deeply invade the mountains. A population of *coronis* in the Black Hills of South Dakota appears to be intermediate between Colorado *halcyone* and northern Wyoming *snyderi*.

Distribution: This subspecies occurs east of the Continental Divide in Colorado and in the Laramie Mountains of southeastern Wyoming. Curiously there appear to be no records to date of *halcyone* on the west slope of the Rocky Mountains in Colorado.

11. **Speyeria zerene** (Boisduval). *Present Concept:* The relationship of *zerene* to other species of *Speyeria*, especially *coronis* has long been confused. There is also wide variability within *zerene* which presents itself in arid regions with marked pallidity. The humidity factor appears to be an especially important one in *zerene*, perhaps greater in this species than in any other *Speyeria*. Parallel variation in the Great Basin is most marked in *zerene*, considerably so in *egleis* and *nevadensis*, somewhat in *electa*, *coronis* and *eurynome*, but hardly at all in *leto*. The cool damp influence of the Pacific Coast results in *zerene* populations in this area being characterized by heavier maculation and greater basal suffusion. The same characteristics prevail to a slightly lesser degree in the cooler and more moist environments in the higher elevations of the Rocky Mountains. Like all other *Speyeria*, adults of *zerene* favor open, sunny glades. The adults of both sexes avidly visit many wild flowers such as *Cirsium*, *Rudbeckia* and *Monarda*. In favorable locations dozens of the adults may be taken in a rather brief period of time visiting such flowers. As in other species of *Speyeria* long series are important in *zerene* and no taxonomic decision can be deemed trustworthy when based upon a single specimen.

Early Stages: These are presently being worked out by David McCorkle of Monmouth, Oregon.

(a) **zerene** (Boisduval). Plate 21, figure 1, ♂; figure 2, ♀.   Males are bright fulvous above and females are paler. Both sexes are unsilvered beneath and are heavily lavender on the apices. The disc is lavender and the outer band is not buff but pale lavender. Typical *zerene* blends with *conchyliatus* to the north and *malcolmi* to the east. Expanse 55 to 60 mm.

Distribution: Nominate *zerene* occurs between 7000 to 8000 feet in the California Sierras. The butterfly is rather widespread but is not abundant anywhere.

(b) **conchyliatus** (J. A. Comstock). Plate 25, figure 14, ♂; figure 15, ♀.   Adults are deeper fulvous above than in nominate *zerene*. The black maculation is somewhat heavier, with heavy basal suffusion, and the spots on the underside are silvered. Ventrally the disc is chestnut or dark maroon; the band is lavender (as in *zerene zerene*). There is a wide blend zone between *conchyliatus* and *zerene* at the northern terminus of the California Sierras. It is *conchyliatus* rather than typical *zerene* that blends so perfectly with *cynna* in the Warner Mountains. Expanse: 55 to 65 mm.

Distribution: Northern California and southern Oregon.

(c) **gloriosa** Moeck. Plate 25, figure 13, ♂; Plate 42, figure 1, ♀.   Moeck discovered this beautiful population of *zerene* while collecting in the Illinois River Valley in Josephine county, Oregon. It is the connecting link between *conchyliatus* to the south and *bremnerii* to the north. The subspecies *gloriosa* combines the more reddish disc and buff outer band of *bremneri* with the large size and heavy maculation of *conchyliatus.* Expanse: 55 to 70 mm.

Distribution: This subspecies occurs in Josephine county, Oregon, intergrading with *conchyliatus* southward.

(d) **malcolmi** (J. A. Comstock). Plate 21, figure 3, ♂; figure 4, ♀. Adults are bright ochreous above and very red basally below on the primaries of the female. Adults may be silvered or unsilvered beneath. The disc is rather pale with much ochreous suffusion; the outer buff band is bright and distinct. Adults appear from late June at lower elevations to late August at higher levels. They visit blooms of Western Pennyroyal, Western Pink Spreading Dogbane, and Western Blue Penstemon. *S. z. malcolmi* blends with Sierran nominate *zerene* as well as with Nevada *cynna.*

Distribution: S. zerene malcolmi is common in the Pine Nuts Mountains and the Carson Ranges in Nevada and in the region about Virginia City. Type locality: Mammoth Lakes in Mono county, California.

(e) **carolae** dos Passos & Grey. Plate 23, figure 1, ♂; figure 2, ♀; figure 4, ♀, underside. Adults are bright fulvous above, lightly marked and with light basal suffusion. The disc is rather pale but shades gradually outward into the buff band. Females are considerably larger than males. The status of *carolae* is not settled. It was originally placed in *coronis* by dos Passos & Grey in their 1947 catalogue, but was later placed by Grey in *zerene.* It does not intergrade to any known population of either *zerene* or *coronis,* but appears to be closer to *zerene malcolmi* than anything else. Carole's Silverspot was named after Miss Carole Lombard, American film actress, who died in a plane crash in 1942 on the slopes of Charleston Peak west of Las Vegas. Expanse: 55 to 60 mm.

Distribution: Upper slopes of Charleston Peak between 6000 to 7800 ft., Clark county, Nevada. Adults fly in late June and July; they are very abundant up Kyle Canyon just above the Charleston Park campgrounds.

(f) **hippolyta** (Edwards). Plate 22, figure 9, ♂; figure 10, ♂, underside; figure 11, ♀; figure 12, ♀, underside. Adults of this subspecies appear as miniature *bremneri,* with the same color and maculation. Its status is not entirely clear. While primarily an inhabitant of the coast side of the Oregon Coast Ranges, examples have been taken inland at Diamond Lake in Douglas county and in several localities inland along the Columbia River. Recently a series taken in the northeastern portion of the Olympic Peninsula, Clallum county, Washington, is apparently transitional between *bremneri* and *hippolyta.* Expanse: 40 to 45 mm.

(g) **behrensi** (Edwards). Plate 21, figure 13, ♂; figure 14, ♀. Adults are slightly paler above than in *conchyliatus* but resemble that subspecies in many respects, and blend with it on the east side of the northern California Coast Ranges. Heavy basal suffusion is evident in a lengthy series of *behrensi.* This subspecies is nearly always silvered. Expanse: 55 to 60 mm.

Distribution: Restricted to the Pacific side of the Coast Ranges, *behrensi* is found from the vicinity of Point Arena, Trinity county, to Cape Mendocino, Mendocino county, California.

(h) **myrtleae** dos Passos & Grey. Plate 21, figure 11, ♂; figure 12, ♀. Adults are bright fulvous above with heavy greenish basal suffusion. They are characterized by extraordinary basal, tornal and body pubescence, more pronounced than in any other western U.S. *Speyeria.* The disc is reddish brown overscaled by yellowish green. The band is bright yellow in contrast with the dull olive band in *behrensi.* Both sexes are very red basally beneath on the primaries, the reddest of all *zerene,* and brightly silvered beneath. The butterfly was named after Mrs. Myrtle Mack of Livermore, California. Adults fly rapidly among the beach dunes appearing briefly during fleeting moments of sunshine between nearly perpetual banks of fog which sweep across the Point Reyes Peninsula all summer long. On a rare sunny day I presume it would be possible to take *myrtleae* in numbers. It intergrades northward with *behrensi* at Stewarts Point.

Distribution: This subspecies is largely restricted to Point Reyes Peninsula just north of San Francisco. Type locality: coastal side of San Mateo county, California, but apparently extirpated by truck gardens.

(i) **bremnerii** (Edwards). Plate 22, figure 5, ♂; figure 6, ♀; Plate 31, figure 5, ♂ ("sordida"). Adults are bright fulvous above and brightly silvered below. The distinction of this subspecies is in the heaviness of the black medial spots above. These spots usually coalesce to form an irregular bent bar. There is deep basal suffusion. The ground color in females is pale but the heaviness of the medial spots gives them an overall dark appearance. Beneath, the disc is richly shaded in deep maroon or rusty red with a distinct, bright outer buff band. The author of *sordida,* W. G. Wright, neglected to put either a locality or a date of capture beneath his specimen, but in his original description he implied Puget Sound, Washington. Furthermore the specimen is so faded and worn that it is nearly impossible to ascertain if it is silvered or unsilvered beneath. It appears, from an examination of Wright's type, that *sordida* is an individual variant within the normal population of *bremneri.* Individual populations vary much in size from one area to another; the figured examples are about average. Expanse: 55 to 60 mm.

Distribution: Subspecies *bremnerii* occurs in coastal British Columbia, Washington and Oregon. It blends toward *garretti* east of the Cascades.

(j) **picta** (McDunnough). Plate 22, figure 7, ♂; figure 8, ♀. This subspecies is a weakly marked intermediate between coastal *bremnerii* and interior *garretti.* The name is of questionable worth. Adults of *picta* are slightly paler above than *bremnerii,* with less heavy black maculation and a paler disc below, but otherwise similar.

(k) **garretti** (Gunder). Plate 25, figure 11, ♂; figure 12, ♀. Adults are fulvous above as in *bremnerii* but with reduced black maculation. The disc is much paler below. It is a variable subspecies and many *bremnerii*-like individuals turn up among *garretti.* Essentially *garretti* is the dry population from the interior of the northwest. It blends southward in Idaho and western Wyoming with *platina.* It is common in Montana and in some localities I have seen as many as thirty individuals gathered about a moist spot. Adults visit *Monarda,* Pink Spreading Dogbane (*Apocynum*) and Blue Penstemon. Expanse: 55 to 60 mm.

Distribution: This subspecies occurs east of the Cascades in southern British Columbia, eastern Washington, northeastern Oregon, Idaho, Montana and southern Alberta.

(l) **sinope** dos Passos & Grey. Plate 21, figure 5, ♂; figure 9, ♀; figure 10, underside, ♀. Adults of *sinope* show a close affinity to both *garretti* and *platina.* However, *sinope* is a trifle smaller than *platina* and the disc, especially in the male, has a slight greenish cast in Colorado examples. Those of the Laramie Range in southern Wyoming are even more greenish. J. D. Eff writes about the adult habits of *sinope:* "It seems to inhabit the more wooded areas, especially the timbered slopes of the passes. The males frequent the edges of openings, roads, etc., but the females are commonly taken on tall *Senecio* found growing in the wet, marshy, shaded bottoms of ravines." Expanse: 55 mm.

Distribution: This subspecies is found in northwestern Colorado and the Laramie Mountains of southeastern Wyoming.

(m) **platina** (Skinner). Plate 22, figure 1, ♂; figure 2, ♀. Adults of *platina* resemble closely both *garretti* and *sinope.* The only consistent difference is a tendency to paleness in *platina,* but this is not particularly marked. *S. zerene sinope* is an apparent isolate, while *platina* is a southerly Wasatch end of a cline from *garretti.* As in *sinope,* many *garretti*-like individuals turn up in Wasatch *platina.* Along the Alpine Loop Road in the Wasatch Mountains I have taken *platina* visiting thistles along roadsides. The adults also favor moist, open meadows at cool, forested levels and visit the flowers of Golden Glow (*Rudbeckia laciniata*).

Distribution: This subspecies occurs at elevations above 7500 ft. in the Wasatch, Uinta and the Stansbury ranges in northern and central Utah, and in southern Idaho.

(n) **pfoutsi** (Gunder). Plate 21, figure 6, ♂; figure 7, ♂, underside; figure 8, ♀, underside; figure 15, ♀. This low elevation subspecies inhabits the deserts, foothills and canyons of the Wasatch Range. It is bright ochreous rather than fulvous. Between 6500 and 7500 ft. this subspecies intergrades with the higher elevation *platina.* Both subspecies are strongly attracted to mints which grow in profusion along the trails in Bear Canyon on the eastern slope of Mount Nebo.

Distribution: S. z. pfoutsi is found in arid foothills and canyons up to 6500 ft. in the Wasatch Mountains in Utah.

(o) **cynna** dos Passos & Grey. Plate 22, figure 3, ♂; figure 4, ♀. Adults are bright ochreous above and below, with no darkening of the disc and little basal suffusion. The pattern above is light with bright silvering below. This extremely well developed phenotype is unlike any other *zerene.* Expanse 55 to 60 mm.

At Patterson Meadows in the Warner Mountains in Modoc county, California, near the Nevada line, Moeck found a locality where the desert mountains *cynna* and Sierran *zerene* meet. He found there all sorts of gradations from typical *zerene* and *conchyliatus* to nearly pure *cynna.* In the next county to the east (Washoe county, Nevada) he encountered on an unnamed ridge certain individuals of *cynna* in which a basal flush of orange occurred ventrally on the primaries, indicating slight influence of the more westerly *zerene.*

Distribution: S. zerene cynna is a resident of the Snake River Plateau. It occurs in Nevada, western Utah and in the Steens Mountains in Harney county, Oregon.

(p) **gunderi** Comstock. Plate 23, figure 6, ♂; figure 8, ♂ (underside); figure 7, ♀. New Combination. The type locality of this butterfly is at the Davis Creek Ranger Station in the Warner Mountains above Alturas in Modoc county, California. In early August, 1972, students who collected among the large *Speyeria* populations around Blue Lake (which is south of the type locality, in the same county) observed a tremendous variation of the species *zerene*. This is thought to be resultant from a very recent contact in the tension zone between yellow Great Basin and red Pacific subspecies. This population produces many intermediates and extremes, among which are large greenish individuals resembling a pallid *coronis,* the species under which *gunderi* customarily has been placed. But at Blue Lake the *coronis* which flew in abundance a month earlier were producing no abnormal or pallid forms. Many further studies are needed, here and in other localities, but the field data noted above are highly suggestive of *gunderi* being tied to the *zerene* introgression. Furthermore, there seems to be no doubt among students that the holotype of *gunderi* actually is a specimen of *zerene*.

This concludes our presentation of *Speyeria zerene.*

The *nevadensis* group

Present Concept: Speyeria nevadensis, once considered a distinct species, was combined with *Speyeria callippe* by more recent authors. However, as large series of *nevadensis* became better known it became apparent that all Great Basin and Rocky Mountain populations were essentially homologous. They are all green or olive-green disced and invariably silvered. In contrast *Speyeria callippe* is almost uniformly brown disced and often unsilvered. The blend zone between the two entities is located in the Sierra Nevada ranges above Lake Tahoe in northern California. Both *nevadensis* and *callippe* might better be considered entities rather than full species since neither fits our rigidly formal species-subspecies concept but something more fluid in between these views. For the present time we had best regard both *callippe* and *nevadensis* as part of the *nevadensis* group until the relationship between the two entities is better understood. Taxonomy is and always must be tentative and subject to the judgements of the future.

12. **Speyeria nevadensis** (Edwards). The ground color of the adults generally is ochreous above rather than fulvous. All populations of this complex are brightly silvered and the disc on the ventral surfaces and the apices are greenish or olive. Although the members of this complex have been treated as part of the species *callippe* by some authors I believe that *nevadensis* may be a distinct species. It will take an intensive study of the early stages to clearly determine this.

Early Stages: These are presently being worked out by David L. Bauer.

Distribution: This species ranges from Nevada to British Columbia east of the Cascades, eastward to the prairies in Alberta and Saskatchewan, southward through western North Dakota, Wyoming, central Colorado and central Utah. This species favors low, sagebrush levels but invades the canyons and foothills of mountains below 8000 ft.

(a) **nevadensis** (Edwards). Plate 28, figure 9,♂; figure 10,♀. A bright, golden green disc beneath with intense silvering characterizes *nevadensis*. It is quite constant throughout most of its range. In eastern Nevada *nevadensis* blends toward *harmonia*. There is reputed to be a narrow zone of contact with *callippe laura* in Washoe county, Nevada, as mentioned under *laura*. Expanse: 50 to 55 mm.

Distribution: Nominate *nevadensis* occurs in western Nevada up to elevations of 10,000 ft. It is common at 7500 ft. on McClellan Peak, Storey county, Nevada, during late June and early July. It is also common at the Mammoth Lakes in Mono county, California. Type locality: Virginia City, Nevada.

(b) **harmonia** dos Passos & Grey. Plate 29, figure 1, ♂; figure 2, ♀. Adults are larger than nominate *nevadensis* but intergrade widely with that subspecies in eastern Nevada. It is green-disced and silvered. It is abundant in the Stansbury, Uinta and Wasatch mountains of Utah where adults frequent mints in association with *S. zerene pfoutsi* and *platina*. Southeastern Oregon, southern Idaho, northeastern Nevada and northern Utah comprise the range of *harmonia*. Type locality: Mount Wheeler, White Pine county, Nevada, in the Snake Range near the Utah boundary. Expanse: 50 to 60 mm.

(c) **calgariana** (McDunnough). Plate 29, figure 12, ♂; figure 13, ♀. Adults are pale ochreous (never fulvous) above; the black maculation is fine, with slight basal suffusion. The disc is pale, dull greenish and is never so bright as in *gallatini* with which it intergrades in northern Montana. It was named after the city of Calgary, Alberta, type locality of the subspecies. This low elevation butterfly is usually associated with dry sagebrush country. It can be confused with *egleis albrighti* in Montana, but *calgariana* has less basal suffusion above, is generally larger and has finer markings on the veins, especially on females. Other differences are mentioned under *albrighti*. Expanse: 50 to 55 mm.

Distribution: This subspecies occurs in the eastern foothills of the Canadian Rockies in Alberta, and in the plains eastward into Saskatchewan, southward into central and northern Montana and eastward into North Dakota (Turtle Mountains and both units of the Roosevelt National Memorial Parks). Adults fly from early July to August.

(d) **gallatini** (McDunnough). Plate 28, figure 3, ♂; figure 4, ♀. This subspecies is named for the Gallatin Range in southern Montana. Adults of *gallatini* are highly silvered beneath, and the green disc color is more intensely saturated than in either *calgariana* or *harmonia*, with which it blends respectively north and south. Its close association with sagebrush has led some workers to suspect this plant as a possible larval host for the subspecies: an hypothesis unverified as yet.

Distribution: This subspecies is found in northwestern Wyoming and southwestern Montana. Type locality: Elkhorn Ranch, Gallatin Canyon, Montana.

(e) **semivirida** (McDunnough). Plate 28, figure 5, ♀; figure 15, ♂. Adults are deep ochreous above, tending toward fulvous in some individuals. The black maculation above inclines to heaviness with considerable suffusion between spots in some examples; moderate to heavy basal suffusion is present, especially in males. Both sexes are quite variable above. The disc is usually olive to greenish beneath but brown disced individuals occasionally turn up in the same area. This subspecies intergrades with nominate *nevadensis* in southeastern Oregon and with *calgariana* in Alberta.

Distribution: This butterfly is found from central Oregon to British Columbia in the Cascades. Type locality: Aspen Grove, British Columbia.

(f) **meadii** (Edwards). Plate 29, figure 9, ♂; figure 10, ♀. *S. nevadensis meadii* represents the southeasterly thrust of *nevadensis* that enters Colorado. Adults are always greenish below but tend strongly to melanism. Adults above have heavy black patterning with considerable suffusion between spots and a dark basal suffusion. In a loose sense *meadii* represents the southern conclusion of Rocky Mountain *nevadensis,* but *meadii* is an isolate that does not intergrade with either *harmonia* or *gallatini* and it is absent from the dry Great Divide basin in central Wyoming. Expanse: 50 to 55 mm.

Distribution: S. nevadensis meadii is an abundant butterfly below 8000 ft. in the Laramie Range in extreme southern Wyoming; in Colorado it inhabits the Front Range, the Park Range, the Collegiates and other mountains. Type locality: Turkey Creek Junction, Jefferson county, Colorado.

13. **Speyeria callippe** (Boisduval). Members of this group inhabit the Sierras and the Coast Ranges from southern California to central Oregon. Whether or not this species extends into Nevada is not known, although it is believed that Morrison captured the type of *callippe laura* in the western part of that state. All populations of *callippe* presently known are brown disced and may be unsilvered or silvered. Males of *callippe* may be recognized by the heavy sex scaling on the veins of the primaries above in contrast to the light markings on *nevadensis.* There is an absence of sharp breaks between subspecies in *callippe* and no isolates are known. The area of greatest taxonomic difficulty is the region north of Lake Tahoe. California, at the northern end of the Sierras where there are no barriers to inhibit the intermingling of Pacific coast *callippe* and Great Basin *nevadensis.* Long series are needed for recognition of *callippe* subspecies.

Early Stages: The eggs of *callippe* are deposited amid the debris and stems of dead violet leaves in August. Larvae do not differ appreciably from those of *coronis.* They hibernate in the first instar and revive in late winter when rains have moistened the dry hills. The violets, however, have long been withered and dried by months of summer drought at the time that the adults are in flight.

Distribution: Speyeria callippe is found in the Coast Ranges of California and western slopes of the Sierras northward to central Oregon.

(a) **callippe** (Boisduval). Plate 28, figure 8, ♀. Nominate *callippe* is confined to the San Francisco peninsula. The encroachment of the city of San Francisco has long exterminated the subspecies from its type locality. Colonies still survive atop Twin Peaks and San Bruno Mountain but it seems probable that these too will ultimately pass into oblivion. The examples of *callippe* taken in the Oakland Hills across the bay and in Contra Costa county appear to be intermediates to the more southerly *comstocki.* As is usual with most San Francisco endemics, nominate *callippe* apparently cannot adapt to the warmer conditions southward on the peninsula where there is less encroachment by human activities. The dark, heavily marked and deeply suffused San Francisco race is unlike any other *callippe.* Adults are brightly silvered beneath and appear in early June. Expanse: 55 to 60 mm.

(b) **comstocki** (Gunder). Plate 28, figure 1, ♂; figure 2, ♀. Adults are smaller and paler than nominate *callippe,* but are always brightly silvered. Adults appear in late May and continue in evidence into July. Expanse: 50 to 55 mm.

Early Stages: These have been carefully described and illustrated by C. M. Dammers. Larvae were reared on wild violets in Bouquet Canyon in Los Angeles county. In captivity *callippe comstocki* has been reared successfully on cultivated pansies.

Distribution: This subspecies occurs in the Coastal Ranges of the southern half of California: south of the Pajaro River in the Santa Lucia Ranges to the moist western foothills of the San Gabriels in Los Angeles county. It is a coastal subspecies ranging not more than twenty miles inland from the Pacific coast at any point. In the Santa Lucias in Monterey county it ascends to 4000 ft. where it flies with *Speyeria coronis coronis* and *S. adiaste clemencei.*

(c) **macaria** (Edwards). Plate 28, figure 6, ♀; figure 7, ♀. Adults of *macaria* are smaller and paler than *comstocki.* They are silvered except where *macaria* blends with *laurina* in the Greenhorn Mountains in Kern county. Adults fly from early to mid June into July.

Distribution: This subspecies is found in the San Gabriel, San Jacinto and Tehachapi ranges in southern California. It is most abundant in the Tehachapi Mountains from 3500 to 4500 ft.

(d) **laurina** (Wright). Plate 28, figure 11, ♀; figure 12, ♂. The ground color is slightly more fulvous in *laurina* than in either *macaria* or *comstocki.* The black maculation is even smaller and slight basal suffusion is present. Adults may be silvered or unsilvered in the same area. On the south slopes of the Greenhorn Mountains they are mostly silvered. On the north side of the Greenhorn crest they appear to be largely unsilvered though there are intermediates on either side. This is a blend zone between *macaria* to the south and *inornata* to the north and northeast. Adults fly from late May into June. Expanse: about 45 mm.

Distribution: This subspecies is found in the Greenhorn Mountains, Kern county, California.

(e) **inornata** (Edwards). Plate 28, figure 13, ♀; figure 14, ♂. Adults are larger than *laurina* with which *inornata* blends. Males are deeper fulvous than the more southerly populations of *callippe,* and there is heavier basal suffusion above than on either *laurina* or *macaria.* Both sexes are completely unsilvered below and have a warm buff ground color. The disc is usually a warm brown in the males, tending to olivaceous in many females. The butterfly is best netted as it visits the blooming spikes of the California Buckeye. It is occasionally rather abundant but is generally an uncommon subspecies. Adults fly from late June into late July.

This subspecies is often called *juba* (Boisduval) in the literature, but this is quite unlike *inornata,* being yellower banded and brightly silvered. Apparently *juba* coexists and blends with the northernmost *inornata*-like unsilvered variants in the Feather River region. The true status of *juba* is uncertain. Expanse: 50 to 55 mm.

Distribution: S. callippe inornata occupies moist areas in the Sierras from 3500 to about 6000 ft., seldom higher. The type locality is Downieville, California. This is unfortunate because in this locality *inornata* blends with the more northerly *sierra.* The true home of *inornata* is from Calaveras to Tulare counties on the west side of the Sierra Nevada in California.

(f) **sierra** dos Passos & Grey. Plate 29, figure 11, ♂. Adults of *sierra* resemble *inornata* above but on the lower surfaces *sierra* is well silvered. The disc is variable: it may be light brown to buff (nearly as pale as the outer band) or greenish in some individuals. Northern Sierran *callippe* is extremely variable. The figured example is from the type locality. Adults fly in late June into July. Expanse: 50 to 55 mm.

Distribution: Collectors desiring to take *sierra* at its type locality may do so at Gold Lake in Sierra county, California. The type series was taken on a hillside above the old Willoughby Mine about five miles from the lake itself.

(g) **laura** (Edwards). Plate 29, figure 3, ♂; figure 4, ♀. This subspecies usually has a pale brown disc and is brightly silvered. The figure of the male is based on the lectotype and that of the female from a lectoparatype. The status of *laura* is not well established. We do not know from what area Morrison collected the lectotype as it bears no locality label other than "Nevada." There are several places in Washoe county, Nevada where green-disced *nevadensis* shows an abrupt transition to *laura.* Expanse: 50 to 55 mm.

Distribution: "Nevada."

(h) **rupestris** (Behr). Plate 29, figure 5, ♀; figure 6, ♂. Adults are deep fulvous above, and heavily marked in black with heavy basal suffusion. Adults are normally unsilvered but there are exceptions, in areas where *rupestris* is blending either to the north with *elaine* or to the south with *liliana.* Expanse: 50 to 55 mm.

Distribution: Typical *rupestris* inhabits Trinity and Siskiyou counties, California. The blend zone between *rupestris* and *elaine* is on Siskiyou Summit in the Siskiyou Mountains in southern Oregon. To the south *rupestris* intergrades with *liliana* in Mendocino county, California.

(i) **elaine** dos Passos & Grey. Plate 29, figure 14, ♀; figure 15, ♂. Plate 42, figure 10, ♂. Adults closely approach *rupestris* in appearance above. They are usually, but not always, silvered beneath. The disc is deeply reddish with some invasion of the outer band by reddish or russet scaling. This subspecies blends with *rupestris* in northern Siskiyou county, California. Expanse: 45 to 55 mm.

Distribution: Southern Oregon west of the Cascade Ranges.

(j) **liliana** (Hy. Edwards). Plate 29, figure 7, ♂; figure 8, ♀. Adults are moderately fulvous above and brightly silvered beneath. The black maculation is variable but usually rather heavy. Females are very red basally below on the primaries. Expanse: 50 to 55 mm.

Distribution: This California Coast Range subspecies occurs in Marin, Napa,

Sonoma, Lake and Mendocino counties; it blends northward in the latter county with the more northerly *rupestris*. There are earlier records indicating a colony intermediate between *liliana* and nominate *callippe* once inhabited an area immediately north of San Pablo Bay in Marin county, but this colony was exterminated by the urban growth of the Bay area. Type locality: Mount St. Helena, Napa county, California. Expanse: 50 to 55 mm.

The *adiaste* group

14. **Speyeria adiaste** (Edwards).   Three subspecies belong to this group; each is confined to mountain summits in the Coast Ranges of southern California. All three are distinct from all other nearctic *Speyeria* including the *egleis* complex with which they have been previously allied. The three subspecies are: *adiaste* of the Santa Cruz Mountains; *clemencei* of the Santa Lucias; and *atossa* of the San Gabriel-Tehachapi-San Jacinto ranges. The three subspecies share several characteristics: they are uniformly pale and unsilvered beneath; the black maculation above is greatly reduced, almost wanting in some examples (*atossa*); and there is little fuscous basal scaling. A pronounced south-north cline is evident, from large and very pale *atossa* in the south through intermediate *clemencei* to much darker, more deeply fulvous *adiaste* at the northern terminus.

Early Stages: The early stages of *adiaste, atossa,* and *clemencei* are all quite similar, but the complete life history has been worked out only for *atossa,* by C. M. Dammers and John A. Comstock. Dammers's excellent watercolor paintings of these early stages, however, were not published. They are preserved in the Los Angeles County Museum.

Distribution: The species occurs in Coast Ranges of Southern California.

(a) **adiaste** (Edwards). Plate 24, figure 5, ♀.   Adults are deep reddish fulvous above with heavier black patterning than others of the complex. Freshly captured females are deep pink basally beneath on the primaries and tinged with pinkish on the disc and apices. This distinctive hue is lost in old, faded specimens. Males are similar above and below to male *clemencei* but a trifle darker. Adults appear in late June and July. This subspecies is common in some seasons and scarce in others, but is very local and usually uncommon. It is more closely associated with forests than either *clemencei* or *atossa*. Expanse: 50 mm.

Distribution: This subspecies inhabits the higher, remote elevations of the Santa Cruz Mountains in Santa Cruz and Santa Clara counties in central California. It is separated from *clemencei* by the low elevation of the Pajaro River and the Salinas Valley where *adiaste* appears unable to exist.

(b) **clemencei** (J. A. Comstock). Plate 24, figure 3, ♀; figure 4, ♂. Another beautiful member of the *adiaste* group, *clemencei* is intermediate in appearance between *atossa* to the south and *adiaste* to the north but is geographically separated from both. The males are constant as figured, but females are more variable: pale fulvous above with a pink tint beneath on fresh examples. The butterflies visit the blooms of the

Yerba Santa, thistles and the creamy spikes of the California Buckeye. Adults fly in June. Expanse: 50 to 55 mm.

Distribution: This subspecies occurs in the Santa Lucia ranges in Monterey and San Luis Obispo counties, California, absent below 3500 ft. Chews Ridge in Monterey county is a good locality.

(c) **atossa** (Edwards). Plate 24, figure 1, ♀; figure 2, ♂. This subspecies is, or was, a beautiful insect. Largest of all the *adiaste* group it was also the most distinctive in appearance, characterized by greatly reduced black maculation above and virtually no basal suffusion. Females are tinged with deep pink basally beneath on the primaries. However, *atossa* may well have become extinct. It has not appeared for a number of years in areas where it was once common. All known localities for *atossa* were in remote parts of the Tehachapi, Tejon and San Jacinto mountains between 4000 and 6500 ft.

It once flew with *S. egleis tehachapina.* The works of man may have indirectly accounted for *atossa*'s disaster. A prolonged and severe drought in the fifties led some ranchers to experiment with foreign grasses with high drought resistance. These grasses swept the area and may have obliterated the food plant of *atossa,* a violet. Since *egleis tehachapina* utilizes a different species of violet at higher altitudes in the Tehachapi Range it has been speculated that the latter violet was unaffected by the imported grass. Another theory is that the drought itself was responsible. Native evergreen oaks have died by the thousands in the area for lack of moisture and it is possible that the host plant of *atossa* perished under these conditions. It is hoped that colonies of *atossa* may still exist but no adults have been taken since 1959. They were most frequently found visiting horse chestnut blossoms in late June.

15. **Speyeria egleis** (Behr).   This protean species not only may be confounded with other species of *Speyeria* with which it is sympatric but may be exasperatingly confusing within itself. It is primarily a Basin-and-Range province butterfly and is largely confined to rather high, cool and moist elevations. This is not absolute, however, because in the vicinity of Rabbit Ears Pass, Routt county, Colorado, *egleis secreta* descends as low as the upper limits of sage brush. The distribution center of *egleis* is the Snake River Plateau of Idaho, southwestern Montana, northwestern Wyoming and northeastern Oregon. Within this area *egleis* is extremely variable. Adults may be greenish disced, brown disced or leaden gray. Others show varying degrees of reddishness. Furthermore the ventral spots may be fully silvered, completely unsilvered, the pale spots may be sprinkled with silver scales, or just the marginal row may be silvered. To add to the confusion, all variations may be encountered in one area, such as in the Beaverhead Mountains of Montana. The species ranges from Colorado to Montana, westward to California and Oregon.

(a) **egleis** (Behr). Plate 24, figure 13, ♂; figure 14, ♀. Adults are rather small, smaller than *coronis, callippe,* or *zerene* with which *egleis* may be sympatric. The butterflies may be silvered or unsilvered in the same locality. Typical *egleis* is brown disced. Adults appear in July and August. Expanse: 50 mm.

Distribution: This subspecies ranges from northern California south in the Sierras to near Mount Whitney. It may be encountered at low elevations in the northern end of the California Sierras but ascends to 8000 ft. or more southward.

(b) **oweni** (Edwards). Plate 24, figure 11, ♂; figure 12, ♀. Adults are similar in size and coloration to nominate *egleis* but average darker in ground color. They may be silvered or unsilvered. *S. egleis oweni* occurs at somewhat lower elevations in the Oregon Cascades than typical *egleis* in the California Sierras.

Distribution: This subspecies is found in extreme northern California and Oregon.

(c) **tehachapina** (J. A. Comstock). Plate 24, figure 8, ♂; figure 15, ♀. Adults are paler fulvous than in Sierran *egleis,* less heavily marked and with less basal suffusion above. They are unsilvered below except for the outer row of spots which may be silvered on some females.

Distribution: This subspecies is confined to the highest summits of the Tehachapi Mountains in Kern county, California, at 7700 ft. This is the southernmost population of *egleis*.

(d) **linda** dos Passos & Grey. Plate 25, figure 3, ♂; figure 4, ♀. Adults are ochreous above rather than fulvous. The disc is olivaceous or greenish below and specimens are usually (but not always) silvered. The black maculation is finer and the basal suffusion is less than among Rocky Mountain populations. Expanse: 50 mm.

Distribution: *S. egleis linda* is an inhabitant of the Sawtooth Mountains in central Idaho. It blends both with *oweni* in northeastern Oregon and with *mcdunnoughi* in southern Montana.

(e) **utahensis** (Skinner). Plate 25, figure 9, ♂; figure 10, ♀. Adults of both sexes are deeper fulvous above and less ochreous than in *linda*. There is only moderate basal suffusion above but the black maculation averages a little heavier; males, at least, seem to average slightly larger than *linda*. Beneath *utahensis* is a warm, pale buff and entirely unsilvered. The disc is only slightly darker than the outer buff band. The greatest darkening of the disc is immediately inward from the medial spot band. Expanse: about 50 mm.

Distribution: This subspecies inhabits the Wasatch and Uinta ranges in Utah at moderately high elevations between 7500 and 9000 ft.

(f) **toiyabe** Howe, **NEW SUBSPECIES.** Plate 31, figure 13, ♂, holotype. Adults are bright ochreous above with only moderate to slight black maculation above with slight basal suffusion. It is distinctive from all other *egleis* populations in that the disc is yellow. It is brightly silvered below. It reveals a marked trend toward pallidity as does *zerene cynna* and *electa greyi*. The subspecies was discovered by John Lane of Los Angeles.

Distribution: Toiyabe Range of central Nevada. Type locality: Kingston Canyon, Lander county, Nevada. Type deposition: Los Angeles County Museum.

(g) **secreta** dos Passos & Grey. Plate 25, figure 5, ♂; figure 6, ♀. Adults closely approximate *electa nikias* with which they can be confused in the field. A lengthy series of *secreta,* however, will reveal the differences clearly. The ventral surfaces of *secreta* (and most *egleis*) in the subapical areas of the primaries is a flat, dead tan and not a bright tan as occurs in *electa* and other sympatric species. This is also true of the band on the secondaries beneath: it is a dead or dull tan and never bright as in *electa*. Adults of *secreta* are most quickly recognized on the underside in which the apices are as strongly reddish as the disc. The band is heavily invaded by red scaling, amounting to a solid suffusion in many examples. Adults are always brightly silvered beneath. Expanse: not over 50 mm.

Distribution: This subspecies occurs at moderate to high elevations in Colorado and southern Wyoming.

(h) **albrighti** (Gunder). Plate 25, figure 1, ♂; figure 2, ♀. Adults are dull ochreous above. The black maculation and basal suffusion are heavier than in *linda* and the general coloration is duller. The disc is dull greenish so the insect might be mistaken for *callippe calgariana*. However, *albrighti* has developed a rather peculiar sort of silvering that to the experienced eye is immediately distinct from that of *calgariana*. *S. egleis albrighti* inhabits a remote area seldom visited by lepidopterists, and is a poorly known subspecies of rather uncertain status. Expanse: about 50 mm.

Distribution: The subspecies occurs in north central Montana. The high prairies just west of Great Falls, Montana, is an easily accessible area where it is possible to take many *albrighti* in early July.

(i) **mcdunnoughi** (Gunder). Plate 25, figure 7, ♂; figure 8, ♀. Adults of *mcdunnoughi* are typically brown disced and may be silvered or unsilvered. This population seems to contain elements of *linda, albrighti, secreta* and *utahensis;* as such the name *mcdunnoughi* can hardly be said to apply to a very definitive entity but I am using the term for the *egleis* populations that inhabit southern and southeastern Montana and northern Wyoming.

In addition to the above subspecies of *egleis,* a distinctive green-disced population has been discovered recently in the Stansbury Mountains in Tooele county, Utah. I have no further information regarding it.

16. **Speyeria hydaspe** (Boisduval).   There are two general groups of subspecies of *hydaspe*. One group ranges down the Cascades and the Sierra Nevada. The second group is found the length of the Rocky Mountains at suitable elevations as far as the latitude of central New Mexico. The center of distribution of the species is north of the Salmon River in Idaho, in southern British Columbia and in Washington. During the Wisconsin glaciation, *hydaspe* probably took refuge in the Great Basin. As the region warmed *hydaspe* became isolated in the mountain ranges of this region where today the butterfly displays its greatest degree of variability and exhibits its widest choice of habitat. In both the Rocky Mountains and the Sierras *hydaspe* is found at rather high, moist elevations. In British Columbia *hydaspe* is abundant at sea level.

In most places *hydaspe* is relatively uniform in appearance and easy to recognize. A glance at the purplish or lavender cast to disc and apices on the underside betrays the species. The disc is variable but is usually wine red, brick red or even blood red while the outer band is suffused with lavender or reddish scales and is rarely buff. On Vancouver Island *hydaspe* may be brightly silvered, unsilvered or partially so. In the Cascade, Sierra and Rocky mountains *hydaspe* is generally unsilvered.

The spots beneath range from cream to pale butter yellow. A north-south cline occurs in the Sierras where *hydaspe* trends toward pallidity southward, ending in the Greenhorn Mountains with the pale *viridicornis*.

Early Stages: These await description.

Distribution: The species ranges from British Columbia southward in the mountains to southern California and northern New Mexico.

(a) **hydaspe** (Boisduval). Plate 30, figure 1, ♂; figure 2, ♀. Adults are fulvous above and rather heavily marked, as are all *hydaspe*. They are unsilvered beneath and the band is lavender; the disc is dull purplish red to medium brick red but not so dark or intense as in *purpurascens,* found farther north. Nominate *hydaspe* is sympatric in the Sierras with *zerene* but distinguishable from it by its paler disc color. Expanse: 55 to 60 mm.

Distribution: Nominate *hydaspe* occurs in the central and southern Sierra Nevada in California from Calaveras to Tulare counties at approximately 6000 to 7500 ft. The insect is seldom abundant.

(b) **viridicornis** (J. A. Comstock). Plate 30, figure 11, ♀; figure 12, ♂. Adults are paler both above and below, but the black maculation is essentially the same as in nominate *hydaspe*. The principal differences are beneath, where the disc is pale lavender as is the outer band, and the spots are unsilvered. This subspecies is the southern termination of a cline ending in the Greenhorn Mountains in Kern county, California. However, individuals closely resembling *viridicornis* turn up in both Yosemite and Kings Canyon national parks where *viridicornis* blends with typical *hydaspe*. I have taken *viridicornis* in certain sections of Yosemite while in other areas within the park I have encountered typical *hydaspe*.

Distribution: This subspecies is found in the southern Sierras of California from Kern county (Greenhorn Mountains) north to the Yosemite Valley. Flight Period: late June into July.

(c) **purpurascens** (Hy. Edwards). Plate 30, figure 5, ♂; figure 9, ♀ *purpurascens/rhodope,* upperside; figure 10, *purpurascens/rhodope,* ♀, underside. Adults are deep fulvous above and heavily marked often with considerable suffusion, especially basally. Females are slightly paler than the males. The spots beneath are unsilvered. The disc is dull brick red, not quite so purplish red as in *rhodope*. There are all manner of intermediates between both forms and a wide blend zone occurs in Oregon and Washington west of the Cascades. Expanse: 50 to 55 mm.

Distribution: This subspecies occurs in southern Oregon and northern California, blending southward in the northern Sierras with nominate *hydaspe*. S. *hydaspe purpurascens* in southern Oregon and northern California inhabits somewhat lower elevations than does Sierran *hydaspe* but does not occur on seacoasts. Usually it is a rather common butterfly between 3500 to 6000 ft. Adults in late June into July.

(d) **rhodope** (Edwards). Plate 30, figure 7, ♂; figure 8, ♂, underside; figure 13, ♀.
Adults are small, deeply fulvous and heavily patterned above with deep basal suffusion, in many examples amounting to nearly solid fuscous shading inward from the median row of black spots. The disc below is deep wine red to purplish, often

with bright silver spots, but other examples from the same area may be unsilvered. This subspecies and *minor* are the only silvered or partially silvered *hydaspe*. Expanse: 50 to 55 mm.

Distribution: West of the Cascades in southern British Columbia, Oregon and Washington *rhodope* occurs, blending with *purpurascens* to the south but differing sharply from *sakuntala* on the dry eastern side of the Cascades in southern British Columbia. There is no sharp boundary between *rhodope* and *purpurascens* and they intergrade with each other as far south as central Oregon. *S. hydaspe rhodope* is a forest subspecies of the broad river bottoms of the Fraser River system in British Columbia.

(e) **minor** (McDunnough). Plate 30, figure 14, ♂; figure 15, ♀. *S. hydaspe minor* is a poorly defined mountain subspecies of British Columbia. It is slightly paler in ground color than *rhodope,* less purplish beneath and likewise not invariably silvered.

Distribution: This subspecies occurs in the mountains of the coastal ranges of southern British Columbia. It is little known and uncommon in collections.

(f) **sakuntala** Skinner. Plate 30, figure 3, ♂; figure 4, ♀. On the eastern side of the Cascade Ranges in southern British Columbia it is dry, even arid, and here we have a subspecies known as *sakuntala,* distinctly paler than either coastal *rhodope* or *purpurascens.* Expanse: 50 to 55 mm.

Distribution: The type locality of *sakuntala* is Kaslo, British Columbia. From here it ranges eastward into southern Alberta and southward into Idaho, Montana, northeastern Utah, Wyoming and northern Colorado. Adults of *sakuntala* are abundant in southern Montana where I have taken them visiting the blooms of western blue penstemons, Blue Mint (*Monarda*), and Pink Spreading Dogbane (*Apocynum androsaemifolium*).

(g) **conquista** dos Passos & Grey. Plate 30, figure 6, ♂. Plate 31, figure 15, ♀. Adults are similar to *sakuntala.* The type, from which the figured male was drawn, is somewhat damaged and did not make the best model for an illustration. *S. hydaspe conquista* is the southern end of the Rocky Mountains cline.

Distribution: This subspecies is confined to the Sangre de Cristo Mountains in northern New Mexico and the San Juan Mountains in southern Colorado.

17. **Speyeria mormonia** (Boisduval). With few exceptions the various populations of this group are the most nearly boreal of all nearctic *Speyeria*. It is the most widespread *Speyeria* of the arctic and alpine zones in western America. Adults are rather small, pale fulvous to ochreous above, with rather fine lines on the veins and small, crisp black spots. Some subspecies are strongly suffused basally and others are quite pubescent especially on the anal angle. Females are nearly always recognizable, regardless of subspecies, by the pale, nearly white row of spots above inward from the first marginal spot band on the primaries. Males are nearly always more deeply fulvous above than the females and are easily confused with *Speyeria egleis* in places where they are sympatric. Members of this group may be silvered or unsilvered beneath. In the Rocky Mountains they are most at home in lofty meadows above timberline, flying with *Parnassius smintheus* and *Colias meadii*. In Colorado

mormonia eurynome is rarely met below 9000 ft. and is found up to 14,000 ft. In Montana, however, *eurynome* may descend as low as 5000 ft. where it flies in sage-brush areas. Ecologically, *eurynome* has a wide tolerance and will be encountered in more different habitats than any other nearctic *Speyeria*. Its general abundance suggests that it is remarkably well adapted to this wide range of environments and that it may possibly have diverse host plants. It is not uncommon to see forty or fifty individuals at one time sipping water at a puddle. It is abundant along the coast of Alaska but farther south in southern British Columbia and the United States *mormonia* avoids seacoasts. As we follow it southward we discover that it occurs at progressively higher and higher elevations. In the southern limits of its distribution it is restricted to treeline levels on some of our loftiest peaks. Most populations of *mormonia* are well known and only in rare instances do they pose any serious taxonomic problems.

Early Stages: These are unstudied as yet.

Distribution: The species ranges from southern Alaska, British Columbia and Alberta southward to the central Sierras of California, the central Great Basin and central Rocky Mountains of Colorado and northern New Mexico.

(a) **mormonia** (Boisduval). Plate 42, figure 12, ♂; Plate 32, figure 17, ♂, underside; figure 15, ♀. Adults are pale fulvous above with fine black maculation. Although similar to the Colorado subspecies, *eurynome,* nominate *mormonia* is smaller and generally paler. There is little basal suffusion and most specimens are brightly silvered below. Adults are frequent flower visitors, as are all *mormonia,* and they are easily netted. Expanse: 40 to 45 mm.

Distribution: Nominate *mormonia* occurs from northeastern California (Warner Mountains) eastward to central Utah. It inhabits rather high elevations and is usually not encountered below 7000 ft.

(b) **eurynome** (Edwards). Plate 32, figure 5, ♂; figure 6, ♀. Adults are larger than *mormonia* and have slightly heavier maculation with considerably more basal suffusion. The disc is much darker than the ground color and may be brown in some individuals, greenish olive in others. Adults are usually (but not always) silvered below. In Colorado *eurynome* is strictly a high mountain butterfly, seldom encountered below 10,000 ft. and from there to far above timberline. It flies with *Colias meadii* from which it is not distinguishable except at close range. Its flight is rapid when the sun is warm and bright, but when clouds sweep across the peaks and a chill wind blows one may see *eurynome* perched, with wings open to the wind, on the barren rocks and tundra, so torpid from the cold that they may be collected with forceps. Expanse: about 45 mm.

Distribution: S. mormonia eurynome occurs at high elevations in alpine habitats of southern Wyoming, Colorado and northern New Mexico; it descends to much lower elevations farther north in extreme northern Wyoming, Montana, Saskatchewan and Alberta. In many areas it is the commonest *Speyeria.*

(c) **clio** (Edwards). Plate 42, figure 11, ♂. This subspecies consistently turns up in a number of geographic areas and I have decided to elevate it from the synonymy once more. It appears to be somewhat distinct from Rocky Mountain *eurynome,* although admittedly the status of *clio* requires further study before it will be well understood. Adults may be recognized by the solid ochreous ground above and a very pale disc. *S. mormonia clio* is closer in appearance to Nevada *artonis* and, like *artonis,* is unsilvered. However, the spots beneath are clearly outlined in *clio* while in *artonis* these outlines are but faintly indicated.

Distribution: The type locality is the vicinity of Jackson Lake, Teton county, Wyoming. This subspecies has also been recorded from the Big Horn Mountains of Wyoming and the Judith Mountains of Montana. It occurs at much lower elevations than *eurynome* and appears to choose different habitats, though this conclusion may be drawn from insufficient data.

(d) **washingtonia** (Barnes & McDunnough). Plate 32, figure 9, ♂; figure 10, ♀. Adults are heavily patterned above with deep basal shading and strongly developed anal and basal pubescence. The subspecies occurs with underside spots both unsilvered and silvered; these spots are greenish yellow and dark, with a greenish disc. It is probably the darkest of all *mormonia* with the possible exception of *opis.* Expanse: 45 mm.

Distribution: *S. mormonia washingtonia* is found in meadows at elevations of between 3500 to 6000 ft. in the Cascade Ranges of Oregon and Washington.

(e) **bischoffii** (Edwards). Plate 42, figure 16, ♀; figure 17, ♂. This is the Alaskan population of *mormonia.* It has strong basal and anal suffusion above and a general duskiness. Adults may be silvered or unsilvered beneath. Edwards's lectotype, in the Carnegie Museum, is figured.

Distribution: This subspecies occurs on the seacoasts of southern Alaska up to 2500 ft.

(f) **erinna** (Edwards). Plate 24, figure 16, ♀; Plate 32, figure 18, ♂ underside; Plate 42, figure 9. ♂. Adults are brightly fulvous above with only moderate black maculation. There is some fuscous shading but little or no anal pubescence. They are brightly silvered beneath and the disc is reddish brown with some olive-green over-scaling.

Distribution: The insect is native to Oregon and Washington on the eastern slopes of the Cascades. It is found between 3000 and 4000 ft. in eastern Washington.

(g) **luski** (Barnes & McDunnough). Plate 32, figure 13, ♂; figure 14, ♀. This is a distinctive isolate among *mormonia.* The spots, greenish yellow rather than silvered, and the disc of the same hue as the ground color, with curious maculation below, all distinguish *luski* from any other *Speyeria.*

Distribution: After the July rains *luski* is sometimes quite abundant in the vicinity of Hannagan Meadows and Greer in the White Mountains of Arizona. It is found only (?) in these mountains at elevations of 8500 to 9500 ft. Common where found from late July into August.

(h) **artonis** (Edwards). Plate 32, figure 7, ♂; figure 8, ♀. Adults are pale fulvous above with reduced basal suffusion. They are unsilvered beneath, with only faint maculation. The entire lower surfaces are ochreous. A similar development toward pallidity is displayed by *zerene cynna* and *electa greyi* from the same general region.

Distribution: This subspecies is found in the Ruby and Jarbidge mountains of northern Nevada and in the Steens Mountains of southeastern Oregon at suitable elevations during the first two weeks in July.

(i) **arge** (Strecker). Plate 32, figure 11, ♂; figure 12, ♀. Adults of this subspecies are small, with variable black maculation above, heavy in some individuals and light in others. The disc below is a warmer buff or brownish than in nominate *mormonia* and is rarely greenish. The ventral surfaces are usually silvered but many times the spots are only sprinkled with silver scales. The basal suffusion is moderate. The subspecies is often sympatric with *S. egleis egleis* and may be confused with it. Adults of *arge* are distinguished by the very fine black lines on the veins above, while in male *egleis egleis* the veins tend to be marked with heavy and suffused lines. Adults of *arge* greatly favor the blooms of the Western Pennyroyal (*Monarda menthaefolium*) upon which they may be netted with ease. Expanse: about 45 mm.

Distribution: This subspecies is common and widespread in the California Sierras from late June to late August. In the Sierras *arge* may be found from 4600 to 12,500 ft. Sometimes *arge* has been referred to (incorrectly) as *Speyeria montivaga*.

(j) **opis** (Edwards). Plate 42, figure 15, ♂. Edwards named *opis* from a series taken on Bald Mountain, near Keithly, in the Cariboo Mining District of British Columbia. The spots beneath on the secondaries are silvered and outlined very heavily in brownish olive. This subspecies is rare in collections.

(k) **jesmondensis** (McDunnough). Plate 42, figure 13, ♂; figure 14, ♀. Adults of this subspecies somewhat resemble *bischoffii* but lack the heavy markings above. The secondaries beneath are unsilvered with only a faint outline of the spots. As in the preceding, *jesmondensis* is rare in collections. Expanse: about 45 mm.

Distribution: This subspecies occurs in southern and central British Columbia.

Genus BOLORIA Reuss

JON H. SHEPARD

The small species that comprise this genus are similar in appearance to the much larger *Speyeria* on the upper surface but they differ considerably beneath. In *Speyeria* most species have a similar pattern of silvered spots on the under surface, but in *Boloria* there is a variety of patterns. The two genera are also separated by characteristics of the male genitalia. The generic name *Boloria* has been employed for North American species in recent years to replace *Brenthis* Hübner, which is restricted to three Palearctic species. Authorities in the Old World consider that what we call *Boloria* represents three genera. Dos Passos (1964) treats the three as subgenera.

The genus *Boloria* is represented in North America by fourteen species of which four are restricted to the Nearctic and ten are also found in the Palearctic region. At least seven additional species are restricted to the Palearctic region, making twenty-one species for the entire genus. Our North American species are restricted to the Arctic north, the Arctic-Alpine mountain summits of the West, and meadows or bogs of the coniferous forest and the northeastern mixed forest, southward to North Carolina in the mountains.

It has been generally assumed that *Boloria* and *Speyeria* share a common and exclusive utilization of violets (*Viola*) as larval food. This assumption has been perpetuated by a lack of knowledge of the life histories of *Boloria* in North America and a lack of familiarity with the literature on the Palearctic species. The life histories of only two species, *Boloria selene* and *B. bellona,* were previously known on this continent. Both species feed on *Viola.* However, several of the Holarctic species have foodplants other than *Viola,* for example: *Salix, Saxifraga* and *Polygonum.* Foodplants for species other than *B. selene* and *B. bellona* are from rearings by the author unless otherwise stated. Most species of *Boloria* are single brooded, but the two best known species, *B. selene* and *B. bellona,* have two or more generations a year. Two species, *B. alberta* and *B. astarte,* have only one generation every two years, at least in certain parts of their ranges.

1. **Boloria napaea** (Hoffmansegg).   This species is characterized by the lack of a row of postmedian, rounded spots on the underside of the secondaries and the angled appearance of the margin of the secondaries. It has frequently appeared in the literature as *Brenthis pales* Denis & Schiffermüller. The nominate subspecies does not occur in our area, but three other subspecies do.

Early Stages: Nothing is known of these in North America. European workers have found *Viola* and *Vaccinium* utilized as larval foodplants.

Distribution: This is a circumpolar species. The Nearctic representatives inhabit the Arctic regions of western North America and the Wind River Range of western Wyoming. Adults appear in July.

(a) **halli** Klots. Plate 33, figure 3, ♂; figure 15, ♀.   This subspecies is characterized by a lack of dark scales on the upper surface of the male and by the lighter appearance of the upper surface of the female. It is found only in the Wind River Mountains of Wyoming, where it is confined to upper Hudsonian and lower Arctic-Alpine bogs and meadows. The type locality is Green River Pass, Wind River Range, Sublette county, Wyoming.

(b) **alaskensis** (Holland). Plate 33, figure 1, ♂.   This subspecies is intermediate in appearance between *halli* and *nearctica.* It has a much wider distribution, being recorded in western and southern Alaska, Yukon and Atlin, British Columbia. The name *reiffi* Reuss is considered a synonym. The type locality is the mountains between 40 Mile and Mission creeks, Alaska.

(c) **nearctica** Verity. Plate 33, figure 2, ♀.   This subspecies is characterized by the heavily dusted and blackish appearance of the upper surfaces. It is apparently restricted to northeastern Alaska. A specimen from Victoria Island in the Northwest Territories also appears to be referable to *nearctica.* The type locality is northeastern Alaska.

2. **Boloria eunomia** (Esper).   *Boloria eunomia* is characterized by Klots as follows: "dark spots in submarginal areas of ventral hind wing . . . and of ventral fore wing . . . regularly round or oval, and sharply defined, with light yellow, white, or silvery centers . . ." Because of the somewhat silvery appearance of both submarginal and postmedian spots it has been confused with *B. selene,* which has more metallic

appearing spots. As in the preceding, nominate *eunomia* is Palearctic and is not found in our area. The species is represented in North America by seven subspecies, some of which are rather poorly defined.

Early Stages: Klots records *Polygonum viviparum* as a foodplant. In Europe it is known to feed upon *Viola* and *Polygonum.* In Alberta I found the larvae may feed on *Viola* and *Polygonum* but prefer *Salix.* The insect overwinters in the larval stage.

Distribution: This is another circumpolar species. It occurs in virtually all of the Arctic and Alpine areas of North America. Specimens from southern Montana are presently not assigned to any subspecies. The species is single brooded, flying in late June and July or early August depending on locality.

(a) **dawsoni** (Barnes & Benjamin). Plate 35, figure 16, ♂; figure 17, ♀. This subspecies represents *eunomia* in southern Manitoba, Ontario, northern Michigan, and near Mount Katahdin, Maine. In northern Michigan *dawsoni* occurs in sphagnum bogs in the Upper Peninsula and is on the wing in late June. The butterfly appears to prefer bogs in which heaths, black spruce, and tamarack are growing. Earlier reports that this subspecies will fly for only one day in a year are not true. The flight period lasts three to five weeks. The type locality is Hymers (near Port Arthur), Ontario.

(b) **triclaris** (Hübner). Plate 34, figure 2, ♀. This subspecies is usually distinguishable from *dawsoni* by the lighter ground color of the upper surface. It ranges from Labrador through northern Manitoba to Alaska and Atlin, British Columbia. Klots reports the larval foodplant is *Polygonum viviparum* at Churchill, Manitoba. The type locality is Labrador.

(c) **denali** (Klots). Plate 34, figure 12, ♂. In *denali* the ground color is lighter than in any other subspecies of *eunomia.* It is distributed through much of Alaska and has been taken on Mount McKinley and in the vicinity of Fairbanks. Specimens from the McKenzie Delta intergrade with *triclaris.* The type locality is McKinley National Park, Alaska.

(d) **nichollae** (Barnes & Benjamin). Plate 34, figure 3, ♂. The type locality of this subspecies is presumed to be in the Rocky Mountains of Alberta. This name has been applied to specimens of *eunomia* taken in the Rocky Mountain region of Alberta and British Columbia. The habitat is similar to that of *dawsoni.*

(e) **laddi** (Klots). *B. eunomia laddi* is slightly smaller than *caelestis* and is unsilvered below. Ladd's Fritillary is found in the Snowy Range in southeastern Wyoming. This subspecies is found in bogs at elevations from 8000 ft. to tree line. The type locality is Lewis Lake, Albany county, Wyoming.

(f) **caelestis** (Hemming). Plate 35, figure 13, ♂; figure 14, ♀. This subspecies is limited to Colorado. The type locality is Hall Valley, Park county, Colorado.

(g) **ursadentis** Ferris and Groothuis. Plate 34, figure 1, ♂. The subspecies has recently been described from material collected at Beartooth Pass, Park county, Wyoming. The ground color of the dorsal surface or the wings is "a more distinct yellow-brown . . . than is found in its congeners." Specimens I have seen from southwestern Montana do not fit this description.

3. **Boloria selene** (Denis & Schiffermüller).   The presence of silver spots on the under surface of the secondaries serves to separate this species from all our other *Boloria*. Six described subspecies are known from our area. Nominate *selene* is Palearctic.

Early Stages: In North America *Viola* has been recorded as a foodplant. In Europe, *Viola, Fragaria* and *Vaccinium* are recorded hosts. At low elevations and in southern localities *selene* may have three broods: May, late July, and from late August to early September. In higher elevations and northern localities two broods, June and August, are usual but sometimes only one brood occurs.

Distribution: This circumpolar species is found in bogs, marshy areas and meadows throughout the coniferous forest and eastern deciduous forest regions of North America except in California and the western portions of Oregon, Washington and British Columbia. It is not found in the truly Arctic regions. In the West isolated colonies are sometimes located in bogs that are maintained by underground springs, these bogs not being in the normal coniferous forest habitat.

(a) **myrina** (Cramer). Plate 35, figure 1, ♂.   The size and appearance of this subspecies are average for the species. There is no yellow in the ground color of the ventral surface of the secondaries. The upper surface has no darkening of either the margin or the basal regions. Most of our knowledge of the life history of North American *selene* is based upon this subspecies, which ranges from Iowa and Minnesota to southern New England, southward in the East to Maryland. The name *marilandica* Clark is considered a synonym. Records of this subspecies from North Carolina require verification. The type locality is New York.

(b) **terraenovae** (Holland). Plate 34, figure 9, ♂.   This subspecies is restricted to Newfoundland. It is characterized by very dark margins on the wings and a dark brown ground color on the underside of the secondaries. The type locality is Newfoundland.

(c) **atrocostalis** (Huard). Plate 34, figure 18, ♂.   This subspecies differs slightly from *myrina* in being smaller and with the margins of the wings more heavily patterned in black. It is intermediate in color and maculation between *myrina* and *terraenovae*. The name *albequina* (Holland) (T. L. Whitehorse, Yukon Territory) has been applied to material from Alberta, the Yukon and northern British Columbia. It is here considered a synonym of *atrocostalis*. *B. selene atrocostalis* replaces *myrina* to the north, and is found from northern New England and northern New York westward through the northern sections of Minnesota, Wisconsin and Michigan to North Dakota, Montana, Washington and hence north to Alaska. The type locality is Chicoutimi, Quebec.

(d) **nebraskensis** (Holland). Plate 35, figure 3, ♂.   This subspecies is similar to *myrina* except that it is extremely large. Females approach *Speyeria mormonia* in wing expanse. The original colony was discovered by Leussler in a marsh just south of Omaha, Nebraska, in Sarpy county. It has since been found in several other Nebraska localities and at one locality in North Dakota. Not all Nebraska material is unusually large.

(e) **tollandensis** (Barnes & Benjamin). Plate 35, figure 2, ♀.   This subspecies is characterized by the yellow ground-color of the under surface of the secondaries. It is known from New Mexico, Colorado, Utah, Wyoming, and areas of Montana bordering northwestern Wyoming. The type locality is Tolland, Moffat county, Colorado.

4. **Boloria bellona** (Fabricius).   This species is easily separated from all others by the "squared off" apical portion of the fore wing. It has been confused with *B. epithore* and *B. frigga* because all three have a purple tone to the under surface of the secondaries. Recent literature has treated this species under the species name *toddi* (Holland).

Early Stages: In the East this species is known to have two and sometimes three generations a year. The subspecies *jenistai* Stallings and Turner apparently is double brooded. Populations from Colorado apparently are single brooded. Species of *Viola* serve as foodplants.

Distribution: This Nearctic species is known from the Canadian and Transition zones of eastern North America and the lower elevations of the northern Rocky Mountains south to Colorado. Specimens from Colorado and the Columbia River watersheds are not referable to any hitherto described subspecies. Where multiple brooded, *bellona* flies from June to August. Single brooded populations appear in June or early July.

(a) **toddi** (Holland). Plate 35, figure 6, ♂.   This subspecies has the basal portion of the upper surface of the wings dark. It ranges from Quebec and northern New England to Manitoba and northern Wisconsin. There is a cline between nominate *bellona* and *toddi*. The type locality is St. Margaret's River, Quebec.

(b) **bellona** (Fabricius). Plate 35, figure 4, ♀.   This subspecies lacks the basal darkening of the upper surfaces of the wings. It ranges from North Dakota to New York and south in the mountains to North Carolina and Tennessee. The name *ammiralis* Hemming is here considered a synonym.

(c) **jenistai** Stallings & Turner. Plate 35, figure 5, ♀.   This subspecies has the wings basally darkened on the upper surface but to a lesser degree than *toddi*. Also *jenistai* has a more reddish tinge to the ground color of the upper surface. It is known from Saskatchewan, Alberta, northern British Columbia and the Northwest Territories. The type locality is Lloydminster, Saskatchewan.

5. **Boloria epithore** (Edwards).   This species can be confused with *B. frigga*, but the latter has a large, basal, rectangular white area on the under surface of the secondaries that is lacking in *epithore*.

Early Stages: I have reared *epithore* on *Viola* sp. in Montana and California. It overwinters as a penultimate instar larva.

Distribution: A Nearctic species, *epithore* is known from British Columbia southward to California and, in the Rockies, to northwestern Wyoming. Persistent records from Colorado are all errors. The species is single brooded, flying in June or July.

(a) **epithore** (Edwards). Plate 34, figure 13, ♂; figure 14, ♀.   This subspecies has a median row of disconnected black markings on the upper surface of the secondaries and its general appearance is larger and lighter than in *chermocki*. It is restricted to the Santa Cruz Mountains of California. The type locality is Saratoga, Santa Cruz county, California.

(b) **chermocki** Perkins & Perkins. Plate 34, figure 15, ♂. The median row of black markings on the upper surface of the secondaries is connected in *chermocki*. This subspecies was proposed after the type locality of *epithore* had been restricted to the Santa Cruz Mountains and it occupies the rest of the range of the species. Specimens from the Sierra Nevada and higher elevations of the Cascade Mountains tend to be reduced in size. The type locality is Dolph, Yamhill county, Oregon.

6. **Boloria kriemhild** (Strecker). Plate 33, figure 17, ♂; figure 18, ♀. The plate will serve to distinguish *kriemhild*. It has at times been confused with *epithore*. There are no subspecies.

Early Stages: I have reared this on *Viola* sp. in Montana. The larva overwinters in the penultimate instar.

Distribution: This Nearctic species is known from northeastern Utah, western Wyoming, southeastern Idaho and southwestern Montana. Strecker's cotypes were supposedly taken in Colorado and Arizona but the butterfly has not been taken within those states since. Adults appear in June.

7. **Boloria frigga** (Thunberg). This is another Holarctic butterfly of which the nominate subspecies does not occur in our territory. Three subspecies are credited to our fauna. Close scrutiny of the plates will usually distinguish *frigga* from *bellona* or *epithore,* both of which on occasion may be confused with it.

Early Stages: I have reared this on *Salix* in Alberta. At Prudhoe Bay, Alaska, Philip saw it ovipositing on *Dryas integrifolia*. In Europe *Rubus chamaemorus* has been recorded as a foodplant.

Distribution: This circumpolar species is similar to *B. selene* and *B. bellona* but it is generally more northern, with one subspecies (*gibsoni*) inhabiting tundra. The species is restricted to sphagnum and willow bogs. The species is single brooded, appearing in June.

(a) **sagata** (Barnes & Benjamin). Plate 33, figure 4, ♂. This subspecies is found in Colorado and southeastern Wyoming. The upper surface is lighter than that of the other subspecies. The type locality is Hall Valley, Park county, Colorado.

(b) **saga** (Staudinger). Plate 33, figure 5, ♀, figure 6, ♂. This subspecies has the basal portion of the upper surfaces suffused with black scales. It is the most widely distributed subspecies, known from Labrador west to Alaska and south in the Rocky Mountains to southern Alberta and central British Columbia. The type locality is Labrador.

(c) **gibsoni** (Barnes & Benjamin). Plate 33, figure 9, ♂. This subspecies is larger and darker than *saga*. It is known from northeastern Alaska eastward to Hudson Bay, its range lying north of that of *saga*. The type locality is Barter Island, North Alaska.

8. **Boloria freija** (Thunberg). This is another circumpolar species originally described from Lapland. This species is recognized by the obvious postmedian band of white and the long, triangular, submedian discal spot on the lower surface of the hind wing.

Early Stages: John Pelman has reared last instar larva on *Vaccinium caespitosum* in Washington. Japanese workers have reared the species on *Rhododendron aureum,* according to Klots. In Europe foodplants include *Arctostaphylos Uva-ursi, Empetrum nigrum, Rubus chamaemorus* and *Vaccinium uliginosum.*

Distribution: This circumpolar species is found from Alaska to Labrador southward to Washington State, northern New Mexico, northern Minnesota and Wisconsin. It is the first *Boloria* to fly in the spring, often as early as April.

(a) **browni** Higgins. Plate 34, figure 4, ♂. This subspecies lacks the dark basal area on the upper surface of the male secondaries. In Colorado, nearly any willow bog from 9000 to 13,000 ft. is likely to harbor *browni,* which also flies widely in open, grassy areas and "tundra." It is probable that *browni* inhabits all mountain ranges in Colorado and Wyoming. It is also recorded from northern New Mexico, Utah and southwestern Montana. The type locality is Independence Pass, Pitkin county, Colorado.

(b) **freija** (Thunberg). Plate 34, figure 5, ♂; figure 6, ♀. The nominate subspecies appears to range across subarctic Eurasia into Alaska, then south to Washington and Manitoba. In North America it is found south of and at lower elevations than *tarquinius.* The type locality is Västerbotten, Sweden.

(c) **tarquinius** (Curtis). Plate 34, figure 7, ♂. This subspecies of *freija* is found in the Arctic tundra of the far north from Alaska to Labrador. It is usually darker than typical *freija.* Curtis described *tarquinius* from specimens collected by the Ross Arctic Expedition in the vicinity of the Boothia Peninsula in the Northwest Territories. Specimens from Labrador, the delta of the Mackenzie, McKinley National Park, Alaska, and from Baffin Island are assigned to this subspecies.

(d) and (e) **natazhati** (Gibson) and **nabokovi** Stallings & Turner. Plate 34, figure 8, ♀, *nabokovi.* I know no more of these two supposed subspecies than what is contained in the original descriptions. The name *natazhati* seems a valid one when applied to large, dark specimens from the Yukon-Alaska border region. The name *nabokovi* was applied to two specimens from Mile 102, Alaska Highway, British Columbia. Other specimens from the area are referable to typical *freija.* The type locality for *natazhati* is north of Mount Natazhat, Yukon Territory.

9. **Boloria titania** (Esper). This is another butterfly whose nominate subspecies is Palearctic. The species is well represented in North America by six subspecies, many of which are widely distributed and abundant. Several of these previously were placed under *chariclea* (Schneider) but are now considered to belong to the species *titania.* The *titania* subspecies of northern North America are similar to those of Europe, while the western subspecies, *helena* and *rainieri,* are closer to *chariclea.* Locality and appearance, as illustrated, are sufficient to separate *chariclea* from *titania* and the various *titania* subspecies from one another.

Early Stages: John Pelman has reared last instar larvae on *Polygonum bistortoides* in the Olympics of Washington. In Europe *titania* is known to feed upon *Viola* and *Polygonum.* Klots (1961) records *Salix arctica, S. herbacea* and *Polygonum viviparum. Solidago* is not a foodplant. This species overwinters as newly hatched first instar larvae.

Distribution: Another circumpolar species, *titania* is found in North America from subarctic Canada south to Maine, Minnesota, Washington, and in the Rocky Mountains to New Mexico. There is one brood which appears from mid July to early August.

(a) **boisduvalii** (Duponchel). Plate 35, figure 15, ♂. This butterfly is distributed from the eastern Arctic south to Labrador and Churchill, Manitoba. At the southern limits it intergrades with the subspecies *grandis.* The type locality is Labrador.

(b) **grandis** (Barnes & McDunnough). Plate 35, figure 7, ♂; figure 8, ♀. The distribution of *grandis* is from New Brunswick and northern Ontario westward to central British Columbia, Alaska and Yukon. Adults frequently visit flowers of the Goldenrod, *Solidago graminifolia,* along forest roadsides, marshy areas and the edges of spruce bogs. The type locality is Hymers, Ontario.

(c) **montinus** (Scudder). Plate 35, figure 18, ♂. This butterfly inhabits the White Mountains of New Hampshire.

(d) **rainieri** (Barnes & McDunnough). Plate 35, figure 9, ♂. This subspecies occurs in the Cascade and Olympic Mountains of Washington and the Hope Mountains of British Columbia. It is similar to the southern Rocky Mountain subspecies *helena.* Their geographic separation by the distinctly different subspecies *ingens,* however, argues for considering *rainieri* and *helena* as distinct. The type locality is Mount Rainier, Washington.

(e) **ingens** (Barnes & McDunnough). Plate 35, figure 12, ♂. This large subspecies is found in southwestern Montana, southeastern Idaho and northwestern Wyoming. It frequents open spaces on the wooded slopes or in the valley bottoms to timberline and is easily netted on the flowers of *Senecio.* The type locality is Yellowstone National Park, Wyoming.

(f) **helena** (Edwards). Plate 35, figure 10, ♂; figure 11, ♀. This is the most abundant and widespread of all southern Rocky Mountain *Boloria.* In Colorado it is not confined to bogs but is encountered in moist meadows and semi-woodlands in every mountain range in the state between 9000 and 12,000 ft. In southern Wyoming *helena* flies at slightly lower elevations, from 6900 to 7000 ft. and is very abundant in the Medicine Bow Range during the month of July. It is also found in northern New Mexico and in the La Sal Mountains in Utah. The type locality is Mosquito Pass, Lake-Park counties, Colorado.

10. **Boloria alberta** (Edwards). Plate 34, figure 10, ♂; figure 11, ♀. The illustration will be sufficient to recognize this species. There are no known subspecies in North America.

Early Stages: Edwards through correspondence with Bean obtained eggs laid on *Dryas* sp., however these did not develop. It is the presumed foodplant.

Distribution: This species is known from high, barren windswept ridges in the Rocky Mountains of Alberta, Glacier National Park, and Lillooet, British Columbia. Early museum records suggested that *alberta* flew only on even-numbered years in Alberta. However observations at Plateau Mountain in southern Alberta show that it flies there every year. The type locality is Laggan, Alberta.

11. **Boloria astarte** (Doubleday). This large species may be recognized at once from the figures. There are two subspecies, each previously considered a distinct species.

Early Stages: I have raised *astarte astarte* on *Saxifraga bronchialis* in Alberta. This same foodplant is known in Siberia. In Alberta adults fly each year, not every two years as previously thought. In Washington the adults fly only in even-numbered years.

Distribution: This species occurs in Washington and Alberta northward to Alaska and Yukon Territory. Adults occur in the south during late July and early August; in the north they occur in June.

(a) **astarte** (Doubleday). Plate 33, figure 10, ♂; figure 11, ♀. This subspecies differs from *distincta* by having a more pointed apex on the fore wing and the submedian row of white spots on the underside of the hind wing free of dark overscaling. This subspecies flies in the Rocky Mountains of Alberta, in the Lillooet region of British Columbia and in Okanogan county, Washington. The type locality is probably near Banff, Alberta.

(b) **distincta** (Gibson). Plate 33, figure 12, ♀; Plate 23, figure 10, underside. This subspecies is known from the barren mountain ridges of northern Alaska and the Yukon. There is diversity of opinion as to whether this should be considered a separate species. Until the two forms are better studied the controversy will not be resolved. The type locality is Harrington Creek, Yukon Territory.

12. **Boloria improba** (Butler). This species is easily recognized from the illustrations.

Early Stages: Unknown in North America. *Salix herbacea* is recorded as a foodplant in Europe.

Distribution: This Holarctic species inhabits the true Arctic regions of North America, flying in July.

(a) **improba** (Butler). Plate 33, figure 7, ♂. This subspecies occurs in the Canadian arctic west to the Yukon. The wings are heavily melanic. The type locality is Winter Cove and Cambridge Bay, Northwest Territories.

(b) **youngi** (Holland). Plate 33, figure 8, ♂. This subspecies occurs in Alaska, and at Atlin, British Columbia. It is characterized by the bright fulvous color of the upper wings. The type locality is mountains between 40 Mile and Mission creeks, Alaska.

13. **Boloria polaris** (Boisduval). Plate 34, figure 16, ♂; figure 17, ♀. This species is immediately recognizable by the very distinctive maculation beneath. It is circumpolar, ranging across the Arctic from Scandinavia to Greenland. In most of its range no subspecies are distinguished (but see *B. p. stellata,* below).

(a) **polaris** (Boisduval). This is the nominate subspecies of the Palaearctic and most of the Nearctic. Adults fly in late July and August.

Early Stages: These are unknown; *Dryas octopetala* is a suspected larval foodplant in Scandinavia.

Distribution: This subspecies ranges from Alaska southward into British Columbia, across arctic Canada to Greenland. The type locality is the Norwegian Alps.

(b) **stellata** Masters. This recently described subspecies is smaller, with brighter fulvous coloration on the upperside and much more contrasty and distinct light markings on the underside.

Distribution: The type locality is Churchill, Manitoba. Its northward boundaries (or intergradation with *p. polaris*) are not known.

14. **Boloria chariclea** (Schneider).   As noted previously, *B. titania helena* and *B. titania rainieri* resemble this species. Nominate *chariclea* is European, but two subspecies represent this butterfly in North America.

Early Stages: Unknown in North America. *Salix arctica* may be a European foodplant.

Distribution: This circumpolar species is restricted to tundra in North America. The adults fly in July.

(a) **arctica** (Zetterstedt). Plate 33, figure 16, ♂.   The distribution of this subspecies in North America is confined to the far north, from Greenland to Yukon Territory. The name *obscurata* (M'Lachlan) is a synonym of *arctica*. The type locality is Greenland.

(b) **butleri** (Edwards). Plate 33, figure 13, ♂; figure 14, ♀.   This subspecies is known only from Alaska. Some individuals have silvery spots on the lower surface of the secondaries. The type locality is Cape Thompson, Alaska.

Family HELICONIIDAE

WILLIAM H. HOWE

The heliconiids are found only in the Americas where all but a few species are confined to the tropical regions. Those that invade the warmer parts of the temperate zones are easily recognized by their elongate fore wings. In addition all heliconiids have greatly reduced fore legs that cannot be used for walking, a large head and a long slender body. The cell of the fore wing is closed and that of the hind wing open. The abdominal margin of the hind wing lacks the body fold found in true nymphalids.

The family is composed of one very large genus, *Heliconius,* and several small genera each containing one to three species. The genus *Heliconius* has long been a favorite among collectors of tropical butterflies. The recognition of many of the Amazonian species is difficult because within the genus itself there are many mimetic pairs of species. Other butterflies and moths that look like heliconiids are also protected from predators by the resemblance. Like the Danaidae and Ithomiidae, the Heliconiidae are distasteful to birds and lizards. So far as we know the larvae of all heliconiids feed on the leaves of passion flower (*Passiflora*), which supply the insects with the bitter substance that makes them distasteful.

Early Stages: These are known for a number of species representing all genera. The eggs are subconical and vary from twice as tall to almost as tall as wide. The sides are decorated with vertical and horizontal ribs. At the crown the ribs give way to a pattern of hexagonal pits. The mature larvae carry six rows of long, spurred spines called scoli. Those of the lowest row are reduced to a few hairs on the thorax but are well developed on the abdomen. The head is surmounted by a pair of coronal horns, barely noticeable on *Dione* but prominent on all other genera. The pupae in profile are "sway-backed" with the wing case projecting ventrad. The surface varies from somewhat warty to decorated with grotesque flaps, spines and processes.

Genus HELICONIUS Kluk

As yet we do not know just how many species are represented in the several hundred names that have been used with this genus. One species breeds in the United States and another occasionally strays into the Brownsville, Texas, area. This is the only genus in the Heliconiidae with the cell on the hind wing closed.

1. **Heliconius charitonius** (Linnaeus). The Zebra appears in our territory as two subspecies, one in the East, the other in the West. Linnaeus's type came from St. Thomas in the Virgin Islands. The species itself ranges from northwestern South America throughout the West Indies and Central America to Florida and northern Mexico.

(a) **tuckeri** Comstock & Brown. Plate 1, figure 9, ♂. This is the Florida subspecies. It is found in breeding colonies from Florida around the Gulf to Louisiana.

Early Stages: These were fully described by W. H. Edwards.

(b) **vazquezae** Comstock & Brown. The Mexican subspecies strays north as far as Colorado and Kansas. Whether or not breeding colonies exist within the United States is yet to be established. The yellow band across the hind wing of *vazquezae* is wider than on *tuckeri.* On *tuckeri* the posterior edge of the band falls inside the cell while on *vazquezae* it is well outside the cell.

2. **Heliconius petiveranus** Doubleday. Plate 1, figure 10, ♂. The Mexican subspecies, nominate *petiveranus,* occasionally occurs in extreme southern Texas. Thus far no breeding colony has been found. The insect was first described from "Mexico and Honduras" and ranges southward into northwestern South America where other subspecies occur.

Genus DRYAS Hübner

A single widely distributed species composes this genus. The antennae of *Dryas* are proportionally shorter than in *Heliconius* and the club is more prominent. As in *Heliconius* androconia are found on the subcostal and radial stalk veins of the hind wing. On the fore wing these specialized male scales are found on the anal, cubital and median branch veins. The cell of the hind wing is open in *Dryas.*

Early Stages: The eggs are buff-yellow, a little taller than wide, with eighteen to twenty-one vertical ribs. The mature larva has coronal horns about as long as the face, and is buffy brown spotted with lighter and darker markings. The head is creamy white with black and dark red markings. The pupa is without grotesque processes or spines but is somewhat warty and with low subdorsal flanges, brownish with a few gold spots.

Distribution: The species occurs throughout the tropical parts of the Americas and the adjacent warm temperate areas.

1. **Dryas julia** Fabricius.

(a) **cillene** (Cramer). Plate 1, figure 11, ♂; figure 12, ♀. There is some question about the proper name to be applied to this, the Cuban subspecies of *julia.* Cramer said the specimen he figured as *cillene* was from Surinam but it does not match specimens from there. It is a rather good match for Cuban specimens. Marston Bates used *nudeola* Stichel for the Cuban subspecies. That name was first applied to an aberration and technically had no standing until Bates used it.

Distribution: This subspecies is found in Cuba and southern Florida, chiefly the Keys.

(b) **moderata** (Stichel).   The Central American subspecies is found in eastern Texas. It differs from the Cuban subspecies in having all of the black markings reduced and sometimes almost absent.

Distribution: This subspecies ranges from Texas south to Panamá.

Genus DIONE Hübner

Three silver-spotted species found in the American tropics compose this genus. Many structural characters separate *Dione* from both *Dryas* and *Agraulis.* The most easily seen of these are: the femora of the mid and hind legs are hairy on *Dione* and scaled on the other two; and the fore wing is markedly angulate at M_3 on *Dione* and smoothly curved on the other two.

Early Stages: The height of the egg is about one and one-half times the diameter; it has thirteen vertical ribs and is dark red. In the mature larva the coronal horns are very short, much shorter than the distance between them, there is a short branched spine on the first thoracic segment (absent from all other Heliconiidae), and the body is dark brown with small orange spots and sprinkled with silver. Pupa: in profile most of the wing case appears to project below the venter; there are many small tubercles.

Distribution: The genus ranges from Mexico south to Bolivia and Argentina. Two species are found north of Costa Rica.

1. **Dione moneta** Hübner. Plate 77, figure 2, ♂.   A single example of this species (the Mexican subspecies, *poeyi* (Butler)) was taken in 1964 near Catarina, in Dimmit county, Texas, the first U.S. record of this species.

Distribution: Central Mexico to Peru.

Genus AGRAULIS Boisduval & Le Conte

A single widespread species constitutes this genus. Numerous subspecies have been recognized, two of which breed in the United States. The two most easily noted morphological characters that separate the two genera of tropical silver-spotted butterflies are noted under *Dione.*

Early Stages: The egg is a little taller than its diameter, with sixteen to seventeen vertical ribs, buff-yellow becoming mottled as eclosion approaches. In the mature larva the coronal horns are about as long as the face, and the body is gray to black with three pairs of orange dorso-lateral stripes the length of the body and a broken white sublateral stripe. The pupa is brown with many small tubercles, the wing cases projecting below the venter.

Distribution: The species occurs from southern United States throughout tropical America to Argentina.

1. **Agraulis vanillae** (Linnaeus).

(a) **nigrior** Michener. Plate 1, figure 13, ♂; figure 14, ♂, underside. This eastern subspecies is less brilliantly colored and the black markings are bolder than on *incarnata,* the western subspecies. The spots in cells M_3, Cu_1 and Cu_2 are larger in *nigrior* than in *incarnata.*

Distribution: This subspecies occurs from Florida west to Louisiana, north to North Carolina (occasionally New York) and on Bermuda (but not the Bahamas or Cuba where ssp *insularis* Maynard is found). In the Mississippi Valley the two subspecies intergrade.

(b) **incarnata** (Riley). The western subspecies is brilliant orange-fulvous with considerably reduced black markings. Some would call this subspecies *comstocki,* but that name was proposed by Gunder in 1925 for an aberration and has no standing in nomenclature. The use of *comstocki* as a valid subspecies name dates from McDunnough (1938), twelve years after Riley proposed *incarnata* for certain Mexican specimens.

Distribution: This subspecies ranges from California and Texas south to Honduras, in the United States east to Missouri and Arkansas. Coastal material from Texas intergrades with *nigrior.*

Family LIBYTHEIDAE

The Snout Butterflies

WILLIAM H. HOWE

As the name implies these butterflies can be recognized by the snoutlike, greatly elongated palpi. The fore wings are apically produced and falcate. The wings are colored dark brown and patterned with white and orange. Two genera are recognized, *Libythea* Fabricius for all of the Old World species and *Libytheana* Michener for the New World species.

Early Stages: The mature caterpillars are cylindrical and without spines. The last abdominal segment is rounded and never bifurcate. The larval host is *Celtis* (Hackberry.)

Distribution: The family, though a small one, is worldwide.

Genus LIBYTHEANA Michener

The American Snout Butterflies have palpi that are longer than the thorax while in the Old World species (Genus *Libythea* Fabricius) the palpi are shorter than the thorax. Three species are found in the Americas. One of these is well established in the region we treat while a second appears to be little more than a casual visitor in the southwestern states.

1. **Libytheana bachmanii** (Kirtland). This distinctive butterfly may be recognized at once from the figures. In the southwest it is easily confused with the next species. Careful study of the figures and the text for *carinenta* will help you decide what you have caught. The butterflies have a rapid flight but settle frequently at mud puddles. They are attracted by bait of fermenting fruits. There are two subspecies.

Occasionally snout butterflies perform mass migrations. On August 9, 1966, these migrants were so numerous that they obscured the sun over Tucson, Arizona, and it was necessary to turn on the street lights!

Early Stages: The first two thoracic segments are notably swollen and the last abdominal segment abruptly tapered. The insects are dark green with yellow lateral and middorsal stripes. On the swollen thoracic segments there is a pair of low, small, black warts circled with yellow. The pupa is green and tapers conically both posteriorly to the cremaster and anteriorly to the head from the thickened thoracic area.

Distribution: From central New England and southern Ontario south to Florida and west to the Rocky Mountains.

(a) **bachmanii** (Kirtland). Plate 47, figure 1, ♂; figure 2, underside. The Eastern Snout Butterfly is easily recognized from the figures.

Early Stages: As above. The host plant is *Celtis occidentalis.*

Distribution: Originally described from Northern Ohio (the vicinity of Cleveland) and found throughout the eastern part of the range westward to about the 100th meridian.

(b) **larvata** (Strecker). This subspecies is larger, darker, less angular in outline and with the margin of the hind wing less undulate than *bachmanii bachmanii*. It is subject to mass migration in Mexico and Arizona.

Early Stages: These need further study.

Distribution: Described from western Texas, this is the form found in the semi-arid southwest from Texas to Arizona and northward to Colorado. Its range extends southward in Mexico and overlaps that of the following species.

2. **Libytheana carinenta** (Cramer). Plate 47, figure 14, ♂, underside; figure 15, ♂ (ssp. *mexicana*). Adults of *L. carinenta mexicana* Michener somewhat resemble *bachmanii* but there are several differences. The outer edge of the hind wing is straight or nearly so and never so indented or scalloped as in *bachmanii*. The apex of the fore wing is not so falcate or produced. The orange patches on *mexicana* are much paler and more diffused than on *bachmanii*. On the lower surfaces the ground color is pale cream or whitish with many fine gray striations and little or none of the purplish iridescence of *bachmanii*.

Early Stages: Not known.

Distribution: The species ranges north from Paraguay to our southwestern states. The subspecies *mexicana* is found occasionally in southern Arizona and southern Texas and ranges from there southward throughout Mexico and Central America. In September and early October, 1971, hundreds of *carinenta* invaded Franklin county, Kansas. They were taken visiting wild asters with three and four individuals taken in a single net swing. Individuals could be observed flying in a due north-northeast direction from the south.

Family RIODINIDAE

The Metalmarks

JERRY A. POWELL

The family Riodinidae is a large assemblage of nearly worldwide distribution which has its greatest diversity in the New World tropics. More than 1000 species have been described, nearly 90% of which are Neotropical, and the few found in the Nearctic for the most part represent northern derivations or extensions of widespread Neotropical genera or species. Thus the twenty-one species treated here are scattered among six genera, most of which have their greatest diversity to the south. Only in *Calephelis* and *Apodemia* is there indication of Nearctic speciation, primarily in austral situations. None of the North American species is strictly boreal.

The butterflies are small to medium sized, having short, broad wings and unusually elongate antennae. Their common name originates from the presence of metallic colored markings on the wings in many genera. Although Nearctic species are for the most part dull colored, appearing cryptic in browns, oranges and black, or checkered with white, a tremendous diversity of form and color has been developed by Neotropical members of the group. There some species have normally shaped wings, others have the hind wing developed into long tails, resembling miniature swallowtails, while others have tail-like extensions at the ends of most of the hind wing veins. Moreover, the fore wing, especially the costal margin, is often modified. In their colors, the Neotropical species far outdistance their diversity of form, with an astonishing display of both pigment and structural (metallic) ornamentation. Included is a wide variety of both mimetic and apparently non-mimetic groups, which often seem to show more similarity to various other butterflies than to other riodinids.

The females are almost invariably larger than the males and have broader wings, with males exhibiting a straighter costal and terminal margin on the fore wing, resulting in a more pointed apex.

This heterogeneous assemblage is united by possession of variously reduced fore legs (often strongly so, being almost brush-like, with one-segmented tarsi) in the male, where they are not used for walking. In the female the fore legs are functional but smaller than the other pairs. Additionally, the long antenna (more than half the fore wing length in all our species), which bears a slender, flattened club, will serve to distinguish the riodinids.

In the field metalmarks can often be recognized by the characteristic manner in which they hold their wings when perched. Instead of closing them together above them, like most butterflies do, members of most riodinid genera hold the wings out laterally, flat against the substrate, in the manner of many geometrid moths. Others (e.g., *Apodemia*) hold them cocked open, at an angle of 45° or so. In addition, many metalmarks, especially those of Neotropical genera, tend to alight on undersides of leaves, or otherwise seek shaded spots, particularly during the warmest part of the day.

Early Stages: The egg, larva and pupa are most similar to those of the Lycaenidae, the group to which riodinids are considered most closely related, even in a subfamilial relationship by some authors. The egg is somewhat flattened, wider than tall, with either a broad, shallow concavity on top, or a somewhat conical rise with a small central depression in the micropylar area. The surface is uniformly reticulated with a network of fine ridges, without the raised vertical ribs which are characteristic of many Lycaenidae.

The larvae are variable but are somewhat stout, with a larger head, and are not so grub-like in appearance as lycaenid caterpillars. In later instars the riodinid larvae bear a series of dorsolateral, lateral and ventrolateral verrucae (raised spots) with numerous secondary setae. In further contrast to the more or less uniformly distributed short secondary setae of lycaenid larvae, the clumped setae of metalmark caterpillars may be very long, especially on the verrucae low on the sides, from which the setae extend out the width of the body or more, brushing the substrate. Probably they aid in protective concealment through a shadow elimination effect, a feature which seems to be common to a wide variety of Lepidoptera caterpillars in the Neotropical Region. Riodinid larvae usually are not green and do not bear a strong cryptic resemblance to their foodplant substrates.

The pupa also is short and stout, although not so robust as in typical lycaenids, with a flattened ventral surface. The head is turned onto the ventral surface, with the prothorax protruded anteriorly. A coating of fine hairs is borne by most species, at least dorsally, which will further serve to distinguish metalmark pupae from those of the Lycaenidae. Pupation usually occurs in debris on the ground or in the base of the plant, with the chrysalis anchored by a frail median girdle and caudal attachment. *Taxonomy:* All the Nearctic species are members of the subfamily Riodininae, which contains the vast majority of Neotropical and world genera. One species, *Euselasia abreas* (Edwards) (Euselasiinae) was originally described as from "Arizona" nearly a century ago. However, according to F. M. Brown, the type specimen is lost, and lack of other reports of this genus anywhere north of Veracruz suggests that *abreas* was based on a mislabelled specimen. Therefore the species is not considered to be a member of our fauna in this treatment.

Genus CALEPHELIS Grote & Robinson

The genus *Calephelis* comprises a group of small, predominantly brown butterflies with orange undersides. The various species are remarkably similar in external appearance. About a dozen entities have been treated as species by taxonomists. Some of the species are widespread and show moderate geographical variation.

Calephelis is the most northern of the New World riodinid genera, with most of the species occurring entirely in or ranging into the Nearctic, and only three species distributed as far south as northern South America.

1. **Calephelis virginiensis** (Guérin-Méneville). Plate 47, figure 16, ♂; figure 17, ♀; figure 26, ♀, underside. This Gulf states species is most easily recognized by its small size and usually uniform rust brown, nearly orange, upperside. The fringes lack white spotting. *C. virginiensis* flies in grassy fields, wet meadows and open places in savannah and hardwood lowland forest and grassland situations. Although widespread, this species is found primarily in localized colonies. Wingspread: 16 to 20 (rarely to 23) mm.

Early Stages: These have not been described in the literature. The species has been reared on *Cirsium horridulum* (Compositae) in Texas by Roy O. Kendall.

Distribution: C. virginiensis occurs in lowland, coastal parts of the southeastern United States from southeastern Virginia (TL) through the Carolinas and the Gulf states to the vicinity of Houston, Texas; it is generally distributed in Florida, Mississippi and Louisiana and northward to northwestern Arkansas. In Virginia there are three broods, flying in April–May, July, and September–October; southward the generations are less well defined, with records for every month in Florida.

2. **Calephelis borealis** (Grote & Robinson). Plate 47, figure 5, ♀; figure 6, ♀, underside; figure 9, ♂. This northeastern species is considerably larger and usually darker brown dorsally than *virginiensis*. *C. borealis* is quite similar to *C. muticum* and differences between them were overlooked until 1937. Thus early records of "*borealis*" in the Midwest actually refer to *muticum*. From the latter, *borealis* is usually distinguishable by a blackish shade across the upperside of both wings, bordered outwardly by the outer, transverse, irregular line. The metallic marks tend to be more crescent-shaped and connected, the outer transverse line marks heavier, more continuous and prominent in *borealis*. There are decisive genitalic differences. This species flies in open woods, along woodland roads and on high ground, especially limestone and shale outcroppings, usually near streams, the colonies widely scattered and localized. Wingspread: 25 to 29 mm.

Early Stages: The life history was described in 1936 by dos Passos and by Randle in 1953. The egg is flattened with large circular polygonal cells formed by the ribbing of the chorion. The larvae normally pass through eight instars, hibernating usually in the fifth or sixth, under leaves on the ground, where pupation occurs. There is a single annual generation, but individuals reared indoors usually emerge in the fall of the same season. The mature larva is greenish with small black dots dorsally and with long whitish hairs dorsally and laterally. Foodplant: *Senecio obovatus* (Compositae).

Distribution: The species occurs in southern New York (TL: Orange county), northern New Jersey and along the Allegheny and Appalachian mountains to central western Virginia; westward in central Pennsylvania through southern Ohio and northern Kentucky to central Indiana. Adults fly from mid-June to early August.

3. **Calephelis muticum** McAlpine. Plate 47, figure 3, ♂; figure 4, ♂, underside; figure 8, ♀. This species is closely related to *borealis,* and differences between the two are discussed above. *C. muticum* has the upperside a more uniform mahogany brown without a distinct inner blackish shade. It lives in wet meadows, swamps and bogs. Wingspread: 23 to 28 (rarely 30) mm.

Early Stages: These were described by McAlpine in 1938. The eggs are deposited on undersides of leaves of smaller individuals of the foodplant. Both the egg and larva are similar in general appearance to those of *borealis.* The black spots of the larva in that species are lacking in *muticum.* The larvae undergo eight or nine instars, hibernating at the base of small, live leaves in the fourth or fifth instar. Pupation occurs near the base of the plant. The pupal stage lasts about twelve to thirteen days, prior to the single annual flight. Foodplant: *Cirsium muticum* (Compositae).

Distribution: Aside from a single record from Bar Harbor, Maine, the species ranges from the vicinity of Pittsburgh, Pennsylvania, westward through central Ohio, southern Michigan (TL: Willis, Washtenaw county), northern Indiana and Illinois, southern Wisconsin to southeastern Minnesota, southward in south central Missouri to northern Arkansas. The flight period is from early July to mid August.

Although general statements in the literature indicate that *muticum* and *borealis* overlap, the above three species are almost, if not completely, allopatric. This suggests a recent divergence, perhaps following the last glacial period, and a careful study should be carried out in the meeting zone (western Pennsylvania, Central Ohio and Indiana to northern Arkansas) to substantiate the consistency of habitat differentiation and degree of isolation, in order to corroborate the slight morphological differences which are presently considered to represent speciation.

4. **Calephelis guadeloupe** (Strecker). Plate 47, figure 29, ♂; figure 30, ♀. This Texas species was long unrecognized after its original description and was redescribed as *rawsoni* McAlpine, 1939, (TL: Kerrville, Texas) and has been so treated in recent literature. The upperside is somewhat variable, dull reddish brown to chocolate brown, not so reddish as the preceding, eastern species and without the definite transverse dark shade of *nemesis.* The outer margin of the fore wing is somewhat undulate, with three white spots in the fringe. The male genitalia are distinguishable from other *Calephelis* by the very elongate transtilla and more extensive spination of the valvae. Wingspread: 21 to 25 mm.

Early Stages: These are not reported in the literature. The larval foods are *Eupatorium havanense* and *E. greggii* (Compositae), according to Roy O. Kendall.

Distribution: The species occurs from south central Texas (TL: vicinity of New Braunfels) to the Big Bend area. It is probably double brooded, with records of adults from June to November.

5. **Calephelis nemesis** (Edwards). Plate 47, figure 18, ♂; figure 19, ♀. This is the most widespread and variable species of *Calephelis* in North America. The upper surface is usually dark brown without much reddish tinge, crossed by a blackish band which is bordered outwardly by the sinuate postmedian line. In Arizona,

however, the color ranges within populations from normal to red-brown or nearly a rust color similar to *wrighti* and *virginiensis,* and the blackish band disappears on these specimens. The metallic markings are typically inconspicuous but become more noticeable in these variable populations. In the male genitalia, the transtilla is shorter than the valvae and attenuate but rounded at the distal end. The colonies are restricted, although evidently not so much as in the eastern species, and occur in chaparral, mountain canyons and riparian associations in arid areas, not in desert areas *per se.* Wing expanse: 20 to 26 (rarely 19 to 28) mm.

Early Stages: These were described by Comstock and Dammers, in 1932, who reared *nemesis* in southern California on *Baccharis glutinosa* (Compositae). The eggs are deposited on the midrib of the leaves, and larvae reared indoors in fall pupated the same winter. The larvae have somewhat shorter, more decumbent hair than in *wrighti.* Foodplants: *Baccharis glutinosa* (Compositae). In southern California probably other composites such as *Encelia* are used. Larvae accepted *Clematis drummondi* (Ranunculaceae) in the laboratory when reared by Kendall in Texas.

Distribution: The species occurs along the Pacific Coast in southern California and Baja California Norte and along the Colorado River north to Parker Dam, thence scattered widely to the south and east, through the mountains of central and southern Arizona (TL: Tucson, Arizona), the southern half of Texas and most of northern Mexico south at least to Oaxaca. There are two generations in coastal southern California, with adults in May–June and August–October; it is multi-brooded to the south, with flight records for every month in Texas.

6. **Calephelis wrighti** Holland. Plate 47, figure 22, ♀; figure 23, ♂. This species is characterized by a more uniform color on the upperside than in any other *Calephelis.* The reddish ground has a smoky cast, with the black markings obscured, the metallic markings conspicuous and the three white marks of the fringes strongly contrasting. The transtilla of the male genitalia is elongate, nearly as long as the valvae, and is hood-like, nearly surrounding the aedeagus, with a truncate distal end. The butterflies are found only in close association with the foodplant, *Bebbia,* a bush which grows along dry washes or rocky slopes in desert or semi-desert situations. Wingspread: 20 to 26 mm.

Early Stages: These were described by Comstock in 1928 under the name *australis.* The egg is about 0.6 mm in diameter with large cells in the chorion reticulation, about 18–20 in the top row and twice that number at the lateral broadest diameter. The larvae, which are covered with very elongate white hairs, feed on the greenish covering of the stems. Pupation occurs in debris at the base of the plant. Foodplant: *Bebbia juncea* (Compositae).

Distribution: The species occurs in southern California and Baja California Norte, from the western tip of Riverside county and other desert-like associations on the coastal side of the mountains into desert canyons east of the peninsular ranges and along the Colorado River north to Parker Dam. There are probably three annual generations, at least in some situations, with flights in February–March, June–July, and September–October.

The species was described on the basis of the figures published by Wright in the *Butterflies of the West Coast*. The types at the California Academy of Sciences bear no locality data.

7. **Calephelis perditalis** Barnes & McDunnough. Plate 47, figure 20, ♂; figure 21, ♀. This Texas butterfly, which has been considered a subspecies of the widespread *nilus* Felder (TL: Venezuela), is distinguishable from other North American members of the genus by the broad fore wing with rounded apex and termen of the male, so that the wing shape is similar in both sexes. *C. nilus* was described originally from a female, but Stichel and others have considered *argyrodines* Bates (TL: Guatemala), a form with pointed fore wing in the male, to be a synonym, so that the alleged conspecificity of *perditalis* with *nilus* seems unlikely. The female of *perditalis* is quite similar in appearance to the female of *guadeloupe*. The male genitalia are similar to those of *nemesis,* with a rather short transtilla which is more pointed than in the latter species. Wingspread: 17.5 to 22.5 mm.

Early Stages: Not reported as yet. Foodplant: *Eupatorium odoratum* (Compositae) according to Roy O. Kendall.

Distribution: The species is found in southern Texas from Nueces county southward (TL: San Benito); in Mexico it ranges throughout the Gulf region, in Chiapas, the Sierra Madre del Sur, Sierra Madre Occidental, and was reported in Arizona by McAlpine in 1961. The record of *perditalis* at Comfort (north of San Antonio) in Holland's *Butterfly Book* probably is referable to *guadeloupe*. Adults fly throughout the year in Texas.

Genus CARIA Hübner

A convexity near the base of the costa which results in a sinuate costal margin is characteristic of both sexes of *Caria*. About fifteen entities have been assigned specific status, and these are about equally divided among northern Central America, southern Central America and northern South America. Most have patches of metallic greenish scales on the upperside, at least in the male, although these may be variable within species as is the case with the single representative which extends into the United States.

1. **Caria ino** Godman & Salvin. Plate 47, figure 27, ♀; figure 28, ♂. *Caria ino melicerta* Schaus is the only subspecies found in our area. The fore wing in the female has a more pronounced sinuation of the costa. The male has the wings blackish on the upperside with or without a metallic greenish bar at the end of the cell; the female upperside is primarily orange-brown with little contrast in the termen or primarily dark with an orange-brown termen, without metallic greenish in either form. The underside in both sexes is bright brick red or rust orange with conspicuous steel-bluish metallic spots. Wingspread: 20 to 24 mm (Texas specimens).

Early Stages: These are not described in the literature. The foodplant is *Celtis pallida* (Ulmaceae) according to Roy O. Kendall.

Distribution: This subspecies occurs from southern Texas (Lake Corpus Christi southward), throughout the thorn forest regions of eastern Mexico to northern Yucatán (TL: Paso de San Juan [east of Jalapa], Veracruz); *ino ino* Godman & Salvin occurs in the thorn forests of western Mexico (TL: Ventanas [= Villa Corona], Durango) south to Oaxaca. Adults are on the wing almost throughout the year in southern Texas.

Genus LASAIA Bates

This genus contains about five species all of which occur in southern Mexico or northern Central America. Four are widespread, ranging into northern South America, including one which also is distributed northward along the Gulf of Mexico into extreme southern Texas. The butterflies are moderately large and showy, with extensive metallic blue on the upperside, especially in the male.

1. **Lasaia sula** Staudinger. Plate 47, figure 37, ♂; figure 38, ♀. Apparently confusion in the identification has resulted in crediting two species of *Lasaia* to Texas. There appears to be only one, usually called either *L. agesilas narses* Staudinger or *L. sessilis* Schaus. Both of these were reported in Texas by Stichel (in *Lepidopterorum Catalogus*) but present lepidopterists in Texas know of just one species. H. K. Clench believes the correct name for this to be *sula,* and this name was applied to the Texas species by Stichel (in *Genera Insectorum*). The banded underside will distinguish *sula* from *narses,* which ranges northward in the Gulf region at least to San Luis Potosí. The latter species has a broad, pale area on the outer margin of the hind wing. Wingspread: 21 to 29 mm.
    Early Stages: Unknown.
    Distribution: Extreme southern Texas (Pharr-Brownsville area) southward through the Gulf region of Mexico, mountains of Michoacán, Chiapas, to Honduras (TL: San Pedro de Sula). In Texas flight records are available for April, June and August to November.

Genus MELANIS Hübner

Some of the largest and most colorful of the New World metalmarks are among the thirty-five species comprising *Melanis*. This genus has been known as *Lymnas* in most literature, but according to Hemming the correct name is *Melanis*. Nearly all are restricted to South America, but a few range into Central America. One of these is represented by a subspecies which is widespread in the more tropical portions of northern Central America and reaches the southern tip of Texas.

1. **Melanis pixe** Boisduval. Plate 48, figure 1, ♀. The nominate subspecies of *pixe* (the one in our area) always has a single red spot at the tornal angle of the fore

wing, but an additional one or two may be present. Males are smaller than females but do not have an appreciably narrower, more pointed fore wing as in other riodinid genera. Wingspread: 42 to 48 mm.

Early Stages: Not described. The foodplant is *Pithecellobium dulce* (Leguminosae) according to Roy O. Kendall, who has reared *pixe* in Texas.

Distribution: M. p. pixe occurs from extreme southern Texas, south in the Gulf region of Mexico to the Yucatán Peninsula, and the isthmus region of Oaxaca (TL: Mexico); *pixe sanguinea* Stichel occurs on the Pacific side of Mexico, from Chiapas southward to Panamá. There are flight records in Texas for January and July.

Genus EMESIS Fabricius

There are nearly forty species in this genus, which has its center of distribution in the northern tier of countries in South America. Nearly all are relatively large butterflies for Riodinidae and most are similar in appearance and pattern, with uppersides more or less uniform bluish gray or brown, marked with transverse black lines. About half the species are either restricted to Central America or are widespread from South America northward. Three species range into parts of our area, in southern Texas and Arizona. Two of these, *cleis* and *ares,* were described as species long ago and were treated as such and well figured in Holland's *Butterfly Book,* but have generally been regarded as forms of one species in the literature. The situation has been clarified by F. M. Brown in 1969.

1. **Emesis zela** Butler. Plate 48, figure 32, ♂; figure 33, ♀ (ssp. *cleis*). The subspecies that occurs in our area is *E. zela cleis* (Edwards). The extent of orange on the hind wing and quality of orange-brown of the fore wing are variable, perhaps seasonally. Some specimens taken in June resemble *ares* in restriction of hind wing orange and color of fore wing. However, the reduced subterminal black markings and the blackish bar at the end of the cell on the fore wing will serve to distinguish *cleis* in both sexes. In the male genitalia *cleis* has a wide, shallow, V-shaped emargination on the uncus, with a distinct, narrow, U-shaped median sclerotized band on its inner side. Adults of this subspecies frequent canyons in Arizona, where males seem to engage in territorial behavior, occupying individual open spots along creeks and roadways. Wingspread: 27 to 37 mm.

Early Stages: Unknown.

Distribution: The subspecies *cleis* occurs in the mountains of central Arizona from Oak Creek Canyon south through the Tonto Basin, in all the mountains of southern Arizona (TL: vic. Fort Grant), the Sierra Madre Occidental in Mexico to about Michoacán. According to Clench, *cleis* is a subspecies of *Emesis zela,* which ranges widely southward (TL: Venezuela). The possible record for *Emesis* in southwestern Colorado given by Brown in *Colorado Butterflies* seems doubtful but would more likely be *cleis* than *emesia* which has been suggested. The subspecies is at least double brooded in Arizona, with flight records for March–April and from June to mid August.

2. **Emesis ares** (Edwards). Plate 47, figure 31, ♀; figure 32, ♂. This species is less variable than *zela cleis* and can be distinguished by its uniform dark gray-brown fore wing, which is crossed by thin transverse black lines which are uniform in development including the subterminal row, without a dark shade between the two rows at the end of the cell. In addition, *ares* is usually larger, has a deeper reddish quality in the costal portion of the hind wing, and this color is generally more restricted than in *cleis*. In the female the fore wing is equally dark (whereas it is paler in female *cleis* than in the male) and has a terminal row of reddish orange spots. In the male genitalia *ares* has a truncate margin of the uncus with a small median notch, subtended by a less well defined sclerotized band on its median, inner side than in cleis. These two species may fly together in August in the mountains of southern Arizona, but records to document this are lacking, in part owing to the failure of collectors to differentiate between *cleis* and *ares*. Expanse: 30 to 37 mm.

Early Stages: The egg was described by Comstock in 1953 but the foodplant is unknown.

Distribution: E. *ares* is distributed from the mountain ranges of southern Arizona (Graham, Santa Rita, Huachuca and Chiricahua [TL: vic. Fort Grant]), into the Sierra Madre Occidental of Mexico, at least to the mountains west of Hidalgo del Parral. This species apparently has only a single generation and flies later than *cleis:* August to mid September in Arizona, and mid July in Chihuahua.

3. **Emesis emesia** (Hewitson). Plate 47, figure 33, ♂. The nominate subspecies, *emesia emesia,* occurs in our area. The strongly produced convexity near the base of the costa will at once distinguish *emesia* from all related species. The wing shape is similar in the two sexes, although the fore wing is narrower and more pointed in the male. Expanse: 25.5 to 32 mm.

Early Stages: Unknown.

Distribution: This butterfly occurs from southern Texas to Nicaragua (TL). It is widespread in Mexico, from the Rio Grande at Brownsville through the Gulf region, Sierra Madre del Sur, Guerrero, and northward on the west coast to Sinaloa. Flight periods are not well documented: October–November in Texas and Nuevo León; August at Mazatlán, Sinaloa.

Genus APODEMIA Felder & Felder

The small to medium sized butterflies of the genus *Apodemia* are checkered with white on the upperside and lack metallic markings. About nine species make up the genus, occupying a disjunct distribution in North America and southern South America, nearly restricted to the Temperate Zones. Several species are widespread without much geographical variation, while others show moderate to extreme poly-typy.

1. **Apodemia mormo** (Felder & Felder).   This is the most widespread and commonly collected metal-mark in North America. Populations typically occur in arid places, such as dry, rocky slopes in the desert or xeric chaparral-covered hills, but the species is extremely tolerant, ranging from sea beach dunes up to 9000 feet. Colonies sometimes are quite local when the foodplant is restricted, but populations often are extensive, ranging over large areas as, for example, where the foodplant is a dominant feature of chaparral. The quick, shadow-like flight, especially of the males, is characteristic. So, too, is their perch behavior, in which they frequently rest in a vertical position with the head upward or downward and the wings cocked in a partially open angle. Their activity takes place in open, often hot sunshine and they do not commonly seek shaded spots to alight as do many other riodinids. Both sexes often visit flowers other than the foodplant, especially Compositae.

The remarkable geographical variation of this species has been summarized by Opler & Powell. Subsequent research has shown that even greater complexity in the color forms exists. Much more collecting must be done in New Mexico and Texas north through the Rocky Mountains and on the adjacent plains to the Dakotas before the eastern array of *mormo* will be as well understood as is the Californian.

Early Stages: These have been described in California by Grundel in 1905, by Coolidge in 1925, and by Comstock and Dammers in 1934. The full grown larva is purplish with rather short setae protruding in bunches from the veruccae. Over-wintering probably takes place either as young or mature larvae on the ground. Pupation occurs in debris at the base of the plant or within the hollow stems of some host species. The foodplants are *Eriogonum* (Polygonaceae), probably many species. *E. fasciculatum* and *E. elongatum* in southern California, *E. inflatum* in the California desert, and *E. latifolium* and *E. wrighti* in central California are known hosts. A report in the literature of *Atriplex* (Chenopodiaceae) probably is in error.

Distribution: The species ranges from eastern Washington, Oregon, southern Idaho and Wyoming to western Texas, westward through the Great Basin and deserts to the Pacific Coast, and from central California south to the mountains of Sinaloa and the Cape district of Baja California.

(a) **mormo** (Felder & Felder). Plate 47, figure 43, ♀; figure 44, ♂.   F. M. Brown believes that, contrary to general belief, the type specimens of *mormo* were not from Salt Lake City but were taken on the eastern slope of the Sierra Nevada at the western edge of what is now the state of Nevada. However, there are at present no known colonies of typical *mormo* on the eastern edge of the Sierra Nevada. The confusion arose because at the time Lorquin collected the types a broad area including this region was called "Utah." Populations of the Great Basin (nominate *mormo*) have the hind wing ground color entirely black with relatively large white spots and extensive whitish on the underside.

Distribution: Nominate *mormo* occurs throughout the Great Basin from southwestern Colorado and southern Wyoming to the eastern edges of California.

(b) **mormonia** (Boisduval). Plate 48, figure 4, ♂, underside; figure 6, ♂; figure 7, ♀.   Individuals from eastern Washington to northeastern California tend to be larger and a little darker. The name *mormonia* (TL: Oregon) applies strictly to these populations.

(c) **langei** Comstock. Plate 48, figure 10, ♀, underside; figure 11, ♂; figure 12, ♀. This name has been applied to an isolated colony on the sand dunes of the San Joaquin-Sacramento River delta. Individuals of this subspecies have more orange on both fore and hind wings and the white spots on the fore wings are reduced. A complex blend zone in which specimens that resemble *langei* are found with the dark-winged coastal form in interior San Luis Obispo county.

Distribution: This subspecies is known only from the type locality, Antioch, Contra Costa county, California.

(d) **virgulti** (Behr). Plate 48, figure 5, ♂, underside; figure 8, ♂; figure 13, ♀; figure 9, ♀; figure 14, ♂. This subspecies is characterized by having the discal area of the hind wing orange and the underside of that wing black without whitish overscaling between the white spots. A dark segregate of *virgulti* without hind wing orange appears south of the range of normal populations, in Baja California. These are illustrated on Plate 48, figures 9 and 14.

Distribution: A. mormo virgulti occurs from Santa Barbara county southward to some 150 miles into Baja California and east through the mountains. It ranges northward through the Tehachapi Mountains and the southern Sierra Nevada to about the latitude of Yosemite. (TL: Los Angeles)

(e) **tuolumnensis** Opler & Powell. Plate 48, figure 15, ♀, underside; figure 16, ♀. This local form has more extensive orange on the fore wing and a brownish-gray underside.

Distribution: The type (and only known) locality is the Grand Canyon of the Tuolumne River, California.

(f) **dialeuca** Opler & Powell. Plate 48, figure 2, ♂; figure 17, ♀; figure 18, ♀, underside. This subspecies, from the mountains of northern Baja California, differs from *mormo mormo* in having reduced orange and larger white spots on both surfaces. On the underside of the hind wing the dark areas between the white spots are strongly suffused with white scales. Phenotypically similar colonies are found in the higher parts of the San Bernardino Mountains of southern California and in the White Mountains of Arizona.

Distribution: True *dialeuca* is found only in the Sierra San Pedro Martir (TL: 5 mi. NE of La Encantada), Baja California Norte, Mexico.

(g) **deserti** Barnes & McDunnough. Plate 47, figure 45, ♀, underside; figure 46, ♀. This is a pale desert subspecies with large white spots including the terminal row and extensive white overscaling on the gray areas of the hind wing.

Distribution: The name applies strictly to populations on the western edge of the Colorado Desert (TL: La Puerta, San Diego county, California). The concept is often enlarged to include populations from the rest of the Colorado and Mojave deserts with somewhat smaller white spots.

(h) **cythera** (Edwards). Plate 48, figure 19, underside; figure 20. This is another orange hind wing subspecies with a whiter underside which blends with *mormo*

Distribution: A. mormo cythera occurs in the foothills of the eastern slope of the *mormo* north of Sherwin Summit, Mono county, California.
Sierra Nevada in the Owens Valley. (TL: 9 miles west of Lone Pine, Inyo county, California)

(i) **mejicana** (Behr). Plate 47, figure 47, ♀, underside; figure 48, ♀; Plate 48, figure 3, ♂. This subspecies is composed of larger individuals than *cythera* and has darker reddish orange markings. The scattered populations with these features probably are not of a single genetic origin and may represent similar general phenotypic manifestations. The orange on *both* sides of the hind wings is variable but all colonies assignable to this name have some orange on the under hind wing.

Distribution: This subspecies ranges from the type locality in the mountains near Mazatlán, Mexico, northward into Arizona, New Mexico and the Davis Mountains of Texas. Some colonies in southern Colorado may be assignable to this name.

(j) **duryi** (Edwards). Plate 77, figure 5, ♂; figure 6, ♀. This local subspecies is found in the foothills of the northern Organ Mountains of New Mexico. It is much paler than *mejicana,* lacks orange on the underside of the hind wing and has the dark markings of the upperside greatly reduced.

Distribution: It is known only from the vicinity of the type locality, near Mesilla, Dona Ana county, New Mexico.

(k) **maxima** Weeks. This subspecies resembles *mejicana* but has less extensive orange above. Its members are the largest in the genus (females to 40 mm wingspread).

Distribution: Baja California Sur, Mexico (TL: San José del Cabo).

2. **Apodemia palmeri** (Edwards). Plate 47, figure 35, ♂; figure 36, ♀. Form "marginalis:" Plate 47, figure 41, ♂; figure 42, ♀. This small checkered butterfly is common around mesquite through much of the southwestern desert area. The blackish wings with orange margins and pale orange underside will identify *palmeri.* Its exceedingly rapid flight about the mesquite bushes is characteristic, and one must often wait until an individual alights before it can be recognized. The name "marginalis" (Skinner) was applied to a pale form with a conspicuous orange marginal band, from California (TL: Acme, nr. Tecopa, Inyo county, California). Wingspread: 18.5 to 20 (rarely to 23) mm.

Early Stages: The egg and first instar were described by Edwards in 1884 and again, along with the full grown larva, by Comstock & Dammers in 1932. The eggs are deposited singly on the leaves of the foodplant, and the larvae live concealed within nests of leaves except when feeding. The larva is pale gray-green and has relatively short setae, as in *A. mormo.* The foodplant is *Prosopis juliflora* (Leguminosae). The numerous reports of this *Apodemia* feeding on *Beloperone* (Acanthaceae) evidently all date back to the erroneous assumption of Wright in 1906 in *Butterflies of the West Coast.*

Distribution: This species ranges from the western desert margins at the mountains in southern California eastward through southern Nevada and Utah (TL: vicinity of St. George), western and southern Arizona eastward to Big Bend National Park, Texas, northward to Albuquerque, New Mexico, southward on the Mexican Plateau at least to Durango, and along the whole of the peninsula of Baja California. It is probably facultatively double or triple brooded, with flight records from April to October.

3. **Apodemia hepburni** Godman & Salvin. Plate 48, figure 25, ♀; figure 26, ♀, underside; figure 27, ♂. This species is quite similar to *palmeri,* and has been regarded as a subspecies of it. However, according to H. K. Clench, *hepburni* is genitalically distinct and has been taken in southern Arizona and western Texas, within the range of *palmeri.* The two species are widely sympatric in Mexico. *A. hepburni* lacks the marginal row of white dots and has reduced white and orange markings generally; in addition, the inner, black edge of the postmedian line on the hind wing, which is strongly disjunct in *palmeri,* is nearly continuous, although irregular, from vein Sc to M, in *hepburni.* Wing expanse: 19 to 22 mm.

Early Stages: Unknown.

Distribution: The range of this species is poorly known: from the Chisos Mountains in Big Bend National Park in west Texas (according to Clench) and southern Arizona (Patagonia) through the Sierra Madre Occidental in Chihuahua (TL: Pinos Altos) to the Cape District of Baja California. The flight period is incompletely known; it is July in Texas.

4. **Apodemia walkeri** Godman & Salvin. Plate 47, figure 10, ♂, underside; figure 11, ♂; figure 12, ♀, underside; figure 13, ♀. This species resembles *hepburni* but lacks orange on the wings. The white markings are somewhat variable and ill-defined. Wing expanse: 18 to 23 mm.

Early Stages: Unknown.

Distribution: A. walkeri is found from Brownsville, Texas, southward through the mountains of Michoacán and the valley of Tehuacán to Oaxaca, Guerrero, and northward on the Pacific side to Mazatlán (TL: Acapulco, Mexico).

5. **Apodemia multiplaga** Schaus. Plate 47, figure 34, ♂. This is another species described from Mexico which ranges north to southern Texas. The narrow, very pointed fore wing in the male and large, round discal spots will distinguish *multiplaga.* Wing expanse: 30 to 34 mm.

Early Stages: Unknown.

Distribution: The range of *multiplaga* is poorly known: extreme southern Texas to Veracruz, Guerrero, Colima, and the Sierra Madre Occidental (TL: Rinconada [Puebla], Mexico). The flight period is also poorly known: November in Texas.

6. **Apodemia phyciodoides** Barnes & Benjamin. Plate 48, figure 31, ♂. This unusual species, which superficially resembles a small nymphalid, remains one of the rarest of North American butterflies. It is known only from two specimens collected before 1924. Wing espanse: 24 to 26 mm.

Early Stages: Unknown.

Distribution: Chiricahua Mountains of southeastern Arizona.

7. **Apodemia nais** (Edwards). Plate 47, figure 39, ♀; figure 40, ♂. The genus *Polystigma* Godman & Salvin was proposed for this species which was thought to be unique among all Riodinidae in having the prothoracic legs nearly perfect, that is,

possessing a tarsal claw and with only a partial fusing of the tarsal segments. However, this feature is variable within *nais,* from that condition to four segments (with a partial division of one) to three segmented. In any case, statements in the general literature that *nais* has the prolegs "well developed" are misleading because even in near perfect condition they are very reduced as in other metalmarks and are nonfunctional in walking. This species is said to frequent moist canyons and it ranges into the higher mountains of the Southwest. Wingspread: 29 to 36 mm.

Early Stages: These were described by Edwards in 1884. The larva is pale green with short, bunched setae on the dorsolateral and dorsoventral verrucae. The food-plant is probably *Ceanothus* (Rhamnaceae). *Prosopis juliflora* (Leguminosae) was the plant sent from Arizona with the eggs that Edwards received, but "wild plum" was the only plant accepted among the selection he offered the larvae in West Virginia. No *Prunus* species has a range similar to that of *nais,* and the butterflies are found in association with *Ceanothus fendleri* in Arizona according to Kilian Roever.

Distribution: This species occurs from Colorado on both flanks of the Rockies, and the mountains of northern New Mexico, throughout the mountains of Arizona from the vicinity of Williams southward (TL: Prescott), to the Sierra del Nido and the Sierra Madre Occidental in Chihuahua. The species is probably single brooded, with records from May to September, mostly in June and July.

8. **Apodemia chisosensis** Freeman. Plate 47, figure 7, ♀; figure 24, ♂; figure 25, ♂, underside.   This recently described species is similar to *nais* in general features, but the condition of the prolegs has not been described. *A. chisosensis* differs from *nais* especially by the lack of orange and by the alignment of the black spots in the discal row on the hind wing underside. There are also minor differences in the male genitalia. Discovery of populations from the intervening region between *nais* and *chisosensis* may shed light on the specific relationship between them. Wing expanse: 27 to 32 mm.

Early Stages: Unknown.

Distribution: This species is known only from the Chisos Mountains (at about 5200 ft.) in Big Bend National Park, Texas; the types were taken in early August.

Family LIPHYRIDAE

WILLIAM H. HOWE

This small family of butterflies reaches its greatest development in the Ethiopian region. The family is not found in Europe nor in the Neotropics. The single North American species is restricted to the eastern states.

Genus FENISECA Grote

1. **Feniseca tarquinius** Fabricius. Plate 54, figure 23, ♂. This species is readily recognized from the figure, which represents the first brood. Later broods have less orange on the upperside. Some would use the name *novascotiae* for these early specimens, especially from north of the 40th parallel where there is only one brood. These butterflies seldom stray far from the immediate vicinity of their birthplace.

Early Stages: This is the only North American butterfly with wholly carnivorous larvae. They feed on woolly aphids belonging to two genera, *Schizoneura* and *Pemphigus*. The aphids are found on many different plants: alder (*Alnus*), ash (*Fraxinus*), beech (*Fagus*), wild currant (*Ribes*), witch hazel (*Hamamelis*), hawthorn (*Crataegus*), maple (*Acer*), and probably elm (*Ulmus*). The pupa is curiously shaped and dorsally looks like a "monkey face."

Distribution: The humid East is the range of this species, from Ontario and the Maritime Provinces to Florida and central Texas.

Family LYCAENIDAE

WILLIAM H. HOWE

The hairstreaks, coppers and blues are the prominent members of this large family of small butterflies. Along with several other families, the Riodinidae for example, the Lycaenidae represent a type of butterfly as distinct as the skippers. The forelegs of the males of most Lycaenidae are reduced and modified and cannot be used for walking. These legs in females are normal, functional walking legs. On this count alone the Lycaenidae and related families differ from other butterflies. The venation is also somewhat different from that of other families; the hind wing lacks a humeral vein and the fore wing usually (always among our species) lacks one or two branches of the radial vein.

Our Lycaenidae are divided among three subfamilies: Theclinae (hairstreaks), Lycaeninae (coppers) and Plebejinae (blues). No single character can be used to separate all these subfamilies. Most hairstreaks have a filamentous tail near the anal angle of the hind wing; some, however, have none and others have several. Most male coppers are coppery colored but some are blue and copper color is not restricted to the Lycaeninae. Most blues are tailless, but the genus *Everes* in our territory is tailed.

Early Stages: Although these are discussed in detail under each of the subfamilies a few familial generalizations are possible. The eggs are broader than tall and the surface usually patterned. The larvae tend to be slug-shaped, flattened, broad and tapering to head and tail. They are covered with short hairs set in tiny sockets. The pupae are compact, more or less rounded and are usually formed in debris at the base of the foodplant. In many cases, especially in the tropics, the larvae are tended by ants for the sweet fluid that is exuded from specialized glands on the back.

Distribution: The family is found on all continents except Antarctica. The Theclinae tend to be tropical while the Lycaeninae and Plebejinae are mainly temperate climate butterflies.

Subfamily THECLINAE

WILLIAM H. HOWE

For many years the generic name *Thecla* was a catch-all for tailed species of these butterflies. Then the term *Strymon* came into general use for North American hairstreaks. Now, primarily since the studies of Clench, many generic names are used for the truly tailed members of the Theclinae in North America. What has not been generally recognized by collectors is that there are two well defined tribes of hairstreaks in America. The tribe Theclini is abundant in the Old World and represented in America by only two western species. The other, the Strymonini, encompasses all of the rest of our hairstreaks.

Among the Theclini the radial vein of the fore wing has four branches. The same condition is found among all the rest of the Lycaenidae except the Strymonini. The Strymonini have only three branches to the fore wing radius. In addition the genitalia are highly characteristic for the two tribes. Males of the Strymonini always have an internal ridge on the dorsum of the tegumen, absent in the Theclini. The ventral margins of the valvae are sometimes fused in the Strymonini; they are free in the Theclini. The juxta and a median uncus are absent in the Strymonini and present in the Theclini. (The uncus rarely is obliterated among the Theclini.) The genital plate is simple on females of the Strymonini and highly complicated in the Theclini.

Early Stages: Although the majority of the larvae of Theclinae are leaf eaters some bore into fruit or flower buds. Some are attended by ants. This part of the life histories needs further study. Few species appear to hibernate as larvae; most pass the winter as eggs or pupae.

Distribution: Hairstreaks are essentially tropical and temperate. Only the subgenus *Callophrys* (*Incisalia*) ranges well into the Hudsonian zone.

Tribe Theclini
Genus HABRODAIS Scudder

FRED THORNE

A single species represents this genus.

1. **Habrodais grunus** (Boisduval). Plate 49, figure 8, ♂; figure 9, ♀. Weakly developed subspeciation which has been recognized by three names occurs in this species. There is little difference in the appearance of the sexes. The upper side is dull brown or brownish yellow with the marginal areas somewhat darker. Beneath, the insect is ochre with faint irregular linear patterning. The hind wings bear short tails near the anal angle.

Early Stages: The mature larva is slug-shaped, lightly haired and bluish green in color. It feeds on oaks, particularly *Quercus chrysolepis,* the Canyon Oak.

Distribution: This subspecies occurs in the foothills and mountains of southern California, and north in the Sierra Nevada Range and in adjacent Nevada.

(a) **grunus** (Boisduval). Plate 49, figure 8, ♂; figure 9, ♀. Above, the discal areas are orange-brown darkening toward the margins. Beneath, the butterfly is light ochre with a faint sinuous mesial band of dark brown, usually with a few distal white scales, extending across both wings. A faint submarginal row of dark crescents is located on the hind wing, sprinkled with blue near the anal angle.

Distribution: This subspecies occurs in the eastern mountains of California and in adjacent Nevada.

(b) **lorquini** W. D. Field.   The subspecies *lorquini* is darker than nominate *grunus* and has wider dark margins above. Beneath, it is darker ochre and the pattern is more prominent. Females are noticeably paler than males.

Distribution: H. g. lorquini is found in the coastal areas of central California.

(c) **herri** W. D. Field.   The light areas on this subspecies are greatly extended and are almost yellow. All markings beneath are very faint, almost obliterated.

Distribution: This subspecies is found in northern California, Oregon and southwestern Idaho.

Genus HYPAUROTIS Scudder

FRED THORNE

A single species represents this genus. With its showy coloration it looks more like a tropical hairstreak than one restricted to the temperate zone.

1. **Hypaurotis crysalus** (Edwards).   There are two subspecies of this purple, black and orange butterfly. It is one of the largest hairstreaks in our territory. The underside is ashy gray with the usual hairstreak pattern.

(a) **crysalus** (Edwards). Plate 49, figure 3, ♀.   This beautiful butterfly can be readily identified from the figure. The male differs from the female (figured) in having the dark patch at the end of the cell extended to the outer margin. Adults are always found on oak trees, resting or flying near the tops. Two people can collect this species more efficiently than one: one shakes the trees, the other stands off and collects the disturbed insects as they fly out. The flight period on the eastern slope of the Continental Divide is late June and July, while it is from early July into September on the western slope.

Early Stages: Dr. C. L. Remington raised this species on *Quercus Gambelii*.

Distribution: The nominate subspecies is found at moderate elevations (7000 to 9000 feet) in Colorado, New Mexico, Arizona and eastern Utah.

(b) **citima** (Hy. Edwards). Plate 56, figure 21, ♂.   This subspecies lacks the orange spots on the upperside and beneath is more ashy gray than in *c. crysalus*.

Distribution: H. c. citima occurs in oak scrub in the mountains of northern Utah.

Tribe Strymonini

Genus EUMAEUS Hübner

FRED THORNE

1. **Eumaeus atala** (Poey). Plate 49, figure 1, ♂ (subspecies *florida*).   The nominate subspecies does not occur in the United States but is found in Cuba and the Bahama Islands.

Our subspecies is *florida* (Röber). This beautiful hairstreak is so distinctive that the illustration makes a description unnecessary. On the fore wing the iridescent blue-green scaling is largely confined to the upper half in females, and covers most of the wing in males.

Early Stages: The caterpillars feed on tender new fronds of cycads, *Zamia* spp., especially *integrifolia*. The gregarious larvae when mature are brick red, with two dorsal rows of seven conspicuous yellow spots.

Distribution: This butterfly was formerly abundant in southern Florida and some of the keys, but by the mid-1930's it was feared that it might have become extinct. Specimens, however, have been seen in recent years in Broward county, and efforts have been made to colonize this fine butterfly in protected areas. It is hoped that such efforts will succeed because habitats suitable for this insect are being rapidly destroyed. There are several broods, with captures recorded for nearly every month of the year.

2. **Eumaeus minyas** Hübner. Plate 49, figure 2, ♀. *E. minyas* is similar to *E. atala* but larger and with white fringes, not black as in *atala*. This tropical species is doubtfully included here. No authentic specimens are known from the southern United States although it has been vaguely reported from Texas in the past. It is common in some places in Mexico.

Early Stages: The life history is similar to that of *atala,* the larvae feeding on new fronds of a cycad, *Zamia loddigesii* var. *angustifolia.*

Genus CHLOROSTRYMON Clench

FRED THORNE

1. **Chlorostrymon simaethis** (Drury). Plate 51, figure 7, ♂; figure 8, ♀ (ssp. *sarita*). The nominate subspecies is not in our area, but is widely distributed in the Antilles, reaching Cuba but not Florida.

Our subspecies is *sarita* (Skinner). The wings above are iridescent purple in the male; the iridescence is largely lacking in the darker female. On the underside the wings are light yellow-green, with a prominent pearly white postmedian line edged with brown scales. This line is nearly straight on the secondaries except at 2A where it forms a sharp V. There is a wide, warm brown, hoary marginal band which tapers to the outer angle of the hind wing.

Distribution: This exquisite little hairstreak has an extensive range from South America to southern Texas and southern California. It is probably resident in southern Texas, but appears to be a straggler in San Diego county, California. It is known to be widely distributed and abundant at times in Baja California where it is found in association with Balloon Vine (*Cardiospermum*), probably the larval foodplant. Most Texas captures have been made in November and December, but in Baja California the species has been taken in the spring also, and is at least double brooded.

2. Chlorostrymon maesites (Herrich-Schäffer). Plate 50, figure 27, ♂; figure 28, ♀. The male of this small butterfly is iridescent purplish blue while the female is dark brown, with the base of the fore wing and most of the hind wing dark blue. The under surface is green, with a single thin black postmedian line on both wings, inwardly edged with white and not forming a W on the hind wing. There is a distinctive marginal patch, reddish brown and overlaid with gray scales on the marginal edge and extending from the anal angle to M_1.

Distribution: This magnificent little butterfly is rare in southern Florida in the Miami area, whence it ranges south to Cuba, Jamaica, Puerto Rico and the Bahamas. It should be sought in hammocks, especially on flowers of Spanish Needles (*Bidens*). Captures have been recorded from January to July so there appear to be at least two broods, although the life history has not been recorded. The butterflies are extremely swift flyers.

3. Chlorostrymon telea (Hewitson). Plate 51, figure 1, ♂. This species is similar to *C. maesites* and is considered by some to be the continental subspecies of it. On the underside of the hind wing of *telea* the postmedian line forms a W and the marginal patch is smaller than that of *maesites,* and extends from the anal angle only to M_3.

Distribution: This beautiful little hairstreak ranges from Brazil through Mexico to Texas, where it is very rare.

Genus PHAEOSTRYMON Clench

FRED THORNE

1. Phaeostrymon alcestis (Edwards).

(a) **alcestis** (Edwards). Plate 52, figure 21, ♂; figure 22, ♀. The wings above are a uniform warm dark brown; the male scent pad is small. The sexes are much alike. The underside is a lighter brown, with white bars at the ends of the cells in both fore and hind wings, outlined with dark brown scales on the inner and outer sides. The prominent white postmedian line is outlined on the inner side, and the white marginal line, on the outer side, with dark scales, almost black on the latter. On the hind wing the postmedian line forms a distinct "VW" at its posterior end. There is a submarginal band of red-orange crescents along the hind wings and halfway up the primaries. The anal lobe is black, capped with a line and an orange crescent. In interspace Cu_2 there is a large bluish marginal spot.

This butterfly is found in close association with its host plant and flies from late April to June.

Early Stages: The eggs are laid on the bark of the foodplant, *Sapindus saponaria* var. *Drummondii* (Soapberry) and hatch the following spring. References to Chinaberry (*Melia*) as the larval foodplant are probably wrong.

Distribution: The butterfly occurs in southern Kansas, Oklahoma and Texas.

(b) **oslari** (Dyar).   This subspecies replaces *a. alcestis* from western Texas (Davis Mountains) to Arizona, and differs in being slightly smaller, the upper surface a grayer brown, and the underside ashen gray, not brown. The submarginal red-orange band is reduced, and the white bars at the ends of the cells are missing. This hairstreak is not common, and must be sought on or near its host plant. The adults fly at their best in May, and tend to perch near the tops of Soapberry trees; hence a long-handled net is advantageous.

Genus HARKENCLENUS dos Passos

FRED THORNE

1. **Harkenclenus titus** (Fabricius).

(a) **titus** (Fabricius). Plate 52, figure 23, ♂; figure 24, ♀.   The wings are uniform gray-brown above, without markings except for a prominent scent pad on the male, a few orange-red spots near the anal angle of the hind wing of some females, and sometimes a single spot on the male. Tails are lacking. The underside is distinctive, characterized by the submarginal band of coral spots on the secondaries which invades the primaries of some specimens.

Early Stages: The eggs are laid on the twigs of wild plum and wild cherry (*Prunus* spp.) and hatch the following spring. The mature larvae are predominantly green with pink markings.

Distribution: This widespread hairstreak occurs in the southern portions of the Canadian provinces, and over most of the United States except for the Gulf Coast and the extreme Southwest. It is common at times in some areas of the East, but in the West it is found in scattered colonies, usually in limited numbers. The flight is rapid but the butterflies are easily taken at flowers, especially those of the Butterfly Weed (*Asclepias tuberosa*) in the East. There is a single brood with its peak in July.

(b) **mopsus** (Hübner). Plate 50, figure 23, ♀; figure 24, ♂.   The wings of this subspecies beneath are lighter, the markings brighter and more prominent. The black spots on the secondaries are ringed with white scales.

Distribution: H. t. mopsus occurs from the District of Columbia south to Georgia and west to Kansas. It flies earlier in the South, in late May and June.

(c) **watsoni** (Barnes and Benjamin). Plate 52, figure 26, ♀.   This uncommon subspecies is somewhat larger, the underside much paler, the black spots ringed with white and the "coral" band on the hind wing is paler, almost orange.

Range: Southern Oklahoma, northeastern New Mexico and Texas.

(d) **immaculosus** (W. P. Comstock). Plate 52, figure 27, ♂; figure 28, ♀.   The scientific name of this subspecies refers to the reduction or absence of the black markings on the under surfaces. Unlike *t. titus,* the upper surfaces may be well marked with fulvous in the limbal areas, especially on the females, and there may be complete submarginal rows of orange-red spots on both wings; but there is much variation. The ground color beneath is usually somewhat paler, with the black markings absent or mere pinpoints. The red markings are retained but are usually slightly smaller and often orange.

Distribution: The range is from Manitoba south to central New Mexico, and west to Vancouver, Washington and northern California. Adults are on the wing in July and early August.

Genus SATYRIUM Scudder

JOHN F. EMMEL

The genus *Satyrium* contains a relatively large number of species, all of which are found in the Holarctic region. These fast-flying butterflies are generally drab brown or gray, marked with orange, red, black or white. Some species have tails on the secondaries, others are tailless. The adults may be taken on flowers, but more commonly perch on leaves or twigs of the host plant or nearby vegetation. Thirteen species are recognized in our area.

1. **Satyrium fuliginosum** (Edwards). This drab tailless hairstreak occurs in scattered localities in the West. It is found typically in sagebrush areas in the Transition and lower Canadian zones, always in association with lupine, the suspected host plant. The species is western (Rockies to the Pacific) but for reasons yet unknown, it is often absent from regions which appear to contain ideal habitats for the insect: most of Nevada, Utah, Montana, Idaho and Oregon.

Early Stages: Undescribed. The species has been observed ovipositing in the ground litter at the base of lupine plants in the Trinity Alps and Sierra Nevada of California.

(a) **fuliginosum** (Edwards). Plate 49, figure 12, ♂. Nominate *fuliginosum* has the maculation reduced on the underside of both wings and often absent on the hind wings.

Distribution: This subspecies occurs from California (Sierra Nevada to Trinity Alps) to southern British Columbia.

(b) **semiluna** Klots. This subspecies is distinguished from nominate *fuliginosum* by having well developed spots on the underside.

Distribution: The subspecies ranges from northwestern Colorado to Alberta.

2. **Satyrium behrii** (Edwards). An easily recognized butterfly, *S. behrii* is often taken in large numbers on flowers where the host plant, *Purshia,* grows abundantly. The insect is widespread in the western U.S., although still unreported from large areas where little collecting has been done. The adults fly from late May to early August. The subspecies are weakly defined.

Early Stages: The larvae have a color pattern resembling that of the *Purshia* leaves, and are difficult to see when on the host plant. The insect winters in the egg stage.

The known host plants are *Purshia tridentata* and *P. glandulosa* (Antelope Bush); records for various legumes are probably erroneous.

Distribution: The species ranges from southern British Columbia south to California (Sierra Nevada, north slope of the San Gabriel and San Bernardino mountains, and the Mount Pinos region), east to Wyoming, Colorado and northern New Mexico. There is a questionable report of an isolated population found in Palo Duro Canyon, Texas.

(a) **behrii** (Edwards).   The nominate subspecies, *behrii,* occurs in the mountains of eastern California (TL: Mono Lake) and is smaller and paler than the other two subspecies.

(b) **crossi** (Field). Plate 49, figure 10, ♂; figure 11, ♀.   The southern Rocky Mountain subspecies (TL: Nederland, Colorado) is somewhat larger and darker on the underside than *behrii behrii.*

(c) **columbia** (McDunnough).   The Pacific Northwest subspecies (TL: Fairview, B.C.) is the largest and darkest within the species. The very heavy black spotting on the underside separates it from *crossi.*

3. **Satyrium auretorum** (Boisduval).   Confined to California, this hairstreak was once regarded as one of our scarcest butterflies; even today it is relatively uncommon in collections. It is found typically in chaparral and oak woodland areas where suitable oaks serve as host plants. The butterfly tends to be cyclic, appearing in large numbers around the host plants in some years, then virtually disappearing for several years. It flies at its best in late June and July.

Early Stages: The life history was described by Comstock and Dammers. The eggs overwinter. The known host plants is *Quercus wislizenii* (Interior Live Oak); *Q. dumosa* is also strongly suspected in southern California.

(a) **auretorum** (Boisduval). Plate 54, figure 21, ♂; figure 22, ♀.   The two subspecies may be recognized by the underside: the northern one, nominate *auretorum,* is darker.

Distribution: This subspecies ranges from the Sierra Nevada foothills and inner Coast Range of California southward to Santa Barbara and Kern counties.

(b) **spadix** (Hy. Edwards). Plate 48, figure 38, ♂, underside; figure 39, ♂; figure 40, ♀.   The southern, lighter colored, subspecies tends to be a mountain rather than a foothill butterfly.

Distribution: S. a. spadix is found in Santa Barbara and Kern counties south to the mountains of San Diego county.

4. **Satyrium saepium** (Boisduval).   This butterfly is widespread in the western states, and is abundant in favored localities. *S. saepium* is a frequent flower visitor, and attractive bushes, such as *Eriodictyon,* are often dotted with the dark silhouettes of the adults. The insect is single brooded, flying from May to June at lower elevations and July to August at higher elevations.

Early Stages: The larval color pattern closely resembles the undersides of the *Ceanothus* leaves on which the larvae feed. Diapause occurs in the egg stage. Host plants: *Ceanothus cuneatus* (Buckbrush), *C. macrocarpus* and *Cercocarpus betuloides.*

(a) **saepium** (Boisduval). Plate 53, figure 9, ♂; figure 10, ♀.   The figure will readily allow recognition of this butterfly.

Distribution: California eastward to Colorado.

(b) **okanagana** (McDunnough).   The northwestern subspecies is darker than the nominate.

Distribution: S. s. okanagana occurs from Washington and British Columbia eastward to Montana.

5. **Satyrium tetra** (Edwards). Plate 53, figure 7, ♂; figure 8, ♀.   Although presently known only from California and extreme western Nevada, this species will probably be found in southern Oregon where its host plant, Mountain Mahogany (*Cercocarpus betuloides*), reaches the northern limits of its range. In some chaparral areas of southern California the butterfly is often common on the flowers of *Eriogonum fasciculatum* in June. The eggs overwinter, and the insect is single brooded. This species was formerly known as *S. adenostomatis* Hy. Edwards.

Early Stages: These were described by Comstock and Dammers. The silvery green larvae, with diagonal rows of golden orange hairs, match the color and venation of the leaves of the host plant to a remarkable degree. The known host plant is *Cercocarpus betuloides; C. minutiflorus* is suspected in San Diego county.

Distribution: S. tetra ranges through California from the southern mountains to the northern border, and also occurs in the Carson Range in western Nevada.

6. **Satyrium liparops** (Boisduval & Le Conte).   The species is recognized by the widely spaced, broken and offset lines on the underside. Despite its extensive range and its wide variety of host plants, *liparops* is generally uncommon and local. The butterfly is occasionally taken on flowers, but more commonly perches on leaves. In the southern part of its range it flies in spring; in the northern part in midsummer. It is single brooded.

Early Stages: The larva is bright green, marked laterally with oblique yellow-green lines. The insect hibernates as an egg. Host plants are *Quercus* (oak), *Salix* (willow), *Amelanchier* (shadbush), *Malus* (apple), *Prunus* (plum), *Vaccinium* (blueberry) and *Rubus* (blackberry). *Crataegus* (hawthorn) is suspected in Colorado.

(a)   **liparops** (Boisduval & Le Conte). Plate 78, figure 21, ♂.   The southeastern subspecies, *liparops liparops,* has brownish orange patches on the fore wings above. It is rare.

Distribution: The nominate subspecies occurs in northern Florida and southern Georgia.

(b) **strigosum** (Harris). Plate 54, figure 5, ♂; figure 6, ♀.   The orange-brown patches on the fore wing upperside of *liparops liparops* are absent or nearly so on *liparops strigosum.* On the underside the white lines are fine but bright. This is the most common subspecies.

Distribution: S. l. strigosum ranges from northern Georgia northward to New England and southern Canada, and westward to Mississippi, eastern Kansas and Wisconsin.

(c) **fletcheri** (Michener & dos Passos). Plate 16, figure 14, ♂. The orange-brown patches on the upperside are prominent and similar to those of *liparops liparops.* The underside, however, is darker brown and the white lines are reduced.

Distribution: Southern Manitoba.

(d) **aliparops** (Michener & dos Passos). The upperside is like that of *strigosum* and the underside like that of *fletcheri.*

Distribution: This subspecies occurs in the foothills of the Rocky Mountains from Colorado north into Montana.

7. **Satyrium kingi** (Klots & Clench). Plate 54, figure 11, ♂; figure 12, ♀. Little is known about this local and uncommon hairstreak. It has a limited distribution in the southeastern states. The insect is probably single brooded, flying in May near the coast, and in July and August inland.

Early Stages: Unknown.

Distribution: S. kingi ranges from southern Virginia south to northern Florida, westward to Mississippi, chiefly in the lowlands but also in the southern uplands.

8. **Satyrium calanus** (Hübner). The butterflies here grouped under *calanus* may represent two species. Only when the life histories of some of the less common populations have been studied will the answer be known. For a long time *calanus calanus* was known as *wittfeldii* Edwards. The butterfly is single brooded in the north, flying from late June through July; in Texas it flies in May and June. In Florida the adults appear earlier, in March and April; a possible second brood may emerge there in June or July.

Early Stages: At least two color forms of the larva are known, one green and one brown; the body is marked with longitudinal lines of lighter and darker shades. Host plants are *Quercus* (oak), *Carya* (hickory), and *Juglans cinerea* (Butternut).

(a) **calanus** (Hübner). The nominate subspecies is recognized by its large size, dark brown ground color and the presence of a large orange lunule on the upperside of the hind wing at the tails.

Distribution: This subspecies ranges from southeastern Georgia to central Florida.

(b) **falacer** (Godart). Plate 54, figure 9, ♂; figure 10, ♀. This common hairstreak differs from *calanus calanus* in lacking the orange spot on the upperside of the hind wing.

Distribution: The subspecies *falacer* ranges from southeastern Canada southward to western Florida and Texas.

(c) **godarti** (Field). Somewhat like *calanus falacer* this subspecies has the markings on the underside reduced.

Distribution: It is found in the Rocky Mountains.

9. **Satyrium caryaevorus** (McDunnough). Plate 54, figure 13, ♂; figure 14, ♀. This species is easily confused with *S. calanus falacer,* which it closely resembles. *S. caryaevorus* is usually rarer and more local than *calanus,* although its habitat and behavior are similar. At times the butterfly can be abundant, visiting the flowers

of *Asclepias* and *Apocynum.* The single brood appears in July. The insect almost certainly hibernates as an egg.

Early Stages: These are poorly known. Host plants are *Carya* (hickory), *Fraxinus nigra* (Black Ash) and *Crataegus* (hawthorn).

Distribution: This subspecies occurs from Vermont and Connecticut west through southern Canada to Minnesota and Iowa, and south to Ohio, Kentucky and western Pennsylvania.

10. **Satyrium edwardsii** (Grote & Robinson). Plate 54, figure 7, ♂; figure 8, ♀. This species is most common in the northeastern parts of its range, becoming scarcer westward and southwestward. It is generally found around Scrub Oak thickets, where the adults perch on leaves and twigs. The butterfly also visits flowers near woods. Single brooded, it emerges in late June and July.

Early Stages: The larva is brown, marked with paler brown, and is covered with numerous blackish warts with brown hairs. Host plants are *Quercus ilicifolia* (Scrub Oak) and probably other oaks.

Distribution: S. edwardsii ranges from the Maritime Provinces west to Manitoba, and south to Georgia and Texas.

11. **Satyrium sylvinus** (Boisduval). This butterfly is one of a group of several similar *Satyrium* species (*sylvinus, californica* and *acadica*) which are often confused with one another. The habitat of *sylvinus* is willow thickets along stream bottoms, ranging in elevation from near sea level is some areas of southern California to 7000 ft. in the Sierra Nevada. The insect is a frequent flower visitor, and can often be taken in large numbers on *Asclepias* (milkweed). Five subspecies are recognized, all but one rather weakly distinguished. The species is single brooded, with adults appearing in late May and June at lower elevations and in late July at higher elevations.

Early Stages: The larva is pale green, blending well with the lower surfaces of the willow leaves on which it feeds. The eggs hibernate. The host plant is *Salix* (willow); which species are utilized has not been determined.

(a) **sylvinus** (Boisduval). Plate 54, figure 17, ♂; figure 18, ♀. The nominate subspecies is found around willows while *californica* is associated with oaks.

Distribution: This subspecies is found west of the Sierra Nevada crest in California and southward into northern Baja California, Mexico.

(b) **itys** (Edwards). This subspecies is paler beneath than *sylvinus sylvinus.*

Distribution: It occurs in Arizona.

(c) **desertorum** (Grinnell). Specimens of this subspecies are very pale beneath.

Distribution: This subspecies is found along the east slope of the Tehachapi Mountains, California.

(d) **putnami** (Hy. Edwards). Slightly paler than *sylvinus sylvinus, S. s. putnami* is also larger.

Distribution: This subspecies flies in the mountain ranges of the Great Basin.

(e) **dryope** (W. H. Edwards). Plate 53, figure 1, ♂; figure 2, ♀. Quite like *sylvinus*

sylvinus but lacking tails on the hind wings. Some authors set *dryope* apart as a separate species.

Distribution: This butterfly occurs in the coastal ranges from San Francisco to Los Angeles.

12. **Satyrium californica** (Edwards). Plate 54, figure 19, ♂; figure 20, ♀. Widespread in the western U.S., this species is often taken on flowers in a variety of habitats. It occurs a few thousand feet above sea level in parts of southern California and is found as high as 9000 ft. in Colorado, but more commonly it inhabits the middle elevations within its range. In some localities, *californica* is sympatric with *sylvinus;* the former may be distinguished by its darker ground color on the underside. Emergence begins in June at lower elevations and in July at higher elevations. The insect is single brooded, and diapause occurs in the egg stage.

Early Stages: The mature larva is predominantly gray-brown. The host plant is *Quercus* (oak).

Distribution: The species ranges from southern British Columbia south to California, eastward to the Rocky Mountains.

13. **Satyrium acadica** (W. H. Edwards). Like *sylvinus, acadica* has been divided into several weakly differentiated subspecies. Just as *sylvinus* and *californica* can be confused in California and the Southwest, *acadica* and *californica* can be confused in the Northwest. There is no sure way to separate them on the basis of pattern. Remember that *californica* is common around oaks and *acadica* is found with willows. In the East *acadica* is readily recognized by the pale gray ground color beneath with rows of round postmedian spots. The single brood flies in late June and July.

Early Stages: The green larvae have two yellowish longitudinal lines. The host plant is *Salix* (willow).

Distribution: The species occurs from Nova Scotia southward to New Jersey and westward to British Columbia.

(a) **acadica** (W. H. Edwards). Plate 54, figure 15, ♂; figure 16, ♀. The submarginal red markings on the underside of the hind wings are crescentic.

Distribution: Nominate *acadica* occurs from southeastern Canada southward to New Jersey and Michigan.

(b) **watrini** (Dufrane). This is a slightly darker and not particularly distinct northern subspecies.

Distribution: It occurs from central Quebec westward to Saskatchewan.

(c) **montanensis** (Watson & Comstock). Plate 48, figure 34, ♂; figure 35, ♂, underside. A paler subspecies, *montanensis* has the postmedian row of spots on the underside of the fore wing much straighter than in *acadica acadica*.

Distribution: This subspecies is found in the Rocky Mountains from Colorado to Montana.

(d) **coolinensis** (Watson & Comstock). The westernmost subspecies is slightly larger and paler than *montanensis*.

Distribution: It is found from Idaho to British Columbia.

Genus CALLOPHRYS Billberg

WILLIAM H. HOWE

Until recently each of the subgenera of *Callophrys* had been considered a good genus in its own right. They have now been grouped together under one genus because structurally they are more closely related than can be accepted for independent genera. The species concerned may easily be placed in their subgenera by the distinctive characters of the wings.

Subgenus INCISALIA Scudder

(The Elfins)

WILLIAM H. HOWE
(with Oakley Shields as a consultant)

The hind wings are nearly always without tails. The male scent pad on the fore wing is absent on one species (*henrici*). The butterflies are brown on the upperside and patterned with gray or dark brown on lighter brown ground on the underside. Some of the species are difficult to separate even by experienced collectors. *Incisalia* are spring fliers; they rarely stray far from their foodplants and do not commonly visit flowers.

1. **Callophrys (Incisalia) augustinus** (Westwood).   This widely distributed butterfly is composed of several subspecies that intergrade to such an extent that boundaries between them are hard to define. On the underside of the hind wing there is no white terminal line, and the terminal band is brick red, sometimes shaded with gray, never mahogany or gray. The outer margin of the basal field never is edged with white, even in part. This spring appearing species is single-brooded. Sometimes the western subspecies are held to be a separate species, *iroides* (Boisduval).

Early Stages: Well known. The larvae are intense green with lighter green markings. Often the markings form a cryptic pattern resembling the foodplant.

Distribution: The species ranges from Newfoundland west and north to Alaska, south along the Pacific coast northern Baja California, in the Rockies to Arizona and New Mexico and in the east to the upland Gulf states.

(a) **augustinus** (Westwood).   This subspecies is dark with a distinctly checkered fringe. Beneath it is orange-brown with no gray. The larval foodplant is blueberry (*Vaccinium* sp.)

Distribution: Nominate *augustinus* ranges from northern New England to Alaska, the Mackenzie River and Alberta. It is essentially a Canadian subspecies.

(b) **helenae** (dos Passos).   This subspecies is golden brown above and the contrasts beneath are greater than those found on nominate *augustinus*.

Distribution: The subspecies *helenae* is restricted to Newfoundland and Cape Breton Island.

(c) **croesioides** (Scudder). Plate 50, figure 1, ♂; figure 2, ♀. This is the common subspecies in the eastern United States. In New York and southern New England there is a broad zone where *augustinus* and *croesioides* intergrade.

Distribution: This subspecies is found from Massachusetts to Georgia west to the edge of the prairies.

(d) **iroides** (Boisduval). Plate 50, figure 3, ♂; figure 4, ♀. This and the next subspecies together are sometimes considered to be a species independent of *augustinus.* They differ in that the foodplants of *iroides* are quite varied: apple (*Malus*), Wild Lilac (*Ceanothus cuneatus*), *Cuscuta, Gaultheria, Arbutus* and *Chlorogalum.* This subspecies is much like *augustinus* but paler and without conspicuously checkered fringes. The outline of the hind wing is more smoothly rounded.

Distribution: It ranges from the Pacific coast eastward to the Rocky Mountains, from southern Canada southward.

(e) **annetteae** (dos Passos). The underside in this subspecies does not show the usual strong contrast between the basal and limbal areas. No indication of checkering is seen on the fringes.

Distribution: New Mexico and Arizona.

2. **Callophrys (Incisalia) fotis** (Strecker). The four subspecies of this spring butterfly are extremely local. There is some suggestion that more than one species may be involved in this complex. The clue to the species is a strong contrast on the underside of the hind wings, with a distinctive whitish area edging the dark basal patch.

(a) **mossii** (Hy. Edwards). Plate 53, figure 3, ♂. This subspecies is rufous brown above with a white fringe and a narrow white line crossing both wings on the underside; the coloring of the underside is the same as above but paler.

Distribution: Vancouver Island.

(b) **schryveri** (Cross). Plate 53, figure 4, ♂. This subspecies looks much like *mossii* but warmer brown above and has much white powdering in the limbal area on the underside of the hind wing.

Distribution: The subspecies *schryveri* is found along the east slope of the Front Range from Colorado Springs, Colorado, northward.

(c) **fotis** (Strecker). Plate 50, figure 13, ♂; figure 14, ♀. The subspecies *fotis* resembles *schryveri* but is grayer and smaller.

Distribution: Nominate *fotis* occurs in southeastern California, northern Arizona and most of Utah, everywhere in the mountains. The following two subspecies are not as contrasty below as the other three. They seem best assigned to *fotis* but may constitute a good species.

(d) **doudoroffi** (dos Passos). Plate 53, figure 5, ♂. Paler than *fotis* and tending to be more yellowish brown beneath, *doudoroffi* is local in the coast ranges of central California south of San Francisco.

(e) **windi** Clench. Similar to *doudoroffi* and probably not a good subspecies this butterfly is from the central Sierras. Type locality: Placer county, California.

3. **Callophrys (Incisalia) polios** (Cook & Watson). Plate 50, figure 11, ♂; figure 12, ♀. On the underside the terminal areas of both wings are hoary. This elfin is very widespread and is one of the first butterflies to emerge in the spring. It always is found close to and often flying low over its foodplant.

Early Stages: These were described as long ago as 1907 and 1908. The dull greenish caterpillars feed on Bearberry (*Arctostaphylos uva-ursi.*)

Distribution: This species ranges from the mountains of Virginia northward and westward to Michigan and the Mackenzie River and eastern Alaska, south through the Rocky Mountains to northern New Mexico.

4. **Callophrys (Incisalia) irus** (Godart). This and the next species, *henrici* (except for *henrici margaretae*), have a distinct but short tail at the end of vein Cu_2 on the hind wing. The males of *irus* have a scent patch on the upperside of the fore wing as do all other males in the genus except *henrici*. The underside of the hind wing is usually ruddy brown.

Early Stages: The usual reference based on Scudder's work applies to *henrici*, not *irus*. The larvae of *irus* feed on the flowers and fruit of *Lupinus perennis* and *Baptisia tinctoria*.

(a) **irus** (Godart). Plate 50, figure 5, ♂; figure 6, ♀. The figure will serve for recognition of this subspecies.

Distribution: Nominate *irus* ranges from southern New England southward to South Carolina and westward to Michigan and northwestern Illinois.

(b) **hadros** (Cook & Watson). Plate 50, figure 7, ♂; figure 8, ♀. This subspecies is larger and was formerly considered a separate species. It is deep chestnut brown on the upperside and quite dark and lacking hoary scaling beneath.

Distribution: This subspecies is known only from east central Texas.

5. **Callophrys (Incisalia) henrici** (Grote & Robinson). This species is much like *irus*. The two differ in that males of *henrici* have no scent patch on the upperside of the fore wing.

Early Stages: These are well known. The young larvae bore into fruit and feed there. The host plants are plums (*Prunus*), blueberries (*Vaccinium*), redbud (*Cercis*), persimmon (*Diospyros*) and probably others.

(a) **henrici** (Grote & Robinson). Nominate *henrici* is characterized by the combination of short tails (unlike *margaretae*), ruddy cast to the underside (unlike *turneri*) and dark, white-edged basal area of the hind wing underside (unlike *solatus*).

Distribution: This subspecies ranges from North Carolina northward to Quebec and westward to Illinois.

(b) **margaretae** (dos Passos). The long tails set this rare subspecies apart from all others. It also is grayer above than nominate *henrici* and has less contrast on the under hind wing.

Distribution: South Carolina to Florida.

(c) **solatus** (Cook & Watson). The fringe of *solatus* is not checkered and the basal area on the underside of the hind wing is paler and not outlined with a white line.

Distribution: Central Texas.

(d) **turneri** Clench. Plate 50, figure 9, ♂; figure 10, ♀. This subspecies has short tails, is orange-brown above and more yellowish and washed out beneath compared to nominate *henrici.*

Distribution: This midwestern subspecies ranges from south central Kansas to northern Texas.

6. **Callophrys (Incisalia) lanoraieensis** (Sheppard). Plate 50, figure 15, ♂; figure 16, ♀. This small species begins a group of three species that are quite different in appearance from the other *Incisalia* in North America: they have a more checkered pattern on the underside and the termen of the hind wing is distinctly wavy but never tailed. In *lanoraieensis* there is a round black spot in the submarginal area of the underside of the hind wing near the anal angle. In *niphon* and *eryphon* there may be a "V" shaped spot in that area. The length of the fore wing of *lanoraieensis* is rarely over 11 mm, always much greater in the other two.

Early Stages: The caterpillars feed on the needles of Black Spruce (*Picea nigra*). During the first instar they are small enough to mine a needle.

Distribution: This species is limited to a few black spruce-tamarack-sphagnum bogs around Lanoraie, Quebec (type locality) and in central Maine.

7. **Callophrys (Incisalia) niphon** (Hübner). This species differs from western *eryphon,* with which it is easily confused, by a constant feature: in addition to the dark bar at the end of the cell of the forewing there is a second bar across the middle of the cell of *niphon.*

Early Stages: These are well known. The green caterpillar is longitudinally striped with whitish and thus "disappears" among the pine needles on which it feeds. Host plants are the "hard" pines—*Pinus virginiana, P. rigida* and others.

(a) **niphon** (Hübner). This rather rare southern subspecies is found in open pine woods. It visits flowers much more frequently than do most *Incisalia.* Females are rarely caught except when flushed from pines by jarring the trees.

Distribution: The nominate subspecies ranges from northern Florida to north-eastern Texas northward to West Virginia and New Jersey.

(b) **clarki** (Freeman). Plate 50, figure 19, ♂; figure 20, ♀. The northern subspecies is much more common than nominate *niphon.* It is smaller, paler on both surfaces and the markings on the underside of the hind wing are not as crisp and contrasty as in the southern subspecies.

Distribution: The subspecies *clarki* is found from New Jersey and Pennsylvania northward to Nova Scotia and westward to southern Manitoba.

8. **Callophrys (Incisalia) eryphon** (Boisduval). This species is much like the preceding and is easily confused with it. The two are sympatric in northern Michigan and possibly in Colorado. *C. eryphon* lacks the mid-cell dark bar on the fore wing underside that is present on *niphon.* Other markings on the underside also differ, particularly the more deeply dentate subterminal line on the hind wing of *eryphon.*

This is a spring butterfly of pine woods.

Early Stages: Like *niphon* the caterpillars feed on pine needles and are cryptically marked green and yellowish white. Host plants are *Pinus ponderosa, P. contorta* and other pines.

Distribution: Confined to pine forests, which usually means mountains in the West, *eryphon* ranges from central California, northern Arizona and New Mexico northward to British Columbia, thence eastward to northern Manitoba and Michigan.

(a) **eryphon** (Boisduval). Plate 50, figure 17, ♂; figure 18, ♀. The figure will serve to identify this butterfly.

(b) **sheltonensis** (Chermock & Frechin). This poorly differentiated subspecies is found on the Olympic peninsula in Washington.

Subgenus SANDIA Clench & Ehrlich

WILLIAM H. HOWE
(with Oakley Shields as a consultant)

This subgenus is characterized by abnormally long palpi for *Callophrys:* they are twice as long as the vertical diameter of the eye compared to 1.0–1.6 times as long in other subgenera. The subgenus and its single species were described in 1960.

9. **Callophrys (Sandia) mcfarlandi** (Ehrlich & Clench). Plate 53, figure 27, ♂; figure 28, ♀. This striking species of *Callophrys* can be recognized easily from the figures. Note that the postmedian line on the underside of the hind wings is displaced toward the margin. There appear to be two broods, one in early to mid May, the other in mid to late June.

Early Stages: The cryptic larvae feed on the flower heads and green seed capsules of the foodplant, beargrass (*Nolina*). They are quite variable in color and are attended by ants.

Distribution: A few scattered colonies are found in the Upper Sonoran zone from the Sandia Mountains, New Mexico to the Chisos Mountains, Texas.

Subgenus XAMIA Clench

WILLIAM H. HOWE
(with Oakley Shields as a consultant)

The hind wings are tailed and the underside of the hind wing is green. The single species in the subgenus previously was considered to be a member of *Mitoura*. Structurally, *Xamia* is closer to *Incisalia*.

10. **Callophrys (Xamia) xami** (Reakirt). Plate 49, figure 20, ♂; figure 21, ♀. This Mexican species is rather uncommon in the United States where it is found along the border.

Early Stages: The pale yellow-green caterpillar has rose colored markings on the back and stripes along the sides. Host plants in Mexico are *Echeveria gibbiflora* and *Sedum allantoides.* Study is needed on the life history in the U.S.

Distribution: From the state of Veracruz and Mexico City north to southern Texas and southern Arizona. There is one record (now considered dubious) from the Providence Mountains in southern California.

Subgenus MITOURA Scudder

WILLIAM H. HOWE
(with Oakley Shields as a consultant)

The subgenera *Mitoura, Callophrys* and *Cyanophrys* form a cluster within the genus *Callophrys* whose genitalia lack a "cap" on the valvae of the male genitalia. The cap is present on the previously noted subgenera. The males of *Mitoura* bear well developed scent pads on the fore wings and the hind wings of all species are tailed.

11. **Callophrys (Mitoura) spinetorum** (Hewitson). Plate 49, figure 13, ♀.   Although this species is usually collected only in small numbers, it is sometimes locally common. For some as yet unexplained reason, females usually outnumber males two to one in collections. The flight is rapid and erratic. Both sexes are attracted to flowers and moisture. The species flies from mid March to mid September in California, July in Wyoming.

Early Stages: The cryptic larvae are sometimes readily collected by beating the foodplant. The larval foodplants are dwarf mistletoes (*Arceuthobium*) parasitic on conifers.

Distribution: This species ranges throughout the West from the Rocky Mountains to the coast and from southern British Columbia to northern Baja California and Jalisco.

12. **Callophrys (Mitoura) johnsoni** (Skinner). Plate 49, figure 14, ♂; figure 15, ♀. This species is extremely rare in collections. Perhaps the best way to obtain it is to rear it, from eggs when a gravid female is caught, or from larvae beaten from the foodplant. Probably there are two broods; records of captures range from May to August. In many ways *johnsoni* is like *spinetorum* in behavior. It also looks somewhat like *spinetorum,* but instead of being steel blue on the upperside *johnsoni* is wholly brownish. On the underside it lacks the lilac tinting found on *nelsoni.*

Early Stages: These have been described in detail. The cryptically colored larvae feed on *Arceuthobium campylopodum,* a dwarf mistletoe parasitic on *Tsuga heterophylla.*

Distribution: The species is local from extreme southern British Columbia to central California in the Cascades and Sierras. There is a single record from Baker, eastern Oregon.

13. **Callophrys (Mitoura) nelsoni** (Boisduval). This species is abundant in stands of Incense Cedar in the Sierras of California. A single brood flies from May to July. Like the two preceding species, *nelsoni* visits flowers, with a preference for Bear Clover and Pussy Paws. In western Nevada it may be associated with juniper, a situation that should be investigated. As in *johnsoni,* the upperside of *nelsoni* is brown but the underside is laved with lilac especially on the hind wing.

Early Stages: The life history has not been published but *nelsoni* has been raised in British Columbia from caterpillars found on *Thuja plicata.* Incense Cedar (*Libocedrus decurrens*) may be its foodplant farther south and in drier regions it may use *Juniperus.*

(a) **nelsoni** (Boisduval). Plate 49, figure 16, ♂; figure 17, ♀. The row of spots on the underside of the wings is straighter on *n. nelsoni* than on *n. muiri.*

Distribution: This subspecies occurs along the west coast from southern British Columbia to southern California and east to western Idaho and Nevada, except for the coastal ranges from the vicinity of San Francisco Bay northward to Oregon. The species also has been reported from Guadeloupe Island, Baja California.

(b) **muiri** (Hy. Edwards). Plate 53, figure 6, ♂. This subspecies occupies a more humid region than does nominate *nelsoni.* The butterflies are darker beneath and the line of light markings is more irregular on *muiri.*

Distribution: The coastal range of Mendocino county, California (type locality) and of southern Oregon.

14. **Callophrys (Mitoura) siva** (W. H. Edwards). This species is closely associated with *Juniperus* and is never found in the absence of that plant. It is widely distributed and somewhat variable. Apparently *siva* has one brood in late spring and another in late summer. The species can be confused with *xami.*

(a) **siva** (W. H. Edwards). Plate 49, figure 18, ♂; figure 19, ♀. Two features on the underside of the hind wing set this subspecies apart from the others: the disc of *siva siva* is green and the white line zigzags into a "W" near the tails.

Distribution: This Rocky Mountain subspecies ranges from extreme southwestern North Dakota and Montana south to New Mexico and northeastern Arizona.

(b) **juniperaria** (J. A. Comstock). This subspecies is smaller than *siva siva* and lacks the "W" on the underside of the hind wing.

Distribution: This butterfly is restricted to the juniper belt in the mountains of southern California.

(c) **mansfieldi** (Tilden). This local subspecies differs from the other two by having the underside of the hind wing brown.

Distribution: It occurs in the coastal ranges of southern California.

15. **Callophrys (Mitoura) loki** (Skinner). Plate 49, figure 22, ♂; figure 23, ♀. This is another juniper hairstreak. It is quite local but sometimes is common in its favored habitat. There appear to be three broods; March, June and September, with the first brood the most abundant. A row of dark subterminal spots in the light limbal zone

on the underside of the hind wings of this species is almost non-existent on *siva,* which may fly with *loki* in a limited area in the Cajon Pass region of southern California.

Early Stages: Not known. The larval foodplant is *Juniperus californica.*

Distribution: The species ranges from Cajon Pass region, San Bernardino county, California, south into northern Baja California.

16. **Callophrys (Mitoura) gryneus** (Hübner). This eastern species may be confused only with *hesseli.* It differs from *hesseli* in these features: on the underside of the fore wing there is never a white dot in the cell near its end which is present on *hesseli;* and on the hind wing just outside the postmedian line dark brown patches occur in cells M_1 and M_2 on *hesseli* but not on *gryneus.* This species is found associated with low Red Cedar trees.

Early Stages: The dark green slug-shaped caterpillars are decorated with chevron shaped bars. Host plant: *Juniperus virginiana* (Red Cedar).

(a) **gryneus** (Hübner). Plate 49, figure 24, ♂; figure 25 ♀. There is considerable orange-brown on the upperside of the spring brood.

Distribution: This subspecies ranges from southern New England to Georgia, west to western Ontario, eastern Nebraska, eastern Kansas and northeastern Texas.

(b) **smilacis** (Boisduval & Le Conte). Plate 51, figure 2, ♀. There is no orange-brown on the upperside of this subspecies in any brood.

Distribution: Central and northern Florida.

(c) **castalis** (W. H. Edwards). This subspecies is similar to *gryneus gryneus* but is paler in color. In the border country between Texas and New Mexico *castalis* and *siva* may be sympatric. The two white postbasal bars and just costad of the cell on the underside of the hind wing of *gryneus* are absent on *siva.*

Distribution: This subspecies occurs in central and western Texas, probably extending into Oklahoma and New Mexico.

17. **Callophrys (Mitoura) hesseli** (Rawson & Ziegler). Plate 49, figure 26, ♂; figure 27, ♀. This sibling species (of *gryneus*) was overlooked until 1950. See *gryneus* above, and the figures, for the points of difference. The present species is always associated with White Cedar.

Early Stages: Undescribed. The host plant is *Chamaecyparis thyoides* (White Cedar).

Distribution: Southern New Hampshire to North Carolina in White Cedar swamps.

Subgenus CALLOPHRYS Billberg

JAMES A. SCOTT

This subgenus, which includes *C. rubi* (L.) and several other palearctic species, contains several western species of similar appearance in which the taxonomy is unsettled. The subgenus is in need of thorough biological study.

Some specimens may be difficult to identify. *C. dumetorum* and *apama* are the only species with brown discs on the fore wing below, and they have darker fringes than the other species. These two and *affinis* are the only species predominantly with fulvous females, although fulvous females occur rarely in the others. In *sheridanii, dumetorum viridis* and *affinis* the green on the fore wings below extends down to vein Cu_2, while in *apama, dumetorum* and *sheridanii comstocki* this green is invaded by brown or gray. The extent of green is associated with the environment; dry areas have forms without green in the disc, and wet cold areas have forms with green in the disc. Two species (*sheridanii* and *dumetorum*) have both forms in different environments. In *sheridanii* the postmedian band on the hind wings below is somewhat straighter than in the other species, and this band is often solid. The species fall into two groups, the superspecies (or species) containing *apama, dumetorum* and *affinis,* and the species *sheridanii.*

18. **Callophrys (Callophrys) apama** (Edwards). *C. apama* is easily recognized by the fulvous females, the brown disc of the fore wing below, and the angled postmedian band (often absent) which is angled outwardly on the hind wing and is bordered inwardly by black, then fulvous. *C. apama, affinis* and *dumetorum* may prove to be conspecific. They replace each other geographically. *C. d. dumetorum* is very similar to *C. a. homoperplexa* in the postmedian band of the hind wing below, the brown disc of the fore wings below, the color of the fringes, and the fulvous color of the females. Phenotypic intergrades between *dumetorum* and *affinis* occur in eastern Washington, and occasional *homoperplexa*-like individuals occur in Colorado *affinis.* In some southern Utah localities individuals resemble *affinis, apama* and *homoperplexa. C. apama* males perch on low vegetation in gullies, whereas males of the other two species perch on hilltops. This situation is similar to that in *Euphydryas editha* where male behavior differs between nearby colonies.

Early Stages: The foodplant in Mexico is *Eriogonum* sp. An observed oviposition on *Ceanothus fendleri* in Colorado may have been a "mistake" by the female.

Distribution: It occurs from Durango, Chihuahua and Sonora in Mexico north to eastern and central Arizona, New Mexico, Colorado, southern Wyoming and southern Utah. Adults of the single brood occur from March through June, and worn individuals rarely live until early August.

(a) **apama** (Edwards).   This subspecies occurs in Arizona and extreme southwestern Colorado. It has a well developed almost continuous macular band on the hind wing below, which is even more strikingly developed in Mexican populations.

(b) **homoperplexa** Barnes & Benjamin. Plate 53, figure 17, ♂; figure 18. ♀.   This subspecies occurs from northern New Mexico to southern Wyoming and southern Utah. The macular band on the hind wing below is usually reduced or absent.

19. **Callophrys (Callophrys) dumetorum** (Boisduval). *C. dumetorum* and *C. viridis* have been recently considered separate species because of slight larval differences, but the foodplants and behavior of the two are the same, and the geographical replacement of *dumetorum* by *viridis* suggests that *viridis* is an ecotype of *dumetorum.*

C. d. viridis resembles *dumetorum oregonensis* in some respects, and both *viridis* and *oregonensis* occur in cooler habitats than *dumetorum*. *C. d. viridis* intergrades with *dumetorum* on the Marina Beach Dunes in Monterey county and in Del Puerto Canyon. At Marina Beach, larvae feed both on *Lotus scoparius* and on *Eriogonum latifolium*, and both green and red larvae occur. *C. d. viridis* also intergrades with *dumetorum* in Del Puerto Canyon and to a lesser extent elsewhere in the range of *viridis*. The pink color of some *viridis* larvae is an adaptation to the red color of mature *Eriogonum* flowers. The postmedian band of all subspecies may be fairly complete or absent. *C. dumetorum* and *C. d. viridis* males are often found on hilltops.

Early Stages: There are four instars. The larvae of *viridis* vary from light green to pink, with pronounced segmental ridges, and with subdorsal ridges which may be laved with red. The larvae of *dumetorum* are usually dark green with two subdorsal white stripes (or paler and without stripes) which are usually lacking in *viridis*, and larvae are smoother than in *viridis*. Foodplants of *dumetorum* are *Lotus scoparius* (the main plant in California), *nevadensis*, and *crassifolius*, *Syrmatium* sp., *Hosackia* sp., and *Erigonum latifolium*. Laboratory hosts are *Eriogonum elatum, heracleoides* and *compositum;* these hosts may not be used in nature. The foodplants of *viridis* are *Eriogonum latifolium* (usually) and *Lotus scoparius.*

Distribution: The species occurs in Baja California Norte, all of California except desert areas, western Nevada, north through Oregon to northern Washington and western Idaho. There is one brood. Adults fly from February to April in California and fly in May and early June northward (one late September record in southern California represents a rare partial second brood). Where sympatric with *sheridanii*, it flies later in the season.

(a) **dumetorum** (Boisduval). Plate 53, figure 13, ♂; figure 14, ♀. This subspecies occurs in California and southern Oregon. It has brown on the disc on the fore wing below. The name *perplexa* Barnes & Benjamin is a synonym.

(b) **viridis** (Edwards). Plate 53, figure 21, ♂; figure 22, ♀. This California subspecies occurs on the immediate coast from Monterey county to Mendocino county, and inland in Del Puerto Canyon, Stanislaus county. Fresh specimens can be recognized by the whiter antennae and broad white fringes, in addition to the characters cited above. Many specimens have a bluish cast to the green below. The postmedian band below may be fairly complete or absent. These characteristics are variable, and some specimens resemble *dumetorum.*

(c) **oregonensis** Gorelick. This Oregon and Washington subspecies is of doubtful validity because of its variability both within and between local populations. Specimens from the type locality have females with less red above, and the fore wing disc below is invaded with gray rather than brown which does not extend as far into the disc as in *dumetorum*. Specimens from Mason county, Washington, however, are identical to California *dumetorum.*

20. **Callophrys (Callophrys) affinis** (Edwards). Individuals are distinguished by the fulvous females (and some males), the usually immaculate yellowish green under-

sides, and the pale contrasting fringes. The species occurs in sage habitats in the Great Basin. Males perch on sagebrush on low hilltops near the foodplant.

Early Stages: Dr. John Emmel raised larvae from *Eriogonum* sp. in northern Nevada. Females oviposit on *Eriogonum umbellatum* in Colorado and adults are associated with this plant in Montana and Nevada. The larvae are grass green to deep red with subdorsal ridges, a light subdorsal line and a supraventral light white line.

Distribution: It occurs in the Great Basin, from western Colorado north to southern Montana, west to central Nevada, eastern Oregon and Washington, and southern British Columbia. It is single brooded. Adults occur from late May to early July.

(a) **affinis** (Edwards). Plate 53, figure 19, ♂; figure 20, ♀. This subspecies occurs throughout most of the range. The ventral green is yellowish.

(b) **washingtonia** Clench. This subspecies occurs in Washington and British Columbia. The green is darker and there is slightly less fulvous shading above. *C. dumetorum oregonensis* possesses these two characteristics, and further collecting will probably show a cline between *oregonensis* and *affinis affinis* through *affinis washingtonia.*

21. **Callophrys (Callophrys) sheridanii** (Edwards). *C. sheridanii* is a small mouse-gray species with the undersides rather dark green, and with the fringes below often dark at the ends of the cubital veins. Colonies of this species are often found on hillsides. It has a wide elevational range, occurring from transition zone foothills to occasionally above timberline (in alpine zone occasionally in Washington, California, and Colorado). The subspecies are mostly clinal. *C. s. lemberti* and *s. comstocki* were formerly considered distinct species, *C. s. lemberti* is a southern extension of *sheridanii newcomeri,* however, and David Bauer has found that *lemberti* and *comstocki* intergrade in western Nevada and the White Mountains of California. The *lemberti* forms predominate at higher elevations in these two areas, and completely mixed populations occur at lower elevations.

Early Stages: The mature larva (*newcomeri*) is green to pink, with well developed segmental ridges; it is similar to *C. dumetorum viridis* in shape. The foodplants are *Eriogonum umbellatum* in Washington and Colorado, a vine-like *Eriogonum* species in eastern Arizona (Kilian Roever), *E. compositum* var. *lieanthum* in Washington (Jon Pelham), and *Eriogonum* sp. in Washington and the Providence Mountains of California and *Eriogonum incanum* in the Sierras of California and *E. jamesii* var. *wootenii* in the Sacramento Mountains, New Mexico.

Distribution: It occurs from New Mexico and eastern Arizona north to Canada, south to California. It is single brooded in most of the range, from late March to early June. It usually flies earlier in the season where sympatric with *dumetorum oregonensis.* In the Sierra Nevada of California it flies usually in May and June, but occurs rarely as late as early August above timberline. In the Mojave desert of California there are two broods, April–May and August–early September.

(a) **sheridanii** (Edwards). Plate 53, figure 23, ♂; figure 24, ♀. It occurs in the Sacramento Mountains of southern New Mexico, the Blue Mountains of eastern Arizona above 8000 feet, and from central Colorado to the Bighorn Mountains of

Wyoming. It is small, and the postmedian band on the hind wing below is solid and unbroken. Specimens from the Sacramento and Blue mountains are larger and have gray extending farther into the green on the underside of the front wing.

(b) **neoperplexa** (Barnes & Benjamin). It occurs from southwestern Colorado and Utah north to Montana and Washington. It is small, and the postmedian line below is narrower and not lined inwardly with black.

(c) **newcomeri** Clench. This subspecies occurs from southern Alberta and British Columbia south to northern Idaho and central Oregon, east of the Cascades. It is slightly larger and the postmedian band on the hind wing below is often broken into separate spots and the band on the fore wing is often absent.

(d) **lemberti** Tilden. Plate 53, figure 16, ♂. It occurs from western Nevada, the Sierras of California, and the Cascades in northern California and southern Oregon, from 7000 to 11,500 feet, at higher elevations that *C. dumetorum*. The macular band below is slightly more convex (varying from the shape of *newcomeri* to the shape of *comstocki*), and usually reduced to a few spots, and the ventral green is usually lighter. Females are rarely slightly fulvous above.

(e) **comstocki** Henne. Plate 53, figure 15, ♂. This subspecies occurs from the Providence Mountains of the Mojave desert in California north in desert mountains to the White Mountains and to southern and western Nevada (Clark, Esmeralda and Douglas counties). The postmedian band below usually protrudes outwardly as in *apama* but is edged only with black as in *sheridanii sheridanii*. The fore wing below has light gray extending into the disc. It is pale green below.

Subgenus CYANOPHRYS Clench

JAMES A. SCOTT

This subgenus consists of many neotropical species only two of which enter our area in southern Texas. They may be confused with *Callophrys* (*Callophrys*) species on the underside but have blue above.

22. **Callophrys (Cyanophrys) miserabilis** Clench. Plate 53, figure 25, ♂; figure 26, ♀. This species was formerly misidentified as *Strymon pastor* Butler & Druce. It is a breeding resident in southern Texas where it is fairly common. The hind wings are tailed. Both wings of the male are steel blue above. On the hind wing below there are often several reddish brown subterminal spots in cells Cu_1 and Cu_2. The frons, the "face" of the head, was formerly used as a distinguishing characteristic but in both species it is green in females and mostly brown in males.

Early Stages: Unknown.

Distribution: The species ranges from Costa Rica north through Mexico to southern Texas. Adults in Texas fly in April–May, July–August, and October–December.

23. **Callophrys (Cyanophrys) goodsoni** (Clench). Plate 52, figure 18, ♀; figure 25, ♂. This species, formerly reported in error as *Strymon facuna* (Hewitson), is an occasionally common breeding resident in southern Texas. It lacks tails. The blue

of the male is pale and silvery and is restricted to the hind wing and to the base of the fore wing. There is a brown submarginal spot on the hind wing below only in cell Cu$_2$ (rarely absent).

Early Stages: Unknown.

Distribution: The species ranges from Costa Rica north to extreme southern Texas. There are Texas records in June and from late July into October

Genus TMOLUS Hübner

THOMAS C. EMMEL

This is another tropical genus with only two species barely occurring within our region. They are small, single tailed hairstreaks that resemble species of *Ministrymon.*

1. **Tmolus echion** (Linnaeus). Plate 52, figure 9, ♂; figure 10, ♀. This species has a light underside with coral red postbasal spots and postmedian line. It is common in tropical America and strays rarely into southern Texas. Males are dark iridescent blue-violet above, only faintly indicated in the figure.

Early Stages: We know nothing of these except that the larva feeds on *Lantana.*

Distribution: The species ranges from South America northward to extreme southern Texas. It has been introduced into Hawaii in hopes that the larvae will control the (also introduced) lantana which is a pest on the islands.

2. **Tmolus azia** (Hewitson). Plate 51, figure 23, ♂; figure 24, ♀. This tiny butterfly resembles *Ministrymon clytie* on the upperside, but is smaller and has a ventral hind wing surface free of striations except for the thin postmedian line. It flies from late March to May in Texas.

Early Stages: Unknown.

Distribution: *T. azia* ranges from South America north to southern Arizona and southern Texas.

Genus MINISTRYMON Clench

THOMAS C. EMMEL

This small genus contains two southwestern species that closely resemble each other. Both are small hairstreaks with a partially blue dorsal surface and a gray ventral surface with a well marked postmedian line.

1. **Ministrymon leda** (Edwards). Plate 51, figure 25, ♂ (form "leda"); figure 26, ♀ (form "leda"); figure 27, ♂ (form "ines"); figure 28, ♀ (form "ines"). For many years the two seasonal forms of this butterfly were considered to be separate subspecies

or even species. Unpublished studies of Roever, however, have indicated otherwise. The spring form, flying from May into July is *leda*, f. "leda." The autumn or "winter" form appears in late September and October and sometimes in late November and is called *leda*, f. "ines." The principal difference between the two is that the winter form lacks the red markings beneath. The blue on the upper side of *leda* is grayer than that of *clytie* and the orange-red spots at the tails on the under surface of the hind wings are less well developed.

Early Stages: We know only that the host plant is mesquite (*Prosopis juliflora* var *glandulosa*).

Distribution: M. leda ranges from southern Arizona and southern California southward into Mexico, including Baja California.

2. **Ministrymon clytie** (Edwards). Plate 51, figure 21, ♂. The underside of this species is whitish with faint transverse lines and spots. The red ventral spots are well developed. The upperside is rather bright lilac-blue. The spring form is darker than the summer one. There are numerous broods throughout the year.

Distribution: This species occurs from southern Texas and Arizona southward into Mexico.

Genus CALYCOPIS Scudder

THOMAS C. EMMEL

Two species of this large tropical genus are found north of Mexico. A recent study of *Calycopis* was published by W. D. Field, in 1967. Our treatment of the genus, as it enters our territory, follows Field's revision.

1. **Calycopis cecrops** (Fabricius). Plate 51, figure 11, ♂; figure 12, ♀. An easily recognized species, the dark brown underside is marked with bright white, red and black lines. The postdiscal line on the underside of the hind wing is continuous, strongly angled from the two tails and has a broad red component. The butterfly is common in the Southeast and is multiple brooded.

Early Stages: Not published. The larval foodplants include *Croton* and Dwarf Sumac (*Rhus copallina*).

Distribution: The species is found from eastern Kansas through southern Ohio to southern New Jersey southward to Florida and Texas. Occasional strays have been reported as far north as southern Michigan and New York. In the Arkansas Ozarks the adults sometimes swarm over the blooms of the Lemonade Sumac (*Rhus serotina*) in early May.

2. **Calycopis isobeon** Butler & Druce. Plate 51, figure 13, ♂; figure 14, ♀. Much resembling *cecrops*, *C. isobeon* differs in these particulars: the postdiscal line on the underside has a narrower red component on the fore wing than on the hind wing

(in *cecrops* they are equal in thickness) and there is more red around the black spot at the base of the tails.

Distribution: C. *isobeon* is found from eastern and southern Texas southward to Panamá. Strays occasionally reach Kansas.

Genus ATLIDES Hübner

THOMAS C. EMMEL

The single species of this genus in our area is one of our most spectacularly colored butterflies, appropriately called the Great Blue Hairstreak. The hind wing carries a long tail on vein Cu_2 and a short, spike-like one on vein Cu_1. The males have a large compound scent patch on the upperside of the fore wing.

1. **Atlides halesus** Cramer.   The dark shining blue of the upperside of this butterfly is a structural color and not produced by a blue pigment. The natural range of the species is from Mexico into the southern United States. Strays, however, have been found as far north as New York, Illinois and Oregon. It is strongly attracted to the nectar of flowers and most easily caught while feeding.

Early Stages: The downy, green, slug shaped caterpillars feed on mistletoe (*Phoradendron flavescens,* parasitic on Live Oak and Western Sycamore in southern California, and *P. californica,* on desert ironwood).

(a) **halesus** Cramer.   This is the eastern subspecies. Males have a definite tail at Cu_1 and both sexes have some red on the underside between the green tornal bars.

Distribution: The nominate subspecies occurs from Florida northward to New Jersey, westward about to Mississippi, much rarer in the north than southward.

(b) **corcorani** Gunder. Plate 49, figure 4, ♂; figure 5, ♀.   This western subspecies has in the male merely a slight projection of the termen at Cu_1, and both sexes lack the red between the tornal green bars on the underside.

Distribution: This subspecies occurs from the Mississippi Valley westward to the Pacific coast, rarely (strays) as far north as southern Illinois or Oregon. It also flies in northern Mexico.

Genus DOLYMORPHA Holland

THOMAS C. EMMEL

One species of this tropical genus occasionally strays into southern Arizona.

1. **Dolymorpha jada** (Hewitson). Plate 50, figure 25, ♂; figure 26, ♀.   The soft, broad, mustard-colored striping on the creamy underside is distinctive among all our hairstreaks.

Early Stages: Unknown.

Distribution: This species is common in Central America, becomes uncommon in northern Mexico and is very rare in southern Arizona.

Genus EURISTRYMON Clench

THOMAS C. EMMEL

The genus is best recognized by the structure of the male genitalia. It is essentially a New World genus, but a few species, *pruni* among them, are Palearctic. The hind wings are tailed and the males usually have a well developed scent patch on the upperside of the fore wing. The known larvae feed on the leaves of trees.

1. **Euristrymon polingi** (Barnes & Benjamin). Plate 52, figure 19, ♂; figure 20, ♀. The upperside of this quite local species is without any fulvous or subterminal orange lunules, and males lack a scent pad, found in both the other species. The wings are noticeably rounded. The butterflies often feed at the yellow flowers of catsclaw (*Acacia greggii*).

Early Stages: Unknown. Because the butterflies frequently sit on oak leaves some have thought oak to be the foodplant of the larvae.

Distribution: Thus far known only from the Davis Mountains in southwestern Texas.

2. **Euristrymon favonius** (J. E. Smith). Plate 54, figure 1, ♂; figure 2, ♀. The large fulvous patches on the upperside are also found on one subspecies of the next species. The two (*favonius* and *ontario*) may really represent only one species; if so it will be called *favonius,* by priority. The clue to *favonius* appears on the underside of the hind wing. There the red in the submarginal area is heavy and continuous, not broken into patches. Specimens intermediate between *favonius* and *ontario* are known from southern Georgia.

Early Stages: The winter is passed as eggs laid on the terminal twigs of oaks (*Quercus* spp.). The larvae feed on the buds and descend to the leaf litter at the base of the tree for pupation.

Distribution: The species ranges from southern Florida northward to southeastern North Carolina, usually near the coast.

3. **Euristrymon ontario** (W. H. Edwards). The fulvous orange patches on the upperside are quite variable, depending on the subspecies, from not a trace to almost as large as on *favonius.* The submarginal red on the underside of the hind wings is broken into well isolated lunules.

Early Stages: These are similar to those of *favonius,* but in the north hawthorn (*Crataegus*) may be used as host plant as well as oaks.

(a) **ontario** (W. H. Edwards). Plate 54, figure 3, ♂; figure 4, ♀. There is no trace of the fulvous orange patch on the upperside of this subspecies. There is a cline from this typical state of *o. ontario* to typical *o. autolycus* that extends from Ontario to Texas. Technically only one name should be used for this, *ontario.*

Distribution: From Ontario to the Ohio River most specimens have at most only a trace of orange on the upperside. From there southward more and more specimens have good orange patches.

(b) **autolycus** (W. H. Edwards). Plate 16, figure 15, ♀. In its typical form this subspecies has large orange patches on the upperside.

Distribution: This subspecies occurs chiefly in eastern Texas; northward, in Kansas and Missouri, it intergrades with *ontario.*

(c) **violae** (Stallings & Turner). This rare subspecies, known only from the type series, is dark gray-brown rather than red-brown above. The orange patches are similar to those on *autolycus* but paler. The tails are very short and only the posterior one is always present.

Distribution: Vicinity of Folsom, New Mexico (type locality). The westernmost specimens from Texas, Oklahoma and Kansas are still *o. autolycus.*

(d) **ilavia** (Beutenmueller). Plate 53, figure 11, ♂. The extreme western subspecies is like a pale version of *autolycus.* The underside is pale fawn, lacks the prominent submarginal red spots and has only faint traces of any pattern.

Distribution: Eastern and western wooded areas of Arizona.

Genus HYPOSTRYMON Clench

THOMAS C. EMMEL

The only species thus far recognized in this genus flies in Mexico and adjacent Arizona. The hind wings are tailed. The wings above are blue, more extensive in males, and there is a large black androconical patch on the disc of the male fore wing on the upperside.

1. **Hypostrymon critola** (Hewitson). Plate 48, figure 28, ♂; figure 29 ♂, underside; figure 30, ♀ (ssp. *festata*). The figured specimens represent the subspecies *festata* Weeks, which occurs in the southern half of Baja California. It much resembles nominate *critola,* the subspecies in our area.

Early Stages: Unknown.

Distribution: Nominate *critola* is confined to the state of Sonora, and the adjacent Patagonia Mountains in Arizona.

Genus PANTHIADES Hübner

THOMAS C. EMMEL

There are many species in this genus in the neotropics. A single one of these invades our area. The hind wings are tailed and the males have a scent patch on the upperside of the fore wing.

1. **Panthiades m-album** (Boisduval & Le Conte). Plate 49, figure 6, ♂; figure 7, ♀. In this widespread species the postmedian line on the ventral hind wing forms a white "M" near the base of the tails. The butterfly occurs in many habitats but is

uncommon in the northern part of its range. The upper surface of both sexes is rich iridescent blue, brighter in the males.

Early Stages: The larvae are light yellowish green with a darker mid stripe and seven slanted lateral stripes. Host plants are oaks (*Quercus* spp.)

Distribution: This species ranges from Connecticut, southern Pennsylvania and the Ohio River watershed southward to Texas and Florida, thence to Guatemala.

Genus STRYMON Hübner

JAMES A. SCOTT

This genus has been restricted by Clench to include only a handful of the species formerly allotted to it. Most of the species are tropical except for one endemic island species, *S. avalona,* and *S. melinus,* which is common and is sometimes an agricultural pest on hops and beans.

1. **Strymon melinus** Hübner.   *S. melinus* is common and is the only species widespread north of Mexico. It is easily recognized by the pattern beneath. Spring individuals are darker beneath than later individuals. Males are often found in the afternoon on shrubs or low trees on hilltops. *S. melinus* is so variable seasonally and individually that the six described subspecies are weakly differentiated. The most divergent phenotype is found on Clarion Island west of mainland Mexico.

Early Stages: The larvae are variable and are either naked or clothed with short brownish setae. They are unmarked reddish brown to green. Larvae bore into fruits and seeds, and sometimes feed on juvenile leaves. They hibernate as pupae, which are delicate brown, heavily maculated with deep brown spots. The larvae are somewhat cannibalistic in the laboratory. The larvae are polyphagous, and are known to feed on 46 genera of plants in 21 families, including Pinaceae (1 genus), Palmae (1), Agavaceae (*Nolina*), Poaceae (corn), Fagaceae (1), Leguminosae (14), Zygophyllaceae (1), Euphorbiaceae (1), Malvaceae (6 including cotton), Passifloraceae (1), Ebenaceae (1), Verbenaceae (1), Rosaceae (6 including apple, blackberry, strawberry), Moraceae (1), Polygonaceae (1), Hypericaceae (1), Apocynaceae (1), Boraginaceae (1), Cactaceae (1), Labiatae (1), Compositae (1).

Distribution: It ranges from Nova Scotia to southern British Columbia, southward throughout the United States to Venezuela. There are at least two broods in the north, three or more southward, from early spring to late fall.

(a) **melinus** Hübner. Plate 48, figure 41 ♂. This subspecies occurs in Florida and the Gulf states, intergrading westward and northward. The underside is pale gray and the orange spot below touches the postmedian band.

(b) **humuli** (Harris). This subspecies is found in eastern U.S. and eastern Canada west to Nebraska. It is slightly browner below.

(c) **franki** Field. Plate 52, figure 3, ♂; figure 4, ♀. This subspecies occurs in the plains states south to Texas, Arizona and Mexico. It is pale gray below and the postmedian band below is narrow and lined with black and often a slight amount of red. The postmedian band is slightly less straight than the band of the previous two subspecies, but this characteristic is variable and can be found in individuals of most populations.

(d) **pudica** (Hy. Edwards). This subspecies ranges from southern Oregon through California to Baja California. It is similar to *franki* except that about half of the specimens of *pudica* have more red in the hind wing postmedian band below.

(e) **setonia** McDunnough. This subspecies ranges in semiarid areas from Oregon to British Columbia eastward in the Great Basin to Colorado. It is similar to *franki* except that the hind wing band below is more broadly edged with black.

(f) **atrofasciata** McDunnough. Plate 52, figure 8, ♂. This subspecies occurs on Vancouver Island, southwestern British Columbia, and western Washington in the high precipitation zone. It is slightly darker than *setonia* below, with the postmedian band even more heavily edged with black.

2. **Strymon avalona** (Wright). Plate 52, figure 1, ♂; figure 2, ♀. This species is similar to *melinus* but the postmedian line beneath is less distinct and the red-orange spot is reduced both above and below.

Early Stages: The foodplants are *Lotus argophyllus* and sometimes *Lotus scoparius*.

Distribution: This species is endemic to Santa Catalina Island, offshore from Los Angeles, California. There are at least three broods (January–April, July–September, late fall).

3. **Strymon bebrycia** (Hewitson). Plate 52, figure 5, ♂; figure 6, ♀. The name *buchholzi* Freeman is a synonym of *bebrycia*. This species is similar to *melinus* but the postmedian line on the hind wing below is edged inwardly only with red, the red spot is reduced especially dorsally, there are white submarginal and subterminal bands on the underside of the hind wing which are similar to those of *alea*, and the male has a black polygonal stigma occupying the distal third of the cell.

Early Stages: Unknown.

Distribution: The species occurs in northern Mexico and southern Texas. It is multiple brooded and has been collected in February, and September to December.

4. **Strymon alea** (Godman & Salvin). Plate 51, figure 22, ♀. The name *laceyi* (Barnes & Benjamin) is a synonym of *alea*. There are two seasonal forms of this uncommon species. The summer form resembles *columella* but has the postmedian spots below coalesced to form a band. The winter form is similar to *yojoa* below but has a large marginal "thecla-spot" capped with orange, and has several postbasal spots in place of the white stripe on the hind wing.

Early Stages: Unknown.

Distribution: It is found in the southern lowlands of Mexico and along both coasts north to south-central Texas where it is endemic but not common. There are four or more broods, in late April–May, late June–July, October–early November, and December.

5. **Strymon yojoa** (Reakirt). Plate 52, figure 15, ♂; figure 16, ♀. This species is recognized by the postbasal transverse white stripe on the hind wing below, by the wide white distal edging to the postmedian line, and by the two marginal black spots on the hind wing above.

Early Stages: Unknown.

Distribution: It occurs in Central America and Mexico, rarely in southern Texas. It is multiple brooded (January, February, April, August, September, December).

6. **Strymon columella** (Fabricius). *S. columella* is easily distinguished by the two dark spots at the anal region of the hind wing above, and by the pattern below, in which the postmedian line is broken into separate spots. *Strymon columella cybira* (Hewitson) is one of the Antillean subspecies and does not occur in the U.S.

Early Stages: The foodplant is *Sida hederacea* in California.

Distribution: The species occurs in the West Indies and in southern Florida, and from Central America north to southern Texas and southern California. Adults fly throughout the year in southern Texas and Florida, and occur in March and July–September in California.

(a) **modesta** (Maynard). The Florida subspecies is larger and browner, with the red spot below well-developed.

(b) **istapa** (Reakirt). Plate 51, figure 15, ♂; figure 16, ♀. This subspecies occurs from Panamá north to Texas and California. It is smaller, paler, and the red spot is poorly developed.

7. **Strymon rufofusca** (Hewitson). Plate 52, figure 11, ♂; figure 12, ♀. This species is recognized by the tan ground color below, with a definite "thecla-spot" capped with orange and a well developed tortuous postmedian line of white edged with red.

Early Stages: Unknown.

Distribution: This is chiefly a tropical continental species found also on the island of St. Vincent in the Lesser Antilles. It ranges northward into southern Texas. It is multiple brooded, flying at least in March and November–December.

8. **Strymon cestri** (Reakirt). Plate 52, figure 13, ♂; figure 14, ♀. This species and *bazochii* are tailless, and the hind wing below is mottled brown and lacks marginal red spots. *S. cestri* can be recognized by the postbasal spots, the postmedian band of black spots, the prominent large white patches, and a small black submarginal spot in cell Cu_1. These features are lacking on *bazochii*.

Early Stages: Unknown.

Distribution: This species occurs in Central America and Mexico and rarely in southern Texas. It is multiple brooded (March, August, September, October).

9. **Strymon bazochii** (Godart). Plate 51, figure 19, ♂; figure 20, ♀. In addition to the points of difference from *cestri* noted above, *bazochii* males are blue above and the hind wing below is darker.

Early Stages: The larvae are dull green and are covered with white and dark bristles. They feed on the flowering heads of several plants, especially *Lantana camara.* The butterfly was introduced into Hawaii to control this introduced pest shrub. Other Hawaiian host plants are *Hyptis pectinata* and *Ocimum basilicum.*

Distribution: This species is found in the Greater Antilles and in the continental tropics from Brazil to southern Texas, where it is a resident. It is multiple brooded (February, March, May, August to December).

10. **Strymon acis bartrami** (Comstock & Huntington). Plate 51, figure 5, ♂; figure 6, ♀. This species is distinguished from *martialis* by the lack of blue above, and by the postbasal white spots on the hind wing below.

Early Stages: The foodplant is recorded as "wild croton."

Distribution: It occurs in southern Florida and the Antilles. It is multiple brooded, in January–May, July–August, and October–December.

11. **Strymon martialis** (Herrich-Schäffer). Plate 51, figure 3, ♂; figure 4, ♀. This species is easy to recognize by the blue above and by the pattern below.

Early Stages: The larva is dull unmarked green, dorsally covered with short white setae. The foodplant is *Trema floridana.*

Distribution: It occurs in southern Florida and the Antilles. It is multiple brooded, and has been recorded in all months except May and September.

12. **Strymon albata sedecia** (Hewitson). This species has recently been found in extreme southern Texas. It is similar to *alea* in the ventral pattern, but it is paler below and the upperside has a white patch at the anal margin of the hind wing and a large patch covering all but the base and apex of the front wing.

Early Stages: Unknown.

Distribution: It occurs southward to Guatemala.

Genus ERORA Scudder

THOMAS C. EMMEL

This small genus is represented by two species in our area. The butterflies lack tails and the males lack scent pads. For many years only one species was recognized and called *laeta.* The two species, however, are amply distinct.

1. **Erora laeta** (W. H. Edwards). Plate 50, figure 21, ♂. This is an extremely rare species. The male is well figured. The fringe of the wings of the female has little or no orange. The range of *laeta* does not approach that of *quaderna* so there is little chance of confusing the two if the place of capture is known.

Early Stages: The host plants are beech (*Fagus*) and possibly Beaked Hazelnut (*Corylus rostrata*). There probably are two broods.

COLOR PLATES

Key to Reproductions

The following illustrations present the large and medium butterflies approximately two thirds the size of an average adult specimen. Very small butterflies of the families Riodinidae, Lycaenidae, and Hesperiidae are shown actual size, as are the adult butterflies of the genus *Boloria*.

Key to Abbreviations

All geographic abbreviations follow the usage in *The Times Atlas of the World*. The museums and private collections that provided specimens for illustration are abbreviated as follows:

AMNH	American Museum of Natural History, New York.		JHS	Jon H. Shepard (Private).
			JL	John Lane (Private).
CAS	California Academy of Sciences, San Francisco.		JMB	John M. Burns (Private).
			JMP	John M. Plomley (Private).
CDM	C. Don MacNeill (Private).		JRH	John R. Heitzman (Private).
CM	Carnegie Museum of Natural History, Pittsburgh.		LACM	Los Angeles County Museum, Los Angeles.
CNC	Canadian National Collection, Ottawa.		LPG	L. Paul Grey (Private).
DLB	David L. Bauer (Private).		MPM	Milwaukee Public Museum, Milwaukee.
DVM	David V. McCorkle (Private).			
E&SP	Edwin M. Jr. and Stephen F. Perkins (formerly private, recently acquired by the Allyn Museum of Entomology).		OS	Oakley Shields (Private).
			RLL	Robert L. Langston (Private).
			RRI	Roderick R. Irwin (Private).
F&JP	Floyd W. and June D. Preston (Private).		RSW	Ronald S. Wielgus (Private).
			S&T	Don B. Stallings & J. R. Turner (Private).
FER	Frank E. Rutkowski (Private).			
FTT	Fred T. Thorne (Private).		SGJ	Stanley G. Jewett, Jr. (Private).
HAF	H. Avery Freeman (formerly private, recently largely acquired by the American Museum of Natural History).		TCE	Thomas C. Emmel (Private).
			TWD	Thomas W. Davies (Private).
			USNM	United States National Museum (now National Museum of Natural History), Washington.
JAP	Jerry A. Powell (Private).			
JCD	John C. Downey (Private).			
JDE	J. Donald Eff (Private).		WJR	Walfried J. Reinthal (Private).

PLATE 1

1 *Danaus plexippus,* ♂. Brimson, Mo., July 18, 1959. USNM.

2 *Danaus gilippus strigosus,* ♂. Madera Canyon, Pima Co., Ariz., Sept. 5, 1951. AMNH.

3 *Danaus gilippus berenice,* ♀. Crystal R., Fla., Aug. 14, 1958. USNM.

4 *Danaus eresimus montezuma,* ♀. Pharr, Tex. S&T.

5 *Limenitis archippus,* ♂. Mears Park, Franklin Co., Kan., Sept. 17, 1942. AMNH.

6 *Limenitis archippus floridensis,* ♂. Okeechobee, Fla., Aug. 12, 1958. FER.

7 *Limenitis archippus obsoleta,* ♂. Blythe, Cal., June 17, 1950. F&JP.

8 *Limenitis archippus watsoni,* ♂. St. Charles Parish, La., May 28, 1954. E&SP.

9 *Heliconius charitonius tuckeri,* ♂. Key Vaca, Fla., Aug. 18, 1958. AMNH.

10 *Heliconius petiveranus,* ♂. Ciudad Valles, San Luis Potosí, June 28, 1968. HAF.

11 *Dryas julia cillene,* ♂. Key Largo, Fla., Aug. 17, 1958. AMNH.

12 *Dryas julia cillene,* ♀. Key Largo, Fla., Aug. 17, 1958. AMNH.

13 *Agraulis vanillae nigrior,* ♂. Chattahoochee, Fla., Aug. 12, 1958. AMNH.

14 *Agraulis vanillae nigrior,* ♂, underside. Same data as fig. 13.

15 *Euptoieta claudia,* ♀. Chippewa Hills, Franklin Co., Kan., Sept. 16, 1944. AMNH.

16 *Euptoieta hegesia hoffmanni,* ♀. Ciudad Mante, Tamaulipas, June 23, 1968. HAF.

17 *Microtia elva,* ♂. Campostela, Nayarit, Sept. 10, 1932. AMNH.

18 *Dymasia chara imperialis,* ♂, paratype. Chino Canyon, Coachella Valley, Imperial Co., Cal., April 1, 1932. LACM.

19 *Dymasia chara imperialis,* ♀, paratype. Borrego Palm Canyon, San Diego Co., Cal., April 14, 1941. LACM.

20 *Poladryas a. arachne,* form "gilensis," ♂. Hwy 83, Santa Cruz Co., Ariz., June 17, 1962. LACM.

PLATE 1

1

2

3

4

5

6

7

8

9

10

11

12

13

14

15

16

17

18

19

20 William H. Howe

PLATE 2

 1   *Lethe creola*, ♂. Suffolk, Va., June 18, 1944. AMNH.
 2   *Lethe creola*, ♀. Suffolk, Va., June 18, 1944. AMNH.
 3   *Lethe creola*, ♀, underside. Same data as fig. 2.
 4   *Lethe portlandia anthedon*, ♂. Spooner, Wis. USNM.
 5   *Gyrocheilus patrobas tritonia*, ♂. Jerome, Ariz. FER.
 6   *Lethe e. eurydice*, ♂. Springdale, N.J. FER.
 7   *Lethe e. eurydice*, ♂. Same data as fig. 6.
 8   *Lethe appalachia*, ♂. Springdale, N.J. FER.
 9   *Lethe appalachia*, ♂, underside. Same data as fig. 8.
10   *Euptychia c. cymela*, ♂. Willis Woods, Franklin Co., Kans. AMNH.
11   *Euptychia c. cymela*, ♂, underside. Same data as fig. 10.
12   *Euptychia areolata septentrionalis*, ♂. Lakehurst, N.J. FER.
13   *Euptychia mitchellii*, ♀. Springdale, N.J. FER.
14   *Euptychia hermes sosybius*, ♂. Siesta Key, Sarasota Co., Fla., Aug. 27, 1948. USNM.
15   *Euptychia rubricata cheneyorum*, ♀. Upper Madera Canyon, Santa Cruz Co., Ariz., July 19, 1950.
     F&JP.
16   *Euptychia dorothea*, ♂. Huachuca Mts., Cochise Co., Ariz., May 13, 1916. LACM.
17   *Euptychia dorothea*, ♀. Rock Creek Saddle Trail, Chiricahua Mts., Cochise Co., Ariz., June 24, 1950.
     F&JP.
18   *Euptychia henshawi*, ♂. Huachuca Mts., Cochise Co., Ariz., May 27, 1916. LACM.
19   *Euptychia gemma freemani*, ♂. Pharr, Tex., Nov. 10, 1946. HAF.
20   *Paramecera xicaque*, ♀. Rustlers Park, Chiricahua Mts., Cochise Co., Ariz. F&JP.
21   *Paramecera xicaque*, ♂. Chiricahua Mts., Ariz., "June." CM.
22   *Euptychia g. gemma*, ♂. Gastonia, N.Car., April 25, 1921. CM.
23   *Neominois r. ridingsii*, ♂. Fountain Valley, Colorado Springs, Colo., June 17, 1949. JDE.
24   *Neominois ridingsii dionysus*, ♂. Black Canyon of the Gunnison, Montrose Co., Colo. FER.
25   *Neominois ridingsii stretchii*, ♀. Table Mt., Bishop Creek, Inyo Co., Cal., July 5, 1935. LACM.
26   *Euptychia g. gemma*, ♂, underside. Gastonia, N.Car., April 25, 1921. CM.
27   *Coenonympha haydeni*, ♂. Luther, Absaroka Range, Carbon Co., Mont., July 15, 1966. USNM.

PLATE 2

1
2
3
4
5
6
7
8
9
10
11
12
13
14
15
16
17
18
19
20
21
22
23
24
25
26
27

William H. Howe

PLATE 3

1 *Ceryonis pegala texana,* ♂. Sand Hills, Franklin Co., Kan., July 7, 1958. USNM.
2 *Cercyonis pegala texana,* ♀. Mears Park, Franklin Co., Kan., July 14, 1956. USNM.
3 *Cercyonis pegala ariane,* ♂. Sunnyside, Yakima Co., Wash., July 22, 1950. USNM.
4 *Cercyonis pegala boopis,* ♀. Shasta Co., Cal. USNM.
5 *Cercyonis pegala boopis,* ♀. Oak Creek Canyon, Coconino Co., Ariz. F&JP.
6 *Cercyonis m. meadii,* ♀. Green Mt. Falls, Teller Co., Colo., Aug. 23, 1948. USNM.
7 *Cercyonis oetus charon,* ♂. Marshall Pass, Saguache Co., Colo., July 23, 1963. FER.
8 *Cercyonis pegala ino,* ♂. Rapid City, S.Dak., July 23, 1966. FER.
9 *Cercyonis pegala ino,* ♀. Bloomington, Dakota Co., Minn., July 21, 1965. FER.
10 *Cercyonis pegala ino,* ♀. Calgary, Alta., July 26, 1958. TCE.
11 *Cercyonis meadii mexicana,* ♂. 9 mi. N. of Jacob Lake, 7200 ft., Coconino Co., Ariz., July 5, 1965. TCE.
12 *Cercyonis sthenele silvestris,* ♀. San Luis Obispo Co., Cal., June 8, 1947. USNM.
13 *Cercyonis s. sthenele,* ♀. "California." CAS.
14 *Cercyonis sthenele masoni,* ♀. Merkley Park, Ashley Creek, nr. Vernal, Ut. TWD.
15 *Cercyonis pegala ariane,* ♀. Minden, Nev. TWD.
16 *Cercyonis p. pegala,* form "alope," ♂. Branford, Conn. FER.
17 *Cercyonis m. meadii,* ♂. Lake George, 8300 ft. Park Co., Colo., Aug. 8, 1965. TCE.

PLATE 3

William H. Howe

PLATE 4

1   *Lethe eurydice fumosus,* ♂, cotype. Omaha, Nebr., July 3, 1915. LACM.
2   *Lethe eurydice fumosus,* ♂, cotype, underside. Same data as fig. 1.
3   *Cercyonis pegala boopis,* ♀, Oregon City, Ore., Aug. 1, 1918. LACM.
4   *Cercyonis pegala boopis,* ♀, underside. Same data as fig. 3.
5   *Cercyonis sthenele paulus,* ♀. Silver City, Lyon Co., Nev., July 24, 1964. TCE.
6   *Cercyonis sthenele paulus,* ♀, underside. Same data as fig. 5.
7   *Cercyonis oetus charon,* ♀. Clear Lake, nr. Union, Dawson Co., Mont., July 16, 1964. TWD.
8   *Cercyonis pegala boopis,* ♂. Siskiyou Nat. Forest, Del Norte Co., Cal., July 14, 1937. LACM.
9   *Cercyonis o. oetus,* ♂. Truckee, Nevada Co., Cal., July 23, 1910. LACM.
10 *Cercyonis o. oetus,* ♀. Truckee, Nevada Co., Cal., July 23, 1909. LACM.
11 *Cercyonis oetus charon,* ♂. Upper Rosebud Creek Trail, 6700 ft., Stillwater Co., Mont., July 19, 1966. LACM.
12 *Cercyonis pegala boopis,* ♂, underside. Same data as fig. 8.
13 *Coenonympha a. ampelos,* form "elko," ♂. Ruby Valley, Elko Co., Nev., May 17, 1931. LACM.
14 *Coenonympha a. ampelos,* form "elko," ♀. Alturas, Modoc Co., Cal., Aug. 14, 1925. LACM.
15 *Coenonympha a. ampelos,* form "elko," ♀, underside. Same data as fig. 14.
16 *Coenonympha i. inornata,* ♂. Miniota, Man., June 22, 1921. LACM.
17 *Coenonympha i. inornata,* ♀. Miniota, Man., July 10, 1921. LACM.
18 *Coenonympha a. ampelos,* form "mono," ♂, topotype. Bridgeport, Cal., July 2, 1956. LACM.
19 *Coenonympha a. ampelos,* form "mono," ♀, topotype. Bridgeport, Cal., July 3, 1956. LACM.
20 *Coenonympha k. kodiak,* ♂, underside. McKinley Nat. Park, Alaska, July 15, 1931. LACM.
21 *Coenonympha k. kodiak,* ♂. Same data as fig. 20.
22 *Coenonympha ochracea brenda,* ♂. Hobble Creek, Utah Co., Ut., July 10, 1969. USNM.
23 *Coenonympha ochracea subfusca,* ♂. White Mts., Greenlee Co., Ariz., June 20, 1925. LACM.
24 *Coenonympha ochracea subfusca,* ♀. White Mts., Greenlee Co., Ariz., June 16, 1935. LACM.
25 *Coenonympha c. california,* form "galactinus," ♀. Alpine Dam, Marin Co., Cal., Aug. 12, 1950. TWD.
26 *Coenonympha c. california,* ♀. Bear Creek Road, Contra Costa Co., Cal., May 4, 1946. TWD.
27 *Erebia m. magdalena,* ♂. East Ridge of Navajo Peak, 12,700 ft., Boulder Co., Colo., July 16, 1946. USNM.
28 *Erebia disa mancinus,* ♂. Lloydminster, Sask., May 30, 1944. TWD.
29 *Oeneis t. taygete,* ♂. Nain, Labrador, July 18, 1940. TWD.
30 *Oeneis t. taygete,* ♂, underside. Same data as fig. 29.

PLATE 4

William H Howe

PLATE 5

1   *Erebia rossii kuskoquima,* ♂. Wonder Lake, McKinley Nat. Park, Alaska. F&JP.

2   *Cercyonis meadii alamosa,* ♂. San Luis Valley, Colo., Aug. 20, 1965. TCE.

3   *Cercyonis pegala ino,* ♂. Calgary, Alta., July 24, 1957. TCE.

4   *Erebia y. youngi,* ♀. Highway Pass Summit, McKinley Nat. Park, Alaska. F&JP.

5   *Erebia y. youngi,* ♂. McKinley Nat. Park, Alaska, July 14, 1959. F&JP.

6   *Cercyonis pegala ino,* ♂, underside. Calgary, Alta., July 24, 1957. TCE.

7   *Erebia e. epipsodea,* ♂. Flagg Ranch, Moran, Wyo., July 17, 1966. USNM.

8   *Erebia e. epipsodea,* ♀. Powder River Pass, Big Horn Range, Johnson Co., Wyo., July 21, 1966. USNM.

9   *Erebia d. discoidalis,* ♂. Sunnydale, Lloydminster, Alta., June 28, 1946. CNC.

10 *Erebia e. epipsodea,* form "brucei," ♂. Loveland Pass Summit, 11,950 ft., Summit Co., Colo. F&JP.

11 *Erebia e. epipsodea,* form "brucei," ♀. Loveland Pass Summit, 11,950 ft., Summit Co., Colo. F&JP.

12 *Erebia epipsodea remingtoni,* ♂, paratype. Atlin, B.C. AMNH.

13 *Erebia vidleri,* ♂. Salmon Meadows, Okanogan Co., Wash., July 12, 1952. TWD.

14 *Erebia theano ethela,* ♂. Slough Lake Trail, Beartooth Range, Stillwater Co., Mont., July 18, 1966. USNM.

15 *Erebia theano alaskensis,* ♂. Teklanika Camp, McKinley Nat. Park, Alaska, June 20, 1957. F&JP.

16 *Erebia theano demmia,* ♂. Lefthand Park, 10,500 ft., Park Co., Colo., July 22, 1962. TWD.

17 *Erebia c. callias,* ♂. Cottonwood Pass, San Isabel Nat. Forest, Colo., Aug. 6, 1963. USNM.

18 *Coenonympha ochracea furcae,* ♂. McNary Road, nr. Springerville, Apache Co., Ariz. F&JP.

19 *Coenonympha ochracea furcae,* ♀. McNary Road, nr. Springerville, Apache Co., Ariz. F&JP.

20 *Coenonympha n. nipisiquit,* ♂, topotype. Bathurst, N.B. F&JP.

21 *Coenonympha a. ampelos,* ♀. Brewster, Wash., May 25, 1945. TWD.

22 *Coenonympha o. ochracea,* ♀. Colorado Springs, Colo., May 23, 1962. AMNH.

23 *Coenonympha o. ochracea* (high altitude), ♂. Tolland, Colo., July 4, 1951. LACM.

24 *Coenonympha o. ochracea* (high altitude), ♀. Caribou, Boulder Co., Colo., July 15, 1957. LACM.

25 *Coenonympha a. ampelos,* ♂. Brewster, Wash., May 27, 1945. TWD.

PLATE 5

William H. Howe

1   *Oeneis n. nevadensis,* ♂. Satus Pass, Simcoe Mts., Klickitat Co., Wash. FER.
2   *Oeneis n. nevadensis,* ♀. Camp Sherman, Jefferson Co., Ore. FER.
3   *Oeneis nevadensis gigas,* ♂. Vancouver I., B.C., May 27, 1918. LACM.
4   *Oeneis nevadensis gigas,* ♀. Vancouver I., B.C. AMNH.
5   *Oeneis nevadensis iduna,* ♂. Buck Creek, Modoc Co., Cal., June 12, 1924. LACM.
6   *Oeneis nevadensis iduna,* ♀. "California." USNM.
7   *Oeneis macounii,* ♂. Sandilands, Man., June 7, 1958. LACM.
8   *Oeneis macounii,* ♀. Richer, Man. TWD.
9   *Oeneis u. uhleri,* ♀. Flagstaff Mt., Boulder Co., Colo., May 23, 1964. AMNH.
10 *Oeneis uhleri varuna,* ♂. Miniota, Man., June 4, 1924. LACM.
11 *Oeneis melissa semidea,* ♂. Mt. Washington, N.H. AMNH.
12 *Oeneis melissa lucilla,* ♂, type. Hall Valley, Colo. USNM.
13 *Oeneis melissa assimilis,* ♂. Fort Churchill, Man., June 29, 1932. LACM.
14 *Oeneis melissa beani,* ♂. Lillooet, B.C., 8000 ft. LACM.
15 *Oeneis melissa beani,* ♀. Summit, Beartooth Mts., 10,942 ft., Park Co., Wyo., July 27, 1959. AMNH.
16 *Oeneis uhleri varuna,* ♀. Didsbury, Alta. AMNH.

PLATE 6

William H. Howe

PLATE 7

1 *Oeneis jutta alaskensis,* ♂. Mile 1105, Alaska Hwy., Burwash Campground, Yukon Terr. F&JP.
2 *Oeneis jutta alaskensis,* ♀. McKinley Nat. Park, Alaska. F&JP.
3 *Oeneis jutta reducta,* ♂. Signal Peak, Grand Teton Nat. Park, Wyo. F&JP.
4 *Oeneis jutta reducta,* ♀. Rock Creek Lake, Powell Co., Mont. TWD.
5 *Oeneis jutta leussleri,* ♂. Didsbury, Alta., June 15, 1927. AMNH.
6 *Oeneis jutta leussleri,* ♀. Fort Churchill, Man., July 4, 1933. LACM.
7 *Oeneis polixenes katahdin,* ♂, topotype. Mt. Katahdin, Me. F&JP.
8 *Oeneis polixenes katahdin,* ♀. Mt. Katahdin, Me. F&JP.
9 *Oeneis polixenes brucei,* ♂. Mt. Evans, Clear Creek Co., Colo. F&JP.
10 *Oeneis polixenes brucei,* ♀. Loveland Pass, Clear Creek Co., Colo., July 9, 1961. LACM.
11 *Oeneis bore mackinleyensis,* ♂. Polychrome Pass Summit, McKinley Nat. Park, Alaska. F&JP.
12 *Oeneis bore mackinleyensis,* ♀. Teklanika Camp, McKinley Nat. Park, Alaska. F&JP.
13 *Oeneis polixenes subhyalina,* ♂, type. USNM.
14 *Oeneis polixenes subhyalina,* ♀. Repulse Bay, N.W.Terr., July 28, 1958. CNC.
15 *Oeneis p. polixenes,* ♂. Churchill, Man. TWD.
16 *Oeneis p. polixenes,* ♀. Churchill, Man., July 1, 1947. AMNH.
17 *Oeneis bore hanburyi,* ♂. Fort Churchill, Man., July 6, 1932. AMNH.
18 *Oeneis t. taygete,* ♀. Wolstenholme, Que., Lat. 62° 25′, Long. 66° 14′, July 10, 1941. AMNH.

PLATE 7

William H. Howe

PLATE 8

1 *Oeneis c. chryxus,* ♂. Flagg Ranch, Moran, Wyo., July 18, 1965. USNM.
2 *Oeneis c. chryxus,* ♀. Signal Peak, Grand Teton Nat. Park, Wyo., July 18, 1965. USNM.
3 *Oeneis c. chryxus* (low elevation population), ♂. Red Rocks Park, Jefferson Co., Colo., May 23, 1964. USNM.
4 *Oeneis chryxus valerata,* ♂, holotype. Hurricane Ridge, Clallum Co., Wash. LACM.
5 *Oeneis chryxus valerata,* ♀, allotype. Hurricane Ridge, Clallum Co., Wash. LACM.
6 *Oeneis chryxus caryi,* ♂, type. Smith Landing, Lake Athabaska, Sask., June 13, 1903. USNM.
7 *Oeneis chryxus stanislaus,* ♂. Sonora Pass, Tuolumne Co., Cal., July 28, 1953. TWD.
8 *Oeneis ivallda,* ♂. Carson Spur, Amador Co., Cal., July 30, 1941. TWD.
9 *Oeneis ivallda,* ♀. Carson Spur, Amador Co., Cal., July 30, 1941. TWD.
10 *Oeneis chryxus strigulosa,* ♂. Manistique, Mich., May 25, 1932. LACM.
11 *Oeneis chryxus strigulosa,* ♀. Manistique, Mich., May 25, 1932. LACM.
12 *Oeneis alberta daura,* ♂. White Mts., Ariz., June 16, 1935. LACM.
13 *Oeneis chryxus calais,* ♂. Cowan, Man., June 10, 1967. JDE.
14 *Oeneis chryxus calais,* ♀. Laurentides Nat. Park, Que., July 12, 1954. AMNH.
15 *Oeneis alberta daura,* ♀. White Mts., Ariz., June 16, 1935. LACM.
16 *Oeneis uhleri nahanni,* ♂. Yellowknife, N.W.Terr., June 30, 1949. CNC.
17 *Euptychia r. rubricata,* ♂, underside. Mt. Scott, Okla., Sept. 2, 1951. FER.
18 *Oeneis a. alberta,* ♂. Miniota, Man., May 10, 1934. LACM.
19 *Oeneis a. alberta,* ♀. Miniota, Man., May 20, 1921. LACM.

PLATE 8

William H Howe

PLATE 9

1   *Oeneis taygete edwardsi,* ♂. Cottonwood Pass, Chaffee Co., Colo., July 17, 1959. LACM.
2   *Oeneis taygete edwardsi,* ♀. Cottonwood Pass, Chaffee Co., Colo., July 17, 1959. LACM.
3   *Oeneis uhleri reinthali,* ♂, paratype. Gothic, Gunnison Co., Colo., July 12, 1949. WJR.
4   *Oeneis uhleri reinthali,* ♀, topotype. Gothic, Gunnison Co., Colo., July 8, 1952. WJR.
5   *Oeneis polixenes yukonensis,* ♂. Alfred Creek Camp, Alaska, July 15, 1922. JDE.
6   *Oeneis polixenes yukonensis,* ♀. Teller, Alaska, July 18, 1928. AMNH.
7   *Oeneis alberta oslari,* ♀. 1 mi. W. of Tabernash, Grand Co., Colo. JDE.
8   *Oeneis alberta oslari,* ♂. 1 mi. W. of Tabernash, Grand Co., Colo. JDE.
9   *Oeneis jutta acerta,* ♂. Temiscouata, Que., June 18, 1964. LACM.
10   *Oeneis jutta acerta,* ♀. Temiscouata, Que., June 18, 1964. LACM.
11   *Oeneis melissa gibsoni,* ♂. Mt. above Wolf Canyon, Pelly River, N.W.Terr., July 17, 1907. CNC.
12   *Oeneis melissa gibsoni,* ♀. Teller, Alaska, July 18, 1928. AMNH.
13   *Oeneis uhleri nahanni,* ♀, type. Nahanni Mts., Dist. of Mackenzie, N.W.Terr., July 16, 1903. USNM.
14   *Oeneis jutta terraenovae,* ♂. Doyle's Station, Nfld., June 11, 1940. AMNH.
15   *Oeneis jutta ridingiana,* ♀. Riding Mts., Man., July 7, 1937. AMNH.
16   *Oeneis jutta ridingiana,* ♂. Riding Mts., Man., July 8, 1938. CNC.
17   *Oeneis jutta terraenovae,* ♀. Doyle's Station, Nfld., June 16, 1940. AMNH.
18   *Oeneis polixenes peartiae,* ♀. Arctic Bay, Baffin I., 84° W., 73° N., Aug. 2, 1942. AMNH.

PLATE 9

William H. Howe

PLATE 10

1   *Cercyonis pegala abbotti*, ♂. St. Augustine, Fla., July 21, 1959. RRI.
2   *Cercyonis pegala abbotti*, ♀. Jacksonville, Fla., July 21, 1959. RRI.
3   *Erebia disa mancinus*, ♀. Lloydminster, Sask., June 5, 1942. JDE.
4   *Erebia magdalena mackinleyensis*, ♀. Richardson Mts., Yukon Terr., July 11, 1962. JDE.
5   *Oeneis uhleri cairnesi*, ♂. Richardson Mts., S.W. of Aklavik, N.W.Terr., July 7, 1955. JDE.
6   *Erebia youngi herscheli*, ♂. Fort McPherson, N.W.Terr., June 25, 1955. JDE.
7   *Oeneis uhleri cairnesi*, ♀. Reindeer Depot, Mackenzie Delta, N.W.Terr., July 7, 1948. CNC.
8   *Erebia disa subarctica*, ♂. Eagle, Alaska, June 5, 1936. JDE.
9   *Oeneis taygete fordi*, ♂. Mile 45, North Fork of Klondike, Yukon Terr., June 28, 1964. JDE.
10 *Oeneis taygete fordi*, ♀. Eagle Plains, Lat. 66° 7′, Long. 138° 28′, Yukon Terr., July 7, 1964. JDE.
11 *Erebia fasciata*, ♂. Richardson Mts., 3300 ft., Lat. 67° 15′; Long. 137° 15′, Yukon Terr., July 4, 1962. JDE.
12 *Erebia rossii ornata*, ♀. Churchill, Man., July 11, 1942. JDE.
13 *Coenonympha inornata benjamini*, ♂. Harlan, Sask., June 14, 1943. JDE.
14 *Coenonympha inornata benjamini*, ♂, underside. Same data as fig. 13.
15 *Coenonympha inornata benjamini*, ♀. Transcona, Man., July 5, 1954. JDE.
16 *Coenonympha nipisiquit heinemani*, ♂, underside. Grindstone I., Clayton, N.Y., Aug. 23, 1957. AMNH.
17 *Coenonympha nipisiquit heinemani*, ♂. Same data as fig. 16.
18 *Coenonympha nipisiquit heinemani*, ♀. Grindstone I., Clayton, N.Y., Aug. 23, 1957. AMNH.
19 *Erebia f. fasciata*, ♀. Eagle Summit, Alaska, June 23, 1955. AMNH.
20 *Coenonympha inornata macisaaci*, ♂, topotype. Doyle's Station, Nfld., June 22, 1937. AMNH.
21 *Coenonympha inornata macisaaci*, ♂, underside. Same data as fig. 20.
22 *Coenonympha inornata macisaaci*, ♀. Doyle's Station, Nfld. AMNH.
23 *Coenonympha kodiak mixturata*, ♂. Alfred Creek Camp, Alaska, July 15, 1922. AMNH.

PLATE 10

PLATE 11

1   *Anaea andria,* ♂. Olney Springs, Crowley Co., Colo., Aug. 31, 1958. USNM.
2   *Anaea andria,* ♀. Carroll Co., Ark., Sept. 30, 1965. AMNH.
3   *Anaea floridalis,* ♂. Big Pine Key, Monroe Co., Fla., Dec. 31, 1962. AMNH.
4   *Anaea pithyusa,* ♂. El Salto, San Luis Potosí, Aug. 19, 1962. HAF.
5   *Anaea pithyusa,* ♂, underside. Same data as fig. 4.
6   *Anaea glycerium,* ♂. El Salto, San Luis Potosí, Aug. 19, 1962. HAF.
7   *Anaea glycerium,* ♂, underside. Same data as fig. 6.
8   *Asterocampa flora,* ♂, underside. Port Orange, Fla., June 30, 1948. LACM.
9   *Asterocampa alicia,* ♂, underside. Ocoee, Orange Co., Fla., June 21, 1935. LACM.
10 *Asterocampa clyton,* ♂, underside. Amherst, Mass., June 2, 1957. WJR.
11 *Asterocampa celtis,* ♀. Mears Park, Franklin Co., Kan., July 7, 1954. USNM.
12 *Asterocampa celtis,* ♂. Rantoul, Kan., Sept. 2, 1968. USNM.
13 *Asterocampa leilia,* ♀. Sabino Canyon, Baboquivari Mts., Ariz., March 10, 1954. LACM.
14 *Asterocampa leilia,* ♂. Sabino Canyon, Baboquivari Mts., Ariz., March 10, 1954. LACM.
15 *Asterocampa leilia,* ♀, underside. Maricopa, Piñal Co., Ariz., Aug. 31, 1959. WJR.
16 *Asterocampa clyton,* ♂. Hudson, N.Y., June 29, 1959, WJR.
17 *Asterocampa clyton,* ♀. Franklin Co., Kan., June 27, 1945. USNM.
18 *Asterocampa flora,* ♂. Port Orange, Fla., June 30, 1948. LACM.
19 *Asterocampa flora,* ♀. Port Orange, Fla., July 10, 1948. USNM.
20 *Hypanartia lethe,* ♂. Soyolopan El Bajo, Comaltepec, Oaxaca, Oct. 12, 1962. E&SP.
21 *Asterocampa montis,* ♀. Canyon Region N. of Harrison, Sioux Co., Nebr., July 21, 1917. LACM.
22 *Asterocampa montis,* ♂. Canyon Region N. of Harrison, Sioux Co., Nebr., July 10, 1911. LACM.
23 *Asterocampa alicia,* ♀. Orlando, Fla., June 4, 1918. LACM.
24 *Asterocampa alicia,* ♂. Ocoee, Orange Co., Fla., June 21, 1935. LACM.
25 *Asterocampa celtis,* ♂, underside. Same data as fig. 12.

PLATE 11

1 2 3 4 5

6 7 8 9 10

11 12 13 14 15

16 17 18 19 20

21 22 23 24 25

William H Howe

PLATE 12

1 *Doxocopa l. laure,* ♂. Xcan, Quintana Roo, Aug. 30, 1960. WJR.
2 *Doxocopa l. laure,* ♀. Presidio, Veracruz, Aug. 15, 1953. WJR.
3 *Limenitis weidemeyerii oberfoelli,* ♂. Lead, S.Dak., July 24, 1958. E&SP.
4 *Limenitis weidemeyerii angustifascia,* ♂. Jerome, Ariz., June 14, 1963. E&SP.
5 *Doxocopa p. pavon,* ♀. Presidio, Veracruz, Aug. 14, 1952. WJR.
6 *Doxocopa p. pavon,* ♂. Tuxtepec, Oaxaca, July 15, 1954. WJR.
7 *Asterocampa texana,* ♂. Addicks, Harris Co., Tex., Aug. 3, 1957. WJR.
8 *Asterocampa texana,* ♀. Terrell, Tex., April 30, 1954. WJR.
9 *Asterocampa louisa,* ♂. Brownsville, Tex., Oct. 20, 1951. WJR.
10 *Asterocampa louisa,* ♀. Brownsville, Tex., Nov. 7, 1959. WJR.
11 *Asterocampa antonia,* ♂. Palo Pinto Co., Tex., April 26, 1953. WJR.
12 *Asterocampa antonia,* ♀. Kerrville, Tex., June 30, 1959. WJR.

PLATE 12

William H. Howe

PLATE 13

1 *Limenitis arthemis rubrofasciata*, ♂. Pine Ridge, Man., June 24, 1961. E&SP.
2 *Limenitis weidemeyerii nevadae*, ♀. Kyle Canyon, Mt. Charleston, Spring Mts., Clark Co., Nev., July 2, 1936. E&SP.
3 *Lethe portlandia androcardia*, ♀. Fayetteville, Ark., Aug. 18, 1968. FER.
4 *Lethe portlandia androcardia*, ♂. Fayetteville, Ark., Aug. 28, 1966. RRI.
5 *Limenitis weidemeyerii latifascia*, ♂. Lamb's Canyon, Salt Lake Co., Ut., July 14, 1964. E&SP.
6 *Asterocampa montis*, ♂. Sabino Canyon, Baboquivari Mts., Pima Co., Ariz., May 3, 1950. WJR.
7 *Asterocampa montis*, ♀. Mt. Graham, Graham Co., Ariz., July 16, 1958. WJR.
8 *Asterocampa subpallida*, ♂. Baboquivari Mts., Pima Co., Ariz., Oct. 1, 1923. WJR.
9 *Asterocampa subpallida*, ♀. Baboquivari Mts., Pima Co., Ariz., Sept. 15, 1924. WJR.
10 *Lethe portlandia anthedon*, ♀. Streator, Ill., Aug. 29, 1954. RRI.
11 *Limenitis archippus lahontani*, ♂, paratype. Fernley, Lyon Co., Nev., July 29, 1966. E&SP.
12 *Speyeria aphrodite whitehousei*, ♂, paratype. Jaffray, B. C., Aug. 7, 1929. CNC.
13 *Lethe portlandia borealis*, ♀. J. W. Wells State Park, Menominee Co., Mich., Aug. 1, 1950. FER.
14 *Lethe p. portlandia*, ♀. Port Orange, Fla. RRI.

PLATE 13

William H. Howe

1 *Limenitis a. arthemis,* ♂. Spooner, Wis. USNM.
2 *Limenitis a. arthemis,* ♀. Rock, Centre Co., Pa., Aug. 28, 1953. F&JP.
3 *Limenitis a. astyanax,* ♂. Baltimore, Md., July 15, 1952. E&SP.
4 *Limenitis astyanax arizonensis,* ♂. Huachuca Mts., Cochise Co., Ariz., Aug. 19, 1964. E&SP.
5 *Limenitis w. weidemeyerii.* San Isabel Nat. Forest, Chaffee Co., Colo. USNM.
6 *Limenitis weidemeyerii* × *lorquini,* hybrid "fridayi," ♂. Mono Lake, Mono Co., Cal., July 10, 1935. LACM.
7 *Limenitis l. lorquini,* ♂. Fallen Leaf Road, El Dorado Co., Cal. USNM.
8 *Limenitis lorquini burrisonii,* ♀. Mallardville, B.C., July 21, 1930. LACM.
9 *Adelpha bredowii californica,* ♀. Yosemite Nat. Park, Tuolumne Co., Cal., June 21, 1964. USNM.
10 *Adelpha bredowii eulalia,* ♀. Pine Valley, Washington Co., Ut., June 13, 1961. E&SP.
11 *Adelpha bredowii eulalia,* ♀, underside. Same data as fig. 10.
12 *Adelpha fessonia,* ♂. Pisté, Yucatán. E&SP.
13 *Myscelia ethusa,* ♂. Tepic, Nayarit. USNM.
14 *Myscelia cyananthe,* ♂. Tehultzingo, Puebla. USNM.
15 *Siproeta stelenes biplagiata,* ♂. Pisté, Yucatán, Aug. 15, 1962. E&SP.
16 *Siproeta stelenes biplagiata,* ♂. Long Beach, Big Pine Key, Monroe Co., Fla., Oct. 23, 1968. FER.

PLATE 14

1

2

3

4

5

6

7

8

9

10

11

12

13

14

15

16

William H. Howe

PLATE 15

1 *Mestra amymone,* ♂. Mears Park, Franklin Co., Kan., Oct. 17, 1950. USNM.
2 *Marpesia coresia.* El Paso, Tex., Oct. 2, 1910. LACM.
3 *Diaethria anna,* ♂. Catemaco, Veracruz, Aug. 11, 1967. HAF.
4 *Marpesia petreus thetys,* ♂. Ciudad Valles, San Luis Potosí, June 9, 1968. HAF.
5 *Diaethria asteria,* ♂, underside. Tehuantepec, Oaxaca, Aug. 16, 1964. HAF.
6 *Diaethria anna,* ♂, underside. Same data as fig. 3.
7 *Eunica tatila tatilista,* ♀. Key Largo, Fla., Sept. 15, 1933. LACM.
8 *Biblis hyperia aganisa,* ♂. El Salto, San Luis Potosí, Aug. 19, 1962. HAF.
9 *Eunica monima,* ♂. Pharr, Tex., June 27, 1948. AMNH.
10 *Poladryas arachne nympha,* ♂. Mt. Graham, Ariz., July 9, 1951. DLB.
11 *Dynamine dyonis,* ♂. Tamazunchale, San Luis Potosí, June 19, 1964. HAF.
12 *Hamadryas feronia farinulenta,* ♂. Ciudad Valles, San Luis Potosí, June 22, 1967. HAF.
13 *Marpesia chiron,* ♀. Ciudad Valles, San Luis Potosí, Aug. 4, 1967. HAF.
14 *Diaethria asteria,* ♂. Same data as fig. 5.
15 *Chlosyne leanira alma,* ♂. Colorado Nat. Mon., Mesa Co., Colo., May 18, 1961. DLB.
16 *Oeneis melissa semplei,* ♂. Churchill, Man., June 29, 1947. AMNH.
17 *Oeneis melissa semplei,* ♀. Churchill, Man., July 10, 1933. AMNH.
18 *Hamadryas fornax,* ♂. Paranã River, Brazil, Jan 4, 1952. LACM.

PLATE 15

William H. Howe

PLATE 16

1 *Smyrna karwinskii,* ♂. Cuernavaca, Morelos. USNM.
2 *Hypolimnas m. misippus,* ♂. "Madagascar." USNM.
3 *Hypolimnas m. misippus,* ♀. "Madagascar." USNM.
4 *Historis odius,* ssp. ♂. "Chapada" [probably Brazil]. USNM.
5 *Pieris napi marginalis,* ♂. Saddle Mt. State Park, Clatsop Co., Ore., May 28, 1965. FER.
6 *Polygonia silvius,* ♀. Angwin, Napa Co., Cal., DLB.
7 *Pieris napi marginalis,* ♀. Saddle Mt. State Park, Clatsop Co., Ore., May 28, 1965. FER.
8 *Erebia epipsodea hopfingeri,* ♀. Black Canyon, 5 mi. S.E. of Methow, Okanogan Co., Wash., May 27, 1956. AMNH.
9 *Phyciodes m. mylitta,* ♂. Fairfax Hills, Marin Co., Cal., March 16, 1964. DLB.
10 *Phyciodes m. mylitta,* ♀. San Jose, Cal., Sept. 15, 1955. DLB.
11 *Phyciodes picta canace,* ♀. Cottonwood, Yavapai Co., Ariz., July 22, 1952. DLB.
12 *Erebia epipsodea freemani,* ♀. Lloydminster, Sask., June 4, 1944. AMNH.
13 *Erebia disa steckeri,* ♂, paratype. Kuskokwim River, Alaska. AMNH.
14 *Satyrium liparops fletcheri,* ♂. Cartwright, Man., July 24, 1904. USNM.
15 *Euristrymon ontario autolycus,* ♀. Shovel Mt., Tex. USNM.
16 *Pieris napi frigida,* ♀. Hamilton Inlet, Labrador, July 15, 1933. CNC.
17 *Pieris napi frigida,* ♂. Hopedale, Labrador, July 15, 1918. CNC.

PLATE 16

William H Howe

PLATE 17

1 *Nymphalis antiopa*, ♂. East Rosebud Cr., Alpine, Carbon Co., Mont., Aug. 18, 1966. USNM.
2 *Nymphalis milberti*, ♂. Ten Sleep Canyon Road, Big Horn Mts., Washakie Co., Wyo., Aug. 19, 1966. AMNH.
3 *Nymphalis californica.* Yosemite Nat. Forest, Tuolumne Co., Cal., June 24, 1964. AMNH.
4 *Nymphalis vau-album*, ♀. Presque Isle Co., Mich., July 7, 1961. USNM.
5 *Polygonia comma,* typical form, ♂. Rantoul, Kan., Oct. 15, 1948. USNM.
6 *Polygonia comma,* form "dryas," ♀. Mears Park, Franklin Co., Kan., July 27, 1949. USNM.
7 *Polygonia interrogationis,* form "umbrosa," ♂. Willis Woods, Franklin Co., Kan., Aug. 21, 1946. AMNH.
8 *Polygonia satyrus, neomarsyas,* ♂. Castro Valley, Alameda Co., Cal., Sept. 15, 1941. USNM.
9 *Polygonia s. satyrus,* ♀. Ruby-Anthracite Cr., Gunnison Co., Colo., July 18, 1964. AMNH.
10 *Polygonia interrogationis,* ♀. Richmond, Kan., Sept. 29, 1942. USNM.
11 *Polygonia zephyrus,* ♂. Gold Creek Camp, Gunnison Co., Colo., July 18, 1964. USNM.
12 *Polygonia faunus,* ♂. Bartibog, N.B. AMNH.
13 *Polygonia progne,* ♂. Baldwin Hill, Kan., Oct. 2, 1949. USNM.
14 *Polygonia progne,* form "l-argenteum," ♀. Mears Park, Franklin Co., Kan., July 27, 1949. USNM.
15 *Polygonia silvius,* ♂. Angwin, Napa Co., Cal. AMNH.

PLATE 17

William H. Howe

PLATE 18

1 *Vanessa atalanta rubria,* ♀. Mears Park, Franklin Co., Kan., Sept. 28, 1944. USNM.
2 *Polygonia gracilis,* ♂. Rangely, Me., Aug. 9, 1936. AMNH.
3 *Polygonia hylas,* ♂. Gibbon River, Yellowstone Nat. Park, Wyo., Aug. 22, 1931. AMNH.
4 *Vanessa cardui,* ♂. Worland, Wyo., July 7, 1966. USNM.
5 *Polygonia oreas silenus,* ♀. Cranbrook, B.C., Oct. 13, 1910. AMNH.
6 *Polygonia silvius,* ♀. Austin Cr., nr. Duncans Mills, Sonoma Co., Cal. LACM.
7 *Vanessa virginiensis,* ♂. Charlottesville, Va. USNM.
8 *Vanessa tameamea,* Mt. Tantalus, Oahu, Hawaii, RSW.
9 *Precis coenia,* form "rosa," ♀. Springfield, Mo., Oct. 2, 1963. AMNH.
10 *Vanessa annabella,* ♂. Salt Lake City, Ut., Sept. 7, 1964. JDE.
11 *Precis evarete zonalis,* ♂. Key Largo, Fla. AMNH.
12 *Anartia jatrophae guantanamo,* ♀. Coral Gables, Fla. AMNH.
13 *Vanessa annabella,* ab. "letcheri," ♂. Hayward, Cal., June 8, 1941. USNM.
14 *Precis coenia nigrosuffusa,* ♂. 2 mi. W. of Peña Blanca Canyon, Ruby Road, Santa Cruz Co., Ariz., April 21, 1951. JDE.
15 *Anartia fatima,* form "venusta," ♂. Tamazunchale, San Luis Potosí, March 26, 1962. USNM.

PLATE 18

William H. Howe

PLATE 19

1 *Speyeria c. cybele,* ♂. Willis Woods, Franklin Co., Kan. USNM.
2 *Speyeria c. cybele,* ♀. Mears Park, Franklin Co., Kan. USNM.
3 *Speyeria diana,* ♂. Fannin Co., Ga. FER.
4 *Speyeria diana,* ♀. Cherokee Res., Swain Co., N.Car. FER.
5 *Speyeria l. leto,* ♂. Camp Sherman, Metolius R., Jefferson Co., Ore. FER.
6 *Speyeria l. leto,* ♀, topotype. Carson City, Ormsby Co., Nev. DLB.
7 *Speyeria edwardsi,* ♂. San Isabel Nat. Forest, Custer Co., Colo. AMNH.
8 *Speyeria edwardsi,* ♀. San Isabel Nat. Forest, Custer Co., Colo. AMNH.

PLATE 19

William H. Howe

PLATE 20

1 *Speyeria a. aphrodite,* ♀. Springdale, N.J., July 5, 1964. FER.
2 *Speyeria a. aphrodite,* ♂. Springdale, N.J. FER.
3 *Speyeria aphrodite ethne/mayae,* ♀. Alpine, Mont., July 19, 1966. USNM.
4 *Speyeria aphrodite ethne/mayae,* ♂. Alpine, Mont., July 19, 1966. USNM.
5 *Speyeria aphrodite alcestis,* ♂. Ann Arbor, Mich., June 30, 1946. F&JP.
6 *Speyeria aphrodite alcestis,* ♀. Milwaukee, Wis., June 27, 1954. MPM.
7 *Speyeria aphrodite columbia,* ♂. Columbia Lake Reg., B.C., July 29, 1940. MPM.
8 *Speyeria aphrodite columbia,* ♀. Columbia Lake Reg., B.C., July 29, 1940. MPM.
9 *Speyeria aphrodite winni,* ♂. Acadia Nat. Park, Mt. Desert I., Me., July 25, 1936. MPM.
10 *Speyeria aphrodite winni,* ♂, underside. Same data as fig. 9.
11 *Speyeria aphrodite winni,* ♀. Green Mts., Vt., July 26, 1951. MPM.
12 *Speyeria aphrodite mayae,* ♀, underside. Little Missouri Valley, Slope Co., N.Dak., July 27, 1954. MPM.
13 *Speyeria aphrodite mayae,* ♀. Same data as fig. 12.

PLATE 20

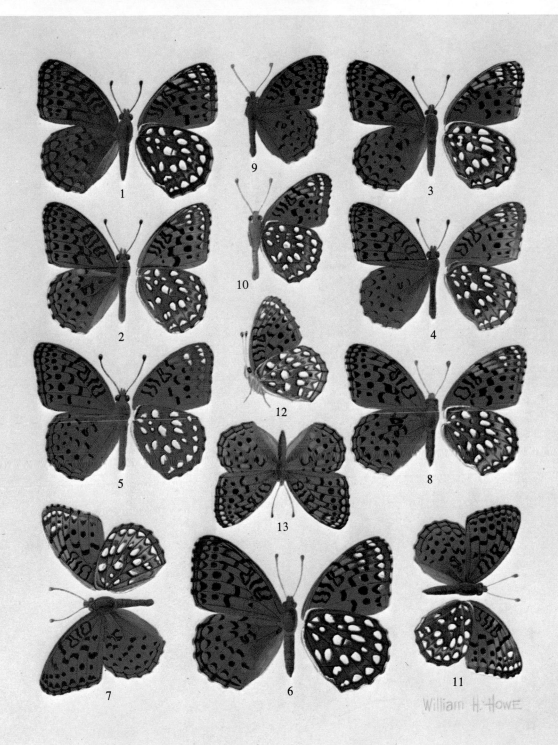

William H. Howe

PLATE 21

 1 *Speyeria z. zerene,* ♂. Yosemite Nat. Park, Tuolumne Co., Cal., USNM.
 2 *Speyeria z. zerene,* ♀. Railroad Flat, Calaveras Co., Cal. TWD.
 3 *Speyeria zerene malcolmi,* ♂, topotype. Mammoth Camp, Mono Co., Cal. TWD.
 4 *Speyeria zerene malcolmi,* ♀. Casa Diablo Hot Springs, Mono Co., Cal. TWD.
 5 *Speyeria zerene sinope,* ♂. Rabbit Ears Pass, Routt Co., Colo., July 5, 1948. LACM.
 6 *Speyeria zerene pfoutsi,* ♂, topotype. Payson Canyon, Payson, Ut., July 20, 1932. LACM.
 7 *Speyeria zerene pfoutsi,* ♂, underside. Same data as fig. 6.
 8 *Speyeria zerene pfoutsi,* ♀, underside. Provo, Ut., Aug. 14, 1916. LACM.
 9 *Speyeria zerene sinope* ♀. Rocky Mt. Nat. Park, Colo., July 7, 1936. LACM.
10 *Speyeria zerene sinope,* ♀, underside. Same data as fig. 9.
11 *Speyeria zerene myrtleae,* ♂. Point Reyes Pen., Marin Co., Cal. USNM.
12 *Speyeria zerene myrtleae,* ♀. Point Reyes Pen., Marin Co., Cal. TWD.
13 *Speyeria zerene behrensi,* ♂. Manchester, Mendocino Co., Cal. TWD.
14 *Speyeria zerene behrensi,* ♀. Manchester, Mendocino Co., Cal. TWD.
15 *Speyeria zerene pfoutsi,* ♀. Provo, Ut., Aug. 14, 1916. LACM.

PLATE 21

1

6

11

2

7

12

3

8

13

4

9

14

5

10

15

William H. Howe

1 *Speyeria zerene platina,* ♂. Provo, Ut., July 30, 1923. LACM.
2 *Speyeria zerene platina,* ♀. Mt. Loafer, Utah Co., Ut., June 2, 1954. LACM.
3 *Speyeria zerene cynna,* ♂, topotype. Ruby Valley, Elko Co., Nev., June 25, 1934. LACM.
4 *Speyeria zerene cynna,* ♀. Angel Lake, 8000 ft., Ruby Mts., Elko Co., Nev., July 30, 1946. MPM.
5 *Speyeria zerene bremnerii,* ♂. Duncans, Vancouver I., B.C. LACM.
6 *Speyeria zerene bremnerii,* ♀. Princeton, B.C., July 12, 1909. LACM.
7 *Speyeria zerene picta,* ♂. Pend Oreille State Park, Pend Oreille Co., Wash., July 31, 1955. MPM.
8 *Speyeria zerene picta,* ♀. Powder River Valley, Wallowa Mts., Union Co., Ore., July 26, 1958. MPM.
9 *Speyeria zerene hippolyta,* ♂, lectotype. Oregon. CM.
10 *Speyeria zerene hippolyta,* ♂, underside. Same data as fig. 9.
11 *Speyeria zerene hippolyta,* ♀. Westport, Wash., Aug. 31, 1950. DVM.
12 *Speyeria zerene hippolyta,* ♀, underside. Same data as fig. 11.
13 *Poladryas a. arachne,* ♂. San Isabel Nat. Forest, Custer Co., Colo., June 16, 1959. USNM.
14 *Speyeria nokomis nitocris,* ♂. White Mts., Apache Co., Ariz., Aug. 15, 1925. LACM.
15 *Speyeria nokomis nitocris,* ♀. White Mts., Apache Co., Ariz., Sept. 1, 1925. LACM.

PLATE 22

William H. Howe

PLATE 23

1   *Speyeria zerene carolae,* ♂. Kyle Canyon, Charleston Peak, Clark Co., Nev., July 1, 1950. F&JP.

2   *Speyeria zerene carolae,* ♀. Kyle Canyon, Charleston Peak, Clark Co., Nev., July 1, 1950. F&JP.

3   *Speyeria c. coronis,* ♂. Mine's Road, Livermore, Cal., May 20, 1947. TWD.

4   *Speyeria zerene carolae,* ♀, underside. Kyle Canyon. Mt. Charleston, Spring Mts., Clark Co., Nev., July 1, 1950. F&JP.

5   *Speyeria c. coronis,* ♀. Redwood Park, Alameda Co., Cal., Aug. 11, 1957. RLL.

6   *Speyeria coronis gunderi,* ♂. Blue Lake, Lassen Co., Cal., Aug. 7, 1962. LACM.

7   *Speyeria coronis gunderi,* ♀. Jess Valley, Blue Lake Road, Warner Mts., Lassen Co., Cal., Aug. 7, 1962. LACM.

8   *Speyeria coronis gunderi,* ♂, underside. Same data as fig. 6.

9   *Speyeria coronis hennei,* ♀. Tehachapi Range, Kern Co., Cal., July 22, 1932. LACM.

10 *Boloria astarte distincta,* underside, paratype. Harrington Cr., Yukon Terr., July 25, 1912. USNM.

11 *Speyeria coronis snyderi,* ♂. Thermopolis, Wyo., July 16, 1965. AMNH.

12 *Speyeria coronis snyderi,* ♀. Alpine, Stillwater Co., Mont., July 15, 1966. AMNH.

13 *Speyeria coronis semiramis,* ♂. Big Bear Lake, San Bernardino Co., Cal. F&JP.

14 *Speyeria coronis semiramis,* ♀. Mt. Laguna Rec. Area, San Diego Co., Cal., July 15, 1951. RLL.

15 *Speyeria coronis hennei,* ♂. Ridge Route, Sierra Madre Range, Los Angeles Co., Cal., June 13, 1932. LACM.

PLATE 23

William H Howe

PLATE 24

1 *Speyeria adiaste atossa*, ♀. Ridge Route Road, Los Angeles Co., Cal. AMNH.
2 *Speyeria adiaste atossa*, ♂. Sierra Madre Mts., Los Angeles Co., Cal. CAS.
3 *Speyeria adiaste clemencei*, ♀. Chews Ridge, Monterey Co., Cal., June 24, 1964. USNM.
4 *Speyeria adiaste clemencei*, ♂. Chews Ridge, Monterey Co., Cal., June 24, 1964. USNM.
5 *Speyeria a. adiaste*, ♀. Santa Cruz Mts., Santa Cruz Co., Cal. CAS.
6 *Speyeria electa dennisi*, ♂, underside. Riding Mts., Man., July 19, 1939. MPM.
7 *Speyeria electa dennisi*, ♂. Same data as fig. 6.
8 *Speyeria egleis tehachapina*, ♂, topotype. Tehachapi Mts., 7994 ft., Kern Co., Cal., July 23, 1932. LACM.
9 *Speyeria electa dennisi*, ♀. Riding Mts., Man., July 13, 1939. MPM.
10 *Speyeria electa dennisi*, ♀, underside. Same data as fig. 9.
11 *Speyeria egleis oweni*, ♂. Westwood, Lassen Co., Cal., July 20, 1960. AMNH.
12 *Speyeria egleis oweni*, ♀. Castle Lake, Siskiyou Co., Cal., July 21, 1960. TWD.
13 *Speyeria e. egleis*, ♂, topotype. Gold Lake, Sierra Co., Cal., July 8, 1947. TWD.
14 *Speyeria e. egleis*, ♀, topotype. Gold Lake, Sierra Co., Cal., July 15, 1935. TWD.
15 *Speyeria egleis tehachapina*, ♀, topotype. Tehachapi Mts., 7994 ft., Kern Co., Cal., July 23, 1932. LACM.
16 *Speyeria mormonia erinna*, ♀. Mark's Cr., 4300 ft., W. of Ochoco Summit, Crook Co., Ore., July 20, 1958. MPH.

PLATE 24

1

2

3

4

5

6

7

8

9

10

11

12

13

14

15

16

William H Howe

PLATE 25

1   *Speyeria egleis albrighti,* ♂. Monarch, Cascade Co., Mont., June 15, 1934. LACM.
2   *Speyeria egleis albrighti,* ♀. Monarch, Cascade Co., Mont., Aug. 16, 1934. LACM.
3   *Speyeria egleis linda,* ♂. Ketchum, Ida., July 27, 1953. LACM.
4   *Speyeria egleis linda,* ♀. Dollarside Summit, Sawtooth Mts., Custer Co., Ida., July 18, 1954. LACM.
5   *Speyeria egleis secreta,* ♂. Rabbit Ears Pass, Routt Co., Colo., July 13, 1955. JDE.
6   *Speyeria egleis secreta,* ♀. Rabbit Ears Pass, Routt Co., Colo., July 25, 1953. JDE.
7   *Speyeria egleis mcdunnoughi,* ♂, topotype. Elkhorn Ranch, Gallatin Co., Mont., July 20, 1932. LPG.
8   *Speyeria egleis mcdunnoughi,* ♀. Teton Glacier Trail, Teton Nat. Park, Wyo., July 18, 1931. LPG.
9   *Speyeria egleis utahensis,* ♂. Bear Creek Canyon, 7000 ft., E. of Mt. Nebo, Juab Co., Ut. MPM.
10   *Speyeria egleis utahensis,* ♀. Bear Canyon, 6500 ft., E. foothills of Mt. Nebo, Juab Co., Ut. MPM.
11   *Speyeria zerene garretti,* ♂. Cranbrook, B.C., July 3, 1912. LACM.
12   *Speyeria zerene garretti,* ♀. Cranbrook, B.C., July 3, 1912. LACM.
13   *Speyeria zerene gloriosa,* ♂. Illinois River Road, Josephine Co., Ore. USNM.
14   *Speyeria zerene conchyliatus,* ♂. Castlelake Road, Siskiyou Co., Cal., July 22, 1960. TWD.
15   *Speyeria zerene conchyliatus,* ♀. Castlelake Road, Siskiyou Co., Cal., July 22, 1960. TWD.

PLATE 25

William H. Howe

PLATE 26

1 *Speyeria a. atlantis,* ♂. Isle Royale, Mich., Aug. 3, 1948. F&JP.
2 *Speyeria a. atlantis,* ♀. Isle Royale, Mich., Aug. 3, 1948. F&JP.
3 *Speyeria electa dorothea,* ♂. Sandia Peak, Bernallilo Co., N.Mex. F&JP.
4 *Speyeria electa chitone,* ♂. Moab, Ut. CAS.
5 *Speyeria electa chitone,* ♀, topotype. Cedar Breaks Nat. Mon., Iron Co., Ut., July 27, 1950. LPG.
6 *Speyeria e. electa,* ♂. Wolf Creek Camp, Mineral Co., Colo., July 20, 1952. F&JP.
7 *Speyeria e. electa,* ♀. Wolf Creek Camp, Mineral Co., Colo., July 20, 1952. F&JP.
8 *Speyeria atlantis hollandi,* ♂, topotype. Riding Mts., Man. CAS.
9 *Speyeria electa tetonia,* ♂. Teton Glacier Trail, Teton Nat. Park, Wyo., July 10, 1946. TWD.
10 *Speyeria electa tetonia,* ♀. Teton Glacier Trail, Teton Nat. Park, Wyo., July 10, 1946. TWD.
11 *Speyeria electa hesperis,* ♀. South Saint Vrain Canyon, Boulder Co., Colo., July 20, 1952. F&JP.
12 *Speyeria electa hesperis,* ♂. South Saint Vrain Canyon, Boulder Co., Colo., July 20, 1952. F&JP.
13 *Speyeria electa nikias,* ♂. Gold Creek Camp, Gunnison Co., Colo., July 9, 1952. USNM.
14 *Speyeria electa nikias,* ♀. Upper Quartz Cr., Gunnison Co., Colo., July 20, 1952. USNM.
15 *Speyeria electa dodgei,* ♂. Castle Lake, Siskiyou Co., Cal., July 21, 1960. TWD.

PLATE 26

William H. Howe

PLATE 27

1 *Speyeria electa greyi,* ♂, topotype. Lamoille Canyon, Ruby Mts., Humboldt Range, Elko Co., Nev., July 10, 1953. MPM.

2 *Speyeria electa greyi,* ♀, paratype. Angel Lake, Ruby Mts., East Humboldt Range, 9500 ft., Elko Co., Nev., July 29, 1946. MPM.

3 *Speyeria electa wasatchia,* ♂. Wasatch Mts., Summit Co., Ut., Aug. 18, 1934. MPM.

4 *Speyeria electa wasatchia,* ♀. Bear Canyon, 6500 ft., Juab Co., Ut. MPM.

5 *Speyeria electa viola,* ♂. Trail Cr., 7500 ft., above Sun Valley, Custer Co., Ida., July 31, 1958. MPM.

6 *Speyeria electa viola,* ♀. Trail Cr., 7500 ft., above Sun Valley, Custer Co., Ida., July 31, 1958. MPM.

7 *Speyeria electa beani,* ♂. Jasper Nat. Park, Alta., July 27, 1940. MPM.

8 *Speyeria electa beani,* ♀. Banff Nat. Park, Alta., July 22, 1940. MPM.

9 *Speyeria electa irene,* ♂. Patterson Meadows, 7300 ft., Warner Mts., Modoc Co., Cal., July 17, 1959. MPM.

10 *Speyeria electa irene,* ♀. Lake Tahoe, Placer Co., Cal., July 17, 1959. MPM.

11 *Speyeria electa helena,* ♂. Lloydminster, Sask., July 7, 1949. MPM.

12 *Speyeria electa helena,* ♀. Lloydminster, Sask., July 7, 1949. MPM.

13 *Speyeria nokomis wenona,* ♂, holotype. Cerro Potosí, Nuevo León, 12,000 ft., subalpine meadow, July 18, 1938. AMNH.

14 *Speyeria nokomis wenona,* ♀, allotype. Cerro Potosí, Nuevo León, 12,000 ft., subalpine meadow, July 18, 1938. AMNH.

15 *Chlosyne palla vallismortis,* ♂. Mahogany Flat, 9500 ft., Panamint Mts., Inyo Co., Cal., June 26, 1966. DLB.

PLATE 27

William H. Howe

PLATE 28

1 *Speyeria callippe comstocki,* ♂. Griffith Park, Los Angeles Co., Cal., May 22, 1938. F&JP.
2 *Speyeria callippe comstocki,* ♀. Griffith Park, Los Angeles Co., Cal., May 22, 1939. F&JP.
3 *Speyeria nevadensis gallatini,* ♂. Signal Mt., Teton Nat. Park, Wyo., July 7, 1965. AMNH.
4 *Speyeria nevadensis gallatini,* ♀. Signal Peak, Teton Nat. Park, Wyo., July 7, 1965. AMNH.
5 *Speyeria nevadensis semivirida,* ♀. Paulina Lakes, Deschutes Co., Ore., July 21, 1961. AMNH.
6 *Speyeria callippe macaria,* ♀. Lebec, Kern Co., Cal., June 11, 1938. F&JP.
7 *Speyeria callippe macaria,* ♂. Lebec, Kern Co., Cal., June 3, 1939. F&JP.
8 *Speyeria c. callippe,* ♀. Visitacion Valley, San Francisco, Cal., CAS.
9 *Speyeria n. nevadensis,* ♂. Ophir Grade, S. of Virginia City, Nev., July 4, 1963. TWD.
10 *Speyeria n. nevadensis,* ♀. Ophir Grade, S. of Virginia City, Nev., July 4, 1963. TWD.
11 *Speyeria callippe laurina,* ♀. Greenhorn Mts., Kern Co., Cal., May 30, 1939. F&JP.
12 *Speyeria callippe laurina,* ♂. Greenhorn Mts., Kern Co., Cal., May 30, 1939. F&JP.
13 *Speyeria callippe inornata,* ♀. Railroad Flat, Calaveras Co., Cal., June 19, 1959. TWD.
14 *Speyeria callippe inornata,* ♂. Railroad Flat, Calaveras Co., Cal., June 19, 1959. TWD.
15 *Speyeria nevadensis semivirida,* ♂. Cricket Cr., Harney Co., Ore., July 11, 1963. MPM.

PLATE 28

1 *Speyeria nevadensis harmonia,* ♂. S. Willow Canyon, 6000 ft., Stansbury Mts., Tooele Co., Ut., July 11, 1959. MPM.
2 *Speyeria nevadensis harmonia,* ♀. S. Willow Canyon; 6800 ft., Stansbury Mts., Tooele Co., Ut., July 11, 1959. MPM.
3 *Speyeria callippe laura,* ♂, lectotype. Nevada. CM.
4 *Speyeria callippe laura,* ♀, lectoparatype. CM.
5 *Speyeria callippe rupestris,* ♀. S.W. side of Mt. Shasta, Siskiyou Co., Cal., July 28, 1956. MPM.
6 *Speyeria callippe rupestris,* ♂. Nr. Minersville, Trinity Co., Cal. TWD.
7 *Speyeria callippe liliana,* ♂. Mt. Vidar, Sonoma Co., Cal. TWD.
8 *Speyeria callippe liliana,* ♀. Lakoya Lodge, Sonoma Co., Cal. TWD.
9 *Speyeria nevadensis meadii,* ♂. Nederland, Colo., July 2, 1949. LACM.
10 *Speyeria nevadensis meadii,* ♀. Turkey Creek Canyon, Jefferson Co., Colo., July 14, 1936. LACM.
11 *Speyeria callippe sierra,* ♂. 5 mi. S. of Gold Lake, Sierra Co., Cal., June 22, 1961. JDE.
12 *Speyeria nevadensis calgariana,* ♂. Spy Hill, Calgary, Alta., July 14, 1963. MPM.
13 *Speyeria nevadensis calgariana,* ♀. Saskatoon, Sask., July 20, 1940. MPM.
14 *Speyeria callippe elaine,* ♀. Applegate Valley, Rogue River Nat. Forest, E. slope of Siskiyou Mts., Jackson Co., Ore., July 24, 1956. MPM.
15 *Speyeria callippe elaine,* ♂. Bolan Mt., 5346 ft., Josephine Co., Ore., July 8, 1958. MPM.

PLATE 29

1

6

11

2

7

12

3

8

13

4

9

14

5

10

15

William H. Howe

1   *Speyeria h. hydaspe,* ♂. Yosemite Valley, Mariposa Co., Cal., July 10, 1910. LPG.

2   *Speyeria h. hydaspe,* ♀. Long Barn, Tuolumne Co., Cal., July 10, 1932. LPG.

3   *Speyeria hydaspe sakuntala,* ♂. Alpine, Absaroka Range, Stillwater Co., Mont., July 18, 1966. AMNH.

4   *Speyeria hydaspe sakuntala,* ♀. Alpine Absaroka Range, Stillwater Co., Mont., July 18, 1966. AMNH.

5   *Speyeria hydaspe purpurascens,* ♂. Nr. Minersville, Trinity Co., Cal., June 26, 1947. TWD.

6   *Speyeria hydaspe conquista,* ♂, holotype. Little Tesuque Canyon, Santa Fe, N.Mex., Aug. 8, 1932. AMNH.

7   *Speyeria hydaspe rhodope,* ♂. Mt. Benson, Vancouver I., B.C., June 28, 1957. TWD.

8   *Speyeria hydaspe rhodope,* ♂, underside. Same data as fig. 7.

9   *Speyeria hydaspe purpurascens/rhodope,* ♀. Canyon Cr., Ochoco Mts., Crook Co., Ore., July 22, 1961. AMNH.

10   *Speyeria hydaspe purpurascens/rhodope,* ♀, underside. Same data as fig. 9.

11   *Speyeria hydaspe viridicornis,* ♀. Cedar Cr., Greenhorn Mts., Kern Co., Cal. AMNH.

12   *Speyeria hydaspe viridicornis,* ♂. Cedar Cr., Greenhorn Mts., Kern Co., Cal. AMNH.

13   *Speyeria hydaspe rhodope,* ♀. Malahat, Vancouver I., B.C., July 13, 1919. LACM.

14   *Speyeria hydaspe minor,* ♂. Spirit Lake, Skamania Co., Wash., Aug. 9, 1958. MPM.

15   *Speyeria hydaspe minor,* ♀. Huckleberry Cr., Pierce Co., Wash., Aug. 29, 1960. MPM.

PLATE 30

1

6

11

2

7

12

3

8

13

4

9

14

5

10

15

William H. Howe

PLATE 31

1   *Speyeria cybele carpenterii,* ♂. Jemez Springs, Sandoval Co., N.Mex., 8500 ft., July 22, 1952. LPG.
2   *Speyeria cybele carpenterii,* ♀. Los Conchas Campground, Jemez Springs, Sandoval Co., N.Mex., Aug. 13, 1951. LPG.
3   *Speyeria aphrodite byblis,* ♂. Hannagan Meadows, Apache Co., Ariz., July 12, 1932. LPG.
4   *Speyeria aphrodite byblis,* ♀. Paradise Park, White Mts., Apache Co., Ariz., Aug. 28, 1932. LPG.
5   *Speyeria zerene bremnerii* ("sordida"), ♂, type of "sordida." CAS.
6   *Speyeria electa hutchinsi* (unsilvered), ♂. Polaris, Mont., June 25, 1940. LPG.
7   *Speyeria electa hutchinsi* (unsilvered), ♀. Polaris, Mont., July 12, 1940. LPG.
8   *Speyeria electa hutchinsi* (silvered), ♀. Polaris, Mont., July 2, 1940. LPG.
9   *Speyeria electa hutchinsi* (silvered), ♂. Polaris, Mont., July 2, 1940. LPG.
10 *Speyeria electa shellbachi,* ♂, topotype. Neal's Spring, North Rim of Grand Canyon, Ariz., July 10, 1953. MPM.
11 *Speyeria electa lurana,* ♂. Harney Peak, Pennington Co., S.Dak., July 24, 1954. MPM.
12 *Speyeria electa lurana,* ♀. Jewel Cave Natl. Mon., Custer Co., S.Dak., July 31, 1953. MPM.
13 *Speyeria electa, "atlantis* type," ♀. Castle Cr., Pennington Co., S.Dak., Aug. 2, 1962. MPM.
14 *Speyeria egleis toiyabe,* ♂, holotype. Kingston Canyon, Toiyabe Range, Lander Co., Nev., Aug. 5, 1965, *ex* John Lane Collection, in LACM.
15 *Speyeria hydaspe conquista,* ♀, allotype. Therma. N.Mex., Aug. 12, 1932. AMNH.

PLATE 31

6

1

11

7

2

12

8

3

13

9

4

14

10

5

15

William H. Howe

1 *Speyeria aphrodite ethne,* ♂. Wet Mts., San Isabel Nat. Forest, Custer Co., Colo., June 16, 1959. USNM.
2 *Speyeria aphrodite ethne,* ♀. Chautauqua Mesa, Boulder Co., Colo., July 9, 1958. USNM.
3 *Speyeria electa nausicaa,* ♂. Pine Flat, Oak Creek Canyon, Coconino Co., Ariz., July 3, 1949. F&JP.
4 *Speyeria electa nausicaa,* ♀. Oak Creek Canyon, Coconino Co., Ariz., July 3, 1949. F&JP.
5 *Speyeria mormonia eurynome,* ♂. Alpine, Mont., July 16, 1966. USNM.
6 *Speyeria mormonia eurynome,* ♀. Beartooth Pass Area, Park Co., Wyo., July 18, 1966. AMNH.
7 *Speyeria mormonia artonis,* ♂. Lamoille Canyon, Ruby Mts., Elko Co., Nev. TWD.
8 *Speyeria mormonia artonis,* ♀. Lamoille Canyon, Ruby Mts., Elko Co., Nev. TWD.
9 *Speyeria mormonia washingtonia,* ♂. Snoqualmie Pass, King Co., Wash., July 7, 1958. RLL.
10 *Speyeria mormonia washingtonia,* ♀. Salmon Meadows, Okanogan Co., Wash., Aug. 2, 1959. DVM.
11 *Speyeria mormonia arge,* ♂. Gaylor Lake Trail, Tioga Pass, 10,750 ft., Tuolumne Co., Cal., Aug. 26, 1956. RLL.
12 *Speyeria mormonia arge,* ♀. Porcupine Flat, 8500 ft., Mariposa Co., Cal., Aug. 25, 1956. RLL.
13 *Speyeria mormonia luski,* ♂. Little Bog Tank, 8 mi. E. of McNary, Apache Co., Ariz., Aug. 19, 1967. RSW.
14 *Speyeria mormonia luski,* ♀. Little Bog Tank, 8 mi. E. of McNary, Apache Co., Ariz., Aug. 19, 1967. RSW.
15 *Speyeria mormonia mormonia,* ♀. Mt. Terrel, 10,500 ft., Sevier Co., Ut., Aug. 13, 1956. MPM.
16 *Speyeria aphrodite mayae,* ♂. Little Missouri Valley, Slope Co., N.Dak., July 27, 1955. MPM.
17 *Speyeria mormonia mormonia,* ♂, underside. Same data as fig. 15.
18 *Speyeria mormonia erinna,* ♂, underside. Trails above Wallowa Lake, 5000 ft., Wallowa Co., Ore., July 25, 1958. MPM.

PLATE 32

William H. Howe

PLATE 33

1 *Boloria napaea alaskensis,* ♂. McKinley Nat. Park, Alaska. LACM.
2 *Boloria napaea nearctica,* ♀. Mt. Dewey, Alaska. LACM.
3 *Boloria napaea halli,* ♂, paratype. Green River Pass, Wind River Range, Sublette Co., Wyo., July 31, 1939. AMNH.
4 *Boloria frigga sagata,* ♂. Tolland, Colo. LACM.
5 *Boloria frigga saga,* ♀. Didsbury, Alta. LACM.
6 *Boloria frigga saga,* ♂. Whitehorse, Yukon Terr. LACM.
7 *Boloria i. improba,* ♂. Kendall I., McKenzie Delta, N.W.Terr., July 7, 1942. CM.
8 *Boloria improba youngi,* ♂, type. Mts. between Mission Cr. and 40 Mile Cr., N.E. Alaska. CM.
9 *Boloria frigga gibsoni,* ♂. Kotzebue, Alaska, June 20, 1956. AMNH.
10 *Boloria a. astarte,* ♂. Lillooet, B.C. LACM.
11 *Boloria a. astarte,* ♀. Slate Peak, Okanogan Co., Wash. JHS.
12 *Boloria astarte distincta,* ♀, paratype. Harrington Cr., Yukon Terr., July 25, 1912. USNM.
13 *Boloria chariclea butleri,* ♂. McKinley Nat. Park, Alaska. LACM.
14 *Boloria chariclea butleri,* ♀. McKinley Nat. Park, Alaska. LACM.
15 *Boloria napaea halli,* ♀, paratype. Green River Pass, Wind River Range, Sublette Co., Wyo., July 31, 1939. AMNH.
16 *Boloria chariclea arctica,* ♂. Mt. Dewey, Alaska, July 15, 1923. LACM.
17 *Boloria kriemhild,* ♂. Timber Lake, Teton Mts., Wyo. LACM.
18 *Boloria kriemhild,* ♀. Mt. Washburn, Yellowstone Nat. Park, Wyo. LACM.

PLATE 33

William H Howe

PLATE 34

1 *Boloria eunomia ursadentis,* ♂. Beartooth Plateau, Mont. LACM.
2 *Boloria eunomia triclaris,* ♀. Hopedale, Labrador. LACM.
3 *Boloria eunomia nichollae,* ♂. Laggan, Alta. LACM.
4 *Boloria freija browni,* ♂. Fremont Pass, 11,316 ft., Summit Co., Colo., June 22, 1954. LACM.
5 *Boloria f. freija,* ♂. Riding Mts., Man. LACM.
6 *Boloria f. freija,* ♀. Riding Mts., Man. LACM.
7 *Boloria freija tarquinius,* ♂. McKinley Nat. Park, Alaska. LACM.
8 *Boloria freija nabokovi,* ♀. Mile 1105, Alaska Hwy., nr. Kluane Lake, Yukon Terr., June 19, 1955. AMNH.
9 *Boloria selene terraenovae,* ♂. Doyles Station, Nfld., July 5, 1935. AMNH.
10 *Boloria alberta,* ♂. Plateau Mt., Alta. LACM.
11 *Boloria alberta,* ♀. Glacier Nat. Park, Mont. LACM.
12 *Boloria eunomia denali,* ♂. Tangle Lakes, Mile 12.5, Denali Hwy., Alaska, June 23, 1957. LACM.
13 *Boloria e. epithore,* ♂. Big Basin Redwoods State Park, Santa Cruz Co., Cal. LACM.
14 *Boloria e. epithore,* ♀. Big Basin Redwoods State Park, Santa Cruz Co., Cal. LACM.
15 *Boloria epithore chermocki,* ♂, paratype. Yamhill, Ore. LACM.
16 *Boloria polaris,* ♂. Meade River, Alaska. LACM.
17 *Boloria polaris,* ♀. Nain, Labrador. LACM.
18 *Boloria selene atrocostalis,* ♂. Edmundston, N.B., June 25, 1961. LACM.

PLATE 34

William H. Howe

PLATE 35

1   *Boloria selene myrina*, ♂. Bloomington, Dakota Co., Minn. FER.
2   *Boloria selene tollandensis*, ♀. Moraing Park, Colo. S&T.
3   *Boloria selene nebraskensis*, ♂. Omaha, Nebr. LACM.
4   *Boloria b. bellona.* Springdale, N.J. FER.
5   *Boloria bellona jenistai*, ♀, paratype. Harlan, Sask. S&T.
6   *Boloria bellona toddi*, ♂. Hideaway Park, Grant Co., Colo., June 23, 1954. LACM.
7   *Boloria titania grandis*, ♂. Riding Mts., Man. S&T.
8   *Boloria titania grandis*, ♀. Riding Mts., Man. S&T.
9   *Boloria titania rainieri*, ♂. Bird Creek Meadows, Mt. Adams Wildlife Area, Yakima Co., Wash. FER.
10 *Boloria titania helena*, ♂. Gold Creek Camp, Gunnison Co., Colo. AMNH.
11 *Boloria titania helena*, ♀. Gold Creek Camp, Gunnison Co., Colo. AMNH.
12 *Boloria titania ingens*, ♂. Little Belt Mts., nr. Neihart, Mont. JDE.
13 *Boloria eunomia caelestis*, ♂. Mt. Kennly, Colo. AMNH.
14 *Boloria eunomia caelestis*, ♀. Hall Valley, Park Co., Colo. AMNH.
15 *Boloria titania boisduvalii*, ♂. Robertson River Bridge, Alaska Hwy., Alaska. LACM.
16 *Boloria eunomia dawsoni*, ♂. Sand Ridge, Riding Mts., Man. LACM.
17 *Boloria eunomia dawsoni*, ♀. Temiscouata, Que., June 26, 1964. LACM.
18 *Boloria titania montinus*, ♂. Mt. Washington, N.H. LACM.

PLATE 35

William H. Howe

PLATE 36

1   *Euphydryas gillettii,* ♀. Highwood Pass, Alta. JDE.
2   *Euphydryas colon perdiccas,* ♀. Sunrise Lodge, Mt. Rainier, Wash. S&T.
3   *Euphydryas c. chalcedona,* ♀. Oakland, Cal. AMNH.
4   *Euphydryas chalcedona quino,* ♂. Jacumba, San Diego Co., Cal. AMNH.
5   *Euphydryas c. colon,* ♂. Cascadia, Ore. JDE.
6   *Euphydryas chalcedona olancha,* ♀. Greenhorn Mts., Kern Co., Cal. JDE.
7   *Euphydryas chalcedona quino,* ♀. Jacumba, San Diego Co., Cal. JDE.
8   *Euphydryas c. colon,* ♀. Cascadia State Park, Linn Co., Ore. JDE.
9   *Euphydryas chalcedona sierra,* ♀. Glen Alpine, El Dorado Co., Cal. DLB.
10 *Euphydryas chalcedona dwinellei,* ♂. 1 mi. E. of Bartle, Siskiyou Co., Cal. JDE.
11 *Euphydryas chalcedona dwinellei,* ♀. 1 mi. E. of Bartle, Siskiyou Co., Cal. JDE.
12 *Euphydryas chalcedona sierra.* Glen Alpine, El Dorado Co., Cal. DLB.
13 *Euphydryas editha rubicunda,* ♂. Incline, Mariposa Co., Cal. JDE.
14 *Euphydryas editha rubicunda,* ♀. Mariposa Canyon, Mariposa Co., Cal. JDE.
15 *Euphydryas chalcedona macglashanii,* ♂. Truckee, Cal. S&T.
16 *Euphydryas chalcedona klotsi,* ♀. Pine Flat, Oak Creek Canyon, Coconino Co., Ariz. F&JP.
17 *Euphydryas chalcedona klotsi,* ♂. Pine Flat, Oak Creek Canyon, Coconino Co., Ariz. F&JP.
18 *Euphydryas phaeton,* ♀. Oak Ridge, Newfoundland, Passaic Co., N.J. FER.

PLATE 36

William H. Howe

PLATE 37

1   *Euphydryas colon wallacensis,* ♀. Rosemary Inn, Lake Crescent, Wash., "1941". AMNH.
2   *Euphydryas colon wallacensis,* ♂, topotype. Wallace, Ida., May 24, 1931. LACM.
3   *Euphydryas colon paradoxa,* ♂. "British Columbia." LACM.
4   *Euphydryas colon paradoxa,* ♀. "British Columbia." LACM.
5   *Euphydryas chalcedona corralensis,* ♂. Rock Corral, San Bernardino Co., Cal., April 1, 1936. LACM.
6   *Euphydryas chalcedona corralensis,* ♀. Rock Corral, San Bernardino Co., Cal., April 1, 1936. LACM.
7   *Euphydryas e. editha,* ♂. Woodstaff Meadows, Piute Mts., Kern Co., Cal., May 24, 1934. LACM.
8   *Euphydryas e. editha,* ♀. Woodstaff Meadows, Piute Mts., Kern Co., Cal., May 24, 1934. LACM.
9   *Euphydryas editha augusta,* ♂. Fish Camp, San Bernardino Co., Cal. LACM.
10 *Euphydryas editha augusta,* ♀. Fish Camp, San Bernardino Co., Cal., June 8, 1936. LACM.
11 *Euphydryas editha lehmani,* ♀, topotype. Lehman Cave, Mt. Wheeler, White Pine Co., Nev., June 4, 1929. LACM.
12 *Euphydryas editha lehmani,* ♂, topotype. Lehman Cave, Mt. Wheeler, White Pine Co., Nev., June 4, 1929. LACM.
13 *Euphydryas anicia carmentis,* ♂. Cedar Breaks, Iron Co., Ut., July 13, 1957. LACM.
14 *Euphydryas anicia carmentis,* ♀. Cedar Breaks, Iron Co., Ut., July 10, 1951. LACM.
15 *Euphydryas anicia maria,* ♂. Empire Canyon, nr. Mt. Nebo, Juab Co., Ut., July 10, 1969. DLB.
16 *Euphydryas anicia maria,* ♀. Empire Canyon, nr. Mt. Nebo, Juab Co., Ut., July 10, 1968. DLB.
17 *Euphydryas anicia windi,* ♀. Yellowstone Nat. Park, Wyo., June 22, 1925. LACM.
18 *Euphydryas anicia morandi,* ♂. Kyle Canyon, Mt. Charleston, Spring Mts., Clark Co., Nev., May 14, 1934. LACM.

PLATE 37

7

1

13

8

2

14

9

3

15

10

4

16

11

5

17

12

6

18

William H. Howe

PLATE 38

1   *Euphydryas anicia alena,* ♂. Black Ridge, Mesa Co., Colo. JDE.
2   *Euphydryas anicia alena,* ♀. Black Ridge, Mesa Co., Colo. JDE.
3   *Euphydryas anicia capella,* ♂. Plainview, Colo. AMNH.
4   *Euphydryas editha bayensis,* ♂. Mt. Diablo, Contra Costa Co., Cal. USNM.
5   *Euphydryas editha bayensis,* ♀. Mt. Diablo, Contra Costa Co., Cal. USNM.
6   *Euphydryas anicia capella,* ♀. Flagstaff Mt., Boulder Co., Colo., June 29, 1953. F&JP.
7   *Euphydryas editha wrighti,* ♂. Gavilan Hills, Riverside Co., Cal. F&JP.
8   *Euphydryas editha wrighti,* ♀. San Diego, Cal., March 7, 1907. AMNH.
9   *Euphydryas editha baroni,* ♀. Clear Lake Oaks, Lake Co., Cal., May 21, 1960. RLL.
10 *Euphydryas editha aurilacus,* ♂. Gold Lake, Sierra Co., Cal. S&T.
11 *Euphydryas editha aurilacus,* ♀. Gold Lake, Sierra Co., Cal. S&T.
12 *Euphydryas editha baroni,* ♂. Alameda Co., Cal., April 10, 1946. AMNH.
13 *Euphydryas editha taylori,* ♀. Victoria, B.C., April 27, 1957. AMNH.
14 *Euphydryas editha colonia,* ♂. Easton, Wash. CAS.
15 *Euphydryas editha colonia,* ♀. Easton, Wash. CAS.
16 *Euphydryas anicia macyi,* ♀. Wildhorse Cr., Alvord Basin, Harney Co., Ore., May 24, 1960. SGJ.
17 *Euphydryas chalcedona dwinellei,* ♀. 1 mi. E. of Bartle, Siskiyou Co., Cal., July 14, 1967. DLB.
18 *Euphydryas chalcedona dwinellei,* ♂. 1 mi. E. of Bartle, Siskiyou Co., Cal., July 30, 1967. DLB.

PLATE 38

William H. Howe

PLATE 39

1 *Euphydryas anicia eurytion,* ♂. Mt. Inabnit, Carbon Co., Mont., July 18, 1966. USNM.
2 *Euphydryas anicia eurytion,* ♀. Slough Lake Trail, Beartooth Range, Stillwater Co., Mont. USNM.
3 *Euphydryas a. anicia,* ♂. Banff, Alta., July 4, 1930. AMNH.
4 *Euphydryas anicia wheeleri,* ♂. Lehman Resort, Mt. Wheeler, White Pine Co., Nev. AMNH.
5 *Euphydryas anicia bernadetta,* ♂. Ashland, Mont. S&T.
6 *Euphydryas anicia bernadetta,* ♀. Ashland, Mont. S&T.
7 *Euphydryas anicia howlandi,* ♂, paratype. Polaris, Mont. S&T.
8 *Euphydryas anicia howlandi,* ♀, paratype. Polaris, Mont. S&T.
9 *Euphydryas anicia bakeri,* ♂, paratype. Durkee, Ore., May 16, 1940. S&T.
10 *Euphydryas anicia bakeri,* ♀, paratype. Durkee, Ore., May 16, 1940. S&T.
11 *Euphydryas chalcedona sierra,* ♂. Silver Lake, Amador Co., Cal. S&T.
12 *Euphydryas chalcedona sierra,* ♀. Silver Lake, Amador Co., Cal. S&T.
13 *Euphydryas anicia hopfingeri,* ♂. Brewster, Wash., May 19, 1929. S&T.
14 *Euphydryas anicia hopfingeri,* ♀. Brewster, Wash., May 19, 1929. S&T.
15 *Euphydryas anicia veazieae,* ♂, paratype. Jackass Mts., Harney Co., Ore., May 22, 1950. SGJ.
16 *Euphydryas anicia magdalena,* ♀. White Mts., Greenlee Co., Ariz. S&T.
17 *Euphydryas anicia magdalena,* ♂. White Mts., Greenlee Co., Ariz. S&T.
18 *Euphydryas anicia veazieae,* ♀, paratype. Jackass Mts., Harney Co., Ore., May 22, 1950. SGJ.

PLATE 39

William H. Howe

PLATE 40

1 *Chlosyne gorgone carlota,* ♂. Caldwell, Kans. S&T.
2 *Chlosyne n. nycteis,* ♂. Chicago, Ill. S&T.
3 *Chlosyne nycteis drusius,* ♂. White Mts., Greenlee Co., Ariz., July 1, 1939. LACM.
4 *Chlosyne h. harrisi,* ♀. Newfoundland, Passaic Co., N.J. FER.
5 *Chlosyne n. neumoegeni,* ♂. Pasadena, Cal. S&T.
6 *Chlosyne n. neumoegeni,* ♀. Cajon Pass, Santa Barbara Co., Cal. S&T.
7 *Chlosyne gabbii,* ♂. San Marcos Pass, Santa Barbara Co., Cal. S&T.
8 *Chlosyne gabbii,* ♀. El Cielo Drive, Santa Ynez Mts., Santa Barbara Co., Cal. S&T.
9 *Chlosyne palla sterope,* ♀. Gypsum, Snake R., Baker Co., Ore., May 28, 1962. DLB.
10 *Poladryas a. arachne,* ♀. Beulah, Pueblo Co., Colo. S&T.
11 *Poladryas a. arachne,* ♂. Beulah, Pueblo Co., Colo. S&T.
12 *Chlosyne palla sterope,* ♂. John Day River, Guilliam Co., Ore., June 2, 1961. DLB.
13 *Chlosyne acastus dorothyi,* ♂. Durkee, Ore., May 16, 1940. LACM.
14 *Chlosyne acastus,* ssp. ♀. Kyle Canyon, 6770 ft., Mt. Charleston, Clark Co., Nev., July 1, 1950. F&JP.
15 *Chlosyne damoetas malcolmi,* ♀. Barney Lake, Mono Co., Cal., July 23, 1933. LACM.
16 *Chlosyne acastus dorothyi,* ♀. Fulton Canyon, Sherman Co., Ore., June 9, 1961. DLB.
17 *Chlosyne leanira oregonensis,* ♀. Mt. Ashland, Loop Road, Jackson Co., Ore., July 6, 1961. LACM.
18 *Chlosyne damoetas malcolmi,* ♂. Upper Gaylord Lake, Yosemite Nat. Park, Cal., July 14, 1960. TWD.

PLATE 40

William H. Howe

PLATE 41

1   *Chlosyne a. acastus,* ♂. Saddlerock, Colorado Nat. Mon., Mesa Co., Colo. JDE.
2   *Chlosyne a. acastus,* ♀. Rogers Mesa, Delta Co., Colo. JDE.
3   *Chlosyne a. acastus,* ♀, underside. Thermopolis, Wyo., July 5, 1966. DLB.
4   *Chlosyne acastus,* ♀. Same data as fig. 3.
5   *Chlosyne palla calydon,* ♂. Mammoth Hot Springs, Yellowstone Nat. Park, Wyo., July 8, 1966. USNM.
6   *Chlosyne palla calydon,* ♀. Durkee, Ore. S&T.
7   *Chlosyne palla,* form "eremita," ♀. Blue Lakes, Cal. S&T.
8   *Chlosyne h. hoffmanni,* ♂. Huntington Lake, Fresno Co., Cal. S&T.
9   *Chlosyne d. damoetas,* ♂. Corona Pass, Boulder Co., Colo. JDE.
10   *Chlosyne d. damoetas,* ♀. Cumberland Pass, Gunnison Co., Colo. USNM.
11   *Chlosyne hoffmanni segregata,* ♂. "Oregon," July 27, 1937. DLB.
12   *Chlosyne h. hoffmanni,* ♀. Silver Lake, Amador Co., Cal., July 19, 1947. TWD.
13   *Chlosyne l. leanira,* ♂. Indian Flat, Mariposa Co., Cal. AMNH.
14   *Chlosyne l. leanira,* ♀. Mt. Hamilton, Santa Clara Co., Cal. JDE.
15   *Chlosyne fulvia,* ♂. Rock Canyon Arch, Pueblo Co., Colo. JDE.
16   *Chlosyne fulvia,* ♀. Trail of the Serpent, Colorado Nat. Mon., Colo. JDE.
17   *Chlosyne leanira wrighti,* ♂. Cajon Pass, San Bernardino Co., Cal. S&T.
18   *Chlosyne leanira wrighti,* ♀. Cajon Pass, San Bernardino Co., Cal. S&T.
19   *Chlosyne theona bolli,* ♂. Del Rio, Tex. S&T.
20   *Chlosyne theona bolli,* ♀. Del Rio, Tex. S&T.
21   *Chlosyne leanira cerrita,* ♀. Cajon Pass, San Bernardino Co., Cal. S&T.
22   *Chlosyne leanira cerrita,* ♂. Cajon Pass, San Bernardino Co., Cal. S&T.
23   *Chlosyne theona bolli,* ♂, underside. Del Rio, Tex., June 29, 1929. LACM.
24   *Chlosyne chinatiensis,* ♂. Van Horn, Tex., Oct. 14, 1950. AMNH.
25   *Texola elada ulrica,* ♂. Pharr, Tex. S&T.
26   *Texola elada ulrica,* ♀. Pharr, Tex. S&T.
27   *Texola elada perse,* ♂. Madera Canyon, Santa Cruz Co., Ariz., Aug. 23, 1946. LACM.
28   *Texola elada perse,* ♀. Madera Canyon, Santa Cruz Co., Ariz., Aug. 23, 1946. LACM.
29   *Dymasia dymas,* ♂. Castle Plain, Yuma Co., Ariz., Sept. 15, 1946. DLB.

PLATE 41

William H. Howe

PLATE 42

1   *Speyeria zerene gloriosa,* ♀, topotype. Illinois R. Valley, Josephine Co., Ore., July 9, 1958. MPM.
2   *Speyeria coronis halcyone,* ♂. Roosevelt Nat. Forest, 6500 ft., Larimer Co., Colo., Aug. 5, 1952. MPM.
3   *Speyeria coronis halcyone,* ♀. Buckhorn Valley, 6000 ft., Larimer Co., Colo., Aug. 28, 1956. MPM.
4   *Speyeria coronis simaetha,* ♂. Above Sun Pass, 5100 ft., Klamath Co., Ore., July 10, 1962. MPM.
5   *Speyeria coronis simaetha,* ♀. Above Sun Pass, Klamath Co., Ore., July 18, 1956. MPM.
6   *Euphydryas anicia effi,* ♂, topotype. Proctor Mt., Ketchum, Ida., July 7, 1944. S&T.
7   *Euphydryas anicia effi,* ♀, paratype. Corral Creek, Ketchum, Ida., July 12, 1944. S&T.
8   *Euphydryas colon nevadensis,* ♀. Wildhorse Creek Campground, Elko Co., Nev., July 6, 1966. DLB.
9   *Speyeria mormonia erinna,* ♂. Camp Sherman, Metolius R., Jefferson Co., Ore., Aug. 16, 1964. FER.
10 *Speyeria callippe elaine,* ♂. Copper Mule Cr., Jackson Co., Ore., May 25, 1965. DLB.
11 *Speyeria mormonia clio,* ♂. Nr. Jackson, Wyo., July 4, 1939. LPG.
12 *Speyeria m. mormonia,* ♂. Mt. Terrel, 10,500 ft., Sevier Co., Ut., Aug. 13, 1956. MPM.
13 *Speyeria mormonia jesmondensis,* ♂. Jesmond, B.C., July 31, 1931. LPG.
14 *Speyeria mormonia jesmondensis,* ♀. Jesmond, B.C., July 31, 1931. LPG.
15 *Speyeria mormonia opis,* ♂. Smithers, B.C., 6000–7000 ft., July 28, 1938. LPG.
16 *Speyeria mormonia bischoffii,* ♀, lectotype. Kodiak I., Alaska. CM.
17 *Speyeria mormonia bischoffii,* ♂. Skagway, Alaska, June 25, 1925. LPG.

PLATE 42

William H. Howe

PLATE 43

1 *Speyeria cybele charlottii,* ♂. Rabbit Ears Pass, Routt Co., Colo., July 24, 1954. LACM.
2 *Speyeria cybele charlottii,* ♀. Rabbit Ears Pass, Routt Co., Colo., July 24, 1954. LACM.
3 *Speyeria leto letona,* ♂. City Creek Canyon, Salt Lake City, Ut., July 12, 1930. LACM.
4 *Speyeria cybele pseudocarpenteri,* ♂. Harlan, Sask., July 10, 1955. MPM.
5 *Speyeria cybele pseudocarpenteri,* ♀. Lloydminster, Sask., July 20, 1945. MPM.
6 *Phyciodes o. orseis,* ♂. Trinity Co., Cal., June 13, 1913. LACM.
7 *Phyciodes pallida barnesi,* ♂. "British Columbia." LACM.
8 *Phyciodes mylitta arizonensis,* ♂. Hannagan Meadows, White Mts., Greenlee Co., Ariz., June 22, 1937. LACM.
9 *Chlosyne harrisii hanhami,* ♂. Riding Mts., Man., June 25, 1932. LACM.
10 *Chlosyne cyneas,* ♂. Cochise Co., Ariz., June 15, 1916. LACM.
11 *Chlosyne cyneas,* ♀. Chiricahua Mts., Cochise Co., Ariz., Oct. 15, 1916. LACM.
12 *Chlosyne p. palla,* ♂. Eldredge, Sonoma Co., Cal., June 6, 1917. LACM.
13 *Poladryas arachne monache,* ♂. Monache Meadows, Tulare Co., Cal., June 20, 1936. LACM.
14 *Poladryas arachne monache,* ♀. Monache Meadows, Tulare Co., Cal., July 6, 1935. LACM.
15 *Euphydryas editha lawrencei,* ♂, topotype. Mt. Thielsen, Douglas Co., Ore., July 13, 1934. LACM.
16 *Euphydryas editha lawrencei,* ♀, topotype. Mt. Thielsen, Douglas Co., Ore., July 17, 1931. LACM.
17 *Euphydryas anicia helvia,* ♂. Whitehorse, Yukon Terr., June 17, 1933. LACM.
18 *Euphydryas anicia helvia,* ♀. Eagle City, Alaska, July 8, 1899. CM.
19 *Chlosyne californica,* ♀. Chino Canyon, San Bernardino Co., Cal., Sept. 19, 1929. TWD.

PLATE 43

William H. Howe

PLATE 44

1 *Speyeria nokomis coerulescens,* ♀. JDE.
2 *Speyeria nokomis apacheana,* ♂. Round Valley, Inyo Co., Cal. TWD.
3 *Speyeria nokomis apacheana,* ♀. Round Valley, Inyo Co., Cal. FER.
4 *Speyeria idalia,* ♀. Baldwin Hill, Kan., July 4, 1951. USNM.
5 *Phyciodes p. pallida,* ♂. Gregory Canyon, Boulder Co., Colo. USNM.
6 *Phyciodes t. tharos,* ♂. Rantoul, Kan. AMNH.
7 *Phyciodes phaon,* form "hiemalis," ♀. Neola, Dade Co., Mo. AMNH.
8 *Phyciodes t. tharos,* ♀. Rantoul, Kan. AMNH.
9 *Phyciodes batesii,* ♀. Montreal, Que. S&T.
10 *Phyciodes c. campestris,* ♂. Alpine, Mont. AMNH.
11 *Phyciodes p. picta,* ♀. Kenton, Okla. S&T.
12 *Phyciodes c. campestris,* ♀. Signal Peak, Teton Nat. Park, Wyo. AMNH.
13 *Chlosyne lacinia adjutrix,* ♀. Lake Corpus Christi, San Patricio Co., Tex. FER.
14 *Phyciodes texana seminole,* ♀. Mears Park, Franklin Co., Kan., Oct. 13, 1953. AMNH.
15 *Chlosyne lacinia crocale,* ♀. Phoenix, Ariz. USNM.
16 *Phyciodes f. frisia,* ♀. Key Vaca, Fla. USNM.
17 *Chlosyne endeis,* ♂. McCook, Hidalgo Co., Tex., Oct. 5, 1956. DLB.
18 *Phyciodes ptolyca,* ♂. Santa Ana Wildlife Refuge, Hidalgo Co., Tex. DLB.
19 *Phyciodes frisia tulcis,* ♂. Tamazunchale, San Luis Potosí, Aug. 4, 1954. DLB.

PLATE 44

William H. Howe

PLATE 45

1   *Speyeria coronis snyderi,* ♂. Mt. Loafer, nr. Payson, Ut., May 28, 1934. LACM.

2   *Speyeria coronis snyderi,* ♀. Payson Canyon, nr. Payson, Ut., July 20, 1933. LACM.

3   *Speyeria n. nokomis,* ♂. Merkeley Park, Vernal, Uintah Co., Ut., July 29, 1964. LACM.

4   *Speyeria n. nokomis,* ♀. Mesa Co., Colo., Sept. 2, 1965. LACM.

5   *Chlosyne neumoegeni sabina,* ♂, topotype. Sabino Canyon, Santa Catalina Mts., Pima Co., Ariz., April 11, 1933. LACM.

6   *Chlosyne neumoegeni sabina,* ♀, topotype. Sabino Canyon, Santa Catalina Mts., Pima Co., Ariz., April 10, 1933. LACM.

7   *Chlosyne theona thekla,* ♂. Peppersauce Canyon, nr. Oracle, Ariz., May 25, 1933. LACM.

8   *Chlosyne theona thekla,* ♀. Mt. Lemmon, nr. Oracle, Ariz., May 25, 1933. LACM.

9   *Phyciodes orseis herlani,* ♂, holotype. Glenbrook Creek, 7000 ft., Douglas Co., Nev., June 17, 1964. DLB.

10   *Phyciodes orseis herlani,* ♀, allotype. Glenbrook Creek, 7000 ft., Douglas Co., Nev., July 7, 1964. DLB.

11   *Euphydryas colon nevadensis,* ♂. Wildhorse Creek Campground, Elko Co., Nev., July 5, 1966. DLB.

12   *Chlosyne harrisii liggetti,* ♂. Slippery Rock, Pa., June 14, 1936. LACM.

13   *Chlosyne harrisii liggetti,* ♀. Slippery Rock, Pa., June 13, 1927. LACM.

14   *Phyciodes vesta,* ♀. Kerrville, Tex., June 16, 1916. LACM.

15   *Phyciodes t. texana,* ♂. Patagonia, Ariz., Aug. 26, 1949. LACM.

16   *Euphydryas a. anicia,* ♀. Kanaskis Forest, Alta., July 16, 1963. JDE.

17   *Chlosyne hoffmanni manchada,* ♀. Bear Canyon, Tieton R., Yakima Co., Wash., June 23, 1961. DLB.

18   *Chlosyne hoffmanni manchada,* ♂, paratype. Leavenworth, Chelan Co., Wash., June 16, 1958. DLB.

PLATE 45

William H. Howe

PLATE 46

1   *Speyeria leto pugetensis,* ♂. McDonald Forest, Corvallis, Ore., July 13, 1965. JDE.
2   *Speyeria leto pugetensis,* ♀. Black Rock Road, Falls City, Ore., Aug. 6, 1966. JDE.
3   *Speyeria electa dorothea,* ♀. Sandia Peak, Bernallilo Co., N.Mex., July 16, 1962. F&JP.
4   *Speyeria cybele krautwurmi,* ♀. Daisy Farm, Isle Royale, Mich., Aug. 2, 1948. F&JP.
5   *Euphydryas editha beani,* ♂. Plateau Mt., Alta., July 8, 1962. JDE.
6   *Euphydryas editha beani,* ♀. Plateau Mtn., Alta., July 14, 1962. JDE.
7   *Euphydryas editha nubigena,* ♂. Duck Lake, Fresno Co., Cal. S&T.
8   *Euphydryas editha nubigena,* ♀. Duck Lake, Fresno Co., Cal. S&T.
9   *Euphydryas editha monoensis,* ♂. Mono Lake, Mono Co., Cal. TWD.
10   *Euphydryas editha monoensis,* ♀. Mono Lake, Mono Co., Cal. TWD.
11   *Chlosyne janais,* ♂. LACM.
12   *Chlosyne definita,* ♂. Esper Ranch, Brownsville, Tex. AMNH.
13   *Poladryas minuta,* ♂. Davis Mts., Presidio Co., Tex., July 20, 1926. LACM.
14   *Euphydryas anicia macyi,* ♂. Wild Horse Cr., Alvord Basin, Ore. TWD.
15   *Euphydryas editha hatchinsi,* ♂. Sylvan Pass, Yellowstone Nat. Park, Wyo., July 24, 1925. LACM.
16   *Euphydryas editha hutchinsi,* ♀. Timber I., Teton Nat. Park, Wyo., June 15, 1931. LACM.
17   *Euphydryas editha remingtoni,* ♂. Diamond Lake, Douglas Co., Ore., July 3, 1930. LACM.
18   *Chlosyne erodyle,* ♂. Veracruz, Mexico, July 31, 1954. CAS.

PLATE 46

William H. Howe

1 *Libytheana bachmanii,* ♂. Franklin Co., Kan., July 7, 1952. USNM.
2 *Libytheana bachmanii,* ♂, underside. Same data as fig. 1.
3 *Calephelis muticum,* ♂. Sidney, Montcalm Co., Mich., July 26, 1950. FER.
4 *Calephelis muticum,* ♂, underside. Same data as fig. 3.
5 *Calephelis borealis,* ♀. Springdale, Essex Co., N.J., July 2, 1966. FER.
6 *Calephelis borealis,* ♀, underside. Same data as fig. 5.
7 *Apodemia chisosensis,* ♀, allotype. Chisos Mts., Brewster Co., Tex., Aug. 3, 1962. HAF.
8 *Calephelis muticum,* ♀. Stoney Creek, Mich., Aug. 1, 1940. HAF.
9 *Calephelis borealis,* ♂. Sussex Co., N.J., July 1, 1943. AMNH.
10 *Apodemia walkeri,* ♂, underside. Pharr, Tex., Nov. 2, 1947. HAF.
11 *Apodemia walkeri,* ♂. Same data as fig. 10.
12 *Apodemia walkeri,* ♀, underside. Pharr, Tex., Dec. 14, 1946. HAF.
13 *Apodemia walkeri,* ♂. Same data as fig. 12.
14 *Libytheana carinenta mexicana,* ♂, underside. Alamos, Sonora, Aug. 7, 1953. LACM.
15 *Libytheana carinenta mexicana,* ♂. Same data as fig. 14.
16 *Calephelis virginiensis,* ♂. Leland, N.Car., June 26, 1939. AMNH.
17 *Calephelis virginiensis,* ♀. Florida City, Fla., April 28, 1946. AMNH.
18 *Calephelis nemesis,* ♂. Del Rio, Tex., Aug. 21, 1951. HAF.
19 *Calephelis nemesis,* ♀. Pharr, Tex., Oct. 10, 1946. HAF.
20 *Calephelis perditalis,* ♂. Pharr, Tex., Oct. 17, 1946. HAF.
21 *Calephelis perditalis,* ♀. Pharr, Tex., Sept. 27, 1946. HAF.
22 *Calephelis wrighti,* ♀. Chino Canyon, Palm Springs, Cal., June 10, 1937. HAF.
23 *Calephelis wrighti,* ♂. Riverside, Cal., Sept. 3, 1939. HAF.
24 *Apodemia chisosensis,* ♂, holotype. Chisos Mts., Tex., Aug. 3, 1962. AMNH.
25 *Apodemia chisosensis,* ♂, underside. Same data as fig. 24.
26 *Calephelis virginiensis,* ♀, underside. Florida City, Fla., Nov. 28, 1946. AMNH.
27 *Caria ino melicerta,* ♀. Pharr, Tex., Sept. 17, 1945. HAF.
28 *Caria ino melicerta,* ♂. Pharr, Tex., Nov. 27, 1945. HAF.
29 *Calephelis guadeloupe,* ♂. New Braunfels, Tex., June 29, 1963. HAF.
30 *Calephelis guadeloupe,* ♀. New Braunfels, Tex., June 30, 1963. HAF.
31 *Emesis ares,* ♀. Onion Saddle, 7500 ft., Chiricahua Mts., Cochise Co., Ariz., July 12, 1960. HAF.
32 *Emesis ares,* ♂. Paradise, 6400 ft., Ariz., July 11, 1960. HAF.
33 *Emesis emesia,* ♂. Pharr, Tex., Oct. 4, 1944. HAF.
34 *Apodemia multiplaga,* ♂. Acatlán, Puebla, Aug. 22, 1964. HAF.
35 *Apodemia palmeri,* ♂. Madera Canyon, Santa Cruz Co., Ariz., Sept. 8, 1950. HAF.
36 *Apodemia palmeri,* ♀. Baboquivari Mts., Pima Co., Ariz., Sept. 9, 1950. HAF.
37 *Lasaia sula.* ♂. Pharr, Tex., Nov. 5, 1944. HAF.
38 *Lasaia sula,* ♀. Pharr, Tex., Nov. 29, 1944. HAF.
39 *Apodemia nais,* ♀. Flagstaff Mt., Boulder Co., Colo., July 4, 1951. HAF.
40 *Apodemia nais,* ♂. Boulder Canyon, Boulder Co., Colo., July 13, 1951. HAF.
41 *Apodemia palmeri* form "marginalis," ♂. Indian Wells, Coachella Valley, Cal., Sept. 30, 1921. LACM.
42 *Apodemia palmeri,* form "marginalis," ♀. Indian Wells, Coachella Valley, Cal., Sept. 30, 1921. LACM.
43 *Apodemia m. mormo,* ♀. 12 mi. N. of Mexican Hat, San Juan Co., Ut., Oct. 2, 1968. JAP.
44 *Apodemia m. mormo,* ♂. 12 mi. N. of Mexican Hat, San Juan Co., Ut., Oct. 2, 1968. JAP.
45 *Apodemia mormo deserti,* ♀, underside. Scissors Crossing, San Diego Co., Cal., Sept. 19, 1954. LACM.
46 *Apodemia mormo deserti,* ♀. Same data as fig. 45.
47 *Apodemia mormo mejicana,* ♀, underside. Ramsey Canyon, Huachuca Mts., Cochise Co., Ariz., Sept. 3, 1952. LACM.
48 *Apodemia mormo mejicana,* ♀. Same data as fig. 47.

PLATE 47

William H. Howe

PLATE 48

1 *Melanis p. pixe,* ♀. Tampico, Tamaulipas, June 21, 1964. HAF.
2 *Apodemia mormo "dialeuca,"* ♂. Sugarloaf Ridge, San Bernardino Co., Cal., June 5, 1966. JAP.
3 *Apodemia mormo mejicana,* ♂. Ramsey Canyon, Huachuca Mts., Cochise Co., Ariz., Sept. 3, 1952. LACM.
4 *Apodemia mormo mormonia,* ♂, underside. Del Puerto Canyon, 22 mi. W. of Patterson, Cal., Sept. 6, 1962. JAP.
5 *Apodemia mormo virgulti,* ♂, underside. El Cajon, Cal., Feb. 2, 1959. OS.
6 *Apodemia mormo mormonia,* ♂. Same data as fig. 4.
7 *Apodemia mormo mormonia,* ♀. Del Puerto Canyon, 22 mi. W. of Patterson, Cal., Sept. 6, 1962. JAP.
8 *Apodemia mormo virgulti,* ♂. Same data as fig. 5.
9 *Apodemia mormo virgulti* (southern segregate), ♀. Sierra San Pedro Martir, Baja Cal., May 26, 1958. JAP.
10 *Apodemia mormo langei,* ♀, underside. Antioch, Cal., Sept. 5, 1954. LACM.
11 *Apodemia mormo langei,* ♂. Antioch, Cal., Sept. 5, 1954. LACM.
12 *Apodemia mormo langei,* ♀. Same data as fig. 10.
13 *Apodemia mormo virgulti,* ♀. El Cajon, Cal., May 20, 1959. OS.
14 *Apodemia mormo virgulti* (southern segregate), ♂. San Simon, Baja Cal., Sept. 10, 1955. JAP.
15 *Apodemia mormo tuolumnensis,* ♀, underside. Hetch Hetchy Dam, Tuolumne Co., Cal., Sept. 9, 1964. OS.
16 *Apodemia mormo tuolumnensis,* ♀. Same data as fig. 15.
17 *Apodemia mormo "dialeuca,"* ♀. Sugarloaf Ridge, San Bernardino Co., Cal., June 5, 1966. JAP.
18 *Apodemia mormo "dialeuca,"* ♀, underside. Same data as fig. 17.
19 *Apodemia mormo cythera,* underside. Bishop Creek, Inyo Co., Cal., July 22, 1934. LACM.
20 *Apodemia mormo cythera.* Same data as fig. 19.
21 *Philotes speciosa bohartorum,* ♂, paratype. Briceburg, Mariposa Co., Cal., May 4, 1968. JL.
22 *Philotes speciosa bohartorum,* ♂, underside. Same data as fig. 21.
23 *Oenomaus ortygnus,* ♂. Catemaco, Veracruz, June 18, 1966. CM.
24 *Oenomaus ortygnus,* ♂, underside. Same data as fig. 23.
25 *Apodemia hepburni,* ♀. Boca de la Sierra, Baja Cal. del Sur, Nov. 22, 1961. CM.
26 *Apodemia hepburni,* ♀, underside. Same data as fig. 25.
27 *Apodemia hepburni,* ♂. Boca de la Sierra, Baja Cal. del Sur, Nov. 17, 1961. CM.
28 *Hypostrymon critola festata,* ♂. Boca de la Sierra, Baja Cal. del Sur, Nov. 24, 1961. CM.
29 *Hypostrymon critola festata,* ♂, underside. Same data as fig. 28.
30 *Hypostrymon critola festata,* ♀. Arroyo Candelaria, Baja Cal. del Sur, Nov. 24, 1961. CM.
31 *Apodemia phyciodoides,* ♂, holotype. Chiricahua Mts., Cochise Co., Ariz. USNM.
32 *Emesis zela cleis,* ♂. Huachuca Mts., Cochise Co., Ariz. USNM.
33 *Emesis zela cleis,* ♀. Reddington, Ariz. USNM.
34 *Satyrium acadica montanensis,* ♂. Fort Lupton, Weld Co., Colo., July 17, 1959. JDE.
35 *Satyrium acadica montanensis,* ♂, underside. Same data as fig. 34.
36 *Hemiargus ceraunus antibubastus,* ♂. Big Pine Key, Monroe Co., Fla., Aug. 7, 1967. FER.
37 *Hemiargus ceraunus antibubastus,* ♀. Big Pine Key, Monroe Co., Fla., Aug. 5, 1967. FER.
38 *Satyrium auretorum spadix,* ♂, underside. Loma Linda, San Bernardino Co., Cal., July 21, 1931. USNM.
39 *Satyrium auretorum spadix,* ♂. Same data as fig. 38.
40 *Satyrium auretorum spadix,* ♀. Pasadena, Cal. USNM.
41 *Strymon m. melinus,* ♂. Miami, Fla., Oct. 1, 1907. USNM.

PLATE 48

William H. Howe

PLATE 49

1   *Eumaeus atala florida,* ♂. Nr. Miami, Dade Co., Fla., Jan. 20, 1917. LACM.
2   *Eumaeus minyas,* ♀. Quirigua, Guatemala. CM.
3   *Hypaurotis c. crysalus,* ♀. White Mts., Ariz., July 3, 1937. LACM.
4   *Atlides halesus corcorani,* ♂. China Ranch, Inyo Co., Cal., Sept. 29, 1955. LACM.
5   *Atlides halesus corcorani,* ♀. Topanga, Cal., July 19, 1955. LACM.
6   *Panthiades m-album,* ♂. Mears Park, Franklin Co., Kan. AMNH.
7   *Panthiades m-album,* ♀. Baldwin Hill, Kan. AMNH.
8   *Habrodais g. grunus,* ♂. Forest Home, San Bernardino Co., Cal., July 10, 1933. LACM.
9   *Habrodais g. grunus,* ♀. Forest Home, San Bernardino Co., Cal., July 2, 1928. LACM.
10 *Satyrium behrii crossi,* ♂. Bergen Park, Jefferson Co., Colo., July 13, 1936. LACM.
11 *Satyrium behrii crossi,* ♀. Bergen Park, Jefferson Co., Colo., July 13, 1936. LACM.
12 *Satyrium f. fuliginosum,* ♂. Virginia Lake, Mono Co., Cal., July 28, 1933. LACM.
13 *Callophrys spinetorum,* ♀. Charleston Peak, Spring Mts., Clark Co., Nev., June 29, 1935. LACM.
14 *Callophyrs johnsoni,* ♂. Mason Co., Wash. AMNH.
15 *Callophrys johnsoni,* ♀. Dead Horse Summit, Siskiyou Co., Cal. CAS.
16 *Callophrys nelsoni,* ♂. Yosemite Nat. Park, Cal., June 25, 1922. LACM.
17 *Callophrys nelsoni,* ♀. Blue Jay, San Bernardino Mts., Cal., June 30, 1955, LACM.
18 *Callophrys siva,* ♂. Wedding of the Waters, Thermopolis, Wyo. AMNH.
19 *Callophrys siva,* ♀. Red Rocks Park, Jefferson Co., Colo. AMNH.
20 *Callophrys xami,* ♂. Corpus Christi, Tex. CM.
21 *Callophrys xami,* ♀. Pharr, Texas, Oct. 28, 1944. AMNH.
22 *Callophrys loki,* ♂. Nr. Jacumba Hot Springs, Cal., June 19, 1924. LACM.
23 *Callophrys loki,* ♀. Gavilan Hills, Riverside Co., Cal., March 25, 1933. LACM.
24 *Callophrys g. gryneus,* ♂. Bloomington, Ind., April 24, 1954. CM.
25 *Callophrys g. gryneus,* ♀. Bloomington, Ind., April 24, 1954. CM.
26 *Callophrys hesseli,* ♂. Lakehurst, Ocean Co., N.J., May 9, 1951. LACM.
27 *Callophrys hesseli,* ♀. Lakehurst, Ocean Co., N.J., May 14, 1951. LACM.

PLATE 49

William H. Howe

PLATE 50

1 *Callophrys augustinus croesioides,* ♂. Lakehurst, N.J. AMNH.
2 *Callophrys augustinus croesioides,* ♀. Lakehurst, N.J. AMNH.
3 *Callophrys augustinus iroides,* ♂. Alpine Lake, Marin Co., Cal. AMNH.
4 *Callophrys augustinus iroides,* ♀. Durkee, Ore. AMNH.
5 *Callophrys i. irus,* ♂. Wallingford, Conn. AMNH.
6 *Callophrys i. irus,* ♀. Center, N.Y. AMNH.
7 *Callophrys irus hadros,* ♂. Tyler State Park, Tyler, Tex. AMNH.
8 *Callophrys irus hadros,* ♀. Tyler State Park, Tyler, Tex. AMNH.
9 *Callophrys henrici turneri,* ♂. Warsaw, Mo. AMNH.
10 *Callophrys henrici turneri,* ♀. Prairie Village, Kan. AMNH.
11 *Callophrys polios,* ♂. Lakehurst, N.J. AMNH.
12 *Callophrys polios,* ♀. Sugarloaf Mtn., Boulder Co., Colo. AMNH.
13 *Callophrys f. fotis,* ♂. Cedar Mts., Tooele Co., Ut. AMNH.
14 *Callophrys f. fotis,* ♀. Cedar Mts., Tooele Co., Ut. AMNH.
15 *Callophrys lanoraieensis,* ♂. Lincoln, Me. AMNH.
16 *Callophrys lanoraieensis,* ♀. Lincoln, Me. AMNH.
17 *Callophrys e. eryphon,* ♂. LaJunta Canyon, Taos Co., N.Mex. AMNH.
18 *Callophrys e. eryphon,* ♀. Gilchrist, Ore. AMNH.
19 *Callophrys niphon clarki,* ♂. Willimantic, Conn. AMNH.
20 *Callophrys niphon clarki,* ♀. Mansfield, Conn. AMNH.
21 *Erora laeta,* ♂. Edmundston, N.B. AMNH.
22 *Erora quaderna sanfordi,* ♀. Madera Canyon, Santa Cruz Co., Ariz. AMNH.
23 *Harkenclenus titus mospus,* ♀. Sleepy Creek, Edgefield Co., S.C. CM.
24 *Harkenclenus titus mopsus,* ♂. Sleepy Creek, Edgefield Co., S.C. CM.
25 *Dolymorpha jada,* ♂. Tancitaro, Michoacán. AMNH.
26 *Dolymorpha jada,* ♀. Guerrero. AMNH.
27 *Chlorostrymon maesites,* ♂. Miami, Fla. AMNH.
28 *Chlorostrymon maesites,* ♀. Miami, Fla. AMNH.

PLATE 50

William H. Howe

PLATE 51

1 *Chlorostrymon telea,* ♂. Ciudad Valles, San Luis Potosí. CM.
2 *Callophrys gryneus smilacis,* ♀. St. Augustine, Fla., June 7, 1954. CM.
3 *Strymon martialis,* ♂. Miami, Fla. JRH.
4 *Strymon martialis,* ♀. Miami, Fla. JRH.
5 *Strymon acis bartrami,* ♂. Miami, Fla. JRH.
6 *Strymon acis bartrami,* ♀. Miami, Fla. JRH.
7 *Chlorostrymon simaethis sarita,* ♂. Brownsville, Tex. S&T.
8 *Chlorostrymon simaethis sarita,* ♀. Brownsville, Tex. S&T.
9 *Oenomaus ortygnus,* ♀. Ciudad Valles, San Luis Potosí, June 16, 1967. CM.
10 *Thereus zebina,* ♀. Pharr, Tex., Dec. 5, 1935. HAF.
11 *Calycopis cecrops,* ♂. Volusia Co., Fla. April 14, 1957. AMNH.
12 *Calycopis cecrops,* ♀. Leesburg, Fla., May 4, 1961. AMNH.
13 *Calycopis isobeon,* ♂. Alamo, Tex., May 29, 1939. AMNH.
14 *Calycopis isobeon,* ♀. Hamilton, Tex. AMNH.
15 *Strymon columella istapa,* ♂. Ajijic, Jalisco, Nov. 17, 1966. CM.
16 *Strymon columella istapa,* ♀. Tampico, Tamaulipas, Jan. 26, 1966. CM.
17 *Vaga blackburni,* ♂. Mt. Tantalus, Oahu, Hawaii. RSW.
18 *Vaga blackburni,* ♀. Mt. Tantalus, Oahu, Hawaii. RSW.
19 *Strymon bazochii,* ♂. Brownsville, Tex. AMNH.
20 *Strymon bazochii,* ♀. Pharr, Tex. AMNH.
21 *Ministrymon clytie,* ♂. Brownsville, Tex. Oct. 25, 1938. AMNH.
22 *Strymon alea,* ♀. Ciudad Mante, Tamaulipas, June 22, 1964. HAF.
23 *Tmolus azia,* ♂. Pharr, Tex., July 25, 1945. AMNH.
24 *Tmolus azia,* ♀. Pharr, Tex., July 25, 1948. AMNH.
25 *Ministrymon leda,* form "leda," ♂. Pima Co., Ariz., Sept. 4, 1950. AMNH.
26 *Ministrymon leda,* form "leda," ♀. Black Dike Prospect, Sierritas, Ariz., July 29, 1916. AMNH.
27 *Ministrymon leda,* form "ines," ♂. Santa Rita Mts., Ariz., Oct. 29, 1923. AMNH.
28 *Ministrymon leda,* form "ines," ♀. Vallecito, San Diego Co., Cal., Oct. 11, 1918. LACM.

PLATE 51

William H. Howe

1 *Strymon avalona,* ♂. Santa Catalina I., Cal., July, 1928. LACM.
2 *Strymon avalona,* ♀. Santa Catalina I., Cal., May 19, 1933. LACM.
3 *Strymon melinus franki,* ♂. Lake Charles, La. JRH.
4 *Strymon melinus franki,* ♀. Lake Charles, La. JRH.
5 *Strymon buchholzi,* ♂. Ciudad Mante, Tamaulipas, June 22, 1964. HAF.
6 *Strymon buchholzi,* ♀. Gómez Farías, Tamaulipas, Jan. 9, 1966. CM.
7 *Thereus zebina,* ♂. Ciudad Valles, San Luis Potosí, June 20, 1964. HAF.
8 *Strymon melinus atrofasciata,* ♂. Vancouver, B.C., April 13, 1904. USNM.
9 *Tmolus echion,* ♂. El Banito, San Luis Potosí. AMNH.
10 *Tmolus echion,* ♀. Presidio, Veracruz. AMNH.
11 *Strymon rufofusca,* ♂. Colima. AMNH.
12 *Strymon rufofusca,* ♀. Matamoros, Tamaulipas. AMNH.
13 *Strymon cestri,* ♂. Ayutla, Guerrero. AMNH.
14 *Strymon cestri,* ♀. Brownsville, Tex. AMNH.
15 *Strymon yojoa,* ♂. Tepescuintle, Tabasco. AMNH.
16 *Strymon yojoa,* ♀. Tepescuintle, Tabasco. AMNH.
17 *Lampides boeticus,* ♂. Honolulu, Hawaii. RSW.
18 *Callophrys goodsoni,* ♀. Pharr, Tex., July 23, 1945. HAF.
19 *Euristrymon polingi,* ♂. Alpine, Tex. AMNH.
20 *Euristrymon polingi,* ♀. Alpine, Tex. AMNH.
21 *Phaeostrymon alcestis,* ♂. Kerrville State Park, Kerrville, Tex., May 25, 1959. CM.
22 *Phaeostrymon a. alcestis,* ♀. Ft. Worth, Tex. AMNH.
23 *Harkenclenus t. titus,* ♂. Presque Isle Co., Mich. JRH.
24 *Harkenclenus t. titus,* ♀. Presque Isle Co., Mich. JRH.
25 *Callophrys goodsoni,* ♂. Ciudad Valles, San Luis Potosí, June 9, 1956. CM.
26 *Harkenclenus titus watsoni,* ♀, topotype. Kerrville, Tex., June 5, 1948. HAF.
27 *Harkenclenus titus immaculosus,* ♂. Copper Lake Trail, Gunnison Co., Colo. AMNH.
28 *Harkenclenus titus immaculosus,* ♀. Copper Lake Trail, Gunnison Co., Colo. AMNH.

PLATE 52

William H. Howe

PLATE 53

1 *Satyrium sylvinus dryope*, ♂. Arroyo Seco, Los Angeles Co., Cal., June 30, 1919. AMNH.
2 *Satyrium sylvinus dryope*, ♀. Suñol, Alameda Co., Cal., June 2, 1940. AMNH.
3 *Callophrys fotis* ssp., probably *mossii*, ♂. 10 mi. S.W. of the Dalles, Wasco Co., Ore. March 31, 1934. LACM.
4 *Callophrys fotis schryveri*, ♂. Coal Creek Canyon, Jefferson Co., Colo. JDE.
5 *Callophrys fotis doudoroffi*, ♂. Partingian Canyon, S. of Big Sur, Monterey Co., Cal., May 26, 1954. LACM.
6 *Callophrys nelsoni muiri*, ♂. St. Helena Creek, Napa Co., Cal., April 30, 1960. RLL.
7 *Satyrium tetra*, ♂. Mint Canyon, Los Angeles Co., Cal., June 16, 1947. AMNH.
8 *Satyrium tetra*, ♀. Mint Canyon, Los Angeles Co., Cal., June 9, 1927. AMNH.
9 *Satyrium s. saepium*, ♂. Frenchman Flat, Los Angeles Co., Cal., May 22, 1939. AMNH.
10 *Satyrium s. saepium*, ♀. Hebron Pass. Siskiyou Co., Cal., July 27, 1953. AMNH.
11 *Euristrymon ontario ilavia*, ♂. Hualapai Mt. Park, Hualapai Mts., Mojave Co., Ariz., June 22, 1921. LACM.
12 *Electrostrymon endymion cyphara*, ♂. Tampico, Tamaulipas, June 21, 1964. HAF.
13 *Callophrys dumetorum* ssp., ♂. Witch Creek, Cal., Feb. 1906. AMNH.
14 *Callophrys dumetorum* ssp., ♀. Witch Creek, Cal., Feb., 1906. AMNH.
15 *Callophrys comstocki*, ♂. Bonanza King Canyon, Providence Mts., San Bernardino Co., Cal. RSW.
16 *Callophrys lemberti*, ♂. Panther Meadow, Mt. Shasta, Siskiyou Co., Cal. AMNH.
17 *Callophrys apama homoperplexa*, ♂. Boulder Co., Colo., May 24, 1958. AMNH.
18 *Callophrys apama homoperplexa*, ♀. Boulder Co., Colo., May 24, 1958. AMNH.
19 *Callophrys a. affinis*, ♂. Virginia City, Mont. AMNH.
20 *Callophrys a. affinis*, ♀. Virginia City, Mont. AMNH.
21 *Callophrys viridis*, ♂. Point Reyes, Marin Co., Cal., April 4, 1932. CM.
22 *Callophrys viridis*, ♀. Twin Peaks, San Francisco, Cal., May 1, 1913. AMNH.
23 *Callophrys s. sheridanii*, ♂. Sunshine Canyon, Boulder Co., Colo., April 4, 1954. AMNH.
24 *Callophrys sheridanii*, ♀. Flagstaff Mt., Boulder Co., Colo., April 11, 1954. AMNH.
25 *Callophrys miserabilis*, ♂. Brownsville, Tex., Nov. 29, 1946. HAF.
26 *Callophrys miserabilis*, ♀. Brownsville, Tex., Nov. 14, 1944. HAF.
27 *Callophrys macfarlandi*, ♂. Sandia Mts., N.Mex., March 12, 1967. AMNH.
28 *Callophrys macfarlandi*, ♀. High Rolls, N.Mex., June 12, 1902. CM.

PLATE 53

William H. Howe

PLATE 54

1   *Euristrymon favonius*, ♂. DeLand, Fla. JRH.
2   *Euristrymon favonius*, ♀. St. Augustine, Fla. JRH.
3   *Euristrymon o. ontario*, ♂. Clifton Forge, Va. CM.
4   *Euristrymon o. ontario*, ♀. Clifton Forge, Va. CM.
5   *Satyrium liparops strigosum*, ♂. Blue Springs, Mo. JRH.
6   *Satyrium liparops strigosum*, ♀. Shawnee Mission Park, Johnson Co., Kan. JRH.
7   *Satyrium edwardsii*, ♂. Holliday, Kan. JRH.
8   *Satyrium edwardsii*, ♀. Holliday, Kan. JRH.
9   *Satyrium calanus falacer*, ♂. Eureka Springs, Ark. JRH.
10 *Satyrium calanus falacer*, ♀. Blue Springs, Mo. JRH.
11 *Satyrium kingi*, ♂. Atlanta, Ga. JRH.
12 *Satyrium kingi*, ♀. Mt. Pleasant, S.C. JRH.
13 *Satyrium caryaevorus*, ♂. New Haven, Conn. JRH.
14 *Satyrium caryaevorus*, ♀. Blue Springs, Jackson Co., Mo. JRH.
15 *Satyrium a. acadica*, ♂. Presque Isle, Mich. JRH.
16 *Satyrium a. acadica*, ♀. Richland, N.Dak. JRH.
17 *Satyrium s. sylvinus*, ♂. Stanbury Mts., Tooele Co., Ut. JRH.
18 *Satyrium s. sylvinus*, ♀. Lone Pine, Inyo Co., Cal. JRH.
19 *Satyrium californica*, ♂. Laguna Mts., San Diego Co., Cal. JRH.
20 *Satyrium californica*, ♀. Jerseydale, Mariposa Co., Cal. JRH.
21 *Satyrium auretorum*, ♂. Arroyo Bayo, Santa Clara Co., Cal. JRH.
22 *Satyrium auretorum*, ♀. Pinecrest, Tuolumne Co., Cal. JRH.
23 *Feniseca tarquinius*, ♂. Baldwin Hill, Kan. JRH.
24 *Lycaena hermes*, ♂. Suncrest, El Cajon, Cal. JRH.
25 *Lycaena c. cupreus*, ♂. Bassetts, Sierra Co., Cal. JRH.
26 *Lycaena c. cupreus*, ♀. Logan Canyon, (Wasatch Mts.) Cache Co., Ut. JRH.
27 *Lycaena cupreus snowi*, ♂. Copper Lake Trail, Gothic, Colo. JRH.
28 *Lycaena cupreus snowi*, ♀. Corona Pass, Gilpin Co., Colo. JRH.

PLATE 54

William H Howe

1   *Lycaena xanthoides dione,* ♂. Prairie Village, Johnson Co., Kan. JRH.
2   *Lycaena xanthoides dione,* ♀. Lee's Summit, Mo. JRH.
3   *Lycaena e. epixanthe,* ♂. Lakehurst, Ocean Co., N.J. JRH.
4   *Lycaena e. epixanthe,* ♀. Lakehurst, Ocean Co., N.J. JRH.
5   *Lycaena phlaeas americana,* ♂. Prairie Village, Johnson Co., Kan. JRH.
6   *Lycaena phlaeas americana,* ♀. Prairie Village, Johnson Co., Kan. JRH.
7   *Lycaena hyllus,* ♂. Lee's Summit, Mo. JRH.
8   *Lycaena hyllus,* ♀. Prairie Village, Johnson Co., Kan. JRH.
9   *Lycaena dorcas claytoni,* ♂. Springfield, Me. JRH.
10 *Lycaena dorcas claytoni,* ♀. Springfield, Me. JRH.
11 *Lycaena dorcas dospassosi,* ♂. Bathurst, N.B. JRH.
12 *Lycaena dorcas dospassosi,* ♀. Bathurst, N.B. JRH.
13 *Lycaena h. helloides,* ♂. Hayward, Cal. JRH.
14 *Lycaena h. helloides,* ♀. Vernal, Ut. JRH.
15 *Lycaena mariposa,* ♂. Salmon Meadows, Okanogan Co., Wash. JRH.
16 *Lycaena mariposa,* ♀. Union Creek Meadow, Yakima Co., Wash. JHR.
17 *Lycaena heteronea gravenotata,* ♂. Central City, Colo. JRH.
18 *Lycaena heteronea gravenotata,* ♀. Gold Creek Camp, Gunnison Co., Colo. JRH.
19 *Lycaena nivalis,* ♂. Rabbit Ears Pass, Routt Co., Colo. JRH.
20 *Lycaena nivalis,* ♀. Copper Lake Trail, Gunnison, Co., Colo. JRH.
21 *Lycaena editha,* ♂. Westwood, Lassen Co., Cal. JRH.
22 *Lycaena editha,* ♀. Mohawk, Plumas Co., Cal. JRH.
23 *Lycaena gorgon,* ♂. Arroyo Bayo, Santa Clara Co., Cal. JRH.
24 *Lycaena gorgon,* ♀. Arroyo Bayo, Santa Clara Co., Cal. JRH.
25 *Lycaena rubidus,* ♂. Durkee, Ore. JRH.
26 *Lycaena rubidus,* ♀. White Mts., Apache Co., Ariz. JRH.
27 *Lycaena a. arota,* ♂. Jerseydale, Mariposa Co., Cal. JRH.
28 *Lycaena a. arota,* ♀. Jerseydale, Mariposa Co., Cal. JRH.

PLATE 55

William H. Howe

PLATE 56

1 *Lycaena arota nubila,* ♂, paratype. Griffith Park, Los Angeles Co., Cal., July 2, 1922. LACM.
2 *Lycaena arota nubila,* ♀, paratype. Griffith Park, Los Angeles Co., Cal., July 2, 1922. LACM.
3 *Lycaena arota virginiensis,* ♂. Walker Canyon, nr. Bridgeport, Cal., Aug. 6, 1922. LACM.
4 *Lycaena arota virginiensis,* ♀, topotype. Virginia City, Nev., July 27, 1923. LACM.
5 *Lycaena arota schellbachi,* ♂, type. Grand Canyon, Ariz. USNM.
6 *Lycaena arota schellbachi,* ♀. Jemez Springs, Sandoval Co., N.Mex., Aug. 6, 1945. LACM.
7 *Lycaena x. xanthoides,* ♂. Berkeley, Cal., July 3, 1920. LACM.
8 *Lycaena x. xanthoides,* ♀. Corona, Cal., May 10, 1935. LACM.
9 *Lycaena heteronea clara,* ♂. Tehachapi, Cal., July 15, 1918. LACM.
10 *Lycaena heteronea clara,* ♀. Tehachapi Mts., Kern Co., Cal., July 26, 1918. LACM.
11 *Lycaena h. heteronea,* ♂. Mammoth Camp, Mono Co., Cal., July 26, 1922. LACM.
12 *Lycaena h. heteronea,* ♀. Mammoth Camp, Mono Co., Cal., July 26, 1922. LACM.
13 *Phaedrotes p. piasus,* ♂. Yosemite Nat. Park, Tuolumne Co., Cal., June 26, 1964. AMNH.
14 *Phaedrotes piasus catalina,* ♀. Glendale, Cal., March 12, 1923. LACM.
15 *Plebejus icarioides evius,* ♂. Laguna Mts., San Diego Co., Cal., May 27, 1951. RLL.
16 *Plebejus icarioides evius,* ♀. Cuyamaca Lake, Laguna Mts., San Diego Co., Calif., May 27, 1951. RLL.
17 *Plebejus icarioides moroensis,* ♂. 5 mi. S. of Oceano, Oso Flaco Lake, San Luis Obispo Co., Cal., June, 1966. RLL.
18 *Plebejus icarioides moroensis,* ♀. 5 mi. S. of Oceano, Oso Flaco Lake, San Luis Obispo Co., Cal., June 6, 1966. RLL.
19 *Glaucopsyche lygdamus australis,* ♂. National City, San Diego Co., Cal., Feb. 24, 1951. RLL.
20 *Glaucopsyche lygdamus australis,* ♀. Chula Vista, San Diego Co., Cal., March 4, 1951. RLL.
21 *Hypaurotis crysalus citima,* ♂. Payson Canyon, Utah Co., Ut., July 20, 1932. LACM.
22 *Plebejus i. icarioides,* ♂. Dutch Flat, Placer Co., Cal., May 29, 1954. JCD.
23 *Plebejus icarioides buchholzi,* ♀. White Mts., Greenlee Co., Ariz., June 24, 1937. JCD.
24 *Plebejus icarioides buchholzi,* ♂. White Mts., Greenlee Co., Ariz., June 18, 1938. JCD.
25 *Everes comyntas,* summer form, ♂. Aspinwall, Pa., July 15, 1928. CM.
26 *Plebejus i. icarioides,* ♀. Mt. Tallac, 7500 ft., El Dorado Co., Cal., July 17, 1909. JCD.
27 *Plebejus icarioides pembina,* ♂. Osoyoos, B.C., May 27, 1938. JCD.
28 *Plebejus icarioides pembina,* ♀. Yahk, B.C., June 15, 1957. JCD.
29 *Everes comyntas,* summer form, ♀. Rantoul, Kan., Aug. 25, 1968. USNM.
30 *Plebejus icarioides montis,* ♂. Mt. Cheam, B.C., Aug. 7, 1903. JCD.
31 *Plebejus icarioides montis,* ♀. Mt. McLean, Lillooet, B.C., July 7, 1921. JCD.
32 *Zizula cyna,* ♂. Gómez Farías, Tamaulipas, Jan. 11, 1966. CM.

PLATE 56

William H. Howe

1   *Philotes enoptes ancilla,* ♂. Signal Peak, Teton Nat. Park, Wyo. USNM.
2   *Philotes enoptes ancilla,* ♀. Signal Peak, Teton Nat. Park, Wyo. USNM.
3   *Philotes sonorensis,* ♂. Scissors Crossing, San Diego Co., Cal., March 11, 1951. RLL.
4   *Philotes sonorensis,* ♀. San Gabriel Canyon, San Gabriel Mts., Los Angeles Co., Cal., Feb. 9, 1936. LACM.
5   *Philotes mojave,* ♂. Morongo Canyon, Argus Mts., Inyo Co., Cal., April 20, 1929. LACM.
6   *Philotes mojave,* ♀. Morongo Canyon, Argus Mts., Inyo Co., Cal., May 17, 1936. LACM.
7   *Philotes spaldingi,* ♂. Shiprock, N.Mex., Aug. 8, 1924. LACM.
8   *Philotes spaldingi,* ♀. Shiprock, N.Mex., Aug. 8, 1924. LACM.
9   *Philotes r. rita,* ♂. Ramsey Canyon, Huachuca Mts., Cochise Co., Ariz., Sept. 1, 1953. LACM.
10 *Philotes r. rita,* ♀. Ramsey Canyon, Huachuca Mts., Cochise Co., Ariz., Sept. 1, 1953. LACM.
11 *Celastrina argiolus lucia,* ♂. Skagway, Alaska, May 9, 1923. LACM.
12 *Celastrina argiolus lucia,* ♀. Skagway, Alaska, May 9, 1923. LACM.
13 *Celastrina argiolus pseudargiolus* form "violacea," ♂. Ottawa, Kan., April 1, 1944. AMNH.
14 *Celastrina argiolus pseudargiolus* form "violacea," ♀. Chippewa Hills, Franklin Co., Kan., April 25, 1950. AMNH.
15 *Celastrina argiolus echo,* ♂. Miller Creek Road, Alameda Co., Cal., March 3, 1940. AMNH.
16 *Celastrina argiolus cinerea,* ♀. Palo Flechado Pass, Colfax Co., N.Mex., June 18, 1959. AMNH.
17 *Phaedrotes piasus daunia,* ♂. Chautauqua Mesa, Boulder Co., Colo. JDE.
18 *Hemiargus ceraunus zachaeina,* ♂. San Pedro, Cameron Co., Texas. JRH.
19 *Celastrina argiolus pseudargiolus,* ♂. Hastings, Mich., July 20, 1946. RLL.
20 *Celastrina argiolus pseudargiolus,* ♀. Ottawa, Kan., Aug. 29, 1945. AMNH.
21 *Leptotes cassius theonus,* ♂. Hollywood, Fla. JRH.
22 *Leptotes cassius theonus,* ♀. Big Pine Key, Fla. JRH.
23 *Leptotes marina,* ♂. Olney Springs, Colo., Aug. 30, 1958. AMNH.
24 *Leptotes marina,* ♀. Franklin Co., Kan., Oct. 14, 1959. AMNH.
25 *Hemiargus bethunebakeri,* ♂. Key Largo, Fla. JRH.
26 *Hemiargus bethunebakeri,* ♀. Key Largo, Fla. JRH.
27 *Hemiargus isola alce,* ♂. Jemez Mts., Los Alamos Co., N.Mex., July 8, 1966. RLL.
28 *Hemiargus isola alce,* ♀. Mears Park, Franklin Co., Kan., Nov. 16, 1944. AMNH.

PLATE 57

William H. Howe

PLATE 58

1 *Plebejus optilete yukona,* ♂. Eagle, Alaska. USNM.
2 *Plebejus optilete yukona,* ♀. Eagle, Alaska. USNM.
3 *Plebejus lupini chlorina,* ♂, type. Tehachapi, Cal., July 1, 1921. LACM.
4 *Plebejus lupini chlorina,* ♀. Ridge Route, Tejon Range, Los Angeles Co., Cal., June 21, 1923. LACM.
5 *Plebejus lupini monticola,* ♂, type. Arroyo Seco, Los Angeles Co., Cal., June 12, 1907. LACM.
6 *Plebejus lupini monticola,* ♀, paratype. Arroyo Seco, Los Angeles Co., Cal., June 3, 1907. LACM.
7 *Plebejus emigdionis,* ♂. Victorville, Cal. F&JP.
8 *Plebejus emigdionis,* ♀. Victorville, Cal. F&JP.
9 *Glaucopsyche lygdamus behri,* ♂. Crockett, Cal. JCD.
10 *Glaucopsyche lygdamus behri,* ♀. Glen Ellen, Sonoma Co., Cal., March 29, 1953. RLL.
11 *Glaucopsyche lygdamus arizonensis,* ♂. Greer, White Mts., Ariz. USNM.
12 *Glaucopsyche lygdamus columbia,* ♀. Salt Lake City, Ut. USNM.
13 *Glaucopsyche xerces,* ♀. San Mateo Co., Cal. USNM.
14 *Glaucopsyche xerces* form "polyphemus," ♂. San Francisco, Cal. USNM.
15 *Glaucopsyche xerces* form "antiacis," ♂. San Francisco, Cal. USNM.
16 *Glaucopsyche lygdamus columbia,* ♂. Signal Mt., Teton Nat. Park, Wyo. USNM.
17 *Plebejus aquilo rustica,* ♂. Below Sandia Crest, 9000 ft., Bernalillo Co., N.Mex., July 7, 1966. RLL.
18 *Plebejus aquilo rustica,* ♀. Las Conchas Campground, Jemez Mts., Sandoval Co., N.Mex., July 8, 1966. RLL.
19 *Plebejus aquilo podarce,* ♂. Mt. Rose, Washoe Co., Nev., July 20, 1964. RLL.
20 *Plebejus aquilo podarce,* ♀. Kyburz, Cal. USNM.
21 *Everes a. amyntula,* ♂. Atascadero, Cal., April 21, 1946. AMNH.
22 *Everes a. amyntula,* ♀. La Honda Road, San Mateo Co., Cal. RSW.
23 *Everes comyntas,* spring form, ♂. Baldwin Hill, Kan., April 16, 1950. USNM.
24 *Everes comyntas,* spring form, ♀. Williamsburg, Kan., April 10, 1967. USNM.
25 *Philotes battoides bernardino,* ♂. Mt. Palomar, San Diego Co., Cal., June 28, 1968. RLL.
26 *Philotes battoides bernardino,* ♀. La Mesa, Cal. JCD.
27 *Philotes battoides centralis,* ♂. El Morro Nat. Mon., Valencia Co., N.Mex., July 10, 1966. RLL.
28 *Philotes battoides centralis,* ♀. Alamosa Reservoir, Conejos Co., Colo. JDE.
29 *Philotes enoptes ancilla,* ♂. City Creek Canyon, Salt Lake Co., Ut. JCD.
30 *Philotes s. speciosa,* ♂. Randsburg, Kern Co., Cal., April 30, 1936. LACM.
31 *Philotes s. speciosa,* ♀. Kramer Junc., San Bernardino Co., Cal., April 30, 1936. LACM.
32 *Brephidium exilis,* ♂. Taft, Cal. (Specimen lost).
33 *Brephidium exilis,* ♀. Amargosa River, 2 mi. S. of Beatty, Nye Co., Nev., April 21, 1958. RLL.
34 *Brephidium pseudofea,* ♂. Ft. George, Fla. JRH.
35 *Brephidium pseudofea,* ♀. Vero Beach, Fla., June 15, 1921. CM.

PLATE 58

William H. Howe

PLATE 59

1 *Plebejus icarioides missionensis,* ♂. San Bruno Mt., nr. Colma, Cal., Apr. 24, 1966. USNM.
2 *Plebejus icarioides missionensis,* ♀. San Bruno Mt., nr. Colma, Cal., Apr. 24, 1966. USNM.
3 *Plebejus saepiolus hilda,* ♂. Idyllwild, San Jacinto Mts., Riverside Co., Cal., June 10, 1925. LACM.
4 *Plebejus saepiolus hilda,* ♀. Idyllwild, San Jacinto Mts., Riverside Co., Cal., June 10, 1925. LACM.
5 *Plebejus saepiolus gertschi,* ♂. Happy Jack, s. of Flagstaff, Coconino Co., Ariz., May 31, 1959. LACM.
6 *Plebejus saepiolus gertschi,* ♀. Alpine, Apache Co., Ariz., June 7, 1937. LACM.
7 *Plebejus saepiolus insulanus,* ♂. Shawnigan, B.C., June 24, 1925. LACM.
8 *Plebejus saepiolus insulanus,* ♀. Victoria, B.C., May 22, 1913. LACM.
9 *Plebejus saepiolus amica,* ♀. Skagway, Alaska, May 22, 1923. LACM.
10 *Plebejus a. aquilo,* ♂. Hopedale, Labrador, June 18, 1924. LACM.
11 *Plebejus a. aquilo,* ♀. Battle Harbor, Labrador, Aug. 2, 1912. LACM.
12 *Plebejus aquilo megalo,* ♂. Cooney Lake, Brewster, Wash. July 24, 1965. CM.
13 *Plebejus aquilo megalo,* ♀. Jesmond, B.C., Sept. 1, 1937. LACM.
14 *Plebejus saepiolus amica,* ♂. Eagle, Alaska, June 29, 1936. LACM.
15 *Plebejus shasta minnehaha,* ♂. Arapahoe Pass Trail, Boulder Co., Colo., Aug. 6, 1953. F&JP.
16 *Plebejus s. shasta (comstocki),* ♀. Deer Cr. Camp Road, Mt. Charleston, Clark Co., Nev., July 1, 1950. F&JP.
17 *Plebejus s. shasta (comstocki),* ♂. S. Fork of Bishop Cr., 8400 ft., Inyo Co., Cal., July 15, 1950. F&JP.
18 *Plebejus s. shasta,* ♂. Donahue Pass, Yosemite Natl. Park. Cal., Aug. 4, 1954. LACM.
19 *Plebejus s. shasta,* ♀. Donahue Pass, Yosemite Nat. Park. Cal., Aug. 6, 1959. LACM.
20 *Glaucopsyche l. lygdamus,* ♂. Elgin, Ill., May 13, 1924. LACM.
21 *Glaucopsyche l. lygdamus,* ♀. Elgin, Ill., May 13, 1924. LACM.
22 *Glaucopsyche lygdamus couperi,* ♂. Eagle, Alaska, June 13, 1936. LACM.
23 *Glaucopsyche lygdamus couperi,* ♀. Laggan, Alta. LACM.
24 *Plebejus argyrognomon empetri,* ♂. Mts. above Pleasant Bay, N.S., July 24, 1941. LACM.
25 *Plebejus melissa inyoensis,* ♂. Olancha, Inyo Co., Cal., June 21, 1937. LACM.
26 *Plebejus melissa inyoensis,* ♀. Olancha, Inyo Co., Cal., June 21, 1937. LACM.
27 *Plebejus melissa pseudosamuelis,* ♂. Cottonwood Lake, Chaffee Co., Colo., July 9, 1959. LACM.
28 *Plebejus melissa pseudosamuelis,* ♀. Cottonwood Lake, Chaffee Co., Colo., July 9, 1959. LACM.
29 *Plebejus argyrognomon empetri,* ♀. Mt. Uniacke, N.S., July 21, 1950. LACM.
30 *Plebejus argyrognomon ferniensis,* ♂. Jesmond, B.C., July 26, 1937. LACM.
31 *Plebejus argyrognomon ferniensis,* ♀. Jesmond, B.C., July 26, 1937. LACM.
32 *Plebejus argyrognomon aster,* ♂. Pokemouche, N.B., July 10, 1940. LACM.
33 *Plebejus argyrognomon longinus,* ♂. Mt. Washburn, Yellowstone Nat. Park, Wyo., July 25, 1925. LACM.
34 *Plebejus argyrognomon longinus,* ♀. Moran, Wyo., July 15, 1925. LACM.
35 *Plebejus argyrognomon alaskensis,* ♂. Eagle, Alaska, June 26, 1936. LACM.
36 *Plebejus argyrognomon alaskensis,* ♀. Eagle, Alaska, July 17, 1936. LACM.
37 *Plebejus argyrognomon aster,* ♀. Tabusintac, N.B., July 19, 1939. LACM.
38 *Plebejus argyrognomon atrapraetextus,* ♂. Priest R., Ida., July 6, 1910. LACM.
39 *Plebejus argyrognomon atrapraetextus,* ♀. Priest R., Ida., July 8, 1910. LACM.

PLATE 59

William H. Howe

PLATE 60

1 *Plebejus argyrognomon ricei,* ♂. Brewster, Wash. JDE.
2 *Plebejus argyrognomon ricei,* ♀. Brewster, Wash. JDE.
3 *Plebejus argyrognomon anna,* ♂. Willamette Pass, Lane Co., Ore. JRH.
4 *Plebejus argyrognomon anna,* ♀. Annie Creek Road, Klamath Co., Ore. JRH.
5 *Plebejus argyrognomon lotis,* ♂. Mendocino Co., Cal., June 18, 1953. JCD.
6 *Plebejus argyrognomon lotis,* ♀. Mendocino Co., Cal., June 18, 1953. JCD.
7 *Plebejus argyrognomon sublivens,* ♂. Cottonwood Pass, Gunnison Co., Colo. JDE.
8 *Plebejus argyrognomon sublivens,* ♀. Emerald Lake, Gothic, Gunnison Co., Colo. JDE.
9 *Plebejus melissa samuelis,* ♂. Karner, N.Y. JRH.
10 *Plebejus melissa samuelis,* ♀. Karner, N.Y. JRH.
11 *Plebejus m. melissa,* ♂. Mineral Springs, Slope Co., N.Dak. JRH.
12 *Plebejus m. melissa,* ♀. Eddy Co., N.Dak. JRH.
13 *Plebejus s. saepiolus,* ♂. Mono Lake, Mono Co., Cal. JRH.
14 *Plebejus s. saepiolus,* form "rufescens," ♀. Strawberry, Tuolumne Co., Cal. JRH.
15 *Plebejus saepiolus whitmeri,* ♂. Caribou Bog, Boulder Co., Colo. JRH.
16 *Plebejus saepiolus whitmeri,* ♀. Caribou Bog, Boulder Co., Colo. JRH.
17 *Plebejus icarioides ardea,* ♂, topotype. Virginia City, Nev. JCD.
18 *Plebejus icarioides ardea,* ♀, topotype. Virginia City, Nev. JCD.
19 *Plebejus icarioides lycea,* ♂. Moran, Wyo. JCD.
20 *Plebejus icarioides lycea,* ♀. Taylor Res., Gunnison Co., Colo. JCD.
21 *Plebejus icarioides pheres,* ♂. Sloat Blvd., San Francisco, Cal., May 26, 1937. USNM.
22 *Plebejus icarioides pheres,* ♀. Sloat Blvd., San Francisco, Cal., May 26, 1937. USNM.
23 *Plebejus icarioides pardalis,* ♂. Green Valley, Solano Co., Cal. USNM.
24 *Plebejus icarioides pardalis,* ♀. Berkeley, Cal. USNM.
25 *Plebejus icarioides blackmorei,* ♂. Fitzgerald, B.C. JCD.
26 *Plebejus icarioides blackmorei,* ♀. Fitzgerald, B.C. JCD.
27 *Plebejus l. lupini,* ♂. Huntington Lake, Fresno Co., Cal., June 27, 1936. LACM.
28 *Plebejus l. lupini,* ♀. Mt. Tallac, El Dorado Co., Cal. USNM.
29 *Plebejus acmon cottlei,* ♂. San Francisco, Cal. USNM.
30 *Plebejus acmon cottlei,* ♀. Lake Merced, San Francisco, Cal. USNM.
31 *Plebejus a. acmon,* ♂. Chelan, Wash. USNM.
32 *Plebejus a. acmon,* ♀. Chelan, Wash. USNM.
33 *Plebejus neurona,* ♀. Mt. Tehachapi, Kern Co., Cal. JRH.

PLATE 60

William H. Howe

PLATE 61

1 *Philotes e. enoptes,* ♂. Kingsbury Grade, Douglas Co., Nev., July 17, 1964. RLL.
2 *Philotes e. enoptes,* ♀. 3 mi. E. of Burney, Shasta Co., Cal., July 15, 1965. RLL.
3 *Philotes enoptes columbiae,* ♂, paratype. Brewster, Okanogan Co., Wash., May 11, 1946. LACM.
4 *Philotes enoptes columbiae,* ♀, paratype. Brewster, Okanogan Co., Wash., May 11, 1946. LACM.
5 *Philotes enoptes bayensis,* ♂, paratype. Tiburon, Marin Co., Cal., June 4, 1963. LACM.
6 *Philotes enoptes bayensis,* ♀, paratype. Carquinez Strait at Glen Cove, Solano Co., Cal., June 2, 1962. LACM.
7 *Philotes enoptes smithi,* ♂, paratype. Burns Cr., State Hwy 1, Monterey Co., Cal., Aug. 20, 1948. LACM.
8 *Philotes enoptes smithi,* ♀, paratype. Dolan Cr., State Hwy 1, Monterey Co., Cal., Aug. 20, 1948. LACM.
9 *Philotes enoptes dammersi,* ♂. Whitewater Canyon, Riverside Co., Cal., Sept. 28, 1933. LACM.
10 *Philotes enoptes dammersi,* ♀. Whitewater Canyon, Riverside Co., Cal., Sept. 28, 1933. LACM.
11 *Philotes rita coloradensis,* ♂, paratype. 7 mi S. of Kendrick, Lincoln Co., Colo., Aug. 20, 1964. LACM.
12 *Philotes rita coloradensis,* ♀, paratype. 7 mi S. of Kendrick, Lincoln Co., Colo., Aug. 20, 1964. LACM.
13 *Philotes b. battoides,* ♂. Mineral King, 11,000 ft., Tulare Co., Cal., July 8, 1915. LACM.
14 *Philotes b. battoides,* ♀. Above Tioga Pass, 11,200 ft., Tuolumne Co., Cal., July 25, 1961. RLL.
15 *Philotes battoides intermedia,* ♂. Castle Lake, Siskiyou Co., Cal., July 10, 1931. LACM.
16 *Philotes battoides intermedia,* ♀. Gold Lake, Sierra Co., Cal., July 15, 1935. LACM.
17 *Philotes battoides oregonensis,* ♂. Mt. Thielsen, Douglas Co., Ore., July 13, 1931. LACM.
18 *Philotes battoides oregonensis,* ♀. Crater Lake, Klamath Co., Ore., Aug. 2, 1923. LACM.
19 *Philotes battoides glaucon,* ♂. Bishop Cr., Inyo Co., Cal., May 17, 1937. LACM.
20 *Philotes battoides glaucon,* ♀. Andrews Camp, Bishop Cr., Inyo Co., Cal., June 10, 1935. LACM.
21 *Philotes battoides martini,* ♂, paratype. Oatman, Mohave Co., Ariz., April 17, 1948. LACM.
22 *Philotes battoides martini,* ♀, paratype. Oatman, Mohave Co., Ariz., April 17, 1948. LACM.
23 *Philotes pallescens elvirae,* ♂, paratype. Juniper Hills, Mojave Desert, Los Angeles Co., Cal., Sept. 16, 1964. LACM.
24 *Philotes pallescens elvirae,* ♀, paratype. S.W. of Pearblossom, Mojave Desert, Los Angeles Co., Cal., Aug. 22, 1963. LACM.
25 *Hemiargus ceraunus gyas,* ♂. Vallecitos Stage Station, Anza Desert, San Diego Co., Cal., Sept. 20, 1950. F&JP.
26 *Hemiargus ceraunus gyas,* ♀. Pinery Canyon, Chiricahua Mts., Cochise Co., Ariz., June 20, 1950. F&JP.
27 *Glaucopsyche lygdamus oro,* ♂. Lefthand Canyon, Boulder Co., Colo., June 9, 1946. LACM.
28 *Glaucopsyche lygdamus oro,* ♀. Gregory Canyon, Boulder Co., Colo., May 30, 1948. LACM.
29 *Philotes enoptes tildeni,* ♂, paratype. Del Puerto Canyon, Stanislaus Co., Cal., Aug. 11, 1962. RLL.
30 *Philotes enoptes tildeni,* ♀. Del Puerto Canyon, Stanislaus Co., Cal., Sept. 11, 1963. RLL.
31 *Philotes p. pallescens,* ♂, paratype. Hickman Canyon, Stansbury Mts., Tooele Co., Ut., Aug. 17, 1953. CAS.
32 *Philotes p. pallescens,* ♀, allotype. Little Granite Mt., Dugway Proving Grounds, Tooele Co., Ut., Aug. 20, 1953. CAS.

PLATE 61

William H. Howe

PLATE 62

1 *Papilio brevicauda bretonensis,* ♀. Tabusintac, N.B. AMNH.
2 *Papilio t. troilus,* ♀. Luray, Va., July 29, 1962. USNM.
3 *Papilio rutulus,* ♂. Palo Flechado Pass, Carson Nat. Forest, Colfax Co., N.Mex., June 18, 1959. USNM.
4 *Papilio g. glaucus,* ♀. Ottawa, Kan., April 30, 1945. AMNH.
5 *Papilio g. glaucus,* ♂. Eureka, Mo., Aug. 5, 1963. AMNH.
6 *Papilio g. glaucus,* normal form "turnus." ♀. Greencastle, Ind., Aug. 7, 1944. USNM.

PLATE 62

William H. Howe

1   *Papilio brevicauda bretonensis,* ♀. Tabusintac, N.B. AMNH.
2   *Papilio b. brevicauda,* ♀. Avalon Peninsula, Nfld. AMNH.
3   *Papilio nitra,* ♂. Green Mt., Boulder Co., Colo. JDE.
4   *Papilio zelicaon,* ♂. Topanga Canyon, Los Angeles Co., Cal. LACM.
5   *Papilio indra kaibabensis,* ♀, paratype. Roaring Springs, North Rim, Grand Canyon, Coconino Co., Ariz., Aug. 17, 1945. LACM.
6   *Papilio i. indra,* ♂. Boulder Canyon, Boulder Co., Colo. AMNH.
7   *Papilio indra minori,* ♂. Colorado Nat. Mon., Colo. FER.
8   *Papilio indra pergamus,* ♂. Borrego Nat. Mon., San Diego Co., Cal. JRH.
9   *Papilio bairdii,* ♂. Mingus Mt., Yavapai Co., Ariz. AMNH.
10 *Papilio bairdii,* ♀. Mingus Mt., Yavapai Co., Ariz. AMNH.
11 *Papilio rudkini,* form "comstocki," ♂. Ivanpah Mts., San Bernardino Co., Cal., Sept. 10, 1934. LACM.
12 *Papilio o. oregonius,* ♂. Priest Rapids Dam, Columbia R., Benton Co., Wash. JRH.
13 *Papilio polyxenes asterius,* ♂. Independence, Mo. JRH.
14 *Papilio polyxenes asterius,* ♀. Independence, Mo. JRH.
15 *Papilio polyxenes asterius,* form "pseudoamericus," ♂. Wheeler Expedition, Ariz. AMNH.
16 *Papilio machaon hudsonianus,* ♂. Riding Mts., Man. JRH.

PLATE 63

1

2

3

4

5

6

7

8

9

10

11

12

13

14

15

16

PLATE 64

1 *Papilio rudkini* form "clarki," ♂. Granite Pass, 18 mi. N.E. of Amboy, San Bernardino Co., Cal., Oct. 8, 1967. LACM.

2 *Papilio rudkini* form "clarki," ♀. Scissors Crossing, 8 mi. N.E. of Julion, San Diego Co., Cal. LACM.

3 *Papilio oregonius dodi.* Red Deer River, Drumheller, Alta., Aug. 10, 1967. E&SP.

4 *Papilio rudkini* form "comstocki," ♀. Ivanpah Mts., San Bernardino Co., Cal., Sept. 12, 1935. LACM.

5 *Papilio brevicauda gaspeensis,* ♂. Gaspé Co., Que., July 10, 1934. LACM.

6 *Papilio kahli,* ♂, paratype. Riding Mts., Man., June 16, 1937. LACM.

7 *Papilio gothica,* ♀. East River, 9000 ft., Gunnison Co., Colo., June 23, 1968. LACM.

8 *Papilio machaon aliaska,* ♀. McKinley Nat. Park, Alaska, June 15, 1931. LACM.

PLATE 64

William H. Howe

PLATE 65

1 *Papilio multicaudatus,* ♀. Mammoth Hot Springs, Yellowstone Nat. Park, Wyo., July 9, 1965. USNM.
2 *Papilio cresphontes,* ♂. Kansas City, Mo., July 27, 1964. AMNH.
3 *Papilio thoas autocles,* ♂. Presidio, Veracruz, July 19, 1947. HAF.
4 *Battus polydamas lucayus,* ♂. Miami, Fla. AMNH.
5 *Papilio ornythion,* ♂. Ciudad Mante, Tamaulipas, June 22, 1964. HAF.
6 *Papilio ornythion,* dimorphic, ♀. Ciudad Valles, San Luis Potosí. HAF.

PLATE 65

1

2

3

4

5

6

William H. Howe

PLATE 66

1 *Graphium marcellus,* ♀. Eureka Springs, Ark., May 1, 1965. AMNH.
2 *Graphium marcellus,* form "lecontei," ♀. Hardfish Cr., Franklin Co., Kan., July 7, 1948. AMNH.
3 *Battus p. philenor,* ♂. Noel, Mo., Aug. 8, 1958. AMNH.
4 *Battus philenor,* ♂, underside. Same data as fig. 3.
5 *Papilio palamedes,* ♂. Lake Okeechobee, Fla., Aug. 19, 1958. AMNH.
6 *Papilio palamedes,* ♂, underside. Same data as fig. 5.
7 *Papilio pilumnus,* ♂. Fernando, Cameron Co., Tex., May 18, 1932. LACM.
8 *Papilio eurymedon,* ♂. Yosemite Nat. Park, Cal., June 22, 1964. AMNH.
9 *Papilio eurymedon,* ♂, underside. Same data as fig. 8.
10 *Papilio aristodemus ponceanus,* ♂. Upper Matecumbe Key, Fla., May 22, 1945. LACM.
11 *Papilio aristodemus ponceanus,* ♂, underside. Same data as fig. 10.

PLATE 66

William H. Howe

PLATE 67

1 *Papilio astyalus pallas,* ♂. Ciudad Victoria, Tamaulipas. S&T.
2 *Papilio astyalus pallas,* ♀. Pharr, Tex. S&T.
3 *Papilio ornythion,* ♀. Monterrey, Mexico. FER.
4 *Papilio ornythion,* ♀, underside. Same data as fig. 3.
5 *Papilio indra fordi,* ♂, holotype. Apple Valley, San Bernardino Co., Cal., April 1, 1951. LACM.
6 *Papilio indra martini,* ♀, allotype. Gilroy Canyon, Providence Mts., San Bernardino Co., Cal., Oct. 10, 1964. LACM.
7 *Papilio astyalus pallas,* ♀. Elkhorn Ranch Canyon, Baboquivari Mts., Pima Co., Ariz., July 28, 1949. LACM.
8 *Papilio bairdi,* form "brucei," ♀. Glenwood Springs, Colo., Oct. 5, 1967. LACM.
9 *Papilio anchisiades,* ♂. Llera, Tamaulipas, June 9, 1966. HAF.
10 *Parnassius phoebus hermodur* ♀. Mt. Evans, Clear Creek Co., Colo., Aug. 8, 1965. JDE.

PLATE 67

William H. Howe

PLATE 68

1 *Parnassius phoebus sayii,* ♂. Mt. Roosevelt, nr. Hebron, N.Dak., June 30, 1930. LACM.
2 *Parnassius phoebus sayii,* ♀. Mt. Roosevelt, nr. Hebron, N.Dak., July 3, 1930. LACM.
3 *Parnassius phoebus maximus,* ♂. Beartooth Plat., Mont., Aug. 2, 1940. LACM.
4 *Parnassius phoebus maximus.* ♀. Beartooth Plat., Mont., Aug. 2, 1940. LACM.
5 *Parnassius phoebus alaskaensis,* ♂. McKinley Nat. Park, Alaska, Aug. 6, 1931. LACM.
6 *Parnassius phoebus alaskaensis,* ♀. McKinley Nat. Park, Alaska, Aug. 6, 1931. LACM.
7 *Parnassius phoebus hermodur,* ♂. Telluride, Colo., 8000 ft., July 15, 1941.
8 *Parnassius phoebus olympianus,* ♀. Hurricane Pass, Clallum Co., Wash., Aug. 11, 1936. LACM.
9 *Parnassius phoebus smintheus,* ♂. Plateau Mt., Alta., June 17, 1935. LACM.
10 *Parnassius phoebus smintheus,* ♀. Plateau Mt., Alta., Aug. 30, 1917. LACM.
11 *Parnassius clodius baldur,* ♀. Donner Summit, nr. Truckee, Cal., July 10, 1960. LACM.
12 *Parnassius clodius baldur,* ♂. Donner Pass, nr. Truckee, Cal., June 27, 1960. LACM.
13 *Parnassius clodius altaurus,* ♀. Base of Tetons, Teton Nat. Park, Wyo., July 13, 1925. LACM.
14 *Parnassius clodius altaurus,* ♂. Mammoth Hot Springs, Yellowstone Nat. Park, Wyo., July 9, 1965. LACM.
15 *Parnassius clodius altaurus,* ♂. Dollarside Summit, Sawtooth Mts., Ida., July 23, 1954. LACM.
16 *Parnassius clodius altaurus,* ♀. Trail Cr., Sawtooth Mts., Ida., July 21, 1954. LACM.

PLATE 68

William H. Howe

PLATE 69

1 *Parnassius eversmanni thor,* ♂. McKinley Nat. Park, Alaska. CAS.
2 *Parnassius eversmanni thor,* ♀. McKinley Nat. Park, Alaska. CAS.
3 *Parnassius phoebus behrii,* ♂. Mt. Dana, Tuolumne Co., Cal. CAS.
4 *Parnassius phoebus behrii,* ♀. Mt. Dana, Tuolumne Co., Cal. CAS.
5 *Parnassius phoebus golovinus,* ♀. Nome, Alaska. CAS.
6 *Parnassius phoebus sayii,* ♂. Gothic, Colo. USNM.
7 *Parnassius phoebus sayii,* ♀. Quartz Cr., Gunnison Co., Colo. USNM.
8 *Parnassius phoebus hermodur,* ♀. Cottonwood Pass, San Isabel Nat. Forest, Chaffee Co., Colo. USNM.
9 *Parnassius phoebus magnus,* ♂. Atlin, B.C., July 25, 1914. LACM.
10 *Parnassius phoebus magnus,* ♀. Atlin, B.C., July 25, 1914. LACM.
11 *Parnassius phoebus sternitzkyi,* ♂. Grey Rocks, Shasta Co., Cal. CAS.
12 *Parnassius phoebus sternitzkyi,* ♀. Grey Rocks, Shasta Co., Cal. CAS.
13 *Parnassius phoebus xanthus,* ♂. Wallace, Ida., June 13, 1926. LACM.
14 *Parnassius phoebus xanthus,* ♀. Wallace, Ida., June 13, 1926. LACM.
15 *Parnassius clodius strohbeeni,* ♂. Ben Lomond, Santa Cruz Co., Cal. CAS.
16 *Parnassius clodius shepardi,* ♂. Wawawai, Wash., May 6, 1965. JHS.
17 *Parnassius clodius claudianus,* ♂. Cowichan Lake, Victoria I., B.C., June 18, 1913. LACM.
18 *Parnassius clodius claudianus,* ♀. Fitzgerald, B.C., July 1, 1919. LACM.
19 *Euchloe creusa,* ♂. Atlin, B.C., June 19, 1921. AMNH.
20 *Euchloe creusa,* ♂, underside. Same data as fig. 19.
21 *Eurema dina helios,* ♂. Goulds, Fla., April 20, 1968. JMP.
22 *Eurema dina helios,* ♀. Goulds, Fla., April 6, 1969. JMP.

PLATE 69

1   2   3   4   5

6   7   8   9   10

11   12   13   14

15   16   17   18

19   20   21   22

William H. Howe

PLATE 70

1 *Enantia melite,* ♂. Fortín de las Flores, Veracruz, Aug. 25, 1969. CM.
2 *Enantia melite,* ♀. Fortín de las Flores, Veracruz, Aug. 25, 1969. CM.
3 *Neophasia menapia,* ♂. Fairfax, Wash. JRH.
4 *Neophasia menapia,* ♀. Fairfax, Wash. JRH.
5 *Appias drusilla neumoegenii,* ♂. Coral Gables, Fla. AMNH.
6 *Appias drusilla neumoegenii,* ♀. Matheson Hammock, Dade Co., Fla. AMNH.
7 *Neophasia terlootii,* ♂. Madera Canyon, Santa Cruz Co., Ariz. JRH.
8 *Neophasia terlootii,* ♀. Southern Arizona. AMNH.
9 *Ascia monuste phileta,* ♂. Broward Co., Fla. JRH.
10 *Ascia monuste phileta,* ♀. Broward Co., Fla. JRH.
11 *Ascia josephina josepha,* ♂. Mexcala River, Mexico, Aug. 2, 1944. JDE.
12 *Ascia josephina josepha,* ♀. Pisté, Yucatán, Sept. 9, 1957. JDE.
13 *Pieris p. protodice,* ♂. Miles City, Mont. AMNH.
14 *Pieris p. protodice,* ♀. Shawnee Mission, Kan. JRH.
15 *Pieris occidentalis,* ♂. Calgary, Alta. JRH.
16 *Pieris rapae,* ♂. Niagara Co., N.Y. AMNH.
17 *Pieris beckerii,* ♂. Ohio City, Colo. AMNH.
18 *Pieris beckerii,* ♀. Richland, Wash. JRH.
19 *Pieris napi oleracea,* ♂. Montmorency Co., Mich. JRH.
20 *Pieris napi pseudobryoniae,* ♀. Site Summit, nr. Anchorage, Alaska. JRH.
21 *Pieris s. sisymbri,* ♂. Mill Creek Canyon, Salt Lake Co., Ut. JRH.
22 *Pieris s. sisymbri,* ♀. Mueller Park, Davis Co., Ut. JRH.
23 *Pieris virginiensis,* ♂. Whately, Mass. JRH.
24 *Pieris napi venosa,* ♂. Boulder Cr., Santa Cruz Co., Cal. JRH.

PLATE 70

William H. Howe

PLATE 71

1 *Anteos clorinde nivifera,* ♂. Patagonia Mts., Santa Cruz Co., Ariz., Aug. 22, 1951. LACM.
2 *Phoebis statira floridensis,* ♂. St. Petersburg, Fla. JRH.
3 *Phoebis statira jada,* ♀. San Antonio, Tex. AMNH.
4 *Kricogonia castalia,* ♂. Pharr, Tex. HAF.
5 *Kricogonia castalia,* ♀. Brownsville, Tex., Nov. 15, 1949. LACM.
6 *Anthocharis s. sara,* ♀. Alum Rock Park, Santa Clara Co., Cal., June 4, 1967. USNM.
7 *Anthocharis cethura* form, "caliente," ♂. Vallecito, San Diego Co., Cal., March 6, 1937. LACM.
8 *Anthocharis s. sara,* ab. "dammersi," ♂, type. Whitewater Canyon, Riverside Co., Cal. LACM.
9 *Anthocharis s. sara,* ♂. Alum Rock Park, Santa Clara Co., Cal., June 4, 1967. USNM.
10 *Anthocharis cethura,* ♂. Sweetwater Lake, San Diego Co., Cal. OS.
11 *Anthocharis cethura,* ♀. Dictionary Hill, Spring Valley, San Diego Co., Cal. OS.
12 *Anthocharis pima,* ♂. "A" Mountain, Tucson, Ariz. JRH.
13 *Anthocharis pima,* ♀. Bumblebee, Yavapai Co., Ariz. JRH.
14 *Anthocharis s. sara,* form "reakirti," ♂. McDonald Forest, Corvallis, Ore. JRH.
15 *Anthocharis s. sara,* form "reakirti," ♀. El Cajon, Cal. FTT.
16 *Anthocharis sara stella,* ♀. Antilon Lake, Chelan Co., Wash. JRH.
17 *Anthocharis midea annickae,* ♂. Rock Ridge [= West Rock?], New Haven, Conn. JRH.
18 *Anthocharis m. midea,* ♀. Sugar Creek, Jackson Co., Mo. JRH.
19 *Anthocharis m. midea,* ♂. Wilmington I., nr. Savannah, Ga., April 11, 1947. AMNH.
20 *Anthocharis lanceolata,* ♂. Mather, Yosemite Nat. Park, Cal. AMNH.
21 *Anthocharis lanceolata,* ♀. Jacumba, San Diego Co., Cal. SRH.
22 *Euchloe h. hyantis,* ♂. Stansbury Mts., Tooele Co., Ut. JRH.
23 *Euchloe creusa,* ♀. Golden B.C. JRH.
24 *Euchloe olympia rosa,* ♂. Chippewa Hills, Franklin Co., Kan., April 30, 1944. AMNH.
25 *Euchloe olympia rosa,* ♀. Chippewa Hills, Franklin Co., Kan., May 5, 1963. AMNH.
26 *Euchloe ausonides,* ♂. Pittsburg, Cal. JRH.
27 *Euchloe ausonides,* ♀. Pittsburg, Cal. JRH.

PLATE 71

William H Howe

1   *Eurema d. daira,* winter form, ♂. Jacksonville, Fla. JRH.
2   *Eurema d. daira,* winter form, ♀. Key Largo, Fla. JRH.
3   *Eurema d. daira,* summer form, ♂. Southern Pines, N.C. JRH.
4   *Eurema d. daira,* summer form, ♀. Southern Pines, N.C. JRH.
5   *Eurema boisduvaliana,* ♂. Brownsville, Tex. JRH.
6   *Eurema boisduvaliana,* ♀. Brownsville, Tex. JRH.
7   *Eurema mexicana,* ♂. California Gulch, Santa Cruz Co., Ariz. JRH.
8   *Eurema mexicana,* ♀. Homewood, Kan. AMNH.
9   *Eurema p. proterpia,* summer form, ♂. California Gulch, Santa Cruz Co., Ariz. JRH.
10 *Eurema p. proterpia,* summer form, ♀. Madera Canyon, Santa Rita Mts., Ariz. JDE.
11 *Eurema p. proterpia,* winter form, ♂. El Salto, San Luis Potosí. AMNH.
12 *Eurema p. proterpia,* winter form, ♀. Hidalgo, Tex., Nov. 7, 1953. JDE.
13 *Eurema messalina blakei,* ♂. New Providence I., Bahamas, June 13, 1960. AMNH.
14 *Eurema daira palmira,* ♂. Coral Gables, Fla., Oct. 22, 1965. JMP.
15 *Eurema daira* × *palmira,* ♀. Upper Largo Key, Fla. July 15, 1967. JMP.
16 *Eurema salome limoneus,* ♂. Yepocapa, Guatemala, Oct. 23, 1947. AMNH.
17 *Eurema l. lisa,* ♂. Garnett, Kans. AMNH.
18 *Eurema l. lisa,* ♀. Roscoe, Mo. JRH.
19 *Eurema l. lisa* albinic ♀. Sugar Creek, Jackson Co., Mo. JRH.
20 *Eurema nise,* ♂. Santa Ana Res., Hidalgo Co., Tex. JRH.
21 *Eurema nise,* ♀. Santa Ana Res., Hidalgo Co., Tex. JRH.
22 *Eurema dina westwoodi,* ♂. Brownsville, Tex. AMNH.
23 *Eurema nicippe,* ♂. Shawnee Mission, Johnson Co., Kan., Oct. 2, 1962. JRH.
24 *Eurema nicippe,* ♀. Holliday, Johnson Co., Kan. Sept. 29, 1962. JRH.

PLATE 72

William H. Howe

PLATE 73

1   *Colias s. scudderii,* ♂. Above Gold Creek Camp, Gunnison Co., Colo. AMNH.
2   *Colias s. scudderii,* ♀. Copper Lake Trail, Gothic, Gunnison Co., Colo. AMNH.
3   *Colias g. gigantea,* ♂. Churchill, Man. AMNH.
4   *Colias a. alexandra,* ♂. Marshall Pass, Saguache Co., Colo. AMNH.
5   *Colias a. alexandra,* ♀. Marshall Pass., Saguache Co., Colo. AMNH.
6   *Colias g. gigantea,* ♀. Churchill, Man. AMNH.
7   *Colias alexandra astraea,* ♂ (orange, *christina*-like form). Mt. Inabnit, Carbon Co., Mont. USNM.
8   *Colias nastes thula,* ♂, paratype. 70° 45′ × 156° 30′, near Meade R., Terr. of Alaska. AMNH.
9   *Colias eurytheme,* melanic, ♀. Mears Park, Franklin Co., Kans. AMNH.
10 *Colias p. pelidne,* ♂. Ungava Bay, Fort Chimo, P.Q. JDE.
11 *Colias p. pelidne,* ♂, underside, same specimen.
12 *Colias p. pelidne,* ♂. Nain, Labrador. JDE.
13 *Colias pelidne minisni,* ♀. Marsh Creek, Custer Co., Idaho. JDE.
14 *Colias palaeno chippewa,* ♂. Knik, Alaska. JDE.
15 *Colias palaeno chippewa,* ♂, underside, same specimen.
16 *Colias palaeno chippewa,* ♀. McKinley Natl. Park, Alaska. JDE.
17 *Colias nastes moina,* ♂. Churchill, Man., July 30, 1942. JDE.
18 *Colias nastes streckeri,* ♂. Plateau Mtn., Alta. JRH.
19 *Colias nastes streckeri,* ♀. Bow Pass, Alta. JRH.
20 *Colias behrii,* ♂. Tioga Pass, Yosemite Natl Park, Calif. AMNH.
21 *Colias behrii,* ♀. Tuolumne Meadows, Yosemite Natl. Park, Calif. AMNH.

PLATE 73

William H. Howe

PLATE 74

1   *Colias m. meadii,* ♂. Copper Lake Trail, Gothic, Gunnison Co., Colo., July 14, 1963. AMNH.
2   *Colias m. meadii,* ♀. Cottonwood Pass, San Isabel Nat. Forest, Chaffee Co., Colo. July 24, 1963. AMNH.
3   *Colias m. meadii,* albinic, ♀. Upper Quartz Creek, Gunnison Co., Colo., July 14, 1963. JRH.
4   *Colias meadii elis,* ♂. Bow Pass, S. of Peyto Lake, Banff Nat. Park, Alta., Aug. 14, 1959. JDE.
5   *Colias meadii elis,* ♀. Bow Pass, Alta. JRH.
6   *Colias hecla glacialis,* ♂. Sable Pass, McKinley Nat. Park, Alaska, July 11, 1956. JDE.
7   *Colias boothii,* ♂. Dist. of Keewatin, N.W.Terr., Aug. 2, 1947.
8   *Colias boothii,* ♀. Baker Lake, N.W.Terr., July, 1960. AMNH.
9   *Colias hecla glacialis,* ♂. McKinley Nat. Park, Alaska, July 12, 1956. JDE.
10 *Colias interior,* ♂. Sudbury, Ont., July 12, 1958. AMNH.
11 *Colias interior,* ♀. Geraldton, Ont., July 16, 1954. AMNH.
12 *Colias harfordii,* ♂. Pine Canyon, Tejon Mts., Los Angeles Co., Cal., May 26, 1934. JDE.
13 *Colias occidentalis chrysomelas,* ♂. Lakoya Lodge, Sonoma Co., Cal., June 8, 1946.
14 *Colias chrysomelas,* ♀. Hoberg's, Lake Co., Cal., June 20, 1961. JDE.
15 *Colias harfordii,* ♀. Laguna Mts., San Diego Co., Cal., May 6, 1962. JDE.
16 *Colias o. occidentalis,* ♂. Naches River, Kittitas Co., Wash., July 11, 1955. JDE.
17 *Colias o. occidentalis* albinic, ♀. Ochoco Mts., Crook Co., Ore., July 23, 1962. JDE.
18 *Colias o. occidentalis,* ♀. Wellington, Victoria I., B.C., June 17, 1956. JDE.

PLATE 74

1

2

3

4

5

6

7

8

9

10

11

12

13

14

15

16

17

18

William H. Howe

1 *Colias eurytheme,* summer form, ♂. St. Joseph, Mo. JRH.
2 *Colias eurytheme,* summer form, ♀. Independence, Mo. JRH.
3 *Colias eurytheme,* albinic, ♀. Pleasant Hill, Mo. JRH.
4 *Colias eurytheme,* spring form, ♂. Independence, Mo.
5 *Colias eurytheme,* spring form, ♀. Willimantic, Conn. AMNH.
6 *Colias f. philodice,* ♂. Prairie Village, Johnson Co., Kan. JRH.
7 *Colias p. philodice,* ♀. Shawnee Mission, Johnson Co., Kan. JRH.
8 *Colias p. philodice,* albinic ♀. Prairie Village, Johnson Co., Kan. JRH.
9 *Colias philodice,* form "eriphyle," ♂. Olney Springs, Colo. JRH.
10 *Colias philodice,* form "eriphyle," ♀. Big Timber, Mont. JRH.
11 *Colias eurytheme × philodice,* ♂. Holliday, Kan. JRH.
12 *Colias eurytheme × philodice,* ♂. Atherton, Mo. JRH.
13 *Colias eurydice,* ♂. Lake Arrowhead, San Bernardino Co., Cal. JRH.
14 *Colias eurydice,* ♂. Roscoe Park, Los Angeles Co., Cal. JRH.
15 *Colias cesonia,* ♂. Baldwin Hill, Kan., July 4, 1951. AMNH.
16 *Colias cesonia,* ♀. Cape Fair, Mo., Aug. 12, 1950. AMNH.
17 *Colias eurydice,* ♀. Atascadero, Cal. AMNH.
18 *Colias eurydice,* form "amorphae," ♀. Pine Mt., Los Padres Nat. Forest, Ventura Co., Cal. JRH.
19 *Colias cesonia,* form "rosa," ♂. Decatur, Ark., Sept. 29, 1963. AMNH.
20 *Colias cesonia,* form "rosa," ♀. Baldwin Hill, Kan., Oct. 2, 1949. AMNH.
21 *Colias cesonia,* form "rosa," ♀, underside. Same data as fig. 20.
22 *Nathalis iole,* ♂. Olney Springs, Colo. AMNH.
23 *Nathalis iole,* ♀. Bazaar, Kan. AMNH.
24 *Eurema chamberlaini,* ♀. Landrail Pt., Crooked I., Bahama Is. AMNH.
25 *Eurema chamberlaini,* ♀. Landrail Pt., Crooked I., Bahama Is. AMNH.

PLATE 75

1

2

3

4

5

6

7

8

9

10

11

12

13

14

15

16

17

18

19

20

21

22

23

24

25

William H. Howe

PLATE 76

1 *Phoebis sennae marcellina,* ♂. Santa Cruz, Cal., Aug. 10, 1941. USNM.
2 *Phoebis sennae marcellina,* ♀. Santa Cruz, Cal., Aug. 23, 1941. USNM.
3 *Phoebis sennae eubule,* ♀. Ottawa, Kan., Aug. 16, 1945. AMNH.
4 *Phoebis senna eubule,* form "browni," ♀. Baldwin Hill, Kan., Sept. 9, 1948. AMNH.
5 *Phoebis philea,* ♂. Jacksonville, Fla. AMNH.
6 *Phoebis philea,* ♀. Jacksonville, Fla. AMNH.
7 *Phoebis agarithe maxima,* ♂. Key Vaca, Fla., Aug. 15, 1958. AMNH.
8 *Phoebis agarithe maxima,* ♀. Key Largo, Fla., Dec. 2, 1940. AMNH.
9 *Phoebis neocypris bracteolata,* ♂. Douglas, Ariz. LACM.
10 *Anteos maerula lacordairei,* ♀. Boca de la Sierra, Baja Cal. Sur, Oct. 13, 1961. CM.
11 *Ascia monuste phileta,* ♀. Big Pine Key, Fla. USNM.
12 *Ascia monuste raza,* ♂. Scammons Lagoon, Baja Cal., May 4, 1926. AMNH.
13 *Anthocharis sara alaskensis,* ♂. Skagway, Alaska, May 22, 1923. LACM.
14 *Anthocharis sara browningi,* ♂. City Creek Canyon, Salt Lake City, Ut., May 29, 1929. LACM.
15 *Anthocharis sara inghami,* ♂. Mayer, Yavapai Co., Ariz., Feb. 22, 1961. AMNH.
16 *Euchloe hyantis lotta,* ♂. Phelan, Cal., March 23, 1931. LACM.
17 *Euchloe ausonides mayi,* ♀. Riding Mts., Man., June 27, 1932. LACM.
18 *Euchloe ausonides andrewsi,* ♂, paratype. Lake Arrowhead, San Bernardino Co., Cal., June 10, 1936. LACM.
19 *Pieris sisymbrii flavitincta,* ♂. Whitehorse, Yukon Terr., June 9, 1923. LACM.
20 *Pieris sisymbrii flavitincta,* ♀. Mt. Robson, B.C., April 28, 1935. LACM.
21 *Pieris sisymbrii elivata,* ♂. Flagstaff Mt., Boulder Co., Colo., April 24, 1954. LACM.
22 *Pieris sisymbrii elivata,* ♀. Jemez Springs, Sandoval Co., N.Mex., April 30, 1924. LACM.
23 *Pieris p. protodice,* form "vernalis," ♀. Willis Woods, Franklin Co., Kan., March 10, 1954. LACM.
24 *Pieris p. protodice,* form "vernalis," ♂. Mears Park, Franklin Co., Kan., April 21, 1951. LACM.

PLATE 76

William H. Howe

PLATE 77

1   *Papilio andraemon bonhotei,* ♂. AMNH.
2   *Dione moneta,* ♂. Chiapas, Mexico. AMNH.
3   *Lycorea ceres atergatis,* ♂. Fortín de las Flores, Veracruz, Aug. 25, 1969. CM.
4   *Anaea aidea,* form "morrisoni," ♀. Mercedes, Tex., Nov. 6, 1968. AMNH.
5   *Apodemia mormo duryi,* ♂. Mesilla Park, Dona Ana Co., N.Mex., Sept. 5, 1961. JAP.
6   *Apodemia mormo duryi,* ♀. Mesilla Park, Dona Ana Co., N.Mex., Sept. 5, 1961. JAP.
7   *Erebia rossii gabrieli,* ♂. Wonder Lake, McKinley Nat. Park, Alaska, July 2, 1955. AMNH.
8   *Erebia youngi rileyi,* ♂. Wonder Lake, McKinley Nat. Park, Alaska, July 2, 1955. AMNH.
9   *Phyciodes tharos pascoensis,* ♂. Buckboard Flat, Abajo Mts., San Juan Co., Ut., July 16, 1969. USNM.
10 *Phyciodes tharos pascoensis,* ♀. Buckboard Flat, Abajo Mts., San Juan Co., Ut., July 16, 1969. USNM.
11 *Chlosyne palla flavula,* ♂. Upper Hobble Creek, Utah Co., Ut., July 4, 1969. DLB.
12 *Chlosyne palla flavula,* ♀. Rabbit Ears Pass, Routt Co., Colo., July 23, 1955.
13 *Erebia r. rossii,* ♂. Whitefish, nr. Tuktoyaktuk, N.W.Terr., July 14, 1955. AMNH.
14 *Chlosyne leanira alma,* ♀. Colorado Nat. Mon., Mesa Co., Colo., May 18, 1961. DLB.
15 *Oeneis polixenes peartiae,* ♂. Norman Wells, N.W.Terr., June 26, 1949. CNC.
16 *Cercyonis pegala damei,* ♂, topotype. Roaring Springs Canyon, 6700 ft., North Kaibab Trail, Grand Canyon, Ariz., Aug. 22, 1964. TCE.
17 *Oeneis m. melissa,* ♂. Frobisher Bay, Baffin I., June 27, 1948. CNC.
18 *Oeneis m. melissa,* ♀. Frobisher Bay, Baffin I., June 23, 1948. CNC.

PLATE 77

5

6

7

8

9

11

10

2

12

13

14

15

3

17

16

4

18

William H. Howe

1   *Coenonympha ampelos insulana,* ♂. Tenino, Thurston Co., Wash., May 18, 1946. JDE.
2   *Coenonympha ampelos insulana,* ♀. Oak Bay, B.C., June 30, 1953. JDE.
3   *Coenonympha california eryngii,* ♂. Yukon Courts, Inyo Co., Cal., Sept. 10, 1944. JDE.
4   *Coenonympha california eryngii,* form "siskiyouensis," ♂. Butte Falls, Ore., May 23, 1931. JDE.
5   *Phyciodes campestris camillus,* ♀. Buckboard Flat, Abajo Mts., San Juan Co., Ut., July 15, 1969. USNM.
6   *Phyciodes pallida barnesi,* ♀. Buckboard Flat, Abajo Mts., San Juan Co., Ut., July 15, 1969. CM.
7   *Erebia vidleri,* ♀. Kelowna, B.C., July, 1916. AMNH.
8   *Papilio glaucus canadensis,* ♂. Chitina, Alaska, May 23, 1953. JDE.
9   *Plebejus aquilo,* ssp. near *bryanti,* ♂. Eagle, Alaska, June 18, 1936. LACM.
10 *Plebejus aquilo,* ssp. near *bryanti,* ♀. Mt. Dewey Glacier, Alaska, July 7, 1923. LACM.
11 *Pieris napi hulda,* ♂. Anchorage, Alaska, July 7, 1951. CNC.
12 *Coenonympha k. kodiak* (ssp. ?), ♂. Anchorage, Alaska, June 27, 1951. CNC.
13 *Coenonympha ochracea mackenziei,* ♂. Fort Smith, N.W.Terr., June 28, 1950. CNC.
14 *Coenonympha ochracea mackenziei,* ♀. Fort Simpson, N.W.Terr., July 17, 1950. CNC.
15 *Dymasia c. chara,* ♂. Yuma, Ariz., Sept. 14, 1946. DLB.
16 *Dymasia c. chara,* ♀. Santa Catalina Mts., Pima Co., Ariz., Sept. 17, 1947. DLB.
17 *Parnassius clodius sol,* ♂. Yosemite Nat. Park, Tuolumne Co., Cal., 5000 ft., June 26, 1964. USNM.
18 *Parnassius clodius menetriesii,* ♂. Bear Canyon, nr. Mt. Nebo, Juab Co., Ut., July 10, 1969. CM.
19 *Colias a. alexandra,* form "emilia," ♂. Alpine Loop Road, 7500 ft., Utah Co., Ut., July 10, 1969. CM.
20 *Colias scudderii ruckesi,* ♂. Santa Fe Ski Area, N.Mex., Aug. 2, 1964. AMNH.
21 *Satyrium l. liparops,* ♂. Statenville, Echols Co., Ga., May 18, 1967. CM.
22 *Thereus palegon,* ♂, underside. Colima, Mexico, March 23, 1967. CM.
23 Same data as fig. 22.
24 *Allosmaitia pion,* ♂. "Guatemala." CM.
25 *Ocaria ocrisia,* ♂. Ciudad Valles, San Luis Potosí, June 7, 1968. CM.

PLATE 78

William H. Howe

PLATE 79

1 *Megathymus ursus violae,* ♀. Carlsbad Nat. Park, N.Mex. S&T.
2 *Agathymus aryxna,* ♀. Sonoita, Ariz. S&T.
3 *Agathymus aryxna,* ♂. Sonoita, Ariz. S&T.
4 *Megathymus u. ursus,* ♀. Madera Canyon, Santa Rita Mts., Santa Cruz Co., Ariz., July 7, 1956. S&T.
5 *Agathymus alliae,* ♀, paratype. 15 mi. W. of Cameron, Ariz., Oct. 3, 1953. S&T.
6 *Agathymus alliae,* ♂, paratype. 15 mi W. of Cameron, Ariz., Sept. 16, 1954. S&T.
7 *Megathymus s. streckeri,* ♀. Petrified Forest, Ariz., May 25, 1949. S&T.
8 *Megathymus yuccae wilsonorum,* ♀, paratype. Ciudad Victoria, Tamaulipas, Feb. 17, 1954. S&T.
9 *Agathymus n. neumoegeni,* ♂. Jerome, Ariz., Sept. 16, 1961. S&T.

PLATE 79

1

2

4

3

5

7

6

8

9

William H. Howe

PLATE 80

1 *Agathymus neumoegeni diabloensis,* ♂, paratype. Victoria Canyon, Tex., Sept. 1, 1960. HAF.
2 *Agathymus neumoegeni diabloensis,* ♀, paratype. Victoria Canyon, Tex., Sept. 15, 1960. HAF.
3 *Megathymus yuccae,* form "winkensis," ♀, paratype. Wink, Tex., April 10, 1963. HAF.
4 *Megathymus yuccae reinthali,* ♀, paratype. Tyler State Park, Smith Co., Tex., March 25, 1963. HAF.
5 *Megathymus yuccae reinthali,* ♂, paratype. Tyler State Park, Smith Co., Tex., March 22, 1950. HAF.
6 *Agathymus m. mariae,* ♂, topotype. El Paso, Tex., Oct. 8, 1950. HAF.
7 *Megathymus yuccae,* form "kendalli," ♂, paratype. San Antonio, Tex., May 9, 1950. HAF.
8 *Megathymus y. yuccae,* ♂. Pensacola, Fla., Feb. 24, 1954. S&T.
9 *Megathymus yuccae,* form "louiseae," ♀, paratype. Del Rio, Tex., May 10, 1960. HAF.
10 *Megathymus yuccae,* form "buchholzi," ♀, paratype. Jupiter, Fla., April 13, 1947. HAF.
11 *Agathymus mariae rindgei,* ♂, paratype. Del Rio, Tex., Oct. 21, 1961. HAF.
12 *Agathymus mariae rindgei,* ♀, paratype. Del Rio, Tex., Oct. 29, 1961. HAF.
13 *Agathymus mariae chinatiensis,* ♂, paratype. Chinati Mts., Presidio Co., Tex., 4350 ft., Oct. 1, 1960. HAF.
14 *Agathymus mariae chinatiensis,* ♀, paratype. Shafter, Tex., Oct. 12, 1957. HAF.
15 *Agathymus mariae lajitaensis,* ♂, paratype. Lajitas, Tex., Oct. 12, 1962. HAF.
16 *Agathymus mariae lajitaensis,* ♀, paratype. Lajitas. Tex., Sept. 28, 1962. HAF.

PLATE 80

6

1

11

7

2

12

8

3

13

9

4

14

10

5

15

16

William H. Howe

1 *Agathymus estelleae valverdiensis,* ♂, allotype. 28 mi. N. of Del Rio, Tex., Oct. 13, 1963. HAF.
2 *Agathymus gilberti,* ♂, paratype. Bracketville, Tex., Oct. 13, 1959. HAF.
3 *Agathymus polingi,* ♂. Mt. Lemmon, nr. Tucson, Ariz., 5500 ft., Oct. 8, 1960. HAF.
4 *Agathymus baueri freemani,* ♂. Hillside, Ariz., Oct. 2, 1961. S&T.
5 *Agathymus stephensi,* ♂. San Felipe Valley, San Diego Co., Cal., Oct. 20, 1956. HAF.
6 *Agathymus polingi,* ♀. Mt. Lemmon, nr. Tucson, Ariz., 5500 ft., Oct. 8, 1960. HAF.
7 *Agathymus baueri freemani,* ♀. Hillside, Ariz., Oct. 15, 1966. S&T.
8 *Agathymus n. neumoegeni,* ♀. Jerome, Ariz., Sept. 13, 1961. S&T.
9 *Agathymus neumoegeni judithae,* ♀, paratype. 10 mi. E. of Hueco, Tex., in Hueco Mts., 5300 ft., Sept. 25, 1954. S&T.
10 *Agathymus neumoegeni florenceae,* ♀, paratype. Ft. Davis, Tex., 6200 ft., Oct. 1, 1954. S&T.
11 *Agathymus b. baueri,* ♀. Verde Hot Springs, Ariz., Sept. 27, 1961. S&T.
12 *Agathymus b. baueri,* ♂. Verde Hot Springs, Ariz., Sept. 27, 1961. S&T.
13 *Agathymus evansi,* ♂. Ramsey Canyon, Ariz., Sept. 3, 1950. S&T.
14 *Megathymus yuccae coloradensis,* ♂. Springfield, Colo., Sept. 9, 1956. S&T.

PLATE 81

William H. Howe

1   *Megathymus yuccae reubeni,* ♀. Hueco Mts., Hudspeth Co., Tex. S&T.
2   *Megathymus y. yuccae,* ♀. Greensboro, Ga. S&T.
3   *Megathymus yuccae coloradensis,* ♀. Springfield, Colo. S&T.
4   *Megathymus streckeri texanus,* ♂. Pampa, Tex. S&T.
5   *Megathymus streckeri texanus,* ♀. Pampa, Tex. S&T.
6   *Megathymus s. streckeri,* ♂. Petrified Forest, Ariz. S&T.
7   *Megathymus c. cofaqui,* ♂. Longboat Key, Sarasota, Fla. S&T.
8   *Megathymus c. cofaqui,* ♀. Longboat Key, Sarasota, Fla. S&T.
9   *Agathymus evansi,* ♀. Ramsey Canyon, Huachuca Mts., Cochise Co., Ariz., Sept. 1, 1950. HAF.
10 *Megathymus cofaqui harrisi,* ♂. Harris Trail, Ga., Aug. 8, 1955, *ex larva.* HAF.
11 *Cogia h. hippalus,* ♂. Nogales, Ariz., July 14, 1964. HAF.
12 *Agathymus neumoegeni mcalpinei,* ♂. Marathon, Tex. HAF.
13 *Agathymus neumoegeni chisosensis,* ♀, topotype. Chisos Mts., Big Bend Nat. Park, Tex. HAF.
14 *Urbanus teleus,* ♂. Ciudad Valles, San Luis Potosi, Aug. 19, 1967. HAF.
15 *Agathymus neumoegeni mcalpinei,* ♀. Marathon, Tex. HAF.

PLATE 82

1

2

3

4

5

6

7

8

9

10

11

12

13

14

15

William H. Howe

PLATE 83

1 *Agathymus neumoegeni carlsbadensis,* ♂. Guadeloupe Mts., nr. Nickle, Tex. S&T.
2 *Agathymus neumoegeni carlsbadensis,* ♀. Guadeloupe Mts., nr. Nickle, Tex. S&T.
3 *Megathymus yuccae navajo,* ♀. Grand Canyon, Ariz. S&T.
4 *Stallingsia maculosus,* ♀. Sinton, Tex. S&T.
5 *Agathymus m. mariae,* ♀. Hueco Mts., Hudspeth Co., Tex. S&T.
6 *Megathymus yuccae martini,* ♀. Little Rock, Cal. S&T.
7 *Thespieus macareus,* ♂. Oaxaca, Mexico, June 23, 1966. HAF.
8 *Panoquina hecebolus,* ♂. Pharr, Tex., Oct. 15, 1944. HAF.
9 *Panoquina hecebolus,* ♂, underside. Same data as fig. 8.
10 *Nyctelius nyctelius,* ♂. Ciudad Valles, San Luis Potosí. S&T.
11 *Panoquina panoquin,* ♂. Ft. George, Duval Co., Fla. JRH.
12 *Panoquina panoquin,* ♀. Ft. George, Duval Co., Fla. JRH.
13 *Panoquina panoquinoides,* ♂. Padre I., Tex. JRH.
14 *Panoquina panoquinoides,* ♀. Padre I., Tex. JRH.
15 *Panoquina ocola,* ♀. Hollywood, Broward Co., Fla. JRH.
16 *Panoquina sylvicola,* ♂. Pharr, Tex. S&T.
17 *Panoquina errans,* ♂. Glendora, Cal., Oct. 1, 1930. HAF.
18 *Pellicia arina,* ♂. Ciudad Valles, San Luis Potosí, June 9, 1966. HAF.
19 *Panoquina ocola,* ♂. Bighton, Fla. JRH.
20 *Panoquina evansi,* ♂. Acahuezotla, Guerrero, July 15, 1960. HAF.
21 *Panoquina evansi,* ♂, underside. Same data as fig. 20.
22 *Calpodes ethlius,* ♂. Lehigh Acres, Lee Co., Fla. JRH.
23 *Calpodes ethlius,* ♀. Coral Gables, Fla. JRH.
24 *Oligoria maculata,* ♂. Jekyll I., Ga. JRH.
25 *Oligoria maculata,* ♀. Pensacola, Fla. JRH.
26 *Lerodea eufala,* ♂. Hollywood, Fla. JRH.
27 *Lerodea eufala,* ♀. Tucson, Ariz. JRH.

PLATE 83

PLATE 84

1   *Lerodea arabus,* ♂. Ciudad Victoria, Tamaulipas. HAF.
2   *Lerodea dysaules,* ♀. Brownsville, Tex. CDM.
3   *Amblyscirtes exoteria,* ♂. Madera Canyon, Santa Cruz Co., Ariz. HAF.
4   *Amblyscirtes exoteria,* ♀. Madera Canyon, Santa Cruz Co., Ariz. HAF.
5   *Amblyscirtes simius,* ♂. Palo Duro Canyon, Tex. HAF.
6   *Amblyscirtes simius,* ♀. Palo Duro Canyon, Tex. HAF.
7   *Amblyscirtes cassus,* ♂. Madera Canyon, Santa Cruz Co., Ariz. JRH.
8   *Amblyscirtes cassus,* ♀. Madera Canyon, Santa Cruz Co., Ariz. JRH.
9   *Amblyscirtes aenus,* ♂. Bluebell Canyon, Boulder Co., Colo. JRH.
10 *Amblyscirtes oslari,* ♂. Red Rocks Canyon, Jefferson Co., Colo. JRH.
11 *Amblyscirtes oslari,* ♀. Red Rocks Canyon Jefferson Co., Colo. JRH.
12 *Amblyscirtes erna,* ♂. Wichita Mts., Okla. S&T.
13 *Amblyscirtes erna,* ♀. Barber Co., Kan. S&T.
14 *Amblyscirtes aenus,* ♀. Eureka Springs, Ark. JRH.
15 *Amblyscirtes hegon,* ♂. Eureka Springs, Ark. JRH.
16 *Amblyscirtes hegon,* ♀. Atlanta, Ga. JRH.
17 *Amblyscirtes texanae,* ♂. Davis Mts., Jeff Davis Co., Tex. HAF.
18 *Amblyscirtes texanae,* ♀. Alpine, Texas. HAF.
19 *Amblyscirtes prenda,* ♂. Tepic, Nayarit. S&T.
20 *Amblyscirtes aesculapius,* ♂. Jericho Ditch, Nansemond Co., Va. HAF.
21 *Amblyscirtes aesculapius,* ♀. Lutie, Ozark Co., Mo. USNM.
22 *Amblyscirtes carolina,* ♂. Wallaceton, Suffolk Co., Va. JRH.
23 *Amblyscirtes carolina,* ♀. Wallaceton, Suffolk Co., Va. JRH.
24 *Amblyscirtes linda,* ♂, paratype. Hope Hill Farm, Faulkner Co., Ark. HAF.
25 *Amblyscirtes nereus,* ♂. Mt. Locke, Davis Mts., Jeff Davis Co., Tex. JRH.
26 *Amblyscirtes nereus,* ♀. Davis Mts., Jeff Davis Co., Tex. HAF.
27 *Amblyscirtes nysa,* ♂. Independence, Mo. JRH.
28 *Amblyscirtes nysa,* ♀. Independence, Mo. JRH.
29 *Amblyscirtes eos,* ♂. Worth Ranch, Palo Pinto Co., Tex. HAF.
30 *Amblyscirtes vialis,* ♂. Mother Cabrini Shrine, Jefferson Co., Colo. HAF.
31 *Amblyscirtes vialis,* ♀. Hermitage, Mo. JRH.
32 *Amblyscirtes celia,* ♂. Brownsville, Tex. HAF.
33 *Amblyscirtes celia,* ♀. Brownsville, Tex. HAF.
34 *Amblyscirtes eos,* ♀. Davis Mts., Jeff Davis Co., Tex. HAF.
35 *Amblyscirtes alternata,* ♂. Tyler State Park, Smith Co., Tex. HAF.
36 *Amblyscirtes alternata,* ♀. Cherry Pt., Craven Co., N.Car. HAF.
37 *Amblyscirtes belli,* ♂, paratype. Vickery, Tex. HAF.
38 *Amblyscirtes phylace,* ♂. Golden, Colo. JRH.
39 *Amblyscirtes fimbriata,* ♂. Hamburg Mine, Huachuca Mts., Cochise Co., Ariz. JRH.

PLATE 84

William H. Howe

1   *Atrytonopsis hianna,* ♂. Cherry Pt., Craven Co., N.Car. S&T.
2   *Atrytonopsis hianna,* ♀. Monroe Canyon, Sioux Co., Nebr. S&T.
3   *Atrytonopsis deva,* ♂. Rustler's Park, Chiricahua Mts., Cochise Co., Ariz. S&T.
4   *Atrytonopsis deva,* ♀. Rustler's Park, Chiricahua Mts., Cochise Co., Ariz. S&T.
5   *Atrytonopsis loammi,* ♂. Orlando, Fla. S&T.
6   *Atrytonopsis loammi,* ♀. Orlando, Fla. S&T.
7   *Atrytonopsis vierecki,* ♂. Folsom, N.Mex. S&T.
8   *Atrytonopsis vierecki,* ♀. Kim, Colo. S&T.
9   *Atrytonopsis lunus,* ♂. Onion Saddle, Chiricahua Mts., Cochise Co., Ariz., July 11, 1960. HAF.
10   *Atrytonopsis lunus,* ♀. Madera Canyon, Santa Rita Mts., Santa Cruz Co., Ariz., July 27, 1958. HAF.
11   *Atrytonopsis pittacus,* ♂. Madera Canyon, Santa Rita Mts., Santa Cruz Co., Ariz. S&T.
12   *Atrytonopsis pittacus,* ♀. Alpine, Tex. HAF.
13   *Atrytonopsis p. python,* ♂. Chiricahua Mts., Cochise Co., Ariz. S&T.
14   *Atrytonopsis p. python,* ♀. Chiricahua Mts., Cochise Co., Ariz. S&T.
15   *Atrytonopsis cestus,* ♂. Sycamore Canyon, W. side of Baboquivari Mts., Pima Co., Ariz., April 25, 1961. HAF.
16   *Atrytonopsis python margarita,* ♂. Jemez Hot Springs, Sandoval Co., N.Mex., June 6, 1923. LACM.
17   *Atrytonopsis ovinia edwardsi,* ♂. Sabino Canyon, Baboquivari Mts., Pima Co., Ariz. S&T.
18   *Atrytonopsis ovinia edwardsi,* ♀. Mt. Locke, Davis Mts., Jeff Davis Co., Tex. S&T.
19   *Asbolis capucinus,* ♂. Lehigh Acres, Lee Co., Fla. JRH.
20   *Asbolis capucinus,* ♀. Hollywood, Broward Co., Fla. S&T.
21   *Euphyes arpa,* ♂. Shalimar, Fla. JRH.
22   *Euphyes arpa,* ♀. Shalimar, Fla. JRH.
23   *Euphyes vestris metacomet,* ♂. Coal Creek Canyon, Clear Creek Co., Colo. JRH.
24   *Euphyes vestris metacomet,* ♀. Monroe Canyon, Sioux Co., Nebr. JRH.
25   *Euphyes c. conspicua,* ♂. Durham Center, Middlesex Co., Conn. JRH.
26   *Euphyes c. conspicua,* ♀. Homer Township, Will Co., Ill. JRH.
27   *Euphyes bimacula,* ♂. Germania, Pa. JRH.
28   *Euphyes bimacula,* ♀. Forks of the Potomac, Hampshire Co., W. Va. JRH.

PLATE 85

William H. Howe

1   *Euphyes dion,* ♂. Coolie Lake, Clay Co., Mo. JRH.
2   *Euphyes dion,* ♀. Coolie Lake, Clay Co., Mo. JRH.
3   *Euphyes berryi,* ♂. Pensacola, Fla. JRH.
4   *Euphyes berryi,* ♀, topotype, Orlando, Fla., Oct. 10, 1941. HAF.
5   *Euphyes palatka,* ♂. Port Everglades, Fla. JRH.
6   *Euphyes palatka,* ♀. Cherry Point, Craven Co., N.Car. JRH.
7   *Euphyes dukesi,* ♂. New Bern, N.Car. JRH.
8   *Euphyes dukesi,* ♀. Indian Creek, Suffolk Co., Va. JRH.
9   *Mellana eulogius,* ♂. Tierra Colorado, Guerrero. HAF.
10 *Choranthus haitensis,* ♂. Santo Domingo, Hispaniola. HAF.
11 *Choranthus radians,* ♀. Havana, Cuba. HAF.
12 *Callimormus saturnus,* ♂. Tepic, Nayarit, Sept. 4, 1964. HAF.
13 *Paratrytone m. melane,* ♂. Foothill Area, San Diego Co., Cal. JRH.
14 *Paratrytone m. melane,* ♀. Strawberry Canyon, Berkeley, Cal. JRH.
15 *Poanes massasoit,* ♂. Bloomington, Dakota Co., Minn. JRH.
16 *Poanes massasoit,* ♀. Reading, Pa. JRH.
17 *Poanes hobomok,* ♂. Taylor's Bush Park, Toronto, Ont. JRH.
18 *Poanes hobomok,* yellow ♀. Eureka Springs, Ark. JRH.
19 *Poanes hobomok,* black ♀. Eureka Springs, Ark. JRH.
20 *Poanes zabulon,* ♂. Shawnee Mission, Johnson Co., Kan. JRH.
21 *Poanes t. taxiles,* ♂. Madera Canyon, Santa Rita Mts., Santa Cruz Co., Ariz. JRH.
22 *Poanes t. taxiles,* ♀. Coronado Trail, Rose Peak, Blue Range in White Mts., Greenlee Co., Ariz. JRH.
23 *Poanes t. taxiles,* ♀, underside. Same data as fig. 22.
24 *Poanes zabulon,* ♀. Independence, Mo. JRH.
25 *Poanes viator,* ♂. Hamden, New Haven Co., Conn. JRH.
26 *Poanes viator,* ♀. Onaway, Montmorency Co., Mich. JRH.
27 *Poanes yehl,* ♂. Suffolk, Va. JRH.
28 *Poanes yehl,* ♀. North Landing, Princess Anne Co., Va. JRH.

PLATE 86

William H. Howe

1   *Poanes aaroni howardi,* ♂. Orlando, Fla. S&T.
2   *Poanes aaroni howardi,* ♀. Orlando, Fla. JRH.
3   *Ochlodes s. snowi,* ♂. Rustler's Park, Chiricahua Mts., Cochise Co., Ariz. JRH.
4   *Ochlodes s. snowi,* ♀. South Turkey Cr., Jefferson Co., Colo. JRH.
5   *Ochlodes yuma,* ♂. Sherman I., Sacramento Co., Cal. JRH.
6   *Ochlodes yuma,* ♀. Jackson Slough Road, Sacramento Co., Cal. JRH.
7   *Ochlodes sylvanoides,* ♂. Turkey Cr., Jefferson Co., Colo. JRH.
8   *Ochlodes sylvanoides,* ♀. Corvallis, Ore. JRH.
9   *Ochlodes agricola,* ♂. Chews Ridge, Monterey Co., Cal. JRH.
10 *Ochlodes agricola,* ♀. Glendora Mtn., Los Angeles Co., Cal. JRH.
11 *Problema bulenta,* ♂. Wilmington, N.Car. JRH.
12 *Problema bulenta,* ♀. Leland, N.Car. JRH.
13 *Problema byssus,* ♀. Holliday, Johnson Co., Kan. JRH.
14 *Problema byssus,* ♀, underside. Mears Park, Franklin Co., Kan. JRH.
15 *Problema byssus,* ♂. Shawnee Mission Park, Johnson Co., Kan. JRH.
16 *Atrytone arogos,* ♂. Welch, Okla. JRH.
17 *Atrytone arogos,* ♀. 17 mi. W. of Lawrence, Kan. JRH.
18 *Atrytone delaware,* ♂. Shawnee Mission Park, Johnson Co., Kan. JRH.
19 *Atrytone delaware,* ♀. Baldwin Hill, Kan. JRH.
20 *Atalopedes campestris,* ♂. Independence, Mo. JRH.
21 *Atalopedes campestris,* ♀. Independence, Mo. JRH.
22 *Wallengrenia otho,* ♂. Ponte Vedra, Fla. JRH.
23 *Wallengrenia otho,* ♀. Brownsville, Tex. JRH.
24 *Wallengrenia egeremet,* ♂. Independence, Mo. JRH.
25 *Wallengrenia egeremet,* ♀. Independence, Mo. JRH.
26 *Pompeius verna,* ♂. Camp Nicholson, Miami Co., Kan. JRH.
27 *Pompeius verna,* ♀. Atherton, Mo. JRH.
28 *Polites vibex praeceps,* ♂. San Pedro, Tex. JRH.
29 *Polites vibex praeceps,* ♀. San Pedro, Tex. JRH.

PLATE 87

William H. Howe

1   *Hesperia comma yosemite*, ♂. Sentinel Dome, Yosemite Nat. Park, Cal., July 3, 1946. AMNH.
2   *Hesperia comma yosemite*, ♀. Buck Meadow, Tuolumne Co., Cal., Sept. 30, 1939. AMNH.
3   *Hesperia comma leussleri*, ♂. Warners Hot Springs, San Diego Co., Cal. LACM.
4   *Hesperia comma luessleri*, ♀. Laguna Mts., San Diego Co., Cal. LACM.
5   *Hesperia comma manitoba*, ♂. Atlin, B.C., June 20, 1929. LACM.
6   *Hesperia comma manitoba*, ♀. South Park, Colo., July 19, 1902. LACM.
7   *Hesperia comma assiniboia*, ♂. Birtle, Man., Aug. 6, 1941. HAF.
8   *Hesperia comma assiniboia*, ♀. Miniota, Man., Aug. 6, 1941. HAF.
9   *Hesperia comma ochracea*, ♂. Bailey, Colo., Aug. 21, 1941. HAF.
10 *Hesperia comma ochracea*, ♀. Boulder, Colo., Aug. 29, 1954. HAF.
11 *Hesperia comma hulbirti*, ♂, topotype. Hurricane Hill, Wash., July 23, 1940. HAF.
12 *Hesperia comma hulbirti*, ♀, topotype. Hurricane Hill, Wash., July 22, 1940. HAF.
13 *Hesperia comma borealis*, ♂. Labrador. CM.
14 *Hesperia comma borealis*, ♀. Labrador. CM.
15 *Hesperia harpalus*, ♂. Kyle Canyon, Mt. Charleston, Clark Co., Nev., June 30, 1950. F&JP.
16 *Hesperia comma harpalus*, ♀. Deer Creek Camp Road, Mt. Charleston, Clark Co., Nev., July 1, 1950. F&JP.
17 *Yvretta rhesus*, ♀. Santa Fe, N.Mex., May 22, 1951. HAF.
18 *Yvretta carus subreticulata*, ♂. Ft. Davis, Tex., July 11, 1949.
19 *Hesperia comma oregonia*, ♂. Mullan, Ida., Aug. 5, 1946. HAF.
20 *Hesperia comma oregonia*, ♀. Minam, Ore., July 27, 1945. HAF.
21 *Hesperia p. pahaska*, ♂. White Mts., Ariz., June 10, 1933. LACM.
22 *Hesperia p. pahaska*, ♀. White Mts., Ariz., Aug. 25, 1930. LACM.
23 *Hesperia pahaska martini*, ♂, paratype. 5 mi. S.E. of Ivanpah, New York Mts., San Bernardino Co., Cal., Sept. 13, 1955. LACM.
24 *Hesperia pahaska martini*, ♀, paratype. 5 mi. S.E. of Ivanpah, New York Mts., San Bernardino Co., Cal., Sept. 12, 1955. LACM.
25 *Hesperia uncas lasus*, ♀. Prescott, Ariz., June 20, 1937. LACM.
26 *Hesperia uncas lasus*, ♂. Chino Canyon, Prescott, Ariz., Aug. 18, 1953. LACM.
27 *Hesperia uncas macswaini*, ♂, paratype. Blancos Corral, White Mts., Mono Co., Cal., June 14, 1954. LACM.
28 *Hesperia uncas macswaini*, ♀, paratype. Blancos Corral, White Mts., Mono Co., Cal., June 14, 1954. LACM.

PLATE 88

1

2

3

4

5

6

7

8

9

10

11

12

13

14

15

16

17

18

19

20

21

22

23

24

25

26

27

28

William H. Howe

PLATE 89

1   *Hesperia u. uncas,* ♂. Sand Dunes, Alamosa Co., Colo. JRH.
2   *Hesperia u. uncas,* ♀. Denver, Colo. JRH.
3   *Hesperia metea licinus,* ♂. Tyler State Park, Smith Co., Tex. USNM.
4   *Hesperia metea licinus,* ♀. Tyler State Park, Smith Co., Tex. JRH.
5   *Hesperia m. metea,* ♂. Otsego Co., Mich. JRH.
6   *Hesperia m. metea,* ♀. Otsego Co., Mich. JRH.
7   *Hesperia ottoe,* ♂. Sioux City, Iowa. AMNH.
8   *Hesperia ottoe,* ♀. Mears Park, Franklin Co., Kan. AMNH.
9   *Hesperia comma colorado,* ♂. Old Monarch Pass Road, 8000 ft., Gunnison Co., Colo. CDM.
10 *Hesperia comma colorado,* ♀. Old Monarch Pass Road, 8000 ft., Gunnison Co., Colo. CDM.
11 *Hesperia woodgatei,* ♂. Mingus Mt., Yavapai Co., Ariz., Sept. 24, 1951. HAF.
12 *Hesperia woodgatei,* ♀. Mingus Mt., Yavapai Co., Ariz. JRH.
13 *Hesperia pahaska williamsi,* ♂. Madera Canyon, Santa Rita Mts., Santa Cruz Co., Ariz., Aug. 20, 1952. LACM.
14 *Hesperia pahaska williamsi,* ♀. Ft. Huachuca, Cochise Co., Ariz., Aug. 26, 1952. CDM.
15 *Hesperia viridis,* ♂. Clear Creek Canyon, Jefferson Co., Colo. AMNH.
16 *Hesperia viridis,* ♀. Jemez Springs, Sandoval Co., N.Mex. AMNH.
17 *Hesperia juba,* ♂. Stansbury Mts., Tooele Co., Ut. JRH.
18 *Hesperia juba,* ♀. Cottonwood Canyon, Salt Lake Co., Ut. JRH.
19 *Hesperia a. attalus,* ♂. Barber Co., Kan. S&T.
20 *Hesperia a. attalus,* ♀. Barber Co., Kan. S&T.
21 *Hesperia meskei,* ♂. Atlanta, Ga. JRH.
22 *Hesperia meskei,* ♀. Orlando, Fla. JRH.
23 *Hesperia dacotae,* ♂. Grinnell, Iowa. S&T.
24 *Hesperia dacotae,* ♀. Grinnell, Iowa. S&T.
25 *Pseudocopaeodes eunus,* ♂. Scissors Crossing, San Diego Co., Cal. S&T.
26 *Pseudocopaeodes eunus,* ♀. Scissors Crossing, San Diego Co., Cal. S&T.
27 *Adopaeoides prittwitzi,* ♀. Davis Mts., Jeff Davis Co., Tex. S&T.
28 *Adopaeoides prittwitzi,* ♀, underside. Same data as fig. 27.
29 *Stinga morrisoni,* ♂. Jemez Springs, Sandoval Co., N.Mex., June 25, 1914. HAF.
30 *Yvretta c. carus,* ♂. Pena Blanca, Santa Cruz Co., Ariz. S&T.
31 *Yvretta c. carus,* ♀. Proctor Ranch, Santa Rita Mts., Pima Co., Ariz. S&T.
32 *Yvretta rhesus,* ♂. Raton Pass, Colfax Co., N.Mex., May 21, 1951. HAF.
33 *Yvretta rhesus,* ♂, underside. Same data as fig. 32.
34 *Stinga morrisoni,* ♀. U.S.A.F. Academy, Colorado Springs, Colo. JRH.

PLATE 89

William H. Howe

PLATE 90

1 *Polites coras,* ♂. St. Joseph, Mo. JRH.
2 *Polites coras,* ♀. St. Joseph, Mo. JRH.
3 *Polites sabuleti,* ♂. Antioch, Cal. JRH.
4 *Polites sabuleti,* ♀. Antioch, Cal. JRH.
5 *Polites draco,* ♂. Wolf Creek Pass, Archuleta Co., Colo. JRH.
6 *Polites themistocles,* ♂. Independence, Mo. JRH.
7 *Polites themistocles,* ♀. Independence, Mo. JRH.
8 *Polites o. origenes,* ♂. Roscoe, Mo. JRH.
9 *Polites o. origenes,* ♀. Roscoe, Mo. JRH.
10 *Polites draco,* ♀. Mt. Goliath, Clear Creek Co., Colo. JRH.
11 *Polites s. sonora,* ♂. Round Valley, Inyo Co., Cal. JRH.
12 *Polites sonora siris,* ♀. Viola, Shasta Co., Cal. JRH.
13 *Polites m. mystic,* ♂. Edmundston, N.B. JRH.
14 *Polites m. mystic,* ♀. Edmundston, N.B. JRH.
15 *Polites mardon,* ♂. Signal Peak, Yakima Co., Wash. JRH.
16 *Hesperia columbia,* ♂. Spring Mt. Road, Sonoma Co., Cal. JRH.
17 *Hesperia columbia,* ♀. Spring Mt. Road, Sonoma Co., Cal. JRH.
18 *Polites baracoa,* ♂. Florida City, Fla., Apr. 29, 1947. HAF.
19 *Polites baracoa,* ♀. Florida City, Fla., Mar. 22, 1946. HAF.
20 *Polites mardon,* ♀. Signal Peak, Yakima Co., Wash. JRH.
21 *Hesperia nevada,* ♂. Mt. Conconully, Okanogan Co., Wash. JRH.
22 *Hesperia nevada,* ♀. Signal Peak, Yakima Co., Wash. JRH.
23 *Hesperia comma laurentina,* ♂. Edmundston, N.B. JRH.
24 *Hesperia comma laurentina,* ♀. Edmundston, N.B. JRH.
25 *Hesperia sassacus,* ♂. Washington, Litchfield Co., Conn. JRH.
26 *Hesperia lindseyi,* ♂. Arroyo Bayo, Santa Clara Co., Cal. JRH.
27 *Hesperia lindseyi,* ♀. Bouquet Canyon, Los Angeles Co., Cal. JRH.
28 *Hesperia miriamae,* ♂. Mammoth Peak Summit, Yosemite Nat. Park, Cal. JRH.
29 *Hesperia miriamae,* ♀, paratype. Mono Pass, Inyo Co., Cal., Aug. 11, 1957. AMNH.
30 *Hesperia sassacus,* ♀. Adamstown, Pa. JRH.
31 *Hesperia comma harpalus,* ♂. Satus Pass, Yakima Co., Wash. JRH.
32 *Hesperia comma harpalus,* ♀. Bear Canyon, nr. Tieton R., Yakima Co., Wash. JRH.
33 *Hesperia comma dodgei,* ♂. Swanton, Santa Cruz Co., Cal. JRH.
34 *Hesperia comma tildeni,* ♂. Arroyo Bayo, Santa Clara Co., Cal. JRH.
35 *Hesperia comma susanae,* ♂. Shannon, Pinaleno Mts., Graham Co., Ariz. JRH.
36 *Hesperia leonardus,* ♂. Mack's Creek, Camdenton Co., Mo. JRH.
37 *Hesperia leonardus,* ♀. Mack's Creek, Camdenton Co., Mo. JRH.
38 *Hesperia pawnee,* ♂. Rocky Flats, Denver, Colo. JRH.
39 *Hesperia pawnee,* ♀. Denver, Colo. JRH.

PLATE 90

William H. Howe

PLATE 91

1   *Hylephila p. phyleus,* ♂. Independence, Mo. JRH.
2   *Hylephila p. phyleus,* ♀. Pleasant Hill, Mo. JRH.
3   *Thymelicus lineola,* ♂. Edmundston, N.B. JRH.
4   *Thymelicus lineola,* ♀. Edmundston, N.B. JRH.
5   *Copaeodes aurantiaca,* ♂. Sentinel Canyon, San Diego Co., Cal. JRH.
6   *Oarisma garita,* ♂. Buckboard Flat, Abajo Mts., San Juan Co., Ut. JRH.
7   *Oarisma garita,* ♀. Buckboard Flat, Abajo Mts., San Juan Co., Ut. JRH.
8   *Copaeodes minima,* ♂. Cameron, La. JRH.
9   *Copaeodes minima,* ♀. Cameron, La. JRH.
10 *Copaeodes aurantiaca,* ♀. Tucson, Ariz. JRH.
11 *Oarisma garita,* ♂. Jacob's Lake, Kaibab Forest, Coconino Co., Ariz. JRH.
12 *Oarisma garita,* ♀. Jacob's Lake, Kaibab Forest, Coconino Co., Ariz. JRH.
13 *Oarisma edwardsii,* ♂. Ruby, Ariz. JRH.
14 *Oarisma edwardsii,* ♀. Madera Canyon, Santa Cruz Co., Ariz. JRH.
15 *Ancyloxypha numitor,* ♂. Baldwin Hill, Kan. JRH.
16 *Piruna polingii,* ♂. Beulah, Colo. S&T.
17 *Piruna pirus,* ♂. Huachuca Mts., Cochise Co., Ariz. S&T.
18 *Ancyloxypha arene,* ♂. Brownsville, Tex. JRH.
19 *Ancyloxypha arene,* ♀. Marathon, Tex. JRH.
20 *Ancyloxypha numitor,* ♀. Salem, Mo. JRH.
21 *Cymaenes odilia trebius,* ♂. Pharr, Tex. HAF.
22 *Cymaenes odilia trebius,* ♂, underside. Pharr, Tex. HAF.
23 *Decinea percosius,* ♂. Southmost, Tex. HAF.
24 *Decinea percosius,* ♂, underside. Same data as fig. 23.
25 *Bolla brennus,* ♂. Santa Rosa, Comitán, Chiapas. HAF.
26 *Nastra lherminier,* ♂. Mansfield, La. JRH.
27 *Nastra lherminier,* ♀. Mansfield, La. JRH.
28 *Nastra neamathla,* ♂. Orlando, Fla. JRH.
29 *Nastra neamathla,* ♂, underside. Same data as fig. 28.
30 *Nastra julia,* ♂. San Antonio, Tex. JRH.
31 *Nastra julia,* ♀. Brownsville, Tex. JRH.
32 *Lerema accius,* ♂. Brownsville, Tex. JRH.
33 *Lerema accius,* ♀. Shalimar, Fla. JRH.
34 *Cymaenes tripunctus,* ♂. West Hollywood, Fla. JRH.
35 *Cymaenes tripunctus,* ♀. West Hollywood, Fla. JRH.
36 *Monca telata tyrtaeus,* ♂. Pharr, Tex. JRH.
37 *Synapte malitiosa pecta,* ♂. Pharr, Tex. JRH.
38 *Ephyriades brunnea floridensis,* ♂. Homestead, Fla. JRH.
39 *Gesta gesta invisus,* ♂. Ciudad Valles, San Luis Potosí. JRH.
40 *Timochares r. ruptifasciatus,* ♀. Pharr, Tex. JRH.

PLATE 91

William H. Howe

PLATE 92

1 *Carterocephalus palaemon mandan,* ♂. So. Milford, N.B. S&T.
2 *Pholisora catullus,* ♀. Gregory Canyon, Boulder Co., Colo. S&T.
3 *Pholisora mejicana,* ♂. Beulah, Colo. S&T.
4 *Pholisora l. libya,* ♂. Fish Springs, Cal. S&T.
5 *Pholisora a. alpheus,* ♂. Palo Duro Canyon, Randall Co., Tex. JMB.
6 *Celotes nessus,* ♂. Davis Mts., Jeff Davis Co., Tex. S&T.
7 *Staphylus ceos,* ♂. Davis Mts., Jeff Davis Co., Tex. S&T.
8 *Staphylus mazans,* ♂. Ciudad Valles, San Luis Potosí, June 10, 1966. HAF.
9 *Staphylus hayhurstii,* ♀. Baldwin Hill, Kan. AMNH.
10 *Pholisora a. alpheus,* ♂, underside. Same data as fig. 5.
11 *Heliopetes laviana,* ♂. Ciudad Victoria, Tamaulipas. S&T.
12 *Heliopetes ericetorum,* ♂. Topanga Canyon, Los Angeles Co., Cal. S&T.
13 *Heliopetes macaira,* ♂. Pharr, Tex. S&T.
14 *Heliopetes d. domicella,* ♂. Dripping Springs, Organ Pipe Cactus Nat. Mon., Ariz. S&T.
15 *Pyrgus centaureae loki,* ♀. Needle Mts., Colo. S&T.
16 *Pyrgus ruralis,* ♂. Brewster, Wash. S&T.
17 *Pyrgus c. communis,* ♂. Caldwell, Kan. S&T.
18 *Pyrgus c. communis,* ♀. Caldwell, Kan. S&T.
19 *Pyrgus xanthus,* ♀. Deming, N.Mex. S&T.
20 *Pyrgus o. oileus,* ♂. Ocoee, Fla. S&T.
21 *Pyrgus scriptura,* ♂. Laguna Dam, Cal. S&T.
22 *Xenophanes trixus,* ♂. Ciudad Valles, San Luis Potosí. S&T.
23 *Polythrix octomaculata,* ♂. Acahuezotla, Guerrero. HAF.
24 *Perichares philetas adela,* ♂. Jalapa, Veracruz. HAF.
25 *Thorybes valeriana,* ♀. Fresnillo, Zacatecas, June 25, 1950. HAF.
26 *Vidius perigenes,* ♂. Los Fresnos, Tex., June 25, 1964. HAF.
27 *Erynnis scudderi,* ♂. Huachuca Mts., Cochise Co., Ariz. AMNH.
28 *Ephyriades brunnea floridensis,* ♀. Big Pine Key, Monroe Co., Fla. FER.
29 *Pyrrhocalles antiqua orientis,* ♀. Cuba. HAF.
30 *Vidius perigenes,* ♂, underside. Same data as fig. 26.
31 *Pyrgus philetas,* ♂. Nogales, Ariz., July 11, 1964. HAF.
32 *Piruna microsticta,* ♂. Monterrey, Mexico, July 25, 1966. HAF.
33 *Pyrgus communis albescens,* ♂. San Francisco, Tamaulipas, Aug. 9, 1964. HAF.
34 *Pyrgus communis albescens,* ♀. Sinaloa, Mexico, Nov. 3, 1967. HAF.
35 *Poanes a. aaroni,* ♂. Cape May, N.J., June 20, 1937. HAF.
36 *Pyrgus philetas,* ♀. Laredo, Tex., June 4, 1940. HAF.

PLATE 92

William H. Howe

PLATE 93

1 *Erynnis icelus,* ♂. Signal Mt., Teton Nat. Park, Wyo. USNM.
2 *Erynnis b. brizo,* ♀. Shawnee Mission Park, Johnson Co., Kan. AMNH.
3 *Erynnis b. brizo,* ♂. Mears Park, Franklin Co., Kan. AMNH.
4 *Erynnis persius,* ♂. Signal Mt., Teton Nat. Park, Wyo. USNM.
5 *Erynnis p. pacuvius,* ♂. Mother Cabrini Shrine area, Jefferson Co., Colo. USNM.
6 *Erynnis martialis,* ♀. Warsaw, Mo. AMNH.
7 *Erynnis baptisiae,* ♂. Sand Hills, Franklin Co., Kan. AMNH.
8 *Erynnis baptisiae,* ♀. Baldwin Hill, Kan. USNM.
9 *Erynnis j. juvenalis,* ♂. Mears Park, Franklin Co., Kan. USNM.
10 *Erynnis j. juvenalis,* ♀. Ottawa, Kan. AMNH.
11 *Erynnis t. tristis,* ♂. Citrus Heights, Sacramento Co., Cal. AMNH.
12 *Erynnis t. tristis,* ♀. Los Angeles, Cal. S&T.
13 *Erynnis telemachus,* ♂. Smith Fork, Delta Co., Colo. USNM.
14 *Erynnis telemachus,* ♀. Palo Flechado Pass, Colfax Co., N.Mex. USNM.
15 *Erynnis horatius,* ♂. Baldwin Hill, Kan. AMNH.
16 *Erynnis horatius,* ♀. Mears Park, Franklin Co., Kan. AMNH.
17 *Erynnis propertius,* ♂. Mt. Veeder, Napa Co., Cal. USNM.
18 *Erynnis propertius,* ♀. Napa, Cal. S&T.
19 *Erynnis brizo lacustra,* ♂. Cajon Pass, San Bernardino Co., Cal. S&T.
20 *Erynnis brizo lacustra,* ♀. Cajon Pass, San Bernardino Co., Cal. S&T.
21 *Erynnis brizo somnus,* ♂. Melbourne, Fla. S&T.
22 *Erynnis brizo somnus,* ♀. Melbourne, Fla. S&T.
23 *Erynnis brizo burgessi,* ♂. Kingman, Ariz. S&T.
24 *Erynnis brizo burgessi,* ♀. Chiricahua Nat. Mon., Ariz. S&T.
25 *Erynnis persius,* ♂. Albany, N.Y. HAF.
26 *Erynnis persius,* ♀. Hess Lake, Newaygo Co., Mich. HAF.
27 *Erynnis lucilius,* ♂. Oxford, Oakland Co., Mich. HAF.
28 *Erynnis lucilius,* ♀. Oxford, Oakland Co., Mich. HAF.
29 *Erynnis afranius,* ♂. Los Angeles, Cal. LACM.
30 *Erynnis afranius,* ♀. Flagstaff, Ariz. LACM.
31 *Erynnis pacuvius pernigra,* ♂. Alpine Lake, Marin Co., Cal. CDM.
32 *Erynnis pacuvius lilius,* ♀. Wawona Road, nr. Yosemite Nat. Park, Cal. LACM.
33 *Erynnis pacuvius callidus,* ♂. Pepper Flat, San Jacinto Mts., Los Angeles Co., Cal. LACM.
34 *Erynnis pacuvius callidus,* ♀. Pepper Flat, San Jacinto Mts., Los Angeles Co., Cal. LACM.
35 *Erynnis juvenalis clitus,* ♂. Chiricahua Mts., Cochise Co., Ariz. LACM.
36 *Erynnis juvenalis clitus,* ♀. Madera Canyon, Santa Cruz Co., Ariz. LACM.
37 *Erynnis funeralis,* ♂. Caldwell, Kan. S&T.
38 *Erynnis funeralis,* ♀. Dripping Springs, Organ Pipe Cactus Nat. Mon., Ariz. S&T.
39 *Erynnis zarucco,* ♂. Augusta, Ga. S&T.
40 *Erynnis zarucco,* ♀. Augusta, Ga. S&T.
41 *Erynnis m. meridianus,* ♂. Chiricahua Nat. Mon., Cochise Co., Ariz. S&T.
42 *Erynnis m. meridianus,* ♀. Miami, N.Mex. S&T.

PLATE 93

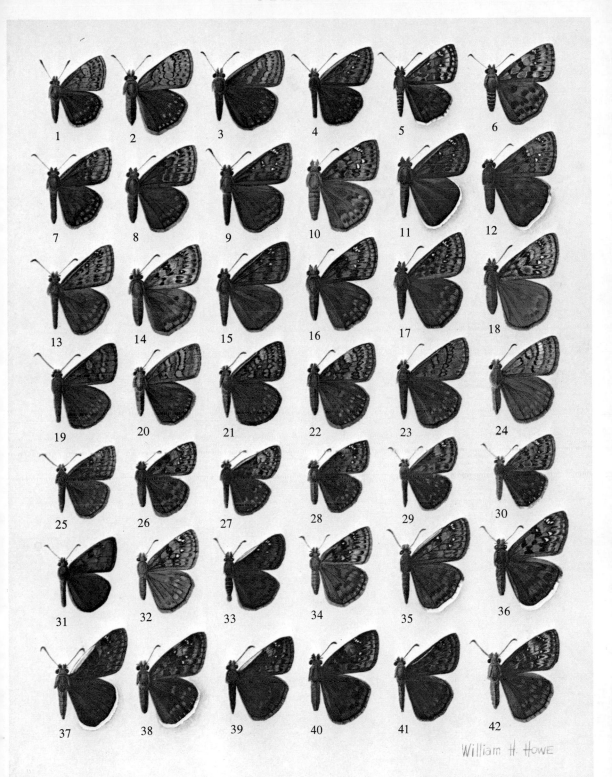

William H. Howe

PLATE 94

1 *Thorybes pylades,* ♀. Billings, Mont., June 15, 1948. CDM.
2 *Thorybes bathyllus,* ♀. Quitman, Ark. S&T.
3 *Achalarus lyciades,* ♂. Hickory Co., Mo., May 29, 1961. HAF.
4 *Thorybes confusis,* ♀. Lake Bennett, Faulkner Co., Ark. July 4, 1941. HAF.
5 *Achalarus toxeus,* ♂. McCall, Tex. S&T.
6 *Achalarus c. casica,* ♂. Davis Mts., Jeff Davis Co., Tex. S&T.
7 *Thorybes m. mexicana,* ♂. México, D.F. S&T.
8 *Autochton cellus,* ♂. Widewater, Md. S&T.
9 *Autochton cellus,* ♀. Palmerlee, Cochise Co., Ariz. S&T.
10 *Thorybes drusius,* ♂. Madera Canyon, Ariz., July 6, 1960. HAF.
11 *Thorybes mexicana nevada,* ♂. S. Fork of Kern River, Tulare Co., Cal. CDM.
12 *Thorybes mexicana dobra,* ♀. Mt. Graham, Ariz., June 19, 1958. CDM.
13 *Thorybes diversus,* ♀. Scott Mt., Trinity Co., Cal., July 5, 1963. CDM.
14 *Cogia calchas,* ♂. Pharr, Tex. S&T.
15 *Cogia outis,* ♂. Vickery, Dallas Co., Tex. S&T.
16 *Cogia caicus moschus,* ♂. Chiricahua Mts., Cochise Co., Ariz. S&T.
17 *Cabares p. potrillo,* ♂. Pharr, Tex. S&T.
18 *Systasea zampa,* ♂. Sabino Canyon, Pima Co., Ariz. S&T.
19 *Systasea pulverulenta,* ♂. Pharr, Tex. S&T.
20 *Achylodes thraso tamenund,* ♂. Pharr, Tex. S&T.
21 *Cabares potrillo,* ♂, underside. Same data as fig. 17.
22 *Nisoniades rubescens,* ♂. Ciudad Valles, San Luis Potosí. S&T.
23 *Chiomara asychis georgina,* ♂. Pharr, Tex. S&T.
24 *Carrhenes c. canescens,* ♀. El Salto, San Luis Potosí, Aug. 19, 1962. HAF.
25 *Gorgythion begga pyralina,* ♂. Ciudad Victoria, Tamaulipas. S&T.

PLATE 94

PLATE 95

1 *Epargyreus c. clarus,* ♂. Baldwin Hill, Kan. AMNH.
2 *Epargyreus zestos,* ♀. Key Largo, Fla. AMNH.
3 *Epargyreus exadeus cruza,* ♂. Tamazunchale, San Luis Potosí. HAF.
4 *Chioides z. zilpa.* Monterrey, Nuevo León. HAF.
5 *Zestusa dorus,* ♂. Cherry Creek, Grant Co., N.Mex. S&T.
6 *Chioides catillus albofasciatus,* ♂. Ciudad Victoria, Tamaulipas. S&T.
7 *Grais s. stigmaticus,* ♀. Pharr, Tex. S&T.
8 *Polygonus l. leo,* ♂. Key Vaca, Fla. HAF.
9 *Polygonus l. leo,* ♀. Key Largo, Fla. HAF.
10 *Aguna a. asander,* ♀. Ciudad Victoria, Tamaulipas. HAF.
11 *Celaenorrhinus stallingsi,* ♂, holotype. Monterrey, Nuevo León. S&T.
12 *Celaenorrhinus fritzgaertneri,* ♀. Ciudad Valles, San Luis Potosí, Aug. 4, 1966. HAF.
13 *Atrytonopsis turneri,* ♀, paratype. Barber Co., Kan., April 26, 1946. HAF.
14 *Typhedanus undulatus,* ♀. Mapastepec, Chiapas, June 19, 1966. HAF.
15 *Astraptes gilberti,* ♂. Ciudad Victoria, Tamaulipas, June 8, 1966. HAF.
16 *Astraptes anaphus annetta,* ♂. Catemaco, Veracruz, June 19, 1966. HAF.

PLATE 95

PLATE 96

1 *Astraptes fulgerator azul,* ♂. Pharr, Tex. S&T.
2 *Phocides pigmalion okeechobee,* ♂. Miami, Fla. S&T.
3 *Phocides polybius lilea,* ♂. Orizaba, Veracruz. S&T.
4 *Phocides urania,* ♂. Cuernavaca, Morelos. S&T.
5 *Codatractus arizonensis,* ♂. El Salto, San Luis Potosí. S&T.
6 *Codatractus a. alcaeus,* ♂. Sierra Blanca, Mexico. S&T.
7 *Codatractus melon,* ♂. Ciudad Valles, San Luis Potosí. S&T.
8 *Urbanus p. proteus,* ♂. Augusta, Ga. S&T.
9 *Urbanus d. doryssus.* ♂. Ciudad Victoria, Tamaulipas. S&T.
10 *Pyrrhopyge araxes arizonae,* ♀. Cochise Co., Ariz. S&T.
11 *Urbanus tanna,* ♂. Pharr, Tex. S&T.
12 *Proteides m. mercurius,* ♂. Sierra Blanca, Mexico. S&T.
13 *Urbanus procne,* ♂. Monterrey, Nuevo León. S&T.
14 *Spathilepia clonius,* ♂. Pharr, Tex. HAF.
15 *Urbanus d. dorantes,* ♂. Ciudad Valles, San Luis Potosí. S&T.

PLATE 96

PLATE 97

1 *Pholisora libya lena,* ♂. Gerlach, Pershing Co., Nev., July 10, 1967. DLB.
2 *Pholisora libya lena,* ♀. Gerlach, Pershing Co., Nev., July 10, 1969. DLB.
3 *Oarisma powesheik,* ♂. Lake Okiboji (Iowa Great Lakes), Dickinson Co., Iowa, June 24, 1921. CDM.
4 *Oarisma powesheik,* ♂, underside. Same data as fig. 3.
5 *Pholisora alpheus oricus,* ♀. Lucerne, San Bernardino Co., Cal., April 15, 1964. CDM.
6 *Plebejus argyrognomon scudderi,* ♂. East Main, Hudson Bay, N.W.Terr., July 23, 1912. CM.
7 *Leptotes cassius striata,* ♂. Ajijic, Jalisco, Sept. 9, 1965. CM.
8 *Leptotes cassius striata,* ♀. Ajijic, Jalisco, Oct. 2, 1965. CM.
9 *Euptychia cymela viola,* ♂, underside. Ocoee, Fla. April 3, 1938. FER.
10 *Pholisora gracielae,* ♂, paratype. Parker, Ariz., April 18, 1964. CDM.
11 *Pholisora gracielae,* ♀, paratype. Parker, Ariz., April 18, 1964. CDM.
12 *Oeneis taygete gaspeensis,* ♂, paratype. Mt. Albert, Gaspé Co., Que., July 19, 1940. AMNH.
13 *Oeneis taygete gaspeensis,* ♀, paratype. Mt. Albert, Gaspé Co., Que., July 18, 1940. AMNH.
14 *Autochton cellus,* ♂. Cave Creek, Cochise Co., Ariz., June 16, 1958. CDM.
15 *Euptychia cymela viola,* ♂. Same data as fig. 9.
16 *Lycaena phlaeas feildeni,* ♂. McKinley Nat. Park, Alaska, July 29, 1930. AMNH.
17 *Autochton pseudocellus,* ♂. Las Adjuntas, Durango, July 1, 1952. CDM.
18 *Lycaena d. dorcas,* ♂. Riding Mts., Man., Aug. 28, 1927. AMNH.
19 *Lycaena phlaeas hypophlaeas,* ♂. North slope of Mt. Dana, 11,500 ft., Mono Co., Cal., Aug. 6, 1966. AMNH.
20 *Colias gigantea harroweri,* ♂, holotype. Green River Lake, Wind River Range, Wyo., July 16, 1939. AMNH.
21 *Colias gigantea harroweri,* ♀, allotype. Clear Creek, Green River Lakes, Wind River Range, Wyo., July 16, 1939. AMNH.
22 *Lycaena d. dorcas,* ♀. Whiteshell Prov. Park, Man., July 24, 1955. AMNH.
23 *Colias alexandra krauthii,* ♂, paratype. Black Hills, S. Dak., July 1, 1931. AMNH.
24 *Colias hecla hela,* ♂. Churchill, Man., July 13, 1933. AMNH.
25 *Lycaena cupreus snowi,* ♀. Rocky Mt. Nat. Park, Colo., 11,000 ft., Aug. 28, 1962. FER.
26 *Polygonus m. manueli,* ♂. British Honduras, July 1, 1935. CDM.
27 *Pieris protodice nelsoni,* ♂. McKinley Nat. Park, Alaska, July 24, 1930. AMNH.
28 *Urbanus simplicius,* ♂, underside. Ocozocoautla, Chiapas, July 26, 1952. CDM.
29 *Urbanus procne,* ♂, underside. "Colombia."
30 *Codatractus c. carlos,* ♂. La Encarnación, Campeche. CDM.

PLATE 97

William H. Howe

Distribution: Erora laeta is found chiefly in beech-maple forest from southern Nova Scotia and southern Quebec west to Michigan and southward in the Appalachians to Tennessee.

2. **Erora quaderna** (Hewitson). Plate 50, figure 22, ♀ (ssp. *sanfordi*).   This species is common in certain canyons in the mountains of southern Arizona where as many as a hundred may be taken in a day. The males have much less blue on the upperside than do the males of *laeta.* That color is either absent or restricted to a line at the tornus of the hind wing. The fringe of the female is distinctly orange. The subspecies in the United States is *sanfordi* dos Passos.

Early Stages: Unknown.

Distribution: The species ranges from Guatemala north through Mexico to western New Mexico, Arizona and southern Utah. In southern Arizona it is common in the oak-pine region (Upper Austral zone) between 4500 and 7800 ft.

Genus ELECTROSTRYMON Clench

THOMAS C. EMMEL

This is a tropical genus of which a single member reaches our area. The hind wings are tailed and the males lack scent pads. The underside of the hind wing bears the characteristic *Strymon* post discal line with a "W" basad of the tails.

1. **Electrostrymon endymion** (Fabricius). Plate 53, figure 12, ♂ (ssp. *cyphara*).   The upperside of this tropical hairstreak vaguely resembles *Mitoura* because of the fulvous patches in the male, while the underside is somewhat like that of *Calycopis cecrops.* Our subspecies is *cyphara* (Hewitson).

Early Stages: Unknown.

Distribution: The species ranges from the southern tip of Texas to southern Brazil. The subspecies *cyphara* occurs from Panamá northward to southern Texas where it may be resident.

Genus OENOMAUS Hübner

HARRY K. CLENCH

So far as known, *Oenomaus* contains only one species. The genus is distinguished primarily by the male genitalia, particularly the large, conical, spiculate cornutus in the penis.

1. **Oenomaus ortygnus** (Cramer). Plate 48, figure 23, ♂; figure 24, ♂, underside; Plate 51, figure 9, ♀.   On the upperside both sexes resemble *Panthiades m-album,* brilliant

blue in the male, duller in the female. The underside, however, is unique: pale rosy gray, with a few scattered black spots and some iridescent green in the terminal and tornal areas. Our subspecies is nominate *ortygnus*.

Early Stages: Unknown.

Distribution: This species occurs widely over the tropical mainland from South America north to central Mexico. A single specimen was taken, and another seen, in Brownsville, Texas, in 1962.

Genus THEREUS Hübner

HARRY K. CLENCH

This strange genus includes a number of neotropical species, some so remarkably similar to one another as to be considered sibling species, others so different that they would never be thought congeneric. The genus is chiefly recognized by its male genital structure, the more unusual aspects of which are the triangular projections, one on each side, on the anterior edge of the vinculum, associated with the presence of coremata, or abdominal tufts of specialized (odor-producing?) scales in the male.

1. **Thereus zebina** (Hewitson) (?). Plate 52, figure 7, ♂; Plate 51, figure 10, ♀. As mentioned above, several species of *Thereus* are so similar as to be separable only with difficulty, and only by subtle differences in male secondary sexual characters. To further complicate the picture, their females are extremely similar and so far neither distinguishable among themselves, nor capable of association with their respective males. Two such females were recorded from extreme southern Texas by H. A. Freeman in 1950, one each under the names *zebina* Hewitson and *spurina* Hewitson. Without much more and better knowledge we cannot be sure whether or not they are different from each other nor what are the correct names they should bear. For the present I unite them under the name "*zebina* (?)." Males are dully iridescent blue with a scent pad at the cell-end, and females are gray and whitish above; both sexes on the underside have a simple hairstreak pattern reminiscent of that of *Panthiades m-album*.

2. **Thereus palegon** (Stoll). Plate 78, figure 22, ♂; figure 23, ♂, underside. This distinctive species is quite unlike the preceding in appearance. The underside pattern is reminiscent of some *Callophrys* (*Incisalia*) but in shades of gray and ochre. The hind wing is tailed and the upperside is blue, somewhat iridescent in males, duller and more restricted in females.

Early Stages: Unknown.

Distribution: Thereus palegon occurs in tropical and subtropical forested areas of the Neotropics, from South America north to central Mexico. A single specimen was taken in 1968 in southernmost Texas.

Genus ALLOSMAITIA Clench

HARRY K. CLENCH

The few members of this genus resemble some *Thereus* in appearance but differ in the complete absence of corematal processes on the anterior vinculum of the male genitalia. They are found in the New World tropics, including several islands of the West Indies.

1. **Allosmaitia pion** (Godman & Salvin). Plate 78, figure 24, ♂. This species is distinctive in the male by having a scent pad, not on the fore wing, but on the hind wing just costad of the discal cell near the base. The fuscous border on the upperside of the male extends basad to the cell-end.

Early Stages: Unknown.

Distribution: This uncommon species is known only from Central America, ranging north, chiefly in montane scrub and low forest, to central Mexico. A single worn specimen was taken in 1968 in southernmost Texas.

Genus OCARIA Clench

HARRY K. CLENCH

This genus is one of the few known tropical members of the *Satyrium* group of genera (*Satyrium* Scudder, *Harkenclenus* dos Passos, *Chlorostrymon* Clench, *Phaeostrymon* Clench, *Ocaria* Clench), characterized by having a serrated keel ventrally at the apex of the penis in the male genitalia. *Ocaria* differs from the others in the triangular shape of the keel and in the presence of an anterior corematal process on the vinculum, similar to that of *Thereus* but smaller and much less conspicuous.

1. **Ocaria ocrisia** (Hewitson). Plate 78, figure 25, ♂. On the upperside the male of this species has a dully shining blue fore wing and a blue terminal border on the hind wing; the female is dimorphic, either uniform brown or with a blue patch on the hind wing. The underside of both sexes is similar, mottled dark brown with the usual hairstreak pattern of thin, pale lines, but faint and readily obscured by wear.

Early Stages: Unknown.

Distribution: The species is found, not commonly, from South America north to central Mexico. A single worn specimen was taken in southernmost Texas in 1968.

Subfamily LYCAENINAE

PAUL A. OPLER

This subfamily encompasses the familiar coppers. Most of these butterflies vary from dull purple to a lustrous red-orange. Some species are not coppery, however, and may have gray, brown, yellow or even blue as the predominant color. Most coppers are stout-bodied and quite capable of rapid flight. Some species frequent marshy areas, meadows or bogs. Several of the western species occur in extremely dry areas. The males of many coppers take up perches from which they dart "aggressively" at passing objects, until a female of the proper species is encountered whereupon courtship and mating usually follow. Most species tend to occur in fairly compact colonies and rarely stray any great distance from the area.

Structurally these butterflies are similar to other lycaenids. The following features characterize the members of the subfamily: androconial scales are usually absent; there are four radial veins on the fore wing; vein M_1 arises from the discal cell; and the spines of the undersides of the tarsi occur in irregular clusters rather than in regular rows. In the male genitalia the lobes of the uncus are always long and digitate.

Early Stages: The life history of these butterflies is similar to other lycaenids in most respects. The winter is passed in many instances as a first instar larva within the egg. The larvae are green and may have faint yellow longitudinal stripes. Many of the host plants upon which the larvae feed belong to the family Polygonaceae (*Eriogonum, Rumex, Polygonum* or *Oxyria*). Plants of such unrelated families as Ericaceae, Rhamnaceae, Rosaceae (particularly *Potentilla*), Rubiaceae and Saxifragaceae are preferred by other species.

Distribution: These butterflies are found primarily in the cooler climates of North America, Europe and temperate Asia, but a few occur in the Ethiopian and the Indo-Australian regions and one is found in the mountains of Guatemala. All Nearctic species are contained in the genus *Lycaena.* Two of our species, *phlaeas* and *cupreus,* belong to the chiefly Old World subgenus *Lycaena* while all of the others are placed in the predominantly New World subgenus *Tharsalea.*

Genus LYCAENA Fabricius

Fifteen species are attributed to our fauna. Some writers devote much space to an exhaustive treatment of subspecies and minor variations, but the scope of this volume, in which many species of diverse families must be treated over a great geographic distance, necessarily precludes my including all of the forms in this genus. With the aid of the color figures, however, the majority of the subspecies of every Nearctic *Lycaena* should be readily identifiable.

1. **Lycaena (Tharsalea) arota** (Boisduval).   This species will be readily recognized by the figures. Note the tails and the linear pattern below. Both sexes visit some kinds of flowers such as *Clematis* and *Merubium.* The butterfly is associated with Upper Sonoran to Canadian zone forests. Its habitat is shaded water courses on north facing slopes, although occasionally it may be encountered upon sagebrush and in open mountain meadows.

Early Stages: The larval foodplant is gooseberry (*Ribes*).

Distribution: The species occurs in montane areas throughout the West from southern Oregon to southern California eastward to the Rocky Mountains of Colorado and central New Mexico.

(a) **arota** (Boisduval). Plate 55, figure 27, ♂; figure 28, ♀. This is the darkest of the Pacific states subspecies.

Distribution: Central California to Oregon on the western side of the Sierras.

(b) **nubila** J. A. Comstock. Plate 56, figure 1, ♂; figure 2, ♀. Specimens from southern California are lighter and have been given this name.

(c) **virginiensis** (W. H. Edwards). Plate 56, figure 3, ♂; figure 4, ♀. This is the lightest colored subspecies.

Distribution: The eastern slopes of the Sierra Nevada in Nevada and California.

(d) **schellbachi** Tilden. Plate 56, figure 5, ♂; figure 6, ♀. The heavier dark brown patterning on the female sets apart this subspecies.

Distribution: Northern Arizona and central New Mexico northward into southern Wyoming.

2. **Lycaena (Tharsalea) gorgon** (Boisduval). Plate 55, figure 23, ♂; figure 24, ♀. Males are strongly purplish above. Females may be mistaken for female *Lycaena xanthoides* by the inexperienced. This attractive butterfly is an inhabitant of the dry oak and digger pine semi-woodlands of the inner ranges of the California Coast Ranges. It is rare or absent in the outer coastal ranges, but is common and quite widespread inland.

Early Stages: The larvae feed upon *Eriogonum elongatum* and *E. latifolium,* members of the family Polygonaceae. There is a single brood of adults from mid May until mid July.

Distribution: This Upper Sonoran species ranges from southern Oregon to northern Baja California.

3. **Lycaena (Tharsalea) heteronea** Boisduval. Males of this species are bright lilac-blue above, in sharp contrast to other species of the genus. Adults favor hilly terrain with a southern exposure, in diverse plant associations.

Early Stages: The larvae feed upon several wild buckwheats, among which are *Eriogonum fasciculatum, E. latifolium nudum, E. microthecum* and *E. umbellatum.* There is one brood in July and August.

Distribution: This species occurs in the Upper Sonoran and Canadian zones from southern British Columbia, Idaho and Montana southward to southern California, northern Arizona and Colorado.

(a) **heteronea** Boisduval. Plate 56, figure 11, ♂; figure 12, ♀. This Sierran form is found from central California northward. Boisduval's original specimens may have come from the vicinity of the old gold diggings in Tuolumne county.

(b) **clara** Hy. Edwards. Plate 56, figure 9, ♂; figure 10, ♀. Southern Californian *heteronea clara* is rather rare. It is somewhat paler than true *heteronea.*

(c) **gravenotata** Klots. Plate 55, figure 17, ♂; figure 18, ♀. Although Gunder's *coloradensis* was described earlier than *gravenotata* the name was specifically applied to an aberration and therefore has no status. This subspecies is more heavily marked on the underside than either of the Californian subspecies. It is found in the southern Rocky Mountains and Great Basin.

(d) **klotsi** Field.   This northern Rocky Mountains subspecies seems to combine the features of the three others. The underside is like nominate *heteronea;* the upperside of the male is like *clara,* violet-blue, not silvery blue; and the upperside of the female is lighter than *gravenotata* but like that subspecies lacks orange-brown lunules on the margin of the hind wings.

4. **Lycaena (Tharsalea) hyllus** (Cramer). Plate 55, figure 7, ♂; figure 8, ♀. Known popularly as the Bronze Copper, this attractive butterfly has no close relatives. It is strongly sexually dimorphic. Its habitat is open, wet meadows, where it tends to be colonial but is seldom abundant. Until recently this species was widely known under the synonymous name *thoe* Guérin-Méneville.

Early Stages: The larva is bright yellowish green, slug shaped and with a blackish stripe dorsally. Larval foodplants include Yellow Dock (*Rumex crispus*), perhaps other water-loving docks.

Distribution: This Upper Austral and Transition zone species ranges from Ontario westward to Alberta and southward to northeastern Colorado, Kansas, Arkansas, Pennsylvania and New Jersey. There is a single record for Mississippi and one for Gainesville, Florida: both are undoubtedly strays. There are two broods, one in late May and June and another in August.

5. **Lycaena (Tharsalea) hermes** (Edwards). Plate 54, figure 24, ♂. This beautiful yellow and brown copper may not be mistaken for any other Nearctic species. It inhabits open chaparral in which its foodplant, *Rhamnus crocea,* is growing.

Early Stages: These have been described recently by Thorne.

Distribution: This species occupies an exceedingly small range, comprising San Diego county, California, and adjacent northern Baja California. One seasonal brood occurs from May to early July.

6. **Lycaena (Tharsalea) xanthoides** (Boisduval).   This grassland species has a curiously discontinuous distribution, the ranges of the two populations being widely separated by the basinrange and Rocky Mountain provinces.

Early Stages: The larval host plant is *Rumex hymenosepalus.* One brood occurs from late May to early July.

(a) **xanthoides** (Boisduval). Plate 56, figure 7, ♂; figure 8, ♀.   The west coast subspecies is found in grasslands and grassy foothills.

Distribution: The nominate subspecies ranges from southern Oregon to northern Baja California. It is especially common in the San Joaquin and Sacramento valleys.

(b) **dione** Scudder. Plate 55, figure 1, ♂; figure 2, ♀. This is the largest Nearctic copper. Adults are lustrous gray-brown above. The subspecies *dione* is entirely restricted to prairie meadows in which *Rumex obtusifolius* grows.

Distribution: This butterfly is found in the midwestern prairies and the Great Plains from Alberta, Saskatchewan and Manitoba southward to northwestern Illinois, Iowa, Missouri and Oklahoma. Adults fly from late May to early July in one brood: usually common where found.

7. **Lycaena (Tharsalea) editha** (Mead). Plate 55, figure 21, ♂; figure 22, ♀. Males of this active species frequently sun themselves, "patrol" dry stream beds and settle on bare rocks. Adults of both sexes visit the flowers of Yarrow (*Achillea*) and Spreading Pink Dogbane (*Apocynum androsaemifolium*). *L. editha* is found in dry sagebrush amid mixed open conifer associations. The subspecies *montana* Field is not separately discussed.

Early Stages: Unknown. Possible hosts are reported to be *Horkelia* and *Potentilla.*

Distribution: Lycaena editha occurs in the Canadian and Hudsonian zones from southeastern Washington, Idaho and Montana southward to California (high Sierra only), Nevada, Utah and northwestern Colorado. It is essentially montane, with one brood from late June to late August.

8. **Lycaena (Tharsalea) rubidus** (Behr). Plate 55, figure 25, ♂; figure 26, ♀. Males of this species are rivaled only by those of *Lycaena cupreus* in the brilliance of their coloration. This species visits flowers frequently, such as those of *Eriogonum, Achillea, Chrysothamnus, Medicago* and others. In habitat *rubidus* favors edges of meadows or streams in sagebrush associations, with or without conifers.

Early Stages: These are incompletely known. *Rumex triangularis* is a reported foodplant in Colorado.

Distribution: L. rubidus ranges from the Transition to the Hudsonian zone, from Alberta and British Columbia to central California, northern and eastern Arizona and Colorado, east to western Nebraska and western South Dakota. There is one annual brood in July and August.

9. **Lycaena (Tharsalea) nivalis** (Boisduval). Plate 55, figure 19, ♂; figure 20, ♀. Usually not common where found, this species is nevertheless widespread in mountainous areas within its range. In the past it was called *zeroe,* actually a synonym of *mariposa.* In flight it cannot be distinguished from *Lycaena helloides,* with which it flies at the upper altitudinal levels of the latter. However, *nivalis* may always be distinguished from *helloides* by the ventral surfaces. In *nivalis* the ground color is bright yellow, with dull pink on the outer margins of the secondaries. The species tends to be quite variable above in both sexes. Some males are dark purplish like *helloides;* others are paler, such as the one illustrated. Low elevation specimens tend toward lightness while higher altitude examples are darker. Females at higher levels are characterized by heavy black maculation above with considerable dark suffusion, especially basally. *L. nivalis* inhabits dry meadows and open areas in coniferous forests.

Early Stages: These were recorded under the name *zeroe.* The larval foodplant is *Polygonum douglasii* in California, Colorado and Washington.

Distribution: L. nivalis occurs in the Canadian Zone from Montana, Idaho, Washington and British Columbia south to Colorado, Utah, Nevada and central California. There is one brood in late July and August.

10. **Lycaena (Tharsalea) mariposa** Reakirt. Plate 55, figure 15, ♂; figure 16, ♀. This is a local species but it may be quite abundant where found. Adults frequent sun-filled glades in late stage meadows almost filled with surrounding conifers (always Lodgepole Pines in California and Ponderosa Pines in southern Montana). Low growing flowers, such as *Fragaria,* are often visited. Males frequent wet patches along shaded or partially sunny trails.

Early Stages: Unknown.

Distribution: This species occurs in the High Canadian zone from southern Alaska and British Columbia to Colorado, Idaho, Nevada and northern California. There is one brood in late July and August.

11. **Lycaena (Tharsalea) helloides** (Boisduval). Plate 55, figure 13, ♂; figure 14, ♀. Geographically and ecologically this species has the widest range of any North American copper. The relationship between this species and *L. dorcas* is still unclear. High altitude populations in Colorado appear intermediate between *helloides* and *dorcas* but are probably best referred to as *helloides* "florus" Edwards. Adults of *helloides* inhabit widely diverse terrains from sea level in California to 10,800 ft. in Colorado.

Early Stages: The larva is bright green covered with a whitish pubescence, with many lateral oblique yellow lines. Larval foodplants include various docks (*Rumex*), knotweed (*Polygonum*) and baby's breath (*Galium*).

Distribution: This species is found from the Transition to the Canadian zone, with occasional extensions into the Hudsonian in Colorado. It ranges from southern British Columbia to Quebec, Michigan and northern Illinois in the east, southward to Iowa, western Kansas, northern New Mexico, southern Utah and northern Baja California (but unknown from Arizona). It is multiple brooded in warm areas (as many as six annually in lowland California) to a single brood at high elevations. It is frequent in yards as well as in open countryside.

12. **Lycaena (Tharsalea) dorcas** Kirby. Adults closely resemble *helloides* "florus" from which they may not be distinguishable without the locality labels! The relationship between *dorcas* and *helloides* remains unresolved as yet. However, the male of *dorcas* is usually characterized with a wide dark brown margin above and both sexes of *dorcas* are consistently smaller than *helloides*. The distributions of the two species overlap in southern Ontario, Michigan and northwestern Ohio, but the figures will enable the reader to separate both in most instances.

Early Stages: Poorly known as yet. Newcomb raised the larvae on *Potentilla fruticosa.*

Distribution: This species occurs in the Canadian and Transition zones from Labrador and Newfoundland to Alaska, southward to Saskatchewan, northern

Minnesota, Michigan, northwestern Ohio, and Maine and New Hampshire. There is one brood in July and August.

(a) **dorcas** Kirby. Plate 97, figure 18, ♂; figure 22, ♀. The major portion of the species range is occupied by this subspecies. Only in northern New England and in New Brunswick are other subspecies as noted below.

(b) **dospassosi** McDunnough. Plate 55, figure 11, ♂; figure 12, ♀. This strikingly distinct subspecies of *dorcas* is called the Salt Marsh Copper because of its restriction to the coastal salt marshes of New Brunswick. Adults are dull ochreous beneath rather than orange-brown. The type and only known locality is Bathurst, N.B.

(c) **claytoni** Brower. Plate 55, figure 9, ♂; figure 10, ♀. This subspecies of *dorcas* is characterized by its small size, the dull coloration above of the females, the reduced spots and markings above and the submarginal orange band on the secondaries being reduced in size, indistinct or absent. Its habitat is old fields in dry uplands, associated with *Potentilla.* It is found in Maine.

13. **Lycaena (Tharsalea) epixanthe** (Boisduval & Le Conte). Plate 55, figure 3, ♂; figure 4, ♀. This diminutive species is quite abundant at times, although extremely local in cranberry bogs. There is a violet gloss above in males, but females are dull gray above.

Early Stages: These are still incompletely known. According to Klots the eggs are laid singly on the lower surfaces of the leaves near the tips of the shoots. The larval foodplant is Wild Cranberry (*Vaccinium macrocarpon*). The species hibernates in the egg, which can withstand periodic flooding.

Distribution: The species is restricted to acid bogs in Transition and Canadian zones from Nova Scotia and Newfoundland to Manitoba, southward to New Jersey, Pennsylvania, northern Ohio, Michigan and Wisconsin.

14. **Lycaena (Lycaena) phlaeas** (Linnaeus). This Palearctic species is represented in North America by the following four subspecies:

(a) **americana** Harris. Plate 55, figure 5, ♂; figure 6, ♀. This brightly colored and distinctive little butterfly occurs in the northeastern and in the cooler portions of the midwestern United States and adjacent southern Canada. Our northeastern subspecies is virtually identical with north European nominate *phlaeas,* but the assertion that it was imported from Europe would be difficult to establish.

Early Stages: These are described in detail by Klots and by Scudder. The larval foodplant is Sheep Sorrel (*Rumex acetosella*) and possibly also Garden Sorrel (*R. acetosa*) and Yellow Dock (*Rumex crispus*).

Distribution: The subspecies *americana* occurs in the Upper Austral, Transition and lower Canadian zones throughout the northeastern United States southward to northern Georgia (mountains), North Carolina, Kentucky and Arkansas, and west to extreme northeastern Kansas and North Dakota. Two to four broods occur, from May to September.

(b) **feildeni** (M'Lachlan). Plate 97, figure 16, ♂. This arctic subspecies is found in few collections. It is nearer in appearance to *phlaeas* of Europe and Siberia than to *americana* or *hypophlaeas,* the two well known subspecies. This subspecies is quite brassy (yellowish, rather than orange) on the upperside.

Distribution: This subspecies is found in northwestern Greenland, Ellesmere Island, Baffin Island and Southampton Island, west along the arctic coast to the mouth of the Mackenzie River and possibly still farther west, along the arctic coast of Alaska. It is strictly a barren ground subspecies.

(c) **arethusa** (Wolley-Dod). This curious subspecies is restricted to the montane regions of southwestern Alberta. It is quite gray above and the fiery red normally seen on male *phlaeas* is obscured.

(d) **hypophlaeas** (Boisduval). Plate 97, figure 19, ♂. This western subspecies of *phlaeas* inhabits sandy flats and "rock gardens" high above timberline or in tundra. Isolated populations occur above 11,000 ft. in the Sierras of California and the Wallowa Mountains in Oregon. Studies now in progress suggest that the butterflies assignable to *phlaeas* from the southern part of Alaska southward to northwestern Wyoming and western British Columbia are doubtfully *hypophlaeas.*

15. **Lycaena (Lycaena) cupreus** (Edwards). This tends to be a high altitude species and ranges from the Transition to the Arctic-alpine zones. The flashing fiery red wings of the males make it one of our most beautiful coppers. Three subspecies are recognized, each associated with a particular group of mountain ranges.

(a) **cupreus** (Edwards). Plate 54, figure 25, ♂; figure 26, ♀. This is the most brilliant of the subspecies. It is found in the Sierra Nevada of California, Nevada and Oregon. A similar butterfly occurs in the high mountains of Utah.

Early Stages: Lembert in 1894 raised this subspecies on *Rumex pauciflorius.* Nothing else is known.

(b) **snowi** (Edwards). Plate 54, figure 27, ♂; figure 28, ♀; Plate 97, figure 25, ♀. The southern and central Rocky Mountain subspecies was named for its original captor, Dr. F. H. Snow, an early chancellor of the University of Kansas. In early spring this butterfly first appears in canyons low on the flanks of the Laramie Mountains of Wyoming. In July the subspecies is found at and above treeline.

Early Stages: All that we know is that Bruce found the mature larvae on *Oxyria digyna* in Hall Valley, Colorado, in 1896.

(c) **henryae** (Cadbury). This subspecies is found in northern British Columbia and extreme southeastern Alaska.

Subfamily PLEBEJINAE

WILLIAM H. HOWE

The Plebejinae, or "blues," are widely distributed in the temperate regions of both hemispheres. Many species are found in the cold north or upon the summits of high mountains. Relatively few are found in the tropics. The hairstreaks, on the contrary, although common in temperate regions, are abundant in tropical areas, only a few species ranging to the far north and alpine summits.

The blues are familiar almost everywhere. They appear in earliest spring and fly until well into autumn. Some species are on the wing all year in the more southerly climates. A few Old World blues have been observed in migration but there is no such record for the New World, although some are suspected. Many blues are found congregating about damp sand or mud on hot, sunny days. Most species freely visit a wide variety of flowers. A few are never found far from their larval foodplant. Compared to most other butterflies blues usually have a weak, fluttery flight but they may fly rather rapidly when alarmed. Together with their small size, this type of flight enables them to easily elude the lepidopterist as they dart over shrubbery or up steep canyons. Thirty-six species are credited to our Nearctic fauna, as well as dozens of named subspecies, varieties and forms.

Early Stages: The eggs are turban shaped, flattened and slightly depressed on top at the micropyle. The outer surfaces are variously sculptured with ribs, ridges and depressions. The eggs are laid most often on the buds or in the flower heads of the foodplant, but sometimes on new growth or on the stems. The caterpillars are often remarkably well camouflaged among the flower buds on which they feed, simulating the texture as well as the color of the buds. As they mature, the caterpillars become slug shaped and their color may change to conform with the petals, bracts or delicate terminal leaves.

In common with many Lycaenidae, the caterpillars of most species studied bear a secretory gland on the dorsal surface of the tenth segment, and a pair of eversible sacs on the eleventh. These larvae are attended by ants which greatly relish the sweet droplets exuded by the gland. It has been theorized that the ants protect the larvae from wasp parasites and other predators in return for the "honey dew" secretion. The ant brushes its antennae or fore legs against the caterpillar's body which stimulates the flow of the secretion.

The pupae are plump and ovoid. They are short and compressed, with the cremaster attached to a silken pad or button on the substrate. The caterpillar spins a silken girdle about the middle, closely fastening the pupa to the surface. Although many pupae appear smooth, they are variously adorned with short hairs, bristles or spines. As with the camouflaged larvae the pupae are often of similar color to their surroundings. On the abdominal segments are "rasp and file" arrangements at one of the sutures. As the abdomen is twitched these produce a creaky sound. The adults are small and the wings of some species are fragile and thin. They are popularly called "blues" because the prevailing ground color above is usually some shade of blue, lavender or aquamarine, especially in the male. Females, usually duller, may be solid gray above; others are brownish, russet or even ochreous. Often some blue scaling appears at the base of the female wings, or they may be mostly blue as in the males. In one North American genus (*Everes*) the adults of both sexes are tailed. The lower surface is reasonably similar in the two sexes and diagnostic for the species.

The generic assignment of butterflies in this subfamily depends in part upon the arrangement of the radial veins of the fore wing.

Genus BREPHIDIUM Scudder

ROBERT L. LANGSTON

In the Nearctic this genus is represented by two species. These are the smallest known butterflies, the fore wing length of some being only 8 mm. The genus is further characterized by the rounded apex and outer margin of the fore wing, and a row of lustrous gold and black circlets in the submarginal area of the hind wings below.

1. **Brephidium exilis** (Boisduval). Plate 58, figure 32, ♂; figure 33, ♀. The Western Pigmy Blue is found commonly from Texas to California and south to Venezuela. Although the major portion of its range is neotropical, strays have been taken northward as far as Kansas, Nebraska, Colorado and Oregon. It is often found in disturbed areas such as roadsides, railroad tracks and vacant lots overgrown with weeds. Because of its foodplants, it is found in low areas such as alkali flats, washes and salt marshes. The species is common in central and southern California and I have collected it below sea level in Death Valley, and also around bays, inlets and the much cooler dunes along the Pacific Ocean.

B. exilis is distinctive on the underside: the ground color is grayish white basally and brown distally; the fringes are mostly white; and the wings above are brown with considerable blue basally, sometimes extending halfway out.

This species is multiple brooded, with one generation often overlapping the next. It flies all year in southern Texas; northern strays have been recorded from July to September. In California it becomes more common as the season progresses, being most abundant in late summer and autumn.

Early Stages: The flattened eggs are a delicate bluish green, with a raised white network. The larvae are pale green to cream colored. Their surface is finely punctate with a yellowish white dorsal line and frequently a bright yellow substigmatal line. The mature larvae are covered with minute brown tubercles tipped with white. This gives them a frosted appearance which simulates the under surfaces of the saltbush leaves, or the mealy flower heads of the pigweed. The pupae are variable in color, the usual type being light brownish yellow, with a fuscous dorsal line. The wing cases are usually a pale yellowish green with a few brownish dots. Larval foodplants are mostly Chenopodiaceae, including *Atriplex bracteosa* (Lamb's Tongue), *Chenopodium album* (White Pigweed) and *Salicornia ambigua* (Pickle Weed). It has also been recorded from a species of Solanaceae, *Petunia parviflora*.

2. **Brephidium pseudofea** (Morrison). Plate 58, figure 34, ♂; figure 35, ♀. The Eastern Pigmy Blue is found in coastal Alabama, Georgia and Florida. It has also been recorded as a stray from Galveston, Texas. There are inland records, but it is never common far from salt water. Because of its foodplants, it is locally common in coastal salt marshes and tidal flats. Its flight is weak and low, hence the butterfly is easily collected.

B. pseudofea is distinctive on the underside, the ground color being uniformly brown and the fringes uniformly dark. The wings above are brown with no blue.

There are apparently at least three broods, with adults appearing most abundantly in February, April and September.

Early Stages: These were described by Rawson. The larvae feed on glasswort (*Salicornia:* Chenopodiaceae). Klots has also associated it environmentally with saltwort (*Batis:* Batidaceae).

Genus LEPTOTES Scudder

ROBERT L. LANGSTON

In the Nearctic this genus is represented by two species. They are characterized on the underside by transverse light and dark bands on both wings. The blue or purplish scaling on the upper surface is thin, with the markings from below showing through. The hind wings below have two submarginal metallic eye spots or ocelli. Both species are neotropical, one of which occurs in our area in the form of two subspecies.

1. **Leptotes cassius** (Cramer).   The nominate subspecies occurs in South America, not in our area.

(a) **theonus** (Lucas). Plate 57, figure 21, ♂; figure 22, ♀.   The West Indian Blue is found in southern Florida, the Bahama Islands, Cuba and Jamaica to Puerto Rico. It is probably the most common blue in southern Florida, often visiting flowers, especially of trees and shrubs.

This butterfly is smaller than the following species, with the blue above rather pure, not purplish. On the fore wings below the transverse dark brownish gray lines tend to fade out below the cell and cubital veins leaving blank white areas down to the inner margin. The submarginal eye spots of the hind wing are large. Males above have distinct whitish along the anal margins of the hind wings. Females have considerable white in the discal areas of both wings. There are several broods annually, with records in winter as well as summer.

Early Stages: The larva is green with a russet red overtone, the skin rough and the head and legs are concealed by an overlapping fringe. Larval foodplants include many Leguminosae, among them *Plumbago* (Leadwort), *Galactia volubilis* (Hairy Milk Pea), *Phaseolus limensis* (Lima Bean), *Crotalaria incana* (Rattle-box) and perhaps *Albizzia*.

(b) **striatus** (Edwards). Plate 97, figure 7, ♂; figure 8, ♀.   The Striated Blue is found from Panamá to southern Texas, rarely straying northward to Kansas and Missouri. The male is more purplish blue above than *theonus,* and the female has more white and less blue. The markings below are paler, brownish. The submarginal eye spots of the hind wing are small, the anal one frequently reduced or absent. There are several broods annually, with more in the tropics.

Early Stages: Oviposition, eggs and larvae have been noted on the buds and blossoms of *Phaseolus vulgaris* (String Bean) in Texas; and oviposition on flowers of *Phaseolus limensis* in Missouri. It probably feeds on many Leguminosae throughout its extensive range.

2. **Leptotes marina** (Reakirt). Plate 57, figure 23, ♂; figure 24, ♀. The Marine Blue occupies an extensive territory from western Illinois and Nebraska west to central California and south through Texas to Central America. In Mexico, southern Texas, southern California and Baja California it fairly swarms during favorable seasons. In the more northerly areas (Kansas, Nebraska) it may breed, but cannot overwinter. The northerly colonies are established annually by summer migrants. Although one male was recorded from Mississippi in 1967, it is apparently absent from the southeastern and eastern states.

Larger than the previous species, the adults are overcast with pronounced purplish above. The females have heavy brown margins invading the outer half of the primaries nearly to the cell. Below, the transverse brown bands and spots cover most of the wings. There are prominent submarginal eye spots on the secondaries.

The species is multiple brooded with adults all year in the tropics and frostfree parts of the U.S. only, during the warmer months in the north and at higher elevations in the mountains, where it is uncommon.

Early Stages: The eggs are a delicate green color, becoming whiter as they mature. The larvae are extremely variable, with intergrades between a light green form with almost no markings, to a rich brown with heavy chocolate colored maculations. The nearly naked chrysalis is pale brownish ochreous, the wing cases pale grayish, semi-transparent, with numerous brown freckles. Larvae are common around ornamentals in cities, found on *Wisteria* in the spring and, after the blossoms fall, on *Plumbago* (leadwort). Other hosts, all Leguminosae, include *Astragalus* (rattle-weed, loco-weed), *Dolichos* (hyacinth bean), *Galactia* (milk pea), *Medicago* (alfalfa, bur clover) and *Phaseolus* (beans). *Lysiloma thornberi* is reported in Arizona.

Genus VAGA Zimmerman

WILLIAM H. HOWE

The single representative of the genus is confined to Hawaii and is one of the few endemic butterflies of these islands.

1. **Vaga blackburni** (Tuely). Plate 51, figure 17, ♂; figure 18, ♀. This distinctive little butterfly may be recognized by the figures. It is an abundant species on all the Hawaiian Islands.

Genus LAMPIDES Hübner

WILLIAM H. HOWE

This Old World genus occurs in our area only in Hawaii.

1. **Lampides boeticus** (Linnaeus). Plate 52, figure 17, ♂. This butterfly is called the Bean Blue because of the preference of the caterpillars for flowers of various legumes. The butterfly was introduced into Hawaii nearly a century ago and has since become one of the most abundant butterflies there. It is also common elsewhere in the Pacific, notably the Philippines, Japan and American Samoa as well as China, India, Africa and southern Europe.

Genus ZIZULA Chapman

ROBERT L. LANGSTON

In the Nearctic this genus is represented by a single species. The wing venation is similar to that of *Brephidium,* but the species lacks the black metallic spots on the ventral hind wings. Our species has been erroneously considered an imported African species, *Z. hylax* Fabricius (= *gaika* Trimen). Genitalia and wing pattern, however, show it to be distinct.

1. **Zizula cyna** (Edwards). Plate 56, figure 32, ♂. The Cyna Blue is found in Arizona, New Mexico and Texas. Common around San Antonio, it has been recorded on the border from Pharr to Big Bend National Park, Texas, and southward through Mexico and Guatemala to Colombia.

This delicate little species has relatively long, slender fore wings and short, rounded hind wings. The upperside is pale lilac blue with broad pale fuscous outer margins. The underside is very pale gray, with small darker spots and ashen fringes. The flight of *cyna* is low and weak. Several broods occur, with records from March through September within the U.S.

Early Stages: Not recorded.

Genus HEMIARGUS Hübner

ROBERT L. LANGSTON

In the Nearctic this genus is represented by three distinct species, which include several named subspecies. Although somewhat variable, all three species endemic to our zone should be recognizable from the figures. Nabokov places each of the three species in a separate genus, whereas dos Passos gives each subgeneric rank within *Hemiargus.* However, Klots and Ehrlich & Ehrlich keep them in a single genus, the arrangement followed here.

The genus *Hemiargus* is characterized on the dorsal surface by at least one prominent black spot near the anal angle of the hind wing. The ventral hind wing has some wavy white lines in addition to black spots.

1. **Hemiargus thomasi** Clench.   This Antillean species is established in southern Florida.

(a) **bethunebakeri** Comstock & Huntington. Plate 57, figure 25, ♂; figure 26, ♀. The Miami Blue occurs in the southern half of Florida and the Keys. It is local and may be common where found. The adults visit a wide assortment of flowers in open, sunny areas.

The Miami Blue is distinctive in the transverse bands and white shading of the wings below, caused by broadening and inward extension of the white edge of the submarginal markings. The larger eye spot of the hind wing is particularly large, and has much orange. The winter–spring adults (which are the examples figured) are bright blue, whereas the summer–fall adults are darker with more invasion of the dark marginal borders. The species is multiple brooded, with the winter pheno-type predominately from December to April and the summer phenotype from May to November.

Early Stages: The larval foodplants include *Pithecolobium guadaloupensis* (Black-bead, Catsclaw) and *Guilandina crista* (Gray Nicker, Holdback), both in the Leguminosae.

2. **Hemiargus ceraunus** (Fabricius).   The nominate subspecies of this Blue is Antil-lean.

(a) **antibubastus** Hübner. Plate 48, figure 36, ♂; figure 37, ♀.   The Florida Blue, as its name implies, flies commonly in Florida, ranging into Alabama and Georgia. The male above is purplish blue, with narrow black outer borders and white fringes. The female is darker. The underside of the hind wing is broadly margined with fuscous, followed inwardly by a pale, more diffuse band of lighter color, in some specimens nearly white. It has a large submarginal ocellate spot, but no orange as in the preceding species. There are at least three broods.

Early Stages: The larvae are dimorphic, either green with a reddish dorsal stripe, or reddish with a green under-shade. The larvae feed on flower buds. Larval food-plants include *Chamaecrista brachiata* (Partridge Pea), *C. aspera* (Hairy Partridge Pea) and *Abrus precatorius* (Crabs-eye Vine, Rosary Pea), all Leguminosae.

(b) **gyas** (Edwards). Plate 61, figure 25, ♂; figure 26, ♀.   Edwards' Blue is the subspecies represented in Arizona, New Mexico and southern California, ranging into adjacent Baja California and northern Mexico. It may be found in fair numbers throughout the deserts and lowlands, and occasionally strays to moderate elevations in the mountains. The upperside of the male is quite pale lilac-blue, and the female is dark brown with some blue basally. In both sexes there is a trace of the dark ocellus on the hind wing near the anal angle. This ocellus is conspicuous on the underside. There are at least three broods, with adults recorded in spring, summer and in the fall as late as November.

Early Stages: Larval foodplants include *Astragalus* (Rattle-weed, Loco-weed), *A. crotalariae* (Salton Loco-weed), *Prosopis juliflora* (Mesquite) and *P. pubescens* (Screw-bean Mesquite), all in the Leguminosae.

(c) **zachaeina** (Butler & Druce). Plate 57, figure 18, ♂. This Central American subspecies enters our area in southern Texas. Of common occurrence in Mexico, this subspecies may connect with *gyas* in Arizona. *H. c. zachaeina* has two black ocellate spots on the underside of the hind wing while *gyas* has only one. In southern Texas *zachaeina* is on the wing all year, appearing in a succession of overlapping broods. As with most tropical species, there is no diapause, and the caterpillars mature rapidly on their foodplants.

Early Stages: Larval foodplants include *Phaseolus* (beans), and in Texas on *Acacia angustissima, A. hirta* and *Rhyncosia minima.*

3. **Hemiargus isola** (Reakirt). Plate 57, figure 27, ♂; figure 28, ♀ (ssp. *alce*). Reakirt's Blue is immediately separable from the other two species of *Hemiargus* found in our territory by the presence on the ventral fore wing of a prominent postmedian row of large, black, roughly circular spots ringed with white. The outer margin of the fore wing is straighter, giving the wing a squarish shape, rather than the rounded wings of the other species. Reakirt's Blue occupies a wide territory from Ohio, Michigan and Minnesota west to British Columbia and southward to Costa Rica. The nominate subspecies is confined to the central Mexican plateau. The subspecies of *isola* that is found within our area, *alce* (Edwards), is well figured and cannot be confused with any other blue. There are many broods in the southern states. Adults appear in summer and early autumn in the more northerly regions.

Early Stages: Larval foodplants include many Leguminosae. The larvae are common on the blossoms and immature seed pods of *Prosopis juliflora* (Mesquite); in Texas it is reported on flower buds of *Acacia hirta,* leaves of *A. roemeriana,* flower buds of *Albizzia julibrissin, Indigofera leptosepala, I. lindheimeriana, I. miniata* (Indigo Plants), *Melilotis indicus* (Sour Clover) and *Dalea pogonanthera.*

Genus PHILOTES Scudder

ROBERT L. LANGSTON

The adults of this genus are small and may be recognized by the outer fringe of the wings having a checkered appearance. This characteristic will distinguish *Philotes* as a group but it will not differentiate among the eight species within the genus. Outwardly these species resemble those of the *Plebejus acmon* complex. Adults of both groups are characterized by a gray ground color beneath with an outer row of black spots on the secondaries inwardly edged with a band or row of orange macules. In *Plebejus* there are bright silvery crescents located within the orange band while in *Philotes* these silvery crescents are wanting. This feature and the checkered fringes are the first thing to look for in the field. Unfortunately, two or more species of *Philotes* may fly together and may look alike. In such situations the examination of the male genitalia will separate the species. The color figures will help in some instances.

Adults are closely associated with their foodplants, various species of wild buck-wheat, and stonecrop which usually grow on steep, hot, dry and rocky slopes, hills, or canyon walls. All species presently known inhabit the western states, western Canada and Baja California.

1. **Philotes battoides** (Behr). *P. battoides* differs from all other nearctic *Philotes* in the deeply bifurcate valvae of the male genitalia, and internal differences in the female.

Early Stages: The young larvae are whitish or cream, being about the color of the flower heads of the host plant upon which they feed. With growth, the larvae become more slug-shaped and vary from cream to yellow to pale rose. The rose coloring increases as the white or yellow flowers get older, turning to pinkish brown as the seeds develop. Pupation takes place in debris at the base of the foodplants. In *battoides* the larvae are either known or suspected to feed on wild buckwheat, *Eriogonum* (Polygonaceae). Adults appear in late spring and summer varying with elevation, latitude and subspecies.

(a) **battoides** (Behr). Plate 61, figure 13, ♂; figure 14, ♀. The Square-spotted Blue is the high elevation representative of the species in the Sierra Nevada of California. The nominate subspecies is recognized by the large black quadrate spots on the underside of both wings. These black spots are much heavier and darker than in any other *Philotes*. There is also much suffusion between the spots as the figures show. Some specimens from mid elevations on the east slopes show intergradation to *glaucon,* but no tendencies toward *intermedia* have been noted on the west slopes. The *type locality* is the San Joaquin River, California, at 11,000 ft., now placed as Mineral King, Tulare county. The types were destroyed in the San Francisco earthquake and fire in 1906.

(b) **intermedia** Barnes & McDunnough. Plate 61, figure 15, ♂; figure 16, ♀. The Intermediate Blue is found primarily in the northern California mountains and on the west slopes of the Sierra Nevada at low to moderate elevations. It is sympatric with the much commoner *P. enoptes enoptes* throughout most of its range. The ventral surfaces of both sexes are distinctive. The small black spots and orange "band" are reduced to series of lunules. The uppersides of most males have rather wide, dark borders, and the females have an orange band in the anal area of the secondaries. The type locality is Shasta county, California.

(c) **glaucon** (Edwards). Plate 61, figure 19, ♂; figure 20, ♀. The Glaucous Blue is the subspecies found in the Great Basin. It has a wide distribution in eastern and northeastern California, southwestern Idaho, northern and western Nevada and eastern Oregon. The underside of both sexes has the black spots a little heavier and the orange-red is wider and more extensive than in *intermedia*. Females have a well developed submarginal orange band on the upperside of the secondaries.

Early Stages: This subspecies has been reared on the Sulphur Flower, *Eriogonum umbellatum* (sens. lat.) in California, Oregon and Idaho.

(d) **centralis** Barnes & McDunnough. Plate 58, figure 27, ♂; figure 28, ♀. The Central Blue is the subspecies in the Rocky Mountains of Arizona, Colorado, New Mexico and Utah. It appears to show north to south clinal variation. Northern examples are darker gray beneath, whereas southern examples display a more extensive development of the orange-red band on the upperside of the secondaries of the female. A limited amount of orange reappears above in some males. Adults of *centralis* are often seen in association with *Plebejus acmon lutzi,* and resemble it closely. The type locality is the vicinity of Salida, Chaffee county, Colorado.

Early Stages: Larval foodplant in Colorado has been reported as the Sulphur Flower, *Eriogonum umbellatum* (sens. lat.).

(e) **oregonensis** Barnes & McDunnough. Plate 61, figure 17, ♂; figure 18, ♀. The Oregon Blue is the subspecies in the Pacific Northwest. At its type locality (Crater Lake, Klamath county, Oregon) and in the Cascades of southern Oregon it occurs at high elevations, but its elevation decreases as it ranges north through Washington and into British Columbia. Some specimens show intergradation with *glaucon* with decreased elevation, particularly in southeast Oregon and along the east slopes of the Cascades. It differs from *glaucon* by the heavier black spots on the underside and by the wide, dark borders on the upperside of the males. In a considerable portion of its range, *oregonensis* is sympatric with *P. enoptes columbiae,* which it resembles closely. Since *columbiae* was described much later (Mattoni, 1955), there is probably a mixture of the two species in some museums and private collections.

(f) **bernardino** Barnes & McDunnough. Plate 58, figure 25, ♂; figure 26, ♀. The San Bernardino Blue is the common spring and early summer subspecies found most often in lower canyons and dry washes in southern California. It ranges north in the Coast Range of central California and in the southern Sierra Nevada, the Tehachapi Mountains and also the western Mojave and the Colorado deserts. It extends southward into Baja California, including Cedros Island, and is recorded from the Sierra San Pedro Mártir. With little variation, it occurs from the coast to the tops of higher mountains in southern California. Adults of *bernardino* are smaller than all the previously discussed subspecies. The spots on the underside are clearly defined on a uniform light gray background. The females have a prominent sub-marginal orange band on the upperside of the secondaries. The type locality is Camp Baldy, San Bernardino Mountains, California.

Early Stages: The larval foodplant is *Eriogonum f. fasciculatum* in coastal southern California, *E. fasciculatum foliosum* throughout most of its range and *E. fasciculatum polifolium* and *E. flavoviride* in the deserts and east slope areas.

(g) **martini** Mattoni. Plate 61, figure 21, ♂; figure 22, ♀. Martin's Blue, named for Lloyd Martin of the LACM (retired), is the subspecies in western Arizona and the eastern and northern Mojave desert of California. It is known from many isolated desert mountain ranges such as the Panamints, the Argus, the Providence, and Ivanpah in eastern California and the Ajo and Hualapai ranges in western Arizona. Intergrades with *bernardino* have been taken in the western parts of its range in California. Also small, *martini* differs from *bernardino* in the lighter blue of the males; it also has a lighter underside than all other subspecies. There is an extremely well developed orange-red band averaging one-eighth of the total wing expanse. Females may (but usually do not) have some blue scales on the upperside of the secondaries at the base. The type locality is Oatman, Mojave county, Arizona.

Early Stages: The larval foodplant is *Eriogonum fasciculatum polifolium.*

2. **Philotes enoptes** (Boisduval). *P. enoptes* has entire, subquadrate valvae of the male genitalia. The distal end has a series of 18 to 22 (usually 21) short spines, giving it a sawtooth appearance. Seven subspecies are presently known.

Early Stages: In many, if not all, of the subspecies the flattened, centrally depressed eggs are deposited on late buds or early flower heads of various species of wild buckwheat, *Eriogonum* (Polygonaceae). The young larvae are well camouflaged, being about the color of the flower heads. Like *battoides,* as the larvae mature they become slug-shaped and vary from cream or yellow to pale rose, matching the color changes of the flowers.

(a) **enoptes** (Boisduval). Plate 61, figure 1, ♂; figure 2, ♀. The Dotted Blue occurs in California and western Nevada in the Cascades and Sierra Nevada, both on the east and west slopes. It has been recorded in all "mountain" counties in California from Siskiyou to Kern. The nominate subspecies is quite distinct on the ventral surfaces in that the orange "band" is reduced to a series of lunules, faint or obsolescent in many specimens. The male is blue above with wide dark borders. The female is dark brown above, occasionally with a few faint orange lunules on the secondaries.

Early Stages: I have associated adults with *Eriogonum latifolium nudum* and *E. saxicola* in parts of California and Nevada. The adults are on the wing in late spring and early summer.

(b) **ancilla** Barnes & McDunnough. Plate 58, figure 29, ♂; Plate 57, figure 1, ♂; figure 2, ♀. The Ancilla Blue is the subspecies in the Rocky Mountains and adjoining valleys and ranges. It has been recorded from Colorado, Idaho, Nevada, Utah, New Mexico and Wyoming. With such a wide range and scattered localities, there may be more than one subspecies involved. Based upon records and specimens examined, it appears to be most abundant in Utah, where the examples are close to typical. Most *ancilla* have a well developed orange-red submarginal band on the underside, with a relatively dark gray ground color and darker suffusion on the primaries. The type locality is Eureka, Juab county, Utah.

Early Stages: Larval foodplant known to be a form of *Eriogonum flavum* in Wyoming.

(c) **columbiae** Mattoni. Plate 61, figure 3, ♂; figure 4, ♀. The Columbia Blue is the subspecies in the Pacific Northwest, named for the type locality in the Columbia River Basin (near Brewster, Okanogan county, Washington). It has since been recorded on the central and eastern slopes of the Cascades of both Oregon and Washington and the ranges to the east. One of the largest *Philotes,* it is distinguished by the marginal band on the male upper hind wing which is often dissociated into a series of spots, the light gray underside ground color and the heavy black terminal line near the fringes. In parts of its range, *columbiae* is sympatric with *P. battoides glaucon* and *P. battoides oregonensis,* which some examples closely resemble. Adults appear in late May and June.

(d) **bayensis** Langston. Plate 61, figure 5, ♂; figure 6, ♀. The Bay Blue is the subspecies found close to San Francisco Bay area and the north coast ranges of California. It is allopatric to all other *Philotes.* At all known colonies *Plebejus acmon* is also present, and usually in greater numbers. Since the ubiquitous *acmon* has a much longer flight period (early spring to late fall), and few lepidopterists bother to collect long series, some *bayensis* colonies may have been overlooked. The male of *bayensis* is distinguished by the narrow marginal borders on the upperside of the hind wings. The ventral surfaces of both sexes have a light gray ground color with small but distinct spots and a prominent row of submarginal red spots on the secondaries. The type locality is China Camp, Marin county, California.

Early Stages: The life history as given by Langston and Comstock emphasizes a short period of adult flight (late May to early July), with oviposition synchronized with the late bud or early flower stage of the foodplant. The mature larvae have much less pinkish coloring, stripes and geometric patterns than other members of the genus that have been studied. Larval foodplants are *Eriogonum latifolium auriculatum* near the Bay, and *E. latifolium nudum* in the north coast ranges. Both plants bloom in late spring to early summer and have white flowers.

(e) **smithi** Mattoni. Plate 61, figure 7, ♂; figure 8, ♀.   Smith's Blue is known only from the coastal fog belt of Monterey county, California. It inhabits the sand dunes area north of Monterey, and ranges southward through the Big Sur country. *Plebejus acmon* is present at all the known colonies of *enoptes smithi*. The male of *smithi* is distinguished by the wide marginal border of the secondaries. The underside of both sexes has a faint terminal line and a light ground color with large prominent spots. The type locality is Burns Creek, State Highway One, Monterey county, California. Adults appear in late summer and early fall.

Early Stages: Adults have been associated with *Eriogonum parvifolium* at most colonies, but are also attracted to *E. latifolium* as a nectar source where it grows in close proximity to the former.

(f) **tildeni** Langston. Plate 61, figure 29, ♂; figure 30, ♀.   Tilden's Blue is found along the inner coast ranges of central California. It inhabits the hot, dry "rain shadow" foothills bordering the San Joaquin Valley. It appears to be a rather scarce insect and is very difficult to collect when there may be several dozen *Plebejus acmon* congregated and flying around the same flowers. The male of *tildeni* is distinguished by the wide dark borders on the upperside of the wings and the dark coloring in the subcostal area of the hind wing, resulting in a reduced amount of blue. The undersides of both sexes have slightly suffused fore wings with proportionately large black spots, and a prominent row of submarginal orange-red spots on the hind wing. The type locality is Del Puerto Canyon, Stanislaus county, California. Adults usually appear in late summer and early autumn, but a few have been taken in late spring.

Early Stages: The larval *foodplants* are late summer and fall blooming forms of *Eriogonum latifolium* with yellow flowers. Depending upon localities, the subspecies of the foodplant have been determined as *auriculatum, indictum, nudum* and *saxicola*.

(g) **dammersi** Comstock & Henne. Plate 61, figure 9, ♂; figure 10, ♀.   Dammers' Blue is the subspecies in the desert and adjacent mountain ranges of southern California and Arizona. It was originally presumed to be an inhabitant of the desert, but several colonies have been discovered at moderately high elevations in the mountains of southern California and in west central Arizona. This subspecies is distinguished on the underside by the extensive dark suffusion of the primaries, sometimes almost obscuring the large black spots. This suffusion is variable, however, and some specimens are lighter, particularly in the northwestern portions of the range.

As with the two previous *enoptes* subspecies, the adults fly from late summer into early autumn. Depending upon the season, elevation and latitude, most records are in August, September and October. The type locality is Snow Creek, Riverside county, California.

Early Stages: As recorded by Comstock & Henne, the light blue-green eggs are echinoid in form, and the top is deeply depressed with a relatively small micropyle. The young larvae are ivory white, with tinges of pink and brown in dashes and stripes. These markings are blurred by a complete covering of short white setae, giving the larvae a frosted appearance. The pupae are uniform pale chestnut color. Oviposition takes place on the buds and flowers of *Eriogonum elongatum* and *E. wrightii trachygonum* upon which the larvae feed.

3. **Philotes mojave** Watson & Comstock. Plate 57, figure 5, ♂; figure 6, ♀. The Mojave Blue is found in the Colorado and Mojave deserts of California and Nevada, and their bordering mountain slopes. It has also been found sparingly northward to the east of the Sierra Nevada: Argus and White mountains, California, eastward to Clark and Lincoln counties, Nevada. This species has extensive blue overscaling on the female, distinguishing it from all other *Philotes*. The male is pale lilac-blue on the upper surfaces.

Early Stages: As recorded by Comstock, the ivory white egg is echinoid in form and the top is deeply depressed with a minute micropyle. The young larvae have a conspicuous dark red middorsal line. The mature larvae are yellow with bars, dashes and spots of deep rose arranged in regular patterns. The pupa is brown, with a slight yellow tinge on the abdominal segments. Oviposition and larval feeding take place on the flowers of *Eriogonum pusillum*. The adult flight period coincides with the spring blooming desert wildflowers, March to early June, with most records in April.

4. **Philotes rita** (Barnes & McDunnough). Two completely allopatric subspecies of this butterfly are known. One is in the southwestern deserts, the other in prairie grassland.

(a) **rita** (Barnes & McDunnough). Plate 57, figure 9, ♂; figure 10, ♀. The Rita Blue is found in Arizona and southwestern New Mexico. According to Clench the type locality may be the vicinity of the Rio Verde Mountains near Phoenix, Arizona. Mattoni speculates that its range may extend into Mexico, the lack of records being the result of poor collecting in that area. I have examined atypical examples indicating a range extension northward into Utah and southwestern Colorado. The nominate subspecies has a broad and extensive red band on the underside of the secondaries, with large, distinct black spots on a creamy white ground. The upperside of the female on the secondaries has a wide, distinct orange-red submarginal band; pink shows in the male above also.

Early Stages: The foodplant is a species of *Eriogonum* close to *wrightii*.

(b) **coloradensis** Mattoni. Plate 61, figure 11, ♂; figure 12, ♀. The Colorado Blue is found in eastern Colorado (type locality, seven miles south of Kendrick, Lincoln county). The types and other specimens were taken in gently rolling prairie grassland. It occurs farther east than any other known *Philotes* in North America and flies in late summer. The subspecies differs from typical *rita* by the darker grayish undersides with clear halos around the spots. The upperside of the male is a darker purplish blue and has wide dark borders.

Early Stages: The larval foodplants are *Eriogonum effusum* in Colorado and a form of *E. flavum* in Wyoming.

5. **Philotes pallescens** Tilden & Downey. As in the preceding species, two subspecies have been described for this butterfly.

(a) **pallescens** Tilden & Downey. Plate 61, figure 31, ♂; figure 32, ♀. The Pale Blue was described from northwestern Utah. Atypical populations, however, have been found in other parts of Utah, and intermediates in Nevada. In reference to a Nevada specimen, Clench stated: "In the sum of its characters it is closest to *pallescens* . . ." and "one character suggests a relationship to *elvirae*." Nominate *pallescens* is known only from the general vicinity of the type locality, Little Granite Mountains, Dugway Proving Grounds, Tooele county, Utah. The female of *pallescens* is distinguished by the gray scales on the basal portions of the upperside of the primaries. The male is light blue with three to six submarginal spots on the upperside of the secondaries. Originally described as a full species, *pallescens* was later classified as a subspecies of *rita*. However, its elevation once again to species status in this volume has been done on advice from both of its describers. The genitalia, though similar to those of *rita*, differ sufficiently.

Early Stages: The larval foodplant is *Eriogonum spp.* Nominate *pallescens* appears to be most frequently recorded in August, although a few examples have been taken in July and September.

(b) **elvirae** Mattoni. Plate 61, figure 23, ♂; figure 24, ♀. The Elvira Blue is found in the Mojave desert and the east slope of the Sierra Nevada in California. The type locality is three and one-half miles southwest of Pearblossom, Los Angeles county, California. The paratypes are all from the southern portion of its range. To the north *elvirae* becomes atypical, grading into the Nevada form of *pallescens* noted above. Subspecies *elvirae* differs from the others in the shape of the hind wing, showing maximum expanse at M_1 instead of M_2 and a rather straight outer margin. Other unique features include the wide ventral marginal band and the strongly subquadrate spots.

Early Stages: As recorded by Comstock & Henne the pale green, echinoid eggs are deposited singly, deep in the flowers of the late blooming buckwheat. The first instar larva is light yellow-green with four longitudinal rows of translucent setae. The mature larva is ivory white turning a uniform orange-yellow. The larval foodplant is *Eriogonum plumatella*. Adults appear from late July to October, with most records in August and September.

6. **Philotes spaldingi** Barnes & McDunnough. Plate 57, figure 7, ♂; figure 8, ♀. Spalding's Blue is generally distributed in the central and eastern Rocky Mountains and in the Great Basin. It has been recorded from Arizona, Colorado, New Mexico and Utah. Adults of *spaldingi* are distinct from all other species of *Philotes* but outwardly resemble Blues in the *Lycaeides melissa* complex because the submarginal orange-red bands on the underside extend to the fore wings in addition to the hind wings. The upperside of the female also has extensive orange on both wings. The type locality is Provo, Utah county, Utah. Adults appear in June and July.

Early Stages: A known larval foodplant in Colorado is *Eriogonum racemosum.*

7. **Philotes speciosa** (Hy. Edwards). This extremely diminutive species contains two subspecies, one of recent discovery.

(a) **speciosa** (Hy. Edwards). Plate 58, figure 30, ♂; figure 31, ♀. The Small Blue is found most commonly in the western Colorado and Mojave deserts in California. It has been taken sparingly in the southern San Joaquin Valley, on the west slopes of the Sierra Nevada and in the White Mountains in eastern California; eastward in Clark county, and northward to Pershing county, Nevada. The type locality is Havilah, Kern county, California. Adults appear in March and April on the deserts, and in May in the more northerly parts of its range and at higher elevations. The adult *speciosa* is distinct from all other *Philotes* by the complete absence of orange-red spots, its very small size, the unicolorous brown of the female and the pale lilac-blue of the male.

Early Stages: Comstock and Dammers have recorded the curious larval habit of feeding only on the small fleshy points which arise from the stem around the leaf junctures of *Oxytheca perfoliata* (Polygonaceae), a principal foodplant. Other hosts include *Oxytheca trilobata* and *Eriogonum reniforme.* Mature larvae have also been found on the flowers of *Eriogonum pusillum.*

(b) **bohartorum** Tilden. Plate 48, figure 21, ♂; figure 22, ♂, underside. The males of this recently described subspecies are characterized by the lavender ground color above and the wide brown margins on the primaries. Females are solid smoky gray-brown above. The butterfly inhabits the foothills of the southern portions of the Sierra Nevada in California. The type locality is Briceburg, Mariposa county.

8. **Philotes sonorensis** (Felder & Felder). Plate 57, figure 3, ♂; figure 4, ♀. The Sonora Blue, one of the most charming of the lycaenids, is unique in appearance. It is found most commonly in lower canyons and dry washes in southern California. It also occurs in the Coast Ranges of central California, the west slopes of the Sierra Nevada and the lower canyons adjoining the western edges of the Mojave and Colorado deserts. It has been recorded southward into Baja California as far as the vicinity of Punta Prieta, Ensenada and the Sierra Juárez. Its northern limit in the California Coast Ranges is Santa Clara county; its northern known limit in the Sierras is Placer county, California.

This is the earliest *Philotes* on the wing. Its major flight is in February and March, both in the north and in the south. It may, however, extend into May at higher elevations or if the season is retarded by rain or snow. The type locality is "Sonora, Mexico," but there are no reports of *sonorensis* from the state of Sonora as it is now known. Butterflies named by the Felders as from Sonora are all found within the present limits of California and thus the true type locality of *sonorensis* must lie somewhere from Los Angeles southward into extreme northern Baja California.

Early Stages: As recorded by Comstock & Coolidge, "The eggs are placed mainly on the undersurface of the leaves, but may also be deposited on the uppersides and even on the stalks. The larvae feed on the thick, juicy leaves, sometimes crawling entirely within, but usually several of the posterior segments are left protruding. The apical portion of the leaves seems to be the preferred part, and even the stalk may be riddled. Pupation takes place in debris about, or at the base of the food-plant." The *foodplants* are various stonecrops (Crassulaceae). In northerly sections of its range it has been associated with *Dudleya c. cymosa, Dudleya cymosa setchellii* and *D. c. minor;* in southern California with *Dudleya lanceolata.* It probably also feeds on other sedums and stonecrops.

Genus PHAEDROTES Scudder

ROBERT L. LANGSTON

There is but a single species of this genus in our fauna. Recent studies by F. M. Brown have shown that the species *piasus* Boisduval (= *sagittigera* Felder & Felder) is genetically similar to *lygdamus* and should be placed with the genus *Glaucopsyche* Scudder. It has also been referred to *Scolitantides* Hübner.

1. **Phaedrotes piasus** (Boisduval).
   (a) **piasus** (Boisduval). Plate 56, figure 13, ♂. The nominate subspecies is paler above and below than other subspecies of *piasus.* It is distinguished by a row of white arrowhead spots below which blend into the pale gray ground color. Adults are larger than most other Plebejinae. Some of the largest examples occur in eastern Oregon and Washington. It may be easily recognized wherever taken by the figures provided. It is commonly called the Arrowhead Blue.
   Early Stages: The eggs are sculptured with deep reticulations, and are slightly flattened in shape. The mature larvae are yellow-brown with a gray-brown dorsal line, and lateral oblique lashes of dull white. In another color phase the larvae are blue-green. The caterpillars are attended by ants, a phenomenon known in other Lycaenidae. All subspecies of *piasus* feed on various types of lupine, *Lupinus* spp. (Leguminosae).
   Distribution: Chiefly montane; the species inhabits the Sierra Nevada of California and the Cascades of Oregon and Washington. It ranges northward in Washington and British Columbia where it is found at lower elevations. While often considered rare by collectors, it may be locally abundant in restricted colonies around perennial

lupine. But it is not found "everywhere lupines grow." In the Sierra Nevada *piasus* may be taken at elevations between 4000 and 8000 ft. Adults are in flight from April to July.

(b) **catalina** (Reakirt). Plate 56, figure 14, ♀.   The Cataline Blue is the subspecies represented in dry washes in southern California. It is distinguished by its smaller size, darker ground color beneath and the rusty outer margins above. It is very lavender above. The white arrowhead spots stand out in sharp contrast against the deep gray ground of the lower surface of the secondaries.

Early Stages: Coolidge found eggs on *Lupinus excubitus hallii* and *Lupinus hirsutissimus,* and reared the caterpillars on these hosts.

Distribution: This butterfly was formerly very common in the lowlands of Los Angeles county, but the disappearance of the wildflowers along with the development of subdivisions has decimated most colonies. Populations are still found in parts of the San Gabriel, Laguna, Santa Ynez, and Tehachapi mountains. A blend zone exists in the southern Sierras where *catalina* and typical *piasus* converge.

(c) **daunia** (Edwards). Plate 57, figure 17, ♂.   The Daunia Blue is darker blue above than other *piasus* and the arrowhead spots below are very distinct contrasting with the dark gray of the secondaries.

Distribution: This subspecies occurs from southern Alberta, Canada, south through western Nebraska to Colorado. It is most frequently encountered in the Front Range of Colorado between 6000 and 9000 ft. As it ranges westward to British Columbia, Washington, eastern Nevada, etc., it blends with the nominate *piasus.* Adults appear from late May to early July in a single brood. The butterfly is usually uncommon and restricted to local colonies.

Genus GLAUCOPSYCHE Scudder

WILLIAM H. HOWE

In the Nearctic this genus is represented by only two species. One of these, however, is composed of a rather extensive array of named subspecies, with much intergradation. Adults of *Glaucopsyche* are recognized on the ventral surfaces by a transverse postmedian row of rounded black spots sharply ringed with white, over a cold, steel gray ground color. Distal to these spots there are no other markings, which is distinctive. The upper surface of the male is characteristically bright, silvery blue. Females are usually brown or gray, or have a varying amount of blue overscaling depending on subspecies.

1. **Glaucopsyche lygdamus** (Doubleday).   This species is widespread, occurring across the northern United States from coast to coast; across all of Canada northward into the boreal regions of Alaska, the Yukon and the Northwest Territories; and south in the Appalachians to Georgia, Alabama and the Ozark Plateau in Arkansas. It is absent entirely in the hot humid belt in eastern Kansas and Missouri. It ranges

down the length of the high western side of the Great Plains to central Kansas and central Oklahoma. In the Rocky Mountains it extends southward to Arizona and New Mexico at higher elevations and from this region west to the Pacific. Its altitudinal distribution extends from sea level to above timberline.

Early Stages: The mature larvae are slug-shaped, and (depending on subspecies and individuals) variably colored—pale green, pale coffee color to purplish. A darker dorsal stripe, often reddish brown with a purplish tinge, characterizes many larvae. There are oblique whitish dashes and a lateral line becoming purplish ventrally. In *lygdamus behrii* the body is covered with roughened, long pale hairs producing a "frosted" appearance. In the middle of the tenth segment there is a gland providing a sweet secretion attractive to ants which tend the larvae. The pupa is formed amid debris and attached to a fixed object by means of both the cremaster and a silken girdle. In *behrii* the pupa is wood brown, with a paler metathorax and wing covers. Larval foodplants include many Leguminosae, including rattleweed and loco-weed (*Astragalus*); everlasting pea, (*Lathyrus*); beach pea (*Lathyrus couperi* and *L. ochroleucus*); also *Vicia caroliniana*, trefoils (*Lotus*), deerweed (*Lotus glaber*); lupines (*Lupinus*, including *Lupinus micranthus*), and vetch (*Vicia*, including *V. cracca* and *V. gigantea*). Other hosts, according to Downey, include *Hedysarum boreale*, *Adenostoma fasciculatum* (Chamise, Greasewood) and also Rosaceae. *Flight Period:* Adults have a brief flight period and are single brooded. They fly from March at sea level and in the far south to early June at timberline and in the far north.

(a) **lygdamus** (Doubleday). Plate 59, figure 20, ♂; figure 21, ♀. The nominate subspecies (*nittanyensis* is a synonym) is known as the Silvery Blue and is the common eastern U.S. representative. It occurs from the Great Lakes region to Georgia. The type locality is Screven county, Georgia.

(b) **couperi** Grote. Plate 59, figure 22, ♂; figure 23, ♀. Adults are small and pale silvery blue above. Below, the black spots are notably reduced in size and in some examples are obsolescent. This northern subspecies occurs in eastern Newfoundland, Canada, Alaska, the Yukon and the Northwest Territories, as well as northern Minnesota, Michigan and Wisconsin. The type locality is Anticosti Island, Quebec.

(c) **mildredae** Chermock. Mildred's Silvery Blue is a distinctive, very local subspecies discovered in northeastern Nova Scotia in 1941. As compared to *couperi* the blue is darker and brighter. On the lower side the black spots are larger, with their white rims broad and conspicuous. The ground color is dark slate, overcast with blue-green scales in the basal area. The type locality is Baddeck, Cape Breton Island, Nova Scotia.

(d) **oro** Scudder. Plate 61, figure 27, ♂; figure 28, ♀. The Oro Blue is the subspecies in the Rocky Mountains and Great Basin. With typical examples in Colorado, it intergrades with *couperi* to the north, *jacki* to the east and *columbia* in the Pacific Northwest. A montane subspecies in the Rockies, *oro* appears early in spring, following the snow melt on the mountain slopes up to timberline. Significantly larger than the previously treated eastern and northern subspecies, *oro* has the undersides more thickly dusted with gray and the hind wing basally greenish. It is pale silvery blue above.

(e) **jacki** Stallings & Turner.   Jack's Silvery Blue is the subspecies in the western Great Plains. The description was based on specimens taken in the Red Hills in Barber county, Kansas (type locality) and in north-central Oklahoma. It is also recorded in southeastern Colorado. Adults are large as are other western subspecies of *lygdamus;* the gray-brown underside is intermediate in color between eastern and western populations. The males are bright blue with metallic luster and the veins are edged distally with black, basally with white. The blue on females is more sparse than either *couperi* or *oro.*

(f) **arizonensis** McDunnough. Plate 58, figure 11, ♂.   The Arizona Silvery Blue is the subspecies in the higher mountains of eastern Arizona. It is the largest of the western subspecies. The upperside of the male is bright blue, deeply cast with purplish iridescence and with a heavy black marginal border. The black spots beneath are very large, each circled prominently with white. The ground color beneath is a warmer gray than all other *lygdamus,* with a pronounced darkening toward the outer edge. The type locality is the White Mountains in Arizona.

(g) **australis** Grinnell. Plate 56, figure 19, ♂; figure 20, ♀.   This subspecies occurs in dry washes and arroyos in southern California (type locality, Pasadena) and northern Baja California. It ranges northward in California intergrading with *behrii* in the central counties. It may be distinguished from *behrii* by a greater amount of blue on the upperside above in the female and smaller black spots beneath on the secondaries.

(h) **behrii** (Edwards). Plate 58, figure 9, ♂; figure 10, ♀.   Behr's Silvery Blue is the subspecies represented in the Coast Ranges of central and northern California. Common in the San Francisco Bay region, specimens from Monterey to Napa and Sonoma counties are close to typical. Examples from the Sierra Nevada and Cascade ranges blend toward *columbia* to the north. Adults are large, the males lustrous blue above with narrow black borders. Beneath there is a normal row of uniform black spots on a gray ground color. The female is dark brown, rarely with a few blue scales on the basal portions of the wings.

Early Stages: The larvae have been reared on *Lupinus micranthus* in Marin county; they are also recorded on *Lotus glaber, Astragalus* and the large yellow lupine, *Lupinus arboreus.*

(i) **columbia** Skinner. Plate 58, figure 12, ♀; figure 16, ♂.   The Columbia Silvery Blue is the subspecies represented in Oregon, Washington and extreme northern California, blending to the east in the Great Basin with *oro.* Intermediates are encountered in Idaho, northwestern Wyoming and western Montana. It averages about the same size as *behrii,* but the underside is paler gray with black spots averaging proportionately smaller. Above, *columbia* is a deeper shade of blue than *couperi,* and typical specimens are larger than the latter with which it blends to the north. The type locality is Port Columbia [= Brewster], Okanogan county, Washington.

2. **Glaucopsyche xerces** (Boisduval). Plate 58, figure 13, ♀; figure 14, ♂ (form "polyphemus"); figure 15, ♂ (form "antiacis").   The Xerces Blue was confined to the San

Francisco Peninsula from near Twin Peaks to North Beach, and from the Presidio southward to Lake Merced. So far as known, Dr. Harry Lange of Davis, California, took the last examples of *xerces* on March 23, 1943, on the beach side of Sloat Boulevard. It has not been collected since and is presumed extinct. There is little or no chance that it will ever "reappear." The species was known from sand dune colonies which were situated too near the city of San Francisco to be left unmolested. As with *Cercyonis sthenele* that preceded it to extinction, *xerces* was not adapted to conditions farther down the peninsula. Cold summer fogs drift constantly over the peninsula from the Pacific, but in nearly every land direction the summers are markedly warmer and sunnier, possibly something the species could not tolerate. Typical *xerces* is the form in which the black spots on the underside are absent, leaving large, white spots on a background of gray. The other forms have increased amounts of black spotting as shown in the figures.

Early Stages: These were recorded in detail by F. X. Williams and repeated by Comstock. Williams found one larva on *Lupinus arboreus,* and larvae readily devoured the leaves and pods of *Lupinus micranthus* and *Astragalus menziesii.* Other reported hosts were *Lotus glaber* and *Hosackia scoparia.* Museum specimens and published records indicate one brood of adults in March and April.

Genus CELASTRINA Tutt

ROBERT L. LANGSTON

In the Nearctic this genus is represented by the single Holarctic species *argiolus* (Linnaeus). The genus *Celastrina* is of circumpolar distribution, but *sensu stricto* the name *argiolus* refers to an entity occurring only in Europe and western Asia. Adult *Celastrina* are recognized on the upper surface by a pale, slightly violet-tinged blue, frequently whitish in the discal area, particularly on the secondaries. The ventral surface is entirely without any orange or metallic markings. In some subspecies the spots are vague or faded against a gray to whitish background, giving a "washed-out" appearance. In others the hind wing has brown blotches in the discal area and/or irregular brownish margins on both wings.

1. **Celastrina argiolus** (Linnaeus).   Nominate *argiolus* is Palearctic and does not occur in North America. The general distribution of those in the New World is from central Alaska to Labrador, south to the Gainesville area of Florida, and on through Mexico to Panamá. It occurs from the Hudsonian Zone to the Lower Austral Zone (= Lower Sonoran). It is apparently absent from southern Florida, the Bahamas and the central parts of the southwestern deserts, but does occur in the Great Plains and in most desert mountain ranges.

Five subspecies have been named from or are recorded in our area in addition to the four treated in detail below. These five are: *argentata* (Fletcher), *nigrescens* (Fletcher), *sidara* (Clench), *bakeri* (Clench) and *gozora* (Boisduval).

Early Stages: The pea-green eggs are turban shaped and studded with pale prominences. They are laid among flower buds, often tucked down out of sight, or on leaves. The larvae are predominately greenish, but may have a wide diversity of color variation by instar, subspecies or individuals. In the eastern U.S. they are whitish, rose-tinted, with a faint, dusky dorsal stripe and very faint lateral oblique greenish stripes. The body is covered with a white pubescence. The caterpillars are much attended by ants. The pupa is of the usual lycaenid form, plump and ovoid, usually brownish in color. The larvae feed on a wide variety of flowering shrubs, trees and plants including *Cornus florida* (Flowering Dogwood), *Ceanothus* (New Jersey Tea, California Lilac, Buckbrush), *Vaccinium* (Blueberries, Huckleberries), *Spiraea* (Meadowsweets), *Actinomeris* (Eastern Sunflowers), *Lotus* (Trefoils, Spanish Clover), *Verbesina* (Crownbeards), *Aesculus* (California Buckeye, Horse Chestnut), *Cimicifuga* (Bugbane, Black snakeroot), *Rhus* (Sumac, Squaw-bush), *Viburnum* and *Hosackia* (Deerweed). One of our earliest species, adults often appear while snow is still on the ground and few flowers are yet in bloom. One brood occurs in the far north, three in much of the eastern area, and perhaps more southward. Specimens have been collected as early as January (southern California) and well into September (Missouri).

(a) **lucia** (Kirby). Plate 57, figure 11, ♂; figure 12, ♀. The Northern Azure is found from Alaska eastward across Canada and south into Michigan and New York. In the far north specimens of the single brood are small and heavily marked with large, brown patches below. Farther south, in southern Canada and northern U.S., specimens appear in the first spring brood resembling *lucia.* Mingled with these, however, is the form "marginata" which lacks the central hind wing patch but possesses a wide, dark border. The type locality of *lucia* is Latitude 54°, Cumberland House, Saskatchewan.

(b) **pseudargiolus** (Boisduval & Le Conte). Plate 57, figure 19, ♂; figure 20, ♀. 57, figure 13, ♂ (form "violacea"); figure 14, ♀ (form "violacea"). The Spring Azure is the widespread subspecies occupying the central and southern latitudes from Michigan and Pennsylvania southward. The name *pseudargiolus* applies to the second or early summer brood, which is a large pale form. The uppersides, especially of the females, are characterized by large white areas in the discal region. Beneath the wings are clear grayish white with clear cut, though often small dark crescent-like markings. The name "violacea" applies to the common spring brood. These spring examples are smaller and more violet-tinged above, with less whitish in the discal areas. The adults appear in early spring from mid March through early April depending on latitude. The name "neglecta" (Plate 57, figure 20, ♀) applies to the late-summer brood. It averages smaller than typical *pseudargiolus.* The dark spots below are more distinct, and the upper hind wings, especially in the female, are paler.

(c) **cinerea** (Edwards). Plate 57, figure 16, ♀. The Arizona Blue is the subspecies common in Arizona and New Mexico in the southern Rocky Mountains and adjacent plateaus. It ranges southward into the mountains of Chihuahua, and occurs northward to central Colorado, Utah and Nevada. Confined mostly to forested, moun-

tainous areas, it is found up to elevations above 10,500 ft. The name *cinerea* applies
to the brood from overwintering pupae, in which the males are bright blue above,
and the mostly dark females more iridescent than in other subspecies. A female
of *cinerea* is shown on Plate 57, figure 16. The name "arizonensis" (Edwards), applies
to the later summer brood, which is more heavily bordered with black in both sexes.
Extreme examples may have very little blue on the female, especially on the secondaries.

(d) **echo** (Edwards). Plate 57, figure 15, ♂. The Echo Blue is the common Pacific
Coast subspecies. It has an extensive range from northern Baja California, California,
Oregon, Washington to British Columbia, Canada. It also extends inland through
the valleys and mountains to the desert and Great Basin areas. In contrast to the
eastern and northern subspecies, the wing pattern of *echo* is remarkably stable, both
geographically and seasonally. The early spring brood adults differ little from the
late spring and summer broods. The males are of a more delicate lavender tint above
than eastern *pseudargiolus*. In both sexes there is little, if any, white scaling on the
upperside, which is so prevalent in other subspecies. The larval foodplants of *echo*
consist of many flowering trees and shrubs, especially the western plants listed above,
under the species. Adult flight is recorded as early as January in Baja and southern
California, and increases from February to late spring. With some overlap of broods,
echo is still on the wing throughout the summer.

Genus PLEBEJUS Kluk

JOHN C. DOWNEY

The flexible parameters of this genus parallel somewhat the plastic classification of
the subfamily; one authority tends to lump many species under this name, while
the next would be more restrictive in its use. I tend to favor the less restrictive
approach, particularly for the non-specialist, since the use of intermediate categories
is still available to the specialist. The latter may wish, by the use of names within
a taxon, to call attention to similarities and differences not all of which have equivalent rank or value. In the treatment below, the more common usages are indicated
as subgenera, in parentheses. Even in the restricted usage, members of *Plebejus* are
found in the temperate regions of Europe, Asia and North America.

Early Stages: Larvae of the genus have been reported from fourteen different plant
species representing five families. Seven genera of Leguminosae are involved. Eggs
are laid singly on the host plant. Mature larvae have a functional honey gland on
the dorsum of the seventh abdominal segment, and a pair of eversible tentacle-like
structures on the eighth segment, just lateral to the spiracles. The larvae are often
found in association with ants. Many larvae are nocturnal feeders. Cannibalism is
common in reared specimens under laboratory conditions. Larvae usually have four
instars before entering the pupal stage. Pupae so far observed possess stridulating
organs, and all species are presumed to be capable of producing tiny creaking or

chirping noises. Most populations have one brood a year, but some subspecies are known to be double-brooded in the southern portions of their ranges.

1. **Plebejus (Lycaeides) argyrognomon** (Bergsträsser).   This species is circumpolar and widely distributed. It was named in the Old World and no fewer than eleven races have been designated in the boreal and arctic regions of North America. Nabokov (1949) has extensively revised the *Lycaeides* group, and the reader should consult his writings for details, particularly the characters of the genitalia. We have followed his taxonomy except for the level of generic groups and the separation of *empetri* from *aster*. Suffice it to say that in this species, as well as the following, there is great morphological diversity both within and among populations. Individuals may be most difficult to place in a typical subspecies. In fact, interpopulation diversity is so great, and environmental influences so marked, that one questions the validity of the trinomial designation. We include illustrations of specimens from these named races with the understanding that they are an indication of geographical diversity, but not necessarily diagnostic of the named subspecies.

Distribution: In North America, *argyrognomon* is restricted to the more northern areas above the latitude of 48°, except in the western United States where it extends southward through the Rocky Mountains to southern Colorado, and on the Pacific Slope to Fresno county, California. There appear to be three geographical groups of named subspecies: (1) a western array ranging from central California to British Columbia (*anna, lotis* and *ricei*); (2) a southern Rocky Mountain group ranging from southern Colorado northward to eastern Oregon, southeastern Washington and southeastern British Columbia (*sublivens, longinus, atrapraetextus* and *ferniensis*); and (3) a northern transcontinental group ranging from Alaska and British Columbia eastward to the Maritime Provinces of Canada (*alaskensis, scudderii, empetri* and *aster*).

(a) **anna** (Edwards). Plate 60, figure 3, ♂; figure 4, ♀.   Northern California, extreme southern Oregon and western Nevada encompass the general distribution of *anna,* which has been continually confused with the more northern subspecies. It intergrades with *ricei* between Mount Shasta, California, and Crater Lake, Oregon. The type locality is given only as "California." This entity has the largest wing expanse of any subspecies and together with *ricei,* shows a general pigment loss, particularly noticeable in the reduced maculation of the secondaries beneath. The underside ground is powdery white, with a tendency toward a yellowish cast in the female. The terminal line is faint and may be lacking between the veins. Females lack blue scaling on the upperside. The orange areas on the female upperside vary considerably and may be a narrow line, arched in each cell to a bar-like shape heavily infused with brown scaling. They may be blurred or faintly indicated in the fore wing, but are distinct in the hind wing.

(b) **ricei** (Cross). Plate 60, figure 1, ♂; figure 2, ♀.   This subspecies is distributed from southern Oregon through the Cascades of Washington to British Columbia, including Vancouver Island. Chermock's *fretchini* may be referred to this subspecies. The type locality of *ricei* is Big Cultus Lake, Deschutes county, Oregon. The larvae feed upon lupine in southern British Columbia, but are also known to utilize *Lathyrus torreyi* and *Vicia exigua* in Oregon. Maculation tends to be reduced but every transition may be found from poorly marked "*anna*-like" specimens, to the "*scudderii*-like" look of the Mount Rainier populations. Males are purplish blue on the upper surface; the ground beneath is grayish, dusted with blue scales; and the macules of the fore wing tend to align so that the posterior spots point basad. In the females the yellowish aurorae may be lacking in the fore wing, and the hind wing bar is marked distally by conspicuous brown insulae.

(c) **lotis** (Lintner). Plate 60, figure 5, ♂; figure 6, ♀. A rather restricted subspecies, *lotis* is known only from the type locality, Mendocino, and Point Arena in Mendocino county, California. Adults are found in sphagnum-willow bogs. The name has been associated incorrectly with populations from the Sierra Nevada of California (which are referable either to *anna,* or *melissa inyoensis*). *L. argyrognomon lotis* is one of the largest-winged of the nearctic *argyrognomon,* and although it is strongly pigmented, the orange of the hind wing underside is narrow. Scattered black scales impart a grayish cast to the ground color beneath, which is also generously coated basally with light blue-green scales.

(d) **alaskensis** (Chermock). Plate 59, figure 35, ♂; figure 36, ♀. This subspecies flies in northern British Columbia and Alaska. The name *kodiak* (Edwards) has been incorrectly used to refer to populations of *argyrognomon* from Alaska; it should be associated with another species entirely (*icarioides*). The type locality of *alaskensis* is Fort Yukon, Alaska. Pigmentation varies greatly from individual to individual, involving both the ground color and the macular components of the wing. A marked feature of most females is the distal extension of the blue scaling over the brown ground color, which, in the hind wing may reach the terminal line. Whitish scales are intermixed with the light blue overlay, particularly noticeable on the ground color, so that the females usually appear much lighter than females of other races. The orange of the female upperside is reduced to individual dots present only on the hind wing.

(e) **scudderii** (Edwards). Plate 97, figure 6, ♂. This entity has a wide distribution, including Alberta, Saskatchewan, southern Manitoba, Minnesota, eastern Quebec and Labrador. The type locality is the mouth of the Saskatchewan River between Cedar Lake and The Pas, Manitoba. This subspecies grades imperceptibly into *alaskensis* in its northeastern limits, and with *aster* in Quebec.

(f) **aster** (Edwards). Plate 59, figure 32, ♂; figure 37, ♀. Typical *aster* occurs in the Hudsonian zone regions of Newfoundland, Quebec and northern New Brunswick. The wing size is reduced in both sexes, and females have the orange markings on the upperside reduced, almost light brown in color, and they may be absent on the fore wing.

(g) **empetri** (Freeman). Plate 59, figure 24, ♂; figure 29, ♀. This subspecies flies in the Canadian zone of Nova Scotia and on Prince Edward Island (type locality). Females oviposit on *Empetrum nigrum, Ledum palustre* and *Kalmia polifolia,* usually restricted to sphagnum bogs. The figures emphasize the distinctive features, including the darkening of the underside ground, reduced blue scaling, enlarged and deeply pigmented macular components, enlarged terminal lines and reduced aurorae on the upperside of the female, with distal brownish black spots very apparent.

(h) **ferniensis** (Chermock). Plate 59, figure 30, ♂; figure 31, ♀. Populations from southeast British Columbia and southwest Alberta are debatably subspecific segregates of *argyrognomon,* and perhaps fall closest to *atrapraetextus.* They also intergrade with *scudderrii.* This subspecies differs from the latter in having better developed limbal macules and from the former in that the wings are more elongate with a more rounded apex in the female. There is great variability in the upperside aurorae of the female. These aurorae may be absent, present on the hind wing only (as in figure 31), or fully developed.

(i) **atrapraetextus** (Field). Plate 59, figure 38, ♂; figure 39, ♀. This subspecies occurs in Idaho, western Montana, eastern Oregon and southwestern Washington. Males above tend to have a purplish cast to the blue, perhaps exaggerated in darkness due to the darkened distal border. The orange aurorae in the female above, and the orange bar of the underside of both sexes, are noticeably sagittate in outline.

(j) **sublivens** Nabokov. Plate 60, figure 7, ♂; figure 8, ♀. This high altitude race occurs in the San Miguel, San Juan and Elk mountains in Colorado. The type locality is Telluride, Colorado. Males are dark blue above, and have a brownish gray ground color on the underside. The orange spots beneath are somewhat reduced in both sexes so that the orange crescents are discontinuous and the yellow-orange of the female above is reduced to crescents, the associated submarginal spots being most pronounced. The fringes of the wings are darkened at each vein tip, producing a checkered appearance. Males are easily confused with *P. melissa pseudosamuelis.*

Early Stages: Colorado larvae feed on *Lupinus parviflorus,* and both adults and immature stages may be sought in the lupine fields at or above timberline.

(k) **longinus** Nabokov. Plate 59, figure 33, ♂; figure 34, ♀. This subspecies was described from Jackson's Hole, northwestern Wyoming. In characters of the genitalia, individuals are intermediate between *argyrognomon* and *melissa.* Everywhere else these species are easily distinguished in genitalic characters, but Nabokov feels that they are transitional in this locality.

2. **Plebejus (Lycaeides) melissa** (Edwards). This attractive butterfly has a wider range of distribution than does New World *argyrognomon,* being sympatric with it over much of the southern part of the latter's territory and extending beyond into most of the western United States and northern Mexico. Five subspecies are presently recognized in our area. One additional subspecies has been described from the mountains of Chihuahua (*mexicana* Clench).

Early Stages: The life history has been recorded by Comstock, who described the egg of *melissa inyoensis* and oviposition by the female. It is interesting to note that females of the former entity laid eggs rather selectively on pebbles close to the host lupine, or on small leaves of the main stem near its juncture to the ground. Eggs of *melissa melissa* were deposited on any portion of the plant or on dead sticks or pebbles in proximity to it. There may be slight behavioral differences between the two entities in this regard. Larvae were taken in the field on *Glycyrrhiza lepidota,* an herbaceous legume, and raised to maturity on *Wistaria,* a climbing shrub of the same family. In addition, Comstock and Gunder name *Astragalus* and *Lotus* as food plants and Wright lists *Hosackia.* I have taken and reared Utah forms of *melissa melissa* on *Hedysarum boreale, Lupinus caudatus* and *L. parviflorus;* and Arizona forms from *Oxytropis lambertii, Lupinus alpestris* and *L. barbiger.* In addition to these, *Lupinus perennis, Medicago sativa* and *Acmispon americanum* are known hosts. The larvae possess honey glands and eversible tubes and are known to be assiduously attended by ants. Five instars are most common in laboratory rearings. There are generally two broods, but three have been indicated in prairie regions.

(a) **melissa** (Edwards). Plate 60, figure 11, ♂; figure 12, ♀. This subspecies occupies a sagebrush-prairie habitat and has a patchy distribution throughout the western United States. The type locality is Park county, Colorado, between Fairplay and California Gulch, but a part of the type series came from Nevada and Arizona. In northern California nominate *melissa* is sympatric with *P. argyrognomon anna,* but here, as in the mountains of Utah and Colorado, high altitude populations are encountered, two of which (*annetta* and *pseudosamuelis*) have been named. Isolated populations extend southward along the California coast throughout Santa Cruz county to Monterey county. It intergrades with *inyoensis* in Mono county, California, and southward. Nabokov claims to be able to recognize a "small form" of *melissa* in San Diego county, entirely within the range of *inyoensis,* but which intergrades with the latter. It is entirely possible that *melissa* does occur in distributional pockets which may be sufficiently isolated that some genetic, but perhaps more likely some ecological, integrity is maintained. The macular variability is known to be so great, however, and so few genitalic comparisons have been made, that extreme care must be taken to insure that the "intergrades" are only morphological intermediates; while they may reflect hybridization, it is equally possible that our parameters of variability for the entities may be too narrow. I suggest that the race *melissa* does not extend southward beyond the northern limits of Los Angeles county where typical *inyoensis* appears firmly entrenched. The range of *inyoensis* is extended to include all the polytypic array of the species *melissa* southward and eastward from Los Angeles county on the west, and south and eastward from Mono county, on a line roughly following the summit of the Sierra Nevada. The eastern limits of *melissa melissa* are in the western margin of the Great Plains from North Dakota to extreme northwestern Kansas.

(b) **pseudosamuelis** Nabokov. Plate 59, figure 27, ♂; figure 28, ♀. This is the high altitude race of *melissa* in Colorado. It is the extreme of an altitudinal cline from the lowland, brightly colored *melissa* to the rather dingy alpine *pseudosamuelis.* It feeds upon *Lupinus parviflorus.*

(c) **inyoensis** Nabokov. Plate 59, figure 25, ♂; figure 26, ♀. This is the California taxon ranging from Mono county through its presumed type locality at Olancha, Inyo county, and southeastward, west of the Sierra Nevada, and from Los Angeles county south and eastward including all the southern California counties. See remarks under *melissa* above. Many foodplants, all of which are legumes, have been reported for this segment of the species.

Nabokov elevated the name *inyoensis* Gunder from its original placement as a "transition form," which had no nomenclatorial validity. As Nabokov was the first to use *inyoensis* as a subspecies, he gets credit for the name. Nabokov did not designate a type or specify a type locality although both Gunder's type and much of Nabokov's material came from Olancha.

The figures show the typical appearance of both sexes, particularly the very white ground color of the under surface, and the almost blue upper surface of the female with its prominent orange aurorae.

(d) **annetta** (Edwards). This high altitude population is restricted to the Wasatch Mountains of north-central Utah. Like *pseudosamuelis* above, it intergrades with populations of *melissa melissa* at lower elevations. It appears more faded in general than the brighter lowland subspecies. Its habitat is characterized by *Lupinus parviflorus,* upon which the larvae feed, and by the ant, *Formica sanguinea subnuda* Emery, with which it is presumably associated.

(e) **samuelis** Nabokov. Plate 60, figure 9, ♂; figure 10, ♀. Known to easterners as the Karner Blue this subspecies represents *melissa* in the Great Lakes area and the Northeast. It occurs in scattered colonies from the Mississippi River eastward and northward. Its type locality is Karner (formerly Center), New York. As with other races, *Lupinus* is the host plant for this subspecies.

3. **Plebejus (Plebejus) saepiolus** Boisduval. This western Nearctic species has pushed its way eastward in the boreal regions of southern Canada. It is common in the mountainous regions from Colorado westward, and from southern California northward to Alaska. In the East it is distributed in isolated pockets throughout southern Canada eastward to Maine, and extends southward into the Great Lakes states. Adult *saepiolus* vary considerably both within and among populations. Sexual dimorphism is more marked in some areas than others, depending on the amount of blue and orange in the female upperside (see Plate 59, figures 4, 8 and 9). Females may show color variation within one population. The iridescent blue of the males is diagnostic and often appears to have a silvery cast. Populations in which the orange maculation of the underside of the hind wing is reduced or rubbed may be momentarily confused with *icarioides*. A dorsal discal spot, however, is usually visible in *saepiolus*. The ground color of the underside of the female of this species is warmer than in associated males, and the macules are consistently larger and better defined. The adults of *saepiolus* fly close to the ground, and congregate by the dozens in damp places along stream banks and sunny trails. It is the commonest blue in the West, with the possible exception of *P. melissa.*

Early Stages: The larvae feed upon *Trifolium* of various species: *T. hybridum* in the eastern parts of its range; *T. breweri* in Plumas county, California; *T. repens* in Gunnison county, Colorado; and *T. monanthum* in Nye county, Nevada. Eggs are laid on the flower heads and are most difficult to find even when the female has been observed to oviposit on them. The larvae, as with most lycaenids, have both green and reddish color phases, even siblings from the same female. They hibernate as larvae. The far eastern populations are associated with bogs. The species is multi-brooded in the southern parts of its range and at lower elevations. This helps account, at least in part, for the great variability observed in large series from one area.

(a) **saepiolus** (Boisduval). Plate 60, figure 13, ♂; figure 14, ♀ (form "rufescens"). This subspecies ranges from the mountains of central California northward to British Columbia where it gives way to *insulanus;* eastward throughout the mountains of the northern Great Basin and Rocky Mountains it contacts *whitmeri* in southern Colorado and *amica* in the northeastern part of its range. Females are rusty brown with occasional reddish orange spots at the anal angle, but only rarely have a reddish submarginal band on the hind wing.

(b) **hilda** (Grinnell & Grinnell). Plate 59, figure 3, ♂; figure 4, ♀. Hilda's Blue is the southern California representative of *saepiolus.* It is characterized by strongly developed macules in both sexes. In the female the hind wings have a well developed reddish submarginal band, which generally is extended to the fore wing. This subspecies has the largest wing expanse of all *saepiolus.*

(c) **insulanus** Blackmore. Plate 59, figure 7, ♂; figure 8, ♀. Restricted to Vancouver Island and western British Columbia, *insulanus* has weakly to moderately developed macules on the under surface. The hind wing lacks the red-orange maculae so prominent in southern populations. Blue females are very rare; only a few scattered blue scales can be found on the basal part of the wing.

(d) **amica** (Edwards). Plate 59, figure 9, ♀; figure 14, ♂. This name is used for populations from eastern British Columbia to Alaska, and eastward through the mountains of Manitoba to eastern Canada and Maine. The subspecies has also pushed southward into the Great Lakes states. The under surface ground color in the male is pale gray, in contrast to the maritime and California populations which are almost white. Under surface macules are weakly developed. Edwards's name *kodiak* belongs in the synonomy of *saepiolus; kodiak* and *amica* are probably not sufficiently distinct to warrant both names.

(e) **gertschi** dos Passos. Plate 59, figure 5, ♂; figure 6, ♀. This subspecies is restricted to the southern mountains of the Great Basin. It is the smallest of the named forms. No completely brown females are known, blue usually being well developed on the upper surface. Dark submarginal lunules are apparent on the hind wings of both sexes, those of the female often containing orange scaling.

(f) **whitmeri** Brown. Plate 60, figure 15, ♂; figure 16, ♀. Brown's Clover Blue is found in the southern Rocky Mountains. The underside has well developed maculae in both sexes. Females have considerably more blue than females of nominate *saepiolus* or *amica* to the north, and have a darker ground color on the under surface than *gertschi* to the west.

4. **Plebejus (Plebulina) emigdionis** (Grinnell). Plate 58, figure 7, ♂; figure 8, ♀. This attractive species, the San Emigdio Blue, is restricted to isolated colonies in southern California, mostly on the southernmost edges of the San Joaquin Valley. It has been reported as far north as the Lower Haiwee Reservoir in Inyo county, California. Adults appear briefly in May. It is normally single brooded, although an abortive second brood has been reported. Eggs are laid singly on the foodplants, which include *Atriplex* and *Hosackia purshiana.* Larvae have a honey gland and eversible tubes, but their possible association with ants and other aspects of their life history are unreported.

5. **Plebejus (Icaricia) icarioides** (Boisduval). This species is limited in distribution to western North America, west of the central Great Plains region. However, in this vast area it occurs in many discontinuous populations, mostly in the Canadian and Transition life zones. It occurs from northern Baja California and Arizona northward to Alaska, and from sea level to over 12,000 ft. Adults are quite locally distributed and are encountered in close proximity to their host plants. In southern Montana, however, they may be encountered by the hundreds as they visit the flowers of lupine in vast stands of these plants.

Early Stages: Newcomer in 1911 first described the complete life cycle using the name *Lycaena fulla* for the Lake Tahoe population. Comstock and Dammers added to the life history of the southern California representative (*evius*). Downey added data on host plants, relationship to ants, parasites and pairing behavior. Briefly, larvae of the species are limited to the plant genus *Lupinus,* with over forty species and subspecies of the plant being used. One butterfly population, however, is generally restricted to one host species of lupine, generally the most pubescent species in the area. There is only one generation per year. The second instar larvae go into diapause through the long summer and winter months. The later instar larvae are associated in a facultative way with ants, some eleven species of which have been identified in this association. Ants often construct chambers at the base of the foodplants just beneath the soil surface for access to the resting larvae or as diurnal resting places for the larvae, or both. Larvae may sometimes be found on leaves or in the lupine blossoms by looking for the more conspicuous ants in attendance. There is a high incidence of parasitism in mature larvae located in the plant during the daytime; healthy larvae tend to be nocturnal feeders.

It is only with reluctance that I give the following trinomial designations. This species exhibits tremendous variation, both within and among populations, and in time as well as space. Further, specimens reared (see under *icarioides* below) under different conditions indicate that most of the color differences diagnostic of populations are markedly affected by environmental conditions. The differences one observes between populations may be real, but they may also be a reflection of the environmental features in a given area. Most of these subspecies then, should be considered on the basis of general locality, and not on any hard and fast morphological criteria.

(a) **icarioides** (Boisduval). Plate 56, figure 22, ♂; figure 26, ♀. The type locality of the nominate subspecies was fixed by Hovanitz as between 2000 and 4000 ft. in El Dorado and Nevada counties, California. The subspecies extends southward in the Sierra Nevada and gradually gives way to subspecies *evius,* showing also some characters of *ardea.* In its northward extension through the central regions of Oregon and Washington there are locally constant maritime populations which may cause taxonomic consternation. On the crest of the Sierras, the Great Basin subspecies *ardea* interdigitates in scattered pockets. It shows a wide range of macular variation.

Several names have been long considered synonyms of *icarioides* (*phileros* Bdv., *fulla* Edw., *maricopa* Reak., *daedalus* Behr, and *spinimaculata* Gunder). Edwards himself acknowledged that his *helios* (sometimes considered by later authors to be a valid subspecies) was a synonym of Boisduval's *phileros,* and I can see no valid reason for distinguishing populations by that name. Edwards's name *kodiak* has been erroneously placed in the synonymy of *icarioides* but it should be placed with *saepiolus.*

Environment no doubt plays a major role in the interpopulation variability of this species. This was convincingly demonstrated to me when adults of *icarioides icarioides* from the high Sierra Nevada were reared at low elevations (in Davis, California) and 100% of the females were of the *evius* variety, typical of populations from hotter, drier climates. Similarly, offspring of Arizona *icarioides buchholzi* females reared in Illinois were markedly different from their parents.

(b) **evius** (Boisduval). Plate 56, figure 15, ♂; figure 16, ♀. This race is restricted to the hotter, drier mountain ranges of southern California, particularly from the Tehachapi Mountains southward, although single populations falling within the limits of this race have been noted in western Arizona. Maculation is large and pronounced and the females are typically almost blue in appearance. The hind wing upperside of the females usually has orange scaling, which may also occur in the tornal angle of the fore wing. Males have a narrow, well defined terminal line.

(c) **moroensis** (Sternitzky). Plate 56, figure 17, ♂; figure 18, ♀. The type locality of this race is Morro Beach, San Luis Obispo county, California. The influence of the maritime climate has imparted a silvery cast to the upper surface of the male. This same feature is observed in males of other coastal populations (*missionensis, pheres* and *blackmorei*) and is due to an infusion of white scales along with the blue, particularly along wing veins. This race also occurs on Pismo Beach, and in scattered localities inland in the same county.

(d) **missionensis** Hovanitz. Plate 59, figure 1, ♂; figure 2, ♀. The Mission Blue occurs only on the San Francisco Peninsula where its type locality is Twin Peaks, San Francisco, California, at 700 ft. These populations were originally separated by only a short distance from beach populations of *pheres* (Boisduval), which appears to have been extirpated by the expansion of the city.

(e) **pardalis** (Behr). Plate 60, figure 23, ♂; figure 24, ♀. Hovanitz was first to correctly associate *pardalis* and *pheres* as subgroups of *icarioides.* No doubt part of the reluctance of others to accept this assignment is the distinctive appearance of "typical" *pardalis* and *pheres* forms, and the tacit assumption that they did not vary as much as nominate *icarioides.* However, the large spotted *pardalis* type can be seen to vary in a cline from near its type locality in Contra Costa county, California, southward into Santa Clara county (San Jose), and northward through the central lowland districts. Males in Sonoma county, for example, have reduced black spots and lighter ground color, and come closer to nominate *icarioides,* while the females from the same populations retain the rich dark brown color and large macules of typical *pardalis.* This entity occurs sporadically northward through Lake county, and in northern California grades inperceptibly into the *icarioides* type of the Sierras. The name *fenderi* Macy, associated with populations from McMinnville, Oregon, falls into the synonymy of *pardalis.* Females from Contra Costa, Alameda and Marin counties, California, lack any indication of a blue overlay in the upper surface.

(f) **pheres** (Boisduval). Plate 60, figure 21, ♂; figure 22, ♀. The Pheres Blue is one of the most distinctive forms of the species because of the light brown upper surface of the female, and the fact that it always has a prominent white discal spot on the fore wing. This is not to say that females from elsewhere always lack such a spot. The whitish halo surrounding this macule in *pheres,* however, imparts a distinguishing touch. The under surface has reduced maculation, particularly on the secondaries, and the white halos around the much reduced (or absent) pupils are made much more apparent and give a white-spotted appearance to the underside. This name has been used in earlier works for specimens and populations associated with sand dunes in San Mateo and Marin counties (Point Reyes). The former populations in the San Francisco area appear to be entirely extinct.

(g) **ardea** (Edwards). Plate 60, figure 17, ♂; figure 18, ♀. This subspecies occurs throughout the Great Basin of Utah and Nevada, extending across the Sierra Nevada on its western limits into El Dorado county, California, and eastward to the Uinta Mountains in Utah, southward to the Navajo Mountains, Utah, and northward into central Idaho. Adults of *ardea* can be distinguished from those of *lycea* by their smaller size and reduced maculation on the underside of the secondaries, particularly the nearly obscure black pupils. This reduction of "eyespots" on the secondaries may also be accompanied by a reduction or lack of the submarginal row of lunules as shown in Plate 60, figure 17. The marked fuscous marginal band of the male fore wing tends to lose intensity in the secondaries.

The type locality is Virginia City, Nevada, and some of the populations on isolated mountain ranges show extreme diversity, caused in part by climatic conditions under which the butterflies live. Many populations outside the range of *ardea* develop a similar under surface appearance but should be considered ecophenotypes rather than belonging to *ardea.*

(h) **lycea** (Edwards). Plate 60, figure 19, ♂; figure 20, ♀. This subspecies occurs from northern Arizona and northern New Mexico northward through the Rocky Mountains to Wyoming and Montana, where it gradually gives way to *pembina.* The latter has smaller wings, a more brownish cast to the under surface ground and more violet in the male upperside. The subspecies *lycea* extends westward into southeastern Utah, and populations with *ardea* characters are noted in several western Colorado and eastern Utah localities. Flourishing colonies occur in Sioux county, Nebraska. Blue scaling in the female is restricted to the basal area.

(i) **buchholzi** dos Passos. Plate 56, figure 23, ♀; figure 24, ♂. This entity flies in the mountainous regions of eastern Arizona and adjacent western New Mexico. Populations in north-central Arizona and northwestern New Mexico tend to show a large percentage of *lycea* characters and are more properly assigned to that entity. The type locality is the White Mountains, Arizona. The upperside of the male is blue-violet with very wide black marginal borders, which are diagnostic. The female often has an orange spot near the anal angle.

(j) **pembina** (Edwards). Plate 56, figure 27, ♂; figure 28, ♀. The northern race of *icarioides* occurs from the mountains of extreme northwestern Wyoming and northern Idaho northward into Alberta and westward into eastern British Columbia, where it grades into the rather similar subspecies, *montis*. Outlying eastern populations of *pembina* are found in the Cypress Hills of Saskatchewan and in Slope county, North Dakota. The type locality (Lake Winnipeg) indicated in the original description is almost certainly an error. Unfortunately the types were lost in shipment during Edwards's time. The neotype locality is in the Bitter Root Mountains, Ravalli county, Montana. The species, so far as known, does not occur in Manitoba, and barely reaches even the western regions of Saskatchewan.

(k) **blackmorei** Barnes & McDunnough. Plate 60, figure 25, ♂; figure 26, ♀. The type locality of this subspecies is Goldstream, Vancouver Island, British Columbia. The subspecies also occurs in the western lowlands of mainland British Columbia. The silvery blue color of the males is characteristic and is produced by the physical arrangement of cyanic overlay and ground color plus a scattering of white scales. The under surface is almost immaculate and most individuals show some reduction in macular components. Wing size in both sexes is large, and is exceeded only by populations from the Sierras in California.

(l) **montis** Blackmore. Plate 56, figure 30, ♂; figure 31, ♀. This subspecies is distributed at higher elevations in central and eastern British Columbia. Maculation of the under surface is much more pronounced than in *blackmorei*. The upperside of the male is a much lighter shade of violaceous blue than in *pembina*, and it also has a much narrower black border.

6. **Plebejus (Icaricia) shasta** (Edwards). The species is widespread throughout the alpine regions of western North America, usually above timberline. Adults fly for only a short time, but may be locally very numerous. Larvae feed on *Astragalus calycosus* in the Toquima Range in Nevada, and are suspected of using lupine in California. There is one generation a year.

(a) **shasta** (Edwards). Plate 59, figure 18, ♂; figure 19, ♀; figure 16, ♀ (form "comstocki"); figure 17, ♂ (form "comstocki"). Widely distributed throughout the higher peaks of California, Oregon and Washington, nominate *shasta* also occurs throughout the mountains of the Great Basin northward into Idaho.

The name "comstocki" Fox has been used for individuals which can be found with populations of nominate *shasta*. Individuals exhibit some variation, which falls within the parameters of the nominate subspecies, so that the name "comstocki" should be considered infrasubspecific and without nomenclatural status.

(b) **minnehaha** (Scudder). Plate 59, figure 15, ♂. This subspecies flies in the high peaks of the Colorado Rockies and ranges northward into Montana and Alberta. It also occurs in western Nebraska.

7. **Plebejus (Icaricia) acmon** (Westwood & Hewitson). This species ranges from the West Coast to the western edges of the Great Plains, and from southern Canada south to northern Baja California and central mainland Mexico, with outlying colonies (representing eastward range extensions) in Minnesota, Nebraska and Kansas. The types are from California. *P. acmon* is separable from most other lycaenids by the orange submarginal band on the upperside of the secondaries in

both sexes. Distally the band contains a series of black or fuscous dots; it is slightly broader in the female. This species has a wide variety of legumes listed as acceptable foodplants, among which are *Astragalus, Acmispon (Hosakia), Lotus* and *Lupinus*. In Colorado *Eriogonum subalpinum* and *E. umbellatum* are reported for *acmon lutzi*. Four broods are known to occur in some areas, and seasonal variation must be considered in accounting for color variations. Cannabalistic tendencies are noted in the larvae.

(a) **acmon** (Westwood & Hewitson). Plate 60, figure 31, ♂; figure 32, ♀. *Butterfly:* Within its broad range from southern California northward to British Columbia, including the intermontane western states, *acmon* is quite variable. Typically it is a small species with a slight lavender cast to the blue of the male fore wing; the orange band on the male secondaries often has a lavender or pinkish cast. Adults fly close to the ground and congregate at mud patches along sunny forest trails, forest openings or clearings.

(b) **cottlei** (Grinnell). Plate 60, figure 29, ♂; figure 30, ♀. This insect is widely distributed in the lowlands and foothills of central California. It emerges in early spring. The female has a rich shade of blue basal on the upperside, more extensive in the fore wing, and the orange bar of the secondaries is much wider than in nominate *acmon*. This may represent only the spring brood of *acmon*, so additional taxonomic work is warranted.

(c) **lutzi** dos Passos. The Rocky Mountain population of *acmon* has a bright lilac-blue male; females rarely have traces of blue on the wing bases. It is abundant in Colorado.

8. **Plebejus (Icaricia) lupini** (Boisduval). Four subspecies are assigned to this species. At present their taxonomy is unsettled. This species has been thought to be a Sierran race of *acmon*, but it appears to be distinct.

(a) **lupini** (Boisduval). Plate 60, figure 27, ♂; figure 28, ♀. This butterfly is larger than *acmon*. Although variable in width, the orange line on the secondaries is usually narrow, and appears to be formed of a series of crescents, one in each interspace. A diagnostic feature of the male is the broad black or fuscous marginal band which fades gradually into the blue. A single brood flies in late June and July and has been associated with the plant *Eriogonum*. Nominate *lupini* occurs in the higher elevations of the Sierra Nevada of California.

(b) **spangelatus** Burdick. Populations in the northern part of the species range may go by this name. It was described from the Olympic Mountains in Washington. It also inhabits the Cascade Range.

(c) **monticola** (Clemence). Plate 58, figure 5, ♂; figure 6, ♀. The taxonomic position of this insect with respect to *lupini* is open to question. Originally it was described as a race of *acmon* occurring in the southern Sierras. It has also been treated as a full species. It is a *lupini* however, whose large size and pale blue in the males give it a unique appearance. Females have much blue on the upper surface, exceeding that of any other member of the subgenus. It flies in mountain ranges around Los Angeles, California.

(d) **chlorina** (Skinner). Plate 58, figure 3, ♂; figure 4, ♀. Limited to small populations in the Tehachapi and Tejon mountains of southern California, this entity is of doubtful taxonomic status and has been considered a full species. It is easily distinct from other *lupini* relatives by the greenish shade in the blue of the upper surface. This cast may be more difficult to ascertain in the female.

9. **Plebejus (Icaricia) neurona** (Skinner). Plate 60, figure 33, ♀. *P. neurona* occurs in small populations at high elevations in the Tehachapi, San Gabriel, San Jacinto and San Bernardino mountains in southern California, as well as in scattered localities in the southern Sierra Nevada. Both sexes are brown above, the male slightly smaller in wing span. As indicated in the figure, orange veining of the upperside, particularly the primaries, is a distinguishing feature. Females show some variation in this character. The species is single brooded with adults in early June. Larvae feed on *Eriogonum wrightii*.

10. **Plebejus (Vacciniina) optilete** (Knoch). Plate 58, figure 1, ♂; figure 2, ♀ (ssp. *yukona*). This is a circumpolar species, our representative of which (ssp. *yukona* (Holland), as figured) is limited to the subarctic from eastern Alaska eastward to the vicinity of Churchill, Manitoba. Adults are usually taken in mid July. Its appearance in the figure is typical: the striking purple of the male upperside; the prominent orange spot in the anal angle of the secondaries; and the chocolate brown female with basal violet scaling. The larvae of *optilete* feed on *Vaccinium myrtillus*. In Europe the larvae lack the honey gland and eversible tubes and are not associated with ants. The larval stage overwinters.

11. **Plebejus (Agriades) aquilo** (Boisduval). The distribution of this arctic species is circumpolar. In North America it extends southward down the western coastal ranges to the central Sierras and in the central Rockies to northern New Mexico and east-central Arizona, and eastward to Manitoba, Ellesmere Island and Labrador. Females have been observed to oviposit on several plants, *Androsace, Soldanella, Diapensia* and *Vaccinium,* and larvae are reported to feed on *Saxifraga appositifolia*. In Europe *aquilo* feeds on *Gregoria*. The butterfly has an "arctic" look about it, particularly its small size and dull colors. There is considerable color variation from population to population.

(a) **aquilo** (Boisduval). Plate 59, figure 10, ♂; figure 11, ♀. Adults are characterized by small size and dull, dingy colors. The wings above have narrow terminal borders. This subspecies extends northward from Churchill, Manitoba, to the limit of land in the Arctic and eastward to Labrador.

(b) **lacustris** Freeman. This subspecies occurs in central Manitoba. It is larger than the preceding, with dark marginal borders above.

(c) **bryanti** Leussler. Plate 78, figure 9, ♂; figure 10, ♀ (both Alaska specimens, subspecies near *bryanti*). This subspecies has a limited range. Its type locality is Black Mountain, near Aklavik, Northwest Territory.

(d) **megalo** McDunnough. Plate 59, figure 12, ♂; figure 13, ♀. This subspecies ranges from British Columbia eastward into Alberta and south to Washington. The cold blue of the male and the brownish ground of the female are accurately shown in the figures.

(e) **rustica** (Edwards). Plate 58, figure 17, ♂; figure 18, ♀. The central and southern Rocky Mountains are the home of *rustica*. Adults are much larger than the more northern races and the dorsal marginal band is large, often diffusing inward some distance and obscuring the line of submarginal spots on the secondaries. Females are a warm dark brown and may also lack traces of submarginal lunules.

(f) **podarce** (Felder & Felder). Plate 58, figure 19, ♂; figure 20, ♀. This subspecies occurs in high mountain meadows throughout the Sierra Nevada, northward into Oregon. The females tend to be russet color on the upperside. The larval foodplant has been recorded as *Vaccinium nivictum*.

Genus EVERES Hübner

The Tailed Blues

JOHN C. DOWNEY

Members of this genus possess a small but distinct tail at vein Cu_2. They also have characters of the wings (R touches Sc), legs (tarsal claws with inner tooth) and genitalia which set the genus apart. In our region the tailed condition of the secondaries is readily apparent and diagnostic. The genus ranges throughout Europe, the Oriental region and Australia. Our two species are endemic to North America. There is no reliable way to distinguish between the two species externally. The genitalia of both sexes are distinct, however, and since the ranges of the species overlap only infrequently, geography may prove an aid in applying trinomial designations. I am grateful to Harry K. Clench for aid in the taxonomic reassignments of the entities here treated. At least nine genera of Leguminosae are known to be utilized as foodplants by *Everes*. The larvae are equipped with honey glands and eversible tubes, but are only infrequently attended by ants in the field. They hibernate as full grown larvae. The species are multiple brooded. The pupae stridulate.

1. **Everes comyntas** (Godart). Plate 56, figure 25, ♂ (summer form); figure 29, ♀ (summer form); Plate 58, figure 23, ♂ (spring form); figure 24, ♀ (spring form). The nominate subspecies is widely distributed east of the 110th meridian, and extends from Montreal, Quebec, southward to Florida. (There is also an isolated population in coastal Oregon and California.) The names *herrii* (Grinnell), *valeriae* Clench and *albrighti* Clench, hitherto associated with *comyntas,* should be transferred to *amyntula.* Nominate *comyntas* is the commonest lycaenid in the eastern area, and one of our most abundant butterflies. The adults are encountered virtually everywhere (except deep forests), especially along roadsides, in open meadows and farmlots as well as in city yards. Contrary to most native butterfly species, *comyntas*

seems to increase with the activities of man. Road and railroad rights-of-way are often kept mowed, or are seeded with plants suitable for this species, and its habitat would thus appear to be increasing.

Early Stages: Eggs and larvae are found on White Clover (*Trifolium repens*), Red Clover (*T. pratensis*) and lespedeza (*Lespedeza stipulaceae*), all cultivated by man, although many other plants may also be used. Eggs are laid on the flower heads and the larvae prefer feeding on the flower parts. Several authors have described the immature stages. Of interest is the fact that some larval characters are variable, just as are the adult characters and character changes also occur from molt to molt.

The species is multiple brooded and some adult characters show seasonal variation. Early spring males are usually pale with narrow black margins while summer generation males are darker with wider margins. Early spring females show moderate to extensive blue scaling above (see figures). In contrast, summer females are dark brown to slate gray above, with little or no blue scaling. This is one of the earliest butterflies to appear in spring and flies until the first freeze of autumn.

The chiefly Mexican and Central American race, *texana* Chermock, may be distinguished by its smaller size, the male with more violet above, and the female with a discal infusion of blue scales. The type locality is San Antonio, Texas.

2. **Everes amyntula** (Boisduval). Plate 58, figure 21, ♂; figure 22, ♀. This is likewise a common species, largely replacing *comyntas* in the West and Northwest. Adults of *amyntula* average larger than those of *comyntas* but resemble the latter closely. The relationship between *amyntula* and *comyntas* is not completely clear. While the two species are distinct, both fly together in several localities such as St. Louis county, Minnesota, and coastal sections of Oregon and California. But *amyntula* is boreal, on the West Coast ranging from northern Baja California to Alaska and the Mackenzie Delta Region, and eastward to the Gaspé Peninsula. It also extends southward in the central Rocky Mountains to Arizona and southern New Mexico. Where the two species are encountered together you may recognize *amyntula* beneath by the chalky white (not gray) ground color, and the rounded (rather than pointed) apex of the wing. The male has a narrow terminal line above; both sexes may have reduced to obsolete maculation, and usually have a much reduced pale orange spot on the secondaries beneath. Females almost always have some blue above.

Early Stages: The larvae have been reported on *Astragalus, Lathyrus* and *Vicia*.

Because of the variability of *amyntula,* many of the populations assigned to it are vague, indistinct and difficult to place. The Canadian, Alaskan and northern Minnesota subspecies has been designated *albrighti* Clench. This northern segregate was distinguished on the basis of the grayish costal shading of the fore wing below (TL: Kings Hill, Montana). The subspecies *valeriae* Clench may be recognized by the very white lower surfaces with little maculation and no orange lunule on the dorsal hind wing (TL: Terry Peak, Black Hills, South Dakota). Additional named subspecies include *herrii* (Grinnell) in Arizona and New Mexico. Nominate *amyntula* is confined to the Pacific states.

Family PIERIDAE
The Sulphurs, Whites and Orange-tips

WILLIAM H. HOWE
(except for *Colias*)

The Pieridae are found on all continents except Antarctica. These common and familiar butterflies are small to medium, occasionally large, in size. Ours are white, yellow or orange variously marked with black. The pigments responsible for the white, yellow and orange coloration are known as pterins and do not occur in the wings of other butterflies. These pigments contain biopterin, a vitamin, and sepiapterin, a pigment playing a photoreceptive role in insects. The Pieridae are rather closely related to the Papilionidae but differ from the latter family in several ways. The following characteristics readily distinguish the pierids from all other butterfly families: (1) the tarsal claws are bifid; (2) the front legs are fully developed in both sexes; (3) an epiphysis is lacking on the front legs; (4) vein M_1 of the fore wing is nearly always stalked with the radius; (5) from three to five radial branches are present, some of which are always stalked and reach the margin of the fore wing; (6) the cell is closed in both wings; and (7) a prespiracular bar at the base of the abdomen is lacking.

Early Stages: The eggs are tall and spindle-shaped and frequently vertically ribbed. The only other family of butterflies with eggs of about this shape is the Danaidae. The larvae are slender, smooth and cylindrical. When full grown they attain a length of between 20 and 40 mm. Frequently the larvae are green with longitudinal stripes. Pierid larvae are superficially similar to hesperiid larvae, but differ in the shape of the head capsule and the absence of a markedly narrow prothoracic segment, the presence of which gives hesperiid larvae the appearance of possessing a distinct "neck." The larvae differ from papilionid larvae by lacking osmeteria and fleshy protuberances. The first instar larvae possess only primary setae (which are present in *all* lepidopterous larvae). Later instars, however, are characterized by the presence of numerous short, fine secondary setae. At least some have blunt, glandular hairs. The crochets on the prolegs are biordinal or triordinal. The described life histories of North American pierids are almost universally inadequate in detail. The pupae are anchored by a silken girdle and by entangling the cremaster in a silken pad, as in the papilionids. There is almost always a forward protuberance from the head. In a number of genera the wing cases are extremely large. The Pieridae are divided into four subfamilies of which only two (Coliadinae, Pierinae) occur north of the Mexican border. A third, the Dismorphiinae, has been vaguely recorded in the southern United States and has been included here only because it needs to be confirmed north of the Mexican border.

Subfamily DISMORPHIINAE

Over a hundred species have been described in this subfamily, nearly confined to the tropics of the Americas. Some adults closely resemble and presumably mimic members of the Heliconiidae. The antennae are extremely long and thin, gradually terminating in a long, spindle-shaped club. In many species the males have very large androconial patches. In Central and South America many exceptionally beautiful forms occur. The shape of the wings, the pattern and ground color may differ radically between the sexes. The primaries of the male are often long, narrow and falcate or quite produced apically; the secondaries are usually wider than the primaries. The females are often duller in color than the males. The lower surfaces of both sexes are often glossy.

Genus ENANTIA Hübner

1. **Enantia melite** (Johansson). Plate 70, figure 1, ♂; figure 2, ♀. The butterfly may be readily recognized from the figures. The species has been credited to our fauna on the authority of Reakirt. There are no recent U.S. records, although it may be expected as a casual stray in southern Texas because the butterfly is quite abundant in Mexico.

Subfamily COLIADINAE

The adults of this subfamily are popularly called Sulphurs. They are among the most widespread of all butterflies and in temperate regions some are on the wing from early spring until the first hard freeze. Adults differ from those of the Pierinae in the following structural features: the antennae are relatively shorter than those of the Pierinae; the third segment of the labial palpus is short and usually not hairy; the wings are frequently yellow or orange; and the humeral vein of the secondaries is weakly developed or absent. The larvae feed primarily on leguminous plants, but some species feed on members of the families Ericaceae (heaths), Salicaceae (willows) or Compositae (composites).

Genus COLIAS Fabricius

ALEXANDER B. KLOTS

Colias is essentially a Holarctic genus with offshoots southward into Africa, southern Asia and tropical America. The Palaearctic Region has the most species, some of the central Asiatic ones being exceedingly beautiful and unusual. At least three species (*hecla, nastes* and *palaeno*) are Holarctic. Several species are quite difficult to distinguish because of hybridization or local or individual variation. The genitalia have been little used taxonomically. Details of the life histories, particularly of the natural foodplants and habits and habitats, are valuable, but are scantily known. Merely collecting a few specimens (which, unfortunately, do not carry samples of their foodplants with them) is fun for the collector, but often little help to the taxonomist.

Most of our species are sexually dimorphic, the dark borders of the males being solid while those of the females contain a row of light spots or are greatly narrowed. *C. nastes* is our only species with such light spots in the male. In one of our species, *C. (C.) meadii,* the males have a sex patch near the humeral angle of the hind wing above. Numerous Palaearctic species and both species of *Colias (Zerene)* have this patch. Dimorphic white females occur as a genetically controlled feature. The white color is a thermoregulator, subject to natural selection in different environments. The proportion of white females in a population is taxonomically important.

Considerable genetic work has been done on some species. Two quite new techniques show great promise for solving problems of species and subspecies relationships. One of these depends on the ultraviolet reflectance of the male (very rarely female) wings, which differ greatly in different species. The other is based on differential esterase analyses of fresh wing pigments. Our ideas about the classification of some species are still fluid. The classification given here is, therefore, tentative in places, and may be modified, perhaps during the next few years.

The larvae, which are very incompletely known, are green with a dense covering of a short pile when mature, and a whitish line, more or less edged ventrally with black (and often containing some red) along each side through the spiracles. Larval characters, when known well enough for comparisons, may be valuable in classification. Most species are univoltine with a one-year egg-to-egg life. *C. hecla,* and perhaps other Arctic species, seems to have a two-year life. Members of the *C. philodice-eurytheme-harfordii* complex may have several more or less overlapping generations annually. Hibernation is as a partly grown larva, a pupa or perhaps in the far South, an adult. A period of aestivation has been recorded in one species.

A great many individual, seasonal and local forms, and some hybrids, have been named; such names have no status in scientific nomenclature. Some populations, named or cited as subspecies, are probably only variations along clines. Validity of names for such clinal populations is a subjective matter.

The species fall into three apparently natural groups according to their foodplants;

these are the legume (Leguminosae), heath (Ericaceae) and willow (Salicaceae) feeders. Some foodplant records need verification, as natural foodplants, not "laboratory" ones.

Two subgenera are recognized in North America. *Colias* (*Colias*) contains most of our species (as well as all the Palaearctic ones). *Colias* (*Zerene*), the "Dogfaces," consists of two endemic species with Neotropical offshoots.

Subgenus COLIAS Fabricius

Group 1. The Legume Feeders

1. **Colias (Colias) philodice** Godart. Plate 75, figure 6, ♂; figure 7, ♀; figure 8, albinic ♀; figure 9, ♂; figure 10, ♀ (*"eriphyle"*). This is our widespread, often abundant, Clouded Sulphur or "Mud Puddle" Butterfly. The classification of it and *eurytheme* has been very confused, since they have been variously considered as separate species; or as conspecific, but separate, subspecies; or as subspecies of the palaearctic *C. chrysotheme*. At present they are regarded as separate (but not entirely separate) species that hybridize widely. The two species probably evolved almost complete specific distinction while geographically mostly separated, with *philodice* ranging from Virginia northward into eastern Canada with a westward extension in Canada; and *eurytheme* ranging over most of central and western North America. Then, as white man cleared the forests and plowed the prairies, and everywhere spread introduced clovers, alfalfas and vetches, both butterflies very largely switched over to these as larval foodplants and rapidly, sometimes almost explosively, became sympatric almost everywhere. They hybridize freely, the hybrids showing many degrees of intermediacy. Phenotypically identifiable hybrids may constitute 5–10% of a population. *C. philodice* does best on clovers (*Trifolium*) while *eurytheme* is more successful on alfalfa (*Medicago sativa*).

Both *philodice* and *eurytheme* are characterized by wide dark borders in both sexes, those of the females having the contained light spots well separated from the orange or yellow ground color basad; by the discal spot of the hind wings beneath being subsilvery with sharply defined reddish rims and a small "satellite" spot; and by the presence of submarginal dark spots on the fore wings and hind wings beneath. *C. philodice* males do not show ultraviolet reflectance; males of *eurytheme* do.

C. philodice shows considerable individual and seasonal variation. White females are common. "Cold weather" forms are frequent in late autumn and early spring populations, being smaller with narrower dark borders; darker, almost greenish hind wings beneath; and a paler yellow ground color. Occasional melanic and suffused aberrations occur. A subspecies, *C. p. guatemalena* Röber, occurs at high altitudes in Chiapas, Mexico, and Guatemala. Some western populations have been regarded as subspecies (e.g., *kootenai* Cockle and *eriphyle* Edwards) but this is argumentative.

Early Stages: The eggs are yellowish green, turning to orange and dark red, slender and fusiform, with longitudinal ribs and many weak cross-ridges between these. The

first instar larvae are pale, with irregular setation and a dark head. The mature larvae
are yellowish green with a darker middorsal line and a whitish line along each side
through the spiracles that is variably edged ventrally with black and contains a quite
variable, broken, red line. A blue-green variety (with blue-green haemolymph, or
blood) is known. The pupa is green, losing color as the adult develops within. The
species is said to be bivoltine even in Alaska, but multivoltine in the far south with
the generations overlapping considerably. The larval foodplants are a great variety
of native and introduced, herbaceous Leguminosae; the species especially favors and
does best on Clovers (*Trifolium*).

Distribution: The range comprises most of North America northward into Hudsonian Zone. The species is rare or absent in peninsular Florida and western California, and in desert and heavily forested areas.

(a) **philodice** Godart.   The data and discussions given above apply almost entirely
to this, the nominate subspecies.

(b) **vitabunda** Hovanitz.   This is probably the only population of *philodice* that
deserves subspecific status. It is characterized by generally narrower dark borders;
more rounded fore wings; a melanic suffusion of the hind wings beneath in females;
distinctly heavier orange-yellow on the apices of the fore wings and the hind wings
beneath in males; and a very large proportion of white or whitish females (running
up to 95% in Alaska and 70% in Yukon Territory). There seems to be some intergradation with northern populations of *p. philodice*.

Distribution: Named from Mount McKinley Park, Alaska, *vitabunda* ranges
widely in Alaska and Yukon Territory, and in adjacent parts of British Columbia
and the Northwest Territories.

2. **Colias (Colias) eurytheme** Boisduval. Plate 75, figure 1, ♂; figure 2, ♀; figure 3,
♀ (summer generation); figure 4, ♂; figure 5, ♀ (spring generation); figure 11, ♂; figure
12 ♂ (hybrids, *eurytheme* × *philodice*).   The interrelationship of *eurytheme* and
philodice is discussed above. *C. eurytheme* shows great normal variation, ranging
from large, richly colored specimens of the hot weather generations to much smaller
ones of cold weather generations; in some of the latter the orange is pale, but in
others it is deep but limited to the discal areas of the wings. Many variants are
probably hybrids. Hybridization with other species than *philodice* is suspected, e.g.,
with *christina* ("*alberta*" Bowman) and *hecla*. Numerous melanic and "smudged"
aberrations are known. White females are common; white males are known, but
extremely rare. A black female is shown on Plate 73, figure 9.

Early Stages: These are essentially as described above for *philodice*. The species
is univoltine in the far north or at high altitudes, multivoltine in the most southern
parts of its range, with overlapping of generations and consequent almost continuous
flight. It may become extremely abundant on Alfalfa, particularly in the Middle
West and West, and is at times injurious to this crop, being called the "Alfalfa
Butterfly." Many other herbaceous legumes are larval foodplants.

Distribution: The range is from southern Mexico northward over most of the
continent into Hudsonian Zone.

3. **Colias (Colias) harfordii** Henry Edwards. Plate 74, figure 12, ♂; figure 15, ♀. *C. harfordii* is an endemic Californian species of uncertain affinity. In appearance and bivoltinism it seems closest to the *C. eurytheme-philodice* complex; but in its ultraviolet reflectance (a large patch on the hind wing) it resembles yellow *alexandra*. The ground color of the wings above is usually a warm, almost orange-tinted yellow not deepening on the hind wings toward the outer borders; there is very little black dusting at the bases of the wings above and on the hind wings beneath; the dark submarginal spots of the wings beneath are usually at least slightly present, sometimes strongly; and the discal spot of the hind wing beneath is well defined, usually at least slightly pearly with a fairly well defined dark rim. Females usually have a well marked outer dark border on the fore wing, which often runs down to, or nearly to, the inner margin. *C. barbara* Hy. Edwards, from Santa Barbara, named from two rather worn females, is almost certainly synonymous.

Early Stages: The larvae resemble those of *philodice* and *eurytheme* and feed on *Astragalus.* The species is largely bivoltine, but a partial third autumn generation has been reported.

Distribution: The species occurs only in the mountains of California, from Contra Costa county southward, and in Baja California.

4. **Colias (Colias) alexandra** Edwards. This is our most complex *Colias* species, or "species complex." Its two most distinctive components are the yellow *C. alexandra* and the orange *C. christina.* These apparently blend over a very large area where many degrees of mixture occur, some as "isolates" or "segregates." The conventional division into subspecies given below is partially an unsatisfactory compromise, since some of the names represent intergrading or mixed populations. A vast amount of study is needed.

Early Stages: Larval foodplants (recorded almost wholly from yellow populations) are: *Astragalus miser, bisulcatus, lentiginosus, eremiticus* and *canadensis; Lathyrus leucanthus; Thermopsis* sp. and *Oxytropis* sp. (mostly from Scott Ellis, MS). Records of *Lupinus, Medicago* and *Trifolium* are somewhat suspect. Most populations are univoltine, but one in North Dakota is bivoltine (T. McCabe, *in litt.*). There may be a larval diapause in hot weather (aestivation) as well as the one in winter. The species flies mostly in upper Transition and Canadian Zones, and has been noted as most successful in plant successional stages following lumbering or burns.

Distribution: See distributions given below.

(a) **alexandra** Edwards. Plate 73, figure 4, ♂; figure 5, ♀. Nominate *a. alexandra* is typically light, bright yellow above, deepening to a warmer yellow outward to the dark border, especially of the hind wing. The fore wing is a little more pointed apically than in most *Colias;* the fringes are yellow. The hind wing has no orange discal spot above, and beneath is gray-green to almost slaty gray with the discal spot lacking any dark rim. Females are predominantly yellow, with great diversity in the fore wing border. The males have a large, discal ultraviolet reflectance patch on the hind wing, none on the fore wing.

Distribution: These yellow populations range over southern central Wyoming, Colorado, New Mexico and eastern Arizona. Great Basin populations tend to be larger and paler above, with the hind wings beneath paler. Eastward populations in Plains country (eastern Colorado, western Nebraska and western North Dakota) are smaller, with more white females and some bivoltinism.

(b) **edwardsii** Edwards and *emilia* Edwards. Plate 78, figure 19, ♂. The yellow Rocky Mountain populations more or less grade into the yellow populations of the southern and western Great Basin, for which the name *edwardsii* (type locality Virginia City, Nevada) can be used, with *emilia* Edwards (type locality Oregon) as a subjective junior synonym. The populations average large and pale, and yellow on the hind wings beneath with the discocellular spot sometimes narrowly rimmed with red. Males average much like *a. alexandra* in ultraviolet reflectance, but northward may also show some reflectance areas on the fore wing.

(c) **columbiensis** Ferris. This is an apparently locally segregated, yellow population from southern British Columbia. The fore wings are apically blunter; the dark outer borders are narrow; the discal spot of the hind wings above is orange; and the males have ultraviolet reflectance on the fore wing, especially along the outer discal veins and inside the outer border, as well as a prominent patch on the hind wing.

(d) **astraea** Edwards. Plate 73, figure 7, ♂. This is a "wastebasket" name for many variously mixed, yellow to orange populations. These occur, blending, or interdigitated, with the yellow *a. alexandra* and *a. edwardsii* populations in parts of Oregon, Washington, British Columbia, Alberta, northern Utah, Idaho, Montana, northern Wyoming, Saskatchewan and Manitoba—in fact, in the general region between the southeastern and southern yellow populations and the northeastern and northern orange ones. Perhaps some southern Alaska and Yukon populations can be lumped here. The yellow, individuals, often predominant locally, have the discocellular spot of the hind wing above orange in males, which also show diverse ultraviolet reflectance areas on the fore wings as well as the hind wings.

(e) **christina** Edwards. *C. christina* was named from Great Slave Lake, Northwest Territories. Presumably this is an all-orange population, but we cannot be sure of this; it may really be mixed. Little material is known to connect it with the southernmost all-orange populations (see below). The males have a large, ultraviolet reflectance patch on the fore wing as well as one on the hind wing.

(f) **krauthii** Klots. Plate 97, figure 23, ♂. This name applies to an all-orange population of the Black Hills, South Dakota, and may be used for the all-orange populations found in southern Manitoba. The Black Hills population has the hind wings beneath greener than in the Manitoba ones. Some specimens show possible hybridization with *C. eurytheme.* The males have a large ultraviolet reflectance patch on both the fore wing and the hind wing.

5. **Colias (Colias) occidentalis** Scudder. *C. occidentalis* is a large species of the Pacific Northwest. The wings beneath usually have some small, but distinct, dark submarginal spots. The discal spot of the hind wings beneath is large, sometimes pearly, with a more or less diffuse pink to red rim, and is often elongated axially.

The fringes are pink. The species flies at relatively low altitudes. The males lack ultraviolet reflectance.

(a) **occidentalis** Scudder. Plate 74, figure 16, ♂; figure 18, ♀; figure 17, albinic, ♀. This, the nominate subspecies, has the dark borders of the wings narrower than in *chrysomelas,* and the dark discal spot of the fore wing above small, often missing.

Early Stages: Reported larval foodplants (in Washington) are Vetch (*Vicia angustifolia*) and Sweet White Clover (*Melilotis alba*); Lupine (*Lupinus* sp.) and *Astragalus* are suspected.

Distribution: Southern Alaska and British Columbia southward through Washington and Oregon.

(b) **chrysomelas** Henry Edwards. Plate 74, figure 13, ♂; figure 14, ♀. The dark borders of the wings are very wide in both sexes; in females they are almost always complete to the anal angle.

Distribution: Northern California, on north or east facing slopes in Douglas Fir forests (Opler). Blending with *o. occidentalis* in southern Oregon.

6. **Colias (Colias) meadii** Edwards. *C. meadii* is distinguished from other Nearctic species by its dark orange ground color, a male sex patch near the humeral angle of the hind wing above, and its Hudsonian to Arctic-Alpine Zone habitat.

(a) **meadii** Edwards. Plate 74, figure 1, ♂; figure 2, ♀; figure 3, pale ♀. The nominate subspecies is often common in Rocky Mountain Hudsonian Zone meadows and "tundra" above timberline, often flying up into Alpine Zone, sometimes down into upper Canadian Zone. It is a fast flier that gives the collector many a hard chase; and when it drops to the ground its greenish undersides camouflage it well. In Colorado it flies from early July until early September.

Early Stages: The larvae are stippled with tiny black tubercles and hairs, and may bear lateral light stripes and black dots. It is univoltine, hibernating in the third instar. Foodplants are alpine Clovers such as *Trifolium dasyphyllum* and *T. parryi.*

Distribution: C. m. meadii occurs typically in the mountains of the Colorado massif, including the Snowy and Medicine Bow ranges of Carbon and Sublette counties, Wyoming and the Uinta Mts. of northeastern Utah. It should occur in the Sangre de Cristo Mts. of northern New Mexico. The populations of western and northern Wyoming are to be considered *m. meadii,* but show some transition to *m. elis.*

(b) **elis** Strecker. Plate 74, figure 4, ♂; figure 5, ♀. This subspecies flies typically in the high Rocky Mountains of Canada. It is distinguished from *m. meadii* by its larger size; proportionately narrower dark borders; a lighter orange ground color; and the almost total absence of white females, which occur regularly in some *m. meadii* populations. Like other alpine species it flies at progressively lower elevations northward, and often occurs in meadows well below timberline. Transitional populations between *m. meadii* and *m. elis* in Montana and Idaho need study.

Distribution: Rocky Mountains of Alberta and British Columbia.

7. **Colias (Colias) hecla** Lefebre. *C. hecla* is a circumpolar species, ranging around the Arctic from Scandinavia to Greenland (it is the only Greenland *Colias*). The color above is orange with well developed dark borders in both sexes. Males have

no sex patch near the humeral angle of the hind wing like that of *C. meadii.* The butterflies have a fast flight, but not as fast as that of *C. nastes,* and fly on lower ground and at lower altitudes than *nastes.* There is much evidence of hybridization between *hecla* and *nastes,* which are sympatric in much of the Arctic (see *C. boothii* and *C. nastes*). *C. hecla* varies greatly individually, but subspecific differences in its true arctic populations are not clear.

Early Stages: There is only one generation annually, but apparently individuals require two seasons to mature. The larval foodplant of the Scandinavian subspecies is *Astragalus alpinus,* which occurs all across Arctic America.

(a) **hecla** Lefebre.   Specimens from Greenland (type locality) average a dull orange above, the females very dark, and the hind wings beneath more often very dark and heavily clouded. White females are very rare.

Distribution: Greenland, Ellesmere and Baffin islands, northern Labrador and across the Canadian Arctic at least to Yukon Territory (cf. *h. glacialis,* below).

(b) **hela** Strecker. Plate 97, figure 24, ♂. This distinct subarctic subspecies, named from Churchill, Manitoba, is brighter and clearer orange, with the wings beneath paler, more yellow. Northward and westward it more or less intergrades to *h. hecla.* White females are extremely rare.

(c) **glacialis** McLachlan. Plate 74, figure 6, ♂; figure 9, ♀. The "normal" individuals are hardly worth distinguishing from *h. hecla*—in appearance perhaps averaging a little lighter and brighter. But many individuals occur (e.g., in Mount McKinley Park, Alaska) with narrow dark borders and a ground color ranging through light orange to orange-tinted yellow. These grade into *C. boothii* and are perhaps a hybrid population. Occasional Alaska and Yukon individuals are very large and bright, phenotypically matching *C. eurytheme.* Perhaps there is hybridization here, also. The whole Alaska-Yukon population needs thorough (not piecemeal) study. White females are often common, up to 68% in some areas (*teste* Hovanitz).

Distribution: Yukon Territory and Alaska, southward in the mountains to northern British Columbia and central Alberta, at relatively low altitudes.

8. **Colias (Colias) boothii** Curtis. Plate 74, figure 7, ♂; figure 8, ♀. *C. boothii* has been considered by different authorities either as a distinct species that perhaps arose long ago as a hybrid between *C. hecla* and *nastes,* or as merely comprising individuals still arising from such continuing hybridization. The colors above are bright, light orange and yellow; the dark borders are narrow with pale yellowish spots along basad of them that suggest the pale spots of *C. nastes.* Field observations show that it flies in more sheltered environments than does *nastes.* A variety with the dark borders lacking is "chione."

9. **Colias (Colias) nastes** Boisduval.   *C. nastes* is a circumpolar species of the "high Arctic," ranging southward chiefly only in high, cold, mountain ranges. It is distinguished from our other species by the light spots in the dark borders of the males; its small size; and its generally greenish and clouded appearance. It is extremely variable, both individually and regionally, so that numerous varieties and subspecies

have been named. Within a local population some individuals may have the fore wings almost solidly clouded with dark scales, while others have the ground color light and contrasting with the dark borders. Whether or not it hybridizes with *C. hecla,* our other "high Arctic" species, is a moot question. Certainly in some regions orange-tinted *nastes* occur regularly. *C. nastes* is a fast flying, very active species that flies in general in higher, more barren environments (where its leguminous foodplants grow best) than other associated *Colias.* Most of its so-called subspecies are not very distinctive and probably intergrade to each other. *C. n. moina* and *C. n. thula* are the most easily distinguished.

Early Stages: Exact descriptions are lacking. Larval foodplants are various Arctic Leguminosae, e.g., *Astragalus alpinus.* The species is univoltine, with hibernation as a young larva.

(a) **nastes** Boisduval. The accepted type locality is Labrador. The populations of the eastern Arctic vary considerably, but in general are a fairly pale grayish-greenish, with the black submarginal spots beneath not prominent, often inconspicuous. An Ungava Peninsula series is much darker beneath, with a heavier hind wing discal spot. A Baffin Island series varies from very dark to very light, some specimens with an orange tint.

Distribution: Eastern Arctic, Labrador, Baffin and Ellesmere islands westward, grading into *n. rossii.*

(b) **rossii** Guenée. The populations from the central Canadian Arctic are very variable from dark to light individuals, often slightly orange tinted. The submarginal dark spots beneath also vary, but are more prominent than in Labrador series.

Distribution: Central Canadian Arctic, north and west of Hudson Bay, Southampton Island, Melville and Boothia peninsulas.

(c) **moina** Strecker. Plate 73, figure 17, ♂. *C. n. moina* from near Churchill, Manitoba, is very distinctive, being very much brighter, lighter and more contrasty; the submarginal black marks beneath are large and consistent.

Early Stages: At Churchill in late July several females were observed (by ABK) ovipositing on *Oxytropis campestris* (favoring low, nonflowering plants), on which many eggs were found. Adults visited the *Oxytropis, Hedysarum mackenziae* and *Astragalus eucosmus* flowers freely. Larvae were reared on the *Oxytropis* until third instar diapause.

(d) **cocandicides** Verity. This represents the populations of the northern and northwestern Barren Grounds. Individuals (with all the usual variations) are not as bright and contrasty as *moina,* but have the submarginal black spots beneath quite prominent.

Distribution: Western Canadian Arctic, westward to, or into, Yukon Territory.

(e) **aliaska** Bang-Haas. This is the population of much of Alaska and Yukon Territory. As usual there is much variation. In general the populations are fairly brightly colored and contrasting. The submarginal light spots on the hind wing beneath are strong.

Distribution: Most of Alaska and Yukon Territory, southward into British Columbia.

(f) **thula** Hovanitz. Plate 73, figure 8, ♂. The dark borders of the wings of males, particularly of the fore wings, are much narrowed, sometimes so as not to contain the usual row of light spots, which are almost merged into the discal area basad. There is little of the general melanin clouding of so many *nastes*. It is possible that *thula* represents a distinctive species.

Distribution: Extreme Arctic Alaska, inland from Point Barrow.

(g) **streckeri** Grum-Grshmaïlo. Plate 73, figure 18, ♂; figure 19, ♀. There is great individual variation above from very dark and clouded to very light, pale yellowish. Beneath, the submarginal dark spots are markedly inconspicuous, and the dark discal spot of the hind wing is rarely large or smeared axially. The submarginal light spots of the hind wing beneath are most commonly inconspicuous.

Distribution: Rocky Mountains of Alberta and British Columbia, northward in Arctic-Alpine Zone.

Group 2. The Heath Feeders

10. **Colias (Colias) palaeno** (Linnaeus). Nominate *C. palaeno,* from Scandinavia, is very pale yellow.

(a) **chippewa** Edwards. Plate 73, figure 14, ♂; figure 15, ♂, underside; figure 16, ♀. All the North American populations belong to one subspecies. The dark borders of the wings above are consistently wide, especially in males. The black discal spot of the fore wing above is almost always minute or absent. The discal spot of the hind wing beneath is small to very small, whitish, and only very rarely has a trace of a dark rim. In males the discal spot of the hind wing above is almost always conspicuously very pale. The fringes are narrowly pink.

Early Stages: The chief larval foodplant is the Arctic Bilberry (*Vaccinium uliginosum*), perhaps also the Dwarf Bilberry (*V. caespitosum*). At Churchill, Manitoba females were watched (by ABK) in early July ovipositing on *V. uliginosum;* larvae were reared on this until 3d instar diapause in mid-August.

Distribution: Alaska and Yukon Territory south into northern British Columbia, Alberta and Manitoba, eastward to the west coast of Hudson Bay; northern Labrador (Ungava) and Baffin Island.

11. **Colias (Colias) behrii** Edwards. Plate 73, figure 20, ♂; figure 21, ♀. Of all our *Colias* this has the most restricted range and is the most unmistakable. It is small and usually so heavily clouded with dark scales as to appear almost green.

Early Stages: Mature larva green, with light middorsal and subdorsal longitudinal lines as well as the usual lateral ones. It is univoltine, flying in late July and August. The larval foodplant is the Dwarf Bilberry (*Vaccinium caespitosum*); a record of *Gentiana newberryi* needs confirmation.

Distribution: High Alpine meadows in the California Sierras, especially about Tioga Pass, from Tuolumne county in the north to Tulare county in the south.

12. **Colias (Colias) interior** Scudder. The "Pink Edged Sulphur" is a Canadian Zone species that ranges nearly across the continent. The head and fringes are markedly pink. The ground color above is a rather warm yellow; the wings have little black dusting, either above or beneath; the discocellular spot of the hind wings beneath is usually simple and pink rimmed; and the dark borders of the females are usually much reduced. White females are very rare.

C. *interior* is quite closely related to C. *pelidne* (see below), and it has been suggested that the two are conspecific. Two supposed subspecies of *interior* (beside the nominate one) bear names. They are characterized below more to draw attention to them than from any deep conviction of their validity.

Early Stages: The larvae feed on *Vaccinium,* definite records being *V. myrtilloides* (= *canadense*), a low, bushy species and (Montana) *V. caespitosum* (Scott Ellis, MS). The species is univoltine; hibernation is as a larva, variously stated to be in the first or the third instar.

Distribution: British Columbia, Washington and Oregon eastward in Canadian Zone to Quebec, the Maritime Provinces and Newfoundland; northern Minnesota, Wisconsin, Michigan, New York and New England; southward in Pennsylvania and Virginia (isolated colonies) in the mountains.

(a) **interior** Scudder. Plate 74, figure 10, ♂; figure 11, ♀. The type locality is along the north shore of Lake Superior, Ontario. The populations westward seem homogeneous enough to be considered all one subspecies, and so do most of those eastward into Quebec (but see *vividior,* below). Central and western populations seem a little larger and paler yellow than the most eastern ones.

(b) **vividior** Berger. This supposed subspecies was named from Oneida, Eagle River, Wisconsin, as being larger and brighter. It is not markedly so there; but a population from the upper peninsula and the northern part of the lower peninsula of Michigan (e.g., Cheboygan) does seem larger and brighter, with wider dark borders in the males and females.

(c) **laurentina** Scudder. The type locality is Cape Breton Island. The name can be used for the populations from Quebec eastward on the basis of slightly smaller size and brighter coloration.

13. **Colias (Colias) pelidne** Boisduval and Leconte. C. *pelidne* has a markedly discontinuous distribution, occurring in the eastern arctic and subarctic, and in the western Rocky Mountains. It is closely related to C. *interior.* The suggestion has been made, in fact, that *interior* and *pelidne* are conspecific, with "a continuous range of morphological and geographical intergradation." This infers a conspecifity something like that of *Limenitis arthemis* and *astyanax,* where there is a definite, narrow zone of intergradation. This has not been clearly demonstrated for *interior* and *pelidne,* but the concept is perfectly possible. "Conspecificity" is, after all, a rather subjective matter. Perhaps esterase and ultraviolet reflectance tests will help settle the dispute.

C. *pelidne* as here considered differs from *interior* in having: a less warm yellow ground color; the discocellular spot of the hind wing above very rarely discernible, not orange; pronounced black basal dusting on the wings above, especially the hind wings; black dusting in the discal area of the fore wings beneath (especially in western populations); considerable black dusting on the hind wings beneath; and a small discocellular spot on the hind wings beneath which frequently has its central light area smaller in diameter than the width of the dark rim. The opposites of these features characterize *interior*. In the east *C. pelidne* extends much farther northward, and in the west regularly flies at much higher altitudes. *C. pelidne* has a faster, more direct flight than *interior*. The ratios of white and yellow females are very different. *C. pelidne* is generally understood to consist of at least two, possibly three, subspecies which are not strongly differentiated.

Early Stages: Females have been recorded ovipositing on a *Vaccinium* (Hovanitz) and in Idaho on *Gaultheria hemifusa* (Scott Ellis, MS).

Distribution: see below.

(a) **pelidne** Boisduval and Leconte. Plate 73, figure 10, ♂; figure 11, underside, ♂; figure 12, ♀.   The type locality ("Arctic Regions") is Labrador, one of the older Moravian Missions (Nain, Okkak or Hopedale). Compared with the western subspecies: the black discal spot of the fore wing above, when present, is smaller; the black basal dusting on the wings above, and the black discal dusting on the fore wings beneath, are weaker; the hind wings beneath are a colder yellow, often appearing greenish. The females are preponderantly white, rarely yellowish white.

Distribution: Baffin Island, Ungava, Labrador Peninsula (at higher altitudes inland) and Newfoundland; southern distribution in Quebec uncertain.

(b) **minisni** Bean. Plate 73, figure 13, ♀.   This population of the Canadian Rockies is not clearly distinct from the more southern populations. It is slightly smaller, the discocellular black spot of the fore wing above is a little smaller, rarely absent; the dark discal clouding of the fore wing beneath is a little heavier; and the hind wing beneath averages a slightly warmer, more orange-yellow. The females are predominantly white (72/4).

Distribution: Canadian Rocky Mountains of western Alberta and eastern British Columbia.

(c) **skinneri** Barnes.   As noted above, this population seems to differ only in averages, and then not greatly, from *minisni*. The Wyoming populations differ the most; probably there is a cline with the extreme at the southern limit. Of 31 Wyoming females at hand 14 are yellow and 17 white. In the Wind River and Wyoming ranges populations chiefly fly in Hudsonian Zone (10,000–11,500 ft. alt.) but individuals occasionally stray down to 7000 ft. A possible hybrid with *C. meadii* is known.

Distribution: Upper Canadian and Hudsonian zones, Montana, Idaho and northern and west-central Wyoming.

Group 3. The Willow Feeders

14. **Colias (Colias) gigantea** Strecker.   *C. gigantea* is a large, subarctic species that ranges southward in acid, moss and willow bogs. These true bogs are isolated southern remnants of the Hudsonian flora and fauna which were left behind after

the recession of the continental Pleistocene glaciers. (Such true bogs must not be confused with ordinary marshes and other wet areas.) *C. gigantea* has relatively narrow black borders; little black dusting at the bases of the wings above; usually no black submarginal spots beneath; and the discal spot of the hind wing beneath usually large and prominent with a pearly center and often a small satellite spot.

(a) **gigantea** Strecker. Plate 73, figure 3, ♂; figure 6, ♀. This, the nominate subspecies, extends more or less continuously from the west shore of Hudson Bay above Churchill (type locality) northwestward following the very irregular Hudsonian Zone boundaries. South of true Hudsonian Zone it is restricted to the increasingly isolated bogs; somewhat diverse populations appear, such as *mayi* Chermock and Chermock from the Riding Mountains, Manitoba. Where to draw a line between *g. gigantea* and *g. harroweri* is not clear.

Early Stages: The larval foodplant has been recorded as a *Salix* species. At Churchill in late July females were watched (by ABK) ovipositing on leaves of *Salix reticulata* (a dwarf, leathery leaved species). The eggs were secured and the larvae reared into third instar diapause in August.

Distribution: West coast of Hudson Bay northwestward, in the very irregular Hudsonian Zone through Yukon Territory and much of Alaska, southward in British Columbia, Alberta, Saskatchewan and Manitoba.

(b) **harroweri** Klots. Plate 97, figure 20, ♂; figure 21, ♀. This subspecies was named from a population in a willow bog near Green River Lake, Sublette county, Wyoming, the southernmost known population of *gigantea.* Compared with *g. gigantea* the size is smaller; the dark borders of the wings of the males are proportionately wider; the hind wings and apices of the fore wings beneath are a more greenish yellow; and the hind wings beneath are more sparsely dark dusted. Individuals do not range widely, but confine their activities to bogs and their very close vicinity.

Early Stages: Natural oviposition by the allotype female was recorded on a shrubby *Salix.*

Distribution: From Sublette county, Wyoming, northward at least in Idaho and Montana.

15. **Colias (Colias) scudderii** Reakirt. *C. scudderii* is a species of the Colorado massif, i.e., of the mountains of Colorado and adjoining parts of other states. It seems most closely related to *C. gigantea,* also a willow feeder but bog-limited. *C. scudderii* flies commonly in open Canadian Zone mountain meadows, sometimes in wet, or even boggy, ones, but more often in dry, grassy ones. It ranges widely up to timberline as the season progresses. It has been suggested that *scudderii* is closely related to *C. pelidne,* but this is very unlikely.

(a) **scudderii** Reakirt. Plate 73, figure 1, ♂; figure 2, ♀. In the nominate subspecies the males have the dark borders of the wings above proportionately narrower than in *s. ruckesi.* White females far outnumber yellow ones, e.g., 3/1 in Colorado.

Early Stages: There are a number of records of Willow (*Salix*) as the larval foodplant. A record of *Vaccinium* has not been confirmed.

Distribution: C. s. scudderii ranges in mid to upper Canadian Zone meadows throughout the Colorado mountains and in the Snowy and Medicine Bow ranges of southern Wyoming and the Uinta Mountains of northeastern Utah. It may occur in the La Sal Mountains of eastern Utah.

(b) **ruckesi** Klots. Plate 78, figure 20, ♂. The males have proportionately wider dark borders than those of *s. scudderii,* and a somewhat brighter yellow ground color. Of 11 females, 5 are bright yellow, 2 are yellowish white and 4 are white.

Early Stages: These are unknown except that a captive female, given a wide choice, oviposited on *Salix.*

Distribution: C. s. ruckesi flies in the Sangre de Cristo Mountains of Santa Fe and San Miguel counties, New Mexico, ranging northward toward or into Colorado.

Subgenus ZERENE Hübner

This subgenus contains two species, both North American. Its most prominent characteristics are: the acutely pointed fore wing; the dog's head marking of the male fore wing; the occasional presence of cross bands on the larvae; and the presence of a sex patch near the humeral angle of the male hind wing above (as in some *C.* (*Colias*) and *Nathalis*).

16. **Colias (Zerene) cesonia** Stoll. Plate 75, figure 15, ♂; figure 16, ♀; figure 19, ♂, winter form; figure 20, ♀, winter form; figure 21, ♀, underside, winter form. *C. cesonia,* the Dog's Head or Dog Face Butterfly, ranges widely across the United States, chiefly southwardly. It is often abundant in the South. Its flight is fast, but it visits flowers and damp soil freely. The "hot weather" generations are yellow beneath, but the "winter form," which emerges in the autumn and hibernates, is often very red beneath. The appearance of populations in northern states is sporadic.

Early Stages: The mature larva is green, but very variable, from individuals with a light lateral line to others cross banded with yellow to orange and black, or lined longitudinally with yellow and black. The chief larval foodplant is False Indigo, or Lead Plant (*Amorpha fruticosa*) but other leguminous herbs such as Clovers (*Trifolium*), Soy Bean (*Glycine*) and Alfalfa (*Medicago*) have been reported. It is at least trivoltine in the South, but breeding irregularly, perhaps univoltine, in the most northern states.

Distribution: Southern California (and Baja California) to Florida, northward (irregularly) to Wyoming, North Dakota, Manitoba, Iowa, Wisconsin, Minnesota, Michigan, Ontario and New York. Southward it ranges to Argentina with some striking subspecies.

17. **Colias (Zerene) eurydice** Boisduval. Plate 75, figure 13, ♂; figure 14, ♂; figure 17, ♀; figure 18, ♀. *C. eurydice,* the California Dog Face, occurs locally, but sometimes commonly, in open oak woodlands and open glades in Douglas Fir forests. As the illustrations show, it is quite variable; numerous varieties have been named.

Early Stages: The mature larva is dull green with black dots, a pale lateral line edged with orange, and dorsad of this a dark mark on each segment. The larval foodplant is False Indigo (*Amorpha californica*).

Distribution: California Coast ranges and occasional in the foothills of the Sierras, from Lake and Napa counties southward to northern Baja California; Arizona (rare); Texas? It is bivoltine, with a "false brood" in late autumn.

The remainder of the Pieridae is by William H. Howe.

Genus ANTEOS Hübner

This genus contains three species and is restricted to tropical America. Both species entering our area belong to the subgenus *Anteos.*

1. **Anteos (Anteos) clorinde** (Godart). Plate 71, figure 1, ♂ (ssp. *Nivifera*). The subspecies of *clorinde* entering our area is *nivifera* Fruhstorfer (as figured); adults from the tropics of Mexico stray into our southwestern states during late summer with regularity, some reaching as far north as Colorado and Kansas. While always rare in our area, it is often incredibly abundant in adjacent Mexico. Its habitat in its native region is tropical scrub forest and clearings. It is a breeding resident in southern Texas. The larval foodplant is *Cassia spectabilis.*

Distribution: In our area this species is a rare straggler in Arizona, resident in Texas and twice recorded in Colorado.

2. **Anteos (Anteos) maerula** (Fabricius). Plate 76, figure 10, ♂ (ssp. *lacordairei*). Nominate *maerula* does not enter our area; individuals taken in the U.S. belong to the subspecies *lacordairei* (Boisduval), as figured. This is another neotropical species which enters the extreme southern parts of Texas and Florida as occasional strays. It is common in Mexico.

Genus PHOEBIS Hübner

The Giant Sulphurs

This group of butterflies of the American tropics has been shown by Klots to be unrelated to Old World butterflies of the genus *Catopsilia,* despite their superficial resemblance. Our species all have a strong, rapid flight but may be collected with ease at flowers or at mud puddles. They are butterflies of open sunny areas. Members of this genus are strongly migratory and their population numbers fluctuate widely. Our species belong to two different subgenera, *Phoebis* and *Aphrissa.*

Subgenus PHOEBIS Hübner

These species display strong sexual dimorphism. Females are also dimorphic, some being normally colored, some albinic.

1. **Phoebis (Phoebis) sennae** (Linnaeus).   Nominate *sennae* (TL Jamaica) enters our area only sporadically as a migrant. The two other subspecies treated below, however, are resident and commonly found in our area.

Early Stages: The larvae are pale yellowish green with a yellowish lateral stripe on each side of the abdomen. On each segment a row of black dots is located crosswise dorsally. The larval foodplants include various species of *Cassia.* The larva lies hidden by day in a tent of the cassia leaf which it folds and ties together with silk. In Louisiana the principal foodplant is Partridge pea (*Chamaecrista cinerea*).

(a) **eubule** (Linnaeus). Plate 76, figure 3, ♀; figure 4, albinic ♀ (form "browni"). Known popularly as the Cloudless Sulphur, males are clear yellow above and unmarked. Beneath there is little or no maculation. Females are fringed with marginal black spots. In both the temperate and tropical zones *sennae* and its subspecies are strong migrators. The stimulus causing the flights is unknown. The butterflies favor open, sunny areas and have a bold, strong flight, visiting many flowers such as thistles and morning glory.

Distribution: This subspecies occurs in the southeastern United States from the Subtropical to the Upper Austral zone. It is also resident in the states adjacent to the Mexican border and the Gulf of Mexico and strays northward as far as Colorado, Nebraska and New York. During some years individuals are frequent in eastern Kansas and Missouri where the adults may be seen flying in a southeast direction in late summer. Mather records similar flights in Mississippi. Two broods occur in the northern part of the range; broods are continuous in the Gulf region and Florida.

(b) **marcellina** (Cramer). Plate 76, figure 1, ♂; figure 2, ♀.   This is the other subspecies of *sennae* widely found in our area. Males are more patterned beneath, with orange-brown scrawls and a background color of orange-yellow rather than pale yellow as in *eubule.* Females are of a much warmer shade of yellow above and more heavily patterned beneath with a ground color of pinkish orange.

Distribution: This is the mainland tropical subspecies of *sennae,* entering the Rio Grande Valley of southern Texas, southern Arizona and southern and central California. Its range extends over most of South America, except Argentina and other subtropical areas where a subspecies similar to *eubule* is found.

2. **Phoebis (Phoebis) philea** (Johansson). Plate 76, figure 5, ♂; figure 6, ♀.   This large species is known as the Orange-barred Sulphur. Adults are so fleet of wing as to be nearly impossible to net unless they are at flowers. This distinctive and beautiful species cannot be confused with any other butterfly. In southern Florida it is more prevalent in city yards and gardens than in the open countryside.

Early Stages: Mature larvae are yellowish green with many fine black granulations, each bearing small, shining black spines. The larval foodplant is *Cassia bicapsularis.*

Distribution: This species occurs in tropical America. About 1930 it became established in southern Florida and has extended its range up the peninsula to Jacksonville. Strays have been found northward as far as Virginia, Arkansas, Colorado and Texas. Strays from adjacent Mexico enter southern Texas every year but apparently *philea* is not established in Texas as it is in Florida.

3. **Phoebis (Phoebis) agarithe** (Boisduval). Plate 76, figure 7, ♂; figure 8, ♀ (ssp. *maxima*). Males are solid, clear bright orange above. Females may be orange like the males or they may be white above with delicate pinkish salmon shading; many individuals have intermediate coloring. The brown markings above are subject to much variation in females both above and below. The straight discal line on the underside of the fore wing of both sexes is continuous. On *argante,* this line is broken and the two parts offset. The butterfly is found in open areas in subtropical scrub. Adults visit puddles and many flowers at which they may be netted with ease despite their strong flight.

Early Stages: Only partially known. The larval foodplants are reported to be *Pithecolobium guadalupensis* and *P. dulcis.* It is not known positively whether or not cassias are a host for this species.

Distribution: This Tropical and Subtropical zone species is resident in our area only in southern Florida where it appears in multiple broods from March through December. There may be movement from population centers during periods of excessive numbers. Our resident subspecies, *maxima* (Neumoegen), is found in southern Florida. Strays occasionally wander as far as Kansas, Arizona and Texas. These may be of the Mexican subspecies, nominate *agarithe.*

4. **Phoebis (Phoebis) argante** (Fabricius). Few individuals have ever been taken in our territory. It is very close to *agarithe,* but on the lower surfaces of the primaries in *argante* the postmedian line of dark brown spots is broken and zigzag; in *agarithe* it is more nearly a straight line. *P. argante* is a neotropical species rarely (if ever) encountered in our area. Many "records" are not trustworthy because they may well be misidentifications of *agarithe.* But *argante* is quite common as near to the U.S. as Tamaulipas, Mexico, and should be expected in southern Texas.

5. **Phoebis (Phoebis) neocypris** (Hübner). Plate 76, figure 9, ♂ (ssp. *bracteolata*). Popularly known as the Giant Tailed Sulphur, this beautiful insect is a creature of the Neotropics and is only rarely encountered in our territory (subspecies *bracteolata* (Butler), as figured). This species is migratory and often flies out to sea in huge numbers. It is a rare straggler in southern Texas and southern Arizona.

Subgenus APHRISSA Butler

Adults of this subgenus closely resemble *Phoebis* in flight habits. Vast swarms of individuals of both *Phoebis* and *Aphrissa* gather on the shores of Venezuela and Brazil and embark upon spectacular sea voyages. The destinations of these flights are as yet unknown. The males of *Aphrissa* are bicolored, the basal two-thirds of the wings being bright yellow (or orange) and the outer third white (or yellowish). This wide white outer border appears mealy and is satiny in texture. On the females no such mealy borders occur. There is a narrow, solid, dark brown or black margin, more extensive on females than on males. In the males there is a characteristic sex patch on the upper surface of the secondaries below the costa and another such patch located on the primaries near the inner margin.

6. **Phoebis (Aphrissa) statira** (Cramer). Plate 71, figure 2, ♂ (ssp. *floridensis*); figure 3, ♀ (ssp. *jada*). Nominate *statira* occurs in South America and does not enter our region. However, the species is sparingly represented in our region by two subspecies. Our only resident subspecies of *statira* is *floridensis* (Neumoegen), in southern Florida. It is similar to nominate *statira*. In the males of *floridensis* the outer pale margins are yellowish and do not contrast greatly with the deeper yellow of the basal two-thirds of the wings. The outer black edging in the apex is not heavy in *floridensis*. Larval foodplants in Florida include *Calliandra* and *Dalbergia exastophyllum*.

Distribution: P. s. *floridensis* occurs in the southern half of Florida. There are two broods: June to September and November to February. The Mexican subspecies, *jada* (Butler), occasionally strays into Texas and even as far north as Kansas.

Genus KRICOGONIA Reakirt

How many species of *Kricogonia* exist? In recent years most lepidopterists have followed the suggestion of W. P. Comstock and considered both *castalia* (Fabricius) 1793 and *lyside* (Godart) 1819 as separate species. One of these bears a peculiar line of thickened scales on the underside of the hind wing, the other does not. What is puzzling about these two is that wherever one appears the other usually is found also. Thomas Turner of Kingston, Jamaica, has solved the problem. There is only one species. Eggs of one type produce offspring of either or both types.

1. **Kricogonia castalia** (Fabricius). Plate 71, figure 4, ♂; figure 5, ♀. Our representative of the genus *Kricogonia* has often been referred to as *lyside*. The adults above are variable, especially females which may be white or yellow in ground color. Huge migrating swarms of this species occur periodically in Mexico and the Neotropics, especially during the autumn months.

Early Stages: These have been described by G. N. Wolcott. The larvae were reared upon Lignum Vitae (*Guaiacum officinale*) in Haiti. In Texas the host plant is *Porliera angustifolia*.

Distribution: This species occurs in the Lower Austral and Subtropical zones. In our area *castalia* is resident in southern Arizona and southern Texas, straying to Colorado, Kansas and Nebraska. It is also a stray in southern Florida. The first large migration reported in our area took place near Catarina in Dimmit county, Texas.

Genus EUREMA Hübner

Members of the genus *Eurema* are small to medium size with yellow, orange or white ground color and dark brown or black outer margins.

Few species inhabit the temperate zone but many occur in the tropical regions of the world. Despite their small size and delicate appearance, some of these butterflies are capable of long sustained flight and periodically engage in tremendous migrations containing millions of individuals. Huge squadrons of *Eurema lisa* have been reported in flight both over land and far at sea. These migrations predate history in the New World and it was probably a swarm of either *Eurema lisa* or *Phoebis eubule* that Columbus and his crew saw about the *Santa Maria* near the south coast of Cuba. Some species are strongly sexually dimorphic. There is also considerable seasonal variation. Some seasonal forms, in fact, have been treated as separate species. Our species belong to three subgenera: *Pyrisitia* Butler, *Abaeis* Hübner and *Eurema* Hübner.

1. **Eurema (Pyrisitia) proterpia** (Fabricius). Plate 72, figure 9, ♂; figure 10, ♀; figure 11, ♂ (winter form); and 12, ♀ (winter form). The winter brood of *proterpia* (the Tailed Sulphur) was formerly considered to be a distinct species, *gundlachia* (Poey). This is an easily recognized species, and the subspecies in our area is nominate *proterpia,* as figured.

Early Stages: Unknown.

Distribution: This species occurs in the Subtropical and Lower Sonoran zones; in our area it occurs as an uncommon resident in southern Arizona and southern Texas. There are two to three broods from July to October. It is common in Mexico.

2. **Eurema (Pyrisitia) lisa** Boisduval & Le Conte. Plate 72, figure 17, ♂; figure 18, ♀; figure 19, albinic ♀. This is our most abundant and widespread *Eurema;* our subspecies is nominate *lisa.* Adults congregate by the hundreds at mud puddles in the South. They sometimes fly over the Caribbean and the Atlantic in huge flocks numbering in the millions. Some have landed as far away as Bermuda. The species is found in open fields and margins of woods as well as sunny trails and roadsides.

In most places in our area *lisa* will not be confused with any other species; however in extreme southern Texas, southern Florida and southern Arizona the range of *lisa* overlaps that of another distinct but quite similar species, *nise* (see below). *E. nise* is somewhat smaller and has much smaller black areas above than *lisa.* Differences in flight behavior are discussed under *nise.*

Early Stages: The mature larvae are grass green, downy and with one or two white lateral stripes. Larval foodplants include Partridge Pea (*Chamaecrista fasciculata*), Sensitive Plant (*Mimosa pudica*), hog peanut (*Amphicarpa*), clovers (*Trifolium*), various cassias and other related Fabaceae.

Distribution: E. lisa occurs on mainland America and in the West Indies from South America northward to Vermont, Quebec, Ontario, Michigan, Iowa, North Dakota and Colorado. It is rare northward but common from Kansas and Virginia southward to Florida, Texas and beyond. Winter hibernation is still uncertain. In more northerly areas (40°N) it seems that neither the adults nor the pupae can withstand the winter. Freshly emerged adults are never seen in early spring and in Missouri do not appear until mid or late May. These late spring individuals are invariably ragged, faded and torn, indicating that they may have flown into the area from the south. In the absence of near freezing temperatures (such as in Florida) there are continuous broods.

3. **Eurema (Pyrisitia) nise** (Cramer). Plate 72, figure 20, ♂; figure 21, ♀. As mentioned above, this species resembles *lisa*. In flight, however, the two species are radically different. Adults of *nise* stay close to scrubby margins of woods and dash into the woods if frightened. Adults of *lisa* stay in open areas and although they often fly near woodland edges they will rarely fly into the woods even when pursued. Other differences have been cited under *lisa*.

Early Stages: The larvae feed upon Sensitive Plant (*Mimosa pudica*).

Distribution: This species ranges from Brazil northward to Mexico, southern Texas and southern Florida where it is perhaps periodically, resident and abundant. It is occasional in southern Arizona. There are at least two broods.

4. **Eurema (Pyrisitia) messalina** (Fabricius). Plate 72, figure 13, ♂ (ssp. *blakei*). This Caribbean species has been recorded (questionably) in southern Florida (subspecies *blakei* (Maynard) as figured). Adults are satiny white with black margins. The species cannot be confounded with any other in our territory.

5. **Eurema (Pyrisitia) dina** (Poey). Occasional specimens of *dina* have been taken in Florida and along the Mexican border in Texas and Arizona. Most of these captures have been made in the Brownsville, Texas, area.

Early Stages: The host plant is reported to be *Picramnia pentandra*.

Distribution: E. dina is widespread in the northern Neotropics.

(a) **westwoodi** (Boisduval). Plate 72, figure 22, ♂. This Central American subspecies on occasion strays into our territory in Texas and Arizona. The specimen figured was captured at Brownsville, Texas. A single male from Madera Canyon, Santa Cruz county, is known from Arizona.

(b) **helios** Bates. Plate 69, figure 21, ♂; figure 22, ♀. A single specimen of this Antillean subspecies was taken on August 23, 1962 at Fairchild Gardens, Matheson Hammock, south of Miami, Florida by J. M. Plomley. Mr. Plomley has since taken additional specimens of *helios* in extreme southern Florida including the examples figured.

6. **Eurema (Pyrisitia) chamberlaini** Butler. Plate 75, figure 24, ♀; figure 25, ♂. This dainty little sulphur is resident in the Bahamas. Charles F. Zeiger discovered a specimen at Castillo Hammock, Dade county, Florida, on March 30, 1963, the sole authentic record to date for the United States.

7. **Eurema (Abaeis) nicippe** (Cramer). Plate 72, figure 23, ♂; figure 24, ♀. Although familiarly known as the Sleepy Yellow, anyone who has tried to net a specimen will not likely want to use this name again for *nicippe*. When frightened *nicippe* flies

in an erratic, zig-zag fashion and is an expert dodger. In the South males congregate at mud puddles and damp sand patches along roadsides and trails. Not infrequently a single assemblage may contain a hundred or more individuals. Adults of *nicippe* are seldom flower visitors. The butterflies prefer open areas, old fields in the East and southern desert scrub associations in the West. In Missouri adults often parallel a woodland edge for many yards but rarely enter the woods.

There are two to three broods annually, with much overlapping particularly in late summer and autumn. Summer brood individuals are yellow beneath, but examples emerging in October and November may be brownish red or even brick red beneath, with many intermediates. In Arkansas and northern Texas the autumn individuals hibernate and reappear early the next spring (April).

Early Stages: The mature larvae are green and slender, with downy pubescence and a lateral yellow line bordered with blackish. Larval foodplants include Partridge Pea (*Chamaecrista fasciculata*), Senna (*Cassia occidentalis*) and *Cassia bicapsularis;* rarely clovers (*Trifolium*) and other Fabaceae.

Distribution: This species ranges from the Subtropical to the Upper Austral zone in the East and the Lower Sonoran zone in the West. In our area it occurs from Florida to southern California and north to New York, Pennsylvania, Ohio, Michigan, Nebraska and Colorado. In Colorado adults fly up to 8000 ft. The species is rare in the North. Winter hibernation occurs as an adult in most instances with an annual influx of migrants to more northerly areas from the South.

8. **Eurema (Eurema) daira** (Godart).

   (a) **daira** (Godart). Plate 72, figure 1, ♂ (winter form "daira"); figure 2, ♀ ("daira"); figure 3, ♂ (summer form "jucunda"); figure 4, ♀ ("jucunda"). The seasonal and geographic forms of this species are numerous and confusing. Careful genetic work is needed to clarify the relationships of each of these forms. At present we are reasonably certain that "jucunda" is merely the summer population of *daira.* This butterfly inhabits open places, including inner ocean beaches, tropical scrub, open fields and waysides.

   Early Stages: The mature larva is dull, light green above covered with fine pubescence, with a paler lateral stripe on each side and an indistinct darker dorsal line. Larval foodplants include Joint Vetch (*Aeschymomene viscidula*), and Pencil Flower (*Stylosanthes biflora*).

   Distribution: This species is resident from Florida to North Carolina, west to Mississippi, Arkansas, Louisiana and eastern Texas. Strays are found as far north as Virginia. Individual strays taken by H. A. Freeman near Pharr, Texas, in the lower Rio Grande Valley, appear to be stragglers of the Mexican subspecies *lydia* (Felder and Felder).

   (b) **palmira** (Poey). Plate 72, figure 14, ♂; figure 15, ♀ (*palmira daira* hybrid). Adults of *palmira* may be recognized at once by the pure white secondaries. This Antillean subspecies occurs in our territory in extreme southern Florida. John Plomley has taken many intermediates between *palmira* and *daira,* an example of which we figure. The subspecies *palmira* has been referred to (incorrectly) as *E.*

elathea (Cramer) in the literature. In *E. elathea* the dark bar on the fore wing of the male is black, not dark gray as in *daira*.

9. **Eurema (Eurema) boisduvaliana** Felder & Felder. Plate 72, figure 5, ♂; figure 6, ♀. This is a common Mexican species. Summer individuals are pale yellow beneath; winter forms are reddish beneath as depicted. According to Klots there are authentic records of *boisduvaliana* from Royal Palm Park in Florida.

Distribution: This species is found in tropical America. It enters our area as a straggler in southern Florida, southern Texas and southern Arizona. It is possibly resident in southern Texas.

10. **Eurema (Eurema) mexicana** (Boisduval). Plate 72, figure 7, ♂; figure 8, ♀. The Mexican Yellow has a well developed "dog's head" on the primaries. Summer individuals are pale yellow beneath, while those of the autumn are pink beneath. In the Southwest it inhabits meadows in Ponderosa Pine forests, southern desert scrub, oak woodlands, ravines and open areas.

Early Stages: These are incompletely known, but *Cassia* is a reported foodplant.

Distribution: This Central American species ranges northward (commonly) as far as Oklahoma, Colorado (breeding), southern Arizona, and southern California. Strays wander as far as Wyoming, North Dakota, Minnesota, Ontario and Michigan. Individuals have been taken occasionally in Louisiana, possibly representing the eastern terminus on the Gulf Coast. In the West *mexicana* breeds in both Lower and Upper Sonoran zones, and adults may stray to even higher levels such as Transition zone forests in Colorado.

11. **Eurema (Eurema) salome** (Felder). Plate 72, figure 16, ♂ (ssp. *limoneus*). This golden yellow species is distinctly patterned and cannot be confused with any other species in our area. The butterfly (subspecies *limoneus* (Felder & Felder) as figured) has been taken occasionally in extreme southern Texas and southern Arizona where individuals straggle into our territory from farther south.

Genus NATHALIS Boisduval

This neotropical genus possesses several exceptional features which distinguish it from all other members of the Pieridae. In the adult the radius of the primaries is three-branched. The larval foodplants are composites rather than legumes or crucifers, and the pupa lacks the frontal projection found on the pupae of other pierids. Perhaps further study will dictate that a separate subfamily be erected for the members of this genus. Only one species occurs in our area.

1. **Nathalis iole** Boisduval. Plate 75, figure 22, ♂; figure 23 ♀. This common species flies in an erratic manner and just a few inches above the ground, visiting flowers frequently. There are several mysteries concerning *iole*. Though a tropical species,

it is found every summer, sometimes commonly, in latitudes too high for winter survival. How does *iole* reach these latitudes? Are several generations involved in the northward movement? It appears incredible that a butterfly so small and fragile could migrate such distances. White males occur, usually very rarely but are sometimes common in local populations.

The habitats of *iole* are dry, open areas. Old fields, ravines, dry hillsides and roadsides are good places to search for it.

Early Stages: The mature larva is dark green with a broad purple stripe and a double yellow and black stripe laterally. Larval foodplants include fetid marigold (*Dysodia*), Sneezeweed (*Helenium autumnale*), Common Chickweed (*Stellaria media*), Bur Marigold (*Bidens pilosa*), Fineleaf Thelosperma (*Thelosperma trifida*) and *Palafoxia linearis.*

Distribution: N. iole occurs in tropical America. In our area it is found from Florida west to southern California, northward to South Carolina, Tennessee, Indiana, Iowa, Minnesota, North Dakota and Wyoming. It is common in the South and the warmer sections of the Great Plains. In southern Arizona *iole* reaches elevations of 8000 ft. It is common in the Colorado Desert of southern California, with four broods annually. There are continuous broods in favorable areas.

Subfamily PIERINAE

This subfamily includes the Whites, Marbles and Orange-tips. Adults of this subfamily may be distinguished from the Coliadinae by the following characteristics: the antennae are longer; the third segment of the labial palp is long and hairy; the ground color of the wings is usually white; the humeral vein of the secondaries is well developed. Adults are common insects and may well be the most abundant of all butterflies.

Early Stages: The caterpillars are smooth, usually green, cylindrical and covered with down or pubescence. The chrysalids have a single, conical, anteriorly directed projection at the bases of the antennae. The larval foodplants are largely members of the family Cruciferae (mustards). Some caterpillars, however, feed upon plants in the Capparidaceae and Pinaceae. Two tribes occur in our area, the Pierini and the Euchloini.

Distribution: Worldwide, except Antarctica.

Tribe Pierini

Butterflies of this tribe are popularly called "whites" because of the prevailing ground color. The antennae are tipped with distinct and rather broad clubs. Adults fly more slowly than members of other tribes and are, therefore, usually more easily netted.

A unique feature of the members of this tribe is that the valva of the male genitalia lacks a well developed armature on the inner face. An important larval characteristic also distinguishes the Pierini from the Euchloini: Pierini larvae feed on the leaves of the foodplant while Euchloini larvae feed on the flowering parts.

Genus NEOPHASIA Behr

There are two species in the genus *Neophasia* and both occur in our territory. The larvae are somewhat gregarious and sometimes seriously defoliate conifers. The humeral vein of the secondaries is straight.

1. **Neophasia menapia** (Felder & Felder). Plate 70, figure 3, ♂; figure 4, ♀. This distinctive species, popularly called the Pine White, may be recognized at once from the figures. The adults flutter weakly about the foliage of pines and rarely visit flowers. It is occasionally an economic pest on pines in the West. Huge flights of *menapia* containing thousands of individuals have been observed in the vicinity of Mount Rainier, Washington (Preston), and elsewhere in the West.

Early Stages: The egg is emerald green, flask-shaped and fluted on the sides with a circle of round beads at the top (Tilden). The caterpillar is dark green with a single broad white band laterally and a narrow white stripe dorsally. The slender chrysalis is dark green with white stripes. Larval foodplants include Western Yellow Pine (*Pinus contorta*), Jeffrey Pine (*P. jeffreyi*) and Ponderosa Pine (*P. ponderosa*); also *Abies balsamea* and *Pseudotsuga menziesii*.

Distribution: This species inhabits the Transition to the Canadian zones, ranging from southern British Columbia and Alberta southward to central California (Napa and Sonoma counties), northern Arizona and central New Mexico. It occurs also in the Black Hills of South Dakota and in Sioux county, Nebraska. There is one record from Itasca Park, Minnesota, probably a stray. There is one annual brood of adults, during July and August.

2. **Neophasia terlootii** Behr. Plate 70, figure 7, ♂; figure 8, ♀. *N. terlootii* is rare in collections and much prized by lepidopterists. Its rarity, however, is largely due to its unusual main flight period (October and November) which comes when most collectors are not in the field to take advantage of the insect's local abundance. Individuals will come down from trees to visit bright objects in the absence of flowers or to drink water from mud puddles.

A form of the female in which the ground color is deep orange was named "princetonia."

Early Stages: The larval foodplant is Ponderosa Pine (*Pinus ponderosa*) and other conifers.

Distribution: This species is found throughout the mountain pine forests of western Mexico northward to Arizona, from the Upper Sonoran to the Transition zone. In the Chiricahua Mountains *terlootii* is associated with pine and Douglas Fir forests at elevations of between 6700 and 7500 ft. The butterfly is common in the Huachuca and Graham mountains during October. It may also occur in New Mexico (White Mountains). One main brood of adults appears in late September and extends into November. There is a partial early brood which appears in June and early July.

Genus PIERIS Schrank

The Whites

The familiar butterflies of this genus are worldwide in distribution. Seven species occur within our faunal limits. On the primaries the cross-vein *ldc* is either straight or nearly so.

1. **Pieris beckerii** Edwards. Plate 70, figure 17, ♂; figure 18, ♀. The strongly marked green veins on the ventral surface of the secondaries, together with the characteristic black markings on the upper surface will readily distinguish Becker's White. It is found on hot, shrubby, semi-arid hillsides, associated with sagebrush and juniper woodland.

Early stages: Larval foodplants include *Stanleya pinnata, Isomeris arborea* and *Brassica nigra.*

Distribution: This species is found from the Upper Sonoran to the Transition zone. Its range includes the intermontane areas from the interior of British Columbia and Idaho southward to northern Baja California, Utah and Colorado. It occurs east of the Continental Divide in Wyoming and Colorado. There are three or more broods during the spring and summer depending upon latitude and elevation.

2. **Pieris sisymbrii** Boisduval. The green markings along the veins on the underside of *sisymbrii* are less bold than on *beckerii;* and *beckerii* is noticeably larger than *sisymbrii.* The black markings on *sisymbrii* are more sharply defined than those on *Pieris occidentalis,* another species that may be confused with it. This single brooded spring butterfly is found in rocky places that are favored by its probable host plant, *Arabis.* There are three rather poorly defined subspecies that intergrade.

Early Stages: These are not well known. Several species of *Arabis* are foodplants for the larvae and it is possible that other crucifers are used.

Distribution: The species ranges from the Yukon Territory and British Columbia eastward to South Dakota and south to Baja California and New Mexico.

(a) **sisymbrii** Boisduval. Plate 70, figure 21, ♂; figure 22, ♀. This subspecies was described from the western slope of the Sierra Nevada in central California. In the basin-and-range region to the east *sisymbrii* tends to intergrade toward the following two subspecies.

Distribution: The range of this subspecies is essentially the Pacific coast states, from western British Columbia to northern Baja California.

(b) **elivata** (Barnes & Benjamin). Plate 76, figure 21, ♂; figure 22, ♀. This name is based upon specimens from Glenwood Springs, Colorado. The markings along the veins on the underside of the hind wings are much stronger on *elivata* than on *sisymbrii*.

Distribution: This subspecies is found in the Rocky Mountains from southwestern North Dakota and Wyoming south to New Mexico, including the Black Hills of South Dakota. Possibly the plains form is sufficiently distinct to warrant a subspecific name. Specimens from Arizona, Nevada and Utah appear to be intermediate between *elivata* and *sisymbrii*.

(c) **flavitincta** J. A. Comstock. Plate 76, figure 19, ♂; figure 20, ♀. There is a strong yellowish cast to members of this subspecies, especially the females. Similar yellowish females ("flava") occur occasionally among *sisymbrii* and *elivata* but should not be confused with *flavitincta*.

Distribution: This subspecies occurs from the Yukon Territory and the interior of southern British Columbia southward to northern Idaho, intergrading with *sisymbrii* southwestward and with *elivata* southeastward.

3. **Pieris protodice** Boisduval & Le Conte. The Checkered White is a common open land butterfly from coast to coast. In the West the first brood ("vernalis") is small and much more sharply marked with black and can be confused with *sisymbrii*. Some lepidopterists have considered *occidentalis* a subspecies of *protodice*. I treat it as a full species (below).

(a) **protodice** Boisduval & Le Conte. Plate 70, figure 13, ♂; figure 14, ♀; Plate 76, figure 23, ♀ (form "vernalis"); figure 24, ♂ (form "vernalis"). There are several broods of nominate *protodice* during the year. The earliest, as mentioned above, resembles the species *sisymbrii*. All other broods are larger and the black markings are much more restricted, as can be seen in the figures. This is a butterfly of open sunny places: dry roadsides, abandoned fields and other disturbed terrain where its weedy host plants abound.

Early Stages: Mature larvae are yellowish, striped with purplish green and have much body pubescence. Larval foodplants include both native and introduced crucifers such as turnips and cabbage, as well as wild mustard (*Brassica*), Golden Mustard (*Selenia aurea*), Shepherd's Purse (*Capsella bursapastoris*), Wild Peppergrass (*Lepidium virginicum*), sweet alyssum (*Lobularia*), fleabane (*Erigeron*), and *Astragalus*.

Distribution: This subspecies occurs from the Lower Sonoran to the Transition zones in the West and both Upper and Lower Austral zones in the East. It ranges abundantly across the southern half of the United States from California to Florida, north to New York, Michigan, North Dakota, Montana and Oregon. It has been taken rarely in southern Alberta and southern Manitoba and is common in Mexico. There are three broods in the north, more in the south. Occasional individuals may emerge on warm midwinter days in some areas.

(b) **nelsoni** Edwards. Plate 97, figure 27, ♂. This subspecies of *protodice,* from the Bering Sea coast of Alaska, is rare in collections. It looks like a slightly dusky spring brood individual of nominate *protodice*. It is single brooded and may prove to be a valid species rather than a subspecies of *protodice*.

4. **Pieris occidentalis** Reakirt. Plate 70, figure 15, ♂. This is a true sibling species. It is close to *protodice* in appearance and in some places flies with it. Chang has shown that this species possesses well defined structural features that distinguish it from *protodice*. Individuals of the spring brood ("calyce") of *occidentalis* are most often confused with early broods of *protodice*. This species favors open, sunny slopes in or near mountains.

Early Stages: The mature caterpillar is dull green with alternate dark and light stripes. Larval foodplants include Spider Plant (*Cleome serrulata*), Western Hedge Mustard (*Sisymbrium altissimum*) and *Thlaspi arvense*. Mustards utilized by *protodice* may also be food sources for *occidentalis*.

Distribution: P. occidentalis ranges from central British Columbia eastward to Alberta and Manitoba, south to central California (Sierra Nevada), northern Arizona and northern New Mexico. There are two broods, one in June and early July and a second in August and September.

The *napi* complex

For years most workers have recognized only two species of this difficult group in North America, *Pieris napi* (Linnaeus) and *Pieris virginiensis* Edwards. Warren, however, suggests that our previous ideas were incorrect and that there may be more than two species in our region. Unfortunately Warren's work is based upon only a single character, the androconial scales. It remains for some worker to study the North American races of the *napi* group, utilizing a number of features of morphology and biology in addition to androconia. Warren's "species" are briefly as follows: (1) *Pieris bryoniae* (Hübner): our arctic populations, represented by the names *hulda* Edwards, *pseudobryoniae* Verity and *frigida* Scudder, are considered to be races of this Old World species. (2) *Pieris napi* (Linnaeus): the race *marginalis* Scudder from Oregon and Washington is considered to be the only North American subspecies of the Palaearctic *napi*. (3) *Pieris oleracea* Harris: this is considered to be a separate species. (4) *Pieris venosa* Scudder: this is also considered a distinct species occurring in California and Alberta. (5) *Pieris mogollon* Burdick: this too is considered a distinct species, inhabiting Arizona. (6) *Pieris virginiensis:* a species unchanged by Warren. I believe that it is best to take a conservative view for the present and follow the "standard" treatment for the *napi* complex until Warren's ideas are either confirmed or discarded.

5. **Pieris napi** (Linnaeus). The following North American subspecies are figured: **hulda** Edwards. Plate 78, figure 11, ♂. **pseudobryoniae** Verity. Plate 70, figure 20, ♀. **marginalis** Scudder. Plate 16, figure 5, ♂; figure 7, ♀. **venosa** Scudder. Plate 70, figure 24, ♂. **oleracea** Harris. Plate 70, figure 19, ♂. **frigida** Scudder. Plate 16, figure 16, ♀; figure 17, ♂. This protean species of circumpolar distribution occupies the cooler portions of Asia, Europe and North America. *P. napi* is not only geographically

variable but varies markedly from one seasonal generation to another. The ecological range of this species has reportedly suffered a severe reduction as a result of competition with *Pieris rapae* and the destruction of its favored habitat, deciduous or mixed coniferous woodland. Adults have a weak and relatively slow flight and favor shaded or partially shaded woodland edges in a cool, moist environment.

Early Stages: Mature larvae are velvety green with a middorsal stripe and a yellow lateral stripe on each side of the abdomen. Host plants include milkmaids and toothworts (*Dentaria*), water cress (*Barbarea*), rock cress (*Arabis*), and Penny Cress (*Thlaspi arvense*).

Distribution: In the north central and eastern states *oleracea* Harris is found in the Transition and Canadian zones and does not extend south of the Catskill Mountains in New York (Klots). In Labrador the subspecies *frigida* Scudder occurs. Some form of *napi* occurs in nearly all Canadian zone forests in the western states. From Montana to northern New Mexico the subspecies *macdunnoughii* Remington ranges. There is little gray veining beneath in this subspecies. The subspecies *mogollon* Burdick is abundant in Canadian zone forests in Arizona. In the California Coast Ranges (southern limit, Lopez Canyon, San Luis Obispo county) the heavily marked subspecies *venosa* Scudder is abundant in February and March. During May a second brood ("castoria") appears in which the black veining and markings are greatly reduced and the underside is nearly immaculate pale yellow. In Oregon and Washington the subspecies *marginalis* Scudder is common. This subspecies has characteristic well defined veining beneath but somewhat less heavy than in *venosa*. There are two or three broods in all areas in which these butterflies occur including northern Canada (ssp. *pseudobryoniae* Verity) and Alaska (chiefly ssp. *hulda* Edwards). *P. napi* is entirely absent in the warmer sections of the Midwest and the South.

6. **Pieris virginiensis** Edwards. Plate 70, figure 23, ♂.   This woodland species of the eastern United States is generally found south of *Pieris napi oleracea*. In southern Vermont and western Massachusetts, however, both species fly together and occupy the same biotope, which confirms the specific distinctness of these two entities. *P. virginiensis* is a local species that inhabits moist woodlands, either deciduous or mixed. Adults fly in a radically different way than do those of *P. napi oleracea*. *P. virginiensis,* if disturbed, flies erratically, is very nervous when approached and when alarmed soars out of net reach. In contrast *napi* is always docile and easily netted whatever the provocation.

Early Stages: Mature larvae are dark yellowish green with a slightly paler narrow dorsal stripe and a pair of lateral stripes. The pupa is slender with an exceptionally thin, curved frontal prominence. Host plants include Toothwort (*Dentaria diphylla*) and possibly other *Dentaria*.

Distribution: This Transition zone species occurs from northern Minnesota and northern Michigan eastward to Quebec and south in the Appalachian Mountains to western North Carolina and northern Georgia. Adults (sometimes locally abundant) appear in a single brood from early to mid May. The species hibernates as a pupa.

7. **Pieris rapae** (Linnaeus). Plate 70, figure 16, ♂. This species was accidentally introduced from Europe into Quebec in about 1860 and rapidly spread throughout most of North America. It now is found in any open area in widely diverse plant associations, including those in cities and towns. It is considered a serious pest in commercial plantings of all cruciferous crops in our area. The larvae of the Cabbage Butterfly also feed upon nasturtiums in household gardens. A tiny braconid wasp, *Apanteles glomeratus* (Linnaeus), frequently parasitizes the caterpillars of this butterfly.

Early Stages: These are well known and described in numerous books and agricultural pamphlets. Larval host plants comprise nearly all Cruciferae and Capparidaceae as well as *Nasturtium cleome.*

Distribution: The species is widespread. In North America it inhabits all life zones from Lower Austral to Canadian, although it is absent or scarce in desert and semidesert regions (except in irrigated areas). It is not found north of the Canadian life zone, nor is it found on the Channel Islands off the coast of southern California. It is now present in the Hawaiian Islands and many other islands of the Pacific where it was formerly absent.

Genus ASCIA Scopoli

This New World genus is composed of four species. Two species, each in a different subgenus, occur in the area treated by this volume.

1. **Ascia (Ascia) monuste** (Linnaeus). Three subspecies of this common tropical species are known from the United States. Two are from the East and Gulf coasts and the other is found in Texas.

Early Stages: Mature larvae are lemon yellow with purplish green to blackish stripes (Klots). Host plants include cultivated Cruciferae (with occasional damage to cabbage and collards in Florida), nasturtium (*Nasturtium*), Spider Flower (*Cleome spinosa*), Saltwort (*Batis maritima*), Beach Cabbage (*Cakile maritima*), Pepper Grass (*Lepidium virginicum*), clammy weed (*Polanisia*) and other wild Cruciferae and Capparidaceae.

(a) **monuste** (Linnaeus). Plate 76, figure 12, ♂ (ssp. *raza*). The common tropical subspecies, nominate *monuste,* invades the Rio Grande Valley of Texas. Just how far it extends along the Gulf Coast we do not know. It is characterized by its large size, the males with wide borders and well marked veins on the underside; females are a little more dusky than the males. The subspecies *raza* Klots, with heavily marked hind wing underside, is found in Baja California and does not reach the U.S.

Distribution: South America northward to southeastern Texas.

(b) **phileta** (Fabricius). Plate 70, figure 9, ♂; figure 10, ♀; Plate 76, figure 11, ♀. This southeastern United States subspecies periodically undergoes population surges which result in emigration. Individuals usually proceed northward from southern Florida along the East Coast. We do not yet know the reasons for such mass movements. The subspecies *phileta* is characterized by somewhat smaller size and less distinctly marked veins beneath. Females may be either white, almost like males, or quite dark and smoky. The latter form is the migratory phase.

Distribution: A. m. phileta ranges along the Gulf Coast from Louisiana (abundant in salt marshes) to Florida, northward into coastal Georgia.

(c) **cleomes** (Boisduval & Le Conte). North of the usual range of *phileta* there is (or was) a subspecies of *monuste, cleomes,* that looks very much like tropical nominate *monuste.* It has white females. At present there are unsolved problems related to *cleomes:* Has it become extinct? Has it been absorbed by *phileta?*

Distribution: This subspecies occurs (or occurred) from Georgia northward to Virginia on the coastal plain.

2. **Ascia (Ganyra) josephina** (Godart). Plate 70, figure 11, ♂; figure 12, ♀ (ssp. *josepha*). The Mexican subspecies, *josephina josepha* (Salvin & Godman), is resident in our region along the Mexican border in southern Texas. There appear to be no authentic records of the insect in Florida.

Early Stages: Not known.

Distribution: The species is found from Central America northward to southeastern Texas (Rio Grande Valley), with strays entering southern Arizona.

Genus APPIAS Hübner

A single American representative of this predominantly Old World tropical genus is encountered in our territory.

1. **Appias drusilla** (Cramer). Plate 70, figure 5, ♂; figure 6, ♀ (ssp. *neumoegeni*). This is our common and familiar Florida White. Both sexes may be recognized by the silky basal sheen on the wings above. Adults are most prevalent in shaded hardwood hammocks. The butterflies tend to avoid open sunshine except when engaged in migratory flights. Out subspecies is *neumoegeni* (Skinner), as figured.

Early Stages: These have been carefully described by R. L. Chermock, who states that the foodplant is the Guiana Plum (*Dryapetes lateriflora*). Other reported hosts are caper (*Capparis*) and allied Capparidaceae.

Distribution: The species is found throughout the Neotropics. The subspecies *neumoegenii* is found in southern Florida and southern Texas. Strays have been reported as far north as New York, Nebraska and Colorado.

Tribe Euchloini

The marbled butterflies and the orange-tips are among the most attractive butterflies of spring. Adults are recognized by the rich greenish yellow marbling beneath; an orange apical patch is found in many species. The males of this tribe have a well developed process on the inner face of the valva.

Early Stages: The eggs are yellow when laid but turn reddish orange in less than a day. They are almost always deposited on or near the flowers of the foodplant. The larvae feed exclusively on the flowers or immature seed pods. The pupal period lasts more than ten months in most instances, with the emerging adults appearing in spring.

Genus ANTHOCHARIS Boisduval, Rambur & Graslin

The Orange Tips

Males have bright orange on the apical area of the primaries in all species except *lanceolata;* females also have orange above except in *midea* and *lanceolata.* The larvae usually feed on the immature seed pods of their cruciferous hosts. Members of this genus are distinguished from *Euchloe* by characteristics of the male genitalia. Other species of *Anthocharis* occur in the Palaearctic region. Representatives of two subgenera, *Anthocharis* and *Falcapica,* occur in our area.

Subgenus ANTHOCHARIS Boisduval, Rambur & Graslin

Members of this subgenus are characterized by the lack of a strongly falcate fore wing and the presence of a black bar at the end of the cell. Three species occur in our territory, all confined to the West.

1. **Anthocharis (Anthocharis) cethura** (Felder & Felder). Plate 71, figure 10, ♂; figure 11, ♀; figure 7, ♂ (form "caliente"). The subspecific names presently applied have little validity. Although closely allied to *pima,* the exact degree of affinity has not been determined. An occasional female lacks the orange tip, to which the designation "deserti" has been applied, but such females appear at low frequencies in most *cethura* populations and do not represent a valid subspecies. Populations from the eastern Mojave Desert are yellow above, but are not considered *pima.* The yellow colored form "caliente" appears regularly throughout most *cethura* populations. This species is found in desert foothills, southern desert shrub and juniper woodland. Host plants are *Descurrainea pinnata, Caulanthus inflatus* and *Streptanthella longirostris.*

Distribution: A. *cethura* occurs in the Lower and Upper Sonoran zones. Its range includes southern California, southern Nevada, western Arizona and northern Baja California. There is one brood from February to mid May.

2. **Anthocharis (Anthocharis) pima** Edwards. Plate 71, figure 12, ♂; figure 13, ♀. The males of this species exhibit strong hilltopping behavior. Females are found on adjacent slopes and creek bottoms before the strong afternoon winds of the desert begin. The favorite habitat is low desert hills.

Early Stages: Unknown.

Distribution: This species is restricted to the Lower Sonoran zone in southern Arizona and northward along the Colorado River to southern Nevada. One brood of adults appears from February to April.

3. **Anthocharis (Anthocharis) sara** Lucas. This western species displays a higher degree of sexual dimorphism than do the two preceding species. Many names have been proposed for local varieties of *sara.* Some of these appear to represent acceptable subspecies, others do not. Yellow females occur in all populations. In some they are universal (*stella*) while in others they are uncommon. The nominate subspecies is double brooded; all other subspecies are single brooded. The species is found in moist areas in at least partially open woodland; also along sunny trails, in open meadows, along stream banks, in canyons and on ridges.

Early Stages: The mature larva is dull grassy green. The head is large and bilobed. Both head and body are covered with short black tubercles or hairs. The pupa is pale silvery gray with the ventral area paler and the wing cases marked in white. Thus far only F. X. Williams has found the pupae in nature and these were suspended at the base of the foodplant. The early stages were carefully described by Coolidge and Newcomer in 1909. Host plants include Hedge Mustard (*Sisymbrium officinale*), Rock Cress (*Arabis sparsiflora arcuata*), Water Cress (*Barbarea vulgaris*), nasturtium (*Nasturtium*); also *Brassica nigra, B. campestris, B. kaber, Descurrainea pinnata* and *Thysanocarpus curvipes.*

(a) **sara** Lucas. Plate 71, figure 6, ♀; figure 9, ♂; figure 14, ♂ (form "reakirtii"); figure 15, ♀ (form "reakirtii"); figure 8, ♂ (ab. "dammersi"). The name *sara* was based on the large, second generation butterfly which appears in late May and June in the California Coast Ranges. The earlier generation was dubbed "reakirtii" by Edwards, a useless name. The single specimen described as "dammersi" by Comstock in 1929 proves to be neither a good species nor a hybrid of *sara* and *lanceolata* but an aberration of *sara.*

Distribution: From Baja California del Norte north to Oregon in the mountains.

(b) **stella** Edwards. Plate 71, figure 16, ♀. This also is a large subspecies, with southern specimens about the same size as in nominate *sara.* It is characterized by having yellow females and by being single brooded.

Distribution: This subspecies ranges from Oregon and Idaho northward into British Columbia; it also occurs in the Tetons of northwestern Wyoming.

(c) **julia** Edwards. The Rocky Mountain subspecies looks like a miniature *sara.* It is nowhere common but is found in small colonies scattered throughout the mountains.

Distribution: A. sara julia occurs in the Rocky Mountains from northern New Mexico and Colorado.

(d) **alaskensis** Gunder. Plate 76, figure 13, ♂. Similar to *julia, alaskensis* is more dusky and apparently separated from the range of *julia.*

Distribution: Coastal mountains of Alaska.

(e) **browningi** Skinner. Plate 76, figure 14, ♂. This subspecies of *sara* occurs in Utah. In *browningi* the orange apical patch is pale, the black patterning is paler and reduced with little marbling beneath. In both sexes there is usually a faint yellow cast to the ground color above.

(f) **inghami** Gunder. Plate 76, figure 15, ♂. Adults of *inghami* may be recognized by the deep, solid orange patch and the heavy black bar in the cell. The maculation beneath is heavier than in *browningi*. The subspecies *inghami* is found in Arizona.

Subgenus FALCAPICA Klots

Adults of this subgenus may be recognized by the black dot at the end of the cell on the primaries above. The apex is falcate. Three species occur in the New World (one of them outside our area) and two species occur in Eurasia.

4. **Anthocharis (Falcapica) midea** Hübner. Plate 71, figure 17, ♂ (ssp. *annickae*); figure 18, ♀ (ssp. *midea*); figure 19, ♂ (ssp. *midea*). This is our well known Falcate Orange-tip. The distribution, geographic variation and population behavior are under study. Some individuals partake in hilltopping behavior. Adult flight is low and erratic, but not fast. The species is nearly always confined to open pine-oak or oak-hickory woodlands and fluctuates widely in abundance from one year to another.

Northern populations have been accorded the name *annickae* dos Passos & Klots. The butterflies are smaller and the orange apical patch of the male is less extensive.

Early Stages: Mature larvae are dull green, finely striped with orange, bluish green, dark blue, white, olive and pale yellow; the orange stripe dorsal, the white stripes lateral and widest (Klots). Host plants include various Cruciferae: Rock Cress (*Arabis perfoliatum*), bitter cress (*Cardamine*), Winter Cress (*Barbarea vulgaris*), Mouse Ear Cress (*Sisymbrium thaliana*) and Shepherd's Purse (*Capsella bursapastoris*). As in the preceding subgenus, the larvae feed only upon the flowers, buds and immature seed pods of the host plants. The pupa is extremely slender with a very long, spinelike process on the head.

Distribution: The species occurs in Upper and Lower Austral zones. It is widespread but local throughout much of the eastern U.S. from central Massachusetts southward to coastal Georgia and westward to northeastern Texas, Arkansas, Kansas and Illinois.

5. **Anthocharis (Falcapica) lanceolata** Lucas. Plate 71, figure 20, ♂; figure 21, ♀. Both sexes lack the orange tip. In addition the ventral surface is gray rather than green. The butterfly is found on open south facing slopes of canyons and desert washes. This species may be recognized by its slow, floating flight and is easily netted if within reach of the collector. Unfortunately, it frequently is out of reach since it flies about the faces of cliffs on which its foodplant occurs. The host plant is *Arabis sparsiflora arcuata* and possibly other *Arabis*.

Distribution: This species inhabits the Upper Sonoran to lower Canadian zones from southern Oregon south to northern Baja California. It occurs also in the Carson Range adjacent to Lake Tahoe in Nevada. There is one brood, from April to June.

Genus EUCHLOE Hübner

The Marble Whites

The members of this Holarctic genus entirely lack an "orange tip." Most, however, are beautifully marbled beneath with a filigree of greenish yellow markings, whence the name "marble whites." When the adults are seated, with wings folded together, on the flowers of yellow mustard the marbling of the lower surfaces successfully camouflages them. In flight all members of this genus may be recognized with experience by the rapid, direct and "purposeful" manner in which they fly. They are more nervous than other pierids and are somewhat more difficult to net. Adults emerge from overwintered pupae in the spring of the year and have a relatively brief flight period. There is only a single brood each year, apparently forced by the food preferences of the caterpillars. They feed solely upon tender green seed pods, flowers or buds of the host plant, which appear only in spring. All our species are in the subgenus *Euchloe*.

The *ausonides* group

The three species in this group are *creusa, ausonides* and *olympia*. There is a scattering of white scales in the black bar in the cell on the upperside of the primaries in all three species. Other characters of the genitalia, larval coloration and oviposition behavior also unite them.

1. **Euchloe (Euchloe) creusa** (Doubleday). Plate 69, figure 19, ♂; figure 20, ♂, underside. Plate 71, figure 23, ♀. This subalpine species has never been taken in the United States although it should be searched for in Glacier National Park. Quite possibly it has been overlooked because of its early flight period. A distinctive population occurs near Prince Albert, Saskatchewan. Subalpine moraines and forest clearings are the habitat of *creusa*. For many years *hyantis* (Edwards) and *lotta* (Beutenmüller) have been considered subspecies of *creusa*, but they represent another species (*hyantis*) in its own species group of *Euchloe* (see below).

Distribution: This species occurs in the upper Hudsonian zone from central Alaska eastward to the mouth of the Mackenzie River in the Northwest Territories, southward into the mountains of Alberta and British Columbia. It flies from mid May to early July in a single brood.

2. **Euchloe (Euchloe) ausonides** Lucas. This is the most widespread *Euchloe* in North America. At present it appears to be extending its range eastward in the Great Lakes region. The species is not particularly variable throughout much of its range and the name *coloradensis* (Hy. Edwards) represents material not different enough to be recognized as a subspecies at this time.

Early Stages: The egg is long and flask-shaped. The mature larva is dark green with a blue-gray dorsal stripe. On either side of this stripe lies a gray-green stripe below which is a yellowish lateral line. Numerous black tubercles are scattered over the body. The chrysalis is at first purplish but turns gray within an hour as does that of *olympia.* Host plants are various mustards, especially *Arabis glabra, A. lyallii, A. duriuscula, A. drummondi* and *A. fendleri spatifolia;* also *Barbarea vulgaris, Descurrainea richardsoni, Brassica nigra, Erysimum capitatum* and *Sisymbrium altissimum.*

(a) **ausonides** Lucas. Plate 71, figure 26, ♂; figure 27, ♀. This rather variable subspecies is found in the mountains of the western United States and southwestern Canada. In California the females are dimorphic: either soiled yellowish or white. This may be sufficient in the eyes of some to restrict the name *ausonides* to the Californian and western mountain populations. If so, then the name *coloradensis* (Hy. Edwards) must be used for the Rocky Mountain populations.

Distribution: The species occurs in a variety of open, mountain habitats throughout the coastal mountains, the Sierras, the basin-and-range and Rocky Mountain systems from central California to northern New Mexico northward into Alberta and British Columbia.

(b) **mayi** Chermock & Chermock. Plate 76, figure 17, ♀. This name is generally applied to northern populations from Alaska and Yukon Territory to the prairie provinces of Canada and eastward into Ontario.

(c) **andrewsi** Martin. Plate 76, figure 18, ♂. The name *andrewsi* represents a local population in southern Utah, and southern California.

3. **Euchloe (Euchloe) olympia** Edwards. Plate 71, figure 24, ♂; figure 25, ♀ (both ssp. *rosa*). The Olympia Marble is a butterfly of the early spring. The species exhibits marked hilltopping behavior in many areas. It flies with *ausonides* in eastern Colorado. The flight of *olympia* is rapid and "purposeful" in contrast to *Pieris rapae* and other whites. Males often fly back and forth, "patroling" an area, especially an open hillside. In the East these butterflies favor open woodland or nearby meadows; in the Great Plains they are found in river woodlands and on river bank bluffs; in eastern Colorado they occur on low, open foothills. Specimens with rosy markings on the underside have been named "rosa" and occur in all populations. They are more common among prairie populations than among those of eastern woodlands.

Early Stages: Mature larvae are deep green with dorsal and lateral lines of slate blue. There is a subdorsal yellowish line on each side of the body. This becomes ashen gray before pupation. The pupa is a beautiful rosy purple when fresh but quickly fades to gray-brown. Host plants include Rock Cress (*Arabis lyrata*) and Hedge Mustard (*Sisymbrium officinale*). One brood of adults appears in April and early May in the East; May and June in Colorado. Hibernation occurs as a pupa.

Distribution: The species ranges from southern Ontario south to Maryland, Kentucky and West Virginia westward to central Montana, eastern Wyoming, eastern Colorado and northern Texas. It is rather local and not a particularly common species.

The *hyantis* group

This group is composed of a single species, only distantly related to the other three species of North American *Euchloe*. There is a strong tendency for vein R_5 to be absent in this species.

4. **Euchloe (Euchloe) hyantis** (Edwards).   This species, like other *Euchloe*, frequently engages in hilltopping or ridge following. It is occasionally difficult to separate *hyantis* from *ausonides* in the Sierra Nevada of California where both species occur. The heavy black bar in the cell of *hyantis* is distinctive. There are usually no white scales in the bar markings of the upper surface in the cell of *hyantis*. The butterfly is partial to rocky, south facing canyon walls, rocky ridges and piñon-juniper woodland. Host plants include *Descurrainea pinnata* (in the Mojave Desert of southern California and in eastern Washington), *Streptanthus tortuosus* (Sierra Nevada of California) and *Streptanthus bernardinus* (San Bernardino Mountains in southern California).

(a) **hyantis** (Edwards). Plate 71, figure 22, ♂.   The notes above apply to this subspecies. It is single brooded, with adults flying from March to June, depending upon climate.

Distribution: Nominate *hyantis* ranges from the Upper Sonoran to the lower Hudsonian zone, in intermontane areas from the interior of British Columbia and Idaho south to northern Baja California, eastward to southern Arizona, northern New Mexico, Colorado and western Wyoming. It also occurs locally in the California Coast Ranges.

(b) **lotta** (Beutenmüller). Plate 76, figure 16, ♂.   The Mojave Desert *lotta* is a rather weakly differentiated subspecies in which the cellular black bar is unusually wide. The butterfly appears in March.

Family PAPILIONIDAE
Swallowtails and Parnassians

WILLIAM H. HOWE

Probably no other butterfly family is as familiar to the layman as this one, which includes many of our largest and most colorful species. The family reaches its greatest development in the tropics, where most of its more than 500 species are found.

Some of the distinguishing characters of the family are easily seen. The prothoracic legs are fully developed and there is only one anal vein (2A) in the hind wing (exception: *Baronia*). The larvae possess an *osmeterium,* an eversible forked organ located on the dorsum of the thorax, just behind the head. It gives off a pungent odor when extruded. Belying their common name, many swallowtails lack a tail on the hind wing.

The family is divided into three subfamilies: Papilioninae, Parnassiinae, and Baroniinae. The majority of species are in the Papilioninae and, until recently, most of the members of this subfamily were placed in the genus *Papilio.* Closer morphological examination revealed that there were more differences than had been previously assumed and for our species four genera, rather than one, are now accepted. The Parnassiinae are restricted to the Northern Hemisphere, and only three species are found in North America. Only one species, *Baronia brevicornis* Salvin, represents the Baroniinae, found south of our area.

Early Stages: The larvae are generally smooth; but in one group of genera there are soft, fleshy projections on the body. Some larvae are covered with short hairs. At this stage of development papilionids have several different ways of protecting themselves. Young larvae in the genus *Papilio* often resemble bird droppings; the malodorous osmeterium may be extruded when the larva is disturbed by a predator; and many of the larval foodplants contain distasteful substances which may render the larvae, pupae and/or adults unpalatable.

The pupae are generally attached to objects by means of a silken pad to which the cremaster is fastened, and a silken girdle around the midsection. The Parnassiinae pupate in crude cocoons in debris on the surface of the ground.

The family is found in tropical, temperate and boreal areas and on all continents and many islands.

Subfamily PAPILIONINAE

Genus BATTUS Scopoli

JOHN F. EMMEL

A common name for the members of this genus is the Aristolochia papilios because all of the known larvae feed on the leaves of that genus or its close allies. These foodplants presumably make the insects unpalatable, thus protecting them. As a result some species in other papilionid genera mimic Aristolochia papilios. This makes it difficult to characterize the genus. Perhaps the best clues are the deep sensory grooves on the underside of the antenna and the four rows of spines on the tarsi, not separated into two groups by a spineless area. Whether *Battus* is a genus or a tribe of genera has not yet been settled.

Early Stages: The larvae are densely clothed with fine hairs which gives them a velvety appearance. They are ornamented with rows of soft, rather long tubercles which are also covered with fine hairs. The pupae are broad in the center, unlike those of the other sections of the papilionids.

Distribution: The Aristolochia papilios are found in the Americas, Eurasia and Australia and adjacent islands. They are absent from Africa except for one species on Madagascar.

1. **Battus philenor** (Linnaeus). Tailless or short tailed individual variants among specimens from the southern United States have erroneously been recorded as *acauda* (Oberthür), a subspecies of southern Mexico.

Distribution: B. philenor is found from southern Mexico northward to southeastern Canada, Colorado and California. It is probably much more extensively distributed now than before European settlement of America and may be expected anywhere where *Aristolochia* (Pipevine) is being cultivated.

(a) **philenor** (Linnaeus). Plate 66, figure 3, ♂; figure 4, ♂, underside. This *Battus* is one of our more strikingly colored species. The hind wing is metallic blue or green dorsally, and has bright red-orange spots ventrally. The butterfly is distasteful to certain predators and serves as a model for several apparently palatable, mimicking species. These include female *Papilio polyxenes, Papilio glaucus* (dark females), *Papilio troilus, Limenitis astyanax* and *Speyeria diana* (females). It is double brooded in the northern parts of its range and probably triple brooded in the south. Diapause occurs in the pupal stage.

Early Stages: The eggs are spherical and reddish brown, and are laid in small clusters. The larvae are dark, with several paired rows of fleshy tentacles; one anterior and three posterior pairs are longer than the others. Host plants include various Aristolochiaceae: in the eastern U.S., *Asarum* (wild ginger), *Aristolochia serpentaria* (Pipevine), *A. macrophylla* and others.

Distribution: In our area *B. p. philenor* ranges from New England and southern

Ontario west to Nebraska, southward to central Florida and westward into Arizona. Occasional strays are taken in southern California, usually in the fall.

(b) **hirsuta** (Skinner).   The adults of this subspecies tend to be slightly smaller than nominate *philenor,* and have slightly longer scales on the thorax and abdomen, giving a "hairy" appearance.

Early Stages: These are essentially the same as for nominate *philenor.* The larval foodplant is *Aristolochia californica.*

Distribution: This subspecies occurs in north-central California, in the Sacramento Valley and San Francisco Bay areas.

2. **Battus polydamas** (Linnaeus).   This is the only other Aristolochia papilio found north of Mexico.

Much individual variation occurs among specimens of *polydamas* and, in the West Indies, there is also geographic variation. Thus far no subspecies have been recognized on the mainland from Texas to Argentina, whereas eleven have been described in the West Indies. A careful study of material from Cuba, the Bahamas, Florida, Texas and Mexico shows that two and possibly three subspecies are involved. The Texas and Mexico material is *B. polydamas polydamas.* Specimens from the Bahamas, Florida and probably Cuba are best assigned to *B. polydamas lucayus.* Rothschild and Jordan were arbitrary and in error when they declared Cuba to be the type locality of *Papilio polydamas* Linnaeus (1758).

(a) **polydamas** (Linnaeus).   The markings on nominate *polydamas* are slightly smaller, the discal bands slightly narrower and the colors slightly darker than on *B. polydamas lucayus.*

Early Stages: These are much like those of *philenor.*

Distribution: Nominate *polydamas* occurs from Texas to northern Argentina.

(b) **lucayus** (Rothschild & Jordan). Plate 65, figure 4, ♂.   There is need for careful study of the material from Cuba, the Bahamas and the eastern Gulf states to clarify the taxonomic situation of *polydamas* in this area.

Distribution: The subspecies *lucayus* occurs in the Bahamas and the east coast of Florida. Probably it also occurs on Cuba and the west coast of Florida. The situation from Florida westward is not clear.

Genus PAPILIO Linnaeus

The common name for this genus is the fluted swallowtails. The features by which members of the genus may be recognized are these: the sensory grooves on the antennae are not easily seen and the antennae are not scaled; the vertical rows of spines on the tarsi are divided clearly into ventral and dorsal rows separated by a smooth spineless area; the abdominal margin of the hind wing of both sexes is bent downward and from beneath appears fluted. This margin is free of scent patches almost always present in *Battus* and *Graphium.*

Early Stages: Mature larvae are without tubercles (except a few species in the Oriental region) and with the third thoracic segment enlarged and often decorated with eyespots. The pupa resembles a weathered splinter of wood. Host plants are not as restricted as in either *Battus* or *Graphium.*

Distribution: The genus is worldwide and ventures farther poleward than either of the other papilionine genera.

1. **Papilio polyxenes** Fabricius. Plate 63, figure 13, ♂; figure 14, ♀; figure 15, ♂ (form "pseudoamericus").   There are at least four subspecies of *Papilio polyxenes,* none of which is clearly distinguished. All of them intergrade, with the possible exception of Cuban *polyxenes polyxenes.* The greatest confusion exists among lepidopterists about the proper name for the strains of this butterfly found in the southern Rocky Mountains. It may be that in time *curvifascia* Skinner will be adopted as the subspecific name for these. The subspecies *stabilis* Rothschild & Jordan, sometimes thought to occur in the southwestern states, is restricted to the mountains from northern Panama to Honduras. The only subspecies in our area is *asterius* Stoll, as figured.

Occasionally a specimen will have a greatly expanded postmedian yellow band, as shown on Plate 63, figure 15 (form "pseudoamericus"), resembling the South American subspecies *P. polyxenes americus;* these should be considered variants of *asterius* rather than representatives of *americus,* because the latter does not reach our area. The species as a whole is extremely variable in the extent of the black and yellow markings, ranging from some specimens which are almost completely black, to individuals from southern Mexico which show a yellow pattern similar to *P. zelicaon.* The black females mimic the distasteful *Battus philenor.*

Early Stages: The larva is green, yellow-green, bluish green, or white, with transverse black bands and yellow, orange or red-orange dots on these bands. Host plants include many species of Umbelliferae (Parsley family); also Rutaceae, including *Ruta graveolens* and *Thamnosma texana.*

Distribution: P. polyxenes asterius is found from southern Canada to Florida, westward to the eastern edge of the Rocky Mountains, through New Mexico to Arizona and southward into Mexico.

2. **Papilio rudkini** J. A. Comstock. Plate 63, figure 11, ♂ (form "comstocki"); Plate 64, figure 1, ♂ (form "clarki"); figure 2, ♀ (form "clarki"); figure 4, ♀ (form "comstocki").   *P. rudkini* is strictly a desert dweller. Recent hybridization studies indicate that *rudkini* is closely related to, or even a subspecies of, *P. polyxenes* rather than *P. bairdii* as was thought previously. It is polymorphic, three forms having been distinguished: the typical form, "rudkini," having facies similar to *P. zelicaon;* a sexually dimorphic black form, "clarki"; and a form in which the postmedian yellow band is intermediate in width between those of the first two forms, known as "comstocki." *P. rudkini* is probably a synonym of *P. coloro* Wright, but the name *rudkini* is retained here pending further investigation. The butterfly has been taken in every month of the year, but is more common in the spring (February-April) and in the fall after late summer rain.

Early Stages: The larva is extremely variable; its pattern is basically like that of *P. polyxenes,* ranging from individuals showing extensive development of the light areas, to examples which are nearly solid black. The host plant is *Thamnosma montana* (Turpentine Broom), a member of the Rutaceae.

Distribution: This species occurs in the desert regions of southern California, western Arizona, southern Nevada and extreme southwestern Utah.

3. **Papilio kahli** Chermock & Chermock. Plate 64, figure 6, ♂. The name *kahli* has been given to a population of a black *Papilio* in the Riding Mountains of Manitoba. The relationship of this butterfly to other members of the *P. machaon* group is poorly understood at present. It has been considered by some authors as a form of *nitra.* It is possibly a variant population of *P. polyxenes,* although many specimens in this population may represent hybrids between *P. polyxenes* and *P. machaon hudsonianus.*

Early Stages: These are similar to those of *P. polyxenes.* The host plant is *Pastinaca sativa* (Parsnip).

4. **Papilio brevicauda** Saunders. This butterfly is easily distinguished from *P. polyxenes* by the shorter tails and stubbier wings. It is sympatric with *polyxenes* in part of its range. The three subspecies that are recognized differ very little and are of questionable value.

Early Stages: The egg, larva, and pupa are similar to *P. polyxenes.* Host plant: *Ligusticum scothicum* (Scotch Lovage).

(a) **brevicauda** Saunders. Plate 63, figure 2, ♀. This is the largest of the subspecies and has the most orange in the postmedian band of spots.

Distribution: Nominate *brevicauda* is found in southern Labrador, Newfoundland, and on Anticosti Island.

(b) **bretonensis** McDunnough. Plate 63, figure 1, ♀. Somewhat smaller than *brevicauda,* this subspecies, also has less orange in the postmedian spots.

Distribution: This subspecies occurs in the Canadian Maritime Provinces.

(c) **gaspeensis** McDunnough. Plate 64, figure 5, ♂. This is the smallest subspecies and the postmedian spots are free, or almost free, of orange.

Distribution: Gaspé Peninsula, Quebec.

5. **Papilio bairdii** Edwards. Plate 63, figure 9, ♂; figure 10, ♀; Plate 67, figure 8, ♀ (form "brucei"). The polymorphic populations of this swallowtail have created some unresolved problems in its taxonomy. The taxon known as *P. brucei* Edwards, somewhat resembling *P. zelicaon,* is variously treated as a subspecies or a form of *P. bairdii,* or even as a separate species. There is roughly a north-south cline of the frequency with which the "brucei" facies occurs in populations. In southern California and Arizona the typical black *bairdii* populations yield only an occasional "brucei," perhaps 1 to 3%. Northward through Colorado and Utah the frequency of "brucei" becomes approximately 50%; north of this area "brucei" predominates, and black forms become rare or absent.

Another form, "hollandi," is infrequently encountered; in this variant the postmedian yellow band is intermediate in width between that of *brucei* and that of *bairdii.* Another taxon in the Pacific Northwest, *P. oregonius,* resembles "brucei" and may be a representative of *bairdii.* It is treated below as a separate species, but hybridization studies now in progress suggest a subspecific affinity to *P. bairdii.* The butterfly is triple brooded southward and double brooded northward.

Early Stages: The larva is similar to *P. polyxenes,* but larger. David L. Bauer has compared the two life histories, as well as the adults. The host plant is *Artemisia dracunculus* (Compositae), an unusual foodplant; most of the other members of the *P. machaon* group feed on Umbelliferae or Rutaceae.

Distribution: This species occurs in southern California (San Bernardino Mountains only), northern Arizona and northern New Mexico, ranging eastward and northward to western Nebraska, western South Dakota, Wyoming, Utah and Nevada.

6. **Papilio oregonius** Edwards.

(a) **oregonius** Edwards. Plate 63, figure 12, ♂. This swallowtail inhabits the arid regions of the Pacific Northwest, where it can be taken from April to September. The spring brood specimens are smaller and lighter than those of the summer brood.

Early Stages: These superficially resemble those of *P. bairdii,* but are geographically variable. In the vicinity of the type locality mature larvae are pale grayish green, with transverse black bands broken by yellow dots. In many other localities the dots are orange. The host plant is *Artemisia dracunculus.*

Distribution: This subspecies is found in southern British Columbia, eastern Washington and Oregon, Idaho and western Montana.

(b) **dodi** McDunnough. Plate 64, figure 3. The biology of this butterfly has been studied in detail by Stephen and Edwin Perkins. Although their work is not completed, preliminary findings suggest that *dodi* is closely related to *P. oregonius,* and it is treated here as a subspecies. It was formerly considered a subspecies of *machaon.* A major difference between *dodi* and *oregonius* is that the cell area of the upper surface of the fore wing of *dodi* lacks the copious yellow scaling found in nominate *oregonius.* It is double brooded, the first brood appearing in May and June and the second brood in late July and August.

Early stages: The mature larvae differ from topotypical *oregonius* larvae mainly in the color of the transverse rows of spots; these are orange-red in topotypical *dodi.* The host plant is *Artemisia dracunculus.*

Distribution: This subspecies occurs in the badlands of south-central Alberta, and in Theodore Roosevelt National Park in western North Dakota.

7. **Papilio machaon** Linnaeus. This is the only holarctic papilionine. Numerous subspecies are recognized across Europe and Asia and two are found in North America. The life histories of the Old World subspecies from across Eurasia have been published. As yet we do not know about the immature stages of our subspecies. It has been reported that *P. machaon aliaska* oviposits on *Artemisia arctica.*

(a) **aliaska** Scudder. Plate 64, figure 8, ♀. Although often taken commonly at localities along the Alaska Highway and other areas accessible by automobile, *aliaska* is still relatively rare in collections because few lepidopterists travel into its territory.

Early Stages: Undescribed. The host plant is reportedly *Artemisia arctica* (Compositae).

Distribution: This subspecies occurs in Alaska and northern areas of Canada.

(b) **hudsonianus** Clark. Plate 63, figure 16, ♂. This subspecies represents *P. machaon* in the southeastern part of its range in North America. In spite of its relatively wide distribution, little is known of its biology.

Early Stages: Unknown.

Distribution: This subspecies occurs in the Hudsonian zone, from James Bay and the east shore of Hudson Bay to the northwest shore of Lake Superior and thence northwestward.

8. **Papilio zelicaon** Lucas. Plate 63, figure 4, ♂. This butterfly is the most common member of the *P. machaon* complex in the western U.S. It breeds from sea level to over 12,000 ft. elevation, and hilltopping males are occasionally taken above the 14,000 ft. level. Over most of its range, *zelicaon* is found in the mountains; along the Pacific Coast it also breeds in lowland areas, especially where imported Fennel (*Foeniculum vulgare*) grows in abundance. In the San Joaquin Valley of California the insect is an economic pest on *Citrus*. It is single brooded at higher elevations, double brooded in the lower mountains, and multiple brooded in the lowlands of California.

Early Stages: These resemble those of *P. polyxenes,* but are extremely variable. Host plants include many Umbelliferae. Some of the more widely used species include: *Foeniculum vulgare* (Fennel), *Tauschia arguta, Pteryxia terebinthina* and *Heracleum lanatum* (Cow Parsnip). *Citrus* (Rutaceae) is also used.

Distribution: The species ranges from northern Baja California to British Columbia. Typical *P. zelicaon* is Californian; the extent of its range is undetermined at present because of our meager understanding of the relationship of this butterfly to *P. gothica.* High altitude specimens from the Sierra Nevada and Cascades may represent *gothica.*

9. **Papilio gothica** Remington. Plate 64, figure 7, ♀. The adults of *P. gothica* are all but indistinguishable from those of *P. zelicaon,* and *gothica* is probably a subspecies of *zelicaon.* It is separated from *zelicaon* on the basis of subtle biological differences rather than on differences in color pattern of the wings. The type locality is Gothic, Gunnison county, Colorado, high on the western slope of the Rocky Mountains; this habitat is in striking contrast to the warm, dry lowlands of California where typical *zelicaon* is taken. The insect is single brooded.

Early Stages: These resemble those of *P. zelicaon,* but in the mature larvae the spots are consistently yellow, while in *zelicaon* larvae the spots range from yellow to red-orange. In the type locality, the following Umbelliferae are used as larval foodplants: *Pseudocymopterus montanus, Angelica ampla, Conioselinum scopulorum, Heracleum lanatum* and *Ligusticum porteri.*

Distribution: Because of its recent naming, the distribution of *P. gothica* is undetermined. I suspect that it is an ecological race of *P. zelicaon* found in the Rocky

Mountains from Alberta and British Columbia to New Mexico, and probably also in the higher mountains of Utah, Nevada and northern Arizona.

10. **Papilio nitra** Edwards. Plate 63, figure 3, ♂. This butterfly has been taken in small numbers along the eastern slope of the Rocky Mountains from Alberta to Colorado. Its range is the approximate area where the ranges of *P. polyxenes* and *P. zelicaon* (or *gothica*) overlap. Some workers have speculated that *nitra* is a hybrid of the two species. However, laboratory hybrids between *polyxenes* and *zelicaon* resemble *polyxenes* rather than *nitra*. Furthermore, specimens of *zelicaon* with *nitra* facies have been taken at Berkeley and San Pedro, California, well outside the range of *polyxenes*. We will be in a better position to understand the status of this insect when *nitra* females are bred in the laboratory and the offspring are studied.

Early Stages: Unknown.

11. **Papilio indra** Reakirt. The *Papilio indra* complex shows a considerable degree of geographic variation, especially in the southern parts of its range. Throughout its range the species is generally uncommon and specimens are rare in collections.

(a) **indra** Reakirt. Plate 63, figure 6, ♂. *P. indra indra* is typically found in arid rocky areas, from near sea level along the Columbia River to over 10,000 ft. in the Sierra Nevada of California. It is single brooded.

Early Stages: Although variable in color pattern, the mature larva is generally salmon pink, with wide transverse black bands and a transverse row of orange dots across each segment. The outline of the pupa is much stubbier and more rounded than that of other members of the *P. machaon* complex. Host plants include *Pteryxia terebinthina, Harbouria trachypleura* (Mountain Parsley) and *Lomatium grayi* (all Umbelliferae). Edwards's record of *Artemisia dracunculus* (Compositae) is undoubtedly erroneous.

Distribution: Nominate *indra* is taken in California (Sierra Nevada and the northern part of the state), Oregon and Washington, eastward through Utah, Idaho and Wyoming to north-central Colorado and western South Dakota.

(b) **pergamus** Hy. Edwards. Plate 63, figure 8, ♂. This subspecies is larger and has longer tails than nominate *indra,* although the pattern of light and dark markings is similar. It is typically found in dry Upper Sonoran and Transition zone habitats in the higher mountains of southern California.

Early Stages: Although the mature larva is morphologically like that of nominate *indra,* the color pattern is strikingly different. The larva of *pergamus* is whitish to pinkish gray and the black markings are reduced considerably. Host plants include *Tauschia arguta, T. parishii* and *Lomatium lucidum* (Umbelliferae).

Distribution: This subspecies occurs in California in the Santa Barbara, San Gabriel, San Bernardino, San Jacinto and Santa Ana ranges, and in the higher mountains of San Diego county.

(c) **fordi** Comstock & Martin. Plate 67, figure 5, ♂. This subspecies shows the greatest development of the yellow markings in comparison to the other members of the *P. indra* complex. It is a desert butterfly, taken in the arid mountains of the Mojave Desert. Males are occasionally observed hilltopping on the higher peaks, while females prefer the wash bottoms and rocky slopes where the foodplant grows. The adults fly in March and April.

Early Stages: The mature larva is somewhat like that of *pergamus,* although the black areas are much more extensive and the light areas show an occasional blue sheen. The host plant is *Cymopterus panamintensis* var. *acutifolius* (Umbelliferae).

Distribution: This subspecies is found in the mountains of the western and southern Mojave Desert, and of the extreme northern Colorado Desert in California.

(d) **martini** Emmel & Emmel. Plate 67, figure 6, ♀. Recently discovered in the Providence Mountains of the eastern Mojave Desert, *martini* represents one of the most variable subspecies of *P. indra.* A series of adults will show individuals resembling *pergamus, minori, kaibabensis,* and some that approach *fordi.* The majority of specimens, however, exhibit a postmedian band that is narrow on the fore wing, whereas on the hind wing it is wide near the costal margin, narrowing to an obsolescent line posteriorly. The habitat is in the piñon-juniper zone. Adults first appear in late March and fly throughout the month of April; there is evidence of a very small second brood in July.

Early Stages: The fourth instar larva most closely resembles that of *P. i. fordi;* the last instar is similar to that of *P. i. minori,* but has a greater development of the black areas. The host plant is *Lomatium parryi* (Umbelliferae).

(e) **kaibabensis** Bauer. Plate 63, figure 5, ♀. The largest known member of the *P. indra* complex, *kaibabensis* occurs in the Grand Canyon region of Arizona. The adults resemble females of *P. bairdii,* but they may be easily separated from that species by the absence of rows of yellow spots on the abdomen. Like *P. indra minori,* the butterfly is double brooded, the first brood flying in May and June, and the second appearing in late July and August.

Early Stages: These are similar to those of *P. i. minori.* The larval foodplant is *Pteryxia petraea* (Umbelliferae).

(f) **minori** Cross. Plate 63, figure 7, ♂. An inhabitant of the wild mesa and canyon country of the upper Colorado River drainage, *minori* is one of our least collected butterflies. For many years it was known only from Black Ridge, near Colorado National Monument in western Colorado. Recently it has been taken elsewhere in this area, and a specimen is also known from northwestern New Mexico. Males have been observed to battle each other fiercely, accounting for the frayed appearance of most specimens. The first brood flies in May and early June; a small second brood appears in July.

Early Stages: The mature larva is pink, with transverse black bands and a transverse row of orange dots on each segment. Larval foodplants are *Lomatium eastwoodae* and *Pteryxia hendersonii* (Umbelliferae).

Distribution: P. indra minori is found in extreme western Colorado, southeastern Utah and northwestern New Mexico.

12. **Papilio cresphontes** Cramer. Plate 65, figure 2, ♂. This is the largest butterfly in our area. It is more commonly taken in the southern parts of its range, becoming scarcer northward. Strays occur in southern Canada. The northern populations have been named *pennsylvanicus* Chermock & Chermock, but this subspecies is only

weakly differentiated. The insect is an economic pest on *Citrus* in some areas.

Early Stages: The mature larva is dark brown with cream markings and an orange osmeterium. Host plants are *Citrus, Dictamnus* (Gas Plant), *Xanthoxylum fagara* (Prickly Ash), *X. Clava-Herculis, Ptelea trifoliata* (Hop Tree) and *Ruta graveolens* (Rue).

Distribution: This species occurs in the eastern United States from the Canadian border to Mexico, and westward along our southern border to southern Arizona.

13. **Papilio thoas** Linnaeus. Plate 65, figure 3, ♂ (ssp. *autocles*). This large and widely distributed yellow and blackish brown butterfly is easily confused with *P. cresphontes.* There is one sure way to separate the two: dorsally near the end of the abdomen of the males there is a notch on *cresphontes* that is absent on *thoas.* You can feel your fingernail drop into the notch as you move it off the posterior edge of the tenth tergite of *cresphontes.* Eight or nine subspecies of *thoas* are recognized. One of these enters our territory, *P. thoas autocles* Rothschild & Jordan, as figured. It is doubtful that *P. t. oviedo* Gundlach, the Cuban subspecies, has ever been taken in Florida. There are no authentic records for that state. Just as doubtful are reputed examples of *P. t. nealces* Rothschild & Jordan, the subspecies that is found in northwestern South America, the northernmost examples coming from Costa Rica.

Early Stages: These are essentially the same as for *cresphontes.*

Distribution: The species ranges from Texas to Argentina. Subspecies *autocles* is not uncommon in southern Texas, with strays found in Kansas and Colorado. Two specimens are known that emerged from wild pupae in central Colorado. The subspecies ranges from there southward to Costa Rica, where it blends with *nealces.*

14. **Papilio aristodemus** Esper. Plate 66, figure 10, ♂; figure 11, ♂, underside (ssp. *ponceanus*). This Antillean papilio occurs in southern Florida. It has been there long enough to have developed as a recognizable subspecies, *ponceanus* Schaus, different from either the Cuban or Hispaniolan subspecies. This Florida subspecies, however, is rare and it is fighting a losing battle in the face of advancing housing developments, highways and airports. It is an inhabitant of the hardwood hammocks of extreme southern Florida.

Early Stages: The egg is spherical and greenish. The mature larva is rich brown with yellow and white lateral markings. The pupa is roughly cylindrical, tapering gradually to the cremaster and more abruptly to the snout with thoracic and cephalic appendages. Host plants: torchwood and wild lime.

Distribution: This subspecies formerly occurred from Miami south through the keys. It is now extinct in the vicinity of Miami. The species ranges from Florida south in the West Indies to Hispaniola, possibly on Puerto Rico but definitely absent from Jamaica.

15. **Papilio andraemon** (Hübner). Plate 77, figure 1, ♂ (ssp. *bonhotei*). This interesting papilio is restricted to Grand Cayman Island, Cuba and most of the large Bahama Islands. A sufficient number of strays, and one specimen that apparently developed

from a caterpillar, have been found in Florida to warrant including the species here. The life history of the Cuban subspecies (*P. a. andraemon*) was sketchily reported by Gundlach. The host plants are *Citrus* and *Ruta*. Florida specimens belong to the subspecies *bonhotei* Sharpe (as figured), which is found on the larger islands of the Bahamas.

16. **Papilio ornythion** Boisduval. Plate 67, figure 3, ♀; figure 4, ♀, underside. Plate 65, figure 5, ♂; figure 6, dimorphic ♀.   This is another subtropical papilio that strays into our territory. It is found in eastern and central Texas adjacent to the Mexican border. The sexes are somewhat different in color and some females are quite dark.

Early Stages: Not known.

Distribution: P. ornythion occurs in Mexico and Guatemala.

17. **Papilio astyalus** Godart. Plate 67, figure 1, ♂; figure 2, ♀; figure 7, ♀ (ssp. *pallas*). The long familiar species name *lycophron* Hübner [1823] must bow to *astyalus* published in 1819. The Mexican subspecies, *pallas* Gray (as figured), strays into southern Texas and southern Arizona. The males and females of *pallas* are quite different in coloring. Both sexes have been found in Texas in late summer and early fall.

Early Stages: These are similar to those of *thoas.*

Distribution: The subspecies *pallas* occurs from northern Mexico to Costa Rica. The species ranges as far south as northern Argentina.

18. **Papilio glaucus** Linnaeus.   The Eastern Tiger Swallowtail probably is the most wide ranging of the tiger swallowtails. Three subspecies are recognized.

Early Stages: The mature larva is green, with a pair of large eyespots on the metathorax, behind which is a transverse yellow stripe bordered by a black stripe. At least seven families are represented in the foodplants of *P. glaucus.* These include *Prunus* (cherry), *Betula* (birch), *Sorbus* (mountain Ash), *Populus* (Poplar), *Salix* (Willow), *Liriodendron* (Tulip Tree), *Fraxinus* (ash), *Tilia* (basswood), *Malus* (apple), *Acer* (maple), and *Magnolia.*

Distribution: The species is found mostly east of the Rocky Mountains, from Alaska and the Hudsonian zone of Canada to the southern United States.

(a) **canadensis** Rothschild & Jordan. Plate 78, figure 8, ♂.   This northern subspecies is smaller and paler than either of the more southern ones. It is single brooded and no dark female form is known to occur.

Distribution: This subspecies ranges through Alaska, Canada, Newfoundland and the northern mountainous parts of New England and New York.

(b) **glaucus** Linnaeus. Plate 62, figure 4, ♀ (dark form); figure 5, ♂; figure 6, ♀ (normal form "turnus").   This is the subspecies found throughout the major portion of the United States east of the Rocky Mountains. In this subspecies the females are dimorphic. The dark form (true glaucus) is uncommon in the northern part of the range but may constitute as much as 95% of the specimens of that sex in the southern part. This subspecies has two or three broods.

Distribution: Nominate *glaucus* occurs from New England to Wisconsin southward to Texas, Louisiana, Alabama and Georgia.

(c) **australis** Maynard. Individuals of this subspecies are quite large and the yellow color is ochraceous and darker than in the more northern subspecies. Dark females are rather scarce in *australis.* It is double or triple brooded.

Distribution: P. glaucus australis is found in Florida and the coastal plain areas of Georgia west to Louisiana and possibly extreme eastern Texas.

19. **Papilio rutulus** Lucas. Plate 62, figure 3, ♂. *P. rutulus* resembles *P. glaucus,* but is generally smaller. The adults prefer canyon bottoms where willows grow abundantly, and occur from sea level to over 10,000 ft. in the mountains of Colorado. Both sexes are strongly attracted to thistle flowers. The species is largely single brooded in the higher mountains, but double or triple brooded at lower elevations. It is questionable whether either *ammoni* Behrens, a dark yellow form, or *arizonensis* Edwards warrants subspecific rank.

Early Stages: These are similar to those of *P. glaucus.* Host plants include *Salix lasiolepis, S. lasiandra* (willow), *Populus tremuloides* (aspen), *P. angustifolia, Platanus* (sycamore), and *Alnus viridis* (alder).

Distribution: P. rutulus ranges from British Columbia to California, east to the high plains east of the Rocky Mountains.

20. **Papilio multicaudatus** Kirby. Plate 65, figure 1, ♀. This species is also found over much of the western part of our area. It is as large as *P. glaucus,* but the black markings are reduced, and the hind wing has two tails rather than one. Like *P. rutulus,* it shows a wide tolerance of elevation although it does not occur as high as *rutulus.* The insect is typically found in canyon bottoms, and thistles seem to be a favorite nectar source.

Early Stages: These are similar to those of *P. glaucus.* Host plants include *Prunus virginiana* (Choke-cherry), *Ptelea trifoliata* (Hop Tree), *P. angustifolia, Fraxinus* (ash), *Ligustrum lucidum* and *L. vulgare.*

Distribution: This species ranges from British Columbia to California, east to Montana, western Nebraska, Colorado and west Texas; south into Mexico.

21. **Papilio eurymedon** Lucas. Plate 66, figure 8, ♂; figure 9, ♂, underside. *P. eurymedon* differs from the other three species in the *P. glaucus* group in that the ground color is white or pale cream rather than yellow. It flies typically in dry mountain areas. Males frequently show hilltopping behavior.

Early Stages: These are similar to those of *P. glaucus.* Larval foodplants include *Ceanothus fendleri, Rhamnus californica* (California Coffeeberry), *Rhamnus crocea* (Redberry) and *Prunus ilicifolia* (Holly-leaved Cherry).

Distribution: P. eurymedon ranges from British Columbia to Baja California, east to Colorado, New Mexico and Montana.

22. **Papilio pilumnus** Boisduval. Plate 66, figure 7, ♂.   *P. pilumnus* is rare in our area, occasionally taken in southern Arizona and southern Texas. Superficially it resembles *P. glaucus,* but morphologically it is more closely related to *P. troilus.*

Early Stages: Probably resemble those of *P. troilus.* I have observed *P. pilumnus* females ovipositing on a species of *Litsea* (Lauraceae) in Chiapas, Mexico.

Distribution: The species ranges from southern Arizona and southern Texas southward to Guatemala.

23. **Papilio troilus** Linnaeus.   The Spicebush Swallowtail is widespread in the eastern United States, flying in shady woods where its foodplants may be found, or visiting flowers in open fields. The females presumably mimic *Battus philenor.* There are three broods in the far south, and two broods in the northern parts of its range.

Early Stages: The larva is green, with two large eyespots on the metathorax and a pair of less prominent ones posteriorly. Host plants include *Benzoin* (spicebush), *Sassafras, Magnolia glauca* (Sweet Bay) and *Xanthoxylum* (prickly ash).

Distribution: P. troilus is found from southern Canada south to Florida, eastern Texas and eastern Kansas, generally east of the Mississippi River.

(a) **troilus** Linnaeus. Plate 62, figure 1, ♂; figure 2, ♀.   The Northern Spicebush Swallowtail is common in wooded areas where its various host plants grow. Toward the southern part of its range it blends with the southern subspecies, *ilioneus.*

Distribution: Nominate *troilus* ranges from southern Canada as far west as Manitoba and south to Texas and Georgia.

(b) **ilioneus** Smith.   This is a larger, brighter insect than *troilus troilus.* It reaches its peak of development in Florida and is found on the coastal plain from southern Georgia to Texas.

24. **Papilio palamedes** Drury. Plate 66, figure 5, ♂; figure 6, ♂, underside.   *P. palamedes* is taken typically in or near swampy woods in the southeastern U.S. It is double to triple brooded.

Early stages: The larva somewhat resembles that of *P. troilus,* having a pair of orange and black eyespots on the metathorax. Host plants include *Persea* (red bay), *Magnolia glauca* and *Sassafras.*

Distribution: This species occurs in Mexico, the Gulf states and Florida, north to Missouri in the Mississippi Valley and on the coastal plain to Virginia and New Jersey.

25. **Papilio anchisiades** Esper. Plate 67, figure 9, ♂ (ssp. *idaeus*).   This distinctive papilio belongs to a neotropical group with short spiky tails. Sometimes the tails are absent in our species. It is the most widely distributed of the group and three subspecies are recognized, two in South America and one in Central America and Mexico. This latter subspecies, *idaeus* (as figured), has become established in the Lower Rio Grande Valley since the planting of citrus groves in that area.

Early Stages: These are somewhat like those of *thoas,* and like that species the larvae are sometimes a pest on citrus.

Distribution: The species ranges from southeastern Texas to Bolivia and northern Argentina. The subspecies *idaeus* Fabricius occurs from Panamá northward. Strays have been taken as far north as Kansas.

Genus GRAPHIUM Scopoli

The kite swallowtails can be recognized by a combination of features. The wings often are less densely scaled than in *Battus* or *Papilio.* The club on the antenna is more distinct and the upper surface of the antenna is loosely scaled on *Graphium* but not on the other genera. The abdominal margin of the hind wing of the males is widened and usually bears a distinct patch of specialized scales as a scent organ. but not on the other genera. The abdominal margin of the hind wing of the males is widened and usually bears a distinct patch of specialized scales as a scent organ.

Although there are over one hundred species in this genus, only one is found in North America north of Mexico. In the tropics one often sees adults of this genus congregating in large numbers at mud puddles.

Early Stages: The mature larva has the third thoracic segment enlarged as in *Papilio* but without the eyespots. The thoracic and anal segments usually bear rather hard tubercles but no true spines; such tubercles are absent on *Battus* and *Papilio.* The pupae are smoother than those of either of the other genera.

Distribution: The genus is found throughout the world in the tropics and into adjacent warm temperate areas.

1. **Graphium marcellus** (Cramer). Plate 66, figure 1, ♀; figure 2, ♀ (form "lecontei"). The only *Graphium* north of Mexico, the Zebra Swallowtail is one of our most distinctive butterflies. It exhibits a high degree of seasonal variation. Specimens of the early spring brood ("marcellus") are the smallest and have the greatest development of the light markings. The later spring specimens are larger and have heavier dark markings; these are known as "telamonides." Summer brood individuals ("lecontei") are still larger with longer tails, and show the greatest development of the dark markings. There are anywhere from two to four broods per year. The subspecies *G. marcellus floridensis* (Holland) is similar to "lecontei" and weakly distinguished; it is found in central Florida.

Early Stages: The larva is smooth and pea green with narrow black and yellow cross bands; there is a wider black band across the last thoracic segment. The pupa is short and stubby in comparison to pupae of other papilionids. The host plant is *Asimina triloba* (Papaw).

Distribution: This species ranges from Massachusetts to southern Ontario and Minnesota, south to the Gulf states and central Florida.

Subfamily PARNASSIINAE

JON H. SHEPARD and SIGRID S. SHEPARD

The Parnassians

This is primarily an Old World subfamily of the Papilionidae. It is recognizable in our fauna by the sphragis that forms during mating on the ventral caudal surface of the abdomen of the female. The number of genera recognized in the Parnassiinae varies from specialist to specialist. We accept the conclusions of Curt Eisner as the most reasonable; he recognizes thirteen genera, only one of which, *Parnassius,* is found in North America.

Genus PARNASSIUS Latreille

The genus *Parnassius* has a circumpolar distribution and ranges southward in western North America through the mountains as far as central California and New Mexico. Because of their great phenotypic variety and beauty Parnassians have been among the favorites of amateur collectors. This has resulted in many names for slightly isolated populations that have no real value in the classification of the butterflies. The early literature is, more than usually, full of mistakes as to type localities. This too has added to the nomenclatural confusion.

Three species of *Parnassius* are known from North America. These are *P. evers-manni* Ménétriés, *P. clodius* Ménétriés and *P. phoebus* Fabricius. *Parnassius evers-manni* is known only from Alaska, Yukon Territory, and northwestern British Columbia. The other two are known from Alaska south to California and Utah with *P. phoebus* extending into New Mexico. Except for *P. phoebus* in the Black Hills of South Dakota none of the species are known east of the Rocky Mountains. *Parnassius clodius* is known only from North America; the other two species are also present in the Palearctic.

The following general account of the biology of *Parnassius* is based on information from the authors' field observations in part and also from information supplied by Mr. Curt Eisner, the European specialist for the Parnassiinae. In early summer, males emerge eight to ten days before the females. Females emerge in the morning. A female almost always copulates before flying, the male seeking her in grassy meadows or on mountain slopes by constant patrolling. During copulation the male releases a liquid substance around the terminal end of the female abdomen. This hardens into a structure called the sphragis. The color and form of this are characteristic for a species. The sphragis is thought to prevent multiple mating of females. According to Eisner only one female specimen is known which has more than one sphragis; in this specimen a second and third sphragis were attached to the middle of the abdomen. Each female lays about sixty eggs, singly, on the ground near the foodplant. The eggs hatch and overwinter as larvae of undetermined instar. Feeding is completed the next spring. Pupation occurs in a loose silk cocoon on the ground. Pupation often occurs some distance from the foodplant. Previous literature on North American Parnassians consistently report *Sedum, Saxifraga,* and sometimes *Viola* as the foodplants for all species. This is absolutely not true. *Sedum* is a foodplant for *P. phoebus* only, the others are not verified. *Parnassius clodius* feeds on *Dicentra* and the foodplant for *P. eversmanni* is unknown in North America.

The following descriptions of subspecies are based on the upper surfaces of the wings unless stated otherwise. The descriptions follow the style of Eisner except that English equivalents replace the German terms. Figure 32 illustrates the use of the special pattern terms, which apply alike to upper and lower surfaces. The lower surface is used in the figure because the basal spots are not present on the upper surface.

1. **Parnassius eversmanni** Ménétriés. Plate 69, figure 1, ♂; figure 2, ♀ (ssp. *thor* Hy. Edwards).   This is a circumpolar butterfly. In North America it can be recognized by its solid black antennae, yellow ground color of the males, and the fact that the anal spot, bar and median ocellus of the hind wing are connected. The females are light yellow to white. Freshly emerged specimens of *clodius* appear slightly yellowish because of yellow hairs. All *Parnassius* may turn dark yellow if left in a moist cyanide jar. This color disappears in fresh air as the cyanide fumes leave the specimen. The sphragis is white.

Early Stages: These are not known in North America. According to Wilson (Ehrlich & Ehrlich, 1961) the caterpillars feed on *Corydalis gigantea.*

Distribution: The North American subspecies *thor* Hy. Edwards (TL: Yukon River, Alaska, 100 miles from mouth) is known from the mountains of Alaska, the Yukon Territory in the drainage area of the Yukon River and northwestern British Columbia.

2. **Parnassius clodius** Ménétriés.   This is the only endemic *Parnassius* species in North America. Both sexes are white to creamy in color and have solid black antennae. The sphragis is white.

Early Stages: The foodplant has recently been found by D. McCorkle to be a *Dicentra* species. Persistent literature citations of *Viola, Sedum* and *Saxifraga* are errors.

Distribution: The species *clodius* is known from southeastern Alaska south to the Santa Cruz Mountains and central Sierras in California. It is also found from Utah north to Montana in the Rocky Mountains but is not known from Colorado or Alberta.

(a) **clodius** Ménétriés.   Male: the anal spot usually is absent; the submarginal spots are weak or present only as a trace; the median ocellus is red. Female: the anal spot is black with sometimes a trace of red; the submarginal spots are medium black; the median ocellus is red. Otherwise the two sexes are similar.

Distribution: This subspecies is found in California, from Marin county (TL: Bear Valley) north to central Trinity county, occuring in coastal mountains from sea level to 6000 ft. Most records are from lower elevations. The flight period is from mid May to mid June.

(b) **strohbeeni** Sternitzky. Plate 69, figure 15, ♂. Male: the anal spot is absent; submarginal spots are present only as traces or are absent; the median ocellus is small with a trace of red; the hind marginal spot is absent. Female: the anal spot is a thin black line; the submarginal spots are weak; both median and costal ocelli are small with a trace of red.

Distribution: In the Santa Cruz Mountains, Santa Cruz county, California (TL: Santa Cruz, California). The flight period is from late May to early July. This subspecies is thought to be extinct. The last known specimen was one female collected in 1956.

(c) **sol** Bryk & Eisner. Plate 78, figure 17, ♂. This subspecies is much larger than the preceding medium sized forms. Male: the anal spot is absent; the submarginal spots are present only as traces or are absent; median and costal ocelli are red with black margins; the hind marginal spot is present; the black on the basal darkening of the hind wing is weak. Female: the anal spot is black or two red spots in black; the submarginal spots are medium; both median and costal ocelli are red with black margins.

Distribution: This subspecies occurs from Eldorado county north to Modoc and Siskiyou counties, California (TL: Baxters, Placer county at elevations of 3000 to 7000 ft. and occasionally to 8000 ft. in the drier northern mountains. The flight period is from early June to mid July.

(d) **baldur** Edwards. Plate 68, figure 11, ♀; figure 12, ♂. This subspecies is the high altitude form from the Sierra Nevada. It is smaller than subspecies *clodius* or *strohbeeni.* Male: like *sol* except that it is smaller and the basal darkening of the hind wing is strong. Female: the anal spot usually has well developed red centers; otherwise like the preceding subspecies except in size.

Distribution: *P. clodius baldur* occurs from Tulare county to Sierra county (TL: Yosemite) in the Sierra Nevada of California above 7000 ft. The flight period is from late June to early August.

(e) **claudianus** Stichel. Plate 69, figure 17, ♂; figure 18, ♀. This subspecies is as large as *sol.* It is much more variable than any of the preceding four subspecies. Male: the anal spot varies from a trace to strong, averaging medium; the submarginal spots are absent to strong, averaging weak; both median and costal ocelli have the black margins very broad. Female: the anal spot is large and black or black with a red center; the submarginal spots are strong; the median and costal ocelli are like those of the male; the hind marginal spot is strong.

Distribution: Subspecies *claudianus* occurs in the Coastal and Cascade mountains from southern Oregon to southwestern mainland British Columbia and southern Vancouver Island (TL: western Washington) below 6000 ft. in the south to below 4500 ft. in the north. The flight period is from early June to early August, depending on the elevation.

(f) **pseudogallatinus** Bryk.   There is considerable question about where in the vicinity of Yale, British Columbia, the types of *pseudogallatinus* were actually taken. Upon this depends the status of *hel* Eisner, which was described from specimens taken at Stevens Pass, King county, Washington, at about 4000 ft. Although Yale itself is only 220 ft. above sea level the mountains on both sides of the Fraser River there rise to 6500 ft. We consider that the two names refer to the same taxon.

Male: the anal spot is medium and black; the submarginal spots are absent to medium; both median and costal ocelli are average in size with red in the center. Female: the anal spot is wide, black or black with a red center; the submarginal spots are medium to strong; both median and costal ocelli are large; the median ocellus sometimes is connected to the anal spot.

Distribution: This subspecies occurs from Mount Rainier northward in the Washington Cascades above 4000 ft., and in the mountains of southwestern British Columbia excluding the immediate coast. The flight period is from mid July to late August.

(g) **incredibilis** Bryk.   This subspecies is known only from the type specimens (TL: Mount St. Elias, Alaska). It resembles *claudianus* but is much more heavily marked. One small specimen from Skagway, Alaska, was determined as *incredibilis* by Eisner. It is similar in size to *pseudogallatinus,* however, and may represent an undescribed subspecies.

(h) **altaurus** Dyar. Plate 68, figures 13 and 16, ♀; figures 14 and 15, ♂.   Male: the anal spot is absent to weak; the submarginal spots are absent; the median ocellus is either small with a red center, or a small black spot. Female: the anal spot is black with sometimes a trace of red; the submarginal spots are medium. The type came from Altaurs Lake, Idaho. *Parnassius clodius gallatinus* Stichel is a synonym.

Distribution: This subspecies is found from southeastern British Columbia, Idaho, Montana west of the continental divide, in the Wallowa Mountains of Oregon and the Teton Mountains of Wyoming at 4500 to 7000 ft. The flight period is from late June to early August.

(i) **shepardi** Eisner. Plate 69, figure 16, ♂.   This is the only inland form which reaches the large size of *sol* and *claudianus.* It is in fact slightly larger than either.

Male: the anal spot is weak to absent; the submarginal spots are weak; the median ocellus is a black spot. Female: the anal spot is large, black or black with red; the submarginal spots are average; both costal and median ocelli are large with wide black borders.

Distribution: This subspecies is known from the Snake River Canyon in Whitman county, Washington (TL: Wawawai, Washington) and Nez Perce county, Idaho, at 600 to 1000 ft. The flight period is May.

(j) **menetriesii** Hy. Edwards. Plate 78, figure 18, ♂.   Male: the anal spot is absent to weak; the submarginal spots are absent; both median and costal ocelli have red centers and an average width border. Female: not examined.

Distribution: This subspecies is known only from the mountains of northeastern Utah (TL: Mount Nebo, Utah). The flight period is from early June to early July.

3. **Parnassius phoebus** Fabricius.   This species is widespread in the Palearctic and in western North America. In our area it can be recognized by the alternately black

and white segments of the antennae, especially at the base. The sphragis is gray or black.

Early Stages: The early stages of *behrii* Edwards (California) and *sayii* Edwards (Colorado) have been described. The principal foodplant of the larvae is *Sedum,* although *Saxifraga* may be used.

Distribution: P. phoebus ranges from northern California and New Mexico northward to Alaska and the Yukon Territory.

(a) **behrii** Edwards. Plate 69, figure 3, ♂; figure 4, ♀. This is the only North American subspecies of *phoebus* in which the costal and median ocelli are normally yellow. In other subspecies yellow ocelli occur rarely as aberrations.

Distribution: This subspecies occurs from Tulare to Plumas counties, California (TL: Sierra Nevada), in the Sierra Nevada from 7500 to 12,000 ft. The flight period is from early July to late August.

(b) **sternitzkyi** McDunnough. Plate 69, figure 11, ♂; figure 12, ♀. Male: the anal spot is weak to absent; the submarginal spots are weak to absent; both costal and median ocelli are red with white centers; there are two red costal spots; the marginal spots are absent. Female: the anal spot consists of two red spots; the submarginal spots are strong; the costal and median ocelli are like those of the male; there are three red subapical spots; the hind marginal spot is red-centered.

Distribution: P. p. sternitzkyi is known from Siskiyou and Shasta counties. California (TL: Castle Rock, Siskiyou county, California). The flight period is July.

(c) **magnus** Wright. Plate 69, figure 9, ♂; figure 10, ♀. Male: the submarginal spots are weak; the costal ocellus is red or red with a white center; the hind marginal spot is small and black; there are two red subapical spots. Female: the anal spot consists of two red spots or two black spots; the submarginal spots are medium; both costal and median ocelli are red with white centers; the marginal spots are weak; the hind marginal spot is black or red.

Distribution: This subspecies is found in the Cascade Mountains of Washington and in the Okanogan region of British Columbia from 3000 to 5000 ft. (TL: Enderby, British Columbia). The flight period is from mid June to late July.

(d) **olympianus** Burdick. Plate 68, figure 8, ♀. This subspecies is smaller than *magnus.* Female: the marginal and submarginal spots are wide; the hind marginal spot is large, black or red. Otherwise *olympianus* is like *magnus.*

Distribution: This subspecies is known from the Olympic Mountains (TL: Hurricane Ridge) and the Cascades north of Stevens Pass in Washington and southwestern British Columbia at and above timberline (6000 ft.). The flight period is from mid July to late August.

(e) **smintheus** Doubleday. Plate 68, figure 9, ♂; figure 10, ♀. This is the first name applied to a Parnassian in North America. Lord Derby probably collected the first specimens in the vicinity of Banff or Lake Louise in the mountains of Alberta. This subspecies differs little in appearance from *olympianus.* Neumoegen's *nanus* from "near Fort Calgarry" is a synonym. If connecting links are found across northern or central British Columbia, then the high altitude material from both the Rockies and the coastal mountains of Washington and British Columbia may be called *smintheus.*

Distribution: The subspecies *smintheus* occurs in the Canadian Rockies of Alberta and British Columbia from Banff northward at least to Jasper. The flight period is from mid July to mid August.

(f) **xanthus** Ehrmann. Plate 69, figure 13, ♂; figure 14, ♀. The names *idahoensis* Bryk & Eisner (TL: Wallace, Idaho) and *montanulus* Bryk & Eisner (TL: Missoula, Montana) are considered synonyms of *xanthus* (TL: Moscow, Idaho). This subspecies differs only slightly from *sayii* Edwards. The geographic separation of *xanthus* and *sayii* by *maximus* Bryk & Eisner is the reason for keeping it a separate subspecies.

Distribution: P. p. xanthus ranges from southeastern British Columbia and southern Alberta south to Idaho, western Montana and the Teton Mountains of Wyoming at elevations of from 3000 ft. to about timberline. The flight period is from late June to early August.

(g) **maximus** Bryk & Eisner. Plate 68, figure 3, ♂; figure 4, ♀. This subspecies is characterized by the large size and melanic appearance of the females. Beartooth Plateau specimens are slightly smaller. The females are exactly like those of *hermodur* Hy. Edwards except for their larger size.

Distribution: This subspecies is known from the Judith Mountains (TL), Castle Mountains, Little Belt Mountains and the Beartooth Plateau of Montana at 4000 to 5000 ft. The flight period is from late June to the end of July.

(h) **sayii** Edwards. Plate 69, figure 6, ♂; figure 7, ♀; Plate 68, figure 1, ♂; figure 2, ♀. Male: the anal spot is absent; the submarginal spots are weak or absent; both median and costal ocelli are smaller than in either *sternitzkyi* or *magnus,* and are either red or red with white centers; there is one red subapical spot. Female: the anal spot consists usually of one black and one red spot; the submarginal spots are medium to strong; both median and costal ocelli are either red or red with white centers; there are either two or three red subapical spots. This subspecies is variable and as a result has numerous synonyms. The names *dakotaensis* Bryk & Eisner (TL: Black Hills), *hollandi* Bryk & Eisner (TL: La Sal Mountains, Utah) and *rubiana* Wyatt (TL: Ruby Mountains, Nevada) are all considered synonyms of *sayii* (TL: "Pikes Peak," Colorado). In Colorado variation has been shown to be directly related to elevation. The altitudes and phenotypes of the above synonymous populations correspond to those known in Colorado.

Distribution: The subspecies *sayii* is known from Colorado, the Black Hills of South Dakota, the Ruby Mountains of Nevada, Utah except the southwest corner, eastern Wyoming and northern New Mexico, occurring below timberline. The flight period is from early July to mid August.

(i) **hermodur** Hy. Edwards. Plate 69, figure 8, ♀; Plate 67, figure 10, ♀; Plate 68, fig. 7, ♂. This subspecies is smaller than *sayii*. The females are melanistic. Otherwise this subspecies is similar to *sayii*. This is the high altitude form of *phoebus* from Colorado (TL: southern Colorado). The names *rotgeri* Bang-Haas and *pseudorotgeri* Eisner are considered synonyms. The flight period is from mid July through August.

(j) **apricatus** Stichel. The following description is based on the illustrations of the type. No other specimens are known. Male: the marginal spots are absent; the submarginal spots are present as a trace; both median and costal ocelli are large;

the hind marginal spot is large. Female: the marginal and submarginal spots are each continuous but the two are not fused. Both sexes: basal darkening extends to the outer margin of the hind wing. The subspecies is large, approaching *magnus* and equalling *golovinus* Holland.

Distribution: This subspecies is known only from Kodiak Island, Alaska (TL). The flight period is unknown.

(k) **golovinus** Holland. Plate 69, figure 5, ♀.   Male: the marginal and submarginal spots are weak; the basal darkening is very wide and extends to the outer margin of the hind wing; both median and costal ocelli are very large and red, the median with a small white center; there is one red and one black subapical spot. Female (based on Holland's type): the marginal spots are very wide and almost fused to the submarginals; there are large red spots in the subapical spots.

Distribution: P. p. golovinus is known from western and northern Alaska (TL: Golovin Bay, near Nome). The flight period is from July to August.

(l) **alaskaensis** Eisner. Plate 68, figure 5, ♂; figure 6 ♀.   Male: The basal darkening extends to the outer margin of the hind wing; the subapical spots are of normal size and black; males are smaller but otherwise like *golovinus*. Female: none examined. Eisner's photograph of the female shows it to be similar to the male.

Distribution: This subspecies is known only from McKinley National Park, Alaska (TL). The flight period is from late July to mid August.

(m) **elias** Bryk.   This subspecies is known from the type and only a few more specimens.

Male: the basal darkening does not extend to the outer margin of the hind wing; the anal spot consists of one median black spot; the submarginal spots are weak; males are the size of *golovinus* and *apricatus*. Female: unknown.

Distribution: This subspecies is known from Mount St. Elias (TL) and Skagway, Alaska. The flight period is July.

(n) **yukonensis** Eisner.   Male: the basal darkening does not extend to the outer margin of the hind wing; there are two red subapical spots; the hind marginal spot is absent; the submarginal spots are present as a trace; the marginal spots are absent; the costal ocellus is red, the median ocellus red with a white center. Female: the basal darkening is like that of the male; there are two red subapical spots; the hind marginal spot is black; the submarginal spots are medium; the marginal spots medium to strong; the median and costal ocelli are like those of the male. Both sexes are similar in size to *behrii* and *sayii*.

Distribution: This subspecies is known from southwestern Yukon Territory (TL) and Atlin, British Columbia. The flight period is from late June to early August.

Superfamily HESPERIOIDEA

Family MEGATHYMIDAE
(The Giant Skippers)

KILIAN ROEVER

Adults of this exclusively New World family are large compared to skippers in general. The venation is hesperioid. The head is clearly narrower than the thorax with clubbed, not hooked, antennae. Foodplants of all species are only in the Agavaceae: the larvae burrow into the leaves or roots. Immature stages are given in detail in the species accounts below.

A review of the Megathymidae, with keys, was published recently (Freeman 1969).

Genus AGATHYMUS Freeman

All species are essentially single brooded, feeding as larvae on species of *Agave*. The eggs lack an adhesive, and thus are free-falling. During the last three instars the larvae are presumably sap feeders with burrows in the leaf base and not in the root system. A trapdoor is constructed over the burrow entrance just before pupation. The pupal cremaster has a pointed tip and lacks conspicuous bristles. Additional characteristics are cited by Roever, 1964.

1. **Agathymus neumoegeni** (Edwards).   Seven named subspecies are included in the present treatment. In central Arizona and western New Mexico the range of *A. neumoegeni* is essentially continuous with little evidence of clinal variation. East of the Rio Grande the disjunct distribution of the foodplants provides an effective barrier to free gene exchange between local populations if the lack of clinal variation and the individual identities of various populations are used as criteria.

Early Stages: Differences in early stages between subspecies are primarily limited to the foodplants. The eggs are light yellow or cream when deposited. Later they turn raspberry red and orange. Eclosion occurs in eighteen to nineteen days. The larval galleries within the foodplant vary, particularly with the size of the plant. In small plants the mesophyll of a large area near the apex of the leaf may be eaten; in large plants only a small apical gallery may be made. Entrance to the basal gallery and trapdoor placement is generally on the upper surface of the leaf. The basal gallery may be confined to one leaf on large plants or extend through several leaves and into the terminal bud when small plants are utilized. Feeding is usually completed in July. It is followed by a resting period of three to six weeks. The tan trapdoors usually have a coarse fringe of silk overlapping the surrounding leaf surface. Larvae of the nominate subspecies frequently occur in extremely small plants, but are by no means limited to them. Whether survival on small plants is the result of a plant's physiological condition or the result of selection pressure by various parasites is not known. I have not observed a marked preference for host plant size in the other subspecies of *A. neumoegeni,* although it was mentioned as occurring in *A. neumoegeni florenceae.*

(a) **neumoegeni** (Edwards). Plate 79, figure 9, ♂; plate 81, figure 8, ♀.

Early Stages: The foodplant is *Agave parryi* (including var. *cousii*).

Distribution: This subspecies occurs in central Arizona (southern Coconino, Yavapai, Gila, southern Navajo, northern Graham, and Greenlee counties) and west central New Mexico (Catron and Grant counties). The type locality was originally stated as southern Arizona, later restricted by Ottolengui in 1895 to about ten miles from Prescott, Arizona. The flight period extends from early September to late October.

(b) **judithae** (Stallings & Turner). Plate 81, figure 9, ♀.

Early Stages: The foodplants are an unnamed *Agave* closely allied to *A. parryi* and hybrids between it and *Agave lecheguilla.*

Distribution: The insect is known only from the Hueco Mountains in northwestern Hudspeth county, Texas, but perhaps will be found in nearby New Mexico. The type locality was restricted by Freeman in 1963 to approximately eight miles east of Hueco, Texas, at an elevation of 5300 ft.

(c) **diabloensis** Freeman. Plate 80, figure 1, ♂; figure 2, ♀.

Early Stages: The recorded foodplant is *Agave gracilipes,* which appears to be a variety of *A. parryi.*

Distribution: This subspecies is known only from the Sierra Diablo and the Sierra Blanca ranges of southeastern Hudspeth county, Texas. The type locality is approximately five miles west of Victoria Canyon, 5700 ft., in the Sierra Diablo range, Hudspeth county, Texas.

(d) **carlsbadensis** (Stallings & Turner). Plate 83, figure 1, ♂; figure 2, ♀.

Early Stages: The foodplants are *Agave parryi* and hybrids between *A. parryi* and *A. lecheguilla* (= *A. glomeruliflora*).

Distribution: This subspecies is at present known only from the Guadalupe Mountains of New Mexico (southwestern Eddy and southeastern Otero counties) and the northwestern section of Culberson county, Texas, comprise the presently known distribution of this subspecies. The type locality is on the mesa at the head of Yucca Canyon at 5740 ft. in the Guadalupe Mountains, Carlsbad Caverns National Park, New Mexico.

(e) **florenceae** (Stallings & Turner). Plate 81, figure 10, ♀.

Early Stages: The foodplant is an undescribed Agave, not *A. neomexicana* but perhaps an intermediate between *A. scabra* and *A. parryi.*

Distribution: Apparently limited to the Davis Mountains, Jeff Davis county, Texas. The type locality has been restricted to the Scenic Drive at 6200 ft., near Mount Locke.

(f) **mcalpinei** (Freeman). Plate 82, figure 12, ♂; figure 15, ♀.

Early Stages: Agave scabra is the foodplant.

Distribution: Known only from the east side of the Glass Mountains in Brewster county, Texas. The type locality is five miles north of Marathon, Texas, at 4300 ft.

(g) **chisosensis** (Freeman). Plate 82, figure 13, ♀.

Early Stages: The foodplant is *Agave scabra.*

Distribution: Indigenous to the Chisos Mountains in southern Brewster county, Texas. The type locality is the Chisos Basin, 5400 ft.

Undescribed populations of *A. neumoegeni* occur in New Mexico in the Organ and Sacramento mountains and in southern Chaves county.

2. **Agathymus polingi** (Skinner). Plate 81, figure 3, ♂; figure 6, ♀. Unlike most *Agathymus,* males of this species do not visit moisture sources. Both sexes, however, may be taken in numbers during mid October where the foodplant abounds. Molino Basin in the Santa Catalina Mountains near Tucson is an easily accessible collecting locality for this butterfly.

Early Stages: The egg coloration and incubation period are similar to those of *A. neumoegeni.* Because the foodplant is a small species, the basal gallery commonly extends through the bases of several leaves and into the caudex. Where two species of *Agave* occur together, *Agathymus* larvae in the more succulent variety usually cease feeding and enter the resting stage well before the larvae of the species in the less succulent plant. Where *A. polingi* and *A. aryxna* are found in the same area the latter generally enters quiescence one to two months before *A. polingi,* which stops feeding in July. *Agave schottii* (amole) is the foodplant.

Distribution: A. polingi occurs in Arizona (Pima, Santa Cruz, southwestern Graham and Cochise counties), New Mexico (southwestern Hidalgo county) and Mexico (northeastern Sonora). The type locality is in the Baboquivari Mountains, Pima county, Arizona. *A. polingi* is on the wing from late September into November. A related (undescribed) species, which feeds on *Agave toumeyana,* occurs in central Arizona north of the Gila River.

3. **Agathymus evansi** (Freeman). Plate 81, figure 13, ♂; Plate 82, figure 9, ♀. This insect is frequently confused with *Agathymus aryxna* with which it is sympatric in the Huachuca Mountains. The genitalia and wing shape offer good characters for distinguishing adults of these two species. Expanse: 50 mm.

Early Stages: The apical galleries are usually placed in the center of the leaf, closer to the base than is common for other species. These galleries result in conspicuous patches of necrotic tissue which aid in the search for infested plants. Feeding in the basal gallery is completed during late June or early July. The trapdoor is usually placed on the lower leaf surface. The outer surface of the trapdoor is jet black with a rough texture. A view of the inner surface of the trapdoor reveals a lip and flange around the perimeter which is more pronounced than in most species. *Agave parryi* var. *huachucensis* serves as the host. The flight period extends from late August into October with the principal period of emergence being the last week of August and the first two weeks of September.

Distribution: This species is limited to the Huachuca Mountains and immediate vicinity in southwestern Cochise and eastern Santa Cruz counties, Arizona. The type was collected in Ramsey Canyon, Huachuca Mountains, Cochise county.

4. **Agathymus aryxna** (Dyar). Plate 79, figure 2, ♀; figure 3, ♂. Confusion concerning the identity of *A. aryxna* amd *A. neumoegeni* persists. Fortunately the lectotypes (and syntypes) and holotype respectively are extant. Biologically and superficially each represents a distinct species. A comparison of the distributions shows that they are allopatric.

Early Stages: The egg is light green when deposited, but within two days a pinkish marbling develops. After five days the egg is dark green with dark red marbling, when viewed under magnification, but to the naked eye it appears gray-green. Eclosion does not occur for at least forty days. Feeding usually ceases in May and the larva remains inactive until just before pupation in late July or August. Trapdoor placement varies between local populations and from year to year, but the majority of trapdoors occur on the lower surfaces of the leaves. The trapdoors have a smooth outer surface and are various shades of brown, usually quite dark. The foodplants are *Agave palmeri* and *A. chrysantha*.

Distribution: This species occurs in southeastern Arizona (southeastern Gila, Graham, southern Greenlee, eastern Pinal, eastern Pima, Santa Cruz and Cochise counties), southwestern New Mexico (Grant and Hidalgo counties) and Mexico (northeastern Sonora). The lectotype bears the label "Mexico," not "northern Sonora." There is a distinct possibility that the type of *A. aryxna* represents a species that does not occur in Arizona. If this proves to be the case the Arizona species would be called *A. drucei* (Skinner), currently regarded as a synonym of *aryxna*. The flight period for *A. aryxna* extends from late August (rarely July) into November.

5. **Agathymus baueri** (Stallings & Turner). This species is closely related to *A. aryxna* amd possibly no more than a subspecies. Breeding studies are currently in progress in an attempt to solve this problem. Populations in eastern Pinal, southwestern Gila and eastern Maricopa counties, Arizona, show intermediate characters.

Early Stages: These are similar to those of *A. aryxna*. *A. baueri* is more consistent in making the apical gallery along the leaf margin and in building the trapdoor on the lower surface of the leaf. The foodplants are *Agave chrysantha* and hybrids between *A. chrysantha* and *A. parryi,* but not *A. parryi* as has been published.

Distribution: Arizona (northeastern Maricopa, western Gila and eastern Yavapai counties). Verde Hot Springs, 4000 ft., Yavapai county, is the type locality. Populations of an undescribed *Agathymus* closely resembling *A. baueri* occur in Arizona (western Pima, western Maricopa and Yuma counties) and California (eastern San Bernardino county), where the foodplant is *A. deserti.*

(a) **baueri** (Stallings & Turner). Plate 81, figure 11, ♀; figure 12, ♂. See above.

(b) **freemani** Stallings, Turner & Stallings. Plate 81, figure 4, ♂; figure 7, ♀. Populations in the vicinity of the Bradshaw Mountains in south-central Yavapai county, Arizona, are transitional to nominate *baueri.* The "ends" of clines in size, maculation and color in *A. baueri* are in northwestern Maricopa and western Mohave counties respectively.

Distribution: Mohave and western Yavapai counties, Arizona. The type locality is near Bagdad at 5000 ft., Yavapai county. This subspecies is on the wing from September into November.

6. **Agathymus estelleae** (Stallings & Turner). Plate 81, figure 1, ♂ (ssp. *valverdiensis*). Nominate *estelleae* is Mexican but one subspecies, *valverdiensis* Freeman, enters the extreme southwestern regions of our territory. This subspecies is of questionable distinctness, as some specimens from the type locality appear identical to the nominate subspecies when superficial characters are considered. Throughout its range this species is sympatric with the *mariae* complex. Expanse: 50 to 55 mm.

Early Stages: The larvae in the last instar are whitish while those of the *mariae* complex are bluish. The trapdoors occur on either surface of the leaf but most commonly on the upperside. The pale tan trapdoors are indistinguishable from those of the *mariae* complex. *Agave lecheguilla* is the larval foodplant.

Distribution: Found in Terrell, Val Verde, Edwards and Kinney counties, Texas. The type locality is 28 miles north of Del Rio, 1450 ft., Val Verde county. The flight period extends from mid September into October and possibly also in April. Pupae were found in March by Kendall, but whether they represent a partial second brood, or an emergence delayed by abnormal weather or growth conditions, remains to be learned.

7. **Agathymus mariae** (Barnes & Benjamin). Four subspecies, including nominate *mariae,* are known in the U.S.

(a) **mariae** (Barnes & Benjamin). Plate 80, figure 6, ♂; Plate 83, figure 5, ♀. This is the most widely distributed subspecies in Texas, and also the most variable. Some of the named subspecies are of questionable worth and much work remains to be done on this species complex as it occurs in both Texas and Mexico. Expanse: 45 to 50 mm.

Early Stages: Burrow length and the feeding area vary widely, depending on the physiological condition and size of the plant. The foodplant of all subspecies is *Agave lecheguilla.* The nominate subspecies also feeds on hybrids between *A. lecheguilla* and *A. scabra* (= *A. chisosensis*), *A. parryi* (= *A. glomeruliflora*) and *A. gracilipes.*

Distribution: Nominate *mariae* occurs in New Mexico (western Eddy, and southern

Chaves, Otero and Dona Ana counties) and in all trans-Pecos counties in Texas. The flight period extends from late September into November.

(b) **chinatiensis** Freeman. Plate 80, figure 13, ♂; figure 14, ♀. This butterfly was named after the Chinati Mountains in Presidio county, Texas, the only known habitat. The type locality is 2.7 miles south of Shafter, Texas, 4000 ft. Expanse: 45 to 50 mm.

(c) **lajitaensis** Freeman. Plate 80, figure 15, ♂; figure 16, ♀.

Distribution: This rather poorly distinguished subspecies is found in the southern part of Presidio county, Texas. Its type locality is 10 miles west of Lajita, 2650 ft. Expanse: 45 to 50 mm.

(d) **rindgei** Freeman. Plate 80, figure 11, ♂; figure 12, ♀.

Distribution: This subspecies has been taken in Val Verde and Kinney counties, Texas. The type is from 14 miles north of Bracketville, 1500 ft., Kinney county.

8. **Agathymus gilberti** Freeman. Plate 81, figure 2, ♂. This species is closely related to *A. mariae*. It is provisionally treated as a separate species because of the reported difference in chromosomes and the untenable position of two subspecies occurring sympatrically.

Distribution: A. gilberti is reported only from Brewster, Terrell and Val Verde counties in Texas where the foodplant is *Agave lecheguilla*. The type locality is 14 miles north of Bracketville, Texas.

9. **Agathymus stephensi** (Skinner). Plate 81, figure 5, ♂. This is the *Agathymus* commonly encountered in California collections.

Early Stages: In the last instar the larvae show considerable color variation (as in several other species) depending apparently on whether they are actively feeding, in the quiescent stage or immediately prepupal. Compared with the other species in this country the basal tunnels of *A. stephensi* are rather bulbous. An obvious area of necrotic tissue is found near the point of larval entry where the burrow lies just beneath the epidermis. When leaves with actively feeding larvae of various *Agathymus* are partly immersed in water or are allowed to dehydrate odd tunnel shapes result as the larvae apparently seek a favorable nutrient or sap flow level. In the summer months the leaves of the foodplant of *A. stephensi* are usually shriveled near the base indicating a stress for water. Perhaps this explains the tunnel shape. The foodplant is *Agave deserti*.

Distribution: This species is found in southern California (eastern San Diego, western Imperial and western Riverside counties), and Baja California. The type was collected at La Puerta (Mason Valley) in San Diego county. The flight period extends from late September into early November.

10. **Agathymus alliae** (Stallings & Turner). Plate 79, figure 5, ♀; figure 6, ♂.

Early Stages: When deposited, the eggs are a pale olive-green, but later turn dull red after a rather intricate series of color changes. As in most *Agathymus* some features of the larvae, particularly the head capsule, are visible within two weeks of oviposition. The incubation period, however, lasts approximately six weeks. Larval feeding is commonly terminated in August, followed by a resting period of one to four weeks. The thin, white trapdoor generally is located on the undersurface of the leaf. The foodplant is *Agave utahensis,* including varieties *eborispina, kaibabensis* and *nevadensis.*

Distribution: This species occurs in Arizona (northern Coconino and Mohave counties), Utah (Washington and perhaps Iron counties); Nevada (Clark and Lincoln counties, perhaps also southern Nye county) and California (northeastern San Bernardino and southeastern Inyo counties). The type locality is 15 miles west of Cameron, Arizona, at 5000 ft. The flight period is from early September through October. No other *Agathymus* occur sympatrically with this species.

Genus STALLINGSIA Freeman

The butterflies of this genus have two broods and the larvae feed on *Manfreda.* Other biological characteristics suggest that the group is quite similar to *Megathymus.* A single representative of the genus enters our territory.

1. **Stallingsia maculosus** (Freeman). Plate 83, figure 4, ♀.
   Early Stages: Eggs are yellow-green when deposited, later turning pure white. Some of the larvae reared in the laboratory burrowed into the leaves and then into the caudex, whereas others penetrated the terminal and proceeded directly into the root stock. When feeding, the larvae maintain a small tent which is enlarged considerably just before pupation. No evidence of trapdoor construction was noted. *Manfreda maculosa* is the foodplant.
   Distribution: S. *maculosus* is reported from southern Texas (south of and including San Patricio, East Bexar and Kinney counties) and Mexico (Nuevo León). The type locality is 2 miles south of Kingsville, Kleberg county, Texas. The butterfly has two broods, flying in April–May and September–October.

Genus MEGATHYMUS Scudder

All members of the genus in the United States are *Yucca* feeders during the larval stage, burrowing in the root system during at least the last three instars. The eggs have an adhesive and are glued to foliage. Tents are constructed prior to pupation. The cremaster of the pupa has a broad tip with conspicuous bristles. Most species are single brooded.

1. **Megathymus yuccae** (Boisduval & Le Conte).
   (a) **yuccae** (Boisduval & Le Conte). Plate 80, figure 8, ♂; Plate 82, figure 2, ♀. See also additional figure citations below. There is evidence, based on chromosomes and superficial characters, that the population assemblages of *M. yuccae* occurring east and west of the Mississippi River respectively may represent separate species. This awaits a definitive study. Because of the polytypic nature of *M. yuccae* no less

than thirty recognizable local populations occur west of the Hundredth Meridian. Naming such populations is creating an unnecessary nomenclatorial burden. Adequate sampling clearly shows these populations are connected by character gradients. Using as reference points a few named populations from the perimeter of the range, a description of clinal trends is possible. On that basis I feel the following subspecific designations can be relegated to the species synonymy: *stallingsi* Freeman; *buchholzi* Freeman (Plate 80, figure 10, ♀); *browni* Stallings & Turner; *louiseae* Freeman (Plate 80, figure 9, ♀); *kendalli* Freeman (Plate 80, figure 7, ♂); *winkensis* Freeman (Plate 80, figure 3, ♀); *maudae* Stallings, Turner & Stallings; and *elidaensis* Stallings, Turner & Stallings. Further restriction may be warranted. Expanse: 60 to 65 mm.

Early Stages: Feeding habits of the larvae vary with the foodplant species. Before entering the caudex, larvae in the first and second instar commonly make a silk shelter and feed near the leaf apex, usually confining themselves to one leaf on the broad-leaved species and webbing together several leaves on the narrow-leaved yuccas; however, they may enter the terminal growth without attempting to feed on the leaf surface. In *Yucca* with trunks or long rhizomes, the larval burrowing habit consists of narrow tunnels which may exceed two feet in length; in plants with a short, massive root system feeding is confined to a short chamber of comparatively large diameter. The tents normally project from the terminal growth of the plant. Not infrequently evidence of the leaves disappears after small plants are attacked. This species is the only member of the genus which, after overwintering as a larva, pupates in the spring without feeding. The foodplants include all species of *Yucca* in the United States except *Y. whipplei*. Two and even three species of *Yucca* may be used by the larvae at a given location. *Megathymus yuccae* is sympatric with all other *Megathymus* in the United States.

Distribution: The species *M. yuccae* is reported from all states south of and including North Carolina, Tennessee, Arkansas, Kansas, Colorado, Utah, Nevada and California. It is also recorded from Mexico in Tamaulipas, Nuevo Leon, Sonora and Baja California. The type was collected in Georgia, probably in Screven county. Why *Y. glauca* apparently is not utilized in the northern Great Plains remains to be learned. The flight period extends from late January to late June depending on location. In any area, with the exception of central Florida, during a given year the flight period probably does not exceed one month.

(b) **reinthali** Freeman. Plate 80, figure 4, ♀; figure 5, ♂.

Distribution: In late March adults may be taken at Tyler State Park in Smith county, Texas, a favorite collecting locality for this subspecies. The type locality is two miles west of Ben Wheeler, Van Zandt county, Texas.

(c) **wilsonorum** Stallings & Turner. Plate 79, figure 8, ♀.   This subspecies enters the United States in a narrow strip extending from Rio Grande City to near Mission, Texas. The foodplant is *Yucca treculiana*. The type locality is near Ciudad Victoria, Tamaulipas, Mexico.

(d) **coloradensis** Riley. Plate 81, figure 14, ♂; Plate 82, figure 3, ♀.

Distribution: This subspecies is found in Colorado east of the Front Range, in western Nebraska, southwestern Kansas, western Oklahoma and the Texas pan-handle. Southward, *coloradensis* intergrades widely with *reinthali* in Texas and *reubeni* in New Mexico. Type locality: Colorado Springs.

(e) **reubeni** Stallings, Turner & Stallings. Plate 82, figure 1, ♀. This strikingly beautiful subspecies is found at 5300 ft. in the Hueco Mountains in Hudspeth county, Texas. The foodplant is *Yucca baccata.*

(f) **navajo** Skinner. Plate 83, figure 3, ♀.

Distribution: This subspecies is encountered in western Colorado, southern Utah, western New Mexico, and northern Arizona. The type locality is Fort Wingate, McKinley county, New Mexico.

(g) **martini** Stallings & Turner. Plate 83, figure 6, ♀. This subspecies occurs in southern California and is sometimes locally abundant in the Mojave desert. The type locality is Little Rock, Los Angeles county, California. Larvae feed on *Yucca brevifolia.* Adults appear in late February and March.

2. **Megathymus ursus** Poling.

(a) **ursus** Poling. Plate 79, figure 4, ♀. This species is readily distinguished from other members of the genus by the pure white scaling on the antennae. The yellow spots (male) and orange-yellow spots (female) separate the nominate form from the following subspecies in which the spotting is orange in both sexes.

Early Stages: Within three days after oviposition the eggs develop an off-white ground color with irregular reddish brown spots. These spots persist after the larvae hatch, although exposure to weathering eventually destroys the pigmentation of the chorion. Eggs of other *Megathymus* do not develop spots on the chorion. First instar larvae are orange-yellow or greenish yellow; those of other species are dark red or orange-red. Subsequent instars are white with a sharply contrasting black head, cervical shield and suranal plate, although second instar larvae when still feeding on leaves may have a greenish tinge. Compared with *M. yuccae* the larvae of *M. ursus* maintain tents which are smaller in both diameter and height, but the diameter of the tents is enlarged just before pupation. Larvae overwinter in the third, fourth or fifth instar, dependent in part on when oviposition occurred. The resting period between the end of feeding and pupation is less than one week. Foodplants include *Y. arizonica,* apparent hybrids between *Y. baccata* and *Y. arizonica* (= *Y. confinis*) *Y. baccata* and *Y. schottii;* the latter is most widely used.

Distribution: Nominate *ursus* occurs in southeastern Arizona (eastern Maricopa, eastern Pinal, eastern Pima, Santa Cruz and Cochise counties); southwestern New Mexico (Hidalgo county) and Sonora, Mexico. The type locality is Pinal county, Arizona, probably in the Santa Catalina Mountains where *Y. schottii* reaches its northern distributional limit. The flight period extends from May to early September, but primarily in July–August.

(b) **violae** Stallings & Turner. Plate 79, figure 1, ♀.

Early Stages: These are essentially the same as the nominate form except that the foodplants are *Y. faxoniana, Y. treculeana,* apparent *Y. baccata* and *torreyi* hybrids and *Y. torreyi.* The latter is the most widely used in the United States.

Distribution: This subspecies occurs in southern New Mexico east of the Rio Grande (Torrance, Dona Ana, Otero and Eddy counties); southwestern Texas (El Paso, Hudspeth, Jeff Davis, Brewster and Kinney counties and presumably other counties in the intervening area) and Coahuila, Mexico. The type locality is Carlsbad Caverns National Park, Eddy county, New Mexico. The flight period extends from late April into late August but appears to vary considerably between localities and years (Big Bend National Park: late April through June; Carlsbad Caverns National Park: late June to late August). It would be interesting to learn if a *M. ursus* relative utilizes *Y. rigida* in Sonora and Chihuahua.

3. Megathymus cofaqui (Strecker).

(a) **cofaqui** (Strecker). Plate 82, figure 7, ♂; figure 8, ♀. Because of sympatric occurrence this species may be confused with *M. yuccae*. In *M. cofaqui* the discal cell spot on the fore wing clearly adjoins the spot in cell Cu_1, whereas in *M. yuccae* these spots are well separated. As can be seen in the illustrations numerous other differences exist. Males of *M. cofaqui* and the following species have conspicuous erect hair-like scales arising from the dorsal surface of the hind wing basad.

Early Stages: Larval behavior in this and the next species is similar. After hatching the larvae crawl to the bases of the leaves and eat their way into the stem. No attempt is made to construct silk shelters or to feed near the apex of the leaves. Larvae proceed quite rapidly down the stem of the offshoot or riser until the rhizomatous root system is reached. Obvious tunnels are excavated in the main root system, and no feces are expelled on the soil surface. During the course of development larvae may either remain solely in the rhizome or burrow up the stems of offshoots from the rhizome. A tent is constructed only upon cessation of feeding with pupation following shortly thereafter. Location of the tent may vary widely within a given population and between populations. Larvae may tunnel vertically from the root system to the soil surface or they may follow an offshoot through the soil surface with the one- to five-inch tent projecting from the bare stem, through leaves below the center of the plant, or (rarely) from the terminal bud area. If the tent is built through the soil surface, particles of soil are often incorporated with silk on the exterior wall, thereby furnishing an effective camouflage. When tents project from aerial portions of a plant, particles of plant matter are generally attached to the outer surface. While this does not provide ideal protective coloration the tent placement alone makes it difficult to locate. Foodplants are *Y. filamentosa* (including *Y. smalliana*) and *Y. aloifolia;* perhaps also *Y. gloriosa,* which may be no more than a form of *Y. aloifolia.*

Distribution: This subspecies is found in the northern two-thirds of Florida and in southeastern Georgia (with most records close to the coastline). The type locality was cited as Georgia. L. H. Harris, Jr. (*in litt.*) informs me that H. K. Morrison, the collector of the holotype, collected in Screven county, Georgia, during the year the species was described. The flight period in Florida extends from February into May and from August into November. Whether this represents two generations per year or an extended flight period interrupted by cold weather remains to be determined. The ranges of this and the following subspecies are inadequately known.

(b) **harrisi** Freeman. Plate 82, figure 10, ♀. The type of *M. c. cofaqui* actually appears intermediate between *M. c. harrisi* and *M. c. cofaqui* as it occurs along the central western coast of Florida. Intermediates from northwestern Florida tend to indicate a north-south cline. Expanse: 55 to 60 mm.

Early Stages: The primary difference from the nominate form is that *M. c. harrisi* seemingly always projects its tents from the soil surface. An excellent account of the life history was given by L. H. Harris, Jr. (1954). The foodplant is *Yucca filamentosa.*

Distribution: The subspecies *harrisi* is found in Georgia, excluding the eastern coastal plain, and perhaps also Tennessee, where tents (no adults) similar to those of this subspecies were found in Madison and Sevier counties. The type locality is Stone Mountain, Dekalb county, Georgia. The flight period extends from early July into September.

4. **Megathymus streckeri** (Skinner).

(a) **streckeri** (Skinner). Plate 79, figure 7, ♀; Plate 82, figure 6, ♂. Rearing, or at least collecting pupae, is the best method for obtaining a series of most *Megathymus*. It is often easier, however, to obtain *streckeri* with a net. In locating pupae of this species a spring-tooth rake is useful where soil and vegetation conditions permit. When raking around clumps of the foodplant the tops of tents may be broken, thereby exposing the white powder used to coat the inside of them; pupae can then be located quite easily. This species is sympatric with *M. yuccae* in many areas and both are occasionally found on the wing together. Generally the main flight period of *M. streckeri* follows that of *M. yuccae* by from two to eight weeks in a given area. The distinct scalloped appearance of the basal edge of the marginal band (secondaries, dorsal surface) separate *streckeri* from *yuccae*. Also in *streckeri* the more distad of the two spots adjoining the subcostal vein (secondaries, ventral surface) is the larger. Expanse: 55 to 75 mm.

Early Stages: The larvae of *M. streckeri* and *M. cofaqui,* in all but the first instar, can be quickly distinguished from those of other species by the color of the suranal plate: off-white, concolorous with the body and not sharply contrasting black or brown as in *M. ursus* and *M. yuccae*. Refer to the previous species for a description of larval behavior. The foodplants are *Yucca baileyi* and *Y. angustissima* as well as apparent hybrids between the two and between *Y. baileyi* and *Y. glauca.*

Distribution: This subspecies occurs in northern Arizona (eastern Mohave, Coconino, Navajo and Apache counties); southeastern Utah (Kane, Emery, Grand and San Juan counties), northwestern New Mexico (San Juan, McKinley, Valencia, Bernalillo, Torrance and Santa Fe counties) and southwestern Colorado (Montezuma, La Plata and Gunnison counties and the San Luis Valley). The type locality is Arizona, further limited by Stallings & Turner to Petrified Forest National Park. The flight period ranges from mid May to mid July, varying with elevation and latitude.

(b) **texanus** Barnes & McDunnough. Plate 82, figure 4, ♂; figure 5, ♀. The variation of external characters is greater in most local populations of this subspecies than in other *Megathymus*.

Early Stages: The foodplants are *Yucca glauca* and *Y. constricta.*

Distribution: The subspecies *texanus* occurs from south-central Texas, north and northwest through eastern New Mexico, western Oklahoma, western Kansas, eastern Colorado, western Nebraska, western South and North Dakota and eastern Montana. It probably occurs also in eastern Wyoming and perhaps western Iowa and south-eastern Saskatchewan where *Y. glauca* is known to occur. In an area extending from southern New Mexico (east of the Rio Grande) northward into the San Luis Valley of Colorado the populations show intermediate tendencies between this and the nominate form. The series on which the description was based comes from "South Texas (Dallas, San Antonio)." Freeman in 1963 restricted the type locality to Kerrville, Texas. The flight period ranges from early April to mid July.

Family HESPERIIDAE

The Skippers

C. DON MACNEILL

Adults are small to medium sized, generally dull colored, butterflies with large heads and stout bodies. Most species have a characteristic very rapid, direct undulating flight with little of the erratic fluttering of most true butterflies; the common name is based upon this skipping flight. The family may be diagnosed as follows:

The head has eyes and antennal bases widely separated, generally with a tufted brush-like "eyelash" at the outer antennal base. The club of the antenna is partly or wholly curved backward hook-like, the terminal recurved segments being called the apiculus. The thorax is hairy, with well developed epaulet-like tegulae and, in males, sometimes provided ventrally with a posterior, divided, flap covering the ventral base of the abdomen. The legs are all well developed, the front pair generally with a specialized modified spur, the epiphysis; the middle and hind legs have at least a pair of terminal tibial spurs. The hind legs of males often have specialized hair-tufts or spines. The wings are short and generally rather narrow in proportion to the massive body, in males frequently bearing specialized folds, pockets, patches or hair-like tufts of modified scales. On the fore wing all veins arise unbranched from the discal cell or the base. The wing membrane is exposed, more or less extensively, free of scales in certain species.

The eggs are hemispherical, often proportionately large, and commonly ornately sculptured. They are deposited singly, usually on or near larval foodplant. The larva has a large head, a constricted "neck" and a body tapered to front and back. There are no conspicuous posterior horns or forked last segment. The abdominal prolegs bear microscopic hook-like crochets of several sizes arranged in a complete circle. The body and head generally appear naked but actually are well clothed with minute, short, occasionally long, hairs, and sometimes are supplemented by waxy or filamentous powdering of special body secretions.

The larvae spin silken tubes or shelters of folded, rolled or connected leaf parts within which they spend most of their time at rest. When feeding, the caterpillars may be exposed some distance from their shelters. A few species are case bearers, the larvae fashioning a cover of leaf tissue or debris and carrying this structure dorsally as they feed.

Larval foodplants of skippers include a broad range of Angiosperms; but two subfamilies, the Trapezitinae of the Australian region and the worldwide Hesperiinae, evidently feed in nature only on monocotyledonous plants (grasses, lilies, orchids, palms, etc.). There is one major exception, a species in southeast Asia. With remarkably few exceptions, larvae of the remaining subfamilies feed only upon various dicotyledonous plants.

The pupae are generally smoothly elongate, sometimes prolonged anteriorly and often with an elongate, free tongue case. While appearing naked, most pupae are covered, on all but the appendage pads, with numerous minute hairs. Many species have a waxy bloom on the pupae. Pupation is generally within a silk cocoon which is sometimes merely a modification of the larval shelter. A few species have exposed pupae, attached like other butterflies to a silken pad or by a median silk girdle.

Many skipper larvae feed principally at night and are inactive by day. A surprising number of adults of certain skippers are normally crepuscular or nocturnal, including a majority of the Old World subfamily Coeliadinae. Several groups of genera in both the Pyrginae and the Hesperiinae are known or suspected to have largely crepuscular or nocturnal adults.

Adults of the Hesperiidae all feed and most species visit flowers. Many visit decaying or fermenting matter or wet mud. It is while attending to these pursuits that adults of most species are collected. There is other business of importance to adults, the business of reproduction, and the several aspects of this may take the individuals away from feeding activities to other parts of the environment. There, by the way, we may learn a great deal about the insects by careful watching, far more than is possible by collecting numbers of adults accumulated at a feeding station.

Adults are critically concerned with mating activities and subsequent reproduction, and both of these activities are intricate, delicate and demanding associations of the animal and particular features of its environment. The elaborate sequence of signaling and responding that is performed between individuals during courtship offers unlimited opportunity for behavioral studies. Generally courtship in skippers involves certain flight features as well as details of behavior after alighting. The biggest danger to understanding courtship behavior is the problem of interpretation.

Not very long ago most collectors refused to bother with skippers because of a long list of difficulties: they are often difficult to catch; they are difficult to handle alive without damage; they are difficult to spread well; they all look dully alike; and they are difficult to identify. Fortunately, most of these complaints greatly exaggerate the problems, which are now looked upon as challenges, and attractions of this group for study. These insects are not difficult to catch if one is patient and careful in stalking a resting specimen. Few skippers are easy to collect on the wing, and the stereotype image of a collector in headlong pursuit of his speeding prize is definitely not a technique of the skipper collector.

Skippers are difficult to handle alive, if they are to be pursued within the net for the purpose of "pinching." The legs and palpi of most skippers are very easily lost, and they may be as important as the wings in identification. Therefore, it is preferable to dispatch the butterfly as quickly as possible, allowing a minimum of flying effort by the specimen. A strong, fast, killing jar filled with loose rumpled tissue gives plenty of walking surface and at the same time reduces abrasion from sliding about after death. Such a fast "knockout" jar, however, should not be allowed to accumulate too many specimens at one time; it should be periodically emptied into a killing jar which is not jostled. If wings flip forward ventrally upon death, these can be reversed if they are carefully tended to soon. If left alone, it is best to wait until the next day to flip back the wings (except in very dry areas).

Skippers are often quite difficult to spread well, and certain genera seem worse than others in this regard. The problem is that the wing muscles are powerful and large, and the wing veins customarily counted upon for strength in moving the wings during mounting are relatively weak. Fresh specimens are seldom a problem, but relaxed specimens can be most difficult. Cutting the wing muscles on larger specimens used to be a recommended technique but this generally damages the specimen somewhat. For such specimens a hypodermic injection of water concurrent with exposure to a humidity chamber usually suffices for adequate relaxing. Practice and patience still seem most necessary.

Many skippers look similar until one becomes familiar with the kinds of differences that exist between taxa. The wing patterns, while fairly reliable generally, are not the only, or even the principal expression of differences that are demonstrated by skippers.

Identification of these insects often requires a magnified view of either legs, antennae, palpi or genitalia, in addition to general appraisal of wing pattern characteristics. Therefore, a device for such examination does become important, whether it be a dissecting microscope or a hand lens. Dissecting microscopes, once coveted tools of the aloof professional, are certainly expensive, but no more so than many other household conveniences that are less essential. There is little pleasure anymore in ribbon matching and butterfly collectors are at last beginning to consider the whole animal, alive and dead, rather than just a set of wings.

Dissecting microscopes are becoming an essential tool for serious collectors, and this should not be a discouraging note to those who have not yet arranged for their scope. A hand lens works fairly well, and either acquaintances or local museums may have a binocular microscope that can be used by serious students upon occasion. Save up specimens to take to a microscope, or save up the money to get your own microscope. There are several references that will be helpful to those particularly interested in skippers. Publications by Burns, Evans, Freeman, Lindsey, MacNeill, et al., are listed in the bibliography and should prove useful.

Three subfamilies of Hesperiidae occur in the Western Hemisphere, and all three of these are represented in America north of Mexico.

Subfamily HESPERIINAE

The Branded Skippers

The eggs of this subfamily appear relatively smooth, although a pit-like reticulation is evident in many species. The eggs are hemispherical, being much broader than high. The head of a mature larva is relatively narrow, often subconical at the summit, and the body is elongate and tapered. This group of skippers generally feeds upon monocotyledons as larvae and in North America includes all the small orange skippers as well as a number of brown ones of tropical affinities. The males of these skippers often have a stigma or brand of specialized scales on the upperside of the fore wing, but never have a tibial tuft of hair or a costal fold of specialized scales. Most species have spines on the middle and hind tibiae, blunt appressed palpi, and generally the antennal club terminates in an abruptly reflexed apiculus. The subfamily is worldwide.

Genus THESPIEUS Godman

A tropical American group of about thirty species, the genus *Thespieus* is comprised of medium to large, rapid flying skippers. Most species are rather similar on the upperside, and have a band of hyaline spots on the hind wings. The lower wing surfaces of most are conspicuously variegated. Nothing is known about the early stages of any of the species. But one species of the genus is attributed to the region covered in this volume.

1. **Thespieus macareus** (Herrich-Schäffer). Plate 83, figure 7, ♂. This dark skipper is easily recognized by the dull gray-blue iridescent body and wing bases above, especially noticeable on the long basal hairs of the hind wing. A band of three hyaline spots is conspicuous on the hind wing. The thoracic tegulae are dark reddish-brown and contrast with the dull blue shade of the remainder of the body. The wings below are distinctively mottled with brown, gray, brick red, lavender and white. The antennae are dark above, but the terminal half of the club is strikingly pale. Males have a slender inconspicuous stigma next to the lower hyaline spots of the fore wing above. Wingspread, 36–42 mm.

Distribution: This species is rarely reported from north of Mexico. It has been taken reputedly in Florida, Texas and Arizona, but its occurrence in the United States requires verification. *Thespieus macareus* is widely distributed from Mexico to Colombia and Venezuela.

Genus NYCTELIUS Hayward

Only two moderately large, dull brown species comprise this neotropical genus. The genus is allied to *Thespieus,* but the species lack a hyaline band on the hind wing, the males have no stigma on the fore wing and the genital structures are technically rather different.

1. **Nyctelius nyctelius** (Latreille). Plate 83, figure 10, ♂. This species is marked very like many species of *Panoquina* on the upper surface: brown with a standard com-

plement and placement of hyaline, often slightly ambered, spots on the fore wings. The lower surface of the hind wings is pale brown with a violet cast and with two darker brown bands. A small but conspicuous dark subcostal spot distinctively punctuates the violet basal half of the hind wing below. Wingspread, 34–40 mm.

Early Stages: The egg is large, 1.5 mm in diameter, colored light green or yellowish. The young larva is pale green with a black head and a conspicuous black "collar." The mature larva is bluish or gray-green with a black collar and a brown head with vertical yellow marks. The pale tawny pupa has brown mottling on the head and is densely short haired, with a long tongue case extending beyond the wing cases but not exceeding the abdomen. The larvae feed on various grasses and on occasion have been considered economic pests of sugar cane and rice.

Distribution: Nyctelius nyctelius recently has been rather common in southern Texas and also is known from southern California. The species is abundant in both agricultural and relatively undisturbed tropical and semitropical areas of Mexico. It is widespread through the American tropics and in the West Indies.

Genus PANOQUINA Hemming

This is a genus of less than two dozen species. All the species are brown on the upper surface with from two to eight hyaline spots on the fore wing and none on the hind wing. Some species have conspicuous ochre hair or scales on the basal half of the wings above. The under surface is generally brown, sometimes with a bluish or purplish wash, and the hind wings frequently bear markings of pale, often white lines of spots, dashes, bands or large patches. Species of this genus lack spines on the tibiae of the middle legs which is not true of closely related genera in the area covered by this book. Most of the species have very long slender legs, and the tarsi of the larger species are unusually long. *Panoquina* species are medium to large. Several are restricted to coastal areas where they are salt marsh inhabitants, the larvae feeding upon certain marsh grasses. Some species feed on a number of grasses, including several agricultural crops like sugar cane and rice. The genus is best represented in tropical America but seven species occur in the United States.

1. **Panoquina panoquin** (Scudder). Plate 83, figure 11, ♂; figure 12, ♀. This skipper is easily recognized. The hind wings underneath have pale yellow veins on a brown ground color and a conspicuous short, whitish, outwardly prolonged dash at the end of the cell. This is one of the coastal species; it is closely associated with certain tidal marshes. Wingspread, 32 mm.

Early Stages: Eggs are hemispherical, pale greenish in color and finely reticulate. The young larvae are cream white with a light brown head. The body becomes greenish yellow shortly after the insect has started feeding. The foodplant is doubtless a salt marsh grass. Shapiro suggests a sedge, *Scirpus* sp., as a foodplant. The early stages were partially reported by Skinner and by Laurent.

Distribution: This species is recorded from the eastern seaboard, from Connecticut to southern Florida, and westward along the Gulf Coast to Mississippi. In the southern part of its range, *P. panoquina* seems to fly from early spring to late fall with two broods indicated.

2. **Panoquina panoquinoides** (Skinner). Plate 83, figure 13, ♂; figure 14, ♀. A dull yellowish brown species, *P. panoquinoides* somewhat resembles the preceding but is slightly smaller. The small yellowish spots on the fore wing are occasionally reduced or even absent above. The lower surface of the hind wings is dull yellowish or grayish brown with three pale spots and often pale veins. This species inhabits coastal marshes but is evidently local and not often encountered. Wingspread, 24–30 mm.

Early Stages: According to Brown the white egg is hemispherical. First instar larvae are vivid green with two fine cream colored lines dorsally. The head is light brown changing to blackish brown. Mature larvae are green with four greenish white dorsal stripes and a pale yellowish lateral stripe. The pupa is translucent green with the stripes of the larva persistent on the abdomen. The larvae are evidently restricted to a particular grass of the salt marshes.

Distribution: Known from Florida and the Gulf Coast of Texas, *P. panoquinoides* is also recorded from the islands of the Caribbean and from South America. In Florida the period of flight seems greatest in spring and fall, suggesting two broods.

3. **Panoquina errans** (Skinner). Plate 83, figure 17, ♂. This is a West Coast counterpart of the preceding species, which it resembles. It is a darker species with usually larger yellowish spots, most of which are hyaline, on the upper surface of the fore wings. The underside of the hind wings is brown, generally with yellow veins and an irregular diffuse band of about four pale spots. Populations from more southern parts of the range tend to have these spots reduced or absent, and the yellow veins more prominent. This species is another maritime representative, being found only along the sea coast adjacent to tidal marshes or behind the beaches where the larval foodplant grows. Wingspread, 24–32 mm.

Early Stages: These have been described by Comstock and by Brown. The egg is hemispherical and pale yellow (Brown) or white (Comstock). First stage larvae are whitish with a blackish head (Brown, and personal observation) or vivid green and semitransparent with a dark brown head (Comstock). There are two fine lateral cream colored lines on each side of the dorsal midline. Half grown larvae are similar, the body being yellowish green with yellowish white longitudinal dorsal stripes. Mature larvae are reddish brown with a dark dorsal line and a thin lateral stripe (Brown), or are green with four longitudinal dorsal greenish white stripes and a yellowish lateral stripe (Comstock, and personal observation). The head is bright green. The pupa is pale whitish green on the head and wing pads and the abdomen is pale brownish yellow (Brown), or it is translucent green with whitish dorsal stripes on the abdomen as occur in the larvae (Comstock). The foodplant is Salt Grass

(*Distichlis spicata*) but the literature has repeatedly indicated the larval foodplant to be Bermuda Grass (*Cynodon dactylon*). Comstock transferred the larvae to the latter plant, with great difficulty, after the fourth instar. It is not the natural foodplant of this species.

Distribution: This species is found only locally along coastal southern California and western Mexico. In California it flies from July to September. In the Cape Region of Baja California, however, it is also on the wing in December and January.

4. **Panoquina ocola** (Edwards). Plate 83, figure 15, ♀; figure 19, ♂. This species, like the three preceding, generally has no pale spot in the cell of the fore wings, and it occasionally has slightly pale veins on the hind wing below. *Panoquina ocola* is usually slightly larger than *P. panoquin,* the wings are more produced than those of the foregoing species and the lower surface of the hind wings is usually brown without conspicuous pale spots or dashes. The species is variable, however, and sometimes has a small white spot in the fore wing cell placed near to the base of the large white hyaline spot. Rarely most of the spots of the fore wing are obsolete, and also rarely there is a faint purple wash on the hind wings below in females. Sometimes the lower surface of the hind wing has a faint band of blurred paler spots. This species seems to be commonly associated with disturbed areas and sometimes appears in large numbers. A mass movement of these skippers was reported by Penn (1955) in Louisiana. According to Freeman it usually flies in late afternoon in Texas. Wingspread, 30–35 mm.

Early Stages: The early stages of this species may have been described under the name of *P. sylvicola.* The immatures are evidently similar to those of that species, to which description the reader is referred. The larval foodplants are grasses, and the species is reported to feed on cultivated rice in Louisiana and Mexico. In the West Indies it also feeds on sugar cane and the grass *Hymenachne amplexicaule.* Shapiro suggests a variety of marsh grass as the foodplant of this species.

Distribution: Panoquina ocola is found through most of the southeastern United States from Virginia to Florida, west to Kentucky, Arkansas and Texas, and has also been reported from New Jersey. It ranges widely through tropical America to Argentina and is common through the West Indies.

5. **Panoquina hecebolus** (Scudder). Plate 83, figure 8, ♂; figure 9, ♂, underside. Formerly this species was thought to be the same as *P. ocola,* which it much resembles. There is always a rounded spot in the cell of the fore wing and the veins of the hind wing underneath are usually slightly pale. In males the fore wing spots are yellowed and the cell spot is distant from the large spot next to the cell, but in females the spots are white and the cell spot is near the large spot. Like *P. ocola* there is seldom a band of pale spots or a purple tint on the lower side of the hind wings, features characteristic of the following species with which it has often been confused. Wingspread, 34–36 mm.

Early Stages: Notes on the early stages of this species may have been reported under the name of the following species. In any event, little is presently known about the biology of *P. hecebolus*, but it is highly probable that grasses serve as the larval foodplant.

Distribution: The species is reported to be common in parts of southern Texas, particularly during fall and winter. It is possible that Florida records, and perhaps many other United States records, of the following species actually pertain to *P. hecebolus*. This species is widely distributed southward from Mexico to Paraguay.

6. **Panoquina sylvicola** (Herrich-Schäffer). Plate 83, figure 16, ♂. This insect is slightly larger than *P. hecebolus* which it resembles on the upper wing surfaces, but the white cell spot on the fore wing of *P. sylvicola* males is generally much more elongate than the slightly amber round cell spot of *P. hecebolus* males. Females of *P. sylvicola* have a smaller cell spot placed very close to the very large central spot, the lower part of which extends conspicuously toward the outer margin of the wing. On the underside of the hind wings this species is marked with a straight band of small white or bluish spots. Females frequently have a blue or purple wash over most of the hind wings below. The underside of males is brown. In Texas this species occasionally has been common in city gardens. Wingspread, 36 mm.

Early Stages: These were described by Dethier. The ivory to white egg is hemispherical, 0.75 mm in diameter. First stage larvae are yellow, becoming light green, and have a black head with a few whitish hairs. Second stage and half grown larvae are green with darker middorsal stripe and four whitish, more lateral, stripes. The head is distinctive in these stages, being light yellowish to green, with two curving lines converging from the front of the ocelli to almost the top of the head and two additional dark lines from the back of the ocelli to the top of the head. Full grown larvae have the first two segments blue-green, the remainder gray-green. There are numerous minute deep greenish spots, a dark dorsal stripe only weakly bordered by dull yellow-green lines, and greenish white lateral stripes. The head is weakly wrinkled and light green without black lines. The ocelli are prominently black. The pupa is slender with a prolongation at the head. It is greenish with at least four yellowish stripes on the upperside of the abdomen and thorax. The tongue case is short, scarcely projecting beyond the wing pads. Normally the larvae feed on wild grasses but this species is one of the more common butterflies attacking sugar cane in Cuba and Puerto Rico.

Distribution: Panoquina sylvicola has been reported to occur in Florida and Texas, but at least the Florida records require verification. The insect is common at times in the lower Rio Grande Valley of Texas from August to December. This species is distributed throughout the West Indies and on the mainland from the United States to Argentina.

7. **Panoquina evansi** (Freeman). Plate 83, figure 20, ♂; figure 21, underside. This species is the largest of the genus in our area. It is a large brown skipper with amber subhyaline spots placed as usual for the genus on the fore wing. The cell spot is

distinctly elongate and projects partly above the very large spot next to the cell. The hind wings on the under surface have a conspicuous bluish violet sheen and there is, in males, an indistinct whitish band extending from the costal margin to near the anal angle. This vague band is almost obsolete in females. *Panoquina evansi* seems to be closely related to *P. fusina* of Central and South America and *P. nero* of the Greater Antilles. Some workers have treated this species as a subspecies of *P. fusina*. Nothing is known of the early stages. Wingspread, 44 mm.

Distribution: This insect is known from less than a dozen specimens. It ranges from the lower Rio Grande Valley of Texas, where it has been collected during October and November, through Mexico, Guatemala, British Honduras where it was taken in July, and Costa Rica, collected in October. It has been reported also from Trinidad.

Genus CALPODES Hübner

This genus includes only one large species, which resembles *Panoquina*. The head is very broad, much broader than one half the total length of the antennae. The tibiae of the middle legs are spined, and a row of four hyaline spots is present on the hind wing.

1. **Calpodes ethlius** (Stoll). Plate 83, figure 22, ♂; figure 23, ♀. A distinctive large brown skipper, *C. ethlius* is easily recognized by the line of hyaline spots on the secondaries. The under surface of the wings is brown, often much lightened by a pale reddish cast in fresh specimens. The fringes are buffy orange. Wingspread, 44–56 mm.

Early Stages: These have been abundantly reported in various ways. The egg is low hemispherical, about 1.25 mm in diameter and dull white with a tint of green which later changes to reddish according to Dyar. The young larvae are whitish translucent, becoming greenish from the ingested leaf material. The head is rounded and very dark brown. Mature caterpillars are pale green and semitransparent with dark orange heads. The pupa is pale green, slender, with a long projection of the head and an extended cremaster at the tip of the abdomen. The tongue case is long, usually extending beyond the tip of the abdomen. The larvae feed on various species of *Canna;* because these plants are widely used as ornamentals and the species has strong powers of flight, this skipper occurs sporadically in many northern cities, but is naturalized and resident in milder southern areas where the foodplant is grown.

Distribution: This species, because of its strong dispersal powers, has been found sporadically in many parts of the United States from Long Island, New York, to St. Louis, Missouri, and west to southern California. This skipper is established, however, in many parts of the South from Texas and Arkansas to Florida. It ranges south through Baja California and mainland Mexico to Argentina, throughout the West Indies and is also one of the few skippers in the Galapagos Islands.

Genus OLIGORIA Scudder

Oligoria includes only one medium sized, dark brown species. The apiculus of the antennal club is rather long, longer than the width of the club. The tibiae of the fore legs have a few short spines on the outer side. The middle and hind tibiae are spined as well. There is no stigma in the male.

1. **Oligoria maculata** (Edwards). Plate 83, figure 24, ♂; figure 25, ♀. This is a rather broad winged, dark brown species with four hyaline spots on the fore wings. The hind wings above are uniform. The lower surface is brown but with a pale reddish overlay in the costal area of the fore wings and over much of the hind wings. In addition there are three conspicuous and distinctive white spots on the hind wings below, two together and one solitary. The species is reportedly common in swamp areas. Wingspread, 32–36 mm.

Early Stages: As described by Chapman the mature larva is pale green with the last two abdominal segments deeper green. The collar is light brown as is the densely pubescent head. The pupa is dull green and pubescent, blunt at the head. The larval foodplant is not known.

Distribution: According to Kimball this species is common throughout Florida. It is also found in Georgia, Alabama, Mississippi, Louisiana and Texas. *Oligoria maculata* has rarely been reported from areas far removed from the Gulf Coast, such as Massachusetts and New York. Throughout most of the range it seems to be double brooded, but in Florida it flies most of the year and is most common in the spring.

Genus LERODEA Scudder

Small, lustrous, often grayish, brown species comprise this genus in the United States. The genus may include fifteen or twenty species but many of the tropical American taxa are not well understood at present. Three species enter our area. The species of this genus have spines on the middle and hind tibiae but not on the fore tibiae. Males have no stigma.

1. **Lerodea eufala** (Edwards). Plate 83, figure 26, ♂; figure 27, ♀. This plain, gray-brown little skipper has from three to five small white hyaline spots on the fore wing but is otherwise virtually unmarked. The basal hairs sometimes give the basal half of the hind wing a slightly paler appearance. The lower surface of the hind wings is brown with a heavy dusting of gray over all but the anal fold, and this dusting is also present on the apical half of the fore wing below. Occasionally a barely discernible row of vague paler spots is present on the underside of the hind wing. Small weakly spotted individuals may resemble some species of the genus *Nastra,* but *L. eufala* usually has distinctly white hyaline spots, and a gray-brown hind wind below. Wingspread, 22–28 mm.

Early Stages: These were described by Coolidge and by Comstock. The egg is hemispherical, glistening delicate pale green and about 1 mm in diameter. The young larva is slender and pale lemon yellow with a black head. Half grown larvae are pale grass green with a fine dark green dorsal line, and several whitish lateral lines. The head is dull whitish with orange-brown blotches. Mature larvae are vivid green with a dark dorsal stripe and several yellowish and one obscure whitish lateral stripes. The pupa is delicate green with abdominal stripes of dark green and yellowish. Hayward reports oviposition but no larval feeding on Cyperaceae (*Cyperus* sp.). Dethier has reared it upon sugarcane in Cuba, and Kendall on St. Augustine Grass (*Stenotaphrum secundatum*) in Texas. In California it commonly feeds on the introduced Johnson Grass (*Sorghum halepense*) and occasionally on cultivated Milo (*Sorghum vulgare*).

Distribution: A widely distributed species, *L. eufala* ranges across most of the southern half of the United States from the middle Atlantic states to the Central Valley in northern California. In the central states it extends north to central Minnesota and Nebraska. It is common through most of its range southward through the Americas to Argentina. It is also present in Cuba. In Chile and Patagonia another subspecies occurs. The species flies most of the year in Texas and Florida, but seems to be primarily one or two brooded in the more northern areas. It flies in September in Iowa.

2. **Lerodea arabus** (Edwards). Plate 84, figure 1, ♂. This is a small brownish skipper with hyaline spots on the fore wing disposed much as in the foregoing species but with the addition of a large or small hyaline spot in the upper part of the cell. Sometimes, but not always, a band of hyaline spots is present on the upper surface of the secondaries. On the lower surface of the hind wings is a conspicuous brownish patch which distinctly contrasts basally with the pale, almost violet-brown basal area. This patch may be outwardly ill defined if no band of pale spots is present on the wing. The fringes on the hind wing appear largely pale brownish, lightening outwardly to buff except near the anal angle where they terminate with a narrow rank of sullied white. The fringes are not conspicuously checkered. This species often has been confused with the following because few examples have been available for study and because this species, at least, seems quite variable. Generally the brown color of the upperside, the conspicuous, contrasting brown patch of the hind wings below, and the placement of the cell spot of the fore wings in the upper part of the cell will serve to separate otherwise similar specimens of the two species. If a suggestion of a band of pale spots is evident on the upper surface of the hind wings the specimen is probably *L. arabus*. Nothing is known of the biology of this seldom collected species. Wingspread, 24–30 mm.

Distribution: Lerodea arabus is known from Arizona, Baja California and Mexico. It probably also occurs in the desert hills of southeastern California. Since Tilden's recent résumé of *L. arabus* and *L. dysaules,* Hoffmann's report of this species from Guerrero, Mexico, is subject to re-evaluation. It is known to fly in April in Arizona. Records for Mexico include January, April and November.

3. **Lerodea dysaules** (Godman). Plate 84, figure 2, ♂.   This is a small dark gray-brown species with an olive brown cast to the wing bases and the body. Like the preceding species, it generally has a complement of hyaline spots on the fore wing similar to *L. eufala.* It often has in addition a cell spot placed in the lower part of the cell and therefore close to the largest hyaline spot of the wing. The hind wings are dark grayish (or basally olive) brown without any band of white spots. The lower surface of the hind wing is vaguely marked with a brown patch that is not in great contrast with a brownish gray basal area. The outer portion of this patch may have a suggestion of whitish edging. The fringes on the hind wing are more broadly whitish than in *L. arabus,* and indistinct checkering may be suggested. Easily confused with the preceding species, *L. dysaules* can be recognized by the darker, grayish brown color above, by the darker basal area of the hind wings below not conspicuously contrasting with the central brown patch which is often pale edged, and by the more broadly pale fringes of the hind wings. The early stages have not been reported. Most United States specimens have been taken in the shade of the canopy of thorn forests. Wingspread, 22–28 mm.

   Distribution: Only recently definitely reported in the United States, *L. dysaules* is known from southern Texas and mainland Mexico. It flies in October and November in Texas.

Genus AMBLYSCIRTES Scudder

This is a rather large genus of about two dozen small brownish or rusty gray species. More than three-fourths of these occur in North America north of Mexico. The wings are often marked with small white spots, or diffuse pale orange marks arranged on the fore wing in a sigmoid curve from the subapical spots to the posterior part of the wing on the upperside, while the lower surface is commonly mottled or grizzled with gray overscaling. The wing fringes are checkered in many species. The fore wing of males of most species is provided with a more or less conspicuous stigma. Most of the species have spines on the middle and hind tibiae. The antennae are conspicuously checkered and the antennal club has a long apiculus in all but one species. Adults fly rapidly, often close to the ground, and evidently engage in nectar feeding infrequently or at times when collectors are not afield. These skippers usually frequent ditches, gravelly streambeds, rocky ravines, canyon entrances or woodland glades, and they generally alight on rocks or the ground. Many of the species are quite local even though widely distributed and little has been learned of their biology. This group is taxonomically difficult and the relationships of the various species are not well understood. Most species are somewhat variable in wing pattern, and the differences between species in terms of maculation are often subtle. Many of the recognizably different populations have not been adequately sampled and it seems certain that with increased field knowledge more new names will be added under this genus. Identification of species of *Amblyscirtes* is therefore difficult for anyone not fairly familiar with the genus.

1. **Amblyscirtes simius** Edwards. Plate 84, figure 5, ♂; figure 6, ♀. This species is generally rather orange on the upper wing surfaces but varies to almost blackish. Characteristically, on the fore wing the entire area basal to the sigmoid discal line of diffuse pale spots is conspicuously darker than the area beyond those spots, but there is usually a pale orange cell spot within this dark region. On the lower surface of the fore wing at least the cell, and usually the adjacent area, is orange. Beyond the line of diffuse spots, at least apically, the wing is heavily dusted with gray scaling, as is most of the hind wing below. The macular band of spots and a few subbasal spots on the hind wing beneath are pale and diffuse. The fringes are pale, not conspicuously checkered. Males have a conspicuous stigma. The apiculus of the antennal club is extremely abbreviated, the fore tibiae are spined and there is only one pair of spurs on the hind tibiae. Because of these structural peculiarities and because the male genitalia are aberrant for this genus, I am not convinced that this species really belongs in *Amblyscirtes*. The species has been placed in *Yvretta* in the past, but that genus also seems unsuitable. According to Freeman and Scott, Ellis & Eff, and Scott (personal communication) this species seems to prefer the open slopes and summits of small hills, another unusual characteristic for the genus. Wingspread, 26 mm.

Early Stages: Nothing is published on the early stages. Scott (personal communication) reports the larval foodplant to be *Bouteloua gracilis* in Colorado.

Distribution: This species is known from Texas, New Mexico and Arizona, north through eastern Wyoming to Nebraska and Saskatchewan and south on the central plateau of Mexico. It is taken in April and May in Texas, June in Colorado and Arizona, and July in Nebraska.

2. **Amblyscirtes exoteria** (Herrich-Schäffer). Plate 84, figure 3, ♂; figure 4, ♀. This species, the largest of the genus in our area, is dark brown above with most of both wings heavily overlaid with dark orange scales. The spots of the fore wing are few, small and pale yellowish. A small cell spot, orange in males and white in females, may or may not be present. The hind wings above sometimes have a band of small orange or buff spots vaguely suggested. The fringes are conspicuously checkered. The lower wing surfaces are dark brown with a loose overscaling of gray scales on the hind wing and the fore wing apex. The cell is sometimes indistinctly dark orange. The hind wings below display numerous distinct, small, separated white spots in a curved series and subbasally. Males have an inconspicuous stigma. The fore wings of males are somewhat more pointed than is usual in this genus. Nothing has been published on the early stages. Wingspread, 26–32 mm.

Distribution: This species is known from southeastern Arizona and Mexico. It flies in June and July in Arizona.

3. **Amblyscirtes cassus** Edwards. Plate 84, figure 7, ♂; figure 8, ♀. This is an orange species with checkered fringes. Males have a prominent small stigma. The fore wings below are mostly orange with whitish subapical spots and a dark apex lightly sprinkled with gray. The hind wings on the lower surface are mottled and grizzled

with gray giving a subtle purplish cast to the darker areas. The whitish spots are diffuse, and part of the vannal fold is orange with minute dark striations. This is an easily recognized species but because it is orange it sometimes has been mistaken for *A. simius*. The antennal apiculus, spurs and spines on the legs and the genitalia are normal for the genus. The early stages have not been reported. Wingspread, 24–28 mm.

   Distribution: This skipper is not uncommon in southeastern Arizona and adjacent Mexico. It is also reported from the Davis Mountains of western Texas. It flies in Arizona from June to August.

4. **Amblyscirtes aenus** Edwards. Plate 84, figure 9, ♂.   This is a brown skipper with subdued orange overscaling on the upper wing surfaces. It is much like *A. cassus* except that the spots of the fore wing are not orange but yellowish and they are much reduced. There is no conspicuous cell spot on the fore wings of this species. The under surface of the wings is like that of *A. cassus* but darker. The cell region of the fore wing below is distinctly dark orange. The fringes of both wings are checkered and the stigma of the male is present but obscure. Nothing has been published on the early stages. This skipper is found, like the preceding species, in rocky ravines or dry boulder strewn slopes of the southwestern mountains and foothills. Wingspread, 22–28 mm.

   Distribution: Amblyscirtes aenus is found from southeastern Arizona east to west Texas and Oklahoma. It ranges northward to central Colorado and Kansas. This species flies from April to July in Texas and is common from June to September in Arizona.

5. **Amblyscirtes linda** Freeman. Plate 84, figure 24, ♂; figure 14, ♀.   A dark skipper with vague orange overscaling on the wings above, this species is similar to *A. aenus*. *Amblyscirtes linda* is darker than *aenus* and the yellowish spots on the fore wing above are fewer and smaller. The cell region on the lower surface is brown like the other dark areas of this surface, not dark orange as in *aenus*. The under side of the hind wings is very like that of the preceding species but darker and the pale spots less well demarked in the male. In females of *A. linda* these spots are more distinct, however, than they are in *A. aenus* females. The male stigma is better developed than in *A. aenus.* Wingspread, 26 mm.

   Early Stages: These are not reported.

   Distribution: Thus far this species is known only from eastern Oklahoma, Arkansas and Tennessee. I have tentatively identified as this species a male specimen from southern Mexico. This example, however, does not have a well developed stigma. The species flies in June and July in Arkansas.

6. **Amblyscirtes oslari** (Skinner). Plate 84, figure 10, ♀; figure 11, ♀.   This species has, in males, somewhat more pointed fore wings than most other species of the genus, excepting *A. exoteria.* This grayish brown skipper has extensive orange overscaling above, providing a dark gray-orange appearance to the upper wing

surfaces. There are no conspicuous pale spots on the upperside of the wings and those of the lower surfaces are only vaguely represented. The cell region of the fore wings below is usually dark orange and the hind wings are liberally dusted with light gray. The fringes are buff and not conspicuously checkered. The male stigma is short but black and rather conspicuous. This obscure little skipper is found in canyons, on slopes of mountain foothills and in small draws or ravines on the prairies. The early stages seem not to have been described. Wingspread, 26–28 mm.

Distribution: The species is known from Arizona east to western Texas and northward through New Mexico, Colorado, Oklahoma, Kansas and Nebraska to North Dakota and Saskatchewan. It has been taken from April to August. In Texas *A. oslari* flies from April to July.

7. **Amblyscirtes erna** Freeman. Plate 84, figure 12, ♂; figure 13, ♀. This obscurely marked little dark skipper is warm maroon-brown on the upper surfaces of the wings with little or no maculation. The lower surface of the fore wings is dark with little orange cast to the cell area. The hind wing appears granulated grayish with a light lavender cast and the band of spots so conspicuous in *A. aenus* is absent or very poorly defined in *erna.* Males have a well developed stigma. The fringes are checkered. This species seems to prefer ravines and rocky stream beds. The early stages of this local skipper have not been described. *A. fluonia* is a related but darker species with different genitalia. Wingspread, 22–26 mm.

Distribution: This insect is known from western Texas, Oklahoma and Kansas. It is also reported from northern Mexico. In Texas it flies from April to July.

8. **Amblyscirtes hegon** (Scudder). Plate 84, figure 15, ♂; figure 16, ♀. This is a black little skipper with a series of whitish spots on the upper surface of the fore wings. The hind wings above are dark with a diffuse band of buff spots which may have a slight greenish cast. Basally on both wings above the hairs and the costal scales of the fore wing are greenish gray. The fore wings on the lower surface are blackish with conspicuous buff spots, and the entire anterior half of the wing is heavily dusted with greenish gray scaling as is all of the hind wing below. A macular band of buff or grayish spots with poorly defined edges is evident on the lower surface of the hind wings. The male stigma is well developed but obscure because it is set in the dark field of the fore wing where there is no contrast. The fringes are light buff, those of the fore wings weakly checkered but those of the hind wings uniform. This is a forest species of the north, usually flying in glades and small clearings in the woods. The name *A. samoset* (Scudder) was recently resurrected for this species by Evans (1955) and this was followed by dos Passos (1964) in his check list. The technical assumption upon which Evans based his change was incorrect (see Brown, 1966:241) and *A. samoset* is here treated as a junior synonym of *A. hegon.* Wingspread, 22–26 mm.

Early Stages: The mature larva is pale whitish green with three slender dorsal stripes of dark green and a whitish lateral stripe. The head is dark brown with two vertical broad pale brown bands on the face and another curved pale brown band on each side running vertically from the back of the ocelli toward the top of the head. The pupa is dull straw yellow, tinged with green especially on the wing pads. The tongue beyond the wing pads is dull orange. The foodplants of the larvae are recorded as *Sorghastrum nutans* (as *Sorghum avenaceum*) and *S. secundum* by Scudder and as *Poa pratensis* by Klots.

Distribution: This species ranges from southeastern Canada southward along the Appalachians to Georgia and westward to Manitoba, Wisconsin, Iowa and, rarely, Mississippi and Arkansas. It has also been reported from Montana and Texas. This skipper has been taken from May to August in the north.

9. **Amblyscirtes texanae** Bell. Plate 84, figure 17, ♂; figure 18, ♀.   This skipper has the upper surfaces of the wings heavily overshaded with yellow fulvous so it appears to be a rather pale species. The pale spots of the fore wing above are yellowish and a rounded pale spot is present in the upper part of the cell. The cell on the lower surface of the fore wing is brown, not at all orange as in *A. aenus*. The wings below are pale gray with the yellow spots as above, and a whitish band is present on the hind wings. The male stigma is poorly developed, if at all, and the fringes are checkered. This species seems to prefer rocky ravines. Nothing is known of the early stages of *A. texanae*. Wingspread, 24–28.

Distribution: To date this species is known only from west Texas and adjacent New Mexico.

10. **Amblyscirtes prenda** Evans. Plate 84, figure 19, ♂.   This is a blackish skipper with many whitish or slightly yellowed hyaline spots on both wings. There is always a large constricted or double spot in the cell of the fore wing. Below the wings are dark with the spots of the upperside conspicuously repeated and well defined. The male has a well developed stigma but it is inconspicuous on the blackish wings. The fringes are pale and generally checkered. This insect is evidently closely allied to *A. tolteca* Scudder of Mexico from which it is said to differ by having an overscaling on the lower wing surfaces of violet-gray, whereas this overscaling in *A. tolteca* is yellowish gray. Nothing is known of the biology of this species. Wingspread, 22–26 mm.

Distribution: Described from southeastern Arizona, *A. prenda* is still known only from that area and from northeastern Mexico.

11. **Amblyscirtes aesculapius** (Fabricius). Plate 84, figure 20, ♂; figure 21, ♀.   This is another dark species above and below. It is most easily recognized by the network of buff or pale yellow veins and irregular spots on the lower surface of the hind wings. On the upper surface of the wings of males the spots are yellowish and in thin bands, only vaguely suggested on the hind wings. Spots of the female above are whitish. The stigma of the males is weakly developed and obscure and the fore wings are slightly more pointed than in most other species. The fringes are checkered. This species seems to prefer cane growth and the flight is not as rapid as that of many other species of this genus. The early stages are unreported. Wingspread, 28 mm.

Distribution: This species inhabits the Southeast from Virginia to Florida and westward to Missouri and Texas. It has been recorded also from Connecticut and New Mexico. The adults have been taken from January to September in various parts of the range, flying during June in Texas, and January, March and April in Florida.

12. Amblyscirtes carolina (Skinner). Plate 84, figure 22, ♂; figure 23, ♀. This little skipper is dark above with distinct yellow spots on the fore wing and often vague spots on the hind wing. The underside of *A. carolina* is distinctive owing to the pale yellowish hind wing and fore wing apex. Darker rusty spots give the hind wing a checkered appearance, while the posterior half of the fore wing is conspicuously blackish. Occasional individuals occur which have the ground color of the hind wings below dark with checker markings of yellow spots, just the reverse of the normal form. The fringes of this species are not checkered, and the male lacks a conspicuous stigma. The species seems to prefer swampy places. The early stages have not been described. Wingspread, 26–28 mm.

Distribution: This insect ranges along the eastern coastal lowlands from Virginia to Georgia and west to Mississippi.

13. Amblyscirtes nereus (Edwards). Plate 84, figure 25, ♂; figure 26, ♀. This is a narrow-winged black species with a slight brassy sheen to the dark upper surface. The spots are white above on both wings but those of the hind wings may be yellowed and reduced or lacking. The fore wings on the lower surface are black on the posterior half and densely overscaled with grayish green in the costal region and the apex. The spots, as on the upper surface, are white. The hind wings below are grayish green with an irregular band of buff spots and several similar spots basally. The fringes are pale buff and uncheckered. The male stigma is obscure. This species is seldom taken in numbers at any given locality and little seems to be known of its habits. The early stages have not been reported. Wingspread, 24–28 mm.

Distribution: Found locally in the southwestern United States and adjacent Mexico, the species is recorded from Texas to Arizona and might be expected in extreme southeastern California as well. It flies during May and June in Texas and from June to August in Arizona.

14. Amblyscirtes nysa Edwards. Plate 84, figure 27, ♂; figure 28, ♀. This is one of the smaller species of the genus. It is black above with three small white subapical spots and occasionally one or two additional small white spots suggesting the sigmoid series so usual in this genus. The lower surface of the hind wings is distinctive; several dark broad areas form a variegated mosaic with patches of lighter grayish and yellow-brown areas. The fringes are checkered, and the male stigma is obscure. This species is not uncommon in city gardens as well as in the remote ravines of the countryside. It is frequently taken at flowers and is able to utilize several weedy lawn grasses as larval foodplants. Wingspread, 22–24 mm.

Early Stages: The immature stages of *A. nysa* have been recorded by Heitzman. The egg is smooth shining white about 1 mm in diameter. The first stage caterpillar is white with a black head. Older larvae are pale green with a darker dorsal line and the head is longitudinally striped with dark brown, light brown and cream. Mature larvae are pale green with a dark green dorsal stripe and numerous minute green blotches. The head is creamy white with orange-brown vertical stripes. The pupa is bright cream becoming light orange-brown on the head. Foodplants include Crab Grass (*Digitaria sanguinalis*) and St. Augustine Grass (*Stenotaphrum secundatum*) in particular, but the grasses *Echinochloa pungens* and *Setaria glauca* are also used.

Distribution: This species ranges from Kansas and Missouri to Texas and westward to Arizona. It is also found on the central plateau of Mexico. In Kansas *nysa* is double brooded, flying during May and June and again during July and August. Texas records range from March to November.

15. **Amblyscirtes eos** (Edwards). Plate 84, figure 29, ♂; figure 34, ♀. This is another black species with a lustrous sheen to the upper wing surfaces. The only marking on the upper side of the wings is a conspicuous set of three white subapical spots, and two to four usually smaller additional spots of the sigmoid series. There is no spot in the cell of the fore wings. The lower wing surfaces are black, that of the fore wing marked like the upper surface. The hind wings are finely overscaled with grayish and there are numerous conspicuous small white spots outlined in black, forming an irregular macular band, and three subbasal spots. The fringes are white and checkered and the male stigma is present but inconspicuous. This species is partial to canyons and ravines, and is also often taken along country roadsides. The early stages have not been reported. Wingspread, 20–26 mm.

Distribution: A. eos is known from Texas to Arizona and from the central plateau of Mexico. It flies from April to July in Texas. It is taken in August and September in Arizona and Mexico.

16. **Amblyscirtes vialis** (Edwards). Plate 84, figure 30, ♂; figure 31, ♀. A small dark species with quite rounded wings, *vialis* is almost unmarked on the upper surface except for the tiny subapical white spots. This species is dark brown on the upper surface, without the lustrous sheen that is characteristic of the more grayish black dark species. The underside of the wings is also dark brown but the fore wing apex and the outer half of the hind wing distinctively overscaled violet-gray. The fringes are buff but conspicuously checkered with dark brown. A small and inconspicuous male stigma is present. This species flies along streambanks and ravines in the woods, and also frequents forest glades. Wingspread, 22–26 mm.

Early stages: These have been detailed by Scudder and by Fletcher. The egg is pale green, hemispherical and distinctly less than 1 mm in diameter. The first stage larva is whitish at first, changing to pale green after some feeding. The head is blackish as is the thoracic collar. Half grown larvae have a slender pale green body with a darker green dorsal stripe and dark brown head which has several paler vertical markings. The head and body are loosely covered by a white waxy powder which clings to the numerous hairs of the head and body. Once this flocculent waxy covering is well accumulated on the larva, the habit of remaining concealed in a shelter is reportedly abandoned, the larva resting on a leaf blade, extended and fully exposed. Mature larvae are pallid green with the body profusely dotted with pale green dots, each of which is at the base of one of the numerous minute hairs. The head is dull frosted white with several vertical stripes of ferruginous. The larva soon acquires the flocculence which obscures the details of the body and head. The pupa is green, becoming yellowish to slightly reddish about the head the cremaster and the tongue beyond the wing pads. Kendall has reported the successful rearing of this species on Bermuda Grass (*Cynodon dactylon*). Shapiro lists *Poa, Avena* and *Agrostis* as foodplants.

Distribution: Known to span the continent in north temperate regions, *vialis* has been reported from virtually every continental state in the U.S. except Alaska. It ranges from British Columbia to Quebec and extends southward to California, Texas and Florida. It has not been reported from Mexico. The species flies from March to September, occurring at different periods in different parts of its range. In Florida it is rare during March and in Texas it is uncommon in April, May and June. It is local but not uncommon in the mountains of California from May to July.

17. **Amblyscirtes celia** Skinner. Plate 84, figure 32, ♂; figure 33, ♀. This dark species has a distinct lustrous sheen to the upper surface. It is a grayish, dark brown insect and thus appears very different from the orange-brown *aenus,* which it otherwise very much resembles. The sigmoid line of spots on the fore wing above is present; the spots are very pale buff, almost white, and there may be a small spot in the cell. The pattern of spots on the upperside of the hind wing is sometimes minutely suggested. The pattern of the lower wing surfaces is somewhat like that of *aenus* but the cell area of the fore wing is brown, and the overscaling of the fore wing apex and the hind wings provides a brown striate appearance rather than the gray-lavender dusting of *aenus.* The whitish spots of the hind wings below are better defined although often smaller in *celia* than they are in *aenus.* The fringes are checkered and the male stigma is obscure. This species is frequently taken at flowers and seems partial to shaded banks of water courses, where it often perches on tree trunks or the ground. *A. celia* is often common and because it can feed upon a common lawn grass as a larva it is to be expected on occasion in city gardens. Wingspread, 24–30 mm.

Early Stages: Kendall reports oviposition on St. Augustine Grass (*Stenotaphrum secundatum*). The immature stages have not been described.

Distribution: This species is at present known only from Texas and northern Mexico. In the lower Rio Grande Valley it is reported to fly nearly every month of the year.

18. **Amblyscirtes belli** Freeman. Plate 84, figure 37, ♂. This dark skipper is much like the preceding species but *belli* is more black and less gray than *celia.* The largest whitish spot of the sigmoid series on the fore wing is generally V-shaped in *belli* and rounded or squared in *celia.* The latter species occasionally has a small spot

in the cell of the fore wing, whereas *belli* never has such a spot. On the lower surface *belli* is darker than *celia,* the whitish overscaling and the pale macular spots being much less conspicuous in *belli.* The band of spots in this species is rather dark hoary gray rather than white, and the spots are occasionally nearly absent. The fringes are whitish, checkered with black, and the stigma is obscure. This species feeds at flowers principally early and late in the day and thus differs in habits somewhat from *celia. A. belli* is primarily an inhabitant of woods, glades and creek beds, but Freeman reports it not uncommon in city flower gardens in late afternoon. Wingspread, 23–32 mm.

Early Stages: These have been reported by Heitzman. The egg is about 1 mm in diameter, white and shiny smooth, hemispherical, with a slightly flattened summit. First stage larvae are pure white with a dense covering of relatively long hairs, an unusual feature in first instar larvae. The head and cervical shield are shiny black. After several days of feeding the larvae become translucent green. Half grown larvae are pale translucent green covered with a rather dense vestiture of short pale and black hairs. The head is pale orange-brown with a broad, grayish white, vertical band in front on each side. Mature larvae are pale translucent green with a whitish overcast. The dorsal median line is darker green. On each side the larva is marked with a lateral greenish white line. The head is creamy white with a neck ring of orange-brown and a marginal and frontal orange-brown vertical stripe on each side. The more anterior stripes converge in the center of the face and are parallel from there to the summit. The pupa is pale orange-brown on the thorax, pale cream on the head and the cases of the appendages and pale yellow with orange intersegmental rings on the abdomen. The body hairs are orange and the tongue case is long and bright orange-brown, free from the wing cases to the tip of the abdomen. The larval foodplant is reported by Heitzman to be *Uniola latifolia* in Missouri.

Distribution: This species ranges from Texas, Oklahoma, Arkansas and Missouri east through Mississippi to Georgia and Florida. The adult is on the wing between March and October in Texas.

19. **Amblyscirtes alternata** (Grote & Robinson). Plate 84, figure 35, ♂; figure 36, ♀. This dark insect is very like *vialis* but the fore wings are much more pointed. The sigmoid series of whitish spots on the fore wings is usually suggested in this species, and the overscaling on the lower surface suggests dull gray tones in *alternata* rather than the lavender-gray of *vialis.* Frequently there is a line of powdery spots on the hind wings below. The fringes are unusually pure white with fine dark checkering, rather than buff as in *vialis.* The male stigma is obscure. This little species tends to inhabit pine woods where it stays rather close to the ground. The early stages remain unknown. Wingspread: 20–26 mm.

Distribution: A. alternata ranges through the Southeast from Texas to Florida and north to North Carolina; it has not been reported from Mexico. This species may be multiple brooded, flying in the extreme south from February to April, again in July and August and finally from September to November.

20. **Amblyscirtes phylace** (Edwards). Plate 84, figure 38, ♂.   This grayish black species with somewhat squared-off wings little resembles the preceding species of the genus. The upper surfaces are unmarked and the fringes are uncheckered buffy tan. The wings below are blackish and unmarked. A distinguishing feature is that the palpi, the top of the head and the collar are conspicuously orange. The palpi of females, however, are whitish ventrally. The males have a dark stigma. Occasionally males of *Euphyes vestris* are mistaken for this species but the antennae are shorter and stouter, the palpi more compact, the middle legs unspined and stigma broader in *vestris*. The relationship of *phylace* to the similar *fimbriata* requires clarification. Coolidge considered them seasonal forms, and others have suggested that they are subspecies, but the literature implies that they are sometimes nearly synchronous as well as partially sympatric. Both of these implications may be misleading. The two are certainly closely related. Little is known about the biology of *phylace*. Wingspread, 26–28 mm.

Distribution: Thus far this species is known only from the southern Rocky Mountain region in Colorado, New Mexico, Arizona and western Texas. It has also been reported from Mexico. In Texas and Colorado it flies in June and July.

21. **Amblyscirtes fimbriata** (Plötz). Plate 84, figure 39, ♂.   This species so closely resembles *phylace* that little additional description is necessary except to note that the fringes are orange in both sexes in *A. fimbriata*, and the palpi of females are orange below. Wingspread, 24–32 mm.

Early Stages: These were partially described by Coolidge. The pale cream-white egg is low hemispherical. First stage larvae are yellow-white at first, becoming greenish white after feeding. The head is large and black. Older larvae are more grass-green in color. The foodplant is a grass but otherwise is not known.

Distribution: This species is known only from the mountains of southeastern Arizona and several widely separated stations in Mexico. In Arizona it has been taken in June, in Mexico during March.

Genus ATRYTONOPSIS Godman

The males of most species of *Atrytonopsis* have very pointed fore wings, a slender, linear, gray stigma and well defined pale hyaline spots. The coloration is generally grayish brown on the upperside; the hind wings below usually are heavily overscaled with grayish and there is a discal series of spots which, in weakly marked species, are dark and narrowly diffuse. In well marked species many or all of these spots are whitish or even hyaline, and visible as well defined spots on the upper surface. The antennal club is long and somewhat slender; the apiculus is moderately long and has many sensory segments but the bare sensory part of the club proper extends over only a few segments. The middle and hind legs have spines on the tibiae. Less than a dozen species comprise this genus, confined to Central and North America.

Most of the species occur in Mexico and the southwestern United States and are treated here. Like members of the preceding genus, some *Atrytonopsis* are more often encountered on rocky hillsides and boulder-strewn stream beds than at flowers. Flowers are visited by most species, however, and sometimes in swarms; but these occasions may be limited and generally missed by collectors.

1. **Atrytonopsis hianna** (Scudder). Plate 85, figure 1, ♂; figure 2, ♀. This is a medium sized brown skipper with pointed fore wings. There are well marked hyaline spots on the fore wing and usually no spot in the cell. Occasionally, however, in females there may even be a double pair of small cell spots. The fringes are uncheckered brown. There are usually no white spots on the hind wing below. The male stigma is absent. Through much of its range this species is evidently a transient because its apparent foodplant is a grass that is a pioneer on recently burned areas. The grass occupies the area disturbed by fire for only a few years until, through succession, it is replaced by other plants. This demands effective dispersal flight of the skippers, for newly burned areas must be quickly located and colonized during the few years that the site is habitable. The grass grows permanently, however, on serpentine barrens, and there *hianna* is possibly resident. Wingspread, 30–36 mm.

Early Stages: The larval foodplant is probably the beard grass *Andropogon scoparius,* because *A. hianna,* like *Hesperia metea,* is closely associated with this grass.

Distribution: This species is found through most of the eastern part of the United States from New England to Manitoba, south to Georgia and Arkansas. It flies in May and June.

2. **Atrytonopsis turneri** Freeman. Plate 95, figure 13, ♀. This is probably a western subspecies of *hianna.* It differs from the more eastern populations in being grayish brown above and grayer on the underside. Like *hianna,* this skipper generally lacks white spots on the hind wings below. The early stages are not described. Wingspread, 30–36 mm.

Distribution: A. turneri is found from Kansas and Oklahoma to Wyoming, Colorado and New Mexico. Adults fly in May.

3. **Atrytonopsis loammi** (Whitney). Plate 85, figure 5, ♂; figure 6, ♀. This is also probably a subspecies of *A. hianna,* representing the extreme southeastern populations. Adults differ from those of *hianna* in having on the lower surface of the hind wing a median row of and several basal, distinct white spots. These spots are not hyaline and therefore are not clearly indicated on the upper surface of the wing. The early stages are not reported. Wingspread, 30–38 mm.

Distribution: In Florida this insect is double brooded, flying in March and April and again in October. Populations are reported north to North Carolina and west to Mississippi, a broad area where intergradation with *hianna* may occur.

4. **Atrytonopsis deva** (Edwards). Plate 85, figure 3, ♂; figure 4, ♀. This fairly large species is light brown above. The spots of the fore wing are hyaline whitish and

there is seldom a spot in the cell. The male has no well developed stigma, the fringes are buff to dirty white and uncheckered. The hind wings above are without white spots and the grayish hind wings generally have only a diffuse slender dark brown macular band on the underside. The early stages are not reported. Wingspread, 38–42 mm.

Distribution: This species is often abundant during June in the mountains of southeastern Arizona. It is also known from Sonora, Mexico.

5. **Atrytonopsis lunus** (Edwards). Plate 85, figure 9, ♂; figure 10, ♀.   A large, dark brown skipper, *lunus* can be distinguished easily from the preceding species by the presence of a large hyaline spot in the cell of the fore wing and the distinctly contrasting white fringe of the hind wing. The fringe of the fore wing is brown, there are no white spots on the hind wings above or below and there is no obvious male stigma. The biology of this species is not recorded. Wingspread, 40-44 mm.

Distribution: This species has been found sparingly in southeastern Arizona and northern Mexico. It flies in June and July.

6. **Atrytonopsis vierecki** (Skinner). Plate 85, figure 7, ♂; figure 8, ♀.   In general appearance this skipper resembles a small *deva,* but it differs from that species in having a well developed hyaline spot crossing the cell of the fore wing, and in having a well developed male stigma. It is a smaller and much paler insect than *lunus* and is also paler than *hianna.* The fringes are buff and not checkered. Nothing is known of the early stages. Wingspread, 34–38 mm.

Distribution: This species is found in prairie and semidesert regions of New Mexico, western Texas, Colorado and Wyoming. It is on the wing in April and May.

7. **Atrytonopsis pittacus** (Edwards). Plate 85, figure 11, ♂; figure 12, ♀.   This small grayish brown species is most easily recognized by the narrow, straight band of hyaline spots on the hind wings. There is a large hyaline spot across the fore wing cell. The fringes are whitish and uncheckered. Males have a stigma. The early stages are not known. This species seems especially partial to rocky slopes and outcrops. Wingspread, 32–34 mm.

Distribution: *A. pittacus* ranges from Arizona to western Texas and into Sonora. It flies in Texas from March to May and in Arizona from April to July.

8. **Atrytonopsis ovinia** (Hewitson). Plate 85, figure 17, ♂; figure 18, ♀ (ssp. *edwardsi* Barnes & McDunnough, as figured).   This skipper is a small, pale brown representative of a Mexican species. The populations in our area are grayish brown above with a conspicuous, almost straight, band of hyaline spots on the hind wings. In this they somewhat resemble the preceding species, but the spots of *o. edwardsi* are usually of several different sizes and not perfectly aligned, and generally not even connected to form a continuous line. There is a large hyaline spot across the cell of the fore wing. The fringes are quite pale and generally at least weakly checkered at the ends of the veins. Males have a stigma, and the antennal club is

shorter than that in *pittacus.* The underside of the hind wings is dusted gray and, in fresh specimens, distinctly striate as in *pittacus.* The early stages are not reported. Wingspread, 34–40 mm.

Distribution: This species occurs from Arizona and west Texas south through Mexico to Nicaragua. It flies in Arizona from March to August and from April to June in Texas.

9. **Atrytonopsis python** (Edwards). Plate 85, figure 13, ♂; figure 14, ♀; figure 16, ♂ (ssp. *margarita*). This is another member of the genus with a large spot across the fore wing cell and distinctly checkered fringes. The spots on both wings are either distinctly yellowish hyaline or whitish hyaline. On the hind wing these spots are of several sizes and distinctly offset from one another so that a very irregular band is formed at best. The hind wings below are heavily overscaled and marbled with a distinctive purple-gray color. The male has a stigma. This species occasionally swarms on particular flowers. Wingspread, 32–38 mm.

Early Stages: The egg (in Arizona) is hemispherical, minutely reticulate and cream colored for the first day or two. Thereafter an orange ring develops around the egg about halfway to the summit. This ring remains for about four days then disappears and soon the dark head capsule of the developing larva is visible in about the upper quarter of the egg, while the remainder is cream-white to dirty cream in color. Newly hatched larvae are pale cream-yellow with a black head. Half grown larvae are pale greenish yellow with vague lateral lines. The head is pale brown with dark markings. Older larvae have a distinctly pinkish cast and a blue-green abdominal region is conspicuous. The pale brown head and the body are densely covered with short blond hairs. The natural foodplant of the larva is not known.

Distribution: The typical form of this species, with yellowed hyaline spots on the upper surface, seems to be found only in southeastern Arizona from March to August, with the greatest numbers of adults in June. Populations from New Mexico and Texas have whitish hyaline spots on the upper surface and are slightly smaller than typical *p. python.* These more eastern populations have been named *python margarita* (Skinner). They are on the wing during June and July.

10. **Atrytonopsis cestus** (Edwards). Plate 85, figure 15, ♂. This species has a large hyaline spot across the cell of the fore wing, checkered fringes and a conspicuous band of hyaline spots on the upperside of the hind wings. The spots of this band are unevenly rectangular and connected to form an irregular band, not a uniform band as in *pittacus* or a disconnected one as in *ovinia edwardsi.* In addition there is a conspicuous, often small, pale subbasal spot in the cell on the upperside of the hind wings. The male has a stigma. Little is known of this species which is still quite rare in collections. Nothing has been published on the immature stages. Wingspread, 36 mm.

Distribution: This insect is known so far only from south central Arizona. It probably also occurs in Sonora.

Genus ASBOLIS Mabille

This genus contains only one Antillean species which has recently become established in Florida. These large skippers are very dark, almost black, on the upperside, and the wings entirely lack distinct pale spots of any sort. The sensory bare portion of the antennal club is about equal to that of the apiculus. The middle and hind tibiae are spined.

1. **Asbolis capucinus** (Lucas). Plate 85, figure 19, ♂; figure 20, ♀. This large dark species is easily recognized by the unmarked blackish brown of the upper surface (females have a diffuse paler region in the discal area) and the black and brick red underside. The males have a conspicuous stigma. A Cuban species, *capucinus* appeared recently (1947–1948) and is now well established in southern Florida where suitable foodplants occur. Wingspread, 42–50 mm.

Early Stages: The larvae feed upon various palms and in Florida, according to Kimball, particularly upon *Sabal palmetto, Cocos nucifera* and the *Phoenix* and *Paurotis* palms.

Distribution: The species is indigenous to Cuba but is now established throughout southern Florida.

Genus EUPHYES Scudder

This is an assemblage of nearly two dozen medium sized tawny or brown skippers. Some species have pointed fore wings while others have broad and rounded wings. Males generally have a conspicuous stigma composed of two oval patches of about the same size forming a short black broken dash on the fore wing. Spines are completely lacking on the tibiae of the middle legs. The antennae are rather short but with a long slender club and prominent apiculus, the length of the club being almost half the remaining length of the antennal shaft. Nearly all of the eight species which occur in our area are associated with swamp or marsh habitats. Five of these are restricted to the southeastern United States and only one extends into the West.

1. **Euphyes arpa** (Boisduval & LeConte). Plate 85, figure 21, ♂; figure 22, ♀. This large species is mostly brown above, but with a bright orange head and collar. In the male there is a large tawny yellow basal and discal area on the fore wing above which does not extend distad beyond the end of the cell. The female is warm brown with the usual discal series of fore wing spots which are pale orange. The wings on the lower surface are striking: the hind wings and the costa and apex of the fore wings are unmarked bright orange; the remainder of the fore wing below is black. Wingspread, 34–40 mm.

Early Stages: According to Chapman the larvae are pale green with yellow stripes. The abdomen is thickly lined with slender yellow and green streaks. The collar is black. The head is black with a white border around the top and sides and two thin white arcs vertically high on the face. The larvae feed from tube-like shelters near the base of the fronds of the foodplant, Saw Palmetto (*Serenoa repens*).

Distribution: E. arpa is found only in Florida, Georgia, Alabama and Mississippi.

2. **Euphyes palatka** (Edwards). Plate 86, figure 5, ♂; figure 6, ♀. Another large species of the genus, this tawny skipper is easily recognized by the extensive yellow fulvous on the fore wing of the male, which includes the costal region and extends well beyond the end of the cell. The head is brownish above, and the hind wings below are plain brownish. Wingspread, 38–44 mm.

Early stages: Chapman reported the larvae to be yellowish green, densely dotted with minute dark tubercles. The head is brownish; the upper part of the face is white with three black stripes. The larval foodplant is Saw-grass (*Mariscus jamaicensis*).

Distribution: This species is the most common representative of the genus through most of Florida where it flies in two fairly well defined broods in spring and fall, though it has been taken during nearly all months of the year. The range extends northward to Virginia and westward to Mississippi.

3. **Euphyes dion** (Edwards). Plate 86, figure 1, ♂; figure 2, ♀. This moderately large brown skipper has restricted areas of orange on the upper side of the wings. In both sexes the orange marks of the hind wings above are restricted to a streak through the end of the cell, corresponding to the anterior of the two distinctive pale rays of the lower surface. Some populations (*dion alabamae*) are very dark above and resemble *dukesi* but always have at least orange subapical spots on the fore wing. The wings below are reddish or orange-brown, with conspicuously pale veins on the hind wings, and two pale orange ray marks in the discal areas, one outward from the cell and the other anterior to the anal fold. This species, like several others of the genus, is extremely local, evidently not wandering more than a few feet from the larval foodplant, which is a marsh inhabitant. Wingspread, 32–40 mm.

Early stages: The larval foodplants are the aquatic sedge *Carex lacustris* and *Scirpus* sp. The egg is light green and finely reticulate. Young larvae are yellowish green with yellowish hairs and a black head and collar.

Distribution: The nominate subspecies ranges from the Carolinas north to New York and Ontario, west to Kansas, Nebraska and Wisconsin. Subspecies *E. dion alabamae* (Lindsey) ranges from Florida to Virginia, and west to Mississippi, Arkansas and Texas. A large geographical region of apparent overlap of these two subspecies suggests the need for much more information concerning their relationships.

4. **Euphyes dukesi** (Lindsey). Plate 86, figure 7, ♂; figure 8, ♀. This distinctive skipper has short rounded wings. Males are dark brown above with no markings except for the stigma, and some vague dark orange regions in the basal areas of both wings. There are no apical spots. Females are similar but with two or three pale orange

spots on the fore wing. The lower surface is rather like that of the preceding species in having the pale rays, but the rays are quite yellow on a brown to tan hind wing. Like *dion,* this insect is exceedingly local and is known only from a few very widely separated colonies, always in swamps. The early stages have not been reported. Wingspread, 32–38 mm.

Distribution: This species is known from Alabama, Mississippi, Louisiana, Arkansas, North Carolina, Virginia, Ohio and Michigan. It flies from August to October in Alabama and during both spring and fall in Virginia.

5. **Euphyes conspicua** (Edwards). Plate 85, figure 25, ♂; figure 26, ♀ (both ssp. *conspicua*). This rather dark species has narrow or broad areas of orange on the upper surface. The orange areas of the hind wings above are always cut by dark veins. Several of the larger spots on the fore wing of females are hyaline. The lower surface is dark reddish brown with a few distinct orange spots on the fore wing of males and a diffuse orange macular band on the hind wing; the spot beyond the end of the cell is distinctly larger than the others. A northern species, *conspicua* is restricted to swampy places or boggy meadows. Wingspread, 26–36 mm.

Early Stages: The immature stages have not been described. According to Shapiro the larvae feed upon *Carex* sp.

Distribution: The nominate subspecies is generally smaller and darker, and ranges from Maryland and New Jersey north through New England, westward to Ontario and Michigan. In Nebraska individuals are very large and broadly orange in males above but darker below. These populations have been named *E. conspicua bucholzi* (Ehrlich & Gillham). Populations occurring in Wisconsin and Iowa are evidently intermediate between the two.

6. **Euphyes berryi** Bell. Plate 86, figure 3, ♂; figure 4, ♀. This little known species is dark above with limited patches of tawny fulvous on both wings. The lower surface is brownish without any trace of the paler spots on the hind wing typical of the preceding species. The veins on the hind wing below are conspicuously lightened, a distinguishing characteristic. The species has only been taken in swampy places. Nothing is known of the early stages. Wingspread, 28–38 mm.

Distribution: This species has been collected in a few swamps in central Florida and once in Georgia. Adults have been taken during March, May, September and October.

7. **Euphyes bimacula** (Grote & Robinson). Plate 85, figure 27, ♂; figure 28, ♀. This dark species has rather pointed fore wings which bear only restricted tawny areas. The hind wings above are without pale regions. On the lower surface of the hind wings, the veins are conspicuously pale on a grayish brown ground color which is basally overscaled with bright orange. The fringes, including the entire vannal edge of the wing, are white. The top of the head and the collar are orange. Another species of northern bogs and swamps, *E. bimacula* is not well understood. Wingspread, 28–32 mm.

Early stages: These are scarcely known. According to Laurent the egg is light green, finely reticulate and hemispherical with the summit slightly flattened.

Distribution: This species is known only locally from New England and Ontario south to Virginia and westward to Wisconsin, Iowa and Nebraska. It flies during July.

8. **Euphyes vestris** (Boisduval). Plate 85, figure 23, ♂; figure 24, ♀ (both ssp. *metacomet*). This small dark brown skipper is characteristically without any pale spots above or below in males. Females generally have a very few pale spots on the fore wing and a diffuse crescent of slightly paler spots on the lower surface of the hind wing. Females may be confused with *Wallengrenia egeremet* females and perhaps also with other dark females of *Pompeius* and *Polites.* Females of those species, however, have well developed spines on the middle tibiae. Most of the populations are dark brown above without much orange overscaling (although there may be considerable orange scaling on top of the head and the palpi below may be orange tinted), and the spots on the fore wings of females are white hyaline. A western series of populations characterized by rather heavy orange overscaling above in males and yellowed fore wing spots of females represents nominate *vestris.* All the remaining populations are referred to the subspecies *E. vestris metacomet* (Harris). Wingspread, 24–30 mm.

Early Stages: The egg is pale green when first deposited, but within a day develops an irregular red encircling band and a red blotch at the apex. The first stage larva is yellow, covered with short white hair; the head is shiny brown. Older larvae are greenish with a white overcast and white hairs on the last segment; the head is orange with creamy vertical stripes. Mature larvae are translucent green with a white overcast from numerous wavy white dashes over the body. The head is caramel brown, black in back, with two cream vertical bands and a velvet black spot at the upper center of the face. The pupa is whitish green, the thorax yellow-green and the wing pads more yellow; the head is pale brownish. The abdomen is blunt with a terminal raised brown ridge bearing two small spikes. The foodplants are sedges (*Cyperus*). Shapiro reports the foodplants as grasses, especially *Tridens flavus.*

Distribution: The nominate subspecies, *v. vestris,* is confined to California and Baja California where it flies during May, June and July. The subspecies *E. v. metacomet* ranges throughout the rest of the United States, southern Canada and doubtless also northern Mexico. In parts of this range the insect is evidently two brooded, flying in late spring and again in late summer.

Genus MELLANA Hayward

This group of fifteen or twenty mostly tawny, tropical American skippers is closely related to *Poanes* and *Paratrytone.* The palpi, however, are more compact and less shaggy and the antennal club is smaller. The front, middle and hind tibiae are spined. There is no stigma in males. Many of the species are extremely similar in wing markings so that examination of male genitalia may be required to correctly identify a specimen. Only one species is at present recorded from our region but it would not be surprising to find that there are, in fact, several similar looking species of this genus occasionally encountered in the Southwest.

1. **Mellana eulogius** (Plötz). Plate 86, figure 9, ♂. This is a tawny orange species with an inwardly well defined brown marginal border on the upperside. The veins through the orange areas are conspicuously brown and, on the fore wings, there is also a distinctive brown line through the middle of the cell longitudinally, beyond which it expands and connects with the brown margin. Another broader but slightly diffuse brown line extends from the base behind the cell out between the veins to the border. The lower surface is mostly dull tawny with a little black basally and vannally on the fore wings, where also the veins forming the posterior edge and the end of the cell are black. The hind wings below are tannish orange with a series of only slightly paler spots, often diffuse, in a poorly defined discal band. The second anal vein is narrowly black. The early stages are not reported. Wingspread, 26–30 mm.

Distribution: Thus far this tropical American species has been reported only from southern Texas, where it was taken in May and November. Some years ago I identified a female from Arizona as the similar *M. mexicana* Bell. This specimen should be re-examined. *M. eulogius* ranges south to Paraguay.

Genus CHORANTHUS Scudder

This genus contains half a dozen tawny species related to *Paratrytone* and *Poanes.* The third segment of the palpi is more prominent than in those two genera and protrudes well beyond the hairs and scales of the second segment. The tibiae of the middle legs have the usual terminal pair of spurs but mostly lack tibial spines. Males of most species have a narrow stigma. The entire genus is West Indian but two species have been reliably reported from Florida and a third species, probably erroneously labeled, is also recorded from Florida.

1. **Choranthus haitensis** (Skinner). Plate 86, figure 10, ♂. This species is bright yellowish fulvous with a diffuse darker border and orange fringes. The underside of the hind wings is pale fulvous gray or orange without any trace of the pale veins so characteristic of the following species. The males have a long slender curved stigma on the fore wing. Wingspread 28–32 mm.

Early Stages: According to Wolcott the full grown larva is opalescent gray-green with two distinct yellow spots dorsally near the end of the abdomen. The head is yellow with brown markings. *C. haitensis* has been reared from sugar cane in Puerto Rico.

Distribution: This species occurs rarely, probably as an introduction, in Florida. It is found principally in Hispaniola.

2. **Choranthus radians** (Lucas). Plate 86, figure 11, ♀. This tawny orange species is much like the preceding but with a more dentate border and a darker basal area above. The lower surface of the hind wing distinguishes this species from all others of the genus because of the pale veins on a grayish olive ground color. Wingspread, 28–32 mm.

Early Stages: These are reported by Dethier for Cuba. The reticulate egg is $\frac{3}{4}$ mm in diameter, lustrous white changing to pink. First stage larvae are yellowish with a black head. Older larvae are grass green with a dull green middorsal line. The head is yellowish with a black vertical median broad line forking and divergent basally to form a W-mark with a parallel pair of long vertical black stripes on the front of the face. The lateral margin also has a black line from the top of the head to the ocellae. The larvae are said to feed upon grasses. Dethier has reared *radians* on sugar cane.

Distribution: This Cuban species occasionally turns up in Florida.

3. **Choranthus vitellius** (Fabricius). This is the only species of *Choranthus* that lacks a stigma in the male. Males are tawny with a darkened border much like the preceding two species. Females of *vitellius* are much more orange on the upperside than are the other species. Wingspread, 28–30 mm.

Distribution: This insect is abundant in Puerto Rico and the Virgin Islands. It has been recorded from Florida, but the record is considered doubtful and in need of confirmation.

Genus PARATRYTONE Godman

This genus of nine or ten species is comprised of dark insects closely allied to the genus *Poanes,* from which they differ in having a shorter antennal club. Half of the species lack a stigma in the male. The fore and middle tibiae are distinctly spined. The palpi are shaggy and the last segment scarcely protrudes beyond the hairs of the second segment. Most of the species inhabit boreal (montane) areas in the Neotropics, particularly in Central America. One species extends north to the southwestern United States.

1. **Paratrytone melane** (Edwards). Plate 86, figure 13, ♂; figure 14, ♀ (both ssp. *melane*). This is a brown skipper with the usual fore wing spots orange in the male, but several are diffusely hyaline in females. The hind wings above are brown, heavily dusted with orange scales, usually with a discal band of orange spots. The wings below are reddish brown, heavily overscaled, especially on the hind wings, with grayish lavender scaling providing a slight purple tint. The spots of the hind wing are orange or yellowish brown. There is no stigma in males. Wingspread, 28–34 mm.

Early Stages: The egg is pale greenish, hemispherical and about 1 mm in diameter. The first stage larvae are dirty yellowish green with darker longitudinal lines; the head is black. Mature larvae are dusky yellowish green with a blackish dorsal line set off by vague yellowish lines, and whitish yellow lateral stripes; the head is yellow-brown, covered with a whitish pile. The pupa is pale straw, changing to darker tan, and there are numerous small black dots on the abdominal segments posterior to the wing cases. The tongue case is long, nearly reaching the end of the abdomen. Several grasses are used by the larvae.

Distribution: This species is distributed from Panamá to California in several different subspecies. The nominate subspecies occurs throughout the lowlands of California and northern Baja California. These populations normally are heavily overscaled with orange on the upperside and the discal band on the hind wings is diffuse and broad. Another subspecies (*P. melane vitellina* Herrich-Schäffer) is essentially Mexican but enters the United States in southeastern Arizona and Texas. This subspecies lacks much of the orange overscaling above and so is much darker; the band of spots on the hind wing is much reduced and well defined.

Genus POANES Scudder

Species of the genus *Poanes* are medium sized yellowish or orange skippers and differ little from *Paratrytone* except that the antennal club is considerably longer. Like *Paratrytone*, the palpi of *Poanes* are shaggy and the third joint scarcely protrudes from the hairs of the second segment. The tibiae of the fore, middle and hind legs are spined. Only two species have a stigma in the male. About a dozen American species comprise the genus, seven of which come within the scope of this book.

1. **Poanes massasoit** (Scudder). Plate 86, figure 15, ♂; figure 16, ♀. This small, dark, stubby-winged species of *Poanes* is chiefly characterized by its dark brown rounded wings. Males may be entirely unmarked or with a few small discal orange spots; in females there are usually a few small spots, those of the fore wing whitish, not orange. The hind wings below have a conspicuous yellowish discal band of squarish connected spots and a broad yellowish dash through the cell to the apex of this band. Occasional specimens have the lower surface of the hind wings suffused with rusty brown, obscuring the yellow markings. This insect occurs locally in the vicinity of bogs or marshes and flies low and weakly through the tall grasses. Wingspread, 24–28 mm.

Early Stages: According to Laurent the eggs are opaque white and nearly round. The first stage larva is dirty yellow with a head of pale brown; the body is covered with long yellow hairs. Second stage larvae are olive green, otherwise similar to the first instar. The larval foodplant, according to Shapiro, is *Carex* sp.

Distribution: Poanes massasoit ranges from Maryland to New England and westward to Nebraska and South Dakota. It has also been reported from Georgia, Colorado and Texas but these records require verification.

2. **Poanes hobomok** (Harris). Plate 86, figure 17, ♂; figure 18, yellow ♀; figure 19, dark ♀. Males of this moderately large species are broadly bright yellow-orange on the upper wing surfaces with a rather broad blackish border on both wings. Some females may be almost as broadly orange above, usually a little less brightly so than males. Other females (form "pocahontas") may be dark brown with a few pale yellow to whitish spots, all of which, save the three subapical spots, are not sharply defined; there is nearly always a spot in the cell of the fore wing. The lower surface of both wings has a continuous purplish brown border. The fore wing below is orange but the hind wing is yellowish, either broadly to a dark basal area, or more narrowly as a broad discal band of connected yellow rectangular spots. In the former case the dark basal area, although not broad, does extend broadly toward the anal angle of the wing; in the latter case the broad basal area also extends halfway into the cell and upward to the costa. There are no dark reddish brown spots in a discal line through the broad yellow area. Males and dark females of this species have been confused with those of *zabulon* but the above diagnosis should permit identification of *hobomok*. In our region this species is usually slightly larger than *zabulon*, but the latter species in Central America is a somewhat larger insect. This is one of the more common skippers of the northeastern states. Wingspread, 26–34 mm.

Early Stages: These have been reported by several early workers, but the past confusion between this species and *zabulon* renders our knowledge uncertain. According to Klots the half grown larva is dark green to brown with transverse lines of numerous small black tubercles bearing black spines. Where these series of lines are absent there are conspicuous naked bands along the sides. The head is black and lustrous with numerous short white hairs. The larval food is grass.

Distribution: This insect is distributed from Nova Scotia to Georgia and westward to Saskatchewan, Kansas, Arkansas and Alabama. It is everywhere single brooded, flying as early as May in Minnesota.

3. **Poanes zabulon** (Boisduval & Le Conte). Plate 86, figure 20, ♂; figure 24, ♀. This skipper is similar to *P. hobomok* in that the males are broadly yellow-orange above with a broad blackish border. Females are always dark brown, with several sharply defined hyaline whitish spots but none in the cell. The lowermost of these spots is yellowed and not hyaline. On the underside males are much like *hobomok* but the dark border on the fore wings is more irregular and inwardly diffuse than in that species; on the hind wings this border is weakly composed of reddish brown spots which are usually interrupted just before the anal fold by an outward extension of the yellow discal color. In the broad yellow discal area a short linear series of small reddish brown spots is generally present. The basal dark area of the wing is usually broadly expanded to the middle of the costal margin in a vague loop that encloses a yellow subbasal spot near the costa, and only a portion of the anal fold is darkened. Females have the lower surface of the hind wings deep reddish brown

with a heavy purplish overscaling on the outer fourth of the wing; the discal band is generally inconspicuous. This species and the preceding are found in woodlands and open fields and both are common. Wingspread, 26–36 mm.

Early Stages: Because of the early confusion of this species with *hobomok,* there is little reliable information on the early stages of *zabulon.* The larval foodplants are the grasses *Tridens* and *Eragrostis* according to Shapiro.

Distribution: This is a more southern insect than *hobomok,* ranging from Massachusetts west to Wisconsin and south to Texas and Georgia. Florida records need confirmation. South of the United States the species ranges from Mexico to Panamá.

4. **Poanes taxiles** (Edwards). Plate 86, figure 21, ♂; figure 22, ♀; figure 23, ♀ underside (all ssp. *taxiles*).   This large brightly yellow-orange species is marked above and below somewhat like *zabulon.* Males are usually more broadly yellow-orange on the upper surface of the fore wing; the subapical spots are not usually distinctly isolated from the discal orange area by dark brown between the costa and the end of the cell as in *zabulon.* The lower surface of the hind wings has the border extending to the costa, and the linear series of red-brown spots in the yellow discal field is more prominent. The anal fold is largely yellowish, or at least not dark brown. Females are dark brown above with broad orange spots and a broad dull orange discal area on the hind wing. The early stages of this insect have not been reported. Wingspread, 32–36 mm.

Distribution: This is a western species, the nominate subspecies ranging from Nevada to Nebraska, Colorado and New Mexico and northwestern Mexico. Another subspecies occurs in central Mexico. Records from Ohio, California, Iowa and Texas are questionable.

5. **Poanes aaroni** (Skinner). Plate 92, figure 35, ♂ (ssp. *aaroni*); Plate 87, figure 1, ♂ (ssp. *howardi*); figure 2, ♀ (ssp. *howardi*).   This is a medium sized orange or dark tawny skipper with broad, sharp edged, dark borders. It has the veins darkened on the upper surface of the hind wings, and males have a very slender, almost obsolete, pale stigma. Some populations slightly resemble *Atrytone arogos,* from which they differ in being less yellow-tawny with dark veins on the hind wings. From *Atrytone delaware* they differ in being deeper orange, having a better defined and broader dark border and in not having such conspicuously dark veins on the fore wing. The lower surface of the hind wings of *P. aaroni* is tawny tan with a diffuse paler ray of dull smoky orange running through the cell toward the outer margin. This species is an inhabitant of salt marshes. Wingspread, 26–38 mm.

Early Stages: According to Laurent the eggs are opaque white, finely reticulate and slightly flattened at the summit. The first instar larva is whitish at first but becomes drab greenish after it begins feeding. The second stage larva is light green. The foodplant is not known but is expected to be a marsh grass.

Distribution: Mostly confined to the Atlantic coastal strip, *P. aaroni* is represented by two subspecies. Nominate *aaroni* is smaller, rather yellowish and represents the populations from New Jersey to Georgia. A larger, more deeply orange, series of populations represents the subspecies *aaroni howardi* (Skinner) from Georgia through Florida.

6. **Poanes yehl** (Skinner). Plate 86, figure 27, ♂; figure 28, ♀.   This good sized, dark orange skipper looks something like a large, broadly fulvous *Euphyes conspicua*. The dark borders are broad and inwardly well defined, the male has a conspicuous large dark stigma and the hind wings have dark veins. The lower surface of the fore wing is orange and this color intrudes along the veins into the dark border, making the border a series of more or less connected dark spots. The posterior two of these spots are frequently darker and more conspicuous than the remainder. The hind wing below is brownish orange with a discal band of three slightly paler spots which are separated at the end of the cell by a scarcely discernible ray of orange. Females are slightly darker and more contrastingly marked below. The species may be separated from *Euphyes conspicua* by the spined middle tibiae and the character of the dark border on the underside of the fore wings. The spots on the hind wings below are much like those of *conspicua,* but are placed closer to the outer margin. This species is an inhabitant of swamps; nothing seems to be known about the early stages. Wingspread, 28–38 mm.

   Distribution: Restricted to the Southeast, this species is reported from Virginia, Tennessee and Arkansas south to Florida, Georgia, Alabama, Mississippi and Texas. It is double brooded in Mississippi, flying in May and June, and again from August to October. Individuals of the earlier brood appear to be rather less dark than those of the fall brood.

7. **Poanes viator** (Edwards). Plate 86, figure 25, ♂; figure 26, ♀.   This skipper is fairly large, broad-winged and orange, with dark veins on the hind wings above. The fore wings of both sexes are mostly brown above with bright orange spots in males largely confined to the posterior half of the wing except for a large cell spot. A pair of small subapical spots is often present. Females have similar but paler spots on the fore wing; most of these are sub-hyaline and whitish. The hind wings above are broadly orange in males, sullied pale orange in females, with a broad brown border. In both sexes a narrow black bar usually marks the end of the short cell on the hind wings above. The male has no stigma. This species seems to prefer salt marsh situations when it inhabits coastal regions, but it is also distributed, locally, through a broad inland area. Kendall suggests that it should be sought near marshes where the foodplant grows. Wingspread, 30–44 mm.

   Early Stages: Little is known of the biology of this species. Laurent reported the eggs to be grayish and finely reticulate with a somewhat flattened summit. The first instar larva is grayish and covered with numerous dark colored spine-like hairs. The head and collar are light yellow, covered with many dark brown spots. The second instar larva is much as in the first stage but brown. According to Kendall the foodplant is Marsh Millet (*Zizaniopsis miliacea*) and Shapiro records wild rice (*Zizania*). Larvae do not build silken shelters, using the natural recess between the sheath and the stem instead.

Distribution: This species is highly local, found thus far in scattered colonies from Massachusetts and Ontario west to Minnesota and Nebraska, south to Florida, Alabama, Louisiana and Texas. It is unrecorded from large areas within the above indicated limits. It has been collected from April to August.

Genus PROBLEMA Skinner & Williams

This genus includes two similar yellowish tawny skippers of the southeastern United States. Closely related to *Atrytone, Problema* differs in considerable detail of the genitalia. The tibiae of the fore and middle legs are generally without spines but the hind tibiae are spined, at least in males. Males have no stigma. The last segment of the palpi extends well beyond the inner or medial scaling of the second segment. Both species of *Problema* are heavy bodied and robust, larger than either species of *Atrytone.*

1. **Problema byssus** (Edwards). Plate 87, figure 13, ♀; figure 14, ♀, underside; figure 15, ♂. A large, yellow-orange species with a dark brown border, males generally have black veins at the apical point of the fore wing cell. In broadly fulvous examples, those with orange overscaling nearly to the wing base, there is usually a pair of minute black longitudinal dashes in the middle of the cell. In darker specimens the dark basal area extends outward in the cell to obscure these dark dashes. The end of the cell on the hind wing above is also usually marked by a short dark line. The veins of the upper surface are often conspicuously darkened, in this respect resembling *Atrytone delaware*. Females above have considerably restricted fulvous areas in which the veins are dark, and females may much resemble large females of *A. delaware.* The markings of the lower surface of the fore wing of males somewhat corresponds to those of the upperside, although the dark border may be nearly obscure. The color of the hind wings below in males is dull olive-yellow or rusty brown with a vague broad crescentic discal band of slightly paler color. Females below are darker and a more pronounced rusty or orange with the same paler band on the hind wings as in the male, but often much better defined. The antennal club is at least narrowly black below the bare sensory area, and it is broadly black elsewhere. This species, at least in Kansas, is an inhabitant of undisturbed prairie regions. Wingspread, 32–38 mm.

Early Stages: The foodplant of the larvae in Missouri is Eastern Gamagrass (*Tripsacum dactyloides*), a perennial bunchgrass. The early stages have been reported in detail by Heitzman. The egg is large, about 1.5 mm in diameter. It is chalky white, hemispherical with a flattened summit, and without apparent reticulation. First stage larvae are pale green with a small white mark dorsally at each intersegmental fold. The hairs are white and the head is dull red-brown. Half grown larvae are pale green or yellow-green covered with tiny black warts and minute white hairs. The head is orange-brown or light reddish brown with two marginal white stripes and a pair of shorter vertical white stripes on the upper face. Mature larvae are dull blue-green, with a yellowish tint dorsally, thickly covered with fine white hair. The head is pale reddish brown with numerous vertical cream colored lines and streaks. The pupa is long and slender, cream colored with a few tiny brown dots. Winter is spent as a fourth instar larva, and the overwintering larvae become pale creamy white, the head purplish black with no pale pattern.

Distribution: The species seems to be local, the adults not often leaving the immediate vicinity of the larval foodplant. For this reason *P. byssus* is not frequently encountered through its wide range in the South and Midwest. Thus far the insect is reported from Florida, Georgia and Alabama north to Illinois, Iowa and Kansas. Field and Heitzman mention Texas also; Mather & Mather and Lambremont list the species as expected in Mississippi and Louisiana respectively. It is single brooded in Missouri, flying in June and July.

2. **Problema bulenta** (Boisduval & Le Conte). Plate 87, figure 11, ♂; figure 12, ♀. This species looks much like the preceding. The fore wings of the male above may be more broadly yellow-fulvous and there is no single or paired longitudinal dash within the cell. The major difference in wing markings between the two species is on the lower surface of the hind wings, where *bulenta* is immaculate yellow in both sexes, without the rusty tint or deep orange or the vague series of spots typical of *byssus*. The antennal club is orange below the sensory area. This exceedingly rare insect in collections has been taken only a few times, and in only a few localities. Nothing is known regarding the biology of this species, other than the fact that several of the colonies seem to be associated with freshwater marshes.

Distribution: The species is presently known only from Virginia, North Carolina, South Carolina and Georgia. It has been taken during May, June, July and August.

Genus ATRYTONE Scudder

This genus in our area comprises of two medium sized, yellow-tawny species which lack a male stigma. The terminal palpal segment protrudes only a little beyond the medial scaling of the second segment. There are at least a few weak spines on the tibiae of the fore and hind legs, although in one species these may be only apical on the fore tibiae and minute and usually hidden on the inside of the hind tibiae. This same species (*A. arogos*) has the tibiae of the middle leg unspined.

1. **Atrytone arogos** (Boisduval & Le Conte). Plate 87, figure 16, ♂; figure 17, ♀. This very yellowish, rather small species has no markings within the broad pale fulvous area in the male. The brown margins are rather broad, quite regular and somewhat diffuse inwardly. The hind wings are similar but the costal region and the anal fold are also brown. The veins are not darkened. Occasionally males are quite dark above with little more than the cell and part of the adjacent discal area fulvous on the fore wing, and the hind wing entirely dark except for a small patch

of pale fulvous in the cell. Females are much like the males above but have broader dark areas. The wings below in both sexes are uniformly unmarked yellow-tawny except for a dusky strip from the base to the outer margin along the posterior part of the fore wing. Wingspread, 22–30 mm.

Early Stages: These have recently been reported by Heitzman. The large (1.2 mm diameter) egg is creamy white, circled by two pale red irregular bands; it is hemispherical with a flattened summit and a protruding micropyle. The first instar larva is pale creamy white changing to green, with a few long white hairs especially on the last segment. The head is pale orange-brown. Half grown larvae are pale grayish green except at the extremes of the body where they are cream. The head is grayish white with the margins orange-brown and four orange-brown vertical curved stripes on the face. The ocelli are dark brown. Mature larvae are pale yellowish green, yellow between the segments, and with orange-brown marginal lines as well as four vertical ventrally joined or forked orange-brown stripes. The ocelli are bright orange. The pupa is pale yellow with the thorax and abdomen dorsally brighter yellow. The wing pads and tongue case are white as are the last two abdominal segments. The head and abdomen have scattered short reddish hairs. The foodplant in Kansas is a beard grass (*Andropogon gerardi*); it may be a species of *Panicum* in Georgia.

Distribution: This species occurs from Florida to Texas, northward to New Jersey, Iowa, Minnesota and Nebraska. Evidently double brooded in the south, *arogos* flies from March to May or June and in August and September. In the north it flies in June and July.

2. **Atrytone delaware** (Edwards). Plate 87, figure 18, ♂; figure 19, ♀. Males are medium sized, brightly yellow-tawny insects with conspicuous black veins and rather narrow dark brown marginal borders. Females are similar but have broad dark marginal borders and the basal half of the wings darkened. The wings on the lower surface are bright orange to yellowish and, in males only, the basal region of the fore wing is darkened; in females, the bases and the posterior part of the margin may be darkened on the fore wing. This species might be confused with *Problema byssus,* especially the females, but *delaware* has tibial spines at least moderately developed on all legs. Wingspread, 26–34 mm.

Early Stages: The mature larva, according to Chapman, is bluish white with a crescent shaped black band on the last two segments. The body is thickly dotted with minute black tubercles. The head is oval but slightly bilobed and white, with a marginal black band around the top and sides and three black vertical streaks on the face. The pupa is slender and greenish white except for the head and the last segment which are black; the head is blunt, tubercled and bristly. The larval foodplant is Woolly Beard Grass (*E. divaricatus*), recorded by Klots and by Chapman (as *E. alopecuroides*). Shapiro adds *Andropogon* and *Panicum virgatum.*

Distribution: This species enjoys a wide range from Massachusetts to Minnesota and the Dakotas south to Florida and Texas. South of northern Mexico, records of *A. delaware* require confirmation.

Genus OCHLODES Scudder

This holarctic genus is comprised of seventeen species. Five of them are found in North America, all but one of which come within the province of this book. The Old World species seem to represent a homogeneous group, but the North American species appear, at least superficially, to be a heterogeneous assemblage of not very closely related entities. The species here are small to medium sized, mostly orange, insects with a prominent male stigma. The antennal apiculus is relatively long, about equal in length to the width of the club. The tibiae of the fore, middle and hind legs are spined in all but one of the four species treated here; the exception, *snowi*, has smooth fore tibiae.

1. **Ochlodes sylvanoides** (Boisduval). Plate 87, figure 7, ♂; figure 8, ♀. One of the smaller species of the genus, *sylvanoides* is rather ruddy orange on the upper surface. Males have a prominent black stigma which often shows a slender gray line in the center, and the usually conspicuous brown border is inwardly well defined and dentate, especially on the hind wings. Usually a broad black dash extends outward from the end of the cell on the fore wing. In both sexes the dark markings, except for the male stigma, are slightly subdued by a more or less heavy overscaling of orange. In neither sex are there ever any whitish or hyaline spots on the fore wing. The lower surface of the hind wings is variable, ranging from yellowish and almost immaculate to nearly chocolate with a conspicuous macular band of squarish yellow spots. This is one of the most common rural skippers of the West but it occurs only rarely in the larger cities. It is ecologically versatile, however, as much at home in extremely disturbed areas as on undisturbed dry hillsides during late summer. Wingspread, 20–28 mm.

Early Stages: The egg is cream, minutely reticulate and small, less than 1 mm in diameter. Half grown larvae are pale greenish with blackish heads which have two broad pale vertical bands on the front of the face. The dorsal line is narrow and darker green and a pale lateral line is vaguely suggested. Mature larvae are similar but the head is more broadly tannish cream except for the margins, the back and a median vertical stripe on the face, which are black. In addition, several pale lateral stripes are evident on the body. According to Comstock, however, the mature larva is buff-yellow with a black head. Different populations or even different broods of this variable species may well have different appearing larvae. The pupa is brownish cream with a grayish bloom over most of the surface. The anterior portions are darker brown and the abdomen is lighter with numerous small dark dots arranged in double bands on the segments. The foodplants of the larvae are grasses, particu- larly several fairly broad bladed, tall species.

Distribution: Abundant and widespread, this skipper ranges through the Pacific states from British Columbia south into northern Baja California. It extends eastward through the Great Basin to Montana and Colorado. The species flies during summer, from June to October in different parts of its range.

2. **Ochlodes agricola** (Boisduval). Plate 87, figure 9, ♂; figure 10, ♀.   A small species, *agricola* is somewhat like *sylvanoides* but the male stigma is proportionately broader and is separated from the broad marginal border by a narrow, generally hyaline, spot. The dark border is more diffuse inwardly than in the preceding species. The lower surface of the hind wings is usually almost immaculate yellow-orange in males, whereas females generally have a pinkish blush to the orange ground color and a more or less conspicuous band of tawny spots. This species frequents some of the same situations as does *sylvanoides* but generally appears a month or two earlier. *O. agricola* more often frequents forest glades and woodland stream courses than *sylvanoides*. Wingspread, 20–26 mm.

Early Stages: The egg is small, less than 1 mm in diameter and nearly as high as wide. It is gray-green (becoming dull white before hatching) and minutely reticulate over most of the surface. First stage larvae are white with a shiny black head. The foodplant is not reported.

Distribution: This species is thus far known only from relatively low elevations in California and northern Baja California. It should be expected in southwestern Oregon as well. Adults fly from May into July, rarely to August.

3. **Ochlodes yuma** (Edwards). Plate 87, figure 5, ♂; figure 6, ♀.   This, the largest species of the genus in the U.S., is easily recognized by the extensive yellow-tawny wings above and below. Females often have a series of diffuse pale, often hyaline, spots on the fore wing above. This lowland southwestern species is local and restricted to colonies of the semi-aquatic reed-grass that serve as the larval food. Wingspread, 28–36 mm.

Early Stages: The pale greenish white eggs are large, about 1.5 mm in diameter, and smoothly hemispherical. The notes on the early stages briefly reported here are derived from unpublished studies made in central California by John Burns and me in 1956. The first stage larva is dull cream yellow or creamy orange with a black head. The larval shelter at this stage is a folded-under edge of the leaf blade. Half grown larvae are pale greenish with a cream head marked by narrow brown marginal and a median vertical stripe. Mature larvae are quite similar, often with less extensive brown vertical marks on the head capsule. Shelters of older larvae are major portions of the leaf blades conspicuously rolled to form a round tube. The pupa is dark brown, almost chocolate on the head, the abdomen transversely spotted with double bands of small dark dots and minute dashes. The tongue case is free beyond the wing cases for about half the distance to the tip of the abdomen. The larval foodplant is Common Reed (*Phragmites communis*), a giant canelike colonial grass of freshwater marshes. Larvae would not accept any substitute.

Distribution: Ochlodes yuma is thus far known only from California, Nevada, Utah, Colorado and Arizona. It may also be found in Sonora, Mexico.

4. **Ochlodes snowi** (Edwards). Plate 87, figure 3, ♂; figure 4, ♀ (both ssp. *snowi*). *Ochlodes snowi* is a dark skipper with a light orange overscaling which imparts a

are all whitish or yellowish hyaline except the orange spot at the posterior end of the band. There is usually an hourglass-shaped spot across the cell. A band of orange spots crosses the hind wing. The undersurface is quite reddish brown with the fore wing spots reproduced; on the hind wings is a conspicuous band of yellow spots and one yellowish spot in the cell. Dark specimens have all the pale spots reduced, occasionally to the point of obsolescence on the hind wing. The fore tibiae are not spined. This is a mountain species of the Southwest. The early stages are not known. Wingspread, 28–36 mm.

Distribution: Adults in the United States are smaller, duller and more vaguely marked than are those of Mexico, and they represent nominate *snowi,* which occurs in the boreal regions of Colorado, New Mexico and Arizona. A large, dark, well marked insect represents another subspecies in the Sierra Madre Occidental and the Sierra Volcanica Transversal of Mexico. The species flies in Colorado from June to August, also in September in Arizona.

Genus ATALOPEDES Scudder

This is a small genus of three species, two of which are essentially orange while the third is dark. Males are easily recognized by the enormously enlarged stigma. Females tend to be darker and rather closely resemble members of the genus *Hesperia,* to which *Atalopedes* is related. The antennae are relatively short with a stout club and short apiculus. All tibiae are spined. Only a single species enters the area covered here and it is restricted to the American mainland. The other two occur in the Greater Antilles and the Bahamas.

1. **Atalopedes campestris** (Boisduval). Plate 87, figure 20, ♂; figure 21, ♀. Males are broadly orange and are quickly identified by the massive stigma. On the underside they are principally yellow with a vague band of paler spots on the hind wings. Females may be broadly orange above, or quite dark, but there is always a distinctive hyaline spot under the end of the fore wing cell. The lower surface of the hind wings is olive or darkly yellow with a macular band of pale, usually yellow, spots very like certain *Hesperia.* Females also are sometimes confused with females of *Hylephila phyleus,* from which they may be separated by the presence of the hyaline spot on the fore wing. This species is as much at home in urban gardens as in rural areas. It seems even more common in such disturbed places than in untouched areas. Wingspread, 24–36 mm.

Early Stages: These have been described by Comstock and by Scudder. The greenish white egg is small, less than 1 mm in diameter, hemispherical and microscopically reticulate. The first stage larva is whitish with a tint of green and a black head. Mature larvae are dark olive-green, profusely covered with minute dark tubercles bearing short black hairs. The middorsal line is dark green and a slightly pale lateral stripe is faintly suggested. The head is black. The pupa is dark blackish brown with a prominent white thoracic spiracle cover. The head, thorax and abdomen are rather densely covered with minute hairs, and a white flocculent powdering covers most of the hairy parts of the pupa. The abdominal segments are dotted with small blackish spots. The species is evidently able to feed upon a variety of grasses. Kendall reports oviposition on Bermuda Grass (*Cynodon dactylon*) and St. Augustine Grass (*Stenotaphrum secundatum*). Comstock and Warren & Roberts cite Bermuda Grass, the latter mentioning an economic infestation of this species in Arkansas pastures.

Distribution: The species ranges from the Atlantic to the Pacific in the southern half of the United States. It occurs (as a non-overwintering wanderer) northward as far as Colorado, Nebraska, Iowa and New York. It also ranges southward to Brazil and Ecuador.

Genus HESPERIA Fabricius

The eighteen species of this large genus are medium sized, mostly tawny insects. The middle legs are spined and the antennal club is large with a rather short apiculus. Many of the species are extremely variable geographically and individually, and a number of species resemble one another, so that identification of these skippers has been discouraging and frustrating for many collectors. Fortunately closely related species, with similar male genitalia, generally do not look much alike and can be recognized by wing markings alone. Several unrelated species look similar, however, and it may occasionally be necessary to examine under a microscope the tip of the abdomen or the fore wing stigma of some males. Enough of the critical structures of the genitalia are usually visible without requiring dissection. This genus is easily recognized in that the male stigma is smoothly arcuate and has a silvery line in the middle. The lower third or, in some species, the lower half or more, of the stigma is bent outward away from the posterior edge of the cell. The majority of the species characteristically have on the hind wing underside a greenish, yellowish or brownish overall color with a chevron-shaped macular band of silvery, white or at least pale, spots. The shape and condition of this macular band is important for identification of species. Normally the posterior arm of the "chevron" is not parallel to the outer wing margin, being a little more basal at the anal end. Sometimes the last anal spot is much offset basally. Hidden, or sometimes exposed, within the central scales of the male stigma is a mass of felt-like material, portions of which can be dipped out with the point of an insect pin. The color of that material, either black, yellow or gray, can help separate some very similar-looking but unrelated species. Females are much more difficult to identify without resort to structural details, but by and large they can be recognized by color pattern together with distributional evidence and the resemblance to associated males.

Many of the species are highly local and several are quite uncommonly encountered. The eggs of all known species are over 1 mm in diameter, and the larvae all look much alike. There are specific differences in the head markings of mature larvae, but the distinctions between young larvae are microscopic and will not be discussed here. First stage larvae are yellowish or cream with a black or brown head.

They all feed, so far as is known, upon particular species of perennial bunchgrasses in nature, but under laboratory conditions will accept a large array of grasses. Older larvae are olive-greenish; they may feed away from the shelter, and often a trail of silk leads from the shelter, which may be partly subterranean, to that part of the grass tuft most recently fed upon. Pupation usually takes place in a loose cocoon, constructed amid debris, often some distance from the larval shelter.

The genus is holarctic, but all eighteen species come within the scope of this book. Several subspecies of one of the North American species (*H. comma*) represent the genus in the Old World, where it occurs south to North Africa. On this continent the genus ranges from Alaska and Labrador south to central Mexico. Most of the species, especially the most confusing ones, occur in western North America (Mac-Neill 1964).

1. **Hesperia uncas** Edwards.   Males have a slender stigma with black interior "felt." The macular band on the hind wings below is complete and composed of white spots arranged "normally" (see generic description). Often, and usually in females, these spots are prolonged along the veins where the white veins contrast with black patches between the basal spots and the macular band. In this respect this species somewhat resembles *Yvretta rhesus,* but that insect is much darker and smaller and its antennae have scarcely any apiculus on the club. *H. uncas* ranges from Saskatchewan to south of Mexico City and from the western Great Plains to the Sierra Nevada of California. Three subspecies occur north of Mexico.

(a) **uncas** Edwards. Plate 89, figure 1, ♂; figure 2, ♀.   The nominate subspecies has restricted dull olive-tawny above and olive-gray or olive-brown on the lower surface. Females may be dark with the spots of the fore wing whitish. The costal margin is usually darkened. The veins are white on the hind wing below and the black patches conspicuous. Wingspread, 26–36 mm.

Early Stages: The larvae of this subspecies feed upon *Bouteloua gracilis* in Colorado, according to Jim Scott (personal communication).

Distribution: Nominate *uncas* ranges from Saskatchewan to Alberta and south through the prairies and the Rocky Mountains to Texas and New Mexico.

(b) **lasus** (Edwards). Plate 88, figure 25, ♀; figure 26, ♂.   This is a larger, more broadly tawny subspecies which otherwise is similar to the nominate subspecies. The light orange overscaling above is extensive, often obliterating most of the dark margin. The color of the underside of the hind wings is pale yellowish or tawny green and the spots are large. The veins are white and the black patches prominent. Wingspread, 28–42 mm.

Distribution: This subspecies inhabits the Great Basin and the Sonoran Desert to the south, from Utah and eastern Nevada through Arizona to northern Mexico.

(c) **macswaini** MacNeill. Plate 88, figure 27, ♂; figure 28, ♀.   A smaller insect, this subspecies is more brightly and more extensively orange above, tending to look much like *H. nevada* in this respect. The hind wings below are grayish green with the white spots in males commonly not extended out along the veins and with the black patches also commonly missing. The normal shape of the band will separate *macswaini* from *nevada,* and the very slender stigma and more blunt fore wings will distinguish it from nearby *H. comma* populations. Usually the costa on the fore wings above is dark. From *H. miriamae,* males may be separated by the lack of dark veins and anal area on the hind wing above, the brighter orange color of the upper surfaces, and the greenish tint and lack of luster on the hind wings below. Females have orange spots above, but generally have black patches and white veins typical of the other subspecies on the hind wings below. Wingspread, 24–34 mm.

Early Stages: The larval foodplant is the recently described Needlegrass, *Stipa nevadensis.* The egg is large, about 1.5 mm in diameter; it is greenish white, smoothly hemispherical, and without evident reticulation except under high magnification.

Distribution: Populations of this subspecies are found locally along the eastern face of the Sierra Nevada, in the White Mountains of California and in somewhat boreal regions of adjacent Nevada.

2. **Hesperia juba** (Scudder). Plate 89, figure 17, ♂; figure 18, ♀. This is a fairly large, boldly marked species of the West. The ground color above is characteristically orange with an inwardly sharply defined, dentate dark border. The male stigma is slender with the interior "felt" black. The lower surface of the hind wings is greenish in fresh specimens; the analmost spot of the macular band is angulate and distinctly offset basally, so that the posterior arm of that band is rather irregular. In this character the species somewhat resembles *H. nevada* and *H. miriamae* but *juba* is larger, has more pointed fore wings, and has a well defined marginal border above. Some females of *H. comma harpalus* may resemble *juba,* but the dark, well defined double spot below the cell on the fore wing above of *juba* is usually distinctive. The antennal club of this species is much shorter and more globose with a very short apiculus, than is true of other species of the genus. Wingspread, 26–38 mm.

Early Stages: These have been described by Lindsey and by MacNeill. The egg is small for this genus, scarcely over 1 mm in diameter. It is smoothly hemispherical in shape with little suggestion of a basal flange, clearly but shallowly reticulate and resembles in nearly all respects the egg of the following species. At first it is shining cream white, soon becoming pinkish, then dull white with a gray cast. The head of the mature larva is black with two short vertical streaks on the upper part of the face. The pupa is brown, darker on the head and thorax, and is covered with a waxy bloom. The abdominal segments each have a double transverse row of dash-like dark spots. The hairs on the head and thorax are hooked. The tongue case is short, scarcely protruding beyond the wing pads.

Distribution: This western species is found from British Columbia to Baja California eastward through the Great Basin to Montana, Wyoming and Colorado.

3. **Hesperia comma** (Linnaeus). This widespread species is nearly impossible to characterize because throughout its range it is represented by many different looking populations, some of which are subject to the most extreme individual variation found in the genus. Many, but not all, of these different looking populations have been named and broad zones of blending exist in some intermediate areas. There

is no point in adding more names to this group; it would only compound the confusion. In order to understand this complex species it is necessary to appreciate the geographical distribution of the many populations relative to one another, because the characteristics of adjacent entities tend to blend in intervening areas. These "in between" examples are to be expected wherever subspecies approach one another and should not disturb the collector who wishes to name every specimen. Names represent populations, not individuals, so specimens should be judged by the population they were sampled from, no matter what they look like and should be labeled accordingly.

At one time I (MacNeill 1964) was inclined to consider this assemblage of populations as four species of a complex, but nothing is to be gained by maintaining that view. The important points in understanding them is that they are all closely related, although different looking, and that there seem to be at least two basic groups in the complex. One group includes all the Old World populations together with those of northern North America. The other group includes the populations of western United States and northern Mexico.

The eggs, so far as known, are conspicuously reticulate, especially upon the upper half. They are rather small, a little more than 1 mm in diameter, and distinctly flanged around the base in some populations. They are colored much like those of the preceding species: creamy white initially, changing to salmon pink then to grayish white with a pearly luster. Mature larvae of Old World and northern American populations have black heads, while those of western United States generally have broad pale marks on the head.

This species in general is characteristically tawny above, with a normal male stigma with black interior "felt." The macular band on the hind wings below, if present, is normally shaped, although the more anal spot of the band in northern American and Eurasian populations may be distinctly offset basally.

(a) **manitoba** (Scudder). Plate 88, figure 5, ♂; figure 6, ♀. This is a dark, short-winged insect, brownish orange with broad dark borders above. The lower surface of the hind wing is usually dark greenish brown or olive-orange with the spots of the macular band lustrous white. The anal spot generally is distinctly offset basally as in *H. juba* or *H. nevada*. This subspecies is darker and has more stubby wings than *juba*. The wing shape is like that of *nevada* but the latter is bright orange and the anal spot of the macular band even more pronouncedly offset basally. Wing-spread, 24–30 mm.

Distribution: This subspecies is distributed principally throughout the more northerly Pacific Northwest, from Alaska south to Washington and east to the Great Slave Lake region of the Northwest Territories, northwestern Wyoming and, possibly, Colorado.

(b) **assiniboia** (Lyman). Plate 88, figure 7, ♂; figure 8, ♀. This is generally a pale tawny insect but females are variable. The tawny, when present, is of a cold tone, and the dark markings are usually well overscaled with this shade. The lower surface is pale yellowish to grayish green and the spots of the band in males are usually yellowish and small; in females they are yellowish or sometimes white. Frequently all these spots are absent. The fringes are rather long and conspicuously white or very pale. Wingspread, 27–33 mm.

Distribution: This northern prairie inhabitant occurs from Alberta to Manitoba and south into North Dakota. It flies from late July to September.

(c) **laurentina** (Lyman). Plate 90, figure 23, ♂; figure 24, ♀. This is a small, dark, but very orange subspecies. The orange above has a slight reddish cast and the broad dark borders are not heavily overscaled. The hind wings below are golden greenish or brownish with the white spots of the macular band appearing almost separated. Wingspread, 25–32 mm.

Early Stages: The eggs are as described for the species. The head of the mature larva is black with a pair of parallel short vertical stripes high on the front. The pupa is "mouse color," with a dull yellow abdomen which has a tinge of blue above.

Distribution: This skipper is found in the northeastern United States and southeastern Canada, from Minnesota to Maine northward to Manitoba and New Brunswick. Adults appear in July and August.

(d) **borealis** Lindsey. Plate 88, figure 13, ♂; figure 14, ♀. This subspecies is much like *laurentina* to the south and west, and may blend with it. Typically *borealis* has the black-edged spots of the macular band below definitely connected into a line, even when the spots are reduced. This subspecies, like *manitoba,* is similar to some of the Old World subspecies.

Distribution: H. c. borealis is known definitely only from Labrador and adjacent Canada. Specimens from northern Manitoba seem closer to *laurentina* although they are often identified as *borealis;* they are typical of neither and may represent an intermediate population.

(e) **harpalus** (Edwards). Plate 88, figure 15, ♂; figure 16, ♀. Plate 90, figure 31, ♂; figure 32, ♀. These brightly tawny insects are generally pale grayish yellow or bright yellowish green on the lower surface of the hind wings. The spots of the macular band are lustrous white and are connected to form a well defined "normal" macular band. The entire anal spot of this band is in line with the rest, although the spot may be expanded to protrude basally. Wingspread, 28–34 mm.

Early Stages: The eggs are particularly like those of *juba,* and a field-collected egg must generally be allowed to hatch in order to identify the species by characters of the first instar larva. Mature larvae have the head broadly marked with pale tan or buff areas. The pupa is brown, with double rows of short small dashes on each abdominal segment. The hairs are gently curved, not hooked at the end as is true of *juba.* Like that species the tongue case is short, scarcely extending beyond the wing pads. There is no grayish bloom covering the pupa. Eggs have been recovered from Thurber Needlegrass (*Stipa thurberiana*) in Mono county, California, and this is presumed to be the preferred foodplant.

Distribution: This subspecies occupies the whole of the Great Basin and the facing slopes of the enclosing mountain ranges. It is found east of the Sierra-Cascade axis from British Columbia to south-central California, and ranges eastward to the slopes of the Rocky Mountains. It flies from June to September.

(f) **yosemite** Leussler. Plate 88, figure 1, ♂; figure 2, ♀. These are small insects which at lower, foothill elevations are pale tawny above and below. Males from these areas are often immaculate yellowish on the hind wings below, while females are pale grayish orange with yellowish or buff square spots forming the underside band. Males, if spotted, have the spots of the band yellowish. Portions of the band are always equally developed, as contrasted with the common condition in *H. c. tildeni*. With increased elevation the upper surface becomes deeper orange and the spots below paler, whitish in females. Where these populations approach those of *harpalus*, i.e., near the Sierran crest, the upper surface becomes tawny and the spots below white. Wingspread, 22–30 mm.

Early Stages: These are described by MacNeill (1964). In most respects these are entirely similar to those of *harpalus*, except that the pupa of this subspecies is covered with a glaucous bloom. The larval foodplant is not known.

Distribution: This subspecies occurs on the western slope of the Sierra Nevada in California. It flies mainly from late July through September, but a few individuals may appear in early July or even in June. Such early flying individuals should be checked carefully. The genitalia may need to be examined, because the rather rare *H. lindseyi* of this region flies at that time and is virtually indistinguishable from local *comma* by wing markings alone.

(g) **leussleri** Lindsey. Plate 88, figure 3, ♂; figure 4, ♀. These skippers are rich orange above and the hind wings below are yellowish green to pale orange. The spots of the macular band are pale orange or cream in males, and in females are white but not lustrous, often extended outward along the veins as in *H. lindseyi*. The latter species, however, is not known from the region inhabited by typical populations of this subspecies. North of these typical populations is a series of blend zone populations which combine features of *leussleri* with those of three other subspecies which converge geographically from the north, introducing characteristics of smaller size, paler color and pearly white spots. Wingspread, 25–34 mm.

Distribution: This subspecies is present in the peninsular ranges of southern California and northern Baja California. Adults fly in early summer.

(h) **tildeni** Freeman. Plate 90, figure 34, ♂. This small subspecies is much like the foothill populations of *yosemite* but is much more variable, and in a different way, on the lower surface of the hind wings. The general color below is pale orange to light brown with a vague purple tint. The spots of the band are variously yellowish or cream, never truly white, and whole sections of the posterior arm of the macular band may be absent while all other spots are of normal size. The dark border of the upper surface may be broad and dark or almost suppressed by a heavy suffusion of tawny scaling. The wings of males are generally more rounded than in other subspecies. Wingspread, 22–30 mm.

Early Stages: The immatue stages are similar to those of *yosemite*. The larval foodplant is Pine Bluegrass (*Poa scabrella*), a small, sparsely tufted bunchgrass.

Distribution: This subspecies occupies the dry inner coast ranges of central California from Lake county south to San Luis Obispo county. Adults fly in late summer, chiefly during August and September.

(i) **dodgei** (Bell). Plate 90, figure 33, ♂. This subspecies is perhaps the most easily recognized of the assemblage owing to the peculiar rich chocolate, or even sooty brown to yellow-brown, of the hind wings below. The spots of the macular band on this surface are yellow-buff or whitish but never lustrous. As in *tildeni* entire sections of the posterior arm of this band may be wanting, and rarely some specimens are immaculate beneath. The upper surface is generally dark with a reddish orange discal area and a broad dark border, but varies to a pale and extensive yellow-orange with a narrow border. Wingspread, 26–34 mm.

Early Stages: The egg is not unlike that of other subspecies except that the reticulation is somewhat more pronounced. The shape of the egg is less smoothly hemispherical, being more prominently angled toward the flattened summit from about half the height of the egg. The pupa lacks a glaucous bloom. In Marin county, California, the preferred larval foodplant is Red Fescue (*Festuca rubra*), an ample, needle-bladed, perennial bunchgrass.

Distribution: This subspecies is confined to the outer coast ranges of central California from Monterey Bay north to Sonoma county. Adults are present from late July to September.

(j) **oregonia** (Edwards). Plate 88, figure 19, ♂; figure 20, ♀. These are rather reddish orange insects above, with the dark borders suffused with orange scaling. The lower surface of the hind wings is fairly uniform dark or light golden olive; the spots of the band are dull whitish to yellowish in males and white or whitish in females but never with the pearly luster of the Great Basin subspecies. Wingspread, 28–36 mm.

Early Stages: The early stages of more northern populations of this subspecies were described by Hardy under the name *H. comma manitoba.* The preferred larval foodplants on Vancouver Island are *Lolium* and *Bromus.*

Distribution: This subspecies is distributed mostly west of the Great Basin in the Cascade Ranges of the Pacific slope from northern California to British Columbia. Populations are also present in northern Idaho. Adults fly mainly during July and August.

(k) **hulbirti** Lindsey. Plate 88, figure 11, ♂; figure 12, ♀. These small skippers with rounded wings are like the preceding subspecies in coloration. They may be distinguished from *oregonia* by the darker tawny above and the rather shaggy appearance of the dark golden hind wings below. The short antennal shaft and long club are more like those of *manitoba,* as is the great length of the hairs on the head, especially the eyelash. Wingspread, 24–30 mm.

Distribution: This subspecies is known only from Olympic National Park in Washington.

(l) **ochracea** Lindsey. Plate 88, figure 9, ♂; figure 10, ♀. Adults are large, broad-winged insects with the orange of the upper surface pale but warm in tone, heavily suffusing the darker markings. Below, the hind wings are uniform rich yellow-orange, often greenish in females. The spots of the macular band vary from pale orange to white in males, always white in females, and not conspicuously outlined in black as are those of most other *comma* subspecies. Often several of these spots are wanting and rarely the entire band is missing. Insects such as these are typical of lower elevations adjacent to the prairies. With increased elevation the populations become more variable in markings and in size. Many populations from somewhat higher elevations closely resemble *leussleri* of southern California and constitute some of the many blend zone populations of *ochracea* with other subspecies to the northeast, to the north and west, and to the southwest. Wingspread, 26–32 mm.

Distribution: This subspecies occurs along the east slope of the Rocky Mountains, in Colorado, New Mexico and Wyoming. It flies during July and August.

(m) **colorado** (Scudder). Plate 89, figure 9, ♂; figure 10, ♀. This subspecies is small and rather dark with pointed fore wings. The hind wings are dark below with distinctly greenish overscaling and have the linear posterior arm of the macular band below forming an acute chevron with the short anterior arm. The spots are lustrous white and usually narrow. Wingspread, 26–30 mm.

Distribution: This is a high elevation inhabitant, known only from higher altitudes in the Rocky Mountains of Colorado. It is to be expected principally between 9000 and 11,000 ft., where it flies in July and August.

(n) **susanae** Miller. Plate 90, figure 35, ♂. Adults are dark, the orange above with a distinct reddish tint and the hind wings below usually dark brownish to golden orange. The spots of the macular band are white in both sexes. This subspecies much resembles *manitoba* in coloration and wing pattern, but it is larger, has pointed wings, the head has shorter hairs, the antennal shaft is long and the club is small, just the reverse of the condition in *manitoba*. Wingspread, 28–34 mm.

Early Stages: The egg is larger and more evenly hemispherical than those of other *comma* subspecies, but otherwise it is quite similar. The preferred larval foodplant is not known.

Distribution: This subspecies ranges through the boreal areas of Arizona and New Mexico and it is also known from western Texas. Adults fly principally from July to September, but there are records for April and June in Arizona, for June in New Mexico and for November in Texas. No records are presently known for Mexico but it unquestionably occurs in the Sierra Madre Occidental.

4. **Hesperia woodgatei** (Williams). Plate 89, figure 11, ♂; figure 12, ♀. These are large insects with a very warm, reddish orange-fulvous color above and a fairly small stigma on broad, rather rounded, wings. The interior "felt" of the stigma is black. The border of the upper surface is rather broad and inwardly diffuse. The hind wing below is brownish to dark yellow-green or olive-brown, with the spots of the macular band small to medium sized, white, rather rounded and generally separated from one another. The posterior arm of the band is not parallel to the outer wing margin, diverging somewhat basad at the anal end. The shaft of the antenna is exceedingly long relative to the very small club, and there is usually (except in Texas) a conspicuous white ring at the base of the antennal club. Wingspread, 30–40 mm.

Early Stages: The egg is large, about 1.4 mm in diameter and smoothly granular without distinct reticulation except under high magnification; it is yellowish cream at first, changing to dull chalky white with an irregular blue-gray blotch which represents the developing head capsule of the young larva within.

Distribution: This species occurs through the boreal mountains of Arizona, New Mexico and probably also northern Mexico. Some isolated populations are known from Kerr and Travis counties in Texas. The species has been rather uncommon in collections, largely because it flies late in the season, in September and October.

5. **Hesperia ottoe** Edwards. Plate 89, figure 7, ♂; figure 8, ♀. This is one of the three pale tawny prairie species with almost unmarked wings below. *H. ottoe* is related to the preceding group of species although it bears little superficial resemblance to them. The male genitalia are like those of that group and, like them, *ottoe* has blackish or gray "felt" within the male stigma. This latter character is one of the simplest ways to separate males of *ottoe* from *pawnee* which has yellow stigma "felt." Females of *ottoe* generally have the inner edge of the marginal border diffuse and vaguely defined. The pale spot on the fore wing below the end of the cell is generally somewhat rounded and whitish hyaline, and at best outwardly edged with pale orange. The spots on the hind wing above are pale orange and vaguely defined, if present. Females of *pawnee* have well defined, squarish white spots on the fore wing above and better demarked spots on the hind wings. Males and females of *dacotae* more closely resemble *ottoe* but are much smaller, with less pointed fore wings. All three of these species are generally smoothly yellow-tawny on the lower surface with little or no indication of a macular band, especially in males. Females of *ottoe* frequently have a few small darker spots on the hind wings, or rarely pale cream spots, and *pawnee* commonly has several squarish pale cream spots in a macular band. Wingspread 30–39 mm.

Early Stages: These have been described by Nielsen for the dark Michigan population under the name of *H. pawnee* (later corrected by him to *ottoe*). The egg is white, smooth and hemispherical, and gradually turns dull yellowish with the dark brown head of the larva visible inside. The head of the mature larva is dark brown. The larval foodplant in Michigan is Fall Witchgrass (*Leptoloma cognatum*).

Distribution: This is a prairie inhabitant, found in generally undisturbed prairies from Iowa to South Dakota, west to Colorado and south to Texas. A dark population is also present in Michigan. The species flies in June, July and into early August. This flight period is generally sufficient to separate *ottoe* from the later flying *pawnee*.

6. **Hesperia leonardus** Harris. Plate 90, figure 36, ♂; figure 37, ♀. This distinctive looking insect is closely related to the three following, very different-appearing, skippers; areas where these species approach one another geographically should be critically collected for evidence of intergradation. Such intergradation has recently been demonstrated between *leonardus* and *pawnee* in Minnesota (Nordin, *in litt.*), and perhaps between *pawnee* and *pahaska* in Colorado (Scott, *in litt.*). Continued careful collecting should provide further information on whether these four (*leonardus, pawnee, pahaska* and *columbia*) are actually as reproductively isolated as was once thought.

This species is large and dark with a reddish cast to the orange of the upper surface. The dark borders are broad and in males the interior "felt" of the stigma is distinctly yellow. The hind wings below are brick red, with white, buff or yellow spots forming a macular band. The females above are mostly dark brown, with the orange restricted to a macular series of spots on both wings. Wingspread, 22–36 mm.

Early Stages: The early stages of *leonardus* have been reported by Scudder, Laurent and Dethier. The egg is large, about 1.3 mm in diameter, dead white with a slight green tint, and minutely reticulate. First stage larvae are cream with a dark reddish brown head. The head of the mature larva is black with two irregular cream patches and a pair of parallel vertical cream stripes on the face. The pupa is nondescript brown and green. The tongue case is free beyond the wing pads for a distance slightly less than halfway to the end of the abdomen. The preferred foodplants of this species in nature are reported to be *Agrostis, Panicum virgatum* and *Eragrostis alba.*

Distribution: This species is eastern, ranging from Ontario to Nova Scotia and Maine and south at least to the Carolinas and Alabama. Early literature also indicates Georgia and Florida but there seem to be no recent records. The species extends westward to Minnesota, Missouri, Arkansas and Louisiana. The northeastern populations in Canada and New England have the spots of the macular band white or slightly yellow, constituting the nominate subspecies. To the west and south populations have those spots increasingly darker yellow to nearly orange, and these have been described as the subspecies *H. leonardus stallingsi* Freeman. The transition from one to the other seems so gradual that subspecies may be less useful than a simple clinal designation. In any case, the western forms (*stallingsi*) both geographically and in color pattern approach eastern populations of *H. pawnee,* and hybrid populations in Minnesota contain all degrees of intermediacy between dark *pawnee* and *stallingsi.* This insect flies during August and September.

7. **Hesperia pawnee** Dodge. Plate 90, figure 38, ♂; figure 39, ♀.   This is another of the large, pale tawny prairie species, long confused with *ottoe* of the same general region. *H. pawnee* has a somewhat longer stigma than *ottoe,* and the interior "felt" is distinctly yellow. Males are often immaculate tawny yellow on the hind wings beneath, but they frequently show traces of whitish or pale yellow separated spots forming a macular band. Females are usually dark above, although the dark areas may be heavily suffused with tawny overscaling. The spots of the fore wings are pale, usually whitish and rather quadrate, and they contrast with the inwardly sharply defined border. The spots on the hind wing may be discrete and contrasting or vague. The hind wings below in females are grayish yellow, bright yellow, or golden with a greenish tint; often, separated squarish white or buff spots from a macular band. Wingspread, 30–38 mm.

Early Stages: These have not been described.

Distribution: This species ranges from Manitoba and Saskatchewan south through the prairie states to Kansas, and from Colorado on the west to Minnesota and Iowa on the east. A supposedly very dark form "montana" has been described. I have seen specimens from Colorado that I suspect are hybrids between *pawnee* and *pahaska* which seem to best match the description of "montana." Scott has recently discovered a Colorado population of possible hybrids between these two species, and these also seem close to my concept of "montana."

8. **Hesperia pahaska** Leussler. This species is geographically variable, with three recognized subspecies. It is orange or tawny above and males have a long stigma, the interior "felt" of which is distinctly yellow. Both sexes have well developed white spots on the lower surface of the hind wing, including a white bar costally over the base of the cell. The shape of the posterior arm of the macular band is commonly linear or concave outward, so that it may be more or less parallel to the wing margin.

(a) **pahaska** Leussler. Plate 88, figure 21, ♂; figure 22, ♀. These insects are dull tawny above with a dark border that is usually broad at the apex and narrow at the anal angle of the male fore wings. Females usually have the tawny orange above restricted by a broad, well defined dark border. The macular band on the hind wing below is composed of joined, angulate white spots which often are larger near the anal angle; the inner edge of the band may diverge from the wing margin, as in the species related to *comma,* while the outer edge of the band is parallel to the wing margin. In females this band may be distinctly concave outwardly, as in *viridis.* The well defined pattern on the upper surface, however, should serve to separate such females from those of *viridis.* Wingspread, 28–38 mm.

Early Stages: Scott (*in litt.*) has found *Bouteloua gracilis* to be the foodplant.

Distribution: This subspecies occupies the western prairie and Rocky Mountain foothills from Canada to Kansas; in New Mexico and boreal central Arizona it approaches, and is modified by, the other two subspecies. It flies during June and July, with a few records for August. It is thus isolated for the most part from *pawnee,* but August flying individuals of each might meet.

(b) **williamsi** Lindsey. Plate 89, figure 13, ♂; figure 14, ♀. This subspecies is extensively pale tawny orange above; the white spots of the macular band are small, often rounded, and separated. Commonly this band is distinctly concave outwardly, much as in *viridis.* Males can be separated readily from that species by the yellow "felt" of the stigma, and females by the contrasting upper wing pattern. Some males with a relatively straight posterior arm of the macular band can closely resemble examples of *columbia* but that species seldom has a white bar over the base of the cell on the hind wing below. Wingspread, 28–36 mm.

Distribution: This subspecies ranges through the high austral regions of southern Arizona, Sonora, Chihuahua and western Texas. It is also present in northern Baja California, where it closely resembles *columbia.*

(c) **martini** MacNeill. Plate 88, figure 23, ♂; figure 24, ♀. This subspecies is characteristically large and brightly marked. The bright, warm, tawny orange above and the large white spots below, contrasting with the distinctly greenish orange overscaling, present a distinctive appearance. The white spots of the macular band, although separated by olive-scaled veins, are larger than those of the nominate subspecies. This band is usually concave outwardly as in *viridis.* Wingspread 28–38 mm.

Early stages: The egg is large, about 1.4 mm in diameter and evenly hemispherical.

It is cream white after oviposition but acquires a green tint within several days. A conspicuous gray darkening of the upper fourth of the egg appears within a week. The head of the half grown larva is dark brown with two short, cream, parallel vertical dashes high on the face and a pale brown patch low on the face in front of the ocelli. The larval foodplant is *Tridens pulchellus,* a small, low-growing desert bunchgrass. The larval shelter of older caterpillars is partly subterranean.

Distribution: This subspecies occurs from the New York, Providence, Ivanpah and Clark mountains of southeastern California across southern Nevada and north-western Arizona, and across southern Utah and into northeastern Arizona. Adults fly in September. Evidently there is a partial spring brood as well, as there are also records for May, June and July.

9. **Hesperia columbia** (Scudder). Plate 90, figure 16, ♂; figure 17, ♀. This distinctive little species is bright or dark orange above. The male stigma seems broad because of a dusky area adjacent outwardly, and the interior "felt" is distinctly yellow. The hind wings below are yellow-orange to greenish golden, with a slender (in males) straight posterior arm of the macular band composed of connected, or in females often disconnected, lustrous white spots. The portions of the macular band anterior to the cell are usually absent, and there is no white bar over the base of the cell. The spots on this wing surface in females are variable in size; that at the end of the cell is often conspicuously larger than the others, some of which may be missing. This species is closely associated with chaparral communities. Wingspread, 22–34 mm.

Early Stages: The large egg (about 1.3 mm in diameter) is white with a greenish tint, changing to dead white. In profile it is smoothly hemispherical and the reticulation is weak, invisible except under high magnification. The head of the mature larva is dark brown with two sets of short parallel cream dashes, high and low on the face, and a pale cream inverted V in front between the two sets. The pupa is pale brown with irregular dark brown mottling. The tongue case is long, extending free beyond the tip of the wing pads nearly half the distance to the end of the abdomen. The hairs on the thorax and abdomen are simple, straight and erect, not terminally hooked. The preferred larval food in Marin county, California, is *Koeleria cristata,* a small bunchgrass common about the dry margins of the chaparral.

Distribution: This species is restricted to the Pacific Slope, ranging from northern Baja California through western California to western Oregon. It is double brooded, flying from March through June, rarely into July, and again in September and October.

10. **Hesperia metea** Scudder. This small dark species has the tawny color above restricted and often of a cold olive tint. Commonly in females the only paler area on the upper surface is a macular series of pale yellowish or white spots, but these may be wanting. The lower surface is blackish, often with a reddish tawny over-scaling; the white macular band spots are extended outward along the veins in paler specimens, somewhat recalling the condition in *uncas.* Some populations are so dark

that many adults, especially females, may be immaculate sooty brown to black above and below. The stigma is slender and distinctly angled away from the cell for more than its lower half. The interior "felt" is black. Most populations represent the typical subspecies. A remarkably dark series of populations comprises a second subspecies.

(a) **metea** Scudder. Plate 89, figure 5, ♂; figure 6, ♀.   Paler adults are brown to sooty black with pale spots and a moderate suffusion of cold olive-tawny. Females often lack this suffusion and the spots are whitish. The lower surface of the hind wings is dark, often with an olive overscaling and the macular band is white, often conspicuously extended along the veins. This skipper, like *Atrytonopsis hianna* with which it is often found, is dependent upon a larval foodplant that is a fire pioneer. This grass appears for a few years following a fire, then, as succession proceeds, the grass is replaced by other plants. Therefore both the grass and the skipper are then transient species, not permanent parts of the biota in such sites. On serpentine barrens, shale barrens and some of the eastern pine barrens, where soil conditions are limiting to competitive plants, the grass evidently does form a stable part of the flora; in such areas *metea* colonies can exist as permanent residents. Wingspread, 24–36 mm.

Early Stages: The larval foodplant is Bluestem Beard Grass (*Andropogon scoparius*). The dead white egg is small, a little over 1 mm in diameter, finely reticulate and hemispherical but flattened at the summit. First stage larvae are as described for the genus. Half grown larvae, according to Laurent, are dark green, almost brown. Mature larvae are brown with a distinct greenish narrow dorsal line. The pupa is at first green but after two days becomes a "drab color."

Distribution: This subspecies occupies most of the range of the species from Maine to Michigan and south to Florida and Mississippi. Adults are present in different parts of the range in April, May or June. According to Shapiro the flight period of any particular colony is generally very short. In Pennsylvania the first males appear about May 6 and are gone by May 25. Females are first seen around May 12 and may still be present as late as June 1.

(b) **licinus** (Edwards). Plate 89, figure 3, ♂; figure 4, ♀.   This blackish insect is much darker both above and below than the nominate subspecies. On the hind wings below the macular band in males varies from an obscure grayish line to a well defined grayish white band, whereas females are usually immaculate. Wingspread, 29–36 mm.

Distribution: This subspecies is known only from Texas and Arkansas. Specimens from Georgia to Mississippi, however, show tendencies toward this subspecies and a careful analysis might well demonstrate a large zone of intergradation between the two east and north of Texas. This subspecies flies in late March and April.

11. **Hesperia viridis** (Edwards). Plate 89, figure 15, ♂; figure 16, ♀.   This species seems to be distantly related to both *metea* and *attalus,* although it superficially looks like neither. This orange-tawny species has a heavy tawny suffusion over the broad, dark, inwardly diffuse borders. The male stigma is slender and more than the lower half is bent away from the posterior edge of the cell. The interior "felt" is black. The

hind wings below are bright greenish orange to yellowish orange and the spots of the macular band are white, usually distinctly outlined with black. The macular band is generally conspicuously outwardly concave, occasionally just parallel to the outer margin in females; in this characteristic *viridis* can only be confused with *pahaska*. Males are easily distinguished from that species by the slender stigma half of which is bent away from the cell, and by the color of the interior "felt" of the stigma (black in *viridis,* yellow in *pahaska*). Females are more difficult to separate from those of *pahaska* without resort to technical details of the genitalia. Generally females of *viridis* are so suffused with tawny orange scaling above that the markings all appear vague, even in dark specimens, whereas females of *pahaska* usually have contrasting, rather well defined markings on the upper surface. The two species frequently fly together, sometimes with males of one species and females of the other dominant, so some care may be necessary to properly identify these two species. Populations of *viridis* from Arizona tend to be slightly larger and darker with a reddish cast than specimens from other areas. Wingspread, 30–40 mm.

Early Stages: The immature stages have not been described. The larval foodplant in nature is presumed to be Blue Grama (*Bouteloua gracilis*) by MacNeill and by Kendall. This has been confirmed as the foodplant in Colorado by the observations of Scott (*in litt.*). Kendall has reared the species successfully in the laboratory on Perennial Ryegrass (*Lolium perenne*), a naturalized native of Europe.

Distribution: This species is found on the hills or prairies of Kansas, Oklahoma and Texas, west into the mountains of Colorado, New Mexico and Arizona. Records for California and western Nevada are based upon mislabeled or misidentified specimens. This species extends southward well into Mexico in the Sierra Madre Occidental. Adults have been taken in April through August, and October. Kendall suggests that the species is double brooded in Texas, the first appearing from April through June, and another from August to October.

12. **Hesperia attalus** (Edwards). Plate 89, figure 19, ♂; figure 20, ♀ (both ssp. *attalus*). This skipper has pointed fore wings and varies from broadly tawny orange above to very dark with broad, well defined borders and the cold tawny restricted to discal spots. Females tend to be dark grayish brown above with tawny or whitish spots. The lower surface of the hind wings in males varies from pale yellowish orange to dusky yellow or dark olive and the spots of the macular band are very small, yellowish or whitish and separated, or they may be wanting. Females are similar but generally a little darker; the spots tend to be whitish and often several are missing. The male stigma is slender and more than the lower half is bent away from the posterior edge of the cell. The interior "felt" of the stigma is black. This species sometimes resembles *meskei* but the tawny orange of the upper surface of *attalus* is much paler and colder, the underside of the secondaries not as richly dusky orange and the anal fold and costal area not contrastingly pure orange as in that species. *H. attalus* is seldom collected and its habits are not well understood. It evidently is partial to pine barrens. Wingspread, 26–36 mm.

Distribution: This species has been reported from Nebraska and Wisconsin east to Massachusetts and south to Georgia and Texas. Populations within the above range are more or less extensively pale tawny above and below and comprise the nominate subspecies. Specimens from Florida are generally much darker above and below with restricted tawny spots above and are referred to the subspecies *H. attalus slossonae* (Skinner). The species is recorded in June in Nebraska and is known to fly in May and September in Texas, during August and September in Mississippi, and in Florida from February to May and in October and November.

13. **Hesperia meskei** (Edwards). Plate 89, figure 21, ♂; figure 22, ♀. This is a dark insect above with restricted but rich orange spots on both wings. The male stigma has the interior "felt" black, and there is usually a diffuse sooty patch broadly bordering the outside of the stigma. On the lower surface of the hind wing orange scaling densely overlies a dark wing providing a rich orange or reddish olive, slightly sooty everywhere but along the anal fold and the costal margin, which are pure orange. A macular band of slightly paler orange spots is usually at least faintly indicated, the spots often ill defined. This is another seldom collected skipper and nothing is known of its life history. Wingspread, 28–36 mm.

Distribution: This species is known from only a few localities, from Arkansas and Texas east to Florida, and Georgia and North Carolina.

14. **Hesperia dacotae** (Skinner). Plate 89, figure 23, ♂; figure 24, ♀. This is a fairly small, broadly tawny species with rather stubby wings. It somewhat resembles a small *ottoe* in general pattern and the female has a hyaline spot on the fore wing below the end of the cell as does female *ottoe*. Both sexes above are generally vaguely marked because of a broad tawny suffusion over the darker markings, distinguishing this species from *sassacus* which it otherwise closely resembles in wing shape and somewhat in maculation below. The male stigma has the interior "felt" black. The lower surface of the hind wings is yellow-tawny in males, golden gray in females, and the spots of the macular band are yellowish, often poorly defined and squarish, or they may be lacking. These spots seldom contrast much with the overall wing color. Females may be immaculate below, or they may have a few or all spots of the band present; such spots may be scarcely discernible or fairly well defined. This species is rare in collections and few colonies are known. It seems to be confined to moist undisturbed prairie. Wingspread, 25–35 mm.

Distribution: H. dakotae is confined to the northern prairie region from Manitoba south into Minnesota, Iowa and Illinois and west to the Dakotas. It flies during June and July.

15. **Hesperia lindseyi** Holland. Plate 90, figure 26, ♂; figure 27, ♀. On the upperside this skipper is exceedingly similar to populations of *comma* that fly in the same area. It is tawny orange with broad or narrow borders that are inwardly diffuse. Females vary from broadly pale and tawny to restricted reddish tawny with heavy, contrasting dark markings above. The male stigma has the interior "felt" black. The hind wings below are brownish tawny to quite greenish; the spots of the macular band are

yellowish to buff in males, whitish in females, and characteristically angulate and extended conspicuously along the veins. The fringes at the ends of the veins are usually cut by black lines. Populations along the west slope of the central Sierra Nevada, however, generally do not have these distinctive pale veins and are thus extremely difficult to distinguish by wing markings from middle elevation populations of *comma yosemite* that fly in the same area. In most instances where both *lindseyi* and a subspecies of *comma* occur in the same locality and tend to look alike, *lindseyi* generally flies earlier and is essentially gone by the time *comma* adults appear. The two species are easily distinguished by characters of the genitalia, as they are not at all closely related. Wingspread, 24–34 mm.

Early Stages: The white to dull white egg is unusual. It is large, about 1.3 mm in diameter, rather low and broadly flattened with a distinctly flanged base. It is heavily reticulate, more so than the eggs of *comma* or *juba*. The head of the mature larva is brown with two short parallel cream vertical bars high on the front of the face, and an inverted V-shaped cream white mark below. The pupa is pale brown without dark mottling. The tongue case is long, extending free beyond the wing pads well over half the distance to the end of the abdomen. The hairs are simple, somewhat gently curved and not terminally hooked. The pupa is covered with a light waxy bloom. This species spends most of both summer and winter as a fully formed larva within the egg in a diapause state; the larva will not hatch unless exposed to special sequences of temperatures. Some populations of this insect are still more remarkable in that the females do not oviposit on the larval foodplant but instead seek out clumps of a particular arboreal lichen (*Usnea florida*), whether on a fence post or forty feet up in a tree, on which to deposit their eggs. Upon hatching the first stage larvae then must travel considerable distances to locate an acceptable foodplant. In Marin county, California, these foodplants are *Festuca idahoensis* and *Danthonia californica*. Where these grasses are close-cropped by grazing, the larvae construct partly subterranean shelters.

Distribution: This species ranges along the Pacific Slope from western Oregon south in the coastal mountains to Riverside county, California. It also occurs along the lower and middle elevations of the Sierra Nevada, in northeastern California, adjacent western Nevada and doubtless also southeastern Oregon. Throughout most of California the species flies during May and June. More northern populations appear in June and fly through July.

16. **Hesperia sassacus** Harris. Plate 90, figure 25, ♂; figure 30, ♀. This fairly small, bright orange skipper has a broad, rather well defined dark, somewhat dentate border above. The hind wing border is particularly deeply dentate. The male stigma has the interior "felt" black. The wings below are yellowish brown or tawny olive with the spots of the macular band usually large and yellow but often not greatly contrasting with the remainder of the wing. These spots are usually, at least outwardly, extended along the veins. This species inhabits open fields and meadows. Wingspread, 26–34 mm.

Early Stages: These have been partly described by Fletcher and by Scudder. The egg is pale greenish, almost chalk white, with a pearly luster. It ultimately changes to sullied yellow. The egg is not large, being scarcely over 1 mm in diameter, and is broadly hemispherical. The first stage larva is as usual for the genus but is more plump than most other *Hesperia*. The larval foodplant in Georgia has been suggested to be Crabgrass (*Digitaria sanguinalis*), an introduced European species. The preferred native foodplant is reported by Comstock to be a species of *Panicum*.

Distribution: This species occurs from Maine and southern Ontario westward to Wisconsin and Iowa and south to Virginia and Tennessee. Reports of *sassacus* from Florida require verification. This is one of the early flying skippers throughout its range, appearing in the north in May; records run through July. It is said to be double brooded in the southern portion of its range.

17. **Hesperia miriamae** MacNeill. Plate 90, figure 28, ♂; figure 29, ♀. This coldly tawny species has a distinctive washed-out appearance above. The apical spots on the fore wing are usually large. Fresh specimens have a distinctive sheen to both surfaces of the wings. The veins and anal fold of the hind wings are dark above. The stigma has black interior "felt." The hind wings below are lustrous grayish blue or lustrous pale gold, and the spots of the macular band are large and lustrous white or lustrous cream. Because of the overall sheen of the hind wings below, the shining macular band often does not greatly contrast with the remainder of the wing even though the spots are bright. This is the most truly alpine species of the genus. It inhabits rocky fell-fields, benches and summits well above timberline and flies usually between the altitudes of 11,000 to over 14,000 ft. Wingspread, 28–34 mm.

Early Stages: The larval foodplant is Bluestem Beard Grass (*Andropogon scoparius*). with a pearly luster changing through dull creamy white with a salmon pink blot, to dirty yellow cream with an irregular gray blot, the head capsule of the developing larva within. The reticulation is uniformly weak, and the egg is rounded hemispherical with a broad summit.

Distribution: Hesperia miriamae is known only from the crest region of the central Sierra Nevada of California and from the equally high White Mountains in eastern California and western Nevada. The species flies in late summer, from late July through August and probably early September.

18. **Hesperia nevada** (Scudder). Plate 90, figure 21, ♂; figure 22, ♀. This small, brightly colored species has tawny orange wings and a narrow or broad inwardly diffuse border. Females vary from broadly tawny orange to rather dark with restricted pale orange above. The male stigma has black interior "felt." The hind wings below are dark grayish green or golden green with lustrous white spots angulate or crescent shaped, forming a very irregular macular band. The most anal spot of this band is much offset basad, and the pair of spots at the vertex of the macular "chevron" are offset outwardly, giving the posterior arm a three-stepped irregularity. *H. juba, comma manitoba* and *miriamae* also often have the more anal spot of the band offset basally, but seldom to the same degree. *H. juba* is larger and has more pointed wings; *H. comma manitoba* is of similar size but is much darker and deeper

orange; and *miriamae* is pale and washed-out above and bluish or pale brassy gold below. *H. uncas macswaini* males often closely resemble *H. nevada* also, but the posterior arm of the macular band is not especially irregular in *macswaini*. Wingspread, 26–34 mm.

Early Stages: The egg is about 1.4 mm in diameter, smoothly hemispherical, weakly reticulate and not lustrous. The color is initially cream white, soon becoming slightly greenish, then changing to dull white with gray above. The head of the nearly grown larva is blackish with several irregular pale brown and creamy white markings on the face. The preferred foodplant in California is Western Needlegrass (*Stipa occidentalis*).

Distribution: This species ranges through the boreal regions of, and the boreal slopes bordering, the Great Basin from interior British Columbia, eastern Washington, Oregon and California eastward through the higher parts of Nevada and Utah and into the Rocky Mountains from Alberta to Colorado, south to New Mexico and Arizona.

Genus POMPEIUS Evans

This genus is comprised of about six species, most of which are tropical American, brown skippers of medium size, the males all with a black stigma. Several, if not all, of the species, seem rather closely related to the genus *Polites,* from which they differ in having slightly larger antennae and a larger apiculus on the club. One species occurs in our area.

1. **Pompeius verna** (Edwards). Plate 87, figure 26, ♂; figure 27, ♀.   This is a blackish or dark brown skipper with distinctive whitish and squarish hyaline spots on the fore wing, particularly the large spot below the end of the cell. This whitish, almost glassy, square spot will help separate females of *verna* from those of other common eastern species of *Polites, Wallengrenia* and from *Euphyes vestris,* with which they may sometimes be confused. *P. verna* is dark brown beneath, with the fore wing spots repeated and the hind wings almost unmarked or with poorly defined small pale spots, often purplish in males and vaguely tinged yellowish in females. Wingspread, 24–32 mm.

Early Stages: The egg is small, about 0.85 mm in diameter and rounded hemispherical. It is bone white or very pale green, and finely reticulate. The first stage larva is cream at first, then greenish; the head is almost black. Half grown larvae are light green with numerous minute black spine-like hairs scattered over the body. There is a dark green dorsal line and a subdorsal line on each side, and the body is covered with numerous whitish spots. The head is blackish. Mature larvae are similar but yellowish green to yellowish brown profusely flecked with minute dark brown spots. The hairs are pale and the body stripes dark, comprised of one mid-dorsal stripe and three pairs on the sides. The head is dark red-brown, edged behind with black. The foodplant is *Tridens flavus.*

Distribution: This widely distributed and rather common eastern species is found from New England and Michigan westward to Nebraska and south to Texas and Georgia. In New England it flies in June, in Mississippi during April, May, July and August. Colorado records require verification.

Genus WALLENGRENIA Berg

This is a small genus of at least three species. The interrelationships of the several South American and West Indian populations are not well understood and there may be more species represented than is now thought. The two recognized here which occur north of Mexico have long been considered as forms of a single species. This genus is closely related to *Polites* and is similar except that the male stigma is complex, with several different regions of scale modification. Superficially, the black part of the stigma appears to be widely divided into two sections by a patch of lustrous plate-like scales. Both species treated here are basically brownish although one species has much orange-tawny scaling on the upper surface.

1. **Wallengrenia otho** (J. E. Smith). Plate 87, figure 22, ♂; figure 23, ♀. This species characteristically has yellow-orange areas on the upper surface in the cell and costal regions of males and in the dorsal spots of females. The lower surface is reddish orange or reddish brown. There is a curved band of small paler spots on the hind wings beneath which may be almost obscure. Wingspread, 24–32 mm.

Early Stages: Reports of immature stages by Scudder and by Laurent probably refer to *egeremet* and will be considered under that name. Kendall reports that the larvae are case-bearers, cutting off circular discs of material (presumably leaf parts in nature; paper facial tissue was utilized in the laboratory) and carrying these over themselves. The larvae readily feed in confinement upon St. Augustine Grass (*Stenotaphrum secundatum*) in Texas.

Distribution: This is a more southern species than the following, although there is a broad region of overlap. *W. otho* is reported from as far north as Maryland and Virginia; otherwise the range seems restricted to Georgia, Florida, the Gulf states, Texas southward through Mexico to Costa Rica. It flies from April to October.

2. **Wallengrenia egeremet** (Scudder). Plate 87, figure 24, ♂; figure 25, ♀. This is much like *otho* but is darker and with little tawny color. The upper surface is sooty brown with just a few yellowish spots in the male, occasionally wanting; the spots of the female are few, and yellowish to whitish rather than orange as in *otho*. The lower surface is brownish with a curved band of buff spots on the hind wings, often barely discernible. Females might be confused with females of *Euphyes vestris metacomet, Pompeius verna* or even *Polites vibex.* The underside of the hind wings will immediately distinguish *vibex.* The large squarish glassy spot on the fore wing of *P. verna* will separate that species. *Euphyes vestris* females are duller brown than *egeremet* and the spots of the fore wing above are usually whiter, smaller and somewhat

hyaline or, if small and slightly yellow, the spot below the end of the cell is not inwardly squarish. The middle tibiae of *E. vestris* lack spines, which are well developed in the other species. Wingspread, 24–32 mm.

Early Stages: Descriptions by Scudder and Laurent of immature stages, under the names *T. aetna* and *P. otho* respectively, are believed to refer to this species. Descriptions of the egg and larva were published also by Dethier. The egg is less than 1 mm in diameter, clearly reticulate and pale green or yellowish white. The first stage larva is whitish, changing to greenish after feeding. The body is uniformly sprinkled with round dark brown spots and short dark hairs; the head is blackish. Half grown larvae are greenish brown with a distinct dorsal line. Mature larvae are pale green with a profuse and uniform mottling of dark green. The dorsal line is dark green, broadly bordered by dull yellowish green, and there are a pair each of indistinct greenish lines and yellowish stripes on the sides. The head is chocolate brown with a central dark streak bordered by pale vertical stripes on the face. The pupa is greenish brown on the head, green on the thorax and yellow-green on the abdomen. The tongue case is long, extending free beyond the wing cases nearly to the end of the abdomen. (This diagnosis of the pupa may actually apply to *otho* as it was taken by Scudder from a drawing of a Georgia specimen.) The larval foodplant is *Panicum* according to Comstock. Shapiro indicates that larger species of *Panicum* are preferred, such as *P. clandestinum.*

Distribution: This species ranges from Quebec and Ontario south to Florida and Texas. It flies from June to August.

Genus POLITES Scudder

This is a genus of ten somewhat small, mostly orange or tawny skippers with generally distinctive patterns on the hind wings below. The antennae are rather short, with a stout club and a moderately long apiculus. The last segment of the palpi does not much protrude beyond the hairs of the second segment. The tibiae of all legs are spined. Males of most species have a prominent, almost S-shaped, stigma. This is an American genus ranging from Canada to Argentina. Some populations of all ten species come within the scope of this book.

1. **Polites coras** (Cramer). Plate 90, figure 1, ♂; figure 2, ♀. This small species has restricted tawny orange marks on the upper surface of both wings. Males have a distinctive broad grayish brown patch of specialized scales next to the outside of the stigma and extending to the dark border. The hind wings below are characteristic, often somewhat reminiscent of some *Poanes,* in that the wing is reddish or orange-brown with very large squarish yellow spots in a broad macular band and about the base. These spots are of different sizes, the one through the end of the cell very elongate. Those of the macular band are sometimes more or less coalesced with the basal spots making the wing essentially yellow, with a reddish brown border and a few similar colored spots or patches in the discal part of the wing. Wingspread, 20–26 mm.

Early Stages: These are described by Scudder and by Dethier. The egg is about 0.75 mm in diameter, globose hemispherical, reticulate and very pale green, nearly white at first. Ultimately it becomes heavily mottled on one side with thread-like branching lines of bright red. The first stage larva is at first whitish, becoming sullied green after feeding; the head is black. Halfgrown larvae are maroon, mottled with dirty white, and the head is black. The mature larva is dark maroon with light brown mottling; the head is black with a pair of short parallel vertical white streaks high on the face, and two whitish patches on each side of the face in front, one below the other. The pupa is dull reddish purple with white cases of the tongue, antennae, legs and wing pads. The tongue is long, extending free beyond the wing pads nearly to the end of the abdomen. The hairs are long and tawny, and there is a bluish bloom on the sides of the abdomen. The larvae have been reared in the laboratory upon a variety of grasses. The preferred foodplants in nature have not been reported.

Distribution: This species is distributed from the Atlantic coast of Canada south to Georgia and westward to British Columbia, Oregon, Montana, Colorado and Arizona. There are several broods in the south where it is not common, and one or two in the north. It is recorded from May to September.

2. **Polites sabuleti** (Boisduval). Plate 90, figure 3, ♂; figure 4, ♀. This small, usually broadly tawny, species has the dark border deeply dentate, especially on the hind wings above. Females generally have a little more extensive brown markings above, and some of the fore wing spots may be yellowish or almost white. The tone of the tawny markings above is variable: pale yellow in some populations, rich reddish orange in others. The hind wings below in males are generally buffy yellow or sandy colored with variable amounts of blackish overscaling except where the macular band and basal pale spots should be. This produces a series of pale spots, which may be so coalesced as to not be recognizable as such, of the same general color as the remainder of the wing but free of black scales. These spots are generally conspicuously extended both inward along the veins and outward toward the margin. Females are similar but the wings are usually darker so the spots are more contrasting. These lower wing surfaces, however, are variable geographically. A large number of different looking populations of the species are known, and some have received names. A few especially well marked populations are reminiscent of a diminutive *Hesperia,* being olive greenish with nearly white spots. Others are nearly chocolate below with conspicuous pale veins. Still others are almost gray, with little trace of tawny. By and large, all these different looking populations have in common a deeply dentate hind wing border above and pale veins outward from the macular band of the hind wing below. The male stigma is broad, and the gray-brown patch of scales on the outer side is no broader than the adjacent width of the stigma. Wingspread, 20–28 mm.

Early Stages: The egg is small, about 0.75 mm in diameter (Newcomer and Comstock report it to be as large as 1 mm), tall hemispherical, finely reticulate and delicate pale green to pale blue green at first, later becoming cream. First stage larvae are cream, becoming light green after feeding; the head is shiny black. Half grown larvae are brownish green or grayish green with brown or dull green mottling or small dots. The middorsal line is clear brown. Two lateral lines on each side are faintly indicated by the absence of mottling. The head is black, occasionally with a dull indistinct pattern. Mature larvae are dull green, heavily mottled with chocolate (central California) or light gray with numerous small brownish patches (southern Washington). The head is black with two whitish, short, parallel bars vertically high on the face, and a pale, interrupted W-shaped mark below. The pupa is initially clear green except on the abdomen where the general color is pale, mottled rusty brown. Later the wing pads and abdomen become yellowish. The tongue case is short, extending free scarcely beyond the tip of the wing pads. Lembert reported eggs of this species deposited in nature on a sedge (*Carex filifolium*) and a clover (*Trifolium*) and these have been cited several times subsequently as the foodplants. Both plants were doubtless "mistakes" made by female, a not uncommon occurrence in nature, but they are almost certainly not normally acceptable foodplants. Newcomer could not get this species to feed either on that sedge or on several clovers. Comstock reported the foodplant to be Bermuda Grass (*Cynodon dactylon*). *P. sabuleti* feeds naturally on several lawn grasses in central California.

Distribution: This western species is found from Washington to southern Baja California on the Pacific slope, eastward through the Great Basin to Colorado, and south through western Arizona well into Mexico on the western mainland. It occurs in California from sea level to well above timberline at elevations of 13,000 ft. or more. Throughout this considerable geographic and ecological range this species presents a great diversity of appearance. A detailed study of the relationships of its many forms has yet to be made. In Washington *sabuleti* is double brooded, flying in May and June, and again in August and September. In central California it may be encountered around urban lawns any time between March or April and November. In the high Sierra it flies from June to September.

3. **Polites draco** (Edwards). Plate 90, figure 5, ♂; figure 10, ♀. This species is a little larger than, but in many respects similar to, some populations of *sabuleti*. The brownish gray patch just outside the male stigma is larger, being somewhat broader than the width of the adjacent stigma. The brown border on the hind wings above in both sexes is usually broad and not as conspicuously and deeply dentate as in *sabuleti*. The orange of the hind wings above is more macular, reflecting the condition of the spots below. The lower surface is brownish to greenish, and the distinct and yellowish or whitish spots are not outwardly extended along the veins. Typically the spot through the end of the cell is much enlarged and elongate and so contrasts greatly with the rather small spots on each side; the anal spot is usually larger than the two preceding it, so the band presents a less uniform configuration than that in *sabuleti*. *P. draco* also resembles a small species of *Hesperia* because of the wing markings below. The early stages of this species have not been reported. Wingspread, 22–26 mm.

Distribution: This is a Rocky Mountain species, ranging from Alberta and Saskatchewan south through Montana, Wyoming, Colorado and New Mexico, west to Idaho, Arizona and Utah. It flies from June to August and in Colorado is found from 8000 to 12,000 ft.

4. **Polites mardon** (Edwards). Plate 90, figure 15, ♂; figure 20, ♀. This is a small orange skipper with stubby wings. The dark borders above are broad and occasionally dentate but not so deeply as are those of *sabuleti*. The male stigma is small; the gray-brown patch outside it is small, sometimes scarcely evident, and no broader than the width of the adjacent stigma. The lower surface of the hind wings is light reddish tan, sometimes rather profusely overscaled with gray-green. The spots are yellow and generally relatively large and squarish, but specimens with the greenish overscaling may have the spots softened at the edges and less contrasting. The lower surface of such specimens tends to have a soft, almost fuzzy, look, in part amplified by the relatively long, soft-looking fringes. This species has been extremely rare in collections, but a good colony was recently located by E. J. Newcomer on open grassy slopes at a relatively high elevation in Washington. Wingspread, 20–24 mm.

Early Stages: The egg, according to Newcomer, is about 1 mm in diameter (this seems large), spherical with a flattened base, and cream at first, eventually becoming yellow-orange. The surface is finely reticulate. The first stage larva is light brown with transverse rows of brown dots; the head is light brown. Half grown larvae are light brown with a dark brown head marked with a darker narrow dorsal stripe. Mature larvae are light gray, sprinkled with irregular dark brown dots and spots, and with a black middorsal line. The head is black with a pair of light dorsal stripes. The pupa is ashy gray with light brown areas on the abdomen and darker spots scattered over thorax abdomen and wing pads.

Distribution: This species was described from northern Oregon. It has been taken since in several localities in Washington.

5. **Polites baracoa** (Lucas). Plate 90, figure 18, ♂; figure 19, ♀. This small dark skipper much resembles *P. themistocles*. Like that species it is brown with only a suggestion of orange as a wash over the hind wings, a conspicuous orange cell and costal region on the fore wings and several orange spots subapically and outside the upper stigmal area. The male stigma is small and slender, sometimes scarcely apparent. Females have less of the cell and costal area orange, and the subapical spots are separated from the orange costal area, not true in males. The hind wings below are brownish, usually somewhat "grizzled" with an overscaling of pale olive or gray which in the discal area is concentrated into a vague but usually fairly broad curved pale band. This band, when present in *themistocles,* is usually composed of narrow and uncontrasting but distinct spots, sometimes vague. The fore wings of male *baracoa* are proportionately broader than are those of *themistocles*. This little insect has a restricted range and is uncommon in collections. Wingspread, 20–25 mm.

Early Stages: The early stages of *baracoa* in Cuba have been described by Dethier. The egg is about 0.75 mm in diameter, tall hemispherical, finely reticulate and at first yellow later becoming buff-pink. First stage larvae are yellow, becoming greenish after feeding; the head is blackish. Half grown larvae are green dorsally and yellow on the sides and below. The head is blackish with lighter markings faintly indicated. Mature larvae are buff-brown with a narrow dark brown middorsal line and, on each side, a broad dark brown line with light borders. The area between the stripes is mottled irregularly with brown. The head is dull gold with a pair of vertical parallel white stripes high on the face and a white spot above the ocelli. Dethier later reported that *baracoa* can be reared on sugarcane. The preferred food plant in nature is a grass.

Distribution: This Antillean species is also found locally from southern Georgia through Florida. In Florida it has been taken from January to November.

6. **Polites themistocles** (Latreille). Plate 90, figure 6, ♂; figure 7, ♀. This common small skipper, resembles *baracoa*. It is a dull brown insect with bright orange in the fore wing cell and the costal area, which in both sexes may be connected to the subapical spots. *P. themistocles* may be distinguished from both *baracoa* and *origenes* by the rather broad black S-shaped stigma of the males. The spots on the lower surface of the hind wings, if present and broad, are as well defined outwardly as they are inwardly, which is not true of *baracoa*. The patch of specialized gray-brown scales adjacent to the male stigma does not conspicuously contrast with the dark brown color of the outer margin. Females, unlike those of the other two species, are generally conspicuously orange in the costal area and in the fore wing cell. Wingspread, 20–26 mm.

Early Stages: The egg is small, a little over 0.75 mm in diameter, finely reticulate and pale green. First stage larvae are whitish with a faint dorsal line and a black head. Half grown larvae are pale brownish yellow with a dorsal greenish tinge, profusely flecked with dark brown dots; the head is black. Mature larvae are rich purplish brown, yellow-brown or chocolate and the head is black with conspicuous short white vertical stripes in front. The pupa is dirty whitish to light brown with the wing pads dusky green and the head dusky. The tongue case scarcely extends free beyond the tip of the wing pads. Comstock gives *Panicum* as the foodplant, and Shapiro states further that small species of *Panicum* are preferred but *P. clandestinum* is sometimes used.

Distribution: This species is found through most of the United States and southern Canada. It ranges from Nova Scotia to British Columbia, south to Florida and California. It is usually single brooded in Canada, the northern United States, and through the West. It is probably double brooded in the South. In California it seems to be a forest species, preferring small glades in the woods to open meadows or grasslands. This is not true in the East where it is much more common.

7. **Polites origenes** (Fabricius). Plate 90, figure 8, ♂; figure 9, ♀. This is a larger skipper than *themistocles,* which it otherwise closely resembles. The male stigma is long, slender and less sinuate; the adjacent patch of specialized scales is grayish and rather conspicuously contrasts with the brown marginal border. Females are generally somewhat darker than those of *themistocles,* the orange is much paler, the spots sometimes almost white, and there is seldom a broad yellow-orange area in the cell and costal area of the fore wing. The spot below the end of the cell of the female fore wing is usually large and squarish. This species is not as common as *themistocles.*

Early Stages: The pale green egg is about 1 mm in diameter, more prominently reticulate than in *themistocles,* hemispherical and broadly flattened at the summit. First stage larvae are pallid green with a black head. Half grown larvae are dull olive-green with dull white mottling. The mature larva is dark chocolate with soiled white mottling, the head dull black without pale markings. The larvae feed upon *Tridens flavus.*

Distribution: There are two recognized subspecies: *P. origenes origenes* ranges through the eastern region from New England to Georgia and west to the Dakotas and Arkansas. *P. origenes rhena* (Edwards) is a little larger, the fulvous markings broader and more yellow than in the nominate subspecies; it is found in the eastern foothills of the Rocky Mountains in Montana, Colorado and New Mexico, where it flies from June to August.

8. **Polites mystic** (Edwards). Plate 90, figure 13, ♂; figure 14, ♀. (both ssp. *mystic*). This is a medium sized orange skipper. Males are broadly tawny orange on the upper surface of both wings. *P. mystic* and *sonora* have a basal loop of brown on the hind wing, running from the base around the end of the cell and back to the base again; this loop usually encloses some orange in the cell. The stigma is black, sinuate and slender, but looks quite broad because the adjacent patch of modified scales is also black and adds apparent width to the stigma. The upper end of the stigma contacts the lower corner of a brown dash connecting the cell end with the border. The lower surface of the hind wings is orange-brown with a curved broad macular band and a basal area of large yellow spots separated by brown veins. Females are brown above with a similar curved broad band of orange spots separated by dark brown veins on the hind wings and more restricted orange fore wing markings than in the males. Wingspread, 26–32 mm.

Early Stages: The egg is pale green, hemispherical and finely reticulate. The first stage larva is pale greenish yellow, nearly white with a black head. Half grown larvae are light milk chocolate, faintly mottled with dull white, with the head reddish brown and covered with whitish hairs. Mature larvae are chocolate with dull white mottling and a dark brown dorsal line; the head is black and roughened. The pupa is blackish or dark brown with long tawny hairs on the head and abdomen. The free part of the tongue case is tawny to almost black and extends free of the wing pads to the tip of the abdomen. The preferred foodplant in nature is reported to be *Poa* by Shapiro.

Distribution: This species ranges from Washington state to New Jersey and north into Canada. Populations east of the Great Plains are well marked with a pale band on the hind wings below and represent the nominate subspecies. In the prairie region from Iowa to Colorado specimens are yellow below and the macular band is less contrasting; these populations are of the subspecies *P. mystic dacotah* (Edwards). I have recently seen, in the collection of Jon Shepard, material of this species from Montana, Idaho, Washington and British Columbia. These specimens do not resemble the prairie populations and seem to represent an unnamed subspecies. In the East the species flies from May to September, in two broods in the south but only one (spring) in the north. Prairie populations are on the wing from May to July.

9. **Polites sonora** (Scudder). Plate 90, figure 11, ♂ (ssp. *sonora*); figure 12, ♀ (ssp. *sonora*). This medium sized, pale tawny to reddish orange species in most populations is broadly marked in both sexes above. It is similar, and closely related, to *mystic*. The male stigma and the adjacent patch of special scales together present a broad black aspect to the stigma, and there is a loop of brown from the base around the cell of the hind wings. The brown borders and other markings are generally heavily suffused with the orange or tawny that is present in the discal areas on the upper surface, so that even females of the darkest populations are broadly reddish orange in overall appearance. The lower surface of the hind wings is pale greenish yellow, light olive or orange-brown to chocolate, with a curved, relatively narrow band of yellow-cream spots separated by darker veins; the under hind wings also have a distinct pair of connected subbasal spots, in the cell and just below, of the same color. The borders on the upper surface, because of the paler suffusion, contrast less with the discal area than is true of *mystic*. Wingspread, 24–32 mm.

Early Stages: These have been reported for nominate *sonora* by Newcomer, although I would expect that the Washington populations to which he refers represent the subspecies *P. sonora siris.* The light green egg is about 1 mm in diameter, almost spherical with a small flattened base. First stage larvae are creamy white with a black head. Half grown larvae are grayish green with a solid black head. The larval foodplant is not known but Newcomer suggests that Idaho Fescue (*Festuca idahoensis*) may be used.

Distribution: This species occurs in several subspecies from British Columbia to northern Baja California, eastward to Wyoming and Colorado. The subspecies *P. sonora siris* (Edwards) is larger than the other populations, dark reddish orange above and dark yellowish brown to chocolate on the hind wings below, with prominent pale spots. It is found along the coast and in the coastal and Cascade mountains from British Columbia to central California. The subspecies *P. sonora sonora* is pale tawny above and yellowish or slightly greenish on the hind wings below. It ranges through the western portion of the Great Basin from British Columbia to southern Nevada, in the Sierra Nevada, and from the southern California mountains southward into the Sierra San Pedro Martir of Baja California. Eastward this subspecies blends fairly broadly with the remaining subspecies, *P. sonora utahensis,* (Skinner) which is like nominate *sonora* above, below tends to be more greenish with whiter spots. This subspecies comprises the Rocky Mountain populations, ranging through the mountainous parts of Idaho, Wyoming, Colorado and Utah. Adults have been taken from May to September.

10. **Polites vibex** (Geyer). Plate 87, figure 28, ♂; figure 29, ♀ (both ssp. *praeceps*). In our populations males are broadly yellow-orange above with a broad, scarcely sinuate, stigma. The adjacent black patch of specialized scales provides the stigma with a very broad aspect. The hind wings above are broadly yellow-orange with dark veins and there is seldom a conspicuous basal loop of brown around the cell, although the end of the cell is often finely darkened. The hind wings of males below

are yellow with a marginal series of brown spots and several basal ones, the last sometimes absent. Females are brown or sooty brown with a short series of discal whitish or yellowish spots. The hind wings below are grayish or sooty yellow with several submarginal or marginal and basal dark spots. Wingspread, 26–30 mm.

Early Stages: The egg is hemispherical, smooth and white. First stage larvae are white with a black head. Half grown larvae are greenish white. The mature larva is pale green with a dark dorsal stripe and an obscure line on either side. The head is blackish, granular, with two yellow-white short vertical stripes high on the face and a pair of yellow-white patches on the sides of the face. The pupa is pale green with a whitish abdomen. The tongue case is long, extending free beyond the end of the wing pads to the end of the abdomen. The fooplant of nominate *vibex* is *Paspalum setaceum* according to Chapman, or *Paspalum ciliatifolium* according to Scudder. Kendall reports that *P. vibex praeceps* in metropolitan areas readily uses Bermuda Grass (*Cynodon dactylon*) and St. Augustine Grass (*Stenotaphrum secundatum*).

Distribution: This species is distributed from Virginia, rarely Connecticut, and Arkansas south through tropical America and the West Indies to Argentina. North of Mexico *P. vibex* is represented by three subspecies. Nominate *vibex* is the most widespread in the United States, ranging from Connecticut to Florida and west to Arkansas and Texas. It is broadly tawny above with a moderately broad and somewhat ill-defined border. Females are more or less dusky yellowish on the hind wing below. Another subspecies, *P. vibex brettoides* (Edwards), has an extremely thin border above and females may have some yellowish scaling on the costa of the fore wing and on the hind wing above. This subspecies occurs in Arizona and New Mexico. In southern Texas a Mexican representative, *P. vibex praeceps* (Scudder), enters our area. It is distinguished by a broader, well defined border in the male, and females with grayish on the hind wings below.

Genus HYLEPHILA Billberg

This genus is comprised of nearly a dozen species of principally orange, small to medium sized skippers. In most the males bear a distinct stigma. The upper surface is similar in nearly all the species. The antennae are short, very short in *phyleus,* and there are spines on the tibiae of all legs. The genus is primarily South American, especially well represented in the Andes from Peru to Chile and Argentina. Only a single species occurs north of South America.

1. **Hylephila phyleus** (Drury). Plate 91, figure 1, ♂; figure 2, ♀ (both ssp. *phyleus*). This well known skipper is easily recognized by the broad expanse of bright yellow-orange and deeply dentate borders on the wings of males. Below, the males are yellowish with a few scattered small dark spots. Females are darker above with the orange restricted to large spots. This species can always be identified by the extremely short antennae which seem scarcely longer than the width of the head. Males

(without antennae) might be confused at first with *Polites vibex* but the spots on that species below are larger and the upper surface is quite different. Females are sometimes confused with those of *Atalopedes campestris* but that species generally has at least the large spot below the end of the fore wing cell partly hyaline, and the antennae much longer. Wingspread, 24-32 mm.

Early Stages: This is one of the more common "lawn skippers" in urban areas of the southern United States. Because the larval shelter is horizontal in the basal parts of the grass the larvae are able to withstand repeated mowing and are highly successful in such places. This species is much less common in areas not so altered by man. The glistening pale blue-green egg is small, less than 0.75 mm in diameter, hemispherical and reticulate. The first stage larva is yellow at first, changing to yellowish green with feeding; the head is black. Half grown larvae are dirty yellowish brown with a prominent dark dorsal line. Mature larvae are dark gray-brown to dark yellow-brown with three dark longitudinal stripes. The head is black with reddish brown stripes. The pupa is yellowish brown, sometimes reddish or greenish, with a prominent blackish dorsal line from head to tip of abdomen, and several black or dark brown dashes and some mottling particularly dorsally. The tongue case extends free of the end of the wing pads nearly half the distance to the end of the abdomen. The larvae feed on a large variety of grasses including sugarcane, Bermuda Grass (*Cynodon dactylon*), bent grass (*Agrostis*) and St. Augustine Grass (*Stenotaphrum secundatum*).

Distribution: This species ranges from Connecticut to California and south through tropical America to Chile. Several subspecies are present in South America, but only a single subspecies occurs north of that continent, *H. phyleus phyleus.* This skipper is common in the southern United States but rare to the north.

Genus YVRETTA Hemming

Both *Yvretta* and *Hylephila* are closely related to *Polites.* These skippers are small to medium sized (some females) and generally somewhat gray-brown with orange, yellowish or whitish spots on the upper surface. These spots may form macular bands on both wings or they may be scarcely evident and only on the fore wings. Below *Yvretta* is generally grayish yellow, frequently with slightly paler veins, and with white or yellowish spots in a macular band and basally. The male stigma is slender, with only the anterior third along the cell; in one species it is almost obscure. The antennae are short and the apiculus on the club is extremely short and stout, scarcely evident. The tibiae of all legs are well spined. The genus is confined to the southwestern United States and from Mexico south to Panamá. It is here considered to be comprised of only two species.

1. **Yvretta rhesus** (Edwards). Plate 88, figure 17, ♀. Plate 89, figure 32, ♂; figure 33, ♂, underside.   This easily recognized species is grayish brown above with white spots which may be much reduced in males. It is said to have only a single pair of spurs

on the hind tibia, but at least some females have a single short spur representing the usual upper pair. Males have a slender, almost obscure, stigma. The fringes are long and white. The hind wings below are distinctive because of the white macular band which extends outward on the veins, and the contrasting black patches in the cell and on both sides of the posterior arm of the macular band. This surface is reminiscent of the markings of *Hesperia uncas* below but on the upper surfaces the two species are readily separated. The early stages are not described. Little is known of its habits as it is not frequently collected. Wingspread, 26–30 mm.

Distribution: Yvretta rhesus has been taken in Wyoming, Colorado, Kansas, New Mexico, Arizona and Mexico. It flies in May.

2. **Yvretta carus** (Edwards). Plate 88, figure 18, ♂ (ssp. *subreticulata*) Plate 89, figure 30, ♂ (ssp. *carus*); figure 31, ♀ (ssp. *carus*). Two subspecies of this skipper are recognized here. Some workers would regard these as distinct species, presumably because there seems to be a wide geographical region of overlap. I am not convinced that the two forms often truly occur together over this broad, apparently common range. If it can be demonstrated that they do, and that there is no blending between them in good samples from such places, then I will agree that they represent separate species. The two subspecies are similar, chiefly distinguishable in that *Y. carus carus* has pale yellow, almost whitish, spots on the upper surface; the hind wings below are yellowish, lightly dusted with scattered blackish scales; and the veins tend to be pale buffy yellow like the spots of the macular band. *Yvretta carus subreticulata* (Plötz) has orange spots above; on the lower surface of the hind wings the dusting of blackish scales is heavier; and the veins are not conspicuously paler so that it appears to be slightly darker below. Both subspecies are variable in the development of the pale spots on the wings above and below, and males of both may have the spots of the upper surfaces reduced to near obsolescence. Females usually have well developed spots on the fore wings but those of the hind wings above are often completely absent. There are two pairs of well developed spurs on the hind tibiae. The male stigma is slender but better developed than that of *rhesus*. The early stages are not known. Wingspread, 22–30 mm.

Distribution: Yvretta carus carus ranges from Texas, New Mexico and Arizona into northern Mexico. According to Roever (*in litt.*) it has been taken in two localities in southern California as well. It flies from April to September. *Yvretta carus subreticulata* ranges from Panamá north through Mexico. A few specimens that appear typical of this subspecies have been taken in West Texas. Adults of *subreticulata* have been taken in January, February, May, July, October and December.

Genus STINGA Evans

This genus was erected to receive a single species which has been shifted about a good deal, never fitting well in any other genus. The species is orange and looks much like some western *Hesperia*. The antennal apiculus is peculiarly short and stout, and the stigma is slender, a little like that of *Yvretta*. The male genitalia seem closer to those of the genus *Ochlodes,* where it once was placed.

1. **Stinga morrisoni** (Edwards). Plate 89, figure 29, ♂; figure 34, ♀. An orange skipper above, very like a *Hesperia, S. morrisoni* has a somewhat darker basal half on the hind wings, although this area may be well suffused with orange scaling. The lower surface of the hind wings is brownish, often with a golden tawny or greenish overscaling, and has lustrous white spots arranged in a conspicuous chevron-shaped macular band. In these respects it is like *Hesperia* below. This species, however, is distinctive in having a lustrous white bar extending from the base lengthwise through the upper half of the cell to its end, a characteristic not seen in any *Hesperia.* This has been a scarce skipper in collections, and nothing is known of its biology. Wingspread, 26–32 mm.

Distribution: This species is presently known only from the mountainous areas of Colorado, New Mexico, Arizona and west Texas. It flies in early spring.

Genus PSEUDOCOPAEODES Skinner & Williams

A single tawny species comprises this genus. The antennae have only a rudimentary apiculus on the club. The terminal joint of the palpus is short and robustly conical. The tibiae of all legs are well spined but there is only a single pair of spurs on the hind tibia rather than the usual two pairs of spurs. The males have a slender stigma on the fore wing. This genus is confined to the southwestern United States and western Mexico.

1. **Pseudocopaeodes eunus** (Edwards); Plate 89, figure 25, ♂; figure 26, ♀. This is a fairly small species, totally tawny orange above except for a narrow uniform border and black veins near the border. Males have a small slender black stigma. The lower surface of the hind wings is pale creamy orange with two cream rays extending from the base to the margin, longitudinally through the cell and alongside the anal fold. Commonly there are dusky suffusions in patches near the cell and along the veins. This species is highly localized, occurring in good colonies only in the immediate vicinity of inland stands of the larval foodplant and is easily overlooked by collectors. Wingspread, 22–28 mm.

Early Stages: The egg is surprisingly large, nearly 1.25 mm in diameter. It is cream, hemispherical to subconical and finely reticulate. The larval foodplant is Desert Salt Grass (*Distichlis stricta*). Confined larvae accepted *D. spicata* with reluctance and did not thrive.

Distribution: This species is known from central and southern California, Nevada, Baja California and western mainland Mexico. It probably also occurs in Arizona, Utah and southeastern Oregon. In California it is taken from April through September.

Genus THYMELICUS Hübner

This is a Palearctic genus of eight species; one was successfully introduced into North America where it has spread considerably. These are pale or bright tawny to golden orange skippers, the males with a slender, small and inconspicuous stigma placed for most of its length close alongside the lower end of the fore wing cell; its orientation is therefore more less horizontal on the wing. The antennal club is elongate and without an apiculus. The last joint of the palpus is long and slender. The tibia of the middle leg is spined but those of the fore and hind legs are not. The hind legs have two pairs of tibial spurs.

1. **Thymelicus lineola** (Ochsenheimer). Plate 91, figure 3, ♂; figure 4, ♀. This orange skipper is easily recognized by the brassy sheen, the rather narrow dark border and the tendency for the veins to be dark. The horizontal orientation of the male stigma occurs in only a few North American species. The hind wings below are dusky or olive-orange, while the fore wings are broadly orange below. This skipper undergoes great fluctuations in density and upon occasion has achieved the proportions of an economic pest. Wingspread, 20–26 mm.

Early Stages: These have been detailed for the American populations by Pengelly. The whitish and finely reticulate egg is about 1 mm in diameter, low and broadly hemispherical with a depressed summit. The first stage larva is yellowish white with a black head. The half grown larva is greenish with a dark middorsal stripe; the head is light brown with two whitish or yellowish patches on the back. The mature larva is similar except that the yellowish patches on the head are extended forward as longitudinal stripes down the front of the face. The pupa is yellowish green on the abdomen with longitudinal striping similar to that of the larva. The thorax is green. The head has a down-curved strong projection or horn in front. The preferred larval foodplant is Timothy (*Phleum pratense*) although several other grasses are also eaten.

Distribution: This species was first discovered on the North American continent at London, Ontario, in 1910. Since then it has spread, very likely primarily through human transport of eggs in hay, in all directions from that point. It is now known from New Brunswick to Michigan and south to Maryland, Kentucky and Illinois. The species is also established in west-central British Columbia: possibly another primary introduction from Eurasia rather than a secondary transplant from eastern American localities. In the Old World the species ranges from Sweden south to Morocco and Algeria, and eastward across Europe and the U.S.S.R. to at least Sakhalin. The North American populations fly during June, July and perhaps August.

Genus ADOPAEOIDES Godman

Of the two species that comprise this genus, one enters the southwestern United States. Adults are tawny with no stigma in the males. The antennal club is long and terminally rather pointed, but there is no reflexed apiculus. The terminal segment of the palpus is long and slender. The tibiae of all legs are unspined but the hind tibia has two pairs of spurs.

1. **Adopaeoides prittwitzi** (Plötz). Plate 89, figure 27, ♀; figure 28, ♀, underside.   This skipper is bright orange with something of a luster on the upper surface. Males have a rather narrow border conspicuously drawn inward along the veins, but the veins are generally not darkened on the central part of the wing. Usually the very short cell, the anal fold and, even more prominently, the costal area of the hind wing above are darkened. The fringes of both wings are conspicuously orange. Females are similar but the veins of both wings are entirely darkened and on the hind wing the cell and anal fold are darker than in males. The lower surface varies from rich reddish golden to pale yellowish orange and a conspicuous yellow ray extends from the base to the margin, passing through the anterior half of the cell. Nothing is known of the life history. Wingspread, 22–28 mm.

Distribution: First found to occur in the United States in 1946, this species is still known from only two small areas north of Mexico: western Texas near Alpine, and southeastern Arizona near Sonoita. Specimens have been taken during May, June and September. The species is widely distributed in Mexico where it also flies during July.

Genus COPAEODES Edwards

This is a genus of three small orange skippers with pointed fore wings. Males have a slender linear stigma oriented horizontally (longitudinally) on the fore wing. The antennae are short and the club lacks an apiculus. The third segment of the palpus is long and slender. The tibiae of the fore and hind legs are unspined, but there are commonly a few spines on the mid tibia. Two pairs of spurs occur on the hind tibia of the two species that come within our region. The third species is South American.

1. **Copaeodes aurantiaca** (Hewitson). Plate 91, figure 5, ♂; figure 10, ♀.   Males are almost unmarked bright tawny orange above and below. The border is a mere line at the base of the fringes and only the extremely slender stigma and some basal dark dusting interrupts the tawny expanse of the fore wing. The hind wings above are usually somewhat dusky along the costa and anal fold. Females may be similar, but usually display a fine dark line behind the cell of the fore wing and a dark posterior margin. Females often also have a series of dusky patches along the outer margin which, in extreme cases, forms a broad dark border broadest near the anal angle. The hind wings below are generally yellowish. Wingspread, 18–22 mm.

Early Stages: The egg is cream, smooth and glistening and shaped like a flattened hemisphere. The first stage larva is green with dark green longitudinal stripes, these stripes coalesce posteriorly in a pinkish red stripe that extends back onto a horn-like posterior projection of the last abdominal segment. The head is conical with a pair of horn-like knobs at the top in front; it is vertically striped with pink and has a large purple area on each side. Older larvae are similar but the dorsal stripes of the body are heavy and purple. The pupa is pale straw with an elongate beak-like projection extending forward from the head. There are brown lines on the wing pads and abdomen. The middorsal line is also brown and is bordered by two narrow white lines, the outermost having pink edges. There is a faint yellow line on each side. The pupa is exposed, suspended by a delicate silk girdle. According to Kendall the preferred foodplant of the larva is Bermuda Grass (*Cynodon dactylon*).

Distribution: This species ranges from Texas west to southern California and north to Nevada, probably also to Utah and Colorado. South of the United States the range extends to Panamá. In some parts of the Southwest *aurantiaca* is on the wing nearly all months of the year.

2. **Copaeodes minima** (Edwards). Plate 91, figure 8, ♂; figure 9, ♀. This is probably the tiniest skipper in North America. Males above are similar to those of the preceding species but the stigma is often more obscure because it is so slender. Females above are also like those of *aurantiaca* except that they have dark veins. The hind wings below are as in the preceding but with a white streak from the base to the outer margin, running longitudinally through the cell. Wingspread, 14–20 mm.

Early Stages: Kendall reports oviposition in nature, and successful rearing in confinement, of this species on Bermuda Grass (*Cynodon dactylon*). No additional information on the immature stages has been published.

Distribution: This skipper, often very common, ranges from Georgia and Florida west to Arkansas and Texas. It is generally distributed through Mexico and extends southward to Panamá. In some parts of its range in the United States it flies all year. Ordinarily adults are taken from March through October or November.

Genus OARISMA Scudder

The genus *Oarisma* contains nine species of rather small orange or brown skippers which have quite broad, squared-off wings. Two of the species occurring beyond our limits possess a male stigma but ours do not. The antennae are short with an elongate blunt club which completely lacks an apiculus. The last joint of the palpus is long and slender. The tibiae of the fore and middle legs are spined and the tibial epiphysis on the fore leg is much reduced in some of the species. The hind tibia has two pairs of spurs. The genus is represented from Canada to northern South America and in the Antilles.

1. **Oarisma powesheik** (Parker). Plate 97, figure 3, ♂; figure 4, ♂, underside. This is the largest species of the genus and is usually easily recognized once one has seen

it. The following species, *garita,* is variable and can be superficially quite similar to *powesheik.* As a result the two species are often confused. Most specimens that I have seen identified as the evidently quite rare *powesheik* are actually just dark examples of the common *garita. O. powesheik* is a blackish species with bigger wings than any of the others. The costal area above the cell on the fore wing is conspicuously orange. This orange sometimes extends, as a suffusion of orange dusting, out over other parts of the upper surface, but is always conspicuously absent from the outer half of the hind wing, which remains quite blackish. The lower surface of the fore wing is broadly black, the orange suffusion being generally limited to the costal area and narrowly to the apical half of the outer margin. The fore wing cell, then, is generally mostly black. The hind wings below are black, but have all save the costal area and broad anal fold heavily dusted with grayish or sometimes whitish-yellow scales. In this area all the veins are conspicuously whitened. The broadly black anal fold is not bordered with an orange or yellowish orange streak, nor is it anywhere dusted with orange scales. The antennae are proportionately shorter than in *garita* and there are additional small morphological differences between the two species in the palpi and legs. Both species have the last palpal segment much shorter than the length of the front tibia, and they both have the epiphysis on that tibia much reduced. The early stages are not known. Wingspread, 26–30 mm.

Distribution: Because of frequent confusion with *garita* it is difficult to determine from published records the actual distribution of *powesheik.* It was described from Iowa and reliable records also include Illinois, Nebraska and the Dakotas. It flies in June and July.

2. **Oarisma garita** (Reakirt). Plate 91, figure 6, ♂; figure 7, ♀; figure 11, ♂; figure 12, ♀. An extremely variable little skipper, *garita* has been confused with both *powesheik* and *edwardsii.* The upperside varies from mostly very dark brown with an orange costal area to almost wholly bright yellow-orange. There is usually as much or more orange suffusion on the outer half of the hind wing above as there is basally. The lower surface is also variable. The fore wing may be quite blackish well into the discal area from the hind margin, but the cell is usually mostly orange, or most of the wing may be suffused with orange. The hind wings below may be creamy buff, decidedly yellowish, or brown dusted with gray scales, and the veins commonly lightened. The anal fold may be broadly orange, partly suffused with blackish scales, brownish or even blackish; in the latter event, however, it is only the anal portion of the fold that is darkened, and it is separated from the pale part of the wing at least near the outer margin by a streak of orange which may be ray-like from the base. The antennae are relatively longer in this species than in the preceding. Like *powesheik, garita* has the third joint of the palpus, much shorter than the length of the front tibiae, and the tibial epiphysis is much reduced. By these latter features, as well as by its shorter, more stubby wings and duller color this species may be separated from *edwardsii.* Wingspread, 20–26 mm.

Early Stages: The egg is creamy white, hemispherical and reticulated. First stage larvae are at first creamy white, changing to pale sea green after feeding. There are three whitish stripes along each side of the body between the lateral fold and the center of the back. The head is slightly bilobed and has an indefinite black triangular band down the front of the face. Older larvae are grass green with a white middorsal line and seven white lines on each side; the head is pale green.

Distribution: This is a common skipper of the northern and western Great Plains and Rocky Mountains, flying from June to August. It ranges from Washington and British Columbia east to Manitoba and Saskatchewan and south through Idaho, Montana and the Dakotas to New Mexico and Arizona, and on into Mexico in the Sierra Madre Occidental. Another subspecies is found in central and southern Mexico.

3. **Oarisma edwardsii** (Barnes). Plate 91, figure 13, ♂; figure 14, ♀.   This skipper varies from pale tawny orange to quite dusky or brownish orange above. The lower surface is generally orange on the fore wing but is broadly blackish on the anal margin. The hind wings are gray-orange, sooty yellowish or dully greenish cream except for the broadly orange area of the anal fold. The veins are seldom if ever conspicuously paler than the rest of the wing. The last segment of the palpus is extremely long and thin, almost as long as the fore tibia. The fore tibial epiphysis is rather well developed and reaches nearly to the end of the tibia. The wings of this species are proportionately longer than in *powesheik* or *garita* and the hind wings, especially, are almost triangular. The early stages have not been described. Wingspread, 22–28 mm.

Distribution: This species ranges from Colorado south through New Mexico, Arizona and Texas to northern Mexico. It flies from April to July.

Genus ANCYLOXYPHA Felder

This genus contains seven species of small, mostly orange skippers with long slender bodies and long rounded wings. Males have no stigma. The antennae are rather short and the club is blunt, the apiculus represented by a tiny pointed terminal segment. The third segment of the palpus is long and slender, about the length of the fore tibia. The tibial epiphysis is well developed and none of the tibiae have spines. There are two pairs of spurs on the hind tibia. The genus ranges from Canada to Patagonia, with two species north of Mexico.

1. **Ancyloxypha numitor** (Fabricius). Plate 91, figure 15, ♂; figure 20, ♀.   The upper surface of the fore wings varies from entirely black to blackish with a heavy orange suffusion along the costa, around the end of the cell broadly and in the discal area below the cell. The hind wings are orange with a broad black marginal border. On the fore wing below, the orange is restricted to the costal region, the apex and the outer margin, the remainder of the wing being conspicuously black. The hind wings below are orange, gold, or creamy orange and unmarked. This species flies low and rather weakly among tall grasses. Wingspread, 20–26 mm.

Early Stages: The egg is about 0.75 mm in diameter, glistening bright yellow at first but soon acquiring patches of orange-red in a band around the middle. The first stage larva is pale yellow with a black head. The half grown larva is straw to pale green, finely mottled with greenish white except on the middorsal line; the head is black and densely granular. The mature larva is light grass green and the head is dark brown with the front of the face ringed with a white line not quite joined at the top and enclosing numerous irregular white spots. Behind the ocelli is a white patch on each side. The pupa is cream with brown patches and lines and a broad, blunt head. Scudder and Kendall suggest that several grasses associated with wet places will be the preferred larval foodplants. Kendall records one grass known to serve the species in nature: Marsh Millet (*Zizaniopsis miliacea*). Ross & Lambremont report the occurrence of *numitor* larvae on cultivated rice in Louisiana, and Shapiro reports this species on *Poa* in the Delaware Valley.

Distribution: This widely distributed species ranges from Nova Scotia and Quebec to Florida, and westward to Saskatchewan and Texas. It has not been recorded from Mexico. In New England *numitor* appears to be triple brooded, flying from May to October. In Texas there are apparently at least four broods and the species flies from April to November.

2. **Ancyloxypha arene** (Edwards). Plate 91, figure 18, ♂; figure 19, ♀. This orange species has a usually broad vague dark border on the fore wings, which sometimes is extended inwardly a short distance along the veins. Usually a slender short dark line indicates the end of the cell and occasionally the cell is vaguely darkened in females. Females, and less often males, tend to have the posterior margin of the fore wing somewhat darkened, at least basally. The costal margin is broadly, and the outer margin narrowly, dark bordered. The lower surface of both wings is rich orange, lustrous on the hind wings which are often golden. There is a black border on the basal three-fourths of the posterior margin of the fore wing, and often there is a discernible pale ray from base to margin through the cell of the hind wing below. The mostly orange fore wings on the lower surface will serve to separate this species from even the most fulvous examples of *numitor*. Nothing is known of the early stages. Wingspread, 18–24 mm.

Distribution: North of the Mexican border *arene* has only been found locally in Arizona and Texas, where it flies from May to August. It ranges south through Mexico to Costa Rica.

Genus DECINEA Evans

This is a tropical American genus of nine brownish, medium sized, broad winged skippers with pale hyaline spots at least on the fore wing and usually also on the hind wing. Males have no stigma. The antennae are long and the club has a conspicuous long apiculus. The last joint of the palpus is short and conical. The tibia of the middle leg is spined. The metropolis of this genus is in South America, but three species reach Mexico and a single species has been reported from United States.

1. **Decinea percosius** (Godman). Plate 91, figure 23, ♂; figure 24, ♀.   This brown species has two conspicuous pale hyaline spots, and usually also two or three sub-apical spots, on the upper surface of the fore wings. The hind wings above may be unspotted, or have one or two spots near the end of the cell. The hind wing below has a spot in the cell, and usually two separated small spots near the end of the cell. These may form a row with several other inconspicuous spots, all bordered with dark brown. The brown area between the median row and the margin may have a vague purple tint. The early stages are not recorded. Wingspread, 22–26 mm.

Distribution: This Central American species ranges from Mexico to northern South America. It has been taken several times in extreme southern Texas in April and November.

Genus PERICHARES Scudder

This tropical American genus comprises large skippers with somewhat pointed fore wings and hind wings. Males of most species have a conspicuous or large curved stigma. The antennae are long and the club is slender with a long apiculus. The tibiae of the fore and middle legs are weakly spined and the hind tibia is densely clothed with reddish hairs in males, orange-brown in females. The abdomen below is yellow in males and brown banded with yellow in females. Many of the species are superficially similar, brown above with a bluish or greenish iridescence on the thorax and wing bases. Whitish or yellowish hyaline spots are usually present on the fore wing in the cell and in a series outward and below the cell spot. There are no subapical spots in the species treated here. The hind wings are unmarked above but on the lower surface are variegated with brown and violet or purple. The fringes are checkered in our species.

1. **Perichares philetes** (Gmelin). Plate 92, figure 24, ♂ (ssp. *adela*).   Our subspecies, *adela* (Hewitson), differs from other subspecies principally in having pale yellowish spots above and in having the lower part of the cell spot nearly as large as the upper part. The male stigma is gray. Females have the pale yellowish spots of the fore wing larger and closer together than those of the male. Adults are said to be principally crepuscular. Wingspread, 46–54 mm.

Early Stages: The half grown larva is yellow-green and noticeably hairy with a whitish pubescence; the head is black. The mature larva is light yellow-green, glossy dorsally, laterally well furnished with light downy hairs. The head is light yellow to green, unmarked but covered with dense long colorless hairs. The elongate pupa is grass green with a pair of dorsal yellow lines; it has a projecting head and the free tongue case extends to slightly beyond the end of the abdomen. The larvae feed on *Panicum maximum* in Jamaica according to Kaye. In Brazil the species is found on the palm, *Desmonicus* sp., and on *Hyospatha elegans* but it appears to favor sugarcane. Wolcott, Dethier and others have indicated that *philetes* is sometimes a minor pest of sugarcane in the West Indies.

Distribution: The species as a whole ranges from southern Texas and the West Indies south to Argentina. The subspecies *adela* occurs on the mainland from Texas south through Central America to Brazil. Texas examples were taken in November and December.

Genus LEREMA Scudder

This is a group of six or eight medium sized, mostly dark brown, tropical American species. The antennae are long and the club has a relatively long apiculus. The middle tibiae are spined but the tibiae of the fore and hind legs are not or are only weakly so. Males have a curved broad stigma. One species is represented in eastern United States.

1. **Lerema accius** (Smith). Plate 91, figure 32, ♂; figure 33, ♀.   This species is dark brown, almost blackish above with a series of three subapical white spots and usually two or more additional ones. In males these are small and include a minute cell spot and one a little larger just below the end of the cell. The gray or blackish curved stigma is sometimes not very conspicuous. The fore wing of females above is similar but the spots are somewhat larger and there are usually one or two additional ones. The hind wings are unmarked above. Below they are brown with three bands of violet-gray or lighter brown parallel to the outer margin. These may be merely slightly lighter than the dark brown intervening areas. In Arkansas *accius* is partial to grassy riparian habitats and may be restricted elsewhere to such stream bottom glades. Wingspread, 26–36 mm.

Early Stages: The reticulate egg is about 1 mm in diameter. Mature larvae are nearly white, mottled with minute darker lines and points, the posterior half of each segment unmottled and more prominent. The head is white with a black band around the top and sides and three black vertical streaks on the front. The pupa is slender, smooth and greenish white with the head tapered into a slender pointed beak. The tongue case is long, extending free to the tip of the abdomen. Larval foodplants are reported to be Woolly Beard Grass (*Erianthus alopecuroides*) by Chapman and St. Augustine Grass (*Stenotaphrum secundatum*) by Kendall. The species has also been reported to feed on "Indian Corn" (*Zea mays*) by Abbot & Smith and on *Echinochloa poiretiana* by Jorgensen.

Distribution: Lerema accius ranges from New England to Florida, westward to Illinois, Arkansas and Texas, and southward to northern South America. The insect is scarce northward but locally not uncommon in the southern states where it may be taken from February to November.

Genus CYMAENES Scudder

This genus comprises about two dozen small to medium sized dark skippers, most of which were formerly included in the genus *Lerodea,* which they rather resemble. Males have no stigma. The antennae and legs are as in *Lerema.* Two species enter our area.

1. **Cymaenes tripunctus** (Herrich-Schäffer). Plate 91, figure 34, ♂; figure 35, ♀. This insect is dark brown above with well defined but small whitish spots on the fore wings. The hind wings below are smooth yellowish brown with a discal series of faint pale spots. *C. tripunctus* somewhat resembles *Lerodea eufala* but is a darker, warmer brown above and does not have the grayish cast of that species. Wingspread, 22–28 mm.

Early Stages: Dethier and Comstock have described the early stages of West Indian populations. The egg is white to light green about 0.8 mm in diameter, hemispherical and faintly reticulate. The first stage larva is whitish, then ivory to yellow with a smooth blackish head. The half grown larva is bluish green with a grayish green dorsal stripe and two or three light green lines separating green and gray-green bands, some of which are dotted with grayish green. The head is variable, ranging from white with dark brown marginal stripes to mostly brown with a white stripe in front on each side. The mature larva is similar. The pupa is narrow and cylindrical with a horn-like projecting front. It is light green except for the free portion of the tongue case which is pinkish and projects free to the end of the abdomen. The larvae feed on Guinea Grass (*Panicum maximum*) according to Comstock; Dethier found that they feed readily upon sugarcane.

Distribution: This species is established in Florida where it flies from February to October. It occurs in the West Indies and on the mainland from southern Mexico to southern Brazil and Argentina.

2. **Cymaenes odilia** (Burmeister). Plate 91, figure 21, ♂; figure 22, ♀, underside (both ssp. *trebius*). This is a dark brown skipper marked much like a small female of *Lerema accius.* The spots on the fore wing are smaller and often fewer. The lower surface is brown, marked similarly to *accius* but without the violet-gray cast to the paler areas. The central dark brown band is directed toward a more posterior part of the anal margin than in *accius.* This species seems to prefer grassy glades at the edges of woods. Adults spend much time resting in the grass and fly only short distances. The early stages are not reported. Wingspread, 24–30 mm.

Distribution: Common but local in southern Texas, this species ranges south to Argentina. Our subspecies, *trebius* (Mabille), as figured, extends through Central America. Four more subspecies occur in South America. In Texas it has been taken from April to December.

Genus NASTRA Evans

This genus consists of about a dozen chiefly neotropical species, three of which occur within our region. The species are similar to those of *Cymaenes* but they are generally less well marked both above and below, and the antennae are shorter so that the club is relatively longer in proportion to the shaft. The range of the genus extends from New York to Argentina.

1. **Nastra lherminier** (Latreille). Plate 91, figure 26, ♂; figure 27, ♀.   This rather small brown skipper looks like a *Lerodea* but it is usually entirely without spots both above and below. Sometimes there are some vague paler areas below the end of the cell but these are rarely sufficiently well developed to be called spots. The wings below are yellowish brown, the fore wings show no spots and the veins of the hind wings are frequently slightly paler yellow. This species is said to be partial to moist meadows. Wingspread, 22–26 mm.

Early Stages: These have been described in part by Laurent under the name *Pamphila fusca.* The egg is shiny, pearl white, finely reticulate and distinctly flattened at the summit. First stage larvae are opaque white with a light brown head. The foodplant is *Andropogon scoparius.*

Distribution: N. lherminier ranges from New York to Florida and west to Missouri and Texas. Macy and Shepard (1941) state that this species further ranges from Mexico to Paraguay, but since neither Hoffman (1941) nor Evans (1955) even mention records of this species from Mexico, its distribution south of the United States requires verification. I have seen one specimen of *lherminier,* however, simply labeled "Brazil." This species flies from May to September in two broods in the north, and appears to be also double brooded in the south, flying from March to June and again from August to October in Florida.

2. **Nastra neamathla** (Skinner & Williams). Plate 91, figure 28, ♂; figure 29, ♂, underside.   This skipper is similar to *lherminier,* being warm olivaceous brown above and rather obscurely marked. Usually there are at least two small dull yellowish spots on the fore wing below the end of the cell and there may or may not be also one or more minute subapical spots. The fore wings below usually have the two larger pale spots more or less clearly indicated. The hind wings below and the costal part and apex of the fore wing are heavily overscaled with dull yellow-brown; the dark discal area and anal margin of the fore wings do not contrast so conspicuously with the overscaling as they do in *julia.* Nothing is known of the early stages. Wingspread, 22–26 mm.

Distribution: This species ranges from Georgia and Florida westward through the Gulf states and Texas to Arizona and southeastern California. It is found in southern Baja California, and on the mainland the species ranges south at least to Costa Rica.

3. **Nastra julia** (Freeman). Plate 91, figure 30, ♂; figure 31, ♀.   *Nastra julia* is difficult to separate from *neamathla.* Generally it is a little larger than that species and the

spots on the fore wing both above and below tend to be a little more conspicuous. The overscaling on the lower surface of the wings is a brighter orange-yellow and, on the fore wings, contrasts with the broad blackish discal area. All three species of this genus are superficially close and individual variation is just enough to make the species difficult to tell apart without examining the male genitalia. Wingspread, 24–28 mm.

Early Stages: The immature stages have not been described. Kendall has reared larvae on St. Augustine Grass (*Stenotaphrum secundatum*). The preferred larval foodplant in nature is not known.

Distribution: This species was described from Texas, where it is widely distributed, and it is also reported from Alabama. The species ranges westward to western Arizona and southeastern California, and southward into Mexico. In southern Texas adults are present all year.

Genus MONCA Evans

This is a small genus of four tropical American skippers which resemble *Cymaenes*. The antennae are relatively long and the shaft is delicately slender. The male lacks a stigma. These insects are dark brown above and always have at least a small whitish or yellowish spot over the cell of the fore wing almost halfway from the tip to the base along the costa. All the species have two conspicuous pale areas on the lower surface of the hind wings, and the pattern may recall that of *Lerema accius* and *Cymaenes odilia*. Only one species occurs in America north of Mexico.

1. **Monca telata** (Herrich-Schäffer). Plate 91 figure 36, ♂ (ssp. *tyrtaeus*). This small black skipper has rather narrow but terminally rounded wings. There is a series of small discal and subapical yellowish white spots and frequently a minute one in the cell under the single or double costal spot. The pattern below is distinctive. The fore wing is broadly blackish with a rusty brown costal area to the apex. Along the apical half of the outer margin is a violet patch. The hind wings are bright rusty brown with two pale violet bands and the brown of the outer margin may also be heavily suffused with violet. This species flies slowly and near the ground. Adults often are found in shaded glades or stream beds within woods. The early stages are not known. Wingspread, 18–24 mm.

Distribution: Monca telata is found in the United States only in the lower Rio Grande Valley of Texas, where it flies from January to May and from October to December. Our subspecies, *tyrtaeus* (Plötz), as figured, ranges southward to Colombia. Two additional subspecies occur in northern South America.

Genus VIDIUS Evans

This genus is a mixed collection of ten variously patterned brown skippers. The antennae are long and slender, from half to less than half the length of the fore wing. As in *Monca*, there is no stigma in the male. The middle tibiae are well spined. The genus is tropical American, only one distinctive species occurring north of Mexico.

1. **Vidius perigenes** (Godman). Plate 92, figure 26, ♂; figure 30, ♂, underside.   This insect is unmarked warm or dark brown above with a vague orange suffusion along the basal half of the costal margin of the fore wing. The fore wing below is blackish with a broad expanse of rusty brown and pale veins along the costa and at the apex. The hind wings below are rusty brown with pale veins, a blackish anal fold and a conspicuous whitish streak extending from near the base through the upper half of the cell to the wing margin. The vein along the upper edge of this streak is white, and even if the streak is only slightly pale, the white vein remains conspicuous. Wingspread, 26–30 mm.

Early stages: The biology of this species is almost unknown. Kendall records oviposition of *perigenes* in confinement on St. Augustine Grass (*Stenotaphrum secundatum*), on which the larvae were successfully reared.

Distribution: Only recently reported to occur north of Mexico, this species is so far known only from grassy areas in mesquite flats of Cameron county, Texas. There are evidently three overlapping broods of the species in south Texas, with adults flying in March, April, June and October. The species is known to the south from Mexico, El Salvador and Colombia.

Genus CALLIMORMUS Scudder

These are rather small dark skippers with long, yellow-checkered antennae, a long slender terminal segment on the palpi and spines on the tibiae of the middle legs. The wings are somewhat rounded, most species have yellowish spots at least on the fore wings above, and the veins on the hind wings below are yellowish. Nine species are currently placed in this tropical American genus. Only one of them has been recorded from north of Mexico.

1. **Callimormus saturnus** (Herrich-Schäffer). Plate 86, figure 12, ♂.   This is a small olive brown species with conspicuous yellow spots discally and subapically on the fore wing above. There is often an additional yellow spot in the cell. The fore wings below are dark brown with a broad orange costal area and two yellow spots below the end of the cell. On the hind wings below the veins are not, or scarcely, pale except through the marginal border, but there is a broad continuous pale discal band that is violet-gray. Much of the wing is overscaled light lavender. The anal fold is yellowish. Nothing is known of the biology of this species. Wingspread, 22–26 mm.

Distribution: *C. saturnus* has been reported to occur in Texas. It is common in Mexico and ranges southward to Argentina.

Genus PYRRHOCALLES Mabille

These are large orange or tawny skippers with a broad dark border above. The antennal apiculus is long, about half as long as the rest of the club. The last segment of the palpi is long and slender, and the tibiae of the middle legs have short spines. The wings are rather broad and the male has no stigma. The two species in the genus are confined to the West Indies. The report of one from the continental United States is subject to doubt.

1. **Pyrrhocalles jamaicensis** Schaus. Compare Plate 92, figure 29, ♀ (*P. antiqua orientis* Skinner). The skipper illustrated is a closely related species, *P. antiqua orientis* Skinner (Cuba). *P. jamaicensis* is similar but brighter tawny and less orange than *P. antiqua.* The early stages are not described. This species was recorded from the United States (Florida) on the basis of a mislabeled specimen and it is extremely doubtful that either species ever reaches this country. Wingspread, 40–44 mm.

Genus SYNAPTE Mabille

These broad-winged skippers are dark brown, mostly yellowish tawny, or dark orange above with variegated or minutely striated hind wings below. The antennae are long and slender; the last palpal segment is also long, although it may not protrude much from the hairs of the second segment. The tibiae of the middle legs are unspined. The wings are rounded and the male has no stigma. Five species and a number of very different looking subspecies are ascribed to the genus. All are tropical American; one species enters the United States.

1. **Synapte malitiosa** (Herrich-Schäffer). Plate 91, figure 37, ♂ (ssp. *pecta*). This subspecies, *pecta* Evans, is dark brownish above with a cold yellowish tawny dusting discally producing a sooty yellow or dull light orange band on the fore wings. The cell region and often also the costa are blackish. The hind wings above are blackish with a suffusion of the cold tawny color that may be scarcely apparent. The hind wings below are light yellowish brown and minutely striated with darker brown. The early stages have not been reported. Wingspread, 26–32 mm.

Distribution: The species ranges from Texas and Cuba south to Argentina. Ssp *pecta* represents the species on the mainland north of Panamá. It flies in the lower Rio Grande Valley of Texas from May to November.

Genus PIRUNA Evans

This genus contains about a dozen small blackish species which have small whitish spots on at least the fore wings above. Males lack a stigma. The terminal segment of the palpi is long and protrudes forward. The antennal club is gently arched and ends in a pointed segment, but no apiculus is formed. The fore tibial epiphysis is reduced to a small scale-like structure. The middle tibiae are spined. The genus is principally distributed through Mexico with a few species extending south to Guatemala. Three species occur in the western United States.

1. **Piruna pirus** (Edwards). Plate 91, figure 17, ♂. This is a plain dark brown little skipper above, with a row of three small subapical white spots and usually one or two more minute spots below the end of the cell of the fore wings. This species, because of the blunt antennae, the forward projecting palpi and the wing markings above, looks something like a species of *Pholisora* or perhaps *Staphylus*. The lower surface is distinctive, however, because of the decidedly rusty cast to the brown, especially on the hind wings. There are no spots on the hind wings above or below. Nothing is known of the biology. Wingspread, 22–26 mm.

Distribution: Known so far from Wyoming, Colorado, Utah, New Mexico and Arizona, *P. pirus* may possibly occur also in Sonora, Mexico. There is one record from coastal southern California. The insect flies during June and July. The California specimen was taken in September.

2. **Piruna polingii** (Barnes). Plate 91, figure 16, ♂. A small warm brown skipper with conspicuous small white spots on the fore wing above, *P. polingii* usually also has two or three larger pale yellowish or whitish spots discally on the upperside of the hind wing. Below, this species is rich reddish brown with a line of three silvery spots and usually a more basal one on the hind wing. The early stages are not known. Wingspread, 20–26 mm.

Distribution: This species is found in the mountains of Arizona and New Mexico, perhaps also Colorado, and in Mexico. It flies in June and July.

3. **Piruna microsticta** (Godman). Plate 92, figure 32, ♂. This small blackish species has numerous small white dots on the fore wing and several on the hind wing above. The fore wing spots below are similar to those of the upperside; the hind wing is blackish, often with an ochre cast and numerous small white dots arranged in two curved lines and one more basal in the middle of the cell. The fringes are checkered at the vein ends. This species closely resembles several Mexican *Piruna* and has often been confused with one or more of them. The only skippers north of Mexico with which this species might be confused, because of the hind wing markings below, are several spotted species of *Amblyscirtes;* but the upper surface of *microsticta* does not resemble any of those. Nothing is known of the biology. Wingspread, 20–22 mm.

Distribution: This species evidently is taken rather rarely in Mexico. There is only a single specimen known from Texas, and Skinner records it with doubt from Arizona. The residence of this skipper in the United States would seem to require verification.

Genus CARTEROCEPHALUS Lederer

This genus contains thirteen species of small to medium sized skippers that are brown or blackish above and have large orange, yellow or white spots. The hind wings below have yellowish or silver spots. The wings are rather broad and males have no stigma. The antennal club is blunt without an apiculus. The last segment of the palpi is long and projects forward. The tibia of the fore leg is long and bears an abbreviated epiphysis. The middle and hind legs have the tibiae spined; there is only a single pair of spurs in our species. All of the species are Asian. Two of these also occur in Europe and one in North America as well.

1. **Carterocephalus palaemon** (Pallas). Plate 92, figure 1, ♂ (ssp. *mandan*). This distinctive insect should not be confused with any other North American skipper. The fore wings above are large-spotted with about equal amounts of black and orange. The hind wings are usually mostly black with large rounded orange spots. The fore wings below are yellowish with black spots, the hind wings reddish brown with distinctly outlined, rounded yellowish spots. This is a boreal insect and, in the West at least, seems to inhabit forest glades rather than open meadows. Wingspread, 20–30 mm.

Early Stages: The early stages have in part been described by Fletcher and by Scudder. The egg is pale greenish white, hemispherical, faintly reticulate and about 0.8 mm in diameter. The first stage larva is yellowish white with a black head. The half grown larva is pale green and translucent with three pale, longitudinal stripes on each side, the middle one of each group more white. The head is whitish with a diffuse dark patch on each side. The mature larva is glaucous green to uniform cream with a darker green middorsal stripe and a whitish or pale yellowish stripe on each side; below these is a line of blackish spots. Eggs were laid in confinement on Kentucky Bluegrass (*Poa pratensis*). Fletcher noted that the larvae fed readily on all grasses offered but seemed to prefer broad-bladed species. The preferred grass for oviposition in Sonoma county, California, is Purple Reedgrass (*Calamagrostis purpurascens*), a broad-bladed grass of forest glades. The larvae are reported to make no shelters after the fourth molt, lying instead upon the upper surface of the leaves.

Distribution: This rather variable species ranges transcontinentally across the northern United States and Canada from Nova Scotia west to Alaska and Washington. The species ranges southward to Pennsylvania, northern Michigan and Minnesota, and in the west through western Oregon to Sonoma and Sierra counties in California. Several subspecific names are available for some of the North American populations, but the differences between them are slight, and a number of additional local populations are equally distinguishable. Because of this, and the considerable individual variation expressed in most populations, I believe that no useful purpose is served by applying those names in this work. I refer all North American populations to the subspecies *mandan* (Edwards). The species tends to fly early in the year. In most places from Alaska to New England and the Cascades of California it flies in June. In central California it is taken in May. It is reported from Michigan in August.

Subfamily PYRGINAE

The skippers of this subfamily generally feed as larvae on dicotyledonous plants. Included here are all of the small to medium sized black-and-white checkered skippers, all of the broad winged dark brown or blackish skippers called dusky-wings or sooty-wings, all of the large brownish tropical skippers with long swallowtail-like extensions of the hind wings, as well as the several tropical species having bright bluish or greenish iridescence on the upper surface. Almost none of the species of this subfamily which occur in our region is orange or tawny. The antennae are generally long, the club often long and curved. The body may be robust, particularly in the larger tropical species, or it may be relatively slender, in which case it does not extend much beyond the margin of the hind wings. The tibiae of the fore and middle legs are not spined. Males never have a stigma on the fore wing, but may have a fold along the upperside of the costal margin, or a dense pencil or brush of hairs of the hind tibia and a paired flap-like extension of the thorax covering the ventral surface of the abdomen at its base. Males in some genera bear a specialized erectile tuft of hairs on the hind wings. The eggs of members of this group are usually vertically ribbed and the ribs are connected by horizontal cross pieces. The head of a mature larva is rounded or expanded above and heart shaped, often with prominent eye-like spots high on the face. The body is generally robust, as is the pupa. The tongue case of the pupa is usually short, not extending free beyond the tip of the wing pads. This large subfamily is world wide, but is best represented in the American tropics. Most of the species are easily recognized by their markings.

Genus PHOLISORA Scudder

This is a small genus of small to medium sized black skippers which have long, forward projecting palpi. The antennae are not long and the club is curved sickle-like and tapered to a blunt tip with no distinct reflexed apiculus. The wings are broad and the outer margin quite rounded. Two of the species have a costal fold in the male but a tibial tuft is not present in this genus. The five species included are all North American and are generally easy to distinguish.

1. **Pholisora catullus** (Fabricius). Plate 92, figure 2, ♀. This small black skipper may have many minute white dots on the fore wing above, or all but two or three subapical dots may be absent. A series of small white spots arranged in a submarginal row may be present on the hind wings but they are commonly lacking. Males have

a costal fold. The hind wings below and the fringes are uniform sooty brown. This is a common skipper in many parts of its range. Wingspread, 22–30 mm.

Early Stages: The yellowish to whitish egg is small, about 0.5 mm in diameter and nearly as high. The upper part is extraordinarily mounded with a few large dome-like tubercles which merge downward into the prominent vertical ribs. The first stage larva is yellow with a black tip and a black head. The half grown larva is pale yellowish green with two thin yellowish lines on each side and a black head. The mature larva is dull pale green, uniformly flecked with pale dots; the head is blackish brown with a thin covering of tawny hairs. The pupa is purplish brown, covered by a glaucous bloom. The foodplants are usually various Chenopodiaceae and Amaranthaceae. Edwards lists *Chenopodium* sp., *Ambrosia* sp., *Monarda punctata* and *Origanum* as foodplants, the latter two of which are in the mint family. Newcomer reports the larvae on *Malva rotundifolia;* Kendall has collected larvae on *Chenopodium album, C. ambrosioides, C. berlandieri, Amaranthus caudatus, A. spinosus* and *A. retroflexus* in Texas; and Shapiro adds to the list *Marrubium, Celosia argentea* var. *cristata* and *Chenopodium paganum,* used in Delaware and New York.

Distribution: This species is found from Quebec to British Columbia and south to Georgia and California, ranging across the entire United States with the exception of Florida. The species extends southward in Baja California and in the northern part of the Central Plateau of Mexico. In the south it flies from March to November; in the north it may appear as early as April, and it may have two broods.

2. **Pholisora mejicana** (Reakirt). Plate 92, figure 3, ♂. This species is exactly like *catullus* on the upper surface, and its markings are nearly as variable. It is easily recognized, however, by the bluish gray luster to the blackish hind wings below, upon which the black veins stand out conspicuously. A costal fold is present on the male fore wing. Nothing is known of the early stages. Wingspread, 20–28 mm.

Distribution: This species is seldom collected north of Mexico. It is known from Colorado, Texas, New Mexico and Arizona. South of the United States it ranges widely in Mexico. It flies from May through August.

3. **Pholisora libya** (Scudder). Plate 92, figure 4, ♂ (ssp. *libya*); Plate 97, figure 1, ♂ (ssp. *lena*); figure 2, ♀ (ssp. *lena*). This species is blackish above with a conspicuous series of three relatively large subapical spots, and usually also a vague series of submarginal spots which may be faint. The marginal area, particularly apically, has a diffuse brassy sheen. Males may have no more markings than those mentioned but females generally have a number of additional small white spots on the fore wing above. The hind wings are unspotted. The fore wings below are black, with subapical white spots and an apical brassy overscaled area. The hind wings below are heavily overscaled with light olive or buff; they have at least a large white spot in the cell and another at the end of the cell, usually also a white spot halfway along the inner edge of the whitish anal fold and a series of conspicuous submarginal white spots. Males of this and the two following species do not have a costal fold. Wingspread, 24–34 mm.

Early Stages: The egg is large, about 1 mm in diameter, low hemispherical, the vertical ribs knobbed at the junction of the cross ridges. It is dull orange at first, changing to soiled ivory white. The first stage larva is pale yellow with a dark head. The mature larva is pale blue-green, profusely dotted with small white papillae, each of which bears a white hair. There are three lines of black dots running longitudinally on each side. The head is black and densely covered with short orange hair. The pupa is stout with the end of the abdomen curved ventrally, light brown, darker on the abdomen; the wing pads are black. The foodplant is *Atriplex canescens* and possibly other species of the same genus.

Distribution: P. libya is a desert species, ranging from Montana west to Oregon and south to Colorado, Arizona and southern California. The more southern populations, in the Mojave and Sonoran deserts, are well marked below, usually with a complete series of conspicuous submarginal spots. These are the nominate subspecies. Populations of the Great Basin, from eastern California to Colorado and northward, are larger and tend to have few white spots on the hind wings below. These have been referred to the subspecies *P. libya lena* (Edwards). The species also ranges southward into Sonora and Baja California, Mexico. In southern California, nominate *libya* flies from March through May, and in September and October; *l. lena* flies during June and July.

4. **Pholisora alpheus** (Edwards). Plate 92, figure 5, ♂ (ssp. *alpheus*); figure 10, ♂, underside (ssp. *alpheus*); Plate 97, figure 5, ♀ (ssp *oricus*). This species and the next are rather closely related to *libya*. A dark brown to blackish species, *alpheus* generally has on the fore wing above a discal series of wedge-shaped black dashes basad of which are often small whitish discal spots; the latter are more often present in females. A subapical series of two or three white or whitish spots is usually present. The fringes may be nearly blackish or very distinctly checkered with white. Even in the darkest examples however, there is usually some checkering on the fore wings. The hind wings above may be unmarked blackish or dark brown, or there may be, especially in females, a small pale line marking the end of the cell and an obscure submarginal series of small whitish spots. The hind wings below are variable but usually have a white line at the end of the cell and a minute white spot halfway to the base within the cell. The wing can be almost entirely blackish or heavily overscaled with white, producing a grizzled aspect. Generally the anal fold is as dark as the rest of the wing. There may be an obscure pale spot or two along the edge of the anal fold near the mark at the end of the cell. If that spot is evident, there is usually a more conspicuous submarginal series of white spots running from the anal fold almost to the costa. Males lack a costal fold. Wingspread, 20–30 mm.

Early Stages: The early stages described by Comstock (1929) under this name refer to *gracielae*. Adults of the subspecies *alpheus oricus* in the Mojave Desert of California were found to be closely associated with *Atriplex canescens,* and females were particularly partial to low young plants of this species. Although oviposition was not observed it is probable that *A. canescens* serves as the larval foodplant in that area. Roever (*in litt.*) has raised larvae of nominate *alpheus* in Arizona on *A. canescens.*

Distribution: This species ranges from the Mojave Desert, and the Great Basin of California and Oregon east to Colorado and south to Texas, Arizona and northern Mexico. Southern populations are dark with almost no white overscaling on the fore wings above or the hind wings below. They represent nominate *alpheus* and occur in Arizona, New Mexico, Colorado, Texas and Mexico. Populations of the Mojave Desert and the Great Basin are quite different because of the heavy white overscaling on the fore wings above, especially outside of the wedge-shaped dashes. The white subapical spots are conspicuous and the fringes are boldly checkered. The hind wings below usually are heavily white overscaled and grizzled, and the submarginal series of spots is commonly well developed. These populations represent *alpheus oricus* Edwards and occur in California, Oregon, Nevada, Utah and Colorado. The nominate subspecies is evidently double brooded, flying from March to July and again in September. Examples of the second brood are generally darker but retain the submarginal spots on the fore wing above. *P. a. oricus* is so far known to fly only from April to June.

5. **Pholisora gracielae** MacNeill. Plate 97, figure 10, ♂; figure 11, ♀. This recently described species has long been confused with *alpheus;* Comstock (1927) figured *gracielae* under the name *alpheus*. *P. gracielae* much resembles nominate *alpheus* but is smaller; the fore wings above have the discal black marks short, seldom clearly elongate into wedge-shaped dashes; and there is a buffy overscaling that is especially prominent in females, making the nondescript black markings conspicuous. The subapical and discal spots when present are seldom white, usually buff, and the fringes are buff-and-black checkered. The hind wings below usually have a scattered buff overscaling that is particularly heavy along the anal fold, making that area somewhat grayer than the remainder of the wing. The two white spots at the end and in the middle of the cell are present, and usually there are also two, sometimes three, conspicuous buff spots separated by dark veins, forming a slightly curved line of spots linking the one at the end of the cell with the anal fold. If a submarginal series of pale spots is present it is obscure and becomes obsolete on the costal half of the wing. The palpi are longer than in *alpheus* and somewhat pendulous. This little skipper seems to be strictly a riparian associate, and its behavior is distinctive. Seldom venturing out into the open, it tends to stay well within the twigs and branches of the large *Atriplex* shrubs that doubtless serve as the larval foodplant. Since these bushes commonly form dense stands, the insect can travel long distances without moving outside of the foliage canopy of the shrubs. While standing on a small, low slash pile that narrowly connected two stands of the *Atriplex* shrub, I watched individuals pass beneath me, well within the tangle of slash, moving from one stand to the other. Not one example made the crossing in the open during a half-hour period. Thus, although the species is extremely abundant in its habitat, it is difficult to collect. Neither *gracielae* nor *alpheus* is commonly observed at flowers. Wingspread, 18–24 mm.

Early Stages: The early stages of this species were described under the name *alpheus* by Comstock (1929). The egg is high hemispherical, about 0.75 mm in diameter, and ivory colored, darker in the depressions. The vertical ribs are knobbed at the junctions of the cross ridges. The mature larva is dull green and covered with small whitish nodules. The head is brownish black with a dense vestiture of wavy yellowish pile. The pupa is straw colored, slightly darker on the abdomen and covered with a powdery white bloom. Comstock lists the foodplant as *Atriplex expansa,* but I have only found the species in close association with *A. lentiformis* which, according to Roever, serves as the larval foodplant.

Distribution: Thus far *gracielae* is known only from the drainage systems of the Colorado River in Arizona and California. It unquestionably occurs also along that river in Mexico. The species flies in April and May, and again from late July to October. Examples of the latter brood are often much darker, and on the upper surface even the subapical spots are commonly wanting. The slightly curved band of spots from the cell end to the pale anal fold on the hind wing below may be the only whitish spots on the insect, although this band may be suggested on the upperside in pale brown.

Genus CELOTES Godman & Salvin

This genus of only one small tannish brown species is similar to *Pholisora* but the rounded fore wings are slightly indented before the anal angle and the hind wings are broad but crenulate. Males have a costal fold and a slender tuft of long hairs on the hind tibia which fits into a ventral pouch between a thoracic flap and the abdomen. The genus is confined to the southern, especially southwestern, United States and Mexico.

1. **Celotes nessus** (Edwards). Plate 92, figure 6, ♂. This species is easily identified by the long narrow V-shaped dark markings projecting inward from the margin, the variegated dark and light brown markings and the distribution of small hyaline spots on both wings. The fringes are conspicuously checkered. *C. nessus* seems partial to dry washes of the foothills, in Arizona. Wingspread, 20–26 mm.

Early Stages: These are not described. Kendall has recorded *Abutilon incanum, Althaea rosea, Sida filipes, Sphaeralcea lobata* and *Wissadula amplissima* as larval foodplants in nature.

Distribution: This species is found in Arizona, New Mexico, Texas and, rarely, Louisiana. It also occurs in northern Mexico. *C. nessus* flies from March to November in Texas.

Genus HELIOPETES Billberg

This genus comprises fourteen or fifteen white and black skippers of about medium size. Most species are broadly whitish but one or two are checkered above like members of the following genus, *Pyrgus.* The wings are rather broad and more or less rounded in some species. The antennae are not long and the club is narrow and curved, conspicuously blunt in some species and in others tapered to a point, but there is no reflexed apiculus. The palpi project forward and the third segment is somewhat long but the species may vary in this respect. In no case are the palpi as long proportionately as they are in *Pholisora* and *Celotes*. Males have both a costal fold and a hair pencil arising at the base of the tibia. This group of skippers is closely related to *Pyrgus* and to several genera of the Palearctic region. *Heliopetes* is primarily tropical American, however, and occurs from Argentina to Washington state. As with *Celotes* and most of *Pyrgus*, as far as known *Heliopetes* seem to prefer malvaceous plants as larval food. Four species occur in our region.

1. **Heliopetes domicella** (Erichson). Plate 92, figure 14, ♂. Easily recognized from the figure, this smaller species looks somewhat like a *Pyrgus* species with a broad white central band on both wings above. The fore wing below is dark near the base and the fringes are checkered. The species may be separated from any *Pyrgus* by the broad dark border of both wings above and by the pattern on the hind wing below; and from other *Heliopetes* north of Mexico by the dark border and dark base of both wings above. The early stages are not described. Wingspread 24–34 mm.

 Distribution: H. domicella ranges from southern Arizona and Texas to Argentina. There are three subspecies in South America and one of these, nominate *domicella*, reaches our area. It is taken in April and from August to October in the United States.

2. **Heliopetes ericetorum** (Boisduval). Plate 92, figure 12, ♂. Males of this species can be separated easily from other *Heliopetes* by the narrow crescents in the border of both wings and the lack of a broadly darkened fore wing apex above. The white is slightly more creamy than in the other species, and this cream becomes rich and yellowish if the specimen has been left in a cyanide jar for very long. Females above are much darker, having a broad bluish gray basal area on both wings, a moderately narrow central white band, and a broad, checkered border. This border has much larger white spots within than does *H. domicella*, which otherwise it somewhat resembles. Females thus appear much like a large *Pyrgus*. The fore wings below do not have a conspicuously dark basal third of the wing, and the pattern on the hind wings is pale brownish. Wingspread, 26–38 mm.

 Early Stages: The egg is high hemispherical, about 0.75 mm in diameter, and pale lemon yellow soon changing to chalky white. First stage larva is pale lemon yellow with a whitish sheen; the head is black with a few scattered hairs. The half grown larva is pale greenish yellow studded with numerous rounded tubercles each bearing white, pronged hairs; the head is black and heavily clothed with similar white hairs. The mature larva is similar, but with a green middorsal line and a single green line, a yellowish line and a broader yellowish band on each side. The body becomes pinkish as pupation approaches. The head is black, densely clothed with branching hairs. The pupa is yellowish brown with pinkish abdominal segments but these colors are obscured by a dense covering of a bright bluish bloom. Coolidge lists *Sphaeralcea fasciculata, S. Davidsonii, S. exilis, S. ambigua, S. rotundifolia, S. angustifolia, Malva borealis*, hollyhock (*Althaea*) and *Amaranthus blitoides*, as larval foodplants for this species. Newcomer notes oviposition on Globe Mallow (*Iliamna rivularis*).

 Distribution: North of Mexico this skipper is known from Washington, Oregon,

California, Nevada, Arizona, New Mexico and Colorado. It also ranges into Mexico in Baja California and on the mainland south to Guerrero. In southern California it flies from December to November in five broods, but to the north and in the mountains it is on the wing for a much shorter period. The species is most abundant in arid regions. It is generally less common to the north.

3. **Heliopetes laviana** (Hewitson). Plate 92, figure 11, ♂. This species is similar to *ericetorum* but usually is colder white above; in males this has a slightly lustrous sheen, and in females a slight pearly iridescence. The border is broadly darkened at the apex of the fore wings, especially so in females. The hind wings below are brownish, often with an olive tint, and there is a deep V-shaped indentation into the subbasal band; the inner edge of the broad outer brown area is straight. Wing-spread, 32–42 mm.

Early Stages: The immature stages of this species are not described. Larval foodplants are given as "Convolvulaceae" by Costa Lima for a Brazilian subspecies. The foodplants utilized by larvae of northern populations are given by Moreno & Bibby as *Abutilon hypoleucum* and *Pseudabutilon Lozani* and by Kendall as *Abutilon abutiloides, Sida filipes, Malvastrum americanum* and, in confinement, *Abutilon incanum* and *Wissadula holosericea.*

Distribution: H. laviana ranges from Texas to Arizona south to Argentina. In South America four subspecies represent *laviana.* In southern Texas it flies throughout the year.

4. **Heliopetes macaira** (Reakirt). Plate 92, figure 13, ♂. This skipper resembles *laviana* but is slightly smaller and has somewhat more rounded wings. The apex of the fore wing in males is less broadly darkened. The lower surface of the hindwing differs from that of *laviana* in that the inner edge of the broad marginal brown border is curved more or less parallel to the wing margin, not inwardly a distinct straight line. This species seems to prefer wooded or brushy areas in Texas. Wingspread, 30–34 mm.

Early Stages: These are not reported. Kendall lists the larval foodplant as *Malvaviscus Drummondii.*

Distribution: This species, like *laviana,* is recorded from Texas west to Arizona and south to Paraguay. Additional subspecies occur in South America. In the lower Rio Grande Valley of Texas this species flies throughout the year.

Genus PYRGUS Hübner

This large genus embraces some thirty-odd species which are characteristically small insects with black-and-white spotted or checkered wings and checkered fringes. The wings are usually rather broad and somewhat rounded. Structurally *Pyrgus* is similar to *Heliopetes* and it is also closely related to several Eurasian and North African genera. Males of most species have a hair pencil on the hind tibia and a number of species also have a costal fold on the fore wing. Several subspecies of one American species (*communis*) are the only populations which lack both of these characters in males. The genus ranges through Europe to northern India and China in the Old World. About a dozen species represent the genus in America, where it is distributed from Alaska and Labrador south to Patagonia. It is also present in the West Indies. Seven species occur within the region covered by this book.

1. **Pyrgus centaureae** (Rambur). Plate 92, figure 15, ♀.   This, like *ruralis, xanthus* and *scriptura,* is generally a small black skipper with white spots above. It closely resembles those three species but may be distinguished in that the two white spots (sometimes just one) near the middle of the hind margin of the fore wing are adjacent and the uppermost is not next to the cell. Therefore no white spot is placed next to the central part of the fore wing cell. The hind wings above usually have a submarginal series and sometimes a large cell spot and other discal spots. Males have a slender costal fold on the fore wing and a brush on the hind tibia. Nothing is known of the early stages. Wingspread, 22–32 mm.

Distribution: This circumpolar species is represented in northern Eurasia by two subspecies and in North America by three. *Pyrgus centaureae wyandot* (Edwards) is small and dark and flies on grassy hillsides from New York south to North Carolina. *P. c. freija* (Warren) is larger with larger squarish spots above and is much more strikingly black-and-white on the under surface. This subarctic subspecies ranges from Alaska to Labrador south to Manitoba and the mountains of the Gaspé Peninsula. A third subspecies, *P. c. loki* Evans (figured), is found in alpine and subalpine situations in the Rocky Mountains from British Columbia to Colorado. It is generally even larger than *freija* and is similarly well spotted above, but below the dark bands are more olive brown than black and the fringes are more strongly checkered. The species flies early in the summer, May in the east, and during June or July in the Rocky Mountains and in the north.

2. **Pyrgus ruralis** (Boisduval). Plate 92, figure 16, ♂.   This little black skipper has squarish white spots on the fore wing above and two bands of white spots on the hind wings. On the fore wing of this and all following species of the genus there is a conspicuous white spot next to the posterior central part of the cell, anterior to the single or double spot near the middle of the hind margin. The submarginal band of hind wing spots is quite variable but is generally comprised of deeply crescentic or V-shaped spots which give the band a zigzag aspect. The band may be reduced on occasion, and in one group of populations is greatly enlarged and almost merges with the discal band, giving the hind wing a broad whitish, rather than blackish, appearance. The hind wings below vary greatly. The dark areas are often distinctly rusty red and they vary to dark sooty brown, olive brown, or dull grayish. Males have both a very slender costal fold on the fore wing and a hair pencil on the hind tibia. This is a mountain species, not ordinarily found on the low valleys and prairies. Wingspread, 20–28 mm.

Early Stages: Little is published concerning the biology of this species. Coolidge described the egg as hemispherical, about 0.5 mm in diameter and about as high, pale greenish at first, changing to light lemon yellow. Lembert lists the foodplant as *Horkelia fusca.* Comstock mentions *Horkelia tenuiloba* and Emmel & Emmel suggest *Potentilla Drummondi.* Shields and J. Emmel (*in litt.*) suggest that the foodplant in southern California is *Horkelia bolanderi clevelandii.*

Distribution: This montane species ranges from British Columbia and Alberta south to southern California, Nevada and Colorado. Although not reported from Mexico it will undoubtedly be found to occur in the northern mountains of Baja California. This species flies from April to July depending upon the locality.

3. **Pyrgus xanthus** Edwards. Plate 92, figure 19, ♀. This may well be a subspecies of *ruralis.* It differs from *ruralis* mainly in the reduced and usually not deeply crescentic submarginal spots of the hind wing above. Males lack a costal fold on the fore wing but do have a tibial tuft of hairs. *P. xanthus* is almost impossible to separate from early spring examples of *scriptura* without examining the genitalia, and these two species have been confused in the literature. *P. xanthus* and its close relative *ruralis* are, however, mountain inhabitants whereas *scriptura* is usually a lowland skipper, particularly at home in agricultural regions. Nothing is known regarding the early stages of *xanthus.* Wingspread, 22–26 mm.

Distribution: P. xanthus inhabits boreal regions of southern Colorado, New Mexico and Arizona. It may extend into Mexico along the Sierra Madre Occidental. It flies from May to July.

4. **Pyrgus scriptura** (Boisduval). Plate 92, figure 21, ♂. This is the smallest species of the genus in our region. Like the three preceding species, *scriptura* is black with small white spots, but it is ordinarily easily recognized. The black above is usually somewhat glossy and generally lacks any bluish gray overscaling, particularly basally where the other species usually are heavily overscaled. The fore wing spots are ordinarily small, the submarginal series on the hind wings weakly developed or absent and the discal series often reduced to a single spot at the end of the cell. The fringes are long and broadly white because of a reduction in the black checkering. The hind wings below are frequently more or less cream, with the dark and light pattern poorly contrasted. *P. scriptura* is variable, however, and early spring examples in particular can closely resemble *xanthus* and *ruralis* in nearly every respect. The males lack a costal fold but have a hind tibial tuft. This lowland species is found in close association with the larval food, a malvaceous plant that is especially opportunistic in disturbed places such as marginal wastelands associated with agriculture and road construction. Wingspread, 16–24 mm.

Early Stages: These have not been described. Comstock suggested the probable foodplant as Alkali Mallow (*Sida hederacea*). J. A. Powell and I have confirmed this on a number of occasions in central California.

Distribution: P. scriptura ranges from Wyoming, Colorado and New Mexico west through Arizona to California and northern Baja California. In California it flies from March to September.

5. **Pyrgus oileus** (Linnaeus). Plate 92, figure 20, ♂. *Pyrgus oileus* has previously been known in most books as *P. syrichtus* (Fabricius). This skipper and the two following species, *philetas* and *communis,* are basically grayish (males) or blackish (females) with a heavy checkering of white spots above. They differ from the preceding four species in having a submarginal and marginal series of spots on the fore wing in addition to the large discal series. The hind wings also have a conspicuous sub-marginal and marginal series of spots. Males of this species are bluish gray above, caused by extensive basal, discal and anal areas of long bluish gray hair. There are usually no white spots between the anal margin and the cell at the basal third of the fore wing, usually present in males of *philetas.* Females are darker, with smaller spots and the basal hair is conspicuous only on the hind wing. The submarginal spots of the hind wing above are generally much larger than the marginal spots. The hind wings below in both sexes are whitish or sometimes suffused smoky brown, with distinct fine black lines outlining the several series of grayish spots. Between the base and the apex along the costal margin (in North American populations) are three dark brown spots; just below the basal and middle of these are two angulate spots defined only by the fine black outlining. *P. philetas* has an almost unmarked costal margin and the subcostal spots are usually only represented by dark dots. Males have a prominent costal fold and a hind tibial brush or hair pencil. Wing-spread, 26–32 mm.

Early Stages: The early stages of this insect have been often described, principally for West Indian populations where the species is abundant. The egg is hemispherical, cream colored and about 0.5 mm in diameter. The first stage larva is cream with a few lines of branched hairs; the head is blackish. The half grown larva is light greenish with cream tubercles bearing terminally flattened hairs; the head is black and wrinkled. The mature larva is green with a faint middorsal line and numerous slightly flattened hairs, each arising from a white rounded tubercle; the head is black with dense short hairs. The pupa is greenish with numerous white hairs, dull yellowish green on the abdomen with a darker middorsal line. Scudder lists *Sida, Malva, Abutilon* and hollyhock (*Althaea*) as foodplants in the United States. Several species of *Sida* are mentioned for West Indian populations.

Distribution: Within the United States *oileus* is known from southern Florida, Mississippi, Arkansas and eastern Texas. It ranges southward to Argentina and through the West Indies. Two subspecies represent the species in South America. Our subspecies is nominate *oileus.* In Florida and southern Texas it flies throughout the year. Skinner's (1911) report of this species from Arizona or southern California is probably based upon a misidentification.

6. **Pyrgus philetas** Edwards. Plate 92, figure 31, ♂; figure 36, ♀. This smaller species resembles *oileus* closely. Males differ in having much less bluish hairy vestiture above and in having one or two white spots between the cell and the anal margin of the fore wing about one-third of the distance from the base. In both sexes the sub-marginal series of spots on the hind wing above is usually somewhat reduced so that they are commonly not much larger than those of the conspicuous marginal

series. The hind wing below is generally whitish with the five bands broken into separate short dashes; the costal margin unmarked except at the apex; and subcostally, above the cell and just beyond, usually only two to four small black dots. This surface is thus much less contrastingly marked than that of *oileus*. Males have both a costal fold and a tibial brush. Nothing is known of the early stages. Wingspread, 22–30 mm.

Distribution: P. philetas ranges from central Texas to southern New Mexico and Arizona. It is widespread in mainland Mexico and is known from Baja California. In Texas it has been collected from February to December.

7. **Pyrgus communis** (Grote). Plate 92, figure 17, ♂ (ssp. *communis*); figure 18, ♀ (ssp. *communis*); figure 33, ♂ (ssp. *albescens*); figure 34, ♀ (ssp. *albescens*). This skipper, like *philetas,* is grayish in males, blackish in females, with numerous white spots providing a checkered aspect. The marginal spots are reduced but the submarginal spots are well developed above. The hind wings below are white with several bands of olive tan or olive brown with a scarcely contrasting fine black outlining. This species lacks a tibial tuft in the male. Males north of Mexico all have a costal fold, but this structure is lacking in some Central and South American populations. *P. communis* is one of the more common skippers throughout most of our region. Wingspread 20–32 mm.

Early Stages: The egg is about 0.5 mm in diameter, rounded hemispherical and greenish white at first, becoming cream just before hatching. The first stage larva is cream and most of the dorsal hairs have forked and recurved tips; the head is black. The half grown larva is light brownish with darker longitudinal lines similar to those of mature larvae; the head is black and densely covered with short, slightly branched, hairs. The mature larva is yellowish white to brownish with a gray-green to dark brownish middorsal line and on each side are two prominent brownish lines and two thin white lateral lines. The surface is peppered with tiny white tubercles each bearing either a long split hair or a short terminally flattened one; the head is black and covered with a dense pile of tawny hairs. The pupa is light greenish anteriorly, light brown on the abdomen which also is marked with transverse bands of blackish dots and streaks. The larval foodplants are several rough-leaved Malvaceae of the genera *Abutilon, Althaea, Anoda, Callirhoe, Hibiscus, Malva, Sida, Sidalcea* and *Sphaeralcea.*

Distribution: P. communis ranges from Canada to Argentina and is represented through its range by half a dozen subspecies. Two of these come within the province of this book; they are superficially indistinguishable although they are genitalically different. The status of these two, as subspecies or something else, is still uncertain. The nominate subspecies is distributed throughout the region from Canada to Mexico and from coast to coast; it extends well into southern Mexico. The subspecies *communis albescens* Plötz occurs from the desert areas of southern California east to Texas. In most regions where both subspecies occur *communis* inhabits the cooler more northern or boreal areas or the more humid sections, whereas *albescens* is an inhabitant of the hotter or more arid lowland areas. Thus, in southeastern Arizona, nominate *communis* occurs in numerous isolated populations in the boreal mountain "islands" of the region, surrounded entirely by populations of *albescens* in the desert lowlands. In Texas *communis* is the most widespread and is absent only from the Rio Grande Plains area east of the Pecos River and on the southern Gulf coast, where it is replaced by *albescens*. In most areas the species flies all year except during the winter.

Genus ERYNNIS Schrank

This is a large genus of medium sized to almost large skippers which are dark brownish above, usually with a few small whitish, often hyaline, spots on the fore wing and some patterns of very dark brown or almost black. A number of populations have white fringes on the hind wings. By and large most of the species tend to look alike, and this, together with individual and seasonal variation makes identification difficult. Detailed collecting data can be an important aid to identification. Males generally are darker, often with a hairy vestiture on the fore wings, and have reduced whitish spots. Females usually have more contrasting patterns and larger hyaline spots. The antennae are not long and the club is bent into a gentle arc with a blunt or pointed tip. The palpi project conspicuously forward from the face. The fore wing is slightly bowed so that the apex is inclined to droop. Males of all our species have a costal fold on the fore wing and several species also have a tibial tuft. The male genitalia, especially the valvae, are highly asymmetrical in all but *icelus* and *brizo*. Most *Erynnis* rest with their wings held more or less horizontally, and sleep with the wings folded down over the body, roof-like, in the manner of many moths. The genus is Holarctic, with four species confined to Eurasia and the remaining eighteen or so confined to the American continent where the range extends from Alaska to Chile and Argentina, including the West Indies and the Galápagos Islands. All the American species but one are found north of Mexico.

Confusion regarding the identity of most of these species in the past makes many of the early descriptions of immature stages of little use. A generalized description of these for the genus follows and only foodplant information is provided at the species level, drawn principally from Burns (1964) and subsequent workers. The egg is small, about 0.75 mm in diameter, high hemispherical with prominent vertical ribbing. It is usually pale greenish, becoming salmon within several days; one species, *pacuvius,* does not undergo such a color change in the egg. The first stage larva is pale greenish yellow with a blackish or yellowish head. The half-grown larva is pale green profusely sprinkled with white dots from which arise the pale short body hairs. The head is broad above, usually depressed at the top and with a suggestion of knobs at the top on each side; the color is blackish with a few reddish spots, or reddish with yellowish spots. The mature larva is similar with a more strongly angulate and more completely spotted head. Winter is usually passed in this stage. The pupa is dark brown to greenish. Eggs of species feeding as larvae on tree foliage may be more concentrated on low sucker shoots or saplings.

1. **Erynnis icelus** (Scudder & Burgess). Plate 93, figure 1, ♂. This small to medium sized skipper is closely related to a Mexican species not treated here. These two, together with *brizo,* are most closely allied to the Old World representatives of the genus and comprise a special subgroup. *E. icelus* and *brizo* generally have no sub-apical white spots or any other white spots on the fore wing. The hind wings usually have a marginal and irregular discal series of pale brown spots. The discal series of black marks on the fore wing usually takes the form of opposed fine black crescents, giving the band a "chain-linked" aspect. The wings of this species are short and rounded. Males have a tibial brush on the hind leg. The palpi of *icelus* are especially long and the tip of the antennal club is sharp. Wingspread, 25–35 mm.

Early Stages: According to Burns the larvae feed chiefly upon species of *Salix* and *Populus.* They also apparently feed upon Black Locust, and Shapiro records *Betula populifolia* as an additional foodplant.

Distribution: This species ranges from Nova Scotia to British Columbia, south in the East to Georgia, Indiana and Minnesota, and west of the prairies south to New Mexico, Arizona, Nevada and California. It has been reported from Mexico but this requires verification. Everywhere this species seems to fly from April to August, being ordinarily more common early in this period.

2. **Erynnis brizo** (Boisduval & Le Conte). This is a brown or grayish skipper without any distinct white spots on the fore wing and with the discal marks "chain-like," as in *icelus.* Males have no tibial tuft on the hind leg. The palpi are much shorter than those of *icelus* and are about the normal length for the genus. The club of the antenna is stout with a blunt tip. The species is represented north of Mexico by four similar subspecies most easily distinguished by the form of the male genitalia.

(a) **brizo** (Boisduval & Le Conte). Plate 93, figure 2, ♀; figure 3, ♂. This subspecies is generally quite brownish with the grayish overscaling most evident within the discal and central "chain-like" dark bands. Females may be quite pale brown on the fore wing between these two darker bands, and the spots on the hind wing above may be almost yellowish. Wingspread, 30–40 mm.

Early Stages: This subspecies has been reared on *Quercus ilicifolia* and like the other populations of the species it is very likely partial to a scrub oak habitat in nature. Shapiro reports it also on American chestnut (*Castanea*).

Distribution: Nominate *brizo* occurs from Manitoba and Massachusetts south to northern Florida and eastern Texas. It is also known from northeastern Mexico. The species as a whole has a very short period of flight, generally early in the spring.

(b) **somnus** (Lintner). Plate 93, figure 21, ♂; figure 22, ♀. This subspecies is like *b. brizo* but are somewhat darker brown above. The gray overscaling seems more whitish and is more restricted than in the nominate subspecies. Wingspread, 29–37 mm.

Early Stages: Kimball (1965) lists the foodplant as *Quercus ilicifolia* but he may have intended that reference to pertain principally to nominate *brizo.*

Distribution: *E. brizo somnus* is restricted to peninsular Florida where it has been taken from January to April.

(c) **burgessi** (Skinner). Plate 93, figure 23, ♂; figure 24, ♀. This subspecies is similar to nominate *brizo* but the entire fore wing is more uniformly grayed. The fringes are usually brown, as in the other subspecies, but some southern examples have a distinct trace of white in the fringes of the hind wings. Wingspread, 31–39 mm.

Early Stages: Adults frequent scrub oak habitats and the larval foodplants are low growing oaks. Burns lists *Quercus turbinella, Q. undulata, Q. Gambelii* and a hybrid, *Q. turbinella* X *Q. arizonica,* as foodplants in nature.

Distribution: This subspecies ranges from Colorado and west Texas west to Utah, Nevada and southeastern California, and south into northern Mexico. Like the other subspecies, *burgessi* flies early in the spring. According to Kendall there is evidently, on occasion, a partial second brood in parts of Texas.

(d) **lacustra** (Wright). Plate 93, figure 19, ♂; figure 20, ♀. This skipper resembles *burgessi* but is often quite evenly gray above except for the dark "chain-like" bands. Females generally are not conspicuously paler than the males. The fringes are brown. Wingspread, 29–35 mm.

Early Stages: The foodplant is probably the scrub oak, *Quercus durata,* a chaparral constituent confined to serpentine soils in central and northern California. In southern California and Baja California the foodplant is likely to be either *Quercus dumosa* or *Q. turbinella,* both close relatives of the presumed foodplant to the north.

Distribution: E. brizo lacustra is restricted to the chaparral communities of the Coast Ranges, Sierran foothills and southern mountains of California, and to the northern ranges in Baja California. It flies from March to May.

3. **Erynnis juvenalis** (Fabricius). Plate 93, figure 9, ♂ (ssp. *juvenalis*); figure 10, ♀ (ssp. *juvenalis*); figure 35, ♂ (ssp. *clitus*); figure 36, ♀ (ssp. *clitus*). Most populations of this and the following two species, *telemachus* and *propertius,* resemble one another closely in wing pattern but differ in genitalic detail. Perhaps the most useful means of distinguishing them without examining the genitalia is careful consideration of the locality data. The only region where any two of these species are known to overlap in distribution is in east-central Arizona, where the two species concerned (*telemachus* and *j. clitus*) are easily distinguished by wing characterics. *E. juvenalis* is one of the larger members of the genus. Males have a more or less conspicuous vestiture of long curved whitish hairs which are elevated above the surface of the fore wing and directed toward the outer margin. The hyaline spots are small and consist of a subapical series, one in the upper part of the cell, and usually one or two within the discal series of darker markings which connect the subapical spots to the hind margin. There are usually two conspicuous pale brown spots on the apical third of the hind wing below, but in one subspecies these are frequently poorly defined. The general aspect of males is dark brown, with minutely grizzled patches on the fore wings, especially bordering darker brown spots. Females are pale brown above with conspicuously contrasting darker blackish brown patches, and hyaline spots similar to those of the male but larger and more numerous. There are no long raised white hairs on the fore wing but appressed scales impart a grayish cast to several pale brown regions, especially outside the subapical spots and the dark band

below, and in the central discal area. The hind wings above have a conspicuous series of pale brown spots marginally and submarginally. The two subapical pale brown spots are very evident on the lower surface of the hind wing. Males lack a hind tibial tuft. The fringes of the hind wings are brown or white. Wingspread, 32–43 mm.

Early Stages: This species feeds on oaks. Burns records the nominate subspecies feeding on *Quercus ilicifolia, mohriana,* and *rubra.* Kendall adds *Q. stellata* and *marilandica* for the same subspecies in Texas, and reports that in confinement larvae feed well on *Q. fusiformis.* Ross & Lambremont reported *Q. nigra* to be the foodplant in Louisiana. Several other plants, chiefly legumes, have been reported to serve as larval foodplants but these are considered doubtful and require verification. The southwestern subspecies, *juvenalis clitus,* is reported by Burns to feed upon *Q. arizonica, Emoryi, hypoleucoides* and probably *Gambelii* in nature. Oviposition seems to be restricted to young leaves.

Distribution: Two subspecies represent *E. juvenalis* through its range. The nominate subspecies is distributed over the eastern half of America north of Mexico, from Nova Scotia to Manitoba, south through eastern Wyoming to Texas and Florida. It is not known from Colorado or New Mexico. Nominate *juvenalis* lacks white fringes on the hind wings and is therefore the subspecies that most closely resembles the two following species. *E. juvenalis clitus* (Edwards) occurs in southeastern Arizona and Mexico. It has a less conspicuous hairy vestiture on the fore wing of males, the two subapical spots of the hind wing below are reduced or absent, and the fringe of the hind wing is white. This subspecies most closely resembles *E. tristis tatius* and *E. scudderi,* but there is never any expansion onto the wing of the white color of the fringes as in *tristis.* It is difficult to distinguish *j. clitus* from *E. scudderi,* however, without a genitalic examination except that *scudderi* is much less commonly encountered. Nominate *juvenalis* has only one brood, early in the spring, except in southern Florida where there is a partial second brood. In southeastern Arizona *clitus* flies from April to September in two broods.

4. **Erynnis telemachus** Burns. Plate 93, figure 13, ♂; figure 14, ♀. Both sexes of this skipper closely resemble *propertius* and *j. juvenalis.* Males have a heavy vestiture of the long curved elevated hairs on the fore wing, and tend to look more like *propertius* in this respect, but the fore wing is more pale brownish gray than dark gray. Both sexes seem paler than *juvenalis.* In most other respects the characteristics are much as in *juvenalis,* to which it is most closely related. This species may be readily identified by locality since none of the other most closely similar forms occurs within its range. Wingspread, 33–42 mm.

Early Stages: Burns reports the larval foodplant to be *Quercus Gambelii* in Arizona and New Mexico.

Distribution: The species ranges through Utah, Colorado, New Mexico, northern Arizona and extreme western Texas. It flies from April to July and has but a single brood.

5. **Erynnis propertius** (Scudder & Burgess). Plate 93, figure 17, ♂; figure 18, ♀. Females of this species are extremely like those of *j. juvenalis*. Males are similar to males of *telemachus,* having a fore wing densely overlaid with copious, long, curved, white hairs giving the wing a dark grayish aspect. The subapical region of the hind wing below bears two pale brown spots as in *telemachus* and *juvenalis*. The hind wing fringes are brown. This species may be recognized by its size and brown fringes alone within the region in which it occurs. Wingspread, 32–45 mm.

Early Stages: Burns lists the known foodplants as *Quercus agrifolia* and *Q. garryana.*

Distribution: This species is restricted to the Pacific states where oaks occur, from southern Vancouver Island south to northern Baja California. In California the species inhabits the mountains and hills west of the Great Basin and the desert, and seems to be absent from the floor of the Central Valley even though oaks are common. Like most *telemachus* and *juvenalis* this is an early flying species and normally has only one brood.

6. **Erynnis meridianus** Bell. Plate 93, figure 41, ♂; figure 42, ♀ (both ssp. *meridianus*). Closely related to *propertius,* this species tends to resemble *juvenalis, telemachus* and *propertius,* especially in the spring brood. Even in the spring, *meridianus* however, has a less contrasting pale and dark brown pattern. Males have elevated white hairs in the fore wing but these are shorter and less raised above the wing surface than in *telemachus* and *propertius,* and the effect is a darker brown with softer markings. The two subapical spots of the hind wings below are usually absent. Males of the second brood can sometimes be very dark and softly patterned, little resembling the several preceding species. The fringes are brown in all populations occurring north of Mexico. Wingspread, 33–43 mm.

Early Stages: Burns indicates that *Quercus arizonica* is a larval foodplant in Arizona, and *Q. fusiformis* is used in Texas.

Distribution: E. meridianus ranges from southern Nevada to northwest Texas, and south at least to central Mexico; it is represented by two subspecies through this range. The nominate subspecies has brown hind wing fringes and occurs in western and central Texas, New Mexico, Arizona and southern Nevada. It may also be found in the eastern ranges of the Mojave Desert in California and the northern portions of the Sierra Madre Occidental in northwest Mexico. A white-fringed subspecies is known only from the Sierra Volcanica Transversal of Mexico. In Arizona the first brood flies in April and May and the second from June to September. Texas records indicate that the first brood flies from March to May, and the second from May to at least July, with additional records of specimens in September suggesting a possible third brood.

7. **Erynnis scudderi** (Skinner). Plate 92, figure 27, ♂. This rather rare member of the genus has white fringes on the hind wings and therefore resembles *E. tristis, juvenalis clitus* and to a lesser extent *p. pacuvius* and *E. funeralis,* all of which also

occur in the Southwest. *E. scudderi* is a fairly dark brown skipper with most of the dark markings merely darker and richer brown and not quite blackish except near the costa. In this respect it resembles *tristis tatius* and *juvenalis clitus* more closely than *p. pacuvius,* but is a slightly smaller species like the latter. *E. scudderi* has no marginal band of broad horizontal white spots on the lower surface of the wing itself near the fringes as is characteristic of *tristis tatius.* There is often, however, a marginal and parallel submarginal series of minute pale spots; the marginal set may be white but the spots are narrow and vertical. Such a condition is not unusual in *juvenalis clitus* and is well expressed in *p. pacuvius.* Males of *scudderi* have a denser vestiture of longer, elevated hairs on the upper surface of the fore wing than *juvenalis clitus,* but a greater proportion of these elevated hairs are brown rather than white. In *juvenalis clitus* most of the elevated hairs are short, rather scattered and white, and most of the brown hairs are not elevated. Males on the fore wing above, then, tend to have softer, slightly blurred markings rather like *tristis,* especially on the basal half of the wing. The round subapical spots on the lower surface of the hind wings are lacking. Females are difficult to separate with certainty from those of *juvenalis clitus* without examination of the genitalia. Wingspread, 31–38 mm.

Early Stages: These are not known. Burns suggests that larvae of *scudderi,* like others of the *juvenalis* group, feed on species of *Quercus.*

Distribution: North of Mexico this species is known only from the high boreal ranges of southeastern Arizona. It may also occur in adjacent montane New Mexico. It ranges south of the United States to the mountains of Chiapas in extreme southern Mexico and probably will be found to extend to southeastern Guatemala. Records of the occurrence of this species in Texas require verification. *E. scudderi* has been taken from May through August and Burns suggests that there may be more than one brood. In Mexico it has also been collected in December.

8. **Erynnis horatius** (Scudder & Burgess). Plate 93, figure 15, ♂; figure 16, ♀. This is a moderately large brown skipper rather like, and often confused with, *juvenalis.* It is a more uniformly brown species, however, with little white overscaling. Males tend to have relatively little contrast between the dark brown markings and the brown ground color of the wing; the fore wing has a dense vestiture of long, slightly elevated hairs, nearly all of which are brown, not white. Females generally have quite large hyaline spots on the fore wing, and the dark markings are conspicuous. There is often a particularly broad dark region from the middle of the costa through the cell. The hind wings are usually conspicuously mottled with vague large spots less well defined than in *juvenalis.* The two pale subapical spots on the lower surface of the hind wing are rarely present. This species has also sometimes been confused with *meridianus,* from which it differs in having much less white scaling outside the dark band of the fore wing that runs from the subapical hyaline spots to the anal margin. In *meridianus* these white scales usually form a conspicuous hoary serrated stripe which outlines the wedge-shaped dark spots of the band. This region is usually merely pale brown in *horatius,* since the white scales are scarce. The fringes of the hind wings are brown. Wingspread, 31–45 mm.

Early Stages: According to Burns this species is known to feed on *Quercus ilicifolia, stellata, texana, fusiformis, shumardis, nigra, virginiana* and *Erythrobalanus* oak. Kendall, in addition to most of these, also adds *Q. hemisphaerica, laurifolia, marilandica, phellos* and, in confinement, *Q. Gambelii.* Burns found this species closely associated with *Q. Gambelii* in the Rocky Mountains and it seems likely that Gambel's Oak is also used in nature. Shapiro gives *Q. Muhlenbergii* as the foodplant in New Jersey.

Distribution: Widely distributed over the eastern half of our region, *horatius* ranges from Massachusetts to southern Florida, west to the Rocky Mountains of Colorado and New Mexico and to eastern Texas. The species, however, is almost absent from the Great Plains. *E. horatius* has been reported in the literature to occur also in Minnesota, which may be valid, and in Washington and Montana, both of which are incorrect. Several records of this species from Arizona pertain to misidentified *meridianus.* This skipper has at least two broods in the northern portion of its range and in the Rocky Mountains, and has three generations a year in the south, where it flies from January to October.

9. **Erynnis tristis** (Boisduval). Plate 93, figure 11, ♂; figure 12, ♀ (both ssp. *tristis*). This close relative of *horatius* is a dark species with a white hind wing fringe, looking rather like a white-fringed *meridianus.* Indeed, a brown-fringed subspecies of *tristis* from Baja California was thought to be *meridianus* until Burns placed it properly. Males of *tristis* are dark with a dense vestiture of somewhat elevated, primarily brown hairs on the fore wing. White scales are few, but most abundant outside the wedge-shaped dark spots of the band running from the subapical hyaline spots to the anal margin. Females have more contrasting dark markings and that in the cell adjacent to the hyaline spot is particularly conspicuous. A basal series of blackish spots is also usually evident. There are no subapical pale spots on the hind wing beneath in either sex. The fringes are white in both our subspecies of *tristis,* and there are conspicuous, broad, white horizontal spots adjacent to the fringe on the lower surface of the hind wing in one of the subspecies, but rarely in the other. The hind wing fringes are generally white nearly to their base, seldom with partial brown checkering of the basal fringe scales, at least in the posterior half of the fringe. The other white-fringed forms, *juvenalis clitus, scudderi,* and *p. pacuvius* all characteristically have the white fringes basally interrupted by intrusive brown partial checkering through most of the fringe. Another white-fringed species, *funeralis,* is relatively easily distinguished from all these species by its narrower fore wings and rather broad triangular hind wings. Wingspread, 29–43 mm.

Early Stages: Burns lists as larval foodplants of nominate *tristis Quercus lobata, agrifolia, douglasii* and the introduced cork oak. Freeman reports *tristis tatius* closely associated with *Q. grisea* and *Emoryi* in western Texas.

Distribution: Two white-fringed subspecies represent *tristis* in our region. The nominate subspecies rarely displays any broad white patches adjacent to the fringes on the hind wings below. This subspecies is essentially Californian, occurring in the Coast Ranges, Central Valley and Sierran foothills. It also undoubtedly ranges into northern Baja California. The subspecies *tristis tatius* (Edwards) is similar but generally larger and has a conspicuous series of horizontal white marginal patches on the lower surface of the hind wing adjacent to the fringes; it occurs from southern Utah, Arizona, southwestern New Mexico and west Texas south through Mexico and Central America to Colombia. A third subspecies, which has brown fringes, inhabits the mountains of southernmost Baja California. This species has three generations a year in Texas and Arizona, flying from March to November. The nominate subspecies also has two or more broods and is on the wing from March to November with occasional specimens taken well into December.

10. **Erynnis martialis** (Scudder). Plate 93, figure 6, ♀.   This species and *pacuvius,* related but dissimilar looking, comprise a group which seems to have no other close relatives within the genus. *E. martialis* is a distinctive, rather small, species that is pale brown, often with a slight lavender cast, and has greatly contrasting darker markings on both wings in both sexes. There are relatively few long hairs, but whitish overscaling provides a pale lavender contrast to the dark spots. The fringes of the hind wings are brown. Males do not have a tibial tuft on the hind leg. Wingspread, 24–36 mm.

Early Stages: An impressive array of larval foodplants for *martialis* has been suggested in the literature but Burns nicely postulated, then subsequently demonstrated, that *Ceanothus americanus* served as its foodplant. Shapiro also found this species closely associated with *C. americanus* in New York.

Distribution: E. martialis inhabits the eastern half of our region, ranging from New England to western South Dakota and the eastern foothills of the Rockies, south to Georgia, Mississippi and central Texas. Reports of the occurrence of this species in New Mexico require verification.

11. **Erynnis pacuvius** (Lintner).   This widely distributed species is represented by four subspecies, some of which bear little superficial resemblance to others. *E. pacuvius* is small to medium sized for the genus and may be relatively pale with contrasting dark markings to almost wholly blackish. Generally the hyaline spots of the fore wings are quite small, occasionally absent in individuals of one of the subspecies (*pernigra*). Males do not have a tibial brush on the hind leg, a useful means of distinguishing this species from similar-looking members of the *persius* group in the West. This species inhabits the western mountain ranges from British Columbia to southern Mexico.

(a) **pacuvius** (Lintner). Plate 93, figure 5, ♂.   This subspecies is pale brown, of variable size and with greatly contrasting dark brown to blackish markings on the fore wings. White hairs and scales are present on the fore wings of males, the scales most dense and conspicuous outside the dark band of spots that connects the subapical hyaline spots with the anal margin. This pale streak is also conspicuous in females. The hind wings are darker brown, scarcely mottled above, and the fringes are white with basal intrusions of brown at the ends of the veins. The hind wings below are dark, with a marginal and submarginal series of small white vertical dashes or ill-defined spots between the veins. This subspecies looks most like *E. scudderi* but is generally much more contrastingly marked on the fore wings above. Wingspread, 30–39 mm.

Early Stages: Eff and Burns both report this subspecies using *Ceanothus Fendleri* as a larval foodplant in Colorado and Arizona.

Distribution: Nominate *pacuvius* ranges through the Rocky Mountain region of north central Colorado south and west into New Mexico, southern Utah and Arizona, thence southward through the mountains of western Mexico to the Sierra Volcanica Transversal of south central Mexico. In Colorado it flies from May to July in only one brood. To the south this subspecies has two broods, and in Arizona has been taken from April to late September.

(b) **lilius** (Dyar). Plate 93, figure 32, ♀. Like the preceding subspecies, *p. lilius* displays a high contrast between the light and dark markings on the fore wings; but the males, particularly, are darker and the light or pale brown areas fewer. There are few to many white, slightly elevated, hairs on the fore wing of males, and females have a conspicuous grayish band distad of the outer discal dark band carrying the hyaline spots. The hind wing above in males is dark brown and scarcely mottled, in females pale brown and mottled or dark with conspicuous large pale brown spots in a sinuate band. The fringes are brown. The hind wings below are dark brown in males, often with a purplish cast in certain lights, and frequently with a submarginal series of small buff spots. Females may also have a marginal series of these spots. Wingspread, 29–35 mm.

Early Stages: The larval foodplant in the central and northern Sierra Nevada is *Ceanothus cordulatus.*

Distribution: E. p. lilius is known from the Rocky Mountains of Idaho and Montana, southern British Columbia, thence southward in the Cascades through Washington to northern California. It extends farther southward through the length of the Sierra Nevada in California. Although not yet reported, it is expected to occur in Wyoming and in certain of the higher Great Basin ranges. Adults are taken from May to July, in a single generation.

(c) **callidus** (Grinnell). Plate 93, figure 33, ♂; figure 34, ♀. This is a distinctly dark brown skipper with the hyaline spots of the fore wing generally minute. The contrast between the brown ground color and the dark markings is not great. The brown wings may acquire a faint purple luster when viewed at an angle. The male hind wings below are dark brown with only a faint indication of the submarginal pale spots. The fringes are brown. Females are paler, resembling those of *p. lilius,* and have a conspicuous gray band inside the submarginal dark band of the fore wings. The white scales on the fore wings of females are flattened and broad as usual, not hair-like as are most in the males. Wingspread, 28–33 mm.

Early Stages: These are not known for *p. callidus* with certainty, but Burns points out that part of the report by Comstock & Dammers on the life history of *E. afranius* undoubtedly pertains to *callidus,* particularly the reference to the foodplant *Ceanothus divaricatus.* This particular plant, now *Ceanothus oliganthus,* is presumed to be the larval foodplant of this subspecies.

Distribution: E. p. callidus occur in California from the coastal mountains of Monterey county south to the Transverse and Peninsular ranges of southern California and the mountains of Baja California Norte. Northward these populations fly only from May to July, but in the southern part of the range there is more than one generation, adults having been taken from April to October.

(d) **pernigra** (Grinnell), Plate 93, figure 31, ♂. This is undoubtedly the darkest member of the genus. Above the fore wings are almost velvet black, the paler areas scarcely contrasting with the blackish marks by virtue of a delicate gray dusting of slightly elevated white hairs scattered amid a fairly heavy vestiture of dark brown hairs. The hyaline spots of males are few and minute, frequently apparently absent, while those of females are very small but at least the subapical are present. The hind wings of both sexes are uniform blackish brown above and the fringes are brown. The lower surface of the hind wings is dark brown generally without a trace of pale submarginal spots in males, and just a trace in females. Females of this subspecies are remarkable in that they much resemble the males above, and are not conspicuously paler with contrasting markings. Further, females from the Marin county population, at least, have abundant white hairs on the fore wings and only marginally are the white scales broad and flat. Females do not have a conspicuous contrasting gray band just inward from a conspicuous submarginal dark band as do females of the other subspecies. Instead, the submarginal dark band is much reduced and the entire region from the margin to the discal dark band leading from the subapical spots is delicately grayed but not contrasting. Wingspread, 28–33 mm.

Early Stages: The foodplant of this subspecies is not known but is inferred to be a species of *Ceanothus.* The only females known from the Marin county population (3) were closely associated with a lush, dense chaparral formation with a high density of *Ceanothus.* Several individuals, perhaps all females, have been seen moving through the tall, dense chaparral well below the canopy.

Distribution: E. pacuvius pernigra is restricted to the central Coast Ranges of California in Sonoma, Marin, San Mateo, Santa Cruz and Santa Clara counties. The darkest populations seem to be in Marin county. Adults are most abundant during May, but examples have been taken from April to July.

12. **Erynnis zarucco** (Lucas). Plate 93, figure 39, ♂; figure 40, ♀. This rather distinctive large brown *Erynnis* is closely related to *funeralis.* The dark fore wings are a little narrower and more apically pointed than those of other *Erynnis* (except *funeralis*) and the hind wings are large and somewhat triangular. The markings on the fore wings above are obscure basally but there is a characteristic broad paler brown patch extending from the costa through the outer end of the cell, and to the subapical spots. The hyaline cell spot, which would be just basal to the pale brown patch, is frequently absent. There are many short, slightly elevated brown hairs on the fore wing of the male. Males have a tibial tuft on the hind leg which fits into a thoracic flap overlapping the basal ventral surface of the abdomen. This species has commonly been confused only with *baptisiae,* from which it differs in the more pointed fore wings and the large triangular hind wings. Wingspread, 28–43 mm.

Early Stages: Larvae of *zarucco* are presumed to feed on a variety of leguminous plants but trustworthy records are few, in a large measure because of confusion with *baptisiae.* Burns reports larvae collected on *Robinia* and cites Kendall's record on *Robinia pseudoacacia.* Gundlach found *zarucco* in Cuba feeding on *Sesbania grandiflora,* an introduced Asian legume, and Kendall found it on *S. exaltata* in Louisiana. Shapiro adds *Lespedeza hirta.* Other reported foodplant records require verification.

Distribution: This species of the southeastern United States also occurs on Cuba, Hispaniola, and possibly Puerto Rico. It ranges on the mainland from Florida north to New Jersey and west to Louisiana and Mississippi. It has been reported to occur as far north as Massachusetts but most such northern records beyond the above range may be based on misidentifications. This skipper flies all months of the year in Florida, and there are several broods.

13. **Erynnis funeralis** (Scudder & Burgess). Plate 93, figure 37, ♂; figure 38, ♀.   This species is almost exactly like *zarucco* but the dark markings are more blackish than brown, the fore wings are narrower, and the hind wing fringe is white. There are usually a few white hair-like scales on the fore wing of males. Males also have a hind tibial tuft. This species, with its distinctive wing shape and white fringes, should not be easily confused with any other member of the genus.

Early Stages: Larvae of *funeralis,* like those of *zarucco* feed on legumes; the growth form (woody or herbaceous) of the plant seems unimportant. Burns has summarized the literature pertaining to valid foodplant records, and mentions the following: *Lotus scoparius, Olneya tesota, Robinia neomexicana, Vicia texana, Indigofera leptosepala, Geoffroca decorticans,* and possibly *Medicago sativa* and *Nemophila membranacea,* the last a non-legume. The larvae of this species and of *zarucco* are distinctively marked with a dorsolateral yellow longitudinal line bearing a bright yellow spot on each abdominal segment.

Distribution: E. *funeralis* ranges from California to Texas and south through tropical America to Argentina and Chile. It is also known from the most distant of the Revillagigedo Islands. This species finds desert expanses no barrier, and the great variety of desert legumes is probably part of the reason. In addition, *funeralis* must have considerable dispersal power for it is at least sometimes associated with distinctly transient plants, like certain *Lotus,* that are pioneers in a successional vegetation series, quick to take advantage of a disturbed situation but soon completely replaced by other vegetation. The presence of this species on several islands also suggests that it can be a traveler. Such a species can be expected to appear sporadically well beyond the generally accepted limits of its range. An apparently valid Florida record of this species, however, is unexplained without obvious considerations of human transport. This skipper flies from February to October in southern California, in three broods.

14. **Erynnis lucilius** (Scudder & Burgess). Plate 93, figure 27, ♂; figure 28, ♀.   With this species we encounter the first of a series of at least four named species which

are closely related, exceedingly difficult to tell apart and relatively little known biologically. There is reason to suspect that the four names do not adequately reflect all of the species comprising this assemblage. The biological differences that are known are impressive but corresponding superficial features in some instances have remained obscure. This group of small to medium sized *Erynnis* is collectively referred to as the *persius* group. The first three species treated here, *lucilius, baptisiae* and *afranius,* are most closely related. *E. lucilius* is a small dark skipper with a blackish basal half of the fore wing and a pale outer half with contrasting dark brown bands, one of which includes some hyaline spots. There are virtually no hair-like scales on the fore wing of males, and the few that are present are appressed, not elevated. Males therefore sometimes resemble females in the wing markings. Males have a hind tibial tuft. The hind wings have a brown fringe. This species is easily confused with *afranius* and some specimens of *baptisiae,* but adults are closely associated with the larval foodplant, which remains the most reliable means of recognizing this species for anyone other than the specialist. Wingspread, 23–31 mm.

Early Stages: The larvae of *lucilius* are known to feed only on columbine (*Aquilegia*), according to Burns usually *A. canadensis.*

Distribution: This is a species of the Northeast. It is known from Quebec and Ontario south to New Jersey and Pennsylvania and west to Michigan and Minnesota. Throughout its range *lucilius* is multiple brooded.

15. **Erynnis baptisiae** (Forbes). Plate 93, Figure 7, ♂; figure 8, ♀. This dark brown skipper is medium to large for the genus but small examples occur which are much like *lucilius.* This species, like the last, is dark on the basal half of the forewings, pale brown with dark bands on the outer half. Between the subapical hyaline spots and the basal darkening in the fore wing cell, is a broad pale brown patch that is like the marking so characteristic of *zarucco.* Large examples do very much recall *zarucco* but the hindwings of *baptisiae* are not enlarged and triangular and the fore wing is not as conspicuously pointed. There are hair-like scales on the fore wing of *baptisiae* males, and a tibial tuft present on the hindlegs. The fringes are brown. Adults of this species are, like *lucilius,* common about the larval foodplants, and this serves as a most important aid to identification. Wingspread, 29–40 mm.

Early Stages: The only foodplants known for this species are various kinds of wild indigo (*Baptisia*). Burns cites *Baptisia tinctoria* and Kendall adds *B. laevicaulis.* It is of interest that some specimens of *E. baptisiae* were reared on columbine in confinement from eggs laid on *Baptisia leucantha.*

Distribution: This is a more southern species than *lucilius,* but the ranges overlap. *E. baptisiae* is known from Massachusetts and eastern New York south to northern Florida and west to Illinois, eastern Nebraska, Kansas and central Texas. It is not to be expected continuously through this region; most specimens have been taken in the Atlantic Coast states and from the region north of the Ohio River. Like the preceding species this skipper is everywhere multiple brooded.

16. **Erynnis afranius** (Lintner). Plate 93, figure 29, ♂; figure 30, ♀. This skipper is small to medium sized for the genus and somewhat similar in appearance to *lucilius.*

It is a blacker species than *lucilius,* however, and the fore wings above are well overscaled with flat white scales but lack the long hair-like scales characteristic of *persius.* The fringes of the hind wings in some populations, particularly in the Southwest, are often tipped with white. Males have a hind tibial tuft. Wingspread, 25–35 mm.

Early Stages: Burns notes that *Lupinus* and *Lotus* are probably foodplants of this species. Scott, Ellis & Eff in 1968 reaffirmed the use of *Lupinus* by *afranius* in Colorado.

Distribution: This mountain species is known to range from Montana and western North Dakota south to New Mexico, Arizona and southwestern California. It also extends well into Mexico, at least as far as the Sierra Volcanica Transversal on the mainland and through the mountains of Baja California Norte. It is multiple brooded throughout its range.

17. **Erynnis persius** (Scudder). Plate 93, figure 4, ♂; figure 25, ♂; figure 26, ♀. This species is small to medium in size for the genus. Adults are dark or light brown skippers with conspicuous but rather small subapical hyaline spots on the fore wings. The fore wings of males have a dense vestiture of somewhat elevated hair-like scales, giving the wing a soft appearance which sometimes blurs the darker markings especially on the basal half of the wing. The proportion of hair-like scales that are white, and therefore very conspicuous, is different in different populations. Males, because of this hairy vestiture of the fore wing, differ in appearance from females of the same populations, a difference not clearly expressed in the three close relatives of *persius.* All four (*persius, lucilius, baptisiae* and *afranius*) lack the two subapical pale brown spots on the hind wing below, so characteristic of several of the *juvenalis* group, but they have a marginal and a submarginal series of small pale spots on the hind wing below. Females have as much gray scaling interior to the discal brown band on the outer half of the wing as they have outward from that band, thus differing from females of *pacuvius,* which have the gray conspicuous only outward of the dark band. Males have a hair tuft at the base of the hind tibia, as do those of the other three members of the group. Several of the *persius* populations look different from others, and some have received subspecific names. The status of these named entities is unclear at present, largely because these populations are biologically unknown; the entire assemblage currently placed under the name *persius* cannot be meaningfully divided until much more is known, at least about the foodplant relationships. The species generally is boreal, occurring in its southern limits principally in the mountains. But in California this species has an extensive ecological range; populations occur from sea level to over 10,000 ft., from the floor of the hot Central Valley to subalpine regions. Wingspread, 26–36 mm.

Early Stages: Burns points out the paucity of data on immature stages of this species and notes that larvae of eastern populations seem to feed on Willow (*Salix*) and several species of *Populus;* and that Arizona populations seem to be restricted to a legume, *Thermopsis pinetorum.* More recently, Paul Opler found females in lowland California ovipositing on a species of *Lotus* that is a frequent pioneer in streamside gravel deposits which are, however, generally near both willows and cottonwoods. Whether most populations treated as *persius* are as restrictive with respect to larval foodplants as are those of the related species is unknown.

Distribution: As presently constituted, *persius* is found from New England, and probably Quebec and Ontario, south in the Appalachian Mountains to Tennessee, westward across the northern United States and probably southern Canada to Alaska; southward in the Rocky Mountains to New Mexico, Arizona and possibly northern Mexico; and on the Pacific Slope to central California. The species is single brooded everywhere except in parts of Oregon and California, where there are at least two broods. In Alaska the species flies in late May and June. In southern Canada it flies from May to July as it does in the Rocky Mountain region. In the eastern United States adults may be present from April to June, while in California the species is taken from March to September.

Genus EPHYRIADES Hübner

This is a small genus of four medium sized to large dark skippers, the males of which may be totally unspotted. The antennal club is arcuate much as in *Erynnis,* and the tip is blunt in two of the species but sharply pointed in the single species that occurs in our region. The palpi are short. Males are either blackish brown with a purple gloss and unspotted, or dark brown without the gloss and generally with a series of small subapical hyaline spots. The costal fold is present, large in some species. Males also have a hind tibial tuft and a dense covering of partly erect, fine, short hair over the basal two-thirds of the wings; the hairs on the hind wing may be slightly different, producing a dark velvety aspect in those species that are lighter brown. Females are paler brown with dark brown bands and larger, more numerous hyaline spots on the fore wing. The genus is primarily distributed through the Antilles but examples of all the species are known from the mainland in Central and South America. Only one species occurs in the United States.

1. **Ephyriades brunnea** (Herrich-Schäffer). Plate 91, figure 38, ♂; Plate 92, figure 28, ♀ (both ssp. *floridensis*).   This skipper should be easily recognized. Males are brown with a darker velvety brown basal half or two-thirds of the wings; they usually have a small rounded hyaline spot in the upper outer part of the cell and an arc of smaller hyaline subapical spots, although these spots vary and some examples may be immaculate. Females look quite different: they are paler brown with three darker brown bands across the wings; the hyaline spots are well developed and extend from the costa to below the end of the cell. *E. brunnea* is found through the Greater Antilles with one subspecies (*floridensis* Bell & Comstock) restricted to southern Florida. This subspecies is much like others of the species but males are a little darker and smaller.

Early Stages: According to Tamburo & Butcher the first stage larva is nearly transparent until feeding, whereupon it assumes the green color of older larvae. The mature larva is green with three longitudinal white stripes along each side of the body. Irregular translucent stripes are present medially between the two most dorsal of three stripes. The foodplant in the vicinity of Miami is reported to be Barbados Cherry (*Malpighia glabra*). Kimball notes that this subspecies has also been reared on *Brysonima*.

Distribution: E. b. floridensis is not uncommon on the Florida Keys but on the mainland it seems to be known only from the vicinities of Florida City and Miami. It has been taken during every month but November.

Genus GESTA Evans

Four brown species which more or less resemble *Erynnis* comprise this genus. The costa of the fore wing is rather strongly bowed convexly but with a slightly concave dip just before the apex. The outer margin of the fore wing is somewhat rounded. Males of all but one species lack a costal fold, but all species have a hind tibial tuft. The palpi are long, as in *Erynnis,* and conspicuously project forward in front of the face. The antennal club is arched, with the tip blunt in some species and appearing sharp in others. This genus is closely allied to both *Erynnis* and *Chiomara*. The species are all tropical American; one extends north to the southwestern United States.

1. **Gesta gesta** (Herrich-Schäffer). Plate 91, figure 39, ♂ (ssp. *invisus*). This brown *Erynnis*-like skipper has a poorly defined darker brown or blackish patch through much of the cell region and the adjacent costa of the fore wing. A submarginal band of brown spots is inwardly bordered by a conspicuous bluish gray band of overscaling which partly overlaps a darker brown band of spots. There are occasionally one or two small subapical hyaline spots costad in the darker band. The hind wings above are brown with vague alternating dark and light brown sinuous bands. The hind wing fringes are white with faint checkering basally, dirty white or brown. Males and females look much alike. The tip of the antennal club appears sharply pointed to the unaided eye. Wingspread, 30–36 mm.

Early Stages: The egg is high hemispherical with almost two dozen vertical ridges, without apparent cross striations. It is lustrous orange-yellow at first, ultimately becoming dull ivory. The first stage larva is yellow with an orange head. The mature larva is yellow-green, greenest anteriorly and fading to nearly white at the end of the abdomen, and there is a median narrow green stripe dorsally on the posterior two-thirds of the body. On each side every segment except for the first two has a bright yellow spot high on the side. The head is dirty white with numerous rounded black spots. The pupa is glistening green paler near the end of the abdomen. The spiracle covers, on the thorax just behind the head are conspicuously black. The larval foodplants are several legumes of the genera *Cassia* and *Indigofera,* particularly *I. suffruticosa* and *I. Lindheimeriana* in Texas. In confinement older larvae accepted *Indigofera leptosepala* but larvae were never found on this plant in nature (Kendall).

Distribution: This species ranges from the southern United States adjacent to Mexico, through tropical America to Argentina. It is also present in the West Indies. Two subspecies are currently recognized. That occurring on the mainland north of Panama is the subspecies *G. gesta invisus* (Butler & Druce). It differs from the South American subspecies only in rarely having hyaline subapical spots and no white spots on the lower surface of the hind wing. Most specimens I have seen have had brownish or dusty white fringes on the hind wings, although Evans suggests that they are generally white. In the United States *invisus* is known to be resident in southern Texas where it may be found from March to November. It is also reported from Arizona.

Genus CHIOMARA Godman & Salvin

This is another small genus of less than six species, allied to *Erynnis*. Most of the species are brown but two have conspicuous whitish or grayish areas above. The costal margin of the fore wing is somewhat bowed and the outer margin is rather rounded, much as in *Gesta*. A costal fold is present in only one species but all have a hind tibial tuft. The antennal club is sickle-shaped and seems to taper to a more or less sharp point to the naked eye. The palpi are moderately long to short and project forward. This genus is tropical American, with one species entering our area.

1. **Chiomara asychis** (Stoll). Plate 94, figure 23, ♂ (ssp. *georgina*). This variable species is basically brownish on the upper surfaces but the white bands and patches of both wings may be so greatly expanded that some individuals, such as that illustrated, appear largely whitish above. Commonly the white banding and spotting of the fore wings above is almost obscured by brownish scaling. The lower surface is basically white except at the outer margins and grayish brown spots are either suggested or well developed on the hind wings. The fore wings below may be extensively brownish gray with the white restricted to several patches and bands on the outer half of the wing. The obscurely checkered fringes are pale brown to buff, sometimes whitish on the hind wings. Wingspread, 30–37 mm.

Early Stages: These are not well documented. According to Miles Moss the larvae (in South America) are plain green and the pupa is greenish. He gives the foodplant only as a "straggling creeper" belonging to the Malpighiaceae.

Distribution: This species occurs from the southwestern United States to Argentina and in certain of the Lesser Antilles; it is represented by eight subspecies. On the mainland north of Panamá is the subspecies *C. asychis georgina* (Reakirt), which differs from the others in genitalic details and by generally having less extensive, or differently developed, white areas on the upper surface. In the United States *georgina* is known from Texas and Arizona, and has been taken from March to June and from August to December. In southern Texas it is frequently found in urban flower gardens.

Genus TIMOCHARES Godman & Salvin

A genus of only two fairly large species, *Timochares* is easily recognized by the rather long narrow fore wings, the slight emargination of the hind wing margin opposite the cell and the pale brown hind wings with an orange or buffy cast. The palpi project conspicuously in front of the face. Males have both a long costal fold and a hind tibial tuft. The genus is tropical American, with a single species occurring as far north as southern Texas.

1. **Timochares ruptifasciatus** (Plötz). Plate 91, figure 40, ♀. This distinctive skipper has a slight orange cast to the pale brown hind wings which are crossed by bands of squarish brown spots. The fore wings may be slightly more grayish, or dark or pale orange-brown, also marked with bands of separated brown spots. Wingspread, 40–44 mm.

Early Stages: The egg is high hemispherical, bearing about fifteen nodulated high ridges running vertically from the summit to the base; it is initially lustrous pearl but gradually turns light orange-yellow. The first stage larva is deep orange. Older larvae are yellow-green with black heads. Mature caterpillars are light green on the thorax and blue-green sprinkled with yellow dots on the abdomen. High on each side of the abdomen is a longitudinal yellow line which bears an orange spot or dash at each segment. The head is broad and flattened, mostly mottled ivory white and olive, with a dark brown line around the margin which extends forward at the crown. There is a mottled yellow area on the cheek next to the marginal line. The pupa is uniform glistening green. Comstock identified the foodplant only as a vine belonging to the Malpighiaceae.

Distribution: This species is found throughout much of Mexico, and in southern Texas. It is also attributed to Arizona (Skinner, 1901). Our subspecies is nominate *ruptifasciatus;* another subspecies has been described from Jamaica. In Texas *ruptifasciatus* has been taken in August and October, especially in city gardens.

Genus GRAIS Godman & Salvin

This genus contains one or possibly two large, long-winged brownish skippers with short antennae and palpi. The antennal club is slender and bent near its base to a long, tapering, pointed apiculus. Males do not have either a costal fold on the fore wing or a hind tibial tuft. The genus is tropical American but extends north to Texas.

.1. **Grais stigmaticus** (Mabille). Plate 95, figure 7, ♀ (ssp. *stigmaticus*). This rather large species somewhat resembles *Timochares ruptifasciatus* in its wing shape and hind wing markings, but it has even longer fore wings and is darker brown. The spotting of the wings varies from dark and conspicuous, as in the example illustrated, to not much darker than the lustrous, almost olive brown of the wings; in the latter examples the spots are scarcely discernible. Males seldom have any hyaline spots on the fore wing but females generally have at least a subapical series and sometimes more, forming a series of isolated spots from the subapical ones to near the anal margin. Well spotted females usually also have a spot in the cell as well as another just below but outside the cell. The palpi are bright orange-yellow beneath, as is the pectus in front of the fore legs. The ventral surface of the abdomen is yellow-buff with a conspicuous, slender, dark median line. According to Freeman this species has a habit of resting on the under surface of large leaves. Nothing is known of the early stages. Wingspread, 44–56 mm.

Distribution: Grais stigmaticus ranges from Texas, rarely Kansas, south to Argentina as a single subspecies, nominate *stigmaticus.* Another subspecies is known from Jamaica. In Texas *stigmaticus* is resident in the lower Rio Grande Valley and the vicinity of Kerrville; it flies in August and September.

Genus ACHLYODES Hübner

This genus of medium sized to large brownish skippers contains six tropical American species. The costa of the fore wing is strongly bowed and the apex is pointed although the outer margin is somewhat to greatly rounded. Two of the species have the apex protruding because of a conspicuous excavation in the outer margin just below the apex. The wings are broad in all the species. The palpi are somewhat short and the antennal club is long, curved and slender. Males do not have a costal fold but those of most populations do have a hind tibial tuft. Only a single, unmistakable, species comes under consideration here.

1. **Achlyodes thraso** (Hübner). Plate 94, figure 20, ♂ (ssp. *tamenund*). *A. thraso* is medium sized and easily recognized by the shape of the fore wings. The males are dark brown with a purple luster which gives some of the scattered paler brown spots a bluish cast. Females are brown with several bands of squarish bluish gray or olive-gray spots. Wingspread, 40–46 mm.

Early Stages: The half grown larva is yellowish green with a reddish brown head. The mature larva (Puerto Rico) is yellow-green with a darker green median line and a broad transverse band on the side of each segment made up of fine irregular spots; the large, heart-shaped head is greenish brown. Miles Moss, however, reported that the full grown larva (Brazil) is plain green with a rotund brown head. The pupa, plain green with a whitish bloom, is partially supported by a silken girdle. The larvae feed on various Rutaceae: *Citrus* (grapefruit, orange, lemon) and *Xanthoxylum* (incl. *Fagara*), notably *X. fagara* in Texas (Kendall).

Distribution: This species, with five or six subspecies, is distributed from Texas to Argentina, and through the Greater Antilles. Evans considered all the mainland populations to be the nominate subspecies and several of the insular populations to be the others. Some workers consider the populations in Texas sufficiently distinct to be recognized, and the name *A. thraso tamenund* (Edwards) applies to them. The skipper flies all year in southern Texas.

Genus SYSTASEA Edwards

This small genus is easily recognized because the species are peculiarly patterned with a patchy blending of olive-gray, lustrous copper and dark striations in the anal region of the hind wing. A band of hyaline spots crosses the fore wing and the outer margin of the hind wing is conspicuously irregular. Only three medium sized species are included and all are North American, two of which occur north of Mexico. They look much alike and can be confused with each other but with no other skippers found in the United States.

1. **Systasea pulverulenta** (R. Felder). Plate 94, figure 19, ♂. This species closely resembles *S. zampa*. It is most easily identified by the relationship of the hyaline cell spot and the one below it in the central band of the fore wing. In *pulverulenta* the inner edges of these two spots form a continuous line, the lower spot not offset basad. This species is generally less light olive-gray on the wings above, the dark markings more often brownish, and the orange or copper color seems more prominent. The excavation in the margin of the hind wing is usually less marked than in *evansi*. Wingspread, 24–32 mm.

Early Stages: Details of the immature stages have not been described. Moreno and Bibby list *Abutilon pedunculare* and *Pseudabutilon Lozani* as larval foodplants. Kendall found that *Wissadula holosericea* seems to be preferred in Texas, but that larvae in nature also utilized *W. amplissima, Sphaeralcea angustifolia, Abutilon Wrightii, A. abutiloides* and *A. incanum,* the latter evidently the least desirable.

Distribution: This species ranges from the southwestern United States to Guatemala. North of Mexico it is found principally in Texas; a few records from Arizona are questionable. It is not known from either California or Baja California. In Texas *pulverulenta* flies from February to November. It seems to be the dominant *Systasea* in southern Texas and mainland Mexico.

2. **Systasea zampa** Edwards. Plate 94, figure 18, ♂. Very like *pulverulenta,* this slightly larger species (formerly known as *evansi* (Bell)) is generally paler above with more light olive-gray areas and with the hind wings a little more prominently excised at the outer margin opposite the cell. The most reliable trait, aside from those of the male genitalia, is that the hyaline spot below the large one in the fore wing cell is shifted basad so that the inner of the two are not in line. Nothing has been published regarding the early stages. Wingspread, 25–38 mm.

Distribution: S. zampa is known from western Texas, New Mexico, Arizona and southern California; in Mexico it is only in the extreme northwest part of the mainland and throughout Baja California. This is the principal *Systasea* in Arizona, where it has been taken from April to October.

Genus XENOPHANES Godman & Salvin

This genus contains only one medium sized, grayish brown, tropical American skipper that has a cluster of hyaline spots of different sizes in the discal part of both fore and hind wings. These spots are bright silvery when viewed at an angle in oblique light. The palpi are fairly short and the antennal club is slender and rather sharply bent at about the middle. Males have a hind tibial tuft but lack a costal fold on the fore wing. The hind wing margin is slightly indented opposite the cell.

1. **Xenophanes trixus** (Stoll). Plate 92, figure 22, ♂. This skipper is not easily confused with any other. The hyaline spots are somewhat variable, the large one in the fore wing cell is usually deeply indented at least outwardly and is generally smaller than that in the example illustrated. The hyaline cell spot of the hind wing is distinctly larger than the others of that wing and there is a grayish dusting on the wing between the hyaline spots and the outer margin. The lower surface of the hind wing is mostly whitish except around the outer margin. Wingspread, 30–35 mm.
   Early Stages: These have been briefly reported for Brazilian populations by Miles Moss. The larva is whitish green, freckled and slightly hairy; the sepia-brown head is rough in texture. The pupa is warm brown, freckled, hairy and powdered with white. The larval foodplants in Brazil are *Malachra fasciata* and another, unidentified, Malvaceous plant, as well as a white-flowering "carapicho."
   Distribution: The species ranges from Mexico to Argentina. It has been recorded from extreme southern Texas, taken in July near Brownsville.

Genus CARRHENES Godman & Salvin

This is a small genus of variable but similar looking, medium sized skippers. The wings are somewhat broad, generally with several small hyaline spots on the fore wing. The antennal club is slender, curved and gradually tapered to a sharp tip. The palpi are rather short. Males have both a costal fold and a hind tibial tuft. Some of the species are dimorphic, a brownish form and a whitish form occurring in the same populations. *Carrhenes* contains four tropical American species, only one of which occurs north of Mexico.

1. **Carrhenes canescens** (Felder). Plate 94, figure 24, ♀. This pale brownish skipper has a slight grayish smoky cast to the lighter brown areas. Both wings have slightly darker brown slender bands and lines, and there are usually eight or nine small, sometimes inconspicuous, hyaline spots on the fore wing. The lower surfaces are lighter, almost buff, with five dark lines forming the bands. A pale form, appearing

rather washed out with the spots and markings somewhat obscure, sometimes occurs. Nothing is known of the early stages. Wingspread, 28–34 mm.

Distribution: C. *canescens* ranges from Texas to Argentina and three subspecies are recognized. The nominate subspecies is the one in the United States. It has only been collected in extreme southern Texas, during February and May.

Genus GORGYTHION Godman & Salvin

This tropical American genus contains four similar-looking species. These are somewhat small brown skippers, sometimes pale brown and sometimes quite dark, but always with bands of broad dark spots on the upper surface. The costal margin of the fore wing is bowed and the outer margin is slightly angled or bent near the middle. There are two small subapical hyaline spots on the fore wing. The palpi are moderately long and protrude well forward. The antennal club is conspicuously and rather abruptly bent to an apiculus that is not longer than the remainder of the club. There is a fringe of long hair on the posterior edges of the tibiae of the middle and hind legs. Males have a tuft on the hind tibiae but lack a costal fold. Only one species has been encountered in the United States.

1. **Gorgythion begga** (Kirby). Plate 94, figure 25, ♂ (ssp. *pyralina*). This small variegated brown skipper is unmistakable in our region. It has a slight violet cast to the wings on the upperside. The lower surface of the hind wings is brown with darker bands and lines in some populations, whereas in others there is a broad white area near the anal angle. The early stages are not described. Wingspread, 22–30 mm.

Distribution: Three subspecies represent *begga* in its range from Mexico to Argentina. The populations in Mexico are referred to the subspecies G. *begga pyralina* (Möschler), which is characteristically brown on the lower surface of the hind wings, with no whitish. This subspecies has been taken once in extreme southern Texas, in March. It is to be looked for in the lower Rio Grande Valley of Texas.

Genus STAPHYLUS Godman & Salvin

This is a large genus of well over three dozen smallish dark skippers that much resemble those of the genus *Pholisora.* Many of the species are difficult to distinguish without dissecting the male genitalia, which differ considerably. Interrelationships among the species of *Staphylus* are not yet well understood, and their relationships to the following genus, *Bolla,* which is also large and relatively devoid of superficial specific characteristics, are also uncertain. There may be a close affinity of certain members to *Pholisora* as well. For the purposes of this book, however, it will suffice to mention that these problems exist and their resolution must await future study. Most of the species of *Staphylus* are tropical American, dark brown or blackish, and with few markings, although some species have small subapical hyaline spots.

The hind wings are generally deeply, but in some species only weakly, excavated on the margin opposite the cell. The palpi are long and protruding, but are slightly to considerably shorter than those of *Pholisora.* The antennal club is a little more slender, more abruptly bent to an apiculus and generally tapered to a sharper point than in *Pholisora.* Males of most species, including all those treated here, have a costal fold on the fore wing but no hind tibial tuft. The three species of the genus that come within our region are, fortunately, relatively easy to recognize by superficial characteristics and locality data.

1. **Staphylus ceos** (Edwards). Plate 92, figure 7, ♂.   This is the only small, broad winged skipper in the Southwest that has bright orange on top of the head and long palpi. *S. ceos* is dark brown, with obscure darker bands above. The outer margin of the fore wings is rounded as in *Pholisora.* The hind wings are nearly smoothly rounded but there is a slight excavation or indentation of the margin opposite the cell; this varies somewhat and occasional examples do not seem to have it. The fringe at the apex of the fore wing is white. There are usually at least two subapical white spots, and females may have a few more white spots in a discal series linked to the subapical spots. The early stages are not reported. Wingspread, 24–28 mm.

Distribution: This species is known only from southern Arizona, New Mexico, western and southern Texas and northern Mexico. A California record in the literature (Evans, 1953) is considered doubtful. In Texas this species is taken from April to October; in Arizona records range from April to September.

2. **Staphylus hayhurstii** (Edwards). Plate 92, figure 9, ♀.   Often considered a subspecies of *mazans,* this skipper appears to be specifically distinct where it meets the northernmost populations of *mazans* in Texas. The genitalia of the two are rather different, and there is no evidence of interbreeding in the contact region. The two species are much alike superficially, both being dark skippers with deeply excavated margins on the hind wings. *S. hayhurstii* is somewhat paler, so that the dark markings are more conspicuous. Wingspread, 24–30 mm.

Early Stages: The egg is small, flattened hemispherical and orange with irregular white vertical ridges. The first stage larva is at first orange, then after fading becomes pale green with orange edges; the head is black. The half grown larva is pale green becoming yellowish and pale brown toward the end of the abdomen; the dense short body hairs are white; the head is deep purple with a dense covering of short white hairs, and the summit and front of the face are conspicuously indented. The mature larva is deep green with a rosy cast, covered with fine white hair; the head is deep purple, almost black, and deeply cleft vertically on the upper half of the face. The pupa is light olive-brown becoming pale orange-brown on the abdomen. The body hairs are orange, and the entire pupa is thickly dusted with a powdery white bloom. According to Heitzman the larvae are found on *Chenopodium* and *Alternanthera* and adults are not found far from such plants.

Distribution: This species is found from Pennsylvania to Colorado and south to central Texas and southern Florida. Evans's (1953) report of specimens from Montana and British Honduras are most doubtful. It has been collected from March to November, evidently in at least three broods.

3. **Staphylus mazans** (Reakirt). Plate 92, figure 8, ♂. This species is like *hayhurstii* but darker and with less noticeable dark banding. The best feature for identification, aside from details of the male genitalia, is the locality. There is only a narrow region of overlap of the two species, from roughly Austin to north of San Antonio, Texas. Wingspread, 25–30 mm.

Early Stages: The immature stages have not been described. Kendall reports the larval foodplants to be *Chenopodium album, C. ambrosioides* and *Amaranthus retroflexus.*

Distribution: The distribution of *mazans* is not entirely clear. In the United States it is found in southern Texas, south of an east-west line roughly through Austin. From San Antonio south in Texas it is the only *Staphylus* with deeply emarginate hind wings. This species is reported to range southward in eastern Mexico and perhaps as far south as Brazil. In Texas the species is on the wing from March to November, probably in three broods.

Genus BOLLA Mabille

A genus of about two dozen species, *Bolla* apparently is closely related to at least some sections of *Staphylus* which the species much resemble. *Bolla* has more evenly rounded wings than *Staphylus,* and the antennal apiculus is slightly longer. The species are generally slightly larger than those of *Staphylus,* and are brown, obscurely marked skippers whose identification usually requires a genitalic examination. The males of most species have a costal fold but lack a tibial tuft. Only one species has been reported from north of Mexico.

1. **Bolla brennus** (Godman & Salvin). Plate 91, figure 25, ♂. This dark brown skipper with obscure markings above is just barely larger than *Staphylus mazans.* The male has a costal fold but no hyaline subapical spots; females usually have two such spots. This species should be confused with no other skipper of the Southwest, but south of our region it is very difficult to identify without dissection. The early stages are not known. Wingspread, 26–30 mm.

Distribution: B. brennus ranges from Mexico to Panamá, but was once reported from Arizona (Skinner, 1901). The occurrence of *brennus* in the United States requires confirmation.

Genus PELLICIA Herrich-Schäffer

This tropical American genus has about a dozen dark brown to blackish species with pointed fore wings and triangular hind wings. The antennal club is long and robust, sharply bent to a rather short slender apiculus. The palpi are gray below, quite long and close together. Males have a long brush of hairs on the upper surface of the hind wing near the base at the costa, but have no costal fold on the fore wing nor a hind tibial tuft. There are no hyaline spots on the fore wing. Many of the species are similar and examination of the male genitalia is necessary to be certain of the specific identity. The single species known from north of Mexico, however, is sufficiently different from other skippers of the region that no serious confusion should exist.

1. **Pellicia arina** Evans. Plate 83, figure 18, ♂.   This dark skipper has rather obscure markings and a slight purplish glaze on the fore wing. The only skipper in the United States that it resembles is *Nisoniades rubescens,* but that species has subapical hyaline spots and the palpi are brown below, unlike the species of *Pellicia.* Nothing is known of the early stages. Wingspread, 30–38 mm.
   Distribution: Pellicia arina ranges from extreme southern Texas to Panama. In Texas it has been collected in March and November.

Genus NISONIADES Hübner

This genus is closely related to *Pellicia* and consists of at least fifteen tropical American, dark brown to blackish species. The wing shape is much like that of *Pellicia,* as are the palpi and antennae. The palpi are usually brown below. Like those of the preceding genus, *Nisoniades* males have a tuft of hair costally near the base on the upper surface of the hind wing, and lack a costal fold and tibial tuft. Skippers of this genus characteristically have at least two small subapical hyaline spots on the fore wing. This is another difficult genus, genitalic examination usually being required for identification. Only a single species is known to occur north of Mexico, however, so that identification in our area should not be difficult.

1. **Nisoniades rubescens** (Möschler). Plate 94, figure 22, ♂.   Like *Pellicia arina* in many respects, this species is at once recognizable by the slightly more rounded hind wing and the hyaline subapical spots on the fore wing. The early stages are not reported. Wingspread, 30–36 mm.
   Distribution: This species has been found from southern Texas to Brazil. It has only been collected in the United States on one occasion, in November near Pharr, Texas.

Genus COGIA Butler

In most of the dozen or so small to large brown species of this genus the males have a tuft of hair on the upper surface of the hind wing near the base of the anal fold, but no costal fold or tibial tuft. The fore wings are somewhat produced, more or less pointed apically in the species treated here, and the hind wings also tend to be elongate toward the anal angle. Some of the species look a little like members of the genera *Thorybes* or *Achalarus*. The palpi are rather short to moderately long, and the last segment projects forward. The antennal club is elongate, robust and sharply bent to a moderately short and slender apiculus. This tropical American genus is distributed from the southwestern United States to Argentina.

1. **Cogia calchas** (Herrich-Schäffer). Plate 94, figure 14, ♂. This brown skipper has produced wings which are nonetheless slightly rounded on the margins in males; in females the wings are much broader and rounded marginally. There are several small vague hyaline spots in a straight line subapically, and on occasion also one in the cell of the fore wing; otherwise this species is unmarked above. The fringes are brown and usually checkered with dark brown. The lower surface of both wings is brown, generally well striated with fine brown lines. The hind wings usually have a broad brown marginal band and a broad almost bluish black or dark gray, discal and subbasal band on the lower surface, often with dark brown mottling in the adjacent lighter brown areas. The hind wings below ordinarily have a very dark aspect. Wingspread, 32–44 mm.

Early Stages: The caterpillar has been described briefly by Miles Moss as being stumpy, yellowish and covered with fine white dots. He mentions that the foodplants in Brazil are species of *Schrankia* and *Indigofera.* Kendall found *Mimosa pigra* var. *berlandieri* to be the foodplant in Texas, and the distribution of the skipper there corresponds well with the distribution of that plant.

Distribution: This widespread species ranges from Texas to Argentina. In Texas it seems to be limited to Cameron and Hidalgo counties where it has been collected from March to November, apparently in three broods.

2. **Cogia hippalus** (Edwards). Plate 82, figure 11, ♂. This rather large member of the genus is easily recognized. The fore wings above have a number of conspicuous hyaline spots, including a large rectangular one in the cell, a larger one below it, and an elongate narrow one near the costa over the cell spot. The fore wing fringes are checkered and those of the hind wing are mostly white with only a basal suggestion of checkering in our populations. The hind wings below are brown with a lavender-gray cast. The dark bands are conspicuous and between the outermost of these and the margin there is often a broad series of brownish marginal spots, sometimes completely obscured by heavy lavender-gray overscaling. The lavender, or in worn specimens purplish brown, cast of the hind wing underside is distinctive. The brown of the upperside is warm, with an almost orange cast basally. The early stages have not been reported. Wingspread, 38–48 mm.

Distribution: This species ranges from the southwestern United States through Mexico, including southern Baja California, south to northern South America. There are at least four recognizable subspecies. The nominate subspecies occurs from central Mexico north into Arizona, New Mexico and western Texas. In the United States the species is taken from April to September, and is often common.

3. **Cogia outis** (Skinner). Plate 94, figure 15, ♂. This skipper resembles *C. hippalus* and is closely related to that species. It differs in being smaller, often with hyaline spots reduced both in number and size on the fore wings, and in having brownish, only faintly grayed, fringes which may or may not be well checkered with darker brown. This species could be considered a subspecies of *hippalus* and some recent workers have treated it so, but both *hippalus* and *outis* occur together in parts of Texas, evidently without interbreeding. The species is apparently local and easily overlooked. It seems to be closely associated with the larval foodplant. Wingspread, 34–40 mm.

Early Stages: Kendall reports the foodplants to be *Acacia angustissima* var. *hirta* and *A. texensis.* The larvae pupate on the ground amid litter or may even burrow below the surface and prepare an earthen, silk-lined, cell.

Distribution: This species is evidently rather widely distributed in Texas but is seldom encountered because its foodplant is so local. *C. outis* has been collected from April to October, apparently in three to five broods.

4. **Cogia caicus** (Herrich-Schäffer). Plate 94, figure 16, ♂ (ssp. *moschus*). This is a dark skipper of medium to moderately large size with white fringes on the hind wings. The margin of the hind wings is more rounded than that of our other *Cogia* and the palpi are slightly longer. The male hair tuft on the hind wing near the base of the anal fold is much less conspicuous than in the other *Cogia.* The hyaline spots of the fore wing may be almost as well developed as they are in *hippalus,* or reduced to near obsolescence, depending on the population. The lower surface of the hind wing is brown and banded as in *C. hippalus* but the dark bands are prominent, almost bluish black, finely outlined with a black line. Between the outermost band and the margin is a lighter, lavender-white area frequently minutely striated with fine brown lines. The lower surface and the white fringes of the hind wings suggest *Achalarus casica* but that species has much shorter palpi and the hind wings are slightly produced and quite angulate at the beginning of the anal fold. The dark markings below in *casica* are not as conspicuous although they are similar in color, because the entire wing of *casica* is much darker brown, and the lavender-white to white submarginal area is broader and more contrasting than in *caicus.* The early stages are not known. Wingspread, 36–42 mm.

Distribution: The species ranges from Arizona to Guatemala. The nominate subspecies (central Mexico to Guatemala) is darker brown and has the hyaline spots on the fore wing reduced or obsolete. Populations from northwestern Mexico and Arizona have well developed hyaline spots on the fore wings and belong to the subspecies *C. caicus moschus* (Edwards). It has been collected from March to August.

Genus SPATHILEPIA Butler

This tropical American genus contains only one distinctive species with peculiarly shaped wings. The palpi are short and the antennal club is slender, long and abruptly bent to a rather long slender apiculus. The male has a short costal fold on the fore wing. The femora and tibiae of all legs are copiously fringed with hair but the hair on the hind tibia is extraordinary: a conspicuous, dense and long, brush-like fringe extending the whole length of the segment. The apex of the fore wing is produced and abruptly truncated, and the outer margin is irregularly indented. The anal angle of the hind wings is produced into a vestigial "tail."

1. **Spathilepia clonius** (Cramer). Plate 96, figure 14, ♂. This rather large black skipper has a band of white hyaline spots across the fore wing. The lower surface of the hind wing is distinctively marked with a vague marbling of violet, subtle blue (near the costa) and several shades of brown. Two groups of rich, dark brown spots are finely outlined in white and form two irregular bands, the more basal of which becomes expanded and prominent near the middle of the costal margin. The thorax above is brownish, weakly iridescent bluish green in certain lights, and the basal hairs on the hind wing above have a dull greenish appearance. Wingspread, 40–44 mm.

Early Stages: Miles Moss briefly described the larva as being bright yellow with an X-shaped dorsal pattern in brown. The pupa was described as stumpy, light brown, and so covered with spikes of a white waxy powder as to appear covered with a fungus. The foodplants were stated to be *Inga edulis* and a wild bean (*Phaseolus* sp.).

Distribution: The species is distributed from southern Texas to Argentina. In Texas it is rare, taken in May and November.

Genus CELAENORRHINUS Hübner

This large genus comprises nearly seventy species, and is one of the comparatively few pan-tropical genera of terrestrial animals. Perhaps thirty-five species occur in southeast Asia, about twenty in Africa and about fifteen in tropical America. This genus is closely related to a number of peculiar appearing, poorly understood skippers of the American tropics. There is good evidence that several of these peculiar species are principally nocturnal, or at least crepuscular, and therefore not as frequently seen as most other skippers. Interestingly, therefore, some American *Celaenorrhinus* have been reported being found in buildings, caves, mineshafts, culverts and the like during daylight hours. They are usually flushed into flight by the intruding collector, and may fly about within the shelter or fly briefly out into the sunlight, after which they return to the shelter. In Mexico I have only occasionally encountered *C. fritzgaertneri* in the open during the day but I have taken more examples under culverts and bridges. I suspect that several *Celaenorrhinus* are mainly crepuscular and that our two species might best be sought in natural or artificial "cave-like" situations during the day. At dusk or dawn they might more commonly be found feeding at flowers.

The American *Celaenorrhinus* are medium to large brown skippers having irregular large or small hyaline spots on the fore wings and small yellowish spots on the hind wings beneath. The wings are broad, and the hind wings in a number of species are angled about the center of the outer margin, although the margin is rather rounded in the species considered here. Males have no costal fold but on the hind tibia there is a tuft of long hairs that are slightly curled near their ends. The antennae are moderately long with a conspicuously bent club, the apiculus or terminal bent portion long and quite robust although the tip is sharply pointed. The palpi are short, directed more dorsally than in the preceding members of this subfamily. A number of the American species can only be identified with certainty by reference to the genitalia but our two species are recognizable by wing markings alone.

1. **Celaenorrhinus fritzgaertneri** (Bailey). Plate 95, figure 12, ♀.   This species and the next can be separated from the other American species in that the hind wings above are vaguely mottled with pale brown and larger dark brown spots. The hind wing fringes of this species are conspicuously checkered. On the fore wing the costal hyaline spot of the central band is quite small and there is a small divided hyaline spot halfway between that band and the wing base, just under the cell. The lower surface of the fore wing is brown. There is much uninterrupted white on the terminal half of the antennal shaft and broadly on the club. The only specimen of this skipper taken north of Mexico was collected in a school building. The early stages are not known. Wingspread, 41–46 mm.

Distribution: C. fritzgaertneri ranges from extreme southern Texas to Costa Rica. The Texas example was collected in February.

2. **Celaenorrhinus stallingsi** Freeman. Plate 95, figure 11, ♂.   This species is a little darker brown than the preceding, and the fringes of the hind wings are brown, not checkered. The hyaline spots of the fore wing band are a little more yellowish in males and the costal spot of this band is long, almost as broad as the cell spot. Halfway from the hyaline band to the wing base there is a vague darker brown spot, never a small hyaline spot. The lower surface of the fore wing is conspicuously pale buff or whitish along the anal region. The outer margin of the hind wings is slightly more angled centrally than in the foregoing species. *C. stallingsi* has seldom been collected, but several of the few known specimens were taken in Texas. Nothing is known of the biology of this species. Wingspread, 44 mm.

Distribution: Examples of this species are known from extreme southern Texas, Mexico and Costa Rica. Texas specimens have been taken in June and November.

Genus CABARES Godman & Salvin

This is a tropical American genus of three medium to moderately large brown skippers. The males have no hind tibial tuft and our species also lacks a costal fold. The hind wings are slightly produced at the anal angle and also in the middle of the outer margin, accented in part by a slight indentation opposite the end of the cell. Separated hyaline spots form a transverse band and a subapical series on the fore wing. The hind wings are crossed by dark bands on the lower surface. The antennae are moderately long with a fairly slender club and long apiculus. The palpi are short, the last segment directed somewhat dorsally. The genus ranges from Texas to Argentina, but only one species inhabits North America.

1. **Cabares potrillo** (Lucas). Plate 94, figure 17, ♂; figure 21, ♂, underside. This distinctive skipper may easily be recognized by the double cell spot that is usually connected to form an irregular U-shape on the fore wing, the angle in the middle of the outer margin of the hind wing, and the two dark brown bands crossing the hind wing on the lower surface. The fringes of both wings may or may not be distinctly checkered on the apical half. Wingspread, 28–38 mm.

Early Stages: The egg was described by Dethier as dark pea green, about 0.8 mm in diameter and bearing eleven prominent vertical ridges connected by low horizontal striations. According to Gundlach the mature larva is light brownish with small brown-orange specks and a brown-orange line high on each side. The dorsal median line is blackish, and each segment is posteriorly tinted black; the head is black. The pupa is light brown with a purple tint and is entirely covered with an ashy powder. The foodplant is not known.

Distribution: The North American populations of *potrillo* are referred to the nominate subspecies, which ranges from extreme southern Texas to Costa Rica, and through the Greater Antilles. Another subspecies, with more reduced markings, is found from Panamá into northern South America. The species flies in Texas from March to May, in June and in November, and is evidently double or triple brooded.

Genus THORYBES Scudder

This genus includes about seven species of brown to dark brown skippers of similar appearance. The wings are rather broad and the hind wing is usually quite rounded on the margin. The fore wings have a number of separated angular hyaline spots distributed in a fashion that is usual among the members of this subfamily which are treated below. These spots consist of a series that often forms a band from the middle of the costa through the cell and extending toward the anal angle, a single spot which lies just outside the middle of the band toward the apex, and a series of subapical spots. In *Thorybes* some of the spots of that central hyaline band are missing in certain species, or all the spots may be reduced and widely separated. The hind wings below are marked with an outer discal dark band of spots, and an inner one that passes through the cell. The antennae are somewhat long with an elongate but conspicuous club bearing a sharply bent apiculus shorter than the remainder of the club and somewhat heavy, not particularly slender, but pointed at the tip. The palpi are short and the third segment scarcely protrudes beyond the hairs of the second segment except in one species that may not belong in the genus. The males of two of the species have a costal fold, but there is no hind tibial tuft.

This genus is a northern representative of a large array of tropical American genera and is distributed from southern Canada to Panamá. Most of the species are confined to the United States and all of them come within the scope of this book.

1. **Thorybes bathyllus** (Smith). Plate 94, figure 2, ♀. This skipper is easily recognized in that all the spots of the central band of the fore wing are normally present and all but the one nearest the anal angle are elongated in the direction of the band. Thus the cell spot is large and hourglass-shaped, and the spot slightly removed and below the cell in the band is rectangular and oriented with the band. The hind wings of males are a little more produced or pointed at the anal angle than in the other species except *T. drusius*. Males have no costal fold. The fringes are pale brown to light buff and are generally partially checkered with dark brown. The palpi are grayish below. This species is often confused with *T. pylades* which occurs in the same region but may be distinguished by the lack of a costal fold and more produced hind wings in males, and by the larger spots of the central hyaline band, especially the cell spot. Wingspread, 33–40 mm.

Early Stages: The egg is broad hemispherical with fourteen or fifteen slender slight vertical ridges connected horizontally by numerous cross striations. Mature larvae are dull mahogany brown with an olivaceous tinge, densely dotted with minute pale wartlets each of which bears a short, slightly clubbed, hair. The dorsal line is faint and dusky and on each side there is a slightly paler lateral line. The head is black, deeply cleft above in the middle, and densely covered with short golden brown hairs. The pupa is dull or greenish brown and rather stout. The veins of the wing pads and the dots on the anterior ventral abdominal segments are dark brown. The foodplants mentioned by Scudder are Wild Bean (*Strophostyles tomentosus*), *Cracca ambigua*, *Bradburya virginiana* and *Lespedeza hirta*. Comstock stated that *Lespedeza capitata* is the preferred foodplant in New Jersey. Kendall adds *Astragalus Engelmanni*, *Desmodium ciliare*, *D. paniculatum* for Texas, and notes rearing in confinement on *Lespedeza texana*. Huber lists the wild beans *Strophostyles helveola* and *S. leiosperma* as foodplants in Minnesota. Shapiro mentions oviposition on *Desmodium rotundifolium* in New York.

Distribution: This species ranges through the eastern United States from Massachusetts west to Minnesota and Nebraska, southward to Florida and Texas. Macy and Shepard attribute *bathyllus* to Arizona, but this is doubtful. In the north there is but one brood and adults are most abundant in late June. In the southern part of the range the species is double brooded and adults are present from March to December.

2. **Thorybes pylades** (Scudder). Plate 94, figure 1, ♀. A variable, widespread skipper, *pylades* can usually be recognized by the numerous but small hyaline spots on the fore wing. The central band of these is generally not developed as such because the cell spot is small or lacking; the spot slightly removed and below the cell may be reduced to one or two small triangular spots which, if connected, are usually oriented out of line with the course of the band. Males have a costal fold on the

fore wing, a feature immediately distinguishing *pylades* from others with which it could be confused. The hind wings below are brown, often darker basally, and the outer of the two discal bands is often not especially dark but finely outlined with an irregular dark brown line. The more basal band is darker, but usually also finely outlined with dark brown. The fringes are light brown to dirty whitish on the hind wings and obscurely to distinctly checkered with dark brown. The palpi are usually brown beneath but in some specimens they are grayish. By and large this dark brown species has an aspect above of numerous small triangular hyaline spots and checkered fringes; below the dark bands of the hind wings are finely outlined. Occasional examples are immaculate above. This is the most common member of the genus almost everywhere except at high elevations in the West. Wingspread, 30–46 mm.

Early Stages: These have been described by Scudder. Comstock & Dammers also described them, under the name *T. mexicanus,* which they later "corrected" to *T. diversus.* The egg is glistening pale greenish to white and is slightly less than 1 mm in diameter (although Comstock & Dammers give the diameter as 1.3 mm). There are twelve to fifteen distinct delicate vertical ridges extending from the summit to just short of the base, horizontally connected by numerous, poorly defined, elevated cross-striations. The first stage larva is whitish at first, becoming yellowish green after feeding; the head is black. Half-grown larvae are dull greenish or yellow-green, irregularly speckled with whitish or yellowish minute warts, each of which bears a short pale hair; the head is black and hoary with dense whitish hairs. Mature larvae are dark green to maroon-green with a thin brownish green to maroon dorsal line and on each side two paler salmon orange lines. The body is profusely covered with minute orange warts, each bearing a pale hair. The head is blackish, dark amber or dark maroon, densely covered with fine pale hairs. The pupae are blackish brown on the head, the front of the thorax and end of the abdomen. The thorax is dark olive mottled with black; the abdomen is tan to brown and each segment has dark posterior margins and an anterior speckling of black dots and blotches. The wing cases are dull buff marked with irregular blackish streaks. The foodplants are various species of *Trifolium, Lespedeza, Desmodium, Medicago, Amorpha, Dolicholus, Astragalus, Hosackia* and perhaps other legumes.

Distribution: This species ranges from Quebec to British Columbia, southward to Florida, Texas and California, and on into Baja California and as far as Oaxaca in south-central Mexico. In the northern part of its range the species is single brooded, flying from late May to early July; in the south it is on the wing from March to December and has three or more broods.

3. **Thorybes diversus** Bell. Plate 94, figure 13, ♀. This small dark brown species much resembles *pylades*. *T. diversus* more often has the hyaline spots of the central band on the fore wing elongate and the band is more or less recognizable, although very slender and broken. The cell spot often extends across the cell; the spot below the cell is usually slender and elongate, although slightly curved, in alignment with the band. This latter is commonly the largest hyaline spot on the fore wing. The relative condition of this spot and its orientation will ordinarily serve to separate

diversus from *pylades*. *T. diversus* has no costal fold in the male. The hind wings below are obscurely marked; dark brown basally, lighter, slightly rosy brown discally, and outwardly gradually more densely overscaled with purplish gray. The two dark bands are poorly defined and are most evident near the anal fold. This species has not been common in collections. It is partial to glades and small clearings in coniferous forest rather than to broad meadows, and therefore has been overlooked. Wingspread, 30–36 mm.

Early Stages: These have not been previously reported in the literature. The reference to *diversus* by Comstock & Dammers applies to *pylades.* During June of 1960 and 1961, John Burns and I studied some features of the biology of this species at moderate elevation in the central Sierra Nevada of California where *diversus* was found to be highly localized in damp glades in a Yellow Pine forest. A detailed discussion of the early stages will be published elsewhere, but a preliminary report of certain aspects can be included here. The egg is small, measuring about 0.8 mm in diameter, sculptured much as is that of *pylades.* The color at first is pale turquoise which changes within hours to leaf green, ultimately to translucent gray with a darkened summit area as the larva within develops. The first stage larva is gray-cream with a black head. Half-grown larvae are yellowish olive-green, the posterior portion of each segment dark green. On each side are two pale lines, the uppermost converging shortly before the end of the abdomen. The entire first thoracic segment appears dark. The head is black. Mature larvae are dark olive-brown with a yellowish cast provided by a dense stippling of minute pale dots from which arise the abundant short hairs. A median dorsal line is dark olive and on each side are two pale lateral stripes. The first thoracic segment is dark reddish brown and the head is black. The larval foodplant is *Trifolium Wormskjoldii,* a semi-aquatic clover.

Distribution: This species is known only from Colorado, Wyoming and California. It will probably be found to occur in Oregon and possibly in Washington and Idaho as well. This early flying species is on the wing in May and June at moderate elevations in the Sierra Nevada of California. In northern California at higher elevations, and in other states where it has been taken, it flies during late June and July. There is evidently only one brood.

4. **Thorybes mexicana** (Herrich-Schäffer).   This species is small to moderate sized, pale or dark brown above with more or less checkered fringes. Males have no costal fold. The principal distinguishing feature of *mexicana* is found on the lower surface of the hind wings, where distad of the outermost dark band the wing is conspicuously paler and densely marked with short, fine, dark striations which also may be apparent over much of the rest of the wing. The species ranges from the mountains of the western United States to southern Mexico. An isolated population in Panamá may represent a separate species. Four subspecies are now recognized and two, possibly three, of these occur north of Mexico.

(a) **mexicana** (Herrich-Schäffer). Plate 94, figure 7, ♂.   This skipper is dark brown above on the basal half of the wing and paler brown on the outer half, especially on the hind wings, where the strong striations of the lower surface faintly show through. The hyaline spots of the fore wing are moderately well developed but the spot of the central band below the cell is not well oriented along the course of the band and may be weakly expressed. The cell spot of the band is usually present but may not extend across the cell. The fringes are pale buffy orange or whitish buff, and the checkering is rudimentary. This subspecies is like the following but more completely spotted on the fore wings, has paler fringes, and is slightly larger. Nothing is known regarding the early stages. The report on the early stages of *T. mexicanus* (sic) by Comstock & Dammers refers to *T. pylades.* Wingspread, 34–36 mm.

Distribution: This subspecies ranges through the boreal mountains from south central Mexico north through the Sierra Madre Occidental to northwestern Mexico. It is reported from Arizona and populations may occur in the extreme southern mountain islands of that state. However, since the similar subspecies *dobra* also occurs near or in that region, the report of nominate *mexicana* north of Mexico requires verification.

(b) **dobra** Evans. Plate 94, figure 12, ♀. This is a small to medium sized dark skipper with reduced markings on the fore wings. Often only the subapical hyaline spots and a small spot in the upper part of the cell are present, but this is variable and these spots are sometimes as well developed as in nominate *mexicana.* The fringes are orange-buff and ordinarily checkered. There is a slight orange tinge to the brown of the hind wings below, at least in fresh specimens. The immature stages have not been described. Wingspread, 30–38 mm.

Distribution: This skipper ranges from the mountains of southeastern Arizona northeastward to New Mexico, southeastern Utah and southwestern Colorado. In Colorado this subspecies intergrades with *T. m. nevada,* and in northern Mexico (or southeastern Arizona) it may intergrade with nominate *mexicana.* Adults may be encountered from May to July, depending upon climatic conditions. Most examples in Arizona are taken in June.

(c) **nevada** Scudder. Plate 94, figure 11, ♂. This small pale brown skipper has well developed hyaline spots on the fore wing above. The spots are usually outlined in darker brown, and the striations of the hind wing below show through the pale brown outer half of the upper surface. The fringes are buff to pinkish buff and well checkered. Poorly marked individuals of this subspecies might be mistaken for *T. diversus* but the latter species never has the distinct fine striation below, and the brown bands are not as well defined as in *nevada.* In general, this subspecies flies at rather higher elevations than do other species of *Thorybes* in the same region. Wingspread, 26–34 mm.

Early Stages: These have not been described, but Lembert reported oviposition on *Trifolium monandrum.*

Distribution: This subspecies occurs in the higher mountains of California, western Nevada and Oregon, and in the fragmented Rocky Mountain system of eastern Utah and Colorado. In California it is principally subalpine and flies from June to August; in Colorado it flies in June and July.

5. **Thorybes confusis** Bell. Plate 94, figure 4, ♀. This large dark species is often difficult to separate from *T. pylades*. Generally the hyaline spots of the central band on the fore wing, if present at all, are somewhat differently shaped. In particular, the spot below the cell, although often entirely lacking, is normally long and aligned with the band. When reduced the spots tend to become minute short lines rather than triangular spots as is the case with *pylades*. Males lack a costal fold and, if the hyaline spots are well developed, this species can also be confused with *T. bathyllus;* the latter species, however, has more pointed wings than does *confusis*. The palpi below are grayish, thus differing from most *pylades*. In wing pattern, even when the hyaline spots are almost absent, as is frequent, the general disposition of spots and the wing shape are similar to those of the smaller and paler populations of *T. mexicana,* but *T. confusis* is not striated on the hind wings below as is *mexicana*. By and large this is a poorly spotted, large, dark *Thorybes* with distinct brown bands on the lower surface of the hind wings; the males lack a costal fold and have rounded hind wings. The early stages are not known. Wingspread, 30–40 mm.

Distribution: This southeastern species ranges from Florida north to Pennsylvania and westward to Texas and Kansas. It flies from February to October in the south, where it is often quite common, and during July and August in the northern portion of its range.

6. **Thorybes drusius** (Edwards). Plate 94, figure 10, ♂. This species is rather large and dark brown with small hyaline spots on the fore wing. The fringes of the hind wing are white and uncheckered. Males have a costal fold, rather pointed fore wings, and anally produced hind wings. The lower surface of the hind wing is brown, becoming grayish outside the outermost brown band. This outer band, in particular, may only be evident by the fine dark brown outline of its position. The inner band is usually darker but is also distinctly outlined by a fine dark line. This species can be confused with no other *Thorybes* but it might be mistaken for *Achalarus toxeus,* which is much larger, has no hyaline spots on the wings and has even more pointed fore and hind wings. It could be confused also with *Achalarus casica* or *Cogia caicus,* but both of these have, in United States populations, well developed hyaline spots on the fore wings and dark, bluish black bands and conspicuous striations on the lower surface of the hind wings. The early stages are not reported. Wingspread, 38–40 mm.

Distribution: T. drusius ranges from western Texas and southeastern Arizona south to southern Mexico. It may also occur in parts of New Mexico. In Arizona it has been taken from June to August, and in Texas from April to June.

7. **Thorybes valeriana** (Plötz). Plate 92, figure 25, ♀. This large, distinctive skipper should be confused with no other member of the genus. It is brown, broad-winged, with a distinct tawny cast and often with a slightly amber tinge to the hyaline spots on the fore wing, especially in females. These spots are usually well developed and, although the figured example lacks it, there is usually at least an upper cell spot. Frequently this spot is double or hourglass-shaped, across the cell. The fringes are

broad, slightly orange-buff and distinctly checkered with dark brown. Males lack a costal fold. In fresh examples the hind wings below are variegated with bands of different shades of brown and irregular fine black lines: at the margin a band of arched dark spots, brown with a bluish overscaling; next basad a band of crescent-shaped light reddish buff spots; a warm brown highly irregular band is next, its basal margin finely edged with black; then a broad irregular area of slightly grayish brown; and finally an inner reddish brown band, outlined by a fine black line. The basal area is darker brown, and there is a red-brown subbasal spot above the cell. Worn specimens tend to show only the fine black outlines of the two dark bands. The palpi are quite pale beneath, the third segment long, projecting conspicuously beyond the hairs of the second segment. The antennae have a stout sickle-shaped club quite different from that of the other members of the genus. On the wing this species presents a distinctly reddish brown aspect, but in my experience it does not fly readily or far. *T. valeriana* has been rather rare in collections and is not well understood. More than one species may currently be included under this name, and the species itself may not properly belong in *Thorybes*. Nothing is known of the life history. Wingspread, 38–48 mm.

Distribution: In the United States *valeriana* is known only from southeastern Arizona, where it has been encountered rarely. It ranges southward along the Sierra Madre Occidental to Oaxaca. It is also known from southern Baja California. In Arizona it has been taken in August.

Genus ACHALARUS Scudder

These are rather large brown skippers, somewhat like the genus *Thorybes* but with a more produced anal angle on the hind wings. The fore wings are marked with either hyaline or obscure brown spots. The hind wings below are brown, marked with two darker, often irregular, bands. Some species are intensely striated on the hind wings below, with a large whitish area between the outer dark band and the margin. Most of the species have white hind wing fringes. A short, slender costal fold is present in males of most species but there is no hind tibial tuft. The antennal club is longer and more slender than in *Thorybes* and is rather abruptly bent to a long tapering apiculus. The palpi are short, with the short, stout last segment slightly protruding beyond the hairs of the second segment. Five or six species are included in *Achalarus,* three of which occur in the United States. The genus ranges south to northern South America.

1. **Achalarus lyciades** (Geyer). Plate 94, figure 3, ♂. This distinctive skipper cannot be confused with any other of the region. The upper surface, with crowded, large, light orange to golden hyaline spots on the fore wing, might suggest either *Autochton cellus* or *Epargyreus clarus,* but the outer broad whitish area on the hind wing below permits easy recognition. *A. lyciades* tends to frequent the edges of woodlands. Wingspread, 38–46 mm.

Early Stages: The egg is opalescent dull white, about 1 mm in diameter, and bears from thirteen to fifteen vertical ridges connected by many raised cross striations. The first stage larva is green, spotted with pale green oval dots arranged in lines across the segments on the folds; the head is blackish. The half-grown larva is yellowish green, covered with minute lemon yellow dots which form a distinct lateral line on each side; the head is blackish, depressed medially at the top, and on each side at the summit is a minute comb-like row of triangular teeth. The mature larva is dark green with a bluish green median line, a profuse speckling of yellowish orange dots which become more orange in a narrow lateral stripe on each side; there is also, more ventrally, another broader, vague stripe on each side; the head is black and the comb-like teeth at the summit are curved forward. The pupa is pale brown, darkest toward the head and dirty yellow-brown on the abdomen; black dots are clustered in irregular patches on the head, sparse and unevenly distributed on the thorax and tending to be arranged in several segmental lines on the abdomen. The larvae feed on *Desmodium* (*Dilleni, paniculatum, ciliare*) and *Lespedeza* (*hirta, texana*), possibly also on *Baptisia* and (doubtfully) "morning glory."

Distribution: This eastern skipper ranges from New Hampshire west to Minnesota and south to the Gulf states from Florida to the northeastern quarter of Texas. It flies from May to July in the north and from April to September, probably into December, in Texas.

2. **Achalarus casica** (Herrich-Schäffer). Plate 94, figure 6, ♂. This skipper is brown above with separated whitish hyaline spots on the fore wing and a white fringe on the hind wing. The aspect of the upper surface suggests either *Thorybes drusius* or *Cogia caicus*. From the former it is distinguished usually by the much larger hyaline spots, and from the latter by the much more pointed hind wings and the shorter palpi. The lower surface is similar to that of *A. lyciades,* and might be mistaken for *Cogia caicus,* but that species has much more contrasting dark bands on the hind wing below and the whitish marginal area is narrower and less intensely white. *A. casica* is somewhat larger than *C. caicus* and the conspicuous, dark brown patch at the anal angle of the hind wing below is poorly defined in *C. caicus.* This species, unlike *A. lyciades,* lacks a costal fold in the male. The early stages are not described. Wingspread, 38–50 mm.

Distribution: A. casica ranges from southeastern Arizona and Texas south to southern Mexico. *A. tehuacana* Draudt was thought, as a subspecies, to represent *casica* from Mexico to Costa Rica. The two broadly overlap without intergradation in central and southern Mexico, however. *A. casica* flies from May to October.

3. **Achalarus toxeus** (Plötz). Plate 94, figure 5, ♂. This large dark brown skipper requires little description: in the United States it is a distinctive insect. From Mexico southward, however, at least two other species are similar. The pointed wings, the scarcely discernible rectangular brown spots of the fore wing above, and the white-fringed hind wing will serve to identify *toxeus.* Males usually have a short, slender costal fold. Wingspread, 42–50 mm.

Early Stages: The immature stages have not been described but Kendall reports that Texas Ebony (*Pithecolobium flexicaule*) is a larval foodplant in Texas. He suggests that several other woody legumes are possible where this skipper occurs outside the range of Texas Ebony.

Distribution: This species ranges from Arizona and Texas south to Panamá. In Texas it has been taken from February to April, in June and July, and from August to November.

Genus AUTOCHTON Hübner

This chiefly tropical American genus includes over a dozen species that are all blackish or dark brown above with the hyaline spots on the fore wing arranged in a continuous central band. The hind wings are rather elongate in a number of species. Generally the fringes of the hind wing, if not the wing itself, are pale, at least along the outer costa and on the apical margin. Males have neither a costal fold nor a hind tibial tuft. The antennae vary within the genus, the club ranging from moderately stout with a long, heavy apiculus to long and slender with a long, fine apiculus. Most species have the blunt last segment of the palpi protruding a little beyond the vestiture of the second segment. In most species the fringes of both wings are not checkered, but our two are exceptions in the genus, superficially quite unlike the others of the group. The genus occurs from the United States to Argentina.

1. **Autochton cellus** (Boisduval & Le Conte). Plate 94, figure 8, ♂; figure 9, ♀; Plate 97, figure 14, ♂.   This large dark brown skipper with a continuous light orange fore wing band (quite brassy under oblique lighting) can only be confused with *A. pseudocellus.* The hind wings above are conspicuously yellowish orange in the apical region and the fringes are checkered on only about the anterior two-thirds of the outer margin, the remainder dark brown and uncheckered. The antennae above are uniformly dark brown and the third segment of the palpi protrudes clearly just beyond the hairs of the second segment. The hind wings below have a broad submarginal black-spotted area conspicuously overscaled with bluish gray and the two central dark brown bands are seldom conspicuously outlined in black. Rarely, individuals occur which are bronze brown above, not blackish, and occasionally the central band may be exceedingly broad or reduced and broken into four well-separated spots. Wingspread, 40–54 mm.

Early Stages: These have been described in detail by Scudder and by Clark. The eggs are deposited in strings of two to seven, a most unusual occurrence, among the Hesperiidae. They are high hemispherical, about 1 mm in diameter and yellow, becoming brownish yellow before hatching. The fifteen to twenty vertical ridges are more elevated near the summit, connected by numerous, fine, slightly raised horizontal lines. The first stage larva is yellow with the first segment pinkish, the head is light yellow-brown. The half-grown larva is yellowish green, the head black with tooth-like prominences on the summit at each side. The mature larva is bright yellow-green with an even speckling of minute yellow dots and a broad lateral line of clear sulphur yellow; the head is reddish brown with two large yellow spots in front. At first the pupa is brilliant green anteriorly and on the wing pads, and the abdomen is straw yellow, green at the tip. Within hours the pupa begins to darken, becoming coffee brown with a green tinge and ultimately entirely blackish shortly before the adult emerges. Clark found this species limited to Hog Peanut (*Amphicarpa pitcheri*) in Maryland.

Distribution: A. cellus has a disjunct distribution. It is found (intensely local) from New York to Ohio and southeastern Missouri, south to northern Florida, Alabama and Mississippi. It is also known from western Texas and from southeastern Arizona where it is not uncommon. South of the United States the species ranges to southern Mexico. In the northern part of its range this species flies from May to July, and again in late July through August. In Arizona and Texas it has been taken from February to September.

2. **Autochton pseudocellus** (Coolidge & Clemence). Plate 97, figure 17, ♂. This skipper is much smaller than most populations of *A. cellus,* but otherwise similar. The hyaline band of the fore wing is paler and tends to have a brassy luster even under direct lighting. The hind wings above are only narrowly or not at all yellowish on the costa near the apex and the fringes are conspicuously checkered from apex to anal angle, although the fringes are somewhat darkened posteriorly. The antennae above have a broad conspicuous whitish ring around the base of the club, hard to see in badly worn or rubbed specimens. The last segment of the palpus just reaches the end of the hairs of the second segment although again, worn specimens may be deceiving. The hind wings below are reddish brown with broad brown spots, poorly defined marginally on the apical half, but with no bluish gray overscaling. The two central dark bands are dark brown with a loose grayish overscaling and outlined by fine black lines. The immature stages are not known. Wingspread, 32–42 mm.

Distribution: This species is uncommon in collections and is known only from southeastern Arizona and in Mexico from Sonora and Chihuahua south to Morelos and Puebla. In Arizona it has been taken from June to September.

Genus ASTRAPTES Hübner

This large tropical American genus is comprised of more than forty species, most of which have lustrous bluish or greenish wings above. The species are large with stout bodies and large heads. The antennae are long and slender, the club thin and elongate with a sharply bent, long apiculus. The fore wings are large and rather broad; the outer margin is usually relatively straight, although some species have a distinctly truncated apex. The hind wings are produced at the anal angle, forming a short tail in a few species. Males of many species have a short and inconspicuous costal fold, but a tibial tuft is lacking. Although a number of *Astraptes* are superficially similar and require genitalic examination for proper determination, our three species cannot be easily confused with each other or with any other skipper treated in this book. The genus is represented from Texas to Argentina.

1. **Astraptes fulgerator** (Walch). Plate 96, figure 1, ♂ (ssp. *azul*).   Except for the following species, *gilberti,* this is the only large, tailless skipper with blackish wings and a broad lustrous blue basal region known to occur in the United States. Like *gilberti,* this species has a conspicuous white costal region on the lower surface of the hind wing. The costal area at the base of the fore wing below, however, is shining blue and there is a conspicuous central band and subapical series of hyaline spots on the fore wing above. The thorax and head are shining blue above. On the ventral side the palpi, the chest and leg bases, and the extreme base of the hind wings on the costal vein are yellowish. Males have a small costal fold. This insect can be mistaken for no other skipper within our area. Wingspread, 48–60 mm.

Early Stages: The half-grown larva is velvety black with transverse bands of brilliant yellow; the neck region, the area below the spiracles and the posterior segments are dark brownish red. The head is also dark reddish brown. The mature larva of our subspecies is velvety black with one or two transverse lemon yellow bands on each abdominal segment and is loosely covered with curved white hairs; the head is large with a slight vertical notch, black or dark brown with reddish brown marks, obscured by a dense vestiture of long white hairs. The full grown larva in Brazilian populations is considerably different. The pupa is dark brown to black but so completely covered by a thin coating of white waxy powder that it appears snowy white except for the intersegmental bands and at the spiracles. Larvae of the northern subspecies fed upon *Vitex mallis* according to Comstock & Vazquez. Populations in Argentina used *Ilex paraguariensis* according to Blanchard. In Brazil, Costa Lima gave the foodplant as *Cassia* sp. and Miles Moss stated that the species feeds upon *Cassia Hoffmanseggi* and *Inga* spp. Several species of *Astraptes* in tropical America have been confused with *A. fulgerator,* so the variations reported for larval features may pertain to different species.

Distribution: A. fulgerator ranges from Texas to Argentina, and two similar appearing subspecies are recognized. The nominate subspecies is South American. Populations from northern South America to Texas belong to the subspecies *A. fulgerator azul* (Reakirt). It is common at times in extreme southern Texas where it has been taken from March to May and from August to December.

2. **Astraptes gilberti** Freeman. Plate 95, figure 15, ♂.   This recently described species is shining blue-green on the body and wing bases above as in *fulgerator,* and like that species has a white costal area near the base on the lower surface of the hind wing. It lacks the hyaline spots of the central band and subapical series on the fore wing, however; the lower surface of the fore wing lacks the blue-green base of the costal area, and has a broad white patch posteriorly. Until recently this species was thought to be *A. alector hopfferi* (Plötz) which it closely resembles. (No examples of that species are known from north of Mexico.) Males do not have a costal fold. The early stages are not known. Wingspread, 50 mm.

Distribution: This species is known only from Texas and Mexico. The single example thus far taken in extreme southern Texas was captured in October.

3. **Astraptes anaphus** (Cramer), Plate 95, figure 16, ♂ (ssp. *annetta*).   This large, warm brown species has dark brown spots arranged in several bands on the wings above and below. There are no hyaline spots. Most populations have a broad yellowish band on the lower surface of the hind wing that extends from the anal angle some distance along the margin; usually the upper surface of the hind wing is rather broadly yellow near the anal angle. Males have no costal fold. This wing pattern, especially that of the lower surface, recurs in a number of unrelated tropical American skippers of both this subfamily and the Hesperiinae, but none of these is known from the United States. Wingspread, 50–58 mm.

Early Stages: According to Miles Moss the larvae of Brazilian populations are plain yellow with large, rounded, brown heads bearing prominent eye spots. They feed on an unidentified creeping wild bean in open country.

Distribution: This species occurs from southern Texas to Argentina, through the Greater Antilles and on Trinidad. Five subspecies are known, that of mainland North America being *A. anaphus annetta* Evans. It was collected once in extreme southern Texas in September, but is abundant in Mexico.

Genus URBANUS Hübner

These are medium sized to large brown skippers with the anal angle of the hind wings greatly prolonged into a tail. The thorax and wing bases may be metallic greenish or bluish and the hind wing tails are white in some species. The fore wings usually have a central band and a subapical series of whitish or amber hyaline spots, and many of the species also have an additional large spot below the end of the cell halfway between the central and subapical spots. The head is large and the body robust. The palpi are short and the antennal club is rather long but stout and sharply bent to a moderately long apiculus. Males of many of the species have a costal fold. This is a large genus of over thirty species, many of which closely resemble one another. It is a tropical American group, represented from the United States to Argentina, through the West Indies and in the Galápagos Islands. Six or seven of these species occur north of Mexico, most of which are superficially quite different from one another. It is of considerable interest that at least four species of this genus have been reported to feed upon monocotyledonous plants (grasses, etc.), contradicting the generalization that the larvae of this entire subfamily feed on dicotyledonous plants.

1. **Urbanus proteus** (Linnaeus). Plate 96, figure 8, ♂ (ssp. *proteus*).   In our area this is the only long-tailed skipper with a conspicuous green head, thorax and wing bases. The green on the hind wing above is extensive. The fringes of both wings are checkered. The central band of the fore wing is composed of four separated squarish

spots, and another squarish large spot is under the end of the cell. In tropical America about a dozen species closely resemble *proteus*. None of these has yet been found north of Mexico, but examples from southern Texas should be checked carefully as one or more of the other greenish species may be found to occur there. The male of *proteus* has a costal fold, and the antennal club is yellowish brown below. Wing-spread, 38–50 mm.

Early Stages: These have been described or figured many times. The egg is light yellow and just under 1 mm in diameter. It is high hemispherical, with about a dozen vertical ridges connected by uniformly spaced cross striations. The first stage larva is pale yellow with a blackish head. The half-grown larva is uniform yellowish green covered with minute, short, dark hairs; the head is black with a cluster of minute tooth-like tubercles on each side of the summit, and with an obscure small reddish spot low on each side between the ocelli and the mandibles. The mature larva is yellowish green with a slender blackish dorsal line and on each side a broad lemon-yellow to reddish stripe and two pale green lines; the head is black with the top part brown. This brown is connected by a thin band on each side to a large orange or yellowish spot low on the face between the ocelli and the mouthparts. The pupa is dark brown, covered with a whitish powder. The list of known foodplants is extensive because this species is widely distributed and is a frequent feeder on agricultural legumes and crucifers. Plants used include several beans (*Phaseolus* spp.), cowpeas, buckeye bean, turnips and cabbage, catnip, wild plum, beggarweed or trefoil (*Desmodium* spp.), mesquite (*Prosopis*), *Clitoria* spp., *Wistaria* spp., *Soja, Vigna, Bauhinia, Kraunhia, Stigmatophyllum lingulatum* and *Canna* sp. The last two are monocotyledons, reported by Wolcott and by Costa Lima. Other records of monocotyledonous plants used by *Urbanus* pertain to another group of species and may not be unusual with them. *U. proteus,* however, usually feeds on dicots, and the use of a monocot by this species is probably rare.

Distribution: This common insect is distributed from the United States to Argentina and through the West Indies. Mainland populations comprise the nominate subspecies, with all of the insular populations falling into a second subspecies. In the United States *p. proteus* is found from Connecticut south to Florida and west to Texas, Arkansas, Arizona and California. To the north and in the extreme west it is only sporadic, but in Florida is abundant and occurs throughout the year. In Texas it may be found from July to December.

2. **Urbanus dorantes** (Stoll). Plate 96, figure 15, ♂ (ssp. *dorantes*).   This brown skipper much resembles *proteus* on the upper surface but lacks the brilliant green head, thorax and wings. Both fore and hind wings are somewhat broader and shorter than those of *proteus*. A considerable amount of geographic variation is expressed by different insular populations, where the fore wing spots may be reduced or absent and the tail of the hind wing very short. Males have a costal fold. Wingspread, 30–49 mm.

Early Stages: The lustrous iridescent green egg is about 0.75 mm in diameter (1 mm in Cuban populations according to Dethier), with a flattened base and summit.

About thirteen vertical ridges are connected by horizontal striations. The first stage larva is clear yellow to greenish with a black head. The half-grown larva is greenish with orange at the neck, the head black and roughened in texture. The mature larva is pale pinkish orange to greenish becoming reddish brown near the end of the abdomen and with a dark reddish brown median line. The head is round, roughened, dark brown to blackish and fuzzy with numerous tawny hairs. The pupa is light brown with a sharp cremaster. Larvae feed upon cultivated and wild beans (*Phaseolus* spp.), *Clitoria* and various other legumes (Fabaceae).

Distribution: This species is distributed from Texas, Arizona and California southward to Argentina, and recently has become established in southern Florida. The mainland populations (including those in Florida) all belong to the nominate subspecies. Five additional subspecies are recognized for the isolated populations in Baja California, the Galápagos Islands, and several islands of the West Indies. In Texas and Arizona this insect has been taken from June to October, and has been collected rarely in southern California in June.

3. **Urbanus procne** (Plötz). Plate 96, figure 13, ♂; Plate 97, figure 29, ♂, underside. This insect is similar to the next three species (*simplicius, teleus, tanna*). All four have rather pointed fore wings, the hyaline spots, if present in a central band, tightly compacted into an extremely slender linear band, and the fringes not checkered. *U. procne* and *simplicius* usually have a poorly developed (or no) central band of hyaline spots on the fore wing and the males have a costal fold. In general *procne* can be separated from *simplicius* by the narrower fore wing and the shorter, more laterally directed, hind wing tails. On the lower surface of the hind wings the basal dark band of this species is between, and does not reach, either of the two dark costal spots, thus differing from *simplicius*. The two species are similar, however, and genitalic examination may be necessary to separate them with certainty. Wingspread, 42–49 mm.

Early Stages: The only report definitely of this species is by Kendall who notes that the larvae are grass feeders and that they make no shelter until ready to pupate. It is noteworthy that *simplicius* and *teleus* have also been reported to feed on monocotyledons, but it is not unlikely that the reports, at least of *simplicius,* actually refer to *procne.* Kendall noted oviposition by this species on two unidentified grasses and on Bermuda Grass (*Cynodon dactylon*), and successfully reared it on the latter.

Distribution: U. procne ranges from southern Texas, and possibly Arizona, south to Argentina. In Texas it has been common in March and October but is on the wing throughout the year, probably in at least three broods. Records of *simplicius* in Arizona are scarce and may refer to *procne.*

4. **Urbanus simplicius** (Stoll). Plate 97, figure 28, ♂, underside. This skipper is much like *procne* and, indeed, the two were only relatively recently recognized as different species. Like *procne,* and thus different from *teleus* and *tanna, simplicius* seldom has a well developed central hyaline band on the fore wing in males, although such a band is often incomplete or obscurely developed. Males have a costal fold. This

species differs from *procne, teleus* and *tanna* in that the basal dark band of the hind wings below extends straight to the central costal spot and joins with it. The short line of dark spots near the subapical spots on the fore wing below is smudged and vaguely defined in *simplicius,* well defined in *procne, teleus* and *tanna.* The fore wings of this species tend to be somewhat shorter and broader than are those of the other three similar species. Wingspread, 38–44 mm.

Early Stages: The larvae are brown and feed upon *Schrankia* in Brazil according to Miles Moss. Costa Lima and Hayward state that the larvae feed on the monocotyledon *Canna* sp., and although Hayward (1947) lists *Canna* as the foodplant he cites Monte (1934b) as part of his authority. I found no reference to *U. simplicius* in Monte's paper.

Distribution: This species ranges from Mexico to Argentina, and it has been reported to occur in Arizona, California (Davis, 1931) and Texas. Recent reexamination of Texas material suggests that if *simplicius* occurs in Texas at all it is very scarce (Tilden, 1965). Skinner (1901) originally reported that this species had been taken in (presumably) Arizona, but if it occurs there it is rare. It seems probable that early records of this species from north of Mexico are based on either misidentified or mislabeled specimens, and its occurrence in the United States requires verification.

5. **Urbanus teleus** (Hübner). Plate 82, figure 14, ♂. This species resembles *procne* and *simplicius* but has, like *tanna,* a well-developed slender hyaline central band across the fore wing and males lack a costal fold. Aside from differences in the male genitalia, this species differs from *tanna* only in that it has four small subapical hyaline spots on the fore wing rather than five. This species is referred to in older literature as *eurycles* (Latreille). Wingspread, 40–46 mm.

Early Stages: Miles Moss states that the larvae, like those of *simplicius,* are brown and feed on the legume *Schrankia* sp. Hayward lists grasses as the foodplants of this species and cites Monte (1934a) as his reference for the statement. I have not seen this paper by Monte.

Distribution: This species is distributed from the United States to Argentina. North of Mexico it has only been reported in Arizona and Texas. It is slightly less common in southern Texas than *procne,* with which it flies, and it has been taken from May to December.

6. **Urbanus tanna** Evans. Plate 96, figure 11, ♂. This skipper is superficially extremely like *teleus,* with which it was confused until rather recently. *U. tanna* has a slender hyaline band on the fore wing and males lack a costal fold. This species has five subapical spots on the fore wing instead of the four which are characteristic of *teleus.* Nothing is known of the early stages. Wingspread, 42–46 mm.

Distribution: *U. tanna* is found from southern Texas to Ecuador. It seems to be much less often collected than the other species of this group. In Texas it has been taken, rarely, in the extreme southern part.

7. **Urbanus doryssus** Swainson. Plate 96, figure 9, ♂ (ssp. *doryssus*). One of the smaller members of the genus, this species is easily recognized when encountered north of Mexico because of the short white tails on the hind wings. The white color extends from the tail as a long marginal patch about halfway to the costa. The fringes of the hind wing are also white to just beyond the white marginal area. On the fore wings a hyaline central band is usually present, composed of separate rectangular spots, and some subapical spots are present as well. Males have a costal fold. The basal hairs of the hind wings and those which clothe the head and thorax above may appear dull grayish green or olive-green under oblique lighting. Several other tropical species with short white tails resemble *doryssus* but none of these is known to occur within the United States. The early stages of this insect have not been reported. Wingspread, 30–44 mm.

Distribution: Two subspecies of this skipper are recognized through its range from Texas to Argentina. All the North American populations belong to the nominate subspecies. In extreme southern Texas *doryssus* has been collected in March and in October.

Genus CODATRACTUS Lindsey

This genus comprises about nine or ten large blackish or brownish skippers with a light brownish or orange-brown basal vestiture on the wings above. Most of the species have a complete set of large amber or bluish white hyaline spots on the fore wing in a central band, a subapical series and a single spot below the end of the cell. The anal angle of the hind wing is slightly produced in most species but several have a long, usually rather broad, tail. The hind wings in particular are rather broad in most species and the fringes more or less checkered. The palpi are short and the third segment extends just a little beyond the hairs of the second segment. The antennal club is evenly sickle-shaped, not abruptly bent to the apiculus. Males have no costal fold. A number of the tailless species are similar in appearance and identification often requires examination of the genitalia. Most of the species occur in Mexico and Central America but the genus is represented from the southwestern United States to Argentina. Three species are listed by dos Passos (1964) as occurring within the United States.

1. **Codatractus melon** (Godman & Salvin). Plate 96, figure 7, ♂. This large darkish skipper has large bluish white hyaline spots on the fore wing. The base of the fore wing and all but the costal third and the margin of the hind wing are overlaid with dark orange-brown hairs. The hind wings below are brown, often with a slight purple tinge, crossed by much darker irregular bands of well defined spots; the submarginal dark band, however, is poorly defined. Between that band and the outermost discal band the wing color is brown like the rest of the wing, but just before the anal area there may be a paler brown or buff streak. Nothing is published on the early stages. Wingspread, 40–60 mm.

Distribution: This species ranges from Mexico south to Nicaragua. It is also reported from Trinidad. I know of no authentic records within the United States and include it here because it might be found in the Southwest. It is a common species in northwest Mexico.

2. **Codatractus arizonensis** (Skinner). Plate 96, figure 5, ♂.   This untailed species is exceedingly like *melon;* indeed, some examples cannot be separated with certainty from it or from some other Mexican species without examining the genitalia. The fore wings have large bluish white spots as is frequent in the genus. The base of the fore wing and most of the hind wing are covered by light tawny brown hairs much as in *melon* but somewhat lighter and yellower. The lower surface of the hind wing is like that of *melon* except that the region between the submarginal and the outermost discal dark bands is paler than the other intervals between bands. This area is usually buff but in some specimens it is conspicuously whitish. The early stages have not been reported. Wingspread, 42–58 mm.

Distribution: C. arizonensis is distributed from the southwestern United States to southern Mexico. In the United States the species is taken in southeastern Arizona from June to October and in western Texas during June.

3. **Codatractus alcaeus** (Hewitson). Plate 96, figure 6, ♂ (ssp. *alcaeus*). (Compare also Plate 97, figure 30, *C. c. carlos*).   This brown, tailed skipper is distinctively marked on the lower surface of the hind wings with a conspicuous whitish patch inside the broadly darkened margin. There is no other tailed skipper in our area with which this species might be confused. *Chioides zilpa* also has a white patch on the hind wings below but it is placed differently and that species also has a rather different shape to the fore wing. One or two Mexican species of *Codatractus* are tailed and have the lower surface of the hind wings marked almost exactly like *C. alcaeus*. One of these, *C. carlos* Evans, is about as common as *alcaeus* and may, in fact, be the species which occasionally is taken in Texas or Arizona. *C. carlos* differs from *alcaeus* superficially only in that the spots of the central hyaline band of the fore wing are slightly smaller and the spot nearest the anal angle is not overlapped by the next spot in the band below the cell. The basal clothing of hairs on the wings is more olive colored in *carlos*. I have not seen any specimens or figures of this species from the United States and am not certain which of these two species, *alcaeus* or *carlos,* actually occurs north of Mexico. It was not known until 1952 that two species were going under the name of *alcaeus,* and most illustrations of this species up to that time were of Mexican specimens of *carlos*. For comparative purposes we illustrate *Codatractus carlos* Evans as well. The immature stages of this species have not been reported. Wingspread, 46–54 mm.

Distribution: C. alcaeus ranges from Mexico to Panamá in two subspecies. The nominate subspecies embraces all the populations north of Costa Rica. The other species, *C. carlos,* ranges from Mexico south to Colombia and Venezuela in three subspecies. Nominate *carlos* ranges from Panamá to Mexico and has been diagnosed above in the discussion of the two species. *C. alcaeus* has been recorded from western Texas and Arizona, where it must be quite rare.

Genus ZESTUSA Lindsey

This is a peculiar genus of two species having rather long palpi which project conspicuously forward in front of the face and a long, stout, sickle-shaped antennal club. The bared sensory part of the club is extraordinarily long, extending the entire length of the club and slightly onto the relatively short antennal shaft. The wings are rather triangular and the anal angle of the hind wing is prolonged into a short, very broad, tail. The placement of the pale spots on the wings is unusual. The hairs of the body and wings are long, and there is a dense linear cluster of these hairs along the length of the anal fold on the hind wing above. Males have a costal fold but no hind tibial tuft. The genus is North American. One species ranges from southern Mexico south perhaps to western Panamá, the other is restricted to the southwestern United States and northwestern Mexico.

1. **Zestusa dorus** (Edwards). Plate 95, figure 5, ♂. This skipper can be confused with no other. The brown of the wings above has a slight reddish tint and the long basal hairs give that part of the wings a greenish gray cast. The spots of both wings on the upper surface are hyaline and pale amber. The hind wings below are hoary bluish gray with two dark brown slender bands converging toward the costa. The anal third of the fore wing below is pale orange-buff. This species, like the other member of the genus, is apt to be local and is not common in collections. Wingspread, 38–42 mm.

Early Stages: According to A. B. Klots (*in litt.*) the larvae of this species feed on *Quercus Emoryi* and *Q. arizonica* in southeastern Arizona.

Distribution: Z. *dorus* is known from western Texas, southwestern Colorado, New Mexico, Arizona and south into Sonora. In the United States it has been collected from April to July.

Genus POLYTHRIX Watson

This is a genus of over a dozen tropical American species. They are moderately large brown skippers which have the central hyaline band of the fore wing rather short; the spot that is usually under the end of the cell outside the band is more or less crowded against or into the band so the fore wing central spots have a clustered aspect. The subapical spots of the fore wing are rather large and arranged in a straight line. The hind wings of most species are broad at the costa but rapidly become narrowed, and all the species have the anal angle greatly prolonged into a conspicuous short or long tail. The palpi are short and the third segment extends slightly beyond the vestiture of the second segment. The antennal club is relatively long and quite stout in some species, and it is usually sharply bent to a long slender apiculus. Males of most species have a costal fold, but it is slender and inconspicuous in some. Males of some species also have specialized hair tufts on the wings, either on the hind wing above near the base of the costal area, on the lower surface of the fore wing below the base of the cell or along the central part of the anal fold on the hind wing below. A number of the species are superficially similar and because individuals vary a little in wing pattern it is frequently necessary to refer to the male genitalia for proper identification. One species of *Polythrix* is known to occur in the United States, its identity only recently resolved by Freeman (1967).

1. **Polythrix octomaculata** (Sepp). Plate 92, figure 23, ♂. The wings of this species are rather narrow. The fore wings are produced apically and the hind wings taper gradually toward the anal region where they are prolonged broadly into a short (male) or longer (female) tail. The central hyaline band on the fore wing is short and the extra spot below the end of the cell is small and does not touch either of the two large spots of the central band. Males do not have a costal fold. The compactly scaled palpi below and the pectus are strikingly light yellow-buff or pale orange-buff, especially near the end of the palpi. The obscure dark bands of the lower surface of the hind wings are vaguely reproduced on the upperside. Wing-spread, 40–46 mm.

Early Stages: The larva is nearly white and marked with minute longitudinal streaks of gray. The extremely flattened, heart-shaped head is yellow with a loop of pale purple or light red across the face. The pupa is light bone colored with reddish streaks at the sides and angular projections near the head. The larval foodplant is given by Draudt and by Hayward as the legume *Pterocarpus indicus.* Miles Moss gives the foodplants as the legumes "mututy" and *Muellera moniliformis.*

Distribution: This species ranges from extreme southern Texas southward to Argentina. A related population is reputed to inhabit Haiti but this is probably a different species. Although Evans considers *P. alciphron* of Mexico a subspecies of *P. octomaculata,* I am convinced that they are separate species. The Texas specimens were taken in March.

Genus TYPHEDANUS Butler

About eight dissimilar looking tropical American species are placed together in this genus. All have a relatively long antennal club that is abruptly bent to a long or short, slender apiculus. The palpi are rather short and the third segment is usually evident. Most species have the fore wing somewhat produced at the apex, at least in males, and most of the species have a long tail at the anal angle of the hind wing. Males have no costal fold but all have an erectile tuft of long hair near the base of the anal fold on the hind wing above. This tuft is the same color as the wing in many species and is thus inconspicuous, but several species have a contrasting yellowish tuft. Only one species is known to occur north of Mexico.

1. **Typhedanus undulatus** (Hewitson). Plate 95, figure 14, ♀. The relatively narrow and apically produced fore wing, the long-tailed hind wing and the pattern of hyaline spots on the fore wing give this insect somewhat the aspect of a *Chioides,* but this skipper is easily recognized by the shorter, more abruptly bent antennal apiculus,

and by the distinctive markings on the lower surfaces. The hind wings below are light brown, densely striate, and are banded with very dark bluish black bands. Wingspread, 41–47 mm.

Early Stages: The egg is "smooth" and about 0.8 mm in diameter. It is at first translucent grayish blue but soon becomes opaque gray and ultimately whitish with a black spot representing the larval head within. The first stage larva is transparent yellowish with a brownish black head. The mature larva is stout and greenish gray with a darker median line. Laterally the dorsal coloring is intensified but below this it abruptly becomes dull yellow with an oblique yellow dash on each segment; the body is sprinkled with short whitish hairs; the head is robust and roughened, dark brown with a small red-brown spot on each side just above the mouthparts. The ocelli are yellow. The pupa is lustrous dark or light brown with dark, almost blackish head, eyes and mouthparts; the tip of the abdomen is sharply pointed. The foodplant is given by Hayward as *Cassia corymbosa* in Argentina. Miles Moss found larvae in Brazil on *C. alata, reticulata,* and *occidentalis.*

Distribution: This is another widely distributed tropical species, ranging from Mexico to Argentina. In Texas it has been collected once, in September.

Genus AGUNA Williams

This tropical American genus comprises over a dozen mostly large, brown, tailed or untailed species. Many are brilliantly green on the head, thorax and wing bases above, and most of them have a white line or band on the lower surface of the hind wings, generally extending from the costa to near the anal angle. The palpi are as in *Typhedanus* above. The antennal club is rather long and stout and is sharply bent to a long slender apiculus. Males have an obscure, slender, rather short costal fold but no specialized hair tufts on the wings or legs. The fore wings are generally quite produced apically and the hind wings, even if not long-tailed, are at least prolonged at the anal angle into a small tail-like projection. Only one species thus far has been collected north of Mexico.

1. **Aguna asander** (Hewitson). Plate 95, figure 10, ♀ (ssp. *asander*).   This large brown skipper with pale orange, brassy golden or amber spots across the fore wing and a large central white patch on the hind wing below, might be mistaken for *Epargyreus clarus* (or some other *Epargyreus* in more southern regions). The spots of the central band on the fore wing of *asander* are paler and more nearly the same size than in *E. clarus.* The hind wings below of *asander* are purplish, often with much white overscaling, and the central white patch, if well defined, is quite different in shape than in any *Epargyreus.* This white marking is variable in *asander:* frequently blurred on the outer edges, variously reduced, or even entirely lacking. Several tropical species of other genera are like *asander* below but none of these comes within our area. North of Mexico this species should not be difficult to recognize. Wingspread, 50–56 mm.

Early Stages: Little seems to have been published concerning the immature stages of this common tropical skipper. Costa Lima states only that the larvae feed on legumes.

Distribution: Nominate *asander* occurs from extreme southern Texas to Argentina. Two additional subspecies are found in the Greater Antilles. In Texas this skipper has been taken during August, October and November. Freeman notes that it seems to prefer deep shade and that individuals tend to rest on the lower surface of large leaves.

Genus CHIOIDES Lindsey

This genus contains less than half a dozen large, brown, tailed skippers that look rather similar above. The fore wing of all species is rather narrow and much produced apically. The apex is abruptly squared off, below which the outer margin is somewhat concave. On the lower surface of the fore wing is a characteristic dark triangular patch on the costa between the subapical spots and the apex. The palpi are rather short but the last segment is conspicuous. The antennal club is robust and usually gently hooked to form the rather thick, long apiculus. Males have a costal fold but no special hair tufts on the wings or legs. The hyaline spots on the fore wing are light amber in all but one species. The genus extends from the southwestern United States to Argentina and is also present in the West Indies where several species and subspecies are endemic. Two species occur north of Mexico, both with long tails on the hind wings.

1. **Chioides catillus** (Cramer). Plate 95, figure 6, ♂ (ssp. *albofasciatus*).   This large species may be recognized immediately by the presence of a pale band on the lower surface of the hind wing which extends from the middle of the costa nearly to the anal angle at the base of the tail. This band may be irregular and brownish gray or straight, evenly narrow and white. The hyaline spots of the fore wing above are light amber and may be squarish and moderately separated in the central band, in some populations large and overlapping. No other skipper north of Panamá can be confused with North American populations of this species. Wingspread, 46–52 mm.

Early Stages: The egg is large, a little over 1 mm in diameter, white at first, becoming yellow within a few days, and bears a surface sculpture of about fourteen vertical ridges. The first stage larva is bright yellow with a black head. The half grown larva is pale bluish green with a bluish median dorsal line, a faint yellowish line on each side and the whole body covered with slightly raised yellow speckles; The first segment of the thorax is deep orange-yellow with a black dorsal shield; the head dull black with an orange-brown spot on each side above the mouthparts. The last stage larva (South America) is at first olive-green, becoming pinkish or purplish with maturity. The lateral lines are deep red-orange and the first thoracic segment reddish with a black collar; the head is dark chocolate brown with an inverted V-mark of dark brown on the front above the mouthparts, and with two black spots on each side of the face. In Mexico the mature larva has a yellow lateral line; the head is scarlet above and marginally, blending to reddish toward the base and with a black central mark on the face suggesting a spread-winged bird. The pupa is dark brown, covered with a whitish waxy bloom. The larvae feed on various legumes: *Mimosa, Rhynchosia senna* and "Soja" (South America); *Tephrosia Lindheimeri, Rhynchosia minima* and *Phaseolus atropurpureus* (Texas).

Distribution: This widely distributed insect is found from southern Arizona and Texas to Argentina and on several islands of the West Indies. Mainland populations north of Panamá all have a deep reddish brown lower surface of the hind wing and the pale stripe is brilliant white, straight, and of nearly uniform width. This is the subspecies *C. catillus albofasciatus* (Hewitson). Seven additional subspecies are known. Kendall has shown that the northern distributional limits in Texas are determined partly by the species' inability to survive through the winter. Too few larvae enter a dormant diapause state to await spring, and pupae produce adults without dormancy. Larval foodplants north of extreme southern Texas are winter defoliated so non-diapausing larvae starve. Only during mild winters can larvae survive winter conditions in most of Texas, and possibly also Arizona, so in these areas the species can be expected to be sporadic in occurrence. In extreme southern Texas adults are present all year.

2. Chioides zilpa (Butler). Plate 95, figure 4, ♀ (ssp. *zilpa*). This species is similar to *catillus* on the upper surface. The hind wings below, however, are mottled dark reddish brown with a conspicuous white patch between the outer half of the cell and the anal fold and a short white bar near the anal angle. Nothing is published concerning the early stages. Wingspread, 48–58 mm.

Distribution: C. zilpa ranges from southeastern Arizona and Texas south to Ecuador. The populations of Arizona and northwestern Mexico are reputed to be much paler on the lower surfaces, with the base of the hind wing costa whitish; these are referred to the subspecies *C. zilpa namba* Evans. The remaining populations, presumably including those of southern Texas, belong to the nominate subspecies, which has the base of the hind wing costa below dark brown. This skipper is much less common than *catillus* and is seldom encountered within the United States. In Arizona it has been collected in May. In Texas it has been taken from September to November.

Genus POLYGONUS Hübner

Two similar tropical American species comprise this genus. They are large, dark brown skippers with narrow, produced fore wings and produced hind wings but with no distinct tail at the anal angle. There is a series of three subapical spots and three larger, more discal, hyaline spots nearly of equal size. Generally there is a faint purplish iridescence on the wing surfaces above and below. Males have neither a costal fold nor a hair tuft on the wings or hind legs. The palpi are short, the third segment visible beyond the compact scaling of the second segment. The antennal club is somewhat slender, but not unusually long, and is abruptly bent to a rather slender, long apiculus. The genus is represented from the southern United States to Argentina, and is widely distributed through the West Indies. Both species occur north of Mexico.

1. **Polygonus leo** (Gmelin). Plate 95, figure 8, ♂; figure 9, ♀ (both ssp. *leo*). This is a slightly larger species than *P. manueli,* with somewhat longer fore wings. The fore wings are basally brown with a faint purplish gloss in oblique light. The hyaline spots of the fore wing are not brilliantly reflective under oblique light on either surface because the translucent scales of these spots are elevated nearly vertical to the wing surface, a characteristic not visible without a microscope. The paler areas of the hind wings are much duller brown above than is usual in *manueli.* The lower surface of the fore wing is usually dark brown from the discal region below the cell all the way to the anal angle, and if a dark spot is discernible outside and below the lowest hyaline spot, it is only faintly indicated. The hind wings below are brown with a grayish purple gloss, usually with a round dark spot near the wing base, and without a conspicuous rust red cast in the pale areas adjacent to the anal fold, at least under ordinary lighting. Males and females are superficially similar. Wingspread, 46–52 mm.

Early Stages: The egg is swollen cylindrical, flat at the summit and the base, about 0.8 mm in diameter and slightly more in height. About fourteen sharp vertical ridges are expanded to form a crown-like crest at the summit enclosing a smooth depressed micropyle. The egg is green changing eventually to reddish with the ridges and crest snowy white. The first stage larva is orange-yellow with a rounded dull black head. The half-grown larva is pale yellowish green dotted with yellow, and with two yellow lines on each side; the black head is broad and slightly heart-shaped on top. The mature larva is yellow-green with a translucent skin bearing an inconspicuous dense, fine, white pile but appearing almost naked; on each side is a straight yellow line and below that a series of striate yellow blotches forming another, indefinite, line; the head is greenish white and rough with a black margin and two black spots on the front near the top. The foodplant in Florida, Puerto Rico and Argentina is *Ichthyomethia piscipula.* Kimball also lists *Pongamia pinnata* (Florida). Gundlach raised larvae from *Lonchocarpus sericeus* (Cuba). *Derris eliptica* was also reported (Puerto Rico) according to Wolcott.

Distribution: This insect is found through the range of the genus from Florida, western Texas, Arizona and southern California south to Peru and Argentina and through the West Indies. It has not been recorded from Baja California but may occur there. Four or five subspecies are recognized. I consider all the mainland populations to be nominate *leo.* Florida material tends to be slightly darker above, especially on the hind wings, and might more appropriately be associated with the subspecies of Cuba and the Bahamas but that is not a matter to be settled here. In Florida *leo* is on the wing throughout the year. In Arizona it has been taken from May to September. In California it is decidedly scarce: it is reported from as far north as Los Angeles county, and I have seen it in San Bernardino and Inyo counties in September.

2. **Polygonus manueli** Bell & Comstock. Plate 97, figure 26, ♂ (ssp. *manueli*).   A smaller skipper than *leo, manueli* is commonly confused with that species, partly because there seem to be some anomalies in the original description. *P. manueli* is not difficult to recognize, however, if the following features are considered in contrast to their condition in *leo*. The fore wings are somewhat shorter, and basally they are distinctly blue glossed in contrast to the faint purplish cast of the dark outer two-thirds of the wing. The hyaline spots of the fore wing are brilliantly reflective under oblique light on both surfaces, because the shiny translucent scales of these spots are not elevated but are flat-shingled against the wing membrane as is usual in other scales, a feature not visible without a microscope. The paler areas of the hind wings above are brown with a slightly more reddish tinge than usual in *leo*. The lower surface of the forewing is blackish brown in the discal area about the cell, but this ordinarily does not extend to the anal angle, where there is a distinct submarginal and marginal pair of squarish dark brown spots. The hind wings below are brown with a distinct bluish purple gloss except near the anal fold where the paler brown areas have a conspicuous rust-red cast. There is often a round black spot near the wing base. The palpi and legs are somewhat darker but with a warmer, yellowish or rusty tint to the brown rather than the gray-brown tone of these structures in *leo*. Males and females are similar. Wingspread, 40–44 mm.

Early Stages: The early stages of this skipper have been briefly recorded by Miles Moss. The mature larva is half green and half yellow, with a patchy aspect owing to the transparent skin. There is a light stripe on the upper part of each side. The head is flattened, glossy light red, darker behind and with black eye spots on the upper part of the face; the mouthparts are pale. The pupa is unmarked brown. In Brazil the species feeds on *Muelleria moniliformis,* a shrub of tidal mud flats.

Distribution: Nominate *manueli* is known from Florida south to Peru and Argentina. A smaller-spotted subspecies inhabits the Lesser Antilles. In southern Florida *m. manueli* has been taken from February to November. This seems to be a skipper of restricted habitats, perhaps tidal flats, as it is rather seldom collected.

Genus EPARGYREUS Hübner

This is a tropical American genus of at least fifteen species, more than half of which are variable, similar looking and difficult to identify. These difficult members of the genus are not well understood and they are currently under study because the interpretations by Evans (1952), while a considerable improvement over earlier concepts, are still not satisfactory. The skippers of this genus are large brown insects with long, apically produced fore wings and a prolonged anal angle on the hind wings. A band of large or moderate sized hyaline spots crosses the fore wing, which is more or less orange in many species. Most species have a large irregular silvery band or group of spots on the lower surface of the hind wing. Males have a costal fold but no hair tuft on the legs or wings. The palpi are short with the stout third segment just visible beyond the scaling of the second. The antennal club is long but robust, usually evenly hooked to the long, rather heavy, apiculus. The genus is confined to the Western Hemisphere, where it extends from Canada to Argentina and through the West Indies. Only three different-appearing species are reported to occur north of Mexico.

1. **Epargyreus clarus** (Cramer). Plate 95, figure 1, ♂ (ssp. *clarus*).   The rather long and narrow fore wing and the shape of the characteristic large central silver spot on the hind wing below will distinguish this, the well known Silver Spotted Skipper, from otherwise similar members of other genera. This distinctive species is brown above with a well developed central band of light to golden orange spots on the fore wing. The hind wing below is chocolate brown with a large, irregularly broad, silver band across the middle of the wing. The fringes are brown or buff and checkered. Wingspread, 44–60 mm.

Early Stages: Immature stages of *clarus* have been abundantly reported since they were first illustrated by Abbot & Smith in 1797. The green egg is hemispherical, a little over 1 mm in diameter. It has from sixteen to nineteen vertical, minutely beaded ridges, every other ridge extending higher on the summit. The ridges are connected by numerous minute raised cross lines. First stage larvae are pale greenish yellow with rounded, dark brown heads. The half-grown larva is dark green above with many narrow yellow-green cross stripes; the head is brownish black. The mature larva is greenish yellow marked with cross-lines, blotches and dots of bright green; the head is brownish red with two large round orange-red spots low on the face. The pupa is dark brown with black and yellow-brown markings, or brown with numerous fine markings of dark brown or black. The wing pads, legs and mouthparts are commonly darker. The larval foodplants known to be used by *clarus* are summarized by Scudder (1889): *Robinia pseudoacacia, R. hispida, R. viscosa, R. neo-mexicana, Amorpha fruticosa, Wisteria frutescens, Lespedeza capitata, Lathyrus paluster, Desmodium nudiflorum, D. canadense, D. marylandicum, Amphicarpaea monoica, Gleditschia* and *Apios tuberosa.* In addition Lembert reported oviposition on *Hosackia grandiflora,* and Fiske gave the foodplant as *Phaseolus perennis.* Clark reported larvae from *Desmodium paniculata, D. Dillenii* and *D. Michauxii.* Kendall noted that although wild females will oviposit on *Erythrina herbacea* and *Rhynchosia minima,* the first stage larvae cannot survive on them. He also stated that *Wisteria sinensis* was an acceptable foodplant, and Sim found that the oriental *Pueria hirsuta* is also utilized by this species. By and large, *Robinia* species seem to be the most usual foodplant of this skipper through its range; Shapiro notes that small trees isolated or in small stands seem to be preferred.

Distribution: This species ranges from Quebec to British Columbia and south to Florida, Texas, northwestern Mexico and Baja California. There is some slight geographic variation through this range, the majority of the populations north of

Mexico being represented by the nominate subspecies. These skippers are large and have the last spot of the central band nearest the anal angle on the fore wing large and generally distinctively overlapped by the next spot in the band. On the hind wings below, the silver band or spot is broad with the upper narrowed part relatively short because its inner margin is gradually expanded to the broadest part of the band. A faint white tracery usually extends above the outer edge of this spot. Populations in Arizona, and perhaps New Mexico and Sonora, may be referred to the subspecies *E. clarus huachuca* Dixon. This subspecies differs from the nominate only in that the lower spot of the central band on the fore wing is usually relatively small and slightly detached from the next forward spot of the band. The fine white lines along the outer edge of the silver patch on the hind wing below are generally only indicated near the anal margin, and the silver spot itself is considerably narrower. California populations differ from the two preceding subspecies in that they are much smaller with broader, shorter wings. The lower spot of the central band on the fore wing is small to absent, but it may be detached or slightly overlapped by the next spot in the band. On the hind wing below the silver spot is relatively narrow, as in *huachuca,* but the upper narrowed part of this spot is a long and rather uniform "neck" because both the inner and outer margins are simultaneously abruptly expanded to the wide portion of the band. The white lines outside the spot are obsolete as in *huachuca.* The name available for this subspecies is *E. clarus californicus* (J. B. Smith). Populations from Baja California, California and perhaps the entire Pacific slope may be referred to this subspecies. *E. clarus* is common in many parts of its range but is apparently local to the north; on the Pacific slope it is rather uncommon and quite local. It generally is most abundant through the summer but is taken from March to September in Texas and from February to December in Florida. Nominate *clarus* is often found in suburban or urban situations because acceptable foodplants (woody legumes) are often planted as ornamentals.

2. **Epargyreus zestos** Geyer. Plate 95, figure 2, ♀.   This insect is similar to *clarus* above, but below the hind wings have no silver spot or band and are simply dark brown with a slight purple tint and several vague paler brown bands. Nothing is published concerning the early stages. Wingspread, 49–59 mm.

    Distribution: In the United States *zestos* is restricted to southern Florida, including the Keys. It is also widely distributed through the West Indies. Mainland records for Arizona, Mexico, Honduras and Surinam are undoubtedly based upon mislabeled specimens. In Florida the species is on the wing from January to September.

3. **Epargyreus exadeus** (Cramer). Plate 95, figure 3, ♂ (ssp. *cruza*).   This skipper is one of a very poorly understood assemblage of similar tropical American species. These species are dark, generally with the body and the basal part of the wings above clothed with yellowish or pale brown hairs. The hind wings below are generally dark chocolate-brown and have one or more large or small silvery spots and whitish lines. The spots of the central band on the fore wing are paler than in *clarus* or *zestos,* being hyaline amber or whitish, and are generally smaller and separated.

Members of this complex which have been reported in the southwestern United States are considered to represent a northern subspecies of *E. exadeus, cruza* Evans. Whether they really belong to the species *exadeus* is debatable; studies now in progress may alter our views.

E. e. cruza is as described above, but with the central hyaline band of the fore wing composed of separated pale amber or nearly whitish spots, and the wing bases above conspicuously tawny brownish. The markings on the lower surface of the hind wing consist of several rather small separated silver spots. Wingspread, 52–58 mm.

Early Stages: According to Comstock & Vazquez the mature larva of *cruza* is olive-green with transverse lines of black spots and blotches intermingled with white dots; the thoracic segments have an opaque orange tint; the collar is scarlet with a broad black border behind; on each side of the abdomen there is a longitudinal yellow stripe; and the head is black with two large round red spots low on the face. The pupa is light brown with a network of fine dark brown wavy lines and spots, most evident on the abdominal segments. Comstock & Vazquez also state that larvae were found on *Cassia* sp. in Mexico. Miles Moss reports larvae on wild beans (*Phaseolus* sp.) and, tentatively, *Lecythis paraënsis* in Brazil.

Distribution: The species *exadeus* is reputed to range from the southwestern United States south to Argentina, the subspecies *cruza* representing populations north of Panamá. Examples of this northern subspecies have been recorded rarely from Arizona (in March), New Mexico and southern California. The reports for the latter two states are questionable.

Genus PROTEIDES Hübner

The two known species of this tropical American genus are like those of *Epargyreus,* being large brown skippers with produced fore wings, a robust head and thorax and with a long robust antennal club. The club is constricted before the more or less abrupt bend to the long, rather slender apiculus. There is a central band of whitish, well-separated hyaline spots across the fore wing of some populations of one of the species, but hyaline spots are often entirely absent. Males have no costal fold and they lack specialized hair tufts on legs or wings. This genus differs from *Epargyreus* in having generally narrower and more produced fore wings, in the form of the antennal club and in the lack of a male costal fold, but the two genera are rather closely related. One of the two species of *Proteides* is endemic to Cuba; the other extends from the southern United States south to Argentina and through the West Indies.

1. **Proteides mercurius** (Fabricius). Plate 96, figure 12, ♂ (ssp. *mercurius*).   This large skipper is easily recognized by its long narrow fore wing, with the outer two-thirds contrastingly dark brown or blackish. The basal portion of both wings and the top of the head and thorax are bright yellowish orange. The abdomen above and on the sides is black with white segmental rings. The hind wing below is dark reddish

brown basally and on the anal fold. The rest of the wing is paler reddish brown, unevenly overscaled with whitish discally and bluish gray marginally. A conspicuous, slightly sinuous, dark reddish brown band extends part way across the wing from the outer half of the anal fold into the paler area. The palpi and pectus below are conspicuously pale pinkish buff. Wingspread, 58–68 mm.

Early Stages: The mature larva is dark olive-green or honey-colored, strewn with dark brown and with brown transverse bands; there is a bright red stripe on each side and the median dorsal line is dark; the head is round and robust, dark brown with red eyespots low on the face. The pupa is robust and dark brown but appears bluish because of a heavy coating of white waxy powder. Gundlach listed *Ecastophyllum, Rhynchosia* and *Vigna* as larval foodplants in Cuba. The foodplants according to Draudt, Kaye and Hayward are *Cassia* spp. and other tree-like legumes. Wolcott reported this species feeding on *Derris eliptica* in Puerto Rico. Miles Moss found it commonly on *Muellera moniliformis,* a tidal flat shrub that is subject to daily inundations.

Distribution: Through the mainland distribution of this insect, from the United States to Argentina, the fore wings are well spotted with separated whitish spots in a central series. These populations are referred to the nominate subspecies which has been collected rarely in Arizona, New Mexico and Texas. In the latter state it has been taken in April. Through the West Indies occur six additional subspecies. The Cuban subspecies, *sanantonio* (Lucas), is characterized by the absence of pale hyaline spots on the fore wings (sometimes a minute subapical spot near the costa) but otherwise it is just like nominate *mercurius.* This subspecies has appeared rarely in Florida. An example was taken in northern Florida in May.

Genus PHOCIDES Hübner

This tropical American genus includes eighteen or more large, heavy-bodied species, nearly all of which bear a remarkable resemblance to certain tropical Pyrrhopyginae. Indeed, some subspecies (or species) of *Phocides* may resemble a pyrrhopygine species more than they resemble other conspecific (or congeneric) populations. Yet, some *Phocides* are so similar superficially that identification depends on genitalic characters. It is also of interest that before the last instar, the larvae of some *Phocides* also resemble the conspicuous larvae of Pyrrhopyginae, but without the conspicuous hairy vestiture of the latter. The wings of Phocides are broad and triangular, pointed at the apex. They are generally blackish or rarely brown above, usually with metallic bluish or greenish ray-like streaks of basal overscaling, but these basal rays may be almost obsolete. The fore wings may be totally unspotted or marked with three hyaline bands: the central, the subapical and one between these. In addition to the basal rays, the hind wings may be marked with lines of blue or green scaling and the body may be striped with blue or green. Males have a costal fold but no specialized clusters of spines or hair tufts on the legs or wings. The palpi are short, stocky and separated, converging at their tips. The antennae are long, with a long robust club that is constricted before the sharp bend to a long slender apiculus. The tibia of the middle leg is spined in a few species. The genus occurs from southern United States to Argentina and in the Greater Antilles and the Bahamas. Only three species occur within the United States.

1. **Phocides pigmalion** (Cramer). Plate 96, figure 2, ♂ (ssp. *okeechobee*). This is a blackish or slightly brownish purple species with a submarginal series of metallic light blue spots on the hind wing above. On the upper surface there may be no hyaline spots on the fore wing or a complete set of three broad hyaline bands. The basal blue ray pattern also varies from virtually obsolete to conspicuous and extensive on both wings above. The blue on the hind wings below varies from a few vague tracings to several bold stripes. The middle tibiae are spined. The species is represented by about half a dozen subspecies from Florida to Argentina and in the Bahamas and Greater Antilles. One of these subspecies is endemic to Florida; *okeechobee* (Worthington).

Superficially quite unlike most other subspecies of pigmalion, *okeechobee* is unmarked blackish or dark brownish above with a distinct bluish purple cast. The only conspicuous markings are a blue submarginal line of spots on the hind wings above, and a faint trace of basal blue rays on the fore wing, especially near the costa. There are several faint blue lines on the hind wings below. The abdomen is generally brown, sometimes with traces of blue segmental rings. Wingspread, 50–62 mm.

Early Stages: The early stages have been reported by Dyar and by Strohecker. The egg is nearly spherical with a slightly flattened base and eighteen vertical ridges, every other ridge shortened and not reaching the summit. The half-grown larva is wine-red to purplish brown with transverse segmental rings of bright yellow or orange; the head is colored as the body with a large round spot of yellow or orange low on each side of the face in front. Soon after molting the mature larva acquires a bright frosted white aspect because of a covering of powdery white exudate which completely masks the markings; the body is distinctly contracted and stout in this stage; the head is pale brown, blackish around the mouth with two large orange or yellow spots low on the front of the face. The pupa is robust with two short prominences between the large eyes; it is creamy white with a greenish cast on the thorax and appendage cases and a yellow stripe on the upper part of the eye. The foodplant is Red Mangrove (*Rhizophora mangle*).

Distribution: P. p. okeechobee is confined to the coast of southern Florida where it flies from November to May. In the southernmost parts of its range it is also taken from June to August.

2. **Phocides polybius** (Fabricius). Plate 96, figure 3, ♂ (ssp. *lilea*). This blackish species has a bright red spot in the cell of the fore wing and usually another adjacent at the costa. The basal metallic ray marks on the fore wings are greenish, nearly obsolete in some populations. The remainder of the upper surface has a blackish blue or green cast in oblique light. The head and palpi are red or orange below, as are the palpi and collar above. The wing fringes are white, those of the hind

wing deep orange normally in some populations (not ours). Wingspread, 50–64 mm.

Early Stages: The half-grown larva is bright crimson or maroon with bright yellow intersegmental rings; the head is colored as the body but dark on the lower half. The mature larva is white, the brown head with a large round yellow spot low on each side of the face in front. The head of the robust larva sometimes appears to be partially withdrawn into the swollen segments behind it. The pupa is smooth, dirty white or pale green, the head produced in front of the eyes as a double crested knob. The head, thorax and appendage cases are sprinkled with minute black dots. Larvae feed upon various species of *Psidium* (e.g., Guava, Araca).

Distribution: The species ranges from Mexico to Argentina in three subspecies. The northernmost, *P. polybius lilea* (Reakirt), includes all of the populations north of Panamá. It differs from the others principally in that the hind wing fringes are entirely white with no orange at the anal angle. The subspecies has long been reported to occur in Texas, but its occurrence there has only recently been verified.

3. **Phocides urania** (Westwood). Plate 96, figure 4, ♂. This unmistakable skipper is basically blackish but the extensive overscaling above gives a distinctive metallic green aspect. The basal green rays are conspicuous and extend to near the central hyaline band on the fore wing, beyond which the outer portion of the wing is copiously overscaled with green. The hind wing has three basal greenish rays and a submarginal series of greenish or bluish spots and some discal spots near the cell. The hyaline spots of the fore wing (absent in some populations) are arranged in two bands and a subapical V-shaped series. The fringes of the hind wings are checkered. Nothing has been reported on the early stages. Wingspread, 54–60 mm.

Distribution: This species ranges from Mexico to Costa Rica. It has been reported several times to have been taken in Texas and Arizona, but these are old records and the specimens were probably mislabeled. The occurrence of this species north of Mexico requires verification.

Subfamily PYRRHOPYGINAE

This is a small subfamily of skippers compared to the other two subfamilies represented in the Western Hemisphere. This group consists of about twenty genera and nearly 150 species. The entire subfamily is confined to the more or less tropical regions of North and South America. The larvae are generally strikingly colored, reddish or purple with yellow segmental rings, usually abundantly clothed with fine long hairs. Larvae feed on dicotyledonous plants. Adults are mostly large skippers, variously patterned; the several basic patterns are duplicated often by numerous species within a genus, by particular species in different genera, and sometimes in less striking departures, by particular subspecies of different species. Several of these basic and often quite different wing patterns are closely approached by species in the Pyrginae and in the Hesperiinae. Red patches on the tip of the abdomen, on the wings or on the head seem to be a common and recurring feature in this group. Pyrrhopygine skippers have extraordinarily massive bodies and generally rather short triangular wings relative to the body size. The hind wings in particular are unusually small in many cases. One species of this subfamily (*Jemadia scomber* Druce) is probably the "largest" American skipper outside of the Megathymidae yet its fore wing length is only 39 mm. The thorax, however, is about 10 mm across at the bases of the wings, so the total "expanse" of this species is nearly 90 mm from wing tip to wing tip. The palpi of pyrrhopygine skippers are extremely short and closely oppressed to the face. The antennae are distinctive: there is no recurved apiculus, but the antennal shaft is often bent at the base of the blunt or somewhat pointed long club so that the entire club is reflexed. In some genera the club is fairly slender and the bend occurs at the thickest but more or less basal part of the club, which may be pointed at the end. The middle tibiae are usually unspined and have a single pair of spurs; the hind tibiae usually have two pairs of spurs. Males of a few species have dense brushes of hair on the opposing surfaces of the femur and tibia of the hind leg. Otherwise there are no secondary sex characters in this subfamily, save for the somewhat broader wings in females. Only one species represents this fascinating and colorful group north of Mexico.

Genus PYRRHOPYGE Hübner

Most of the nearly sixty species in this genus are blackish insects with a bluish or greenish luster above. Most species have no hyaline spots on the wings but a large number have the end of the abdomen conspicuously red (whence the generic name). Some species have red on the head, collar, tegulae or wings. Species of other genera are often similar to certain *Pyrrhopyge,* and sometimes such species may be placed in the proper genus most readily by reference to the genitalic structures. Males of most *Pyrrhopyge* have narrower, more pointed, wings than females, but this is not always conspicuous. Structurally and in wing markings this is a diverse assemblage of species. The genus ranges from the southwestern United States to Argentina. Our only member is relatively drab.

1. **Pyrrhopyge araxes** (Hewitson). Plate 96, figure 10, ♀.   This large brown skipper is immediately recognizable in that the entire antennal club is bent back. The head is partly yellowish above, and in some populations the entire head, body and legs are yellowish orange beneath. Often the abdomen is dorsally somewhat banded with yellowish rings. The wings above are brown with large hyaline spots on the fore wing. The lower surface is brown with at least the basal parts orange or yellow-orange. Wingspread, 44–61 mm.

Early Stages: The early stages have been partially described by Comstock. The stout mature larva is red-brown with transverse narrow bright yellow stripes, the body covered with scattered long white hairs. The head is black with a dense covering of long hairs. Most of the hairs are white but on each side in front the hairs are orange, appearing as two orange spots. The pupa is brownish red on the head, wing pads and thorax. The abdomen is dull orange with a maroon margin on each segment clothed everywhere but on the appendage pads with long white hairs; a few hairs on the top of the head are orange. The pupa within several days becomes covered with a white flaky powder which obscures the body. Comstock merely gave oak as the foodplant. Burns reported finding a larva of this species on *Quercus arizonica*.

Distribution: This species is known from the southern United States south to Oaxaca. There are two subspecies, the northernmost being that found in southeastern Arizona and rarely in Texas. This subspecies, *P. araxes arizonae* (Godman & Salvin), has much more yellow-orange on the lower surface of the body and wings than the somewhat larger and darker nominate subspecies of central Mexico.

Doubtful Records

The following six tropical American skippers are enumerated in the dos Passos (1964) check list but are not considered here to be adequately recorded from north of the Mexican boundary:

> *Heliopetes domicella willi* (Plötz)
> *Pellicia angra* Evans
> *Dyscophellus euribates* (Stoll)
> *Achalarus albociliatus* (Mabille)
> *Astraptes alector hopfferi* (Plötz)
> *Astraptes galesus cassius* Evans

ADDENDA

Several additional species have been captured in southern Texas since the original manuscripts were received. Most are strays from Mexico but one is a valid resident in the eastern United states.

1. **Graphium philolaus** Boisduval.   A specimen of the Mexican Zebra Swallowtail was taken by Mr. Jack Lipes. He took the specimen on Padre Island, Port Isabel, Cameron county, Texas, on July 21, 1958. The specimen has been donated to the Allyn Entomological Museum at Sarasota, Florida. Source: Journal of the Lepidopterists Society, Vol. 24, No. 24, 1970, p. 233. Author: Raymond J. Jae.

2. **Eueides cleobaea zorcaon** (Reakirt).   A specimen of this common Mexican butterfly was taken on June 11, 1968, on the blooms of *Acacia greggi* at Big Bend National Park, Brewster county, Texas, in the Chisos Mountains basin. The collector was Mr. David A. Easterla. Since then, other examples have been taken at the park suggesting that a colony may exist.

3. **Celastrina ebenina** Clench.   This newly described species is carefully documented in the Annals of the Carnegie Museum, Vol. 44, Dec. 20, 1972, Art. 4, pp. 33–44, *"Celastrina ebenina,* A New Species of Lycaenidae (Lepidoptera) from the Eastern United States" by Harry K. Clench. It is too late for us to include a summary but the interested student may refer to the cited paper.

William H. Howe

GLOSSARY

The content of this Glossary has been kept to a minimum. Words in ordinary English usage may be found in any good dictionary and are omitted; words fully explained in the Introduction are listed in the Index (referring to the Introduction) and are also excluded here.

Arcuate – Curved; in the form of an arc (esp. the stigma of Hesperiinae).

Aurora (pl. **aurorae**) – Orange submarginal crescent, on the hind wing (chiefly the underside) of Plebejinae (Nabokov, 1944).

Bifid – Branching into two parts; forking.

Bifurcate – Same as *bifid.*

Biordinal – Units of two different lengths, occurring alternately in a single row. Applied to the crotchets on larval prolegs (see *triordinal*).

Caudex – The central stalk of an *Agave* plant.

Cervical shield – A sclerotized dorsal plate on the first thoracic segment of a larva.

Chaparral – A plant formation consisting of dense, rigid, evergreen shrubs usually much less than twelve feet high. Typically composed of oaks, chamise, manzanita and *Ceanothus* and largely confined to the western states.

Chorion – The outer covering (shell) of an insect egg.

Conspecific – Belonging to the same species.

Coronal horns – Hornlike processes on the dorsal part of the head of some larvae.

Costa – The dorsal edge of the valva in the male genitalia. Also part of a wing (see Index).

Deciduous – Easily dislodged; naturally falling off. In some species of Lepidoptera scales on parts of the wings or body are deciduous and fall off at, or soon after, emergence from the pupa.

Diapause – A state of "suspended animation" particularly in the larval or pupal state, when normal functions are reduced to a minimum and development is arrested. Diapause is induced and terminated by various environmental signals (such as a particular day length or temperature level) and functions both to carry the individual through unfavorable conditions and to coordinate the whole life history schedule with the seasonal cycle.

Disjunct – Interrupted or disjoined (e.g., in a row of spots on a wing, particularly if one or more are displaced inward or outward relative to the rest); separated by a gap (e.g., in the range of a species; for example, montane species are often disjunct, areas of occurrence being separated by the lowland gaps between mountain ranges).

Dorsum – The back; the upper surface or side away from the legs. See *venter.*

Endemic – Restricted to a given region; generally used to indicate an unusual degree of restriction (e.g., *Strymon avalona* is an endemic species on Santa Catalina Island off the coast of southern California).

f – Form (q.v.)

Facies – External appearance: esp. size, wing shape, color and pattern.

Ferruginous – Rusty red-brown.

Form – (1) One of two or more different aspects of a single population, such as a seasonal form or dimorphic form (see Index). (2) An unspecified taxon of species level or less.

Fulvous – Tawny; brownish orange-yellow or brownish yellow.

Glaucous – Pale grayish blue; whitish.

Hibernaculum – A shelter constructed by a larva, in which it spends the winter.

Hilltopping – The congregation of individuals, of Lepidoptera and other orders of insects, on the summits of hills, ridges and mountain tops. See esp. Shields (1968).

Host specific – Feeding upon only one species or on a limited group of plants or animals.

Hyaline – Nearly or quite transparent; "glassy."

Insula (pl. **insulae**) – A subterminal fuscous spot on the hind wing upperside of some Plebejinae (Nabokov, 1944).

Lunule – A crescent-shaped spot between the veins on a wing, usually concave outward.

Maculation – Markings: the spots, bars, etc., in the wing pattern.

Macule – A spot, as part of the wing pattern (Nabokov, 1944).

Melanotic – Blackish, invaded by black color.

Mesonotum – The dorsal part of the mesothorax or second thoracic segment.

Nymotypical – Nominate: of subspecies, the first-named of a polytypic species; of subgenera, the first-named of several subgenera in a genus. *Nominate* **is now the preferred term.**

Ocellation – A series of ocelli or eyespots in a wing pattern.

Ocellus (pl. **ocelli**) – (1) A simple eye (see Index). (2) A circular eye-like spot, with a different-colored center and sometimes several concentric rings of different colors, usually confined to, or centered on, one or more particular interspaces (esp. common in the Satyridae and some Nymphalidae).

Ochreous – Yellowish tan.

Oviposit – To lay an egg. The term means literally to "place" an egg, whence its common use in insects, because females typically apply and affix the egg to a selected spot.

Pantropical – Occurring in the tropical regions all around the earth.

Pectus – The ventral part of the anterior thorax, particularly its vestiture.

Pyriform – In the shape of a pear: globose at one end, slender at the other.

Sclerotized – Invested with chitin or similar hard cuticular material.

Scolus (pl. **scoli**) – A spiniferous, sclerotized outgrowth of the body wall in the larvae of some saturniid moths and some butterflies. Often (incorrectly) termed "branched spines."

Serpentine soils – Soils derived from the decomposition of serpentine (a metamorphic rock, usually greenish, with high content of magnesium silicate and iron). Such soils are unsuitable to many plants, but others are more or less confined to them. Vegetation on serpentine soils is usually of a "barrens" type, similar to that on sand and shale barrens.

Stalked – Of a wing vein: on a common stalk with another vein.

Subhyaline – Inclining to transparency; not quite hyaline (q.v.).

Suranal plate – A sclerotized dorsal plate near the end of the abdomen of some larvae.

Tegula (pl. **tegulae**) – A small, articulating, scaled sclerite of the thorax, lying over the extreme base of the fore wing like an epaulet. Its presumed function is to protect the delicate, complex hinge mechanism of the fore wing.

Thecla spot – A recurrent combination of pattern elements on the hind wing underside in interspace Cu_1-Cu_2 of most hairstreaks (whence the name) and some blues (Lycaenidae): an enlarged, black, circular segment of the subterminal line, capped by a yellow (or orange or red) crescent, and that, in turn, occasionally by a black line.

Transtilla – Part of the male genitalia: a sclerotized, transverse structure in the dorsal part of the diaphragma or fultura superior.

Triordinal – Units of three different lengths occurring repetitively in a single row. Applied to the crotchets on the larval prolegs (see *biordinal*).

Tubercle – A small sclerotized area on the larval cuticle bearing one or a few setae.

Typical – (1) Average or normal. (2) Nominate, the first described of several subspecies of a species, or the first described of several subgenera of a genus. The term *nominate* is preferred.

Vannal fold – The anal area of the hind wing, the part traversed by the anal (or vannal) veins. It is commonly of a color contrasting with the rest of the wing and often deflexed and embracing the abdomen when the wings are in a folded position.

Venter – The ventral part of the thorax or abdomen.

Ventrum – Venter (q.v.). The term *venter* is preferred.

Verruca (pl. **verrucae**) – A tubercle (q.v.) bearing many setae.

BIBLIOGRAPHY

This bibliography is primarily a highly selective list of the most important reference works that every serious student should sooner or later get to know. It was impracticable to include the hundreds of small articles on which most of our knowledge is really based. However, a few of these have been included as samples. Publications on the Neotropical and Palaearctic butterflies include species also found in North America. We have in general omitted papers that have appeared in the *Journal of the Lepidopterists' Society* (before 1959 called *The Lepidopterists' News*) or the *Journal of Research on the Lepidoptera.* These and other journals are essential sources of information.

ABBOT, JOHN, & JAMES EDWARD SMITH

1797. A natural history of the rarer lepidopterous insects of Georgia. London, 2 vols., xv + 214 pp., 104 pls. [In nomenclature, Smith is the sole author of the names.]

BARNES, WILLIAM, & COAUTHORS (J. H. McDUNNOUGH, A. BUSCK, A. W. LINDSEY OR F. H. BENJAMIN)

1911-1924. Contributions to the natural history of the Lepidoptera of North America. Decatur, Ill.: author. 5 vols., in all 1477 pp., ill.

BELL, E. L.

1938. A catalogue of the original descriptions of the Rhopalocera found north of the Mexican border. Part one, the Hesperioidea. Bull. Cheyenne Mtn. Mus. **1**: 35 pp.

BEUTENMÜLLER, WILLIAM

1893. Descriptive catalogue of the butterflies found within fifty miles of New York City, together with a brief account of their life histories and habits. Bull. American Mus. Nat. Hist. **5**: 241–310.

BOISDUVAL, J. A., & JOHN E. LE CONTE

[1829-1834]. Histoire générale et iconographie des Lépidoptères et des chenilles de l'Amérique Septentrionale. Vol. **1** [all publ.]: [iv] + 228 pp., 78 pls.

BROWN, F. MARTIN

1931. A revision of the genus *Aphrissa*. American Mus. Novit., **454**: 14 pp., ill.

1955. Studies of Nearctic *Coenonympha tullia* (Rhopalocera, Satyridae). *Coenonympha tullia inornata* Edwards. Bull. American Mus. Nat. Hist. **105**: 359–410, ill.

1961. *Coenonympha tullia* on islands in the St. Lawrence River. Canadian Ent. **93**: 107–117, ill.

1964-1970 [incomplete]. The types of butterflies described by William Henry Edwards. Trans. American Ent. Soc. **90** (1964): 323–413 (Satyridae); **91** (1965): 233–350 (Nymphalidae: Argynninae); **92** (1966); 357–468 (Nymphalidae: Melitaeinae); **93** (1967): 319–393 (Nymphalidae: Nymphalinae, Limenitidinae, Apaturinae, Charaxinae); **94** (1968); 111–136 (Riodinidae); **95** (1969): 161–179 (Lycaenidae: Lycaeninae); **96** (1970) 19–77 (Lycaenidae: Theclinae, Strymoninae); 353–433 (Lycaenidae: Plebejinae). All ill.

1966. The authorship of *Polites mystic,* Edwards or Scudder? (Hesperiidae). J. Lepid. Soc. **20**: 239–242.

Brown, F. Martin, J. Donald Eff & Bernard Rotger

1954-1957. Colorado butterflies. Denver: Denver Mus. Nat. Hist. viii × 368 pp., ill.

Brown, F. Martin & Bernard Heineman

1972. Jamaica and its butterflies. E. W. Classey, London. xv + 478 pp., 10 col. pls., maps.

Burns, John M.

1964. Evolution of skipper butterflies in the genus *Erynnis*. Univ. California Publ. Ent. **37**: 1–216, ill.

1966. Expanding distribution and evolutionary potential of *Thymelicus lineola* (Lepidoptera: Hesperiidae), an introduced skipper, with special reference to its appearance in British Columbia. Canadian Ent. **98**: 859–866, ill.

Cardé. Ring T., Arthur M. Shapiro & Harry K. Clench.

1970. Sibling species in the *eurydice* group of *Lethe* (Lepidoptera: Satyridae). Psyche **77**: 70–103, ill.

Clark, Austin H.

1932. The butterflies of the District of Columbia and vicinity. U. S. Nat. Mus., Bull. **157**: ix + 337 pp., ill.

1936. The Gold-banded Skipper (Rhabdoides cellus). Smithsonian Misc. Coll. **95** (7): 50 pp., ill.

1948. Classification of the butterflies, with the allocation of the genera occurring in North America north of Mexico. Proc. Biol. Soc. Washington **61**: 77–81.

Clark, Austin H., & Leila F. Clark

1951. The butterflies of Virginia. Smithsonian Misc. Coll. **116** (7): vii + 239 pp., ill.

Clench, Harry K.

1944. Notes on lycaenid butterflies. (a) the genus Callophrys in North America; (b) The acaste group of the genus Thecla. Bull. Mus. Comp. Zool. (Harvard) **94**: 217–245.

1955. Revised classification of the butterfly family Lycaenidae and its allies. Ann. Carnegie Mus. **33**: 261–274, ill.

1961. *Panthiades m-album* (Lycaenidae); remarks on its early stages and its occurrence in Pennsylvania. J. Lepid. Soc. **15**: 226–232, ill.

1966. Behavioral thermoregulation in butterflies. Ecology **47**: 1021–1034, ill.

1967. Temporal dissociation and population regulation in certain hesperiine butterflies. Ecology **48**: 1000–1006, ill.

Comstock, John Adams

1927. The butterflies of California. Los Angeles: author. 335 pp., ill.

1929. Studies in Pacific Coast Lepidoptera (continued). Bull. S. California Acad. Sci. **28**: 22–32, ill.

Comstock, William P.

1940. Butterflies of New Jersey. J. New York Ent. Soc. **48**: 47–84.

1961. Butterflies of the American Tropics. The genus *Anaea*, Lepidoptera Nymphalidae. New York: American Mus. Nat. Hist. xii + 214 pp., ill.

Comstock, William P., & E. Irving Huntington

1943. Lycaenidae of the Antilles. Ann. New York Acad. Sci. **45**: 49–130, ill.

1958-1964. An annotated list of the Lycaenidae (Lepidoptera, Rhopalocera) of the Western Hemisphere. J. New York Ent. Soc. **66**: 103–118 [foreword; part I, genera]; **67**: 59–96, 163–212; **68**: 49–62, 105–122, 176–186, 232–240; **69**: 54–58, 105–118, 157–176, 191–200; **70**: 39–46, 100–118, 177–179; **71**: 45–57, 115–119, 189–197, 262–264; **72**: 62–64, 120–130, 173–192 [all part II, species].

COOLIDGE, KARL R.

1908. The Rhopalocera of Santa Clara county, California. Canadian Ent. **40:** 425–431.

1909. Further notes on the Rhopalocera of Santa Clara county. Canadian Ent. **41:** 187–188.

D'ALMEIDA, ROMUALDO F.

1966. Catálogo dos Papilionidae Americanos. São Paulo: Soc. Brasiliera Ent. [v] + 366 pp.

DAVENPORT, DEMOREST

1941. The butterflies of the satyrid genus Coenonympha. Bull. Mus. Comp. Zool. (Harvard) **87:** 215–349, ill.

DAVIS, W. B.

1931. New records of diurnal Lepidoptera for California. Bull. S. California Acad. Sci. **30:** 93.

DOS PASSOS, CYRIL F.

1964. A synonymic list of the nearctic Rhopalocera. Lepid. Soc., Mem. **1:** v + 145 pp.

DOS PASSOS, CYRIL F., & L. PAUL GREY

1947. Systematic catalogue of *Speyeria* (Lepidoptera, Nymphalidae) with designations of types and fixations of type localities. American Mus. Novit. #**1370:** 30 pp.

DOWNEY, JOHN C.

1962. Myrmecophily in *Plebejus* (*Icaricia*) *icarioides* (Lepidoptera: Lycaenidae). Ent. News **73:** 57–66.

DYAR, HARRISON G.

1903 ("1902"). A list of North American Lepidoptera and key to the literature of this order of insects. U. S. Nat. Mus., Bull. **52:** xix + 723 pp.

EDWARDS, WILLIAM HENRY

1862–1897. The butterflies of North America. Philadelphia: American Ent. Soc. (vol. 1); Boston: Houghton Mifflin Co. (reprint of vol. 1; vols. 2 and 3). 3 vols.: vol. **1,** 218 pp., 50 pls.; vol. **2,** 357 pp., 51 pls.; vol. **3,** 431 pp., 51 pls. (Pages largely unnumbered; vols. 1 and 2 each include a check list of North American butterflies at the end.)

EHRLICH, PAUL R.

1955. The distribution and subspeciation of *Erebia epipsodea* Butler (Lepidoptera: Satyridae). Univ. Kansas Sci. Bull. **37** (1): 175–194, ill.

EHRLICH, PAUL R., & ANNE H. EHRLICH

1961. How to know the butterflies. Dubuque, Iowa: W. C. Brown Co. (Pictured Key Nature Series). [vii] + 262 pp., ill. (Sections contributed by: D. L. Bauer; H. K. Clench; C. F. dos Passos; J. C. Downey; L. P. Grey; A. B. Klots; W. S. McAlpine; K. H. Wilson.)

EMMEL, THOMAS C., & JOHN F. EMMEL

1973. The butterflies of Southern California. Nat. Hist. Mus. of Los Angeles Co., Sci. Series **26:** 148 pp.

EVANS, W. H.

1951–1955. A catalogue of the American Hesperiidae. London: British Mus. (Nat. Hist.). Part I (1951), x + 92 pp. (Introduction; Pyrrhopyginae); Part II (1952), v + 178 pp. (Pyrginae, section 1); part III (1953), v + 246 pp. (Pyrginae, section 2); Part IV (1955), v + 499 pp. (Hesperiinae and Megathyminae). All ill. + Addenda and corrigenda, 4 pp.

FERGUSON, DOUGLAS C.

1955. The Lepidoptera of Nova Scotia. Part I (Macrolepidoptera) [all publ.]. Proc. Nova

Scotian Inst. Sci. **23:** 161–375 + 4 pp. corrigenda and addenda, ill. (Nova Scotia Mus. Sci., Bull. 2.)

FERRIS, CLIFFORD D.

1971. A key to the Rhopalocera (butterflies) of Wyoming. Science Monograph 21, Agr. Exp. Sta., Univ. of Wyoming, Laramie.

1972. Notes on certain species of Colias (Lepidoptera, Pieridae) found in Wyoming and associated regions. Bull. Allyn Mus., No. 6.

FIELD, WILLIAM D.

1938. A manual of the butterflies and skippers of Kansas. Bull. Univ. Kansas **39** (10): 328 pp.

1971. Butterflies of the genus Vanessa and of the resurrected genera Bassaris and Cynthia (Lepidoptera: Nymphalidae). Smithsonian Contrib. Zool., #84: 105 pp., ill.

FORBES, WILLIAM T. M.

1944. The genus Phyciodes (Lepidoptera, Nymphalidae). Entom. Americana (n.s.) **24:** 139–207, ill.

1960. Lepidoptera of New York and neighboring states. Part IV. Cornell Univ. Agr. Exp. Sta., Mem. **371:** 188 pp., ill.

FORSTER, WALTER

1964. Beiträge zur Kenntnis der Insektenfauna Boliviens XIX. Lepidoptera III, Satyridae. Veröff. Staatssamml. München **8:** 51–188, ill.

FREEMAN, H. AVERY

1951. Ecological and systematic study of the Hesperioidea of Texas (Lepidoptera, Hesperioidea). So. Methodist Univ. Studies, #6: 67 pp.

1969. Systematic review of the Megathymidae. J. Lepid. Soc. **23,** suppl. 1: 59 pp., ill.

GARTH, JOHN S.

1950. Butterflies of Grand Canyon National Park. Grand Canyon Nat. Hist. Assoc., Bull. **11:** [iv] + 52 pp., ill.

GREY, L. PAUL, & ARTHUR MOECK

1962. Notes on overlapping subspecies. I. An example in *Speyeria zerene* (Nymphalidae). J. Lepid. Soc. **16:** 81–97.

GREY, L. PAUL, ARTHUR H. MOECK & W. H. EVANS

1963. Notes on overlapping subspecies. II. Segregation in the *Speyeria atlantis* ("*electa*") of the Black Hills (Argynninae). J. Lepid. Soc. **17:** 129–147.

HALL, ARTHUR

1928–1930. A revision of the genus *Phyciodes* Hübn. (Lepidoptera Nymphalidae). Bull. Hill Mus. (suppl. to vols. 2–4): 206 pp., ill. + 1 p. Additions and corrections.

HARRIS, LUCIEN, JR.

1954. An account of the unusual life history of a rare yucca skipper (Megathymidae). Lepid. News **8:** 153–162.

1972. Butterflies of Georgia. U. of Oklahoma Press, Norman. xx + 326 pp., col. frontispiece, 24 pls. (10 col.), maps.

HAYWARD, KENNETH J.

1947. Algunas plantas huespedes de las larvas de los Hesperidos Americanos (Lepidoptera, Rhopalocera, Hesperiidae). Acta Zool. Lilloana **4:** 19–54.

HEMMING, FRANCIS

1967. The generic names of the butterflies and their type-species (Lepidoptera: Rhopalocera). Bull. British Mus. Nat. Hist. (Ent.), Suppl. **9:** 509 pp.

HIGGINS, LIONEL G.

1960. A revision of the Melitaeine genus *Chlosyne* and allied species (Lepidoptera: Nymphalinae). Trans. R. Ent. Soc. London **112:** 381–467, ill.

HIGGINS, LIONEL G. & NORMAN D. RILEY

1970. A field guide to the butterflies of Britain and Europe. Collins, London. 380 pp., 760 col. ills., maps.

HOLLAND, WILLIAM J.

1898. The butterfly book. New York: Doubleday, Page & Co. xx + 382 pp., ill.

1932. The butterfly book, new and thoroughly revised edition. New York: Doubleday, Doran & Co. xii + 424 pp., ill.

INTERNATIONAL COMMISSION ON ZOOLOGICAL NOMENCLATURE

1961. International code of zoological nomenclature adopted by the XV International Congress of Zoology. London, for the Int. Comm. Zool. Nomencl.: xx + 176 pp.

KIMBALL, CHARLES P.

1965. The Lepidoptera of Florida. Gainesville, Fla.: Fla. Dept. Agr. (Arthropods of Florida and neighboring land areas, vol. 1): v + 363 pp., ill.

KLOTS, ALEXANDER B.

1933. A generic revision of the Pieridae (Lepidoptera). Ent. Americana (n.s.) **12:** 139–242, ill.

1951. A field guide to the butterflies of North America, east of the Great Plains. Boston: Houghton Mifflin Co. xvi + 349 pp., ill.

1957. The world of butterflies and moths. Harrap, London & McGraw-Hill, New York. 207 pp., 88 pls. (24 col.).

1970. Lepidoptera (in) Taxonomists' glossary of insect genitalia, S. L. Tuxen, ed., 2d edition. Munksgaard, Copenhagen. pp. 115–130, figs. 143–154.

LANGSTON, ROBERT L.

1964. *Philotes* of central coastal California (Lycaenidae). J. Lepid. Soc. **17** ("1963"): 201–223.

1969. *Philotes* of North America: synonymic list and distribution (Lycaenidae). J. Lepid. Soc. **23:** 49–62.

LEIGHTON, BEN V.

1946. The butterflies of Washington. Univ. Washington Publ. Biol. **9:** 47–63.

LINDSEY, ARTHUR W.

1921. The Hesperioidea of America north of Mexico. Univ. Iowa Studies Nat. Hist. **9** (4): 114 pp., ill.

1942. A preliminary revision of *Hesperia*. Denison Univ. Bull., J. Sci. Lab. **37:** 1–150, ill.

LINDSEY, ARTHUR W., E. L. BELL & ROSWELL C. WILLIAMS

1931. The Hesperioidea of North America. Denison Univ. Bull., J. Sci. Lab. **26:** 1–142, ill.

MacNEILL, C. DON

1964. The skippers of the genus *Hesperia* in western North America with special reference to California (Lepidoptera: Hesperiidae). Univ. California Publ. Ent. **35:** 1–130, ill.

MACY, RALPH W., & HAROLD H. SHEPARD

1941. Butterflies. Minneapolis: Univ. Minnesota Press. 247 pp., ill.

MATHER, BRYANT, & KATHERINE MATHER

1958. The butterflies of Mississippi. Tulane Studies Zool. **6:** 63–109, ill.

MATTONI, R. H. T.

1955. Notes on the genus *Philotes* (Lycaenidae: Lepidoptera). I. Descriptions of three new subspecies and a synoptic list. Bull. S. California Acad. Sci. **53** ("1954"): 157–165.

McALPINE, WILBUR S., STEPHEN P. HUBBELL & THOMAS E. PLISKE

1960. The distribution, habits, and life history of *Euptychia mitchelli* (Satyridae). J. Lepid. Soc. **14**: 209–226.

McDUNNOUGH, JAMES H.

1938. Checklist of the Lepidoptera of Canada and the United States of America. Part I, Macrolepidoptera. Mem. S. California Acad. Sci. **1**: 1–272, + 3 pp. corrigenda.

MICHENER, CHARLES D.

1942. A generic revision of the Heliconiinae (Lepidoptera, Nymphalidae). American Mus. Novit. #**1197**: 8 pp., ill.

MILLER, LEE D.

1968. The higher classification, phylogeny and zoogeography of the Satyridae (Lepidoptera). Mem. American Ent. Soc. #**24**: [6] + iii + 174 pp., ill.

MILLER, LEE D., & HARRY K. CLENCH

1968. Some aspects of mating behavior in butterflies. J. Lepid. Soc. **22**: 125–132, ill.

MONTE, OSCAR

1934 a. Publ. Ser. Agricola no. 31 (Secr. Agric. Est. Minas Gerais). [not seen].

1934 b. Borboletas que viven en plantas cultivadas. Bol. Agric., Zootec., Vet. (Minas Gerais) **7**: 337–363.

NABOKOV, VLADIMIR

1944. Notes on the morphology of the genus Lycaeides (Lycaenidae, Lepidoptera). Psyche **51**: 104–138, ill.

1945. Notes on neotropical Plebejinae (Lepidoptera: Lycaenidae). Psyche **52**: 1–61, ill.

1949. The nearctic members of the genus *Lycaeides* Hübner (Lycaenidae, Lepidoptera). Bull. Mus. Comp. Zool. (Harvard) **101**: 479–541, ill.

NEWCOMER, E. J.

1967. Early stages of *Chlosyne hoffmanni manchada* (Nymphalidae). J. Lepid. Soc. **21**: 71–73.

OPLER, PAUL A., & JERRY A. POWELL

1961. Taxonomic and distributional studies on the western components of the *Apodemia mormo* complex (Riodinidae). J. Lepid. Soc. **15**: 145–171, ill.

PENGELLY, D. H.

1961. *Thymelicus lineola* (Ochsenheimer) (Lepidoptera: Hesperiidae): a pest of hay and pasture grasses in southern Ontario. Proc. Ent. Soc. Ontario **91**: 189–197.

PENN, GEORGE H.

1955. Mass flight of Ocola Skippers (*Panoquina ocola* Edwards). Lepid. News **9**:79.

PLATT, AUSTIN P., & LINCOLN P. BROWER

1968. Mimetic versus disruptive coloration in intergrading populations of *Limenitis arthemis* and *astyanax* butterflies. Evolution **22**: 699–718, ill.

ROEVER, KILIAN

1962. Notes on *Erora* (Lycaenidae). J. Lepid. Soc. **16**: 1–4.

ROSS, GARY N., & EDWARD N. LAMBREMONT

1963. An annotated supplement to the state list of Louisiana butterflies and skippers. J. Lepid. Soc. **17**: 148–158.

SCHWANWITSCH, B. N.

1924. On the ground-plan of wing-pattern in Nymphalids and certain other families of the Rhopalocerous Lepidoptera. Proc. Zool. Soc. London **1924:** 509–528, ill.

SCOTT, JAMES A., SCOTT L. ELLIS & DONALD EFF
1968. New records, range extensions, and field data for Colorado butterflies and skippers. J. Lepid. Soc. **22:** 159–171.

SCUDDER, SAMUEL H.
1889. The butterflies of the eastern United States and Canada with special reference to New England. Cambridge: author. 3 vols. xxiv, xi, vii + 1958 pp., ill.

SEITZ, ADALBERT (ed.)
1907–1924. Die Grossschmetterlinge der Erde. Vol. 5, Die Amerikanishen Tagfalter. viii + 1141 pp., ill. (Also in English language edition.)

SHAPIRO, ARTHUR M.
1965. Ecological and behavioral notes on *Hesperia metea* and *Atrytonopsis hianna* (Hesperiidae). J. Lepid. Soc. **19:** 215–221.
1966. Butterflies of the Delaware Valley. American Ent. Soc., Special Publ. vi + 79 pp., ill.

SHIELDS, OAKLEY
1968. Hilltopping. J. Res. Lepid. **6** ("1967"): 69–178, ill.

SHIROZU, TAKASHI, & HIDEHO YAMAMOTO
1956. A generic revision and the phylogeny of the tribe Theclini (Lepidoptera; Lycaenidae). Sieboldia **1:** 329–421, ill.

SKINNER, HENRY
1901. On a small collection of butterflies made in California and Arizona. Ent. News **12:** 170–171.
1911. A new variety of Megathymus yuccae (Lepid.). Ent. News **22:** 300.

STRECKER, HERMAN
1872–1878. Lepidoptera, Rhopaloceres and Heteroceres, indigenous and exotic; with descriptions and colored illustrations. Reading, Penna.: author. 143 pp., ill. Suppl. 1 (1898), 12 pp.; suppl. 2 (1899), 11 pp.; suppl. 3 (1900), pp. 13–37.

TILDEN, J. W.
1965. Butterflies of the San Francisco Bay region. Berkeley, Calif.: Univ. California Press (Calif. Nat. Hist. Guides: 12). 88 pp., ill.

URQUHART, F. A.
1960. The Monarch Butterfly. Toronto: Univ. Toronto Press. xxiv + 361 pp., ill.

WHITTAKER, ROBERT H.
1969. New concepts of kingdoms of organisms. Science **163:** 150–160, ill.

WILLIAMS, C. B.
1930. The migration of butterflies. Edinburgh: Oliver & Boyd. xi + 473 pp.

WRIGHT, W. G.
1905. The butterflies of the West Coast of the United States. San Francisco. 257 + vii pp., ill. (The second edition [1906], published by the author, is more easily found; most copies of the first edition were destroyed in the San Francisco earthquake.)

COLLECTIONS

The chief North American collections of Lepidoptera are in the following institutions:
Allyn Museum of Entomology, Sarasota, Florida
American Museum of Natural History, New York City, New York
Academy of Natural Sciences, Philadelphia
California Academy of Science, San Francisco, California
Carnegie Museum of Natural History, Pittsburgh, Pennsylvania
Canadian National Collection, Ottawa, Ontario
Cornell University, Ithaca, New York
Field Museum, Chicago, Illinois
Illinois Natural History Survey, Urbana, Illinois
Los Angeles County Museum, Los Angeles, California
Museum of Comparative Zoology, Cambridge, Massachusetts
University of California, Berkeley, California
United States National Museum, Washington, District of Columbia

Some of the European museums are especially important because they contain types of North American species named by the older authors; some of these are:
British Museum (Natural History), London
Linnaean Society, London
Zoologisches Museum, Humboldt-Universität, Berlin, East Germany
Museum National d'Histoire Naturelle, Paris
Rijksmuseum van Natuurlijke Historie, Leiden
Universitetets Zoologiske Museum, Copenhagen

Nearly all of the North American institutions listed contain, not only large and broadly representative study collections, but also many types of species-group names. They also have very extensive libraries. Most of them have one or more professional lepidopterists on their staffs who not only care for the collections but also carry on and publish research, aid students and answer queries.

Many other important collections are maintained by local museums, colleges and universities. Most of these collections are somewhat narrower in scope than those of the chief museums. Many of the collections are fundamentally for teaching. Such institutions frequently deposit types in the larger institutions.

It cannot be emphasized enough that all type specimens are to be regarded as the property of science and are to be deposited in a major museum where they will be preserved for study. *No type should ever be retained in a private collection.* Moreover, every collector should do all in his power to help build up the great study collections that are the repositories of most of our taxonomic knowledge and the fountainhead of most of our research.

INDEX TO FOODPLANTS

References made to larval foodplants are combined with adult nectar sources and each is summarized here. Both common and Latin botanical names are included, which is the way that most authors wrote them in their sections. All plant families are written in capitals.

INDEX TO BUTTERFLIES AND OTHER FEATURES

EDITORS' NOTE: Common, or vernacular, names, which have no formal status, pose special problems. Some people like to use them but others do not. Many of them, such as Monarch, Mourning Cloak, Painted Lady and Red Admiral, are hallowed by tradition. So are many group names such as Arctics, Anglewings, Hackberry Butterflies and Checkerspots. Many, however, are merely translations or repeitions of scientific names and so serve little purpose. In the preparation of this book each of the twenty-one authors was privileged to use common names as he chose. Inevitably, there were variations in the number the various writers used. In making the index the editors followed the definitive texts. Common names used by an author were included. The editors have added a few traditional common names which it seemed a pity to leave out.

Numbers in bold-face type refer to the plate numbers of the color illustrations.

William H. Howe
at Fortin de los Flores,
VERA CRUZ